MEANS PLUMBING COST DATA 1990

TABLE OF CONTENTS

Foreword	ii
How To Use This Book	iii
Section A Unit Price	
Crew Listings	viii
Unit Price Pages	1
Section B Assemblies	237
Section C Reference	333
Section D Appendix	
Historical Cost Index	368
City Cost Indexes	369
Abbreviations	378
Index	381

Editor-In-Chief
William D. Mahoney

Senior Editor
John J. Moylan

First Printing

Contributing Editors
Allan B. Cleveland
Donald D. Denzer
Jeffrey M. Goldman
Dwayne R. Lehigh
Alan E. Lew
Melville J. Mossman
Jeannene D. Murphy
Kenneth M. Randall
Kornelis Smit
Edward B. Wetherill
Ernest T. Williams
Rory Woolsey
David M. Zuniga

Technical Coordinators
Marion Schofield
Wayne D. Anderson

Graphics
Carl W. Linde

FOREWORD

THE COMPANY AND THE EDITORS

Since 1942, R.S. Means Company, Inc. has been actively engaged in construction cost publishing and consulting throughout North America. The primary objective of the company is to provide the construction industry professional — the contractor, the owner, the architect, the engineer, the facilities manager — with current and comprehensive construction cost data.

A thoroughly experienced and highly qualified staff of professionals at R.S. Means work daily at collecting, analyzing and disseminating reliable cost information for your needs. These staff members have years of practical construction experience and engineering training prior to joining the firm. Each contributes to the maintenance of a complete, continually-updated construction cost data system.

With the constant flow of new construction methods and materials, the construction professional often cannot find enough time to examine and evaluate all the diverse construction cost possibilities. R.S. Means performs this function by analyzing all facets of the industry. Data is collected and organized into a format that is instantly accessible. The data is useful for all phases of construction cost determination — from the preliminary budget to the detailed unit price estimate.

The Means organization is always prepared to assist you and help in the solution of construction problems through the services of its four major divisions; Construction and Cost Data Publishing, Computer Data and Software Services, Consulting Services and Educational Seminars.

DEVELOPMENT OF COST DATA

The staff at R.S. Means Company, Inc. continuously monitors developments in the construction industry in order to ensure reliable, thorough and up-to-date cost information. While *overall* construction costs may vary relative to general economic conditions, price fluctuations within the industry are dependent upon many other factors. Individual price variations may, in fact, be opposite to overall economic trends. Therefore, costs are monitored and updated and new items are added in response to industry changes.

All costs represent U.S. national averages and are given in U.S. dollars. The Means City Cost Indexes can be used to convert costs to a particular location. The City Cost Indexes for Canada can be used to convert U.S. national averages to local costs in Canadian dollars.

Material Costs are determined by contacting manufacturers, dealers, distributors, and contractors throughout the United States. If current material costs are available for a specific location, adjustments can be made to reflect differences from the national average. Material costs do not include sales tax.

Labor Costs are based on the average of wage rates from 30 major U.S. cities. Rates are determined from agreements or prevailing wages for construction trades for the current year. Rates are listed on the inside back cover of this book. If wage rates in your area vary from those used in this book, or if rate increases are expected within a given year, labor costs should be adjusted accordingly.

Labor costs reflect productivity based on actual working conditions. These figures include time spent during a normal work day on items other than actual installation such as material receiving and handling, mobilization, site movement, breaks, and cleanup. Productivity data is developed over an extended period so as not to be influenced by abnormal variations, and reflects a typical average.

Equipment Costs as presented include not only rental costs, but also operating costs. Equipment prices are obtained from industry sources throughout the country — contractors, suppliers, dealers and manufacturers.

FACTORS AFFECTING COSTS

Quality: The prices for materials and the workmanship upon which productivity is based are in line with U.S. Government specifications and represent good sound construction.

Overtime: No allowance has been made for overtime. If premium time or work during other than normal working hours is anticipated, adjustments to labor costs should be made accordingly.

Productivity: The productivity, daily output and man-hour figures for each line item are based on working an eight hour day in daylight hours. For other than normal work hours, productivity may decrease.

Size of Project: The size and type of construction project can have a significant impact on cost. Economy of scale can reduce costs for large projects. Conversely, costs may be higher for small projects due to higher percentage overhead costs, small quantity material purchases and minimum labor and/or equipment charges. Costs in this book are intended for the size and type of project as described in the "How To Use This Book" pages. Costs for projects of a significantly different size or type should be adjusted accordingly.

Location: Material prices are for metropolitan areas. Beyond a 20 mile radius of large cities, extra trucking or other transportation charges will increase the material costs slightly. This material increase may be offset by lower wage rates. Both of these factors should be considered when preparing an estimate, especially if the job site is remote. Highly specialized subcontract items may require high travel and per diem expenses for mechanics.

Other factors affecting costs are season of year, contractor management, weather, local union restrictions, building code requirements, and the availability of adequate energy, skilled labor, and building materials. General business conditions influence the "in-place" cost of all items. Substitute materials and construction methods may have to be employed, and these may increase the installed cost and/or life cycle costs. Such factors are difficult to evaluate and cannot be predicted on the basis of the job's location in a particular section of the country. Thus, there may be a significant, but unavoidable cost variation where these factors are concerned.

HOW TO USE THIS BOOK

HOW THE BOOK IS ARRANGED

Means Plumbing Cost Data 1990 is divided into four major sections: A, B, C and D. The A Section is the unit price portion, and is numbered in accordance with the CSI Format divisions. The B section contains the "assembly" pricing information. It is numbered by divisions as shown under the Assembly Format heading. Section C is a grouping of code extracts and useful technical/engineering data for sizing and quantifying construction components. It is also numbered by divisions as shown under the Assembly Format heading. Section D is an appendix containing the Historical and City Cost Indexes, a comprehensive list of abbreviations and the index for the book.

The table on the following page lists the CSI format for unit prices and the corresponding "assembly" format used for this book.

Numbering System: The basic numbering format used for unit prices is 16 major divisions of building construction plus a S.F. & C.F. Cost Division. These divisions are patterned after the MASTERFORMAT adopted by the American Institute of Architects, Associated General Contractors of America, Inc., and developed by the Construction Specifications Institute, Inc. The system is widely used by most segments of the building construction industry. The major divisions are then divided into their major component parts shown in bold face type at the top of each page along with the major component subdivision number. The individual items making up the major component part are then listed alphabetically. Subdivisions and other sizes are indented below each descriptive item. An outline of the major components and their numbering system is shown on the first page of Section A.

Unit Price Arrangement: The cost and descriptive information for each item in the unit price portions of the book is arranged as follows:

Line Number: Each item has its own 3 part line number. The subdivision number at the top of the page is the first part of the number (153 for the example). **Water Cooler** has a bold type face number **105** associated with it. The appropriate line number for a fully recessed water cooler is 3400. The entire 3 part line number for the item is thus 153-105-3400 (see also page vi of the book for a pictorial analysis).

Crew Costs: As illustrated in the Foreword of the book, the Crew Tables are listed two ways, one with bare labor rates, the other with billing rates as shown in Div. C10 and the inside rear cover. Local labor rates may be substituted to arrive at precise local daily crew costs. Abbreviations for the individual trades are shown on the inside rear cover. The power equipment required for each crew is included in the particular crew cost. The daily equipment costs are usually the sum of the weekly rental rate divided by 5 plus the hourly operating cost times 8. (See Div. C10 for further discussion.) For daily costs incl. Subs O & P, 10% is added to the bare costs to allow for the contractors mark-up on the equipment costs.

Description Major items of each subdivision are listed in bold type face within the subdivisions. Components of the major items are listed after the major items with more individual sizes listed after each particular description.

Crew To the right of the item described is the typical crew needed to install the item. Typical crews are tabulated in the Foreword. When installations are made by one trade and require no power equipment, the appropriate trade is listed directly in the crew column. For instance "2 Plum" would indicate that the installation is made with 2 Plumbers. If the installing crew was Q-2 (shown in the Foreword) this would be made up of 2 Plumbers and 1 Apprentice.

Daily Output To the right of the crew column is the Daily Output columns. This is the number of units that a given crew will install in an 8 hour day. In other words, the total daily crew cost divided by the Daily Output will produce the unit installation costs. To calculate the unit equipment costs, divide the daily equipment costs by the Daily Output.

Man-Hours The column following "Daily Output" is "Man-hours". This figure represents the man-hours required to install one "unit" of work. Unit man-hours are calculated by dividing the total daily crew hours (as seen in the Crew Tables) by the Daily Output.

Unit To the right of the Daily Output column is the Unit column which describes the unit upon which the price, and crew are based, as S.F. (square foot), etc. See the list of abbreviations in the back of the book.

Bare Costs The next 4 columns contain costs that do not include the Subcontractors Overhead and Profit. The first column under the "Bare Cost" heading is MAT. which is the unit material cost for the item (without Subs O & P). The next column is the LABOR figures. This column is the installation cost. As mentioned above, this cost is arrived at by dividing the daily crew or labor cost (using bare costs in both cases) by the Daily Output. The third column under the "Bare Cost" heading lists the unit EQUIP. This figure is the daily equipment cost divided by the daily output. The last column under the BARE COST heading is TOTAL which is the arithmetical sum of the three previous columns. The last column is the TOTAL INCL O&P. This column is the sum of the bare material and equipment costs plus 10%, which is then added to the installation costs incl. Subs O & P. In this case the crew costs and the labor costs used would include the Subs O & P. When these costs are divided by the Daily Output, a unit installation cost incl. Subs O & P is developed.

General Arrangement: Following the item there are frequently found numbers in squares which are reference numbers. These refer to "assembly" information and supplementary engineering design and code data in the rear portion of the book.

The breakdowns and "assembly" costs show how the editors arrived at the tabulated figure and also indicate the cost of typical complete systems commonly encountered in building construction. The breakdowns and "assemblies" information in the rear is generally arranged in the same sequence as the items in the unit price portion of each section.

CROSS REFERENCES

Numerous cross references are included to aid in the rapid location of items that could logically be listed under two or more subdivisions. A cross reference referring to say, Division 152, would mean that the entire division (Plumbing Fixtures) was the intended cross reference. A cross reference of 152-148 would indicate showers, and a cross reference of 152-148-3000 would indicate line 3000, Division 152-148, or, in this case, Fiberglass showers.

Major Sections of This Book	CSI Format		Assemblies Format	
	Division	Description	Division	Description
Mechanical Related Items Items have been rearranged to be consistent with major sections of this book.	1	General Requirements	1	Foundation/Substructure
	2	Site Work	2	Substructure
	3	Concrete	3	Superstructure
	4	Masonry		
	5	Metals	4	Exterior Closure
	6	Wood & Plastics	5	Roofing
	7	Moisture Protection	6	Interior Construction
	8	Doors, Windows & Glass	7	Conveying
	9	Finishes		
	10	Specialties	10	General Conditions
	11	Equipment	11	Specialties
	12	Furnishings	12	Site Work
	13	Special Construction		
	14	Conveying Systems		
Mechanical	15	Mechanical	8	Mechanical
Electrical	16	Electrical	9	Electrical
Cost Modifications	17 Appendix	Square Foot City Cost Index	14	Square Foot Costs

ROUNDING OF COSTS

In general, all unit prices in excess of $5.00 have been rounded to make them easier to use and still maintain adequate precision of the results. The rounding rules generally followed in this book are as follows:

Price from $.01 to $5.00 rounded to nearest 1¢

Price from $5.01 to $20.00 rounded to nearest 5¢

Price from $20.01 to $100.00 rounded to nearest $1

Price from $100.01 to $1,000.00 rounded to nearest $5

Price from $1,000.01 to $10,000.00 rounded to nearest $25

Price from $10,000.01 to $50,000.00 rounded to nearest $100

Price over $50,000.01 rounded to nearest $500

SQUARE FOOT AND CUBIC FOOT BUILDING COSTS

The figures in Division A17 are included to facilitate rapid preliminary budget estimates. See Division C14 for details of how the figures were derived.

There are two times when square foot costs are useful. The first is in the schematic stage when no details are available, when square foot costs make a useful starting point. The second is after the bids are in and the costs can be worked back into their appropriate units for information purposes. As soon as details become available in the project design, the square foot approach should be discontinued and the project priced by its particular components.

In using the figures in Division A17, it is recommended that the median column be used for preliminary figures if no additional information is available. The median figures, when multiplied by the total city construction cost index figures in Section D and then multiplied by the project size modifier in Division C14, should present a fairly accurate base figure which would then have to be adjusted in view of the estimator's experience, local economic conditions, code requirements, and the owner's particular requirements. There is no need to factor the percentage figures, as these remain constant from city to city. All tabulations mentioning air conditioning had at least partial air conditioning.

OVERHEAD, PROFIT, CONTINGENCIES

General: Prices given in this book are of two kinds: (1) BARE COSTS to which an allowance for Contractor Overhead and Profit must be added, and (2) COSTS INCL. SUBS O & P, to which an allowance covering only the general contractors mark-up must be applied. The general contractor includes this price in his bid with a normal mark-up ranging from 0 to 15%. This mark-up depends on economic conditions plus the supervision and trouble-shooting expected by the general contractor. For purposes of this book it is best to add an allowance of 10% to the figures including O & P. In using the bare cost figures, experience shows that an addition of 35% for general contractors O & P gives best results.

The figures in the column on the right, TOTAL INCL. O & P, contain the subcontractor's overhead and profit, thus it is necessary to add a percentage for all subcontracted items unless the owner is receiving multiple prime contracts.

Overhead and Profit: Subcontractors' overhead and profit allowances are detailed in Division C10. These are general figures and local deviations are certainly to be expected. A subcontractor should be able to tell from records very closely what his own overhead will be. He will then add whatever profit and contingency percentage circumstances dictate.

Subcontractors: Usually a considerable portion of all large jobs is subcontracted. In fact the percentage done by subs is constantly increasing and may run over 90%. Since the workmen employed by these companies do nothing else but install their particular product they soon become experts in that line. The result is that installation by these firms is accomplished so efficiently that the total in-place cost, even with the subcontractor's overhead and profit, is no more and often less than if the principal contractor had handled the installation himself. There is, moreover, the advantage of having the work done right. Companies who sell specialties are anxious that their product perform well and, consequently, the installation will be the best possible.

Contingencies: The allowance for contingencies generally is to provide for unforeseen construction difficulties. On alterations or repair jobs 20% is none too much. If drawings are final and only field contingencies are being considered 2% or 3% is probably sufficient and often nothing need be added. As far as the contract is concerned, future changes in plans will be covered by extras. The contractor should consider inflationary price trends and possible material shortages during the course of the job. If drawings are not complete or approved or a budget cost wanted, it is wise to add 10% to 15%. Contingencies, then, are a matter of judgment. Additional allowances are shown in Division A010-020 for contingencies and job conditions and Division A010-032 for factors to convert prices for repair and remodeling jobs.

SIZE OF JOB

The book is aimed primarily at industrial and commercial buildings costing $500,000 and up or large housing developments. The costs are also for new construction of complete buildings rather than repairs and minor alterations. Material prices given are usually trade quantity purchases. With reasonable exercise of judgment the figures can be used for any building work, but do not apply to civil engineering structures such as bridges, dams, highways or the like.

The "productivity," or daily output of each craftsman, includes mobilization and clean-up time, break time, plan layout time, as well as an allowance to carry stock from the storage trailer or location on the job site up to 200' into the building and on the first or second floor. If material has to be transported over greater distances or to higher floors, an additional allowance should be considered by the estimator. An allowance has also been included in the piping and fittings installation time for a leak check and minor tightening. Equipment installation time includes start-up with associated adjustments.

ESTIMATING GUIDELINES

The following suggestions are made to enable the estimator to perform unit price estimating in a logical, easy to check and thorough manner.

1. Use pre-printed forms for orderly lists and for recording of material telephone quotations.
2. Use only the front side of each paper or form except for certain pre-printed summary forms.
3. Use printed (rather than measured) dimensions when both are given.
4. Add up multiple numbers for a single entry where possible.
5. Measure all dimensions carefully.
6. Do not "round off" quantities until the final summary, round off to purchasing quantities.
7. Mark drawings with different colors as items are taken off.
8. Keep similar items together; different items separate.
9. Identify function and drawing numbers to aid in future checking for completeness.
10. Measure or list everything on the drawings or mentioned in the specifications.
11. It will be necessary to list items not called for to make the job complete.
12. Be alert for: notes on plans such as N.T.S. (not to scale); changes in scale throughout the drawings; reduced size drawings; discrepancies between the specifications and the drawings.
13. Develop a consistent pattern of performing a takeoff. For example:
    a. Start the quantity take-off at the lower floor and move to the next higher floor.
    b. Proceed from the main section of the building to the wings.
    c. Proceed from south to north or vice versa, clockwise or counterclockwise.
    d. Take off floor plan quantities first, elevations next, then detail drawings.
    e. Be consistent.
14. Utilize design symmetry or repetition (repetitive floors, repetitive wings, symmetrical design around a center line, similar room layouts, etc.). Note: extreme caution is needed here so as not to omit or duplicate an area.

DOING THE WORK

In preparing an estimate ignore the cents column. Just give total to the nearest dollar. The cents will average up in a column of figures. An estimate of $457,323.37 is ridiculous; $457,325 is certainly more sensible and $457,000 is better and just as likely to be right.

If you follow this simple instruction the time saved is tremendous with an added important advantage: using round numbers your mind is left free to exercise judgment and common sense rather than being overcome and befuddled by a mass of computations.

When you have finished, roughly check the big items for location of the decimal point. That is important. A large error can creep in if you write down $300 when it should be $3,000. Also check the list to be sure you have not omitted any large item. A common error is to overlook, let us say, insulation or to forget cleaning or testing or otherwise commit a gross omission. No amount of accuracy in prices can compensate for such an oversight.

It is important to keep the bare costs and costs that already include the Subs O & P separate since different mark-ups will have to be applied to each category. Organize your estimating procedures to minimize confusion and simplify checking to insure against omissions and/or duplications.

By using pre-printed forms listing the usual plumbing items, the chance of omissions and duplications is lessened, but never completely eliminated.

THE EDITORS
Plumbing

John J. Moylan, a former commercial/industrial mechanical contractor with over 40 years of experience in estimating, project managing, purchasing and ownership. A seminar lecturer and member of ASHRAE, ASPE, AEE, and IDHA and a former contractor member of MCAA.

Melville J. Mossman, a registered professional engineer and seminar lecturer, member of ASHRAE, ASPE, AACE and AEE.

HOW TO USE UNIT PRICE PAGES

Important
Prices in this section are listed in two ways: as bare costs and as costs including overhead and profit of the installing contractor. In most cases, if the work is to be subcontracted, it is best for a general contractor to add an additional 10% to the figures found in the column titled **"TOTAL INCL. O&P"**.

Unit
The unit of measure listed here reflects the material being used in the line item. For example: Water coolers are expressed as each (Ea.).

Productivity
The daily output represents typical total daily amount of work that the designated crew will produce. Man-hours are a unit of measure for the labor involved in performing a task. To derive the total man-hours for a task, multiply the quantity of the item involved times the man-hour figure shown.

Line Number Determination
Each line item is identified by a unique ten-digit number.

MASTERFORMAT
Division
153 105 3400
Subdivision

Mediumscope
153 105
153 **105** 3400
Major Classification

153 105 **3400**
Individual Line Number

Description
The meaning of this line item shows a recessed water cooler will be installed by a Q-1 crew at a rate of 3.5 per day. (4.57 man-hours each)

C8.1 403 Reference Number
These reference numbers refer to charts, tables, estimating data, cost derivations and other information which may be useful to the user of this book. These references may direct the reader to any section within the book.

Bare Costs are developed as follows for line no. **153-105-3400**
Mat. is **Bare Material Cost ($765)**
Labor for Crew Q1 = Man-hour Cost **($22.83)** × Man-hour Units **(4.570)** = **$100.00**
Equip. for Crew Q1 = Equip. Hour Cost **($0)** × Man-hour Units **(9.600)** = **$0**
Total = **Mat. Cost ($765)** + **Labor Cost ($100.00)** + **Equip. Cost ($0)** = **$865** each.
(**Note:** Where a Crew is indicated Equipment and Labor costs are derived from the Crew Tables. See example above.)

Total Costs Including O&P are developed as follows:
Mat. is **Bare Material Cost** + 10% = **$765** + **$76.50** = **$841.50**
Labor for Crew Q1 = Man-hour Cost **($32.55)** × Man-hour Units **(4.570)** = **$148.75**
Equip. for Crew Q1 = Equip. Hour Cost **($0)** × Man-hour Units **(4.570)** = **$0**
Total = **Mat. Cost ($841.50)** + **Labor Cost ($148.75)** + **Equip. Cost ($0)** = **$990.00**
(**Note:** Where a crew is indicated, Equipment and Labor costs are derived from the Crew Tables. See example above. **"Total Inc. O&P"** costs are rounded.)

Crew Q-1

Crew Q-1	Hr.	Daily	Hr.	Daily	Bare Costs	Incl. O&P
1 Plumber	$24.70	$197.60	$36.65	$293.20	$22.23	$32.97
1 Plumber Apprentice	19.76	158.08	29.30	234.40		
16 M.H., Daily Totals		$355.68		$527.60	$22.23	$32.97

153 | Plumbing Appliances

	153 100	Water Appliances		CREW	DAILY OUTPUT	MAN-HOURS	UNIT	MAT.	LABOR	EQUIP.	TOTAL	TOTAL INCL O&P	
105	0010	WATER COOLER											105
	0030	See line 153-105-9800 for rough-in, waste & vent											
	0040	for all water coolers											
	0100	Wall mounted, non-recessed											
	0140	4 GPH		Q-1	4	4	Ea.	291	89		380	450	
	0180	8.2 GPH			4	4		347	89		436	515	
	0220	14.3 GPH			4	4		367	89		456	535	
	0260	16.1 GPH			4	4		390	89		479	560	
	0600	For hot and cold water, add						160			160	175	
	0640	For stainless steel cabinet, add						41.50			41.50	46	
	1040	14.3 GPH		Q-1	3.80	4.210		504	94		598	695	
	1240	For stainless steel cabinet, add						78			78	86	
	2600	Wheelchair type, 8 GPH		Q-1	4	4		875	89		964	1,100	
	3000	Simulated recessed, 8 GPH			4	4		416	89		505	590	
	3040	11.5 GPH			4	4		440	89		529	615	
	3200	For glass filler in addition to bubbler, add						69			69	76	
	3240	For stainless steel cabinet, add						27			27	30	
	3300	Semi-recessed, 8.1 GPH		Q-1	4	4		468	89		557	645	
	3320	12 GPH		Q-1	4	4	Ea.	490	89		579	670	
	3340	For glass filler, add						69			69	76	
	3360	For stainless steel cabinet, add						27			27	30	
	3400	Full recessed, stainless steel, 8 GPH		Q-1	3.50	4.570		765	100		865	990	
	3420	11.5 GPH		*	3.50	4.570		825	100		925	1,050	
	3460	For glass filler, add						69			69	76	
	3600	For mounting can only						180			180	200	
	4600	Floor mounted, flush-to-wall											
	4640	4 GPH		1 Plum	3	2.670	Ea.	312	66		378	440	
	4680	8.2 GPH			3	2.670		354	66		420	485	
	4720	14.3 GPH			3	2.670		370	66		436	505	
	4960	For hot and cold water, add						132			132	145	
	4980	For stainless steel cabinet, add						65.50			65.50	72	
	5040	14.3 GPH		1 Plum	2	4		540	99		639	740	

SECTION A
UNIT PRICE COSTS

TABLE OF CONTENTS

DIV. NO.		PAGE
010	Overhead	1
013	Submittals	3
015	Construction Facilities & Temporary Controls	4
016	Material & Equipment	7
017	Contract Closeout	11
020	Subsurface Investigation & Demolition	11
021	Site Preparation	16
022	Earthwork	17
026	Piped Utilities	19
027	Sewerage & Drainage	22
028	Site Improvements	28
031	Concrete Formwork	29
033	Cast-in-Place Concrete	29
050	Metal Materials, Finishes & Fastenings	29
051	Structural Metal Framing	30
061	Rough Carpentry	31
064	Custom Casework	31
076	Flashing & Sheet Metal	32
101	Chalkboards, Compartments & Cubicles	33
108	Toilet and Bath Accessories and Scales	35
110	Equipment	37
111	Mercantile, Commercial & Detention Equipment	37
114	Food Service, Residential, Darkroom, Athletic Equipment	38
116	Laboratory, Planetarium, Observatory Equipment	40
117	Medical Equipment	41
130	Special Construction	41
131	Pre-Eng. Structures, Pools & Ice Rinks	42
146	Hoists & Cranes	43
151	Pipe & Fittings	43
152	Plumbing Fixtures	149
153	Plumbing Appliances	162
154	Fire Extinguishing Systems	169
155	Heating	179
156	HVAC Piping Specialties	199
157	Air Conditioning/Ventilating	207
160	Raceways	215
163	Starters, Boards, & Switches	218
168	Special Systems	219
171	S.F., C.F. & % of Total Costs	228

CREWS

Crew No.	Bare Costs		Incl. Subs O & P		Cost Per Man-hour	
Crew A-1	Hr.	Daily	Hr.	Daily	Bare Costs	Incl. O&P
1 Building Laborer	$17.15	$137.20	$26.05	$208.40	$17.15	$26.05
1 Gas Eng. Power Tool		53.20		58.50	6.65	7.31
8 M.H., Daily Totals		$190.40		$266.90	$23.80	$33.36
Crew A-1A	Hr.	Daily	Hr.	Daily	Bare Costs	Incl. O&P
1 Laborer	$17.15	$137.20	$26.05	$208.40	$17.15	$26.05
1 Power Equipment		115.40		126.95	14.42	15.86
8 M.H., Daily Totals		$252.60		$335.35	$31.57	$41.91
Crew A-2	Hr.	Daily	Hr.	Daily	Bare Costs	Incl. O&P
2 Building Laborers	$17.15	$274.40	$26.05	$416.80	$17.36	$26.23
1 Truck Driver (light)	17.80	142.40	26.60	212.80		
1 Light Truck, 1.5 Ton		138.20		152.00	5.75	6.33
24 M.H., Daily Totals		$555.00		$781.60	$23.11	$32.56
Crew A-3	Hr.	Daily	Hr.	Daily	Bare Costs	Incl. O&P
1 Truck Driver (heavy)	$18.10	$144.80	$27.05	$216.40	$18.10	$27.05
1 Dump Truck, 12 ton		282.80		311.10	35.35	38.88
8 M.H., Daily Totals		$427.60		$527.50	$53.45	$65.93
Crew A-4	Hr.	Daily	Hr.	Daily	Bare Costs	Incl. O&P
2 Carpenters	$21.60	$345.60	$32.80	$524.80	$21.16	$31.88
1 Painter, Ordinary	20.30	162.40	30.05	240.40		
24 M.H., Daily Totals		$508.00		$765.20	$21.16	$31.88
Crew A-5	Hr.	Daily	Hr.	Daily	Bare Costs	Incl. O&P
2 Building Laborers	$17.15	$274.40	$26.05	$416.80	$17.22	$26.11
.25 Truck Driver (light)	17.80	35.60	26.60	53.20		
.25 Light Truck, 1.5 Ton		34.55		38.00	1.91	2.11
18 M.H., Daily Totals		$344.55		$508.00	$19.13	$28.22
Crew A-6	Hr.	Daily	Hr.	Daily	Bare Costs	Incl. O&P
1 Chief Of Party	$21.10	$168.80	$31.50	$252.00	$19.95	$29.80
1 Instrument Man	18.80	150.40	28.10	224.80		
16 M.H., Daily Totals		$319.20		$476.80	$19.95	$29.80
Crew A-7	Hr.	Daily	Hr.	Daily	Bare Costs	Incl. O&P
1 Chief Of Party	$21.10	$168.80	$31.50	$252.00	$18.88	$28.45
1 Instrument Man	18.80	150.40	28.10	224.80		
1 Rodman/Chainman	16.75	134.00	25.75	206.00		
24 M.H., Daily Totals		$453.20		$682.80	$18.88	$28.45
Crew A-8	Hr.	Daily	Hr.	Daily	Bare Costs	Incl. O&P
1 Chief Of Party	$21.10	$168.80	$31.50	$252.00	$18.35	$27.77
1 Instrument Man	18.80	150.40	28.10	224.80		
2 Rodmen/Chainmen	16.75	268.00	25.75	412.00		
32 M.H., Daily Totals		$587.20		$888.80	$18.35	$27.77
Crew A-9	Hr.	Daily	Hr.	Daily	Bare Costs	Incl. O&P
1 Asbestos Foreman	$24.45	$195.60	$37.70	$301.60	$24.01	$37.00
7 Asbestos Workers	23.95	1341.20	36.90	2066.40		
4 Airless Sprayers		101.60		111.75		
3 HDPA Vacs., 16 Gal.		72.00		79.20	2.71	2.98
64 M.H., Daily Totals		$1710.40		$2558.95	$26.72	$39.98

Crew No.	Bare Costs		Incl. Subs O & P		Cost Per Man-hour	
Crew A-10	Hr.	Daily	Hr.	Daily	Bare Costs	Incl. O&P
1 Asbestos Foreman	$24.45	$195.60	$37.70	$301.60	$24.01	$37.00
7 Asbestos Workers	23.95	1341.20	36.90	2066.40		
2 HEPA Vacs., 16 Gal.		48.00		52.80	.75	.82
64 M.H., Daily Totals		$1584.80		$2420.80	$24.76	$37.82
Crew A-11	Hr.	Daily	Hr.	Daily	Bare Costs	Incl. O&P
1 Asbestos Foreman	$24.45	$195.60	$37.70	$301.60	$24.01	$37.00
7 Asbestos Workers	23.95	1341.20	36.90	2066.40		
4 Airless Sprayers		101.60		111.75		
2 HEPA Vacs., 16 Gal.		48.00		52.80		
2 Chipping Hammers		18.40		20.25	2.62	2.88
64 M.H., Daily Totals		$1704.80		$2552.80	$26.63	$39.88
Crew A-12	Hr.	Daily	Hr.	Daily	Bare Costs	Incl. O&P
1 Asbestos Foreman	$24.45	$195.60	$37.70	$301.60	$24.01	$37.00
7 Asbestos Workers	23.95	1341.20	36.90	2066.40		
4 Airless Sprayers		101.60		111.75		
2 HEPA Vacs., 16 Gal.		48.00		52.80		
1 Large Prod. Vac. Loader		440.80		484.90	9.22	10.14
64 M.H., Daily Totals		$2127.20		$3017.45	$33.23	$47.14
Crew B-1	Hr.	Daily	Hr.	Daily	Bare Costs	Incl. O&P
1 Labor Foreman (outside)	$19.15	$153.20	$29.05	$232.40	$17.81	$27.05
2 Building Laborers	17.15	274.40	26.05	416.80		
24 M.H., Daily Totals		$427.60		$649.20	$17.81	$27.05
Crew B-2	Hr.	Daily	Hr.	Daily	Bare Costs	Incl. O&P
1 Labor Foreman (outside)	$19.15	$153.20	$29.05	$232.40	$17.55	$26.65
4 Building Laborers	17.15	548.80	26.05	833.60		
40 M.H., Daily Totals		$702.00		$1066.00	$17.55	$26.65
Crew B-3	Hr.	Daily	Hr.	Daily	Bare Costs	Incl. O&P
1 Labor Foreman (outside)	$19.15	$153.20	$29.05	$232.40	$18.62	$28.04
2 Building Laborers	17.15	274.40	26.05	416.80		
1 Equip. Oper. (med.)	22.10	176.80	33.00	264.00		
2 Truck Drivers (heavy)	18.10	289.60	27.05	432.80		
F.E. Loader, T.M., 2.5 C.Y.		769.60		846.55		
2 Dump Trucks, 16 Ton		692.80		762.10	30.46	33.51
48 M.H., Daily Totals		$2356.40		$2954.65	$49.08	$61.55
Crew B-4	Hr.	Daily	Hr.	Daily	Bare Costs	Incl. O&P
1 Labor Foreman (outside)	$19.15	$153.20	$29.05	$232.40	$17.64	$26.71
4 Building Laborers	17.15	548.80	26.05	833.60		
1 Truck Driver (heavy)	18.10	144.80	27.05	216.40		
1 Tractor, 4 x 2, 195 H.P.		255.60		281.15		
1 Platform Trailer		124.80		137.30	7.92	8.71
48 M.H., Daily Totals		$1227.20		$1700.85	$25.56	$35.42
Crew B-5	Hr.	Daily	Hr.	Daily	Bare Costs	Incl. O&P
1 Labor Foreman (outside)	$19.15	$153.20	$29.05	$232.40	$19.44	$29.31
4 Building Laborers	17.15	548.80	26.05	833.60		
2 Equip. Oper. (med.)	22.10	353.60	33.00	528.00		
1 Mechanic	23.60	188.80	35.25	282.00		
1 Air Compr., 250 C.F.M.		84.00		92.40		
Air Tools & Accessories		27.60		30.35		
2-50 Ft. Air Hoses, 1.5" Dia.		9.60		10.55		
F.E. Loader, T.M., 2.5 C.Y.		769.60		846.55	13.91	15.31
64 M.H., Daily Totals		$2135.20		$2855.85	$33.35	$44.62

CREWS

Crew No.	Bare Costs		Incl. Subs O & P		Cost Per Man-hour	
Crew B-6	Hr.	Daily	Hr.	Daily	Bare Costs	Incl. O&P
2 Building Laborers	$17.15	$274.40	$26.05	$416.80	$18.46	$27.86
1 Equip. Oper. (light)	21.10	168.80	31.50	252.00		
1 Backhoe Loader, 48 H.P.		181.40		199.55	7.55	8.31
24 M.H., Daily Totals		$624.60		$868.35	$26.01	$36.17
Crew B-7	Hr.	Daily	Hr.	Daily	Bare Costs	Incl. O&P
1 Labor Foreman (outside)	$19.15	$153.20	$29.05	$232.40	$18.30	$27.70
4 Building Laborers	17.15	548.80	26.05	833.60		
1 Equip. Oper. (med.)	22.10	176.80	33.00	264.00		
1 Chipping Machine		169.20		186.10		
F.E. Loader, T.M., 2.5 C.Y.		769.60		846.55		
2 Chain Saws		79.60		87.55	21.21	23.33
48 M.H., Daily Totals		$1897.20		$2450.20	$39.51	$51.03
Crew B-7A	Hr.	Daily	Hr.	Daily	Bare Costs	Incl. O&P
2 Laborers	$17.15	$274.40	$26.05	$416.80	$18.46	$27.86
1 Equip. Oper. (light)	21.10	168.80	31.50	252.00		
1 Rake w/Tractor		178.60		196.45		
2 Chain Saws		38.80		42.70	9.05	9.96
24 M.H., Daily Totals		$660.60		$907.95	$27.51	$37.82
Crew B-8	Hr.	Daily	Hr.	Daily	Bare Costs	Incl. O&P
1 Labor Foreman (outside)	$19.15	$153.20	$29.05	$232.40	$19.08	$28.66
2 Building Laborers	17.15	274.40	26.05	416.80		
2 Equip. Oper. (med.)	22.10	353.60	33.00	528.00		
1 Equip. Oper. Oiler	18.80	150.40	28.10	224.80		
2 Truck Drivers (heavy)	18.10	289.60	27.05	432.80		
1 Hyd. Crane, 25 Ton		476.00		523.60		
F.E. Loader, T.M., 2.5 C.Y.		769.60		846.55		
2 Dump Trucks, 16 Ton		692.80		762.10	30.28	33.31
64 M.H., Daily Totals		$3159.60		$3967.05	$49.36	$61.97
Crew B-9	Hr.	Daily	Hr.	Daily	Bare Costs	Incl. O&P
1 Labor Foreman (outside)	$19.15	$153.20	$29.05	$232.40	$17.55	$26.65
4 Building Laborers	17.15	548.80	26.05	833.60		
1 Air Compr., 250 C.F.M.		84.00		92.40		
Air Tools & Accessories		27.60		30.35		
2-50 Ft. Air Hoses, 1.5" Dia.		9.60		10.55	3.03	3.33
40 M.H., Daily Totals		$823.20		$1199.30	$20.58	$29.98
Crew B-10	Hr.	Daily	Hr.	Daily	Bare Costs	Incl. O&P
1 Equip. Oper. (med.)	$22.10	$176.80	$33.00	$264.00	$20.45	$30.68
.5 Building Laborer	17.15	68.60	26.05	104.20		
12 M.H., Daily Totals		$245.40		$368.20	$20.45	$30.68
Crew B-10A	Hr.	Daily	Hr.	Daily	Bare Costs	Incl. O&P
1 Equip. Oper. (med.)	$22.10	$176.80	$33.00	$264.00	$20.45	$30.68
.5 Building Laborer	17.15	68.60	26.05	104.20		
1 Roll. Compact., 2K Lbs.		71.60		78.75	5.96	6.56
12 M.H., Daily Totals		$317.00		$446.95	$26.41	$37.24
Crew B-10B	Hr.	Daily	Hr.	Daily	Bare Costs	Incl. O&P
1 Equip. Oper. (med.)	$22.10	$176.80	$33.00	$264.00	$20.45	$30.68
.5 Building Laborer	17.15	68.60	26.05	104.20		
1 Dozer, 200 H.P.		762.60		838.85	63.55	69.90
12 M.H., Daily Totals		$1008.00		$1207.05	$84.00	$100.58
Crew B-10C	Hr.	Daily	Hr.	Daily	Bare Costs	Incl. O&P
1 Equip. Oper. (med.)	$22.10	$176.80	$33.00	$264.00	$20.45	$30.68
.5 Building Laborer	17.15	68.60	26.05	104.20		
1 Dozer, 200 H.P.		762.60		838.85		
1 Vibratory Roller, Towed		86.80		95.50	70.78	77.86
12 M.H., Daily Totals		$1094.80		$1302.55	$91.23	$108.54
Crew B-10D	Hr.	Daily	Hr.	Daily	Bare Costs	Incl. O&P
1 Equip. Oper. (med.)	$22.10	$176.80	$33.00	$264.00	$20.45	$30.68
.5 Building Laborer	17.15	68.60	26.05	104.20		
1 Dozer, 200 H.P.		762.60		838.85		
1 Sheepsft. Roller, Towed		113.80		125.20	73.03	80.33
12 M.H., Daily Totals		$1121.80		$1332.25	$93.48	$111.01
Crew B-10E	Hr.	Daily	Hr.	Daily	Bare Costs	Incl. O&P
1 Equip. Oper. (med.)	$22.10	$176.80	$33.00	$264.00	$20.45	$30.68
.5 Building Laborer	17.15	68.60	26.05	104.20		
1 Tandem Roller, 5 Ton		113.00		124.30	9.41	10.35
12 M.H., Daily Totals		$358.40		$492.50	$29.86	$41.03
Crew B-10F	Hr.	Daily	Hr.	Daily	Bare Costs	Incl. O&P
1 Equip. Oper. (med.)	$22.10	$176.80	$33.00	$264.00	$20.45	$30.68
.5 Building Laborer	17.15	68.60	26.05	104.20		
1 Tandem Roller, 10 Ton		179.00		196.90	14.91	16.40
12 M.H., Daily Totals		$424.40		$565.10	$35.36	$47.08
Crew B-10G	Hr.	Daily	Hr.	Daily	Bare Costs	Incl. O&P
1 Equip. Oper. (med.)	$22.10	$176.80	$33.00	$264.00	$20.45	$30.68
.5 Building Laborer	17.15	68.60	26.05	104.20		
1 Sheepsft. Roll., 130 H.P.		462.40		508.65	38.53	42.38
12 M.H., Daily Totals		$707.80		$876.85	$58.98	$73.06
Crew B-10H	Hr.	Daily	Hr.	Daily	Bare Costs	Incl. O&P
1 Equip. Oper. (med.)	$22.10	$176.80	$33.00	$264.00	$20.45	$30.68
.5 Building Laborer	17.15	68.60	26.05	104.20		
1 Diaphr. Water Pump, 2"		14.00		15.40		
1-20 Ft. Suction Hose, 2"		4.40		4.85		
2-50 Ft. Disch. Hoses, 2"		5.20		5.70	1.96	2.16
12 M.H., Daily Totals		$269.00		$394.15	$22.41	$32.84
Crew B-10I	Hr.	Daily	Hr.	Daily	Bare Costs	Incl. O&P
1 Equip. Oper. (med.)	$22.10	$176.80	$33.00	$264.00	$20.45	$30.68
.5 Building Laborer	17.15	68.60	26.05	104.20		
1 Diaphr. Water Pump, 4"		49.40		54.35		
1-20 Ft. Suction Hose, 4"		10.90		12.00		
2-50 Ft. Disch. Hoses, 4"		7.60		8.35	5.65	6.22
12 M.H., Daily Totals		$313.30		$442.90	$26.10	$36.90
Crew B-10J	Hr.	Daily	Hr.	Daily	Bare Costs	Incl. O&P
1 Equip. Oper. (med.)	$22.10	$176.80	$33.00	$264.00	$20.45	$30.68
.5 Building Laborer	17.15	68.60	26.05	104.20		
1 Centr. Water Pump, 3"		26.00		28.60		
1-20 Ft. Suction Hose, 3"		6.60		7.25		
2-50 Ft. Disch. Hoses, 3"		6.80		7.50	3.28	3.61
12 M.H., Daily Totals		$284.80		$411.55	$23.73	$34.29

CREWS

Crew No.	Bare Costs		Incl. Subs O & P		Cost Per Man-hour	
Crew B-10K	Hr.	Daily	Hr.	Daily	Bare Costs	Incl. O&P
1 Equip. Oper. (med.)	$22.10	$176.80	$33.00	$264.00	$20.45	$30.68
.5 Building Laborer	17.15	68.60	26.05	104.20		
1 Centr. Water Pump, 6"		141.80		156.00		
1-20 Ft. Suction Hose, 6"		22.40		24.65		
2-50 Ft. Disch. Hoses, 6"		25.20		27.70	15.78	17.36
12 M.H., Daily Totals		$434.80		$576.55	$36.23	$48.04
Crew B-10L	Hr.	Daily	Hr.	Daily	Bare Costs	Incl. O&P
1 Equip. Oper. (med.)	$22.10	$176.80	$33.00	$264.00	$20.45	$30.68
.5 Building Laborer	17.15	68.60	26.05	104.20		
1 Dozer, 75 H.P.		268.00		294.80	22.33	24.56
12 M.H., Daily Totals		$513.40		$663.00	$42.78	$55.24
Crew B-10M	Hr.	Daily	Hr.	Daily	Bare Costs	Incl. O&P
1 Equip. Oper. (med.)	$22.10	$176.80	$33.00	$264.00	$20.45	$30.68
.5 Building Laborer	17.15	68.60	26.05	104.20		
1 Dozer, 300 H.P.		819.20		901.10	68.26	75.09
12 M.H., Daily Totals		$1064.60		$1269.30	$88.71	$105.77
Crew B-10N	Hr.	Daily	Hr.	Daily	Bare Costs	Incl. O&P
1 Equip. Oper. (med.)	$22.10	$176.80	$33.00	$264.00	$20.45	$30.68
.5 Building Laborer	17.15	68.60	26.05	104.20		
F.E. Loader, T.M., 1.5 C.Y.		337.60		371.35	28.13	30.94
12 M.H., Daily Totals		$583.00		$739.55	$48.58	$61.62
Crew B-10O	Hr.	Daily	Hr.	Daily	Bare Costs	Incl. O&P
1 Equip. Oper. (med.)	$22.10	$176.80	$33.00	$264.00	$20.45	$30.68
.5 Building Laborer	17.15	68.60	26.05	104.20		
F.E. Loader, T.M., 2.25 C.Y.		413.05		454.35	34.42	37.86
12 M.H., Daily Totals		$658.45		$822.55	$54.87	$68.54
Crew B-10P	Hr.	Daily	Hr.	Daily	Bare Costs	Incl. O&P
1 Equip. Oper. (med.)	$22.10	$176.80	$33.00	$264.00	$20.45	$30.68
.5 Building Laborer	17.15	68.60	26.05	104.20		
F.E. Loader, T.M., 2.5 C.Y.		769.60		846.55	64.13	70.54
12 M.H., Daily Totals		$1015.00		$1214.75	$84.58	$101.22
Crew B-10Q	Hr.	Daily	Hr.	Daily	Bare Costs	Incl. O&P
1 Equip. Oper. (med.)	$22.10	$176.80	$33.00	$264.00	$20.45	$30.68
.5 Building Laborer	17.15	68.60	26.05	104.20		
F.E. Loader, T.M., 5 C.Y.		957.20		1052.90	79.76	87.74
12 M.H., Daily Totals		$1202.60		$1421.10	$100.21	$118.42
Crew B-10R	Hr.	Daily	Hr.	Daily	Bare Costs	Incl. O&P
1 Equip. Oper. (med.)	$22.10	$176.80	$33.00	$264.00	$20.45	$30.68
.5 Building Laborer	17.15	68.60	26.05	104.20		
F.E. Loader, W.M., 1 C.Y.		215.60		237.15	17.96	19.76
12 M.H., Daily Totals		$461.00		$605.35	$38.41	$50.44
Crew B-10S	Hr.	Daily	Hr.	Daily	Bare Costs	Incl. O&P
1 Equip. Oper. (med.)	$22.10	$176.80	$33.00	$264.00	$20.45	$30.68
.5 Building Laborer	17.15	68.60	26.05	104.20		
F.E. Loader, W.M., 1.5 C.Y.		294.40		323.85	24.53	26.98
12 M.H., Daily Totals		$539.80		$692.05	$44.98	$57.66

Crew No.	Bare Costs		Incl. Subs O & P		Cost Per Man-hour	
Crew B-10T	Hr.	Daily	Hr.	Daily	Bare Costs	Incl. O&P
1 Equip. Oper. (med.)	$22.10	$176.80	$33.00	$264.00	$20.45	$30.68
.5 Building Laborer	17.15	68.60	26.05	104.20		
F.E. Loader, W.M., 2.5 C.Y.		426.80		469.50	35.56	39.12
12 M.H., Daily Totals		$672.20		$837.70	$56.01	$69.80
Crew B-10U	Hr.	Daily	Hr.	Daily	Bare Costs	Incl. O&P
1 Equip. Oper. (med.)	$22.10	$176.80	$33.00	$264.00	$20.45	$30.68
.5 Building Laborer	17.15	68.60	26.05	104.20		
F.E. Loader, W.M., 5.5 C.Y.		909.80		1000.80	75.81	83.40
12 M.H., Daily Totals		$1155.20		$1369.00	$96.26	$114.08
Crew B-10V	Hr.	Daily	Hr.	Daily	Bare Costs	Incl. O&P
1 Equip. Oper. (med.)	$22.10	$176.80	$33.00	$264.00	$20.45	$30.68
.5 Building Laborer	17.15	68.60	26.05	104.20		
1 Dozer, 700 H.P.		2371.20		2608.30	197.60	217.35
12 M.H., Daily Totals		$2616.60		$2976.50	$218.05	$248.03
Crew B-10W	Hr.	Daily	Hr.	Daily	Bare Costs	Incl. O&P
1 Equip. Oper. (med.)	$22.10	$176.80	$33.00	$264.00	$20.45	$30.68
.5 Building Laborer	17.15	68.60	26.05	104.20		
1 Dozer, 105 H.P.		392.80		432.10	32.73	36.00
12 M.H., Daily Totals		$638.20		$800.30	$53.18	$66.68
Crew B-10X	Hr.	Daily	Hr.	Daily	Bare Costs	Incl. O&P
1 Equip. Oper. (med.)	$22.10	$176.80	$33.00	$264.00	$20.45	$30.68
.5 Building Laborer	17.15	68.60	26.05	104.20		
1 Dozer, 410 H.P.		1106.00		1216.60	92.16	101.38
12 M.H., Daily Totals		$1351.40		$1584.80	$112.61	$132.06
Crew B-10Y	Hr.	Daily	Hr.	Daily	Bare Costs	Incl. O&P
1 Equip. Oper. (med.)	$22.10	$176.80	$33.00	$264.00	$20.45	$30.68
.5 Building Laborer	17.15	68.60	26.05	104.20		
1 Vibratory Drum Roller		287.00		315.70	23.91	26.30
12 M.H., Daily Totals		$532.40		$683.90	$44.36	$56.98
Crew B-11	Hr.	Daily	Hr.	Daily	Bare Costs	Incl. O&P
1 Equipment Oper. (med.)	$22.10	$176.80	$33.00	$264.00	$19.62	$29.52
1 Building Laborer	17.15	137.20	26.05	208.40		
16 M.H., Daily Totals		$314.00		$472.40	$19.62	$29.52
Crew B-11A	Hr.	Daily	Hr.	Daily	Bare Costs	Incl. O&P
1 Equipment Oper. (med.)	$22.10	$176.80	$33.00	$264.00	$19.62	$29.52
1 Building Laborer	17.15	137.20	26.05	208.40		
1 Dozer, 200 H.P.		762.60		838.85	47.66	52.42
16 M.H., Daily Totals		$1076.60		$1311.25	$67.28	$81.94
Crew B-11B	Hr.	Daily	Hr.	Daily	Bare Costs	Incl. O&P
1 Equipment Oper. (med.)	$22.10	$176.80	$33.00	$264.00	$19.62	$29.52
1 Building Laborer	17.15	137.20	26.05	208.40		
1 Dozer, 200 H.P.		762.60		838.85		
1 Air Powered Tamper		12.80		14.10		
1 Air Compr. 365 C.F.M.		197.40		217.15		
2-50 Ft. Air Hoses, 1.5" Dia.		9.60		10.55	61.40	67.54
16 M.H., Daily Totals		$1296.40		$1553.05	$81.02	$97.06

CREWS

Crew No.	Bare Costs		Incl. Subs O & P		Cost Per Man-hour	
Crew B-11C	Hr.	Daily	Hr.	Daily	Bare Costs	Incl. O&P
1 Equipment Oper. (med.)	$22.10	$176.80	$33.00	$264.00	$19.62	$29.52
1 Building Laborer	17.15	137.20	26.05	208.40		
1 Backhoe Loader, 48 H.P.		181.40		199.55	11.33	12.47
16 M.H., Daily Totals		$495.40		$671.95	$30.95	$41.99
Crew B-11K	Hr.	Daily	Hr.	Daily	Bare Costs	Incl. O&P
1 Equipment Oper. (med.)	$22.10	$176.80	$33.00	$264.00	$19.62	$29.52
1 Building Laborer	17.15	137.20	26.05	208.40		
1 Trencher, 8' D., 16" W.		402.00		442.20	25.12	27.63
16 M.H., Daily Totals		$716.00		$914.60	$44.74	$57.15
Crew B-11L	Hr.	Daily	Hr.	Daily	Bare Costs	Incl. O&P
1 Equipment Oper. (med.)	$22.10	$176.80	$33.00	$264.00	$19.62	$29.52
1 Building Laborer	17.15	137.20	26.05	208.40		
1 Grader, 30,000 Lbs.		513.40		564.75	32.08	35.29
16 M.H., Daily Totals		$827.40		$1037.15	$51.70	$64.81
Crew B-11M	Hr.	Daily	Hr.	Daily	Bare Costs	Incl. O&P
1 Equipment Oper. (med.)	$22.10	$176.80	$33.00	$264.00	$19.62	$29.52
1 Building Laborer	17.15	137.20	26.05	208.40		
1 Backhoe Loader, 80 H.P.		281.00		309.10	17.56	19.31
16 M.H., Daily Totals		$595.00		$781.50	$37.18	$48.83
Crew B-12	Hr.	Daily	Hr.	Daily	Bare Costs	Incl. O&P
1 Equip. Oper. (crane)	$22.90	$183.20	$34.20	$273.60	$20.85	$31.15
1 Equip. Oper. Oiler	18.80	150.40	28.10	224.80		
16 M.H., Daily Totals		$333.60		$498.40	$20.85	$31.15
Crew B-12A	Hr.	Daily	Hr.	Daily	Bare Costs	Incl. O&P
1 Equip. Oper. (crane)	$22.90	$183.20	$34.20	$273.60	$20.85	$31.15
1 Equip. Oper. Oiler	18.80	150.40	28.10	224.80		
1 Hyd. Excavator, 1 C.Y.		556.60		612.25	34.78	38.26
16 M.H., Daily Totals		$890.20		$1110.65	$55.63	$69.41
Crew B-12B	Hr.	Daily	Hr.	Daily	Bare Costs	Incl. O&P
1 Equip. Oper. (crane)	$22.90	$183.20	$34.20	$273.60	$20.85	$31.15
1 Equip. Oper. Oiler	18.80	150.40	28.10	224.80		
1 Hyd. Excavator, 1.5 C.Y.		668.00		734.80	41.75	45.92
16 M.H., Daily Totals		$1001.60		$1233.20	$62.60	$77.07
Crew B-12C	Hr.	Daily	Hr.	Daily	Bare Costs	Incl. O&P
1 Equip. Oper. (crane)	$22.90	$183.20	$34.20	$273.60	$20.85	$31.15
1 Equip. Oper. Oiler	18.80	150.40	28.10	224.80		
1 Hyd. Excavator, 2 C.Y.		927.00		1019.70	57.93	63.73
16 M.H., Daily Totals		$1260.60		$1518.10	$78.78	$94.88
Crew B-12D	Hr.	Daily	Hr.	Daily	Bare Costs	Incl. O&P
1 Equip. Oper. (crane)	$22.90	$183.20	$34.20	$273.60	$20.85	$31.15
1 Equip. Oper. Oiler	18.80	150.40	28.10	224.80		
1 Hyd. Excavator, 3.5 C.Y.		1981.80		2180.00	123.86	136.25
16 M.H., Daily Totals		$2315.40		$2678.40	$144.71	$167.40
Crew B-12E	Hr.	Daily	Hr.	Daily	Bare Costs	Incl. O&P
1 Equip. Oper. (crane)	$22.90	$183.20	$34.20	$273.60	$20.85	$31.15
1 Equip. Oper. Oiler	18.80	150.40	28.10	224.80		
1 Hyd. Excavator, .5 C.Y.		331.60		364.75	20.72	22.79
16 M.H., Daily Totals		$665.20		$863.15	$41.57	$53.94
Crew B-12F	Hr.	Daily	Hr.	Daily	Bare Costs	Incl. O&P
1 Equip. Oper. (crane)	$22.90	$183.20	$34.20	$273.60	$20.85	$31.15
1 Equip. Oper. Oiler	18.80	150.40	28.10	224.80		
1 Hyd. Excavator, .75 C.Y.		449.60		494.55	28.10	30.90
16 M.H., Daily Totals		$783.20		$992.95	$48.95	$62.05
Crew B-12G	Hr.	Daily	Hr.	Daily	Bare Costs	Incl. O&P
1 Equip. Oper. (crane)	$22.90	$183.20	$34.20	$273.60	$20.85	$31.15
1 Equip. Oper. Oiler	18.80	150.40	28.10	224.80		
1 Power Shovel, .5 C.Y.		358.00		393.80		
1 Clamshell Bucket, .5 C.Y.		46.40		51.05	25.27	27.80
16 M.H., Daily Totals		$738.00		$943.25	$46.12	$58.95
Crew B-12H	Hr.	Daily	Hr.	Daily	Bare Costs	Incl. O&P
1 Equip. Oper. (crane)	$22.90	$183.20	$34.20	$273.60	$20.85	$31.15
1 Equip. Oper. Oiler	18.80	150.40	28.10	224.80		
1 Power Shovel, 1 C.Y.		411.60		452.75		
1 Clamshell Bucket, 1 C.Y.		59.20		65.10	29.42	32.36
16 M.H., Daily Totals		$804.40		$1016.25	$50.27	$63.51
Crew B-12I	Hr.	Daily	Hr.	Daily	Bare Costs	Incl. O&P
1 Equip. Oper. (crane)	$22.90	$183.20	$34.20	$273.60	$20.85	$31.15
1 Equip. Oper. Oiler	18.80	150.40	28.10	224.80		
1 Power Shovel, .75 C.Y.		382.40		420.65		
1 Dragline Bucket, .75 C.Y.		28.60		31.45	25.68	28.25
16 M.H., Daily Totals		$744.60		$950.50	$46.53	$59.40
Crew B-12J	Hr.	Daily	Hr.	Daily	Bare Costs	Incl. O&P
1 Equip. Oper. (crane)	$22.90	$183.20	$34.20	$273.60	$20.85	$31.15
1 Equip. Oper. Oiler	18.80	150.40	28.10	224.80		
1 Gradall, 3 Ton, .5 C.Y.		528.00		580.80	33.00	36.30
16 M.H., Daily Totals		$861.60		$1079.20	$53.85	$67.45
Crew B-12K	Hr.	Daily	Hr.	Daily	Bare Costs	Incl. O&P
1 Equip. Oper. (crane)	$22.90	$183.20	$34.20	$273.60	$20.85	$31.15
1 Equip. Oper. Oiler	18.80	150.40	28.10	224.80		
1 Gradall, 3 Ton, 1 C.Y.		734.80		808.30	45.92	50.51
16 M.H., Daily Totals		$1068.40		$1306.70	$66.77	$81.66
Crew B-12L	Hr.	Daily	Hr.	Daily	Bare Costs	Incl. O&P
1 Equip. Oper. (crane)	$22.90	$183.20	$34.20	$273.60	$20.85	$31.15
1 Equip. Oper. Oiler	18.80	150.40	28.10	224.80		
1 Power Shovel, .5 C.Y.		358.00		393.80		
1 F.E. Attachment, .5 C.Y.		45.00		49.50	25.18	27.70
16 M.H., Daily Totals		$736.60		$941.70	$46.03	$58.85
Crew B-12M	Hr.	Daily	Hr.	Daily	Bare Costs	Incl. O&P
1 Equip. Oper. (crane)	$22.90	$183.20	$34.20	$273.60	$20.85	$31.15
1 Equip. Oper. Oiler	18.80	150.40	28.10	224.80		
1 Power Shovel, .75		382.40		420.65		
1 F.E. Attachment, .75 C.Y.		84.80		93.30	29.20	32.12
16 M.H., Daily Totals		$800.80		$1012.35	$50.05	$63.27
Crew B-12N	Hr.	Daily	Hr.	Daily	Bare Costs	Incl. O&P
1 Equip. Oper. (crane)	$22.90	$183.20	$34.20	$273.60	$20.85	$31.15
1 Equip. Oper. Oiler	18.80	150.40	28.10	224.80		
1 Power Shovel, 1 C.Y.		411.60		452.75		
1 F.E. Attachment, 1 C.Y.		119.40		131.35	33.18	36.50
16 M.H., Daily Totals		$864.60		$1082.50	$54.03	$67.65

CREWS

Crew No.	Bare Costs		Incl. Subs O & P		Cost Per Man-hour	
Crew B-12O	Hr.	Daily	Hr.	Daily	Bare Costs	Incl. O&P
1 Equip. Oper. (crane)	$22.90	$183.20	$34.20	$273.60	$20.85	$31.15
1 Equip. Oper. Oiler	18.80	150.40	28.10	224.80		
1 Power Shovel, 1.5 C.Y.		630.40		693.45		
1 F.E. Attachment, 1.5 C.Y.		133.80		147.20	47.76	52.54
16 M.H., Daily Totals		$1097.80		$1339.05	$68.61	$83.69
Crew B-12P	Hr.	Daily	Hr.	Daily	Bare Costs	Incl. O&P
1 Equip. Oper. (crane)	$22.90	$183.20	$34.20	$273.60	$20.85	$31.15
1 Equip. Oper. Oiler	18.80	150.40	28.10	224.80		
1 Crawler Crane, 40 Ton		630.40		693.45		
1 Dragline Bucket, 1.5 C.Y.		39.80		43.80	41.88	46.07
16 M.H., Daily Totals		$1003.80		$1235.65	$62.73	$77.22
Crew B-12Q	Hr.	Daily	Hr.	Daily	Bare Costs	Incl. O&P
1 Equip. Oper. (crane)	$22.90	$183.20	$34.20	$273.60	$20.85	$31.15
1 Equip. Oper. Oiler	18.80	150.40	28.10	224.80		
1 Hyd. Excavator, 5/8 C.Y.		344.60		379.05	21.53	23.69
16 M.H., Daily Totals		$678.20		$877.45	$42.38	$54.84
Crew B-12R	Hr.	Daily	Hr.	Daily	Bare Costs	Incl. O&P
1 Equip. Oper. (crane)	$22.90	$183.20	$34.20	$273.60	$20.85	$31.15
1 Equip. Oper. Oiler	18.80	150.40	28.10	224.80		
1 Hyd. Excavator, 1.5 C.Y.		668.00		734.80	41.75	45.92
16 M.H., Daily Totals		$1001.60		$1233.20	$62.60	$77.07
Crew B-12S	Hr.	Daily	Hr.	Daily	Bare Costs	Incl. O&P
1 Equip. Oper. (crane)	$22.90	$183.20	$34.20	$273.60	$20.85	$31.15
1 Equip. Oper. Oiler	18.80	150.40	28.10	224.80		
1 Hyd. Excavator, 2.5 C.Y.		1587.40		1746.15	99.21	109.13
16 M.H., Daily Totals		$1921.00		$2244.55	$120.06	$140.28
Crew B-12T	Hr.	Daily	Hr.	Daily	Bare Costs	Incl. O&P
1 Equip. Oper. (crane)	$22.90	$183.20	$34.20	$273.60	$20.85	$31.15
1 Equip. Oper. Oiler	18.80	150.40	28.10	224.80		
1 Crawler Crane, 75 Ton		852.00		937.20		
1 F.E. Attachment, 3 C.Y.		249.00		273.90	68.81	75.69
16 M.H., Daily Totals		$1434.60		$1709.50	$89.66	$106.84
Crew B-12V	Hr.	Daily	Hr.	Daily	Bare Costs	Incl. O&P
1 Equip. Oper. (crane)	$22.90	$183.20	$34.20	$273.60	$20.85	$31.15
1 Equip. Oper. Oiler	18.80	150.40	28.10	224.80		
1 Crawler Crane, 75 Ton		852.00		937.20		
1 Dragline Bucket, 3 C.Y.		71.60		78.75	57.72	63.49
16 M.H., Daily Totals		$1257.20		$1514.35	$78.57	$94.64
Crew B-13	Hr.	Daily	Hr.	Daily	Bare Costs	Incl. O&P
1 Labor Foreman (outside)	$19.15	$153.20	$29.05	$232.40	$18.49	$27.93
4 Building Laborers	17.15	548.80	26.05	833.60		
1 Equip. Oper. (crane)	22.90	183.20	34.20	273.60		
1 Equip. Oper. Oiler	18.80	150.40	28.10	224.80		
1 Hyd. Crane, 25 Ton		476.00		523.60	8.50	9.35
56 M.H., Daily Totals		$1511.60		$2088.00	$26.99	$37.28
Crew B-14	Hr.	Daily	Hr.	Daily	Bare Costs	Incl. O&P
1 Labor Foreman (outside)	$19.15	$153.20	$29.05	$232.40	$18.14	$27.45
4 Building Laborers	17.15	548.80	26.05	833.60		
1 Equip. Oper. (light)	21.10	168.80	31.50	252.00		
1 Backhoe Loader, 48 H.P.		181.40		199.55	3.77	4.15
48 M.H., Daily Totals		$1052.20		$1517.55	$21.91	$31.60

Crew No.	Bare Costs		Incl. Subs O & P		Cost Per Man-hour	
Crew B-15	Hr.	Daily	Hr.	Daily	Bare Costs	Incl. O&P
1 Equipment Oper. (med)	$22.10	$176.80	$33.00	$264.00	$19.10	$28.60
.5 Building Laborer	17.15	68.60	26.05	104.20		
2 Truck Drivers (heavy)	18.10	289.60	27.05	432.80		
2 Dump Trucks, 16 Ton		692.80		762.10		
1 Dozer, 200 H.P.		762.60		838.85	51.97	57.17
28 M.H., Daily Totals		$1990.40		$2401.95	$71.07	$85.77
Crew B-16	Hr.	Daily	Hr.	Daily	Bare Costs	Incl. O&P
1 Labor Foreman (outside)	$19.15	$153.20	$29.05	$232.40	$17.88	$27.05
2 Building Laborers	17.15	274.40	26.05	416.80		
1 Truck Driver (heavy)	18.10	144.80	27.05	216.40		
1 Dump Truck, 16 Ton		346.40		381.05	10.82	11.90
32 M.H., Daily Totals		$918.80		$1246.65	$28.70	$38.95
Crew B-17	Hr.	Daily	Hr.	Daily	Bare Costs	Incl. O&P
2 Building Laborers	$17.15	$274.40	$26.05	$416.80	$18.37	$27.66
1 Equip. Oper. (light)	21.10	168.80	31.50	252.00		
1 Truck Driver (heavy)	18.10	144.80	27.05	216.40		
1 Backhoe Loader, 48 H.P.		181.40		199.55		
1 Dump Truck, 12 Ton		282.80		311.10	14.50	15.95
32 M.H., Daily Totals		$1052.20		$1395.85	$32.87	$43.61
Crew B-18	Hr.	Daily	Hr.	Daily	Bare Costs	Incl. O&P
1 Labor Foreman (outside)	$19.15	$153.20	$29.05	$232.40	$17.81	$27.05
2 Building Laborers	17.15	274.40	26.05	416.80		
1 Vibrating Compactor		40.60		44.65	1.69	1.86
24 M.H., Daily Totals		$468.20		$693.85	$19.50	$28.91
Crew B-19	Hr.	Daily	Hr.	Daily	Bare Costs	Incl. O&P
1 Pile Driver Foreman	$23.80	$190.40	$39.35	$314.80	$21.95	$35.00
4 Pile Drivers	21.80	697.60	36.05	1153.60		
2 Equip. Oper. (crane)	22.90	366.40	34.20	547.20		
1 Equip. Oper. Oiler	18.80	150.40	28.10	224.80		
1 Crane, 40 Ton & Access.		630.40		693.45		
60 L.F. Leads, 15K Ft. Lbs.		63.00		69.30		
1 Hammer, 15K Ft. Lbs.		246.40		271.05		
1 Air Compr., 600 C.F.M.		261.60		287.75		
2-50 Ft. Air Hoses, 3" Dia.		20.40		22.45	19.09	21.00
64 M.H., Daily Totals		$2626.60		$3584.40	$41.04	$56.00
Crew B-20	Hr.	Daily	Hr.	Daily	Bare Costs	Incl. O&P
1 Labor Foreman (out)	$19.15	$153.20	$29.05	$232.40	$19.46	$29.58
1 Skilled worker	22.10	176.80	33.65	269.20		
1 Building Laborer	17.15	137.20	26.05	208.40		
24 M.H., Daily Totals		$467.20		$710.00	$19.46	$29.58
Crew B-21	Hr.	Daily	Hr.	Daily	Bare Costs	Incl. O&P
1 Labor Foreman (out)	$19.15	$153.20	$29.05	$232.40	$19.95	$30.24
1 Skilled worker	22.10	176.80	33.65	269.20		
1 Building Laborer	17.15	137.20	26.05	208.40		
.5 Equip. Oper. (crane)	22.90	91.60	34.20	136.80		
.5 S.P. Crane, 5 Ton		102.20		112.40	3.65	4.01
28 M.H., Daily Totals		$661.00		$959.20	$23.60	$34.25

CREWS

Crew No.	Bare Costs		Incl. Subs O & P		Cost Per Man-hour	
Crew B-22	Hr.	Daily	Hr.	Daily	Bare Costs	Incl. O&P
1 Labor Foreman (out)	$19.15	$153.20	$29.05	$232.40	$20.15	$30.50
1 Skilled worker	22.10	176.80	33.65	269.20		
1 Building Laborer	17.15	137.20	26.05	208.40		
.75 Equip. Oper. (crane)	22.90	137.40	34.20	205.20		
.75 S.P. Crane, 5 Ton		153.30		168.65	5.11	5.62
30 M.H., Daily Totals		$757.90		$1083.85	$25.26	$36.12
Crew B-23	Hr.	Daily	Hr.	Daily	Bare Costs	Incl. O&P
1 Labor Foreman (outside)	$19.15	$153.20	$29.05	$232.40	$17.55	$26.65
4 Building Laborers	17.15	548.80	26.05	833.60		
1 Drill Rig		378.40		416.25		
1 Light Truck, 3 Ton		140.60		154.65	12.97	14.27
40 M.H., Daily Totals		$1221.00		$1636.90	$30.52	$40.92
Crew B-24	Hr.	Daily	Hr.	Daily	Bare Costs	Incl. O&P
1 Cement Finisher	$21.05	$168.40	$30.60	$244.80	$19.93	$29.81
1 Building Laborer	17.15	137.20	26.05	208.40		
1 Carpenter	21.60	172.80	32.80	262.40		
24 M.H., Daily Totals		$478.40		$715.60	$19.93	$29.81
Crew B-25	Hr.	Daily	Hr.	Daily	Bare Costs	Incl. O&P
1 Labor Foreman	$19.15	$153.20	$29.05	$232.40	$18.68	$28.21
7 Laborers	17.15	960.40	26.05	1458.80		
3 Equip. Oper. (med.)	22.10	530.40	33.00	792.00		
1 Asphalt Paver, 130 H.P		1038.60		1142.45		
1 Tandem Roller, 10 Ton		179.00		196.90		
1 Roller, Pneumatic Wheel		232.20		255.40	16.47	18.12
88 M.H., Daily Totals		$3093.80		$4077.95	$35.15	$46.33
Crew B-25B	Hr.	Daily	Hr.	Daily	Bare Costs	Incl. O&P
1 Labor Foreman	$19.15	$153.20	$29.05	$232.40	$18.96	$28.61
7 Laborers	17.15	960.40	26.05	1458.80		
4 Equip. Oper. (medium)	22.10	707.20	33.00	1056.00		
1 Asphalt Paver, 130 H.P.		1038.60		1142.45		
2 Rollers, Steel Wheel		358.00		393.80		
1 Roller, Pneumatic Wheel		232.20		255.40	16.96	18.66
96 M.H., Daily Totals		$3449.60		$4538.85	$35.92	$47.27
Crew B-26	Hr.	Daily	Hr.	Daily	Bare Costs	Incl. O&P
1 Labor Foreman (outside)	$19.15	$153.20	$29.05	$232.40	$19.14	$29.10
6 Building Laborers	17.15	823.20	26.05	1250.40		
2 Equip. Oper. (med.)	22.10	353.60	33.00	528.00		
1 Rodman (reinf.)	23.30	186.40	38.25	306.00		
1 Cement Finisher	21.05	168.40	30.60	244.80		
1 Grader, 30,000 Lbs.		513.40		564.75		
1 Paving Mach. & Equip.		1121.40		1233.55	18.57	20.43
88 M.H., Daily Totals		$3319.60		$4359.90	$37.71	$49.53
Crew B-27	Hr.	Daily	Hr.	Daily	Bare Costs	Incl. O&P
1 Labor Foreman (outside)	$19.15	$153.20	$29.05	$232.40	$17.65	$26.80
3 Building Laborers	17.15	411.60	26.05	625.20		
1 Berm Machine		44.60		49.05	1.39	1.53
32 M.H., Daily Totals		$609.40		$906.65	$19.04	$28.33
Crew B-28	Hr.	Daily	Hr.	Daily	Bare Costs	Incl. O&P
2 Carpenters	$21.60	$345.60	$32.80	$524.80	$20.11	$30.55
1 Building Laborer	17.15	137.20	26.05	208.40		
24 M.H., Daily Totals		$482.80		$733.20	$20.11	$30.55

Crew No.	Bare Costs		Incl. Subs O & P		Cost Per Man-hour	
Crew B-29	Hr.	Daily	Hr.	Daily	Bare Costs	Incl. O&P
1 Labor Foreman (outside)	$19.15	$153.20	$29.05	$232.40	$18.49	$27.93
4 Building Laborers	17.15	548.80	26.05	833.60		
1 Equip. Oper. (crane)	22.90	183.20	34.20	273.60		
1 Equip. Oper. Oiler	18.80	150.40	28.10	224.80		
1 Gradall, 3 Ton, 1/2 C.Y.		528.00		580.80	9.42	10.37
56 M.H., Daily Totals		$1563.60		$2145.20	$27.91	$38.30
Crew B-30	Hr.	Daily	Hr.	Daily	Bare Costs	Incl. O&P
1 Equip. Oper. (med.)	$22.10	$176.80	$33.00	$264.00	$19.43	$29.03
2 Truck Drivers (heavy)	18.10	289.60	27.05	432.80		
1 Hyd. Excavator, 1.5 C.Y.		668.00		734.80		
2 Dump Trucks, 16 Ton		692.80		762.10	56.70	62.37
24 M.H., Daily Totals		$1827.20		$2193.70	$76.13	$91.40
Crew B-31	Hr.	Daily	Hr.	Daily	Bare Costs	Incl. O&P
1 Labor Foreman (outside)	$19.15	$153.20	$29.05	$232.40	$18.44	$28.00
3 Building Laborers	17.15	411.60	26.05	625.20		
1 Carpenter	21.60	172.80	32.80	262.40		
1 Air Compr., 250 C.F.M.		84.00		92.40		
1 Sheeting Driver		8.80		9.70		
2-50 Ft Air Hoses, 1.5" Dia.		9.60		10.55	2.56	2.81
40 M.H., Daily Totals		$840.00		$1232.65	$21.00	$30.81
Crew B-32	Hr.	Daily	Hr.	Daily	Bare Costs	Incl. O&P
1 Highway Laborer	$17.15	$137.20	$26.05	$208.40	$20.86	$31.26
3 Equip. Oper. (med.)	22.10	530.40	33.00	792.00		
1 Grader, 30,000 lbs.		513.40		564.75		
1 Tandem Roller, 10 Ton		179.00		196.90		
1 Dozer, 200 H.P.		762.60		838.85	45.46	50.01
32 M.H., Daily Totals		$2122.60		$2600.90	$66.32	$81.27
Crew B-32A	Hr.	Daily	Hr.	Daily	Bare Costs	Incl. O&P
1 Laborer	$17.15	$137.20	$26.05	$208.40	$20.45	$30.68
2 Equip. Oper. (medium)	22.10	353.60	33.00	528.00		
1 Grader, 30,000 lbs		513.40		564.75		
1 Roll., Vibratory, 29,000 lbs		336.40		370.05	35.40	38.95
24 M.H., Daily Totals		$1340.60		$1671.20	$55.85	$69.63
Crew B-32B	Hr.	Daily	Hr.	Daily	Bare Costs	Incl. O&P
1 Laborer	$17.15	$137.20	$26.05	$208.40	$20.45	$30.68
2 Equip. Oper. (medium)	22.10	353.60	33.00	528.00		
1 Dozer, 200 H.P.		762.60		838.85		
1 Roll., Vibratory, 29,000 lbs		336.40		370.05	45.79	50.37
24 M.H., Daily Totals		$1589.80		$1945.30	$66.24	$81.05
Crew B-32C	Hr.	Daily	Hr.	Daily	Bare Costs	Incl. O&P
1 Labor Foreman	$19.15	$153.20	$29.05	$232.40	$19.95	$30.02
2 Laborers	17.15	274.40	26.05	416.80		
3 Equip. Oper. (medium)	22.10	530.40	33.00	792.00		
1 Grader, 30,000 lbs		513.40		564.75		
1 Roller, Steel Wheel		179.00		196.90		
1 Dozer, 200 H.P.		762.60		838.85	30.31	33.34
48 M.H., Daily Totals		$2413.00		$3041.70	$50.26	$63.36
Crew B-33	Hr.	Daily	Hr.	Daily	Bare Costs	Incl. O&P
1 Equip. Oper. (med.)	$22.10	$176.80	$33.00	$264.00	$20.68	$31.01
.5 Building Laborer	17.15	68.60	26.05	104.20		
.25 Equip. Oper. (med.)	22.10	44.20	33.00	66.00		
14 M.H., Daily Totals		$289.60		$434.20	$20.68	$31.01

xiii

CREWS

Crew No.	Bare Costs		Incl. Subs O & P		Cost Per Man-hour	
Crew B-33A	Hr.	Daily	Hr.	Daily	Bare Costs	Incl. O&P
1 Equip. Oper. (med.)	$22.10	$176.80	$33.00	$264.00	$20.68	$31.01
.5 Building Laborer	17.15	68.60	26.05	104.20		
.25 Equip. Oper. (med.)	22.10	44.20	33.00	66.00		
1 Scraper, Towed, 7 C.Y.		59.40		65.35		
1 Dozer, 300 H.P.		819.20		901.10		
.25 Dozer, 300 H.P.		204.80		225.30	77.38	85.12
14 M.H., Daily Totals		$1373.00		$1625.95	$98.06	$116.13
Crew B-33B	Hr.	Daily	Hr.	Daily	Bare Costs	Incl. O&P
1 Equip. Oper. (med.)	$22.10	$176.80	$33.00	$264.00	$20.68	$31.01
.5 Building Laborer	17.15	68.60	26.05	104.20		
.25 Equip. Oper. (med.)	22.10	44.20	33.00	66.00		
1 Scraper, Towed, 10 C.Y.		162.60		178.85		
1 Dozer, 300 H.P.		819.20		901.10		
.25 Dozer, 300 H.P.		204.80		225.30	84.75	93.23
14 M.H., Daily Totals		$1476.20		$1739.45	$105.43	$124.24
Crew B-33C	Hr.	Daily	Hr.	Daily	Bare Costs	Incl. O&P
1 Equip. Oper. (med.)	$22.10	$176.80	$33.00	$264.00	$20.68	$31.01
.5 Building Laborer	17.15	68.60	26.05	104.20		
.25 Equip. Oper. (med.)	22.10	44.20	33.00	66.00		
1 Scraper, Towed, 12 C.Y.		162.60		178.85		
1 Dozer, 300 H.P.		819.20		901.10		
.25 Dozer, 300 H.P.		204.80		225.30	84.75	93.23
14 M.H., Daily Totals		$1476.20		$1739.45	$105.43	$124.24
Crew B-33D	Hr.	Daily	Hr.	Daily	Bare Costs	Incl. O&P
1 Equip. Oper. (med.)	$22.10	$176.80	$33.00	$264.00	$20.68	$31.01
.5 Building Laborer	17.15	68.60	26.05	104.20		
.25 Equip. Oper. (med.)	22.10	44.20	33.00	66.00		
1 S.P. Scraper, 14 C.Y.		1321.20		1453.30		
.25 Dozer, 300 H.P.		204.80		225.30	109.00	119.90
14 M.H., Daily Totals		$1815.60		$2112.80	$129.68	$150.91
Crew B-33E	Hr.	Daily	Hr.	Daily	Bare Costs	Incl. O&P
1 Equip. Oper. (med.)	$22.10	$176.80	$33.00	$264.00	$20.68	$31.01
.5 Building Laborer	17.15	68.60	26.05	104.20		
.25 Equip. Oper. (med.)	22.10	44.20	33.00	66.00		
1 S.P. Scraper, 24 C.Y.		1578.20		1736.00		
.25 Dozer, 300 H.P.		204.80		225.30	127.35	140.09
14 M.H., Daily Totals		$2072.60		$2395.50	$148.03	$171.10
Crew B-33F	Hr.	Daily	Hr.	Daily	Bare Costs	Incl. O&P
1 Equip. Oper. (med.)	$22.10	$176.80	$33.00	$264.00	$20.68	$31.01
.5 Building Laborer	17.15	68.60	26.05	104.20		
.25 Equip. Oper. (med.)	22.10	44.20	33.00	66.00		
1 Elev. Scraper, 11 C.Y.		562.60		618.85		
.25 Dozer, 300 H.P.		204.80		225.30	54.81	60.29
14 M.H., Daily Totals		$1057.00		$1278.35	$75.49	$91.30
Crew B-33G	Hr.	Daily	Hr.	Daily	Bare Costs	Incl. O&P
1 Equip. Oper. (med.)	$22.10	$176.80	$33.00	$264.00	$20.68	$31.01
.5 Building Laborer	17.15	68.60	26.05	104.20		
.25 Equip. Oper. (med.)	22.10	44.20	33.00	66.00		
1 Elev. Scraper, 20 C.Y.		735.00		808.50		
.25 Dozer, 300 H.P.		204.80		225.30	67.12	73.84
14 M.H., Daily Totals		$1229.40		$1468.00	$87.80	$104.85

Crew No.	Bare Costs		Incl. Subs O & P		Cost Per Man-hour	
Crew B-34	Hr.	Daily	Hr.	Daily	Bare Costs	Incl. O&P
1 Truck Driver (heavy)	$18.10	$144.80	$27.05	$216.40	$18.10	$27.05
8 M.H., Daily Totals		$144.80		$216.40	$18.10	$27.05
Crew B-34A	Hr.	Daily	Hr.	Daily	Bare Costs	Incl. O&P
1 Truck Driver (heavy)	$18.10	$144.80	$27.05	$216.40	$18.10	$27.05
1 Dump Truck, 12 Ton		282.80		311.10	35.35	38.88
8 M.H., Daily Totals		$427.60		$527.50	$53.45	$65.93
Crew B-34B	Hr.	Daily	Hr.	Daily	Bare Costs	Incl. O&P
1 Truck Driver (heavy)	$18.10	$144.80	$27.05	$216.40	$18.10	$27.05
1 Dump Truck, 16 Ton		346.40		381.05	43.30	47.63
8 M.H., Daily Totals		$491.20		$597.45	$61.40	$74.68
Crew B-34C	Hr.	Daily	Hr.	Daily	Bare Costs	Incl. O&P
1 Truck Driver (heavy)	$18.10	$144.80	$27.05	$216.40	$18.10	$27.05
1 Truck Tractor, 40 Ton		331.20		364.30		
1 Dump Trailer, 16.5 C.Y.		103.40		113.75	54.32	59.75
8 M.H., Daily Totals		$579.40		$694.45	$72.42	$86.80
Crew B-34D	Hr.	Daily	Hr.	Daily	Bare Costs	Incl. O&P
1 Truck Driver (heavy)	$18.10	$144.80	$27.05	$216.40	$18.10	$27.05
1 Truck Tractor, 40 Ton		331.20		364.30		
1 Dump Trailer, 20 C.Y.		104.40		114.85	54.45	59.89
8 M.H., Daily Totals		$580.40		$695.55	$72.55	$86.94
Crew B-34E	Hr.	Daily	Hr.	Daily	Bare Costs	Incl. O&P
1 Truck Driver (heavy)	$18.10	$144.80	$27.05	$216.40	$18.10	$27.05
1 Truck, Off Highway, 25 Ton		525.20		577.70	65.65	72.21
8 M.H., Daily Totals		$670.00		$794.10	$83.75	$99.26
Crew B-34F	Hr.	Daily	Hr.	Daily	Bare Costs	Incl. O&P
1 Truck Driver (heavy)	$18.10	$144.80	$27.05	$216.40	$18.10	$27.05
1 Truck, Off Hwy, 22 C.Y.		802.00		882.20	100.25	110.27
8 M.H., Daily Totals		$946.80		$1098.60	$118.35	$137.32
Crew B-34G	Hr.	Daily	Hr.	Daily	Bare Costs	Incl. O&P
1 Truck Driver (heavy)	$18.10	$144.80	$27.05	$216.40	$18.10	$27.05
1 Truck, Off Hwy, 34 C.Y.		1048.00		1152.80	131.00	144.10
8 M.H., Daily Totals		$1192.80		$1369.20	$149.10	$171.15
Crew B-34H	Hr.	Daily	Hr.	Daily	Bare Costs	Incl. O&P
1 Truck Driver (heavy)	$18.10	$144.80	$27.05	$216.40	$18.10	$27.05
1 Truck, Off Hwy, 42 C.Y.		1304.60		1435.05	163.07	179.38
8 M.H., Daily Totals		$1449.40		$1651.45	$181.17	$206.43
Crew B-34J	Hr.	Daily	Hr.	Daily	Bare Costs	Incl. O&P
1 Truck Driver (heavy)	$18.10	$144.80	$27.05	$216.40	$18.10	$27.05
1 Truck, Off Hwy, 60 C.Y.		1771.80		1949.00	221.47	243.62
8 M.H., Daily Totals		$1916.60		$2165.40	$239.57	$270.67
Crew B-34K	Hr.	Daily	Hr.	Daily	Bare Costs	Incl. O&P
1 Truck Driver (heavy)	$18.10	$144.80	$27.05	$216.40	$18.10	$27.05
1 Truck Tractor, 240 H.P.		419.00		460.90		
1 Low Bed Trailer		250.60		275.65	83.70	92.06
8 M.H., Daily Totals		$814.40		$952.95	$101.80	$119.11

CREWS

Crew No.	Bare Costs		Incl. Subs O & P		Cost Per Man-hour	
Crew B-35	Hr.	Daily	Hr.	Daily	Bare Costs	Incl. O&P
1 Laborer Foreman (out)	$19.15	$153.20	$29.05	$232.40	$20.80	$31.28
1 Skilled Worker	22.10	176.80	33.65	269.20		
1 Welder (plumber)	24.70	197.60	36.65	293.20		
1 Laborer	17.15	137.20	26.05	208.40		
1 Equip. Oper. (crane)	22.90	183.20	34.20	273.60		
1 Equip. Oper. Oiler	18.80	150.40	28.10	224.80		
1 Electric Welding Mach.		38.20		42.00		
1 Hyd. Excavator, .75 C.Y.		449.60		494.55	10.16	11.17
48 M.H., Daily Totals		$1486.20		$2038.15	$30.96	$42.45
Crew B-36	Hr.	Daily	Hr.	Daily	Bare Costs	Incl. O&P
1 Labor Foreman (outside)	$19.15	$153.20	$29.05	$232.40	$19.53	$29.43
2 Highway Laborers	17.15	274.40	26.05	416.80		
2 Equip. Oper. (med.)	22.10	353.60	33.00	528.00		
1 Dozer, 200 H.P.		762.60		838.85		
1 Aggregate Spreader		55.80		61.40		
1 Tandem Roller, 10 Ton		179.00		196.90	24.93	27.42
40 M.H., Daily Totals		$1778.60		$2274.35	$44.46	$56.85
Crew B-36A	Hr.	Daily	Hr.	Daily	Bare Costs	Incl. O&P
1 Labor Foreman	$19.15	$153.20	$29.05	$232.40	$20.26	$30.45
2 Laborers	17.15	274.40	26.05	416.80		
4 Equip. Oper. (medium)	22.10	707.20	33.00	1056.00		
1 Dozer, 200 H.P.		762.60		838.85		
1 Aggregate Spreader		55.80		61.40		
1 Roller, Steel Wheel		179.00		196.90		
1 Roller, Pneumatic Wheel		232.20		255.40	21.95	24.15
56 M.H., Daily Totals		$2364.40		$3057.75	$42.21	$54.60
Crew B-37	Hr.	Daily	Hr.	Daily	Bare Costs	Incl. O&P
1 Labor Foreman (outside)	$19.15	$153.20	$29.05	$232.40	$18.14	$27.45
4 Building Laborers	17.15	548.80	26.05	833.60		
1 Equip. Oper. (light)	21.10	168.80	31.50	252.00		
1 Tandem Roller, 5 Ton		113.00		124.30	2.35	2.58
48 M.H., Daily Totals		$983.80		$1442.30	$20.49	$30.03
Crew B-38	Hr.	Daily	Hr.	Daily	Bare Costs	Incl. O&P
1 Labor Foreman (outside)	$19.15	$153.20	$29.05	$232.40	$19.33	$29.13
2 Building Laborers	17.15	274.40	26.05	416.80		
1 Equip. Oper. (light)	21.10	168.80	31.50	252.00		
1 Equip. Oper. (medium)	22.10	176.80	33.00	264.00		
1 Backhoe Loader, 48 H.P.		181.40		199.55		
1 Demol. Hammer, (1000 lb)		319.80		351.80		
1 F.E. Loader (170 H.P.)		538.40		592.25		
1 Pavt. Rem. Bucket		36.20		39.80	26.89	29.58
40 M.H., Daily Totals		$1849.00		$2348.60	$46.22	$58.71
Crew B-39	Hr.	Daily	Hr.	Daily	Bare Costs	Incl. O&P
1 Labor Foreman (outside)	$19.15	$153.20	$29.05	$232.40	$18.14	$27.45
4 Building Laborers	17.15	548.80	26.05	833.60		
1 Equipment Oper. (light)	21.10	168.80	31.50	252.00		
1 Air Compr., 250 C.F.M.		84.00		92.40		
Air Tools & Accessories		27.60		30.35		
2-50 Ft. Air Hoses, 1.5" Dia		9.60		10.55	2.52	2.77
48 M.H., Daily Totals		$992.00		$1451.30	$20.66	$30.22

Crew No.	Bare Costs		Incl. Subs O & P		Cost Per Man-hour	
Crew B-40	Hr.	Daily	Hr.	Daily	Bare Costs	Incl. O&P
1 Pile Driver Foreman	$23.80	$190.40	$39.35	$314.80	$21.95	$35.00
4 Pile Drivers	21.80	697.60	36.05	1153.60		
2 Equip. Oper. (crane)	22.90	366.40	34.20	547.20		
1 Equip. Oper. Oiler	18.80	150.40	28.10	224.80		
1 Crane, 40 Ton		630.40		693.45		
Vibratory Hammer & Gen.		1016.60		1118.25	25.73	28.30
64 M.H., Daily Totals		$3051.80		$4052.10	$47.68	$63.30
Crew B-41	Hr.	Daily	Hr.	Daily	Bare Costs	Incl. O&P
1 Labor Foreman (outside)	$19.15	$153.20	$29.05	$232.40	$17.85	$27.05
4 Building Laborers	17.15	548.80	26.05	833.60		
.25 Equip. Oper. (crane)	22.90	45.80	34.20	68.40		
.25 Equip. Oper. Oiler	18.80	37.60	28.10	56.20		
.25 Crawler Crane, 40 Ton		157.60		173.35	3.58	3.93
44 M.H., Daily Totals		$943.00		$1363.95	$21.43	$30.98
Crew B-42	Hr.	Daily	Hr.	Daily	Bare Costs	Incl. O&P
1 Labor Foreman (outside)	$19.15	$153.20	$29.05	$232.40	$19.11	$29.42
4 Building Laborers	17.15	548.80	26.05	833.60		
1 Equip. Oper. (crane)	22.90	183.20	34.20	273.60		
1 Equip. Oper. Oiler	18.80	150.40	28.10	224.80		
1 Welder	23.45	187.60	39.85	318.80		
1 Hyd. Crane, 25 Ton		476.00		523.60		
1 Gas Welding Machine		64.40		70.85		
1 Horz. Boring Csg. Mch.		403.80		444.20	14.75	16.22
64 M.H., Daily Totals		$2167.40		$2921.85	$33.86	$45.64
Crew B-43	Hr.	Daily	Hr.	Daily	Bare Costs	Incl. O&P
1 Labor Foreman (outside)	$19.15	$153.20	$29.05	$232.40	$18.71	$28.25
3 Building Laborers	17.15	411.60	26.05	625.20		
1 Equip. Oper. (crane)	22.90	183.20	34.20	273.60		
1 Equip. Oper. Oiler	18.80	150.40	28.10	224.80		
1 Drill Rig & Augers		712.35		783.60	14.84	16.32
48 M.H., Daily Totals		$1610.75		$2139.60	$33.55	$44.57
Crew B-44	Hr.	Daily	Hr.	Daily	Bare Costs	Incl. O&P
1 Pile Driver Foreman	$23.80	$190.40	$39.35	$314.80	$21.74	$34.75
4 Pile Drivers	21.80	697.60	36.05	1153.60		
2 Equip. Oper. (crane)	22.90	366.40	34.20	547.20		
1 Building Laborer	17.15	137.20	26.05	208.40		
1 Crane, 40 Ton, & Access.		1103.20		1213.50		
45 L.F. Leads, 15K Ft. Lbs.		47.25		52.00	17.97	19.77
64 M.H., Daily Totals		$2542.05		$3489.50	$39.71	$54.52
Crew B-45	Hr.	Daily	Hr.	Daily	Bare Costs	Incl. O&P
1 Equip. Oper. (med.)	$22.10	$176.80	$33.00	$264.00	$20.10	$30.02
1 Truck Driver (heavy)	18.10	144.80	27.05	216.40		
1 Dist. Tank Truck, 3K Gal.		294.60		324.05		
1 Tractor, 4 x 2, 250 H.P.		298.20		328.00	37.05	40.75
16 M.H., Daily Totals		$914.40		$1132.45	$57.15	$70.77
Crew B-46	Hr.	Daily	Hr.	Daily	Bare Costs	Incl. O&P
1 Pile Driver Foreman	$23.80	$190.40	$39.35	$314.80	$19.80	$31.60
2 Pile Drivers	21.80	348.80	36.05	576.80		
3 Building Laborers	17.15	411.60	26.05	625.20		
1 Chain Saw, 36" Long		39.80		43.80	.82	.91
48 M.H., Daily Totals		$990.60		$1560.60	$20.62	$32.51

XV

CREWS

Crew No.	Bare Costs		Incl. Subs O & P		Cost Per Man-hour	
Crew B-47	Hr.	Daily	Hr.	Daily	Bare Costs	Incl. O&P
1 Blast Foreman	$19.15	$153.20	$29.05	$232.40	$19.13	$28.86
1 Driller	17.15	137.20	26.05	208.40		
1 Equip. Oper. (light)	21.10	168.80	31.50	252.00		
1 Crawler Type Drill, 4"		207.20		227.90		
1 Air Compr., 600 C.F.M.		261.60		287.75		
2-50 Ft. Air Hoses, 3" Dia.		20.40		22.45	20.38	22.42
24 M.H., Daily Totals		$948.40		$1230.90	$39.51	$51.28
Crew B-47A	Hr.	Daily	Hr.	Daily	Bare Costs	Incl. O&P
1 Drilling Foreman	$19.15	$153.20	$29.05	$232.40	$20.28	$30.45
1 Equip. Oper. (heavy)	22.90	183.20	34.20	273.60		
1 Oiler	18.80	150.40	28.10	224.80		
1 Quarry Drill		431.60		474.75	17.98	19.78
24 M.H., Daily Totals		$918.40		$1205.55	$38.26	$50.23
Crew B-48	Hr.	Daily	Hr.	Daily	Bare Costs	Incl. O&P
1 Labor Foreman (outside)	$19.15	$153.20	$29.05	$232.40	$19.05	$28.71
3 Building Laborers	17.15	411.60	26.05	625.20		
1 Equip. Oper. (crane)	22.90	183.20	34.20	273.60		
1 Equip. Oper. Oiler	18.80	150.40	28.10	224.80		
1 Equip. Oper. (light)	21.10	168.80	31.50	252.00		
1 Centr. Water Pump, 6"		141.80		156.00		
1-20 Ft. Suction Hose, 6"		22.40		24.65		
1-50 Ft. Disch. Hose, 6"		12.60		13.85		
1 Drill Rig & Augers		712.35		783.60	15.87	17.46
56 M.H., Daily Totals		$1956.35		$2586.10	$34.92	$46.17
Crew B-49	Hr.	Daily	Hr.	Daily	Bare Costs	Incl. O&P
1 Labor Foreman (outside)	$19.15	$153.20	$29.05	$232.40	$19.88	$30.49
3 Building Laborers	17.15	411.60	26.05	625.20		
2 Equip. Oper. (crane)	22.90	366.40	34.20	547.20		
2 Equip. Oper. Oilers	18.80	300.80	28.10	449.60		
1 Equip. Oper. (light)	21.10	168.80	31.50	252.00		
2 Pile Drivers	21.80	348.80	36.05	576.80		
1 Hyd. Crane, 25 Ton		476.00		523.60		
1 Centr. Water Pump, 6"		141.80		156.00		
1-20 Ft. Suction Hose, 6"		22.40		24.65		
1-50 Ft. Disch. Hose, 6"		12.60		13.85		
1 Drill Rig & Augers		712.35		783.60	15.51	17.06
88 M.H., Daily Totals		$3114.75		$4184.90	$35.39	$47.55
Crew B-50	Hr.	Daily	Hr.	Daily	Bare Costs	Incl. O&P
2 Pile Driver Foremen	$23.80	$380.80	$39.35	$629.60	$21.03	$33.54
6 Pile Drivers	21.80	1046.40	36.05	1730.40		
2 Equip. Oper. (crane)	22.90	366.40	34.20	547.20		
1 Equip. Oper. Oiler	18.80	150.40	28.10	224.80		
3 Building Laborers	17.15	411.60	26.05	625.20		
1 Crane, 40 Ton		630.40		693.45		
60 L.F. Leads, 15K Ft. Lbs.		63.00		69.30		
1 Hammer, 15K Ft. Lbs.		246.40		271.05		
1 Air Compr., 600 C.F.M.		261.60		287.75		
2-50 Ft. Air Hoses, 3" Dia.		20.40		22.45		
1 Chain Saw, 36" Long		39.80		43.80	11.26	12.39
112 M.H., Daily Totals		$3617.20		$5145.00	$32.29	$45.93

Crew No.	Bare Costs		Incl. Subs O & P		Cost Per Man-hour	
Crew B-51	Hr.	Daily	Hr.	Daily	Bare Costs	Incl. O&P
1 Labor Foreman (outside)	$19.15	$153.20	$29.05	$232.40	$17.59	$26.64
4 Building Laborers	17.15	548.80	26.05	833.60		
1 Truck Driver (light)	17.80	142.40	26.60	212.80		
1 Light Truck, 1.5 Ton		138.20		152.00	2.87	3.16
48 M.H., Daily Totals		$982.60		$1430.80	$20.46	$29.80
Crew B-52	Hr.	Daily	Hr.	Daily	Bare Costs	Incl. O&P
1 Carpenter Foreman	$23.60	$188.80	$35.85	$286.80	$20.05	$30.43
1 Carpenter	21.60	172.80	32.80	262.40		
3 Building Laborers	17.15	411.60	26.05	625.20		
1 Cement Finisher	21.05	168.40	30.60	244.80		
.5 Rodman (reinf.)	23.30	93.20	38.25	153.00		
.5 Equip. Oper. (med.)	22.10	88.40	33.00	132.00		
.5 F.E. Ldr., T.M., 2.5 C.Y.		384.80		423.30	6.87	7.55
56 M.H., Daily Totals		$1508.00		$2127.50	$26.92	$37.98
Crew B-53	Hr.	Daily	Hr.	Daily	Bare Costs	Incl. O&P
1 Equip. Oper. (light)	$21.10	$168.80	$31.50	$252.00	$21.10	$31.50
1 Trencher, Chain, 12 H.P.		50.40		55.45	6.30	6.93
8 M.H., Daily Totals		$219.20		$307.45	$27.40	$38.43
Crew B-54	Hr.	Daily	Hr.	Daily	Bare Costs	Incl. O&P
1 Equip. Oper. (light)	$21.10	$168.80	$31.50	$252.00	$21.10	$31.50
1 Trencher, Chain, 40 H.P.		128.40		141.25	16.05	17.65
8 M.H., Daily Totals		$297.20		$393.25	$37.15	$49.15
Crew B-55	Hr.	Daily	Hr.	Daily	Bare Costs	Incl. O&P
2 Building Laborers	$17.15	$274.40	$26.05	$416.80	$17.36	$26.23
1 Truck Driver (light)	17.80	142.40	26.60	212.80		
1 Flatbed Truck w/Auger		378.40		416.25		
1 Truck, 3 Ton		140.60		154.65	21.62	23.78
24 M.H., Daily Totals		$935.80		$1200.50	$38.98	$50.01
Crew B-56	Hr.	Daily	Hr.	Daily	Bare Costs	Incl. O&P
1 Building Laborer	$17.15	$137.20	$26.05	$208.40	$19.12	$28.77
1 Equip. Oper. (light)	21.10	168.80	31.50	252.00		
1 Crawler Type Drill, 4"		207.20		227.90		
1 Air Compr., 600 C.F.M.		261.60		287.75		
1-50 Ft. Air Hose, 3" Dia.		10.20		11.20	29.93	32.92
16 M.H., Daily Totals		$785.00		$987.25	$49.05	$61.69
Crew B-57	Hr.	Daily	Hr.	Daily	Bare Costs	Incl. O&P
1 Labor Foreman (outside)	$19.15	$153.20	$29.05	$232.40	$19.37	$29.15
2 Building Laborers	17.15	274.40	26.05	416.80		
1 Equip. Oper. (crane)	22.90	183.20	34.20	273.60		
1 Equip. Oper. (light)	21.10	168.80	31.50	252.00		
1 Equip. Oper. Oiler	18.80	150.40	28.10	224.80		
1 Power Shovel, 1 C.Y.		411.60		452.75		
1 Clamshell Bucket, 1 C.Y.		59.20		65.10		
1 Centr. Water Pump, 6"		141.80		156.00		
1-20 Ft. Suction Hose, 6"		22.40		24.65		
20-50 Ft. Disch. Hoses, 6"		252.00		277.20	18.47	20.32
48 M.H., Daily Totals		$1817.00		$2375.30	$37.84	$49.47

CREWS

Crew No.	Bare Costs		Incl. Subs O & P		Cost Per Man-hour	
Crew B-58	**Hr.**	**Daily**	**Hr.**	**Daily**	**Bare Costs**	**Incl. O&P**
2 Building Laborers	$17.15	$274.40	$26.05	$416.80	$18.46	$27.86
1 Equip. Oper. (light)	21.10	168.80	31.50	252.00		
1 Backhoe Loader, 48 H.P.		181.40		199.55		
1 Small Helicopter		2137.50		2351.25	96.62	106.28
24 M.H., Daily Totals		$2762.10		$3219.60	$115.08	$134.14
Crew B-59	**Hr.**	**Daily**	**Hr.**	**Daily**	**Bare Costs**	**Incl. O&P**
1 Truck Driver (heavy)	$18.10	$144.80	$27.05	$216.40	$18.10	$27.05
1 Truck, 30 ton		255.60		281.15		
1 Water Tank, 5000 gal.		176.20		193.80	53.97	59.36
8 M.H., Daily Totals		$576.60		$691.35	$72.07	$86.41
Crew B-60	**Hr.**	**Daily**	**Hr.**	**Daily**	**Bare Costs**	**Incl. O&P**
1 Labor Foreman (outside)	$19.15	$153.20	$29.05	$232.40	$19.62	$29.49
2 Building Laborers	17.15	274.40	26.05	416.80		
1 Equip. Oper. (crane)	22.90	183.20	34.20	273.60		
2 Equip. Oper. (light)	21.10	337.60	31.50	504.00		
1 Equip. Oper. Oiler	18.80	150.40	28.10	224.80		
1 Crawler Crane, 40 Ton		630.40		693.45		
45 L.F. Leads, 15K Ft. Lbs.		47.25		52.00		
1 Backhoe Loader, 48 H.P.		181.40		199.55	15.34	16.87
56 M.H., Daily Totals		$1957.85		$2596.60	$34.96	$46.36
Crew B-61	**Hr.**	**Daily**	**Hr.**	**Daily**	**Bare Costs**	**Incl. O&P**
1 Labor Foreman (outside)	$19.15	$153.20	$29.05	$232.40	$18.34	$27.74
3 Building Laborers	17.15	411.60	26.05	625.20		
1 Equip. Oper. (light)	21.10	168.80	31.50	252.00		
1 Cement Mixer, 2 C.Y.		220.00		242.00		
1 Air Compr., 160 C.F.M.		80.20		88.20	7.50	8.25
40 M.H., Daily Totals		$1033.80		$1439.80	$25.84	$35.99
Crew B-62	**Hr.**	**Daily**	**Hr.**	**Daily**	**Bare Costs**	**Incl. O&P**
2 Building Laborers	$17.15	$274.40	$26.05	$416.80	$18.46	$27.86
1 Equip. Oper. (light)	21.10	168.80	31.50	252.00		
1 Loader, Skid Steer		84.40		92.85	3.51	3.86
24 M.H., Daily Totals		$527.60		$761.65	$21.97	$31.72
Crew B-63	**Hr.**	**Daily**	**Hr.**	**Daily**	**Bare Costs**	**Incl. O&P**
4 Building Laborers	$17.15	$548.80	$26.05	$833.60	$17.94	$27.14
1 Equip. Oper. (light)	21.10	168.80	31.50	252.00		
1 Loader, Skid Steer		84.40		92.85	2.11	2.32
40 M.H., Daily Totals		$802.00		$1178.45	$20.05	$29.46
Crew B-64	**Hr.**	**Daily**	**Hr.**	**Daily**	**Bare Costs**	**Incl. O&P**
1 Building Laborer	$17.15	$137.20	$26.05	$208.40	$17.47	$26.32
1 Truck Driver (light)	17.80	142.40	26.60	212.80		
1 Power Mulcher (small)		84.60		93.05		
1 Light Truck, 1.5 Ton		138.20		152.00	13.92	15.31
16 M.H., Daily Totals		$502.40		$666.25	$31.39	$41.63
Crew B-65	**Hr.**	**Daily**	**Hr.**	**Daily**	**Bare Costs**	**Incl. O&P**
1 Building Laborer	$17.15	$137.20	$26.05	$208.40	$17.47	$26.32
1 Truck Driver (light)	17.80	142.40	26.60	212.80		
1 Power Mulcher (large)		192.80		212.10		
1 Light Truck, 1.5 Ton		138.20		152.00	20.68	22.75
16 M.H., Daily Totals		$610.60		$785.30	$38.15	$49.07

Crew No.	Bare Costs		Incl. Subs O & P		Cost Per Man-hour	
Crew B-66	**Hr.**	**Daily**	**Hr.**	**Daily**	**Bare Costs**	**Incl. O&P**
1 Equip. Oper. (light)	$21.10	$168.80	$31.50	$252.00	$21.10	$31.50
1 Backhoe Ldr. w/Attchmt.		155.40		170.95	19.42	21.36
8 M.H., Daily Totals		$324.20		$422.95	$40.52	$52.86
Crew B-67	**Hr.**	**Daily**	**Hr.**	**Daily**	**Bare Costs**	**Incl. O&P**
1 Millwright	$22.40	$179.20	$32.70	$261.60	$21.75	$32.10
1 Equip. Oper. (light)	21.10	168.80	31.50	252.00		
1 Forklift		179.80		197.80	11.23	12.36
16 M.H., Daily Totals		$527.80		$711.40	$32.98	$44.46
Crew B-68	**Hr.**	**Daily**	**Hr.**	**Daily**	**Bare Costs**	**Incl. O&P**
2 Millwrights	$22.40	$358.40	$32.70	$523.20	$21.96	$32.30
1 Equip. Oper. (light)	21.10	168.80	31.50	252.00		
1 Forklift		179.80		197.80	7.49	8.24
24 M.H., Daily Totals		$707.00		$973.00	$29.45	$40.54
Crew B-69	**Hr.**	**Daily**	**Hr.**	**Daily**	**Bare Costs**	**Incl. O&P**
1 Labor Foreman (outside)	$19.15	$153.20	$29.05	$232.40	$18.71	$28.25
3 Highway Laborers	17.15	411.60	26.05	625.20		
1 Equip Oper. (crane)	22.90	183.20	34.20	273.60		
1 Equip Oper. Oiler	18.80	150.40	28.10	224.80		
1 Truck Crane, 80 Ton		1052.00		1157.20	21.91	24.10
48 M.H., Daily Totals		$1950.40		$2513.20	$40.62	$52.35
Crew B-69A	**Hr.**	**Daily**	**Hr.**	**Daily**	**Bare Costs**	**Incl. O&P**
1 Labor Foreman	$19.15	$153.20	$29.05	$232.40	$18.95	$28.46
3 Laborers	17.15	411.60	26.05	625.20		
1 Equip. Oper. (medium)	22.10	176.80	33.00	264.00		
1 Concrete Finisher	21.05	168.40	30.60	244.80		
1 Curb Paver		374.60		412.05	7.80	8.58
48 M.H., Daily Totals		$1284.60		$1778.45	$26.75	$37.04
Crew B-69B	**Hr.**	**Daily**	**Hr.**	**Daily**	**Bare Costs**	**Incl. O&P**
1 Labor Foreman	$19.15	$153.20	$29.05	$232.40	$18.95	$28.46
3 Laborers	17.15	411.60	26.05	625.20		
1 Equip. Oper. (medium)	22.10	176.80	33.00	264.00		
1 Cement Finisher	21.05	168.40	30.60	244.80		
1 Curb/Gutter Paver		818.40		900.25	17.05	18.75
48 M.H., Daily Totals		$1728.40		$2266.65	$36.00	$47.21
Crew B-70	**Hr.**	**Daily**	**Hr.**	**Daily**	**Bare Costs**	**Incl. O&P**
1 Labor Foreman (outside)	$19.15	$153.20	$29.05	$232.40	$19.55	$29.45
3 Highway Laborers	17.15	411.60	26.05	625.20		
3 Equip. Oper. (med.)	22.10	530.40	33.00	792.00		
1 Motor Grader, 30,000 Lb.		513.40		564.75		
1 Grader Attach., Ripper		48.80		53.70		
1 Road Sweeper, S.P.		140.60		154.65		
1 F.E. Loader, 1-3/4 C.Y.		294.40		323.85	17.80	19.58
56 M.H., Daily Totals		$2092.40		$2746.55	$37.35	$49.03
Crew B-71	**Hr.**	**Daily**	**Hr.**	**Daily**	**Bare Costs**	**Incl. O&P**
1 Labor Foreman (outside)	$19.15	$153.20	$29.05	$232.40	$19.55	$29.45
3 Highway Laborers	17.15	411.60	26.05	625.20		
3 Equip. Oper. (med.)	22.10	530.40	33.00	792.00		
1 Pvmt. Profiler, 450 H.P.		3310.00		3641.00		
1 Road Sweeper, S.P.		140.60		154.65		
1 F.E. Loader, 1-3/4 C.Y.		294.40		323.85	66.87	73.56
56 M.H., Daily Totals		$4840.20		$5769.10	$86.42	$103.01

CREWS

Crew No.	Bare Costs		Incl. Subs O & P		Cost Per Man-hour	
Crew B-72	Hr.	Daily	Hr.	Daily	Bare Costs	Incl. O&P
1 Labor Foreman (outside)	$19.15	$153.20	$29.05	$232.40	$19.87	$29.90
3 Highway Laborers	17.15	411.60	26.05	625.20		
4 Equip. Oper. (med.)	22.10	707.20	33.00	1056.00		
1 Pvmt. Profiler, 450 H.P.		3310.00		3641.00		
1 Hammermill, 250 H.P.		897.40		987.15		
1 Windrow Loader		895.40		984.95		
1 Mix Paver 165 H.P.		1175.40		1292.95		
1 Roller, Pneu. Tire, 12 T.		232.20		255.40	101.72	111.89
64 M.H., Daily Totals		$7782.40		$9075.05	$121.59	$141.79
Crew B-73	Hr.	Daily	Hr.	Daily	Bare Costs	Incl. O&P
1 Labor Foreman (outside)	$19.15	$153.20	$29.05	$232.40	$20.49	$30.76
2 Highway Laborers	17.15	274.40	26.05	416.80		
5 Equip. Oper. (med.)	22.10	884.00	33.00	1320.00		
1 Road Mixer, 310 H.P.		834.60		918.05		
1 Roller, Tandem, 12 Ton		179.00		196.90		
1 Hammermill, 250 H.P.		897.40		987.15		
1 Motor Grader, 30,000 Lb.		513.40		564.75		
.5 F.E. Loader, 1-3/4 C.Y.		147.20		161.90		
.5 Truck, 30 ton		127.80		140.60		
.5 Water Tank, 5000 gal.		88.10		96.90	43.55	47.91
64 M.H., Daily Totals		$4099.10		$5035.45	$64.04	$78.67
Crew B-74	Hr.	Daily	Hr.	Daily	Bare Costs	Incl. O&P
1 Labor Foreman (outside)	$19.15	$153.20	$29.05	$232.40	$20.11	$30.15
1 Highway Laborer	17.15	137.20	26.05	208.40		
4 Equip. Oper. (med.)	22.10	707.20	33.00	1056.00		
2 Truck Drivers (heavy)	18.10	289.60	27.05	432.80		
1 Motor Grader, 30,000 Lb.		513.40		564.75		
1 Grader Attach., Ripper		48.80		53.70		
2 Stabilizers, 310 H.P.		1142.80		1257.10		
1 Flatbed Truck, 3 Ton		140.60		154.65		
1 Chem. Spreader, Towed		84.80		93.30		
1 Vibr. Roller, 29,000 Lb.		336.40		370.05		
1 Water Tank, 5000 gal.		176.20		193.80		
1 Truck, 30 Ton		255.60		281.15	42.16	46.38
64 M.H., Daily Totals		$3985.80		$4898.10	$62.27	$76.53
Crew B-75	Hr.	Daily	Hr.	Daily	Bare Costs	Incl. O&P
1 Labor Foreman (outside)	$19.15	$153.20	$29.05	$232.40	$20.40	$30.59
1 Highway Laborer	17.15	137.20	26.05	208.40		
4 Equip. Oper. (med.)	22.10	707.20	33.00	1056.00		
1 Truck Driver (heavy)	18.10	144.80	27.05	216.40		
1 Motor Grader, 30,000 Lb.		513.40		564.75		
1 Grader Attach., Ripper		48.80		53.70		
2 Stabilizers, 310 H.P.		1142.80		1257.10		
1 Dist. Truck, 3000 Gal.		294.60		324.05		
1 Vibr. Roller, 29,000 Lb.		336.40		370.05	41.71	45.88
56 M.H., Daily Totals		$3478.40		$4282.85	$62.11	$76.47

Crew No.	Bare Costs		Incl. Subs O & P		Cost Per Man-hour	
Crew B-76	Hr.	Daily	Hr.	Daily	Bare Costs	Incl. O&P
1 Dock Builder Foreman	$23.80	$190.40	$39.35	$314.80	$21.93	$35.12
5 Dock Builders	21.80	872.00	36.05	1442.00		
2 Equip. Oper. (crane)	22.90	366.40	34.20	547.20		
1 Equip. Oper. Oiler	18.80	150.40	28.10	224.80		
1 Crawler Crane, 50 Ton		722.40		794.65		
1 Barge, 400 Ton		367.20		403.90		
1 Hammer, 15K. Ft. Lbs.		246.40		271.05		
60 L.F. Leads, 15K. Ft. Lbs.		63.00		69.30		
1 Air Compr., 600 C.F.M.		261.60		287.75		
2-50 Ft. Air Hoses, 3" Dia.		20.40		22.45	23.34	25.68
72 M.H., Daily Totals		$3260.20		$4377.90	$45.27	$60.80
Crew B-77	Hr.	Daily	Hr.	Daily	Bare Costs	Incl. O&P
1 Labor Foreman	$19.15	$153.20	$29.05	$232.40	$17.68	$26.76
3 Laborers	17.15	411.60	26.05	625.20		
1 Truck Driver (light)	17.80	142.40	26.60	212.80		
1 Crack Cleaner, 25 H.P.		68.00		74.80		
1 Crack Filler, Trailer Mtd.		120.80		132.90		
1 Flatbed Truck, 3 Ton		140.60		154.65	8.23	9.05
40 M.H., Daily Totals		$1036.60		$1432.75	$25.91	$35.81
Crew B-78	Hr.	Daily	Hr.	Daily	Bare Costs	Incl. O&P
1 Labor Foreman	$19.15	$153.20	$29.05	$232.40	$17.59	$26.64
4 Laborers	17.15	548.80	26.05	833.60		
1 Truck Driver (light)	17.80	142.40	26.60	212.80		
1 Paint Striper, S.P.		172.80		190.10		
1 Flatbed Truck, 3 Ton		140.60		154.65		
1 Pickup Truck, 3/4 Ton		100.60		110.65	8.62	9.48
48 M.H., Daily Totals		$1258.40		$1734.20	$26.21	$36.12
Crew B-79	Hr.	Daily	Hr.	Daily	Bare Costs	Incl. O&P
1 Labor Foreman	$19.15	$153.20	$29.05	$232.40	$17.68	$26.76
3 Laborers	17.15	411.60	26.05	625.20		
1 Truck Driver (light)	17.80	142.40	26.60	212.80		
1 Thermo. Striper, T.M.		216.00		237.60		
1 Flatbed Truck, 3 Ton		140.60		154.65		
2 Pickup Trucks, 3/4 Ton		201.20		221.30	13.94	15.33
40 M.H., Daily Totals		$1265.00		$1683.95	$31.62	$42.09
Crew B-80	Hr.	Daily	Hr.	Daily	Bare Costs	Incl. O&P
1 Labor Foreman	$19.15	$153.20	$29.05	$232.40	$18.80	$28.30
1 Laborer	17.15	137.20	26.05	208.40		
1 Truck Driver (light)	17.80	142.40	26.60	212.80		
1 Equip. Oper. (light)	21.10	168.80	31.50	252.00		
1 Flatbed Truck, 3 Ton		140.60		154.65		
1 Post Driver, T.M.		244.80		269.30	12.04	13.24
32 M.H., Daily Totals		$987.00		$1329.55	$30.84	$41.54
Crew B-81	Hr.	Daily	Hr.	Daily	Bare Costs	Incl. O&P
1 Laborer	$17.15	$137.20	$26.05	$208.40	$19.11	$28.70
1 Equip. Oper. (med.)	22.10	176.80	33.00	264.00		
1 Truck Driver (heavy)	18.10	144.80	27.05	216.40		
1 Hydromulcher, T.M.		228.20		251.00		
1 Tractor Truck, 4x2		255.60		281.15	20.15	22.17
24 M.H., Daily Totals		$942.60		$1220.95	$39.26	$50.87

CREWS

Crew No.	Bare Costs		Incl. Subs O & P		Cost Per Man-hour	
Crew B-82	Hr.	Daily	Hr.	Daily	Bare Costs	Incl. O&P
1 Highway Laborer	$17.15	$137.20	$26.05	$208.40	$19.12	$28.77
1 Equip. Oper. (light)	21.10	168.80	31.50	252.00		
1 Horiz. Borer, 6 H.P.		35.20		38.70	2.20	2.41
16 M.H., Daily Totals		$341.20		$499.10	$21.32	$31.18
Crew B-83	Hr.	Daily	Hr.	Daily	Bare Costs	Incl. O&P
1 Tugboat Captain	$22.10	$176.80	$33.00	$264.00	$19.62	$29.52
1 Tugboat Hand	17.15	137.20	26.05	208.40		
1 Tugboat, 250 H.P.		428.60		471.45	26.78	29.46
16 M.H., Daily Totals		$742.60		$943.85	$46.40	$58.98
Crew B-84	Hr.	Daily	Hr.	Daily	Bare Costs	Incl. O&P
1 Equip. Oper. (med.)	$22.10	$176.80	$33.00	$264.00	$22.10	$33.00
1 Rotary Mower/Tractor		223.40		245.75	27.92	30.71
8 M.H., Daily Totals		$400.20		$509.75	$50.02	$63.71
Crew B-85	Hr.	Daily	Hr.	Daily	Bare Costs	Incl. O&P
3 Highway Laborers	$17.15	$411.60	$26.05	$625.20	$18.33	$27.64
1 Equip. Oper. (med.)	22.10	176.80	33.00	264.00		
1 Truck Driver (heavy)	18.10	144.80	27.05	216.40		
1 Aerial Lift Truck		492.80		542.10		
1 Brush Chipper, 130 H.P.		169.20		186.10		
1 Pruning Saw, Rotary		14.20		15.60	16.90	18.59
40 M.H., Daily Totals		$1409.40		$1849.40	$35.23	$46.23
Crew B-86	Hr.	Daily	Hr.	Daily	Bare Costs	Incl. O&P
1 Equip. Oper. (med.)	$22.10	$176.80	$33.00	$264.00	$22.10	$33.00
1 Stump Chipper, S.P.		145.80		160.40	18.22	20.05
8 M.H., Daily Totals		$322.60		$424.40	$40.32	$53.05
Crew B-86A	Hr.	Daily	Hr.	Daily	Bare Costs	Incl. O&P
1 Equip. Oper. (medium)	$22.10	$176.80	$33.00	$264.00	$22.10	$33.00
1 Grader, 30,000 lbs		513.40		564.75	64.17	70.59
8 M.H., Daily Totals		$690.20		$828.75	$86.27	$103.59
Crew B-86B	Hr.	Daily	Hr.	Daily	Bare Costs	Incl. O&P
1 Equip. Oper. (medium)	$22.10	$176.80	$33.00	$264.00	$22.10	$33.00
1 Dozer, 200 H.P.		762.60		838.85	95.32	104.85
8 M.H., Daily Totals		$939.40		$1102.85	$117.42	$137.85
Crew B-87	Hr.	Daily	Hr.	Daily	Bare Costs	Incl. O&P
1 Common Laborer	$17.15	$137.20	$26.05	$208.40	$21.11	$31.61
4 Equip. Oper. (med.)	22.10	707.20	33.00	1056.00		
2 Feller Bunchers, 50 H.P.		588.00		646.80		
1 Log Chipper, 22" Tree		1702.00		1872.20		
1 Dozer, 105 H.P.		268.00		294.80		
1 Chainsaw, Gas, 36" Long		39.80		43.80	64.94	71.44
40 M.H., Daily Totals		$3442.20		$4122.00	$86.05	$103.05
Crew B-88	Hr.	Daily	Hr.	Daily	Bare Costs	Incl. O&P
1 Common Laborer	$17.15	$137.20	$26.05	$208.40	$21.39	$32.00
6 Equip. Oper. (med.)	22.10	1060.80	33.00	1584.00		
2 Feller Bunchers, 50 H.P.		588.00		646.80		
1 Log Chipper, 22" Tree		1702.00		1872.20		
2 Log Skidders, 50 H.P.		608.40		669.25		
1 Dozer, 105 H.P.		268.00		294.80		
1 Chainsaw, Gas, 36" Long		39.80		43.80	57.25	62.97
56 M.H., Daily Totals		$4404.20		$5319.25	$78.64	$94.97

Crew No.	Bare Costs		Incl. Subs O & P		Cost Per Man-hour	
Crew B-89	Hr.	Daily	Hr.	Daily	Bare Costs	Incl. O&P
1 Equip. Oper. (light)	$21.10	$168.80	$31.50	$252.00	$19.45	$29.05
1 Truck Driver (light)	17.80	142.40	26.60	212.80		
1 Truck, Stake Body, 3 Ton		140.60		154.65		
1 Concrete Saw		90.00		99.00		
1 Water Tank, 65 Gal.		6.40		7.05	14.81	16.29
16 M.H., Daily Totals		$548.20		$725.50	$34.26	$45.34
Crew B-89A	Hr.	Daily	Hr.	Daily	Bare Costs	Incl. O&P
1 Skilled Worker	$22.10	$176.80	$33.65	$269.20	$19.62	$29.85
1 Laborer	17.15	137.20	26.05	208.40		
1 Core Drill (large)		46.40		51.05	2.90	3.19
16 M.H., Daily Totals		$360.40		$528.65	$22.52	$33.04
Crew B-90	Hr.	Daily	Hr.	Daily	Bare Costs	Incl. O&P
1 Labor Foreman (outside)	$19.15	$153.20	$29.05	$232.40	$18.62	$28.03
3 Highway Laborers	17.15	411.60	26.05	625.20		
2 Equip. Oper. (light)	21.10	337.60	31.50	504.00		
2 Truck Drivers (heavy)	18.10	289.60	27.05	432.80		
1 Road Mixer, 310 H.P.		834.60		918.05		
1 Dist. Truck, 2000 Gal.		271.80		299.00	17.28	19.01
64 M.H., Daily Totals		$2298.40		$3011.45	$35.90	$47.04
Crew B-90A	Hr.	Daily	Hr.	Daily	Bare Costs	Incl. O&P
1 Labor Foreman	$19.15	$153.20	$29.05	$232.40	$20.26	$30.45
2 Laborers	17.15	274.40	26.05	416.80		
4 Equip. Oper. (medium)	22.10	707.20	33.00	1056.00		
2 Graders, 30,000 lbs		1026.80		1129.50		
1 Roller, Steel Wheel		179.00		196.90		
1 Roller, Pneumatic Wheel		232.20		255.40	25.67	28.24
56 M.H., Daily Totals		$2572.80		$3287.00	$45.93	$58.69
Crew B-90B	Hr.	Daily	Hr.	Daily	Bare Costs	Incl. O&P
1 Labor Foreman	$19.15	$153.20	$29.05	$232.40	$19.95	$30.02
2 Laborers	17.15	274.40	26.05	416.80		
3 Equip. Oper. (medium)	22.10	530.40	33.00	792.00		
1 Roller, Steel Wheel		179.00		196.90		
1 Roller, Pneumatic Wheel		232.20		255.40		
1 Road Mixer, 310 H.P.		834.60		918.05	25.95	28.54
48 M.H., Daily Totals		$2203.80		$2811.55	$45.90	$58.56
Crew B-91	Hr.	Daily	Hr.	Daily	Bare Costs	Incl. O&P
1 Labor Foreman (outside)	$19.15	$153.20	$29.05	$232.40	$19.99	$30.02
2 Highway Laborers	17.15	274.40	26.05	416.80		
4 Equip. Oper. (med.)	22.10	707.20	33.00	1056.00		
1 Truck Driver (heavy)	18.10	144.80	27.05	216.40		
1 Dist. Truck, 3000 Gal.		294.60		324.05		
1 Aggreg. Spreader, S.P.		536.00		589.60		
1 Roller, Pneu. Tire, 12 Ton		232.20		255.40		
1 Roller, Steel, 10 Ton		179.00		196.90	19.40	21.34
64 M.H., Daily Totals		$2521.40		$3287.55	$39.39	$51.36
Crew B-92	Hr.	Daily	Hr.	Daily	Bare Costs	Incl. O&P
1 Labor Foreman (outside)	$19.15	$153.20	$29.05	$232.40	$17.65	$26.80
3 Highway Laborers	17.15	411.60	26.05	625.20		
1 Crack Cleaner, 25 H.P.		68.00		74.80		
1 Air Compressor		60.00		66.00		
1 Tar Kettle, T.M.		17.00		18.70		
1 Flatbed Truck, 3 Ton		140.60		154.65	8.92	9.81
32 M.H., Daily Totals		$850.40		$1171.75	$26.57	$36.61

CREWS

Crew No.	Bare Costs		Incl. Subs O & P		Cost Per Man-hour	
Crew B-93	Hr.	Daily	Hr.	Daily	Bare Costs	Incl. O&P
1 Equip. Oper. (med.)	$22.10	$176.80	$33.00	$264.00	$22.10	$33.00
1 Feller Buncher, 50 H.P.		294.00		323.40	36.75	40.42
8 M.H., Daily Totals		$470.80		$587.40	$58.85	$73.42
Crew C-1	Hr.	Daily	Hr.	Daily	Bare Costs	Incl. O&P
3 Carpenters	$21.60	$518.40	$32.80	$787.20	$20.48	$31.11
1 Building Laborer	17.15	137.20	26.05	208.40		
Power Tools		23.40		25.75	.73	.80
32 M.H., Daily Totals		$679.00		$1021.35	$21.21	$31.91
Crew C-1A	Hr.	Daily	Hr.	Daily	Bare Costs	Incl. O&P
1 Carpenter	$21.60	$172.80	$32.80	$262.40	$21.60	$32.80
1 Circular Saw, 7"		7.80		8.60	.97	1.07
8 M.H., Daily Totals		$180.60		$271.00	$22.57	$33.87
Crew C-2	Hr.	Daily	Hr.	Daily	Bare Costs	Incl. O&P
1 Carpenter Foreman (out)	$23.60	$188.80	$35.85	$286.80	$21.19	$32.18
4 Carpenters	21.60	691.20	32.80	1049.60		
1 Building Laborer	17.15	137.20	26.05	208.40		
Power Tools		31.20		34.30	.65	.71
48 M.H., Daily Totals		$1048.40		$1579.10	$21.84	$32.89
Crew C-3	Hr.	Daily	Hr.	Daily	Bare Costs	Incl. O&P
1 Rodman Foreman	$25.30	$202.40	$41.50	$332.00	$21.73	$34.76
4 Rodmen (reinf.)	23.30	745.60	38.25	1224.00		
1 Equip. Oper. (light)	21.10	168.80	31.50	252.00		
2 Building Laborers	17.15	274.40	26.05	416.80		
Stressing Equipment		34.80		38.30		
Grouting Equipment		109.80		120.80	2.25	2.48
64 M.H., Daily Totals		$1535.80		$2383.90	$23.98	$37.24
Crew C-4	Hr.	Daily	Hr.	Daily	Bare Costs	Incl. O&P
1 Rodman Foreman	$25.30	$202.40	$41.50	$332.00	$23.80	$39.06
3 Rodmen (reinf.)	23.30	559.20	38.25	918.00		
Stressing Equipment		34.80		38.30	1.08	1.19
32 M.H., Daily Totals		$796.40		$1288.30	$24.88	$40.25
Crew C-5	Hr.	Daily	Hr.	Daily	Bare Costs	Incl. O&P
1 Rodman Foreman	$25.30	$202.40	$41.50	$332.00	$22.88	$36.68
4 Rodmen (reinf.)	23.30	745.60	38.25	1224.00		
1 Equip. Oper. (crane)	22.90	183.20	34.20	273.60		
1 Equip. Oper. Oiler	18.80	150.40	28.10	224.80		
1 Hyd. Crane, 25 Ton		476.00		523.60	8.50	9.35
56 M.H., Daily Totals		$1757.60		$2578.00	$31.38	$46.03
Crew C-6	Hr.	Daily	Hr.	Daily	Bare Costs	Incl. O&P
1 Labor Foreman (outside)	$19.15	$153.20	$29.05	$232.40	$18.13	$27.30
4 Building Laborers	17.15	548.80	26.05	833.60		
1 Cement Finisher	21.05	168.40	30.60	244.80		
2 Gas Engine Vibrators		61.20		67.30	1.27	1.40
48 M.H., Daily Totals		$931.60		$1378.10	$19.40	$28.70

Crew No.	Bare Costs		Incl. Subs O & P		Cost Per Man-hour	
Crew C-7	Hr.	Daily	Hr.	Daily	Bare Costs	Incl. O&P
1 Labor Foreman (outside)	$19.15	$153.20	$29.05	$232.40	$18.50	$27.86
5 Building Laborers	17.15	686.00	26.05	1042.00		
1 Cement Finisher	21.05	168.40	30.60	244.80		
1 Equip. Oper. (med.)	22.10	176.80	33.00	264.00		
2 Gas Engine Vibrators		61.20		67.30		
1 Concrete Bucket, 1 C.Y.		16.20		17.80		
1 Hyd. Crane, 55 Ton		692.40		761.65	12.02	13.23
64 M.H., Daily Totals		$1954.20		$2629.95	$30.52	$41.09
Crew C-8	Hr.	Daily	Hr.	Daily	Bare Costs	Incl. O&P
1 Labor Foreman (outside)	$19.15	$153.20	$29.05	$232.40	$19.25	$28.77
3 Building Laborers	17.15	411.60	26.05	625.20		
2 Cement Finishers	21.05	336.80	30.60	489.60		
1 Equip. Oper. (med.)	22.10	176.80	33.00	264.00		
1 Concrete Pump (small)		489.80		538.80	8.74	9.62
56 M.H., Daily Totals		$1568.20		$2150.00	$27.99	$38.39
Crew C-9	Hr.	Daily	Hr.	Daily	Bare Costs	Incl. O&P
1 Cement Finisher	$21.05	$168.40	$30.60	$244.80	$21.05	$30.60
1 Gas Finishing Mach.		33.40		36.75	4.17	4.59
8 M.H., Daily Totals		$201.80		$281.55	$25.22	$35.19
Crew C-10	Hr.	Daily	Hr.	Daily	Bare Costs	Incl. O&P
1 Building Laborer	$17.15	$137.20	$26.05	$208.40	$19.75	$29.08
2 Cement Finishers	21.05	336.80	30.60	489.60		
2 Gas Finishing Mach.		66.80		73.50	2.78	3.06
24 M.H., Daily Totals		$540.80		$771.50	$22.53	$32.14
Crew C-11	Hr.	Daily	Hr.	Daily	Bare Costs	Incl. O&P
1 Struc. Steel Foreman	$25.45	$203.60	$43.25	$346.00	$23.09	$38.29
6 Struc. Steel Workers	23.45	1125.60	39.85	1912.80		
1 Equip. Oper. (crane)	22.90	183.20	34.20	273.60		
1 Equip. Oper. Oiler	18.80	150.40	28.10	224.80		
1 Truck Crane, 150 Ton		1319.20		1451.10	18.32	20.15
72 M.H., Daily Totals		$2982.00		$4208.30	$41.41	$58.44
Crew C-12	Hr.	Daily	Hr.	Daily	Bare Costs	Incl. O&P
1 Carpenter Foreman (out)	$23.60	$188.80	$35.85	$286.80	$21.40	$32.41
3 Carpenters	21.60	518.40	32.80	787.20		
1 Building Laborer	17.15	137.20	26.05	208.40		
1 Equip. Oper. (crane)	22.90	183.20	34.20	273.60		
1 Hyd. Crane, 12 Ton		342.00		376.20	7.12	7.83
48 M.H., Daily Totals		$1369.60		$1932.20	$28.52	$40.24
Crew C-13	Hr.	Daily	Hr.	Daily	Bare Costs	Incl. O&P
1 Struc. Steel Worker	$23.45	$187.60	$39.85	$318.80	$22.83	$37.50
1 Welder	23.45	187.60	39.85	318.80		
1 Carpenter	21.60	172.80	32.80	262.40		
1 Gas Welding Machine		64.40		70.85	2.68	2.95
24 M.H., Daily Totals		$612.40		$970.85	$25.51	$40.45

CREWS

Crew No.	Bare Costs		Incl. Subs O & P		Cost Per Man-hour	
Crew C-14	Hr.	Daily	Hr.	Daily	Bare Costs	Incl. O&P
1 Carpenter Foreman (out)	$23.60	$188.80	$35.85	$286.80	$20.95	$32.25
5 Carpenters	21.60	864.00	32.80	1312.00		
4 Building Laborers	17.15	548.80	26.05	833.60		
4 Rodmen (reinf.)	23.30	745.60	38.25	1224.00		
2 Cement Finishers	21.05	336.80	30.60	489.60		
1 Equip. Oper. (crane)	22.90	183.20	34.20	273.60		
1 Equip. Oper. Oiler	18.80	150.40	28.10	224.80		
1 Crane, 80 Ton, & Tools		1052.00		1157.20		
Power Tools		23.40		25.75		
2 Gas Finishing Mach.		66.80		73.50	7.93	8.72
144 M.H., Daily Totals		$4159.80		$5900.85	$28.88	$40.97
Crew C-15	Hr.	Daily	Hr.	Daily	Bare Costs	Incl. O&P
1 Carpenter Foreman (out)	$23.60	$188.80	$35.85	$286.80	$20.40	$31.00
2 Carpenters	21.60	345.60	32.80	524.80		
3 Building Laborers	17.15	411.60	26.05	625.20		
2 Cement Finishers	21.05	336.80	30.60	489.60		
1 Rodman (reinf.)	23.30	186.40	38.25	306.00		
Power Tools		15.60		17.15		
1 Gas Finishing Mach.		33.40		36.75	.68	.74
72 M.H., Daily Totals		$1518.20		$2286.30	$21.08	$31.74
Crew C-16	Hr.	Daily	Hr.	Daily	Bare Costs	Incl. O&P
1 Labor Foreman (outside)	$19.15	$153.20	$29.05	$232.40	$20.15	$30.87
3 Building Laborers	17.15	411.60	26.05	625.20		
2 Cement Finishers	21.05	336.80	30.60	489.60		
1 Equip. Oper. (med.)	22.10	176.80	33.00	264.00		
2 Rodmen (reinf.)	23.30	372.80	38.25	612.00		
1 Concrete Pump (small)		489.80		538.80	6.80	7.48
72 M.H., Daily Totals		$1941.00		$2762.00	$26.95	$38.35
Crew C-17	Hr.	Daily	Hr.	Daily	Bare Costs	Incl. O&P
2 Skilled Worker Foremen	$24.10	$385.60	$36.70	$587.20	$22.50	$34.26
8 Skilled Workers	22.10	1414.40	33.65	2153.60		
80 M.H., Daily Totals		$1800.00		$2740.80	$22.50	$34.26
Crew C-17A	Hr.	Daily	Hr.	Daily	Bare Costs	Incl. O&P
2 Skilled Worker Foremen	$24.10	$385.60	$36.70	$587.20	$22.50	$34.26
8 Skilled Workers	22.10	1414.40	33.65	2153.60		
.125 Equip. Oper. (crane)	22.90	22.90	34.20	34.20		
.125 Crane, 80 Ton, & Tools		136.75		150.45		
.125 Hand Held Power Tools		1.00		1.10		
.125 Walk Behind Pwr. Tools		4.35		4.80	1.75	1.93
81 M.H., Daily Totals		$1965.00		$2931.35	$24.25	$36.19
Crew C-17B	Hr.	Daily	Hr.	Daily	Bare Costs	Incl. O&P
2 Skilled Worker Foremen	$24.10	$385.60	$36.70	$587.20	$22.50	$34.26
8 Skilled Workers	22.10	1414.40	33.65	2153.60		
.25 Equip. Oper. (crane)	22.90	45.80	34.20	68.40		
.25 Crane, 80 Ton, & Tools		263.00		289.30		
.25 Hand Held Power Tools		1.95		2.15		
.25 Walk Behind Pwr. Tools		8.35		9.20	3.33	3.66
82 M.H., Daily Totals		$2119.10		$3109.85	$25.83	$37.92

Crew No.	Bare Costs		Incl. Subs O & P		Cost Per Man-hour	
Crew C-17C	Hr.	Daily	Hr.	Daily	Bare Costs	Incl. O&P
2 Skilled Worker Foremen	$24.10	$385.60	$36.70	$587.20	$22.50	$34.26
8 Skilled Workers	22.10	1414.40	33.65	2153.60		
.375 Equip. Oper. (crane)	22.90	68.70	34.20	102.60		
.375 Crane, 80 Ton & Tools		399.75		439.75		
.375 Hand Held Power Tools		2.95		3.25		
.375 Walk Behind Pwr. Tools		12.70		13.95	5.00	5.50
83 M.H., Daily Totals		$2284.10		$3300.35	$27.50	$39.76
Crew C-17D	Hr.	Daily	Hr.	Daily	Bare Costs	Incl. O&P
2 Skilled Worker Foremen	$24.10	$385.60	$36.70	$587.20	$22.50	$34.26
8 Skilled Workers	22.10	1414.40	33.65	2153.60		
.5 Equip. Oper. (crane)	22.90	91.60	34.20	136.80		
.5 Crane, 80 Ton & Tools		526.00		578.60		
.5 Hand Held Power Tools		3.90		4.30		
.5 Walk Behind Pwr. Tools		16.70		18.35	6.50	7.15
84 M.H., Daily Totals		$2438.20		$3478.85	$29.00	$41.41
Crew C-17E	Hr.	Daily	Hr.	Daily	Bare Costs	Incl. O&P
2 Skilled Worker Foremen	$24.10	$385.60	$36.70	$587.20	$22.50	$34.26
8 Skilled Workers	22.10	1414.40	33.65	2153.60		
1 Hyd. Jack with Rods		52.40		57.65	.65	.72
80 M.H., Daily Totals		$1852.40		$2798.45	$23.15	$34.98
Crew C-18	Hr.	Daily	Hr.	Daily	Bare Costs	Incl. O&P
.125 Labor Foreman (out)	$19.15	$19.15	$29.05	$29.05	$17.37	$26.38
1 Building Laborer	17.15	137.20	26.05	208.40		
1 Concrete Cart, 10 C.F.		43.60		47.95	4.84	5.32
9 M.H., Daily Totals		$199.95		$285.40	$22.21	$31.70
Crew C-19	Hr.	Daily	Hr.	Daily	Bare Costs	Incl. O&P
.125 Labor Foreman (out)	$19.15	$19.15	$29.05	$29.05	$17.37	$26.38
1 Building Laborer	17.15	137.20	26.05	208.40		
1 Concrete Cart, 18 C.F.		104.60		115.05	11.62	12.78
9 M.H., Daily Totals		$260.95		$352.50	$28.99	$39.16
Crew C-20	Hr.	Daily	Hr.	Daily	Bare Costs	Incl. O&P
1 Labor Foreman (outside)	$19.15	$153.20	$29.05	$232.40	$18.50	$27.86
5 Building Laborers	17.15	686.00	26.05	1042.00		
1 Cement Finisher	21.05	168.40	30.60	244.80		
1 Equip. Oper. (med.)	22.10	176.80	33.00	264.00		
2 Gas Engine Vibrators		61.20		67.30		
1 Concrete Pump (small)		489.80		538.80	8.60	9.47
64 M.H., Daily Totals		$1735.40		$2389.30	$27.10	$37.33
Crew C-21	Hr.	Daily	Hr.	Daily	Bare Costs	Incl. O&P
1 Labor Foreman (outside)	$19.15	$153.20	$29.05	$232.40	$18.50	$27.86
5 Building Laborers	17.15	686.00	26.05	1042.00		
1 Cement Finisher	21.05	168.40	30.60	244.80		
1 Equip. Oper. (med.)	22.10	176.80	33.00	264.00		
2 Gas Engine Vibrators		61.20		67.30		
1 Concrete Conveyer		125.40		137.95	2.91	3.20
64 M.H., Daily Totals		$1371.00		$1988.45	$21.41	$31.06

CREWS

Crew No.	Bare Costs		Incl. Subs O & P		Cost Per Man-hour	
Crew C-22	Hr.	Daily	Hr.	Daily	Bare Costs	Incl. O&P
1 Rodman Foreman	$25.30	$202.40	$41.50	$332.00	$23.56	$38.53
4 Rodmen (reinf.)	23.30	745.60	38.25	1224.00		
.125 Equip. Oper. (crane)	22.90	22.90	34.20	34.20		
.125 Equip. Oper. Oiler	18.80	18.80	28.10	28.10		
.125 Hyd. Crane, 25 Ton		61.90		68.05	1.47	1.62
42 M.H., Daily Totals		$1051.60		$1686.35	$25.03	$40.15
Crew C-23	Hr.	Daily	Hr.	Daily	Bare Costs	Incl. O&P
2 Skilled Worker Foremen	$24.10	$385.60	$36.70	$587.20	$22.25	$33.76
6 Skilled Workers	22.10	1060.80	33.65	1615.20		
1 Equip. Oper. (crane)	22.90	183.20	34.20	273.60		
1 Equip. Oper. Oiler	18.80	150.40	28.10	224.80		
1 Crane, 90 Ton		1050.20		1155.20	13.12	14.44
80 M.H., Daily Totals		$2830.20		$3856.00	$35.37	$48.20
Crew C-24	Hr.	Daily	Hr.	Daily	Bare Costs	Incl. O&P
2 Skilled Worker Foremen	$24.10	$385.60	$36.70	$587.20	$22.25	$33.76
6 Skilled Workers	22.10	1060.80	33.65	1615.20		
1 Equip. Oper. (crane)	22.90	183.20	34.20	273.60		
1 Equip. Oper. Oiler	18.80	150.40	28.10	224.80		
1 Truck Crane, 150 Ton		1319.20		1451.10	16.49	18.13
80 M.H., Daily Totals		$3099.20		$4151.90	$38.74	$51.89
Crew D-1	Hr.	Daily	Hr.	Daily	Bare Costs	Incl. O&P
1 Bricklayer	$22.15	$177.20	$33.05	$264.40	$19.70	$29.40
1 Bricklayer Helper	17.25	138.00	25.75	206.00		
16 M.H., Daily Totals		$315.20		$470.40	$19.70	$29.40
Crew D-2	Hr.	Daily	Hr.	Daily	Bare Costs	Incl. O&P
3 Bricklayers	$22.15	$531.60	$33.05	$793.20	$20.31	$30.37
2 Bricklayer Helpers	17.25	276.00	25.75	412.00		
.5 Carpenter	21.60	86.40	32.80	131.20		
44 M.H., Daily Totals		$894.00		$1336.40	$20.31	$30.37
Crew D-3	Hr.	Daily	Hr.	Daily	Bare Costs	Incl. O&P
3 Bricklayers	$22.15	$531.60	$33.05	$793.20	$20.25	$30.25
2 Bricklayer Helpers	17.25	276.00	25.75	412.00		
.25 Carpenter	21.60	43.20	32.80	65.60		
42 M.H., Daily Totals		$850.80		$1270.80	$20.25	$30.25
Crew D-4	Hr.	Daily	Hr.	Daily	Bare Costs	Incl. O&P
1 Bricklayer	$22.15	$177.20	$33.05	$264.40	$19.43	$29.01
2 Bricklayer Helpers	17.25	276.00	25.75	412.00		
1 Equip. Oper. (light)	21.10	168.80	31.50	252.00		
1 Grout Pump		84.00		92.40		
1 Hoses & Hopper		23.20		25.50		
1 Accessories		9.80		10.80	3.65	4.02
32 M.H., Daily Totals		$739.00		$1057.10	$23.08	$33.03
Crew D-5	Hr.	Daily	Hr.	Daily	Bare Costs	Incl. O&P
1 Bricklayer	$22.15	$177.20	$33.05	$264.40	$22.15	$33.05
1 Power Tool		30.80		33.90	3.85	4.23
8 M.H., Daily Totals		$208.00		$298.30	$26.00	$37.28

Crew No.	Bare Costs		Incl. Subs O & P		Cost Per Man-hour	
Crew D-6	Hr.	Daily	Hr.	Daily	Bare Costs	Incl. O&P
3 Bricklayers	$22.15	$531.60	$33.05	$793.20	$19.77	$29.53
3 Bricklayer Helpers	17.25	414.00	25.75	618.00		
.25 Carpenter	21.60	43.20	32.80	65.60		
50 M.H., Daily Totals		$988.80		$1476.80	$19.77	$29.53
Crew D-7	Hr.	Daily	Hr.	Daily	Bare Costs	Incl. O&P
1 Tile Layer	$21.55	$172.40	$31.10	$248.80	$19.35	$27.92
1 Tile Layer Helper	17.15	137.20	24.75	198.00		
16 M.H., Daily Totals		$309.60		$446.80	$19.35	$27.92
Crew D-8	Hr.	Daily	Hr.	Daily	Bare Costs	Incl. O&P
3 Bricklayers	$22.15	$531.60	$33.05	$793.20	$20.19	$30.13
2 Bricklayer Helpers	17.25	276.00	25.75	412.00		
40 M.H., Daily Totals		$807.60		$1205.20	$20.19	$30.13
Crew D-9	Hr.	Daily	Hr.	Daily	Bare Costs	Incl. O&P
3 Bricklayers	$22.15	$531.60	$33.05	$793.20	$19.70	$29.40
3 Bricklayer Helpers	17.25	414.00	25.75	618.00		
48 M.H., Daily Totals		$945.60		$1411.20	$19.70	$29.40
Crew D-10	Hr.	Daily	Hr.	Daily	Bare Costs	Incl. O&P
1 Bricklayer Foreman	$24.15	$193.20	$36.05	$288.40	$20.74	$30.96
1 Bricklayer	22.15	177.20	33.05	264.40		
2 Bricklayer Helpers	17.25	276.00	25.75	412.00		
1 Equip. Oper. (crane)	22.90	183.20	34.20	273.60		
1 Truck Crane, 12.5 Ton		397.00		436.70	9.92	10.91
40 M.H., Daily Totals		$1226.60		$1675.10	$30.66	$41.87
Crew D-11	Hr.	Daily	Hr.	Daily	Bare Costs	Incl. O&P
1 Bricklayer Foreman	$24.15	$193.20	$36.05	$288.40	$21.18	$31.61
1 Bricklayer	22.15	177.20	33.05	264.40		
1 Bricklayer Helper	17.25	138.00	25.75	206.00		
24 M.H., Daily Totals		$508.40		$758.80	$21.18	$31.61
Crew D-12	Hr.	Daily	Hr.	Daily	Bare Costs	Incl. O&P
1 Bricklayer Foreman	$24.15	$193.20	$36.05	$288.40	$20.20	$30.15
1 Bricklayer	22.15	177.20	33.05	264.40		
2 Bricklayer Helpers	17.25	276.00	25.75	412.00		
32 M.H., Daily Totals		$646.40		$964.80	$20.20	$30.15
Crew D-13	Hr.	Daily	Hr.	Daily	Bare Costs	Incl. O&P
1 Bricklayer Foreman	$24.15	$193.20	$36.05	$288.40	$20.88	$31.26
1 Bricklayer	22.15	177.20	33.05	264.40		
2 Bricklayer Helpers	17.25	276.00	25.75	412.00		
1 Carpenter	21.60	172.80	32.80	262.40		
1 Equip. Oper. (crane)	22.90	183.20	34.20	273.60		
1 Truck Crane, 12.5 Ton		397.00		436.70	8.27	9.09
48 M.H., Daily Totals		$1399.40		$1937.50	$29.15	$40.35
Crew E-1	Hr.	Daily	Hr.	Daily	Bare Costs	Incl. O&P
1 Welder Foreman	$25.45	$203.60	$43.25	$346.00	$23.33	$38.20
1 Welder	23.45	187.60	39.85	318.80		
1 Equip. Oper. (light)	21.10	168.80	31.50	252.00		
1 Gas Welding Machine		64.40		70.85	2.68	2.95
24 M.H., Daily Totals		$624.40		$987.65	$26.01	$41.15

CREWS

Crew No.	Bare Costs		Incl. Subs O & P		Cost Per Man-hour	
Crew E-2	**Hr.**	**Daily**	**Hr.**	**Daily**	**Bare Costs**	**Incl. O&P**
1 Struc. Steel Foreman	$25.45	$203.60	$43.25	$346.00	$22.99	$37.85
4 Struc. Steel Workers	23.45	750.40	39.85	1275.20		
1 Equip. Oper. (crane)	22.90	183.20	34.20	273.60		
1 Equip. Oper. Oiler	18.80	150.40	28.10	224.80		
1 Crane, 90 Ton		1050.20		1155.20	18.75	20.62
56 M.H., Daily Totals		$2337.80		$3274.80	$41.74	$58.47
Crew E-3	**Hr.**	**Daily**	**Hr.**	**Daily**	**Bare Costs**	**Incl. O&P**
1 Struc. Steel Foreman	$25.45	$203.60	$43.25	$346.00	$24.11	$40.98
1 Struc. Steel Worker	23.45	187.60	39.85	318.80		
1 Welder	23.45	187.60	39.85	318.80		
1 Gas Welding Machine		64.40		70.85		
1 Torch, Gas & Air		59.20		65.10	5.15	5.66
24 M.H., Daily Totals		$702.40		$1119.55	$29.26	$46.64
Crew E-4	**Hr.**	**Daily**	**Hr.**	**Daily**	**Bare Costs**	**Incl. O&P**
1 Struc. Steel Foreman	$25.45	$203.60	$43.25	$346.00	$23.95	$40.70
3 Struc. Steel Workers	23.45	562.80	39.85	956.40		
1 Gas Welding Machine		64.40		70.85	2.01	2.21
32 M.H., Daily Totals		$830.80		$1373.25	$25.96	$42.91
Crew E-5	**Hr.**	**Daily**	**Hr.**	**Daily**	**Bare Costs**	**Incl. O&P**
2 Struc. Steel Foremen	$25.45	$407.20	$43.25	$692.00	$23.33	$38.79
5 Struc. Steel Workers	23.45	938.00	39.85	1594.00		
1 Equip. Oper. (crane)	22.90	183.20	34.20	273.60		
1 Welder	23.45	187.60	39.85	318.80		
1 Equip. Oper. Oiler	18.80	150.40	28.10	224.80		
1 Crane, 90 Ton		1050.20		1155.20		
1 Gas Welding Machine		64.40		70.85		
1 Torch, Gas & Air		59.20		65.10	14.67	16.13
80 M.H., Daily Totals		$3040.20		$4394.35	$38.00	$54.92
Crew E-6	**Hr.**	**Daily**	**Hr.**	**Daily**	**Bare Costs**	**Incl. O&P**
3 Struc. Steel Foreman	$25.45	$610.80	$43.25	$1038.00	$23.35	$38.87
9 Struc. Steel Workers	23.45	1688.40	39.85	2869.20		
1 Equip. Oper. (crane)	22.90	183.20	34.20	273.60		
1 Welder	23.45	187.60	39.85	318.80		
1 Equip. Oper. Oiler	18.80	150.40	28.10	224.80		
1 Equip. Oper. (light)	21.10	168.80	31.50	252.00		
1 Crane, 90 Ton		1050.20		1155.20		
1 Gas Welding Machine		64.40		70.85		
1 Torch, Gas & air		59.20		65.10		
1 Air Compr., 160 C.F.M.		80.20		88.20		
2 Impact Wrenches		55.60		61.15	10.23	11.25
128 M.H., Daily Totals		$4298.80		$6416.90	$33.58	$50.12
Crew E-7	**Hr.**	**Daily**	**Hr.**	**Daily**	**Bare Costs**	**Incl. O&P**
1 Struc. Steel Foreman	$25.45	$203.60	$43.25	$346.00	$23.33	$38.79
4 Struc. Steel Workers	23.45	750.40	39.85	1275.20		
1 Equip. Oper. (crane)	22.90	183.20	34.20	273.60		
1 Equip. Oper. Oiler	18.80	150.40	28.10	224.80		
1 Welder Foreman	25.45	203.60	43.25	346.00		
2 Welders	23.45	375.20	39.85	637.60		
1 Crane, 90 Ton		1050.20		1155.20		
2 Gas Welding Machines		128.80		141.70	14.73	16.21
80 M.H., Daily Totals		$3045.40		$4400.10	$38.06	$55.00

Crew No.	Bare Costs		Incl. Subs O & P		Cost Per Man-hour	
Crew E-8	**Hr.**	**Daily**	**Hr.**	**Daily**	**Bare Costs**	**Incl. O&P**
1 Struc. Steel Foreman	$25.45	$203.60	$43.25	$346.00	$23.17	$38.39
4 Struc. Steel Workers	23.45	750.40	39.85	1275.20		
1 Welder Foreman	25.45	203.60	43.25	346.00		
4 Welders	23.45	750.40	39.85	1275.20		
1 Equip. Oper. (crane)	22.90	183.20	34.20	273.60		
1 Equip. Oper. Oiler	18.80	150.40	28.10	224.80		
1 Equip. Oper. (light)	21.10	168.80	31.50	252.00		
1 Crane, 90 Ton		1050.20		1155.20		
4 Gas Welding Machines		257.60		283.35	12.57	13.83
104 M.H., Daily Totals		$3718.20		$5431.35	$35.74	$52.22
Crew E-9	**Hr.**	**Daily**	**Hr.**	**Daily**	**Bare Costs**	**Incl. O&P**
2 Struc. Steel Foremen	$25.45	$407.20	$43.25	$692.00	$23.35	$38.87
5 Struc. Steel Workers	23.45	938.00	39.85	1594.00		
1 Welder Foreman	25.45	203.60	43.25	346.00		
5 Welders	23.45	938.00	39.85	1594.00		
1 Equip. Oper. (crane)	22.90	183.20	34.20	273.60		
1 Equip. Oper. Oiler	18.80	150.40	28.10	224.80		
1 Equip. Oper. (light)	21.10	168.80	31.50	252.00		
1 Crane, 90 Ton		1050.20		1155.20		
5 Gas Welding Machines		322.00		354.20		
1 Torch, Gas & Air		59.20		65.10	11.18	12.30
128 M.H., Daily Totals		$4420.60		$6550.90	$34.53	$51.17
Crew E-10	**Hr.**	**Daily**	**Hr.**	**Daily**	**Bare Costs**	**Incl. O&P**
1 Welder Foreman	$25.45	$203.60	$43.25	$346.00	$24.45	$41.55
1 Welder	23.45	187.60	39.85	318.80		
4 Gas Welding Machines		257.60		283.35		
1 Truck, 3 Ton		140.60		154.65	24.88	27.37
16 M.H., Daily Totals		$789.40		$1102.80	$49.33	$68.92
Crew E-11	**Hr.**	**Daily**	**Hr.**	**Daily**	**Bare Costs**	**Incl. O&P**
2 Painters, Struc. Steel	$21.00	$336.00	$36.70	$587.20	$20.06	$32.73
1 Building Laborer	17.15	137.20	26.05	208.40		
1 Equip. Oper. (light)	21.10	168.80	31.50	252.00		
1 Air compressor 250 cfm		84.00		92.40		
1 Sand blaster		23.20		25.50		
1 Sand blasting accessories		9.80		10.80	3.65	4.02
32 M.H., Daily Totals		$759.00		$1176.30	$23.71	$36.75
Crew E-12	**Hr.**	**Daily**	**Hr.**	**Daily**	**Bare Costs**	**Incl. O&P**
1 Welder Foreman	$25.45	$203.60	$43.25	$346.00	$23.27	$37.37
1 Equip. Oper. (light)	21.10	168.80	31.50	252.00		
1 Gas Welding Machine		64.40		70.85	4.02	4.42
16 M.H., Daily Totals		$436.80		$668.85	$27.29	$41.79
Crew E-13	**Hr.**	**Daily**	**Hr.**	**Daily**	**Bare Costs**	**Incl. O&P**
1 Welder Foreman	$25.45	$203.60	$43.25	$346.00	$24.00	$39.33
.5 Equip. Oper. (light)	21.10	84.40	31.50	126.00		
1 Gas Welding Machine		64.40		70.85	5.36	5.90
12 M.H., Daily Totals		$352.40		$542.85	$29.36	$45.23
Crew E-14	**Hr.**	**Daily**	**Hr.**	**Daily**	**Bare Costs**	**Incl. O&P**
1 Welder Foreman	$25.45	$203.60	$43.25	$346.00	$25.45	$43.25
1 Gas Welding Machine		64.40		70.85	8.05	8.85
8 M.H., Daily Totals		$268.00		$416.85	$33.50	$52.10

CREWS

Crew No.	Bare Costs		Incl. Subs O & P		Cost Per Man-hour	
Crew E-15	Hr.	Daily	Hr.	Daily	Bare Costs	Incl. O&P
2 Painters, Struc. Steel	$21.00	$336.00	$36.70	$587.20	$21.00	$36.70
1 Paint Sprayer, 17 C.F.M.		25.40		27.95	1.58	1.74
16 M.H., Daily Totals		$361.40		$615.15	$22.58	$38.44
Crew F-1	Hr.	Daily	Hr.	Daily	Bare Costs	Incl. O&P
1 Carpenter	$21.60	$172.80	$32.80	$262.40	$21.60	$32.80
Power Tools		7.80		8.60	.97	1.07
8 M.H., Daily Totals		$180.60		$271.00	$22.57	$33.87
Crew F-2	Hr.	Daily	Hr.	Daily	Bare Costs	Incl. O&P
2 Carpenters	$21.60	$345.60	$32.80	$524.80	$21.60	$32.80
Power Tools		15.60		17.15	.97	1.07
16 M.H., Daily Totals		$361.20		$541.95	$22.57	$33.87
Crew F-3	Hr.	Daily	Hr.	Daily	Bare Costs	Incl. O&P
4 Carpenters	$21.60	$691.20	$32.80	$1049.60	$21.86	$33.08
1 Equip. Oper. (crane)	22.90	183.20	34.20	273.60		
1 Hyd. Crane, 12 Ton		342.00		376.20		
Power Tools		15.60		17.15	8.94	9.83
40 M.H., Daily Totals		$1232.00		$1716.55	$30.80	$42.91
Crew F-4	Hr.	Daily	Hr.	Daily	Bare Costs	Incl. O&P
4 Carpenters	$21.60	$691.20	$32.80	$1049.60	$21.35	$32.25
1 Equip. Oper. (crane)	22.90	183.20	34.20	273.60		
1 Equip. Oper. Oiler	18.80	150.40	28.10	224.80		
1 Hyd. Crane, 55 Ton		692.40		761.65		
Power Tools		15.60		17.15	14.75	16.22
48 M.H., Daily Totals		$1732.80		$2326.80	$36.10	$48.47
Crew F-5	Hr.	Daily	Hr.	Daily	Bare Costs	Incl. O&P
1 Carpenter Foreman	$23.60	$188.80	$35.85	$286.80	$22.10	$33.56
3 Carpenters	21.60	518.40	32.80	787.20		
Power Tools		15.60		17.15	.48	.53
32 M.H., Daily Totals		$722.80		$1091.15	$22.58	$34.09
Crew F-6	Hr.	Daily	Hr.	Daily	Bare Costs	Incl. O&P
2 Carpenters	$21.60	$345.60	$32.80	$524.80	$20.08	$30.38
2 Building Laborers	17.15	274.40	26.05	416.80		
1 Equip. Oper. (crane)	22.90	183.20	34.20	273.60		
1 Hyd. Crane, 12 Ton		342.00		376.20		
Power Tools		15.60		17.15	8.94	9.83
40 M.H., Daily Totals		$1160.80		$1608.55	$29.02	$40.21
Crew F-7	Hr.	Daily	Hr.	Daily	Bare Costs	Incl. O&P
2 Carpenters	$21.60	$345.60	$32.80	$524.80	$19.37	$29.42
2 Building Laborers	17.15	274.40	26.05	416.80		
Power Tools		15.60		17.15	.48	.53
32 M.H., Daily Totals		$635.60		$958.75	$19.85	$29.95
Crew G-1	Hr.	Daily	Hr.	Daily	Bare Costs	Incl. O&P
1 Roofer Foreman	$21.85	$174.80	$35.90	$287.20	$18.67	$30.68
4 Roofers, Composition	19.85	635.20	32.60	1043.20		
2 Roofer Helpers	14.75	236.00	24.25	388.00		
Application Equipment		104.00		114.40	1.85	2.04
56 M.H., Daily Totals		$1150.00		$1832.80	$20.52	$32.72

Crew No.	Bare Costs		Incl. Subs O & P		Cost Per Man-hour	
Crew G-2	Hr.	Daily	Hr.	Daily	Bare Costs	Incl. O&P
1 Plasterer	$21.35	$170.80	$31.80	$254.40	$18.68	$28.00
1 Plasterer Helper	17.55	140.40	26.15	209.20		
1 Building Laborer	17.15	137.20	26.05	208.40		
Grouting Equipment		219.60		241.55	9.15	10.06
24 M.H., Daily Totals		$668.00		$913.55	$27.83	$38.06
Crew G-3	Hr.	Daily	Hr.	Daily	Bare Costs	Incl. O&P
2 Sheet Metal Workers	$24.35	$389.60	$36.80	$588.80	$20.75	$31.42
2 Building Laborers	17.15	274.40	26.05	416.80		
Power Tools		24.50		26.95	.76	.84
32 M.H., Daily Totals		$688.50		$1032.55	$21.51	$32.26
Crew G-4	Hr.	Daily	Hr.	Daily	Bare Costs	Incl. O&P
1 Labor Foreman (outside)	$19.15	$153.20	$29.05	$232.40	$17.81	$27.05
2 Building Laborers	17.15	274.40	26.05	416.80		
1 Light Truck, 1.5 Ton		138.20		152.00		
1 Air Compr., 160 C.F.M.		80.20		88.20	9.10	10.00
24 M.H., Daily Totals		$646.00		$889.40	$26.91	$37.05
Crew G-5	Hr.	Daily	Hr.	Daily	Bare Costs	Incl. O&P
1 Roofer Foreman	$21.85	$174.80	$35.90	$287.20	$18.21	$29.92
2 Roofers, Composition	19.85	317.60	32.60	521.60		
2 Roofer Helpers	14.75	236.00	24.25	388.00		
Application Equipment		104.00		114.40	2.60	2.86
40 M.H., Daily Totals		$832.40		$1311.20	$20.81	$32.78
Crew H-1	Hr.	Daily	Hr.	Daily	Bare Costs	Incl. O&P
2 Glaziers	$22.10	$353.60	$32.65	$522.40	$22.77	$36.25
2 Struc. Steel Workers	23.45	375.20	39.85	637.60		
32 M.H., Daily Totals		$728.80		$1160.00	$22.77	$36.25
Crew H-2	Hr.	Daily	Hr.	Daily	Bare Costs	Incl. O&P
2 Glaziers	$22.10	$353.60	$32.65	$522.40	$20.45	$30.45
1 Building Laborer	17.15	137.20	26.05	208.40		
24 M.H., Daily Totals		$490.80		$730.80	$20.45	$30.45
Crew J-1	Hr.	Daily	Hr.	Daily	Bare Costs	Incl. O&P
3 Plasterers	$21.35	$512.40	$31.80	$763.20	$19.83	$29.54
2 Plasterer Helpers	17.55	280.80	26.15	418.40		
1 Mixing Machine, 6 C.F.		32.80		36.10	.82	.90
40 M.H., Daily Totals		$826.00		$1217.70	$20.65	$30.44
Crew J-2	Hr.	Daily	Hr.	Daily	Bare Costs	Incl. O&P
3 Plasterers	$21.35	$512.40	$31.80	$763.20	$20.13	$29.88
2 Plasterer Helpers	17.55	280.80	26.15	418.40		
1 Lather	21.65	173.20	31.60	252.80		
1 Mixing Machine, 6 C.F.		32.80		36.10	.68	.75
48 M.H., Daily Totals		$999.20		$1470.50	$20.81	$30.63
Crew J-3	Hr.	Daily	Hr.	Daily	Bare Costs	Incl. O&P
1 Terrazzo Worker	$21.50	$172.00	$31.05	$248.40	$19.22	$27.75
1 Terrazzo Helper	16.95	135.60	24.45	195.60		
1 Terrazzo Grinder, Electric		33.40		36.75		
1 Terrazzo Mixer		53.00		58.30	5.40	5.94
16 M.H., Daily Totals		$394.00		$539.05	$24.62	$33.69

CREWS

Crew No.	Bare Costs		Incl. Subs O & P		Cost Per Man-hour	
Crew J-4	Hr.	Daily	Hr.	Daily	Bare Costs	Incl. O&P
1 Tile Layer	$21.55	$172.40	$31.10	$248.80	$19.35	$27.92
1 Tile Layer Helper	17.15	137.20	24.75	198.00		
16 M.H., Daily Totals		$309.60		$446.80	$19.35	$27.92
Crew K-1	Hr.	Daily	Hr.	Daily	Bare Costs	Incl. O&P
1 Carpenter	$21.60	$172.80	$32.80	$262.40	$19.70	$29.70
1 Truck Driver (light)	17.80	142.40	26.60	212.80		
1 Truck w/Power Equip.		369.80		406.75	23.11	25.42
16 M.H., Daily Totals		$685.00		$881.95	$42.81	$55.12
Crew K-2	Hr.	Daily	Hr.	Daily	Bare Costs	Incl. O&P
1 Struc. Steel Foreman	$25.45	$203.60	$43.25	$346.00	$22.23	$36.56
1 Struc. Steel Worker	23.45	187.60	39.85	318.80		
1 Truck Driver (light)	17.80	142.40	26.60	212.80		
1 Truck w/Power Equip.		369.80		406.75	15.40	16.94
24 M.H., Daily Totals		$903.40		$1284.35	$37.63	$53.50
Crew L-1	Hr.	Daily	Hr.	Daily	Bare Costs	Incl. O&P
1 Electrician	$24.35	$194.80	$35.85	$286.80	$24.52	$36.25
1 Plumber	24.70	197.60	36.65	293.20		
16 M.H., Daily Totals		$392.40		$580.00	$24.52	$36.25
Crew L-2	Hr.	Daily	Hr.	Daily	Bare Costs	Incl. O&P
1 Carpenter	$21.60	$172.80	$32.80	$262.40	$19.17	$29.27
1 Helper	16.75	134.00	25.75	206.00		
16 M.H., Daily Totals		$306.80		$468.40	$19.17	$29.27
Crew L-3	Hr.	Daily	Hr.	Daily	Bare Costs	Incl. O&P
1 Carpenter	$21.60	$172.80	$32.80	$262.40	$22.97	$34.56
.5 Electrician	24.35	97.40	35.85	143.40		
.5 Sheet Metal Worker	24.35	97.40	36.80	147.20		
16 M.H., Daily Totals		$367.60		$553.00	$22.97	$34.56
Crew L-4	Hr.	Daily	Hr.	Daily	Bare Costs	Incl. O&P
2 Skilled Workers	$22.10	$353.60	$33.65	$538.40	$20.31	$31.01
1 Helper	16.75	134.00	25.75	206.00		
24 M.H., Daily Totals		$487.60		$744.40	$20.31	$31.01
Crew L-5	Hr.	Daily	Hr.	Daily	Bare Costs	Incl. O&P
1 Struc. Steel Foreman	$25.45	$203.60	$43.25	$346.00	$23.65	$39.52
5 Struc. Steel Workers	23.45	938.00	39.85	1594.00		
1 Equip. Oper. (crane)	22.90	183.20	34.20	273.60		
1 Hyd. Crane, 25 Ton		476.00		523.60	8.50	9.35
56 M.H., Daily Totals		$1800.80		$2737.20	$32.15	$48.87
Crew L-6	Hr.	Daily	Hr.	Daily	Bare Costs	Incl. O&P
1 Plumber	$24.70	$197.60	$36.65	$293.20	$24.58	$36.38
.5 Electrician	24.35	97.40	35.85	143.40		
12 M.H., Daily Totals		$295.00		$436.60	$24.58	$36.38
Crew L-7	Hr.	Daily	Hr.	Daily	Bare Costs	Incl. O&P
2 Carpenters	$21.60	$345.60	$32.80	$524.80	$20.72	$31.30
1 Building Laborer	17.15	137.20	26.05	208.40		
.5 Electrician	24.35	97.40	35.85	143.40		
28 M.H., Daily Totals		$580.20		$876.60	$20.72	$31.30

Crew No.	Bare Costs		Incl. Subs O & P		Cost Per Man-hour	
Crew L-8	Hr.	Daily	Hr.	Daily	Bare Costs	Incl. O&P
2 Carpenters	$21.60	$345.60	$32.80	$524.80	$22.22	$33.57
.5 Plumber	24.70	98.80	36.65	146.60		
20 M.H., Daily Totals		$444.40		$671.40	$22.22	$33.57
Crew L-9	Hr.	Daily	Hr.	Daily	Bare Costs	Incl. O&P
1 Labor Foreman (inside)	$17.65	$141.20	$26.80	$214.40	$19.46	$30.37
2 Building Laborers	17.15	274.40	26.05	416.80		
1 Struc. Steel Worker	23.45	187.60	39.85	318.80		
.5 Electrician	24.35	97.40	35.85	143.40		
36 M.H., Daily Totals		$700.60		$1093.40	$19.46	$30.37
Crew M-1	Hr.	Daily	Hr.	Daily	Bare Costs	Incl. O&P
3 Elevator Constructors	$24.55	$589.20	$36.55	$877.20	$23.32	$34.72
1 Elevator Apprentice	19.64	157.12	29.25	234.00		
Hand Tools		72.00		79.20	2.25	2.47
32 M.H., Daily Totals		$818.32		$1190.40	$25.57	$37.19
Crew M-2	Hr.	Daily	Hr.	Daily	Bare Costs	Incl. O&P
2 Millwrights	$22.40	$358.40	$32.70	$523.20	$22.40	$32.70
Power Tools		15.60		17.15	.97	1.07
16 M.H., Daily Totals		$374.00		$540.35	$23.37	$33.77
Crew Q-1	Hr.	Daily	Hr.	Daily	Bare Costs	Incl. O&P
1 Plumber	$24.70	$197.60	$36.65	$293.20	$22.23	$32.97
1 Plumber Apprentice	19.76	158.08	29.30	234.40		
16 M.H., Daily Totals		$355.68		$527.60	$22.23	$32.97
Crew Q-2	Hr.	Daily	Hr.	Daily	Bare Costs	Incl. O&P
2 Plumbers	$24.70	$395.20	$36.65	$586.40	$23.05	$34.20
1 Plumber Apprentice	19.76	158.08	29.30	234.40		
24 M.H., Daily Totals		$553.28		$820.80	$23.05	$34.20
Crew Q-3	Hr.	Daily	Hr.	Daily	Bare Costs	Incl. O&P
1 Plumber Foreman (ins)	$25.20	$201.60	$37.40	$299.20	$23.59	$35.00
2 Plumbers	24.70	395.20	36.65	586.40		
1 Plumber Apprentice	19.76	158.08	29.30	234.40		
32 M.H., Daily Totals		$754.88		$1120.00	$23.59	$35.00
Crew Q-4	Hr.	Daily	Hr.	Daily	Bare Costs	Incl. O&P
1 Plumber Foreman (ins)	$25.20	$201.60	$37.40	$299.20	$23.59	$35.00
1 Plumber	24.70	197.60	36.65	293.20		
1 Welder (plumber)	24.70	197.60	36.65	293.20		
1 Plumber Apprentice	19.76	158.08	29.30	234.40		
1 Electric Welding Mach.		38.20		42.00	1.19	1.31
32 M.H., Daily Totals		$793.08		$1162.00	$24.78	$36.31
Crew Q-5	Hr.	Daily	Hr.	Daily	Bare Costs	Incl. O&P
1 Steamfitter	$24.75	$198.00	$36.75	$294.00	$22.27	$33.07
1 Steamfitter Apprentice	19.80	158.40	29.40	235.20		
16 M.H., Daily Totals		$356.40		$529.20	$22.27	$33.07
Crew Q-6	Hr.	Daily	Hr.	Daily	Bare Costs	Incl. O&P
2 Steamfitters	$24.75	$396.00	$36.75	$588.00	$23.10	$34.30
1 Steamfitter Apprentice	19.80	158.40	29.40	235.20		
24 M.H., Daily Totals		$554.40		$823.20	$23.10	$34.30

CREWS

Crew No.	Bare Costs		Incl. Subs O & P		Cost Per Man-hour	
Crew Q-7	Hr.	Daily	Hr.	Daily	Bare Costs	Incl. O&P
1 Steamfitter Foreman (ins)	$25.25	$202.00	$37.45	$299.60	$23.63	$35.08
2 Steamfitters	24.75	396.00	36.75	588.00		
1 Steamfitter Apprentice	19.80	158.40	29.40	235.20		
32 M.H., Daily Totals		$756.40		$1122.80	$23.63	$35.08
Crew Q-8	Hr.	Daily	Hr.	Daily	Bare Costs	Incl. O&P
1 Steamfitter Foreman (ins)	$25.25	$202.00	$37.45	$299.60	$23.63	$35.08
1 Steamfitter	24.75	198.00	36.75	294.00		
1 Welder (steamfitter)	24.75	198.00	36.75	294.00		
1 Steamfitter Apprentice	19.80	158.40	29.40	235.20		
1 Electric Welding Mach.		38.20		42.00	1.19	1.31
32 M.H., Daily Totals		$794.60		$1164.80	$24.82	$36.39
Crew Q-9	Hr.	Daily	Hr.	Daily	Bare Costs	Incl. O&P
1 Sheet Metal Worker	$24.35	$194.80	$36.80	$294.40	$21.91	$33.12
1 Sheet Metal Apprentice	19.48	155.84	29.45	235.60		
16 M.H., Daily Totals		$350.64		$530.00	$21.91	$33.12
Crew Q-10	Hr.	Daily	Hr.	Daily	Bare Costs	Incl. O&P
2 Sheet Metal Workers	$24.35	$389.60	$36.80	$588.80	$22.72	$34.35
1 Sheet Metal Apprentice	19.48	155.84	29.45	235.60		
24 M.H., Daily Totals		$545.44		$824.40	$22.72	$34.35
Crew Q-11	Hr.	Daily	Hr.	Daily	Bare Costs	Incl. O&P
1 Sheet Metal Foreman (ins)	$24.85	$198.80	$37.55	$300.40	$23.25	$35.15
2 Sheet Metal Workers	24.35	389.60	36.80	588.80		
1 Sheet Metal Apprentice	19.48	155.84	29.45	235.60		
32 M.H., Daily Totals		$744.24		$1124.80	$23.25	$35.15
Crew Q-12	Hr.	Daily	Hr.	Daily	Bare Costs	Incl. O&P
1 Sprinkler Installer	$25.65	$205.20	$38.20	$305.60	$23.08	$34.37
1 Sprinkler Apprentice	20.52	164.16	30.55	244.40		
16 M.H., Daily Totals		$369.36		$550.00	$23.08	$34.37
Crew Q-13	Hr.	Daily	Hr.	Daily	Bare Costs	Incl. O&P
1 Sprinkler Foreman (ins)	$26.15	$209.20	$38.95	$311.60	$24.49	$36.47
2 Sprinkler Installers	25.65	410.40	38.20	611.20		
1 Sprinkler Apprentice	20.52	164.16	30.55	244.40		
32 M.H., Daily Totals		$783.76		$1167.20	$24.49	$36.47
Crew Q-14	Hr.	Daily	Hr.	Daily	Bare Costs	Incl. O&P
1 Asbestos Worker	$23.95	$191.60	$36.90	$295.20	$21.55	$33.22
1 Asbestos Apprentice	19.16	153.28	29.55	236.40		
16 M.H., Daily Totals		$344.88		$531.60	$21.55	$33.22
Crew Q-15	Hr.	Daily	Hr.	Daily	Bare Costs	Incl. O&P
1 Plumber	$24.70	$197.60	$36.65	$293.20	$22.23	$32.97
1 Plumber Apprentice	19.76	158.08	29.30	234.40		
1 Electric Welding Mach.		38.20		42.00	2.38	2.62
16 M.H., Daily Totals		$393.88		$569.60	$24.61	$35.59
Crew Q-16	Hr.	Daily	Hr.	Daily	Bare Costs	Incl. O&P
2 Plumbers	$24.70	$395.20	$36.65	$586.40	$23.05	$34.20
1 Plumber Apprentice	19.76	158.08	29.30	234.40		
1 Electric Welding Mach.		38.20		42.00	1.59	1.75
24 M.H., Daily Totals		$591.48		$862.80	$24.64	$35.95

Crew No.	Bare Costs		Incl. Subs O & P		Cost Per Man-hour	
Crew Q-17	Hr.	Daily	Hr.	Daily	Bare Costs	Incl. O&P
1 Steamfitter	$24.75	$198.00	$36.75	$294.00	$22.27	$33.07
1 Steamfitter Apprentice	19.80	158.40	29.40	235.20		
1 Electric Welding Mach.		38.20		42.00	2.38	2.62
16 M.H., Daily Totals		$394.60		$571.20	$24.65	$35.69
Crew Q-18	Hr.	Daily	Hr.	Daily	Bare Costs	Incl. O&P
2 Steamfitters	$24.75	$396.00	$36.75	$588.00	$23.10	$34.30
1 Steamfitter Apprentice	19.80	158.40	29.40	235.20		
1 Electric Welding Mach.		38.20		42.00	1.59	1.75
24 M.H., Daily Totals		$592.60		$865.20	$24.69	$36.05
Crew Q-19	Hr.	Daily	Hr.	Daily	Bare Costs	Incl. O&P
1 Steamfitter	$24.75	$198.00	$36.75	$294.00	$22.96	$34.00
1 Steamfitter Apprentice	19.80	158.40	29.40	235.20		
1 Electrician	24.35	194.80	35.85	286.80		
24 M.H., Daily Totals		$551.20		$816.00	$22.96	$34.00
Crew Q-20	Hr.	Daily	Hr.	Daily	Bare Costs	Incl. O&P
1 Sheet Metal Worker	$24.35	$194.80	$36.80	$294.40	$22.40	$33.67
1 Sheet Metal Apprentice	19.48	155.84	29.45	235.60		
.5 Electrician	24.35	97.40	35.85	143.40		
20 M.H., Daily Totals		$448.04		$673.40	$22.40	$33.67
Crew Q-21	Hr.	Daily	Hr.	Daily	Bare Costs	Incl. O&P
2 Steamfitters	$24.75	$396.00	$36.75	$588.00	$23.41	$34.68
1 Steamfitter Apprentice	19.80	158.40	29.40	235.20		
1 Electrician	24.35	194.80	35.85	286.80		
32 M.H., Daily Totals		$749.20		$1110.00	$23.41	$34.68
Crew Q-22	Hr.	Daily	Hr.	Daily	Bare Costs	Incl. O&P
1 Plumber	$24.70	$197.60	$36.65	$293.20	$22.23	$32.97
1 Plumber Apprentice	19.76	158.08	29.30	234.40		
1 Truck Crane, 12 Ton		342.00		376.20	21.37	23.51
16 M.H., Daily Totals		$697.68		$903.80	$43.60	$56.48
Crew R-1	Hr.	Daily	Hr.	Daily	Bare Costs	Incl. O&P
1 Electrician Foreman	$24.85	$198.80	$36.60	$292.80	$21.90	$32.60
3 Electricians	24.35	584.40	35.85	860.40		
2 Helpers	16.75	268.00	25.75	412.00		
48 M.H., Daily Totals		$1051.20		$1565.20	$21.90	$32.60
Crew R-2	Hr.	Daily	Hr.	Daily	Bare Costs	Incl. O&P
1 Electrician Foreman	$24.85	$198.80	$36.60	$292.80	$22.04	$32.83
3 Electricians	24.35	584.40	35.85	860.40		
2 Helpers	16.75	268.00	25.75	412.00		
1 Equip. Oper. (crane)	22.90	183.20	34.20	273.60		
1 S.P. Crane, 5 Ton		204.40		224.85	3.65	4.01
56 M.H., Daily Totals		$1438.80		$2063.65	$25.69	$36.84
Crew R-3	Hr.	Daily	Hr.	Daily	Bare Costs	Incl. O&P
1 Electrician Foreman	$24.85	$198.80	$36.60	$292.80	$24.26	$35.82
1 Electrician	24.35	194.80	35.85	286.80		
.5 Equip. Oper. (crane)	22.90	91.60	34.20	136.80		
.5 S.P. Crane, 5 Ton		102.20		112.40	5.11	5.62
20 M.H., Daily Totals		$587.40		$828.80	$29.37	$41.44

CREWS

Crew No.	Bare Costs		Incl. Subs O & P		Cost Per Man-hour	
Crew R-4	Hr.	Daily	Hr.	Daily	Bare Costs	Incl. O&P
1 Struc. Steel Foreman	$25.45	$203.60	$43.25	$346.00	$24.03	$39.73
3 Struc. Steel Workers	23.45	562.80	39.85	956.40		
1 Electrician	24.35	194.80	35.85	286.80		
1 Gas Welding Machine		64.40		70.85	1.61	1.77
40 M.H., Daily Totals		$1025.60		$1660.05	$25.64	$41.50
Crew R-5	Hr.	Daily	Hr.	Daily	Bare Costs	Incl. O&P
1 Electrician Foreman	$24.85	$198.80	$36.60	$292.80	$21.63	$32.24
4 Electrician Lineman	24.35	779.20	35.85	1147.20		
2 Electrician Operators	24.35	389.60	35.85	573.60		
4 Electrician Groundmen	16.75	536.00	25.75	824.00		
1 Crew Truck		152.00		167.20		
1 Tool Van		277.40		305.15		
1 Pick-up Truck		100.60		110.65		
.2 Crane, 55 Ton		138.50		152.35		
.2 Crane, 12 Ton		68.40		75.25		
.2 Auger, Truck Mtd		283.35		311.70		
1 Tractor w/Winch		237.80		261.60	14.29	15.72
88 M.H., Daily Totals		$3161.65		$4221.50	$35.92	$47.96
Crew R-6	Hr.	Daily	Hr.	Daily	Bare Costs	Incl. O&P
1 Electrician Foreman	$24.85	$198.80	$36.60	$292.80	$21.63	$32.24
4 Electrician Linemen	24.35	779.20	35.85	1147.20		
2 Electrician Operators	24.35	389.60	35.85	573.60		
4 Electrician Groundmen	16.75	536.00	25.75	824.00		
1 Crew Truck		152.00		167.20		
1 Tool Van		277.40		305.15		
1 Pick-up Truck		100.60		110.65		
.2 Crane, 55 Ton		138.50		152.35		
.2 Crane, 12 Ton		68.40		75.25		
.2 Auger, Truck Mtd		283.35		311.70		
1 Tractor w/Winch		237.80		261.60		
3 Cable Trailers		356.40		392.05		
.5 Tensioning Rig		117.80		129.60		
.5 Cable Pulling Rig		691.40		760.55	27.54	30.29
88 M.H., Daily Totals		$4327.25		$5503.70	$49.17	$62.53
Crew R-7	Hr.	Daily	Hr.	Daily	Bare Costs	Incl. O&P
1 Electrician Foreman	$24.85	$198.80	$36.60	$292.80	$18.10	$27.55
5 Electrician Groundmen	16.75	670.00	25.75	1030.00		
1 Crew Truck		152.00		167.20	3.16	3.48
48 M.H., Daily Totals		$1020.80		$1490.00	$21.26	$31.03

Crew No.	Bare Costs		Incl. Subs O & P		Cost Per Man-hour	
Crew R-8	Hr.	Daily	Hr.	Daily	Bare Costs	Incl. O&P
1 Electrician Foreman	$24.85	$198.80	$36.60	$292.80	$21.90	$32.60
3 Electrician Linemen	24.35	584.40	35.85	860.40		
2 Electrician Groundmen	16.75	268.00	25.75	412.00		
1 Pick-up Truck		100.60		110.65		
1 Crew Truck		152.00		167.20	5.26	5.78
48 M.H., Daily Totals		$1303.80		$1843.05	$27.16	$38.38
Crew R-9	Hr.	Daily	Hr.	Daily	Bare Costs	Incl. O&P
1 Electrician Foreman	$24.85	$198.80	$36.60	$292.80	$20.61	$30.89
1 Electrician Lineman	24.35	194.80	35.85	286.80		
2 Electrician Operators	24.35	389.60	35.85	573.60		
4 Electrician Groundmen	16.75	536.00	25.75	824.00		
1 Pick-up Truck		100.60		110.65		
1 Crew Truck		152.00		167.20	3.94	4.34
64 M.H., Daily Totals		$1571.80		$2255.05	$24.55	$35.23
Crew R-10	Hr.	Daily	Hr.	Daily	Bare Costs	Incl. O&P
1 Electrician Foreman	$24.85	$198.80	$36.60	$292.80	$23.16	$34.29
4 Electrician Linemen	24.35	779.20	35.85	1147.20		
1 Electrician Groundman	16.75	134.00	25.75	206.00		
1 Crew Truck		152.00		167.20		
3 Tram Cars		411.60		452.75	11.74	12.91
48 M.H., Daily Totals		$1675.60		$2265.95	$34.90	$47.20
Crew R-11	Hr.	Daily	Hr.	Daily	Bare Costs	Incl. O&P
1 Electrician Foreman	$24.85	$198.80	$36.60	$292.80	$22.30	$33.11
4 Electricians	24.35	779.20	35.85	1147.20		
1 Helper	16.75	134.00	25.75	206.00		
1 Common Laborer	17.15	137.20	26.05	208.40		
1 Crew Truck		152.00		167.20		
1 Crane, 12 Ton		342.00		376.20	8.82	9.70
56 M.H., Daily Totals		$1743.20		$2397.80	$31.12	$42.81
Crew R-12	Hr.	Daily	Hr.	Daily	Bare Costs	Incl. O&P
1 Carpenter Foreman	$22.10	$176.80	$33.55	$268.40	$20.24	$31.07
4 Carpenters	21.60	691.20	32.80	1049.60		
4 Common Laborers	17.15	548.80	26.05	833.60		
1 Equip. Oper. (med.)	22.10	176.80	33.00	264.00		
1 Steel Worker	23.45	187.60	39.85	318.80		
1 Dozer, 200 H.P.		762.60		838.85		
1 Pick-up Truck		100.60		110.65	9.80	10.78
88 M.H., Daily Totals		$2644.40		$3683.90	$30.04	$41.85

010 | Overhead

	010 000	Overhead	CREW	DAILY OUTPUT	MAN-HOURS	UNIT	BARE COSTS MAT.	LABOR	EQUIP.	TOTAL	TOTAL INCL O&P	
004	0011	**ARCHITECTURAL FEES**										004
	0020	For work to $10,000				Project					15%	
	0060	To $100,000									10%	
	0090	To $1,000,000									7%	
	0100	For alteration work, to $500,000, add to fee									50%	
	0150	Over $500,000, add to fee				↓					25%	
012	0011	**CONSTRUCTION COST INDEX** For 162 major U.S. and										012
	0020	Canadian cities, total cost, min. (Greensboro, NC)				%					79.2%	
	0050	Average									100%	
	0100	Maximum (Anchorage, AK)				↓					127.9%	
016	0010	**CONSTRUCTION MANAGEMENT FEES** $1,000,000 job, minimum				Project					4.50%	016
	0050	Maximum									7.50%	
	0300	$5,000,000 job, minimum									2.50%	
	0350	Maximum									4%	
020	0010	**CONTINGENCIES** Allowance to add at conceptual stage									15%	020
	0050	Schematic stage									10%	
	0100	Preliminary working drawing stage									7%	
	0150	Final working drawing stage				↓					2%	
022	0010	**CONTRACTOR EQUIPMENT** See division 016 [C10.3-200]										022
024	0010	**CREWS** For building construction, see How To Use This Book										024
028	0010	**ENGINEERING FEES** Educational planning consultant, minimum				Project					.50%	028
	0100	Maximum				"					2.50%	
	0200	Electrical, minimum [C10.1-103]				Contrct					4.10%	
	0300	Maximum									10.10%	
	0400	Elevator & conveying systems, minimum									2.50%	
	0500	Maximum									5%	
	0600	Food service & kitchen equipment, minimum									8%	
	0700	Maximum									12%	
	0800	Landscaping & site development, minimum									2.50%	
	0900	Maximum									6%	
	1000	Mechanical (plumbing & HVAC), minimum									4.10%	
	1100	Maximum				↓					10.10%	
	1200	Structural, minimum				Project					1%	
	1300	Maximum				"					2.50%	
032	0010	**FACTORS** To be added to construction costs for particular job [C18.1-100]										032
	0200											
	0500	Cut & patch to match existing construction, add, minimum				Costs	2%	3%				
	0550	Maximum					5%	9%				
	0800	Dust protection, add, minimum					1%	2%				
	0850	Maximum					4%	11%				
	1100	Equipment usage curtailment, add, minimum					1%	1%				
	1150	Maximum					3%	10%				
	1400	Material handling & storage limitation, add, minimum					1%	1%				
	1450	Maximum					6%	7%				
	1700	Protection of existing work, add, minimum					2%	2%				
	1750	Maximum					5%	7%				
	2000	Shift work requirements, add, minimum						5%				
	2050	Maximum						30%				
	2300	Temporary shoring and bracing, add, minimum					2%	5%				
	2350	Maximum				↓	5%	12%				
036	0010	**FIELD PERSONNEL** Clerk average				Week		212		212	325	036
	0100	Field engineer, minimum						490		490	745	
	0120	Average						655		655	995	
	0140	Maximum						735		735	1,125	
	0160	General purpose laborer, average						680		680	1,025	
	0180	Project manager, minimum				↓		935		935	1,425	

1

010 | Overhead

		010 000	Overhead	CREW	DAILY OUTPUT	MAN-HOURS	UNIT	BARE COSTS MAT.	BARE COSTS LABOR	BARE COSTS EQUIP.	BARE COSTS TOTAL	TOTAL INCL O&P	
036	0200		Average				Week		1,040		1,040	1,575	036
	0220		Maximum						1,180		1,180	1,800	
	0240		Superintendent, minimum						885		885	1,350	
	0260		Average						985		985	1,500	
	0280		Maximum						1,105		1,105	1,675	
	0290		Timekeeper, average				↓		535		535	815	
038	0011	**HISTORICAL COST INDEXES** Back to 1946											038
040	0010	**INSURANCE** Builders risk, standard, minimum					Job					.22%	040
	0050		Maximum									.59%	
	0200		All-risk type, minimum	C10.1-301								.25%	
	0250		Maximum				↓					.62%	
	0400		Contractor's equipment floater, minimum				Value					.50%	
	0450		Maximum				"					1.50%	
	0600		Public liability, average				Job					1.55%	
	0800		Workers' compensation & employer's liability, average										
	0850		by trade, carpentry, general	C10.2-200			Payroll		15.09%				
	1000		Electrical						5.53%				
	1150		Insulation						12.38%				
	1450		Plumbing						6.74%				
	1550		Sheet metal work (HVAC)				↓		9.44%				
042	0010	**JOB CONDITIONS** Modifications to total											042
	0020		project cost summaries										
	0100		Economic conditions, favorable, deduct				Project					2%	
	0200		Unfavorable, add									5%	
	0300		Hoisting conditions, favorable, deduct									2%	
	0400		Unfavorable, add									5%	
	0700		Labor availability, surplus, deduct									1%	
	0800		Shortage, add									10%	
	0900		Material storage area, available, deduct									1%	
	1000		Not available, add									2%	
	1100		Subcontractor availability, surplus, deduct									5%	
	1200		Shortage, add									12%	
	1300		Work space, available, deduct									2%	
	1400		Not available, add				↓					5%	
046	0011	**LABOR INDEX** For 162 major U.S. and Canadian cities											046
	0020		Minimum (Charleston, S.C.)				%		62.8%				
	0050		Average						100%				
	0100		Maximum (San Francisco, CA)				↓		144.8%				
048	0010	**MAIN OFFICE EXPENSE** Average for General Contractors											048
	0020		As a percentage of their annual volume										
	0050		Annual volume under 1 million dollars				% Vol.				13.60%		
	0100		Up to 2.5 million dollars								8%		
	0150		Up to 4.0 million dollars								6.80%		
	0200		Up to 7.0 million dollars								5.60%		
	0250		Up to 10 million dollars								5.10%		
	0300		Over 10 million dollars				↓				3.90%		
052	0010	**MARK-UP** For General Contractors for change											052
	0100		of scope of job as bid										
	0200		Extra work, by subcontractors, add				%					10%	
	0250		By General Contractor, add									15%	
	0400		Omitted work, by subcontractors, deduct									5%	
	0450		By General Contractor, deduct									7.50%	
	0600		Overtime work, by subcontractors, add									15%	
	0650		By General Contractor, add									10%	
	1000		Installing contractors, on their own labor, minimum	C10.3-200					43%				
	1100		Maximum						68%				

010 | Overhead

010 000 | Overhead

			CREW	DAILY OUTPUT	MAN-HOURS	UNIT	MAT.	LABOR	EQUIP.	TOTAL	TOTAL INCL O&P	
054	0011	**MATERIAL INDEX** For 162 major U.S. and Canadian cities										054
	0020	Minimum (San Antonio, TX)				%	94.3%					
	0040	Average					100%					
	0060	Maximum (Anchorage, AK)					125.7%					
058	0010	**OVERHEAD** As percent of direct costs, minimum								5%		058
	0050	Average								12%		
	0100	Maximum								22%		
062	0010	**OVERHEAD & PROFIT** Allowance to add to items in this										062
	0020	book that do not include Subs O&P, average				%				25%		
	0100	Allowance to add to items in this book that										
	0110	do include Subs O&P, minimum				%					5%	
	0150	Average									10%	
	0200	Maximum									15%	
	0300	Typical, by size of project, under $100,000									30%	
	0350	$500,000 project									25%	
	0400	$2,000,000 project									20%	
	0450	Over $10,000,000 project									15%	
064	0010	**OVERTIME** For early completion of projects or where										064
	0020	labor shortages exist, add to usual labor, up to				Costs		100%				
068	0010	**PERFORMANCE BOND** For buildings, minimum				Job					.60%	068
	0100	Maximum									2.50%	
070	0010	**PERMITS** Rule of thumb, most cities, minimum									.50%	070
	0100	Maximum									2%	
082	0010	**SMALL TOOLS** As % of contractor's work, minimum				Total					.50%	082
	0100	Maximum				"					2%	
086	0010	**TAXES** Sales tax, State, County & City, average				%	4.41%					086
	0050	Maximum					7.50%					
	0200	Social Security, on first $48,000 of wages						7.56%				
	0300	Unemployment, MA, combined Federal and State, minimum						2.20%				
	0350	Average						6.20%				
	0400	Maximum						6.40%				
094	0010	**WINTER PROTECTION** Reinforced plastic on wood										094
	0100	framing to close openings	2 Clab	750	.021	S.F.	.27	.37		.37	.85	
	0200	Tarpaulins hung over scaffolding, 8 uses, not incl. scaffolding		1,500	.011		.14	.18		.18	.40	
	0300	Prefab, fiberglass panels, steel frame, 8 uses		1,200	.013		.52	.23		.23	.90	

013 | Submittals

013 300 | Survey Data

			CREW	DAILY OUTPUT	MAN-HOURS	UNIT	MAT.	LABOR	EQUIP.	TOTAL	TOTAL INCL O&P	
306	0010	**SURVEYING** Conventional, topographical, minimum	A-7	3.30	7.270	Acre	12.75	135		147.75	220	306
	0100	Maximum	A-8	.60	53.330		39	980		1,019	1,525	
	0300	Lot location and lines, minimum, for large quantities	A-7	2	12		21	225		246	365	
	0320	Average	"	1.25	19.200		39	365		404	590	
	0400	Maximum, for small quantities	A-8	1	32		63	585		648	960	
	0600	Monuments, 3' long	A-7	10	2.400	Ea.	9.05	45		54.05	78	
	0800	Property lines, perimeter, cleared land	"	1,000	.024	L.F.	.03	.45		.48	.71	
	0900	Wooded land	A-8	875	.037	"	.03	.67		.70	1.05	
	1500	Aerial surveying, including ground control, minimum fee, 10 acres				Total					4,250	
	1510	100 acres									4,575	
	1550	From existing photography, deduct									700	
	1600	2' contours, 10 acres				Acre					355	

013 | Submittals

013 300 | Survey Data

			CREW	DAILY OUTPUT	MAN-HOURS	UNIT	BARE COSTS MAT.	LABOR	EQUIP.	TOTAL	TOTAL INCL O&P	
306	1650	20 acres				Acre					235	306
	1800	50 acres									77	
	1850	100 acres									65	
	2000	1000 acres									14.75	
	2050	10,000 acres				↓					9.45	
	2150	For 1' contours and										
	2160	dense urban areas, add to above				Acre					40%	

013 800 | Construction Photos

			CREW	DAILY OUTPUT	MAN-HOURS	UNIT	MAT.	LABOR	EQUIP.	TOTAL	INCL O&P	
804	0010	PHOTOGRAPHS 8" x 10", 4 shots, 2 prints ea., std. mounting				Set	92			92	100	804
	0100	Hinged linen mounts					105			105	115	
	0200	8" x 10", 4 shots, 2 prints each, in color					185			185	205	
	0300	For I.D. slugs, add to all above					2.55			2.55	2.81	
	1500	Time lapse equipment, camera and projector, buy					3,500			3,500	3,850	
	1550	Rent per month				↓	495			495	545	
	1700	Cameraman and film, including processing, B.&W.				Day	510			510	560	
	1720	Color				"	575			575	635	

015 | Construction Facilities and Temporary Controls

015 100 | Temporary Utilities

			CREW	DAILY OUTPUT	MAN-HOURS	UNIT	MAT.	LABOR	EQUIP.	TOTAL	INCL O&P	
104	0010	TEMPORARY UTILITIES										104
	0100	Heat, incl. fuel and operation, per week, 12 hrs. per day	1 Skwk	8.75	.914	CSF Flr	15.95	20		35.95	48	
	0200	24 hrs. per day	"	4.50	1.780		21	39		60	83	
	0350	Lighting, incl. service lamps, wiring & outlets, minimum	1 Elec	34	.235		2.16	5.75		7.91	10.80	
	0360	Maximum	"	17	.471		4.87	11.45		16.32	22	
	0400	Power for temporary lighting only, per month, minimum/month								.98	1.02	
	0450	Maximum/month								2.49	2.61	
	0600	Power for job duration incl. elevator, etc., minimum								45	50	
	0650	Maximum				↓				98	100	
	1000	Toilet, portable, see Division 016-420-6410										

015 200 | Temporary Construction

			CREW	DAILY OUTPUT	MAN-HOURS	UNIT	MAT.	LABOR	EQUIP.	TOTAL	INCL O&P	
204	0010	PROTECTION Stair tread, 2" x 12" planks, 1 use	1 Carp	75	.107	Tread	.98	2.30		3.28	4.57	204
	0100	Exterior plywood, ½" thick, 1 use		65	.123		.45	2.66		3.11	4.53	
	0200	¾" thick, 1 use	↓	60	.133	↓	.82	2.88		3.70	5.25	
208	0010	TEMPORARY CONSTRUCTION See division 010-094 & 015-300										208

015 250 | Construction Aids

			CREW	DAILY OUTPUT	MAN-HOURS	UNIT	MAT.	LABOR	EQUIP.	TOTAL	INCL O&P	
254	0010	SCAFFOLD Steel tubular, regular, buy										254
	0090	Building exterior, 1 to 5 stories	3 Carp	16.80	1.430	C.S.F.	13	31		44	61	
	0200	To 12 stories	4 Carp	15	2.130		12.20	46		58.20	83	
	0310	13 to 20 stories	5 Carp	16.75	2.390		11.40	52		63.40	91	
	0460	Building interior walls, (area) up to 16' high	3 Carp	22.70	1.060		12.50	23		35.50	48	
	0560	16' to 40' high		18.70	1.280		12.75	28		40.75	56	
	0800	Building interior floor area, up to 30' high	↓	90	.267	C.C.F.	3.90	5.75		9.65	13.05	
	0900	Over 30' high	4 Carp	100	.320	"	4.40	6.90		11.30	15.35	
	6000	Scaffold steel tubular, suspended slab form supports to 8'-2" high										
	6100	1 use per month	4 Carp	31	1.030	C.S.F.	11.10	22		33.10	46	

Note: Row 0200/0310 contains marking "C10.3-300"

015 | Construction Facilities and Temporary Controls

015 250 | Construction Aids

			CREW	DAILY OUTPUT	MAN-HOURS	UNIT	BARE COSTS MAT.	LABOR	EQUIP.	TOTAL	TOTAL INCL O&P	
254	6150	2 uses per month	4 Carp	43	.744	C.S.F.	5.53	16.05		21.58	30	254
	6500	Steel tubular, suspended slab form supports to 14'-8" high										
	6600	1 use per month	4 Carp	16	2	C.S.F.	17.35	43		60.35	85	
	6650	2 uses per month	"	22	1.450	"	8.65	31		39.65	57	
255	0011	**SCAFFOLDING SPECIALTIES**										255
	0050											
	1200	Sidewalk bridge, heavy duty steel posts & beams, including										
	1210	parapet protection & waterproofing										
	1220	8' to 10' wide, 2 posts	3 Carp	15	1.600	L.F.	10.80	35		45.80	64	
	1230	3 posts	"	10	2.400	"	16.50	52		68.50	97	
	1500	Sidewalk bridge using tubular steel										
	1510	scaffold frames, including planking	3 Carp	45	.533	L.F.	3.71	11.50		15.21	22	
	1600	For 2 uses per month, deduct from all above					50%					
	1700	For 1 use every 2 months, add to all above					100%					
	1900	Catwalks, 32" wide, no guardrails, 6' span, buy				Ea.	115			115	125	
	2000	10' span, buy				"	180			180	200	
	2800	Hand winch-operated masons										
	2810	scaffolding, no plank moving required										
	2900	98' long, 10'-6" high, buy				Ea.	4,950			4,950	5,450	
	3000	Rent per month					300			300	330	
	3100	28'-6" high, buy					8,500			8,500	9,350	
	3200	Rent per month					450			450	495	
	3400	196' long, 28'-6" high, buy					16,500			16,500	18,200	
	3500	Rent per month					885			885	975	
	3600	64'-6" high, buy					28,000			28,000	30,800	
	3700	Rent per month					1,775			1,775	1,950	
	3720	Putlog, standard, 8' span, with hangers, buy					85			85	94	
	3730	Rent per month					12.35			12.35	13.60	
	3750	12' span, buy					125			125	140	
	3760	Trussed type, 14' span, buy					195			195	215	
	3770	Rent per month					18			18	19.80	
	3790	20' span, buy					230			230	255	
	3795	Rent per month					26			26	29	
	3800	Rolling ladders with handrails, 30" wide, buy, 2 step					155			155	170	
	4000	7 step					335			335	370	
	4050	10 step					465			465	510	
	4100	Rolling towers, buy, 5' wide, 7' long, 9' high					925			925	1,025	
	4200	For 5' high added sections, add					180			180	200	
	4300	Complete incl. wheels, railings, etc.										
	4400	up to 20' high, rent per month				Ea.	105			105	115	
	6500	Stair unit, interior, for scaffolding, buy					285			285	315	
	6550	Rent per month					26			26	29	

015 300 | Barriers And Enclosures

			CREW	DAILY OUTPUT	MAN-HOURS	UNIT	MAT.	LABOR	EQUIP.	TOTAL	INCL O&P	
302	0010	**BARRICADES** 5' high, 3 rail @ 2" x 8", fixed	2 Carp	30	.533	L.F.	9.15	11.50		20.65	28	302
	0150	Movable		20	.800		9.90	17.30		27.20	37	
	1000	Guardrail, wooden, 3' high, 1" x 6", on 2" x 4" posts		200	.080		1.42	1.73		3.15	4.18	
	1100	2" x 6", on 4" x 4" posts		165	.097		2.35	2.09		4.44	5.75	
	1200	Portable metal with base pads, buy					11.50			11.50	12.65	
	1250	Typical installation, assume 10 reuses	2 Carp	600	.027		1.35	.58		1.93	2.36	
304	0010	**FENCING** Chain link, 5' high	2 Clab	100	.160		4.60	2.74		7.34	9.20	304
	0100	6' high		75	.213		5.85	3.66		9.51	12	
	0200	Rented chain link, 6' high, to 500'		100	.160		1.89	2.74		4.63	6.25	
	0250	Over 1000' (up to 12 mo.)		110	.145		1.58	2.49		4.07	5.50	
	0350	Plywood, painted, 2" x 4" frame, 4' high	A-4	135	.178		3.73	3.76		7.49	9.75	
	0400	4" x 4" frame, 8' high	"	110	.218		6.35	4.62		10.97	13.95	
	0500	Wire mesh on 4" x 4" posts, 4' high	2 Carp	100	.160		4.05	3.46		7.51	9.70	
	0550	8' high	"	80	.200		6.10	4.32		10.42	13.25	

015 | Construction Facilities and Temporary Controls

015 400 | Security

			DAILY	MAN-		BARE COSTS				TOTAL	
			CREW	OUTPUT	HOURS	UNIT	MAT.	LABOR	EQUIP.	TOTAL	INCL O&P
480	0010	**WATCHMAN** Service, monthly basis, uniformed man, minimum				Hr.					6.55	480
	0100	Maximum									12.40	
	0200	Man and command dog (man dog), minimum									9.35	
	0300	Maximum				↓					14	
	0500	Sentry dog, leased, with job patrol (yard dog), 1 dog				Week					175	
	0600	2 dogs				"					245	
	0800	Purchase, trained sentry dog, minimum				Ea.					870	
	0900	Maximum				"					1,650	

015 500 | Access Roads

			CREW	DAILY OUTPUT	MAN-HOURS	UNIT	MAT.	LABOR	EQUIP.	TOTAL	INCL O&P	
552	0010	**ROADS AND SIDEWALKS** Temporary										552
	0050	Roads, gravel fill, no surfacing, 4″ gravel depth	B-14	715	.067	S.Y.	1	1.22	.25	2.47	3.22	
	0100	8″ gravel depth	"	615	.078	"	2.19	1.42	.29	3.90	4.88	
	1000	Ramp, ¾″ plywood on 2″ x 6″ joists, 16″ O.C.	2 Carp	300	.053	S.F.	1.15	1.15		2.30	3.01	
	1100	On 2″ x 10″ joists, 16″ O.C.	"	275	.058		1.40	1.26		2.66	3.45	
	2200	Sidewalks, 2″ x 12″ planks, 2 uses	1 Carp	350	.023		.31	.49		.80	1.09	
	2300	Exterior plywood, 2 uses, ½″ thick		750	.011		.21	.23		.44	.58	
	2400	⅝″ thick		650	.012		.27	.27		.54	.70	
	2500	¾″ thick	↓	600	.013	↓	.31	.29		.60	.78	

015 600 | Temporary Controls

						UNIT	MAT.	LABOR	EQUIP.	TOTAL	INCL O&P	
602	0010	**TARPAULINS** Cotton duck, 10 oz. to 13.13 oz. per S.Y., minimum				S.F.	.26			.26	.29	602
	0050	Maximum					.45			.45	.50	
	0100	Polyvinyl coated nylon, 14 oz. to 18 oz., minimum					.35			.35	.39	
	0150	Maximum					.45			.45	.50	
	0200	Reinforced polyethylene 3 mils thick, white					.05			.05	.06	
	0300	4 mils thick, white, clear or black					.06			.06	.07	
	0400	5.5 mils thick, clear					.07			.07	.08	
	0500	White, fire retardant					.12			.12	.13	
	0600	7.5 mils, oil resistant, fire retardant					.13			.13	.14	
	0700	8.5 mils, black					.16			.16	.18	
	0710	Woven polyethylene, 6 mils thick					.28			.28	.31	
	0740	Mylar polyester, non-reinforced, 7 mils thick				↓	.86			.86	.95	

015 800 | Project Signs

						UNIT	MAT.	LABOR	EQUIP.	TOTAL	INCL O&P	
804	0010	**SIGNS** Hi-intensity reflectorized, no posts, buy				S.F.	9			9	9.90	804

015 900 | Field Offices And Sheds

			CREW	DAILY OUTPUT	MAN-HOURS	UNIT	MAT.	LABOR	EQUIP.	TOTAL	INCL O&P	
904	0010	**OFFICE** Trailer, furnished, no hookups, 20′ x 8′, buy	2 Skwk	1	16	Ea.	4,000	355		4,355	4,950	904
	0250	Rent per month					150			150	165	
	0300	32′ x 8′, buy	2 Skwk	.70	22.860		6,000	505		6,505	7,375	
	0350	Rent per month					200			200	220	
	0400	50′ x 10′, buy	2 Skwk	.60	26.670		11,300	590		11,890	13,300	
	0450	Rent per month					365			365	400	
	0500	50′ x 12′, buy	2 Skwk	.50	32		12,400	705		13,105	14,700	
	0550	Rent per month					390			390	430	
	0700	For air conditioning, rent per month, add				↓	37			37	41	
	0800	For delivery, add per mile				Mile	1.54			1.54	1.69	
	1000	Portable buildings, prefab, on skids, economy, 8′ x 8′	2 Carp	265	.060	S.F.	60	1.30		61.30	68	
	1100	Deluxe, 8′ x 12′	"	150	.107	"	75	2.30		77.30	86	
	1200	Storage vans, trailer mounted, 16′ x 8′, buy	2 Skwk	1.80	8.890	Ea.	2,500	195		2,695	3,050	
	1250	Rent per month					89			89	98	
	1300	28′ x 10′, buy	2 Skwk	1.40	11.430		2,925	255		3,180	3,600	
	1350	Rent per month				↓	89			89	98	

016 | Material and Equipment

016 400 | Equipment Rental

		Description	UNIT	HOURLY OPER. COST.	RENT PER DAY	RENT PER WEEK	RENT PER MONTH	CREW EQUIPMENT COST	
408	0010	**EARTHWORK EQUIPMENT RENTAL** Without operators							408
	0050	Augers for truck or trailer mounting, vertical drilling							
	0060	4" to 36" diam., 54 H.P., gas, 10' spindle travel	Ea.	12.30	465	1,400	4,200	378.40	
	0070	14' spindle travel		13.35	535	1,600	4,800	426.80	
	0080	Auger, horizontal boring machine, 12" to 36" diameter, 45 H.P.		5.65	270	815	2,450	208.20	
	0090	12" to 48" diameter, 65 H.P.		9.85	540	1,625	4,875	403.80	
	0100	Backhoe, diesel hydraulic, crawler mounted, ½ C.Y. cap.		8.95	435	1,300	3,900	331.60	
	0120	⅝ C.Y. capacity		12.45	410	1,225	3,675	344.60	
	0140	¾ C.Y. capacity		13.70	565	1,700	5,100	449.60	
	0150	1 C.Y. capacity		17.70	690	2,075	6,225	556.60	
	0200	1-½ C.Y. capacity		21	835	2,500	7,500	668	
	0300	2 C.Y. capacity		35.25	1,075	3,225	9,675	927	
	0320	2-½ C.Y. capacity		47.80	2,000	6,025	18,100	1,587	
	0340	3-½ C.Y. capacity		63.35	2,450	7,375	22,100	1,981	
	0350	Gradall type, truck mounted, 3 ton @ 15' radius, ⅝ C.Y.		21	600	1,800	5,400	528	
	0370	1 C.Y. capacity		23.10	920	2,750	8,250	734.80	
	0400	Backhoe-loader, wheel type, 40 to 45 H.P., ⅝ C.Y. capacity		5.80	180	545	1,625	155.40	
	0450	45 H.P. to 60 H.P., ¾ C.Y. capacity		6.80	210	635	1,900	181.40	
	0460	80 H.P., 1-¼ C.Y. capacity		10.25	330	995	2,975	281	
	0470	112 H.P.,1-¾ C.Y. loader, ½ C.Y. backhoe		12.30	320	970	2,900	292.40	
	0750	Bucket, clamshell, general purpose, ⅜ C.Y.		.65	57	170	520	39.20	
	0800	½ C.Y.		.80	67	200	600	46.40	
	0850	¾ C.Y.		.90	78	235	700	54.20	
	0900	1 C.Y.		1.15	83	250	750	59.20	
	0950	1-½ C.Y.		1.35	120	360	1,050	82.80	
	1000	2 C.Y.		1.55	135	400	1,200	92.40	
	1200	Compactor, roller, 2 drum, 2000 lb., operator walking		1.45	100	300	900	71.60	
	1250	Rammer compactor, gas, 1000 lb. blow		.35	33	100	300	22.80	
	1300	Vibratory plate, gas, 13" plate, 1000 lb. blow		.40	27	81	245	19.40	
	1350	24" plate, 5000 lb. blow		1.45	48	145	435	40.60	
	1950	Hammer, pavement demo., hyd., gas, self-prop., 1000 to 1250 lb.		14.35	340	1,025	3,075	319.80	
	2000	Diesel 1300 to 1500 lb.		7.25	370	1,125	3,325	283	
	4900	Trencher, chain, boom type, gas, operator walking, 12 H.P.		1.55	63	190	570	50.40	
	4910	Operator riding, 40 H.P.		5.05	145	440	1,325	128.40	
	5000	Wheel type, diesel, 4' deep, 12" wide		10.65	390	1,175	3,500	320.20	
	5100	Diesel, 6' deep, 20" wide		11.45	590	1,775	5,300	446.60	
	5150	Ladder type, diesel, 5' deep, 8" wide		7.50	295	875	2,650	235	
	5200	Diesel, 8' deep, 16" wide		14	485	1,450	4,350	402	
	5250	Truck, dump, tandem, 12 ton payload		14.10	285	850	2,550	282.80	
	5300	Three axle dump, 16 ton payload		15.80	365	1,100	3,300	346.40	
	5350	Dump trailer only, rear dump, 16-½ C.Y.		2.80	135	405	1,225	103.40	
	5400	20 C.Y.		2.80	140	410	1,250	104.40	
	5450	Flatbed, single axle, 1-½ ton rating		8.90	110	335	1,000	138.20	
	5500	3 ton rating		8.95	115	345	1,025	140.60	
	5550	Off highway rear dump, 25 ton capacity		15.65	665	2,000	6,000	525.20	
	5600	35 ton capacity		25	1,000	3,000	9,000	800	
420	0010	**GENERAL EQUIPMENT RENTAL**							420
	0150	Aerial lift, scissor type, to 15' high, 1000 lb. cap., electric	Ea.	.88	80	240	715	55.05	
	0160	To 25' high, 2000 lb. capacity		1.35	125	380	1,150	86.80	
	0170	Telescoping boom to 40' high, 750 lb. capacity, gas		5.25	345	1,025	3,100	247	
	0180	2000 lb. capacity		6.85	460	1,375	4,125	329.80	
	0190	To 60' high, 750 lb. capacity		7.30	535	1,625	4,825	383.40	
	0200	Air compressor, portable, gas engine, 60 C.F.M.		4.25	43	130	390	60	
	0300	160 C.F.M.		5.65	58	175	525	80.20	
	0400	Diesel engine, rotary screw, 250 C.F.M.		4.50	80	240	720	84	
	0500	365 C.F.M.		7.80	225	675	2,025	197.40	
	0600	600 C.F.M.		13.45	255	770	2,300	261.60	
	0700	750 C.F.M.		14.80	285	850	2,575	288.40	

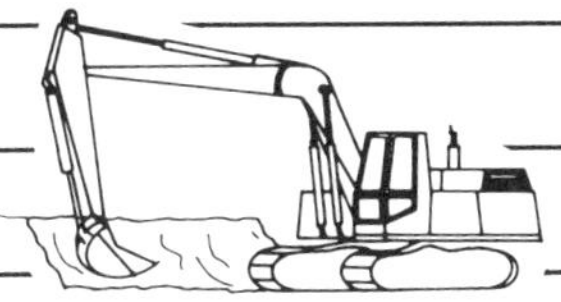

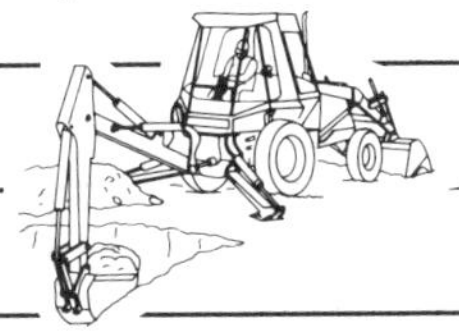

016 | Material and Equipment

016 400 | Equipment Rental

420			UNIT	HOURLY OPER. COST.	RENT PER DAY	RENT PER WEEK	RENT PER MONTH	CREW EQUIPMENT COST	
	0800	For silenced models, small sizes, add	Ea.	3%	5%	5%	5%		420
	0900	Large sizes, add	"	4%	7%	7%	7%		
	0920	Air tools and accessories							
	0930	Breaker, pavement, 60 lb.	Ea.	.10	22	65	195	13.80	
	0940	80 lb.		.11	21	71	195	15.10	
	0950	Drills, hand (jackhammer) 65 lb.		.17	22	65	195	14.35	
	0980	Dust control per drill		.15	9	27	81	6.60	
	1000	Hose, air with couplings, 50' long, ¾" diameter		.36	3	8	25	4.50	
	1100	1" diameter		.94	4	11	34	9.70	
	1200	1-½" diameter		.05	7	22	65	4.80	
	1300	2" diameter		.11	14	42	125	9.30	
	1400	2-½" diameter		.12	15	44	130	9.75	
	1410	3" diameter		.10	16	47	140	10.20	
	1450	Drill, steel, ⅞" x 2'			2.10	6.25	18.75	1.25	
	1460	⅞" x 6'			3.10	9.35	28	1.85	
	1520	Moil points		.70	1.05	4.15	12.50	6.40	
	1560	Tamper, single, 35 lb.		.10	20	60	180	12.80	
	1570	Triple, 140 lb.		1.55	35	110	330	34.40	
	1580	Wrenches, impact, air powered, up to ¾" bolt		.15	17	50	150	11.20	
	1590	Up to 1-¼" bolt		.35	42	125	375	27.80	
	1600	Barricades, barrels, reflectorized, 1 to 50 barrels			.51	1.53	4.59	.30	
	1610	100 to 200 barrels			.45	1.33	4	.25	
	1620	Barrels with flashers, 1 to 50 barrels			.82	2.48	7.45	.50	
	1630	100 to 200 barrels			.75	2.24	6.70	.45	
	1640	Barrels with steady burn type C lights			.84	2.54	7.60	.50	
	1850	Drill, rotary hammer, electric, 1-½" diameter		.10	19.10	57	170	12.20	
	1860	Carbide bit for above			5.20	15.60	47	3.10	
	2100	Generator, electric, gas engine, 1.5 KW to 3 KW		.88	29	87	260	24.45	
	2200	5 KW		1.10	47	140	420	36.80	
	2300	10 KW		1.90	115	350	1,050	85.20	
	2400	25 KW		5.65	115	345	1,025	114.20	
	2500	Diesel engine, 20 KW		3.40	81	245	735	76.20	
	2600	50 KW		5.25	99	295	890	101	
	2700	100 KW		10.10	145	440	1,325	168.80	
	2800	250 KW		24	255	760	2,275	344	
	2900	Heaters, space, oil or electric, 50 MBH		.10	20	59	175	12.60	
	3000	100 MBH		.05	17	49	145	10.20	
	3100	300 MBH		.10	40	120	360	24.80	
	3150	500 MBH		.16	55	165	500	34.30	
	3200	Hose, water, suction with coupling, 20' long, 2" diameter		.05	7	20	59	4.40	
	3210	3" diameter		.05	10	31	92	6.60	
	3220	4" diameter		.05	17	52	155	10.80	
	3230	6" diameter		.05	37	110	330	22.40	
	3240	8" diameter		.05	51	145	460	29.40	
	3250	Discharge hose with coupling, 50' long, 2" diameter		.05	4	11	33	2.60	
	3260	3" diameter		.05	5	15	46	3.40	
	3270	4" diameter		.05	6	17	52	3.80	
	3280	6" diameter		.05	20	61	185	12.60	
	3290	8" diameter		.05	27	81	245	16.60	
	3300	Ladders, extension type, 16' to 36' long			8.30	24	72	4.80	
	3400	40' to 60' long			19.75	60	180	12	
	3500	Light towers, towable, with diesel generator, 2000 watt		1.30	105	315	950	73.40	
	3600	4000 watt		1.60	120	360	1,075	84.80	
	4100	Pump, centrifugal gas pump, 1-½", 4 MGPH		.35	18.40	55	165	13.80	
	4200	2", 8 MGPH		.35	20	60	180	14.80	
	4300	3", 15 MGPH		.95	31	92	275	26	
	4400	6", 90 MGPH		7.85	130	395	1,175	141.80	
	4500	Submersible electric pump, 1-¼", 55 GPM		.25	30	90	270	20	

016 | Material and Equipment

016 400 | Equipment Rental

		UNIT	HOURLY OPER. COST.	RENT PER DAY	RENT PER WEEK	RENT PER MONTH	CREW EQUIPMENT COST	
420	4600	1-½", 83 GPM	Ea.	.25	33	100	300	22	420
	4700	2", 120 GPM		.25	35	105	315	23	
	4800	3", 300 GPM		.50	44	130	390	30	
	4900	4", 560 GPM		.95	59	180	535	43.60	
	5000	6", 1590 GPM		4.35	165	500	1,500	134.80	
	5100	Diaphragm pump, gas, single, 1-½" diameter		.40	16	48	145	12.80	
	5200	2" diameter		.45	17	52	155	14	
	5300	3" diameter		.55	30	90	270	22.40	
	5400	Double, 4" diameter		1.30	65	195	585	49.40	
	5500	Trash pump, self-priming, gas, 2" diameter		.90	27	80	240	23.20	
	5600	Diesel, 4" diameter		1.40	81	245	735	60.20	
	5650	Diesel, 6" diameter		3.85	140	420	1,275	114.80	
	5700	Salamanders, L.P. gas fired, 100,000 B.T.U.		.55	12	36	110	11.60	
	5800	Saw, chain, gas engine, 18" long		.40	27	81	240	19.40	
	5900	36" long		.85	55	165	495	39.80	
	5950	60" long		.90	55	165	495	40.20	
	6000	Masonry, table mounted, 14" diameter, 5 H.P.		1.40	33	98	295	30.80	
	6100	Circular, hand held, electric, 7" diameter		.15	11	33	98	7.80	
	6200	12" diameter		.20	21	63	190	14.20	
	6350	Torch, cutting, acetylene-oxygen, 150' hose		6	19	56	165	59.20	
	6360	Hourly operating cost includes tips and gas		6.30	16.65	50	150	60.40	
	6410	Toilet, portable chemical			8.30	25	75	5	
	6420	Recycle flush type			10.80	31	93	6.20	
	6430	Toilet, fresh water flush, garden hose,			16.20	49	145	9.80	
	6440	Hoisted, non-flush, for high rise			8.65	26	78	5.20	
	6450	Toilet, trailers, minimum			20	60	180	12	
	6460	Maximum			81	245	730	49	
	6500	Trailers, platform, flush deck, 2 axle, 25 ton capacity		1.10	125	380	1,150	84.80	
	6600	40 ton capacity		1.35	190	570	1,700	124.80	
	6700	3 axle, 50 ton capacity		2.45	220	660	1,975	151.60	
	6800	75 ton capacity		3.10	320	970	2,900	218.80	
	7100	Truck, pickup, ¾ ton, 2 wheel drive		8.45	55	165	495	100.60	
	7200	4 wheel drive		9.60	60	175	530	111.80	
	7300	Tractor, 4 x 2, 30 ton capacity, 195 H.P.		8.45	315	940	2,825	255.60	
	7410	250 H.P.		11.65	340	1,025	3,075	298.20	
	7700	Welder, electric, 200 amp		.75	18	54	160	16.80	
	7800	300 amp		1.65	42	125	375	38.20	
	7900	Gas engine, 200 amp		3.80	35	105	315	51.40	
	8000	300 amp		4.05	53	160	480	64.40	
	8100	Wheelbarrow, any size			6.65	20	60	4	
460	0010	**LIFTING & HOISTING EQUIPMENT RENTAL**							460
	0100	without operators							
	0200	Crane, climbing, 106' jib, 6000 lb. capacity, 410 FPM	Ea.	21	1,075	3,225	9,675	813	
	0300	101' jib, 10,250 lb. capacity, 270 FPM	"	28	1,375	4,100	12,300	1,044	
	0400	Tower, static, 130' high, 106' jib,							
	0500	6200 lb. capacity at 400 FPM	Ea.	45	1,275	3,800	11,400	1,120	
	0600	Crawler, cable, ½ C.Y., 15 tons at 12' radius		14.75	400	1,200	3,600	358	
	0700	¾ C.Y., 20 tons at 12' radius		15.30	435	1,300	3,900	382.40	
	0800	1 C.Y., 25 tons at 12' radius		16.45	465	1,400	4,200	411.60	
	0900	1-½ C.Y., 40 tons at 12' radius		23.80	735	2,200	6,600	630.40	
	1000	2 C.Y., 50 tons at 12' radius		27.80	835	2,500	7,500	722.40	
	1100	3 C.Y., 75 tons at 12' radius		34	965	2,900	8,700	852	
	1200	100 ton capacity, standard boom		33	1,350	4,025	12,100	1,069	
	1300	165 ton capacity, standard boom		52	2,150	6,500	19,500	1,716	
	1400	200 ton capacity, 150' boom		98	2,350	7,075	21,200	2,199	
	1500	450' boom		110	2,950	8,850	26,500	2,650	
	1600	Truck mounted, cable operated, 6 x 4, 20 tons at 10' radius		10.80	590	1,800	5,400	446.40	
	1700	25 tons at 10' radius		16.45	980	2,950	8,850	721.60	

016 | Material and Equipment

016 400 | Equipment Rental

			UNIT	HOURLY OPER. COST.	RENT PER DAY	RENT PER WEEK	RENT PER MONTH	CREW EQUIPMENT COST	
460	1800	8 x 4, 30 tons at 10' radius	Ea.	22.15	575	1,725	5,175	522.20	460
	1900	40 tons at 12' radius		23.20	725	2,175	6,525	620.60	
	2000	8 x 4, 60 tons at 15' radius		35.15	790	2,375	7,125	756.20	
	2050	82 tons at 15' radius		28	1,525	4,625	13,800	1,149	
	2100	90 tons at 15' radius		38.15	1,250	3,725	11,200	1,050	
	2200	115 tons at 15' radius		40	1,825	5,450	16,400	1,410	
	2300	150 tons at 18' radius		59.90	1,400	4,200	12,600	1,319	
	2350	165 tons at 18' radius		61	2,025	6,050	18,200	1,698	
	2400	Truck mounted, hydraulic, 12 ton capacity		17.75	335	1,000	3,000	342	
	2500	25 ton capacity		18.25	550	1,650	4,950	476	
	2550	33 ton capacity		19.05	885	2,340	7,950	620.40	
	2600	55 ton capacity		26.55	800	2,400	7,200	692.40	
	2700	80 ton capacity		29	1,375	4,100	12,300	1,052	
	2800	Self-propelled, 4 x 4, with telescoping boom, 5 ton		6.80	250	750	2,250	204.40	
	2900	12-½ ton capacity		12.75	490	1,475	4,425	397	
	3000	15 ton capacity		14.45	430	1,300	3,900	375.60	
	3100	25 ton capacity		16.50	605	1,825	5,425	497	
	3200	Derricks, guy, 20 ton capacity, 60' boom, 75' mast		7.30	265	790	2,375	216.40	
	3300	100' boom, 115' mast		13.30	470	1,400	4,200	386.40	
	3400	Stiffleg, 20 ton capacity, 70' boom, 37' mast		9.35	355	1,050	3,200	284.80	
	3500	100' boom, 47' mast		14.80	575	1,750	5,200	468.40	
	3550	Helicopter, small, lift to 1250 lbs. maximum		200	2,075	6,250	18,800	2,850	
	3600	Hoists, chain type, overhead, manual, ¾ ton		.05	5.20	14.55	42.65	3.30	
	3900	10 ton		.20	21	64	190	14.40	
	4000	Hoist and tower, 5000 lb. cap., portable electric, 40' high		3.45	150	455	1,375	118.60	
	4100	For each added 10' section, add			7.30	21	62	4.20	
	4200	Hoist and single tubular tower, 5000 lb. electric, 100' high		4.25	210	625	1,875	159	
	4300	For each added 6'-6" section, add		.05	18	52	155	10.80	
	4400	Hoist and double tubular tower, 5000 lb., 100' high		4.52	225	680	2,050	172.15	
	4500	For each added 6'-6" section, add		.05	11	33	99	7	
	4550	Hoist and tower, mast type, 6000 lb., 100' high		4.35	245	740	2,225	182.80	
	4570	For each added 10' section, add		.10	8.30	25	75	5.80	
	4600	Hoist and tower, personnel, electric, 2000 lb., 100' @ 125 FPM (C10.3-300)		8.10	605	1,825	5,450	429.80	
	4700	3000 lb., 100' @ 200 FPM		8.70	660	1,975	5,925	464.60	
	4800	3000 lb., 150' @ 300 FPM		9.30	710	2,125	6,400	499.40	
	4900	4000 lb., 100' @ 300 FPM		9.95	765	2,275	6,875	534.60	
	5000	6000 lb., 100' @ 275 FPM		10.55	825	2,475	7,400	579.40	
	5100	For added heights up to 500', add	L.F.		1.05	3	9	.60	
	5200	Jacks, hydraulic, 20 ton	Ea.	.10	2	6	18	2	
	5500	100 ton	"	.15	17	52	155	11.60	
	6000	Jacks, hydraulic, climbing with 50' jackrods							
	6010	and control consoles, minimum 3 mo. rental							
	6100	30 ton capacity	Ea.	.05	87	260	780	52.40	
	6150	For each added 10' jackrod section, add			2	6	18	1.20	
	6300	50 ton capacity			150	460	1,375	92	
	6350	For each added 10' jackrod section, add			3.12	9	27	1.80	
	6500	125 ton capacity			435	1,300	3,900	260	
	6550	For each added 10' jackrod section, add			22	65	195	13	
	6600	Cable jack, 10 ton capacity with 200' cable			74	225	670	45	
	6650	For each added 50' of cable, add			4.50	13.50	41	2.70	
490	0010	WELLPOINT EQUIPMENT RENTAL See also division 021-444							490
	0020	Based on 2 months rental							
	0100	Combination jetting & wellpoint pump, 60 H.P. diesel	Ea.	2.75	225	660	1,975	154	
	0200	High pressure gas jet pump, 200 H.P., 300 psi	"	7.60	180	545	1,650	169.80	
	0300	Discharge pipe, 8" diameter	L.F.		.30	.90	2.70	.20	
	0350	12" diameter			.43	1.28	3.68	.25	
	0400	Header pipe, flows up to 150 G.P.M., 4" diameter			.19	.55	1.65	.10	
	0500	400 G.P.M., 6" diameter			.25	.75	2.25	.15	

016 | Material and Equipment

016 400 | Equipment Rental

		UNIT	HOURLY OPER. COST.	RENT PER DAY	RENT PER WEEK	RENT PER MONTH	CREW EQUIPMENT COST	
490	0600	800 G.P.M., 8" diameter	L.F.		.43	1.28	3.68	.25	490
	0700	1500 G.P.M., 10" diameter			.45	1.33	4	.25	
	0800	2500 G.P.M., 12" diameter			.58	1.77	5.30	.35	
	0900	4500 G.P.M., 16" diameter			.92	2.76	8.25	.55	
	0950	For quick coupling aluminum and plastic pipe, add	↓		1.23	3.68	11	.70	
	1100	Wellpoint, 25' long, with fittings & riser pipe, 1-½" or 2" diameter	Ea.		2.67	8	25	1.60	
	1200	Wellpoint pump, diesel powered, 4" diameter, 20 H.P.		3.14	115	335	1,000	92.10	
	1300	6" diameter, 30 H.P.		4.42	150	450	1,350	125.35	
	1400	8" suction, 40 H.P.		5.10	200	600	1,800	160.80	
	1500	10" suction, 75 H.P.		5.50	245	730	2,175	190	
	1600	12" suction, 100 H.P.		7.80	395	1,200	3,600	302.40	
	1700	12" suction, 175 H.P.		8.55	430	1,300	3,900	328.40	

017 | Contract Closeout

017 100 | Final Cleaning

		CREW	DAILY OUTPUT	MAN-HOURS	UNIT	MAT.	LABOR	EQUIP.	TOTAL	TOTAL INCL O&P	
104	0011	CLEANING UP After job completion, minimum				Project					.30%	104
	0040	Maximum				"					1%	
	0050	Cleanup of floor area, continuous, per day	A-5	12	1.500	M.S.F.	1.50	26	2.88	30.38	44	
	0100	Final	"	11.50	1.570	"	1.60	27	3	31.60	46	
	1000	Mechanical demolition, see division 020										

020 | Subsurface Investigation and Demolition

020 120 | Std Penetration Tests

		CREW	DAILY OUTPUT	MAN-HOURS	UNIT	MAT.	LABOR	EQUIP.	TOTAL	TOTAL INCL O&P	
125	0010	DRILLING, CORE Reinforced concrete slab, up to 6" thick slab										125
	0020	Including layout and set up										
	0100	1" diameter core	B-89A	48	.333	Ea.	2.10	6.55	.97	9.62	13.30	
	0150	Each added inch thick, add		400	.040		.35	.79	.12	1.26	1.71	
	0300	3" diameter core		40	.400		4.67	7.85	1.16	13.68	18.35	
	0350	Each added inch thick, add		267	.060		.78	1.18	.17	2.13	2.84	
	0500	4" diameter core		37	.432		6.25	8.50	1.25	16	21	
	0550	Each added inch thick, add		242	.066		1.04	1.30	.19	2.53	3.32	
	0700	6" diameter core		29	.552		7.60	10.85	1.60	20.05	27	
	0750	Each added inch thick, add		200	.080		1.26	1.57	.23	3.06	4.03	
	0900	8" diameter core		21	.762		10.40	14.95	2.21	27.56	37	
	0950	Each added inch thick, add	↓	133	.120		1.74	2.36	.35	4.45	5.90	
	1100	10" diameter core	A-1	19	.421		14.05	7.20	2.80	24.05	30	
	1150	Each added inch thick, add		114	.070		2.34	1.20	.47	4.01	4.91	
	1300	12" diameter core		16	.500		16.95	8.60	3.33	28.88	35	
	1350	Each added inch thick, add		96	.083		2.83	1.43	.55	4.81	5.90	
	1500	14" diameter core		13.80	.580		21	9.95	3.86	34.81	42	
	1550	Each added inch thick, add		80	.100		3.50	1.72	.67	5.89	7.20	
	1700	18" diameter core		6.80	1.180		27	20	7.80	54.80	69	
	1750	Each added inch thick, add	↓	40	.200		4.69	3.43	1.33	9.45	11.85	

020 | Subsurface Investigation and Demolition

020 120 | Std Penetration Tests

		CREW	DAILY OUTPUT	MAN-HOURS	UNIT	MAT.	LABOR	EQUIP.	TOTAL	TOTAL INCL O&P
125	1760	For horizontal holes, add to above				Ea.				30%	30%
	1770	Prestressed hollow core plank, 6" thick									
	1780	1" diameter core	B-89A	65	.246	Ea.	1.36	4.83	.71	6.90	9.65
	1790	Each added inch thick, add		432	.037		.22	.73	.11	1.06	1.46
	1800	3" diameter core		66	.242		3.07	4.76	.70	8.53	11.40
	1810	Each added inch thick, add		296	.054		.52	1.06	.16	1.74	2.36
	1820	4" diameter core		63	.254		4.10	4.98	.74	9.82	12.90
	1830	Each added inch thick, add		271	.059		.69	1.16	.17	2.02	2.71
	1840	6" diameter core		52	.308		4.98	6.05	.89	11.92	15.65
	1850	Each added inch thick, add		222	.072		.83	1.41	.21	2.45	3.29
	1860	8" diameter core		37	.432		6.80	8.50	1.25	16.55	22
	1870	Each added inch thick, add		147	.109		1.12	2.14	.32	3.58	4.83
	1880	10" diameter core	A-1	32	.250		9.15	4.29	1.66	15.10	18.40
	1890	Each added inch thick, add		124	.065		1.12	1.11	.43	2.66	3.38
	1900	12" diameter core		28	.286		11.10	4.90	1.90	17.90	22
	1910	Each added inch thick, add		107	.075		1.85	1.28	.50	3.63	4.53
	1950	Minimum charge for above, 3" diameter core	B-89A	7.45	2.150			42	6.25	48.25	71
	2000	4" diameter core		7.15	2.240			44	6.50	50.50	74
	2050	6" diameter core		6.40	2.500			49	7.25	56.25	83
	2100	8" diameter core		5.80	2.760			54	8	62	91
	2150	10" diameter core		5	3.200			63	9.30	72.30	105
	2200	12" diameter core		4.10	3.900			77	11.30	88.30	130
	2250	14" diameter core		3.55	4.510			88	13.05	101.05	150
	2300	18" diameter core		3.30	4.850			95	14.05	109.05	160

020 550 | Site Demolition

		CREW	DAILY OUTPUT	MAN-HOURS	UNIT	MAT.	LABOR	EQUIP.	TOTAL	TOTAL INCL O&P
554	0010	SITE DEMOLITION No hauling, abandon catch basin or manhole	B-6	7	3.430	Ea.		63	26	89	125
	0020	Remove existing catch basin or manhole		4	6			110	45	155	215
	0030	Catch basin or manhole frames and covers stored		13	1.850			34	13.95	47.95	67
	0040	Remove and reset		7	3.430			63	26	89	125
	0900	Hydrants, fire, remove only	2 Plum	4.70	3.400			84		84	125
	0950	Remove and reset	"	1.40	11.430			280		280	420
	1710	Pavement removal, bituminous, 3" thick	B-38	690	.058	S.Y.		1.12	1.56	2.68	3.40
	1750	4" to 6" thick	"	420	.095	"		1.84	2.56	4.40	5.60
	2900	Pipe removal, concrete, no excavation, 12" diameter	B-6	175	.137	L.F.		2.53	1.04	3.57	4.96
	2930	15" diameter		150	.160			2.95	1.21	4.16	5.80
	2960	24" diameter		120	.200			3.69	1.51	5.20	7.25
	3000	36" diameter		90	.267			4.92	2.02	6.94	9.65
	3200	Steel, welded connections, 4" diameter		160	.150			2.77	1.13	3.90	5.45
	3300	10" diameter		80	.300			5.55	2.27	7.82	10.85
	4000	Sidewalk removal, bituminous, 2-½" thick		325	.074	S.Y.		1.36	.56	1.92	2.67
	4100	Concrete, plain		160	.150	"		2.77	1.13	3.90	5.45

020 600 | Building Demolition

		CREW	DAILY OUTPUT	MAN-HOURS	UNIT	MAT.	LABOR	EQUIP.	TOTAL	TOTAL INCL O&P
620	0010	RUBBISH HANDLING The following are to be added to the									620
	0020	selective demolition prices									
	0400	Chute, circular, prefabricated steel, 18" diameter	B-1	40	.600	L.F.	9.65	10.70		20.35	27
	0440	30" diameter	"	30	.800	"	18.70	14.25		32.95	42
	0600	Dumpster, (debris box container), 5 C.Y., rent per week				Ea.					160
	0700	10 C.Y. capacity									200
	0800	30 C.Y. capacity									275
	0840	40 C.Y. capacity									330
	1000	Dust partition, 6 mil polyethylene, 4' x 8' panels, 1" x 3" frame	2 Carp	2,000	.008	S.F.	.17	.17		.34	.45
	1080	2" x 4" frame	"	2,000	.008	"	.28	.17		.45	.57
	2000	Load, haul to chute & dumping into chute, 50' haul	2 Clab	24	.667	C.Y.		11.45		11.45	17.35
	2040	100' haul		16.50	.970			16.65		16.65	25
	2080	Over 100' haul, add per 100 L.F.		35.50	.451			7.75		7.75	11.75
	2120	In elevators, per 10 floors, add		140	.114			1.96		1.96	2.97

020 | Subsurface Investigation and Demolition

020 600 | Building Demolition

		Description	CREW	DAILY OUTPUT	MAN-HOURS	UNIT	MAT.	LABOR	EQUIP.	TOTAL	TOTAL INCL O&P	
620	3000	Loading & trucking, including 2 mile haul, chute loaded	B-16	32	1	C.Y.		17.90	10.85	28.75	39	620
	3040	Hand loaded, 50' haul	2 Clab	21.50	.744			12.75		12.75	19.35	
	3080	Machine loaded	B-6	80	.300			5.55	2.27	7.82	10.85	
	3120	Wheeled 50' and ramp dump loaded	2 Clab	24	.667			11.45		11.45	17.35	
	5000	Haul, per mile, up to 8 C.Y. truck	B-34B	1,165	.007			.12	.30	.42	.51	
	5100	Over 8 C.Y. truck	"	1,550	.005			.09	.22	.31	.39	

020 700 | Selective Demolition

		Description	CREW	DAILY OUTPUT	MAN-HOURS	UNIT	MAT.	LABOR	EQUIP.	TOTAL	TOTAL INCL O&P	
717	0010	**HAZARDOUS WASTE CLEANUP/PICKUP/DISPOSAL**										717
	0100	For contractor equipment, i.e. dozer,										
	0110	front end loader, dump truck, etc., see div. 016-408										
	1000	Solid pickup										
	1100	55 gal. drums				Ea.					135	
	1120	Bulk material, minimum				Ton					120	
	1130	Maximum				"					270	
	1200	Transportation to disposal site										
	1220	Truckload = 80 drums or 25 C.Y. or 18 tons										
	1260	Minimum				Mile					3	
	1270	Maximum				"					3.95	
	3000	Liquid pickup, vacuum truck, stainless steel tank										
	3100	Minimum charge, 4 hours										
	3110	1 compartment, 2200 gallon				Hr.					88	
	3120	2 compartment, 5000 gallon				"					99	
	3400	Transportation in 6900 gallon bulk truck				Mile					4	
	3410	In teflon lined truck				"					4.62	
	5000	Heavy sludge or dry vacuumable material				Hr.					99	
	6000	Dumpsite disposal charge, minimum				Ton					115	
	6020	Maximum				"					230	
724	0010	**PLUMBING DEMOLITION**										724
	1020	Fixtures, including 10' piping										
	1100	Bath tubs, cast iron	1 Plum	4	2	Ea.		49		49	73	
	1120	Fiberglass		6	1.330			33		33	49	
	1140	Steel		5	1.600			40		40	59	
	1200	Lavatory, wall hung		10	.800			19.75		19.75	29	
	1220	Counter top		8	1			25		25	37	
	1300	Sink, steel or cast iron, single		8	1			25		25	37	
	1320	Double		7	1.140			28		28	42	
	1400	Water closet, floor mounted		8	1			25		25	37	
	1420	Wall mounted		7	1.140			28		28	42	
	1500	Urinal, floor mounted		4	2			49		49	73	
	1520	Wall mounted		7	1.140			28		28	42	
	1600	Water fountains, free standing		8	1			25		25	37	
	1620	Recessed		6	1.330			33		33	49	
	2000	Piping, metal, to 2" diameter		200	.040	L.F.		.99		.99	1.47	
	2050	To 4" diameter		150	.053			1.32		1.32	1.95	
	2100	To 8" diameter	2 Plum	100	.160			3.95		3.95	5.85	
	2150	To 16" diameter	"	60	.267			6.60		6.60	9.75	
	2160	Deduct for salvage, aluminum scrap				Ton					700	
	2170	Brass scrap									550	
	2180	Copper scrap									1,000	
	2200	Lead scrap									175	
	2220	Steel scrap									45	
	2250	Water heater, 40 gal.	1 Plum	6	1.330	Ea.		33		33	49	
	6000	Remove and reset fixtures, minimum		6	1.330			33		33	49	
	6100	Maximum		4	2			49		49	73	
730	0010	**TORCH CUTTING** Steel, 1" thick plate	A-1A	95	.084	L.F.		1.44	1.21	2.65	3.53	730
	0040	1" diameter bar	"	210	.038	Ea.		.65	.55	1.20	1.60	

020 | Subsurface Investigation and Demolition

020 700 | Selective Demolition

			CREW	DAILY OUTPUT	MAN-HOURS	UNIT	BARE COSTS MAT.	BARE COSTS LABOR	BARE COSTS EQUIP.	BARE COSTS TOTAL	TOTAL INCL O&P	
730	1000	Oxygen lance cutting, reinforced concrete walls										730
	1040	12" to 16" thick walls	A-1A	10	.800	L.F.		13.70	11.55	25.25	34	
	1080	24" thick walls	"	6	1.330	"		23	19.25	42.25	56	
732	0010	**WALLS AND PARTITIONS DEMOLITION**										732
	3800	Toilet partitions, slate or marble	1 Clab	5	1.600	Ea.		27		27	42	
	3820	Hollow metal	"	8	1	"		17.15		17.15	26	

020 800 | Asbestos Removal

			CREW	DAILY OUTPUT	MAN-HOURS	UNIT	MAT.	LABOR	EQUIP.	TOTAL	INCL O&P	
810	0010	**ASBESTOS ABATEMENT EQUIPMENT** and supplies, buy										810
	0200	Air filtration device, 2000 C.F.M.				Ea.	2,250			2,250	2,475	
	0250	Large volume air sampling pump, minimum					500			500	550	
	0260	Maximum					850			850	935	
	0300	Airless sprayer unit, 2 gun					4,000			4,000	4,400	
	0350	Light stand, 500 watt					265			265	290	
	0400	Personal respirators										
	0410	Negative pressure, ½ face, dual operation, min.				Ea.	14			14	15.40	
	0420	Maximum					18			18	19.80	
	0450	P.A.P.R., full face, minimum					450			450	495	
	0460	Maximum					650			650	715	
	0470	Supplied air, full face, incl. air line, minimum					350			350	385	
	0480	Maximum					500			500	550	
	0500	Personnel sampling pump, minimum					400			400	440	
	0510	Maximum					600			600	660	
	1500	Power panel, 20 unit, incl. G.F.I.					1,600			1,600	1,750	
	1600	Shower unit, including pump and filters					2,500			2,500	2,750	
	1700	Supplied air system (type C)					9,400			9,400	10,300	
	1750	Vacuum cleaner, HEPA, 16 gal., stainless steel, wet/dry					1,225			1,225	1,350	
	1760	55 gallon					1,975			1,975	2,175	
	1800	Vacuum loader, 9-18 ton/hr				Ea.	80,000			80,000	88,000	
	1900	Water atomizer unit, including 55 gal. drum					200			200	220	
	2000	Worker protection, whole body, foot and head cover, gloves					10			10	11	
	2500	Respirator, single use					10			10	11	
	2550	Cartridge for respirator					2.85			2.85	3.14	
	2570	Glove bag, 7 mil, 50" x 64"					12			12	13.20	
	2580	10 mil, 44" x 60"					6.25			6.25	6.90	
	3000	HEPA vacuum for work area, minimun					1,000			1,000	1,100	
	6000	Disposable polyethelene bags, 6 mil, 3 C.F.					.60			.60	.66	
	6300	Disposable fiber drums, 3 C.F.					5.75			5.75	6.35	
	6400	Pressure sensitive caution lables, 3" x 5"					.12			.12	.13	
	6450	11" x 17"					.15			.15	.17	
820	0010	**ASBESTOS ABATEMENT WORK AREA** Containment and preparation.										820
	0100	Pre-cleaning, HEPA vacuum and wet wipe	A-10	14,400	.004	S.F.		.11		.11	.17	
	0200	Protect carpeted area, 2 layers 6 mil poly on ¾" plywood	"	1,000	.064		.86	1.54	.05	2.45	3.37	
	0300	Separation barrier, 2" x 4" @ 16", ½" plywood ea. side, 8' high	F-2	400	.040		.73	.86	.04	1.63	2.15	
	0310	12' high		320	.050		.85	1.08	.05	1.98	2.63	
	0320	16' high		200	.080		1.05	1.73	.08	2.86	3.87	
	0400	Personnel decontam. chamber, 2" x 4" @ 16", ¾" ply ea. side		280	.057		1.36	1.23	.06	2.65	3.44	
	0450	Waste decontam. chamber, 2" x 4" studs @ 16", ¾" ply ea side		360	.044		1.36	.96	.04	2.36	3.01	
	0500	Cover surfaces with polyethelene sheeting,										
	0501	Including glue and tape										
	0550	Floors, each layer, 6 mil	A-10	8,000	.008	S.F.	.04	.19	.01	.24	.34	
	0551	4 mil		9,000	.007		.03	.17	.01	.21	.30	
	0560	Walls, each layer, 6 mil		6,000	.011		.04	.26	.01	.31	.44	
	0561	4 mil		7,000	.009		.03	.22	.01	.26	.38	
	0570	For heights above 12', add				%		20%				
	0575	For heights above 20', add				"		30%				

020 | Subsurface Investigation and Demolition

020 800 | Asbestos Removal

			CREW	DAILY OUTPUT	MAN-HOURS	UNIT	BARE COSTS MAT.	LABOR	EQUIP.	TOTAL	TOTAL INCL O&P	
820	0580	For fire retardant poly, add				S.F.	100%					820
	0590	For large open areas, deduct				%	10%	20%				
	0600	Seal floor penetrations with foam firestop, to 36 Sq. In.	F-2	200	.080	S.F.	2.25	1.73	.08	4.06	5.20	
	0610	36 Sq. In. to 72 Sq. In.		125	.128		5.50	2.76	.12	8.38	10.40	
	0615	72 Sq. In. to 144 Sq. In.		80	.200	↓	11	4.32	.20	15.52	18.85	
	0620	Seal wall penetrations with foam firestop to 36 Sq. In.		180	.089	Ea.	2.25	1.92	.09	4.26	5.50	
	0630	36 Sq. In. to 72 Sq. In.		100	.160		5.50	3.46	.16	9.12	11.45	
	0640	72 Sq. In. to 144 Sq. In.	↓	60	.267	↓	11	5.75	.26	17.01	21	
	0800	Caulk seams with latex	1 Carp	230	.035	L.F.	.11	.75		.86	1.26	
830	0010	**DEMOLITION IN ASBESTOS CONTAMINATED AREA**										830
	0200	Ceiling, including suspension system, plaster and lath	A-9	2,100	.030	S.F.		.73	.08	.81	1.22	
	0210	Finished plaster, leaving wire lath		585	.109			2.63	.30	2.93	4.37	
	0220	Suspended acoustical tile		3,500	.018			.44	.05	.49	.73	
	0230	Splined tile grid system		3,000	.021			.51	.06	.57	.85	
	0240	Metal pan grid system		1,500	.043			1.02	.12	1.14	1.71	
	0250	Gypsum board		2,500	.026	↓		.61	.07	.68	1.02	
	0260	Lighting fixtures up to 2' x 4'		72	.889	Ea.		21	2.41	23.41	36	
	0400	Partitions, non load bearing							.25			
	0410	Plaster, lath, and studs	A-9	690	.093	S.F.		2.23	.25	2.48	3.71	
	0450	Gypsum board and studs	"	1,390	.046	"		1.11	.12	1.23	1.84	
	9000	For type C respirator equipment, add				%					10%	
840	0010	**BULK ASBESTOS REMOVAL**										840
	0020	Includes disposable tools and 4 suits and respirators/day/man	A-9	480	.133	S.F.		3.20	.36	3.56	5.35	
	0200	Boiler insulation	"	480	.133	"		3.20	.36	3.56	5.35	
	0210	With metal lath add				%				50%		
	0300	Boiler breeching or flue insulation	A-9	520	.123	S.F.		2.96	.33	3.29	4.92	
	0310	For active boiler, add				%				100%		
	0400	Duct or AHU insulation	A-9	720	.089	S.F.		2.13	.24	2.37	3.55	
	0500	Duct vibration isolation joints, up to 24 Sq. In. duct		56	1.140	Ea.		27	3.10	30.10	46	
	0520	25 Sq. In. to 48 Sq. In. duct		48	1.330			32	3.62	35.62	53	
	0530	49 Sq. In. to 76 Sq. In. duct		40	1.600	↓		38	4.34	42.34	64	
	0600	Pipe insulation up to 4" diameter pipe		900	.071	L.F.		1.71	.19	1.90	2.84	
	0610	4" to 8" diameter pipe		800	.080			1.92	.22	2.14	3.20	
	0620	10" to 12" diameter pipe		700	.091			2.20	.25	2.45	3.66	
	0630	14" to 16" diameter pipe		550	.116	↓		2.79	.32	3.11	4.65	
	0650	Over 16" diameter pipe		650	.098	S.F.		2.36	.27	2.63	3.94	
	0700	With glove bag up to 3" diameter pipe		100	.640	L.F.	4.80	15.35	1.74	21.89	31	
	1000	Pipe fitting insulation up to 4" diameter pipe		320	.200	Ea.		4.80	.54	5.34	8	
	1100	6" to 8" diameter pipe		304	.211			5.05	.57	5.62	8.40	
	1110	10" to 12" diameter pipe		192	.333			8	.90	8.90	13.35	
	1120	14" to 16" diameter pipe		128	.500	↓		12	1.36	13.36	20	
	1130	Over 16" diameter pipe		176	.364	S.F.		8.75	.99	9.74	14.55	
	1200	With glove bag, up to 8" diameter pipe		40	1.600	Ea.	12	38	4.34	54.34	77	
	2000	Scrape foam fireproofing from flat surface		2,400	.027	S.F.		.64	.07	.71	1.07	
	2100	Irregular surfaces		1,200	.053			1.28	.14	1.42	2.13	
	3000	Remove cementitious material from flat surface		800	.080			1.92	.22	2.14	3.20	
	3100	Irregular surface		400	.160			3.84	.43	4.27	6.40	
	6000	Remove contaminated soil from crawl space by hand	↓	400	.160	C.F.		3.84	.43	4.27	6.40	
	6100	With large production vacuum loader	A-12	700	.091	"		2.20	.84	3.04	4.31	
	7000	Radiator backing, not including radiator removal	A-9	1,200	.053	S.F.		1.28	.14	1.42	2.13	
	9000	For type C respirator equipment, add				%					10%	
850	0010	**WASTE PACKAGING, HANDLING, & DISPOSAL**										850
	0100	Collect and bag bulk material, 3 C.F. bags, by hand	A-9	400	.160	Ea.	.60	3.84	.43	4.87	7.05	
	0200	Large production vacuum loader	A-12	880	.073		.60	1.75	.67	3.02	4.09	
	1000	Double bag and decontaminate	A-9	960	.067		.60	1.60	.18	2.38	3.33	
	2000	Containerize bagged material, per bag	"	800	.080		2	1.92	.22	4.14	5.40	
	3000	Cart bags 50' to dumpster	2 Asbe	400	.040	↓		.96		.96	1.48	

020 | Subsurface Investigation and Demolition

020 800 | Asbestos Removal

			CREW	DAILY OUTPUT	MAN-HOURS	UNIT	MAT.	LABOR	EQUIP.	TOTAL	TOTAL INCL O&P	
850	5000	Disposal charges, not including haul, minimum				C.Y.					40	850
	5020	Maximum				"					150	
	9000	For type C respirator equipment, add				%					10%	
860	0010	**DECONTAMINATION CONTAINMENT AREA DEMOLITION** and clean-up										860
	0100	Spray exposed substrate with surfactant (bridging)										
	0200	Flat surfaces	A-9	6,000	.011	S.F.	.25	.26	.03	.54	.71	
	0250	Irregular surfaces		4,000	.016	"	.30	.38	.04	.72	.97	
	0300	Pipes, beams, and columns		2,000	.032	L.F.	.50	.77	.09	1.36	1.83	
	1000	Spray encapsulate polyethelene sheeting		8,000	.008	S.F.	.20	.19	.02	.41	.54	
	1100	Roll down polyethelene sheeting		8,000	.008	"		.19	.02	.21	.32	
	1500	Bag polyethelene sheeting		400	.160	Ea.	.60	3.84	.43	4.87	7.05	
	2000	Fine clean exposed substrate, with nylon brush		2,400	.027	S.F.		.64	.07	.71	1.07	
	2500	Wet wipe substrate		4,800	.013			.32	.04	.36	.53	
	2600	Vacuum surfaces, fine brush	↓	6,400	.010	↓		.24	.03	.27	.40	
	3000	Structural demolition										
	3100	Wood stud walls	A-9	2,800	.023	S.F.		.55	.06	.61	.91	
	3500	Window manifolds, not incl. window replacement		4,200	.015			.37	.04	.41	.61	
	3600	Plywood carpet protection		2,000	.032			.77	.09	.86	1.28	
	5000	HEPA vacuum and shampoo carpeting		4,800	.013		.02	.32	.04	.38	.55	
	9000	Final cleaning of protected surfaces	↓	8,000	.008	↓		.19	.02	.21	.32	
870	0010	**ENCAPSULATION WITH SEALANTS**										870
	0100	Ceilings and walls, minimum	A-9	21,000	.003	S.F.	.20	.07	.01	.28	.34	
	0110	Maximum		10,600	.006	"	.31	.14	.02	.47	.58	
	0300	Pipes to 12" diameter including minor repairs, minimum		800	.080	L.F.	.30	1.92	.22	2.44	3.53	
	0310	Maximum	↓	400	..160	"	.95	3.84	.43	5.22	7.45	
890	0010	**OSHA TESTING**										890
	0100	Certified technician, minimum				Day		275		275		
	0110	Maximum				"		450		450		
	0200	Personal sampling, PCM analysis, minimum				Ea.	2.40	23		25.40		
	0210	Maximum				"	2.40	48		50.40		
	0300	Industrial hygienist, minimum				Day		350		350		
	0310	Maximum				"		500		500		
	1000	Cleaned area samples				Ea.	2.40	23		25.40		
	1100	PCM analysis, minimum					2.40	23		25.40		
	1110	Maximum					2.40	48		50.40		
	1200	TEM analysis, minimum								400		
	1210	Maximum				↓				1,000		

021 | Site Preparation

021 400 | Dewatering

			CREW	DAILY OUTPUT	MAN-HOURS	UNIT	MAT.	LABOR	EQUIP.	TOTAL	TOTAL INCL O&P	
404	0010	**DEWATERING** Excavate drainage trench, 2' wide, 2' deep	B-11C	90	.178	C.Y.		3.49	2.02	5.51	7.45	404
	0100	2' wide, 3' deep, with backhoe loader	"	135	.119			2.33	1.34	3.67	4.98	
	0200	Excavate sump pits by hand, light soil	1 Clab	7.10	1.130			19.30		19.30	29	
	0300	Heavy soil	"	3.50	2.290	↓		39		39	60	
	0500	Pumping 8 hr., attended 2 hrs. per day, including 20 L.F.										
	0550	of suction hose & 100 L.F. discharge hose										
	0600	2" diaphragm pump used for 8 hours	B-10H	4	3	Day		61	5.90	66.90	99	
	0650	4" diaphragm pump used for 8 hours	B-10I	4	3	"		61	17	78	110	

021 | Site Preparation

021 400 | Dewatering

		CREW	DAILY OUTPUT	MAN-HOURS	UNIT	BARE COSTS MAT.	LABOR	EQUIP.	TOTAL	TOTAL INCL O&P	
404	0800	8 hrs. attended, 2" diaphragm pump	B-10H	1	12	Day		245	24	269	395	404
	0900	3" centrifugal pump	B-10J	1	12			245	39	284	410	
	1000	4" diaphragm pump	B-10I	1	12			245	68	313	445	
	1100	6" centrifugal pump	B-10K	1	12			245	190	435	575	
	1300	Re-lay CMP, incl. excavation 3' deep, 12" diameter	B-6	115	.209	L.F.	5.30	3.85	1.58	10.73	13.40	
	1400	18" diameter		100	.240	"	7.95	4.43	1.81	14.19	17.45	
	1600	Sump hole construction, incl. excavation and gravel, pit		1,250	.019	C.F.	.27	.35	.15	.77	.99	
	1700	With 12" gravel collar, 12" pipe, corrugated, 16 ga.		70	.343	L.F.	8.80	6.35	2.59	17.74	22	
	1800	15" pipe, corrugated, 16 ga.		55	.436		10.80	8.05	3.30	22.15	28	
	1900	18" pipe, corrugated, 16 ga.		50	.480		12.65	8.85	3.63	25.13	31	
	2000	24" pipe, corrugated, 14 ga.		40	.600		19.10	11.10	4.54	34.74	43	
	2200	Wood lining, up to 4' x 4', add		300	.080	SFCA	.85	1.48	.60	2.93	3.83	
	9950	See Div. 021-444 for wellpoints										
	9960	See Div. 021-484 for deep well systems										

021 440 | Wellpoints

		CREW	DAILY OUTPUT	MAN-HOURS	UNIT	BARE COSTS MAT.	LABOR	EQUIP.	TOTAL	TOTAL INCL O&P	
444	0010	WELLPOINTS For wellpoint equipment rental, see div. 016-490										444
	0100	Installation and removal of single stage system										
	0110	Labor only, .75 man-hours per L.F., minimum	1 Clab	10.70	.748	LF Hdr		12.80		12.80	19.45	
	0200	2.0 man-hours per L.F., maximum	"	4	2	"		34		34	52	
	0400	Pump operation, 4 @ 6 hr. shifts										
	0410	Per 24 hour day	4 Eqlt	1.27	25.200	Day		530		530	795	
	0500	Per 168 hour week, 160 hr. straight, 8 hr. double time		.18	178	Week		3,750		3,750	5,600	
	0550	Per 4.3 week month		.04	800	Month		16,900		16,900	25,200	
	0600	Complete installation, operation, equipment rental, fuel &										
	0610	removal of system with 2" wellpoints 5' O.C.										
	0700	100' long header, 6" diameter, first month	4 Eqlt	3.23	9.910	LF Hdr	87	210		297	410	
	0800	Thereafter, per month		4.13	7.750		68	165		233	320	
	1000	200' long header, 8" diameter, first month		6	5.330		50	115		165	225	
	1100	Thereafter, per month		8.39	3.810		32	80		112	155	
	1300	500' long header, 8" diameter, first month		10.63	3.010		26	64		90	125	
	1400	Thereafter, per month		20.91	1.530		17	32		49	67	
	1600	1,000' long header, 10" diameter, first month		11.62	2.750		21	58		79	110	
	1700	Thereafter, per month		41.81	.765		12.50	16.15		28.65	38	
	1900	Note: above figures include pumping 168 hrs. per week										
	1910	and include the pump operator and one stand-by pump.										

021 480 | Relief Wells

		CREW	DAILY OUTPUT	MAN-HOURS	UNIT	BARE COSTS MAT.	LABOR	EQUIP.	TOTAL	TOTAL INCL O&P	
484	0010	WELLS For dewatering 10' to 20' deep, 2' diameter										484
	0020	with steel casing, minimum	B-6	165	.145	V.L.F.	1.73	2.69	1.10	5.52	7.15	
	0050	Average		98	.245		3.41	4.52	1.85	9.78	12.60	
	0100	Maximum		49	.490		8.95	9.05	3.70	21.70	28	
	0300	For pumps for dewatering, see division 016-420-4100 to 4400										
	0500	For domestic water wells, see division 026-704										

022 | Earthwork

022 200 | Excav, Backfill, Compact

		CREW	DAILY OUTPUT	MAN-HOURS	UNIT	BARE COSTS MAT.	LABOR	EQUIP.	TOTAL	TOTAL INCL O&P	
254	0010	EXCAVATING, TRENCH or continuous footing, common earth										254
	0020	No sheeting or dewatering included										
	0050	1' to 4' deep, ⅜ C.Y. tractor loader/backhoe	B-11C	150	.107	C.Y.		2.09	1.21	3.30	4.48	
	0060	½ C.Y. tractor loader/backhoe	B-11M	200	.080	"		1.57	1.41	2.98	3.91	

022 | Earthwork

022 200 | Excav, Backfill, Compact

		CREW	DAILY OUTPUT	MAN-HOURS	UNIT	BARE COSTS MAT.	LABOR	EQUIP.	TOTAL	TOTAL INCL O&P	
254											254
0090	4' to 6' deep, ½ C.Y. tractor loader/backhoe	B-11M	200	.080	C.Y.		1.57	1.41	2.98	3.91	
0100	⅝ C.Y. hydraulic backhoe	B-12Q	250	.064			1.33	1.38	2.71	3.51	
0300	½ C.Y. hydraulic excavator, truck mounted	B-12J	200	.080			1.67	2.64	4.31	5.40	
0500	6' to 10' deep, ¾ C.Y. hydraulic backhoe	B-12F	225	.071			1.48	2	3.48	4.41	
0600	1 C.Y. hydraulic excavator, truck mounted	B-12K	400	.040			.83	1.84	2.67	3.27	
0900	10' to 14' deep, ¾ C.Y. hydraulic backhoe	B-12F	200	.080			1.67	2.25	3.92	4.96	
1000	1-½ C.Y. hydraulic backhoe	B-12B	540	.030			.62	1.24	1.86	2.28	
1300	14' to 20' deep, 1 C.Y. hydraulic backhoe	B-12A	320	.050			1.04	1.74	2.78	3.47	
1400	By hand with pick and shovel to 6' deep, light soil	1 Clab	8	1			17.15		17.15	26	
1500	Heavy soil	"	4	2			34		34	52	
1700	For tamping backfilled trenches, air tamp, add	A-1	100	.080			1.37	.53	1.90	2.67	
1900	Vibrating plate, add		90	.089			1.52	.59	2.11	2.97	
2100	Trim sides and bottom for concrete pours, common earth		600	.013	S.F.		.23	.09	.32	.44	
2300	Hardpan		180	.044	"		.76	.30	1.06	1.48	
258											258
0010	**EXCAVATING, UTILITY TRENCH** Common earth										
0050	Trenching with chain trencher, 12 H.P., operator walking										
0100	4" wide trench, 12" deep	B-53	800	.010	L.F.		.21	.06	.27	.38	
0150	18" deep		750	.011			.23	.07	.30	.41	
0200	24" deep		700	.011			.24	.07	.31	.44	
0300	6" wide trench, 12" deep		650	.012			.26	.08	.34	.47	
0350	18" deep		600	.013			.28	.08	.36	.51	
0400	24" deep		550	.015			.31	.09	.40	.56	
0450	36" deep		450	.018			.38	.11	.49	.68	
0600	8" wide trench, 12" deep		475	.017			.36	.11	.47	.65	
0650	18" deep		400	.020			.42	.13	.55	.77	
0700	24" deep		350	.023			.48	.14	.62	.88	
0750	36" deep		300	.027			.56	.17	.73	1.02	
1000	Backfill by hand including compaction, add										
1050	4" wide trench, 12" deep	A-1	800	.010	L.F.		.17	.07	.24	.33	
1100	18" deep		530	.015			.26	.10	.36	.50	
1150	24" deep		400	.020			.34	.13	.47	.67	
1300	6" wide trench, 12" deep		540	.015			.25	.10	.35	.49	
1350	18" deep		405	.020			.34	.13	.47	.66	
1400	24" deep		270	.030			.51	.20	.71	.99	
1450	36" deep		180	.044			.76	.30	1.06	1.48	
1600	8" wide trench, 12" deep		400	.020			.34	.13	.47	.67	
1650	18" deep		265	.030			.52	.20	.72	1.01	
1700	24" deep		200	.040			.69	.27	.96	1.33	
1750	36" deep		135	.059			1.02	.39	1.41	1.98	
2000	Chain trencher, 40 H.P. operator riding										
2050	6" wide trench and backfill, 12" deep	B-54	1,200	.007	L.F.		.14	.11	.25	.33	
2100	18" deep		1,000	.008			.17	.13	.30	.39	
2150	24" deep		975	.008			.17	.13	.30	.40	
2200	36" deep		900	.009			.19	.14	.33	.44	
2250	48" deep		750	.011			.23	.17	.40	.52	
2300	60" deep		650	.012			.26	.20	.46	.60	
2400	8" wide trench and backfill, 12" deep		1,000	.008			.17	.13	.30	.39	
2450	18" deep		950	.008			.18	.14	.32	.41	
2500	24" deep		900	.009			.19	.14	.33	.44	
2550	36" deep		800	.010			.21	.16	.37	.49	
2600	48" deep		650	.012			.26	.20	.46	.60	
2700	12" wide trench and backfill, 12" deep		975	.008			.17	.13	.30	.40	
2750	18" deep		860	.009			.20	.15	.35	.46	
2800	24" deep		800	.010			.21	.16	.37	.49	
2850	36" deep		725	.011			.23	.18	.41	.54	
3000	16" wide trench and backfill, 12" deep		835	.010			.20	.15	.35	.47	
3050	18" deep		750	.011			.23	.17	.40	.52	
3100	24" deep		700	.011			.24	.18	.42	.56	

022 | Earthwork

022 200 | Excav, Backfill, Compact

			CREW	DAILY OUTPUT	MAN-HOURS	UNIT	MAT.	LABOR	EQUIP.	TOTAL	TOTAL INCL O&P	
258	3200	Compaction with vibratory plate, add								50%	50%	258
262	0010	**FILL** Spread dumped material, by dozer, no compaction	B-10B	1,000	.012	C.Y.		.25	.76	1.01	1.21	262
	0100	By hand	1 Clab	12	.667	"		11.45		11.45	17.35	
	0500	Gravel fill, compacted, under floor slabs, 4" deep	B-37	10,000	.005	S.F.	.11	.09	.01	.21	.26	
	0600	6" deep		8,600	.006		.17	.10	.01	.28	.36	
	0700	9" deep		7,200	.007		.26	.12	.02	.40	.49	
	0800	12" deep		6,000	.008		.34	.15	.02	.51	.61	
	1000	Alternate pricing method, 4" deep		120	.400	C.Y.	9.10	7.25	.94	17.29	22	
	1100	6" deep		160	.300		9.10	5.45	.71	15.26	19	
	1200	9" deep		200	.240		9.10	4.35	.57	14.02	17.20	
	1300	12" deep		220	.218		9.10	3.96	.51	13.57	16.55	
266	0010	**HAULING** Earth 6 C.Y. dump truck, ¼ mile round trip, 5.0 loads/hr.	B-34A	240	.033			.60	1.18	1.78	2.20	266
	0030	½ mile round trip, 4.1 loads/hr.		197	.041			.74	1.44	2.18	2.68	
	0040	1 mile round trip, 3.3 loads/hr.		160	.050			.91	1.77	2.68	3.30	
	0100	2 mile round trip, 2.6 loads/hr.		125	.064			1.16	2.26	3.42	4.22	
	0150	3 mile round trip, 2.1 loads/hr.		100	.080			1.45	2.83	4.28	5.25	
	0200	4 mile round trip, 1.8 loads/hr.		85	.094			1.70	3.33	5.03	6.20	
	0300	12 C.Y. dump truck, 1 mile round trip, 2.7 loads/hr.	B-34B	260	.031			.56	1.33	1.89	2.30	
	0400	2 mile round trip, 2.2 loads/hr.		210	.038			.69	1.65	2.34	2.84	
	0450	3 mile round trip, 1.9 loads/hr.		180	.044			.80	1.92	2.72	3.32	
	1300	Hauling in medium traffic, add								20%	20%	
	1400	Heavy traffic, add								30%	30%	
	1600	Grading at dump, or embankment if required, by dozer	B-10B	1,000	.012			.25	.76	1.01	1.21	
	1800	Spotter at fill or cut, if required	1 Clab	8	1	Hr.		17.15		17.15	26	
270	0010	**HORIZONTAL BORING** Casing only, 100' minimum,										270
	0020	not incl. jacking pits or dewatering										
	0100	Roadwork, ½" thick wall, 24" diameter casing	B-42	10	6.400	L.F.	40	120	94	254	335	
	0200	36" diameter		9.50	6.740		56	130	99	285	370	
	0300	48" diameter		9	7.110		95	135	105	335	430	
	0500	Railroad work, 24" diameter		7	9.140		40	175	135	350	460	
	0600	36" diameter		6.50	9.850		56	190	145	391	510	
	0700	48" diameter		6	10.670		95	205	155	455	590	
	0900	For ledge, add								125	155	

026 | Piped Utilities

026 010 | Piped Utilities

			CREW	DAILY OUTPUT	MAN-HOURS	UNIT	MAT.	LABOR	EQUIP.	TOTAL	TOTAL INCL O&P	
012	0010	**BEDDING** For pipe and conduit, not incl. compaction										012
	0050	Crushed or screened bank run gravel	B-6	150	.160	C.Y.	10.55	2.95	1.21	14.71	17.40	
	0100	Crushed stone ¾" to ½"		150	.160		11.50	2.95	1.21	15.66	18.45	
	0200	Sand, dead or bank,		150	.160		3.30	2.95	1.21	7.46	9.40	
	0500	Compacting bedding in trench	A-1	90	.089			1.52	.59	2.11	2.97	
014	0010	**EXCAVATION AND BACKFILL** See division 022-204 & 254										014
	0100	Hand excavate and trim for pipe bells after trench excavation										
	0200	8" pipe	1 Clab	155	.052	L.F.		.89		.89	1.34	
	0300	18" pipe	"	130	.062	"		1.06		1.06	1.60	

026 | Piped Utilities

026 050 | Manholes And Cleanouts

			CREW	DAILY OUTPUT	MAN-HOURS	UNIT	MAT.	LABOR	EQUIP.	TOTAL	TOTAL INCL O&P	
054	0010	UTILITY VAULTS Precast concrete, 6" thick										054
	0050	5' x 10' x 6' high, I.D. [B12.3 .710]	B-13	2	28	Ea.	1,550	520	240	2,310	2,750	
	0100	6' x 10' x 6' high, I.D.		2	28		1,650	520	240	2,410	2,850	
	0150	5' x 12' x 6' high, I.D.		2	28		1,750	520	240	2,510	2,975	
	0200	6' x 12' x 6' high, I.D.		1.80	31.110		1,895	575	265	2,735	3,250	
	0250	6' x 13' x 6' high, I.D.		1.50	37.330		2,450	690	315	3,455	4,075	
	0300	8' x 14' x 7' high, I.D.		1	56		2,650	1,025	475	4,150	5,000	
	0350	Hand hole, precast concrete, 1-½" thick										
	0400	1'-0" x 2'-0" x 1'-9", I.D., light duty	B-1	4	6	Ea.	250	105		355	435	
	0450	4'-6" x 3'-2" x 2'-0", O.D., heavy duty	B-6	3	8	"	525	150	60	735	865	

026 450 | Hydrants

			CREW	DAILY OUTPUT	MAN-HOURS	UNIT	MAT.	LABOR	EQUIP.	TOTAL	TOTAL INCL O&P	
454	0010	PIPING, WATER DISTRIBUTION Mech. joints unless noted										454
	1000	Fire hydrants, two way; excavation and backfill not incl.										
	1100	4-½" valve size, depth 2'-0" [B12.3 .922]	B-21	10	2.800	Ea.	810	56	10.20	876.20	985	
	1200	4'-6"		9	3.110		902	62	11.35	975.35	1,100	
	1260	6'-0"		7	4		956	80	14.60	1,050	1,200	
	1340	8'-0"		6	4.670		1,030	93	17.05	1,140	1,300	
	1420	10'-0"		5	5.600		1,110	110	20	1,240	1,425	
	2000	5-¼" valve size, depth 2'-0"		10	2.800		885	56	10.20	951.20	1,075	
	2080	4'-0"		9	3.110		982	62	11.35	1,055	1,175	
	2160	6'-0"		7	4		1,080	80	14.60	1,174	1,325	
	2240	8'-0"		6	4.670		1,190	93	17.05	1,300	1,475	
	2320	10'-0"		5	5.600		1,215	110	20	1,345	1,525	
	2350	For threeway valves, add					7%					
	2400	Lower barrel extensions with stems, 1'-0"	B-20	14	1.710		190	33		223	260	
	2440	2'-0"		13	1.850		245	36		281	325	
	2480	3'-0"		12	2		310	39		349	400	
	2520	4'-0"		10	2.400		370	47		417	480	
	3200	Post type, non freeze, 4' depth of bury, ¾" conn.	2 Plum	4	4		150	99		249	310	
	4000	1" connection	1 Plum	8	1		188	25		213	245	
	4020	1-¼" connection		8	1		380	25		405	455	
	4040	1-½" connection		7	1.140		535	28		563	630	
	4060	2" connection		7	1.140		670	28		698	780	
	5000	Indicator post										
	5020	Adjustable, valve size 4" to 14", 4' bury	B-21	10	2.800	Ea.	497	56	10.20	563.20	645	
	5060	8' bury		8	3.500		570	70	12.80	652.80	745	
	5080	10' bury		8	3.500		640	70	12.80	722.00	825	
	5100	12' bury		6	4.670		700	93	17.05	810.05	930	
	5500	Non-adjustable, valve size 4" to 14", 3' bury		10	2.000		840	56	10.20	906.20	1,025	

026 650 | Water Systems

			CREW	DAILY OUTPUT	MAN-HOURS	UNIT	MAT.	LABOR	EQUIP.	TOTAL	TOTAL INCL O&P	
652	0010	CORROSION RESISTANCE Wrap & coat, add to pipe, 4" dia.				L.F.	1.10			1.10	1.21	652
	0040	6" diameter					1.17			1.17	1.29	
	0060	8" diameter					1.80			1.80	1.98	
	0100	12" diameter					2.65			2.65	2.92	
	0200	24" diameter					5			5	5.50	
	0500	Coating, bituminous, per diameter inch, 1 coat, add					.20			.20	.22	
	0540	3 coat					.30			.30	.33	
	0560	Coal tar epoxy, per diameter inch, 1 coat, add					.17			.17	.19	
	0600	3 coat					.25			.25	.28	
686	0010	PIPING, WATER DISTRIBUTION SYSTEMS Pipe laid in trench,										686
	0020	excavation and backfill not included										
	1400	Ductile Iron pipe, class 50 water piping, 18' lengths										
	1410	Mechanical joint, 4" diameter	B-20	144	.167	L.F.	6.50	3.24		9.74	12.10	
	1420	6" diameter	"	126	.190		8	3.71		11.71	14.45	
	1430	8" diameter	B-21	108	.259		10.90	5.15	.95	17	21	

026 | Piped Utilities

026 650 | Water Systems

		CREW	DAILY OUTPUT	MAN-HOURS	UNIT	BARE COSTS MAT.	BARE COSTS LABOR	BARE COSTS EQUIP.	BARE COSTS TOTAL	TOTAL INCL O&P
1440	10" diameter	B-21	90	.311	L.F.	14.40	6.20	1.14	21.74	27
1450	12" diameter		72	.389		18.10	7.75	1.42	27.27	33
1460	14" diameter		54	.519		21.50	10.35	1.89	33.74	41
1470	16" diameter		46	.609		24.90	12.15	2.22	39.27	48
1480	18" diameter	B-22	38	.789		28.40	15.90	4.03	48.33	60
1490	24" diameter	"	36	.833		42	16.80	4.26	63.06	76
1550	Tyton joint, 4" diameter	B-20	158	.152		5.90	2.96		8.86	11
1560	6" diameter	"	138	.174		7.35	3.39		10.74	13.25
1570	8" diameter	B-21	118	.237		10.30	4.74	.87	15.91	19.45
1580	10" diameter		100	.280		13.75	5.60	1.02	20.37	25
1590	12" diameter		80	.350		17	7	1.28	25.28	31
1600	14" diameter		60	.467		20.30	9.30	1.70	31.30	38
1610	16" diameter		54	.519		23.80	10.35	1.89	36.04	44
1620	18" diameter	B-22	44	.682		26.75	13.75	3.48	43.98	54
1630	20" diameter		42	.714		31.50	14.40	3.65	49.55	60
1640	24" diameter		40	.750		41	15.10	3.83	59.93	72
2650	Polyvinyl chloride pipe, class 160, S.D.R.-26, 1-½" diameter	B-20	300	.080		.35	1.56		1.91	2.76
2700	2" diameter		250	.096		.55	1.87		2.42	3.45
2750	2-½" diameter		250	.096		.80	1.87		2.67	3.72
2800	3" diameter		200	.120		1.20	2.34		3.54	4.87
2850	4" diameter		200	.120		1.95	2.34		4.29	5.70
2900	6" diameter		180	.133		4.20	2.60		6.80	8.55
2950	8" diameter	B-21	160	.175		9.50	3.49	.64	13.63	16.45
8000	Fittings, ductile iron, mechanical joint, cement lined									
8010	90° bend 4" diameter	B-20	37	.649	Ea.	86	12.65		98.65	115
8020	6" diameter		25	.960		115	18.70		133.70	155
8040	8" diameter		21	1.140		170	22		192	220
8060	10" diameter	B-21	21	1.330		240	27	4.87	271.87	310
8080	12" diameter		18	1.560		320	31	5.70	356.70	405
8100	14" diameter		16	1.750		520	35	6.40	561.40	630
8120	16" diameter		14	2		590	40	7.30	637.30	720
8140	18" diameter		10	2.800		898	56	10.20	964.20	1,075
8160	20" diameter		8	3.500		1,030	70	12.80	1,112	1,250
8180	24" diameter		6	4.670		1,850	93	17.05	1,960	2,200
8200	Wye or tee, 4" diameter	B-20	25	.960		126	18.70		144.70	165
8220	6" diameter		17	1.410		175	27		202	235
8240	8" diameter		14	1.710		247	33		280	320
8260	10" diameter	B-21	14	2		395	40	7.30	442.30	505
8280	12" diameter		12	2.330		515	47	8.50	570.50	645
8300	14" diameter		10	2.800		630	56	10.20	696.20	790
8320	16" diameter		8	3.500		880	70	12.80	962.80	1,100
8340	18" diameter		6	4.670		1,320	93	17.05	1,430	1,600
8360	20" diameter		4	7		1,510	140	26	1,676	1,900
8380	24" diameter		3	9.330		2,640	185	34	2,859	3,225

026 700 | Water Wells

		CREW	DAILY OUTPUT	MAN-HOURS	UNIT	MAT.	LABOR	EQUIP.	TOTAL	INCL O&P
0010	WELLS Domestic water, drilled and cased, including casing									
0100	4" to 6" diameter	B-23	160	.250	V.L.F.	7.75	4.39	3.24	15.38	18.75
0200	8" diameter	"	127	.315	"	9.75	5.55	4.09	19.39	24
0400	Gravel pack well, 40' deep, incl. gravel & casing, complete									
0500	24" diameter casing x 18" diameter screen	B-23	.13	308	Total	18,800	5,400	4,000	28,200	33,300
0600	36" diameter casing x 18" diameter screen		.12	333	"	20,000	5,850	4,325	30,175	35,600
0800	Observation wells, 1-¼" riser pipe		163	.245	V.L.F.	9.75	4.31	3.18	17.24	21
0900	For flush Buffalo roadway box, add	1 Skwk	16.60	.482	Ea.	26	10.65		36.65	45
1200	Test well, 2-½" diameter, up to 50' deep (15 to 50 GPM)	B-23	1.51	26.490	"	430	465	345	1,240	1,550
1300	Over 50' deep, add	"	121.80	.328	L.F.	13	5.75	4.26	23.01	28
1500	Pumps, installed in wells to 100' deep, 4" submersible									
1510	½ H.P.	Q-1	3.22	4.970	Ea.	305	110		415	500

026 | Piped Utilities

026 700 | Water Wells

		CREW	DAILY OUTPUT	MAN-HOURS	UNIT	MAT.	LABOR	EQUIP.	TOTAL	TOTAL INCL O&P	
704	1520	¾ H.P.	Q-1	2.66	6.020	Ea.	370	135		505	605	704
	1600	1 H.P.	"	2.29	6.990		380	155		535	650	
	1700	1-½ H.P.	Q-22	1.60	10		510	220	215	945	1,125	
	1800	2 H.P.		1.33	12.030		760	265	255	1,280	1,525	
	1900	3 H.P.		1.14	14.040		725	310	300	1,335	1,600	
	2000	5 H.P.		1.14	14.040		760	310	300	1,370	1,625	
	3000	6" submersible, 25' to 150' deep, 25 H.P., 249 to 297 GPM		.89	17.980		3,590	400	385	4,375	4,975	
	3100	25' to 500' deep, 30 H.P., 100 to 300 GPM		.73	21.920		4,170	485	470	5,125	5,825	
	9950	See Div. 021-444 for wellpoints										
	9960	See Div. 021-484 for drainage wells										

026 850 | Gas Distribution System

			CREW	DAILY OUTPUT	MAN-HOURS	UNIT	MAT.	LABOR	EQUIP.	TOTAL	TOTAL INCL O&P	
852	0010	**GAS SERVICE & DISTRIBUTION** Not including excavation										852
	0050	or backfill										
	0100	Polyethylene, 60 psi, coils, ½" diameter, SDR 7	B-20	450	.053	L.F.	.15	1.04		1.19	1.75	
	0150	1-¼" diameter, SDR 10		400	.060		.55	1.17		1.72	2.39	
	0200	2" diameter, SDR 11		360	.067		.90	1.30		2.20	2.96	
	0250	3" diameter, SDR 11.5		300	.080		1.80	1.56		3.36	4.35	
	0300	40' joints with coupling, 3" diameter, SDR 11.5	B-21	300	.093		1.95	1.86	.34	4.15	5.35	
	0350	4" diameter, SDR 11		260	.108		3.25	2.15	.39	5.79	7.25	
	0400	6" diameter, SDR 21		240	.117		3.60	2.33	.43	6.36	7.95	
	0450	8" diameter, SDR 21		200	.140		6.75	2.79	.51	10.05	12.25	
	0500	Steel, schedule 40, plain end, tar coated & wrapped										
	0550	1" diameter	Q-4	300	.107	L.F.	2.96	2.52	.13	5.61	7.15	
	0600	2" diameter		280	.114		3.37	2.70	.14	6.21	7.85	
	0650	3" diameter		260	.123		6.51	2.90	.15	9.56	11.65	
	0700	4" diameter	B-35	255	.188		9.32	3.92	1.91	15.15	18.25	
	0750	5" diameter		220	.218		13.43	4.54	2.22	20.19	24	
	0800	6" diameter		180	.267		17.11	5.55	2.71	25.37	30	
	0850	8" diameter		140	.343		25.64	7.15	3.48	36.27	43	

027 | Sewerage & Drainage

027 100 | Subdrainage Systems

			CREW	DAILY OUTPUT	MAN-HOURS	UNIT	MAT.	LABOR	EQUIP.	TOTAL	TOTAL INCL O&P	
106	0010	**PIPING, SUBDRAINAGE, BITUMINOUS**										106
	0021	Not including excavation and backfill										
	2000	Perforated underdrain, 3" diameter	B-20	800	.030	L.F.	1.20	.58		1.78	2.21	
	2020	4" diameter		760	.032		1.50	.61		2.11	2.58	
	2040	5" diameter		720	.033		2.60	.65		3.25	3.85	
	2060	6" diameter		680	.035		2.90	.69		3.59	4.23	
108	0010	**PIPING, SUBDRAINAGE, CONCRETE**										108
	0021	Not including excavation and backfill										
	3000	Porous wall concrete underdrain, std. strength, 4" diameter	B-20	335	.072	L.F.	1.50	1.39		2.89	3.77	
	3020	6" diameter	"	315	.076		1.60	1.48		3.08	4.01	
	3040	8" diameter	B-21	310	.090		2.60	1.80	.33	4.73	5.95	
	3100	18" diameter	"	165	.170		8.25	3.39	.62	12.26	14.90	
	4000	Extra strength, 6" diameter	B-20	315	.076		1.95	1.48		3.43	4.40	
	4020	8" diameter	B-21	310	.090		2.90	1.80	.33	5.03	6.30	
	4040	10" diameter		285	.098		5.70	1.96	.36	8.02	9.65	
	4060	12" diameter		230	.122		6.20	2.43	.44	9.07	11	
	4080	15" diameter		200	.140		7	2.79	.51	10.30	12.50	
	4100	18" diameter		165	.170		10.20	3.39	.62	14.21	17.05	

027 | Sewerage & Drainage

027 100 | Subdrainage Systems

			CREW	DAILY OUTPUT	MAN-HOURS	UNIT	MAT.	LABOR	EQUIP.	TOTAL	TOTAL INCL O&P	
110	0010	**PIPING, SUBDRAINAGE, CORRUGATED METAL**										110
	0021	Not including excavation and backfill										
	2010	Aluminum or steel, perforated, asphalt coated										
	2020	6" diameter, 18 ga.	B-20	380	.063	L.F.	4.75	1.23		5.98	7.10	
	2200	8" diameter, 16 ga.	"	370	.065		5.40	1.26		6.66	7.85	
	2220	10" diameter, 16 ga.	B-21	360	.078		6.65	1.55	.28	8.48	10	
	2240	12" diameter, 16 ga.		285	.098		7.75	1.96	.36	10.07	11.90	
	2260	18" diameter, 16 ga.		205	.137		11.75	2.73	.50	14.98	17.60	
	3000	Uncoated										
	3020	6" diameter, 18 ga.	B-20	380	.063	L.F.	4.46	1.23		5.69	6.80	
	3200	8" diameter, 16 ga.	"	370	.065		4.83	1.26		6.09	7.25	
	3220	10" diameter, 16 ga.	B-21	360	.078		6.14	1.55	.28	7.97	9.40	
	3240	12" diameter, 16 ga.		285	.098		7.40	1.96	.36	9.72	11.50	
	3260	18" diameter, 16 ga.		205	.137		10.90	2.73	.50	14.13	16.65	
112	0010	**PIPING, SUBDRAINAGE, VITRIFIED CLAY**										112
	0020	Not including excavation and backfill										
	3000	Perforated, 5' lengths, C700, 4" diameter	B-20	400	.060	L.F.	1.15	1.17		2.32	3.05	
	3020	6" diameter		315	.076		1.68	1.48		3.16	4.10	
	3040	8" diameter		290	.083		2.62	1.61		4.23	5.35	
	3060	12" diameter	B-21	275	.102		5.45	2.03	.37	7.85	9.50	
	4000	Channel pipe, 4" diameter	B-20	430	.056		1.36	1.09		2.45	3.15	
	4020	6" diameter		335	.072		1.90	1.39		3.29	4.21	
	4060	8" diameter		295	.081		3.05	1.58		4.63	5.75	
	4080	12" diameter	B-21	280	.100		5.90	2	.37	8.27	9.90	
114	0010	**PIPING, SUBDRAINAGE, POLYVINYL CHLORIDE**										114
	0020	Perforated, price as solid pipe, division 027-168										
152	0010	**CATCH BASINS OR MANHOLES** Including footing & excavation,										152
	0020	not including frame and cover										
	0050	Brick, 4' inside diameter, 4' deep	D-1	1	16	Ea.	378	315		693	885	
	0100	6' deep		.70	22.860		525	450		975	1,250	
	0150	8' deep		.50	32		667	630		1,297	1,675	
	0200	For depths over 8', add		4	4	V.L.F.	86	79		165	210	
	0400	Concrete blocks (radial), 4' I.D., 4' deep		1.50	10.670	Ea.	250	210		460	590	
	0500	6' deep		1	16		335	315		650	840	
	0600	8' deep		.70	22.860		435	450		885	1,150	
	0700	For depths over 8', add		5.50	2.910	V.L.F.	63	57		120	155	
	0800	Concrete, cast in place, 4' x 4', 8" thick, 4' deep	B-6	2	12	Ea.	323	220	91	634	790	
	0900	6' deep		1.50	16		435	295	120	850	1,050	
	1000	8' deep		1	24		570	445	180	1,195	1,500	
	1100	For depths over 8', add		8	3	V.L.F.	75	55	23	153	190	
	1110	Precast, 4' I.D., 4' deep		4.10	5.850	Ea.	258	110	44	412	495	
	1120	6' deep		3	8		358	150	60	568	685	
	1130	8' deep		2	12		446	220	91	757	925	
	1140	For depths over 8', add		16	1.500	V.L.F.	63	28	11.35	102.35	125	
	1150	5' I.D., 4' deep		3	8	Ea.	388	150	60	598	715	
	1160	6' deep		2	12		525	220	91	836	1,000	
	1170	8' deep		1.50	16		667	295	120	1,082	1,325	
	1180	For depths over 8', add		12	2	V.L.F.	86	37	15.10	138.10	165	
	1190	6' I.D., 4' deep		2	12	Ea.	635	220	91	946	1,125	
	1200	6' deep		1.50	16		825	295	120	1,240	1,475	
	1210	8' deep		1	24		1,030	445	180	1,655	2,000	
	1220	For depths over 8', add		8	3	V.L.F.	133	55	23	211	255	
	1250	Slab tops, precast, 8" thick										
	1300	4' diameter manhole	B-6	8	3	Ea.	93.50	55	23	171.50	210	
	1400	5' diameter manhole		7.50	3.200		105	59	24	188	230	
	1500	6' diameter manhole		7	3.430		178.50	63	26	267.50	320	
	1600	Frames and covers, C.I., 24" square, 500 lb.		7.80	3.080		172.20	57	23	252.20	300	
	1700	26" D shape, 600 lb.		7	3.430		194.50	63	26	283.50	340	

027 | Sewerage & Drainage

027 100 | Subdrainage Systems

			CREW	DAILY OUTPUT	MAN-HOURS	UNIT	MAT.	LABOR	EQUIP.	TOTAL	TOTAL INCL O&P	
152	1800	Light traffic, 18" diameter, 100 lb.	B-6	10	2.400	Ea.	70.95	44	18.15	133.10	165	152
	1900	24" diameter, 300 lb.		8.70	2.760		137	51	21	209	250	
	2000	36" diameter, 900 lb.		5.80	4.140		350	76	31	457	535	
	2100	Heavy traffic, 24" diameter, 400 lb.		7.80	3.080		172	57	23	252	300	
	2200	36" diameter, 1150 lb.		3	8		475	150	60	685	810	
	2300	Mass. State standard, 26" diameter, 475 lb.		7	3.430		190	63	26	279	335	
	2400	30" diameter, 620 lb.		7	3.430		240	63	26	329	390	
	2500	Watertight, 24" diameter, 350 lb.		7.80	3.080		280	57	23	360	420	
	2600	26" diameter, 500 lb.		7	3.430		335	63	26	424	495	
	2700	32" diameter, 575 lb.		6	4		356	74	30	460	535	
	2800	3 piece cover & frame, 10" deep,										
	2900	1200 lbs., for heavy equipment	B-6	3	8	Ea.	470	150	60	680	805	
	3000	Raised for paving 1-¼" to 2" high,										
	3100	4 piece expansion ring										
	3200	20" to 26" diameter	1 Clab	3	2.670	Ea.	92	46		138	170	
	3300	30" to 36" diameter	"	3	2.670	"	126	46		172	210	
	3320	Frames and covers, existing, raised for paving 2", including										
	3340	row of brick, concrete collar, up to 12" wide frame	B-9	18	2.220	Ea.	26.75	39	6.75	72.50	96	
	3360	20" to 26" wide frame		11	3.640		32.25	64	11	107.25	145	
	3380	30" to 36" wide frame		9	4.440		46.75	78	13.45	138.20	185	
	3400	Inverts, single channel brick	D-1	3	5.330		50	105		155	210	
	3500	Concrete		5	3.200		40.10	63		103.10	140	
	3600	Triple channel, brick		2	8		72.15	160		232.15	315	
	3700	Concrete		3	5.330		45.50	105		150.50	205	
	3800	Steps, heavyweight cast iron, 7" x 9"	1 Bric	40	.200		6.90	4.43		11.33	14.20	
	3900	8" x 9"		40	.200		10.30	4.43		14.73	17.95	
	4000	Standard sizes, galvanized steel		40	.200		10.40	4.43		14.83	18.05	
	4100	Aluminum		40	.200		9.10	4.43		13.53	16.60	
160	0010	**PIPING, DRAINAGE & SEWAGE, BITUMINOUS FIBER**										160
	2000	Plain, 2" diameter	2 Clab	400	.040	L.F.	.93	.69		1.62	2.06	
	2040	3" diameter		400	.040		1.16	.69		1.85	2.32	
	2080	4" diameter		380	.042		1.48	.72		2.20	2.72	
	2120	5" diameter		360	.044		2.54	.76		3.30	3.95	
	2200	6" diameter		340	.047		2.81	.81		3.62	4.32	
	2240	8" diameter		300	.053		6.60	.91		7.51	8.65	
162	0010	**PIPING, DRAINAGE & SEWAGE, CONCRETE**										162
	0020	Not including excavation or backfill										
	1000	Non-reinforced pipe, extra strength, B&S or T&G joints										
	1010	6" diameter	B-20	150	.160	L.F.	2.95	3.11		6.06	8	
	1020	8" diameter	B-21	200	.140		3.25	2.79	.51	6.55	8.40	
	1030	10" diameter		173	.162		3.60	3.23	.59	7.42	9.50	
	1040	12" diameter		173	.162		4.40	3.23	.59	8.22	10.40	
	1050	15" diameter		167	.168		5.10	3.35	.61	9.06	11.35	
	1060	18" diameter		167	.168		6.36	3.35	.61	10.32	12.75	
	1070	21" diameter		153	.183		7.85	3.65	.67	12.17	14.90	
	1080	24" diameter		153	.183		9.50	3.65	.67	13.82	16.70	
	2000	Reinforced culvert, class 3, no gaskets										
	2010	12" diameter	B-21	190	.147	L.F.	5.20	2.94	.54	8.68	10.75	
	2020	15" diameter		155	.181		6.50	3.61	.66	10.77	13.35	
	2030	18" diameter		122	.230		8.30	4.58	.84	13.72	17	
	2035	21" diameter		105	.267		10.50	5.30	.97	16.77	21	
	2040	24" diameter		88	.318		13.50	6.35	1.16	21.01	26	
	2045	27" diameter		84	.333		16.25	6.65	1.22	24.12	29	
	2050	30" diameter	B-13	80	.700		18.50	12.95	5.95	37.40	46	
	2060	36" diameter		60	.933		26.75	17.25	7.95	51.95	64	
	2070	42" diameter		55	1.020		34.50	18.85	8.65	62	76	
	2080	48" diameter		50	1.120		43.65	21	9.50	74.15	90	

027 | Sewerage & Drainage

027 100 | Subdrainage Systems

			CREW	DAILY OUTPUT	MAN-HOURS	UNIT	BARE COSTS MAT.	LABOR	EQUIP.	TOTAL	TOTAL INCL O&P	
162	2090	60" diameter	B-13	35	1.600	L.F.	65.75	30	13.60	109.35	130	162
	2100	72" diameter		30	1.870		92.25	35	15.85	143.10	170	
	2120	84" diameter		24	2.330		148.50	43	19.85	211.35	250	
	2140	96" diameter		20	2.800		180	52	24	256	300	
	2200	With gaskets, class 3, 12" diameter	B-21	210	.133		6.25	2.66	.49	9.40	11.45	
	2220	15" diameter		175	.160		7.50	3.19	.58	11.27	13.75	
	2230	18" diameter		150	.187		9.45	3.73	.68	13.86	16.80	
	2240	24" diameter		100	.280		14.80	5.60	1.02	21.42	26	
	2260	30" diameter	B-13	85	.659		19.80	12.20	5.60	37.60	46	
	2270	36" diameter		70	.800		28.60	14.80	6.80	50.20	61	
	2290	48" diameter		58	.966		46.50	17.85	8.20	72.55	87	
	2310	72" diameter		38	1.470		126.50	27	12.55	166.05	195	
	2330	Flared ends, 6'-1" long, 12" diameter	B-21	190	.147	L.F.	34.10	2.94	.54	37.58	43	
	2340	15" diameter		155	.181		38.50	3.61	.66	42.77	49	
	2400	6'-2" long, 18" diameter		122	.230		45.10	4.58	.84	50.52	57	
	2420	24" diameter		88	.318		55	6.35	1.16	62.51	71	
	2430	30" diameter	B-13	80	.700		68.20	12.95	5.95	87.10	100	
	2440	36" diameter	"	60	.933		95.70	17.25	7.95	120.90	140	
	3040	Vitrified plate lined, add to above, 30" to 36" diameter				SFCA	2.91			2.91	3.20	
	3050	42" to 54" diameter, add					2.71			2.71	2.98	
	3060	60" to 72" diameter, add					2.48			2.48	2.73	
	3070	Over 72" diameter, add					2.31			2.31	2.54	
	3080	Radius pipe, add to pipe prices, 12" to 60" diameter				L.F.	50%					
	3090	Over 60" diameter, add				"	20%					
	3500	Reinforced elliptical, 8' lengths, C507 class 3										
	3520	14" x 23" inside, round equivalent 18" diameter	B-21	82	.341	L.F.	37.40	6.80	1.25	45.45	53	
	3530	24" x 38" inside, round equivalent 30" diameter	B-22	58	.517		48.40	10.40	2.64	61.44	72	
	3540	29" x 45" inside, round equivalent 36" diameter		52	.577		60.50	11.65	2.95	75.10	87	
	3550	38" x 60" inside, round equivalent 48" diameter		38	.789		88	15.90	4.03	107.93	125	
	3560	48" x 76" inside, round equivalent 60" diameter		26	1.150		126.50	23	5.90	155.40	180	
	3570	58" x 91" inside, round equivalent 72" diameter		22	1.360		187	27	6.95	220.95	255	
164	0010	**PIPING, DRAINAGE & SEWAGE, CORRUGATED METAL**										164
	0020	Not including excavation or backfill										
	2000	Corrugated Metal Pipe, galv. or aluminum,										
	2020	Bituminous coated with paved invert, 20' to 30' lengths										
	2040	8" diameter 16 ga. [B12.3-510]	B-20	330	.073	L.F.	4.95	1.42		6.37	7.60	
	2060	10" diameter 16 ga.		260	.092		6.25	1.80		8.05	9.60	
	2080	12" diameter 16 ga.		210	.114		7.65	2.22		9.87	11.80	
	2100	15" diameter 16 ga.	B-21	210	.133		9.40	2.66	.49	12.55	14.90	
	2120	18" diameter 16 ga.		190	.147		11.10	2.94	.54	14.58	17.25	
	2140	24" diameter 14 ga.		160	.175		17.75	3.49	.64	21.88	26	
	2160	30" diameter 14 ga.		120	.233		21.30	4.66	.85	26.81	31	
	2180	36" diameter 12 ga.		100	.280		32.70	5.60	1.02	39.32	46	
	2200	48" diameter 12 ga.	B-13	100	.560		43	10.35	4.76	58.11	68	
	2220	60" diameter 10 ga.		75	.747		64.75	13.80	6.35	84.90	99	
	2240	72" diameter 8 ga.		45	1.240		94	23	10.60	127.60	150	
	2500	Plain, 20' to 30' lengths										
	2520	8" diameter 16 ga.	B-20	355	.068	L.F.	3.45	1.32		4.77	5.80	
	2540	10" diameter 16 ga.		280	.086		4.65	1.67		6.32	7.65	
	2560	12" diameter 16 ga.		220	.109		5.15	2.12		7.27	8.90	
	2580	15" diameter 16 ga.	B-21	220	.127		6.40	2.54	.46	9.40	11.40	
	2600	18" diameter 16 ga.		205	.137		7.60	2.73	.50	10.83	13.05	
	2620	24" diameter 14 ga.		175	.160		12.90	3.19	.58	16.67	19.65	
	2640	30" diameter 14 ga.		130	.215		15.40	4.30	.79	20.49	24	
	2660	36" diameter 12 ga.	B-13	130	.431		24.75	7.95	3.66	36.36	43	
	2680	48" diameter 12 ga.		110	.509		33.70	9.40	4.33	47.43	56	
	2700	60" diameter 10 ga.		78	.718		52.25	13.30	6.10	71.65	84	

027 | Sewerage & Drainage

027 100 | Subdrainage Systems

			Crew	Daily Output	Man-Hours	Unit	Bare Costs Mat.	Labor	Equip.	Total	Total Incl O&P	
164	2800	End sections, 18" diameter	B-21	16	1.750	Ea.	77.25	35	6.40	118.65	145	164
	2820	30" diameter	"	12	2.330	"	154.50	47	8.50	210	250	
	3000	Corrugated steel or alum. oval arch culverts, coated & paved										
	3020	17" x 13" 16 ga., 15" equivalent	B-22	200	.150	L.F.	10.80	3.02	.77	14.59	17.30	
	3040	21" x 15" 16 ga., 18" equivalent		150	.200		12.75	4.03	1.02	17.80	21	
	3060	28" x 20" 14 ga., 24" equivalent		125	.240		20.15	4.84	1.23	26.22	31	
	3080	35" x 24" 14 ga., 30" equivalent		100	.300		23.90	6.05	1.53	31.48	37	
	3100	42" x 29" 12 ga., 36" equivalent	B-13	100	.560		35.80	10.35	4.76	50.91	60	
	3120	49" x 33" 12 ga., 42" equivalent		90	.622		41.35	11.50	5.30	58.15	69	
	3140	57" x 38" 12 ga., 48" equivalent		70	.800		46.90	14.80	6.80	68.50	81	
	3160	Steel, plain oval arch culverts, plain										
	3180	17" x 13" 16 ga., 15" equivalent	B-22	225	.133	L.F.	7.10	2.69	.68	10.47	12.65	
	3200	21" x 15" 16 ga., 18" equivalent		175	.171		8.40	3.45	.88	12.73	15.45	
	3220	28" x 20" 14 ga., 24" equivalent		150	.200		13.40	4.03	1.02	18.45	22	
	3240	35" x 24" 14 ga., 30" equivalent		108	.278		16.75	5.60	1.42	23.77	28	
	3260	42" x 29" 12 ga., 36" equivalent	B-13	108	.519		32.20	9.60	4.41	46.21	55	
	3280	49" x 33" 12 ga., 42" equivalent		92	.609		38.75	11.25	5.15	55.15	65	
	3300	57" x 38" 12 ga., 48" equivalent		75	.747		35.60	13.80	6.35	55.75	67	
	3320	End sections, 17" x 13"		22	2.550	Ea.	30.90	47	22	99.90	130	
	3340	42" x 29"		17	3.290	"	158.60	61	28	247.60	295	
	3360	Multi-plate arch, steel	B-20	1,690	.014	Lb.	.55	.28		.83	1.03	
168	0010	**PIPING, DRAINAGE & SEWAGE, POLYVINYL CHLORIDE**										168
	0020	Not including excavation or backfill										
	2000	10' lengths, S.D.R. 35, 4" diameter	B-20	375	.064	L.F.	.57	1.25		1.82	2.52	
	2040	6" diameter	"	350	.069		1.22	1.33		2.55	3.37	
	2120	10" diameter	B-21	330	.085		2.80	1.69	.31	4.80	6	
	2160	12" diameter		320	.088		3.95	1.75	.32	6.02	7.35	
	2200	15" diameter		190	.147		6.15	2.94	.54	9.63	11.80	
172	0010	**PIPING, DRAINAGE & SEWAGE, VITRIFIED CLAY** C700										172
	0020	Not including excavation or backfill, 4' & 5' lengths										
	4030	Extra strength, compression joints, C425										
	5000	4" diameter	B-20	265	.091	L.F.	1.03	1.76		2.79	3.81	
	5020	6" diameter	"	200	.120		1.71	2.34		4.05	5.45	
	5040	8" diameter	B-21	200	.140		2.67	2.79	.51	5.97	7.75	
	5060	10" diameter		190	.147		4.43	2.94	.54	7.91	9.90	
	5080	12" diameter		150	.187		5.85	3.73	.68	10.26	12.85	
	5100	15" diameter		110	.255		10.90	5.10	.93	16.93	21	
	5120	18" diameter		88	.318		16.40	6.35	1.16	23.91	29	
	5140	24" diameter		45	.622		30.50	12.40	2.27	45.17	55	
	5160	30" diameter	B-22	31	.968		35.50	19.50	4.95	59.95	74	
	5180	00" diameter	"	20	1.500		54.60	30	7.65	92.25	115	
	6000	3' lengths, add to above						30%				
	6020	2' lengths, add to above						40%				
	6040	For die cast slip joints compared to premium joints						90%				
	6060	For plain joints compared to compression joints						75%				
	7060	2' lengths, add to above						40%				
174	0010	**SEWAGE PUMPING STATIONS** Prefabricated steel, concrete										174
	0020	or fiberglass, 200 GPM	C-17D	.17	494	Total	25,100	11,100	3,225	39,425	48,100	
	0200	1,000 GPM		.07	200		37,200	27,000	7,800	72,000	90,500	
	0500	Add for generator unit, 200 GPM, steel		.34	247		19,200	5,575	1,600	26,375	31,400	
	0600	Concrete		.51	165		12,000	3,700	1,075	16,775	20,000	
	1000	Add for generator unit, 1,000 GPM, steel		.30	280		20,400	6,300	1,825	28,525	34,000	
	1200	Concrete		.38	221		17,100	4,975	1,450	23,525	28,000	
	1500	For wet well, if required, add	B-23	.50	80		4,920	1,400	1,050	7,370	8,675	
176	0010	**SEWAGE TREATMENT** Not incl. fencing or external piping										176
	0020	Steel packaged, blown air aeration plants										

027 | Sewerage & Drainage

027 100 | Subdrainage Systems

		CREW	DAILY OUTPUT	MAN-HOURS	UNIT	MAT.	LABOR	EQUIP.	TOTAL	TOTAL INCL O&P
0100	1,000 GPD				Gal.					12
0200	5,000 GPD									7.90
0300	15,000 GPD									4.35
0400	30,000 GPD									4.25
0500	50,000 GPD									3.10
0600	100,000 GPD									2.85
0700	200,000 GPD									2
0800	500,000 GPD									2.20
1000	Concrete, extended aeration, primary and secondary treatment									
1010	10,000 GPD				Gal.					9.10
1100	30,000 GPD									4.30
1200	50,000 GPD									4.40
1400	100,000 GPD									2.85
1500	500,000 GPD									2.05
1700	Municipal wastewater treatment facility									
1720	1.0 MGD				Gal.					3.50
1740	1.5 MGD									3.45
1760	2.0 MGD									2.95
1780	3.0 MGD									2.30
1800	5.0 MGD									2.10
2000	Holding tank system, not incl. excavation or backfill									
2010	Recirculating chemical water closet	2 Plum	4	4	Ea.	628.50	99		727.50	840
2100	For voltage converter, add	"	16	1		154.50	25		179.50	205
2200	For high level alarm, add	1 Plum	7.80	1.030		74	25		99	120

027 350 | Wastewater System

		CREW	DAILY OUTPUT	MAN-HOURS	UNIT	MAT.	LABOR	EQUIP.	TOTAL	TOTAL INCL O&P
0010	WASTEWATER TREATMENT SYSTEM Fiberglass, 1,000 gallon	B-21	1.29	21.710	Ea.	2,340	435	79	2,854	3,325
0100	1,500 gallon	"	1.03	27.180	"	5,270	545	99	5,914	6,725

027 400 | Septic Systems

		CREW	DAILY OUTPUT	MAN-HOURS	UNIT	MAT.	LABOR	EQUIP.	TOTAL	TOTAL INCL O&P
0010	SEPTIC TANKS Not incl. excav. or piping, precast, 1,000 gallon	B-21	8	3.500	Ea.	420	70	12.80	502.80	580
0100	2,000 gallon		5	5.600		795	110	20	925	1,075
0200	5,000 gallon		1.70	16.470		3,500	330	60	3,890	4,425
0300	15,000 gallon	B-13	1.30	43.080		9,680	795	365	10,840	12,300
0400	25,000 gallon		.80	70		14,300	1,300	595	16,195	18,300
0500	40,000 gallon		.60	93.330		22,000	1,725	795	24,520	27,700
0600	Fiberglass, 1,000 gallon	B-21	6	4.670		475	93	17.05	585.05	680
0700	1,500 gallon	"	4	7		595	140	26	761	895
1000	Distribution boxes, concrete, 7 outlets	2 Clab	16	1		50	17.15		67.15	81
1100	9 outlets	"	8	2		295	34		329	375
1150	Leaching field chambers, 13' x 3'-7" x 1'-4", standard	B-13	16	3.500		295	65	30	390	455
1200	Heavy duty, 8' x 4' x 1'-6"		14	4		200	74	34	308	370
1300	13' x 3'-9" x 1'-6"		12	4.670		250	86	40	376	450
1350	20' x 4' x 1'-6"		5	11.200		550	205	95	850	1,025
1400	Leaching pit, precast concrete, 3' dia, 3' deep	B-21	8	3.500		220	70	12.80	302.80	360
1500	6' dia, 3' section		4.70	5.960		330	120	22	472	565
2000	Velocity reducing pit, precast conc., 6' diameter, 3' deep		4.70	5.960		200	120	22	342	425
2200	Excavation for septic tank, ¾ C.Y. backhoe	B-12F	145	.110	C.Y.		2.30	3.10	5.40	6.85
2400	4' trench for disposal field, ¾ C.Y. backhoe	"	335	.048	L.F.		1	1.34	2.34	2.96
2600	Gravel fill, run of bank	B-6	150	.160	C.Y.	10.55	2.95	1.21	14.71	17.40
2800	Crushed stone, ¾"	"	150	.160	"	11.50	2.95	1.21	15.66	18.45

027 660 | Relining Exist. Pipelines

		CREW	DAILY OUTPUT	MAN-HOURS	UNIT	MAT.	LABOR	EQUIP.	TOTAL	TOTAL INCL O&P
0010	LINING PIPE with cement, incl. bypass and cleaning									
0020	Less than 10,000 L.F., urban, 6" to 10"	C-17E	130	.615	L.F.	5.40	13.85	.40	19.65	27
0200	24" to 36"		90	.889		8.70	20	.58	29.28	41
0300	48" to 72"		80	1		13.85	23	.66	37.51	50

028 | Site Improvements

028 100 | Irrigation Systems

		CREW	DAILY OUTPUT	MAN-HOURS	UNIT	BARE COSTS MAT.	LABOR	EQUIP.	TOTAL	TOTAL INCL O&P	
104	0010	**SPRINKLER IRRIGATION SYSTEM** For lawns										104
	0100	Golf course with fully automatic system	C-17	.05	600	9 Holes	73,750	36,000		109,750	136,000	
	0200	24' diam. head at 15' O.C incl. piping, minimum	B-20	70	.343	Head	16	6.65		22.65	28	
	0300	Maximum		40	.600		37	11.70		48.70	58	
	0500	60' diameter head, automatic operation, minimum		28	.857		50	16.70		66.70	80	
	0600	Maximum		23	1.040		135	20		155	180	
	0800	Residential system, custom, 1" supply		2,619	.009	S.F.	.22	.18		.40	.51	
	0900	1-½" supply		2,311	.010	"	.20	.20		.40	.53	
	0905	Commercial system includes piping, heads, controller										
	0906	Backflow prevention and all fittings and valves										
	0910	Flood bubbler to individual trees				Ea.					64	
	0920	4" pop-up to shrub bed, plastic									57	
	0930	6" pop-up to shrub bed, plastic									64	
	0940	12" pop-up to shrub bed, plastic									72	
	0990	For renovation work, add to above						50%				
	1000	Sprinkler heads										
	2000	Pop-up spray, head & nozzle, low/medium volume, plastic	1 Skwk	30	.267	Ea.	2.91	5.90		8.81	12.15	
	2200	Brass, economy		30	.267		5.35	5.90		11.25	14.85	
	2400	Heavy duty		30	.267		8.95	5.90		14.85	18.80	
	3000	Riser mounted spray, head, low/medium volume, plastic		30	.267		1.90	5.90		7.80	11.05	
	3200	Brass		30	.267		2.20	5.90		8.10	11.40	
	4000	Pop-up impact sprinkler, body & case, plastic low/medium volume		30	.267		15.15	5.90		21.05	26	
	4200	Brass, high/medium volume		30	.267		22	5.90		27.90	33	
	4400	High volume		30	.267		66	5.90		71.90	82	
	5000	Quick coupling valve and key, brass, thread type		25	.320		28	7.05		35.05	42	
	5200	Lug type		25	.320		31	7.05		38.05	45	
	5400	Pop-up gear drive sprinkler, nozzle & case plastic, medium volume		30	.267		16.75	5.90		22.65	27	
	6000	Riser mounted gear drive sprinkler, nozzle and case										
	6200	Plastic, medium volume	1 Skwk	30	.267	Ea.	10.15	5.90		16.05	20	
	7000	Riser mounted impact sprinkler, body, part or										
	7200	Full circle plastic, low/medium volume	1 Skwk	25	.320	Ea.	10.05	7.05		17.10	22	
	7400	Brass, low/medium volume		25	.320		18.60	7.05		25.65	31	
	7600	Medium volume		25	.320		22	7.05		29.05	35	
	7800	Female thread		25	.320		46	7.05		53.05	61	
	8000	Riser mounted impact sprinkler, body, full circle only										
	8200	Plastic, low/medium volume	1 Skwk	25	.320	Ea.	6.20	7.05		13.25	17.60	
	8400	Brass, low/medium volume		25	.320		11.15	7.05		18.20	23	
	8600	High volume		25	.320		40	7.05		47.05	55	
	8800	Very high volume		25	.320		70	7.05		77.05	88	

028 200 | Fountains

		CREW	DAILY OUTPUT	MAN-HOURS	UNIT	MAT.	LABOR	EQUIP.	TOTAL	TOTAL INCL O&P	
204	0010	**FOUNTAINS** Incl. fiberglass pools, pumps, piping and lights										204
	0200	4' diameter pool, 18" diameter spray ring	Q-1	2	8	Ea.	600	180		780	925	
	0300	6' diameter pool, 24" diameter spray ring		1.50	10.670		1,000	235		1,235	1,450	
	0400	7.5' diameter pool, 48" diameter spray ring		1	16		1,525	355		1,880	2,200	
	0500	Rain curtains, 3' rain bar, 2' x 4' x 1' pool		2	8		570	180		750	890	
	0600	7' rain bar, 2' x 8' x 1' pool		1	16		1,225	355		1,580	1,875	

031 | Concrete Formwork

031 100 | Struct C.I.P. Formwork

			CREW	DAILY OUTPUT	MAN-HOURS	UNIT	BARE COSTS MAT.	BARE COSTS LABOR	BARE COSTS EQUIP.	BARE COSTS TOTAL	TOTAL INCL O&P	
154	0010	FORMS IN PLACE, EQUIPMENT FOUNDATIONS 1 use	C-2	160	.300	SFCA	1.52	6.35	.20	8.07	11.55	154
	0050	2 use		190	.253		.85	5.35	.16	6.36	9.25	
	0100	3 use		200	.240		.64	5.10	.16	5.90	8.60	
	0150	4 use		205	.234		.55	4.96	.15	5.66	8.30	

033 | Cast-In-Place Concrete

033 100 | Structural Concrete

			CREW	DAILY OUTPUT	MAN-HOURS	UNIT	BARE COSTS MAT.	BARE COSTS LABOR	BARE COSTS EQUIP.	BARE COSTS TOTAL	TOTAL INCL O&P	
130	0011	CONCRETE IN PLACE Including forms (4 uses), reinforcing										130
	0020	steel, and finishing										
	3901	Footings, strip, 18" x 9", plain				C.Y.					165	
	3951	36" x 12", reinforced									140	
	4001	Foundation mat, under 10 C.Y.									210	
	4051	Over 20 C.Y.									170	
	4651	Slab on grade, not including finish, 4" thick									115	
	4701	6" thick									98	
172	0010	PLACING CONCRETE and vibrating, including labor & equipment										172
	1900	Footings, continuous, shallow, direct chute	C-6	120	.400	C.Y.		7.25	.51	7.76	11.50	
	1950	Pumped	C-20	100	.640			11.85	5.50	17.35	24	
	2000	With crane and bucket	C-7	90	.711			13.15	8.55	21.70	29	
	2100	Deep continuous footings, direct chute	C-6	155	.310			5.60	.39	5.99	8.90	
	2150	Pumped	C-20	120	.533			9.85	4.59	14.44	19.90	
	2200	With crane and bucket	C-7	110	.582			10.75	7	17.75	24	
	2900	Foundation mats, over 20 C.Y., direct chute	C-6	350	.137			2.49	.17	2.66	3.94	
	2950	Pumped	C-20	325	.197			3.64	1.70	5.34	7.35	
	3000	With crane and bucket	C-7	300	.213			3.95	2.57	6.52	8.75	

033 450 | Concrete Finishing

			CREW	DAILY OUTPUT	MAN-HOURS	UNIT	BARE COSTS MAT.	BARE COSTS LABOR	BARE COSTS EQUIP.	BARE COSTS TOTAL	TOTAL INCL O&P	
454	0011	FINISHING FLOORS Monolithic, screed finish	1 Cefi	900	.009	S.F.		.19		.19	.27	454
	0101	Float finish	C-9	725	.011			.23	.05	.28	.39	
	0151	Broom finish	"	675	.012			.25	.05	.30	.42	

050 | Metal Materials, Finishes and Fastenings

050 500 | Metal Fastening

			CREW	DAILY OUTPUT	MAN-HOURS	UNIT	BARE COSTS MAT.	BARE COSTS LABOR	BARE COSTS EQUIP.	BARE COSTS TOTAL	TOTAL INCL O&P	
570	0010	WELD ROD Steel, type E6010, -11, ⅛" diameter, less than 500#				Lb.	.81			.81	.89	570
	0100	500# to 2000#					.78			.78	.86	
	0200	2000# to 5000#					.74			.74	.81	
	0400	Steel, type E6011, 3/16" diameter, less than 500#					.78			.78	.86	
	0500	500# to 2000#					.74			.74	.81	
	0600	2000# to 5000#					.70			.70	.77	
	0650	Steel, type E7018, (low hydrogen) ⅛" diam., less than 500#					.74			.74	.81	
	0660	500# to 2000#					.70			.70	.77	
	0670	2000# to 5000#					.66			.66	.73	
	0700	Steel, type E7024, (jet weld) ⅛" diam., less than 500#					.70			.70	.77	

050 | Metal Materials, Finishes and Fastenings

050 500 | Metal Fastening

			CREW	DAILY OUTPUT	MAN-HOURS	UNIT	BARE COSTS MAT.	LABOR	EQUIP.	TOTAL	TOTAL INCL O&P	
570	0710	500# to 2000#				Lb.	.66			.66	.73	570
	0720	2000# to 5000#					.62			.62	.68	
	0800	Deduct for 5/32" diameter, type E6010 or type E6011					.02			.02	.02	
	0810	Semi-automatic coils, 1/16" diameter, 3000# lots					.68			.68	.75	
	1550	Aluminum, type 4043, 1/8" diameter					3.65			3.65	4.02	
	1600	5/32" diameter					3.50			3.50	3.85	
	1810	3/16" diameter					3.35			3.35	3.69	
	1900	Cast iron, 1/8" diameter					.75			.75	.83	
	2000	Stainless steel, type 308-15, 1/8" diam., less than 499#					4.70			4.70	5.15	
	2100	500# to 999#					4.25			4.25	4.68	
	2220	Over 1000#				↓	3.80			3.80	4.18	
575	0010	WELDING Field. Cost per welder, no operating engineer	E-14	8	1	Hr.	2.43	25	8.05	35.48	55	575
	0200	With 1/2 operating engineer	E-13	8	1.500		2.43	36	8.05	46.48	71	
	0300	With 1 operating engineer	E-12	8	2	↓	2.43	47	8.05	57.48	86	
	0500	With no operating engineer, minimum	E-14	13.30	.602	Ton	1.93	15.30	4.84	22.07	33	
	0600	Maximum	"	2.50	3.200		7.70	81	26	114.70	175	
	0800	With one operating engineer per welder, minimum	E-12	13.30	1.200		1.93	28	4.84	34.77	52	
	0900	Maximum	"	2.50	6.400	↓	7.70	150	26	183.70	275	
	1200	Continuous fillet, stick welding, incl. equipment										
	1300	Single pass, 1/8" thick, 0.1#/L.F.	E-14	240	.033	L.F.	.09	.85	.27	1.21	1.84	
	1400	3/16" thick, 0.2#/L.F.		120	.067		.17	1.70	.54	2.41	3.66	
	1500	1/4" thick, 0.3#/L.F.		80	.100		.25	2.55	.81	3.61	5.50	
	1610	5/16" thick, 0.4#/L.F.		60	.133		.34	3.39	1.07	4.80	7.30	
	1800	3 passes, 3/8" thick, 0.5#/L.F.		48	.167		.42	4.24	1.34	6	9.15	
	2010	4 passes, 1/2" thick, 0.7#/L.F.		34	.235		.59	6	1.89	8.48	12.90	
	2200	5 to 6 passes, 3/4" thick, 1.3#/L.F.		19	.421		1.07	10.70	3.39	15.16	23	
	2400	8 to 11 passes, 1" thick, 2.4#/L.F.	↓	10	.800		1.99	20	6.45	28.44	44	
	2600	For all position welding, add, minimum						20%				
	2700	Maximum						300%				
	2900	For semi-automatic welding, deduct, minimum						5%				
	3000	Maximum				↓		15%				
	4000	Cleaning and welding plates, bars, or rods										
	4010	to existing beams, columns, or trusses	E-14	12	.667	L.F.	.40	16.95	5.35	22.70	35	

051 | Structural Metal Framing

051 200 | Structural Steel

			CREW	DAILY OUTPUT	MAN-HOURS	UNIT	BARE COSTS MAT.	LABOR	EQUIP.	TOTAL	TOTAL INCL O&P	
230	0010	LIGHTWEIGHT FRAMING										230
	0400	Angle framing, 4" and larger	E-4	3,000	.011	Lb.	.72	.26	.02	1	1.25	
	0450	Less than 4" angles		1,800	.018		.75	.43	.04	1.22	1.59	
	0600	Channel framing, 8" and larger		3,500	.009		.75	.22	.02	.99	1.22	
	0650	Less than 8" channels	↓	2,000	.016		.78	.38	.03	1.19	1.55	
	1000	Continuous slotted channel framing system, minimum	2 Sswk	2,400	.007		1.15	.16		1.31	1.53	
	1200	Maximum	"	1,600	.010	↓	2	.23		2.23	2.60	
250	0010	STRUCTURAL STEEL MEMBERS Common WF sizes, spans 10' to 45'										250
	0020	including bolted connections and erection										
	0100	W 6 x 9	E-2	600	.093	L.F.	6.55	2.15	1.75	10.45	12.65	
	0300	W 8 x 10	"	600	.093	"	7	2.15	1.75	10.90	13.15	

055 | Metal Fabrications

055 300 | Gratings & Floor Plates

			CREW	DAILY OUTPUT	MAN-HOURS	UNIT	MAT.	LABOR	EQUIP.	TOTAL	TOTAL INCL O&P	
302	0010	CHECKERED PLATE ¼" & ⅜", 2000 to 5000 S.F., bolted	E-4	2,900	.011	Lb.	.50	.26	.02	.78	1.02	302
	0100	Welded		4,400	.007	"	.48	.17	.01	.66	.84	
	0300	Pit or trench cover and frame, ¼" plate, 2' to 3' wide	↓	100	.320	S.F.	12.50	7.65	.64	20.79	27	
	0400	For galvanizing, add				Lb.	.25			.25	.28	
	0500	Platforms, ¼" plate, no handrails included, rectangular	E-4	4,200	.008		.80	.18	.02	1	1.21	
	0600	Circular	"	2,500	.013	↓	1.10	.31	.03	1.44	1.76	

061 | Rough Carpentry

061 100 | Wood Framing

			CREW	DAILY OUTPUT	MAN-HOURS	UNIT	MAT.	LABOR	EQUIP.	TOTAL	TOTAL INCL O&P	
116	0010	FRAMING, MISCELLANEOUS										116
	0020											
	8500	Firestops, 2" x 4"	F-2	.51	31.370	M.B.F.	380	680	31	1,091	1,475	
	8520	2" x 6"		.60	26.670		375	575	26	976	1,325	
	8600	Nailers, treated, wood construction, 2" x 4"	↓	.53	30.190		505	650	29	1,184	1,575	
	8620	2" x 6"		.75	21.330		500	460	21	981	1,275	

061 150 | Sheathing

			CREW	DAILY OUTPUT	MAN-HOURS	UNIT	MAT.	LABOR	EQUIP.	TOTAL	TOTAL INCL O&P	
154	0200	⅝" thick	F-2	1,300	.012	S.F.	.33	.27	.01	.61	.78	154
	0300	¾" thick		1,200	.013		.39	.29	.01	.69	.88	
	0700	⅝" thick		1,050	.015		.33	.33	.01	.67	.88	
	0800	¾" thick	↓	975	.016	↓	.39	.35	.02	.76	.99	

064 | Architectural Woodwork

064 100 | Custom Casework

			CREW	DAILY OUTPUT	MAN-HOURS	UNIT	MAT.	LABOR	EQUIP.	TOTAL	TOTAL INCL O&P	
102	0010	CABINETS Corner china cabinets, stock pine,										102
	0020	80" high, unfinished, minimum	2 Carp	6.60	2.420	Ea.	240	52		292	345	
	0100	Maximum	"	4.40	3.640	"	540	79		619	715	
	0700	Kitchen base cabinets, hardwood, not incl. counter tops,										
	0710	24" deep, 35" high, prefinished										
	0800	One top drawer, one door below, 12" wide	2 Carp	24.80	.645	Ea.	95	13.95		108.95	125	
	0840	18" wide		23.30	.687		105	14.85		119.85	140	
	0880	24" wide	↓	22.30	.717	↓	125	15.50		140.50	160	
	0890											
	1000	Four drawers, 12" wide	2 Carp	24.80	.645	Ea.	105	13.95		118.95	135	
	1040	18" wide		23.30	.687		120	14.85		134.85	155	
	1060	24" wide		22.30	.717		140	15.50		155.50	180	
	1200	Two top drawers, two doors below, 27" wide		22	.727		160	15.70		175.70	200	
	1260	36" wide		20.30	.788		180	17		197	225	
	1300	48" wide		18.90	.847		205	18.30		223.30	255	
	1500	Range or sink base, two doors below, 30" wide		21.40	.748		105	16.15		121.15	140	
	1540	36" wide		20.30	.788		135	17		152	175	
	1580	48" wide		18.90	.847		160	18.30		178.30	205	
	1800	For sink front units, deduct					45			45	50	
	9000	For deluxe models of all cabinets, add to above					40%					

064 | Architecture Woodwork

064 100 | Custom Casework

			CREW	DAILY OUTPUT	MAN-HOURS	UNIT	MAT.	LABOR	EQUIP.	TOTAL	TOTAL INCL O&P	
102	9500	For custom built in place, add to above				Ea.	25%	10%				102
	9550	Rule of thumb, kitchen cabinets not including										
	9560	appliances & counter top, minimum	2 Carp	30	.533	L.F.	60	11.50		71.50	83	
	9600	Maximum	"	25	.640	"	125	13.80		138.80	160	
140	0010	**VANITIES**										140
	0020											
	8000	Vanity bases, 2 doors, 30" high, 21" deep, 24" wide	2 Carp	11	1.450	Ea.	142	31		173	205	
	8050	30" wide		9.80	1.630		175	35		210	245	
	8100	36" wide		8	2		220	43		263	310	
	8150	48" wide	↓	6.60	2.420		305	52		357	415	
	9000	For deluxe models of all vanities, add to above					40%					
	9500	For custom built in place, add to above				↓	25%	10%				

076 | Flashing and Sheet Metal

076 200 | Sheet Mtl Flash & Trim

			CREW	DAILY OUTPUT	MAN-HOURS	UNIT	MAT.	LABOR	EQUIP.	TOTAL	TOTAL INCL O&P	
204	0011	**FLASHING** Aluminum, mill finish, .013" thick	1 Shee	145	.055	S.F.	.26	1.34		1.60	2.32	204
	0030	.016" thick		145	.055		.30	1.34		1.64	2.36	
	0060	.019" thick		145	.055		.65	1.34		1.99	2.74	
	0100	.032" thick		145	.055		.78	1.34		2.12	2.89	
	0200	.040" thick		145	.055		1.32	1.34		2.66	3.48	
	0300	.050" thick	↓	145	.055		1.60	1.34		2.94	3.79	
	0400	Painted finish, add					.15			.15	.17	
	0500	Fabric-backed 2 sides, .004" thick	1 Shee	330	.024		.35	.59		.94	1.28	
	0700	.016" thick		330	.024		.95	.59		1.54	1.94	
	0750	Mastic-backed, self adhesive		460	.017		1.85	.42		2.27	2.67	
	0800	Mastic-coated 2 sides, .004" thick		330	.024		.40	.59		.99	1.33	
	1000	.005" thick		330	.024		.52	.59		1.11	1.46	
	1100	.016" thick	↓	330	.024	↓	.95	.59		1.54	1.94	
	1300	Asphalt flashing cement, 5 gallon				Gal.	6.50			6.50	7.15	
	1600	Copper, 16 oz., sheets, under 6000 lbs.	1 Shee	115	.070	S.F.	2.60	1.69		4.29	5.40	
	1700	Over 6000 lbs.		155	.052		2.60	1.26		3.86	4.76	
	1900	20 oz. sheets, under 6000 lbs.		110	.073		3.25	1.77		5.02	6.25	
	2000	Over 6000 lbs.		145	.055		3.25	1.34		4.59	5.60	
	2200	24 oz. sheets, under 6000 lbs.		105	.076		3.90	1.86		5.76	7.10	
	2300	Over 6000 lbs.		135	.059		3.90	1.44		5.34	6.45	
	2500	32 oz. sheets, under 6000 lbs.		100	.080		5.05	1.95		7	8.50	
	2600	Over 6000 lbs.		130	.062		5.05	1.50		6.55	7.80	
	2800	Copper, paperbacked 1 side, 2 oz.		330	.024		1	.59		1.59	1.99	
	2900	3 oz.		330	.024		1.35	.59		1.94	2.38	
	3100	Paperbacked 2 sides, copper, 2 oz.		330	.024		1	.59		1.59	1.99	
	3150	3 oz.		330	.024		1.45	.59		2.04	2.49	
	3200	5 oz.		330	.024		2.25	.59		2.84	3.37	
	3250	7 oz.		330	.024		2.55	.59		3.14	3.70	
	3400	Mastic-backed 2 sides, copper, 2 oz.		330	.024		1.15	.59		1.74	2.16	
	3500	3 oz.		330	.024		1.65	.59		2.24	2.71	
	3700	5 oz.		330	.024		2.40	.59		2.99	3.53	
	3800	Fabric-backed 2 sides, copper, 2 oz.		330	.024		1.30	.59		1.89	2.32	
	4000	3 oz.		330	.024		1.70	.59		2.29	2.76	
	4100	5 oz.		330	.024		2.45	.59		3.04	3.59	
	4300	Copper-clad stainless steel, .015" thick, under 500 lbs.		115	.070		3	1.69		4.69	5.85	
	4400	Over 2000 lbs.	↓	155	.052	↓	2.88	1.26		4.14	5.05	

076 | Flashing and Sheet Metal

076 200 | Sheet Mtl Flash & Trim

		CREW	DAILY OUTPUT	MAN-HOURS	UNIT	MAT.	LABOR	EQUIP.	TOTAL	TOTAL INCL O&P
4600	.018" thick, under 500 lbs.	1 Shee	100	.080	S.F.	3.90	1.95		5.85	7.25
4700	Over 2000 lbs.	"	145	.055		2.65	1.34		3.99	4.94
5800	Lead, 2.5 lb. per S.F., up to 12" wide	1 Rofc	135	.059		3.15	1.18		4.33	5.40
5900	Over 12" wide	"	135	.059		3.15	1.18		4.33	5.40
8500	Shower pan, bituminous membrane, 7 oz.	1 Shee	155	.052		1.05	1.26		2.31	3.05
8550	3 ply copper and fabric, 3 oz.		155	.052		1.85	1.26		3.11	3.93
8600	7 oz.		155	.052		3.40	1.26		4.66	5.65
8650	Copper, 16 oz.		100	.080		2.70	1.95		4.65	5.90
8700	Lead on copper and fabric, 5 oz.		155	.052		2.15	1.26		3.41	4.26
8800	7 oz.		155	.052		2.45	1.26		3.71	4.59
8850	Polyvinyl chloride, .030" thick		160	.050		.27	1.22		1.49	2.14
8900	Stainless steel sheets, 32 ga., .010" thick		155	.052		1.85	1.26		3.11	3.93
9000	28 ga., .015" thick		155	.052		2.30	1.26		3.56	4.43
9100	26 ga., .018" thick		155	.052		2.85	1.26		4.11	5.05
9200	24 ga., .025" thick		155	.052		3.45	1.26		4.71	5.70
9301										
9400	Terne coated stainless steel, .015" thick, 28 ga.	1 Shee	155	.052	S.F.	1.60	1.26		2.86	3.66
9500	.018" thick, 26 ga.		155	.052		1.80	1.26		3.06	3.88
9600	Zinc and copper alloy, .020" thick		155	.052		1.35	1.26		2.61	3.38
9700	.027" thick		155	.052		1.80	1.26		3.06	3.88
9800	.032" thick		155	.052		2.10	1.26		3.36	4.21
9900	.040" thick		155	.052		2.55	1.26		3.81	4.70

101 | Chalkboards, Compartments and Cubicles

101 600 | Toilet Compartments

		CREW	DAILY OUTPUT	MAN-HOURS	UNIT	MAT.	LABOR	EQUIP.	TOTAL	TOTAL INCL O&P
0010	PARTITIONS, TOILET									
0100	Cubicles, ceiling hung, marble	2 Marb	2	8	Ea.	705	175		880	1,050
0200	Painted metal	2 Carp	4	4		285	86		371	445
0300	Plastic laminate on particle board		4	4		340	86		426	505
0400	Porcelain enamel		4	4		685	86		771	885
0500	Stainless steel		4	4		745	86		831	950
0600	For handicap units, add					80			80	88
0700										
0800	Floor & ceiling anchored, marble	2 Marb	2.50	6.400	Ea.	700	140		840	980
1000	Painted metal	2 Carp	5	3.200		275	69		344	405
1100	Plastic laminate on particle board		5	3.200		335	69		404	475
1200	Porcelain enamel		5	3.200		680	69		749	855
1300	Stainless steel		5	3.200		740	69		809	920
1400	For handicap units, add					80			80	88
1600	Floor mounted, marble	2 Marb	3	5.330		680	115		795	925
1700	Painted metal	2 Carp	7	2.290		245	49		294	345
1800	Plastic laminate on particle board		7	2.290		325	49		374	430
1900	Porcelain enamel		7	2.290		675	49		724	815
2000	Stainless steel		7	2.290		740	49		789	890
2100	For handicap units, add					80			80	88
2200	For juvenile units, deduct					20			20	22
2300										
2400	Floor mounted, headrail braced, marble	2 Marb	3	5.330	Ea.	670	115		785	910
2500	Painted metal	2 Carp	6	2.670		250	58		308	360
2600	Plastic laminate on particle board		6	2.670		335	58		393	455
2700	Porcelain enamel		6	2.670		670	58		728	825

101 | Chalkboards, Compartments and Cubicles

101 600 | Toilet Compartments

			CREW	DAILY OUTPUT	MAN-HOURS	UNIT	BARE COSTS MAT.	LABOR	EQUIP.	TOTAL	TOTAL INCL O&P	
602	2800	Stainless steel ♿	2 Carp	6	2.670	Ea.	735	58		793	895	602
	2900	For handicap units, add					80			80	88	
	3000	Wall hung partitions, painted metal	2 Carp	7	2.290		360	49		409	470	
	3200	Porcelain enamel		7	2.290		680	49		729	825	
	3300	Stainless steel ♿	↓	7	2.290		735	49		784	885	
	3400	For handicap units, add				↓	80			80	88	
	4000	Screens, entrance, floor mounted, 54" high										
	4100	Marble	D-1	35	.457	L.F.	195	9		204	230	
	4200	Painted metal	2 Carp	60	.267		120	5.75		125.75	140	
	4300	Plastic laminate on particle board		60	.267		135	5.75		140.75	155	
	4400	Porcelain enamel		60	.267		240	5.75		245.75	275	
	4500	Stainless steel	↓	60	.267		265	5.75		270.75	300	
	4600	Urinal screen, 18" wide, ceiling braced, marble	D-1	6	2.670	Ea.	290	53		343	395	
	4700	Painted metal	2 Carp	8	2		135	43		178	215	
	4800	Plastic laminate on particle board		8	2		165	43		208	245	
	4900	Porcelain enamel		8	2		245	43		288	335	
	5000	Stainless steel	↓	8	2		340	43		383	440	
	5050											
	5100	Floor mounted, head rail braced										
	5200	Marble	D-1	6	2.670	Ea.	275	53		328	380	
	5300	Painted metal	2 Carp	8	2		135	43		178	215	
	5400	Plastic laminate on particle board		8	2		165	43		208	245	
	5500	Porcelain enamel		8	2		255	43		298	345	
	5600	Stainless steel	↓	8	2		340	43		383	440	
	5700	Pilaster, flush, marble	D-1	9	1.780		325	35		360	410	
	5800	Painted metal	2 Carp	10	1.600		70	35		105	130	
	5900	Plastic laminate on particle board		10	1.600		90	35		125	150	
	6000	Porcelain enamel		10	1.600		180	35		215	250	
	6100	Stainless steel	↓	10	1.600	↓	230	35		265	305	
	6150											
	6200	Post braced, marble	D-1	9	1.780	Ea.	310	35		345	395	
	6300	Painted metal	2 Carp	10	1.600		75	35		110	135	
	6400	Plastic laminate on particle board		10	1.600		90	35		125	150	
	6500	Porcelain enamel		10	1.600		180	35		215	250	
	6600	Stainless steel	↓	10	1.600		230	35		265	305	
	6700	Wall hung, bracket supported										
	6800	Painted metal	2 Carp	10	1.600	Ea.	75	35		110	135	
	6900	Plastic laminate on particle board		10	1.600		95	35		130	155	
	7000	Porcelain enamel		10	1.600		210	35		245	285	
	7100	Stainless steel		10	1.600		220	35		255	295	
	7400	Flange supported, painted metal		10	1.600		120	35		155	185	
	7500	Plastic laminate on particle board		10	1.600		120	35		155	185	
	7000	Porcelain enamel		10	1.600		260	35		295	340	
	7700	Stainless steel		10	1.600		315	35		350	400	
	7800	Wedge type, painted metal		10	1.600		145	35		180	210	
	8000	Porcelain enamel		10	1.600		235	35		270	310	
	8100	Stainless steel	↓	10	1.600	↓	300	35		335	380	

101 850 | Shower Compartments

			CREW	DAILY OUTPUT	MAN-HOURS	UNIT	MAT.	LABOR	EQUIP.	TOTAL	INCL O&P	
852	0010	**PARTITIONS, SHOWER** Floor mounted, no plumbing										852
	0100	Cabinet, incl. base, no door, painted steel, 1" thick walls	2 Shee	5	3.200	Ea.	450	78		528	615	
	0300	With door, fiberglass		4.50	3.560		295	87		382	455	
	0600	Galvanized and painted steel, 1" thick walls		5	3.200		485	78		563	650	
	0800	Stall, 1" thick wall, no base, enameled steel		5	3.200		400	78		478	560	
	1100	Porcelain enameled steel		5	3.200		485	78		563	650	
	1200	Stainless steel	↓	5	3.200		545	78		623	715	
	1400	For double entry type, no doors, deduct					10%					

101 | Chalkboards, Compartments and Cubicles

101 850	Shower Compartments	CREW	DAILY OUTPUT	MAN-HOURS	UNIT	MAT.	LABOR	EQUIP.	TOTAL	TOTAL INCL O&P	
852	1500	Circular fiberglass, cabinet 36" diameter,	2 Shee	4	4	Ea.	290	97		387	465	852
	1700	One piece, 36" diameter, less door		4	4		305	97		402	485	
	1800	With door		3.50	4.570		475	110		585	690	
	2000	Curved shell shower, no door needed		3	5.330		465	130		595	710	
	2300	For fiberglass seat, add to both above					60			60	66	
	2400	Glass stalls, with doors, no receptors, chrome on brass	2 Shee	3	5.330		705	130		835	970	
	2700	Anodized aluminum	"	4	4		455	97		552	650	
	2900	Marble shower stall, stock design, with shower door	2 Marb	1.20	13.330		1,095	295		1,390	1,650	
	3000	With curtain		1.30	12.310		1,100	270		1,370	1,625	
	3200	Receptors, precast terrazzo, 32" x 32"		14	1.140		175	25		200	230	
	3300	48" x 34"		12	1.330		210	29		239	275	
	3500	Plastic, simulated terrazzo receptor, 32" x 32"		14	1.140		75	25		100	120	
	3600	32" x 48"		12	1.330		95	29		124	150	
	3800	Precast concrete, colors, 32" x 32"		14	1.140		119	25		144	170	
	3900	48" x 48"		12	1.330		140	29		169	200	
	4100	Shower doors, economy plastic, 24" wide	1 Shee	9	.889		70	22		92	110	
	4200	Tempered glass door, economy		8	1		115	24		139	165	
	4400	Folding, tempered glass, aluminum frame		6	1.330		155	32		187	220	
	4500	Sliding, tempered glass, 48" opening		6	1.330		110	32		142	170	
	4700	Deluxe, tempered glass, chrome on brass frame, minimum		5	1.600		265	39		304	350	
	4800	Maximum		1	8		490	195		685	835	
	4850	On anodized aluminum frame, minimum		2	4		80	97		177	235	
	4900	Maximum		1	8		265	195		460	585	
	5100	Shower enclosure, tempered glass, anodized alum. frame										
	5120	2 panel & door, corner unit, 32" x 32"	1 Shee	2	4	Ea.	240	97		337	410	
	5140	Neo-angle corner unit, 16" x 24" x 16"	"	2	4		340	97		437	520	
	5200	Shower surround, 3 wall, polypropylene, 32" x 32"	1 Carp	4	2		100	43		143	175	
	5220	PVC, 32" x 32"		4	2		155	43		198	235	
	5240	Fiberglass		4	2		180	43		223	265	
	5250	2 wall, polypropylene, 32" x 32"		4	2		110	43		153	185	
	5270	PVC		4	2		155	43		198	235	
	5290	Fiberglass		4	2		170	43		213	255	
	5300	Tub doors, tempered glass & frame, minimum	1 Shee	8	1		65	24		89	110	
	5400	Maximum		6	1.330		220	32		252	290	
	5600	Chrome plated, brass fframe, minimum		8	1		130	24		154	180	
	5700	Maximum		6	1.330		280	32		312	355	
	5900	Tub/shower enclosure, temp. glass, alum. frame, minimum		2	4		185	97		282	350	
	6200	Maximum		1.50	5.330		375	130		505	610	
	6500	On chrome-plated brass frame, minimum		2	4		275	97		372	450	
	6600	Maximum		1.50	5.330		575	130		705	830	
	6800	Tub surround, 3 wall, polypropylene	1 Carp	4	2		85	43		128	160	
	6900	PVC		4	2		135	43		178	215	
	7000	Fiberglass, minimum		4	2		190	43		233	275	
	7100	Maximum		3	2.670		325	58		383	445	

108 | Toilet and Bath Accessories and Scales

108 200	Bath Accessories	CREW	DAILY OUTPUT	MAN-HOURS	UNIT	MAT.	LABOR	EQUIP.	TOTAL	TOTAL INCL O&P	
204	0010	BATHROOM ACCESSORIES										204
	0200	Curtain rod, stainless steel, 5' long, 1" diameter	1 Carp	13	.615	Ea.	20	13.30		33.30	42	
	0300	1-¼" diameter	"	13	.615	"	25	13.30		38.30	48	

108 | Toilet and Bath Accessories and Scales

108 200 | Bath Accessories

			CREW	DAILY OUTPUT	MAN-HOURS	UNIT	BARE COSTS MAT.	LABOR	EQUIP.	TOTAL	TOTAL INCL O&P	
204	0500	Dispenser units, combined soap & towel dispensers,										204
	0510	mirror and shelf, flush mounted	1 Carp	10	.800	Ea.	215	17.30		232.30	265	
	0600	Towel dispenser and waste receptacle,										
	0610	flush mounted	1 Carp	10	.800	Ea.	335	17.30		352.30	395	
	0800	Grab bar, straight, 1-¼" diameter, stainless steel, 18" long		24	.333		20	7.20		27.20	33	
	0900	24" long		23	.348		22	7.50		29.50	36	
	1000	30" long		22	.364		23	7.85		30.85	37	
	1100	36" long		20	.400		25	8.65		33.65	41	
	1200	1-½" diameter, 24" long		23	.348		28	7.50		35.50	42	
	1300	36" long		20	.400		33	8.65		41.65	49	
	1500	Tub bar, 1" diameter, horizontal, 72" long		14	.571		50	12.35		62.35	74	
	1600	Plus vertical arm		12	.667		70	14.40		84.40	99	
	1900	End tub bar, 1" diameter, 90° angle, 16" x 32"		12	.667		50	14.40		64.40	77	
	2000	For 1-¼" diameter bars, add					15%					
	2100	For 1-½" diameter bars, add					25%					
	2300	Hand dryer, surface mounted, electric, 110 volt	1 Carp	4	2		375	43		418	480	
	2400	220 volt		4	2		375	43		418	480	
	2600	Hat and coat strip, stainless steel, 4 hook, 36" long		24	.333		45	7.20		52.20	60	
	2700	6 hook, 60" long		20	.400		75	8.65		83.65	96	
	3000	Mirror with stainless steel, ¾" square frame, 18" x 24"		20	.400		80	8.65		88.65	100	
	3100	36" x 24"		15	.533		138	11.50		149.50	170	
	3200	48" x 24"		10	.800		168	17.30		185.30	210	
	3300	72" x 24"		6	1.330		240	29		269	310	
	3500	Mirror with 5" stainless steel shelf, ¾" sq. frame, 18" x 24"		20	.400		105	8.65		113.65	130	
	3600	36" x 24"		15	.533		180	11.50		191.50	215	
	3700	48" x 24"		10	.800		255	17.30		272.30	305	
	3800	72" x 24"		6	1.330		368	29		397	450	
	4100	Mop holder strip, stainless steel, 6 holders, 60" long		20	.400		58	8.65		66.65	77	
	4200	Napkin/tampon dispenser, surface mounted		15	.533		285	11.50		296.50	330	
	4300	Robe hook, single, regular		36	.222		6	4.80		10.80	13.90	
	4400	Heavy duty, concealed mounting		36	.222		10	4.80		14.80	18.30	
	4600	Soap dispenser, chrome, surface mounted, liquid		20	.400		52	8.65		60.65	70	
	4700	Powder		20	.400		45	8.65		53.65	63	
	5000	Recessed stainless steel, liquid		10	.800		76	17.30		93.30	110	
	5100	Powder		10	.800		70	17.30		87.30	105	
	5300	Soap tank, stainless steel, 1 gallon		10	.800		80	17.30		97.30	115	
	5400	5 gallon		5	1.600		125	35		160	190	
	5600	Shelf, stainless steel, 5" wide, 18 ga., 24" long		24	.333		30	7.20		37.20	44	
	5700	72" long		16	.500		70	10.80		80.80	93	
	5800	8" wide shelf, 18 ga., 24" long		22	.364		38	7.85		45.85	54	
	5900	72" long		14	.671		98	12.35		110.35	125	
	6000	Toilet seat cover dispenser, stainless steel, recessed		20	.400		65	8.65		73.65	85	
	6050	Surface mounted		15	.533		34	11.50		45.50	55	
	6100	Toilet tissue dispenser, surface mounted, S.S., single roll		30	.267		20	5.75		25.75	31	
	6200	Double roll		24	.333		25	7.20		32.20	38	
	6400	Towel bar, stainless steel, 18" long		23	.348		17	7.50		24.50	30	
	6500	30" long		21	.381		19	8.25		27.25	33	
	6700	Towel dispenser, stainless steel, surface mounted		16	.500		57	10.80		67.80	79	
	6800	Flush mounted, recessed		10	.800		110	17.30		127.30	145	
	7000	Towel holder, hotel type, 2 guest size		20	.400		13	8.65		21.65	27	
	7200	Towel shelf, stainless steel, 24" long, 8" wide		20	.400		40	8.65		48.65	57	
	7400	Tumbler holder, tumbler only		30	.267		10.10	5.75		15.85	19.85	
	7500	Soap, tumbler & toothbrush		30	.267		17.50	5.75		23.25	28	
	7700	Wall urn ash receiver, recessed, 14" long		12	.667		90	14.40		104.40	120	
	7800	Surface, 8" long		18	.444		55	9.60		64.60	75	
	8000	Waste receptacles, stainless steel, with top, 13 gallon		10	.800		110	17.30		127.30	145	
	8100	36 gallon		8	1		240	22		262	295	

108 | Toilet and Bath Accessories and Scales

108 200 | Bath Accessories

			CREW	DAILY OUTPUT	MAN-HOURS	UNIT	BARE COSTS MAT.	LABOR	EQUIP.	TOTAL	TOTAL INCL O&P	
208	0010	MEDICINE CABINETS With mirror, stock, 16" x 22", unlighted	1 Carp	14	.571	Ea.	50	12.35		62.35	74	208
	0100	Lighted		6	1.330		120	29		149	175	
	0300	Sliding mirror doors, 36" x 22", unlighted		7	1.140		140	25		165	190	
	0400	Lighted		5	1.600		185	35		220	255	
	0600	Center mirror, 2 end cabinets, unlighted, 48" long		7	1.140		180	25		205	235	
	0700	72" long		5	1.600		220	35		255	295	
	0900	For lighting, 48" long, add	1 Elec	3.50	2.290		75	56		131	165	
	1000	72" long, add	"	3	2.670		110	65		175	215	
	1200	Hotel cabinets, stainless, with lower shelf, unlighted	1 Carp	10	.800		150	17.30		167.30	190	
	1300	Lighted	"	5	1.600		220	35		255	295	

110 | Equipment

110 100 | Maintenance Equipment

			CREW	DAILY OUTPUT	MAN-HOURS	UNIT	BARE COSTS MAT.	LABOR	EQUIP.	TOTAL	TOTAL INCL O&P	
121	0010	VACUUM CLEANING Central, 3 inlet, residential	1 Skwk	.90	8.890	Total	600	195		795	960	121
	0200	Commercial		.70	11.430		1,200	255		1,455	1,700	
	0400	5 inlet system, residential		.50	16		690	355		1,045	1,300	
	0600	7 inlet system		.40	20		780	440		1,220	1,525	
	0800	9 inlet system		.30	26.670		870	590		1,460	1,850	

110 400 | Ecclesiastical Equip

			CREW	DAILY OUTPUT	MAN-HOURS	UNIT	BARE COSTS MAT.	LABOR	EQUIP.	TOTAL	TOTAL INCL O&P	
401	0010	CHURCH EQUIPMENT Altar, wood, custom design, plain	1 Carp	1.40	5.710	Ea.	1,200	125		1,325	1,500	401
	0050	Deluxe	"	.20	40	"	6,625	865		7,490	8,600	
	0150	Baptistry, fiberglass, 3'-6" deep, x 13'-7" long,										
	0160	steps at both ends, incl. plumbing, minimum	L-8	1	20	Ea.	1,350	445		1,795	2,150	
	0200	Maximum	"	.70	28.570		3,100	635		3,735	4,375	
	0250	Add for filter, heater and lights					950			950	1,050	

111 | Mercantile, Commercial and Detention Equipment

111 020 | Barber Shop Equipment

			CREW	DAILY OUTPUT	MAN-HOURS	UNIT	BARE COSTS MAT.	LABOR	EQUIP.	TOTAL	TOTAL INCL O&P	
021	0010	BARBER EQUIPMENT Chair, hydraulic, movable, minimum	1 Carp	24	.333	Ea.	400	7.20		407.20	450	021
	0050	Maximum	"	16	.500		2,000	10.80		2,010	2,225	
	0500	Sink, hair washing basin, rough plumbing not incl.	1 Plum	8	1		315	25		340	385	
	1000	Sterilizer, liquid solution for tools					80			80	88	

111 100 | Laundry/Dry Cleaning

			CREW	DAILY OUTPUT	MAN-HOURS	UNIT	BARE COSTS MAT.	LABOR	EQUIP.	TOTAL	TOTAL INCL O&P	
101	0010	LAUNDRY EQUIPMENT Not incl. rough-in. Dryers, gas fired										101
	0500	Residential, 16 lb. capacity, average	1 Plum	3	2.670	Ea.	450	66		516	595	
	1000	Commercial, 30 lb. capacity, coin operated, single		3	2.670		1,750	66		1,816	2,025	
	1100	Double stacked		2	4		1,400	99		1,499	1,675	
	1500	Industrial, 30 lb. capacity		2	4		1,750	99		1,849	2,075	
	1600	50 lb. capacity		1.70	4.710		1,975	115		2,090	2,350	
	5000	Washers, residential, 4 cycle, average		3	2.670		560	66		626	715	
	5300	Commercial, coin operated, average		3	2.670		680	66		746	845	

111 | Mercantile, Commercial and Detention Equipment

111 100 | Laundry/Dry Cleaning

			CREW	DAILY OUTPUT	MAN-HOURS	UNIT	BARE COSTS MAT.	LABOR	EQUIP.	TOTAL	TOTAL INCL O&P	
101	6000	Combination washer/extractor, 20 lb. capacity	L-6	1.50	8	Ea.	2,400	195		2,595	2,925	101
	6100	30 lb. capacity		.80	15		5,500	370		5,870	6,600	
	6200	50 lb. capacity		.68	17.650		7,200	435		7,635	8,550	
	6300	75 lb. capacity		.30	40		14,000	985		14,985	16,900	
	6350	125 lb. capacity	↓	.16	75	↓	19,000	1,850		20,850	23,600	

111 400 | Service Station Equip

			CREW	DAILY OUTPUT	MAN-HOURS	UNIT	MAT.	LABOR	EQUIP.	TOTAL	INCL O&P	
401	0010	AUTOMOTIVE Compressors, electric, 1-½ H.P., standard controls	L-4	1.50	16	Ea.	2,450	325		2,775	3,200	401
	0550	Dual controls		1.50	16		2,650	325		2,975	3,400	
	0600	5 H.P., 115/230 volt, standard controls		1	24		3,250	490		3,740	4,325	
	0650	Dual controls		1	24		3,450	490		3,940	4,550	
	1000	Gasoline pumps, conventional, lighted, single		2.50	9.600		2,100	195		2,295	2,600	
	1010	Double		2	12		4,000	245		4,245	4,775	
	2200	Hoists, single post, 8000# capacity, swivel arms	↓	.40	60	↓	3,500	1,225		4,725	5,700	
	2210											
	2400	Two posts, adjustable frames, 11,000# capacity	L-4	.25	96	Ea.	3,900	1,950		5,850	7,275	
	2500	24,000# capacity		.15	160		5,300	3,250		8,550	10,800	
	2700	7500# capacity, frame supports		.50	48		4,575	975		5,550	6,525	
	2800	Four post, roll on ramp		.50	48	↓	4,200	975		5,175	6,100	
	3000	Lube equipment, 3 reel type, with pumps, not including piping		.50	48	Set	5,200	975		6,175	7,200	
	4000	Spray painting booth, 26' long, complete		.40	60	Ea.	9,200	1,225		10,425	12,000	

111 900 | Detention Equipment

			CREW	DAILY OUTPUT	MAN-HOURS	UNIT	MAT.	LABOR	EQUIP.	TOTAL	INCL O&P	
901	0010	DETENTION EQUIPMENT Bar front, rolling, ⅞" bars,										901
	0500	4" O.C., 7' high, 5' wide, with hardware	E-4	2	16	Ea.	3,275	385	32	3,692	4,300	
	2000	Cells, prefab., 5' to 6' wide, 7' to 8' high, 7' to 8' deep,										
	2010	bar front, cot, not incl. plumbing	E-4	1.50	21.330	Ea.	4,450	510	43	5,003	5,800	
	3000	Toilet apparatus including wash basin, average	L-8	1.50	13.330	"	1,600	295		1,895	2,200	

114 | Food Service, Residential, Darkroom, Athletic Equipment

114 000 | Food Service Equipment

			CREW	DAILY OUTPUT	MAN-HOURS	UNIT	BARE COSTS MAT.	LABOR	EQUIP.	TOTAL	TOTAL INCL O&P	
002	0010	APPLIANCES Cooking range, 30" free standing, 1 oven, minimum	2 Clab	10	1.600	Ea.	270	27		297	340	002
	0050	Maximum		4	4		1,200	69		1,269	1,425	
	0150	2 oven, minimum		10	1.600		660	27		687	770	
	0200	Maximum	↓	4	4		1,500	69		1,569	1,750	
	1500	Combination range, refrigerator and sink, 30" wide, minimum	L-1	2	8		520	195		715	860	
	1550	Maximum		1	16		1,180	390		1,570	1,875	
	1570	60" wide, average		1.40	11.430		1,875	280		2,155	2,475	
	1590	72" wide, average		1.20	13.330		2,100	325		2,425	2,800	
	1600	Office model, 48" wide		2	8		1,575	195		1,770	2,025	
	1620	Refrigerator and sink only		2.40	6.670		1,625	165		1,790	2,025	
	1640	Combination range, refrigerator, sink, microwave										
	1660	oven and ice maker	L-1	.80	20	Ea.	3,175	490		3,665	4,225	
	2450	Dehumidifier, portable, automatic, 15 pint					175			175	195	
	2550	30 pint					255			255	280	
	2750	Dishwasher, built-in, 2 cycles, minimum	L-1	4	4		230	98		328	400	
	2800	Maximum		2	8		390	195		585	720	
	2950	4 or more cycles, minimum		4	4		360	98		458	540	
	3000	Maximum	↓	2	8		700	195		895	1,050	

114 | Food Service, Residential, Darkroom, Athletic Equipment

114 000 | Food Service Equipment

			CREW	DAILY OUTPUT	MAN-HOURS	UNIT	MAT.	LABOR	EQUIP.	TOTAL	TOTAL INCL O&P	
002	3200	Dryer, automatic, minimum	L-2	3	5.330	Ea.	250	100		350	430	002
	3250	Maximum	"	2	8		730	155		885	1,025	
	3300	Garbage disposer, sink type, minimum	L-1	10	1.600		55	39		94	120	
	3350	Maximum	"	10	1.600		195	39		234	275	
	3550	Heater, electric, built-in, 1250 watt, ceiling type, minimum	1 Elec	4	2		40	49		89	115	
	3600	Maximum		3	2.670		100	65		165	205	
	3700	Wall type, minimum		4	2		40	49		89	115	
	3750	Maximum		3	2.670		75	65		140	180	
	3900	1500 watt wall type, with blower		4	2		75	49		124	155	
	3950	3000 watt		3	2.670		130	65		195	240	
	4150	Hood for range, 2 speed, vented, 30" wide, minimum	L-3	5	3.200		40	74		114	155	
	4200	Maximum		3	5.330		260	125		385	470	
	4300	42" wide, minimum		5	3.200		155	74		229	280	
	4350	Maximum		3	5.330		300	125		425	515	
	4500	For ventless hood, 2 speed, add					12			12	13.20	
	4650	For vented 1 speed, deduct from maximum					25			25	28	
	4850	Humidifier, portable, 7 gallons per day					80			80	88	
	5000	15 gallons per day					160			160	175	
	5200	Icemaker, automatic, 13 lb. per day	1 Plum	7	1.140		430	28		458	515	
	5350	51 lb. per day		2	4		750	99		849	970	
	6400	Sump pump cellar drainer, 1/3 H.P., minimum		3	2.670		90	66		156	195	
	6450	Maximum		2	4		300	99		399	475	
	6460	Sump pump, see also division 152-480										
	6650	Washing machine, automatic, minimum	1 Plum	3	2.670	Ea.	300	66		366	430	
	6700	Maximum	"	1	8		890	200		1,090	1,275	
	6900	Water heater, electric, glass lined, 30 gallon, minimum	L-1	5	3.200		135	78		213	265	
	6950	Maximum		3	5.330		315	130		445	540	
	7100	80 gallon, minimum		2	8		225	195		420	540	
	7150	Maximum		1	16		535	390		925	1,175	
	7180	Water heater, gas, glass lined, 30 gallon, minimum	2 Plum	5	3.200		155	79		234	290	
	7220	Maximum		3	5.330		465	130		595	705	
	7260	50 gallon, minimum		2.50	6.400		205	160		365	460	
	7300	Maximum		1.50	10.670		465	265		730	900	
	7310	Water heater, see also division 153-110										
	7350	Water softener, automatic, to 30 grains per gallon	2 Plum	5	3.200	Ea.	335	79		414	485	
	7400	To 75 grains per gallon	"	4	4		655	99		754	865	
	7450	Vent kits for dryers	1 Carp	10	.800		12	17.30		29.30	39	
004	0010	KITCHEN EQUIPMENT Bake oven gas, one section	Q-1	8	2	Ea.	2,860	44		2,904	3,200	004
	0300	Two sections		7	2.290		5,590	51		5,641	6,225	
	0600	Three sections		6	2.670		8,320	59		8,379	9,250	
	0900	Electric convection, 40" x 45" x 57"	L-7	4	7		2,625	145		2,770	3,100	
	2350	Cooler, reach-in, beverage, 6' long	Q-1	6	2.670		2,200	59		2,259	2,500	
	2700	Dishwasher, commercial, rack type										
	2720	10 to 12 racks per hour	Q-1	3.20	5	Ea.	2,000	110		2,110	2,375	
	2750	Semi-automatic 38 to 50 racks per hour	"	1.30	12.310		4,200	275		4,475	5,025	
	2800	Automatic 190 to 230 racks per hour	Q-2	.70	34.290		9,000	790		9,790	11,100	
	2820	235 to 275 racks per hour		.50	48		13,000	1,100		14,100	15,900	
	2840	8750 to 12,500 dishes per hour		.20	120		33,900	2,775		36,675	41,400	
	4300	Freezers, reach-in, 44 C.F.	Q-1	4	4		5,425	89		5,514	6,100	
	4500	68 C.F.		3	5.330		6,850	120		6,970	7,700	
	5800	Ice cube maker, 50 pounds per day		6	2.670		1,375	59		1,434	1,600	
	6050	500 pounds per day		4	4		3,500	89		3,589	3,975	
	6350	Kettles, steam-jacketed, 20 gallons	L-7	7	4		5,150	83		5,233	5,800	
	6600	60 gallons	"	6	4.670		6,575	97		6,672	7,375	
	7950	Hood fire protection system, minimum	Q-1	3	5.330		2,300	120		2,420	2,700	
	8050	Maximum		1	16		17,000	355		17,355	19,200	
	8300	Refrigerators, reach-in type, 44 C.F.		5	3.200		3,950	71		4,021	4,450	

114 | Food Service, Residential, Darkroom, Athletic Equipment

114 000 | Food Service Equipment

			DAILY	MAN-		\multicolumn{4}{c	}{BARE COSTS}	TOTAL	
		CREW	OUTPUT	HOURS	UNIT	MAT.	LABOR	EQUIP.	TOTAL	INCL O&P	
004	8550	With glass doors, 68 C.F.	Q-1	4	4	Ea.	5,075	89		5,164	5,725	004

114 740 | Darkroom Processing

				DAILY	MAN-		BARE COSTS				TOTAL	
			CREW	OUTPUT	HOURS	UNIT	MAT.	LABOR	EQUIP.	TOTAL	INCL O&P	
741	0010	DARKROOM EQUIPMENT Developing tanks, 5" deep, 24"x 48"	Q-1	2	8	Ea.	860	180		1,040	1,200	741
	0050	48" x 52"		1.70	9.410		1,545	210		1,755	2,000	
	0200	10" deep, 24" x 48"		1.70	9.410		970	210		1,180	1,375	
	0250	24" x 108"		1.50	10.670		1,750	235		1,985	2,275	
	3500	Washers, round, maximum sheet 11" x 14"		2	8		1,080	180		1,260	1,450	
	3550	Maximum sheet 20" x 24"		1	16		1,280	355		1,635	1,925	
	3800	Square, maximum sheet 20" x 24"		1	16		1,170	355		1,525	1,825	
	3900	Maximum sheet 50" x 56"		.80	20		1,850	445		2,295	2,700	
	4500	Combination tank sink, tray sink, washers, with										
	4510	dry side tables, average	Q-1	1	16	Ea.	3,800	355		4,155	4,700	

116 | Laboratory, Planetarium, Observatory Equipment

116 000 | Laboratory Equipment

				DAILY	MAN-		BARE COSTS				TOTAL	
			CREW	OUTPUT	HOURS	UNIT	MAT.	LABOR	EQUIP.	TOTAL	INCL O&P	
001	0010	LABORATORY EQUIPMENT Cabinets, base, door units, metal	2 Carp	18	.889	L.F.	82	19.20		101.20	120	001
	0300	Drawer units	"	18	.889	"	153	19.20		172.20	195	
	2300	Service fixtures, average				Ea.	34			34	37	
	2500	For sink assembly with hot and cold water, add	1 Plum	1.40	5.710		376	140		516	625	
	2550	Glassware washer, distilled water rinse, minimum	L-1	1.80	8.890		2,625	220		2,845	3,200	
	2600	Maximum	"	1	16		15,400	390		15,790	17,500	
	2800	Sink, one piece plastic, flask wash, hose, free standing	1 Plum	1.60	5		1,000	125		1,125	1,275	
	2850	Epoxy resin sink, 25" x 16" x 10"	"	2	4		111	99		210	270	
	4200	Alternate pricing method: as percent of lab furniture										
	4400	Installation, not incl. plumbing & duct work				% Furn.					22%	
	4800	Plumbing, final connections, simple system									10%	
	5000	Moderately complex system									15%	
	5200	Complex system									20%	
	5400	Electrical, simple system									10%	
	5600	Moderately complex system									20%	
	5800	Complex system									35%	
	6000	Safety equipment, eye wash, hand held				Ea.	206			206	225	
	6200	Deluge shower				"	122			122	135	
	0300	Rule of thumb: lab furniture including installation & connection										
	6320	High school				S.F.					23	
	6340	College									34	
	6360	Clinical, health care									29	
	6380	Industrial									47	

117 | Medical Equipment

117 000 | Medical Equipment

			CREW	DAILY OUTPUT	MAN-HOURS	UNIT	BARE COSTS MAT.	LABOR	EQUIP.	TOTAL	TOTAL INCL O&P	
001	0010	MEDICAL EQUIPMENT Autopsy table, standard	1 Plum	1	8	Ea.	5,500	200		5,700	6,350	001
	0200	Deluxe		.60	13.330		7,500	330		7,830	8,750	
	0700	Distiller, water, steam heated, 50 gal. capacity	↓	1.40	5.710		12,500	140		12,640	14,000	
	1800	Heat therapy unit, humidified, 26" x 78" x 28"					1,600			1,600	1,750	
	2100	Hubbard tank with accessories, stainless steel,										
	2110	125 GPM at 45 psi water pressure				Ea.	14,000			14,000	15,400	
	2150	For electric overhead hoist, add				"	1,500			1,500	1,650	
	2350											
	3600	Paraffin bath, 126°F, auto controlled				Ea.	1,200			1,200	1,325	
	4200	Refrigerator, blood bank, 28.6 C.F. emergency signal					4,050			4,050	4,450	
	4210	Reach-in, 16.9 C.F.					4,300			4,300	4,725	
	4600	Station, dietary, medium, with ice					10,200			10,200	11,200	
	5000	Scrub, surgical, minimum					3,200			3,200	3,525	
	5100	Maximum					4,300			4,300	4,725	
	5600	Sterilizers, floor loading, 28" x 67" x 52", single door, steam					85,000			85,000	93,500	
	5650	Double door, steam					130,000			130,000	143,000	
	5800	General purpose, 20" x 20" x 28", single door					6,000			6,000	6,600	
	6000	Portable, counter top, steam, minimum					945			945	1,050	
	6020	Maximum					3,000			3,000	3,300	
	6050	Portable, counter top, gas					10,000			10,000	11,000	
	6150	Automatic washer/sterilizer	1 Plum	2	4	↓	21,500	99		21,599	23,800	
	6200	Steam generators, electric 10 KW to 180 KW										
	6250	Minimum	1 Elec	3	2.670	Ea.	2,100	65		2,165	2,400	
	6300	Maximum	"	.70	11.430		18,000	280		18,280	20,200	
	8100	Utensil washer-sanitizer	1 Plum	2	4		4,800	99		4,899	5,425	
	8400	Whirlpool bath, mobile, 18" x 24" x 60"					2,500			2,500	2,750	
	8450	Fixed, incl. mixing valves	1 Plum	2	4	↓	3,000	99		3,099	3,450	

117 400 | Dental Equipment

			CREW	DAILY OUTPUT	MAN-HOURS	UNIT	MAT.	LABOR	EQUIP.	TOTAL	INCL O&P	
401	0010	DENTAL EQUIPMENT Central suction system, minimum	1 Plum	1.20	6.670	Ea.	1,600	165		1,765	2,000	401
	0100	Maximum	"	.90	8.890		6,295	220		6,515	7,250	
	0300	Air compressor, minimum	1 Skwk	.80	10		1,300	220		1,520	1,775	
	0400	Maximum		.50	16		6,000	355		6,355	7,150	
	0600	Chair, electric or hydraulic, minimum		.50	16		2,900	355		3,255	3,725	
	0700	Maximum		.25	32		6,700	705		7,405	8,450	
	2000	Light, floor or ceiling mounted, minimum		3.60	2.220		895	49		944	1,050	
	2100	Maximum	↓	1.20	6.670		2,000	145		2,145	2,425	
	2300	Sterilizers, steam portable, minimum					1,695			1,695	1,875	
	2350	Maximum					4,700			4,700	5,175	
	2600	Steam, institutional					8,850			8,850	9,725	
	2650	Dry heat, electric, portable, 3 trays				↓	615			615	675	

130 | Special Construction

130 520 | Saunas

			CREW	DAILY OUTPUT	MAN-HOURS	UNIT	MAT.	LABOR	EQUIP.	TOTAL	INCL O&P	
521	0010	SAUNA Prefabricated, incl. heater & controls, 7' high, 6' x 4'	L-7	2.20	12.730	Ea.	2,675	265		2,940	3,350	521
	0400	6' x 5'		2	14		2,975	290		3,265	3,700	
	0600	6' x 6'		1.80	15.560		3,300	320		3,620	4,125	
	0800	6' x 9'		1.60	17.500		4,325	365		4,690	5,300	
	1000	8' x 12'		1.10	25.450		5,375	525		5,900	6,700	
	1200	8' x 8'	↓	1.40	20	↓	4,225	415		4,640	5,275	

130 | Special Construction

130 520 | Saunas

		Crew	Daily Output	Man-Hours	Unit	Mat.	Labor	Equip.	Total	Total Incl O&P	
521	1400 8' x 10'	L-7	1.20	23.330	Ea.	5,250	485		5,735	6,500	521
	1600 10' x 12'	"	1	28		6,025	580		6,605	7,500	
	2500 Heaters only (incl. above), wall mounted, to 200 C.F.					365			365	400	
	2750 To 300 C.F.					465			465	510	
	3000 Floor standing, to 720 C.F., 10,000 watts	1 Elec	3	2.670		700	65		765	865	
	3250 To 1,000 C.F., 12,500 watts	"	3	2.670		760	65		825	930	

130 540 | Steam Baths

		Crew	Daily Output	Man-Hours	Unit	Mat.	Labor	Equip.	Total	Total Incl O&P	
541	0010 STEAM BATH Heater, timer & head, single, to 140 C.F.	1 Plum	1.20	6.670	Ea.	770	165		935	1,100	541
	0500 To 300 C.F.		1.10	7.270		875	180		1,055	1,225	
	1000 Commercial size, to 800 C.F.		.90	8.890		1,435	220		1,655	1,900	
	1500 To 2500 C.F.		.80	10		4,025	245		4,270	4,800	
	2000 Multiple baths, motels, apartment, 2 baths	Q-1	1.30	12.310		1,160	275		1,435	1,675	
	2500 4 baths	"	.70	22.860		1,440	510		1,950	2,350	
	2700 Conversion unit for residential tub, including door					925			925	1,025	

131 | Pre-Eng. Structures, Pools and Ice Rinks

131 240 | Portable Buildings

		Crew	Daily Output	Man-Hours	Unit	Mat.	Labor	Equip.	Total	Total Incl O&P	
242	0010 COMFORT STATIONS Prefab., stock, w/doors, windows & fixt.										242
	0100 Not incl. interior finish or electrical										
	0300 Mobile, on steel frame, minimum				S.F.	27			27	30	
	0350 Maximum					41			41	45	
	0400 Permanent, including concrete slab, minimum	B-12J	50	.320		138	6.65	10.55	155.20	175	
	0500 Maximum	"	43	.372		185	7.75	12.30	205.05	230	
	0600 Alternate pricing method, mobile, minimum				Fixture	1,725			1,725	1,900	
	0650 Maximum					2,575			2,575	2,825	
	0700 Permanent, minimum	B-12J	.70	22.860		9,900	475	755	11,130	12,400	
	0750 Maximum	"	.50	32		16,500	665	1,050	18,215	20,300	

131 520 | Swimming Pools

		Crew	Daily Output	Man-Hours	Unit	Mat.	Labor	Equip.	Total	Total Incl O&P	
523	0010 SWIMMING POOL EQUIPMENT Diving stand, stainless steel, 3 meter	2 Carp	.40	40	Ea.	3,050	865		3,915	4,675	523
	0300 1 meter	"	2.70	5.930	"	2,050	130		2,180	2,450	
	0900 Filter system, sand or diatomite type, incl. pump, 6000 gal./hr.	2 Plum	1.80	8.890	Total	815	220		1,035	1,225	
	1020 Add for chlorination system, 000 S.F. pool		3	5.330	Ea.	270	130		400	490	
	1040 5000 S.F. pool		3	5.330	"	560	130		690	810	
	1100 Gutter system, stainless steel, with grating, stock,										
	1110 contains supply and drainage system	E-1	20	1.200	L.F.	170	28	3.22	201.22	235	
	1120 Integral gutter and 5' high wall system, stainless steel	"	10	2.400	"	220	56	6.45	282.45	340	
	2100 Lights, underwater, 12 volt, with transformer, 300 watt	1 Elec	.40	20	Ea.	205	485		690	940	
	2200 110 volt, 500 watt, standard		.40	20		73	485		558	795	
	2400 Low water cutoff type		.40	20		73	485		558	795	
	2800 Heaters, see division 155-150										
525	0010 SWIMMING POOLS Residential in-ground, vinyl lined, concrete sides										525
	0020 Sides including equipment, sand bottom				SF Surf					16.75	
	0100 Metal or polystyrene sides	B12.7-950								12	
	0200 Add for vermiculite bottom					.65			.65	.72	
	0500 Gunite bottom and sides, white plaster finish										
	0600 350 S.F.				SF Surf					28	
	0750 800 S.F.				"					16	

131 | Pre-Eng. Structures, Pools and Ice Rinks

131 520 | Swimming Pools

		CREW	DAILY OUTPUT	MAN-HOURS	UNIT	BARE COSTS MAT.	LABOR	EQUIP.	TOTAL	TOTAL INCL O&P	
525	1100 Motel, gunite with plaster finish, incl. medium										525
	1150 capacity filtration & chlorination				SF Surf					35	
	1200 Municipal, gunite with plaster finish, incl. high										
	1250 capacity filtration & chlorination				SF Surf					40	
	1350 Add for formed gutters				L.F.	46			46	51	
	1360 Add for stainless steel gutters				"	125			125	140	
	1700 Filtration and deck equipment only, as % of total				Total				20%	20%	
	1800 Deck equipment, rule of thumb, 20′ x 40′ pool				SF Pool					1.30	
	1900 5000 S.F. pool				"					1.90	
	3000 Painting pools, preparation + 3 coats, 20′ x 40′ pool, epoxy	2 Pord	.33	48.480	Total	525	985		1,510	2,025	
	3100 Rubber base paint, 18 gallons	"	.33	48.480		395	985		1,380	1,900	
	3500 42′ x 82′ pool, 75 gallons, epoxy paint	3 Pord	.14	171		2,425	3,475		5,900	7,825	
	3600 Rubber base paint	"	.14	171	↓	1,700	3,475		5,175	7,025	

146 | Hoists and Cranes

146 010 | Hoists And Cranes

		CREW	DAILY OUTPUT	MAN-HOURS	UNIT	BARE COSTS MAT.	LABOR	EQUIP.	TOTAL	TOTAL INCL O&P	
011	0010 MATERIAL HANDLING										011
	1500 Cranes, portable hydraulic, floor type, 2,000 lb. capacity				Ea.	1,800			1,800	1,975	
	1600 4,000 lb. capacity					2,500			2,500	2,750	
	1800 Movable gantry type, 12′ to 15′ range, 2,000 lb. capacity					2,500			2,500	2,750	
	1900 6,000 lb. capacity					3,800			3,800	4,175	
	2100 Hoists, electric overhead, chain, hook hung, 15′ lift, 1 ton cap.					1,350			1,350	1,475	
	2200 2 ton capacity					1,600			1,600	1,750	
	2500 5 ton capacity					3,000			3,000	3,300	
	2600 For hand-pushed trolley, add					15%					
	2700 For geared trolley, add					30%					
	2800 For motor trolley, add				↓	60%					
	3000 For lifts over 15′, 1 ton, add				L.F.	25			25	28	
	3100 5 ton, add				"	40			40	44	
	3300 Lifts, scissor type, portable, electric, 36″ high, 1000 lb.				Ea.	2,400			2,400	2,650	
	3400 42″ high, 2000 lb.				"	2,950			2,950	3,250	

151 | Pipe and Fittings

151 100 | Miscellaneous Fittings

		CREW	DAILY OUTPUT	MAN-HOURS	UNIT	BARE COSTS MAT.	LABOR	EQUIP.	TOTAL	TOTAL INCL O&P	
101	0010 AVERAGE Square foot and percent of total										101
	0100 job cost for plumbing, see division 171										
105	0010 BACKFLOW PREVENTER Includes gate valves,										105
	0020 and four test cocks, corrosion resistant, automatic operation										
	1000 Double check principle										
	1080 Threaded										
	1100 ¾″ pipe size	1 Plum	16	.500	Ea.	135	12.35		147.35	165	
	1120 1″ pipe size	"	14	.571	"	155	14.10		169.10	190	

151 | Pipe and Fittings

151 100 | Miscellaneous Fittings

			CREW	DAILY OUTPUT	MAN-HOURS	UNIT	MAT.	LABOR	EQUIP.	TOTAL	TOTAL INCL O&P	
105	1140	1-½" pipe size	1 Plum	10	.800	Ea.	210	19.75		229.75	260	105
	1160	2" pipe size	"	7	1.140	"	270	28		298	340	
	1300	Flanged										
	1380	3" pipe size	Q-1	4.50	3.560	Ea.	1,200	79		1,279	1,425	
	1400	4" pipe size	"	3	5.330		1,725	120		1,845	2,075	
	1420	6" pipe size	Q-2	3	8		2,900	185		3,085	3,475	
	4000	Reduced pressure principle										
	4100	Threaded										
	4120	¾" pipe size	1 Plum	16	.500	Ea.	215	12.35		227.35	255	
	4140	1" pipe size		14	.571		270	14.10		284.10	320	
	4150	1-¼" pipe size		12	.667		345	16.45		361.45	405	
	4160	1-½" pipe size		10	.800		400	19.75		419.75	470	
	4180	2" pipe size	↓	7	1.140	↓	480	28		508	570	
	5000	Flanged, bronze										
	5060	2-½" pipe size	Q-1	5	3.200	Ea.	1,725	71		1,796	2,000	
	5080	3" pipe size		4.50	3.560		1,900	79		1,979	2,200	
	5100	4" pipe size	↓	3	5.330		3,450	120		3,570	3,975	
	5120	6" pipe size	Q-2	3	8		6,150	185		6,335	7,050	
	5600	Flanged, iron										
	5660	2-½" pipe size	Q-1	5	3.200	Ea.	1,550	71		1,621	1,800	
	5680	3" pipe size		4.50	3.560		1,750	79		1,829	2,050	
	5700	4" pipe size	↓	3	5.330		2,425	120		2,545	2,850	
	5720	6" pipe size	Q-2	3	8		3,725	185		3,910	4,375	
	5740	8" pipe size		2	12		8,000	275		8,275	9,200	
	5760	10" pipe size	↓	1	24	↓	10,575	555		11,130	12,500	
110	0010	**CLEANOUTS**										110
	0060	Floor type										
	0080	Round or square, scoriated nickel bronze top										
	0100	2" pipe size	1 Plum	10	.800	Ea.	41	19.75		60.75	74	
	0120	3" pipe size		8	1		48	25		73	89	
	0140	4" pipe size		6	1.330		59	33		92	115	
	0160	5" pipe size	↓	4	2		98	49		147	180	
	0180	6" pipe size	Q-1	6	2.670		115	59		174	215	
	0200	8" pipe size	"	4	4	↓	130	89		219	275	
	0340	Recessed for tile, same price										
	0980	Round top, recessed for terrazzo										
	1000	2" pipe size	1 Plum	9	.889	Ea.	74	22		96	115	
	1080	3" pipe size		6	1.330		74	33		107	130	
	1100	4" pipe size	↓	4	2		87	49		136	170	
	1120	5" pipe size	Q-1	6	2.670		140	59		199	240	
	1140	6" pipe size		5	3.200		145	71		216	265	
	1160	8" pipe size	↓	4	4	↓	180	89		269	330	
	2000	Round scoriated nickel bronze top, extra heavy duty										
	2060	2" pipe size	1 Plum	9	.889	Ea.	59	22		81	97	
	2080	3" pipe size		6	1.330		65	33		98	120	
	2100	4" pipe size	↓	4	2		75	49		124	155	
	2120	5" pipe size	Q-1	6	2.670		135	59		194	235	
	2140	6" pipe size		5	3.200		150	71		221	270	
	2160	8" pipe size	↓	4	4	↓	220	89		309	375	
	4000	Wall type, square smooth cover, over wall frame										
	4060	2" pipe size	1 Plum	14	.571	Ea.	35	14.10		49.10	59	
	4080	3" pipe size		12	.667		40	16.45		56.45	68	
	4100	4" pipe size		10	.800		55	19.75		74.75	90	
	4120	5" pipe size		9	.889		100	22		122	145	
	4140	6" pipe size	↓	8	1		155	25		180	205	
	4160	8" pipe size	Q-1	11	1.450	↓	185	32		217	250	
	5000	Extension, C.I., bronze countersunk plug, 8" long										

151 | Pipe and Fittings

151 100 | Miscellaneous Fittings

			CREW	DAILY OUTPUT	MAN-HOURS	UNIT	BARE COSTS MAT.	LABOR	EQUIP.	TOTAL	TOTAL INCL O&P	
110	5040	2" pipe size	1 Plum	16	.500	Ea.	5.25	12.35		17.60	24	110
	5060	3" pipe size		14	.571		8.85	14.10		22.95	31	
	5080	4" pipe size		13	.615		15.35	15.20		30.55	39	
	5100	5" pipe size		12	.667		30	16.45		46.45	57	
	5120	6" pipe size	↓	11	.727	↓	40	17.95		57.95	71	
115	0010	**CLEANOUT TEE** Cast iron with countersunk plug										115
	0200	2" pipe size	1 Plum	4	2	Ea.	11	49		60	85	
	0220	3" pipe size		3.60	2.220		23	55		78	105	
	0240	4" pipe size		3.30	2.420		25	60		85	115	
	0260	5" pipe size	Q-1	5.50	2.910		36	65		101	135	
	0280	6" pipe size	"	5	3.200		50	71		121	160	
	0300	8" pipe size	Q-3	5	6.400		80	150		230	310	
	0500	For round smooth access cover, add					20%					
	0600	For round scoriated access cover, add					75%					
	0700	For square smooth access cover, add				↓	200%					
120	0010	**CONNECTORS** Flexible, corrugated, ⅞" O.D., ½" I.D.										120
	0050	Gas, seamless brass, steel fittings										
	0200	12" long	1 Plum	36	.222	Ea.	6.10	5.50		11.60	14.85	
	0220	18" long		36	.222		7.55	5.50		13.05	16.45	
	0240	24" long		34	.235		8.95	5.80		14.75	18.45	
	0260	30" long		34	.235		9.65	5.80		15.45	19.25	
	0280	36" long		32	.250		10.65	6.20		16.85	21	
	0320	48" long		30	.267		13.55	6.60		20.15	25	
	0340	60" long		30	.267		16.10	6.60		22.70	27	
	0360	72" long	↓	30	.267	↓	18.65	6.60		25.25	30	
	2000	Water, copper tubing, dielectric separators										
	2100	12" long	1 Plum	36	.222	Ea.	5.35	5.50		10.85	14.05	
	2220	15" long		36	.222		5.95	5.50		11.45	14.70	
	2240	18" long		36	.222		6.45	5.50		11.95	15.25	
	2260	24" long	↓	34	.235	↓	7.95	5.80		13.75	17.35	
125	0010	**DRAINS**										125
	0140	Cornice, C.I., 45° or 90° outlet										
	0180	1-½" & 2" pipe size	Q-1	14	1.140	Ea.	50	25		75	93	
	0200	3" and 4" pipe size	"	12	1.330		68	30		98	120	
	0260	For galvanized body, add					9.25			9.25	10.20	
	0280	For polished bronze dome, add				↓	7.95			7.95	8.75	
	0400	Deck, auto park, C.I., 13" top										
	0440	3", 4", 5", and 6" pipe size	Q-1	8	2	Ea.	165	44		209	245	
	0480	For galvanized body, add				"	75			75	83	
	0800	Promenade, heelproof grate, C.I., 14" top										
	0840	2", 3", and 4" pipe size	Q-1	10	1.600	Ea.	79	36		115	140	
	0860	5" and 6" pipe size		9	1.780		98	40		138	165	
	0880	8" pipe size	↓	8	2		115	44		159	190	
	0940	For galvanized body, add					52			52	57	
	0960	For polished bronze top, add				↓	54			54	59	
	1200	Promenade, heelproof grate, C.I., lateral, 14" top										
	1240	2", 3" and 4" pipe size	Q-1	10	1.600	Ea.	105	36		141	170	
	1260	5" and 6" pipe size		9	1.780		135	40		175	205	
	1280	8" pipe size	↓	8	2		155	44		199	235	
	1340	For galvanized body, add					52			52	57	
	1360	For polished bronze top, add				↓	54			54	59	
	1500	Promenade, slotted grate, C.I., 11" top										
	1540	2", 3", 4", 5", and 6" pipe size	Q-1	12	1.330	Ea.	72	30		102	125	
	1600	For galvanized body, add					29			29	32	
	1640	For polished bronze top, add				↓	42			42	46	
	2000	Floor, medium duty, C.I., deep flange, 7" top										

151 | Pipe and Fittings

151 100 | Miscellaneous Fittings

			CREW	DAILY OUTPUT	MAN-HOURS	UNIT	BARE COSTS MAT.	LABOR	EQUIP.	TOTAL	TOTAL INCL O&P	
125	2040	2" and 3" pipe size	Q-1	12	1.330	Ea.	29	30		59	76	125
	2080	For galvanized body, add					12.35			12.35	13.60	
	2120	For polished bronze top, add				↓	15.95			15.95	17.55	
	2160	Heavy duty, C.I., 12" antitilt grate										
	2180	2", 3", 4", 5" and 6" pipe size	Q-1	10	1.600	Ea.	67	36		103	125	
	2220	For galvanized body, add					36			36	40	
	2240	For polished bronze top, add				↓	41			41	45	
	2300	X-Heavy duty, C.I., 15" antitilt grate										
	2320	4", 5", 6", and 8" pipe size	Q-1	8	2	Ea.	180	44		224	265	
	2360	For galvanized body, add					61			61	67	
	2380	For polished bronze top, add				↓	72			72	79	
	2400	Heavy duty, with sediment bucket, C.I., 12" loose grate										
	2420	3", 4", 5", and 6" pipe size	Q-1	9	1.780	Ea.	100	40		140	170	
	2440	For galvanized body, add					45			45	50	
	2460	For polished bronze top, add				↓	41			41	45	
	2500	Heavy duty, cleanout & trap w/bucket, C.I., 15" top										
	2540	2", 3", and 4" pipe size	Q-1	6	2.670	Ea.	720	59		779	880	
	2560	For galvanized body, add					210			210	230	
	2580	For polished bronze top, add				↓	220			220	240	
	2600	Medium duty, with perforated SS basket, C.I., body,										
	2610	18" top for refuse container washing area										
	2620	2" thru 6" pipe size	Q-1	4	4	Ea.	1,225	89		1,314	1,475	
	2630	Polyethylene, corrosion-resistant										
	2640	3" and 4" pipe size	Q-1	16	1	Ea.	215	22		237	270	
	2650	PVC or ABS thermoplastic										
	2660	3" and 4" pipe size	Q-1	16	1	Ea.	38	22		60	75	
	2680	Extra heavy duty, oil intercepting, gas seal cone,										
	2690	with cleanout, loose grate, C.I., body 16" top										
	2700	3" and 4" diameter outlet, 4" slab depth	Q-1	4	4	Ea.	795	89		884	1,000	
	2720	3" and 4" diameter outlet, 8" slab depth		3	5.330		860	120		980	1,125	
	2740	3" and 4" dia. outlet, 10"-12" slab depth	↓	2	8	↓	890	180		1,070	1,250	
	2780	Shower, with strainer, uniform diam. trap, bronze top										
	2800	1-½", 2" and 3" pipe size	Q-1	8	2	Ea.	62	44		106	135	
	2820	4" pipe size	"	7	2.290		72	51		123	155	
	2840	For galvanized body, add				↓	25			25	28	
	2860	With strainer, backwater valve, drum trap										
	2880	1-½", 2", and 3" pipe size	Q-1	8	2	Ea.	75	44		119	150	
	2890	4" pipe size	"	7	2.290		110	51		161	195	
	2900	For galvanized body, add					28			28	31	
	2910	Prison cell, vandal-proof, 1-½", and 2" diam. pipe	Q-1	12	1.330		44	30		74	92	
	2920	3" pipe size	"	10	1.600	↓	52	36		88	110	
	2930	Trap drain, light duty, backwater valve C.I. top										
	2950	8" diameter top, 2" pipe size	Q-1	12	1.330	Ea.	36	30		66	84	
	2960	10" diameter top, 3" pipe size		10	1.600		76	36		112	135	
	2970	12" diameter top, 4" pipe size	↓	8	2		110	44		154	185	
	2990	Pool main discharge, polished bronze top, C.I. body										
	3000	8" diam. grate, 2", 3" & 4" pipe size	Q-1	8	2	Ea.	67	44		111	140	
	3100	12" diam. grate, 4", 5" & 6" pipe size	"	8	2		150	44		194	230	
	3160	For galvanized body, add				↓	31			31	34	
	3200	Gutter, bronze body, polished bronze top										
	3220	9" grate, 1-½" & 2" pipe size	Q-1	8	2	Ea.	26	44		70	95	
	3240	12" grate, 2", 2-½" & 3" pipe size	"	7	2.290	"	62	51		113	145	
	3380	Overflow, 5" dome & 6" high pipe polished bronze,										
	3400	cast iron body, 2", 3", & 4" pipe size	Q-1	10	1.600	Ea.	99	36		135	160	
	3580	Recirculating inlet, 6" sq face polished bronze,										
	3600	C.I. body, 1-½", 2", 3" & 4" pipe size	Q-1	10	1.600	Ea.	41.20	36		77.20	98	
	3620	For galvanized body, add				"	10.10			10.10	11.10	
	3860	Roof, flat metal deck, C.I. body, 10" aluminum dome										

151 | Pipe and Fittings

151 100 | Miscellaneous Fittings

		CREW	DAILY OUTPUT	MAN-HOURS	UNIT	BARE COSTS MAT.	LABOR	EQUIP.	TOTAL	TOTAL INCL O&P
3880	2" pipe size	Q-1	15	1.070	Ea.	100	24		124	145
3890	3" pipe size		14	1.140		105	25		130	155
3900	4" pipe size		13	1.230		110	27		137	160
3910	5" pipe size		12	1.330		135	30		165	190
3920	6" pipe size	↓	10	1.600	↓	185	36		221	255
3980	Precast plank deck, C.I. body, aluminum dome									
4000	10" top, 2" pipe size	Q-1	14	1.140	Ea.	46	25		71	88
4100	10" top, 3" pipe size		13	1.230		58	27		85	105
4120	13" top, 4" pipe size		12	1.330		75	30		105	125
4140	13" top, 5" pipe size		10	1.600		88	36		124	150
4160	16" top, 6" pipe size		8	2		105	44		149	180
4180	16" top, 8" pipe size	↓	7	2.290		150	51		201	240
4220	For galvanized body, add				↓	40			40	44
4280	Integral expansion joint, C.I. body, 12" polypropylene dome									
4300	2" pipe size	Q-1	8	2	Ea.	88	44		132	165
4320	3" pipe size		7	2.290		93	51		144	180
4340	4" pipe size		6	2.670		98	59		157	195
4360	5" pipe size		4	4		140	89		229	285
4380	6" pipe size		3	5.330		150	120		270	340
4400	8" pipe size	↓	3	5.330		235	120		355	435
4440	For galvanized body, add				↓	62			62	68
4480	Flexible neoprene bellows, no-hub connection									
4500	3" and 4" pipe size	Q-1	5	3.200	Ea.	105	71		176	220
4520	5" and 6" pipe size	"	4	4	"	115	89		204	260
4620	Main, all aluminum, 12" low profile dome									
4640	2", 3" and 4" pipe size	Q-1	14	1.140	Ea.	150	25		175	205
4660	5" and 6" pipe size		13	1.230		165	27		192	220
4680	8" pipe size		10	1.600		205	36		241	280
4690	Main, CI body, 12" polyprop. dome, 2", 3", & 4" pipe size		8	2		46	44		90	115
4710	5" and 6" pipe size		6	2.670		62	59		121	155
4720	8" pipe size		4	4		82	89		171	220
4730	For underdeck clamp, add	↓	22	.727		17	16.15		33.15	43
4740	For vandalproof dome, add					7.45			7.45	8.20
4750	For galvanized body, add					52			52	57
4760	Main, PVC body and dome, 2" pipe size	Q-1	14	1.140	Ea.	35	25		60	76
4780	3" pipe size		14	1.140		35	25		60	76
4800	4" pipe size		14	1.140		40	25		65	82
4820	For underdeck clamp, add	↓	24	.667	↓	9.25	14.80		24.05	32
4900	Terrace planting area, with perforated overflow, C.I.									
4920	2", 3" and 4" pipe size	Q-1	8	2	Ea.	120	44		164	200
4980	Scupper floor, oblique strainer, C.I.									
5000	6" x 7" top, 2", 3" and 4" pipe size	Q-1	16	1	Ea.	40	22		62	77
5100	8" x 12" top, 5" and 6" pipe size	"	14	1.140		77	25		102	120
5160	For galvanized body, add					40%				
5200	For polished bronze strainer, add				↓	100%				
5980	Trench, floor, heavy duty, modular, C.I., 12" x 12" top									
6000	2", 3", 4", 5", & 6" pipe size	Q-1	8	2	Ea.	125	44		169	205
6100	For polished bronze top, add					62			62	68
6200	For 12" extension section, C.I. top, add					125			125	140
6240	For polished bronze top, add				↓	62			62	68
6960	Backwater valve, soil pipe, C.I. body									
6980	Bronze gate and automatic flapper valves									
7000	3" and 4" pipe size	Q-1	13	1.230	Ea.	245	27		272	310
7100	5" and 6" pipe size	"	13	1.230	"	390	27		417	470
7240	Bronze flapper valve, bolted cover									
7260	2" pipe size	Q-1	16	1	Ea.	82	22		104	125
7280	3" pipe size		14.50	1.100		130	25		155	180
7300	4" pipe size	↓	13	1.230		160	27		187	215

151 | Pipe and Fittings

151 100 | Miscellaneous Fittings

			CREW	DAILY OUTPUT	MAN-HOURS	UNIT	BARE COSTS MAT.	BARE COSTS LABOR	BARE COSTS EQUIP.	BARE COSTS TOTAL	TOTAL INCL O&P	
125	7320	5" pipe size	Q-2	18	1.330	Ea.	190	31		221	255	125
	7340	6" pipe size	"	17	1.410		225	33		258	295	
	7360	8" pipe size	Q-3	10	3.200		320	75		395	465	
	7380	10" pipe size	"	9	3.560		480	84		564	650	
	7500	For threaded cover, same cost										
	7540	Revolving disk type, same cost as flapper type										
	9000	Sewer control system, valve unit, guardrail, leak detector										
	9010	With fittings, monitor, 40' cable. No pit fabrication										
	9020	4" pipe size	Q-2	.25	96	Ea.	4,500	2,225		6,725	8,225	
	9120	5" pipe size		.22	109		4,800	2,525		7,325	9,000	
	9140	6" pipe size		.20	120		5,700	2,775		8,475	10,400	
	9160	8" pipe size		.17	141		6,500	3,250		9,750	12,000	
130	0010	**DIELECTRIC UNIONS** Standard gaskets for water and air										130
	0020	250 psi maximum pressure										
	0280	Female IPT to sweat, straight										
	0300	½" pipe size	1 Plum	24	.333	Ea.	2.32	8.25		10.57	14.75	
	0340	¾" pipe size		20	.400		2.32	9.90		12.22	17.20	
	0360	1" pipe size		19	.421		4.42	10.40		14.82	20	
	0380	1-¼" pipe size		15	.533		7.20	13.15		20.35	27	
	0400	1-½" pipe size		13	.615		10.80	15.20		26	34	
	0420	2" pipe size		11	.727		15.15	17.95		33.10	43	
	0580	Female IPT to brass pipe thread, straight										
	0600	½" pipe size	1 Plum	24	.333	Ea.	4.48	8.25		12.73	17.15	
	0640	¾" pipe size		20	.400		5.70	9.90		15.60	21	
	0660	1" pipe size		19	.421		8.60	10.40		19	25	
	0680	1-¼" pipe size		15	.533		12.85	13.15		26	34	
	0700	1-½" pipe size		13	.615		17.65	15.20		32.85	42	
	0720	2" pipe size		11	.727		23	17.95		40.95	52	
	0780	Female IPT to female IPT, straight										
	0800	½" pipe size	1 Plum	24	.333	Ea.	3.60	8.25		11.85	16.20	
	0840	¾" pipe size		20	.400		4	9.90		13.90	19.05	
	0860	1" pipe size		19	.421		5.30	10.40		15.70	21	
	0880	1-¼" pipe size		15	.533		7.20	13.15		20.35	27	
	0900	1-½" pipe size		13	.615		11.15	15.20		26.35	35	
	0920	2" pipe size		11	.727		16.20	17.95		34.15	44	
	2000	175 psi maximum pressure, flanged										
	2180	Female IPT to sweat										
	2200	1-½" pipe size	1 Plum	11	.727	Ea.	29	17.95		46.95	59	
	2240	2" pipe size	"	9	.889		33	22		55	69	
	2260	2-½" pipe size	Q-1	15	1.070		36	24		60	75	
	2280	3" pipe size		14	1.140		49	25		74	92	
	2300	4" pipe size		11	1.450		130	32		162	190	
	2320	5" pipe size	Q-2	14	1.710		215	40		255	295	
	2340	6" pipe size		12	2		250	46		296	345	
	2360	8" pipe size		10	2.400		740	55		795	895	
	2480	Female IPT to brass pipe										
	2500	1-½" pipe size	1 Plum	11	.727	Ea.	43	17.95		60.95	74	
	2540	2" pipe size	"	9	.889		52	22		74	90	
	2560	2-½" pipe size	Q-1	15	1.070		75	24		99	120	
	2580	3" pipe size		14	1.140		87	25		112	135	
	2600	4" pipe size		11	1.450		150	32		182	215	
	2620	5" pipe size	Q-2	14	1.710		170	40		210	245	
	2640	6" pipe size		12	2		195	46		241	285	
	2680	8" pipe size		10	2.400		315	55		370	430	
	2880	Female IPT to female IPT										
	2900	1-½" pipe size	1 Plum	11	.727	Ea.	26	17.95		43.95	55	
	2940	2" pipe size	"	9	.889		28	22		50	63	
	2960	2-½" pipe size	Q-1	15	1.070		35	24		59	74	

151 | Pipe and Fittings

151 100 | Miscellaneous Fittings

			CREW	DAILY OUTPUT	MAN-HOURS	UNIT	MAT.	LABOR	EQUIP.	TOTAL	TOTAL INCL O&P	
130	2980	3" pipe size	Q-1	14	1.140	Ea.	44	25		69	86	130
	3000	4" pipe size	"	11	1.450		66	32		98	120	
	3020	5" pipe size	Q-2	14	1.710		76	40		116	140	
	3040	6" pipe size		12	2		98	46		144	175	
	3060	8" pipe size	↓	10	2.400	↓	110	55		165	205	
	3380	Copper to copper										
	3400	1-½" pipe size	1 Plum	11	.727	Ea.	34	17.95		51.95	64	
	3440	2" pipe size	"	9	.889		40	22		62	77	
	3460	2-½" pipe size	Q-1	15	1.070		44	24		68	84	
	3480	3" pipe size	"	14	1.140		54	25		79	97	
	3500	4" pipe size	↓	11	1.450		165	32		197	230	
	3520	5" pipe size	Q-2	14	1.710		265	40		305	350	
	3540	6" pipe size		12	2		335	46		381	435	
	3560	8" pipe size	↓	10	2.400		900	55		955	1,075	
141	0010	**FAUCETS/FITTINGS**										141
	0150	Bath, faucets, diverter spout combination, sweat	1 Plum	8	1	Ea.	45	25		70	86	
	0200	For integral stops, IPS unions, add					17.85			17.85	19.65	
	0300	Three valve combinations, spout, head, arm, flange, sweat	1 Plum	6	1.330		45	33		78	98	
	0400	For integral stops, IPS unions, add					19			19	21	
	0500	Drain, central lift, 1-½" IPS male	1 Plum	20	.400		28	9.90		37.90	45	
	0600	Trip lever, 1-½" IPS male		20	.400		28	9.90		37.90	45	
	0700	Pop up, 1-½" IPS male		18	.444		33	11		44	53	
	0800	Chain and stopper, 1-½" IPS male	↓	24	.333	↓	23	8.25		31.25	38	
	0840	Flush valves, with vacuum breaker										
	0850	Water closet										
	0860	Exposed, rear spud	1 Plum	8	1	Ea.	78	25		103	120	
	0870	Top spud		8	1		73	25		98	115	
	0880	Concealed, rear spud		8	1		78	25		103	120	
	0890	Top spud		8	1		88	25		113	135	
	0900	Wall hung	↓	8	1	↓	78	25		103	120	
	0920	Urinal										
	0930	Exposed, stall	1 Plum	8	1	Ea.	70	25		95	115	
	0940	Wall, (washout)		8	1		70	25		95	115	
	0950	Pedestal, top spud		8	1		72	25		97	115	
	0960	Concealed, stall		8	1		72	25		97	115	
	0970	Wall (washout)	↓	8	1	↓	72	25		97	115	
	0971	Automatic flush sensor and operator for										
	0972	Urinals or water closets, add	1 Plum	16	.500	Ea.	70	12.35		82.35	95	
	1000	Kitchen sink faucets, top mount, cast spout	"	10	.800		33	19.75		52.75	66	
	1100	For spray, add					10	10%				
	1200	Wall type, swing tube spout	1 Plum	10	.800		41	19.75		60.75	74	
	1240	For soap dish, add					1.80			1.80	1.98	
	2000	Laundry faucets, shelf type, IPS or copper unions	1 Plum	12	.667		28	16.45		44.45	55	
	2100	Lavatory faucet, centerset, without drain	"	10	.800		24	19.75		43.75	56	
	2200	For pop-up drain, add					10	15%				
	2250	For acrylic handles, add					3.50			3.50	3.85	
	2400	Concealed, 12" centers	1 Plum	10	.800		56	19.75		75.75	91	
	2450	For pop-up drain, add					8	15%				
	2600	Shelfback, 4" to 6" centers, 17 Ga. tailpiece	1 Plum	10	.800		41	19.75		60.75	74	
	2650	For pop-up drain, add					10	15%				
	2700	For shampoo faucet with supply tube, add					28	10%				
	2800	Self-closing, center set	1 Plum	10	.800		68	19.75		87.75	105	
	2850	Medical, bedpan cleanser, with pedal valve,		12	.667		340	16.45		356.45	400	
	2860	With screwdriver stop valve		12	.667		180	16.45		196.45	220	
	2870	With self-closing spray valve		12	.667		140	16.45		156.45	180	
	2900	Faucet, gooseneck spout, wrist handles, grid drain		10	.800		150	19.75		169.75	195	
	2940	Mixing valve, knee action, screwdriver stops		4	2		265	49		314	365	
	3000	Service sink faucet, cast spout, pail hook, hose end	↓	14	.571	↓	47	14.10		61.10	73	

151 | Pipe and Fittings

151 100 | Miscellaneous Fittings

			CREW	DAILY OUTPUT	MAN-HOURS	UNIT	MAT.	LABOR	EQUIP.	TOTAL	TOTAL INCL O&P	
141	4000	Shower by-pass valve with union	1 Plum	18	.444	Ea.	35	11		46	55	141
	4100	Shower arm with flange and head		22	.364		12	9		21	27	
	4200	Shower thermostatic mixing valve, concealed		8	1		160	25		185	215	
	4300	For inlet strainer, check, and stops, add					52	5%				
	5000	Sillcock, compact, brass, IPS or copper to hose	1 Plum	24	.333		4.50	8.25		12.75	17.15	
	6000	Stop and waste valves, bronze										
	6100	Angle, solder end ½"	1 Plum	24	.333	Ea.	5.20	8.25		13.45	17.95	
	6110	¾"		20	.400		5.20	9.90		15.10	20	
	6300	Straightway, solder end ⅜"		24	.333		3.25	8.25		11.50	15.80	
	6310	½"		24	.333		3	8.25		11.25	15.50	
	6320	¾"		20	.400		3.25	9.90		13.15	18.25	
	6330	1"		19	.421		10.50	10.40		20.90	27	
	6400	Straightway, threaded ⅜"		24	.333		3.50	8.25		11.75	16.05	
	6410	½"		24	.333		3.25	8.25		11.50	15.80	
	6420	¾"		20	.400		3.50	9.90		13.40	18.50	
	6430	1"		19	.421		10.50	10.40		20.90	27	
	8000	Water supply stops, polished chrome plate										
	8200	Angle, ⅜"	1 Plum	24	.333	Ea.	12	8.25		20.25	25	
	8300	½"		22	.364		13.50	9		22.50	28	
	8400	Straight, ⅜"		26	.308		12	7.60		19.60	24	
	8500	½"		24	.333		13.50	8.25		21.75	27	
	8600	Water closet, angle, w/flex riser, ⅜"		24	.333		15.75	8.25		24	30	
146	0010	**FLOOR RECEPTORS** For connection to 2", 3" & 4" diameter pipe										146
	0200	12-½" square top, 25 sq. in. open area	Q-1	10	1.600	Ea.	200	36		236	275	
	0300	For grate with 4" diam. x 3-¾" high funnel, add					32			32	35	
	0400	For grate with 6" diameter x 6" high funnel, add					42			42	46	
	0500	For full hinged grate with open center, add					38			38	42	
	0600	For aluminum bucket, add 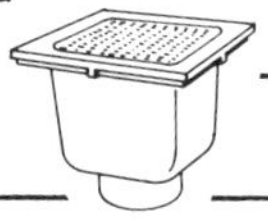					21			21	23	
	0700	For acid-resisting bucket, add					43			43	47	
	0800	For galvanized bucket, add					28			28	31	
	0900	For stainless steel mesh bucket liner, add					32			32	35	
	1000	For bronze antisplash dome strainer, add					18			18	19.80	
	1100	For partial solid cover, add					18			18	19.80	
	1200	For trap primer connection, add					16			16	17.60	
	2000	12-⅝" diameter top, 40 sq. in. open area 	Q-1	10	1.600		160	36		196	230	
	2100	For options, add same prices as square top										
	3000	8" x 4" rectangular top, 7.5 sq. in. open area	Q-1	14	1.140		120	25		145	170	
	3100	For trap primer connections, add					13			13	14.30	
	4000	24" x 16" rectangular top, 70 sq. in. open area	Q-1	4	4		455	89		544	630	
	4100	For trap primer connection, add					27			27	30	
156	0010	**HYDRANTS**										156
	0050	Wall type, moderate climate, bronze encased										
	0200	¾" IPS connection	1 Plum	16	.500	Ea.	115	12.35		127.35	145	
	0300	1" IPS connection	"	14	.571		130	14.10		144.10	165	
	0400	For ¾" adapter type vacuum breaker, add					52			52	57	
	0500	For anti-siphon type, add					63			63	69	
	1000	Non-freeze, bronze, exposed										
	1100	¾" IPS connection, 4" to 9" thick wall	1 Plum	14	.571	Ea.	96	14.10		110.10	125	
	1120	10" to 14" thick wall		12	.667		110	16.45		126.45	145	
	1140	15" to 19" thick wall		12	.667		120	16.45		136.45	155	
	1160	20" to 24" thick wall		10	.800		130	19.75		149.75	170	
	1200	For 1" IPS connection, add					19	10%				
	1240	For ¾" adapter type vacuum breaker, add 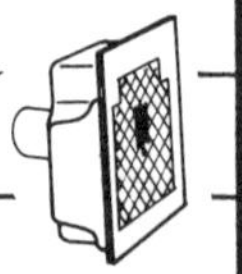					13			13	14.30	
	1280	For anti-siphon type, add					22			22	24	
	2000	Non-freeze bronze, encased										
	2100	¾" IPS connection, 5" to 9" thick wall	1 Plum	14	.571	Ea.	165	14.10		179.10	200	
	2120	10" to 14" thick wall		12	.667		175	16.45		191.45	215	
	2140	15" to 19" thick wall		12	.667		185	16.45		201.45	230	

151 | Pipe and Fittings

151 100 | Miscellaneous Fittings

			CREW	DAILY OUTPUT	MAN-HOURS	UNIT	BARE COSTS MAT.	LABOR	EQUIP.	TOTAL	TOTAL INCL O&P	
156	2160	20" to 24" thick wall	1 Plum	10	.800	Ea.	195	19.75		214.75	245	156
	2200	For 1" IPS connection, add					19	10%				
	2240	For ¾" adapter type vacuum breaker, add					45			45	50	
	2280	For anti-siphon type, add					53			53	58	
	3000	Ground box type, bronze frame, ¾" IPS connection										
	3080	Non-freeze, all bronze, polished face, set flush										
	3100	2 feet depth of bury	1 Plum	8	1	Ea.	175	25		200	230	
	3120	3 feet depth of bury		8	1		190	25		215	245	
	3140	4 feet depth of bury		8	1		205	25		230	260	
	3160	5 feet depth of bury		7	1.140		220	28		248	285	
	3180	6 feet depth of bury		7	1.140		230	28		258	295	
	3200	7 feet depth of bury		6	1.330		245	33		278	320	
	3220	8 feet depth of bury		5	1.600		260	40		300	345	
	3240	9 feet depth of bury		4	2		270	49		319	370	
	3260	10 feet depth of bury		4	2		285	49		334	385	
	3400	For 1" IPS connection, add					19	10%				
	3450	For 1-¼" IPS connection, add					325	14%				
	3500	For 1-½" connection, add					415	18%				
	3550	For 2" connection, add					560	24%				
	3600	For tapped drain port in box, add					16			16	17.60	
	4000	Non-freeze, CI body, bronze frame & scoriated cover										
	4010	with hose storage										
	4100	2 feet depth of bury	1 Plum	7	1.140	Ea.	335	28		363	410	
	4120	3 feet depth of bury		7	1.140		350	28		378	425	
	4140	4 feet depth of bury		7	1.140		360	28		388	440	
	4160	5 feet depth of bury		6.50	1.230		365	30		395	445	
	4180	6 feet depth of bury		6	1.330		370	33		403	455	
	4200	7 feet depth of bury		5.50	1.450		390	36		426	480	
	4220	8 feet depth of bury		5	1.600		400	40		440	500	
	4240	9 feet depth of bury		4.50	1.780		410	44		454	515	
	4260	10 feet depth of bury		4	2		415	49		464	530	
	4280	For 1" IPS connection, add					59			59	65	
	4300	For tapped drain port in box, add					16			16	17.60	
	5000	Moderate climate, all bronze, polished face										
	5020	and scoriated cover, set flush										
	5100	¾" IPS connection	1 Plum	16	.500	Ea.	140	12.35		152.35	170	
	5120	1" IPS connection	"	14	.571		155	14.10		169.10	190	
	5200	For tapped drain port in box, add					16			16	17.60	
	6000	Ground post type, all non-freeze, all bronze, aluminum casing										
	6010	guard, exposed head, ¾" IPS connection										
	6100	2 feet depth of bury	1 Plum	8	1	Ea.	135	25		160	185	
	6120	3 feet depth of bury		8	1		145	25		170	195	
	6140	4 feet depth of bury		8	1		150	25		175	200	
	6160	5 feet depth of bury		7	1.140		160	28		188	220	
	6180	6 feet depth of bury		7	1.140		170	28		198	230	
	6200	7 feet depth of bury		6	1.330		180	33		213	245	
	6220	8 feet depth of bury		5	1.600		190	40		230	270	
	6240	9 feet depth of bury		4	2		205	49		254	300	
	6260	10 feet depth of bury		4	2		215	49		264	310	
	6300	For 1" IPS connection, add					41	10%				
	6350	For 1-¼" IPS connection, add					250	14%				
	6400	For 1-½" IPS connection, add					415	18%				
	6450	For 2" IPS connection, add					560	24%				
165	0010	**SHOCK ABSORBERS**										165
	0500	¾" male I.P.S. For 1 to 11 fixtures	1 Plum	12	.667	Ea.	31	16.45		47.45	59	
	0600	1" male I.P.S., For 12 to 32 fixtures		8	1		63	25		88	105	
	0700	For 33 to 60 fixtures		8	1		95	25		120	140	

151 | Pipe and Fittings

151 100	Miscellaneous Fittings	CREW	DAILY OUTPUT	MAN-HOURS	UNIT	BARE COSTS MAT.	LABOR	EQUIP.	TOTAL	TOTAL INCL O&P	
165	0800	For 61 to 113 fixtures	1 Plum	8	1	Ea.	230	25		255	290	165
	0900	For 114 to 154 fixtures		8	1		290	25		315	355	
	1000	For 155 to 330 fixtures	↓	4	2	↓	330	49		379	435	
170	0010	**SUPPORTS/CARRIERS** For plumbing fixtures										170
	0500	Drinking fountain, wall mounted										
	0600	Plate type with studs, top back plate	1 Plum	7	1.140	Ea.	13	28		41	56	
	0700	Top front and back plate		7	1.140		20	28		48	64	
	0800	Top & bottom, front & back plates, w/bearing jacks	↓	7	1.140	↓	23	28		51	67	
	3000	Lavatory, concealed arm										
	3050	Floor mounted, single										
	3100	High back fixture	1 Plum	6	1.330	Ea.	70	33		103	125	
	3200	Flat slab fixture		6	1.330		82	33		115	140	
	3220	Paraplegic	↓	6	1.330		68	33		101	125	
	3250	Floor mounted, back to back										
	3300	High back fixtures	1 Plum	5	1.600	Ea.	100	40		140	170	
	3400	Flat slab fixtures		5	1.600		120	40		160	190	
	3430	Paraplegic	↓	5	1.600		84	40		124	150	
	3500	Wall mounted, in stud or masonry										
	3600	High back fixture	1 Plum	6	1.330	Ea.	42	33		75	95	
	3700	Flat slab fixture	"	6	1.330	"	53	33		86	105	
	4000	Exposed arm type, floor mounted										
	4100	Single high back or flat slab fixture	1 Plum	6	1.330	Ea.	100	33		133	160	
	4200	Back to back, high back or flat slab fixtures		5	1.600		160	40		200	235	
	4300	Wall mounted, High back or flat slab lavatory	↓	6	1.330	↓	69	33		102	125	
	4600	Sink, floor mounted										
	4650	Exposed arm system										
	4700	Single heavy fixture	1 Plum	5	1.600	Ea.	110	40		150	180	
	4750	Single heavy sink with slab		5	1.600		155	40		195	230	
	4800	Back to back, standard fixtures		5	1.600		150	40		190	225	
	4850	Back to back, heavy fixtures		5	1.600		165	40		205	240	
	4900	Back to back, heavy sink with slab	↓	5	1.600	↓	165	40		205	240	
	4950	Exposed offset arm system										
	5000	Single heavy deep fixture	1 Plum	5	1.600	Ea.	115	40		155	185	
	5100	Plate type system										
	5200	With bearing jacks, single fixture	1 Plum	5	1.600	Ea.	85	40		125	150	
	5300	With exposed arms, single heavy fixture		5	1.600		120	40		160	190	
	5400	Wall mounted, exposed arms, single heavy fixture		5	1.600		58	40		98	120	
	6000	Urinal, floor mounted, 2" or 3" coupling, blowout type		6	1.330		74	33		107	130	
	6100	With fixture or hanger bolts, blowout or washout		6	1.330		53	33		86	105	
	6200	With bearing plate		6	1.330		59	33		92	115	
	6300	Wall mounted, plate type system	↓	6	1.330	↓	59	33		92	115	
	6980	Water closet, siphon jet										
	7000	Horizontal, adjustable, caulk										
	7040	Single, 4" pipe size	1 Plum	6	1.330	Ea.	100	33		133	160	
	7050	4" pipe size, paraplegic		6	1.330		100	33		133	160	
	7060	5" pipe size		6	1.330		130	33		163	190	
	7100	Double, 4" pipe size		5	1.600		185	40		225	260	
	7110	4" pipe size, paraplegic		5	1.600		185	40		225	260	
	7120	5" pipe size		5	1.600		245	40		285	330	
	7160	Horizontal, adjustable, extended, caulk										
	7180	Single, 4" pipe size	1 Plum	6	1.330	Ea.	130	33		163	190	
	7200	5" pipe size		6	1.330		175	33		208	240	
	7240	Double, 4" pipe size		5	1.600		220	40		260	300	
	7260	5" pipe size	↓	5	1.600	↓	280	40		320	365	
	7400	Vertical, adjustable, caulk or thread										
	7440	Single, 4" pipe size	1 Plum	6	1.330	Ea.	120	33		153	180	
	7460	5" pipe size	"	6	1.330	"	155	33		188	220	

151 | Pipe and Fittings

151 100 | Miscellaneous Fittings

			CREW	DAILY OUTPUT	MAN-HOURS	UNIT	BARE COSTS MAT.	LABOR	EQUIP.	TOTAL	TOTAL INCL O&P	
170	7480	6" pipe size	1 Plum	5	1.600	Ea.	175	40		215	250	170
	7520	Double, 4" pipe size		5	1.600		200	40		240	280	
	7540	5" pipe size		5	1.600		235	40		275	315	
	7560	6" pipe size		4	2		265	49		314	365	
	7600	Vertical, adjustable, extended, caulk										
	7620	Single, 4" pipe size	1 Plum	6	1.330	Ea.	175	33		208	240	
	7640	5" pipe size		6	1.330		195	33		228	265	
	7680	6" pipe size		5	1.600		300	40		340	390	
	7720	Double, 4" pipe size		5	1.600		270	40		310	355	
	7740	5" pipe size		5	1.600		320	40		360	410	
	7760	6" pipe size		4	2		420	49		469	535	
	7780	Water closet, blow out										
	7800	Vertical offset, caulk or thread										
	7820	Single, 4" pipe size	1 Plum	6	1.330	Ea.	100	33		133	160	
	7840	Double, 4" pipe size	"	5	1.600	"	175	40		215	250	
	7880	Vertical offset, extended, caulk										
	7900	Single, 4" pipe size	1 Plum	6	1.330	Ea.	135	33		168	195	
	7920	Double, 4" pipe size	"	5	1.600	"	190	40		230	270	
	7960	Vertical, for floor mounted back-outlet										
	7980	Single, 4" thread, 2" vent	1 Plum	6	1.330	Ea.	90	33		123	150	
	8000	Double, 4" thread, 2" vent	"	6	1.330	"	180	33		213	245	
	8040	Vertical, for floor mounted back-outlet, extended										
	8060	Single, 4" caulk, 2" vent	1 Plum	6	1.330	Ea.	120	33		153	180	
	8080	Double, 4" caulk, 2" vent	"	6	1.330	"	170	33		203	235	
	8200	Water closet, residential										
	8220	Vertical centerline, floor mount										
	8240	Single, 3" caulk, 2" or 3" vent	1 Plum	6	1.330	Ea.	58	33		91	115	
	8260	4" caulk, 2" or 4" vent		6	1.330		80	33		113	135	
	8280	3" copper sweat, 3" vent		6	1.330		63	33		96	120	
	8300	4" copper sweat, 4" vent		6	1.330		115	33		148	175	
	8400	Vertical offset, floor mount										
	8420	Single, 3" or 4" caulk, vent	1 Plum	4	2	Ea.	100	49		149	185	
	8440	3" or 4" copper sweat, vent		5	1.600		165	40		205	240	
	8460	Double, 3" or 4" caulk, vent		4	2		175	49		224	265	
	8480	3" or 4" copper sweat, vent		5	1.600		245	40		285	330	
	9000	Water cooler (electric), floor mounted										
	9100	Plate type with bearing plate, single	1 Plum	6	1.330	Ea.	56	33		89	110	
	9120	Plate type with bearing plate, double		4	2		80	49		129	160	
	9140	Plate type with bearing plate, back to back		4	2		76	49		125	155	
181	0010	**TRAPS**										181
	0030	Cast iron, service weight										
	0050	Long P trap, 2" pipe size										
	1100	12" long	Q-1	16	1	Ea.	6.70	22		28.70	40	
	1140	18" long	"	16	1	"	10.90	22		32.90	45	
	1180	Running trap, single hub, with vent										
	2080	3" pipe size, 3" vent	Q-1	14	1.140	Ea.	14.10	25		39.10	53	
	2120	4" pipe size, 4" vent	"	13	1.230		19.20	27		46.20	62	
	2140	5" pipe size, 4" vent	Q-2	11	2.180		32	50		82	110	
	2160	6" pipe size, 4" vent		10	2.400		55	55		110	145	
	2180	6" pipe size, 6" vent		8	3		60	69		129	170	
	2200	8" pipe size, 4" vent	Q-3	10	3.200		125	75		200	250	
	2220	8" pipe size, 6" vent	"	8	4		135	94		229	290	
	2300	For double hub, vent, add					10%	20%				
	2800	S trap, extra heavy weight, 2" pipe size	Q-1	15	1.070		15.35	24		39.35	52	
	2840	3" pipe size		14	1.140		26.25	25		51.25	67	
	2850	4" pipe size		13	1.230		44	27		71	89	
	3000	P trap, 2" pipe size		16	1		7.50	22		29.50	41	

151 | Pipe and Fittings

151 100 | Miscellaneous Fittings

			DAILY	MAN-		\multicolumn{4}{c}{BARE COSTS}	TOTAL
		CREW	OUTPUT	HOURS	UNIT	MAT.	LABOR	EQUIP.	TOTAL	INCL O&P
3040	3" pipe size	Q-1	14	1.140	Ea.	12.90	25		37.90	52
3060	4" pipe size	"	13	1.230		15.25	27		42.25	57
3080	5" pipe size	Q-2	18	1.330		26	31		57	74
3100	6" pipe size	"	17	1.410		35	33		68	87
3120	8" pipe size	Q-3	11	2.910		100	69		169	210
3130	10" pipe size	"	10	3.200		185	75		260	315
3150	P trap, no hub, 1-½" pipe size	Q-1	17	.941		4.05	21		25.05	36
3160	2" pipe size		16	1		4.05	22		26.05	37
3170	3" pipe size		14	1.140		9.20	25		34.20	48
3180	4" pipe size		13	1.230		15.75	27		42.75	58
3190	6" pipe size	Q-2	17	1.410		27	33		60	78
3350	Deep seal trap									
3400	1-¼" pipe size	Q-1	14	1.140	Ea.	9.05	25		34.05	48
3410	1-½" pipe size		14	1.140		9.05	25		34.05	48
3420	2" pipe size		14	1.140		9.45	25		34.45	48
3440	3" pipe size		12	1.330		15.10	30		45.10	61
3460	4" pipe size		11	1.450		19.25	32		51.25	69
3500	For trap primer connection, add					11.35			11.35	12.50
3540	For trap with floor cleanout, add					22.10	5%			
3580	For trap with adjustable cleanout, add					43			43	47
3800	Drum trap, 4" x 5", 1-½" tapping	Q-2	17	1.410	Ea.	12.50	33		45.50	62
3820	2" tapping	"	17	1.410		11.50	33		44.50	61
3840	For galvanized, add					100%				
4700	Copper, drainage, drum trap									
4800	3" x 5" solid, 1-½" pipe size	1 Plum	16	.500	Ea.	16.60	12.35		28.95	37
4840	3" x 6" swivel, 1-½" pipe size		16	.500		23	12.35		35.35	44
4900	4" x 8" swivel, 1-½" pipe size		13	.615		65	15.20		80.20	94
4920	2" pipe size		13	.615		72	15.20		87.20	100
5100	P trap, standard pattern									
5200	1-¼" pipe size	1 Plum	18	.444	Ea.	13.30	11		24.30	31
5240	1-½" pipe size		17	.471		15.55	11.60		27.15	34
5260	2" pipe size		15	.533		30	13.15		43.15	53
5280	3" pipe size		11	.727		39	17.95		56.95	70
5340	With cleanout and slip joint									
5360	1-¼" pipe size	1 Plum	18	.444	Ea.	13.65	11		24.65	31
5400	1-½" pipe size		17	.471		12.90	11.60		24.50	31
5420	2" pipe size		15	.533		24.50	13.15		37.65	47
5460	For swivel, add					2.80			2.80	3.08
5750	Chromed brass, tubular, P trap, without cleanout, 20 Ga.									
5800	1-¼" pipe size	1 Plum	18	.444	Ea.	6.25	11		17.25	23
5840	1-½" pipe size	"	17	.471	"	7.10	11.60		18.70	25
5900	With cleanout, 20 Ga.									
5940	1-¼" pipe size	1 Plum	18	.444	Ea.	9.80	11		20.80	27
6000	1-½" pipe size	"	17	.471	"	10.55	11.60		22.15	29
6350	S trap, without cleanout, 20 Ga.									
6400	1-¼" pipe size	1 Plum	18	.444	Ea.	10.85	11		21.85	28
6440	1-½" pipe size	"	17	.471	"	12	11.60		23.60	30
6550	With cleanout, 20 Ga.									
6600	1-¼" pipe size	1 Plum	18	.444	Ea.	16.20	11		27.20	34
6640	1-½" pipe size	"	17	.471		18.95	11.60		30.55	38
6660	Corrosion resistant, glass, P trap, 1-½" pipe size	Q-1	17	.941		25	21		46	59
6670	2" pipe size		16	1		33	22		55	69
6680	3" pipe size		14	1.140		68	25		93	110
6690	4" pipe size		13	1.230		105	27		132	155
6700	6" pipe size	Q-2	17	1.410		390	33		423	475
6710	ABS DWV P trap, solvent weld joint									
6720	1-½" pipe size	1 Plum	18	.444	Ea.	2.52	11		13.52	19.05
6730	2" pipe size	"	17	.471	"	3.75	11.60		15.35	21

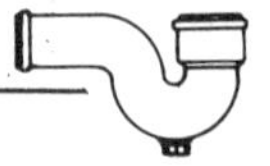

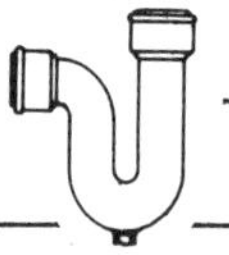

151 | Pipe and Fittings

151 100 | Miscellaneous Fittings

			CREW	DAILY OUTPUT	MAN-HOURS	UNIT	BARE COSTS MAT.	LABOR	EQUIP.	TOTAL	TOTAL INCL O&P	
181	6740	3" pipe size	1 Plum	15	.533	Ea.	21	13.15		34.15	43	181
	6750	4" pipe size		14	.571		42	14.10		56.10	67	
	6760	PP DWV, dilution trap, 1-½" pipe size		16	.500		110	12.35		122.35	140	
	6770	P trap, 1-½" pipe size		17	.471		16.70	11.60		28.30	36	
	6780	2" pipe size		16	.500		18.30	12.35		30.65	38	
	6790	3" pipe size		14	.571		45.30	14.10		59.40	71	
	6800	4" pipe size		13	.615		82.70	15.20		97.90	115	
	6810	Running trap, 1-½" pipe size		16	.500		14.50	12.35		26.85	34	
	6820	2" pipe size		15	.533		20	13.15		33.15	42	
	6830	S trap, 1-½" pipe size		16	.500		26.70	12.35		39.05	48	
	6840	2" pipe size		15	.533		36.70	13.15		49.85	60	
	6850	Universal trap, 1-½" pipe size		14	.571		23	14.10		37.10	46	
	6860	PVC DWV hub x hub, basin trap, 1-¼" pipe size		18	.444		3.50	11		14.50	20	
	6870	Sink P trap, 1-½" pipe size		18	.444		3	11		14	19.60	
	6880	Tubular S trap, 1-½" pipe size	↓	17	.471	↓	3.70	11.60		15.30	21	
	6890	PVC sch. 40 DWV, drum trap										
	6900	1-½" pipe size	1 Plum	16	.500	Ea.	5.75	12.35		18.10	25	
	6910	P trap, 1-½" pipe size		18	.444		1.85	11		12.85	18.30	
	6920	2" pipe size		17	.471		2	11.60		13.60	19.45	
	6930	3" pipe size		15	.533		7.50	13.15		20.65	28	
	6940	4" pipe size		14	.571		18.15	14.10		32.25	41	
	6950	P trap w/clean out, 1-½" pipe size		18	.444		3	11		14	19.60	
	6960	2" pipe size		17	.471		4.50	11.60		16.10	22	
	6970	P trap adjustable, 1-½" pipe size		17	.471		1.52	11.60		13.12	18.90	
	6980	P trap adj. w/union & cleanout, 1-½" pipe size		16	.500		2.25	12.35		14.60	21	
	6990	P trap fixture, 1-½" pipe size		18	.444		2.85	11		13.85	19.40	
	7000	Trap primer, flow through type, ½" diameter		24	.333		29	8.25		37.25	44	
	7100	With sediment strainer	↓	22	.364	↓	33	9		42	50	
	7450	Trap primer distribution unit										
	7500	2 opening	1 Plum	18	.444	Ea.	33	11		44	53	
	7540	3 opening		17	.471		35	11.60		46.60	56	
	7560	4 opening	↓	16	.500	↓	40	12.35		52.35	62	
	7850	Trap primer manifold										
	7900	2 outlet	1 Plum	18	.444	Ea.	46	11		57	67	
	7940	4 outlet		16	.500		71	12.35		83.35	96	
	7960	6 outlet		15	.533		90	13.15		103.15	120	
	7980	8 outlet	↓	13	.615	↓	112	15.20		127.20	145	
185	0010	**VACUUM BREAKERS** Hot or cold water										185
	1030	Anti-siphon, brass										
	1040	¼" size	1 Plum	24	.333	Ea.	12.45	8.25		20.70	26	
	1050	⅜" size		24	.333		12.45	8.25		20.70	26	
	1060	½" size		24	.333		14.10	8.25		22.35	28	
	1080	¾" size		20	.400		16.75	9.90		26.65	33	
	1100	1" size		19	.421		26	10.40		36.40	44	
	1120	1-¼" size		15	.533		43	13.15		56.15	67	
	1140	1-½" size		13	.615		51	15.20		66.20	79	
	1160	2" size		11	.727		79	17.95		96.95	115	
	1180	2-½" size		9	.889		230	22		252	285	
	1200	3" size	↓	7	1.140		305	28		333	375	
	1300	For polished chrome, (¼" thru 1"), add				↓	45%					
	1900	Vacuum relief, water service, bronze										
	2000	½" size	1 Plum	30	.267	Ea.	11.85	6.60		18.45	23	
	2040	¾" size	"	28	.286	"	14.85	7.05		21.90	27	
195	0010	**VENT FLASHING**										195
	1000	Aluminum with lead ring										
	1020	1-¼" pipe	1 Plum	20	.400	Ea.	4.35	9.90		14.25	19.45	
	1030	1-½" pipe	"	20	.400	"	4.35	9.90		14.25	19.45	

151 | Pipe and Fittings

151 100 | Miscellaneous Fittings

			CREW	DAILY OUTPUT	MAN-HOURS	UNIT	BARE COSTS MAT.	LABOR	EQUIP.	TOTAL	TOTAL INCL O&P	
195	1040	2" pipe	1 Plum	18	.444	Ea.	4.65	11		15.65	21	195
	1050	3" pipe		17	.471		5.25	11.60		16.85	23	
	1060	4" pipe	↓	16	.500	↓	6.35	12.35		18.70	25	
	1350	Copper with neoprene ring										
	1400	1-¼" pipe	1 Plum	20	.400	Ea.	13.40	9.90		23.30	29	
	1430	1-½" pipe		20	.400		13.40	9.90		23.30	29	
	1440	2" pipe		18	.444		14.15	11		25.15	32	
	1450	3" pipe		17	.471		16.60	11.60		28.20	36	
	1460	4" pipe	↓	16	.500	↓	18.30	12.35		30.65	38	
	2000	Galvanized with neoprene ring										
	2020	1-¼" pipe	1 Plum	20	.400	Ea.	3.85	9.90		13.75	18.90	
	2030	1-½" pipe		20	.400		3.85	9.90		13.75	18.90	
	2040	2" pipe		18	.444		4.05	11		15.05	21	
	2050	3" pipe		17	.471		4.45	11.60		16.05	22	
	2060	4" pipe	↓	16	.500	↓	5.70	12.35		18.05	25	
	2980	Neoprene, one piece										
	3000	1-¼" pipe	1 Plum	24	.333	Ea.	3.65	8.25		11.90	16.25	
	3030	1-½" pipe		24	.333		3.65	8.25		11.90	16.25	
	3040	2" pipe		23	.348		3.85	8.60		12.45	17	
	3050	3" pipe		21	.381		4.60	9.40		14	19	
	3060	4" pipe	↓	20	.400	↓	5.80	9.90		15.70	21	
200	0010	**PIPING** See also divisions 026 & 027 for sitework										200
	1000	Add to labor for elevated installation										
	1080	10' to 15' high						10%				
	1100	15' to 20' high						20%				
	1120	20' to 25' high						25%				
	1140	25' to 30' high						35%				
	1160	30' to 35' high						40%				
	1180	35' to 40' high						50%				
	1200	Over 40' high						55%				

151 210 | Aluminum Pipe

			CREW	DAILY OUTPUT	MAN-HOURS	UNIT	MAT.	LABOR	EQUIP.	TOTAL	INCL O&P	
215	0010	**PIPE, ALUMINUM** Prices for 1 to 2-½ ton quantity										215
	0850	For 5 or more tons, deduct				L.F.	10%					
	0900	Does not include hangers or fittings										
	0980	Schedule 5, type 6063-T6										
	1000	1-¼" diameter				L.F.	1.09			1.09	1.20	
	1100	1-½" diameter					1.25			1.25	1.38	
	1120	2" diameter					1.57			1.57	1.73	
	1140	2-½" diameter					2.28			2.28	2.51	
	1160	3" diameter					2.75			2.75	3.03	
	1180	4" diameter					3.71			3.71	4.08	
	1200	5" diameter					5.80			5.80	6.40	
	1220	6" diameter					7.35			7.35	8.10	
	2000	Schedule 10, type 6063-T6, ¾" diameter					1.28			1.28	1.41	
	2100	1" diameter					1.25			1.25	1.38	
	2120	1-¼" diameter					1.60			1.60	1.76	
	2140	1-½" diameter					1.86			1.86	2.05	
	2160	2" diameter					2.40			2.40	2.64	
	2180	2-½" diameter					3.14			3.14	3.45	
	2200	3" diameter					3.76			3.76	4.14	
	2220	4" diameter					4.90			4.90	5.40	
	2240	5" diameter					6.85			6.85	7.55	
	2260	6" diameter					8.85			8.85	9.75	
	3000	Schedule 40, type 6063-T6, 1" diameter					1.51			1.51	1.66	
	3100	1-¼" diameter					2			2	2.20	

151 | Pipe and Fittings

151 210	Aluminum Pipe	CREW	DAILY OUTPUT	MAN-HOURS	UNIT	BARE COSTS MAT.	LABOR	EQUIP.	TOTAL	TOTAL INCL O&P
3120	1-½" diameter				L.F.	2.37			2.37	2.61
3140	2" diameter					3.17			3.17	3.49
3160	2-½" diameter					5.05			5.05	5.55
3180	3" diameter					6.55			6.55	7.20
3200	3-½" diameter					7.80			7.80	8.60
3220	4" diameter					9.30			9.30	10.25
3240	5" diameter					12.95			12.95	14.25
3260	6" diameter					18			18	19.80
3280	8" diameter					27			27	30
3300	10" diameter					41			41	45
3320	12" diameter				↓	84			84	92
3980	Type 6061-T6									
4000	¼" diameter				L.F.	.83			.83	.91
4100	⅜" diameter					1.09			1.09	1.20
4120	½" diameter					1.43			1.43	1.57
4140	¾" diameter					1.63			1.63	1.79
4160	1" diameter					1.64			1.64	1.80
4180	1-¼" diameter					2.12			2.12	2.33
4200	1-½" diameter					2.55			2.55	2.81
4220	2" diameter					3.42			3.42	3.76
4240	2-½" diameter					5.45			5.45	6
4260	3" diameter					7.15			7.15	7.85
4280	3-½" diameter					8.55			8.55	9.40
4300	4" diameter					10.10			10.10	11.10
4320	5" diameter					13.79			13.79	15.15
4340	6" diameter					19.45			19.45	21
4360	8" diameter					30			30	33
4380	10" diameter					46			46	51
4400	12" diameter					90			90	99
4420	14" diameter					125			125	140
4440	16" diameter				↓	150			150	165
6000	Schedule 80, type 6063-T6									
6020	1" diameter				L.F.	1.92			1.92	2.11
6100	1-¼" diameter					2.61			2.61	2.87
6120	1-½" diameter					3.16			3.16	3.48
6140	2" diameter					4.38			4.38	4.82
6160	2-½" diameter					6.70			6.70	7.35
6180	3" diameter					8.85			8.85	9.75
6200	3-½" diameter					10.75			10.75	11.85
6220	4" diameter					12.95			12.95	14.25
6240	5" diameter					16.85			16.85	18.55
6260	6" diameter					27			27	30
6280	8" diameter					41			41	45
6300	10" diameter					64			64	70
6320	12" diameter				↓	135			135	150
6980	Type 6061-T6									
7000	1" diameter				L.F.	2.12			2.12	2.33
7100	1-¼" diameter					2.82			2.82	3.10
7120	1-½" diameter					3.39			3.39	3.73
7140	2" diameter					4.73			4.73	5.20
7160	2-½" diameter					7.20			7.20	7.90
7180	3" diameter					9.65			9.65	10.60
7200	3-½" diameter					11.75			11.75	12.95
7220	4" diameter					14.10			14.10	15.50
7240	5" diameter					20			20	22
7260	6" diameter					30			30	33
7280	8" diameter					46			46	51
7300	10" diameter				↓	69			69	76

151 | Pipe and Fittings

151 210 | Aluminum Pipe

			CREW	DAILY OUTPUT	MAN-HOURS	UNIT	BARE COSTS MAT.	LABOR	EQUIP.	TOTAL	TOTAL INCL O&P	
215	7320	12" diameter				L.F.	140			140	155	215

151 250 | Brass Pipe

			CREW	DAILY OUTPUT	MAN-HOURS	UNIT	MAT.	LABOR	EQUIP.	TOTAL	INCL O&P	
251	0010	**PIPE, BRASS** Plain end,										251
	0900	Field threaded, coupling & clevis hanger 10' O.C.										
	0920	Regular weight										
	0980	⅛" diameter	1 Plum	62	.129	L.F.	1.39	3.19		4.58	6.25	
	1000	¼" diameter		57	.140		1.87	3.47		5.34	7.20	
	1100	⅜" diameter		52	.154		2.34	3.80		6.14	8.20	
	1120	½" diameter		48	.167		3.03	4.12		7.15	9.45	
	1140	¾" diameter		46	.174		4.13	4.30		8.43	10.90	
	1160	1" diameter	↓	43	.186		5.86	4.60		10.46	13.25	
	1180	1-¼" diameter	Q-1	72	.222		8.78	4.94		13.72	17	
	1200	1-½" diameter		65	.246		10.30	5.45		15.75	19.45	
	1220	2" diameter		53	.302		13.57	6.70		20.27	25	
	1240	2-½" diameter		41	.390		20.25	8.70		28.95	35	
	1260	3" diameter	↓	31	.516		28.83	11.45		40.28	49	
	1280	3-½" diameter	Q-2	39	.615		46.29	14.20		60.49	72	
	1300	4" diameter		37	.649		46.36	14.95		61.31	73	
	1320	5" diameter		31	.774		70.92	17.85		88.77	105	
	1340	6" diameter		24	1		92.51	23		115.51	135	
	1360	8" diameter	↓	20	1.200	↓	190.28	28		218.28	250	
	1930	To delete coupling & hanger, subtract										
	1940	⅛" diam. to ½" diam.					14%	46%				
	1950	¾" diam. to 1-½" diam.					8%	47%				
	1960	2" diam. to 5" diam.					10%	37%				
	1970	6" diam. to 8" diam.					13%	29%				
	2000	Extra heavy weight										
	2100	⅛" diameter	1 Plum	58	.138	L.F.	1.78	3.41		5.19	7	
	2120	¼" diameter		55	.145		2.53	3.59		6.12	8.10	
	2140	⅜" diameter		50	.160		3.13	3.95		7.08	9.30	
	2160	½" diameter		46	.174		4.28	4.30		8.58	11.10	
	2180	¾" diameter		44	.182		5.83	4.49		10.32	13.10	
	2200	1" diameter	↓	41	.195		8.51	4.82		13.33	16.50	
	2220	1-¼" diameter	Q-1	69	.232		11.83	5.15		16.98	21	
	2240	1-½" diameter		62	.258		14.25	5.75		20	24	
	2260	2" diameter		51	.314		19.17	6.95		26.12	31	
	2280	2-½" diameter		39	.410		28.75	9.10		37.85	45	
	2300	3" diameter	↓	30	.533		39.68	11.85		51.53	61	
	2320	3-½" diameter	Q-2	39	.615		61.29	14.20		75.49	88	
	2340	4" diameter	"	35	.686		62.36	15.80		78.16	92	
	2950	To delete coupling & hanger, subtract										
	2960	⅛" diam. to ½" diam.					16%	46%				
	2970	¾" diam. to 1-½" diam.					10%	47%				
	2980	2" diam. to 4" diam.					12%	37%				
258	0010	**PIPE, BRASS, FITTINGS** Rough bronze, threaded										258
	1000	Standard wt., 90° Elbow										
	1040	⅛"	1 Plum	13	.615	Ea.	1.75	15.20		16.95	24	
	1060	¼"		13	.615		1.75	15.20		16.95	24	
	1080	⅜"		13	.615		1.75	15.20		16.95	24	
	1100	½"		12	.667		2.13	16.45		18.58	27	
	1120	¾"		11	.727		3.13	17.95		21.08	30	
	1140	1"	↓	10	.800		4.38	19.75		24.13	34	
	1160	1-¼"	Q-1	17	.941		7.80	21		28.80	40	
	1180	1-½"		16	1		9.25	22		31.25	43	
	1200	2"		14	1.140		15.95	25		40.95	55	
	1220	2-½"		11	1.450	↓	36	32		68	88	

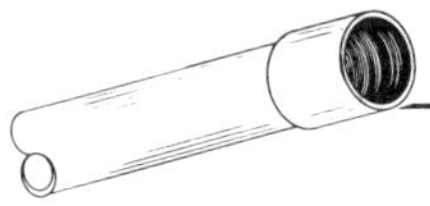

151 | Pipe and Fittings

151 250 | Brass Pipe

		CREW	DAILY OUTPUT	MAN-HOURS	UNIT	BARE COSTS MAT.	BARE COSTS LABOR	BARE COSTS EQUIP.	BARE COSTS TOTAL	TOTAL INCL O&P
1240	3"	Q-1	8	2	Ea.	56	44		100	130
1260	4"	Q-2	11	2.180		125	50		175	210
1280	5"		8	3		265	69		334	395
1300	6"		7	3.430		365	79		444	520
1320	8"	↓	5	4.800		720	110		830	955
1500	45° Elbow, ⅛"	1 Plum	13	.615		2.25	15.20		17.45	25
1540	¼"		13	.615		2.25	15.20		17.45	25
1560	⅜"		13	.615		2.25	15.20		17.45	25
1580	½"		12	.667		2.25	16.45		18.70	27
1600	¾"		11	.727		3.75	17.95		21.70	31
1620	1"	↓	10	.800		6.50	19.75		26.25	36
1640	1-¼"	Q-1	17	.941		10	21		31	42
1660	1-½"		16	1		12.45	22		34.45	47
1680	2"		14	1.140		12.80	25		37.80	52
1700	2-½"		11	1.450		40	32		72	92
1720	3"	↓	8	2		62.50	44		106.50	135
1740	4"	Q-2	11	2.180		145	50		195	235
1760	5"		8	3		270	69		339	400
1780	6"	↓	7	3.430		400	79		479	555
2000	Tee, ⅛"	1 Plum	9	.889		2.25	22		24.25	35
2040	¼"		9	.889		2.25	22		24.25	35
2060	⅜"		9	.889		2.25	22		24.25	35
2080	½"		8	1		2.25	25		27.25	39
2100	¾"		7	1.140		3.88	28		31.88	46
2120	1"	↓	6	1.330		6.90	33		39.90	56
2140	1-¼"	Q-1	10	1.600		12.50	36		48.50	67
2160	1-½"		9	1.780		13.50	40		53.50	73
2180	2"		8	2		17.65	44		61.65	85
2200	2-½"		7	2.290		51	51		102	130
2220	3"	↓	5	3.200		75	71		146	190
2240	4"	Q-2	7	3.430		175	79		254	310
2260	5"		5	4.800		300	110		410	495
2280	6"	↓	4	6		515	140		655	770
2500	Coupling, ⅛"	1 Plum	26	.308		2.24	7.60		9.84	13.75
2540	¼"		22	.364		2.24	9		11.24	15.80
2560	⅜"		18	.444		2.24	11		13.24	18.75
2580	½"		15	.533		2.24	13.15		15.39	22
2600	¾"		14	.571		3.15	14.10		17.25	24
2620	1"	↓	13	.615		5.40	15.20		20.60	28
2640	1-¼"	Q-1	22	.727		8.95	16.15		25.10	34
2660	1-½"		20	.800		11.65	17.80		29.45	39
2680	2"		18	.889		19.25	19.75		39	50
2700	2-½"		14	1.140		31	25		56	72
2720	3"	↓	10	1.600		44	36		80	100
2740	4"	Q-2	12	2		90	46		136	165
2760	5"		10	2.400		155	55		210	255
2780	6"		9	2.670		220	61		281	335
2790	8"	↓	8	3	↓	355	69		424	495
3000	Union, 150 lb									
3020	⅛"	1 Plum	12	.667	Ea.	7.20	16.45		23.65	32
3040	¼"		12	.667		7.20	16.45		23.65	32
3060	⅜"		12	.667		7.20	16.45		23.65	32
3080	½"		11	.727		7.20	17.95		25.15	35
3100	¾"		10	.800		9.90	19.75		29.65	40
3120	1"	↓	9	.889		13	22		35	47
3140	1-¼"	Q-1	16	1		18.80	22		40.80	54
3160	1-½"		15	1.070		22.40	24		46.40	60
3180	2"	↓	13	1.230	↓	35	27		62	79

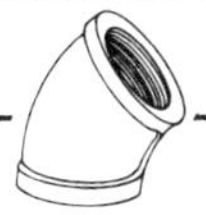

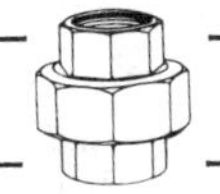

151 | Pipe and Fittings

151 250 | Brass Pipe

			CREW	DAILY OUTPUT	MAN-HOURS	UNIT	BARE COSTS MAT.	BARE COSTS LABOR	BARE COSTS EQUIP.	BARE COSTS TOTAL	TOTAL INCL O&P
3200	2-½"		Q-1	10	1.600	Ea.	90	36		126	150
3220	3"		"	7	2.290		140	51		191	230
3240	4"		Q-2	10	2.400	↓	305	55		360	420
5000	Extra heavy, 90° Elbow										
5040	⅛"		1 Plum	13	.615	Ea.	4.19	15.20		19.39	27
5060	¼"			13	.615		4.19	15.20		19.39	27
5080	⅜"			13	.615		4.19	15.20		19.39	27
5100	½"			12	.667		6.70	16.45		23.15	32
5120	¾"			11	.727		9.05	17.95		27	37
5140	1"		↓	10	.800		13.45	19.75		33.20	44
5160	1-¼"		Q-1	17	.941		24	21		45	57
5180	1-½"			16	1		36	22		58	73
5200	2"			14	1.140		60	25		85	105
5220	2-½"			11	1.450		98	32		130	155
5240	3"		↓	8	2		140	44		184	220
5260	4"		Q-2	11	2.180		305	50		355	410
5500	45° Elbow, ⅛"		1 Plum	13	.615		5	15.20		20.20	28
5540	¼"			13	.615		5	15.20		20.20	28
5560	⅜"			13	.615		5	15.20		20.20	28
5580	½"			12	.667		6.95	16.45		23.40	32
5600	¾"			11	.727		9.55	17.95		27.50	37
5620	1"		↓	10	.800		16.70	19.75		36.45	48
5640	1-¼"		Q-1	17	.941		26	21		47	60
5660	1-½"			16	1		39	22		61	76
5680	2"			14	1.140		63	25		88	105
5700	2-½"			11	1.450		100	32		132	160
5720	3"		↓	8	2		170	44		214	255
5740	4"		Q-2	11	2.180		300	50		350	405
6000	Tee, ⅛"		1 Plum	9	.889		7.20	22		29.20	41
6040	¼"			9	.889		7.20	22		29.20	41
6060	⅜"			9	.889		7.20	22		29.20	41
6080	½"			8	1		8.05	25		33.05	46
6100	¾"			7	1.140		13.15	28		41.15	56
6120	1"			6	1.330		17.95	33		50.95	69
6140	1-¼"		Q-1	10	1.600		34	36		70	90
6160	1-½"			9	1.780		49	40		89	115
6180	2"			8	2		70	44		114	145
6200	2-½"			7	2.290		123	51		174	210
6220	3"		↓	5	3.200		195	71		266	320
6240	4"		Q-2	7	3.430		250	79		329	390
6500	Coupling, ⅛"		1 Plum	26	.308		5.60	7.60		13.20	17.45
6540	¼"			22	.364		5.60	9		14.60	19.50
6560	⅜"			18	.444		5.60	11		16.60	22
6580	½"			15	.533		7.90	13.15		21.05	28
6600	¾"			14	.571		9.80	14.10		23.90	32
6620	1"			13	.615		15.05	15.20		30.25	39
6640	1-¼"		Q-1	22	.727		22	16.15		38.15	48
6660	1-½"			20	.800		29	17.80		46.80	58
6680	2"			18	.889		45	19.75		64.75	79
6700	2-½"			14	1.140		74	25		99	120
6720	3"			10	1.600		105	36		141	170
6730	3-½"		↓	8	2		155	44		199	235
6740	4"		Q-2	12	2	↓	155	46		201	240
7000	Union, 300 lb										
7020	⅛"		1 Plum	12	.667	Ea.	22	16.45		38.45	49
7040	¼"			12	.667		22	16.45		38.45	49
7060	⅜"			12	.667		22	16.45		38.45	49
7080	½"		↓	11	.727		25	17.95		42.95	54

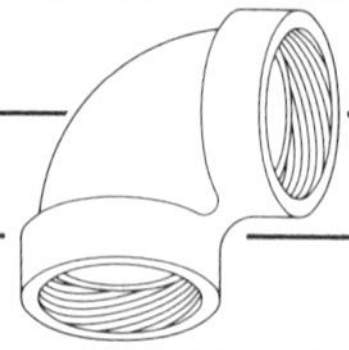

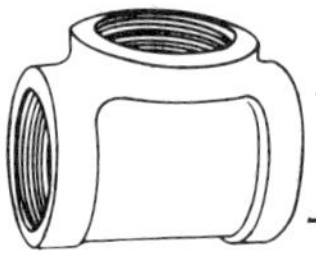

151 | Pipe and Fittings

151 250 | Brass Pipe

			CREW	DAILY OUTPUT	MAN-HOURS	UNIT	BARE COSTS MAT.	LABOR	EQUIP.	TOTAL	TOTAL INCL O&P	
258	7100	¾"	1 Plum	10	.800	Ea.	35	19.75		54.75	68	258
	7120	1"	"	9	.889		49	22		71	86	
	7140	1-¼"	Q-1	16	1		69	22		91	110	
	7160	1-½"		15	1.070		85	24		109	130	
	7180	2"	↓	13	1.230	↓	125	27		152	180	

151 300 | Cast Iron Pipe

			CREW	DAILY OUTPUT	MAN-HOURS	UNIT	MAT.	LABOR	EQUIP.	TOTAL	INCL O&P	
301	0010	**PIPE, CAST IRON** Soil, on hangers 5' O.C.										301
	0020	Single hub, service wt., lead & oakum joints 10' O.C.										
	2120	2" diameter	Q-1	63	.254	L.F.	2.20	5.65		7.85	10.80	
	2140	3" diameter		60	.267		3.11	5.95		9.06	12.20	
	2160	4" diameter	↓	55	.291		4.02	6.45		10.47	14	
	2180	5" diameter	Q-2	76	.316		5.44	7.30		12.74	16.80	
	2200	6" diameter	"	73	.329		6.52	7.60		14.12	18.40	
	2220	8" diameter	Q-3	59	.542		10.76	12.80		23.56	31	
	2240	10" diameter		54	.593		16.93	14		30.93	39	
	2260	12" diameter		48	.667		24.55	15.75		40.30	50	
	2261	15" diameter	↓	40	.800		41	18.85		59.85	73	
	2320	For service weight, double hub, add					44%					
	2340	For extra heavy, single hub, add					47%	4%				
	2360	For extra heavy, double hub, add					95%	4%				
	2400	Lead for caulking				Lb.	.75			.75	.83	
	2420	Oakum for caulking				"	1.82			1.82	2	
	2960	To delete hangers, subtract										
	2970	2" diam. to 4" diam.					16%	19%				
	2980	5" diam. to 8" diam.					14%	14%				
	2990	10" diam. to 15" diam.					13%	19%				
	3000	Single hub, service wt, push-on gasket joints 10' O.C.										
	3010	2" diameter	Q-1	66	.242	L.F.	2.36	5.40		7.76	10.60	
	3020	3" diameter		63	.254		3.32	5.65		8.97	12	
	3030	4" diameter	↓	57	.281		4.28	6.25		10.53	13.95	
	3040	5" diameter	Q-2	79	.304		5.84	7		12.84	16.80	
	3050	6" diameter	"	75	.320		6.94	7.40		14.34	18.55	
	3060	8" diameter	Q-3	62	.516		11.69	12.20		23.89	31	
	3070	10" diameter		56	.571		18.37	13.50		31.87	40	
	3080	12" diameter	↓	49	.653	↓	26.37	15.40		41.77	52	
	3100	For service weight, double hub, add					10%					
	3110	For extra heavy, single hub, add					25%	4%				
	3120	For extra heavy, double hub, add					20%	4%				
	3130	To delete hangers, subtract										
	3140	2" diam. to 4" diam.					12%	21%				
	3150	5" diam. to 8" diam.					10%	16%				
	3160	10" diam. to 12" diam.					9%	21%				
	4000	No hub, couplings 10' O.C.										
	4100	1-½" diameter	Q-1	71	.225	L.F.	2.74	5		7.74	10.45	
	4120	2" diameter		67	.239		2.84	5.30		8.14	11	
	4140	3" diameter		64	.250		3.73	5.55		9.28	12.35	
	4160	4" diameter	↓	58	.276		5.07	6.15		11.22	14.70	
	4180	5" diameter	Q-2	83	.289		7.13	6.65		13.78	17.75	
	4200	6" diameter	"	79	.304		8.97	7		15.97	20	
	4220	8" diameter	Q-3	69	.464		14.71	10.95		25.66	32	
	4240	10" diameter	"	61	.525	↓	23.73	12.40		36.13	44	
	4280	To delete hangers, subtract										
	4290	1-½" diam. to 6" diam.					22%	47%				
	4300	8" diam. to 10" diam.					21%	44%				
320	0010	**PIPE, CAST IRON, FITTINGS,** Soil										320
	0040	Hub and spigot, service weight, lead & oakum joints										

151 | Pipe and Fittings

151 300 | Cast Iron Pipe

		CREW	DAILY OUTPUT	MAN-HOURS	UNIT	BARE COSTS MAT.	LABOR	EQUIP.	TOTAL	TOTAL INCL O&P	
320	0080	¼ Bend, 2"	Q-1	16	1	Ea.	3.20	22		25.20	37	320
	0120	3"		14	1.140		5.90	25		30.90	44	
	0140	4"		13	1.230		8.70	27		35.70	50	
	0160	5"	Q-2	18	1.330		11.90	31		42.90	59	
	0180	6"	"	17	1.410		15.05	33		48.05	65	
	0200	8"	Q-3	11	2.910		46.25	69		115.25	155	
	0220	10"		10	3.200		68	75		143	185	
	0240	12"		9	3.560		88	84		172	220	
	0241	15"		7	4.570		250	110		360	435	
	0250	Closet bend, 3" diameter with ring 10" x 16"	Q-1	14	1.140		24	25		49	64	
	0260	16"x16"		12	1.330		27	30		57	74	
	0270	Closet bend, 4" diameter, 1" x 4" ring, 6" x 16"		13	1.230		27	27		54	70	
	0280	8" x 16"		13	1.230		25	27		52	68	
	0290	10" x 12"		12	1.330		23	30		53	69	
	0300	10" x 18"		11	1.450		31	32		63	82	
	0310	12" x 16"		11	1.450		28	32		60	79	
	0330	16" x 16"		10	1.600		32	36		68	88	
	0340	⅛ Bend, 2"		16	1		2.46	22		24.46	36	
	0350	3"		14	1.140		5.05	25		30.05	43	
	0360	4"		13	1.230		7	27		34	48	
	0380	5"	Q-2	18	1.330		9.55	31		40.55	56	
	0400	6"	"	17	1.410		11.80	33		44.80	61	
	0420	8"	Q-3	11	2.910		34	69		103	140	
	0440	10"		10	3.200		53	75		128	170	
	0460	12"		9	3.560		85	84		169	220	
	0461	15"		7	4.570		150	110		260	325	
	0500	Sanitary Tee, 2"	Q-1	10	1.600		5.50	36		41.50	59	
	0540	3"		9	1.780		10.25	40		50.25	70	
	0620	4"		8	2		12.25	44		56.25	79	
	0700	5"	Q-2	12	2		22	46		68	93	
	0800	6"	"	11	2.180		27	50		77	105	
	0880	8"	Q-3	7	4.570		70	110		180	235	
	0881	10"		7	4.570		120	110		230	290	
	0882	12"		6	5.330		170	125		295	375	
	0883	15"		4	8		295	190		485	605	
	0884	Sanitary Tee, reducing										
	0885	3" x 2"	Q-1	8	2	Ea.	9.60	44		53.60	77	
	0886	4" x 2"	"	9	1.780		11.40	40		51.40	71	
	0887	5" x 3"	Q-2	9	2.670		17.95	61		78.95	110	
	0888	6" x 3"	"	8	3		22	69		91	125	
	0889	8" x 5"	Q-3	9	3.560		55	84		139	185	
	0890	10" x 6"		8	4		96	94		190	245	
	0891	12" x 8"		7	4.570		160	110		270	335	
	0892	15" x 10"		5	6.400		255	150		405	505	
	1000	Tee, 2"	Q-1	10	1.600		6.70	36		42.70	60	
	1060	3"		9	1.780		10.50	40		50.50	70	
	1120	4"		8	2		14.25	44		58.25	82	
	1200	5"	Q-2	12	2		22	46		68	93	
	1300	6"	"	11	2.180		28	50		78	105	
	1380	8"	Q-3	7	4.570		66	110		176	235	
	1400	Combination Y and ⅛ Bend										
	1420	2"	Q-1	10	1.600	Ea.	7.75	36		43.75	61	
	1460	3"		9	1.780		11.60	40		51.60	71	
	1520	4"		8	2		16	44		60	84	
	1540	5"	Q-2	12	2		30	46		76	100	
	1560	6"		11	2.180		37	50		87	115	
	1580	8"		7	3.430		91	79		170	215	
	1600	Double Y, 2"	Q-1	8	2		8.40	44		52.40	75	

151 | Pipe and Fittings

151 300 | Cast Iron Pipe

			CREW	DAILY OUTPUT	MAN-HOURS	UNIT	BARE COSTS MAT.	LABOR	EQUIP.	TOTAL	TOTAL INCL O&P
320	1610	3"	Q-1	7	2.290	Ea.	14.15	51		65.15	91
	1620	4"	"	6.50	2.460		21	55		76	105
	1630	5"	Q-2	9	2.670		30	61		91	125
	1640	6"	"	8	3		45	69		114	150
	1650	8"	Q-3	5.50	5.820		110	135		245	325
	1660	10"		5	6.400		155	150		305	395
	1670	12"		4.50	7.110		223	170		393	495
	1740	Reducer, 3" x 2"	Q-1	15	1.070		4.05	24		28.05	40
	1750	4" x 2"		14.50	1.100		4.20	25		29.20	41
	1760	4" x 3"		14	1.140		5.45	25		30.45	44
	1770	5" x 2"		14	1.140		6.50	25		31.50	45
	1780	5" x 3"		13.50	1.190		6.50	26		32.50	46
	1790	5" x 4"		13	1.230		6.70	27		33.70	48
	1800	6" x 2"		13.50	1.190		7.70	26		33.70	48
	1810	6" x 3"		13	1.230		8.75	27		35.75	50
	1840	6" x 5"		11	1.450		9.80	32		41.80	59
	1860	8" x 2"	Q-2	14	1.710		17.30	40		57.30	78
	1880	8" x 3"		13	1.850		17.50	43		60.50	82
	1900	8" x 4"		13	1.850		18	43		61	83
	1920	8" x 5"		12	2		18.15	46		64.15	88
	1940	8" x 6"		12	2		18.35	46		64.35	89
	1960	Increaser, 2" x 3"	Q-1	15	1.070		5.50	24		29.50	41
	1980	2" x 4"		14	1.140		7.40	25		32.40	46
	2000	2" x 5"		13	1.230		9.30	27		36.30	51
	2020	3" x 4"		13	1.230		7.95	27		34.95	49
	2040	3" x 5"		13	1.230		8.60	27		35.60	50
	2060	3" x 6"		12	1.330		10.10	30		40.10	55
	2070	4" x 5"		13	1.230		9.75	27		36.75	51
	2080	4" x 6"		12	1.330		12.70	30		42.70	58
	2090	4" x 8"	Q-2	13	1.850		26	43		69	92
	2100	5" x 6"	Q-1	11	1.450		18.65	32		50.65	68
	2110	5" x 8"	Q-2	12	2		29	46		75	100
	2120	6" x 8"		12	2		31	46		77	105
	2130	6" x 10"		8	3		43	69		112	150
	2140	8" x 10"		6.50	3.690		52	85		137	185
	2150	10" x 12"		5.50	4.360		80	100		180	235
	2500	Y, 2"	Q-1	10	1.600		5.55	36		41.55	59
	2510	3"		9	1.780		10.30	40		50.30	70
	2520	4"		8	2		13.20	44		57.20	80
	2530	5"	Q-2	12	2		23	46		69	94
	2540	6"	"	11	2.180		31	50		81	110
	2550	8"	Q-3	7	4.570		77	110		187	245
	2560	10"		6	5.330		118	125		243	315
	2570	12"		5	6.400		175	150		325	415
	3000	For extra heavy, add					33%	4%			
	3600	Hub and spigot, service weight gasket joint									
	3605	Note: gaskets and joint labor have									
	3606	Been included with all listed fittings.									
	3610	¼ bend, 2"	Q-1	20	.800	Ea.	4.55	17.80		22.35	31
	3620	3"		17	.941		7.45	21		28.45	39
	3630	4"		15	1.070		11.05	24		35.05	47
	3640	5"	Q-2	21	1.140		14.75	26		40.75	55
	3650	6"	"	19	1.260		18	29		47	63
	3660	8"	Q-3	12	2.670		46	63		109	145
	3670	10"		11	2.910		71	69		140	180
	3680	12"		10	3.200		96	75		171	220
	3700	Closet bend, 3" diameter with ring 10" x 16"	Q-1	17	.941		24.50	21		45.50	58
	3710	16" x 16"	"	15	1.070		27.15	24		51.15	65

151 | Pipe and Fittings

151 300 | Cast Iron Pipe

			CREW	DAILY OUTPUT	MAN-HOURS	UNIT	BARE COSTS MAT.	LABOR	EQUIP.	TOTAL	TOTAL INCL O&P	
320	3730	Closet bend, 4" diameter, 1" x 4" ring, 6" x 16"	Q-1	15	1.070	Ea.	28	24		52	66	320
	3740	8" x 16"		15	1.070		25.50	24		49.50	63	
	3750	10" x 12"		14	1.140		24.55	25		49.55	65	
	3760	10" x 18"		13	1.230		31.50	27		58.50	75	
	3770	12" x 16"		13	1.230		28	27		55	71	
	3780	16" x 16"		12	1.330		32.25	30		62.25	79	
	3800	⅛ bend, 2"		20	.800		4.10	17.80		21.90	31	
	3810	3"		17	.941		6.05	21		27.05	38	
	3820	4"		15	1.070		8.70	24		32.70	45	
	3830	5"	Q-2	21	1.140		12.15	26		38.15	52	
	3840	6"	"	19	1.260		14.15	29		43.15	59	
	3850	8"	Q-3	12	2.670		36.50	63		99.50	135	
	3860	10"		11	2.910		54	69		123	160	
	3870	12"		10	3.200		89	75		164	210	
	3900	Sanitary Tee, 2"	Q-1	12	1.330		7.60	30		37.60	52	
	3910	3"		10	1.600		13.50	36		49.50	68	
	3920	4"		9	1.780		16	40		56	76	
	3930	5"	Q-2	13	1.850		30.25	43		73.25	96	
	3940	6"	"	11	2.180		44	50		94	125	
	3950	8"	Q-3	8	4		93	94		187	240	
	3980	Tee, 2"	Q-1	12	1.330		7.85	30		37.85	53	
	3990	3"		10	1.600		13.70	36		49.70	68	
	4000	4"		9	1.780		17.50	40		57.50	78	
	4010	5"	Q-2	13	1.850		27.25	43		70.25	93	
	4020	6"	"	11	2.180		33	50		83	110	
	4030	8"	Q-3	8	4		67	94		161	215	
	4060	Combination Y and ⅛ bend										
	4070	2"	Q-1	12	1.330	Ea.	9.65	30		39.65	55	
	4080	3"		10	1.600		16.15	36		52.15	71	
	4090	4"		9	1.780		21	40		61	82	
	4100	5"	Q-2	13	1.850		36	43		79	105	
	4110	6"	"	11	2.180		41	50		91	120	
	4120	8"	Q-3	8	4		92	94		186	240	
	4160	Double Y, 2"	Q-1	10	1.600		12.40	36		48.40	66	
	4170	3"		8	2		19	44		63	87	
	4180	4"		7	2.290		24	51		75	100	
	4190	5"	Q-2	10	2.400		36	55		91	120	
	4200	6"	"	9	2.670		47	61		108	145	
	4210	8"	Q-3	6	5.330		115	125		240	315	
	4220	10"		5	6.400		175	150		325	415	
	4230	12"		4.50	7.110		250	170		420	525	
	4260	Reducer, 3" x 2"	Q-1	17	.941		4.55	21		25.55	36	
	4270	4" x 2"		16.50	.970		5.65	22		27.65	38	
	4280	4" x 3"		16	1		8	22		30	42	
	4290	5" x 2"		16	1		8.05	22		30.05	42	
	4300	5" x 3"		15.50	1.030		8.60	23		31.60	44	
	4310	5" x 4"		15	1.070		9.15	24		33.15	45	
	4320	6" x 2"		15.50	1.030		8.85	23		31.85	44	
	4330	6" x 3"		15	1.070		11	24		35	47	
	4340	6" x 5"		13	1.230		11.70	27		38.70	53	
	4350	8" x 2"	Q-2	16	1.500		20	35		55	73	
	4360	8" x 3"	Q-1	15	1.070		21	24		45	58	
	4370	8" x 4"	Q-2	15	1.600		21	37		58	78	
	4380	8" x 5"		14	1.710		23	40		63	84	
	4390	8" x 6"		14	1.710		23	40		63	84	
	4430	Increaser, 2" x 3"	Q-1	17	.941		7.45	21		28.45	39	
	4440	2" x 4"		16	1		11.40	22		33.40	46	
	4450	2" x 5"		15	1.070		13.60	24		37.60	50	

151 | Pipe and Fittings

151 300 | Cast Iron Pipe

			CREW	DAILY OUTPUT	MAN-HOURS	UNIT	BARE COSTS				TOTAL INCL O&P	
							MAT.	LABOR	EQUIP.	TOTAL		
320	4460	3" x 4"	Q-1	15	1.070	Ea.	12.15	24		36.15	49	320
	4470	3" x 5"		15	1.070		12.55	24		36.55	49	
	4480	3" x 6"		14	1.140		13.40	25		38.40	52	
	4490	4" x 5"		15	1.070		16.30	24		40.30	53	
	4500	4" x 6"	↓	14	1.140		18.55	25		43.55	58	
	4510	4" x 8"	Q-2	15	1.600		35	37		72	93	
	4520	5" x 6"	Q-1	13	1.230		36	27		63	80	
	4530	5" x 8"	Q-2	14	1.710		43	40		83	105	
	4540	6" x 8"		14	1.710		44	40		84	105	
	4550	6" x 10"		10	2.400		59	55		114	145	
	4560	8" x 10"		8.50	2.820		71	65		136	175	
	4570	10" x 12"	↓	7.50	3.200		115	74		189	235	
	4600	Y, 2"	Q-1	12	1.330		6.10	30		36.10	51	
	4610	3"		10	1.600		13.70	36		49.70	68	
	4620	4"	↓	9	1.780		18	40		58	78	
	4630	5"	Q-2	13	1.850		26	43		69	92	
	4640	6"	"	11	2.180		36	50		86	115	
	4650	8"	Q-3	8	4		76	94		170	225	
	4660	10"		7	4.570		130	110		240	305	
	4670	12"		6	5.330	↓	205	125		330	410	
	4900	For extra heavy, add					8%	4%				
	4940	Gasket and making push-on joint										
	4950	2"	Q-1	40	.400	Ea.	1.55	8.90		10.45	14.90	
	4960	3"		35	.457		2.05	10.15		12.20	17.35	
	4970	4"	↓	32	.500		2.60	11.10		13.70	19.35	
	4980	5"	Q-2	43	.558		4	12.85		16.85	23	
	4990	6"	"	40	.600		4.15	13.85		18	25	
	5000	8"	Q-3	32	1		9.25	24		33.25	45	
	5010	10"		29	1.100		14.35	26		40.35	54	
	5020	12"	↓	25	1.280	↓	18.20	30		48.20	65	
	5030	Note: gaskets and joint labor have										
	5040	Been included with all listed fittings.										
	5990	No hub										
	6000	Cplg. & labor required at joints not incl. in fitting										
	6010	price. Add 1 coupling per joint for installed price										
	6020	¼ Bend, 1-½"				Ea.	2.55			2.55	2.81	
	6060	2"					2.70			2.70	2.97	
	6080	3"					3.55			3.55	3.91	
	6120	4"					5.35			5.35	5.90	
	6140	5"					12.45			12.45	13.70	
	6160	6"					12.90			12.90	14.20	
	6180	8"					31			31	34	
	6181	10"					68			68	75	
	6200	⅛ Bend, 1-½"					2			2	2.20	
	6240	2"					2.05			2.05	2.26	
	6260	3"					2.90			2.90	3.19	
	6280	4"					3.85			3.85	4.24	
	6300	5"					8			8	8.80	
	6320	6"					8.75			8.75	9.65	
	6340	8"					20			20	22	
	6360	10"					39			39	43	
	6400	Sanitary Tee, 1-½"					3.40			3.40	3.74	
	6460	2"					3.80			3.80	4.18	
	6520	3"					4.55			4.55	5	
	6600	4"					7.10			7.10	7.80	
	6680	5"					18			18	19.80	
	6700	6"					21			21	23	
	6720	8"				↓	47			47	52	

151 | Pipe and Fittings

151 300 | Cast Iron Pipe

			CREW	DAILY OUTPUT	MAN-HOURS	UNIT	BARE COSTS MAT.	LABOR	EQUIP.	TOTAL	TOTAL INCL O&P	
320	6721	10"				Ea.	91			91	100	320
	6724	Sanitary Tee, reducing										
	6725	3" x 2"				Ea.	5.60			5.60	6.15	
	6726	4" x 3"					6.15			6.15	6.75	
	6727	5" x 4"					14.25			14.25	15.70	
	6728	6" x 3"					13.75			13.75	15.15	
	6729	8" x 4"					36			36	40	
	6730	Y, 1-½"					3.65			3.65	4.02	
	6740	2"					3.65			3.65	4.02	
	6750	3"					4.85			4.85	5.35	
	6760	4"					7.90			7.90	8.70	
	6770	5"					17.20			17.20	18.90	
	6780	6"					21			21	23	
	6790	8"					41			41	45	
	6800	Double Y, 2"					5.15			5.15	5.65	
	6920	3"					9.25			9.25	10.20	
	7000	4"					19			19	21	
	7100	6"					33			33	36	
	7120	8"					83			83	91	
	7200	Combination Y and ⅛ Bend										
	7220	1-½"				Ea.	3.60			3.60	3.96	
	7260	2"					3.85			3.85	4.24	
	7320	3"					6			6	6.60	
	7400	4"					11.05			11.05	12.15	
	7480	5"					23			23	25	
	7500	6"					28			28	31	
	7520	8"					66			66	73	
	7600	Reducer, 3" x 2"					3.20			3.20	3.52	
	7820	4" x 2"					4.25			4.25	4.68	
	7840	4" x 3"					4.85			4.85	5.35	
	8000	Coupling, standard (by CISPI Mfrs.)										
	8020	1-½"	Q-1	48	.333	Ea.	2.30	7.40		9.70	13.50	
	8040	2"		44	.364		2.30	8.10		10.40	14.50	
	8080	3"		38	.421		2.68	9.35		12.03	16.85	
	8120	4"		33	.485		3.09	10.80		13.89	19.40	
	8160	5"	Q-2	44	.545		7.80	12.55		20.35	27	
	8180	6"	"	40	.600		8.15	13.85		22	29	
	8200	8"	Q-3	33	.970		15.80	23		38.80	51	
	8220	10"	"	26	1.230		22	29		51	67	
	8300	Coupling, cast iron clamp & neoprene gasket (by MG)										
	8310	1-½"	Q-1	48	.333	Ea.	6.50	7.40		13.90	18.15	
	8320	2"		44	.364		6.75	8.10		14.85	19.40	
	8330	3"		38	.421		7.20	9.35		16.55	22	
	8340	4"		33	.485		9	10.80		19.80	26	
	8350	5"	Q-2	44	.545		18.90	12.55		31.45	39	
	8360	6"	"	40	.600		25	13.85		38.85	48	
	8380	8"	Q-3	33	.970		44	23		67	82	
	8400	10"	"	26	1.230		70	29		99	120	
	8600	Coupling, Stainless steel, by Clamp-All Corp.										
	8620	1-½"	Q-1	48	.333	Ea.	7.35	7.40		14.75	19.10	
	8630	2"		44	.364		7.90	8.10		16	21	
	8640	2" x 1-½"		44	.364		8.50	8.10		16.60	21	
	8650	3"		38	.421		8.50	9.35		17.85	23	
	8660	4"		33	.485		9.75	10.80		20.55	27	
	8670	4" x 3"		33	.485		11	10.80		21.80	28	
	8680	5"	Q-2	44	.545		21	12.55		33.55	42	
	8690	6"	"	40	.600		22	13.85		35.85	45	
	8700	8"	Q-3	33	.970		36	23		59	74	

151 | Pipe and Fittings

151 300 | Cast Iron Pipe

			CREW	DAILY OUTPUT	MAN-HOURS	UNIT	BARE COSTS MAT.	LABOR	EQUIP.	TOTAL	TOTAL INCL O&P	
320	8710	10"	Q-3	26	1.230	Ea.	47	29		76	95	320

151 400 | Copper Pipe & Tubing

			CREW	DAILY OUTPUT	MAN-HOURS	UNIT	MAT.	LABOR	EQUIP.	TOTAL	INCL O&P	
401	0010	**PIPE, COPPER** Solder joints										401
	0020	Type K tubing, couplings & clevis hangers 10' O.C.										
	1100	¼" diameter	1 Plum	84	.095	L.F.	.78	2.35		3.13	4.35	
	1120	⅜" diameter		82	.098		1.24	2.41		3.65	4.94	
	1140	½" diameter		78	.103		1.28	2.53		3.81	5.15	
	1160	⅝" diameter		77	.104		1.61	2.57		4.18	5.60	
	1180	¾" diameter		74	.108		2.24	2.67		4.91	6.45	
	1200	1" diameter		66	.121		2.87	2.99		5.86	7.60	
	1220	1-¼" diameter		56	.143		3.64	3.53		7.17	9.25	
	1240	1-½" diameter		50	.160		4.65	3.95		8.60	11	
	1260	2" diameter		40	.200		6.95	4.94		11.89	15	
	1280	2-½" diameter	Q-1	60	.267		10.15	5.95		16.10	19.95	
	1300	3" diameter		54	.296		14.19	6.60		20.79	25	
	1320	3-½" diameter		42	.381		19.02	8.45		27.47	33	
	1330	4" diameter		38	.421		23.32	9.35		32.67	40	
	1340	5" diameter		32	.500		64.92	11.10		76.02	88	
	1360	6" diameter	Q-2	38	.632		95.01	14.55		109.56	125	
	1380	8" diameter	"	34	.706		155.28	16.25		171.53	195	
	1390	For other than full hard temper, add					25%					
	1440	For silver solder, add						15%				
	1800	For medical clean, (oxygen class), add					3.50%					
	1950	To delete cplgs. & hngrs., ¼"-1" pipe, subtract					27%	60%				
	1960	1-¼"-3" pipe, subtract					14%	52%				
	1970	3-½"-5" pipe, subtract					10%	60%				
	1980	6"-8" pipe, subtract					19%	53%				
	2000	Type L tubing, couplings & hangers 10' O.C.										
	2100	¼" diameter	1 Plum	88	.091	L.F.	.71	2.25		2.96	4.11	
	2120	⅜" diameter		84	.095		.99	2.35		3.34	4.58	
	2140	½" diameter		81	.099		1.10	2.44		3.54	4.83	
	2160	⅝" diameter		79	.101		1.62	2.50		4.12	5.50	
	2180	¾" diameter		76	.105		1.65	2.60		4.25	5.65	
	2200	1" diameter		68	.118		2.29	2.91		5.20	6.85	
	2220	1-¼" diameter		58	.138		3.07	3.41		6.48	8.45	
	2240	1-½" diameter		52	.154		3.89	3.80		7.69	9.90	
	2260	2" diameter		42	.190		5.80	4.70		10.50	13.35	
	2280	2-½" diameter	Q-1	62	.258		8.50	5.75		14.25	17.85	
	2300	3" diameter		56	.286		11.69	6.35		18.04	22	
	2320	3-½" diameter		43	.372		16.32	8.25		24.57	30	
	2340	4" diameter		39	.410		19.57	9.10		28.67	35	
	2360	5" diameter		34	.471		59.92	10.45		70.37	81	
	2380	6" diameter	Q-2	40	.600		77.01	13.85		90.86	105	
	2400	8" diameter	"	36	.667		125.28	15.35		140.63	160	
	2410	For other than full hard temper, add					25%					
	2590	For silver solder, add						15%				
	2900	For medical clean, (oxygen class), add					3.50%					
	2940	To delete cplgs. & hngrs., ¼"-1" pipe, subtract					37%	63%				
	2960	1-¼"-3" pipe, subtract					12%	53%				
	2970	3-½"-5" pipe, subtract					12%	63%				
	2980	6"-8" pipe, subtract					24%	55%				
	3000	Type M tubing, couplings & hangers 10' O.C.										
	3100	¼" diameter	1 Plum	90	.089	L.F.	.67	2.20		2.87	3.99	
	3120	⅜" diameter		87	.092		.76	2.27		3.03	4.21	
	3140	½" diameter		84	.095		.80	2.35		3.15	4.37	
	3160	⅝" diameter		81	.099		1.05	2.44		3.49	4.77	

151 | Pipe and Fittings

151 400 | Copper Pipe & Tubing

		CREW	DAILY OUTPUT	MAN-HOURS	UNIT	BARE COSTS MAT.	LABOR	EQUIP.	TOTAL	TOTAL INCL O&P	
3180	¾" diameter	1 Plum	78	.103	L.F.	1.19	2.53		3.72	5.05	401
3200	1" diameter		70	.114		1.65	2.82		4.47	6	
3220	1-¼" diameter		60	.133		2.36	3.29		5.65	7.50	
3240	1-½" diameter		54	.148		3.23	3.66		6.89	9	
3260	2" diameter		44	.182		4.98	4.49		9.47	12.15	
3280	2-½" diameter	Q-1	64	.250		6.98	5.55		12.53	15.90	
3300	3" diameter		58	.276		9.17	6.15		15.32	19.20	
3320	3-½" diameter		45	.356		12.85	7.90		20.75	26	
3340	4" diameter		40	.400		16.37	8.90		25.27	31	
3360	5" diameter		36	.444		51.92	9.90		61.82	72	
3370	6" diameter	Q-2	42	.571		67.01	13.15		80.16	93	
3380	8" diameter	"	38	.632		104.28	14.55		118.83	135	
3390	For other than full hard temper, add					25%					
3440	For silver solder, add						15%				
3950	For medical clean, (oxygen class), add					3.50%					
3960	To delete cplgs. & hngrs., ¼"-1" pipe, subtract					35%	65%				
3970	1-¼"-3" pipe, subtract					19%	56%				
3980	3-½"-5" pipe, subtract					13%	65%				
3990	6"-8" pipe, subtract					28%	58%				
4000	Type DWV tubing, couplings & hangers 10' O.C.										
4100	1-¼" diameter	1 Plum	60	.133	L.F.	2.78	3.29		6.07	7.95	
4120	1-½" diameter		54	.148		3.44	3.66		7.10	9.20	
4140	2" diameter		44	.182		4.56	4.49		9.05	11.70	
4160	3" diameter	Q-1	58	.276		7.68	6.15		13.83	17.55	
4180	4" diameter		40	.400		13.93	8.90		22.83	29	
4200	5" diameter		36	.444		46.92	9.90		56.82	66	
4220	6" diameter	Q-2	42	.571		67.01	13.15		80.16	93	
4240	8" diameter	"	38	.632		144.78	14.55		159.33	180	
4260	For other than full hard temper, add					25%					
4730	To delete cplgs. & hngrs., 1-¼"-2" pipe, subtract					16%	53%				
4740	2-½"-4" pipe, subtract					13%	60%				
4750	5"-8" pipe, subtract					23%	58%				
5200	ACR tubing, type L, hard temper, cleaned and										
5220	capped, no couplings or hangers										
5240	⅜" OD				L.F.	.52			.52	.57	
5250	½" OD					.75			.75	.83	
5260	⅝" OD					.96			.96	1.06	
5270	¾" OD					1.26			1.26	1.39	
5280	⅞" OD					1.48			1.48	1.63	
5290	1-⅛" OD					2.10			2.10	2.31	
5300	1-⅜" OD					2.90			2.90	3.19	
5310	1-⅝" OD					3.66			3.66	4.03	
5320	2-⅛" OD					5.60			5.60	6.15	
5330	2-⅝" OD					7.90			7.90	8.70	
5340	3-⅛" OD					10.95			10.95	12.05	
5350	3-⅝" OD					16.50			16.50	18.15	
5360	4-⅛" OD					19			19	21	
5440	For soft temper, add					25%					
5800	Refrigeration tubing, dryseal, 50' coils										
5840	⅛" OD				Coil	15.60			15.60	17.15	
5850	3/16" OD					16.75			16.75	18.45	
5860	¼" OD					19.20			19.20	21	
5870	5/16" OD					25			25	28	
5880	⅜" OD					28			28	31	
5890	½" OD					36			36	40	
5900	⅝" OD					48			48	53	
5910	¾" OD					57			57	63	
5920	⅞" OD					84			84	92	

151 | Pipe and Fittings

	151 400	Copper Pipe & Tubing	CREW	DAILY OUTPUT	MAN-HOURS	UNIT	BARE COSTS				TOTAL INCL O&P	
							MAT.	LABOR	EQUIP.	TOTAL		
401	5930	1-⅛" OD				Coil	120			120	130	401
	5940	1-⅜" OD					170			170	185	
	5950	1-⅝" OD				↓	215			215	235	
430	0010	**PIPE, COPPER, FITTINGS,** Wrought unless otherwise noted										430
	0040	Solder joints, copper x copper										
	0070	90° Elbow, ¼"	1 Plum	22	.364	Ea.	.64	9		9.64	14.05	
	0090	⅜"		22	.364		.60	9		9.60	14	
	0100	½"		20	.400		.23	9.90		10.13	14.90	
	0110	⅝"		19	.421		1.57	10.40		11.97	17.15	
	0120	¾"		19	.421		.52	10.40		10.92	16	
	0130	1"		16	.500		1.24	12.35		13.59	19.70	
	0140	1-¼"		15	.533		2.39	13.15		15.54	22	
	0150	1-½"		13	.615		2.99	15.20		18.19	26	
	0160	2"	↓	11	.727		5.60	17.95		23.55	33	
	0170	2-½"	Q-1	13	1.230		11.60	27		38.60	53	
	0180	3"		11	1.450		16.40	32		48.40	66	
	0190	3-½"		10	1.600		48	36		84	105	
	0200	4"		9	1.780		38	40		78	100	
	0210	5" cast brass	↓	6	2.670		90	59		149	185	
	0220	6" cast brass	Q-2	9	2.670		130	61		191	235	
	0230	8" cast brass	"	8	3		550	69		619	710	
	0250	45° Elbow, ¼"	1 Plum	22	.364		1.53	9		10.53	15	
	0270	⅜"		22	.364		1.29	9		10.29	14.75	
	0280	½"		20	.400		.47	9.90		10.37	15.20	
	0290	⅝"		19	.421		2.36	10.40		12.76	18.05	
	0300	¾"		19	.421		.80	10.40		11.20	16.30	
	0310	1"		16	.500		2.06	12.35		14.41	21	
	0320	1-¼"		15	.533		2.83	13.15		15.98	23	
	0330	1-½"		13	.615		3.41	15.20		18.61	26	
	0340	2"	↓	11	.727		5.65	17.95		23.60	33	
	0350	2-½"	Q-1	13	1.230		12.10	27		39.10	54	
	0360	3"		13	1.230		17.95	27		44.95	60	
	0370	3-½"		10	1.600		17.95	36		53.95	73	
	0380	4"		9	1.780		38	40		78	100	
	0390	5" cast brass	↓	6	2.670		85	59		144	180	
	0400	6" cast brass	Q-2	9	2.670		130	61		191	235	
	0410	8" cast brass	"	8	3		670	69		739	840	
	0450	Tee, ¼"	1 Plum	14	.571		1.90	14.10		16	23	
	0470	⅜"		14	.571		1.45	14.10		15.55	23	
	0480	½"		13	.615		.40	15.20		15.60	23	
	0490	⅝"		12	.667		2.84	16.45		19.29	28	
	0500	¾"		12	.667		.91	16.45		17.36	25	
	0510	1"		10	.800		3.15	19.75		22.90	33	
	0520	1-¼"		9	.889		5	22		27	38	
	0530	1-½"		8	1		6.95	25		31.95	44	
	0540	2"	↓	7	1.140		10.85	28		38.85	54	
	0550	2-½"	Q-1	8	2		22	44		66	90	
	0560	3"		7	2.290		34	51		85	115	
	0570	3-½"		6	2.670		82	59		141	180	
	0580	4"		5	3.200		72	71		143	185	
	0590	5" cast brass	↓	4	4		140	89		229	285	
	0600	6" cast brass	Q-2	6	4		190	92		282	345	
	0610	8" cast brass	"	5	4.800		1,050	110		1,160	1,325	
	0650	Coupling, ¼"	1 Plum	24	.333		.16	8.25		8.41	12.40	
	0670	⅜"		24	.333		.28	8.25		8.53	12.50	
	0680	½"		22	.364		.22	9		9.22	13.55	
	0690	⅝"	↓	21	.381		.64	9.40		10.04	14.65	

151 | Pipe and Fittings

151 400 | Copper Pipe & Tubing

			Daily Output	Man-Hours	Unit	Bare Costs Mat.	Bare Costs Labor	Bare Costs Equip.	Bare Costs Total	Total Incl O&P	
430	0700	¾"	1 Plum	21	.381	Ea.	.37	9.40		9.77	14.35	430
	0710	1"		18	.444		.88	11		11.88	17.25	
	0720	1-¼"		17	.471		1.54	11.60		13.14	18.95	
	0730	1-½"		15	.533		2.06	13.15		15.21	22	
	0740	2"	↓	13	.615		3.05	15.20		18.25	26	
	0750	2-½"	Q-1	15	1.070		5.50	24		29.50	41	
	0760	3"		13	1.230		10.10	27		37.10	52	
	0770	3-½"		8	2		17.30	44		61.30	85	
	0780	4"		7	2.290		19.60	51		70.60	97	
	0790	5"	↓	6	2.670		125	59		184	225	
	0800	6"	Q-2	8	3		195	69		264	315	
	0810	8"	"	7	3.430		620	79		699	800	
	0850	Unions, ¼"	1 Plum	21	.381		6.65	9.40		16.05	21	
	0870	⅜"		21	.381		6.65	9.40		16.05	21	
	0880	½"		19	.421		1.89	10.40		12.29	17.50	
	0890	⅝"		18	.444		8.85	11		19.85	26	
	0900	¾"		18	.444		2.48	11		13.48	19	
	0910	1"		15	.533		4.29	13.15		17.44	24	
	0920	1-¼"		14	.571		6.20	14.10		20.30	28	
	0930	1-½"		12	.667		8.60	16.45		25.05	34	
	0940	2"	↓	10	.800		14.50	19.75		34.25	45	
	0950	2-½" cast brass	Q-1	12	1.330		38	30		68	86	
	0960	3" cast brass	"	10	1.600		98	36		134	160	
	0980	Adapter, copper x male, ¼" IPS	1 Plum	24	.333		2.71	8.25		10.96	15.20	
	0990	⅜" IPS		24	.333		1.34	8.25		9.59	13.70	
	1000	½" IPS		22	.364		.49	9		9.49	13.85	
	1010	¾" IPS		21	.381		.75	9.40		10.15	14.80	
	1020	1" IPS		18	.444		2.33	11		13.33	18.85	
	1030	1-¼" IPS		17	.471		3.46	11.60		15.06	21	
	1040	1-½" IPS		15	.533		3.97	13.15		17.12	24	
	1050	2" IPS	↓	13	.615		6.75	15.20		21.95	30	
	1060	2-½" IPS	Q-1	15	1.070		11.35	24		35.35	48	
	1070	3" IPS		13	1.230		18.40	27		45.40	61	
	1080	3-½" IPS		8	2		39	44		83	110	
	1090	4" IPS		7	2.290		39	51		90	120	
	1200	5" IPS	↓	6	2.670		145	59		204	245	
	1210	6" IPS	Q-2	8	3		175	69		244	295	
	1250	Cross, ½"	1 Plum	10	.800		3.19	19.75		22.94	33	
	1260	¾"		9.50	.842		6.18	21		27.18	38	
	1270	1"		8	1		10.40	25		35.40	48	
	1280	1-¼"		7.50	1.070		14.15	26		40.15	55	
	1290	1-½"		6.50	1.230		21	30		51	68	
	1300	2"	↓	5.50	1.450		40	36		76	97	
	1310	2-½"	Q-1	6.50	2.460		77	55		132	165	
	1320	3"		5.50	2.910		180	65		245	295	
	1340	4"		4.70	3.400		370	76		446	520	
	1350	5"	↓	3.20	5		900	110		1,010	1,150	
	1360	6"	Q-2	4.70	5.110		1,450	120		1,570	1,775	
	1500	Tee, mechanically formed, ⅜"	1 Plum	80	.100			2.47		2.47	3.67	
	1520	½"		80	.100			2.47		2.47	3.67	
	1530	¾"		60	.133			3.29		3.29	4.89	
	1540	1"		48	.167			4.12		4.12	6.10	
	1550	1-¼"		48	.167			4.12		4.12	6.10	
	1560	1-½"		40	.200			4.94		4.94	7.35	
	1570	2"	↓	24	.333	↓		8.25		8.25	12.20	
	2000	DWV, solder joints, copper x copper										
	2030	90° Elbow, 1-¼"	1 Plum	13	.615	Ea.	2.53	15.20		17.73	25	
	2050	1-½"	"	12	.667	"	2.59	16.45		19.04	27	

151 | Pipe and Fittings

151 400 | Copper Pipe & Tubing

		CREW	DAILY OUTPUT	MAN-HOURS	UNIT	BARE COSTS MAT.	LABOR	EQUIP.	TOTAL	TOTAL INCL O&P	
430	2070	2"	1 Plum	10	.800	Ea.	4.88	19.75		24.63	35	430
	2090	3"	Q-1	10	1.600		6.75	36		42.75	60	
	2100	4"	"	9	1.780		40	40		80	105	
	2150	45° Elbow, 1-¼"	1 Plum	13	.615		2.25	15.20		17.45	25	
	2170	1-½"		12	.667		1.90	16.45		18.35	27	
	2180	2"	↓	10	.800		4.48	19.75		24.23	34	
	2190	3"	Q-1	10	1.600		9.10	36		45.10	63	
	2200	4"	"	9	1.780		25	40		65	86	
	2250	Tee, Sanitary, 1-¼"	1 Plum	9	.889		4.23	22		26.23	37	
	2270	1-½"		8	1		3.89	25		28.89	41	
	2290	2"	↓	7	1.140		7.20	28		35.20	50	
	2310	3"	Q-1	7	2.290		14.15	51		65.15	91	
	2330	4"	"	6	2.670		41	59		100	135	
	2400	Coupling, 1-¼"	1 Plum	14	.571		1.66	14.10		15.76	23	
	2420	1-½"		13	.615		1.46	15.20		16.66	24	
	2440	2"	↓	11	.727		2	17.95		19.95	29	
	2460	3"	Q-1	11	1.450		3.34	32		35.34	52	
	2480	4"	"	10	1.600		8.54	36		44.54	62	
	2600	Traps, see division 151-181-4700 thru 5460										
	6990	Polybutylene/polyethylene pipe, See 151-558-7990, plastic ftng.										
	7000	Insert type Brass/copper, 100 psi @ 180°F, CTS										
	7010	Adapter MPT ⅜" x ⅜" CTS 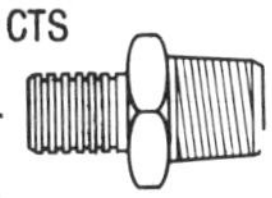	1 Plum	29	.276	Ea.	.48	6.80		7.28	10.65	
	7020	½" x ½"		26	.308		.51	7.60		8.11	11.85	
	7030	¾" x ½"		26	.308		.82	7.60		8.42	12.20	
	7040	¾" x ¾"		25	.320		.78	7.90		8.68	12.60	
	7050	Adapter CTS ½" x ½" sweat 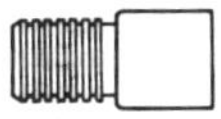		24	.333		.34	8.25		8.59	12.60	
	7060	¾" x ¾" sweat		22	.364		.43	9		9.43	13.80	
	7070	Coupler center set ⅜" CTS		25	.320		.21	7.90		8.11	11.95	
	7080	½" CTS		23	.348		.27	8.60		8.87	13.05	
	7090	¾" CTS 		22	.364		.44	9		9.44	13.80	
	7100	Elbow 90°, copper ⅜"		25	.320		.28	7.90		8.18	12.05	
	7110	½" CTS		23	.348		.33	8.60		8.93	13.10	
	7120	¾" CTS 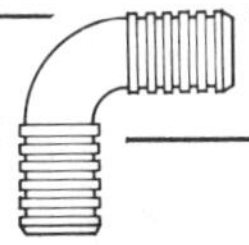		22	.364		.36	9		9.36	13.70	
	7130	Tee copper ⅜" CTS		17	.471		.42	11.60		12.02	17.70	
	7140	½" CTS		15	.533		.36	13.15		13.51	19.95	
	7150	¾" CTS		14	.571		.46	14.10		14.56	21	
	7160	⅜" x ⅜" x ½"		16	.500		.62	12.35		12.97	19	
	7170	½" x ⅜" x ½" 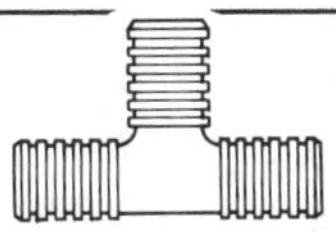		15	.533		.52	13.15		13.67	20	
	7180	¾" x ½" x ¾"	↓	14	.571	↓	.46	14.10		14.56	21	

151 450 | Corrosion Resistant Pipe

		CREW	DAILY OUTPUT	MAN-HOURS	UNIT	MAT.	LABOR	EQUIP.	TOTAL	TOTAL INCL O&P	
451	0010	**PIPE, CORROSION RESISTANT** No couplings or hangers										451
	0020	Iron alloy, drain, mechanical joint										
	1000	1-½" diameter	Q-1	70	.229	L.F.	15	5.10		20.10	24	
	1100	2" diameter		66	.242		17.50	5.40		22.90	27	
	1120	3" diameter		60	.267		25	5.95		30.95	36	
	1140	4" diameter	↓	52	.308	↓	30	6.85		36.85	43	
	1980	Iron alloy, drain, B&S joint										
	2000	2" diameter	Q-1	54	.296	L.F.	21	6.60		27.60	33	
	2100	3" diameter		52	.308		31	6.85		37.85	44	
	2120	4" diameter		48	.333		41	7.40		48.40	56	
	2140	6" diameter	Q-2	59	.407		68	9.40		77.40	89	
	2160	8" diameter	"	54	.444		122	10.25		132.25	150	
	2980	Plastic, Epoxy, fiberglass filament wound										
	3000	2" diameter	Q-1	62	.258	L.F.	5.70	5.75		11.45	14.80	
	3100	3" diameter		51	.314		8.05	6.95		15	19.20	
	3120	4" diameter	↓	45	.356	↓	10.30	7.90		18.20	23	

151 | Pipe and Fittings

151 450 | Corrosion Resistant Pipe

			CREW	DAILY OUTPUT	MAN-HOURS	UNIT	BARE COSTS MAT.	LABOR	EQUIP.	TOTAL	TOTAL INCL O&P	
451	3140	6" diameter	Q-1	32	.500	L.F.	15.20	11.10		26.30	33	451
	3160	8" diameter	Q-2	38	.632		26	14.55		40.55	50	
	3180	10" diameter		32	.750		39	17.30		56.30	69	
	3200	12" diameter		28	.857		56	19.75		75.75	91	
	3980	Polyester, fiberglass filament wound										
	4000	2" diameter	Q-1	62	.258	L.F.	9.10	5.75		14.85	18.50	
	4100	3" diameter		51	.314		12.20	6.95		19.15	24	
	4120	4" diameter		45	.356		14.50	7.90		22.40	28	
	4140	6" diameter		32	.500		21	11.10		32.10	40	
	4160	8" diameter	Q-2	38	.632		28	14.55		42.55	52	
	4180	10" diameter		32	.750		35	17.30		52.30	64	
	4200	12" diameter		28	.857		40	19.75		59.75	73	
	4980	Polypropylene, acid resistant, Schedule 40										
	5000	1-½" diameter	Q-1	68	.235	L.F.	1.55	5.25		6.80	9.45	
	5100	2" diameter		62	.258		2	5.75		7.75	10.70	
	5120	3" diameter		51	.314		3.55	6.95		10.50	14.25	
	5140	4" diameter		45	.356		5.35	7.90		13.25	17.60	
	5160	6" diameter		32	.500		10.15	11.10		21.25	28	
	5980	Proxylene, fire retardent, Schedule 40										
	6000	1-½" diameter	Q-1	68	.235	L.F.	3.36	5.25		8.61	11.45	
	6100	2" diameter		62	.258		4.24	5.75		9.99	13.15	
	6120	3" diameter		51	.314		7.66	6.95		14.61	18.80	
	6140	4" diameter		45	.356		11.05	7.90		18.95	24	
	6160	6" diameter		32	.500		21.75	11.10		32.85	40	
	6600	Polyvinylidene fluoride, Schedule 40										
	6640	½" diameter	1 Plum	44	.182	L.F.	5.30	4.49		9.79	12.50	
	6660	¾" diameter		34	.235		6.95	5.80		12.75	16.25	
	6680	1" diameter		31	.258		9.35	6.35		15.70	19.75	
	6700	1-½" diameter		25	.320		14.85	7.90		22.75	28	
	6720	2" diameter		22	.364		19.65	9		28.65	35	
	6820	For Schedule 80, add					30%	2%				
	7100	Steel pipe, plastic lined for temperature and chemical										
	7120	resistance, flanged joints										
	7140	Polypropylene lining for temperatures to 225°F.										
	7160	1" diameter	Q-1	76	.211	L.F.	8.80	4.68		13.48	16.60	
	7180	1-½" diameter		64	.250		10.20	5.55		15.75	19.45	
	7200	2" diameter		51	.314		11.50	6.95		18.45	23	
	7220	3" diameter		34	.471		20	10.45		30.45	38	
	7240	4" diameter		29	.552		28	12.25		40.25	49	
	7260	6" diameter	Q-2	26	.923		50	21		71	87	
	7280	8" diameter		23	1.040		80	24		104	125	
	7300	10" diameter		20	1.200		95	28		123	145	
	7600	Fluorinated ethylene propylene lining										
	7620	for temperatures to 300°F.										
	7640	1" diameter	Q-1	76	.211	L.F.	23	4.68		27.68	32	
	7660	1-½" diameter		64	.250		28	5.55		33.55	39	
	7680	2" diameter		51	.314		31	6.95		37.95	44	
	7700	3" diameter		34	.471		50	10.45		60.45	71	
	7720	4" diameter		29	.552		75	12.25		87.25	100	
	7740	6" diameter	Q-2	26	.923		140	21		161	185	
	7760	8" diameter		23	1.040		260	24		284	320	
	7780	10" diameter		20	1.200		365	28		393	445	
	8000	Polytetrafluoroethylene lining										
	8020	for temperatures to 500°F.										
	8040	1" diameter	Q-1	76	.211	L.F.	30	4.68		34.68	40	
	8060	1-½" diameter		64	.250		37	5.55		42.55	49	
	8080	2" diameter		51	.314		41	6.95		47.95	55	
	8100	3" diameter		34	.471		62	10.45		72.45	84	

151 | Pipe and Fittings

151 450	Corrosion Resistant Pipe	CREW	DAILY OUTPUT	MAN-HOURS	UNIT	BARE COSTS MAT.	LABOR	EQUIP.	TOTAL	TOTAL INCL O&P	
451	8120	4" diameter	Q-1	29	.552	L.F.	91	12.25		103.25	120	451
	8140	6" diameter	Q-2	26	.923		170	21		191	220	
	8160	8" diameter		23	1.040		305	24		329	370	
	8180	10" diameter		20	1.200		425	28		453	510	
	8300	For heavy duty series, add					5%					
	9000	External pipe protection										
	9040	Bituminous coating, per diameter inch, 1 coat, add				L.F.	.25			.25	.28	
	9050	3 coat, add					.38			.38	.42	
	9080	Coal tar epoxy coating, per diameter inch, 1 coat, add					.22			.22	.24	
	9100	3 coat, add					.31			.31	.34	
	9200	Coating and wrapping, 1" diameter, add					3.05			3.05	3.36	
	9210	2" diameter, add					1.20			1.20	1.32	
	9220	2-½" diameter, add					1.34			1.34	1.47	
	9230	3" diameter, add					1.34			1.34	1.47	
	9240	4" diameter, add					1.34			1.34	1.47	
	9250	5" diameter, add					1.40			1.40	1.54	
	9260	6" diameter, add					2.20			2.20	2.42	
	9270	8" diameter, add					2.20			2.20	2.42	
	9280	10" diameter, add					3.20			3.20	3.52	
	9290	12" diameter, add					3.20			3.20	3.52	
	9300	14" diameter, add					3.50			3.50	3.85	
	9310	16" diameter, add					3.98			3.98	4.38	
	9320	18" diameter, add					4.40			4.40	4.84	
	9330	20" diameter, add					4.90			4.90	5.40	
	9340	24" diameter, add					5.95			5.95	6.55	
	9380	Fittings are covered in field				S.F.	6.65			6.65	7.30	
	9390	Minimum cost per fitting				Ea.	50			50	55	
	9540	Polyethylene high density coating,										
	9550	extruded and bonded, yellow										
	9560	½" diam. pipe, .025" plastic thkns, add				L.F.	.26			.26	.29	
	9570	¾" diam. pipe, .025" plastic thkns, add					.26			.26	.29	
	9580	1" diam. pipe, .025" plastic thkns, add					.28			.28	.31	
	9590	1-¼" diam. pipe, .025" plastic thkns, add					.33			.33	.36	
	9600	1-½" diam. pipe, .025" plastic thkns, add					.37			.37	.41	
	9610	2" diam. pipe, .030" plastic thkns, add					.41			.41	.45	
	9620	2-½" diam. pipe, .030" plastic thkns, add					.50			.50	.55	
	9630	3" diam. pipe, .035" plastic thkns, add					.60			.60	.66	
	9640	3-½" diam. pipe, .035" plastic thkns, add					.70			.70	.77	
	9650	4" diam. pipe, .035" plastic thkns, add					.78			.78	.86	
	9660	5" diam. pipe, .040" plastic thkns, add					1.08			1.08	1.19	
	9670	6" diam. pipe, .040" plastic thkns, add					1.10			1.10	1.21	
	9680	8" diam. pipe, .040" plastic thkns, add					1.44			1.44	1.58	
	9690	10" diam. pipe, .040" plastic thkns, add					1.75			1.75	1.93	
	9700	12" diam. pipe, .040" plastic thkns, add					2.09			2.09	2.30	
	9710	14" diam. pipe, .060" plastic thkns, add					2.90			2.90	3.19	
	9720	16" diam. pipe, .060" plastic thkns, add					3.34			3.34	3.67	
	9730	18" diam. pipe, .060" plastic thkns, add					4			4	4.40	
	9740	20" diam. pipe, .060" plastic thkns, add					4.51			4.51	4.96	
	9770	Fittings are wrapped in field				S.F.	13			13	14.30	
454	0010	**PIPE, CORROSION RESISTANT, FITTINGS**										454
	0030	Iron alloy										
	0050	Mechanical joint										
	0060	¼ Bend, 1-½"	Q-1	12	1.330	Ea.	24	30		54	70	
	0080	2"		10	1.600		30	36		66	86	
	0090	3"		9	1.780		43	40		83	105	
	0100	4"		8	2		59	44		103	130	
	0110	⅛ Bend, 1-½"		12	1.330		24	30		54	70	

151 | Pipe and Fittings

151 450	Corrosion Resistant Pipe	CREW	DAILY OUTPUT	MAN-HOURS	UNIT	BARE COSTS MAT.	LABOR	EQUIP.	TOTAL	TOTAL INCL O&P
0130	2"	Q-1	10	1.600	Ea.	30	36		66	86
0140	3"		9	1.780		41	40		81	105
0150	4"	↓	8	2	↓	59	44		103	130
0160	Tee and Y, sanitary, straight									
0170	1-½"	Q-1	8	2	Ea.	31	44		75	100
0180	2"		7	2.290		42	51		93	120
0190	3"		6	2.670		63	59		122	155
0200	4"		5	3.200		110	71		181	225
0360	Coupling, 1-½"		14	1.140		22	25		47	62
0380	2"		12	1.330		26	30		56	73
0390	3"		11	1.450		27	32		59	78
0400	4"	↓	10	1.600		30	36		66	86
0500	Bell & Spigot									
0510	¼ and 1/16 Bend, 2"	Q-1	16	1	Ea.	36	22		58	73
0520	3"		14	1.140		54	25		79	97
0530	4"	↓	13	1.230		70	27		97	120
0540	6"	Q-2	17	1.410		250	33		283	325
0550	8"	"	12	2		610	46		656	740
0620	⅛ Bend, 2"	Q-1	16	1		36	22		58	73
0640	3"		14	1.140		54	25		79	97
0650	4"	↓	13	1.230		70	27		97	120
0660	6"	Q-2	17	1.410		170	33		203	235
0680	8"	"	12	2		500	46		546	620
0700	Tee, sanitary, 2"	Q-1	10	1.600		48	36		84	105
0710	3"		9	1.780		68	40		108	135
0720	4"	↓	8	2		105	44		149	180
0730	6"	Q-2	11	2.180		210	50		260	305
0740	8"	"	8	3		760	69		829	940
1800	Y, sanitary, 2"	Q-1	10	1.600		47	36		83	105
1820	3"		9	1.780		79	40		119	145
1830	4"	↓	8	2		105	44		149	180
1840	6"	Q-2	11	2.180		210	50		260	305
1850	8"	"	8	3	↓	985	69		1,054	1,175
3000	Epoxy, filament wound									
3030	Quick-lock joint									
3040	90° Elbow, 2"	Q-1	28	.571	Ea.	27	12.70		39.70	49
3060	3"		16	1		37	22		59	74
3070	4"		13	1.230		46	27		73	91
3080	6"	↓	8	2		125	44		169	205
3090	8"	Q-2	9	2.670		240	61		301	355
3100	10"		7	3.430		335	79		414	485
3110	12"	↓	6	4		450	92		542	630
3120	45° Elbow, 2"	Q-1	28	.571		27	12.70		39.70	49
3130	3"		16	1		37	22		59	74
3140	4"		13	1.230		46	27		73	91
3150	6"	↓	8	2		125	44		169	205
3160	8"	Q-2	9	2.670		240	61		301	355
3170	10"		7	3.430		335	79		414	485
3180	12"	↓	6	4		450	92		542	630
3190	Tee, 2"	Q-1	19	.842		49	18.70		67.70	82
3200	3"		11	1.450		57	32		89	110
3210	4"		9	1.780		67	40		107	130
3220	6"	↓	5	3.200		180	71		251	305
3230	8"	Q-2	6	4		330	92		422	500
3240	10"		5	4.800		535	110		645	755
3250	12"	↓	4	6	↓	660	140		800	930
4000	Polypropylene, acid resistant									
4020	Non-pressure									

151 | Pipe and Fittings

151 450 | Corrosion Resistant Pipe

			CREW	DAILY OUTPUT	MAN-HOURS	UNIT	BARE COSTS MAT.	BARE COSTS LABOR	BARE COSTS EQUIP.	BARE COSTS TOTAL	TOTAL INCL O&P	
454	4050	¼ Bend, 1-½"	1 Plum	16	.500	Ea.	6.10	12.35		18.45	25	454
	4060	2"	Q-1	28	.571		7.75	12.70		20.45	27	
	4080	3"		17	.941		15.25	21		36.25	48	
	4090	4"		14	1.140		25	25		50	65	
	4110	6"	↓	8	2	↓	60	44		104	130	
	4150	¼ Bend, long sweep										
	4170	1-½"	1 Plum	16	.500	Ea.	6.50	12.35		18.85	25	
	4180	2"	Q-1	28	.571		8.10	12.70		20.80	28	
	4200	3"		17	.941		16.20	21		37.20	49	
	4210	4"		14	1.140		27	25		52	67	
	4250	⅛ Bend, 1-½"	1 Plum	16	.500		6.05	12.35		18.40	25	
	4260	2"	Q-1	28	.571		7.50	12.70		20.20	27	
	4280	3"		17	.941		16	21		37	49	
	4290	4"		14	1.140		18.35	25		43.35	58	
	4310	6"	↓	8	2		50	44		94	120	
	4400	Tee, sanitary										
	4420	1-½"	1 Plum	10	.800	Ea.	7.75	19.75		27.50	38	
	4430	2"	Q-1	17	.941		9.20	21		30.20	41	
	4450	3"		11	1.450		21	32		53	71	
	4460	4"		9	1.780		32	40		72	94	
	4480	6"	↓	5	3.200	↓	55	71		126	165	
	4500	Tee/wye, long turn										
	4520	1-½"	1 Plum	10	.800	Ea.	10.50	19.75		30.25	41	
	4530	2"	Q-1	17	.941		14.25	21		35.25	47	
	4550	3"		11	1.450		30	32		62	81	
	4570	4"		9	1.780		38	40		78	100	
	4650	Wye 45°, 1-½"	1 Plum	10	.800		7.75	19.75		27.50	38	
	4670	2"	Q-1	17	.941		11.30	21		32.30	43	
	4680	3"		11	1.450		24	32		56	74	
	4700	4"		9	1.780		34	40		74	96	
	4720	6"		5	3.200		85	71		156	200	
	4800	Wye, double 45°										
	4820	1-½"	1 Plum	8	1	Ea.	14.05	25		39.05	52	
	4830	2"	Q-1	14	1.140		23	25		48	63	
	4850	3"		9	1.780		40	40		80	105	
	4870	4"	↓	4	4		52	89		141	190	
	6000	Plastic lined, ductile iron, flanged (for bolt sets see 151-720)										
	6010	Polypropylene (PP) lined,										
	6020	90° Elbow, 1"	Q-1	16	1	Ea.	88	22		110	130	
	6030	1-½"		14	1.140		100	25		125	150	
	6040	2"		13	1.230		120	27		147	175	
	6060	3"		11	1.450		165	32		197	230	
	6070	4"	↓	8	2		225	44		269	315	
	6090	6"	Q-2	9	2.670		420	61		481	555	
	6100	8"		8	3		680	69		749	850	
	6110	10"	↓	7	3.430		1,000	79		1,079	1,225	
	6190	45° Elbow, 1"	Q-1	16	1		86	22		108	130	
	6210	1-½"		14	1.140		105	25		130	155	
	6220	2"		13	1.230		110	27		137	160	
	6240	3"		11	1.450		165	32		197	230	
	6250	4"		8	2		225	44		269	315	
	6270	6"		9	1.780		425	40		465	525	
	6280	8"	↓	8	2		650	44		694	780	
	6290	10"	Q-2	7	3.430		915	79		994	1,125	
	6370	Tee, 1"	Q-1	11	1.450		130	32		162	190	
	6390	1-½"		10	1.600		160	36		196	230	
	6400	2"		9	1.780		170	40		210	245	
	6420	3"	↓	7	2.290		215	51		266	310	

151 | Pipe and Fittings

151 450	Corrosion Resistant Pipe	CREW	DAILY OUTPUT	MAN-HOURS	UNIT	BARE COSTS MAT.	LABOR	EQUIP.	TOTAL	TOTAL INCL O&P
6430	4"	Q-1	5	3.200	Ea.	320	71		391	460
6450	6"	Q-2	6	4		550	92		642	740
6460	8"		5	4.800		870	110		980	1,125
6470	10"	↓	4	6		1,500	140		1,640	1,850
6560	Reducer, 1-½"	Q-1	16	1		100	22		122	145
6570	2"		15	1.070		110	24		134	155
6590	3"		13	1.230		150	27		177	205
6660	4"	↓	10	1.600		200	36		236	275
6680	6"	Q-2	11	2.180		315	50		365	420
6690	8"		10	2.400		610	55		665	755
6700	10"	↓	9	2.670	↓	1,000	61		1,061	1,200
6800	Fluorinated ethylene propylene (FEP) lined									
6810	90° Elbow, 1"	Q-1	16	1	Ea.	140	22		162	185
6830	1-½"		14	1.140		150	25		175	205
6840	2"		13	1.230		175	27		202	235
6860	3"		11	1.450		280	32		312	355
6870	4"	↓	8	2		415	44		459	520
6890	6"	Q-2	9	2.670		850	61		911	1,025
6900	8"		8	3		1,300	69		1,369	1,525
6910	10"	↓	7	3.430		2,125	79		2,204	2,450
7000	45° Elbow, 1"	Q-1	16	1		125	22		147	170
7020	1-½"		14	1.140		145	25		170	195
7030	2"		13	1.230		155	27		182	210
7050	3"		11	1.450		270	32		302	345
7060	4"	↓	8	2		350	44		394	450
7080	6"	Q-2	9	2.670		725	61		786	890
7090	8"		8	3		1,135	69		1,204	1,350
7100	10"	↓	7	3.430		1,900	79		1,979	2,200
7180	Tee, 1"	Q-1	11	1.450		225	32		257	295
7200	1-½"		10	1.600		300	36		336	385
7210	2"		9	1.780		315	40		355	405
7230	3"		7	2.290		450	51		501	570
7240	4"	↓	5	3.200		575	71		646	740
7260	6"	Q-2	6	4		1,050	92		1,142	1,300
7270	8"		5	4.800		1,475	110		1,585	1,775
7280	10"	↓	4	6		2,525	140		2,665	2,975
7370	Reducer, 1-½"	Q-1	16	1		165	22		187	215
7380	2"		15	1.070		185	24		209	240
7400	3"		13	1.230		260	27		287	325
7410	4"	↓	10	1.600		350	36		386	440
7430	6"	Q-2	11	2.180		550	50		600	680
7440	8"		10	2.400		950	55		1,005	1,125
7450	10"	↓	9	2.670	↓	1,700	61		1,761	1,950
7550	Polytetrafluoroethylene (TFE) lined									
7560	90° Elbow, 1"	Q-1	16	1	Ea.	175	22		197	225
7580	1-½"		14	1.140		180	25		205	235
7590	2"		13	1.230		205	27		232	265
7610	3"		11	1.450		310	32		342	390
7620	4"	↓	8	2		475	44		519	590
7640	6"	Q-2	9	2.670		1,000	61		1,061	1,200
7650	8"		8	3		1,500	69		1,569	1,750
7660	10"	↓	7	3.430		2,200	79		2,279	2,525
7740	45° Elbow, 1"	Q-1	16	1		180	22		202	230
7760	1-½"		14	1.140		200	25		225	260
7770	2"		13	1.230		210	27		237	270
7790	3"		11	1.450		315	32		347	395
7800	4"	↓	8	2		475	44		519	590
7820	6"	Q-2	9	2.670		1,000	61		1,061	1,200

151 | Pipe and Fittings

151 450 | Corrosion Resistant Pipe

			CREW	DAILY OUTPUT	MAN-HOURS	UNIT	BARE COSTS MAT.	LABOR	EQUIP.	TOTAL	TOTAL INCL O&P	
454	7830	8"	Q-2	8	3	Ea.	1,500	69		1,569	1,750	454
	7840	10"	"	7	3.430		2,200	79		2,279	2,525	
	7920	Tee, 1"	Q-1	11	1.450		310	32		342	390	
	7940	1-½"		10	1.600		315	36		351	400	
	7950	2"		9	1.780		375	40		415	470	
	7970	3"		7	2.290		575	51		626	710	
	7980	4"		5	3.200		710	71		781	885	
	8000	6"	Q-2	6	4		1,235	92		1,327	1,500	
	8010	8"		5	4.800		1,650	110		1,760	1,975	
	8020	10"		4	6		2,775	140		2,915	3,250	
	8110	Reducer, 1-½"	Q-1	16	1		215	22		237	270	
	8120	2"		15	1.070		265	24		289	325	
	8140	3"		13	1.230		325	27		352	400	
	8150	4"		10	1.600		435	36		471	530	
	8170	6"	Q-2	11	2.180		690	50		740	835	
	8180	8"		10	2.400		1,000	55		1,055	1,175	
	8190	10"		9	2.670		1,650	61		1,711	1,900	

151 500 | Glass Pipe

			CREW	DAILY OUTPUT	MAN-HOURS	UNIT	MAT.	LABOR	EQUIP.	TOTAL	TOTAL INCL O&P	
501	0010	**PIPE, GLASS** Borosilicate, couplings & hangers 10' O.C.										501
	0020	Drainage										
	1100	1-½" diameter	Q-1	52	.308	L.F.	4.83	6.85		11.68	15.45	
	1120	2" diameter		44	.364		6.46	8.10		14.56	19.10	
	1140	3" diameter		39	.410		8.67	9.10		17.77	23	
	1160	4" diameter		30	.533		14.98	11.85		26.83	34	
	1180	6" diameter		26	.615		26.52	13.70		40.22	49	
	1870	To delete coupling & hanger, subtract										
	1880	1-½" diam. to 2" diam.					19%	22%				
	1890	3" diam. to 6" diam.					20%	17%				
	2000	Process supply (pressure), beaded joints										
	2040	½" diameter	1 Plum	36	.222	L.F.	3.99	5.50		9.49	12.55	
	2060	¾" diameter		31	.258		4.91	6.35		11.26	14.85	
	2080	1" diameter		27	.296		6.41	7.30		13.71	17.90	
	2100	1-½" diameter	Q-1	47	.340		7.96	7.55		15.51	20	
	2120	2" diameter		39	.410		10.71	9.10		19.81	25	
	2140	3" diameter		34	.471		14.58	10.45		25.03	32	
	2160	4" diameter		25	.640		21.68	14.25		35.93	45	
	2180	6" diameter		21	.762		36.22	16.95		53.17	65	
	2860	To delete coupling & hanger, subtract										
	2870	½" diam. to 1" diam.					25%	33%				
	2880	1-½" diam. to 3" diam.					22%	21%				
	2890	4" diam. to 6" diam.					23%	15%				
	3000	Beaded joint, armored, translucent										
	3040	½" diameter	1 Plum	36	.222	L.F.	9.87	5.50		15.37	19	
	3060	¾" diameter		31	.258		11.32	6.35		17.67	22	
	3080	1" diameter		27	.296		12.08	7.30		19.38	24	
	3100	1-½" diameter	Q-1	47	.340		14.77	7.55		22.32	27	
	3120	2" diameter		39	.410		18.87	9.10		27.97	34	
	3140	3" diameter		34	.471		30.03	10.45		40.48	49	
	3160	4" diameter		25	.640		47.73	14.25		61.98	74	
	3180	6" diameter		21	.762		81.82	16.95		98.77	115	
	3710	To delete coupling & hanger, subtract										
	3720	½" diam. to ¾" diam.					30%	27%				
	3730	1" diam. to 3" diam.					28%	22%				
	3740	4" diam. to 6" diam.					24%	15%				
	3800	Conical joint, transparent										
	3880	1" diameter	1 Plum	27	.296	L.F.	7	7.30		14.30	18.55	

151 | Pipe and Fittings

		151 500	Glass Pipe	CREW	DAILY OUTPUT	MAN-HOURS	UNIT	BARE COSTS MAT.	LABOR	EQUIP.	TOTAL	TOTAL INCL O&P	
501	3900		1-½" diameter	Q-1	47	.340	L.F.	9.24	7.55		16.79	21	501
	3920		2" diameter		39	.410		11.75	9.10		20.85	26	
	3940		3" diameter		34	.471		19.43	10.45		29.88	37	
	3960		4" diameter		25	.640		28.43	14.25		42.68	52	
	3980		6" diameter	↓	21	.762	↓	48.92	16.95		65.87	79	
	4500		To delete couplings & hangers, subtract										
	4510		1" diam.					23%	27%				
	4520		1-½" diam. to 4" diam.					17%	23%				
	4530		6" diam.					22%	26%				
512	0010	**PIPE, GLASS, FITTINGS**											512
	0020		Drainage, beaded ends										
	0040		Cplg. & labor required at joints not incl. in fitting										
	0050		price. Add 1 per joint for installed price										
	0070		90° Bend or sweep, 1-½"				Ea.	11.35			11.35	12.50	
	0090		2"					14.35			14.35	15.80	
	0100		3"					25			25	28	
	0110		4"					37			37	41	
	0120		6" (sweep only)				↓	115			115	125	
	0200		45° Bend or sweep same as 90°										
	0350		Tee, single sanitary, 1-½"				Ea.	18.40			18.40	20	
	0370		2"					18.40			18.40	20	
	0380		3"					28			28	31	
	0390		4"					51			51	56	
	0400		6"					130			130	145	
	0410		Tee, straight, 1-½"					24			24	26	
	0430		2"					24			24	26	
	0440		3"					33			33	36	
	0450		4"					57			57	63	
	0460		6"				↓	145			145	160	
	0500		Coupling, stainless steel, TFE seal ring										
	0520		1-½"	Q-1	32	.500	Ea.	7.50	11.10		18.60	25	
	0530		2"		30	.533		9.60	11.85		21.45	28	
	0540		3"		25	.640		12.85	14.25		27.10	35	
	0550		4"		23	.696		23	15.45		38.45	48	
	0560		6"	↓	20	.800	↓	51	17.80		68.80	82	
	0600		Coupling, stainless steel, bead to plain end										
	0610		1-½"	Q-1	36	.444	Ea.	9.85	9.90		19.75	26	
	0620		2"		34	.471		12.35	10.45		22.80	29	
	0630		3"		29	.552		23	12.25		35.25	43	
	0640		4"		27	.593		37	13.15		50.15	60	
	0650		6"	↓	24	.667		120	14.80		134.80	155	
	2000		Process supply (pressure), beaded ends										
	2050		90° Sweep elbow, ½"				Ea.	12			12	13.20	
	2070		¾"					14.25			14.25	15.70	
	2080		1"					13.60			13.60	14.95	
	2090		1-½"					20			20	22	
	2100		2"					27			27	30	
	2120		3"					42			42	46	
	2130		4"					59			59	65	
	2140		6"				↓	160			160	175	
	2150		45° Sweep elbow, same as 90°										
	2250		Tee, straight, ½"				Ea.	21			21	23	
	2270		¾"					21			21	23	
	2280		1"					24			24	26	
	2290		1-½"					34			34	37	
	2300		2"					39			39	43	
	2310		3"					49			49	54	

151 | Pipe and Fittings

151 500 | Glass Pipe

			CREW	DAILY OUTPUT	MAN-HOURS	UNIT	BARE COSTS MAT.	LABOR	EQUIP.	TOTAL	TOTAL INCL O&P	
512	2320	4"				Ea.	82			82	90	512
	2330	6"				"	145			145	160	
	2350	Coupling, Hydrin liner, for temperatures to 300°F										
	2370	½"	Q-1	40	.400	Ea.	9.20	8.90		18.10	23	
	2380	¾"		37	.432		10.85	9.60		20.45	26	
	2390	1"		35	.457		10.85	10.15		21	27	
	2400	1-½"		32	.500		13.80	11.10		24.90	32	
	2410	2"		30	.533		16.55	11.85		28.40	36	
	2420	3"		25	.640		26	14.25		40.25	50	
	2430	4"		23	.696		38	15.45		53.45	65	
	2440	6"	↓	20	.800		58	17.80		75.80	90	
	2500	Coupling, for systems to 400°F, add					100%					
	2550	For beaded joint armored fittings, add				↓	200%					
	2600	Conical ends. Flange set, gasket & labor not incl. in fitting										
	2620	price. Add 1 per joint for installed price.										
	2650	90° Sweep elbow, 1"				Ea.	31			31	34	
	2670	1-½"					47			47	52	
	2680	2"					50			50	55	
	2690	3"					73			73	80	
	2700	4"					115			115	125	
	2750	Cross (straight), add					50%					
	2850	Tee, add					20%					
	2950	Lateral "Y", 1"					56			56	62	
	2970	1-½"					64			64	70	
	2980	2"					78			78	86	
	2990	3"					110			110	120	
	3000	4"					175			175	195	
	3010	6"					365			365	400	
	3050	Flange set and Gasket, 1"	Q-1	28	.571		13.25	12.70		25.95	33	
	3070	1-½"		26	.615		13.60	13.70		27.30	35	
	3080	2"		24	.667		16.50	14.80		31.30	40	
	3090	3"		22	.727		30	16.15		46.15	57	
	3100	4"		16	1		51	22		73	89	
	3110	6"	↓	12	1.330	↓	115	30		145	170	

151 550 | Plastic Pipe

			CREW	DAILY OUTPUT	MAN-HOURS	UNIT	MAT.	LABOR	EQUIP.	TOTAL	TOTAL INCL O&P	
551	0010	**PIPE, PLASTIC** See also division 151-451										551
	0020	Fiberglass reinforced, couplings 10' O.C., hangers 3 per 10'										
	0080	General service										
	0120	2" diameter	Q-1	59	.271	L.F.	6.01	6.05		12.06	15.55	
	0140	3" diameter		52	.308		7.52	6.85		14.37	18.40	
	0150	4" diameter		48	.333		9.73	7.40		17.13	22	
	0160	6" diameter	↓	39	.410		14.23	9.10		23.33	29	
	0170	8" diameter	Q-2	49	.490		22.83	11.30		34.13	42	
	0180	10" diameter		41	.585		34.41	13.50		47.91	58	
	0190	12" diameter	↓	36	.667	↓	46.32	15.35		61.67	74	
	0200	High strength										
	0240	2" diameter	Q-1	58	.276	L.F.	7.44	6.15		13.59	17.30	
	0260	3" diameter		51	.314		9.81	6.95		16.76	21	
	0280	4" diameter		47	.340		12.23	7.55		19.78	25	
	0300	6" diameter	↓	38	.421		18.21	9.35		27.56	34	
	0320	8" diameter	Q-2	48	.500		28.78	11.55		40.33	49	
	0340	10" diameter		40	.600		43.16	13.85		57.01	68	
	0360	12" diameter	↓	36	.667	↓	55.30	15.35		70.65	84	
	0550	To delete coupling & hangers, subtract										
	0560	2" diam. to 6" diam.					33%	56%				
	0570	8" diam. to 12" diam.					31%	52%				
	0600	PVC, high impact/pressure, cplgs. 10' O.C., hangers 3 per 10'										

151 | Pipe and Fittings

151 550 | Plastic Pipe

		CREW	DAILY OUTPUT	MAN-HOURS	UNIT	BARE COSTS MAT.	BARE COSTS LABOR	BARE COSTS EQUIP.	BARE COSTS TOTAL	TOTAL INCL O&P	
551	0620	Schedule 40										551
	0670	½" diameter	1 Plum	54	.148	L.F.	.66	3.66		4.32	6.15	
	0680	¾" diameter		51	.157		.72	3.87		4.59	6.55	
	0690	1" diameter		46	.174		.85	4.30		5.15	7.30	
	0700	1-¼" diameter		42	.190		.97	4.70		5.67	8.05	
	0710	1-½" diameter		36	.222		1.04	5.50		6.54	9.30	
	0720	2" diameter	Q-1	59	.271		1.27	6.05		7.32	10.35	
	0730	2-½" diameter		56	.286		2.06	6.35		8.41	11.70	
	0740	3" diameter		53	.302		2.67	6.70		9.37	12.90	
	0750	4" diameter		48	.333		3.70	7.40		11.10	15.05	
	0760	5" diameter		43	.372		5.77	8.25		14.02	18.60	
	0770	6" diameter		39	.410		7.93	9.10		17.03	22	
	0780	8" diameter	Q-2	48	.500		12.34	11.55		23.89	31	
	0790	10" diameter		43	.558		25.06	12.85		37.91	47	
	0800	12" diameter		42	.571		31.92	13.15		45.07	55	
	0930	To delete coupling & hangers, subtract										
	0940	½" diameter					64%	81%				
	0950	¾" diam. to 1-¼" diam.					61%	72%				
	0960	1-½" diam. to 6" diam.					44%	57%				
	0970	8" diam. to 12" diam.					46%	53%				
	1020	Schedule 80										
	1040	¼" diameter	1 Plum	58	.138	L.F.	.93	3.41		4.34	6.10	
	1060	⅜" diameter		55	.145		1.04	3.59		4.63	6.45	
	1070	½" diameter		50	.160		.78	3.95		4.73	6.70	
	1080	¾" diameter		47	.170		.89	4.20		5.09	7.20	
	1090	1" diameter		43	.186		1.04	4.60		5.64	7.95	
	1100	1-¼" diameter		39	.205		1.35	5.05		6.40	9	
	1110	1-½" diameter		34	.235		1.46	5.80		7.26	10.25	
	1120	2" diameter	Q-1	55	.291		1.75	6.45		8.20	11.50	
	1130	2-½" diameter		52	.308		2.19	6.85		9.04	12.55	
	1140	3" diameter		50	.320		3.17	7.10		10.27	14.05	
	1150	4" diameter		46	.348		4.28	7.75		12.03	16.20	
	1160	5" diameter		42	.381		5.96	8.45		14.41	19.10	
	1170	6" diameter		38	.421		7.49	9.35		16.84	22	
	1180	8" diameter	Q-2	47	.511		12.48	11.75		24.23	31	
	1190	10" diameter		42	.571		18.51	13.15		31.66	40	
	1200	12" diameter		38	.632		23.97	14.55		38.52	48	
	1730	To delete coupling & hangers, subtract										
	1740	¼" diam. to ½" diam.					62%	80%				
	1750	¾" diam. to 1-¼" diam.					58%	73%				
	1760	1-½" diam. to 6" diam.					40%	57%				
	1770	8" diam. to 12" diam.					34%	50%				
	1800	PVC, couplings 10' O.C., hangers 3 per 10'										
	1820	Schedule 40										
	1860	½" diameter	1 Plum	54	.148	L.F.	.64	3.66		4.30	6.15	
	1870	¾" diameter		51	.157		.69	3.87		4.56	6.50	
	1880	1" diameter		46	.174		.82	4.30		5.12	7.30	
	1890	1-¼" diameter		42	.190		.96	4.70		5.66	8.05	
	1900	1-½" diameter		36	.222		1.02	5.50		6.52	9.25	
	1910	2" diameter	Q-1	59	.271		1.31	6.05		7.36	10.40	
	1920	2-½" diameter		56	.286		1.87	6.35		8.22	11.50	
	1930	3" diameter		53	.302		2.34	6.70		9.04	12.50	
	1940	4" diameter		48	.333		3.28	7.40		10.68	14.60	
	1950	5" diameter		43	.372		4.77	8.25		13.02	17.50	
	1960	6" diameter		39	.410		5.98	9.10		15.08	20	
	1970	8" diameter	Q-2	48	.500		9.56	11.55		21.11	28	
	1980	10" diameter		43	.558		20.16	12.85		33.01	41	
	1990	12" diameter		42	.571		25.52	13.15		38.67	48	

151 | Pipe and Fittings

151 550 | Plastic Pipe

		CREW	DAILY OUTPUT	MAN-HOURS	UNIT	BARE COSTS MAT.	LABOR	EQUIP.	TOTAL	TOTAL INCL O&P	
551	2000	14" diameter	Q-2	31	.774	L.F.	51.52	17.85		69.37	83	551
	2010	16" diameter	"	23	1.040	"	60.70	24		84.70	100	
	2340	To delete coupling & hangers, subtract										
	2360	½" diam. to 1-¼" diam.					65%	74%				
	2370	1-½" diam. to 6" diam.					44%	57%				
	2380	8" diam. to 12" diam.					41%	53%				
	2390	14" diam. to 16" diam.					48%	45%				
	2420	Schedule 80										
	2440	¼" diameter	1 Plum	58	.138	L.F.	.93	3.41		4.34	6.10	
	2450	⅜" diameter		55	.145		1.04	3.59		4.63	6.45	
	2460	½" diameter		50	.160		.78	3.95		4.73	6.70	
	2470	¾" diameter		47	.170		.89	4.20		5.09	7.20	
	2480	1" diameter		43	.186		1.04	4.60		5.64	7.95	
	2490	1-¼" diameter		39	.205		1.35	5.05		6.40	9	
	2500	1-½" diameter		34	.235		1.46	5.80		7.26	10.25	
	2510	2" diameter	Q-1	55	.291		1.75	6.45		8.20	11.50	
	2520	2-½" diameter		52	.308		2.19	6.85		9.04	12.55	
	2530	3" diameter		50	.320		3.17	7.10		10.27	14.05	
	2540	4" diameter		46	.348		4.28	7.75		12.03	16.20	
	2550	5" diameter		42	.381		5.96	8.45		14.41	19.10	
	2560	6" diameter		38	.421		7.49	9.35		16.84	22	
	2570	8" diameter	Q-2	47	.511		12.48	11.75		24.23	31	
	2580	10" diameter		42	.571		18.46	13.15		31.61	40	
	2590	12" diameter		38	.632		23.97	14.55		38.52	48	
	2830	To delete coupling & hangers, subtract										
	2840	¼" diam. to ½" diam.					66%	80%				
	2850	¾" diam. to 1-¼" diam.					61%	73%				
	2860	1-½" diam. to 6" diam.					41%	57%				
	2870	8" diam. to 12" diam.					31%	50%				
	2900	Schedule 120										
	2910	½" diameter	1 Plum	50	.160	L.F.	.88	3.95		4.83	6.85	
	2950	¾" diameter		47	.170		1.01	4.20		5.21	7.35	
	2960	1" diameter		43	.186		1.23	4.60		5.83	8.15	
	2970	1-¼" diameter		39	.205		1.61	5.05		6.66	9.30	
	2980	1-½" diameter		33	.242		1.78	6		7.78	10.85	
	2990	2" diameter	Q-1	54	.296		2.21	6.60		8.81	12.20	
	3000	2-½" diameter		52	.308		3.24	6.85		10.09	13.70	
	3010	3" diameter		49	.327		4.13	7.25		11.38	15.30	
	3020	4" diameter		45	.356		6.08	7.90		13.98	18.40	
	3030	6" diameter		37	.432		10.80	9.60		20.40	26	
	3240	To delete coupling & hangers, subtract										
	3250	½" diam. to 1-¼" diam.					52%	74%				
	3260	1-½" diam. to 4" diam.					30%	57%				
	3270	6" diam.					17%	50%				
	3300	PVC, pressure, couplings 10' O.C., hangers 3 per 10'										
	3310	SDR 26, 160 psi										
	3350	1-¼" diameter	1 Plum	42	.190	L.F.	.75	4.70		5.45	7.80	
	3360	1-½" diameter	"	36	.222		.81	5.50		6.31	9.05	
	3370	2" diameter	Q-1	59	.271		1.01	6.05		7.06	10.05	
	3380	2-½" diameter		56	.286		1.43	6.35		7.78	11	
	3390	3" diameter		53	.302		1.84	6.70		8.54	11.95	
	3400	4" diameter		48	.333		2.75	7.40		10.15	14	
	3420	6" diameter		39	.410		5.56	9.10		14.66	19.65	
	3430	8" diameter	Q-2	48	.500		9.42	11.55		20.97	27	
	3660	To delete coupling & hangers, subtract										
	3670	1-¼" diam.					63%	68%				
	3680	1-½" diam. to 4" diam.					48%	57%				
	3690	6" diam. to 8" diam.					60%	54%				

151 | Pipe and Fittings

151 550 | Plastic Pipe

		CREW	DAILY OUTPUT	MAN-HOURS	UNIT	BARE COSTS MAT.	BARE COSTS LABOR	BARE COSTS EQUIP.	BARE COSTS TOTAL	TOTAL INCL O&P
551 3720	SDR 21, 200 psi, ½" diameter	1 Plum	54	.148	L.F.	.67	3.66		4.33	6.15
3740	¾" diameter		51	.157		.71	3.87		4.58	6.55
3750	1" diameter		46	.174		.79	4.30		5.09	7.25
3760	1-¼" diameter		42	.190		1.01	4.70		5.71	8.10
3770	1-½" diameter		36	.222		1.08	5.50		6.58	9.35
3780	2" diameter	Q-1	59	.271		1.28	6.05		7.33	10.35
3790	2-½" diameter		56	.286		1.94	6.35		8.29	11.55
3800	3" diameter		53	.302		2.28	6.70		8.98	12.45
3810	4" diameter		48	.333		3.15	7.40		10.55	14.45
3830	6" diameter		39	.410		5.74	9.10		14.84	19.85
3840	8" diameter	Q-2	48	.500		10.73	11.55		22.28	29
4000	To delete coupling & hangers, subtract									
4010	½" diam. to ¾" diam.					71%	77%			
4020	1" diam. to 1-¼" diam.					63%	70%			
4030	1-½" diam. to 6" diam.					44%	57%			
4040	8" diam.					46%	54%			
4100	DWV type, schedule 40, couplings 10' O.C., hangers 3 per 10'									
4120	ABS									
4140	1-¼" diameter	1 Plum	42	.190	L.F.	.96	4.70		5.66	8.05
4150	1-½" diameter	"	36	.222		1.05	5.50		6.55	9.30
4160	2" diameter	Q-1	59	.271		1.27	6.05		7.32	10.35
4170	3" diameter		53	.302		2.31	6.70		9.01	12.50
4180	4" diameter		48	.333		3.22	7.40		10.62	14.55
4190	6" diameter		39	.410		5.89	9.10		14.99	20
4360	To delete coupling & hangers, subtract									
4370	1-¼" diam.					64%	68%			
4380	1-½" diam. to 6" diam.					54%	57%			
4400	PVC									
4410	1-¼" diameter	1 Plum	42	.190	L.F.	.96	4.70		5.66	8.05
4420	1-½" diameter	"	36	.222		1.09	5.50		6.59	9.35
4460	2" diameter	Q-1	59	.271		1.27	6.05		7.32	10.35
4470	3" diameter		53	.302		2.31	6.70		9.01	12.50
4480	4" diameter		48	.333		3.20	7.40		10.60	14.50
4490	6" diameter		39	.410		5.89	9.10		14.99	20
4750	To delete coupling & hangers, subtract									
4760	1-¼" diam. to 1-½" diam.					71%	64%			
4770	2" diam. to 6" diam.					60%	57%			
4800	PVC, clear pipe, cplgs. 10' O.C., hangers 3 per 10', Sched. 40									
4840	¼" diameter	1 Plum	59	.136	L.F.	.81	3.35		4.16	5.85
4850	⅜" diameter		56	.143		.92	3.53		4.45	6.25
4860	½" diameter		54	.148		1.16	3.66		4.82	6.70
4870	¾" diameter		51	.157		1.40	3.87		5.27	7.30
4880	1" diameter		46	.174		1.90	4.30		6.20	8.45
4890	1-¼" diameter		42	.190		2.42	4.70		7.12	9.65
4900	1-½" diameter		36	.222		2.79	5.50		8.29	11.20
4910	2" diameter	Q-1	59	.271		3.60	6.05		9.65	12.90
4920	2-½" diameter		56	.286		5.57	6.35		11.92	15.55
4930	3" diameter		53	.302		7.18	6.70		13.88	17.85
4940	3-½" diameter		50	.320		10.58	7.10		17.68	22
4950	4" diameter		48	.333		10.62	7.40		18.02	23
5250	To delete coupling & hangers, subtract									
5260	¼" diam. to ⅜" diam.					60%	81%			
5270	½" diam. to ¾" diam.					41%	77%			
5280	1" diam. to 1-½" diam.					26%	67%			
5290	2" diam. to 4" diam.					16%	58%			
5360	CPVC, couplings 10' O.C., hangers 3 per 10'									
5380	Schedule 40									
5460	½" diameter	1 Plum	54	.148	L.F.	1.27	3.66		4.93	6.85

151 | Pipe and Fittings

151 550 | Plastic Pipe

			CREW	DAILY OUTPUT	MAN-HOURS	UNIT	BARE COSTS MAT.	BARE COSTS LABOR	BARE COSTS EQUIP.	BARE COSTS TOTAL	TOTAL INCL O&P	
551	5470	¾" diameter	1 Plum	51	.157	L.F.	1.52	3.87		5.39	7.40	551
	5480	1" diameter		46	.174		1.94	4.30		6.24	8.50	
	5490	1-¼" diameter		42	.190		2.71	4.70		7.41	9.95	
	5500	1-½" diameter		36	.222		3.47	5.50		8.97	11.95	
	5510	2" diameter	Q-1	59	.271		4.03	6.05		10.08	13.35	
	5520	2-½" diameter		56	.286		5.95	6.35		12.30	15.95	
	5530	3" diameter		53	.302		7.83	6.70		14.53	18.55	
	5540	4" diameter		48	.333		10.78	7.40		18.18	23	
	5550	6" diameter		43	.372		17.83	8.25		26.08	32	
	5730	To delete coupling & hangers, subtract										
	5740	½" diam. to ¾" diam.					37%	77%				
	5750	1" diam. to 1-¼" diam.					27%	70%				
	5760	1-½" diam. to 3" diam.					21%	57%				
	5770	4" diam. to 6" diam.					16%	57%				
	5800	Schedule 80										
	5860	½" diameter	1 Plum	50	.160	L.F.	1.28	3.95		5.23	7.25	
	5870	¾" diameter		47	.170		1.57	4.20		5.77	7.95	
	5880	1" diameter		43	.186		2.10	4.60		6.70	9.15	
	5890	1-¼" diameter		39	.205		2.78	5.05		7.83	10.60	
	5900	1-½" diameter		34	.235		3.30	5.80		9.10	12.25	
	5910	2" diameter	Q-1	55	.291		4.24	6.45		10.69	14.25	
	5920	2-½" diameter		52	.308		6.94	6.85		13.79	17.80	
	5930	3" diameter		50	.320		8.68	7.10		15.78	20	
	5940	4" diameter		46	.348		12.13	7.75		19.88	25	
	5950	6" diameter		38	.421		24.18	9.35		33.53	40	
	5960	8" diameter	Q-2	47	.511		43.83	11.75		55.58	66	
	6060	To delete couplings & hangers, subtract										
	6070	½" diam. to ¾" diam.					44%	77%				
	6080	1" diam. to 1-¼" diam.					32%	71%				
	6090	1-½" diam. to 4" diam.					25%	58%				
	6100	6" diam. to 8" diam.					20%	53%				
	6240	CTS, ½" diameter	1 Plum	54	.148	L.F.	.83	3.66		4.49	6.35	
	6250	¾" diameter		51	.157		1.09	3.87		4.96	6.95	
	6260	1" diameter		46	.174		.99	4.30		5.29	7.45	
	6270	1 ¼"		42	.190		1.23	4.70		5.93	8.35	
	6280	1 ½" diameter		36	.222		1.48	5.50		6.98	9.75	
	6290	2" diameter	Q-1	59	.271		2.14	6.05		8.19	11.30	
	6370	To delete coupling & hangers, subtract										
	6380	½" diam.					51%	79%				
	6390	¾" diam.					40%	76%				
	6392	1" thru 2" diam.					72%	68%				
	6410	Polybutylene, flexible, no couplings or hangers, 100' coils										
	6420	For plastic hangers see 151-901-8000										
	6430	Cold water										
	6440	SDR 13.5, 160 psi @ 73°F, ¾" CTS	1 Plum	250	.032	L.F.	.18	.79		.97	1.37	
	6450	1" CTS		204	.039		.28	.97		1.25	1.75	
	6460	1-¼" CTS		151	.053		.43	1.31		1.74	2.41	
	6470	1-½" CTS		107	.075		.58	1.85		2.43	3.38	
	6480	2" CTS		87	.092		.98	2.27		3.25	4.45	
	6500	SDR 9, 250 psi @ 73°F, ¾" CTS		250	.032		.26	.79		1.05	1.46	
	6510	1" CTS		204	.039		.41	.97		1.38	1.89	
	6520	1-¼" CTS		151	.053		.60	1.31		1.91	2.60	
	6530	1-½" CTS		107	.075		.86	1.85		2.71	3.69	
	6540	2" CTS		87	.092		1.44	2.27		3.71	4.95	
	6560	SDR 11.5, 160 psi @ 73°F, ¾" IPS		239	.033		.22	.83		1.05	1.47	
	6570	1" IPS		195	.041		.34	1.01		1.35	1.88	
	6580	1-¼" IPS		143	.056		.60	1.38		1.98	2.71	
	6590	1-½" IPS		102	.078		.82	1.94		2.76	3.78	

151 | Pipe and Fittings

151 550 | Plastic Pipe

			CREW	DAILY OUTPUT	MAN-HOURS	UNIT	BARE COSTS MAT.	BARE COSTS LABOR	BARE COSTS EQUIP.	BARE COSTS TOTAL	TOTAL INCL O&P	
551	6600	2" IPS	1 Plum	83	.096	L.F.	1.37	2.38		3.75	5.05	551
	6820	Hot and cold water										
	6830	SDR 11, 100 psi @ 180°F, ⅛" CTS	1 Plum	395	.020	L.F.	.12	.50		.62	.87	
	6840	¼" CTS		390	.021		.13	.51		.64	.89	
	6850	⅜" CTS		342	.023		.15	.58		.73	1.02	
	6860	½" CTS		294	.027		.16	.67		.83	1.17	
	6870	¾" CTS		212	.038		.29	.93		1.22	1.70	
	6900	SDR 11, 100 psi @ 180°F, fusion jts, ¾" CTS		164	.049		.29	1.20		1.49	2.11	
	6910	1" CTS		157	.051		.49	1.26		1.75	2.41	
	6920	1-¼" CTS		117	.068		.70	1.69		2.39	3.28	
	6930	1-½" CTS		83	.096		.99	2.38		3.37	4.62	
	6940	2" CTS		67	.119		1.66	2.95		4.61	6.20	
	6950	3" CTS	↓	61	.131	↓	5.45	3.24		8.69	10.80	
	7100	Straight lengths same price as coil										
	7280	Polyethylene, flexible, no couplings or hangers										
	7300	SDR 15, 125 psi										
	7310	¾" diameter				L.F.	.11			.11	.12	
	7350	1" diameter					.15			.15	.17	
	7360	1-¼" diameter					.26			.26	.29	
	7370	1-½" diameter					.35			.35	.39	
	7380	2" diameter				↓	.58			.58	.64	
	7700	SDR 11.5, 160 psi										
	7710	½" diameter				L.F.	.08			.08	.09	
	7750	¾" diameter					.13			.13	.14	
	7760	1" diameter					.20			.20	.22	
	7770	1-¼" diameter					.34			.34	.37	
	7780	1-½" diameter					.46			.46	.51	
	7790	2" diameter				↓	.77			.77	.85	
	8120	SDR 9, 200 psi										
	8150	¾" diameter				L.F.	.17			.17	.19	
	8160	1" diameter					.26			.26	.29	
	8170	1-¼" diameter				↓	.45			.45	.50	
	8420	SDR 7										
	8440	¾" diameter				L.F.	.22			.22	.24	
	8450	1" diameter					.35			.35	.39	
	8460	1-¼" diameter				↓	.61			.61	.67	
	8800	PVC, type PSP, drain & sewer, belled end gasket jnt., no hngr.										
	8840	3" diameter				L.F.	.32			.32	.35	
	8850	4" diameter					.40			.40	.44	
	8860	6" diameter				↓	.90			.90	.99	
	9000	Perforated										
	9040	4" diameter				L.F.	.40			.40	.44	
558	0010	**PIPE, PLASTIC, FITTINGS**										558
	0030	Epoxy resin, fiberglass reinforced, general service										
	0090	Elbow, 90°, 2"	Q-1	23	.696	Ea.	36	15.45		51.45	63	
	0100	3"		16	1		44	22		66	81	
	0110	4"		13	1.230		61	27		88	110	
	0120	6"	↓	8	2		125	44		169	205	
	0130	8"	Q-2	9	2.670		185	61		246	295	
	0140	10"		7	3.430		235	79		314	375	
	0150	12"	↓	5	4.800	↓	280	110		390	470	
	0160	45° Elbow, same as 90°										
	0290	Tee, 2"	Q-1	17	.941	Ea.	36	21		57	71	
	0300	3"		10	1.600		44	36		80	100	
	0310	4"		8	2		61	44		105	135	
	0320	6"		5	3.200		125	71		196	245	
	0330	8"	Q-2	6	4		185	92		277	340	
	0340	10"	"	5	4.800	↓	340	110		450	540	

151 | Pipe and Fittings

151 550 | Plastic Pipe

		CREW	DAILY OUTPUT	MAN-HOURS	UNIT	BARE COSTS MAT.	BARE COSTS LABOR	BARE COSTS EQUIP.	BARE COSTS TOTAL	TOTAL INCL O&P
0350	12"	Q-2	4	6	Ea.	410	140		550	655
0380	Couplings									
0410	2"	Q-1	28	.571	Ea.	14.40	12.70		27.10	35
0420	3"		20	.800		17.20	17.80		35	45
0430	4"		17	.941		20	21		41	53
0440	6"		12	1.330		25	30		55	71
0450	8"	Q-2	15	1.600		30	37		67	88
0460	10"		11	2.180		50	50		100	130
0470	12"		10	2.400		65	55		120	155
0490	High corrosion resistant couplings, add					30%				
0500	PVC, high impact/pressure, Schedule 40									
0530	90° Elbow, ½"	1 Plum	20	.400	Ea.	.22	9.90		10.12	14.90
0550	¾"		19	.421		.25	10.40		10.65	15.70
0560	1"		16	.500		.42	12.35		12.77	18.80
0570	1-¼"		15	.533		.58	13.15		13.73	20
0580	1-½"		14	.571		.68	14.10		14.78	22
0590	2"	Q-1	23	.696		1.10	15.45		16.55	24
0600	3"		16	1		4.35	22		26.35	38
0610	4"		13	1.230		7.75	27		34.75	49
0620	6"		8	2		26	44		70	95
0630	8"	Q-2	9	2.670		62	61		123	160
0660	45° Elbow, ½"	1 Plum	20	.400		.35	9.90		10.25	15.05
0680	¾"		19	.421		.50	10.40		10.90	16
0690	1"		16	.500		.70	12.35		13.05	19.10
0700	1-¼"		15	.533		.91	13.15		14.06	21
0710	1-½"		14	.571		1.10	14.10		15.20	22
0720	2"	Q-1	23	.696		1.40	15.45		16.85	24
0730	3"		16	1		5.65	22		27.65	39
0740	4"		13	1.230		10.20	27		37.20	52
0750	6"		8	2		26	44		70	95
0760	8"	Q-2	9	2.670		60	61		121	155
0800	Tee, ½"	1 Plum	13	.615		.26	15.20		15.46	23
0820	¾"		12	.667		.30	16.45		16.75	25
0830	1"		11	.727		.58	17.95		18.53	27
0840	1-¼"		10	.800		.92	19.75		20.67	30
0850	1-½"		10	.800		1.04	19.75		20.79	30
0860	2"	Q-1	17	.941		1.60	21		22.60	33
0870	3"		10	1.600		7.60	36		43.60	61
0880	4"		8	2		12.65	44		56.65	80
0890	6"		5	3.200		43	71		114	155
0900	8"	Q-2	6	4		99	92		191	245
0910	10"		4	6		470	140		610	720
0920	12"		3	8		675	185		860	1,025
1070	Coupling, ½"	1 Plum	22	.364		.15	9		9.15	13.50
1080	¾"		21	.381		.19	9.40		9.59	14.15
1090	1"		18	.444		.26	11		11.26	16.55
1100	1-¼"		17	.471		.37	11.60		11.97	17.65
1110	1-½"		16	.500		.41	12.35		12.76	18.80
1120	2"	Q-1	28	.571		.62	12.70		13.32	19.50
1130	2-½"		25	.640		1.46	14.25		15.71	23
1140	3"		22	.727		2.45	16.15		18.60	27
1150	3-½"		19	.842		4.70	18.70		23.40	33
1160	4"		17	.941		4.10	21		25.10	36
1170	5"		14	1.140		7.60	25		32.60	46
1180	6"		12	1.330		13	30		43	58
1190	8"	Q-2	14	1.710		25	40		65	86
1200	10"		13	1.850		94	43		137	165
1210	12"		12	2		120	46		166	200

151 | Pipe and Fittings

151 550 | Plastic Pipe

			CREW	DAILY OUTPUT	MAN-HOURS	UNIT	BARE COSTS MAT.	BARE COSTS LABOR	BARE COSTS EQUIP.	BARE COSTS TOTAL	TOTAL INCL O&P
	1220	14"	Q-2	10	2.400	Ea.	320	55		375	435
	1230	16"	"	7	3.430	"	350	79		429	500
	2100	Schedule 80									
	2110	90° Elbow, ½"	1 Plum	18	.444	Ea.	.65	11		11.65	17
	2130	¾"		17	.471		.84	11.60		12.44	18.15
	2140	1"		15	.533		1.41	13.15		14.56	21
	2150	1-¼"		14	.571		1.80	14.10		15.90	23
	2160	1-½"		13	.615		1.90	15.20		17.10	25
	2170	2"	Q-1	22	.727		2.12	16.15		18.27	26
	2180	3"		14	1.140		5.40	25		30.40	44
	2190	4"		12	1.330		9.25	30		39.25	54
	2200	6"		7	2.290		21	51		72	98
	2210	8"	Q-2	8	3		49	69		118	155
	2250	45° Elbow, ½"	1 Plum	18	.444		1.25	11		12.25	17.65
	2270	¾"		17	.471		1.90	11.60		13.50	19.35
	2280	1"		15	.533		2.80	13.15		15.95	23
	2290	1-¼"		14	.571		3.60	14.10		17.70	25
	2300	1-½"		13	.615		3.60	15.20		18.80	27
	2310	2"	Q-1	22	.727		3.80	16.15		19.95	28
	2320	3"		14	1.140		8	25		33	46
	2330	4"		12	1.330		15	30		45	60
	2340	6"		7	2.290		32	51		83	110
	2350	8"	Q-2	8	3		62	69		131	170
	2400	Tee, ½"	1 Plum	12	.667		1.65	16.45		18.10	26
	2420	¾"		11	.727		1.65	17.95		19.60	28
	2430	1"		10	.800		1.82	19.75		21.57	31
	2440	1-¼"		9	.889		6.70	22		28.70	40
	2450	1-½"		8	1		6.70	25		31.70	44
	2460	2"	Q-1	14	1.140		7.10	25		32.10	46
	2470	3"		9	1.780		8.25	40		48.25	68
	2480	4"		8	2		13.80	44		57.80	81
	2490	6"		5	3.200		30	71		101	140
	2500	8"	Q-2	6	4		58	92		150	200
	2550	Coupling, ½"	1 Plum	18	.444		1.27	11		12.27	17.70
	2570	¾"		17	.471		1.60	11.60		13.20	19
	2580	1"		15	.533		1.60	13.15		14.75	21
	2590	1-¼"		14	.571		2.85	14.10		16.95	24
	2600	1-½"		13	.615		2.85	15.20		18.05	26
	2610	2"	Q-1	22	.727		3	16.15		19.15	27
	2620	3"		19	.842		6.10	18.70		24.80	34
	2630	4"		16	1		6.65	22		28.65	40
	2640	6"		12	1.330		11.20	30		41.20	56
	2650	8"	Q-2	14	1.710		28	40		68	89
	2660	10"		13	1.850		31	43		74	97
	2670	12"		12	2		37	46		83	110
	2700	PVC (white), Schedule 40, socket joints									
	2760	Elbow 90°, ½"	1 Plum	22	.364	Ea.	.17	9		9.17	13.50
	2770	¾"		21	.381		.19	9.40		9.59	14.15
	2780	1"		18	.444		.33	11		11.33	16.65
	2790	1-¼"		17	.471		.58	11.60		12.18	17.90
	2800	1-½"		16	.500		.62	12.35		12.97	19
	2810	2"	Q-1	28	.571		.97	12.70		13.67	19.90
	2820	2-½"		22	.727		2.94	16.15		19.09	27
	2830	3"		17	.941		3.52	21		24.52	35
	2840	4"		14	1.140		6.30	25		31.30	45
	2850	5"		12	1.330		18.75	30		48.75	65
	2860	6"		8	2		20	44		64	88
	2870	8"	Q-2	10	2.400		51	55		106	140

151 | Pipe and Fittings

151 550 | Plastic Pipe

			CREW	DAILY OUTPUT	MAN-HOURS	UNIT	BARE COSTS MAT.	LABOR	EQUIP.	TOTAL	TOTAL INCL O&P	
558	2980	Elbow 45°, ½"	1 Plum	22	.364	Ea.	.27	9		9.27	13.60	558
	2990	¾"		21	.381		.42	9.40		9.82	14.40	
	3000	1"		18	.444		.50	11		11.50	16.85	
	3010	1-¼"		17	.471		.70	11.60		12.30	18	
	3020	1-½"	↓	16	.500		.87	12.35		13.22	19.30	
	3030	2"	Q-1	28	.571		1.14	12.70		13.84	20	
	3040	2-½"		22	.727		2.95	16.15		19.10	27	
	3050	3"		17	.941		4.57	21		25.57	36	
	3060	4"		14	1.140		8.20	25		33.20	47	
	3070	5"		12	1.330		17	30		47	63	
	3080	6"	↓	8	2		21	44		65	89	
	3090	8"	Q-2	10	2.400		49	55		104	135	
	3180	Tee, ½"	1 Plum	14	.571		.21	14.10		14.31	21	
	3190	¾"		13	.615		.23	15.20		15.43	23	
	3200	1"		12	.667		.43	16.45		16.88	25	
	3210	1-¼"		11	.727		.68	17.95		18.63	27	
	3220	1-½"	↓	10	.800		.83	19.75		20.58	30	
	3230	2"	Q-1	17	.941		1.20	21		22.20	32	
	3240	2-½"		14	1.140		3.93	25		28.93	42	
	3250	3"		11	1.450		5.60	32		37.60	54	
	3260	4"		9	1.780		9.35	40		49.35	69	
	3270	5"		8	2		23	44		67	91	
	3280	6"	↓	5	3.200		32	71		103	140	
	3290	8"	Q-2	6	4		74	92		166	220	
	3380	Coupling, ½"	1 Plum	22	.364		.11	9		9.11	13.45	
	3390	¾"		21	.381		.15	9.40		9.55	14.15	
	3400	1"		18	.444		.25	11		11.25	16.55	
	3410	1-¼"		17	.471		.35	11.60		11.95	17.65	
	3420	1-½"	↓	16	.500		.37	12.35		12.72	18.75	
	3430	2"	Q-1	28	.571		.58	12.70		13.28	19.50	
	3440	2-½"		20	.800		1.28	17.80		19.08	28	
	3450	3"		19	.842		2	18.70		20.70	30	
	3460	4"		16	1		2.85	22		24.85	36	
	3470	5"		14	1.140		8.55	25		33.55	47	
	3480	6"	↓	12	1.330		9.15	30		39.15	54	
	3490	8"	Q-2	14	1.710		17	40		57	77	
	3600	Cap sch 40 PVC socket ½"	1 Plum	44	.182		.10	4.49		4.59	6.75	
	3610	¾"		42	.190		.16	4.70		4.86	7.15	
	3620	1"		36	.222		.21	5.50		5.71	8.40	
	3630	1-¼"		34	.235		.36	5.80		6.16	9	
	3640	1-½"	↓	32	.250		.40	6.20		6.60	9.60	
	3650	2"	Q-1	56	.286		.48	6.35		6.83	9.95	
	3660	2-½"		46	.348		1.68	7.75		9.43	13.30	
	3670	3"		36	.444		1.45	9.90		11.35	16.25	
	3680	4"		30	.533		3.34	11.85		15.19	21	
	3690	6"	↓	20	.800		10	17.80		27.80	37	
	3700	8"	Q-2	22	1.090	↓	18.85	25		43.85	58	
	4500	DWV, ABS, non pressure, socket joints										
	4540	¼ Bend, 1-¼"	1 Plum	17	.471	Ea.	.85	11.60		12.45	18.20	
	4560	1-½"	"	16	.500		.61	12.35		12.96	19	
	4570	2"	Q-1	28	.571		.65	12.70		13.35	19.55	
	4580	3"		17	.941		1.85	21		22.85	33	
	4590	4"		14	1.140		3.20	25		28.20	41	
	4600	6"	↓	8	2	↓	28	44		72	97	
	4650	⅛ Bend, same as ¼ Bend										
	4800	Tee, sanitary										
	4820	1-¼"	1 Plum	11	.727	Ea.	1.80	17.95		19.75	29	
	4830	1-½"	"	10	.800	"	.90	19.75		20.65	30	

151 | Pipe and Fittings

151 550 | Plastic Pipe

		CREW	DAILY OUTPUT	MAN-HOURS	UNIT	BARE COSTS MAT.	LABOR	EQUIP.	TOTAL	TOTAL INCL O&P
4840	2"	Q-1	17	.941	Ea.	1.15	21		22.15	32
4850	3"		11	1.450		2.85	32		34.85	51
4860	4"	↓	9	1.780	↓	5.50	40		45.50	65
5000	PVC, Schedule 40, socket joints									
5040	¼ Bend, 1-¼" diameter	1 Plum	17	.471	Ea.	.65	11.60		12.25	17.95
5060	1-½"	"	16	.500		.71	12.35		13.06	19.10
5070	2"	Q-1	28	.571		1.08	12.70		13.78	20
5080	3"		17	.941		4.10	21		25.10	36
5090	4"		14	1.140		7.25	25		32.25	46
5100	6"	↓	8	2		24	44		68	92
5150	⅛ Bend, 1-¼"	1 Plum	17	.471		.80	11.60		12.40	18.15
5170	1-½"	"	16	.500		.97	12.35		13.32	19.40
5180	2"	Q-1	28	.571		1.46	12.70		14.16	20
5190	3"		17	.941		4.21	21		25.21	36
5200	4"		14	1.140		7.05	25		32.05	45
5210	6"	↓	8	2		26	44		70	95
5250	Tee, sanitary 1-¼"	1 Plum	11	.727		.80	17.95		18.75	28
5270	1-½"	"	10	.800		.94	19.75		20.69	30
5280	2"	Q-1	17	.941		1.45	21		22.45	33
5290	3"		11	1.450		6.55	32		38.55	55
5300	4"	↓	9	1.780		11	40		51	71
5350	Coupling, 1-¼"	1 Plum	17	.471		.42	11.60		12.02	17.70
5360	1-½"	"	16	.500		.45	12.35		12.80	18.80
5370	2"	Q-1	28	.571		.68	12.70		13.38	19.60
5380	3"		22	.727		2.05	16.15		18.20	26
5390	4"		17	.941		3.30	21		24.30	35
5400	6"	↓	12	1.330		11	30		41	56
5450	Solvent cement for PVC, industrial grade, per quart				↓	8.45			8.45	9.30
5500	CPVC, Schedule 80, threaded joints									
5540	90° Elbow, ¼"	1 Plum	20	.400	Ea.	4.40	9.90		14.30	19.50
5560	½"		18	.444		1.95	11		12.95	18.45
5570	¾"		17	.471		2.48	11.60		14.08	20
5580	1"		15	.533		3.94	13.15		17.09	24
5590	1-¼"		14	.571		8.55	14.10		22.65	30
5600	1-½"	↓	13	.615		9.50	15.20		24.70	33
5610	2"	Q-1	22	.727		14.50	16.15		30.65	40
5620	2-½"		18	.889		27	19.75		46.75	59
5630	3"		14	1.140		30	25		55	71
5640	4"		12	1.330		54	30		84	105
5650	6"	↓	7	2.290	↓	110	51		161	195
5700	45° Elbow same as 90° Elbow									
5850	Tee, ¼"	1 Plum	14	.571	Ea.	4.91	14.10		19.01	26
5870	½"		12	.667		2.91	16.45		19.36	28
5880	¾"		11	.727		4.64	17.95		22.59	32
5890	1"		10	.800		5.70	19.75		25.45	36
5900	1-¼"		9	.889		12	22		34	46
5910	1-½"	↓	8	1		14	25		39	52
5920	2"	Q-1	14	1.140		16	25		41	55
5930	2-½"		12	1.330		39	30		69	87
5940	3"		9	1.780		39	40		79	100
5950	4"		8	2		52	44		96	125
5960	6"	↓	5	3.200		135	71		206	255
6000	Coupling, ¼"	1 Plum	20	.400		5.30	9.90		15.20	20
6020	½"		18	.444		2.05	11		13.05	18.55
6030	¾"		17	.471		2.87	11.60		14.47	20
6040	1"		15	.533		3.87	13.15		17.02	24
6050	1-¼"		14	.571		5.75	14.10		19.85	27
6060	1-½"	↓	13	.615	↓	7.30	15.20		22.50	31

151 | Pipe and Fittings

151 550 | Plastic Pipe

			CREW	DAILY OUTPUT	MAN-HOURS	UNIT	BARE COSTS MAT.	LABOR	EQUIP.	TOTAL	TOTAL INCL O&P	
558	6070	2"	Q-1	22	.727	Ea.	8.50	16.15		24.65	33	558
	6080	2-½"		20	.800		19	17.80		36.80	47	
	6090	3"		19	.842		21	18.70		39.70	51	
	6100	4"		16	1		27	22		49	63	
	6110	6"	↓	12	1.330		64	30		94	115	
	6120	8"	Q-2	14	1.710		85	40		125	150	
	6200	CTS, 100 psi at 180°F, hot and cold water										
	6230	90° Elbow, ½"	1 Plum	20	.400	Ea.	.09	9.90		9.99	14.75	
	6250	¾"		19	.421		.23	10.40		10.63	15.70	
	6251	1"		16	.500		.72	12.35		13.07	19.10	
	6252	1-¼"		15	.533		1.15	13.15		14.30	21	
	6253	1-½"	↓	14	.571		1.45	14.10		15.55	23	
	6254	2"	Q-1	23	.696		3.10	15.45		18.55	26	
	6260	45° Elbow, ½"	1 Plum	20	.400		.15	9.90		10.05	14.85	
	6280	¾"		19	.421		.26	10.40		10.66	15.70	
	6281	1"		16	.500		.68	12.35		13.03	19.05	
	6282	1-¼"		15	.533		1.22	13.15		14.37	21	
	6283	1-½"		14	.571		1.96	14.10		16.06	23	
	6284	2"	Q-1	23	.696		4.10	15.45		19.55	27	
	6290	Tee, ½"	1 Plum	13	.615		.15	15.20		15.35	23	
	6310	¾"		12	.667		.35	16.45		16.80	25	
	6311	1"		11	.727		1.63	17.95		19.58	28	
	6312	1-¼"		10	.800		2.36	19.75		22.11	32	
	6313	1-½"		10	.800		3.09	19.75		22.84	33	
	6314	2"	Q-1	17	.941		5	21		26	37	
	6320	Coupling, ½"	1 Plum	22	.364		.13	9		9.13	13.45	
	6340	¾"		21	.381		.16	9.40		9.56	14.15	
	6341	1"		18	.444		.63	11		11.63	17	
	6342	1-¼"		17	.471		.72	11.60		12.32	18.05	
	6343	1-½"	↓	16	.500		.99	12.35		13.34	19.40	
	6344	2"	Q-1	28	.571		2.07	12.70		14.77	21	
	6360	Solvent cement for CPVC, commercial grade, per quart						10.40			10.40	11.45	
	7340	PVC flange, slip-on, ½"	1 Plum	22	.364		2.45	9		11.45	16	
	7350	¾"		21	.381		2.60	9.40		12	16.80	
	7360	1"		18	.444		2.89	11		13.89	19.45	
	7370	1-¼"		17	.471		2.98	11.60		14.58	21	
	7380	1-½"	↓	16	.500		3.04	12.35		15.39	22	
	7390	2"	Q-1	26	.615		4.05	13.70		17.75	25	
	7400	2-½"		24	.667		6.25	14.80		21.05	29	
	7410	3"		18	.889		6.90	19.75		26.65	37	
	7420	4"		15	1.070		8.75	24		32.75	45	
	7430	6"	↓	10	1.600		13.75	36		49.75	68	
	7440	8"	Q-2	11	2.180		25	50		75	100	
	7550	Union, sch 40, socket joints, ½"	1 Plum	19	.421		1.63	10.40		12.03	17.20	
	7560	¾"		18	.444		2.07	11		13.07	18.55	
	7570	1"		15	.533		2.36	13.15		15.51	22	
	7580	1-¼"		14	.571		4.70	14.10		18.80	26	
	7590	1-½"	↓	13	.615		5.30	15.20		20.50	28	
	7600	2"	Q-2	27	.889	↓	7.25	20		27.25	38	
	7990	Polybutyl/polyethyl pipe, for copper fittings see 151-430-7000										
	8000	Compression type, PVC, 160 psi cold water										
	8010	Coupling, ¾" CTS	1 Plum	21	.381	Ea.	3.96	9.40		13.36	18.30	
	8020	1" CTS		18	.444		4.95	11		15.95	22	
	8030	1-¼" CTS		17	.471		7.70	11.60		19.30	26	
	8040	1-½" CTS		16	.500		8.90	12.35		21.25	28	
	8050	2" CTS		15	.533		11.80	13.15		24.95	33	
	8060	Female adapter, ¾" FPT x ¾" CTS		23	.348		2.90	8.60		11.50	15.95	
	8070	¾" FPT x 1" CTS	↓	21	.381	↓	4.35	9.40		13.75	18.75	

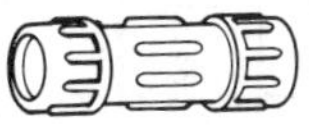

151 | Pipe and Fittings

151 550 | Plastic Pipe

			CREW	DAILY OUTPUT	MAN-HOURS	UNIT	BARE COSTS MAT.	LABOR	EQUIP.	TOTAL	TOTAL INCL O&P	
558	8080	1" FPT x 1" CTS	1 Plum	20	.400	Ea.	4.35	9.90		14.25	19.45	558
	8090	1-¼" FPT x 1-¼" CTS 		18	.444		5.75	11		16.75	23	
	8100	1-½" FPT x 1-½" CTS		16	.500		6.40	12.35		18.75	25	
	8110	2" FPT x 2" CTS		13	.615		10	15.20		25.20	34	
	8130	Male adapter, ¾" MPT x ¾" CTS		23	.348		2.62	8.60		11.22	15.65	
	8140	¾" MPT x 1" CTS		21	.381		3.27	9.40		12.67	17.55	
	8150	1" MPT x 1" CTS		20	.400		3.27	9.90		13.17	18.25	
	8160	1-¼" MPT x 1-¼" CTS 		18	.444		5.10	11		16.10	22	
	8170	1-½" MPT x 1-½" CTS		16	.500		5.90	12.35		18.25	25	
	8180	2" MPT x 2" CTS		13	.615		9.40	15.20		24.60	33	
	8200	Spigot adapter, ¾" IPS x ¾" CTS		23	.348		2.60	8.60		11.20	15.60	
	8210	¾" IPS x 1" CTS 		21	.381		2.60	9.40		12	16.80	
	8220	1" IPS x 1" CTS		20	.400		2.85	9.90		12.75	17.80	
	8230	1-¼" IPS x 1-¼" CTS		18	.444		5.10	11		16.10	22	
	8240	1-½" IPS x 1-½" CTS		16	.500		5.90	12.35		18.25	25	
	8250	2" IPS x 2" CTS		13	.615		9.40	15.20		24.60	33	
	8270	Price includes insert stiffeners										
	8280	250 psi is same price as 160 psi										
	8300	Insert type, nylon, 160 & 250 psi, cold water										
	8310	Clamp ring stainless steel, ¾" IPS	1 Plum	115	.070	Ea.	.53	1.72		2.25	3.13	
	8320	1" IPS		107	.075		.53	1.85		2.38	3.32	
	8330	1-¼" IPS 		101	.079		.53	1.96		2.49	3.49	
	8340	1-½" IPS		95	.084		.53	2.08		2.61	3.67	
	8350	2" IPS		85	.094		.53	2.32		2.85	4.03	
	8370	Coupling, ¾" IPS		22	.364		.27	9		9.27	13.60	
	8380	1" IPS 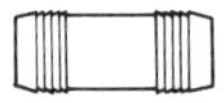		19	.421		.29	10.40		10.69	15.75	
	8390	1-¼" IPS		18	.444		.43	11		11.43	16.75	
	8400	1-½" IPS		17	.471		.51	11.60		12.11	17.80	
	8410	2" IPS		16	.500		.86	12.35		13.21	19.25	
	8430	Elbow, 90°, ¾" IPS		22	.364		.47	9		9.47	13.85	
	8440	1" IPS		19	.421		.51	10.40		10.91	16	
	8450	1-¼" IPS 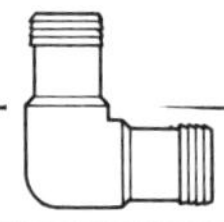		18	.444		.58	11		11.58	16.95	
	8460	1-½" IPS		17	.471		.68	11.60		12.28	18	
	8470	2" IPS		16	.500		.94	12.35		13.29	19.35	
	8490	Male adapter, ¾" IPS x ¾" MPT		25	.320		.27	7.90		8.17	12.05	
	8500	1" IPS x 1" MPT 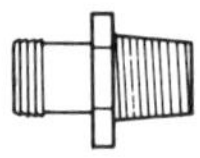		21	.381		.29	9.40		9.69	14.30	
	8510	1-¼" IPS x 1-¼" MPT		20	.400		.65	9.90		10.55	15.40	
	8520	1-½" IPS x 1-½" MPT		18	.444		.89	11		11.89	17.25	
	8530	2" IPS x 2" MPT		15	.533		1.16	13.15		14.31	21	
	8550	Tee, ¾" IPS 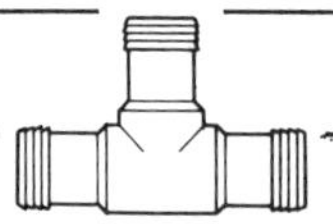		14	.571		.61	14.10		14.71	22	
	8560	1" IPS		13	.615		1.01	15.20		16.21	24	
	8570	1-¼" IPS		12	.667		1.61	16.45		18.06	26	
	8580	1-½" IPS		11	.727		2.22	17.95		20.17	29	
	8590	2" IPS		10	.800		2.99	19.75		22.74	33	
	8610	Insert type, acetal, 100 psi @ 180°F, hot & cold water										
	8620	Coupler, male, ⅜" CTS x ⅜" MPT	1 Plum	29	.276	Ea.	.33	6.80		7.13	10.45	
	8630	⅜" CTS x ½" MPT		28	.286		.33	7.05		7.38	10.85	
	8640	½" CTS x ½" MPT 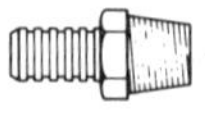		27	.296		.35	7.30		7.65	11.25	
	8650	½" CTS x ¾" MPT		26	.308		.41	7.60		8.01	11.75	
	8660	¾" CTS x ½" MPT		25	.320		.41	7.90		8.31	12.20	
	8670	¾" CTS x ¾" MPT		25	.320		.41	7.90		8.31	12.20	
	8700	Coupling, ⅜" CTS x ½" CTS		25	.320		.20	7.90		8.10	11.95	
	8710	½" CTS 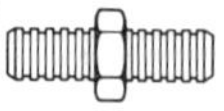		23	.348		.20	8.60		8.80	12.95	
	8720	½" CTS x stub		23	.348		.27	8.60		8.87	13.05	
	8730	¾" CTS		22	.364		.31	9		9.31	13.65	
	8750	Elbow 90°, ⅜" CTS 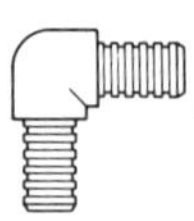		25	.320		.32	7.90		8.22	12.10	
	8760	½" CTS		23	.348		.32	8.60		8.92	13.10	
	8770	¾" CTS		22	.364		.46	9		9.46	13.85	

151 | Pipe and Fittings

151 550 | Plastic Pipe

			CREW	DAILY OUTPUT	MAN-HOURS	UNIT	BARE COSTS MAT.	LABOR	EQUIP.	TOTAL	TOTAL INCL O&P
558	8800	Rings, crimp, copper, ⅜" CTS	1 Plum	120	.067	Ea.	.10	1.65		1.75	2.55
	8810	½" CTS		117	.068		.11	1.69		1.80	2.63
	8820	¾" CTS		115	.070		.13	1.72		1.85	2.69
	8850	Reducer tee, ⅜" x ⅜" x ½" CTS 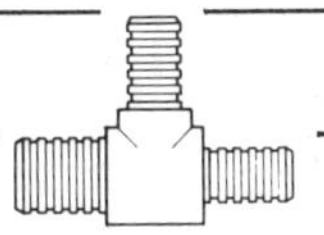		17	.471		.40	11.60		12	17.70
	8860	½" x ⅜" x ½" CTS		15	.533		.40	13.15		13.55	20
	8870	¾" x ½" x ½" CTS		14	.571		.57	14.10		14.67	22
	8890	¾" x ¾" x ½" CTS		14	.571		.57	14.10		14.67	22
	8900	¾" x ½" x ⅜" CTS		14	.571		.57	14.10		14.67	22
	8930	Tee, ⅜" CTS 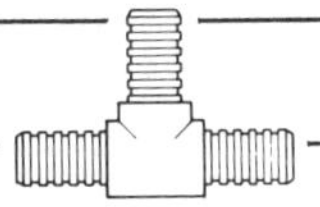		17	.471		.57	11.60		12.17	17.85
	8940	½" CTS		15	.533		.57	13.15		13.72	20
	8950	¾" CTS		14	.571		.57	14.10		14.67	22
	8960	Copper rings included in fitting price									
	9000	Flare type, assembled, acetal, hot & cold water									
	9010	Coupling, ¼" & ⅜" CTS	1 Plum	24	.333	Ea.	1.21	8.25		9.46	13.55
	9020	½" CTS 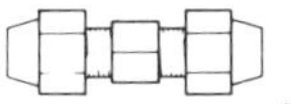		22	.364		1.72	9		10.72	15.20
	9030	¾" CTS		21	.381		2.66	9.40		12.06	16.90
	9040	1" CTS 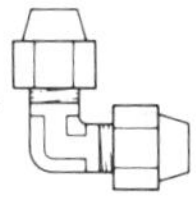		18	.444		3.52	11		14.52	20
	9050	Elbow 90°, ¼" CTS		26	.308		1.75	7.60		9.35	13.20
	9060	⅜" CTS		24	.333		1.88	8.25		10.13	14.30
	9070	½" CTS		22	.364		2.23	9		11.23	15.80
	9080	¾" CTS		21	.381		3.40	9.40		12.80	17.70
	9090	1" CTS		18	.444		4.30	11		15.30	21
	9110	Tee, ¼" & ⅜" CTS 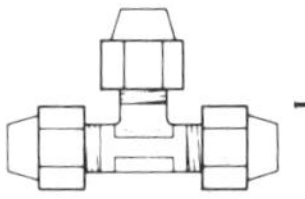		15	.533		1.94	13.15		15.09	22
	9120	½" CTS		14	.571		2.54	14.10		16.64	24
	9130	¾" CTS		13	.615		3.88	15.20		19.08	27
	9140	1" CTS		12	.667		5.10	16.45		21.55	30
	9160	Fusion weld fittings, "hot and cold water"									
	9250	Coupling, 1" CTS 	1 Plum	19	.421	Ea.	1.44	10.40		11.84	17
	9260	1" IPS		19	.421		1.52	10.40		11.92	17.10
	9270	1-¼" IPS		18	.444		1.52	11		12.52	17.95
	9280	1-½" IPS		17	.471		1.76	11.60		13.36	19.20
	9290	2" IPS		16	.500		2.48	12.35		14.83	21
	9300	3" IPS 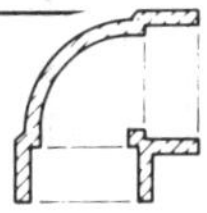		10	.800		10.80	19.75		30.55	41
	9310	Elbow, 90°, 1" CTS		19	.421		1.53	10.40		11.93	17.10
	9320	1" IPS		19	.421		1.92	10.40		12.32	17.55
	9330	1-¼" IPS		18	.444		1.92	11		12.92	18.40
	9340	1-½" IPS		17	.471		2.15	11.60		13.75	19.60
	9350	2" IPS		16	.500		3.26	12.35		15.61	22
	9360	3" IPS		10	.800		40	19.75		59.75	73
	9370	Elbow, 45°, 1" CTS		19	.421		1.53	10.40		11.93	17.10
	9380	1" IPS .		19	.421		1.53	10.40		11.93	17.10
	9390	1-¼" IPS		18	.444		1.92	11		12.92	18.40
	9400	1-½" IPS		17	.471		2.36	11.60		13.96	19.85
	9410	2" IPS		16	.500		3.73	12.35		16.08	22
	9420	3" IPS		10	.800		29	19.75		48.75	61
	9430	Flange, 1" CTS		40	.200		7.35	4.94		12.29	15.40
	9440	1" IPS 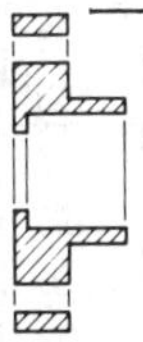		38	.211		7.35	5.20		12.55	15.80
	9450	1-¼" IPS		36	.222		9.45	5.50		14.95	18.55
	9460	1-½" IPS		34	.235		10	5.80		15.80	19.60
	9470	2" IPS		32	.250		10.60	6.20		16.80	21
	9480	Tee, 1" CTS		13	.615		2.66	15.20		17.86	25
	9490	1" IPS		13	.615		4.18	15.20		19.38	27
	9500	1-¼" IPS 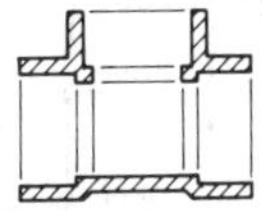		12	.667		4.58	16.45		21.03	29
	9510	1-½" IPS		11	.727		5.80	17.95		23.75	33
	9520	2" IPS		10	.800		9.35	19.75		29.10	40
	9530	3" IPS		7	1.140		43	28		71	89
	9550	For plastic hangers see 151-901-8000									
	9560	For copper/brass fittings see 151-430-7000									

151 | Pipe and Fittings

151 600 | Stainless Steel Pipe

			CREW	DAILY OUTPUT	MAN-HOURS	UNIT	BARE COSTS MAT.	LABOR	EQUIP.	TOTAL	TOTAL INCL O&P
601	0010	**PIPE, STAINLESS STEEL**										601
	0020	Welded, with clevis type hangers 10' O.C.									
	0500	Schedule 5, type 304									
	0540	½" diameter	Q-15	128	.125	L.F.	2.45	2.78	.30	5.53	7.15
	0550	¾" diameter		116	.138		2.88	3.07	.33	6.28	8.10
	0560	1" diameter		103	.155		3.49	3.45	.37	7.31	9.35
	0570	1-¼" diameter		93	.172		4.17	3.82	.41	8.40	10.70
	0580	1-½" diameter		85	.188		4.68	4.18	.45	9.31	11.85
	0590	2" diameter		69	.232		5.69	5.15	.55	11.39	14.50
	0600	2-½" diameter		53	.302		8.15	6.70	.72	15.57	19.70
	0610	3" diameter		48	.333		9.83	7.40	.80	18.03	23
	0620	4" diameter		44	.364		12.61	8.10	.87	21.58	27
	0630	5" diameter		36	.444		20.17	9.90	1.06	31.13	38
	0640	6" diameter	Q-16	42	.571		23.51	13.15	.91	37.57	46
	0650	8" diameter		34	.706		34.68	16.25	1.12	52.05	64
	0660	10" diameter		26	.923		59.14	21	1.47	81.61	98
	0670	12" diameter		21	1.140		75.28	26	1.82	103.10	125
	0700	To delete hangers, subtract									
	0710	½" diam. to 1-½" diam.					8%	19%			
	0720	2" diam. to 5" diam.					4%	9%			
	0730	6" diam. to 12" diam.					3%	4%			
	0750	For small quantities, add				L.F.	10%				
	1250	Schedule 5, type 316									
	1290	½" diameter	Q-15	128	.125	L.F.	3.13	2.78	.30	6.21	7.90
	1300	¾" diameter		116	.138		3.74	3.07	.33	7.14	9
	1310	1" diameter		103	.155		4.32	3.45	.37	8.14	10.30
	1320	1-¼" diameter		93	.172		5.12	3.82	.41	9.35	11.75
	1330	1-½" diameter		85	.188		5.83	4.18	.45	10.46	13.10
	1340	2" diameter		69	.232		7.29	5.15	.55	12.99	16.30
	1350	2-½" diameter		53	.302		10.55	6.70	.72	17.97	22
	1360	3" diameter		48	.333		13.18	7.40	.80	21.38	26
	1370	4" diameter		44	.364		16.26	8.10	.87	25.23	31
	1380	5" diameter		36	.444		28.42	9.90	1.06	39.38	47
	1390	6" diameter	Q-16	42	.571		30.51	13.15	.91	44.57	54
	1400	8" diameter		34	.706		44.68	16.25	1.12	62.05	75
	1410	10" diameter		26	.923		73.14	21	1.47	95.61	115
	1420	12" diameter		21	1.140		94.28	26	1.82	122.10	145
	1490	For small quantities, add					10%				
	1940	To delete hanger, subtract									
	1950	½" diam. to 1-½" diam.					5%	19%			
	1960	2" diam. to 5" diam.					3%	9%			
	1970	6" diam. to 12" diam.					2%	4%			
	2000	Schedule 10, type 304									
	2040	¼" diameter	Q-15	131	.122	L.F.	2.20	2.72	.29	5.21	6.75
	2050	⅜" diameter		128	.125		2.34	2.78	.30	5.42	7
	2060	½" diameter		125	.128		2.98	2.85	.31	6.14	7.85
	2070	¾" diameter		113	.142		3.49	3.15	.34	6.98	8.90
	2080	1" diameter		100	.160		5.15	3.56	.38	9.09	11.35
	2090	1-¼" diameter		91	.176		6.33	3.91	.42	10.66	13.20
	2100	1-½" diameter		83	.193		6.98	4.29	.46	11.73	14.55
	2110	2" diameter		67	.239		8.74	5.30	.57	14.61	18.10
	2120	2-½" diameter		51	.314		10.95	6.95	.75	18.65	23
	2130	3" diameter		46	.348		13.43	7.75	.83	22.01	27
	2140	4" diameter		42	.381		17.46	8.45	.91	26.82	33
	2150	5" diameter		35	.457		24.42	10.15	1.09	35.66	43
	2160	6" diameter	Q-16	40	.600		28.51	13.85	.96	43.32	53
	2170	8" diameter		33	.727		41.68	16.75	1.16	59.59	72
	2180	10" diameter		25	.960		64.14	22	1.53	87.67	105

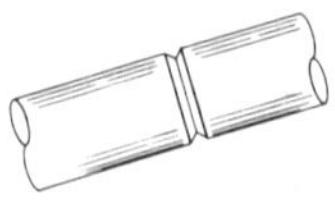

151 | Pipe and Fittings

151 600 | Stainless Steel Pipe

			DAILY	MAN-		\multicolumn{4}{c}{BARE COSTS}	TOTAL	
		CREW	OUTPUT	HOURS	UNIT	MAT.	LABOR	EQUIP.	TOTAL	INCL O&P	
601	2190	12" diameter	Q-16	21	1.140	L.F.	78.28	26	1.82	106.10	125	601
	2250	For small quantities, add				"	10%					
	2650	To delete hanger, subtract										
	2660	¼" diam. to ¾" diam.					9%	22%				
	2670	1" diam. to 2" diam.					4%	15%				
	2680	2-½" diam. to 5" diam.					3%	8%				
	2690	6" diam. to 12" diam.					3%	4%				
	2750	Schedule 10, type 316										
	2790	¼" diameter	Q-15	131	.122	L.F.	2.44	2.72	.29	5.45	7.05	
	2800	⅜" diameter		128	.125		2.76	2.78	.30	5.84	7.50	
	2810	½" diameter		125	.128		3.77	2.85	.31	6.93	8.70	
	2820	¾" diameter		113	.142		4.29	3.15	.34	7.78	9.75	
	2830	1" diameter		100	.160		6.37	3.56	.38	10.31	12.70	
	2840	1-¼" diameter		91	.176		7.98	3.91	.42	12.31	15.05	
	2850	1-½" diameter		83	.193		8.79	4.29	.46	13.54	16.55	
	2860	2" diameter		67	.239		10.94	5.30	.57	16.81	21	
	2870	2-½" diameter		51	.314		14.05	6.95	.75	21.75	27	
	2880	3" diameter		46	.348		18.08	7.75	.83	26.66	32	
	2890	4" diameter		42	.381		22.36	8.45	.91	31.72	38	
	2900	5" diameter		35	.457		32.42	10.15	1.09	43.66	52	
	2910	6" diameter	Q-16	40	.600		35.51	13.85	.96	50.32	61	
	2920	8" diameter		33	.727		57.68	16.75	1.16	75.59	90	
	2930	10" diameter		25	.960		80.14	22	1.53	103.67	125	
	2940	12" diameter		21	1.140		111.28	26	1.82	139.10	165	
	2990	For small quantities, add					10%					
	3430	To delete hanger, subtract										
	3440	¼" diam. to ¾" diam.					6%	22%				
	3450	1" diam. to 2" diam.					3%	15%				
	3460	2-½" diam. to 5" diam.					2%	8%				
	3470	6" diam. to 12" diam.					2%	4%				
	3500	Threaded, couplings and hangers 10' O.C.										
	3520	Schedule 40, type 304										
	3540	¼" diameter	1 Plum	54	.148	L.F.	2.74	3.66		6.40	8.45	
	3550	⅜" diameter		53	.151		3.17	3.73		6.90	9	
	3560	½" diameter		52	.154		4.16	3.80		7.96	10.20	
	3570	¾" diameter		51	.157		5.06	3.87		8.93	11.30	
	3580	1" diameter		45	.178		6.60	4.39		10.99	13.80	
	3590	1-¼" diameter	Q-1	76	.211		8.38	4.68		13.06	16.15	
	3600	1-½" diameter		69	.232		9.88	5.15		15.03	18.50	
	3610	2" diameter		57	.281		13.39	6.25		19.64	24	
	3620	2-½" diameter		44	.364		21.15	8.10		29.25	35	
	3630	3" diameter		38	.421		27.58	9.35		36.93	44	
	3640	4" diameter	Q-2	51	.471		39.16	10.85		50.01	59	
	3740	For small quantities, add					10%					
	4200	To delete couplings & hangers, subtract										
	4210	¼" diam. to ¾" diam.					15%	56%				
	4220	1" diam. to 2" diam.					18%	49%				
	4230	2-½" diam. to 4" diam.					34%	40%				
	4250	Schedule 40, type 316										
	4290	¼" diameter	1 Plum	54	.148	L.F.	3.20	3.66		6.86	8.95	
	4300	⅜" diameter		53	.151		3.82	3.73		7.55	9.75	
	4310	½" diameter		52	.154		5.23	3.80		9.03	11.40	
	4320	¾" diameter		51	.157		6.03	3.87		9.90	12.40	
	4330	1" diameter		45	.178		8.43	4.39		12.82	15.80	
	4340	1-¼" diameter	Q-1	76	.211		10.71	4.68		15.39	18.70	
	4350	1-½" diameter		69	.232		12.50	5.15		17.65	21	
	4360	2" diameter		57	.281		16.73	6.25		22.98	28	
	4370	2-½" diameter		44	.364		26.93	8.10		35.03	42	

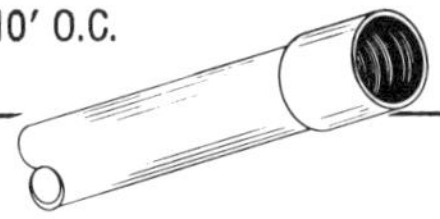

151 | Pipe and Fittings

151 600 | Stainless Steel Pipe

			CREW	DAILY OUTPUT	MAN-HOURS	UNIT	BARE COSTS MAT.	LABOR	EQUIP.	TOTAL	TOTAL INCL O&P	
601	4380	3" diameter	Q-1	38	.421	L.F.	35.64	9.35		44.99	53	601
	4390	4" diameter	Q-2	51	.471		49.72	10.85		60.57	71	
	4490	For small quantities, add				↓	10%					
	4900	To delete couplings & hangers, subtract										
	4910	¼" diam. to ¾" diam.					12%	56%				
	4920	1" diam. to 2" diam.					14%	49%				
	4930	2-½" diam. to 4" diam.					27%	40%				
	5000	Schedule 80, type 304										
	5040	¼" diameter	1 Plum	53	.151	L.F.	3.38	3.73		7.11	9.25	
	5050	⅜" diameter		52	.154		4.01	3.80		7.81	10.05	
	5060	½" diameter		51	.157		5.16	3.87		9.03	11.45	
	5070	¾" diameter		48	.167		6.66	4.12		10.78	13.45	
	5080	1" diameter	↓	43	.186		9.27	4.60		13.87	17	
	5090	1-¼" diameter	Q-1	73	.219		12.98	4.87		17.85	22	
	5100	1-½" diameter		67	.239		14.78	5.30		20.08	24	
	5110	2" diameter	↓	54	.296		19.49	6.60		26.09	31	
	5190	For small quantities, add				↓	10%					
	5700	To delete couplings & hangers, subtract										
	5710	¼" diam. to ¾" diam.					10%	53%				
	5720	1" diam. to 2" diam.					14%	47%				
	5750	Schedule 80, type 316										
	5790	¼" diameter	1 Plum	53	.151	L.F.	4.22	3.73		7.95	10.15	
	5800	⅜" diameter		52	.154		4.96	3.80		8.76	11.10	
	5810	½" diameter		51	.157		6.82	3.87		10.69	13.25	
	5820	¾" diameter		48	.167		8.14	4.12		12.26	15.05	
	5830	1" diameter	↓	43	.186		11.27	4.60		15.87	19.20	
	5840	1-¼" diameter	Q-1	73	.219		16.18	4.87		21.05	25	
	5850	1-½" diameter		67	.239		18.58	5.30		23.88	28	
	5860	2" diameter	↓	54	.296		24.39	6.60		30.99	37	
	5950	For small quantities, add				↓	10%					
	7000	To delete couplings & hangers, subtract										
	7010	¼" diam. to ¾" diam.					9%	53%				
	7020	1" diam. to 2" diam.					14%	47%				
	8000	Weld joints with clevis type hangers 10' O.C.										
	8010	Schedule 40, type 304										
	8050	⅛" pipe size	Q-15	126	.127	L.F.	1.99	2.82	.30	5.11	6.70	
	8060	¼" pipe size		125	.128		2.56	2.85	.31	5.72	7.40	
	8070	⅜" pipe size		122	.131		2.96	2.92	.31	6.19	7.95	
	8080	½" pipe size		118	.136		3.87	3.01	.32	7.20	9.10	
	8090	¾" pipe size		109	.147		4.67	3.26	.35	8.28	10.35	
	8100	1" pipe size		95	.168		5.97	3.74	.40	10.11	12.55	
	8110	1-¼" pipe size		86	.186		7.48	4.14	.44	12.06	14.85	
	8120	1-½" pipe size		78	.205		8.78	4.56	.49	13.83	16.95	
	8130	2" pipe size		62	.258		11.69	5.75	.62	18.06	22	
	8140	2-½" pipe size		49	.327		17.25	7.25	.78	25.28	31	
	8150	3" pipe size		44	.364		22.28	8.10	.87	31.25	37	
	8160	3-½" pipe size		44	.364		26.36	8.10	.87	35.33	42	
	8170	4" pipe size		39	.410		31.36	9.10	.98	41.44	49	
	8180	5" pipe size	↓	32	.500		43.42	11.10	1.19	55.71	66	
	8190	6" pipe size	Q-16	37	.649		53.51	14.95	1.03	69.49	82	
	8200	8" pipe size		29	.828		85.68	19.10	1.32	106.10	125	
	8210	10" pipe size		24	1		171.14	23	1.59	195.73	225	
	8220	12" pipe size	↓	20	1.200	↓	191.28	28	1.91	221.19	255	
	8300	Schedule 40, type 316										
	8310	⅛" pipe size	Q-15	126	.127	L.F.	2.49	2.82	.30	5.61	7.25	
	8320	¼" pipe size		125	.128		2.98	2.85	.31	6.14	7.85	
	8330	⅜" pipe size		122	.131		3.56	2.92	.31	6.79	8.60	
	8340	½" pipe size	↓	118	.136		4.88	3.01	.32	8.21	10.20	

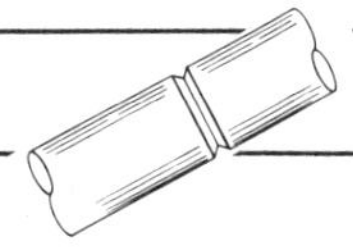

151 | Pipe and Fittings

151 600 | Stainless Steel Pipe

			DAILY	MAN-		\multicolumn{4}{c}{BARE COSTS}	TOTAL
		CREW	OUTPUT	HOURS	UNIT	MAT.	LABOR	EQUIP.	TOTAL	INCL O&P
601	8350	¾" pipe size	Q-15	109	.147	L.F.	5.57	3.26	.35	9.18	11.35	601
	8360	1" pipe size		95	.168		7.67	3.74	.40	11.81	14.45
	8370	1-¼" pipe size		86	.186		9.63	4.14	.44	14.21	17.20
	8380	1-½" pipe size		78	.205		11.18	4.56	.49	16.23	19.60
	8390	2" pipe size		62	.258		14.69	5.75	.62	21.06	25
	8400	2-½" pipe size		49	.327		22.25	7.25	.78	30.28	36
	8410	3" pipe size		44	.364		29.28	8.10	.87	38.25	45
	8420	3-½" pipe size		44	.364		35.36	8.10	.87	44.33	52
	8430	4" pipe size		39	.410		40.36	9.10	.98	50.44	59
	8440	5" pipe size		32	.500		59.42	11.10	1.19	71.71	83
	8450	6" pipe size	Q-16	37	.649		69.51	14.95	1.03	85.49	100
	8460	8" pipe size		29	.828		110.68	19.10	1.32	131.10	150
	8470	10" pipe size		24	1		196.14	23	1.59	220.73	250
	8480	12" pipe size		20	1.200		246.28	28	1.91	276.19	315
	8500	Schedule 80, type 304									
	8510	¼" pipe size	Q-15	110	.145	L.F.	3.16	3.23	.35	6.74	8.65
	8520	⅜" pipe size		109	.147		3.76	3.26	.35	7.37	9.35
	8530	½" pipe size		106	.151		4.77	3.36	.36	8.49	10.60
	8540	¾" pipe size		96	.167		6.07	3.71	.40	10.18	12.60
	8550	1" pipe size		87	.184		8.27	4.09	.44	12.80	15.65
	8560	1-¼" pipe size		81	.198		10.68	4.39	.47	15.54	18.80
	8570	1-½" pipe size		74	.216		12.18	4.81	.52	17.51	21
	8580	2" pipe size		58	.276		15.69	6.15	.66	22.50	27
	8590	2-½" pipe size		46	.348		30.25	7.75	.83	38.83	46
	8600	3" pipe size		41	.390		43.28	8.70	.93	52.91	62
	8610	4" pipe size		33	.485		65.36	10.80	1.16	77.32	89
	8630	6" pipe size	Q-16	30	.800		145.51	18.45	1.27	165.23	190
	8640	Schedule 80, type 316									
	8650	¼" pipe size	Q-15	110	.145	L.F.	3.96	3.23	.35	7.54	9.55
	8660	⅜" pipe size		109	.147		4.68	3.26	.35	8.29	10.40
	8670	½" pipe size		106	.151		6.37	3.36	.36	10.09	12.40
	8680	¾" pipe size		96	.167		7.47	3.71	.40	11.58	14.15
	8690	1" pipe size		87	.184		10.17	4.09	.44	14.70	17.75
	8700	1-¼" pipe size		81	.198		13.68	4.39	.47	18.54	22
	8710	1-½" pipe size		74	.216		15.68	4.81	.52	21.01	25
	8720	2" pipe size		58	.276		20.19	6.15	.66	27	32
	8730	2-½" pipe size		46	.348		49.25	7.75	.83	57.83	67
	8740	3" pipe size		41	.390		60.28	8.70	.93	69.91	80
	8760	4" pipe size		33	.485		81.36	10.80	1.16	93.32	105
	8770	6" pipe size	Q-16	30	.800		215.51	18.45	1.27	235.23	265
	8790	Schedule 160, type 304									
	8800	½" pipe size	Q-15	96	.167	L.F.	6.32	3.71	.40	10.43	12.90
	8810	¾" pipe size		88	.182		7.42	4.04	.43	11.89	14.65
	8820	1" pipe size		80	.200		12.67	4.45	.48	17.60	21
	8840	1-½" pipe size		67	.239		17.43	5.30	.57	23.30	28
	8850	2" pipe size		53	.302		25.19	6.70	.72	32.61	38
	8870	3" pipe size		37	.432		41.28	9.60	1.03	51.91	61
	8900	Schedule 160, type 316									
	8910	½" pipe size	Q-15	96	.167	L.F.	9.42	3.71	.40	13.53	16.30
	8920	¾" pipe size		88	.182		9.92	4.04	.43	14.39	17.40
	8930	1" pipe size		80	.200		14.17	4.45	.48	19.10	23
	8940	1-¼" pipe size		73	.219		20.18	4.87	.52	25.57	30
	8950	1-½" pipe size		67	.239		23.18	5.30	.57	29.05	34
	8960	2" pipe size		53	.302		32.19	6.70	.72	39.61	46
	8990	4" pipe size		30	.533		81.36	11.85	1.27	94.48	110
	9250	Welding labor per joint for stainless steel									
	9260	Schedule 5 and 10									
	9270	¼" pipe size	Q-15	36	.444	Ea.		9.90	1.06	10.96	15.80

151 | Pipe and Fittings

151 600 | Stainless Steel Pipe

			CREW	DAILY OUTPUT	MAN-HOURS	UNIT	MAT.	LABOR	EQUIP.	TOTAL	TOTAL INCL O&P	
601	9280	3/8" pipe size	Q-15	35	.457	Ea.		10.15	1.09	11.24	16.25	601
	9290	1/2" pipe size		35	.457			10.15	1.09	11.24	16.25	
	9300	3/4" pipe size		28	.571			12.70	1.36	14.06	20	
	9310	1" pipe size		25	.640			14.25	1.53	15.78	23	
	9320	1-1/4" pipe size		22	.727			16.15	1.74	17.89	26	
	9330	1-1/2" pipe size		21	.762			16.95	1.82	18.77	27	
	9340	2" pipe size		18	.889			19.75	2.12	21.87	32	
	9350	2-1/2" pipe size		14	1.140			25	2.73	27.73	41	
	9360	3" pipe size		13	1.230			27	2.94	29.94	44	
	9370	4" pipe size		12	1.330			30	3.18	33.18	47	
	9380	5" pipe size		10	1.600			36	3.82	39.82	57	
	9390	6" pipe size		9	1.780			40	4.24	44.24	63	
	9400	8" pipe size		6	2.670			59	6.35	65.35	95	
	9410	10" pipe size		4	4			89	9.55	98.55	140	
	9420	12" pipe size	↓	3	5.330	↓		120	12.75	132.75	190	
	9500	Schedule 40										
	9510	1/4" pipe size	Q-15	35	.457	Ea.		10.15	1.09	11.24	16.25	
	9520	3/8" pipe size		35	.457			10.15	1.09	11.24	16.25	
	9530	1/2" pipe size		34	.471			10.45	1.12	11.57	16.75	
	9540	3/4" pipe size		28	.571			12.70	1.36	14.06	20	
	9550	1" pipe size		24	.667			14.80	1.59	16.39	24	
	9560	1-1/4" pipe size		21	.762			16.95	1.82	18.77	27	
	9570	1-1/2" pipe size		20	.800			17.80	1.91	19.71	28	
	9580	2" pipe size		17	.941			21	2.25	23.25	34	
	9590	2-1/2" pipe size		14	1.140			25	2.73	27.73	41	
	9600	3" pipe size		13	1.230			27	2.94	29.94	44	
	9610	4" pipe size		11	1.450			32	3.47	35.47	52	
	9620	5" pipe size		9	1.780			40	4.24	44.24	63	
	9630	6" pipe size		8	2			44	4.78	48.78	71	
	9640	8" pipe size		5	3.200			71	7.65	78.65	115	
	9650	10" pipe size		4	4			89	9.55	98.55	140	
	9660	12" pipe size	↓	3	5.330	↓		120	12.75	132.75	190	
	9750	Schedule 80										
	9760	1/4" pipe size	Q-15	28	.571	Ea.		12.70	1.36	14.06	20	
	9770	3/8" pipe size		28	.571			12.70	1.36	14.06	20	
	9780	1/2" pipe size		28	.571			12.70	1.36	14.06	20	
	9790	3/4" pipe size		24	.667			14.80	1.59	16.39	24	
	9800	1" pipe size		21	.762			16.95	1.82	18.77	27	
	9810	1-1/4" pipe size		20	.800			17.80	1.91	19.71	28	
	9820	1-1/2" pipe size		19	.842			18.70	2.01	20.71	30	
	9830	2" pipe size		16	1			22	2.39	24.39	36	
	9840	2-1/2" pipe size		13	1.230			27	2.94	29.94	44	
	9850	3" pipe size		12	1.330			30	3.18	33.18	47	
	9860	4" pipe size		8	2			44	4.78	48.78	71	
	9870	5" pipe size		6	2.670			59	6.35	65.35	95	
	9880	6" pipe size		5	3.200			71	7.65	78.65	115	
	9890	8" pipe size		3	5.330			120	12.75	132.75	190	
	9900	10" pipe size		2	8			180	19.10	199.10	285	
	9910	12" pipe size		1	16			355	38	393	570	
	9920	Schedule 160, 1/2" pipe size		25	.640			14.25	1.53	15.78	23	
	9930	3/4" pipe size		22	.727			16.15	1.74	17.89	26	
	9940	1" pipe size		19	.842			18.70	2.01	20.71	30	
	9950	1-1/4" pipe size		18	.889			19.75	2.12	21.87	32	
	9960	1-1/2" pipe size		17	.941			21	2.25	23.25	34	
	9970	2" pipe size		14	1.140			25	2.73	27.73	41	
	9980	3" pipe size		11	1.450			32	3.47	35.47	52	
	9990	4" pipe size	↓	7	2.290	↓		51	5.45	56.45	81	

151 | Pipe and Fittings

151 600 | Stainless Steel Pipe

		CREW	DAILY OUTPUT	MAN-HOURS	UNIT	BARE COSTS				TOTAL INCL O&P
						MAT.	LABOR	EQUIP.	TOTAL	
0010	PIPE, STAINLESS STEEL, FITTINGS									
0100	Butt weld joint, schedule 5, type 304									
0120	90° Elbow, long									
0140	½"	Q-15	16	1	Ea.	7.28	22	2.39	31.67	44
0150	¾"		16	1		7.28	22	2.39	31.67	44
0160	1"		15	1.070		7.28	24	2.55	33.83	46
0170	1-¼"		14	1.140		12	25	2.73	39.73	54
0180	1-½"		13	1.230		10.48	27	2.94	40.42	55
0190	2"		11	1.450		13.04	32	3.47	48.51	66
0200	2-½"		8	2		20	44	4.78	68.78	93
0210	3"		6	2.670		21.60	59	6.35	86.95	120
0220	3-½"		5	3.200		132	71	7.65	210.65	260
0230	4"		4	4		42.40	89	9.55	140.95	190
0240	5"		3	5.330		332	120	12.75	464.75	555
0250	6"	Q-16	4	6		120	140	9.55	269.55	350
0260	8"		3	8		200	185	12.75	397.75	510
0270	10"		2	12		464	275	19.10	758.10	940
0280	12"		1.57	15.290		740	350	24	1,114	1,375
0320	For schedule 5, type 316, add					30%				
0600	45° Elbow, long									
0620	½"	Q-15	16	1	Ea.	10.48	22	2.39	34.87	47
0630	¾"		16	1		10.48	22	2.39	34.87	47
0640	1"		15	1.070		10.48	24	2.55	37.03	50
0650	1-¼"		14	1.140		16	25	2.73	43.73	58
0660	1-½"		13	1.230		10.72	27	2.94	40.66	56
0670	2"		11	1.450		12.32	32	3.47	47.79	65
0680	2-½"		8	2		21	44	4.78	69.78	94
0690	3"		6	2.670		19.20	59	6.35	84.55	115
0700	3-½"		5	3.200		135	71	7.65	213.65	260
0710	4"		4	4		34	89	9.55	132.55	180
0720	5"		3	5.330		235	120	12.75	367.75	450
0730	6"	Q-16	4	6		80	140	9.55	229.55	305
0740	8"		3	8		140	185	12.75	337.75	440
0750	10"		2	12		315	275	19.10	609.10	780
0760	12"		1.57	15.290		495	350	24	869	1,100
0800	For schedule 5, type 316, add					25%				
1100	Tee, straight									
1130	½"	Q-15	10	1.600	Ea.	30	36	3.82	69.82	90
1140	¾"		10	1.600		30	36	3.82	69.82	90
1150	1"		10	1.600		27.20	36	3.82	67.02	87
1160	1-¼"		9	1.780		48	40	4.24	92.24	115
1170	1-½"		8	2		28	44	4.78	76.78	100
1180	2"		7	2.290		28.80	51	5.45	85.25	115
1190	2-½"		5	3.200		84	71	7.65	162.65	205
1200	3"		4	4		54.40	89	9.55	152.95	200
1210	3-½"		3	5.330		110	120	12.75	242.75	310
1220	4"		2	8		76.80	180	19.10	275.90	370
1230	5"		2	8		308	180	19.10	507.10	625
1240	6"	Q-16	2.60	9.230		195	215	14.70	424.70	545
1250	8"		2	12		485	275	19.10	779.10	965
1260	10"		1.80	13.330		800	305	21	1,126	1,350
1270	12"		1.40	17.140		1,025	395	27	1,447	1,750
1320	For schedule 5, type 316, add					25%				
2000	Butt weld joint, schedule 10, type 304									
2020	90° Elbow, long									
2040	½"	Q-15	16	1	Ea.	6.88	22	2.39	31.27	43
2050	¾"		16	1		6.88	22	2.39	31.27	43
2060	1"		15	1.070		6.88	24	2.55	33.43	46

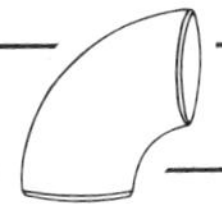

151 | Pipe and Fittings

151 600 | Stainless Steel Pipe

			CREW	DAILY OUTPUT	MAN-HOURS	UNIT	BARE COSTS MAT.	LABOR	EQUIP.	TOTAL	TOTAL INCL O&P	
612	2070	1-¼"	Q-15	14	1.140	Ea.	11.44	25	2.73	39.17	53	612
	2080	1-½"		13	1.230		10	27	2.94	39.94	55	
	2090	2"		11	1.450		12.40	32	3.47	47.87	65	
	2100	2-½"		8	2		19.20	44	4.78	67.98	92	
	2110	3"		6	2.670		21	59	6.35	86.35	120	
	2120	3-½"		5	3.200		125	71	7.65	203.65	250	
	2130	4"		4	4		40	89	9.55	138.55	185	
	2140	5"		3	5.330		315	120	12.75	447.75	535	
	2150	6"	Q-16	4	6		115	140	9.55	264.55	340	
	2160	8"		3	8		190	185	12.75	387.75	495	
	2170	10"		2	12		440	275	19.10	734.10	915	
	2180	12"		1.57	15.290		705	350	24	1,079	1,325	
	2220	For schedule 10, type 316, add					30%					
	2500	45° Elbow, long										
	2520	½"	Q-15	16	1	Ea.	9.76	22	2.39	34.15	46	
	2530	¾"		16	1		9.76	22	2.39	34.15	46	
	2540	1"		15	1.070		9.76	24	2.55	36.31	49	
	2550	1-¼"		14	1.140		15.20	25	2.73	42.93	57	
	2560	1-½"		13	1.230		10	27	2.94	39.94	55	
	2570	2"		11	1.450		11.45	32	3.47	46.92	64	
	2580	2-½"		8	2		19.20	44	4.78	67.98	92	
	2590	3"		6	2.670		18.40	59	6.35	83.75	115	
	2600	3-½"		5	3.200		125	71	7.65	203.65	250	
	2610	4"		4	4		31	89	9.55	129.55	175	
	2620	5"		3	5.330		220	120	12.75	352.75	430	
	2630	6"	Q-16	4	6		75	140	9.55	224.55	300	
	2640	8"		3	8		130	185	12.75	327.75	430	
	2650	10"		2	12		295	275	19.10	589.10	755	
	2660	12"		1.57	15.290		470	350	24	844	1,075	
	2700	For schedule 10, type 316, add					30%					
	3000	Tee, straight										
	3030	½"	Q-15	10	1.600	Ea.	26	36	3.82	65.82	86	
	3040	¾"		10	1.600		26	36	3.82	65.82	86	
	3050	1"		10	1.600		24	36	3.82	63.82	83	
	3060	1-¼"		9	1.780		43	40	4.24	87.24	110	
	3070	1-½"		8	2		27	44	4.78	75.78	100	
	3080	2"		7	2.290		28	51	5.45	84.45	110	
	3090	2-½"		5	3.200		80	71	7.65	158.65	200	
	3100	3"		4	4		52	89	9.55	150.55	200	
	3110	3-½"		3	5.330		110	120	12.75	242.75	310	
	3120	4"		2	8		74	180	19.10	273.10	365	
	3130	5"		2	8		295	180	19.10	494.10	610	
	3140	6"	Q-16	2.60	9.230		190	215	14.70	419.70	540	
	3150	8"		2	12		460	275	19.10	754.10	935	
	3160	10"		1.80	13.330		760	305	21	1,086	1,325	
	3170	12"		1.40	17.140		960	395	27	1,382	1,675	
	3220	For schedule 10, type 316, add					25%					
	3250	Butt weld joint, schedule 40, type 304										
	3260	90° Elbow, long, ½"	Q-15	14	1.140	Ea.	8.48	25	2.73	36.21	50	
	3270	¾"		14	1.140		8.48	25	2.73	36.21	50	
	3280	1"		12	1.330		8.48	30	3.18	41.66	57	
	3290	1-¼"		11	1.450		14.40	32	3.47	49.87	68	
	3300	1-½"		10	1.600		12	36	3.82	51.82	70	
	3310	2"		9	1.780		16	40	4.24	60.24	81	
	3320	2-½"		7	2.290		33.60	51	5.45	90.05	120	
	3330	3"		6	2.670		38.40	59	6.35	103.75	135	
	3340	3-½"		5.50	2.910		200	65	6.95	271.95	325	
	3350	4"		5	3.200		72	71	7.65	150.65	195	

151 | Pipe and Fittings

151 600 | Stainless Steel Pipe

		CREW	DAILY OUTPUT	MAN-HOURS	UNIT	BARE COSTS				TOTAL INCL O&P
						MAT.	LABOR	EQUIP.	TOTAL	
3360	5"	Q-15	4	4	Ea.	328	89	9.55	426.55	505
3370	6"	Q-16	6	4		240	92	6.35	338.35	410
3380	8"		4	6		450	140	9.55	599.55	710
3390	10"		3	8		945	185	12.75	1,142	1,325
3400	12"	↓	2	12	↓	1,225	275	19.10	1,519	1,775
3410	For schedule 40, type 316, add					25%				
3460	45° Elbow, long, ½"	Q-15	14	1.140	Ea.	12	25	2.73	39.73	54
3470	¾"		14	1.140		12	25	2.73	39.73	54
3480	1"		12	1.330		12	30	3.18	45.18	61
3490	1-¼"		11	1.450		16	32	3.47	51.47	69
3500	1-½"		10	1.600		12	36	3.82	51.82	70
3510	2"		9	1.780		16	40	4.24	60.24	81
3520	2-½"		7	2.290		32	51	5.45	88.45	115
3530	3"		6	2.670		28	59	6.35	93.35	125
3540	3-½"		5.50	2.910		200	65	6.95	271.95	325
3550	4"		5	3.200		54	71	7.65	132.65	175
3560	5"	↓	4	4		230	89	9.55	328.55	395
3570	6"	Q-16	6	4		155	92	6.35	253.35	315
3580	8"		4	6		292	140	9.55	441.55	535
3590	10"		3	8		564	185	12.75	761.75	910
3600	12"	↓	2	12	↓	735	275	19.10	1,029	1,250
3610	For schedule 40, type 316, add					25%				
3660	Tee, straight ½"	Q-15	11	1.450	Ea.	28	32	3.47	63.47	83
3670	¾"		9	1.780		28	40	4.24	72.24	94
3680	1"		8	2		28	44	4.78	76.78	100
3690	1-¼"		7	2.290		46	51	5.45	102.45	130
3700	1-½"		6.50	2.460		28	55	5.90	88.90	120
3710	2"		6	2.670		30	59	6.35	95.35	130
3720	2-½"		5	3.200		80	71	7.65	158.65	200
3730	3"		4	4		64	89	9.55	162.55	215
3740	3-½"		3.70	4.320		88	96	10.30	194.30	250
3750	4"		3.50	4.570		88	100	10.90	198.90	260
3760	5"	↓	3	5.330		320	120	12.75	452.75	540
3770	6"	Q-16	4	6		255	140	9.55	404.55	495
3780	8"		3	8		635	185	12.75	832.75	985
3790	10"		2	12		565	275	19.10	859.10	1,050
3800	12"	↓	1.50	16	↓	735	370	25	1,130	1,375
3810	For schedule 40, type 316, add					25%				
6000	Threaded companion flange									
6010	Stainless steel, 150 lb., type 304									
6020	½" diam.	1 Plum	30	.267	Ea.	15.25	6.60		21.85	27
6030	¾" diam.		28	.286		23	7.05		30.05	36
6040	1" diam.	↓	27	.296		26	7.30		33.30	39
6050	1-¼" diam.	Q-1	44	.364		35	8.10		43.10	50
6060	1-½" diam.		40	.400		37	8.90		45.90	54
6070	2" diam.		36	.444		40	9.90		49.90	59
6080	2-½" diam.		28	.571		62	12.70		74.70	87
6090	3" diam.		20	.800		64	17.80		81.80	97
6110	4" diam.	↓	12	1.330		105	30		135	160
6130	6" diam.	Q-2	14	1.710		200	40		240	280
6140	8" diam.	"	12	2	↓	440	46		486	550
6150	For type 316 add					40%				
6260	Weld flanges, stainless steel, type 304									
6270	Slip on, 150 lb. (welded, front and back)									
6280	½" diam.	Q-15	16	1	Ea.	21	22	2.39	45.39	59
6290	¾" diam.		16	1		23	22	2.39	47.39	61
6300	1" diam.		13	1.230		26	27	2.94	55.94	72
6310	1-¼" diam.	↓	12	1.330	↓	35	30	3.18	68.18	86

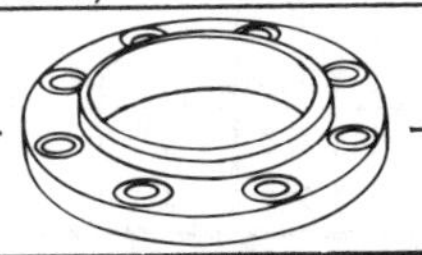

151 | Pipe and Fittings

151 600 | Stainless Steel Pipe

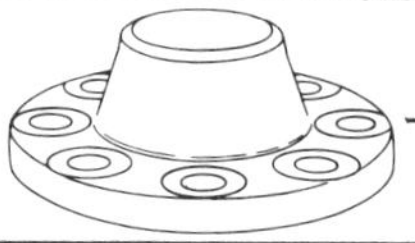

			CREW	DAILY OUTPUT	MAN-HOURS	UNIT	BARE COSTS MAT.	LABOR	EQUIP.	TOTAL	TOTAL INCL O&P	
612	6320	1-½" diam.	Q-15	11	1.450	Ea.	37	32	3.47	72.47	92	612
	6330	2" diam.		10	1.600		41	36	3.82	80.82	100	
	6340	2-½" diam.		9	1.780		62	40	4.24	106.24	130	
	6350	3" diam.		8	2		68	44	4.78	116.78	145	
	6370	4" diam.		6	2.670		105	59	6.35	170.35	210	
	6390	6" diam.	Q-16	6	4		205	92	6.35	303.35	370	
	6400	8" diam.	"	4	6		455	140	9.55	604.55	715	
	6410	For type 316 add					40%					
	6530	Weld neck 150 lb.										
	6540	½" diam.	Q-15	35	.457	Ea.	45	10.15	1.09	56.24	66	
	6550	¾" diam.		32	.500		45	11.10	1.19	57.29	67	
	6560	1" diam.		24	.667		49	14.80	1.59	65.39	78	
	6570	1-¼" diam.		23	.696		72	15.45	1.66	89.11	105	
	6580	1-½" diam.		20	.800		76	17.80	1.91	95.71	110	
	6590	2" diam.		18	.889		88	19.75	2.12	109.87	130	
	6600	2-½" diam.		14	1.140		145	25	2.73	172.73	200	
	6610	3" diam.		12	1.330		145	30	3.18	178.18	205	
	6630	4" diam.		9	1.780		210	40	4.24	254.24	295	
	6650	6" diam.	Q-16	9	2.670		435	61	4.24	500.24	575	
	6670	For type 316 add					23%					
	7000	Threaded joint, 150 lb., type 304										
	7030	90° Elbow										
	7040	⅛"	1 Plum	13	.615	Ea.	4.16	15.20		19.36	27	
	7050	¼"		13	.615		4.16	15.20		19.36	27	
	7070	⅜"		13	.615		5.60	15.20		20.80	29	
	7080	½"		12	.667		5.10	16.45		21.55	30	
	7090	¾"		11	.727		5.60	17.95		23.55	33	
	7100	1"		10	.800		7.70	19.75		27.45	38	
	7110	1-¼"	Q-1	17	.941		11.50	21		32.50	44	
	7120	1-½"		16	1		13	22		35	47	
	7130	2"		14	1.140		19	25		44	59	
	7140	2-½"		11	1.450		53	32		85	105	
	7150	3"		8	2		65	44		109	135	
	7160	4"	Q-2	11	2.180		130	50		180	220	
	7180	45° Elbow										
	7190	⅛"	1 Plum	13	.615	Ea.	5.67	15.20		20.87	29	
	7200	¼"		13	.615		5.67	15.20		20.87	29	
	7210	⅜"		13	.615		6.47	15.20		21.67	30	
	7220	½"		12	.667		6.97	16.45		23.42	32	
	7230	¾"		11	.727		7.52	17.95		25.47	35	
	7240	1"		10	.800		8.32	19.75		28.07	38	
	7250	1-¼"	Q-1	17	.941		10.50	21		31.50	43	
	7260	1-½"		16	1		13	22		35	47	
	7270	2"		14	1.140		19.50	25		44.50	59	
	7280	2-½"		11	1.450		65	32		97	120	
	7290	3"		8	2		93	44		137	170	
	7300	4"	Q-2	11	2.180		165	50		215	255	
	7320	Tee, straight										
	7330	⅛"	1 Plum	9	.889	Ea.	6.40	22		28.40	40	
	7340	¼"		9	.889		6.40	22		28.40	40	
	7350	⅜"		9	.889		8.22	22		30.22	42	
	7360	½"		8	1		7.65	25		32.65	45	
	7370	¾"		7	1.140		8.15	28		36.15	51	
	7380	1"		6.50	1.230		9.65	30		39.65	56	
	7390	1-¼"	Q-1	11	1.450		16	32		48	66	
	7400	1-½"		10	1.600		20	36		56	75	
	7410	2"		9	1.780		29	40		69	91	
	7420	2-½"		7	2.290		75	51		126	160	

151 | Pipe and Fittings

	151 600	Stainless Steel Pipe	CREW	DAILY OUTPUT	MAN-HOURS	UNIT	BARE COSTS				TOTAL INCL O&P	
							MAT.	LABOR	EQUIP.	TOTAL		
612	7430	3"	Q-1	5	3.200	Ea.	115	71		186	230	612
	7440	4"	Q-2	7	3.430	"	185	79		264	320	
	7460	Coupling, straight										
	7470	1/8"	1 Plum	19	.421	Ea.	1.48	10.40		11.88	17.05	
	7480	1/4"		19	.421		1.81	10.40		12.21	17.40	
	7490	3/8"		19	.421		2.13	10.40		12.53	17.75	
	7500	1/2"		19	.421		2.90	10.40		13.30	18.60	
	7510	3/4"		18	.444		3.87	11		14.87	21	
	7520	1"	↓	15	.533		6.32	13.15		19.47	27	
	7530	1-1/4"	Q-1	26	.615		9	13.70		22.70	30	
	7540	1-1/2"		24	.667		11	14.80		25.80	34	
	7550	2"		21	.762		17	16.95		33.95	44	
	7560	2-1/2"		18	.889		39	19.75		58.75	72	
	7570	3"	↓	14	1.140		53	25		78	96	
	7580	4"	Q-2	16	1.500	↓	78	35		113	135	
	7710	Union										
	7720	1/8"	1 Plum	12	.667	Ea.	7.10	16.45		23.55	32	
	7730	1/4"		12	.667		7.10	16.45		23.55	32	
	7740	3/8"		12	.667		8.52	16.45		24.97	34	
	7750	1/2"		11	.727		10.50	17.95		28.45	38	
	7760	3/4"		10	.800		14.50	19.75		34.25	45	
	7770	1"	↓	9	.889		21	22		43	56	
	7780	1-1/4"	Q-1	16	1		39	22		61	76	
	7790	1-1/2"		15	1.070		45.50	24		69.50	85	
	7800	2"		13	1.230		57.50	27		84.50	105	
	7810	2-1/2"		10	1.600		140	36		176	205	
	7820	3"	↓	7	2.290		165	51		216	255	
	7830	4"	Q-2	10	2.400		240	55		295	345	
	7850	For 150 lb., type 316, add				↓	25%					

	151 700	Steel Pipe										
701	0010	**PIPE, STEEL**										701
	0020	All pipe sizes are to Spec. A-53										
	0030	Schedule 10, see 151-801-0500										
	0050	Schedule 40, threaded, with couplings, and clevis type										
	0060	hangers sized for covering, 10' O.C.										
	0540	Black, 1/4" diameter	1 Plum	66	.121	L.F.	.74	2.99		3.73	5.25	
	0550	3/8" diameter		65	.123		.83	3.04		3.87	5.40	
	0560	1/2" diameter		63	.127		.90	3.14		4.04	5.65	
	0570	3/4" diameter		61	.131		1.05	3.24		4.29	5.95	
	0580	1" diameter	↓	53	.151		1.47	3.73		5.20	7.15	
	0590	1-1/4" diameter	Q-1	89	.180		1.84	4		5.84	7.95	
	0600	1-1/2" diameter		80	.200		2.15	4.45		6.60	8.95	
	0610	2" diameter		64	.250		2.89	5.55		8.44	11.40	
	0620	2-1/2" diameter		50	.320		4.70	7.10		11.80	15.70	
	0630	3" diameter		43	.372		6.10	8.25		14.35	19	
	0640	3-1/2" diameter		40	.400		8.41	8.90		17.31	22	
	0650	4" diameter		36	.444		9.56	9.90		19.46	25	
	0660	5" diameter	↓	26	.615		16.73	13.70		30.43	39	
	0670	6" diameter	Q-2	31	.774		21.54	17.85		39.39	50	
	0680	8" diameter		27	.889		30.38	20		50.38	64	
	0690	10" diameter		23	1.040		48.23	24		72.23	89	
	0700	12" diameter	↓	18	1.330	↓	60.34	31		91.34	110	
	0809	A-106, gr. A/B, seamless w/cplgs. & hangers										
	0811	1/4" diameter	1 Plum	66	.121	L.F.	1.97	2.99		4.96	6.60	
	0812	3/8" diameter		65	.123		2.14	3.04		5.18	6.85	
	0813	1/2" diameter	↓	63	.127	↓	2.47	3.14		5.61	7.35	

151 | Pipe and Fittings

151 700 | Steel Pipe

		CREW	DAILY OUTPUT	MAN-HOURS	UNIT	BARE COSTS MAT.	BARE COSTS LABOR	BARE COSTS EQUIP.	BARE COSTS TOTAL	TOTAL INCL O&P	
701 0814	¾" diameter	1 Plum	61	.131	L.F.	3.45	3.24		6.69	8.60	701
0815	1" diameter	"	53	.151		3.28	3.73		7.01	9.15	
0816	1-¼" diameter	Q-1	89	.180		3.98	4		7.98	10.30	
0817	1-½" diameter		80	.200		4.49	4.45		8.94	11.55	
0819	A-53, 2" diameter		64	.250		5.22	5.55		10.77	14	
0821	2-½" diameter		50	.320		7.15	7.10		14.25	18.40	
0822	3" diameter		43	.372		9.39	8.25		17.64	23	
0823	4" diameter		36	.444		13.41	9.90		23.31	29	
1220	To delete coupling & hanger, subtract										
1230	¼" diam. to ¾" diam.					31%	56%				
1240	1" diam. to 1-½" diam.					23%	51%				
1250	2" diam. to 4" diam.					23%	41%				
1260	5" diam. to 12" diam.					21%	45%				
1290	Galvanized, ¼" diameter	1 Plum	66	.121	L.F.	1	2.99		3.99	5.55	
1300	⅜" diameter		65	.123		1.16	3.04		4.20	5.80	
1310	½" diameter		63	.127		1.10	3.14		4.24	5.85	
1320	¾" diameter		61	.131		1.30	3.24		4.54	6.25	
1330	1" diameter		53	.151		1.81	3.73		5.54	7.50	
1340	1-¼" diameter	Q-1	89	.180		2.26	4		6.26	8.40	
1350	1-½" diameter		80	.200		2.74	4.45		7.19	9.60	
1360	2" diameter		64	.250		3.53	5.55		9.08	12.10	
1370	2-½" diameter		50	.320		5.67	7.10		12.77	16.80	
1380	3" diameter		43	.372		7.39	8.25		15.64	20	
1390	3-½" diameter		40	.400		9.71	8.90		18.61	24	
1400	4" diameter		36	.444		11.29	9.90		21.19	27	
1410	5" diameter		26	.615		20.93	13.70		34.63	43	
1420	6" diameter	Q-2	31	.774		26.54	17.85		44.39	56	
1430	8" diameter		27	.889		38.48	20		58.48	73	
1440	10" diameter		23	1.040		55.23	24		79.23	96	
1450	12" diameter		18	1.330		67.34	31		98.34	120	
1750	To delete coupling & hanger, subtract										
1760	¼" diam. to ¾" diam.					31%	56%				
1770	1" diam. to 1-½" diam.					23%	51%				
1780	2" diam. to 4" diam.					23%	41%				
1790	5" diam. to 12" diam.					21%	45%				
2000	Welded, sch. 40, on yoke & roll hangers, sized for covering,										
2010	10' O.C. (no hangers incl. for 14" diam. and up)										
2040	Black, 1" diameter	Q-15	93	.172	L.F.	1.47	3.82	.41	5.70	7.75	
2050	1-¼" diameter		84	.190		1.88	4.23	.45	6.56	8.85	
2060	1-½" diameter		76	.211		2.11	4.68	.50	7.29	9.80	
2070	2" diameter		61	.262		2.68	5.85	.63	9.16	12.30	
2080	2-½" diameter		47	.340		3.74	7.55	.81	12.10	16.25	
2090	3" diameter		43	.372		4.69	8.25	.89	13.83	18.40	
2100	3-½" diameter		39	.410		5.82	9.10	.98	15.90	21	
2110	4" diameter		37	.432		6.77	9.60	1.03	17.40	23	
2120	5" diameter		32	.500		11.33	11.10	1.19	23.62	30	
2130	6" diameter	Q-16	36	.667		13.54	15.35	1.06	29.95	39	
2140	8" diameter		29	.828		18.16	19.10	1.32	38.58	50	
2150	10" diameter		24	1		24.84	23	1.59	49.43	63	
2160	12" diameter		19	1.260		28.84	29	2.01	59.85	77	
2170	14" diameter		15	1.600		40	37	2.55	79.55	100	
2180	16" diameter		13	1.850		46	43	2.94	91.94	115	
2190	18" diameter		11	2.180		59	50	3.47	112.47	145	
2200	20" diameter		9	2.670		65	61	4.24	130.24	165	
2220	24" diameter		8	3		80	69	4.78	153.78	195	
2230	26" diameter		7.50	3.200		90	74	5.10	169.10	215	
2240	30" diameter		6	4		95	92	6.35	193.35	250	
2260	36" diameter		4.50	5.330		110	125	8.50	243.50	315	

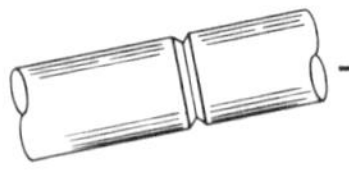

151 | Pipe and Fittings

151 700 | Steel Pipe

			CREW	DAILY OUTPUT	MAN-HOURS	UNIT	BARE COSTS MAT.	LABOR	EQUIP.	TOTAL	TOTAL INCL O&P	
701	2560	To delete hanger, subtract										701
	2570	1" diam. to 1-½" diam.					15%	34%				
	2580	2" diam. to 3-½" diam.					9%	21%				
	2590	4" diam. to 12" diam.					5%	12%				
	3250	Flanged, 150 lb. weld neck, on yoke & roll hangers										
	3260	size for covering, 10' O.C.										
	3290	Black, 1" diameter	Q-15	70	.229	L.F.	3.86	5.10	.55	9.51	12.40	
	3300	1-¼" diameter		64	.250		4.35	5.55	.60	10.50	13.70	
	3310	1-½" diameter		58	.276		4.58	6.15	.66	11.39	14.85	
	3320	2" diameter		45	.356		5.25	7.90	.85	14	18.45	
	3330	2-½" diameter		36	.444		6.65	9.90	1.06	17.61	23	
	3340	3" diameter		32	.500		7.97	11.10	1.19	20.26	27	
	3350	3-½" diameter		29	.552		11.76	12.25	1.32	25.33	33	
	3360	4" diameter		26	.615		10.51	13.70	1.47	25.68	33	
	3370	5" diameter 		21	.762		17.26	16.95	1.82	36.03	46	
	3380	6" diameter	Q-16	25	.960		20.33	22	1.53	43.86	57	
	3390	8" diameter		19	1.260		28.35	29	2.01	59.36	77	
	3400	10" diameter		16	1.500		45.04	35	2.39	82.43	105	
	3410	12" diameter		14	1.710		58.54	40	2.73	101.27	125	
	3470	For 300 lb. flanges, add					63%					
	3480	For 600 lb. flanges, add					310%					
	3960	To delete flanges & hanger, subtract										
	3970	1" diam. to 2" diam.					76%	65%				
	3980	2-½" diam. to 4" diam.					62%	59%				
	3990	5" diam. to 12" diam.					60%	46%				
	4750	Schedule 80, threaded, with couplings, and clevis type hangers										
	4760	sized for covering, 10' O.C.										
	4790	Black, ¼" diameter	1 Plum	54	.148	L.F.	.78	3.66		4.44	6.30	
	4800	⅜" diameter		53	.151		.98	3.73		4.71	6.60	
	4810	½" diameter		52	.154		.94	3.80		4.74	6.65	
	4820	¾" diameter		50	.160		1.13	3.95		5.08	7.10	
	4830	1" diameter		45	.178		1.56	4.39		5.95	8.25	
	4840	1-¼" diameter	Q-1	75	.213		2	4.74		6.74	9.25	
	4850	1-½" diameter		69	.232		2.36	5.15		7.51	10.25	
	4860	2" diameter		56	.286		3.20	6.35		9.55	12.95	
	4870	2-½" diameter		44	.364		5.24	8.10		13.34	17.75	
	4880	3" diameter		38	.421		6.98	9.35		16.33	22	
	4890	3-½" diameter		35	.457		9.15	10.15		19.30	25	
	4900	4" diameter		32	.500		10.60	11.10		21.70	28	
	4910	5" diameter		23	.696		23.73	15.45		39.18	49	
	4920	6" diameter	Q-2	28	.857		27.84	19.75		47.59	60	
	4930	8" diameter		23	1.040		42.18	24		66.18	82	
	4940	10" diameter		20	1.200		56.23	28		84.23	105	
	4950	12" diameter		15	1.600		67.34	37		104.34	130	
	5430	To delete coupling & hanger, subtract										
	5440	¼" diam. to ½" diam.					31%	54%				
	5450	¾" diam. to 1-½" diam.					28%	49%				
	5460	2" diam. to 4" diam.					21%	40%				
	5470	5" diam. to 12" diam.					17%	43%				
	5510	Galvanized, ¼" diameter	1 Plum	54	.148	L.F.	.94	3.66		4.60	6.45	
	5520	⅜" diameter		53	.151		1.13	3.73		4.86	6.80	
	5530	½" diameter		52	.154		1.15	3.80		4.95	6.90	
	5540	¾" diameter		50	.160		1.39	3.95		5.34	7.40	
	5550	1" diameter		45	.178		1.94	4.39		6.33	8.65	
	5560	1-¼" diameter	Q-1	75	.213		2.50	4.74		7.24	9.80	
	5570	1-½" diameter		69	.232		2.96	5.15		8.11	10.90	
	5580	2" diameter		56	.286		4.05	6.35		10.40	13.90	
	5590	2-½" diameter		44	.364		6.51	8.10		14.61	19.15	

151 | Pipe and Fittings

151 700 | Steel Pipe

		CREW	DAILY OUTPUT	MAN-HOURS	UNIT	BARE COSTS MAT.	LABOR	EQUIP.	TOTAL	TOTAL INCL O&P	
701 5600	3" diameter	Q-1	38	.421	L.F.	8.57	9.35		17.92	23	701
5610	3-½" diameter		35	.457		11.19	10.15		21.34	27	
5620	4" diameter		32	.500		13.11	11.10		24.21	31	
5630	5" diameter		23	.696		30.23	15.45		45.68	56	
5640	6" diameter	Q-2	28	.857		35.14	19.75		54.89	68	
5650	8" diameter		23	1.040		55.38	24		79.38	97	
5660	10" diameter		20	1.200		74.23	28		102.23	125	
5670	12" diameter		15	1.600		87.84	37		124.84	150	
5930	To delete coupling & hanger, subtract										
5940	¼" diam. to ½" diam.					31%	54%				
5950	¾" diam. to 1-½" diam.					28%	49%				
5960	2" diam. to 4" diam.					21%	40%				
5970	5" diam. to 12" diam.					17%	43%				
6000	Welded, on yoke & roller hangers										
6010	sized for covering, 10' O.C.										
6040	Black, 1" diameter	Q-15	85	.188	L.F.	1.69	4.18	.45	6.32	8.55	
6050	1-¼" diameter		79	.203		2.23	4.50	.48	7.21	9.65	
6060	1-½" diameter		72	.222		2.55	4.94	.53	8.02	10.70	
6070	2" diameter		57	.281		3.30	6.25	.67	10.22	13.60	
6080	2-½" diameter		44	.364		4.95	8.10	.87	13.92	18.40	
6090	3" diameter		40	.400		6.39	8.90	.96	16.25	21	
6100	3-½" diameter		34	.471		7.89	10.45	1.12	19.46	25	
6110	4" diameter		33	.485		9.34	10.80	1.16	21.30	28	
6120	5" diameter		26	.615		21.33	13.70	1.47	36.50	45	
6130	6" diameter	Q-16	30	.800		25.09	18.45	1.27	44.81	56	
6140	8" diameter		25	.960		37.66	22	1.53	61.19	76	
6150	10" diameter		20	1.200		49.84	28	1.91	79.75	98	
6160	12" diameter		15	1.600		59.14	37	2.55	98.69	125	
6540	To delete hanger, subtract										
6550	1" diam. to 1-½" diam.					30%	14%				
6560	2" diam. to 3" diam.					23%	9%				
6570	3-½" diam. to 5" diam.					12%	6%				
6580	6" diam. to 12" diam.					10%	4%				
7250	Flanged, 300 lb. weld neck, on yoke & roll hangers										
7260	sized for covering, 10' O.C.										
7290	Black, 1" diameter	Q-15	66	.242	L.F.	4.32	5.40	.58	10.30	13.40	
7300	1-¼" diameter		61	.262		5.02	5.85	.63	11.50	14.85	
7310	1-½" diameter		54	.296		5.54	6.60	.71	12.85	16.65	
7320	2" diameter		42	.381		6.44	8.45	.91	15.80	21	
7330	2-½" diameter		33	.485		8.61	10.80	1.16	20.57	27	
7340	3" diameter		29	.552		10.41	12.25	1.32	23.98	31	
7350	3-½" diameter		24	.667		14.08	14.80	1.59	30.47	39	
7360	4" diameter		23	.696		15.57	15.45	1.66	32.68	42	
7370	5" diameter		19	.842		31.31	18.70	2.01	52.02	64	
7380	6" diameter	Q-16	23	1.040		35.43	24	1.66	61.09	76	
7390	8" diameter		17	1.410		54.90	33	2.25	90.15	110	
7400	10" diameter		14	1.710		87.04	40	2.73	129.77	155	
7410	12" diameter		12	2		104.54	46	3.18	153.72	185	
7470	For 600 lb. flanges, add					35%					
7940	To delete flanges & hanger, subtract										
7950	1" diam. to 1-½" diam.					75%	66%				
7960	2" diam. to 3" diam.					62%	60%				
7970	3-½" diam. to 5" diam.					54%	66%				
7980	6" diam. to 12" diam.					55%	62%				
9000	Threading pipe labor, one end, all schedules through 80										
9010	¼" through ¾" pipe size	1 Plum	80	.100	Ea.		2.47		2.47	3.67	
9020	1" through 2" pipe size		73	.110			2.71		2.71	4.02	
9030	2-½" pipe size		53	.151			3.73		3.73	5.55	

151 | Pipe and Fittings

151 700 | Steel Pipe

			CREW	DAILY OUTPUT	MAN-HOURS	UNIT	MAT.	BARE COSTS LABOR	EQUIP.	TOTAL	TOTAL INCL O&P	
701	9040	3" pipe size	1 Plum	50	.160	Ea.		3.95		3.95	5.85	701
	9050	3-½" pipe size	Q-1	89	.180			4		4	5.95	
	9060	4" pipe size		73	.219			4.87		4.87	7.25	
	9070	5" pipe size		53	.302			6.70		6.70	9.95	
	9080	6" pipe size		46	.348			7.75		7.75	11.45	
	9090	8" pipe size		29	.552			12.25		12.25	18.20	
	9100	10" pipe size		21	.762			16.95		16.95	25	
	9110	12" pipe size		13	1.230			27		27	41	
	9200	Welding labor per joint										
	9210	Schedule 40,										
	9230	½" pipe size	Q-15	32	.500	Ea.		11.10	1.19	12.29	17.80	
	9240	¾" pipe size		27	.593			13.15	1.41	14.56	21	
	9250	1" pipe size		23	.696			15.45	1.66	17.11	25	
	9260	1-¼" pipe size		20	.800			17.80	1.91	19.71	28	
	9270	1-½" pipe size		19	.842			18.70	2.01	20.71	30	
	9280	2" pipe size		16	1			22	2.39	24.39	36	
	9290	2-½" pipe size		13	1.230			27	2.94	29.94	44	
	9300	3" pipe size		12	1.330			30	3.18	33.18	47	
	9310	4" pipe size		10	1.600			36	3.82	39.82	57	
	9320	5" pipe size		9	1.780			40	4.24	44.24	63	
	9330	6" pipe size		8	2			44	4.78	48.78	71	
	9340	8" pipe size		5	3.200			71	7.65	78.65	115	
	9350	10" pipe size		4	4			89	9.55	98.55	140	
	9360	12" pipe size		3	5.330			120	12.75	132.75	190	
	9370	14" pipe size		2.60	6.150			135	14.70	149.70	220	
	9380	16" pipe size		2.20	7.270			160	17.35	177.35	260	
	9390	18" pipe size		2	8			180	19.10	199.10	285	
	9400	20" pipe size		1.80	8.890			200	21	221	315	
	9410	22" pipe size		1.70	9.410			210	22	232	335	
	9420	24" pipe size		1.50	10.670			235	25	260	380	
	9450	Schedule 80,										
	9460	½" pipe size	Q-15	27	.593	Ea.		13.15	1.41	14.56	21	
	9470	¾" pipe size		23	.696			15.45	1.66	17.11	25	
	9480	1" pipe size		20	.800			17.80	1.91	19.71	28	
	9490	1-¼" pipe size		19	.842			18.70	2.01	20.71	30	
	9500	1-½" pipe size		18	.889			19.75	2.12	21.87	32	
	9510	2" pipe size		15	1.070			24	2.55	26.55	38	
	9520	2-½" pipe size		12	1.330			30	3.18	33.18	47	
	9530	3" pipe size		11	1.450			32	3.47	35.47	52	
	9540	4" pipe size		8	2			44	4.78	48.78	71	
	9550	5" pipe size		6	2.670			59	6.35	65.35	95	
	9560	6" pipe size		5	3.200			71	7.65	78.65	115	
	9570	8" pipe size		4	4			89	9.55	98.55	140	
	9580	10" pipe size		3	5.330			120	12.75	132.75	190	
	9590	12" pipe size		2	8			180	19.10	199.10	285	
	9600	14" pipe size	Q-16	2.60	9.230			215	14.70	229.70	330	
	9610	16" pipe size		2.30	10.430			240	16.60	256.60	375	
	9620	18" pipe size		2	12			275	19.10	294.10	430	
	9630	20" pipe size		1.80	13.330			305	21	326	480	
	9640	22" pipe size		1.60	15			345	24	369	540	
	9650	24" pipe size		1.50	16			370	25	395	575	
716	0010	**PIPE, STEEL, FITTINGS,** Threaded											716
	0020	Cast Iron,											
	0040	Standard weight, black											
	0060	90° Elbow, straight											
	0070	¼"	1 Plum	16	.500	Ea.	.79	12.35		13.14	19.20	
	0080	⅜"	"	16	.500	"	.79	12.35		13.14	19.20	

151 | Pipe and Fittings

151 700 | Steel Pipe

		CREW	DAILY OUTPUT	MAN-HOURS	UNIT	BARE COSTS MAT.	BARE COSTS LABOR	BARE COSTS EQUIP.	BARE COSTS TOTAL	TOTAL INCL O&P	
716	0090	½"	1 Plum	15	.533	Ea.	.79	13.15		13.94	20	716
	0100	¾"		14	.571		.79	14.10		14.89	22	
	0110	1"	↓	13	.615		1.20	15.20		16.40	24	
	0120	1-¼"	Q-1	22	.727		1.85	16.15		18	26	
	0130	1-½"		20	.800		2.40	17.80		20.20	29	
	0140	2"		18	.889		3.78	19.75		23.53	33	
	0150	2-½"		14	1.140		7.40	25		32.40	46	
	0160	3"		10	1.600		12.95	36		48.95	67	
	0170	3-½"		8	2		21	44		65	89	
	0180	4"		6	2.670		24	59		83	115	
	0190	5"	↓	5	3.200		39	71		110	150	
	0200	6"	Q-2	7	3.430		50	79		129	170	
	0210	8"	"	6	4	↓	100	92		192	245	
	0250	45° Elbow, straight										
	0260	¼"	1 Plum	16	.500	Ea.	1.26	12.35		13.61	19.70	
	0270	⅜"		16	.500		1.26	12.35		13.61	19.70	
	0280	½"		15	.533		1.26	13.15		14.41	21	
	0300	¾"		14	.571		1.26	14.10		15.36	22	
	0320	1"	↓	13	.615		1.50	15.20		16.70	24	
	0330	1-¼"	Q-1	22	.727		2.05	16.15		18.20	26	
	0340	1-½"		20	.800		3.22	17.80		21.02	30	
	0350	2"		18	.889		3.90	19.75		23.65	34	
	0360	2-½"		14	1.140		9.05	25		34.05	48	
	0370	3"		10	1.600		13.80	36		49.80	68	
	0380	3-½"		8	2		22	44		66	90	
	0400	4"		6	2.670		25	59		84	115	
	0420	5"	↓	5	3.200		44	71		115	155	
	0440	6"	Q-2	7	3.430		56	79		135	180	
	0460	8"	"	6	4	↓	115	92		207	265	
	0500	Tee, straight										
	0510	¼"	1 Plum	10	.800	Ea.	1.15	19.75		20.90	31	
	0520	⅜"		10	.800		1.45	19.75		21.20	31	
	0530	½"		9	.889		1.10	22		23.10	34	
	0540	¾"		9	.889		1.60	22		23.60	34	
	0550	1"	↓	8	1		1.65	25		26.65	38	
	0560	1-¼"	Q-1	14	1.140		3	25		28	41	
	0570	1-½"		13	1.230		2.35	27		29.35	43	
	0580	2"		11	1.450		5.05	32		37.05	54	
	0590	2-½"		9	1.780		10.10	40		50.10	70	
	0600	3"		6	2.670		16.05	59		75.05	105	
	0610	3-½"		5	3.200		28	71		99	135	
	0620	4"		4	4		31	89		120	165	
	0630	5"	↓	3	5.330		55	120		175	235	
	0640	6"	Q-2	4	6		67	140		207	280	
	0650	8"	"	3	8	↓	135	185		320	420	
	0660	Tee, reducing run and outlet										
	0661	½"	1 Plum	9	.889	Ea.	1.15	22		23.15	34	
	0662	¾"		9	.889		1.76	22		23.76	35	
	0663	1"	↓	8	1		1.83	25		26.83	39	
	0664	1-¼"	Q-1	14	1.140		3.28	25		28.28	41	
	0665	1-½"		13	1.230		3.67	27		30.67	45	
	0666	2"		11	1.450		5.55	32		37.55	54	
	0667	2-½"		9	1.780		11.95	40		51.95	72	
	0668	3"		6	2.670		18.50	59		77.50	110	
	0669	3-½"		5	3.200		30	71		101	140	
	0670	4"		4	4		35	89		124	170	
	0671	5"	↓	3	5.330		60	120		180	240	
	0672	6"	Q-2	4	6		76	140		216	290	

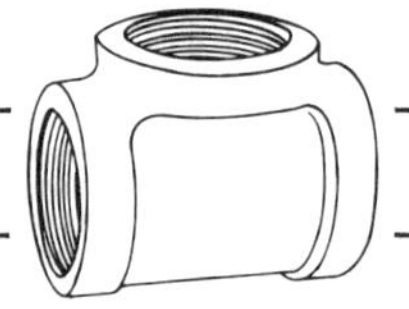

151 | Pipe and Fittings

151 700 | Steel Pipe

			DAILY	MAN-		\multicolumn{4}{c}{BARE COSTS}	TOTAL
		CREW	OUTPUT	HOURS	UNIT	MAT.	LABOR	EQUIP.	TOTAL	INCL O&P
0673	8"	Q-2	3	8	Ea.	155	185		340	445
0674	Reducer, concentric									
0675	¾"	1 Plum	18	.444	Ea.	1.55	11		12.55	18
0676	1"	"	15	.533		1.39	13.15		14.54	21
0677	1-¼"	Q-1	26	.615		2.98	13.70		16.68	24
0678	1-½"		24	.667		4.08	14.80		18.88	26
0679	2"		21	.762		5.42	16.95		22.37	31
0680	2-½"		18	.889		7.69	19.75		27.44	38
0681	3"		14	1.140		9.45	25		34.45	48
0682	3-½"		12	1.330		13.50	30		43.50	59
0683	4"		10	1.600		16.50	36		52.50	71
0684	5"		6	2.670		23	59		82	115
0685	6"	Q-2	8	3		30	69		99	135
0686	8"	"	7	3.430		66	79		145	190
0687	Reducer, eccentric									
0688	¾"	1 Plum	16	.500	Ea.	2.99	12.35		15.34	22
0689	1"	"	14	.571		3.45	14.10		17.55	25
0690	1-¼"	Q-1	25	.640		5.45	14.25		19.70	27
0691	1-½"		22	.727		6.89	16.15		23.04	32
0692	2"		20	.800		9.90	17.80		27.70	37
0693	2-½"		16	1		13.75	22		35.75	48
0694	3"		12	1.330		16.85	30		46.85	63
0695	3-½"		10	1.600		24	36		60	79
0696	4"		9	1.780		31	40		71	93
0697	5"		5	3.200		37	71		108	145
0698	6"	Q-2	8	3		48	69		117	155
0699	8"	"	7	3.430		89	79		168	215
0700	Standard weight, galvanized									
0720	90° Elbow, straight									
0730	¼"	1 Plum	16	.500	Ea.	1.43	12.35		13.78	19.90
0740	⅜"		16	.500		1.43	12.35		13.78	19.90
0750	½"		15	.533		1.43	13.15		14.58	21
0760	¾"		14	.571		1.83	14.10		15.93	23
0770	1"		13	.615		2.13	15.20		17.33	25
0780	1-¼"	Q-1	22	.727		3.45	16.15		19.60	28
0790	1-½"		20	.800		4.52	17.80		22.32	31
0800	2"		18	.889		6.55	19.75		26.30	37
0810	2-½"		14	1.140		13.20	25		38.20	52
0820	3"		10	1.600		20	36		56	75
0830	3-½"		8	2		32	44		76	100
0840	4"		6	2.670		35	59		94	125
0850	5"		5	3.200		62	71		133	175
0860	6"	Q-2	7	3.430		80	79		159	205
0870	8"	"	6	4		165	92		257	320
0900	45° Elbow, straight									
0910	¼"	1 Plum	16	.500	Ea.	2.78	12.35		15.13	21
0920	⅜"		16	.500		2.03	12.35		14.38	21
0930	½"		15	.533		2.80	13.15		15.95	23
0940	¾"		14	.571		2.05	14.10		16.15	23
0950	1"		13	.615		2.45	15.20		17.65	25
0960	1-¼"	Q-1	22	.727		3.85	16.15		20	28
0970	1-½"		20	.800		5.25	17.80		23.05	32
0980	2"		18	.889		7.30	19.75		27.05	37
0990	2-½"		14	1.140		9.25	25		34.25	48
1000	3"		10	1.600		23	36		59	78
1010	3-½"		8	2		30	44		74	99
1020	4"		6	2.670		39	59		98	130
1030	5"		5	3.200		68	71		139	180

151 | Pipe and Fittings

151 700 | Steel Pipe

			CREW	DAILY OUTPUT	MAN-HOURS	UNIT	BARE COSTS MAT.	LABOR	EQUIP.	TOTAL	TOTAL INCL O&P	
716	1040	6"	Q-2	7	3.430	Ea.	87	79		166	215	716
	1050	8"	"	6	4	"	185	92		277	340	
	1100	Tee, straight										
	1110	¼"	1 Plum	10	.800	Ea.	1.95	19.75		21.70	31	
	1120	⅜"		10	.800		1.95	19.75		21.70	31	
	1130	½"		9	.889		1.99	22		23.99	35	
	1140	¾"		9	.889		2.58	22		24.58	35	
	1150	1"	↓	8	1		2.99	25		27.99	40	
	1160	1-¼"	Q-1	14	1.140		4.99	25		29.99	43	
	1170	1-½"		13	1.230		6.25	27		33.25	47	
	1180	2"		11	1.450		8.10	32		40.10	57	
	1190	2-½"		9	1.780		16	40		56	76	
	1200	3"		6	2.670		31	59		90	120	
	1210	3-½"		5	3.200		41	71		112	150	
	1220	4"		4	4		46	89		135	185	
	1230	5"	↓	3	5.330		85	120		205	270	
	1240	6"	Q-2	4	6		105	140		245	320	
	1250	8"	"	3	8	↓	225	185		410	520	
	1300	Extra heavy weight, black										
	1310	Couplings, steel straight										
	1320	¼"	1 Plum	19	.421	Ea.	.47	10.40		10.87	15.95	
	1330	⅜"		19	.421		.56	10.40		10.96	16.05	
	1340	½"		19	.421		.57	10.40		10.97	16.05	
	1350	¾"		18	.444		.73	11		11.73	17.10	
	1360	1"	↓	15	.533		1.02	13.15		14.17	21	
	1370	1-¼"	Q-1	26	.615		1.30	13.70		15	22	
	1380	1-½"		24	.667		1.65	14.80		16.45	24	
	1390	2"		21	.762		2.37	16.95		19.32	28	
	1400	2-½"		18	.889		6.55	19.75		26.30	37	
	1410	3"		14	1.140		9.60	25		34.60	48	
	1420	3-½"		12	1.330		17.40	30		47.40	63	
	1430	4"		10	1.600		17.40	36		53.40	72	
	1440	5"	↓	6	2.670		31	59		90	120	
	1450	6"	Q-2	8	3		38	69		107	145	
	1460	8"		7	3.430		60	79		139	185	
	1470	10"		6	4		95	92		187	240	
	1480	12"	↓	4	6	↓	120	140		260	335	
	1510	90° Elbow, straight										
	1520	½"	1 Plum	15	.533	Ea.	3.98	13.15		17.13	24	
	1530	¾"		14	.571		4.37	14.10		18.47	26	
	1540	1"	↓	13	.615		5.05	15.20		20.25	28	
	1550	1-¼"	Q-1	22	.727		6.15	16.15		22.30	31	
	1560	1-½"		20	.800		7.80	17.80		25.60	35	
	1580	2"		18	.889		10.30	19.75		30.05	41	
	1590	2-½"		14	1.140		16.40	25		41.40	56	
	1600	3"		10	1.600		23	36		59	78	
	1610	4"	↓	6	2.670		49	59		108	140	
	1620	6"	Q-2	7	3.430	↓	92	79		171	220	
	1650	45° Elbow, straight										
	1660	½"	1 Plum	15	.533	Ea.	3.52	13.15		16.67	23	
	1670	¾"		14	.571		3.95	14.10		18.05	25	
	1680	1"	↓	13	.615		4.70	15.20		19.90	28	
	1690	1-¼"	Q-1	22	.727		6.35	16.15		22.50	31	
	1700	1-½"		20	.800		8.40	17.80		26.20	36	
	1710	2"		18	.889		11.85	19.75		31.60	42	
	1720	2-½"		14	1.140		18.20	25		43.20	58	
	1800	Tee, straight										
	1810	½"	1 Plum	9	.889	Ea.	4.60	22		26.60	38	

151 | Pipe and Fittings

151 700 | Steel Pipe

			CREW	DAILY OUTPUT	MAN-HOURS	UNIT	BARE COSTS MAT.	LABOR	EQUIP.	TOTAL	TOTAL INCL O&P	
716	1820	¾"	1 Plum	9	.889	Ea.	4.90	22		26.90	38	716
	1830	1"	"	8	1		5.95	25		30.95	43	
	1840	1-¼"	Q-1	14	1.140		8.10	25		33.10	47	
	1850	1-½"		13	1.230		10.45	27		37.45	52	
	1860	2"		11	1.450		13.90	32		45.90	63	
	1870	2-½"		9	1.780		24	40		64	85	
	1880	3"		6	2.670		36	59		95	130	
	1890	4"		4	4		69	89		158	210	
	1900	6"	Q-2	4	6		134	140		274	355	
	1950	Extra heavy weight, galvanized										
	1970	90° Elbow, straight										
	1980	½"	1 Plum	15	.533	Ea.	4.80	13.15		17.95	25	
	1990	¾"		14	.571		5.70	14.10		19.80	27	
	2000	1"		13	.615		6.95	15.20		22.15	30	
	2010	1-¼"	Q-1	22	.727		9.65	16.15		25.80	35	
	2020	1-½"		20	.800		12.75	17.80		30.55	40	
	2030	2"		18	.889		17.50	19.75		37.25	49	
	2040	2-½"		14	1.140		28	25		53	68	
	2050	3"		10	1.600		40	36		76	97	
	2060	4"		6	2.670		81	59		140	175	
	2070	6"	Q-2	7	3.430		155	79		234	290	
	2100	45° Elbow, straight										
	2110	½"	1 Plum	15	.533	Ea.	5.65	13.15		18.80	26	
	2120	¾"		14	.571		6.70	14.10		20.80	28	
	2130	1"		13	.615		7.65	15.20		22.85	31	
	2140	1-¼"	Q-1	22	.727		10.70	16.15		26.85	36	
	2150	1-½"		20	.800		14.05	17.80		31.85	42	
	2160	2"		18	.889		20	19.75		39.75	51	
	2170	2-½"		14	1.140		36	25		61	77	
	2250	Tee, straight										
	2260	½"	1 Plum	9	.889	Ea.	7.45	22		29.45	41	
	2270	¾"		9	.889		8.30	22		30.30	42	
	2280	1"		8	1		9.70	25		34.70	47	
	2290	1-¼"	Q-1	14	1.140		13.60	25		38.60	53	
	2300	1-½"		13	1.230		17.55	27		44.55	60	
	2310	2"		11	1.450		24	32		56	74	
	2320	2-½"		9	1.780		39	40		79	100	
	2330	3"		6	2.670		58	59		117	150	
	2340	4"		4	4		105	89		194	245	
	2360	6"	Q-2	4	6		215	140		355	440	
	2500	Couplings, steel straight										
	2510	¼"	1 Plum	19	.421	Ea.	.57	10.40		10.97	16.05	
	2520	⅜"		19	.421		.66	10.40		11.06	16.15	
	2530	½"		19	.421		.66	10.40		11.06	16.15	
	2540	¾"		18	.444		.92	11		11.92	17.30	
	2550	1"		15	.533		1.30	13.15		14.45	21	
	2560	1-¼"	Q-1	26	.615		1.55	13.70		15.25	22	
	2570	1-½"		24	.667		1.95	14.80		16.75	24	
	2580	2"		21	.762		3.05	16.95		20	28	
	2590	2-½"		18	.889		7.35	19.75		27.10	37	
	2600	3"		14	1.140		9.95	25		34.95	49	
	2610	3-½"		12	1.330		18.25	30		48.25	64	
	2620	4"		10	1.600		18.95	36		54.95	74	
	2630	5"		6	2.670		36	59		95	130	
	2640	6"	Q-2	8	3		41	69		110	150	
	2650	8"		7	3.430		82	79		161	205	
	2660	10"		6	4		135	92		227	285	
	2670	12"		4	6		165	140		305	385	

151 | Pipe and Fittings

151 700 | Steel Pipe

		CREW	DAILY OUTPUT	MAN-HOURS	UNIT	BARE COSTS MAT.	BARE COSTS LABOR	BARE COSTS EQUIP.	BARE COSTS TOTAL	TOTAL INCL O&P
5000	Malleable iron, 150 lb.									
5020	Black									
5040	90° Elbow, straight									
5060	¼"	1 Plum	16	.500	Ea.	.69	12.35		13.04	19.10
5070	⅜"		16	.500		.69	12.35		13.04	19.10
5080	½"		15	.533		.51	13.15		13.66	20
5090	¾"		14	.571		.56	14.10		14.66	22
5100	1"		13	.615		1.05	15.20		16.25	24
5110	1-¼"	Q-1	22	.727		1.75	16.15		17.90	26
5120	1-½"		20	.800		2.32	17.80		20.12	29
5130	2"		18	.889		3.45	19.75		23.20	33
5140	2-½"		14	1.140		8.60	25		33.60	47
5150	3"		10	1.600		12.90	36		48.90	67
5160	3-½"		8	2		25	44		69	93
5170	4"		6	2.670		23	59		82	115
5180	5"		5	3.200		60	71		131	170
5190	6"	Q-2	7	3.430		72	79		151	195
5250	45° Elbow, straight									
5270	¼"	1 Plum	16	.500	Ea.	.93	12.35		13.28	19.35
5280	⅜"		16	.500		.85	12.35		13.20	19.25
5290	½"		15	.533		.79	13.15		13.94	20
5300	¾"		14	.571		.94	14.10		15.04	22
5310	1"		13	.615		1.23	15.20		16.43	24
5320	1-¼"	Q-1	22	.727		2.14	16.15		18.29	26
5330	1-½"		20	.800		2.65	17.80		20.45	29
5340	2"		18	.889		3.55	19.75		23.30	33
5350	2-½"		14	1.140		10.70	25		35.70	49
5360	3"		10	1.600		14.95	36		50.95	69
5370	3-½"		8	2		28	44		72	97
5380	4"		6	2.670		28	59		87	120
5390	5"		5	3.200		68	71		139	180
5400	6"	Q-2	7	3.430		78	79		157	205
5450	Tee, straight									
5470	¼"	1 Plum	10	.800	Ea.	1.02	19.75		20.77	30
5480	⅜"		10	.800		1.02	19.75		20.77	30
5490	½"		9	.889		.63	22		22.63	33
5500	¾"		9	.889		.90	22		22.90	34
5510	1"		8	1		1.65	25		26.65	38
5520	1-¼"	Q-1	14	1.140		2.68	25		27.68	41
5530	1-½"		13	1.230		3.29	27		30.29	44
5540	2"		11	1.450		4.87	32		36.87	53
5550	2-½"		9	1.780		11.45	40		51.45	71
5560	3"		6	2.670		16.50	59		75.50	105
5570	3-½"		5	3.200		30	71		101	140
5580	4"		4	4		32	89		121	165
5590	5"		3	5.330		70	120		190	255
5600	6"	Q-2	4	6		95	140		235	310
5601	Tee, reducing, run and outlet									
5602	½"	1 Plum	9	.889	Ea.	2.50	22		24.50	35
5603	¾"		9	.889		2.70	22		24.70	36
5604	1"		8	1		3.65	25		28.65	41
5605	1-¼"	Q-1	14	1.140		6.05	25		31.05	44
5606	1-½"		13	1.230		7.35	27		34.35	49
5607	2"		11	1.450		9.35	32		41.35	58
5608	2-½"		9	1.780		21	40		61	82
5609	3"		6	2.670		34	59		93	125
5610	3-½"		5	3.200		45	71		116	155
5611	4"		4	4		51	89		140	190

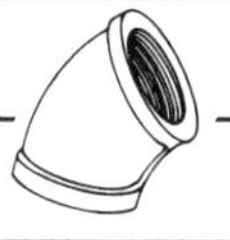

151 | Pipe and Fittings

151 700 | Steel Pipe

		CREW	DAILY OUTPUT	MAN-HOURS	UNIT	MAT.	LABOR	EQUIP.	TOTAL	TOTAL INCL O&P
5612	5"	Q-1	3	5.330	Ea.	91	120		211	275
5613	6"	Q-2	5	4.800	"	110	110		220	285
5650	Coupling, straight									
5670	¼"	1 Plum	19	.421	Ea.	.78	10.40		11.18	16.30
5680	⅜"		19	.421		.78	10.40		11.18	16.30
5690	½"		19	.421		.68	10.40		11.08	16.20
5700	¾"		18	.444		.82	11		11.82	17.20
5710	1" 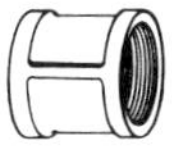		15	.533		1.24	13.15		14.39	21
5720	1-¼"	Q-1	26	.615		1.60	13.70		15.30	22
5730	1-½"		24	.667		2.08	14.80		16.88	24
5740	2"		21	.762		3.10	16.95		20.05	29
5750	2-½"		18	.889		7.30	19.75		27.05	37
5760	3"		14	1.140		10.15	25		35.15	49
5770	3-½"		12	1.330		20	30		50	66
5780	4"		10	1.600		20	36		56	75
5790	5"		6	2.670		38	59		97	130
5800	6"	Q-2	8	3		51	69		120	160
5810	8"		7	3.430		71	79		150	195
5820	10"		6	4		115	92		207	265
5830	12"		4	6		160	140		300	380
5840	Reducer, concentric, ¼"	1 Plum	19	.421		1	10.40		11.40	16.55
5850	⅜"		19	.421		1	10.40		11.40	16.55
5860	½"		19	.421		1	10.40		11.40	16.55
5870	¾"		16	.500		1.10	12.35		13.45	19.55
5880	1"		15	.533		1.62	13.15		14.77	21
5890	1-¼"	Q-1	26	.615		2.03	13.70		15.73	23
5900	1-½"		24	.667		2.55	14.80		17.35	25
5910	2"		21	.762		3.80	16.95		20.75	29
5911	2-½"		18	.889		5.90	19.75		25.65	36
5912	3"		14	1.140		8.05	25		33.05	47
5913	3-½"		12	1.330		13.50	30		43.50	59
5914	4"		10	1.600		16.45	36		52.45	71
5915	5"		6	2.670		30	59		89	120
5916	6"	Q-2	8	3		40	69		109	145
5989	Cap, ¼"	1 Plum	38	.211		.64	5.20		5.84	8.40
5991	⅜"		38	.211		.64	5.20		5.84	8.40
5992	½"		38	.211		.69	5.20		5.89	8.45
5993	¾"		32	.250		.85	6.20		7.05	10.10
5994	1"		30	.267		1.13	6.60		7.73	11
5995	1-¼"	Q-1	52	.308		1.45	6.85		8.30	11.75
5996	1-½"		48	.333		1.93	7.40		9.33	13.10
5997	2"		42	.381		2.47	8.45		10.92	15.30
6000	For galvanized elbows, tees, and couplings add					23%				
7000	Union, with brass seat									
7010	¼"	1 Plum	15	.533	Ea.	2.10	13.15		15.25	22
7020	⅜"		15	.533		2.10	13.15		15.25	22
7030	½"		14	.571		1.99	14.10		16.09	23
7040	¾" 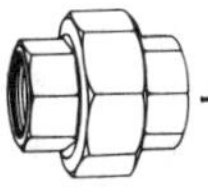		13	.615		2.03	15.20		17.23	25
7050	1"		12	.667		3.01	16.45		19.46	28
7060	1-¼"	Q-1	21	.762		4.17	16.95		21.12	30
7070	1-½"		19	.842		5.05	18.70		23.75	33
7080	2"		17	.941		6.30	21		27.30	38
7090	2-½"		13	1.230		14.90	27		41.90	57
7100	3"		9	1.780		21	40		61	82
7110	Union, all iron, ¼"	1 Plum	15	.533		3.01	13.15		16.16	23
7130	⅜"		15	.533		3.01	13.15		16.16	23
7140	½"		14	.571		3.10	14.10		17.20	24
7150	¾"		13	.615		3.29	15.20		18.49	26

151 | Pipe and Fittings

151 700 | Steel Pipe

			CREW	DAILY OUTPUT	MAN-HOURS	UNIT	BARE COSTS MAT.	LABOR	EQUIP.	TOTAL	TOTAL INCL O&P	
716	7160	1"	1 Plum	12	.667	Ea.	4.50	16.45		20.95	29	716
	7170	1-¼"	Q-1	21	.762		6.15	16.95		23.10	32	
	7180	1-½"		19	.842		7.45	18.70		26.15	36	
	7190	2"		17	.941		9.35	21		30.35	41	
	7200	2-½"		13	1.230		20	27		47	63	
	7210	3"		9	1.780		31	40		71	93	
	7250	For galvanized unions, add					5%					
	7500	Malleable iron, 300 lb										
	7520	Black										
	7540	90° Elbow, straight, ¼"	1 Plum	16	.500	Ea.	2.25	12.35		14.60	21	
	7560	⅜"		16	.500		1.98	12.35		14.33	21	
	7570	½"		15	.533		2.89	13.15		16.04	23	
	7580	¾"		14	.571		3.35	14.10		17.45	25	
	7590	1"		13	.615		4.34	15.20		19.54	27	
	7600	1-¼"	Q-1	22	.727		5.90	16.15		22.05	30	
	7610	1-½"		20	.800		7.25	17.80		25.05	34	
	7620	2"		18	.889		10.20	19.75		29.95	41	
	7630	2-½"		14	1.140		19.15	25		44.15	59	
	7640	3"		10	1.600		23	36		59	78	
	7650	4"		6	2.670		51	59		110	145	
	7660	5"		5	3.200		105	71		176	220	
	7670	6"	Q-2	7	3.430		130	79		209	260	
	7680	8"	"	6	4		260	92		352	425	
	7700	45° Elbow, straight, ¼"	1 Plum	16	.500		3.11	12.35		15.46	22	
	7720	⅜"		16	.500		3.11	12.35		15.46	22	
	7730	½"		15	.533		3.75	13.15		16.90	24	
	7740	¾"		14	.571		4.22	14.10		18.32	26	
	7750	1"		13	.615		4.59	15.20		19.79	28	
	7760	1-¼"	Q-1	22	.727		7.20	16.15		23.35	32	
	7770	1-½"		20	.800		9.45	17.80		27.25	37	
	7780	2"		18	.889		14.15	19.75		33.90	45	
	7790	2-½"		14	1.140		23	25		48	63	
	7800	3"		10	1.600		30	36		66	86	
	7810	4"		6	2.670		56	59		115	150	
	7850	Tee, straight, ¼"	1 Plum	10	.800		2.87	19.75		22.62	32	
	7870	⅜"		10	.800		2.87	19.75		22.62	32	
	7880	½"		9	.889		4.05	22		26.05	37	
	7890	¾"		9	.889		4.49	22		26.49	38	
	7900	1"		8	1		5.35	25		30.35	43	
	7910	1-¼"	Q-1	14	1.140		7.25	25		32.25	46	
	7920	1-½"		13	1.230		8.90	27		35.90	50	
	7930	2"		11	1.450		13.20	32		45.20	62	
	7940	2-½"		9	1.780		24	40		64	85	
	7950	3"		6	2.670		41	59		100	135	
	7960	4"		4	4		70	89		159	210	
	7980	6"	Q-2	4	6		195	140		335	420	
	7990	8"	"	3	8		375	185		560	685	
	8050	Couplings, straight, ¼"	1 Plum	19	.421		1.90	10.40		12.30	17.50	
	8070	⅜"		19	.421		1.90	10.40		12.30	17.50	
	8080	½"		19	.421		2.19	10.40		12.59	17.85	
	8090	¾"		18	.444		2.62	11		13.62	19.15	
	8100	1"		15	.533		3.07	13.15		16.22	23	
	8110	1-¼"	Q-1	26	.615		3.63	13.70		17.33	24	
	8120	1-½"		24	.667		5.35	14.80		20.15	28	
	8130	2"		21	.762		7.40	16.95		24.35	33	
	8140	2-½"		18	.889		11.20	19.75		30.95	42	
	8150	3"		14	1.140		15.50	25		40.50	55	
	8500	For galvanized elbows, tees and couplings add					50%					

151 | Pipe and Fittings

151 700 | Steel Pipe

			CREW	DAILY OUTPUT	MAN-HOURS	UNIT	MAT.	LABOR	EQUIP.	TOTAL	TOTAL INCL O&P	
716	9500	Union with brass seat, ¼"	1 Plum	15	.533	Ea.	3.84	13.15		16.99	24	716
	9530	⅜"		15	.533		3.84	13.15		16.99	24	
	9540	½"		14	.571		3.60	14.10		17.70	25	
	9550	¾"		13	.615		4.07	15.20		19.27	27	
	9560	1"		12	.667		5.25	16.45		21.70	30	
	9570	1-¼"	Q-1	21	.762		8.20	16.95		25.15	34	
	9580	1-½"		19	.842		8.80	18.70		27.50	37	
	9590	2"		17	.941		10.10	21		31.10	42	
	9600	2-½"		13	1.230		26	27		53	69	
	9610	3"		9	1.780		43	40		83	105	
	9620	4"		5	3.200		85	71		156	200	
	9630	Union, all iron, ¼"	1 Plum	15	.533		4.71	13.15		17.86	25	
	9650	⅜"		15	.533		4.71	13.15		17.86	25	
	9660	½"		14	.571		5	14.10		19.10	26	
	9670	¾"		13	.615		5.25	15.20		20.45	28	
	9680	1"		12	.667		6.55	16.45		23	32	
	9690	1-¼"	Q-1	21	.762		10.10	16.95		27.05	36	
	9700	1-½"		19	.842		12.45	18.70		31.15	41	
	9710	2"		17	.941		15.85	21		36.85	48	
	9720	2-½"		13	1.230		32	27		59	76	
	9730	3"		9	1.780		51	40		91	115	
	9750	For galvanized unions, add					10%					
718	0010	**PIPE, STEEL, FITTINGS** Special										718
	0020	Cast iron, drainage, threaded, black										
	0030	90° Elbow, straight										
	0031	1-½" pipe size	Q-1	20	.800	Ea.	3.16	17.80		20.96	30	
	0032	2" pipe size		18	.889		4.77	19.75		24.52	35	
	0033	3" pipe size		10	1.600		16.75	36		52.75	71	
	0034	4" pipe size		6	2.670		35	59		94	125	
	0040	90° Long turn elbow, straight										
	0041	1-½" pipe size	Q-1	20	.800	Ea.	4.10	17.80		21.90	31	
	0042	2" pipe size		18	.889		6.05	19.75		25.80	36	
	0043	3" pipe size		10	1.600		19.90	36		55.90	75	
	0044	4" pipe size		6	2.670		35	59		94	125	
	0050	90° Street elbow, straight										
	0051	1-½" pipe size	Q-1	20	.800	Ea.	4.02	17.80		21.82	31	
	0052	2" pipe size	"	18	.889	"	5.55	19.75		25.30	35	
	0060	45° Elbow										
	0061	1-½" pipe size	Q-1	20	.800	Ea.	3.18	17.80		20.98	30	
	0062	2" pipe size		18	.889		4.75	19.75		24.50	35	
	0063	3" pipe size		10	1.600		16.75	36		52.75	71	
	0064	4" pipe size		6	2.670		28	59		87	120	
	0070	45° Street elbow										
	0071	1-½" pipe size	Q-1	20	.800	Ea.	5.75	17.80		23.55	33	
	0072	2" pipe size	"	18	.889	"	6.65	19.75		26.40	37	
	0092	Tees, straight										
	0093	1-½" pipe size	Q-1	13	1.230	Ea.	4.98	27		31.98	46	
	0094	2" pipe size	"	11	1.450	"	8.25	32		40.25	57	
	0100	TY's, straight										
	0101	1-½" pipe size	Q-1	13	1.230	Ea.	4.91	27		31.91	46	
	0102	2" pipe size		11	1.450		8.25	32		40.25	57	
	0103	3" pipe size		6	2.670		26	59		85	115	
	0104	4" pipe size		4	4		43	89		132	180	
	0120	45° Y branch, straight										
	0121	1-½" pipe size	Q-1	13	1.230	Ea.	6.65	27		33.65	48	
	0122	2" pipe size		11	1.450		11.25	32		43.25	60	
	0123	3" pipe size		6	2.670		33	59		92	125	
	0124	4" pipe size		4	4		61	89		150	200	

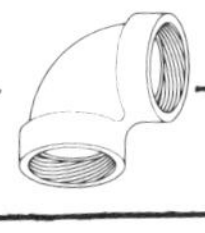

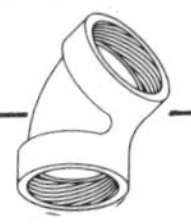

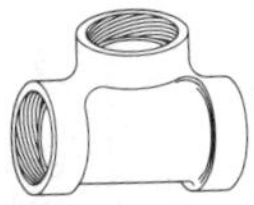

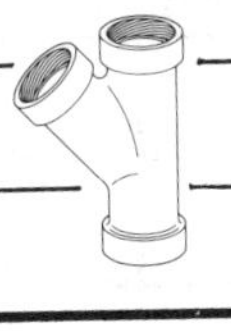

151 | Pipe and Fittings

151 700 | Steel Pipe

		CREW	DAILY OUTPUT	MAN-HOURS	UNIT	BARE COSTS MAT.	LABOR	EQUIP.	TOTAL	TOTAL INCL O&P
0147	Double Y branch, straight									
0148	1-½" pipe size	Q-1	10	1.600	Ea.	7.45	36		43.45	61
0149	2" pipe size	"	7	2.290	"	12.40	51		63.40	89
0160	P trap									
0161	1-½" pipe size	Q-1	15	1.070	Ea.	8.98	24		32.98	45
0162	2" pipe size		13	1.230		15.70	27		42.70	58
0163	3" pipe size		7	2.290		38	51		89	115
0164	4" pipe size		5	3.200		96	71		167	210
0180	Tucker connection									
0181	1-½" pipe size	Q-1	24	.667	Ea.	7.20	14.80		22	30
0182	2" pipe size	"	21	.762	"	8.90	16.95		25.85	35
0205	Cast iron, drainage, threaded, galvanized									
0206	90° Elbow, straight									
0207	1-½" pipe size	Q-1	20	.800	Ea.	4.24	17.80		22.04	31
0208	2" pipe size		18	.889		6.05	19.75		25.80	36
0209	2" pipe size		10	1.600		21	36		57	76
0210	4" pipe size		6	2.670		36	59		95	130
0216	90° Long turn elbow, straight									
0217	1-½" pipe size	Q-1	20	.800	Ea.	5.15	17.80		22.95	32
0218	2" pipe size		18	.889		8	19.75		27.75	38
0219	3" pipe size		10	1.600		26	36		62	81
0220	4" pipe size		6	2.670		46	59		105	140
0226	90° Street elbow, straight									
0227	1-½" pipe size	Q-1	20	.800	Ea.	5.25	17.80		23.05	32
0228	2" pipe size	"	18	.889	"	8.60	19.75		28.35	39
0236	45° Elbow									
0237	1-½" pipe size	Q-1	20	.800	Ea.	4.22	17.80		22.02	31
0238	2" pipe size		18	.889		6.10	19.75		25.85	36
0239	3" pipe size		10	1.600		21	36		57	76
0240	4" pipe size		6	2.670		36	59		95	130
0246	45° Street elbow									
0247	1-½" pipe size	Q-1	20	.800	Ea.	4.80	17.80		22.60	32
0248	2" pipe size	"	18	.889	"	8.05	19.75		27.80	38
0268	Tees, straight									
0269	1-½" pipe size	Q-1	13	1.230	Ea.	6.50	27		33.50	48
0270	2" pipe size	"	11	1.450	"	10.90	32		42.90	60
0276	TY's, straight									
0277	1-½" pipe size	Q-1	13	1.230	Ea.	6.50	27		33.50	48
0278	2" pipe size		11	1.450		10.85	32		42.85	60
0279	3" pipe size		6	2.670		34	59		93	125
0280	4" pipe size		4	4		56	89		145	195
0296	45° Y branch, straight									
0297	1-½" pipe size	Q-1	13	1.230	Ea.	9.05	27		36.05	51
0298	2" pipe size		11	1.450		14.50	32		46.50	64
0299	3" pipe size		6	2.670		42	59		101	135
0300	4" pipe size		4	4		80	89		169	220
0323	Double Y branch, straight									
0324	1-½" pipe size	Q-1	10	1.600	Ea.	10.25	36		46.25	64
0325	2" pipe size	"	7	2.290	"	15.50	51		66.50	92
0336	P Trap									
0337	1-½" pipe size	Q-1	15	1.070	Ea.	11.75	24		35.75	48
0338	2" pipe size		13	1.230		20	27		47	63
0339	3" pipe size		7	2.290		50	51		101	130
0340	4" pipe size		5	3.200		129	71		200	245
0356	Tucker connection									
0357	1-½" pipe size	Q-1	24	.667	Ea.	9.45	14.80		24.25	32
0358	2" pipe size	"	21	.762	"	11.55	16.95		28.50	38

151 | Pipe and Fittings

151 700 | Steel Pipe

				DAILY	MAN-		BARE COSTS				TOTAL
			CREW	OUTPUT	HOURS	UNIT	MAT.	LABOR	EQUIP.	TOTAL	INCL O&P
720	0010	**PIPE, STEEL, FITTINGS** Flanged, welded and special type									720
	0020	Flanged joints, C.I., standard weight, black. One gasket & bolt									
	0040	set required at each joint, not included (see line 0620)									
	0060	90° Elbow, straight, 1-½" pipe size	Q-1	14	1.140	Ea.	36	25		61	77
	0080	2" pipe size		13	1.230		36	27		63	80
	0090	2-½" pipe size		12	1.330		34	30		64	81
	0100	3" pipe size		11	1.450		33	32		65	84
	0110	4" pipe size		8	2		43	44		87	115
	0120	5" pipe size		7	2.290		64	51		115	145
	0130	6" pipe size	Q-2	9	2.670		72	61		133	170
	0140	8" pipe size		8	3		115	69		184	230
	0150	10" pipe size		7	3.430		220	79		299	360
	0160	12" pipe size		6	4		360	92		452	535
	0171	90° Elbow, reducing									
	0172	2-½" by 2" pipe size	Q-1	12	1.330	Ea.	72	30		102	125
	0173	3" by 2-½" pipe size		11	1.450		74	32		106	130
	0174	4" by 3" pipe size		8	2		78	44		122	150
	0175	5" by 3" pipe size		7	2.290		120	51		171	205
	0176	6" by 4" pipe size	Q-2	9	2.670		125	61		186	230
	0177	8" by 6" pipe size		8	3		155	69		224	275
	0178	10" by 8" pipe size		7	3.430		280	79		359	425
	0179	12" by 10" pipe size		6	4		495	92		587	680
	0200	45° Elbow, straight, 1-½" pipe size	Q-1	14	1.140		45	25		70	87
	0220	2" pipe size		13	1.230		45	27		72	90
	0230	2-½" pipe size		12	1.330		46	30		76	95
	0240	3" pipe size		11	1.450		47	32		79	100
	0250	4" pipe size		8	2		61	44		105	135
	0260	5" pipe size		7	2.290		89	51		140	175
	0270	6" pipe size	Q-2	9	2.670		87	61		148	185
	0280	8" pipe size		8	3		130	69		199	245
	0290	10" pipe size		7	3.430		270	79		349	415
	0300	12" pipe size		6	4		380	92		472	555
	0310	Cross, straight									
	0311	2-½" pipe size	Q-1	6	2.670	Ea.	93	59		152	190
	0312	3" pipe size		5	3.200		98	71		169	215
	0313	4" pipe size		4	4		135	89		224	280
	0314	5" pipe size		3	5.330		190	120		310	385
	0315	6" pipe size	Q-2	5	4.800		215	110		325	400
	0316	8" pipe size		4	6		335	140		475	575
	0317	10" pipe size		3	8		530	185		715	855
	0318	12" pipe size		2	12		805	275		1,080	1,300
	0350	Tee, straight, 1-½" pipe size	Q-1	10	1.600		45	36		81	100
	0370	2" pipe size		9	1.780		45	40		85	110
	0380	2-½" pipe size		8	2		49	44		93	120
	0390	3" pipe size		7	2.290		54	51		105	135
	0400	4" pipe size		5	3.200		71	71		142	185
	0410	5" pipe size		4	4		115	89		204	260
	0420	6" pipe size	Q-2	6	4		105	92		197	250
	0430	8" pipe size		5	4.800		165	110		275	345
	0440	10" pipe size		4	6		330	140		470	570
	0450	12" pipe size		3	8		475	185		660	795
	0459	Tee, reducing on outlet									
	0460	2-½" by 2" pipe size	Q-1	8	2	Ea.	82	44		126	155
	0461	3" by 2-½" pipe size		7	2.290		66	51		117	150
	0462	4" by 3" pipe size		5	3.200		105	71		176	220
	0463	5" by 4" pipe size		4	4		145	89		234	290
	0464	6" by 4" pipe size	Q-2	6	4		160	92		252	315
	0465	8" by 6" pipe size	"	5	4.800		220	110		330	405

151 | Pipe and Fittings

151 700 | Steel Pipe

			CREW	DAILY OUTPUT	MAN-HOURS	UNIT	BARE COSTS MAT.	BARE COSTS LABOR	BARE COSTS EQUIP.	BARE COSTS TOTAL	TOTAL INCL O&P
720	0466	10" by 8" pipe size	Q-2	4	6	Ea.	400	140		540	645
	0467	12" by 10" pipe size	"	3	8	"	630	185		815	965
	0476	Reducer, concentric									
	0477	3" by 2-½"	Q-1	12	1.330	Ea.	62	30		92	110
	0478	4" by 3"		9	1.780		77	40		117	145
	0479	5" by 4"	↓	8	2		105	44		149	180
	0480	6" by 4"	Q-2	10	2.400		120	55		175	215
	0481	8" by 6"		9	2.670		135	61		196	240
	0482	10" by 8"		8	3		270	69		339	400
	0483	12" by 10"	↓	7	3.430		460	79		539	625
	0492	Reducer, eccentric									
	0493	4" by 3"	Q-1	8	2	Ea.	98	44		142	175
	0494	5" by 4"	"	7	2.290		130	51		181	220
	0495	6" by 4"	Q-2	9	2.670		120	61		181	225
	0496	8" by 6"		8	3		150	69		219	270
	0497	10" by 8"		7	3.430		300	79		379	445
	0498	12" by 10"	↓	6	4		460	92		552	645
	0500	For galvanized elbows and tees, add					40%				
	0520	For extra heavy weight elbows and tees, add					17%				
	0620	Gasket and 4 to 20 bolt set, ½" thru 1-½" pipe size	1 Plum	30	.267		2.45	6.60		9.05	12.45
	0630	2" pipe size		30	.267		4	6.60		10.60	14.15
	0640	2-½" pipe size		30	.267		4.10	6.60		10.70	14.30
	0650	3" pipe size		30	.267		4.20	6.60		10.80	14.40
	0660	3-½" pipe size		28	.286		7.90	7.05		14.95	19.15
	0670	4" pipe size		27	.296		8.30	7.30		15.60	20
	0680	5" pipe size		26	.308		11.75	7.60		19.35	24
	0690	6" pipe size		24	.333		11.85	8.25		20.10	25
	0700	8" pipe size		20	.400		12.85	9.90		22.75	29
	0710	10" pipe size		18	.444		32	11		43	51
	0720	12" pipe size		16	.500		34	12.35		46.35	56
	0730	14" pipe size		14	.571		73	14.10		87.10	100
	0740	16" pipe size		13	.615		100	15.20		115.20	135
	0750	18" pipe size		12	.667		130	16.45		146.45	165
	0760	20" pipe size		11	.727		165	17.95		182.95	210
	0780	24" pipe size		10	.800		170	19.75		189.75	215
	0790	26" pipe size		9	.889		200	22		222	255
	0810	30" pipe size		8	1		250	25		275	310
	0830	36" pipe size	↓	7	1.140	↓	310	28		338	385
	0850	For 300 Lb. gasket set, add					10%				
	2000	Unions, 125 lb., black, ½" pipe size	1 Plum	17	.471	Ea.	7.40	11.60		19	25
	2040	¾" pipe size		17	.471		8.80	11.60		20.40	27
	2050	1" pipe size	↓	16	.500		8.20	12.35		20.55	27
	2060	1-¼" pipe size	Q-1	28	.571		9.85	12.70		22.55	30
	2070	1-½" pipe size		27	.593		10.95	13.15		24.10	32
	2080	2" pipe size		26	.615		14.25	13.70		27.95	36
	2090	2-½" pipe size		24	.667		18.55	14.80		33.35	42
	2100	3" pipe size		22	.727		24	16.15		40.15	50
	2110	3-½" pipe size		18	.889		36	19.75		55.75	69
	2120	4" pipe size		16	1		33	22		55	69
	2130	5" pipe size	↓	14	1.140		47	25		72	89
	2140	6" pipe size	Q-2	19	1.260		59	29		88	110
	2150	8" pipe size	"	16	1.500		105	35		140	165
	2200	For galvanized unions, add				↓	100%				
	2290	Threaded companion flange,									
	2300	Cast iron,									
	2310	Black 125 lb., per flange,									
	2320	1" pipe size	1 Plum	27	.296	Ea.	5.20	7.30		12.50	16.60
	2330	1-¼" pipe size	Q-1	44	.364	"	5.65	8.10		13.75	18.20

151 | Pipe and Fittings

151 700 | Steel Pipe

			CREW	DAILY OUTPUT	MAN-HOURS	UNIT	BARE COSTS MAT.	LABOR	EQUIP.	TOTAL	TOTAL INCL O&P	
720	2340	1-½" pipe size	Q-1	40	.400	Ea.	5.85	8.90		14.75	19.65	720
	2350	2" pipe size		36	.444		6.50	9.90		16.40	22	
	2360	2-½" pipe size		28	.571		7.15	12.70		19.85	27	
	2370	3" pipe size		20	.800		9.60	17.80		27.40	37	
	2380	3-½" pipe size		16	1		13.15	22		35.15	47	
	2390	4" pipe size		12	1.330		13.15	30		43.15	58	
	2400	5" pipe size		10	1.600		16.70	36		52.70	71	
	2410	6" pipe size	Q-2	14	1.710		21	40		61	82	
	2420	8" pipe size		12	2		32	46		78	105	
	2430	10" pipe size		10	2.400		48	55		103	135	
	2440	12" pipe size		8	3		72	69		141	180	
	2460	For galvanized flanges, add					40%					
	2580	Forged steel,										
	2590	Black 150 lb., per flange										
	2600	½" pipe size	1 Plum	30	.267	Ea.	10.50	6.60		17.10	21	
	2610	¾" pipe size		28	.286		10.75	7.05		17.80	22	
	2620	1" pipe size		27	.296		11.60	7.30		18.90	24	
	2630	1-¼" pipe size	Q-1	44	.364		11.60	8.10		19.70	25	
	2640	1-½" pipe size		40	.400		15.70	8.90		24.60	30	
	2650	2" pipe size		36	.444		16.15	9.90		26.05	32	
	2660	2-½" pipe size		28	.571		17.35	12.70		30.05	38	
	2670	3" pipe size		20	.800		18.90	17.80		36.70	47	
	2690	4" pipe size		12	1.330		22	30		52	68	
	2700	5" pipe size		10	1.600		30	36		66	86	
	2710	6" pipe size	Q-2	14	1.710		36	40		76	98	
	2720	8" pipe size		12	2		63	46		109	140	
	2730	10" pipe size		10	2.400		100	55		155	190	
	2860	Black 300 lb., per flange										
	2870	½" pipe size	1 Plum	30	.267	Ea.	12.50	6.60		19.10	24	
	2880	¾" pipe size		28	.286		14.25	7.05		21.30	26	
	2890	1" pipe size		27	.296		15.05	7.30		22.35	27	
	2900	1-¼" pipe size	Q-1	44	.364		17.85	8.10		25.95	32	
	2910	1-½" pipe size		40	.400		17.85	8.90		26.75	33	
	2920	2" pipe size		36	.444		17.85	9.90		27.75	34	
	2930	2-½" pipe size		28	.571		23	12.70		35.70	44	
	2940	3" pipe size		20	.800		27	17.80		44.80	56	
	2960	4" pipe size		12	1.330		40	30		70	88	
	2970	6" pipe size	Q-2	14	1.710		63	40		103	130	
	3000	Weld joint, butt, carbon steel, standard weight										
	3040	90° Elbow, long										
	3050	½" pipe size	Q-15	16	1	Ea.	4.60	22	2.39	28.99	41	
	3060	¾" pipe size		16	1		4.60	22	2.39	28.99	41	
	3070	1" pipe size		16	1		4.60	22	2.39	28.99	41	
	3080	1-¼" pipe size		14	1.140		4.60	25	2.73	32.33	46	
	3090	1-½" pipe size		13	1.230		4.60	27	2.94	34.54	49	
	3100	2" pipe size		10	1.600		5.15	36	3.82	44.97	63	
	3110	2-½" pipe size		8	2		8.30	44	4.78	57.08	80	
	3120	3" pipe size		7	2.290		9	51	5.45	65.45	91	
	3130	4" pipe size		5	3.200		14.90	71	7.65	93.55	130	
	3140	6" pipe size	Q-16	5	4.800		37	110	7.65	154.65	215	
	3150	8" pipe size		4	6		66	140	9.55	215.55	290	
	3160	10" pipe size		3	8		125	185	12.75	322.75	425	
	3170	12" pipe size		2.50	9.600		175	220	15.30	410.30	540	
	3180	14" pipe size		2	12		350	275	19.10	644.10	815	
	3190	16" pipe size		1.50	16		490	370	25	885	1,125	
	3191	18" pipe size		1.25	19.200		650	445	31	1,126	1,400	
	3192	20" pipe size		1.15	20.870		870	480	33	1,383	1,700	
	3194	24" pipe size		1.02	23.530		1,275	540	37	1,852	2,250	

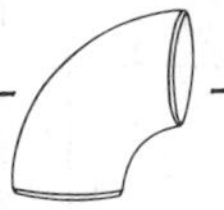

151 | Pipe and Fittings

151 700 | Steel Pipe

		CREW	DAILY OUTPUT	MAN-HOURS	UNIT	BARE COSTS MAT.	LABOR	EQUIP.	TOTAL	TOTAL INCL O&P
720 3195	26" pipe size	Q-16	.85	28.240	Ea.	1,300	650	45	1,995	2,450
3196	30" pipe size		.45	53.330		1,400	1,225	85	2,710	3,450
3198	36" pipe size	↓	.38	63.160	↓	2,225	1,450	100	3,775	4,725
3200	45° Elbow, long									
3210	½" pipe size	Q-15	16	1	Ea.	4.60	22	2.39	28.99	41
3220	¾" pipe size		16	1		4.60	22	2.39	28.99	41
3230	1" pipe size		16	1		4.60	22	2.39	28.99	41
3240	1-¼" pipe size		14	1.140		4.60	25	2.73	32.33	46
3250	1-½" pipe size		13	1.230		4.60	27	2.94	34.54	49
3260	2" pipe size		10	1.600		4.70	36	3.82	44.52	62
3270	2-½" pipe size		8	2		5.80	44	4.78	54.58	78
3280	3" pipe size		7	2.290		6.60	51	5.45	63.05	89
3290	4" pipe size	↓	5	3.200		10.90	71	7.65	89.55	125
3300	6" pipe size	Q-16	5	4.800		24	110	7.65	141.65	200
3310	8" pipe size		4	6		43	140	9.55	192.55	265
3320	10" pipe size		3	8		69	185	12.75	266.75	365
3330	12" pipe size		2.50	9.600		100	220	15.30	335.30	455
3340	14" pipe size		2	12		210	275	19.10	504.10	660
3341	16" pipe size		1.50	16		280	370	25	675	885
3342	18" pipe size		1.25	19.200		405	445	31	881	1,125
3343	20" pipe size		1.15	20.870		510	480	33	1,023	1,300
3345	24" pipe size		1.05	22.860		795	525	36	1,356	1,700
3346	26" pipe size		.85	28.240		880	650	45	1,575	1,975
3347	30" pipe size		.45	53.330		975	1,225	85	2,285	3,000
3349	36" pipe size	↓	.38	63.160	↓	1,550	1,450	100	3,100	3,975
3350	Tee, straight									
3352	For reducing tees and concentrics see 151-720-4600									
3360	½" pipe size	Q-15	10	1.600	Ea.	13.10	36	3.82	52.92	71
3370	¾" pipe size		10	1.600		13.10	36	3.82	52.92	71
3380	1" pipe size		10	1.600		13.10	36	3.82	52.92	71
3390	1-¼" pipe size		9	1.780		15.90	40	4.24	60.14	81
3400	1-½" pipe size		8	2		19	44	4.78	67.78	92
3410	2" pipe size		6	2.670		14.10	59	6.35	79.45	110
3420	2-½" pipe size		5	3.200		17.50	71	7.65	96.15	135
3430	3" pipe size		4	4		20	89	9.55	118.55	165
3440	4" pipe size	↓	3	5.330		27	120	12.75	159.75	220
3450	6" pipe size	Q-16	3	8		50	185	12.75	247.75	345
3460	8" pipe size		2.50	9.600		91	220	15.30	326.30	445
3470	10" pipe size		2	12		155	275	19.10	449.10	600
3480	12" pipe size		1.60	15		360	345	24	729	935
3481	14" pipe size		1.30	18.460		585	425	29	1,039	1,300
3482	16" pipe size		1	24		705	555	38	1,298	1,650
3483	18" pipe size		.80	30		1,125	690	48	1,863	2,325
3484	20" pipe size		.75	32		1,670	740	51	2,461	2,975
3486	24" pipe size		.70	34.290		2,225	790	55	3,070	3,675
3487	26" pipe size		.55	43.640		2,325	1,000	69	3,394	4,125
3488	30" pipe size		.30	80		2,525	1,850	125	4,500	5,650
3490	36" pipe size	↓	.20	120		3,900	2,775	190	6,865	8,600
3491	Eccentric reducer, 1-½" pipe size	Q-15	14	1.140		19	25	2.73	46.73	62
3492	2" pipe size		11	1.450		16.50	32	3.47	51.97	70
3493	2-½" pipe size		9	1.780		18.10	40	4.24	62.34	83
3494	3" pipe size		8	2		19	44	4.78	67.78	92
3495	4" pipe size	↓	6	2.670		26	59	6.35	91.35	125
3496	6" pipe size	Q-16	5	4.800		47	110	7.65	164.65	225
3497	8" pipe size		4	6		70	140	9.55	219.55	295
3498	10" pipe size		3	8		130	185	12.75	327.75	430
3499	12" pipe size	↓	2.50	9.600		180	220	15.30	415.30	545
3501	Cap, 1-½" pipe size	Q-15	28	.571		9.35	12.70	1.36	23.41	31

151 | Pipe and Fittings

151 700 | Steel Pipe

			DAILY	MAN-		\multicolumn{4}{c	}{BARE COSTS}	TOTAL
		CREW	OUTPUT	HOURS	UNIT	MAT.	LABOR	EQUIP.	TOTAL	INCL O&P
3502	2" pipe size	Q-15	22	.727	Ea.	8.20	16.15	1.74	26.09	35
3503	2-½" pipe size		18	.889		8.70	19.75	2.12	30.57	41
3504	3" pipe size		16	1		9.20	22	2.39	33.59	46
3505	4" pipe size		12	1.330		11.90	30	3.18	45.08	61
3506	6" pipe size	Q-16	10	2.400		20	55	3.82	78.82	110
3507	8" pipe size		8	3		32	69	4.78	105.78	145
3508	10" pipe size		6	4		52	92	6.35	150.35	200
3509	12" pipe size		5	4.800		64	110	7.65	181.65	245
3511	14" pipe size		4	6		84	140	9.55	233.55	310
3512	16" pipe size		4	6		120	140	9.55	269.55	350
3517	Weld joint, butt, carbon steel, extra strong									
3519	90° Elbow, long									
3520	½" pipe size	Q-15	16	1	Ea.	5.40	22	2.39	29.79	42
3530	¾" pipe size		16	1		5.40	22	2.39	29.79	42
3540	1" pipe size		16	1		5.40	22	2.39	29.79	42
3550	1-¼" pipe size		14	1.140		6.20	25	2.73	33.93	48
3560	1-½" pipe size		13	1.230		6.80	27	2.94	36.74	51
3570	2" pipe size		10	1.600		7	36	3.82	46.82	65
3580	2-½" pipe size		8	2		10.10	44	4.78	58.88	82
3590	3" pipe size		7	2.290		13	51	5.45	69.45	96
3600	4" pipe size		5	3.200		22	71	7.65	100.65	140
3610	6" pipe size	Q-16	5	4.800		55	110	7.65	172.65	235
3620	8" pipe size		4	6		100	140	9.55	249.55	325
3630	10" pipe size		3	8		180	185	12.75	377.75	485
3640	12" pipe size		2.50	9.600		255	220	15.30	490.30	625
3650	45° Elbow, long									
3660	½" pipe size	Q-15	16	1	Ea.	5.40	22	2.39	29.79	42
3670	¾" pipe size		16	1		5.40	22	2.39	29.79	42
3680	1" pipe size		16	1		5.40	22	2.39	29.79	42
3690	1-¼" pipe size		14	1.140		5.90	25	2.73	33.63	47
3700	1-½" pipe size		13	1.230		6.35	27	2.94	36.29	51
3710	2" pipe size		10	1.600		5.60	36	3.82	45.42	63
3720	2-½" pipe size		8	2		8	44	4.78	56.78	80
3730	3" pipe size		7	2.290		9.90	51	5.45	66.35	92
3740	4" pipe size		5	3.200		14.70	71	7.65	93.35	130
3750	6" pipe size	Q-16	5	4.800		38	110	7.65	155.65	215
3760	8" pipe size		4	6		63	140	9.55	212.55	285
3770	10" pipe size		3	8		100	185	12.75	297.75	400
3780	12" pipe size		2.50	9.600		150	220	15.30	385.30	510
3800	Tee, straight									
3810	½" pipe size	Q-15	10	1.600	Ea.	17	36	3.82	56.82	76
3820	¾" pipe size		10	1.600		17	36	3.82	56.82	76
3830	1" pipe size		10	1.600		17	36	3.82	56.82	76
3840	1-¼" pipe size		9	1.780		17	40	4.24	61.24	82
3850	1-½" pipe size		8	2		20	44	4.78	68.78	93
3860	2" pipe size		6	2.670		16.50	59	6.35	81.85	115
3870	2-½" pipe size		5	3.200		22	71	7.65	100.65	140
3880	3" pipe size		4	4		27	89	9.55	125.55	170
3890	4" pipe size		3	5.330		45	120	12.75	177.75	240
3900	6" pipe size	Q-16	3	8		71	185	12.75	268.75	365
3910	8" pipe size		2.50	9.600		140	220	15.30	375.30	500
3920	10" pipe size		2	12		230	275	19.10	524.10	685
3930	12" pipe size		1.60	15		330	345	24	699	900
4200	Welding ring w/spacer pins, 2" pipe size					1.55			1.55	1.71
4210	2-½" pipe size					1.60			1.60	1.76
4220	3" pipe size					1.70			1.70	1.87
4230	4" pipe size					2.10			2.10	2.31
4240	6" pipe size					2.80			2.80	3.08

151 | Pipe and Fittings

151 700 | Steel Pipe

		CREW	DAILY OUTPUT	MAN-HOURS	UNIT	BARE COSTS MAT.	LABOR	EQUIP.	TOTAL	TOTAL INCL O&P
4250	8" pipe size				Ea.	4.60			4.60	5.05
4260	10" pipe size					5.45			5.45	6
4270	12" pipe size					6.35			6.35	7
4280	14" pipe size					6.35			6.35	7
4290	16" pipe size					7.95			7.95	8.75
4300	18" pipe size					8.60			8.60	9.45
4310	20" pipe size					10			10	11
4330	24" pipe size					11.50			11.50	12.65
4340	26" pipe size					11.75			11.75	12.95
4350	30" pipe size					14.25			14.25	15.70
4370	36" pipe size					18.25			18.25	20
4600	Tee, reducing on outlet									
4601	2-½" by 2" pipe size	Q-15	5	3.200	Ea.	24	71	7.65	102.65	140
4602	3" by 2-½" pipe size		4	4		26	89	9.55	124.55	170
4603	3-½" by 3" pipe size		3.50	4.570		31	100	10.90	141.90	195
4604	4" by 3" pipe size		3	5.330		31	120	12.75	163.75	225
4605	5" by 4" pipe size		2.50	6.400		65	140	15.30	220.30	300
4606	6" by 5" pipe size	Q-16	3	8		65	185	12.75	262.75	360
4607	8" by 6" pipe size		2.50	9.600		120	220	15.30	355.30	475
4608	10" by 8" pipe size		2	12		210	275	19.10	504.10	660
4609	12" by 10" pipe size		1.60	15		370	345	24	739	945
4618	Reducer, concentric									
4619	2-½" by 2" pipe size	Q-5	10	1.600	Ea.	15	36		51	69
4620	3" by 2-½" pipe size	Q-15	9	1.780		20	40	4.24	64.24	85
4621	3-½" by 3" pipe size		8	2		25	44	4.78	73.78	99
4622	4" by 2-½" pipe size		7	2.290		28	51	5.45	84.45	110
4623	5" by 3" pipe size		7	2.290		40	51	5.45	96.45	125
4624	6" by 4" pipe size	Q-16	6	4		50	92	6.35	148.35	200
4625	8" by 6" pipe size		5	4.800		75	110	7.65	192.65	255
4626	10" by 8" pipe size		4	6		125	140	9.55	274.55	355
4627	12" by 10" pipe size		3	8		190	185	12.75	387.75	495
5630	T-O-L, ¼" pipe size, nozzle	Q-15	23	.696		3.45	15.45	1.66	20.56	29
5631	⅜" pipe size, nozzle		23	.696		3.45	15.45	1.66	20.56	29
5632	½" pipe size, nozzle		22	.727		3.45	16.15	1.74	21.34	30
5633	¾" pipe size, nozzle		21	.762		4.15	16.95	1.82	22.92	32
5634	1" pipe size, nozzle		20	.800		4.75	17.80	1.91	24.46	34
5635	1-¼" pipe size, nozzle		18	.889		6.40	19.75	2.12	28.27	39
5636	1-½" pipe size, nozzle		16	1		7.10	22	2.39	31.49	43
5637	2" pipe size, nozzle		12	1.330		8.05	30	3.18	41.23	56
5640	W-O-L, ¼" pipe size, nozzle		23	.696		6.25	15.45	1.66	23.36	32
5641	⅜" pipe size, nozzle		23	.696		6.25	15.45	1.66	23.36	32
5642	½" pipe size, nozzle		22	.727		6.25	16.15	1.74	24.14	33
5643	¾" pipe size, nozzle		21	.762		6.55	16.95	1.82	25.32	34
5644	1" pipe size, nozzle		20	.800		6.80	17.80	1.91	26.51	36
5645	1-¼" pipe size, nozzle		18	.889		7.60	19.75	2.12	29.47	40
5646	1-½" pipe size, nozzle		16	1		8.20	22	2.39	32.59	45
5647	2" pipe size, nozzle		12	1.330		8.55	30	3.18	41.73	57
6000	Weld-on flange, forged steel									
6020	Slip-on, 150 lb. flange, (welded front and back)									
6050	½" pipe size	Q-15	18	.889	Ea.	8	19.75	2.12	29.87	40
6060	¾" pipe size		18	.889		8	19.75	2.12	29.87	40
6070	1" pipe size		17	.941		8	21	2.25	31.25	42
6080	1-¼" pipe size		16	1		8	22	2.39	32.39	44
6090	1-½" pipe size		15	1.070		8	24	2.55	34.55	47
6100	2" pipe size		12	1.330		8	30	3.18	41.18	56
6110	2-½" pipe size		10	1.600		10.50	36	3.82	50.32	69
6120	3" pipe size		9	1.780		11.60	40	4.24	55.84	76
6130	3-½" pipe size		7	2.290		14.80	51	5.45	71.25	98

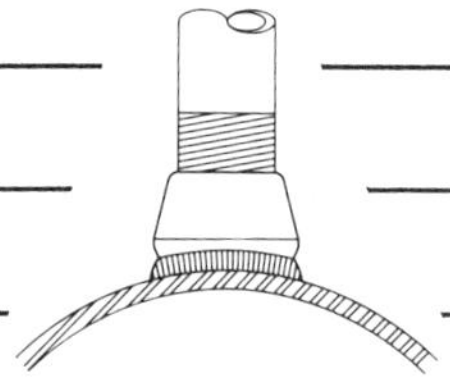

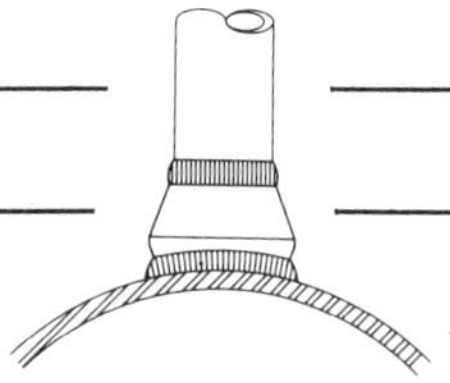

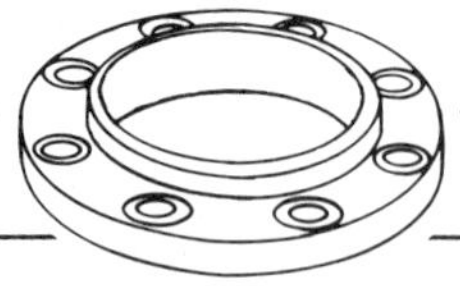

151 | Pipe and Fittings

151 700 | Steel Pipe

		Crew	Daily Output	Man-Hours	Unit	Mat.	Labor	Equip.	Total	Total Incl O&P	
720	6140	4" pipe size	Q-15	6	2.670	Ea.	14.80	59	6.35	80.15	110	720
	6150	5" pipe size	"	5	3.200		20	71	7.65	98.65	135	
	6160	6" pipe size	Q-16	6	4		24	92	6.35	122.35	170	
	6170	8" pipe size		5	4.800		36	110	7.65	153.65	210	
	6180	10" pipe size		4	6		65	140	9.55	214.55	285	
	6190	12" pipe size		3	8		95	185	12.75	292.75	390	
	6191	14" pipe size		2.50	9.600		165	220	15.30	400.30	525	
	6192	16" pipe size		1.80	13.330		200	305	21	526	700	
	6200	300 lb. flange										
	6210	½" pipe size	Q-15	17	.941	Ea.	8.70	21	2.25	31.95	43	
	6220	¾" pipe size		17	.941		9	21	2.25	32.25	43	
	6230	1" pipe size		16	1		9.40	22	2.39	33.79	46	
	6240	1-¼" pipe size		13	1.230		10.50	27	2.94	40.44	55	
	6250	1-½" pipe size		12	1.330		11.20	30	3.18	44.38	60	
	6260	2" pipe size		11	1.450		11.20	32	3.47	46.67	64	
	6270	2-½" pipe size		9	1.780		13.40	40	4.24	57.64	78	
	6280	3" pipe size		7	2.290		15.90	51	5.45	72.35	99	
	6290	4" pipe size		6	2.670		25	59	6.35	90.35	120	
	6300	5" pipe size		4	4		40	89	9.55	138.55	185	
	6310	6" pipe size	Q-16	5	4.800		40	110	7.65	157.65	215	
	6320	8" pipe size		4	6		67	140	9.55	216.55	290	
	6330	10" pipe size		3.40	7.060		130	165	11.25	306.25	395	
	6340	12" pipe size		2.80	8.570		155	200	13.65	368.65	480	
	6400	Welding neck, 150 lb. flange										
	6410	½" pipe size	Q-15	40	.400	Ea.	10.50	8.90	.96	20.36	26	
	6420	¾" pipe size		36	.444		10.80	9.90	1.06	21.76	28	
	6430	1" pipe size		32	.500		10.80	11.10	1.19	23.09	30	
	6440	1-¼" pipe size		29	.552		11.20	12.25	1.32	24.77	32	
	6450	1-½" pipe size		26	.615		11.20	13.70	1.47	26.37	34	
	6460	2" pipe size		20	.800		11.20	17.80	1.91	30.91	41	
	6470	2-½" pipe size		16	1		12.30	22	2.39	36.69	49	
	6480	3" pipe size		14	1.140		14.10	25	2.73	41.83	56	
	6490	3-½" pipe size		12	1.330		26	30	3.18	59.18	76	
	6500	4" pipe size		10	1.600		14.80	36	3.82	54.62	73	
	6510	5" pipe size		8	2		24	44	4.78	72.78	98	
	6520	6" pipe size	Q-16	10	2.400		28	55	3.82	86.82	115	
	6530	8" pipe size		7	3.430		45	79	5.45	129.45	175	
	6540	10" pipe size		6	4		85	92	6.35	183.35	235	
	6550	12" pipe size		5	4.800		125	110	7.65	242.65	310	
	6551	14" pipe size		4.50	5.330		270	125	8.50	403.50	490	
	6552	16" pipe size		3	8		340	185	12.75	537.75	660	
	6553	18" pipe size		2.50	9.600		555	220	15.30	790.30	955	
	6554	20" pipe size		2.30	10.430		660	240	16.60	916.60	1,100	
	6556	24" pipe size		2	12		870	275	19.10	1,164	1,400	
	6557	26" pipe size		1.70	14.120		950	325	22	1,297	1,550	
	6558	30" pipe size		.90	26.670		1,225	615	42	1,882	2,300	
	6559	36" pipe size		.75	32		1,500	740	51	2,291	2,800	
	6560	300 lb. flange										
	6570	½" pipe size	Q-15	36	.444	Ea.	10.90	9.90	1.06	21.86	28	
	6580	¾" pipe size		34	.471		11.20	10.45	1.12	22.77	29	
	6590	1" pipe size		30	.533		11.90	11.85	1.27	25.02	32	
	6600	1-¼" pipe size		28	.571		12.70	12.70	1.36	26.76	34	
	6610	1-½" pipe size		24	.667		13.70	14.80	1.59	30.09	39	
	6620	2" pipe size		18	.889		13.70	19.75	2.12	35.57	47	
	6630	2-½" pipe size		14	1.140		16.25	25	2.73	43.98	59	
	6640	3" pipe size		12	1.330		18	30	3.18	51.18	67	
	6650	4" pipe size		8	2		27	44	4.78	75.78	100	
	6660	5" pipe size		7	2.290		44	51	5.45	100.45	130	

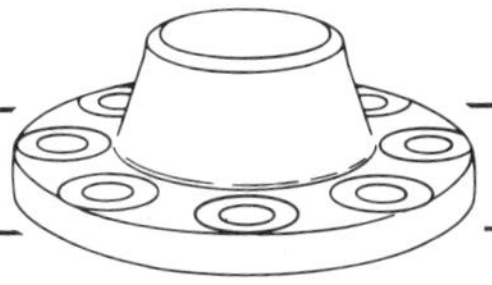

151 | Pipe and Fittings

151 700 | Steel Pipe

		CREW	DAILY OUTPUT	MAN-HOURS	UNIT	BARE COSTS MAT.	LABOR	EQUIP.	TOTAL	TOTAL INCL O&P	
6670	6" pipe size	Q-16	9	2.670	Ea.	48	61	4.24	113.24	150	
6680	8" pipe size		6	4		82	92	6.35	180.35	235	
6690	10" pipe size		5	4.800		170	110	7.65	287.65	360	
6700	12" pipe size		4	6		210	140	9.55	359.55	445	
7740	Plain ends for plain end pipe, mechanically coupled										
7750	Cplg & labor required at joints not included add 1 per										
7760	joint for installed price, see 151-720-9180										
7770	Malleable iron, black, unless noted otherwise										
7800	90° Elbow 1"				Ea.	5.85			5.85	6.45	
7810	1-½"					8.20			8.20	9	
7820	2"					8.20			8.20	9	
7830	2-½"					11.20			11.20	12.30	
7840	3"					14.75			14.75	16.25	
7860	4"					22			22	24	
7870	5" welded steel					73			73	80	
7880	6"					62			62	68	
7890	8" welded steel					125			125	140	
7900	10" welded steel					155			155	170	
7910	12" welded steel					200			200	220	
7970	45° Elbow 1"					5.85			5.85	6.45	
7980	1-½"					8.20			8.20	9	
7990	2"					8.20			8.20	9	
8000	2-½"					11.20			11.20	12.30	
8010	3"					14.75			14.75	16.25	
8030	4"					22			22	24	
8040	5" welded steel					73			73	80	
8050	6"					62			62	68	
8060	8"					125			125	140	
8070	10" welded steel					155			155	170	
8080	12" welded steel					200			200	220	
8140	Tee, straight 1"					8.20			8.20	9	
8150	1-½"					10.25			10.25	11.30	
8160	2"					12.70			12.70	13.95	
8170	2-½"					17.25			17.25	19	
8180	3"					25			25	28	
8200	4"					37			37	41	
8210	5" welded steel					72			72	79	
8220	6"					100			100	110	
8230	8" welded steel					125			125	140	
8240	10" welded steel					185			185	205	
8250	12" welded steel					425			425	470	
8340	Segmentally welded steel										
8390	Wye 2"				Ea.	56			56	62	
8400	2-½"					66			66	73	
8410	3"					79			79	87	
8430	4"					105			105	115	
8440	5"					150			150	165	
8450	6"					185			185	205	
8460	8"					270			270	295	
8470	10"					390			390	430	
8480	12"					435			435	480	
8540	Wye, lateral 2"					31			31	34	
8550	2-½"					69			69	76	
8560	3"					60			60	66	
8580	4"					120			120	130	
8590	5"					175			175	195	
8600	6"					225			225	250	
8610	8"					230			230	255	

151 | Pipe and Fittings

151 700 | Steel Pipe

		CREW	DAILY OUTPUT	MAN-HOURS	UNIT	BARE COSTS MAT.	BARE COSTS LABOR	BARE COSTS EQUIP.	TOTAL	TOTAL INCL O&P
8620	10"				Ea.	450			450	495
8630	12"					500			500	550
8690	Cross, 2"					22			22	24
8700	2-½"					82			82	90
8710	3"					57			57	63
8730	4"					95			95	105
8740	5"					195			195	215
8750	6"					250			250	275
8760	8"					325			325	360
8770	10"					475			475	525
8780	12"					690			690	760
8800	Tees, reducing 2" x 1"					15.20			15.20	16.70
8810	2" x 1-½"					29			29	32
8820	3" x 1"					33			33	36
8830	3" x 1-½"					33			33	36
8840	3" x 2"					33			33	36
8850	4" x 1"					45			45	50
8860	4" x 1-½"					45			45	50
8870	4" x 2"					45			45	50
8880	4" x 2-½"					45			45	50
8890	4" x 3"					45			45	50
8900	6" x 2"					105			105	115
8910	6" x 3"					105			105	115
8920	6" x 4"					105			105	115
8930	8" x 2"					155			155	170
8940	8" x 3"					155			155	170
8950	8" x 4"					225			225	250
8960	8" x 5"					225			225	250
8970	8" x 6"					225			225	250
8980	10" x 4"					240			240	265
8990	10" x 6"					245			245	270
9000	10" x 8"					250			250	275
9010	12" x 6"					365			365	400
9020	12" x 8"					375			375	415
9030	12" x 10"					385			385	425
9080	Adapter nipples 3" long				Ea.					
9090	1"					3.64			3.64	4
9100	1-½"					3.73			3.73	4.10
9110	2"					5.35			5.35	5.90
9120	2-½"					6.40			6.40	7.05
9130	3"					7.90			7.90	8.70
9140	4"					13.30			13.30	14.65
9150	6"					37			37	41
9180	Coupling, mechanical, plain end pipe to plain end pipe or fitting									
9190	1"	Q-1	29	.552	Ea.	8.65	12.25		20.90	28
9200	1-½"		28	.571		8.65	12.70		21.35	28
9210	2"		27	.593		8.75	13.15		21.90	29
9220	2-½"		26	.615		11.10	13.70		24.80	33
9230	3"		25	.640		13.05	14.25		27.30	35
9240	3-½"		24	.667		18.55	14.80		33.35	42
9250	4"		22	.727		18.55	16.15		34.70	44
9260	5"	Q-2	28	.857		27	19.75		46.75	59
9270	6"		24	1		33	23		56	71
9280	8"		19	1.260		57	29		86	105
9290	10"		16	1.500		80	35		115	140
9300	12"		12	2		91	46		137	170
9310	Outlets for precut holes through pipe wall									
9311	Hook type, FIPS, single bolt, w/gasket									

151 | Pipe and Fittings

151 700 | Steel Pipe

		CREW	DAILY OUTPUT	MAN-HOURS	UNIT	BARE COSTS MAT.	BARE COSTS LABOR	BARE COSTS EQUIP.	BARE COSTS TOTAL	TOTAL INCL O&P	
720	9313	1-¼" x ½ or ¾"	1 Spri	30	.267	Ea.	5.20	6.85		12.05	15.90	720
	9314	1-¼" x 1"		30	.267		5.40	6.85		12.25	16.10	
	9315	1-½" x ½ or ¾" 		29	.276		5.45	7.10		12.55	16.55	
	9316	1-½" x 1"		29	.276		6.10	7.10		13.20	17.25	
	9317	2" x ½ or ¾"		28	.286		5.75	7.35		13.10	17.25	
	9318	2" x 1"		28	.286		6.40	7.35		13.75	17.95	
	9319	2-½" x ½ or ¾"		27	.296		6.10	7.60		13.70	18.05	
	9320	2-½" x 1"		27	.296		7.25	7.60		14.85	19.30	
	9331	Strapless type, with gasket, FIPS 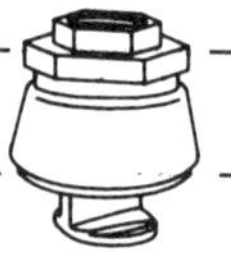										
	9332	4" to 8" pipe x ½"	1 Plum	13	.615	Ea.	4.21	15.20		19.41	27	
	9333	4" to 8" pipe x ¾"		13	.615		4.54	15.20		19.74	28	
	9334	10" pipe and larger x ½"		11	.727		4.21	17.95		22.16	31	
	9335	10" pipe and larger x ¾"		11	.727		4.54	17.95		22.49	32	
	9341	Thermometer wells with gasket 										
	9342	4" to 8" pipe, 6" stem	1 Plum	14	.571	Ea.	2.59	14.10		16.69	24	
	9343	8" pipe and larger, 6" stem	"	13	.615	"	2.59	15.20		17.79	25	
	9400	Mechanical joint ends for plain end pipe										
	9410	Malleable iron, black										
	9420	90° Elbows, 1-¼" 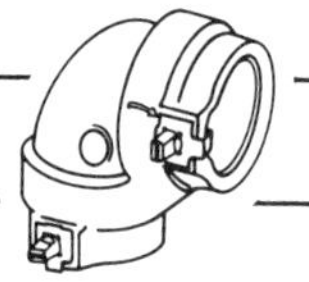	Q-1	29	.552	Ea.	10.70	12.25		22.95	30	
	9430	1-½"		27	.593		11.65	13.15		24.80	32	
	9440	2"		24	.667		13.70	14.80		28.50	37	
	9490	Tee, reducing outlet										
	9510	1-¼" x ½" 	Q-1	18	.889	Ea.	8.53	19.75		28.28	39	
	9520	1-¼" x ¾"		18	.889		8.53	19.75		28.28	39	
	9530	1-¼" x 1"		18	.889		8.53	19.75		28.28	39	
	9540	1-½" x ½"		17	.941		9	21		30	41	
	9550	1-½" x ¾"		17	.941		9	21		30	41	
	9560	1-½" x 1"		17	.941		9	21		30	41	
	9570	2" x ½"		15	1.070		11.10	24		35.10	47	
	9580	2" x ¾"		15	1.070		11.10	24		35.10	47	
	9590	2" x 1"		15	1.070		11.10	24		35.10	47	
	9640	Tee, reducing run and outlet										
	9660	1-¼" x 1" x ½"	Q-1	18	.889	Ea.	9.05	19.75		28.80	39	
	9670	1-¼" x 1" x ¾"		18	.889		9.05	19.75		28.80	39	
	9680	1-¼" x 1" x 1" 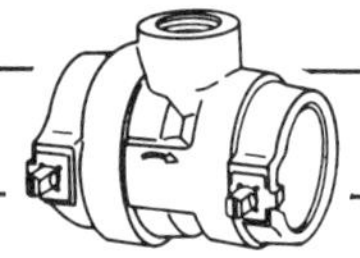		18	.889		9.05	19.75		28.80	39	
	9690	1-½" x 1-¼" x ½"		17	.941		9.70	21		30.70	42	
	9700	1-½" x 1-¼" x ¾"		17	.941		9.70	21		30.70	42	
	9710	1-½" x 1-¼" x 1"		17	.941		9.70	21		30.70	42	
	9720	2" x 1-½" x ½"		15	1.070		11.75	24		35.75	48	
	9730	2" x 1-½" x ¾"		15	1.070		11.75	24		35.75	48	
	9740	2" x 1-½" x 1"		15	1.070		11.75	24		35.75	48	
	9790	Tee, outlet 										
	9810	3" x 1-¼"	Q-1	29	.552	Ea.	23	12.25		35.25	43	
	9820	3" x 1-½"		28	.571		23	12.70		35.70	44	
	9830	3" x 2"		26	.615		25	13.70		38.70	48	
	9840	4" x 1-¼"		28	.571		25	12.70		37.70	46	
	9850	4" x 1-½"		26	.615		27	13.70		40.70	50	
	9860	4" x 2"		24	.667		27	14.80		41.80	52	
	9940	For galvanized fittings for plain end pipe, add					14%					

151 800 | Grooved-Joint Steel Pipe

		CREW	DAILY OUTPUT	MAN-HOURS	UNIT	MAT.	LABOR	EQUIP.	TOTAL	INCL O&P	
801	0010	**PIPE, GROOVED-JOINT STEEL FITTINGS & VALVES**									801
	0020	Pipe includes coupling & clevis type hanger 10' O.C.									
	0500	Schedule 10, black									
	0550	2" diameter	1 Plum	43	.186	L.F.	2.44	4.60		7.04	9.50	
	0560	2-½" diameter	Q-1	61	.262		3.11	5.85		8.96	12.05	
	0570	3" diameter	"	55	.291		3.65	6.45		10.10	13.60	

151 | Pipe and Fittings

151 800 | Grooved-Joint Steel Pipe

		CREW	DAILY OUTPUT	MAN-HOURS	UNIT	BARE COSTS MAT.	LABOR	EQUIP.	TOTAL	TOTAL INCL O&P	
801	0580	3-½" diameter	Q-1	53	.302	L.F.	4.13	6.70		10.83	14.50	801
	0590	4" diameter		49	.327		4.95	7.25		12.20	16.20	
	0600	5" diameter	↓	40	.400		7.11	8.90		16.01	21	
	0610	6" diameter	Q-2	46	.522		8.45	12.05		20.50	27	
	0620	8" diameter		41	.585		14.03	13.50		27.53	35	
	0630	10" diameter		34	.706		18.69	16.25		34.94	45	
	0640	12" diameter	↓	30	.800	↓	21.58	18.45		40.03	51	
	0700	To delete couplings & hangers, subtract										
	0710	2" diam. to 5" diam.					25%	20%				
	0720	6" diam. to 12" diam.					27%	15%				
	1000	Schedule 40, black										
	1040	¾" diameter	1 Plum	71	.113	L.F.	1.53	2.78		4.31	5.80	
	1050	1" diameter		63	.127		1.71	3.14		4.85	6.55	
	1060	1-¼" diameter		58	.138		2.16	3.41		5.57	7.45	
	1070	1-½" diameter		51	.157		2.45	3.87		6.32	8.45	
	1080	2" diameter	↓	40	.200		3.07	4.94		8.01	10.70	
	1090	2-½" diameter	Q-1	57	.281		4.37	6.25		10.62	14.05	
	1100	3" diameter		50	.320		5.48	7.10		12.58	16.60	
	1110	4" diameter		45	.356		7.92	7.90		15.82	20	
	1120	5" diameter	↓	37	.432		13.17	9.60		22.77	29	
	1130	6" diameter	Q-2	42	.571		15.71	13.15		28.86	37	
	1140	8" diameter		37	.649		21.13	14.95		36.08	45	
	1150	10" diameter		31	.774		27.74	17.85		45.59	57	
	1160	12" diameter		27	.889		32.68	20		52.68	66	
	1170	14" diameter		20	1.200		69	28		97	115	
	1180	16" diameter		17	1.410		80	33		113	135	
	1190	18" diameter		14	1.710		96	40		136	165	
	1200	20" diameter		12	2		115	46		161	195	
	1210	24" diameter	↓	10	2.400	↓	140	55		195	235	
	1740	To delete coupling & hanger, subtract										
	1750	¾" diam. to 2" diam.					35%	27%				
	1760	2-½" diam. to 5" diam.					18%	18%				
	1770	6" diam. to 12" diam.					14%	13%				
	1800	Galvanized										
	1840	¾" diameter	1 Plum	71	.113	L.F.	1.69	2.78		4.47	6	
	1850	1" diameter		63	.127		1.91	3.14		5.05	6.75	
	1860	1-¼" diameter		58	.138		2.46	3.41		5.87	7.75	
	1870	1-½" diameter		51	.157		2.82	3.87		6.69	8.85	
	1880	2" diameter	↓	40	.200		3.54	4.94		8.48	11.20	
	1890	2-½" diameter	Q-1	57	.281		5.16	6.25		11.41	14.95	
	1900	3" diameter		50	.320		6.54	7.10		13.64	17.75	
	1910	4" diameter		45	.356		9.38	7.90		17.28	22	
	1920	5" diameter	↓	37	.432		17.47	9.60		27.07	33	
	1930	6" diameter	Q-2	42	.571		21.81	13.15		34.96	44	
	1940	8" diameter		37	.649		29.48	14.95		44.43	55	
	1950	10" diameter		31	.774		37.84	17.85		55.69	68	
	1960	12" diameter	↓	27	.889	↓	44.88	20		64.88	80	
	2540	To delete coupling & hanger, subtract										
	2550	¾" diam. to 2" diam.					36%	27%				
	2560	2-½" diam. to 5" diam.					19%	18%				
	2570	6" diam. to 12" diam.					14%	13%				
	2600	Schedule 80, black										
	2610	¾" diameter	1 Plum	65	.123	L.F.	1.62	3.04		4.66	6.30	
	2650	1" diameter		61	.131		1.95	3.24		5.19	6.95	
	2660	1-¼" diameter		55	.145		2.53	3.59		6.12	8.10	
	2670	1-½" diameter		49	.163		2.91	4.03		6.94	9.20	
	2680	2" diameter	↓	38	.211		3.76	5.20		8.96	11.85	
	2690	2-½" diameter	Q-1	54	.296	↓	5.54	6.60		12.14	15.85	

151 | Pipe and Fittings

151 800	Grooved-Joint Steel Pipe	CREW	DAILY OUTPUT	MAN-HOURS	UNIT	MAT.	LABOR	EQUIP.	TOTAL	TOTAL INCL O&P
801 2700	3" diameter	Q-1	48	.333	L.F.	7.14	7.40		14.54	18.85	801
2710	4" diameter		44	.364		10.54	8.10		18.64	24
2720	5" diameter	↓	35	.457		23.22	10.15		33.37	41
2730	6" diameter	Q-2	40	.600		26.81	13.85		40.66	50
2740	8" diameter		35	.686		40.28	15.80		56.08	68
2750	10" diameter		29	.828		52.74	19.10		71.84	86
2760	12" diameter	↓	24	1	↓	61.68	23		84.68	100
3240	To delete coupling & hanger, subtract									
3250	¾" diam. to 2" diam.					30%	25%			
3260	2-½" diam. to 5" diam.					14%	17%			
3270	6" diam. to 12" diam.					12%	12%			
3300	Galvanized									
3310	¾" diameter	1 Plum	65	.123	L.F.	1.77	3.04		4.81	6.45
3350	1" diameter		61	.131		2.21	3.24		5.45	7.25
3360	1-¼" diameter		55	.145		2.92	3.59		6.51	8.55
3370	1-½" diameter		46	.174		3.39	4.30		7.69	10.10
3380	2" diameter	↓	38	.211		4.41	5.20		9.61	12.55
3390	2-½" diameter	Q-1	54	.296		6.61	6.60		13.21	17.05
3400	3" diameter		48	.333		8.54	7.40		15.94	20
3410	4" diameter		44	.364		12.68	8.10		20.78	26
3420	5" diameter	↓	35	.457		28.92	10.15		39.07	47
3430	6" diameter	Q-2	40	.600		33.41	13.85		47.26	57
3440	8" diameter		35	.686		51.48	15.80		67.28	80
3450	10" diameter		29	.828		66.84	19.10		85.94	100
3460	12" diameter	↓	24	1	↓	77.88	23		100.88	120
3920	To delete coupling & hanger, subtract									
3930	¾" diam. to 2" diam.					30%	25%			
3940	2-½" diam. to 5" diam.					15%	17%			
3950	6" diam. to 12" diam.					11%	12%			
4000	Elbow, 90° or 45°, black steel									
4030	¾" diameter	1 Plum	50	.160	Ea.	3.91	3.95		7.86	10.15
4040	1" diameter		50	.160		3.91	3.95		7.86	10.15
4050	1-¼" diameter		40	.200		4.99	4.94		9.93	12.80
4060	1-½" diameter		33	.242		5.35	6		11.35	14.75
4070	2" diameter	↓	25	.320		5.35	7.90		13.25	17.60
4080	2-½" diameter	Q-1	40	.400		7.55	8.90		16.45	22
4090	3" diameter		33	.485		9.70	10.80		20.50	27
4100	4" diameter		25	.640		14	14.25		28.25	37
4110	5" diameter	↓	20	.800		35	17.80		52.80	65
4120	6" diameter	Q-2	25	.960		40	22		62	77
4130	8" diameter		21	1.140		84	26		110	130
4140	10" diameter		18	1.330		130	31		161	190
4150	12" diameter		15	1.600		210	37		247	285
4170	14" diameter		12	2		400	46		446	510
4180	16" diameter	↓	11	2.180		665	50		715	805
4190	18" diameter	Q-3	15	2.130		972	50		1,022	1,150
4200	20" diameter		13	2.460		1,275	58		1,333	1,500
4210	24" diameter	↓	11	2.910		1,825	69		1,894	2,100
4250	For galvanized elbows, add				↓	15%				
4690	Tee, black steel									
4700	¾" diameter	1 Plum	38	.211	Ea.	5.50	5.20		10.70	13.75
4740	1" diameter		33	.242		5.50	6		11.50	14.95
4750	1-¼" diameter		27	.296		6.25	7.30		13.55	17.75
4760	1-½" diameter		22	.364		6.70	9		15.70	21
4770	2" diameter	↓	17	.471		8.25	11.60		19.85	26
4780	2-½" diameter	Q-1	27	.593		12	13.15		25.15	33
4790	3" diameter		22	.727		16.20	16.15		32.35	42
4800	4" diameter	↓	17	.941	↓	25	21		46	59

151 | Pipe and Fittings

151 800 | Grooved-Joint Steel Pipe

		CREW	DAILY OUTPUT	MAN-HOURS	UNIT	BARE COSTS MAT.	LABOR	EQUIP.	TOTAL	TOTAL INCL O&P	
801	4810	5" diameter	Q-1	13	1.230	Ea.	57	27		84	105	801
	4820	6" diameter	Q-2	17	1.410		66	33		99	120	
	4830	8" diameter		14	1.710		165	40		205	240	
	4840	10" diameter		12	2		250	46		296	345	
	4850	12" diameter		10	2.400		360	55		415	480	
	4851	14" diameter		9	2.670		525	61		586	670	
	4852	16" diameter	↓	8	3		670	69		739	840	
	4853	18" diameter	Q-3	11	2.910		830	69		899	1,025	
	4854	20" diameter		10	3.200		1,225	75		1,300	1,450	
	4855	24" diameter	↓	8	4	↓	1,825	94		1,919	2,150	
	4900	For galvanized tees, add					15%					
	4940	Couplings, standard, black steel										
	4950	¾" diameter	1 Plum	100	.080	Ea.	5.80	1.98		7.78	9.30	
	4960	1" diameter		100	.080		5.80	1.98		7.78	9.30	
	4970	1-¼" diameter		80	.100		7.50	2.47		9.97	11.90	
	4980	1-½" diameter		67	.119		8.10	2.95		11.05	13.30	
	4990	2" diameter	↓	50	.160		9	3.95		12.95	15.75	
	5000	2-½" diameter	Q-1	80	.200		10.75	4.45		15.20	18.45	
	5010	3" diameter		67	.239		12.10	5.30		17.40	21	
	5020	3-½" diameter		57	.281		16.75	6.25		23	28	
	5030	4" diameter		50	.320		17.80	7.10		24.90	30	
	5040	5" diameter		40	.400		28	8.90		36.90	44	
	5050	6" diameter	Q-2	50	.480		33	11.05		44.05	53	
	5070	8" diameter		42	.571		46	13.15		59.15	70	
	5090	10" diameter		35	.686		66	15.80		81.80	96	
	5110	12" diameter		32	.750		74	17.30		91.30	105	
	5120	14" diameter		24	1		98	23		121	140	
	5130	16" diameter		20	1.200		130	28		158	185	
	5140	18" diameter		18	1.330		155	31		186	215	
	5150	20" diameter		16	1.500		235	35		270	310	
	5160	24" diameter	↓	13	1.850		260	43		303	350	
	5200	For galvanized couplings, add				↓	26%					
	5220	Tee, reducing black iron										
	5226	2-½" x 2" diameter	Q-1	28	.571	Ea.	26	12.70		38.70	47	
	5227	3" x 2-½" diameter		23	.696		22	15.45		37.45	47	
	5228	4" x 3" diameter		18	.889		30	19.75		49.75	62	
	5229	5" x 4" diameter	↓	15	1.070		67	24		91	110	
	5230	6" x 4" diameter	Q-2	18	1.330		73	31		104	125	
	5231	8" x 6" diameter		15	1.600		165	37		202	235	
	5232	10" x 8" diameter		13	1.850		170	43		213	250	
	5233	12" x 10" diameter	↓	11	2.180		260	50		310	360	
	5240	Coupling, reducing concentric, black iron										
	5241	2-½" x 2" diameter	Q-1	43	.372	Ea.	7.95	8.25		16.20	21	
	5242	3" x 2-½" diameter		35	.457		7.95	10.15		18.10	24	
	5243	4" x 3" diameter		29	.552		11.65	12.25		23.90	31	
	5244	5" x 4" diameter	↓	22	.727		18.65	16.15		34.80	45	
	5245	6" x 4" diameter	Q-2	26	.923		32	21		53	67	
	5246	8" x 6" diameter		23	1.040		56	24		80	97	
	5247	10" x 8" diameter		20	1.200		98	28		126	150	
	5248	12" x 10" diameter		16	1.500		170	35		205	240	
	5255	Eccentric black iron										
	5256	2-½" x 2" diameter	Q-1	42	.381	Ea.	41	8.45		49.45	58	
	5257	3" x 2-½" diameter		34	.471		48	10.45		58.45	68	
	5258	4" x 3" diameter		28	.571		63	12.70		75.70	88	
	5259	5" x 4" diameter	↓	21	.762		100	16.95		116.95	135	
	5260	6" x 4" diameter	Q-2	25	.960		105	22		127	150	
	5261	8" x 6" diameter		22	1.090		155	25		180	210	
	5262	10" x 8" diameter		19	1.260	↓	205	29		234	270	

151 | Pipe and Fittings

		151 800	Grooved-Joint Steel Pipe	CREW	DAILY OUTPUT	MAN-HOURS	UNIT	MAT.	LABOR	EQUIP.	TOTAL	TOTAL INCL O&P	
801	5263		12" x 10" diameter	Q-2	15	1.600	Ea.	335	37		372	425	801
	5750		Flange, w/groove gasket, black steel(see 151-720-0620, bolt sets)										
	5780		2" pipe size	1 Plum	23	.348	Ea.	23	8.60		31.60	38	
	5790		2-½" pipe size	Q-1	37	.432		28	9.60		37.60	45	
	5800		3" pipe size		31	.516		30	11.45		41.45	50	
	5820		4" pipe size		23	.696		40	15.45		55.45	67	
	5830		5" pipe size		19	.842		46	18.70		64.70	78	
	5840		6" pipe size	Q-2	23	1.040		50	24		74	91	
	5850		8" pipe size		17	1.410		65	33		98	120	
	5860		10" pipe size		14	1.710		101	40		141	170	
	5870		12" pipe size		12	2		125	46		171	205	
	5880		14" pipe size		10	2.400		345	55		400	460	
	5890		16" pipe size		9	2.670		405	61		466	535	
	5900		18" pipe size		6	4		495	92		587	680	
	5910		20" pipe size		5	4.800	L.F.	595	110		705	820	
	5920		24" pipe size		4.50	5.330	Ea.	765	125		890	1,025	
	8000		Butterfly valve, with standard trim										
	8010		1-½" pipe size	Q-1	35	.457	Ea.	53	10.15		63.15	73	
	8020		2" pipe size		34	.471		53	10.45		63.45	74	
	8030		3" pipe size		33	.485		87	10.80		97.80	110	
	8050		4" pipe size		25	.640		115	14.25		129.25	150	
	8070		6" pipe size	Q-2	25	.960		260	22		282	320	
	8080		8" pipe size		21	1.140		440	26		466	525	
	8090		10" pipe size		18	1.330		780	31		811	905	
	8200		With stainless steel trim										
	8240		1-½" pipe size	Q-1	35	.457	Ea.	80	10.15		90.15	105	
	8250		2" pipe size		34	.471		80	10.45		90.45	105	
	8270		3" pipe size		33	.485		125	10.80		135.80	155	
	8280		4" pipe size		25	.640		160	14.25		174.25	195	
	8300		6" pipe size	Q-2	25	.960		315	22		337	380	
	8310		8" pipe size		21	1.140		640	26		666	745	
	8320		10" pipe size		18	1.330		895	31		926	1,025	
	9000		Cut one groove, labor										
	9010		¾" pipe size	Q-1	152	.105	Ea.		2.34		2.34	3.47	
	9020		1" pipe size		140	.114			2.54		2.54	3.77	
	9030		1-¼" pipe size		124	.129			2.87		2.87	4.25	
	9040		1-½" pipe size		114	.140			3.12		3.12	4.63	
	9050		2" pipe size		104	.154			3.42		3.42	5.05	
	9060		2-½" pipe size		96	.167			3.71		3.71	5.50	
	9070		3" pipe size		88	.182			4.04		4.04	6	
	9080		3-½" pipe size		83	.193			4.29		4.29	6.35	
	9090		4" pipe size		78	.205			4.56		4.56	6.75	
	9100		5" pipe size		72	.222			4.94		4.94	7.35	
	9110		6" pipe size		70	.229			5.10		5.10	7.55	
	9120		8" pipe size		54	.296			6.60		6.60	9.75	
	9130		10" pipe size		38	.421			9.35		9.35	13.90	
	9140		12" pipe size		30	.533			11.85		11.85	17.60	
	9150		14" pipe size		20	.800			17.80		17.80	26	
	9160		16" pipe size		19	.842			18.70		18.70	28	
	9170		18" pipe size		18	.889			19.75		19.75	29	
	9180		20" pipe size		17	.941			21		21	31	
	9190		24" pipe size		15	1.070			24		24	35	
	9210		Roll one groove										
	9220		¾" pipe size	Q-1	266	.060	Ea.		1.34		1.34	1.98	
	9230		1" pipe size		228	.070			1.56		1.56	2.31	
	9240		1-¼" pipe size		200	.080			1.78		1.78	2.64	
	9250		1-½" pipe size		178	.090			2		2	2.96	
	9260		2" pipe size		116	.138			3.07		3.07	4.55	

151 | Pipe and Fittings

151 800 | Grooved-Joint Steel Pipe

			CREW	DAILY OUTPUT	MAN-HOURS	UNIT	BARE COSTS MAT.	LABOR	EQUIP.	TOTAL	TOTAL INCL O&P	
801	9270	2-½" pipe size	Q-1	110	.145	Ea.	3.23			3.23	4.80	801
	9280	3" pipe size		100	.160		3.56			3.56	5.30	
	9290	3-½" pipe size		94	.170		3.78			3.78	5.60	
	9300	4" pipe size		86	.186		4.14			4.14	6.15	
	9310	5" pipe size		84	.190		4.23			4.23	6.30	
	9320	6" pipe size		80	.200		4.45			4.45	6.60	
	9330	8" pipe size		66	.242		5.40			5.40	8	
	9340	10" pipe size		58	.276		6.15			6.15	9.10	
	9350	12" pipe size		46	.348		7.75			7.75	11.45	
	9360	14" pipe size		30	.533		11.85			11.85	17.60	
	9370	16" pipe size		28	.571		12.70			12.70	18.85	
	9380	18" pipe size		27	.593		13.15			13.15	19.55	
	9390	20" pipe size		25	.640		14.25			14.25	21	
	9400	24" pipe size		23	.696		15.45			15.45	23	

151 850 | Prefab Pipe Conduit

			CREW	DAILY OUTPUT	MAN-HOURS	UNIT	MAT.	LABOR	EQUIP.	TOTAL	TOTAL INCL O&P	
851	0010	PIPE CONDUIT, PREFABRICATED										851
	0020	Does not include trenching, fittings or crane.										
	0300	For cathodic protection, add 12 to 14%										
	0310	of total built-up price (casing plus service pipe)										
	0580	Polyurethane insulated system, 250°F. max. temp.										
	0620	Black steel service pipe, standard wt., ½" insulation										
	0660	¾" diam. pipe size	Q-17	54	.296	L.F.	9.20	6.60	.71	16.51	21	
	0670	1" diam. pipe size		50	.320		10.15	7.15	.76	18.06	23	
	0680	1-¼" diam. pipe size		47	.340		11.30	7.60	.81	19.71	25	
	0690	1-½" diam. pipe size		45	.356		12.25	7.90	.85	21	26	
	0700	2" diam. pipe size		42	.381		12.70	8.50	.91	22.11	28	
	0710	2-½" diam. pipe size		34	.471		12.90	10.50	1.12	24.52	31	
	0720	3" diam. pipe size		28	.571		14.95	12.75	1.36	29.06	37	
	0730	4" diam. pipe size		22	.727		18.60	16.20	1.74	36.54	46	
	0740	5" diam. pipe size		18	.889		23.90	19.80	2.12	45.82	58	
	0750	6" diam. pipe size	Q-18	23	1.040		28.10	24	1.66	53.76	69	
	0760	8" diam. pipe size		19	1.260		40.50	29	2.01	71.51	90	
	0770	10" diam. pipe size		16	1.500		54.10	35	2.39	91.49	115	
	0780	12" diam. pipe size		13	1.850		66.50	43	2.94	112.44	140	
	0790	14" diam. pipe size		11	2.180		74.90	50	3.47	128.37	160	
	0800	16" diam. pipe size		10	2.400		85.30	55	3.82	144.12	180	
	0810	18" diam. pipe size		8	3		98.80	69	4.78	172.58	215	
	0820	20" diam. pipe size		7	3.430		109	79	5.45	193.45	245	
	0830	24" diam. pipe size		6	4		135	92	6.35	233.35	295	
	0900	For 1" thick insulation, add					10%					
	0940	For 1-½" thick insulation, add					13%					
	0980	For 2" thick insulation, add					20%					
	1500	Gland seal for system, ¾" diam. pipe size	Q-17	32	.500	Ea.	151	11.15	1.19	163.34	185	
	1510	1" diam. pipe size		32	.500		151	11.15	1.19	163.34	185	
	1540	1-¼" diam. pipe size		30	.533		161	11.90	1.27	174.17	195	
	1550	1-½" diam. pipe size		30	.533		161	11.90	1.27	174.17	195	
	1560	2" diam. pipe size		28	.571		187	12.75	1.36	201.11	225	
	1570	2-½" diam. pipe size		26	.615		203	13.70	1.47	218.17	245	
	1580	3" diam. pipe size		24	.667		218	14.85	1.59	234.44	265	
	1590	4" diam. pipe size		22	.727		260	16.20	1.74	277.94	310	
	1600	5" diam. pipe size		19	.842		317	18.75	2.01	337.76	380	
	1610	6" diam. pipe size	Q-18	26	.923		340	21	1.47	362.47	405	
	1620	8" diam. pipe size		25	.960		395	22	1.53	418.53	470	
	1630	10" diam. pipe size		23	1.040		480	24	1.66	505.66	565	
	1640	12" diam. pipe size		21	1.140		530	26	1.82	557.82	625	
	1650	14" diam. pipe size		19	1.260		595	29	2.01	626.01	700	
	1660	16" diam. pipe size		18	1.330		695	31	2.12	728.12	815	

151 | Pipe and Fittings

151 850 | Prefab Pipe Conduit

			CREW	DAILY OUTPUT	MAN-HOURS	UNIT	BARE COSTS MAT.	LABOR	EQUIP.	TOTAL	TOTAL INCL O&P	
851	1670	18" diam. pipe size	Q-18	16	1.500	Ea.	745	35	2.39	782.39	875	851
	1680	20" diam. pipe size		14	1.710		850	40	2.73	892.73	995	
	1690	24" diam. pipe size	↓	12	2	↓	940	46	3.18	989.18	1,100	
	2000	Elbow, 45° for system										
	2020	¾" diam. pipe size	Q-17	14	1.140	Ea.	93.60	25	2.73	121.33	145	
	2040	1" diam. pipe size		13	1.230		96.70	27	2.94	126.64	150	
	2050	1-¼" diam. pipe size		11	1.450		109	32	3.47	144.47	170	
	2060	1-½" diam. pipe size		9	1.780		125	40	4.24	169.24	200	
	2070	2" diam. pipe size		6	2.670		120	59	6.35	185.35	225	
	2080	2-½" diam. pipe size		4	4		130	89	9.55	228.55	285	
	2090	3" diam. pipe size		3.50	4.570		151	100	10.90	261.90	330	
	2100	4" diam. pipe size		3	5.330		172	120	12.75	304.75	380	
	2110	5" diam. pipe size	↓	2.80	5.710		225	125	13.65	363.65	450	
	2120	6" diam. pipe size	Q-18	4	6		255	140	9.55	404.55	495	
	2130	8" diam. pipe size		3	8		370	185	12.75	567.75	695	
	2140	10" diam. pipe size		2.40	10		470	230	15.90	715.90	880	
	2150	12" diam. pipe size		2	12		620	275	19.10	914.10	1,125	
	2160	14" diam. pipe size		1.80	13.330		770	310	21	1,101	1,325	
	2170	16" diam. pipe size		1.60	15		915	345	24	1,284	1,550	
	2180	18" diam. pipe size		1.30	18.460		1,140	425	29	1,594	1,925	
	2190	20" diam. pipe size		1	24		1,460	555	38	2,053	2,475	
	2200	24" diam. pipe size	↓	.70	34.290		1,980	790	55	2,825	3,425	
	2260	For elbow, 90°, add					25%					
	2300	For tee, straight, add					85%	30%				
	2340	For tee, reducing, add					170%	30%				
	2380	For weldolet, straight, add				↓	50%					
	2800	Calcium silicate insulated system, high temp. (1200°F)										
	2840	Steel casing with protective exterior coating										
	2850	6-⅝" diameter	Q-18	52	.462	L.F.	17.20	10.65	.73	28.58	36	
	2860	8-⅝" diameter		50	.480		18.80	11.10	.76	30.66	38	
	2870	10-¾" diameter		47	.511		21.80	11.80	.81	34.41	42	
	2880	12-¾" diameter		44	.545		23.90	12.60	.87	37.37	46	
	2890	14" diameter		41	.585		27	13.50	.93	41.43	51	
	2900	16" diameter		39	.615		29.10	14.20	.98	44.28	54	
	2910	18" diameter		36	.667		32.20	15.40	1.06	48.66	59	
	2920	20" diameter		34	.706		35.40	16.30	1.12	52.82	64	
	2930	22" diameter		32	.750		49.90	17.35	1.19	68.44	82	
	2940	24" diameter		29	.828		57.20	19.10	1.32	77.62	93	
	2950	26" diameter		26	.923		64.50	21	1.47	86.97	105	
	2960	28" diameter		23	1.040		81.10	24	1.66	106.76	125	
	2970	30" diameter		21	1.140		86.30	26	1.82	114.12	135	
	2980	32" diameter		19	1.260		96.70	29	2.01	127.71	150	
	2990	34" diameter		18	1.330		97.80	31	2.12	130.92	155	
	3000	36" diameter	↓	16	1.500		104	35	2.39	141.39	170	
	3040	For multi-pipe casings, add					10%					
	3060	For oversize casings, add				↓	2%					
	3400	Steel casing gland seal, single pipe										
	3420	6-⅝" diameter	Q-18	25	.960	Ea.	239	22	1.53	262.53	300	
	3440	8-⅝" diameter		23	1.040		280	24	1.66	305.66	345	
	3450	10-¾" diameter		21	1.140		315	26	1.82	342.82	390	
	3460	12-¾" diameter		19	1.260		375	29	2.01	406.01	460	
	3470	14" diameter		17	1.410		410	33	2.25	445.25	500	
	3480	16" diameter		16	1.500		480	35	2.39	517.39	580	
	3490	18" diameter		15	1.600		535	37	2.55	574.55	645	
	3500	20" diameter		13	1.850		590	43	2.94	635.94	715	
	3510	22" diameter		12	2		665	46	3.18	714.18	805	
	3520	24" diameter		11	2.180		745	50	3.47	798.47	900	
	3530	26" diameter	↓	10	2.400	↓	850	55	3.82	908.82	1,025	

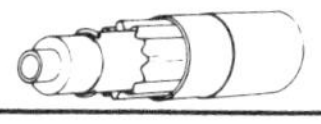

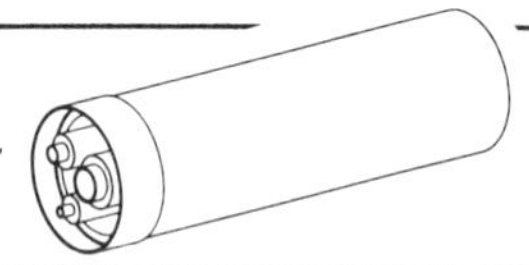

151 | Pipe and Fittings

151 850 | Prefab Pipe Conduit

		CREW	DAILY OUTPUT	MAN-HOURS	UNIT	BARE COSTS MAT.	LABOR	EQUIP.	TOTAL	TOTAL INCL O&P	
851	3540	28" diameter	Q-18	9.50	2.530	Ea.	960	58	4.02	1,022	1,150	851
	3550	30" diameter		9	2.670		980	62	4.24	1,046	1,175	
	3560	32" diameter		8.50	2.820		1,090	65	4.49	1,159	1,300	
	3570	34" diameter		8	3		1,200	69	4.78	1,273	1,425	
	3580	36" diameter	↓	7	3.430		1,270	79	5.45	1,354	1,525	
	3620	For multi-pipe casings, add					5%					
	4000	Steel casing anchors, single pipe										
	4020	6-⅝" diameter	Q-18	8	3	Ea.	218	69	4.78	291.78	350	
	4040	8-⅝" diameter		7.50	3.200		225	74	5.10	304.10	365	
	4050	10-¾" diameter		7	3.430		295	79	5.45	379.45	450	
	4060	12-¾" diameter		6.50	3.690		315	85	5.90	405.90	480	
	4070	14" diameter		6	4		370	92	6.35	468.35	550	
	4080	16" diameter		5.50	4.360		430	100	6.95	536.95	630	
	4090	18" diameter		5	4.800		485	110	7.65	602.65	705	
	4100	20" diameter		4.50	5.330		535	125	8.50	668.50	780	
	4110	22" diameter		4	6		595	140	9.55	744.55	870	
	4120	24" diameter		3.50	6.860		650	160	10.90	820.90	960	
	4130	26" diameter		3	8		735	185	12.75	932.75	1,100	
	4140	28" diameter		2.50	9.600		805	220	15.30	1,040	1,225	
	4150	30" diameter		2	12		855	275	19.10	1,149	1,375	
	4160	32" diameter		1.50	16		1,020	370	25	1,415	1,700	
	4170	34" diameter		1	24		1,140	555	38	1,733	2,125	
	4180	36" diameter	↓	1	24		1,250	555	38	1,843	2,250	
	4220	For multi-pipe, add					5%	20%				
	4800	Steel casing elbow										
	4820	6-⅝" diameter	Q-18	15	1.600	Ea.	295	37	2.55	334.55	380	
	4830	8-⅝" diameter		15	1.600		315	37	2.55	354.55	405	
	4850	10-¾" diameter		14	1.710		380	40	2.73	422.73	480	
	4860	12-¾" diameter		13	1.850		450	43	2.94	495.94	560	
	4870	14" diameter		12	2		480	46	3.18	529.18	600	
	4880	16" diameter		11	2.180		525	50	3.47	578.47	655	
	4890	18" diameter		10	2.400		600	55	3.82	658.82	745	
	4900	20" diameter		9	2.670		640	62	4.24	706.24	800	
	4910	22" diameter		8	3		690	69	4.78	763.78	865	
	4920	24" diameter		7	3.430		760	79	5.45	844.45	960	
	4930	26" diameter		6	4		830	92	6.35	928.35	1,050	
	4940	28" diameter		5	4.800		895	110	7.65	1,012	1,150	
	4950	30" diameter		4	6		900	140	9.55	1,049	1,200	
	4960	32" diameter		3	8		1,030	185	12.75	1,227	1,425	
	4970	34" diameter		2	12		1,110	275	19.10	1,404	1,650	
	4980	36" diameter	↓	2	12	↓	1,200	275	19.10	1,494	1,750	
	5500	Black steel service pipe, std. wt., 1" thick insulation										
	5510	¾" diameter pipe size	Q-17	54	.296	L.F.	7.50	6.60	.71	14.81	18.85	
	5540	1" diameter pipe size		50	.320		7.80	7.15	.76	15.71	20	
	5550	1-¼" diameter pipe size		47	.340		8.75	7.60	.81	17.16	22	
	5560	1-½" diameter pipe size		45	.356		9.55	7.90	.85	18.30	23	
	5570	2" diameter pipe size		42	.381		10.60	8.50	.91	20.01	25	
	5580	2-½" diameter pipe size		34	.471		11.15	10.50	1.12	22.77	29	
	5590	3" diameter pipe size		28	.571		12.70	12.75	1.36	26.81	34	
	5600	4" diameter pipe size		22	.727		16.25	16.20	1.74	34.19	44	
	5610	5" diameter pipe size	↓	18	.889		21.80	19.80	2.12	43.72	56	
	5620	6" diameter pipe size	Q-18	23	1.040	↓	23.90	24	1.66	49.56	64	
	6000	Black steel service pipe, std. wt., 1-½" thick insul.										
	6010	¾" diameter pipe size	Q-17	54	.296	L.F.	7.60	6.60	.71	14.91	18.95	
	6040	1" diameter pipe size		50	.320		8.50	7.15	.76	16.41	21	
	6050	1-¼" diameter pipe size		47	.340		9.55	7.60	.81	17.96	23	
	6060	1-½" diameter pipe size		45	.356		10.40	7.90	.85	19.15	24	
	6070	2" diameter pipe size	↓	42	.381	↓	11.30	8.50	.91	20.71	26	

151 | Pipe and Fittings

151 850 | Prefab Pipe Conduit

			CREW	DAILY OUTPUT	MAN-HOURS	UNIT	BARE COSTS MAT.	LABOR	EQUIP.	TOTAL	TOTAL INCL O&P	
851	6080	2-½" diameter pipe size	Q-17	34	.471	L.F.	12.05	10.50	1.12	23.67	30	851
	6090	3" diameter pipe size		28	.571		13.50	12.75	1.36	27.61	35	
	6100	4" diameter pipe size		22	.727		17.25	16.20	1.74	35.19	45	
	6110	5" diameter pipe size		18	.889		21.80	19.80	2.12	43.72	56	
	6120	6" diameter pipe size	Q-18	23	1.040		25	24	1.66	50.66	65	
	6130	8" diameter pipe size		19	1.260		35.40	29	2.01	66.41	84	
	6140	10" diameter pipe size		16	1.500		46.80	35	2.39	84.19	105	
	6150	12" diameter pipe size		13	1.850		56.20	43	2.94	102.14	130	
	6190	For 2" thick insulation, add					15%					
	6220	For 2-½" thick insulation, add					25%					
	6260	For 3" thick insulation, add					30%					
	6800	Black steel service pipe, ex. hvy. wt., 1" thick insul.										
	6820	¾" diameter pipe size	Q-17	50	.320	L.F.	7.90	7.15	.76	15.81	20	
	6840	1" diameter pipe size		47	.340		8.40	7.60	.81	16.81	21	
	6850	1-¼" diameter pipe size		44	.364		9.70	8.10	.87	18.67	24	
	6860	1-½" diameter pipe size		42	.381		10.30	8.50	.91	19.71	25	
	6870	2" diameter pipe size		40	.400		10.90	8.90	.96	20.76	26	
	6880	2-½" diameter pipe size		31	.516		13.50	11.50	1.23	26.23	33	
	6890	3" diameter pipe size		27	.593		15.20	13.20	1.41	29.81	38	
	6900	4" diameter pipe size		21	.762		20	16.95	1.82	38.77	49	
	6910	5" diameter pipe size		17	.941		28.10	21	2.25	51.35	65	
	6920	6" diameter pipe size	Q-18	22	1.090		31.20	25	1.74	57.94	74	
	7400	Black steel service pipe, ex. hvy. wt., 1-½" thick insul.										
	7420	¾" diameter pipe size	Q-17	50	.320	L.F.	7.90	7.15	.76	15.81	20	
	7440	1" diameter pipe size		47	.340		9	7.60	.81	17.41	22	
	7450	1-¼" diameter pipe size		44	.364		10.45	8.10	.87	19.42	24	
	7460	1-½" diameter pipe size		42	.381		11.45	8.50	.91	20.86	26	
	7470	2" diameter pipe size		40	.400		11.55	8.90	.96	21.41	27	
	7480	2-½" diameter pipe size		31	.516		13.70	11.50	1.23	26.43	34	
	7490	3" diameter pipe size		27	.593		16.10	13.20	1.41	30.71	39	
	7500	4" diameter pipe size		21	.762		20.80	16.95	1.82	39.57	50	
	7510	5" diameter pipe size		17	.941		29.10	21	2.25	52.35	66	
	7520	6" diameter pipe size	Q-18	22	1.090		32.20	25	1.74	58.94	75	
	7530	8" diameter pipe size		18	1.330		47.80	31	2.12	80.92	100	
	7540	10" diameter pipe size		15	1.600		57.20	37	2.55	96.75	120	
	7550	12" diameter pipe size		13	1.850		69.70	43	2.94	115.64	145	
	7590	For 2" thick insulation, add					13%					
	7640	For 2-½" thick insulation, add					18%					
	7680	For 3" thick insulation, add					24%					

151 900 | Pipe Supports/Hangers

			CREW	DAILY OUTPUT	MAN-HOURS	UNIT	MAT.	LABOR	EQUIP.	TOTAL	INCL O&P	
901	0010	**PIPE HANGERS AND SUPPORTS**										901
	0050	Brackets										
	0060	Beam side or wall, malleable iron 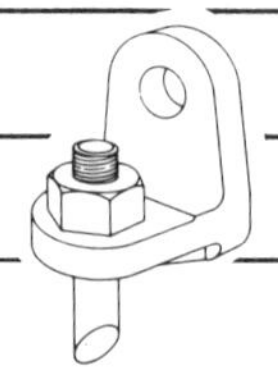										
	0070	⅜" threaded rod size	1 Plum	48	.167	Ea.	.95	4.12		5.07	7.15	
	0080	½" threaded rod size		48	.167		1.35	4.12		5.47	7.60	
	0090	⅝" threaded rod size		48	.167		2.18	4.12		6.30	8.50	
	0100	¾" threaded rod size		48	.167		3.35	4.12		7.47	9.80	
	0110	⅞" threaded rod size		48	.167		4.31	4.12		8.43	10.85	
	0120	For concrete installation, add						30%				
	0150	Wall, welded steel 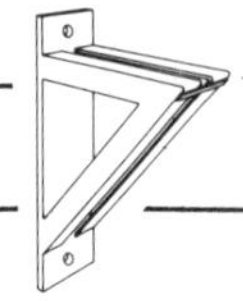										
	0160	0 size, 12" wide, 18" deep	1 Plum	34	.235	Ea.	55	5.80		60.80	69	
	0170	1 size, 18" wide 24" deep		34	.235		66	5.80		71.80	81	
	0180	2 size, 24" wide, 30" deep		34	.235		86	5.80		91.80	105	
	0300	Clamps										
	0310	C-clamp, for mounting on steel beam flange, w/locknut										
	0320	⅜" threaded rod size	1 Plum	160	.050	Ea.	.92	1.24		2.16	2.84	

151 | Pipe and Fittings

151 900 | Pipe Supports/Hangers

		CREW	DAILY OUTPUT	MAN-HOURS	UNIT	BARE COSTS MAT.	BARE COSTS LABOR	BARE COSTS EQUIP.	BARE COSTS TOTAL	TOTAL INCL O&P	
901	0330	½" threaded rod size 	1 Plum	160	.050	Ea.	1.08	1.24		2.32	3.02	901
	0340	⅝" threaded rod size		160	.050		1.63	1.24		2.87	3.63	
	0350	¾" threaded rod size		160	.050		2.36	1.24		3.60	4.43	
	0400	High temperature to 1050°F, alloy steel										
	0410	4" pipe size	Q-1	106	.151	Ea.	38	3.36		41.36	47	
	0420	6" pipe size		106	.151		59	3.36		62.36	70	
	0430	8" pipe size 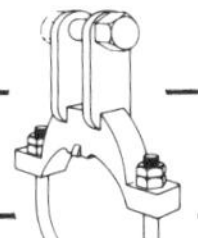		97	.165		71	3.67		74.67	84	
	0440	10" pipe size		84	.190		96	4.23		100.23	110	
	0450	12" pipe size		72	.222		155	4.94		159.94	180	
	0460	14" pipe size		64	.250		185	5.55		190.55	210	
	0470	16" pipe size		56	.286		245	6.35		251.35	280	
	0500	I-beam, for mounting on bottom flange, strap iron										
	0510	2" flange size	1 Plum	96	.083	Ea.	1.86	2.06		3.92	5.10	
	0520	3" flange size		95	.084		2.01	2.08		4.09	5.30	
	0530	4" flange size 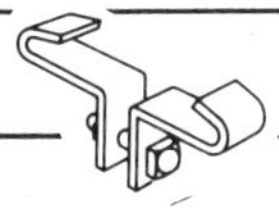		93	.086		2.08	2.12		4.20	5.45	
	0540	5" flange size		92	.087		2.12	2.15		4.27	5.50	
	0550	6" flange size		90	.089		2.19	2.20		4.39	5.65	
	0560	7" flange size		88	.091		2.25	2.25		4.50	5.80	
	0570	8" flange size		86	.093		2.33	2.30		4.63	5.95	
	0600	One hole, vertical mounting, malleable iron										
	0610	½" pipe size 	1 Plum	160	.050	Ea.	.19	1.24		1.43	2.04	
	0620	¾" pipe size		145	.055		.23	1.36		1.59	2.28	
	0630	1" pipe size		136	.059		.35	1.45		1.80	2.54	
	0640	1-¼" pipe size		128	.063		.40	1.54		1.94	2.73	
	0650	1-½" pipe size		120	.067		.47	1.65		2.12	2.96	
	0660	2" pipe size		112	.071		.69	1.76		2.45	3.38	
	0670	2-½" pipe size		104	.077		1.34	1.90		3.24	4.29	
	0680	3" pipe size		96	.083		2.04	2.06		4.10	5.30	
	0690	3-½" pipe size		90	.089		2.78	2.20		4.98	6.30	
	0700	4" pipe size		84	.095		3.75	2.35		6.10	7.60	
	0750	Riser or extension pipe, carbon steel										
	0760	¾" pipe size	1 Plum	48	.167	Ea.	1.43	4.12		5.55	7.70	
	0770	1" pipe size		47	.170		1.45	4.20		5.65	7.85	
	0780	1-¼" pipe size		46	.174		1.82	4.30		6.12	8.40	
	0790	1-½" pipe size		45	.178		1.96	4.39		6.35	8.65	
	0800	2" pipe size		43	.186		2.01	4.60		6.61	9.05	
	0810	2-½" pipe size 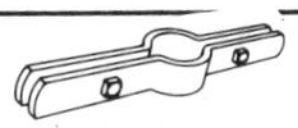		41	.195		2.11	4.82		6.93	9.45	
	0820	3" pipe size		40	.200		2.25	4.94		7.19	9.80	
	0830	3-½" pipe size		39	.205		2.78	5.05		7.83	10.60	
	0840	4" pipe size		38	.211		2.84	5.20		8.04	10.85	
	0850	5" pipe size		37	.216		4.10	5.35		9.45	12.45	
	0860	6" pipe size		36	.222		4.75	5.50		10.25	13.35	
	0870	8" pipe size		34	.235		7.65	5.80		13.45	17.05	
	0880	10" pipe size		32	.250		9.45	6.20		15.65	19.55	
	0890	12" pipe size		28	.286		12.85	7.05		19.90	25	
	0900	For plastic coating ¾" to 4", add					190%					
	0910	For copper plating ¾" to 4", add					58%					
	0950	Two piece, complete, carbon steel, medium weight										
	0960	½" pipe size	Q-1	137	.117	Ea.	.83	2.60		3.43	4.76	
	0970	¾" pipe size		134	.119		.83	2.65		3.48	4.85	
	0980	1" pipe size		132	.121		.85	2.69		3.54	4.94	
	0990	1-¼" pipe size		130	.123		1.14	2.74		3.88	5.30	
	1000	1-½" pipe size		126	.127		1.14	2.82		3.96	5.45	
	1010	2" pipe size		124	.129		1.20	2.87		4.07	5.55	
	1020	2-½" pipe size		120	.133		1.27	2.96		4.23	5.80	
	1030	3" pipe size		117	.137		1.44	3.04		4.48	6.10	
	1040	3-½" pipe size		114	.140		1.44	3.12		4.56	6.20	
	1050	4" pipe size		110	.145		1.98	3.23		5.21	7	

151 | Pipe and Fittings

151 900 | Pipe Supports/Hangers

			CREW	DAILY OUTPUT	MAN-HOURS	UNIT	BARE COSTS MAT.	BARE COSTS LABOR	BARE COSTS EQUIP.	BARE COSTS TOTAL	TOTAL INCL O&P	
901	1060	5" pipe size	Q-1	106	.151	Ea.	3.24	3.36		6.60	8.55	901
	1070	6" pipe size		104	.154		4.95	3.42		8.37	10.50	
	1080	8" pipe size		100	.160		5.90	3.56		9.46	11.75	
	1090	10" pipe size		96	.167		10.65	3.71		14.36	17.20	
	1100	12" pipe size		89	.180		16.65	4		20.65	24	
	1110	14" pipe size		82	.195		27	4.34		31.34	36	
	1120	16" pipe size		68	.235		29	5.25		34.25	40	
	1130	For galvanized, add					45%					
	1150	Insert, concrete										
	1160	Wedge type, carbon steel body, malleable iron nut										
	1170	¼" threaded rod size	1 Plum	96	.083	Ea.	.88	2.06		2.94	4.02	
	1180	⅜" threaded rod size		96	.083		.89	2.06		2.95	4.03	
	1190	½" threaded rod size		96	.083		.93	2.06		2.99	4.08	
	1200	⅝" threaded rod size		96	.083		.99	2.06		3.05	4.14	
	1210	¾" threaded rod size		96	.083		1.04	2.06		3.10	4.20	
	1220	⅞" threaded rod size		96	.083		1.20	2.06		3.26	4.37	
	1230	For galvanized, add					.88			.88	.97	
	1250	Pipe guide sized for insulation										
	1260	No. 1, 1" pipe size, 1" thick insulation	1 Stpi	26	.308	Ea.	59	7.60		66.60	76	
	1270	No. 2, 1-¼"-2" pipe size, 1" thick insulation		23	.348		68	8.60		76.60	88	
	1280	No. 3, 1-¼"-2" pipe size, 1-½" thick insulation		21	.381		77	9.45		86.45	99	
	1290	No. 4, 2-½"-3-½" pipe size, 1-½" thick insulation		18	.444		110	11		121	135	
	1300	No. 5, 4"-5" pipe size, 1-½" thick insulation		16	.500		135	12.40		147.40	165	
	1310	No. 6, 5"-6" pipe size, 2" thick insulation	Q-5	21	.762		185	16.95		201.95	230	
	1320	No. 7, 8" pipe size, 2" thick insulation		16	1		240	22		262	295	
	1330	No. 8, 10" pipe size, 2" thick insulation		12	1.330		295	30		325	370	
	1340	No. 9, 12" pipe size, 2" thick insulation	Q-6	17	1.410		350	33		383	435	
	1350	No. 10, 12"-14" pipe size, 2-½" thick insulation		16	1.500		440	35		475	535	
	1360	No. 11, 16" pipe size, 2-½" thick insulation		10.50	2.290		505	53		558	635	
	1370	No. 12, 16"-18" pipe size, 3" thick insulation		9	2.670		550	62		612	695	
	1380	No. 13, 20" pipe size, 3" thick insulation		7.50	3.200		580	74		654	750	
	1390	No. 14, 24" pipe size, 3" thick insulation		7	3.430		745	79		824	935	
	1400	Bands										
	1410	Adjustable band, carbon steel, for non-insulated pipe										
	1420	½" pipe size	Q-1	142	.113	Ea.	.32	2.50		2.82	4.07	
	1430	¾" pipe size		140	.114		.32	2.54		2.86	4.12	
	1440	1" pipe size		137	.117		.36	2.60		2.96	4.25	
	1450	1-¼" pipe size		134	.119		.36	2.65		3.01	4.34	
	1460	1-½" pipe size		131	.122		.43	2.72		3.15	4.50	
	1470	2" pipe size		129	.124		.59	2.76		3.35	4.74	
	1480	2-½" pipe size		125	.128		.62	2.85		3.47	4.90	
	1490	3" pipe size		122	.131		.69	2.92		3.61	5.10	
	1500	3-½" pipe size		119	.134		1.07	2.99		4.06	5.60	
	1510	4" pipe size		114	.140		1.07	3.12		4.19	5.80	
	1520	5" pipe size		110	.145		1.15	3.23		4.38	6.05	
	1530	6" pipe size		108	.148		1.35	3.29		4.64	6.40	
	1540	8" pipe size		104	.154		2.18	3.42		5.60	7.45	
	1550	For copper plated, add					50%					
	1560	For galvanized, add					30%					
	1570	For plastic coating, add					30%					
	1600	Adjusting nut malleable iron, steel band										
	1610	½" pipe size, galvanized band	Q-1	137	.117	Ea.	.60	2.60		3.20	4.51	
	1620	¾" pipe size, galvanized band		135	.119		.60	2.63		3.23	4.57	
	1630	1" pipe size, gavanized band		132	.121		.62	2.69		3.31	4.68	
	1640	1-¼" pipe size, galvanized band		129	.124		.62	2.76		3.38	4.77	
	1650	1-½" pipe size, galvanized band		126	.127		.72	2.82		3.54	4.98	
	1660	2" pipe size, galvanized band		124	.129		.77	2.87		3.64	5.10	
	1670	2-½" pipe size, galvanized band		120	.133		1.44	2.96		4.40	6	

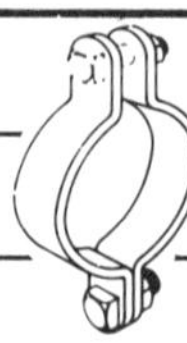

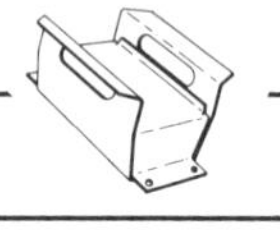

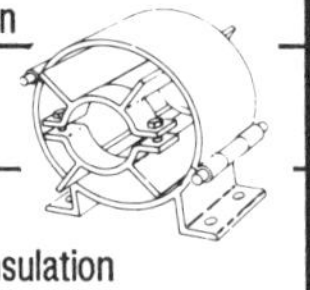

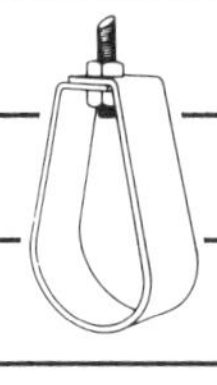

151 | Pipe and Fittings

151 900 | Pipe Supports/Hangers

			CREW	DAILY OUTPUT	MAN-HOURS	UNIT	BARE COSTS MAT.	LABOR	EQUIP.	TOTAL	TOTAL INCL O&P	
901	1680	3" pipe size, galvanized band	Q-1	117	.137	Ea.	1.57	3.04		4.61	6.25	901
	1690	3-½" pipe size, galvanized band		114	.140		1.68	3.12		4.80	6.50	
	1700	4" pipe size, cadmium plated band		110	.145		2.54	3.23		5.77	7.60	
	1710	5" pipe size, cadmium plated band		106	.151		2.95	3.36		6.31	8.25	
	1720	6" pipe size, cadmium plated band		104	.154		4.65	3.42		8.07	10.20	
	1730	8" pipe size, cadmium plated band	↓	100	.160		6.85	3.56		10.41	12.80	
	1740	For plastic coated band, add					35%					
	1750	For completely copper coated, add				↓	45%					
	1800	Clevis, adjustable, carbon steel, for non-insulated pipe										
	1810	½" pipe size	Q-1	137	.117	Ea.	.45	2.60		3.05	4.35	
	1820	¾" pipe size		135	.119		.45	2.63		3.08	4.41	
	1830	1" pipe size		132	.121		.48	2.69		3.17	4.53	
	1840	1-¼" pipe size		129	.124		.55	2.76		3.31	4.70	
	1850	1-½" pipe size		126	.127		.60	2.82		3.42	4.85	
	1860	2" pipe size		124	.129		.72	2.87		3.59	5.05	
	1870	2-½" pipe size		120	.133		1.11	2.96		4.07	5.60	
	1880	3" pipe size		117	.137		1.37	3.04		4.41	6	
	1890	3-½" pipe size		114	.140		1.45	3.12		4.57	6.25	
	1900	4" pipe size		110	.145		1.69	3.23		4.92	6.65	
	1910	5" pipe size		106	.151		2.29	3.36		5.65	7.50	
	1920	6" pipe size		104	.154		2.69	3.42		6.11	8.05	
	1930	8" pipe size		100	.160		4.41	3.56		7.97	10.15	
	1940	10" pipe size		96	.167		8	3.71		11.71	14.30	
	1950	12" pipe size		89	.180		9.35	4		13.35	16.20	
	1960	14" pipe size		82	.195		13.85	4.34		18.19	22	
	1970	16" pipe size	↓	68	.235		19.95	5.25		25.20	30	
	1980	For galvanized, add					66%					
	1990	For copper plated ½" to 4", add					77%					
	2000	For light weight ½" to 4", deduct					13%					
	2010	Insulated pipe type, ¾" to 12" pipe, add					180%					
	2020	Insulated pipe type, chrome-moly U-strap				↓	530%					
	2250	Split ring, malleable iron, for non-insulated pipe										
	2260	½" pipe size	Q-1	137	.117	Ea.	.73	2.60		3.33	4.65	
	2270	¾" pipe size		135	.119		.82	2.63		3.45	4.81	
	2280	1" pipe size		132	.121		.82	2.69		3.51	4.90	
	2290	1-¼" pipe size		129	.124		.92	2.76		3.68	5.10	
	2300	1-½" pipe size		126	.127		1.15	2.82		3.97	5.45	
	2310	2" pipe size		124	.129		1.23	2.87		4.10	5.60	
	2320	2-½" pipe size		120	.133		1.26	2.96		4.22	5.80	
	2330	3" pipe size		117	.137		1.47	3.04		4.51	6.15	
	2340	3-½" pipe size		114	.140		1.54	3.12		4.66	6.30	
	2350	4" pipe size		110	.145		1.54	3.23		4.77	6.50	
	2360	5" pipe size		106	.151		3.32	3.36		6.68	8.65	
	2370	6" pipe size		104	.154		5	3.42		8.42	10.55	
	2380	8" pipe size	↓	100	.160	↓	6.10	3.56		9.66	12	
	2390	For copper plated, add					8%					
	2650	Rods, carbon steel										
	2660	Continuous thread										
	2670	¼" thread size	1 Plum	144	.056	L.F.	.14	1.37		1.51	2.19	
	2680	⅜" thread size		144	.056		.20	1.37		1.57	2.26	
	2690	½" thread size		144	.056		.32	1.37		1.69	2.39	
	2700	⅝" thread size		144	.056		.60	1.37		1.97	2.70	
	2710	¾" thread size		144	.056		.90	1.37		2.27	3.03	
	2720	⅞" thread size		144	.056		1.45	1.37		2.82	3.63	
	2730	For galvanized add				↓	33%					
	2750	Both ends machine threaded 18" length										
	2760	⅜" thread size	1 Plum	240	.033	Ea.	1.16	.82		1.98	2.50	
	2770	½" thread size	"	240	.033	"	1.87	.82		2.69	3.28	

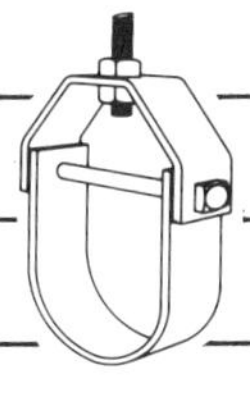

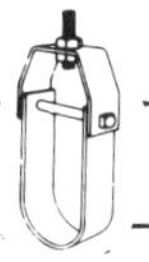

151 | Pipe and Fittings

151 900 | Pipe Supports/Hangers

			CREW	DAILY OUTPUT	MAN-HOURS	UNIT	BARE COSTS MAT.	LABOR	EQUIP.	TOTAL	TOTAL INCL O&P	
901	2780	5/8" thread size	1 Plum	240	.033	Ea.	2.69	.82		3.51	4.18	901
	2790	3/4" thread size		240	.033		3.95	.82		4.77	5.55	
	2800	7/8" thread size		240	.033		5.80	.82		6.62	7.60	
	2810	1" thread size		240	.033		8.05	.82		8.87	10.10	
	2900	Rolls										
	2910	Adjustable yoke, carbon steel with CI roll										
	2920	2-1/2" pipe size	Q-1	137	.117	Ea.	3.51	2.60		6.11	7.70	
	2930	3" pipe size		131	.122		3.65	2.72		6.37	8.05	
	2940	3-1/2" pipe size		124	.129		5.10	2.87		7.97	9.85	
	2950	4" pipe size		117	.137		5.10	3.04		8.14	10.10	
	2960	5" pipe size		110	.145		6	3.23		9.23	11.40	
	2970	6" pipe size		104	.154		7.50	3.42		10.92	13.30	
	2980	8" pipe size		96	.167		11.35	3.71		15.06	18	
	2990	10" pipe size		80	.200		14	4.45		18.45	22	
	3010	14" pipe size		56	.286		45	6.35		51.35	59	
	3020	16" pipe size		48	.333		58	7.40		65.40	75	
	3050	Chair, carbon steel with CI roll										
	3060	2" pipe size	1 Plum	68	.118	Ea.	4.94	2.91		7.85	9.75	
	3070	2-1/2" pipe size		65	.123		5.20	3.04		8.24	10.25	
	3080	3" pipe size		62	.129		5.25	3.19		8.44	10.50	
	3090	3-1/2" pipe size		60	.133		7.55	3.29		10.84	13.20	
	3100	4" pipe size		58	.138		7.55	3.41		10.96	13.35	
	3110	5" pipe size		56	.143		8.20	3.53		11.73	14.25	
	3120	6" pipe size		53	.151		11.40	3.73		15.13	18.05	
	3130	8" pipe size		50	.160		15.20	3.95		19.15	23	
	3140	10" pipe size		48	.167		19.40	4.12		23.52	27	
	3150	12" pipe size		46	.174		27	4.30		31.30	36	
	3170	Trapeze w/roller, (see line 2650 for rods), 1" pipe size	Q-1	137	.117		3.58	2.60		6.18	7.80	
	3180	1-1/4" pipe size		131	.122		3.58	2.72		6.30	7.95	
	3190	1-1/2" pipe size		129	.124		3.70	2.76		6.46	8.15	
	3200	2" pipe size		124	.129		3.79	2.87		6.66	8.40	
	3210	2-1/2" pipe size		118	.136		4.15	3.01		7.16	9.05	
	3220	3" pipe size		115	.139		4.35	3.09		7.44	9.40	
	3230	3-1/2" pipe size		113	.142		5.05	3.15		8.20	10.25	
	3240	4" pipe size		112	.143		6.10	3.18		9.28	11.40	
	3250	5" pipe size		110	.145		6.75	3.23		9.98	12.25	
	3260	6" pipe size		101	.158		8.90	3.52		12.42	15	
	3270	8" pipe size		90	.178		13.70	3.95		17.65	21	
	3280	10" pipe size		80	.200		15.35	4.45		19.80	23	
	3290	12" pipe size		68	.235		23	5.25		28.25	33	
	3300	Saddles (add vertical pipe riser, usually 3" diameter)										
	3310	Pipe support, complete, adjustable, CI saddle										
	3320	2-1/2" pipe size	1 Plum	96	.083	Ea.	41	2.06		43.06	48	
	3330	3" pipe size		88	.091		42	2.25		44.25	50	
	3340	3-1/2" pipe size		79	.101		42	2.50		44.50	50	
	3350	4" pipe size		68	.118		54	2.91		56.91	64	
	3360	5" pipe size		64	.125		56	3.09		59.09	66	
	3370	6" pipe size		59	.136		58	3.35		61.35	69	
	3380	8" pipe size		53	.151		60	3.73		63.73	72	
	3390	10" pipe size		50	.160		67	3.95		70.95	80	
	3400	12" pipe size		48	.167		70	4.12		74.12	83	
	3450	For standard pipe support, one piece, CI deduct					34%					
	3460	For stanchion support, CI with steel yoke, deduct					60%					
	3500	Multiple pipe support 2' long strut	1 Plum	30	.267		7.40	6.60		14	17.90	
	3510	3' long strut		20	.400		10.65	9.90		20.55	26	
	3520	4' long strut		17	.471		15.40	11.60		27	34	
	3550	Insulation shield 1" thick, 1/2" pipe size	1 Asbe	100	.080		2.33	1.92		4.25	5.50	
	3560	3/4" size	"	100	.080		2.65	1.92		4.57	5.85	

151 | Pipe and Fittings

151 900 | Pipe Supports/Hangers

			CREW	DAILY OUTPUT	MAN-HOURS	UNIT	BARE COSTS MAT.	LABOR	EQUIP.	TOTAL	TOTAL INCL O&P	
901	3570	1" pipe size	1 Asbe	98	.082	Ea.	2.65	1.96		4.61	5.95	901
	3580	1-¼" pipe size		98	.082		2.90	1.96		4.86	6.20	
	3590	1-½" pipe size		96	.083		3.10	2		5.10	6.50	
	3600	2" pipe size		96	.083		3.23	2		5.23	6.65	
	3610	2-½" pipe size		94	.085		3.36	2.04		5.40	6.85	
	3620	3" pipe size		94	.085		4.24	2.04		6.28	7.80	
	3630	2" thick, 3-½" pipe size		92	.087		4.24	2.08		6.32	7.85	
	3640	4" pipe size		92	.087		5.85	2.08		7.93	9.65	
	3650	5" pipe size		90	.089		5.85	2.13		7.98	9.70	
	3660	6" pipe size		90	.089		6.90	2.13		9.03	10.85	
	3670	8" pipe size		88	.091		9.70	2.18		11.88	14	
	3680	10" pipe size		88	.091		16.10	2.18		18.28	21	
	3690	12" pipe size		86	.093		18.35	2.23		20.58	24	
	3700	14" pipe size		86	.093		29	2.23		31.23	35	
	3710	16" pipe size		84	.095		31	2.28		33.28	38	
	3720	18" pipe size		84	.095		37	2.28		39.28	44	
	3730	20" pipe size		82	.098		41	2.34		43.34	49	
	3732	24" pipe size		80	.100		42	2.40		44.40	50	
	3733	30" pipe size		78	.103		43	2.46		45.46	51	
	3735	36" pipe size		75	.107		49	2.55		51.55	58	
	3750	Covering protection saddle										
	3760	1" covering size										
	3770	¾" pipe size	1 Plum	68	.118	Ea.	3.25	2.91		6.16	7.90	
	3780	1" pipe size		68	.118		3.25	2.91		6.16	7.90	
	3790	1-¼" pipe size		68	.118		3.25	2.91		6.16	7.90	
	3800	1-½" pipe size		66	.121		3.43	2.99		6.42	8.20	
	3810	2" pipe size		66	.121		4.53	2.99		7.52	9.45	
	3820	2-½" pipe size		64	.125		4.53	3.09		7.62	9.55	
	3830	3" pipe size		64	.125		5.05	3.09		8.14	10.15	
	3840	3-½" pipe size		62	.129		5.40	3.19		8.59	10.65	
	3850	4" pipe size		62	.129		5.40	3.19		8.59	10.65	
	3860	5" pipe size		60	.133		5.40	3.29		8.69	10.85	
	3870	6" pipe size		60	.133		6.40	3.29		9.69	11.95	
	3900	1-½" covering size										
	3910	¾" pipe size	1 Plum	68	.118	Ea.	5.75	2.91		8.66	10.65	
	3920	1" pipe size		68	.118		5.75	2.91		8.66	10.65	
	3930	1-¼" pipe size		68	.118		5.75	2.91		8.66	10.65	
	3940	1-½" pipe size		66	.121		5.75	2.99		8.74	10.75	
	3950	2" pipe size		66	.121		6.55	2.99		9.54	11.65	
	3960	2-½" pipe size		64	.125		6.55	3.09		9.64	11.80	
	3970	3" pipe size		64	.125		6.80	3.09		9.89	12.05	
	3980	3-½" pipe size		62	.129		6.80	3.19		9.99	12.20	
	3990	4" pipe size		62	.129		6.80	3.19		9.99	12.20	
	4000	5" pipe size		60	.133		6.80	3.29		10.09	12.35	
	4010	6" pipe size		60	.133		10.80	3.29		14.09	16.75	
	4020	8" pipe size		58	.138		11.75	3.41		15.16	18	
	4200	Sockets										
	4210	Rod end, malleable iron										
	4220	¼" thread size	1 Plum	240	.033	Ea.	.38	.82		1.20	1.64	
	4230	⅜" thread size		240	.033		.39	.82		1.21	1.65	
	4240	½" thread size		230	.035		.49	.86		1.35	1.81	
	4250	⅝" thread size		225	.036		.91	.88		1.79	2.30	
	4260	¾" thread size		220	.036		1.46	.90		2.36	2.94	
	4270	⅞" thread size		210	.038		2.06	.94		3	3.66	
	4290	Strap, ½" pipe size	Q-1	142	.113		.10	2.50		2.60	3.83	
	4300	¾" pipe size		140	.114		.14	2.54		2.68	3.92	
	4310	1" pipe size		137	.117		.26	2.60		2.86	4.14	
	4320	1-¼" pipe size		134	.119		.37	2.65		3.02	4.35	

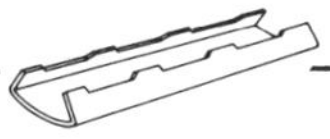

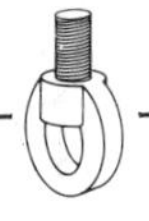

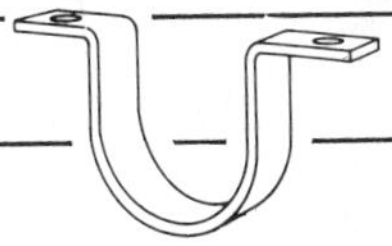

151 | Pipe and Fittings

151 900 | Pipe Supports/Hangers

			CREW	DAILY OUTPUT	MAN-HOURS	UNIT	BARE COSTS MAT.	LABOR	EQUIP.	TOTAL	TOTAL INCL O&P	
901	4330	1-½" pipe size	Q-1	131	.122	Ea.	.45	2.72		3.17	4.53	901
	4340	2" pipe size		129	.124		.62	2.76		3.38	4.77	
	4350	2-½" pipe size		125	.128		1.28	2.85		4.13	5.65	
	4360	3" pipe size		122	.131		1.32	2.92		4.24	5.75	
	4370	3-½" pipe size		119	.134		1.65	2.99		4.64	6.25	
	4380	4" pipe size		114	.140		1.65	3.12		4.77	6.45	
	4400	U-bolt, carbon steel										
	4410	Standard, with nuts										
	4420	½" pipe size	1 Plum	160	.050	Ea.	.43	1.24		1.67	2.31	
	4430	¾" pipe size		158	.051		.44	1.25		1.69	2.34	
	4450	1" pipe size		152	.053		.45	1.30		1.75	2.42	
	4460	1-¼" pipe size 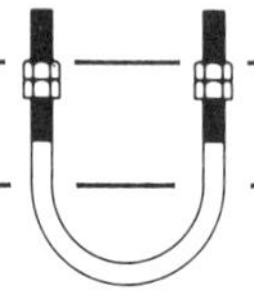		148	.054		.81	1.34		2.15	2.87	
	4470	1-½" pipe size		143	.056		.84	1.38		2.22	2.97	
	4480	2" pipe size		139	.058		.86	1.42		2.28	3.06	
	4490	2-½" pipe size		134	.060		1.40	1.47		2.87	3.73	
	4500	3" pipe size		128	.063		1.48	1.54		3.02	3.92	
	4510	3-½" pipe size		122	.066		1.55	1.62		3.17	4.11	
	4520	4" pipe size		117	.068		1.57	1.69		3.26	4.23	
	4530	5" pipe size		114	.070		1.73	1.73		3.46	4.47	
	4540	6" pipe size		111	.072		2.98	1.78		4.76	5.90	
	4550	8" pipe size		109	.073		3.40	1.81		5.21	6.45	
	4560	10" pipe size		107	.075		6.15	1.85		8	9.50	
	4570	12" pipe size		104	.077		8.25	1.90		10.15	11.90	
	4580	For plastic coating on ½" thru 6" size add					150%					
	4700	U-hook, carbon steel, requires mounting screws or bolts										
	4710	¾" thru 2" pipe size 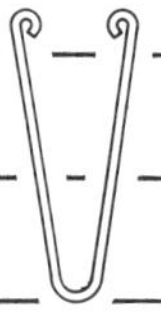										
	4720	6" long	1 Plum	96	.083	Ea.	.82	2.06		2.88	3.96	
	4730	8" long		96	.083		.94	2.06		3	4.09	
	4740	10" long		96	.083		1.10	2.06		3.16	4.26	
	4750	12" long		96	.083		1.16	2.06		3.22	4.33	
	4760	For copper plated, add					50%					
	8000	Pipe clamp, plastic, ½ CTS	1 Plum	80	.100		.17	2.47		2.64	3.85	
	8010	¾" CTS		73	.110		.17	2.71		2.88	4.20	
	8020	1" CTS		68	.118		.25	2.91		3.16	4.59	
	8080	Economy clamp, ¼" CTS 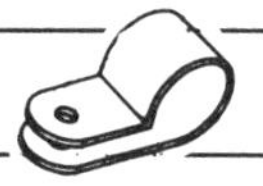		175	.046		.07	1.13		1.20	1.75	
	8090	⅜" CTS		168	.048		.07	1.18		1.25	1.82	
	8100	½" CTS		160	.050		.07	1.24		1.31	1.91	
	8110	¾" CTS		145	.055		.08	1.36		1.44	2.11	
	8200	Half clamp, ½" CTS		80	.100		.10	2.47		2.57	3.78	
	8210	¾" CTS		73	.110		.11	2.71		2.82	4.14	
	8300	Suspension clamp, ½" CTS 		80	.100		.20	2.47		2.67	3.89	
	8310	¾" CTS		73	.110		.23	2.71		2.94	4.27	
	8320	1" CTS		68	.118		.39	2.91		3.30	4.74	
	8400	Insulator, ½" CTS		80	.100		.34	2.47		2.81	4.04	
	8410	¾" CTS		73	.110		.34	2.71		3.05	4.39	
	8420	1" CTS		68	.118		.44	2.91		3.35	4.80	
	8500	J hook clamp with nail ½" CTS		240	.033		.06	.82		.88	1.29	
	8501	¾" CTS		240	.033		.07	.82		.89	1.30	

151 950 | Valves

			CREW	DAILY OUTPUT	MAN-HOURS	UNIT	MAT.	LABOR	EQUIP.	TOTAL	TOTAL INCL O&P	
951	0010	VALVES, BRASS										951
	0030	For motorized valves, see Division 157-420										
	0500	Gas stops, without checks										
	0510	¼" size	1 Plum	26	.308	Ea.	6	7.60		13.60	17.90	
	0520	⅜" size		24	.333		6.45	8.25		14.70	19.30	
	0530	½" size		24	.333		7.35	8.25		15.60	20	
	0540	¾" size		22	.364		8.05	9		17.05	22	
	0550	1" size		19	.421		11	10.40		21.40	28	

151 | Pipe and Fittings

151 950 | Valves

		CREW	DAILY OUTPUT	MAN-HOURS	UNIT	BARE COSTS MAT.	BARE COSTS LABOR	BARE COSTS EQUIP.	BARE COSTS TOTAL	TOTAL INCL O&P	
951	0560	1-¼" size	1 Plum	15	.533	Ea.	16.50	13.15		29.65	38	951
	0570	1-½" size		13	.615		23	15.20		38.20	48	
	0580	2" size	↓	11	.727	↓	38	17.95		55.95	68	
	0660	For stop with check, add					5%					
	0670	For larger sizes use lubricated plug valve, Section 151-990										
955	0010	**VALVES, BRONZE**										955
	1020	Angle, 150 lb., rising stem, threaded 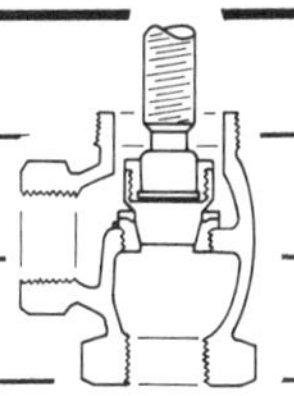										
	1030	⅛" size	1 Plum	24	.333	Ea.	16.60	8.25		24.85	30	
	1040	¼" size		24	.333		16.60	8.25		24.85	30	
	1050	⅜" size		24	.333		21	8.25		29.25	35	
	1060	½" size		22	.364		21	9		30	36	
	1070	¾" size		20	.400		25	9.90		34.90	42	
	1080	1" size		19	.421		36	10.40		46.40	55	
	1090	1-¼" size		15	.533		48	13.15		61.15	72	
	1100	1-½" size		13	.615		65	15.20		80.20	94	
	1110	2" size	↓	11	.727		99	17.95		116.95	135	
	1380	Ball, 150 psi, threaded 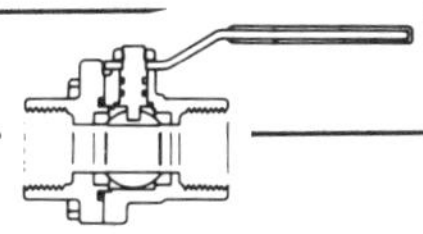										
	1400	¼" size	1 Plum	24	.333	Ea.	4.35	8.25		12.60	17	
	1430	⅜" size		24	.333		4.35	8.25		12.60	17	
	1450	½" size		22	.364		4.35	9		13.35	18.10	
	1460	¾" size		20	.400		7.15	9.90		17.05	23	
	1470	1" size		19	.421		8.80	10.40		19.20	25	
	1480	1-¼" size		15	.533		15.50	13.15		28.65	37	
	1490	1-½" size		13	.615		19.65	15.20		34.85	44	
	1500	2" size	↓	11	.727		24	17.95		41.95	53	
	1600	Butterfly, 175 psi, full port, solder or threaded ends										
	1610	Stainless steel disc and stem										
	1620	¼" size	1 Plum	24	.333	Ea.	4.53	8.25		12.78	17.20	
	1630	⅜" size		24	.333		4.53	8.25		12.78	17.20	
	1640	½" size		22	.364		4.30	9		13.30	18.05	
	1650	¾" size		20	.400		6.65	9.90		16.55	22	
	1660	1" size		19	.421		7.55	10.40		17.95	24	
	1670	1-¼" size		15	.533		14.45	13.15		27.60	35	
	1680	1-½" size		13	.615		18	15.20		33.20	42	
	1690	2" size	↓	11	.727		21	17.95		38.95	50	
	1750	Check, swing, class 150, regrinding disc, threaded										
	1800	⅛" size	1 Plum	24	.333	Ea.	9	8.25		17.25	22	
	1830	¼" size		24	.333		9	8.25		17.25	22	
	1840	⅜" size 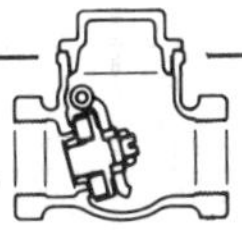		24	.333		9	8.25		17.25	22	
	1850	½" size		24	.333		9.40	8.25		17.65	23	
	1860	¾" size		20	.400		10.90	9.90		20.80	27	
	1870	1" size		19	.421		14.30	10.40		24.70	31	
	1880	1-¼" size		15	.533		21	13.15		34.15	43	
	1890	1-½" size		13	.615		23	15.20		38.20	48	
	1900	2" size	↓	11	.727		36	17.95		53.95	66	
	1910	2-½" size	Q-1	15	1.070		72	24		96	115	
	1920	3" size	"	13	1.230		105	27		132	155	
	2000	For 200 lb., add					20%	10%				
	2040	For 300 lb., add					60%	15%				
	2060	Check swing, 125#, sweat, ⅜" size	1 Plum	24	.333		11	8.25		19.25	24	
	2070	½" size		24	.333		11	8.25		19.25	24	
	2080	¾" size		20	.400		12.25	9.90		22.15	28	
	2090	1" size		19	.421		17.15	10.40		27.55	34	
	2100	1-¼" size		15	.533		23	13.15		36.15	45	
	2110	1-½ size		13	.615		28	15.20		43.20	53	
	2120	2" size	↓	11	.727		72	17.95		89.95	105	
	2130	2-½" size	Q-1	15	1.070		76	24		100	120	

151 | Pipe and Fittings

151 950 | Valves

			DAILY	MAN-		\multicolumn{4}{c}{BARE COSTS}	TOTAL	
		CREW	OUTPUT	HOURS	UNIT	MAT.	LABOR	EQUIP.	TOTAL	INCL O&P	
955	2140	3" size	Q-1	13	1.230	Ea.	110	27		137	160	955
	2850	Gate, N.R.S., soldered, 300 psi										
	2900	3/8" size	1 Plum	24	.333	Ea.	11.15	8.25		19.40	24	
	2920	1/2" size		24	.333		10.90	8.25		19.15	24	
	2940	3/4" size		20	.400		14.40	9.90		24.30	31	
	2950	1" size		19	.421		17.50	10.40		27.90	35	
	2960	1-1/4" size		15	.533		23	13.15		36.15	45	
	2970	1-1/2" size		13	.615		29	15.20		44.20	54	
	2980	2" size	↓	11	.727		39	17.95		56.95	70	
	2990	2-1/2" size	Q-1	15	1.070		86	24		110	130	
	3000	3" size	"	13	1.230	↓	130	27		157	185	
	3350	Threaded, class 150										
	3400	1/8" size	1 Plum	24	.333	Ea.	9.40	8.25		17.65	23	
	3410	1/4" size		24	.333		9.40	8.25		17.65	23	
	3420	3/8" size		24	.333		9.40	8.25		17.65	23	
	3430	1/2" size		24	.333		9.40	8.25		17.65	23	
	3440	3/4" size		20	.400		12	9.90		21.90	28	
	3450	1" size		19	.421		15	10.40		25.40	32	
	3460	1-1/4" size		15	.533		19.30	13.15		32.45	41	
	3470	1-1/2" size		13	.615		24	15.20		39.20	49	
	3480	2" size	↓	11	.727		35	17.95		52.95	65	
	3490	2-1/2" size	Q-1	15	1.070		75	24		99	120	
	3500	3" size	"	13	1.230	↓	110	27		137	160	
	3850	Rising stem, soldered, 300 psi										
	3900	3/8" size	1 Plum	24	.333	Ea.	12.05	8.25		20.30	25	
	3920	1/2" size		24	.333		11.85	8.25		20.10	25	
	3940	3/4" size		20	.400		14.15	9.90		24.05	30	
	3950	1" size		19	.421		17.65	10.40		28.05	35	
	3960	1-1/4" size		15	.533		25	13.15		38.15	47	
	3970	1-1/2" size		13	.615		30	15.20		45.20	56	
	3980	2" size	↓	11	.727		46	17.95		63.95	77	
	3990	2-1/2" size	Q-1	15	1.070		88	24		112	130	
	4000	3" size	"	13	1.230	↓	130	27		157	185	
	4250	Threaded, class 150										
	4300	1/8" size	1 Plum	24	.333	Ea.	9.40	8.25		17.65	23	
	4310	1/4" size		24	.333		9.40	8.25		17.65	23	
	4320	3/8" size		24	.333		9.40	8.25		17.65	23	
	4330	1/2" size		24	.333		9.40	8.25		17.65	23	
	4340	3/4" size		20	.400		12	9.90		21.90	28	
	4350	1" size		19	.421		14.50	10.40		24.90	31	
	4360	1-1/4" size		15	.533		19.35	13.15		32.50	41	
	4370	1-1/2" size		13	.615		24	15.20		39.20	49	
	4380	2" size	↓	11	.727		35	17.95		52.95	65	
	4390	2-1/2" size	Q-1	15	1.070		75	24		99	120	
	4400	3" size	"	13	1.230		110	27		137	160	
	4500	For 300 psi, threaded, add					100%	15%				
	4540	For chain operated type, add				↓	15%					
	4850	Globe, class 150, rising stem, threaded										
	4900	1/8" size	1 Plum	24	.333	Ea.	12.45	8.25		20.70	26	
	4920	1/4" size		24	.333		12.45	8.25		20.70	26	
	4940	3/8" size		24	.333		12.80	8.25		21.05	26	
	4950	1/2" size		24	.333		13.90	8.25		22.15	28	
	4960	3/4" size		20	.400		16.55	9.90		26.45	33	
	4970	1" size		19	.421		27	10.40		37.40	45	
	4980	1-1/4" size		15	.533		40	13.15		53.15	64	
	4990	1-1/2" size		13	.615		51	15.20		66.20	79	
	5000	2" size	↓	11	.727		74	17.95		91.95	110	
	5010	2-1/2" size	Q-1	15	1.070		145	24		169	195	

151 | Pipe and Fittings

151 950 | Valves

			CREW	DAILY OUTPUT	MAN-HOURS	UNIT	BARE COSTS MAT.	BARE COSTS LABOR	BARE COSTS EQUIP.	BARE COSTS TOTAL	TOTAL INCL O&P	
955	5020	3" size	Q-1	13	1.230	Ea.	205	27		232	265	955
	5120	For class 300, threaded, add				"	150%	15%				
	5600	Relief, pressure & temperature, self-closing, ASME										
	5640	¾" size	1 Plum	28	.286	Ea.	44	7.05		51.05	59	
	5650	1" size		24	.333		61	8.25		69.25	79	
	5660	1-¼" size		20	.400		118	9.90		127.90	145	
	5670	1-½" size		18	.444		225	11		236	265	
	5680	2" size		16	.500		240	12.35		252.35	280	
	5950	Pressure, poppet type, threaded										
	6000	½" size	1 Plum	30	.267	Ea.	13.10	6.60		19.70	24	
	6040	¾" size	"	28	.286	"	13.70	7.05		20.75	26	
	6400	Pressure, water, ASME, threaded										
	6440	¾" size	1 Plum	28	.286	Ea.	29	7.05		36.05	42	
	6450	1" size		24	.333		53	8.25		61.25	71	
	6460	1-¼" size		20	.400		81	9.90		90.90	105	
	6470	1-½" size		18	.444		115	11		126	145	
	6480	2" size		16	.500		165	12.35		177.35	200	
	6900	Reducing, water pressure										
	6920	300 psi to 25-75 psi, threaded or sweat										
	6940	½" size	1 Plum	24	.333	Ea.	53	8.25		61.25	71	
	6950	¾" size		20	.400		63	9.90		72.90	84	
	6960	1" size		19	.421		97	10.40		107.40	120	
	6970	1-¼" size		15	.533		205	13.15		218.15	245	
	6980	1-½" size		13	.615		225	15.20		240.20	270	
	6990	2" size		11	.727		320	17.95		337.95	380	
	7100	For built-in by-pass or 10-35 psi, add					7			7	7.70	
	7700	High capacity, 250 psi to 25-75 psi, threaded										
	7740	½" size	1 Plum	24	.333	Ea.	70	8.25		78.25	89	
	7780	¾" size		20	.400		70	9.90		79.90	92	
	7790	1" size		19	.421		110	10.40		120.40	135	
	7800	1-¼" size		15	.533		195	13.15		208.15	235	
	7810	1-½" size		13	.615		295	15.20		310.20	345	
	7820	2" size		11	.727		425	17.95		442.95	495	
	7830	2-½" size		9	.889		465	22		487	545	
	7840	3" size		8	1		755	25		780	865	
	7850	3" flanged (iron body)	Q-1	10	1.600		690	36		726	810	
	7860	4" flanged (iron body)	"	8	2		1,000	44		1,044	1,175	
	7920	For higher pressure, add					25%					
	8000	Silent check, bronze trim										
	8010	Compact wafer type, for 125 or 150 lb. flanges										
	8020	1-½" size	1 Plum	11	.727	Ea.	185	17.95		202.95	230	
	8021	2" size	"	9	.889		190	22		212	240	
	8022	2-½" size	Q-1	9	1.780		200	40		240	280	
	8023	3" size		8	2		235	44		279	325	
	8024	4" size		5	3.200		305	71		376	440	
	8025	5" size	Q-2	6	4		395	92		487	570	
	8026	6" size	"	5	4.800		530	110		640	745	
	8050	For 250 or 300 lb flanges, thru 6" no change										
	8060	Full flange wafer type, 150 lb.										
	8063	1-½" size	1 Plum	11	.727	Ea.	240	17.95		257.95	290	
	8064	2" size	"	9	.889		320	22		342	385	
	8065	2-½" size	Q-1	9	1.780		365	40		405	460	
	8066	3" size		8	2		405	44		449	510	
	8067	4" size		5	3.200		595	71		666	760	
	8068	5" size	Q-2	6	4		775	92		867	990	
	8069	6" size	"	5	4.800		775	110		885	1,025	
	8080	For 300 lb., add					40%	10%				
	8100	Globe type, 150 lb.										

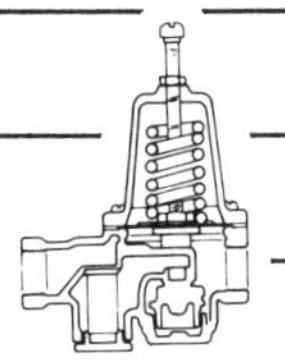

151 | Pipe and Fittings

151 950 | Valves

		CREW	DAILY OUTPUT	MAN-HOURS	UNIT	BARE COSTS MAT.	LABOR	EQUIP.	TOTAL	TOTAL INCL O&P	
955											**955**
8110	2" size	1 Plum	9	.889	Ea.	360	22		382	430	
8111	2-½" size	Q-1	9	1.780		430	40		470	530	
8112	3" size		8	2		515	44		559	630	
8113	4" size		5	3.200		710	71		781	885	
8114	5" size	Q-2	6	4		870	92		962	1,100	
8115	6" size	"	5	4.800		1,170	110		1,280	1,450	
8130	For 300 lb., add					20%	10%				
8140	Screwed end type, 300 lb.										
8141	½" size	1 Plum	24	.333	Ea.	90	8.25		98.25	110	
8142	¾" size		20	.400		96	9.90		105.90	120	
8143	1" size		19	.421		112	10.40		122.40	140	
8144	1-¼" size		15	.533		120	13.15		133.15	150	
8145	1-½" size		13	.615		136	15.20		151.20	170	
8146	2" size		11	.727		158	17.95		175.95	200	
8350	Tempering, water, sweat connections										
8400	½" size	1 Plum	24	.333	Ea.	25	8.25		33.25	40	
8440	¾" size	"	20	.400	"	29	9.90		38.90	47	
8650	Threaded connections										
8700	½" size	1 Plum	24	.333	Ea.	29	8.25		37.25	44	
8740	¾" size		20	.400		36	9.90		45.90	54	
8750	1" size		19	.421		105	10.40		115.40	130	
8760	1-¼" size		15	.533		175	13.15		188.15	210	
8770	1-½" size		13	.615		190	15.20		205.20	230	
8780	2" size		11	.727		285	17.95		302.95	340	
960	**VALVES, IRON BODY**										**960**
0010											
0020	For grooved joint, see Division 151-801										
1020	Butterfly, wafer type, lever actuator										
1030	2" size	1 Plum	14	.571	Ea.	59	14.10		73.10	86	
1040	2-½" size	Q-1	9	1.780		62	40		102	125	
1050	3" size		8	2		68	44		112	140	
1060	4" size		5	3.200		89	71		160	205	
1070	5" size	Q-2	5	4.800		110	110		220	285	
1080	6" size		5	4.800		130	110		240	305	
1090	8" size		4.50	5.330		170	125		295	370	
1100	10" size		4	6		210	140		350	435	
1110	12" size		3	8		315	185		500	620	
1180	For gear actuator, add					65%					
1200	Lug type, lever actuator										
1220	2" size	1 Plum	14	.571	Ea.	68	14.10		82.10	96	
1230	2-½" size	Q-1	9	1.780		73	40		113	140	
1240	3" size		8	2		80	44		124	155	
1250	4" size		5	3.200		94	71		165	210	
1260	5" size	Q-2	5	4.800		130	110		240	305	
1270	6" size		5	4.800		155	110		265	335	
1280	8" size		4.50	5.330		200	125		325	400	
1290	10" size		4	6		260	140		400	490	
1300	12" size		3	8		370	185		555	680	
1320	For gear actuator, add					60%					
1650	Gate, 125 lb., N.R.S., threaded										
1700	2" size	1 Plum	11	.727	Ea.	140	17.95		157.95	180	
1740	2-½" size	Q-1	15	1.070		160	24		184	210	
1760	3" size		13	1.230		185	27		212	245	
1780	4" size		10	1.600		370	36		406	460	
2150	Flanged										
2200	2" size	1 Plum	5	1.600	Ea.	84	40		124	150	
2240	2-½" size	Q-1	5	3.200		110	71		181	225	
2260	3" size		4.50	3.560		115	79		194	245	
2280	4" size		3	5.330		190	120		310	385	

151 | Pipe and Fittings

151 950 | Valves

			CREW	DAILY OUTPUT	MAN-HOURS	UNIT	BARE COSTS MAT.	LABOR	EQUIP.	TOTAL	TOTAL INCL O&P	
960	2290	5" size	Q-2	3.40	7.060	Ea.	325	165		490	600	960
	2300	6" size		3	8		359	185		544	670	
	2320	8" size		2.50	9.600		620	220		840	1,000	
	2340	10" size		2.20	10.910		1,100	250		1,350	1,575	
	2360	12" size	↓	1.70	14.120		1,520	325		1,845	2,150	
	2420	For 250 lb., flanged, add				↓	200%	10%				
	3550	OS&Y, flanged										
	3600	2" size	1 Plum	5	1.600	Ea.	130	40		170	200	
	3640	2-½" size	Q-1	5	3.200		135	71		206	255	
	3660	3" size		4.50	3.560		150	79		229	280	
	3670	3-½" size		3	5.330		215	120		335	410	
	3680	4" size		3	5.330		215	120		335	410	
	3690	5" size	Q-2	3.40	7.060		355	165		520	630	
	3700	6" size		3	8		355	185		540	665	
	3720	8" size		2.50	9.600		630	220		850	1,025	
	3740	10" size		2.20	10.910		1,125	250		1,375	1,600	
	3760	12" size	↓	1.70	14.120		1,500	325		1,825	2,125	
	3900	For 250 lb flanged, add				↓	120%	10%				
	4350	Globe, OS&Y, class 125, threaded										
	4400	2" size	1 Plum	11	.727	Ea.	350	17.95		367.95	410	
	4450	3" size	Q-1	13	1.230		440	27		467	525	
	4460	4" size	"	10	1.600	↓	650	36		686	770	
	4540	Class 125, flanged										
	4550	2" size	1 Plum	5	1.600	Ea.	260	40		300	345	
	4560	2-½" size	Q-1	5	3.200		275	71		346	410	
	4570	3" size		4.50	3.560		320	79		399	470	
	4580	4" size	↓	3	5.330		460	120		580	680	
	4590	5" size	Q-2	3.40	7.060		820	165		985	1,150	
	4600	6" size		3	8		820	185		1,005	1,175	
	4610	8" size	↓	2.50	9.600	↓	1,600	220		1,820	2,100	
	4850	Class 250, threaded										
	4940	2-½" size	Q-1	13	1.230	Ea.	600	27		627	700	
	5040	Class 250, flanged										
	5050	2" size	1 Plum	4.50	1.780	Ea.	400	44		444	505	
	5060	2-½" size	Q-1	4.50	3.560		490	79		569	655	
	5070	3" size		4	4		530	89		619	715	
	5080	4" size	↓	2.70	5.930		755	130		885	1,025	
	5090	5" size	Q-2	3	8		1,350	185		1,535	1,750	
	5100	6" size		2.70	8.890		1,350	205		1,555	1,800	
	5110	8" size		2.20	10.910		2,925	250		3,175	3,600	
	5120	10" size		2	12		5,000	275		5,275	5,900	
	5130	12" size	↓	1.60	15		8,200	345		8,545	9,525	
	5240	Valve sprocket rim w/chain 2" valve	1 Stpi	30	.267		30	6.60		36.60	43	
	5250	2-½" valve		27	.296		37	7.35		44.35	52	
	5260	3-½" valve		25	.320		45	7.90		52.90	61	
	5270	6" valve		20	.400		60	9.90		69.90	81	
	5280	8" valve		18	.444		70	11		81	93	
	5290	12" valve		16	.500		100	12.40		112.40	130	
	5300	16" valve		12	.667		120	16.50		136.50	155	
	5310	20" valve		10	.800		180	19.80		199.80	225	
	5320	36" valve	↓	8	1		230	25		255	290	
	5330	Valve bypass, up to 4" valve					155			155	170	
	5340	5" to 8" valve					170			170	185	
	5350	10" to 24" valve				↓	280			280	310	
	5450	Swing check, 125 lb., threaded										
	5500	2" size	1 Plum	11	.727	Ea.	105	17.95		122.95	140	
	5540	2-½" size	Q-1	15	1.070		120	24		144	165	
	5550	3" size	"	13	1.230		140	27		167	195	

151 | Pipe and Fittings

151 950 | Valves

		CREW	DAILY OUTPUT	MAN-HOURS	UNIT	BARE COSTS MAT.	LABOR	EQUIP.	TOTAL	TOTAL INCL O&P	
960	5560	4" size	Q-1	10	1.600	Ea.	205	36		241	280	960
	5950	Flanged										
	6000	2" size	1 Plum	5	1.600	Ea.	86	40		126	155	
	6040	2-½" size	Q-1	5	3.200		110	71		181	225	
	6050	3" size		4.50	3.560		120	79		199	250	
	6060	4" size	↓	3	5.330		190	120		310	385	
	6070	6" size	Q-2	3	8		325	185		510	630	
	6080	8" size		2.50	9.600		615	220		835	1,000	
	6090	10" size		2.20	10.910		1,050	250		1,300	1,525	
	6100	12" size	↓	1.70	14.120		1,600	325		1,925	2,250	
	6160	For 250 lb., flanged, add				↓	200%	20%				
	6600	Silent check, bronze trim										
	6610	Compact wafer type, for 125 or 150 lb. flanges										
	6630	1-½" size	1 Plum	11	.727	Ea.	85	17.95		102.95	120	
	6640	2" size	"	9	.889		80	22		102	120	
	6650	2-½" size	Q-1	9	1.780		92	40		132	160	
	6660	3" size		8	2		105	44		149	180	
	6670	4" size	↓	5	3.200		135	71		206	255	
	6680	5" size	Q-2	6	4		185	92		277	340	
	6690	6" size		6	4		240	92		332	400	
	6700	8" size		4.50	5.330		360	125		485	580	
	6710	10" size		4	6		575	140		715	840	
	6720	12" size	↓	3	8		1,370	185		1,555	1,775	
	6740	For 250 or 300 lb. flanges, thru 6" no change										
	6741	For 8" and 10", add				Ea.	11%	10%				
	6800	Full flange type, 150 lb.										
	6900	Globe type, 125 lb.										
	6911	2-½" size	Q-1	9	1.780	Ea.	185	40		225	260	
	6912	3" size		8	2		200	44		244	285	
	6913	4" size	↓	5	3.200		270	71		341	405	
	6914	5" size	Q-2	6	4		350	92		442	520	
	6915	6" size		5	4.800		435	110		545	645	
	6916	8" size		4.50	5.330		800	125		925	1,050	
	6917	10" size		4	6		975	140		1,115	1,275	
	6918	12" size	↓	3	8		1,675	185		1,860	2,125	
	6940	For 250 lb., add				↓	40%	10%				
	6980	Screwed end type, 250 lb.										
	6981	1" size	1 Plum	19	.421	Ea.	93.75	10.40		104.15	120	
	6982	1-¼" size		15	.533		107	13.15		120.15	135	
	6983	1-½" size		13	.615		112	15.20		127.20	145	
	6984	2" size	↓	11	.727	↓	120	17.95		137.95	160	
970	0010	**VALVES, LINED, CORROSION RESISTANT/HIGH PURITY**										970
	2000	Butterfly 150 lb. ductile iron,										
	2010	Wafer type										
	2030	FEP lined 3" lever handle	Q-1	8	2	Ea.	660	44		704	790	
	2050	4" lever handle	"	5	3.200		935	71		1,006	1,125	
	2070	6" gear operated	Q-2	4.50	5.330		1,425	125		1,550	1,750	
	2080	8" gear operated		4	6		2,000	140		2,140	2,400	
	2090	10" gear operated		3.50	6.860		2,750	160		2,910	3,250	
	2100	12" gear operated	↓	2.50	9.600	↓	3,275	220		3,495	3,925	
	3500	Check lift, 125 lb., cast iron flanged										
	3510	Horizontal PPL or SL lined										
	3530	1" size	1 Plum	14	.571	Ea.	250	14.10		264.10	295	
	3540	1-½" size		11	.727		300	17.95		317.95	355	
	3550	2" size	↓	8	1		340	25		365	410	
	3560	2-½" size	Q-1	5	3.200		455	71		526	605	
	3570	3" size	"	4.50	3.560	↓	575	79		654	750	

151 | Pipe and Fittings

151 950 | Valves

			CREW	DAILY OUTPUT	MAN-HOURS	UNIT	MAT.	LABOR	EQUIP.	TOTAL	TOTAL INCL O&P	
970	3590	4" size	Q-1	3	5.330	Ea.	750	120		870	1,000	970
	3610	6" size	Q-2	3	8		1,250	185		1,435	1,650	
	3620	8" size	"	2.50	9.600		2,700	220		2,920	3,300	
	4250	Vertical PPL or SL lined										
	4270	1" size	1 Plum	14	.571	Ea.	225	14.10		239.10	270	
	4290	1-½" size		11	.727		285	17.95		302.95	340	
	4300	2" size		8	1		320	25		345	390	
	4310	2-½" size	Q-1	5	3.200		425	71		496	575	
	4320	3" size		4.50	3.560		495	79		574	660	
	4340	4" size		3	5.330		600	120		720	835	
	4360	6" size	Q-2	3	8		1,000	185		1,185	1,375	
	4370	8" size	"	2.50	9.600		2,325	220		2,545	2,875	
	5000	Clamp type, ductile iron, 150 lb. flanged										
	5010	TFE lined										
	5030	1" size, lever handle	1 Plum	9	.889	Ea.	535	22		557	620	
	5050	1-½" size, lever handle		6	1.330		700	33		733	820	
	5060	2" size, lever handle		5	1.600		850	40		890	995	
	5080	3" size, lever handle	Q-1	4.50	3.560		1,075	79		1,154	1,300	
	5100	4" size, gear operated	"	3	5.330		1,535	120		1,655	1,875	
	5120	6" size, gear operated	Q-2	3	8		4,350	185		4,535	5,050	
	5130	8" size, gear operated	"	2.50	9.600		4,600	220		4,820	5,400	
	6000	Diaphragm type, cast iron, 125 lb. flanged										
	6010	PPL or SL, lined										
	6030	1" size, handwheel operated	1 Plum	9	.889	Ea.	105	22		127	150	
	6050	1-½" size, handwheel operated		6	1.330		140	33		173	205	
	6060	2" size, handwheel operated		5	1.600		155	40		195	230	
	6070	2-½" size, handwheel operated	Q-1	5	3.200		220	71		291	350	
	6080	3" size, handwheel operated		4.50	3.560		255	79		334	400	
	6100	4" size, handwheel operated		3	5.330		415	120		535	630	
	6120	6" size, handwheel operated	Q-2	3	8		810	185		995	1,175	
	6130	8" size, handwheel operated	"	2.50	9.600		1,750	220		1,970	2,250	
	8000	Plug, 150 lb. ductile iron flanged										
	8020	FEP lined 1" lever handle	1 Plum	14	.571	Ea.	455	14.10		469.10	520	
	8040	1-½" lever handle		11	.727		600	17.95		617.95	685	
	8050	2" lever handle		8	1		750	25		775	860	
	8070	3" lever handle	Q-1	4.50	3.560		800	79		879	995	
	8090	4" lever handle	"	3	5.330		1,100	120		1,220	1,375	
	8110	6" gear operated	Q-2	3	8		2,275	185		2,460	2,775	
	8120	8" gear operated	"	2.50	9.600		4,175	220		4,395	4,925	
975	0010	**VALVES, PLASTIC**										975
	1100	Angle, PVC, threaded										
	1110	¼" size	1 Plum	26	.308	Ea.	13.30	7.60		20.90	26	
	1120	½" size		26	.308		19.55	7.60		27.15	33	
	1130	¾" size		25	.320		27	7.90		34.90	41	
	1140	1" size		23	.348		30	8.60		38.60	46	
	1150	Ball, PVC, socket or threaded, single union										
	1200	¼" size	1 Plum	26	.308	Ea.	5.05	7.60		12.65	16.85	
	1220	⅜" size		26	.308		5.05	7.60		12.65	16.85	
	1230	½" size		26	.308		5.05	7.60		12.65	16.85	
	1240	¾" size		25	.320		6.35	7.90		14.25	18.70	
	1250	1" size		23	.348		7.55	8.60		16.15	21	
	1260	1-¼" size		21	.381		14	9.40		23.40	29	
	1270	1-½" size		20	.400		14	9.90		23.90	30	
	1280	2" size		17	.471		18.90	11.60		30.50	38	
	1290	2-½" size	Q-1	26	.615		30	13.70		43.70	53	
	1300	3" size		24	.667		40	14.80		54.80	66	
	1310	4" size		20	.800		76	17.80		93.80	110	

151 | Pipe and Fittings

151 950 | Valves

		CREW	DAILY OUTPUT	MAN-HOURS	UNIT	BARE COSTS MAT.	BARE COSTS LABOR	BARE COSTS EQUIP.	BARE COSTS TOTAL	TOTAL INCL O&P
1360	For PVC, flanged, add				Ea.	45%	15%			
1400	For true union, socket or threaded, add				"	40%	5%			
1650	CPVC, socket or threaded, single union									
1700	½" size	1 Plum	26	.308	Ea.	6.20	7.60		13.80	18.10
1720	¾" size		25	.320		8.20	7.90		16.10	21
1730	1" size		23	.348		10.30	8.60		18.90	24
1750	1-¼" size		21	.381		20	9.40		29.40	36
1760	1-½" size		20	.400		20	9.90		29.90	37
1770	2" size		17	.471		27	11.60		38.60	47
1780	3" size	Q-1	24	.667		76	14.80		90.80	105
1840	For CPVC, flanged, add					65%	15%			
1880	For true union, socket or threaded, add					50%	5%			
2050	Polypropylene, threaded									
2100	¼" size	1 Plum	26	.308	Ea.	19.95	7.60		27.55	33
2120	⅜" size		26	.308		19.95	7.60		27.55	33
2130	½" size		26	.308		19.95	7.60		27.55	33
2140	¾" size		25	.320		23	7.90		30.90	37
2150	1" size		23	.348		29	8.60		37.60	45
2160	1-¼" size		21	.381		37	9.40		46.40	55
2170	1-½" size		20	.400		47	9.90		56.90	66
2180	2" size		17	.471		65	11.60		76.60	89
2190	3" size	Q-1	24	.667		175	14.80		189.80	215
2200	4" size	"	20	.800		315	17.80		332.80	375
2550	PVC, three way, socket or threaded									
2600	½" size	1 Plum	26	.308	Ea.	33	7.60		40.60	48
2640	¾" size		25	.320		36	7.90		43.90	51
2650	1" size		23	.348		40	8.60		48.60	57
2660	1-½" size		20	.400		81	9.90		90.90	105
2670	2" size		17	.471		110	11.60		121.60	140
2680	3" size	Q-1	24	.667		265	14.80		279.80	315
2740	For flanged, add					60%	15%			
3150	Ball check, PVC, socket or threaded									
3200	¼" size	1 Plum	26	.308	Ea.	18	7.60		25.60	31
3220	⅜" size		26	.308		18	7.60		25.60	31
3240	½" size		26	.308		18	7.60		25.60	31
3250	¾" size		25	.320		20	7.90		27.90	34
3260	1" size		23	.348		26	8.60		34.60	41
3270	1-¼" size		21	.381		34	9.40		43.40	51
3280	1-½" size		20	.400		42	9.90		51.90	61
3290	2" size		17	.471		57	11.60		68.60	80
3310	3" size	Q-1	24	.667		135	14.80		149.80	170
3320	4" size	"	20	.800		225	17.80		242.80	275
3360	For PVC, flanged, add					50%	15%			
3750	CPVC, socket or threaded									
3800	½" size	1 Plum	26	.308	Ea.	23	7.60		30.60	37
3840	¾" size		25	.320		28	7.90		35.90	43
3850	1" size		23	.348		33	8.60		41.60	49
3860	1-½" size		20	.400		58	9.90		67.90	78
3870	2" size		17	.471		75	11.60		86.60	100
3880	3" size	Q-1	24	.667		200	14.80		214.80	240
3920	4" size	"	20	.800		285	17.80		302.80	340
3930	For CPVC, flanged, add					40%	15%			
4340	Polypropylene, threaded									
4360	½" size	1 Plum	26	.308	Ea.	35	7.60		42.60	50
4400	¾" size		25	.320		48	7.90		55.90	65
4440	1" size		23	.348		62	8.60		70.60	81
4450	1-½" size		20	.400		95	9.90		104.90	120
4460	2" size		17	.471		180	11.60		191.60	215

151 | Pipe and Fittings

151 950 | Valves

			Crew	Daily Output	Man-Hours	Unit	Bare Costs Mat.	Labor	Equip.	Total	Total Incl O&P	
975	4500	For polypropylene flanged, add				Ea.	55%	15%				975
	4850	Foot valve, PVC, socket or threaded										
	4900	½" size	1 Plum	34	.235	Ea.	29	5.80		34.80	41	
	4930	¾" size		32	.250		33	6.20		39.20	45	
	4940	1" size		28	.286		42	7.05		49.05	57	
	4950	1-¼" size		27	.296		78	7.30		85.30	97	
	4960	1-½" size		26	.308		78	7.60		85.60	97	
	4970	2" size		24	.333		95	8.25		103.25	115	
	4980	3" size		20	.400		220	9.90		229.90	255	
	4990	4" size	↓	18	.444	↓	325	11		336	375	
	5000	For flanged, add					25%	10%				
	5050	CPVC, socket or threaded										
	5060	½" size	1 Plum	34	.235	Ea.	37	5.80		42.80	49	
	5070	¾" size		32	.250		50	6.20		56.20	64	
	5080	1" size		28	.286		63	7.05		70.05	80	
	5090	1-¼" size		27	.296		95	7.30		102.30	115	
	5100	1-½" size		26	.308		110	7.60		117.60	130	
	5110	2" size		24	.333		135	8.25		143.25	160	
	5120	3" size		20	.400		320	9.90		329.90	365	
	5130	4" size	↓	18	.444	↓	455	11		466	515	
	5140	For flanged, add					25%	10%				
	5280	Needle valve, PVC, threaded										
	5300	¼" size	1 Plum	26	.308	Ea.	11.65	7.60		19.25	24	
	5340	⅜" size		26	.308		14.25	7.60		21.85	27	
	5360	½" size	↓	26	.308	↓	14.25	7.60		21.85	27	
	5380	For polypropylene, add					20%					
	5800	Y check, PVC, socket or threaded										
	5820	½" size	1 Plum	26	.308	Ea.	27	7.60		34.60	41	
	5840	¾" size		25	.320		28	7.90		35.90	43	
	5850	1" size		23	.348		31	8.60		39.60	47	
	5860	1-¼" size		21	.381		51	9.40		60.40	70	
	5870	1-½" size		20	.400		56	9.90		65.90	76	
	5880	2" size		17	.471		70	11.60		81.60	94	
	5890	2-½" size	↓	15	.533		155	13.15		168.15	190	
	5900	3" size	Q-1	24	.667		145	14.80		159.80	180	
	5910	4" size	"	20	.800		240	17.80		257.80	290	
	5960	For PVC flanged, add				↓	45%	15%				
	6350	Y sediment strainer, PVC, socket or threaded										
	6400	½" size	1 Plum	26	.308	Ea.	20	7.60		27.60	33	
	6440	¾" size		24	.333		25	8.25		33.25	40	
	6450	1" size		23	.348		27	8.60		35.60	42	
	6460	1-¼" size		21	.381		51	9.40		60.40	70	
	6470	1-½" size		20	.400		51	9.90		60.90	71	
	6480	2" size		17	.471		62	11.60		73.60	85	
	6490	2-½" size	↓	15	.533		125	13.15		138.15	155	
	6500	3" size	Q-1	24	.667		125	14.80		139.80	160	
	6510	4" size	"	20	.800	↓	210	17.80		227.80	255	
	6560	For PVC, flanged, add					55%	15%				
985	0010	**VALVES, STAINLESS STEEL**										985
	1000	Butterfly, 175 lb., full port, threaded										
	1020	Type 316 stainless steel	C8.1-081									
	1030	¼" size	1 Plum	24	.333	Ea.	25	8.25		33.25	40	
	1040	⅜" size		24	.333		25	8.25		33.25	40	
	1050	½" size		22	.364		25	9		34	41	
	1060	¾" size		20	.400		40	9.90		49.90	59	
	1070	1" size		19	.421		45	10.40		55.40	65	
	1080	1-¼" size		15	.533		90	13.15		103.15	120	
	1090	1-½" size		13	.615		110	15.20		125.20	145	

151 | Pipe and Fittings

151 950 | Valves

		CREW	DAILY OUTPUT	MAN-HOURS	UNIT	BARE COSTS MAT.	LABOR	EQUIP.	TOTAL	TOTAL INCL O&P	
985 1100	2" size	1 Plum	11	.727	Ea.	120	17.95		137.95	160	985
1700	Check, 200 lb., threaded										
1710	¼" size	1 Plum	24	.333	Ea.	130	8.25		138.25	155	
1720	½" size		22	.364		130	9		139	155	
1730	¾" size		20	.400		145	9.90		154.90	175	
1750	1" size		19	.421		200	10.40		210.40	235	
1760	1-½" size		13	.615		295	15.20		310.20	345	
1770	2" size		11	.727		360	17.95		377.95	425	
1800	150 lb., flanged										
1810	2-½" size	Q-1	5	3.200	Ea.	675	71		746	850	
1820	3" size		4.50	3.560		755	79		834	950	
1830	4" size		3	5.330		1,125	120		1,245	1,425	
1840	6" size	Q-2	3	8		2,075	185		2,260	2,550	
1850	8" size	"	2.50	9.600		3,900	220		4,120	4,625	
2100	Gate, OS&Y, 150 lb., flanged										
2120	½" size	1 Plum	18	.444	Ea.	200	11		211	235	
2140	¾" size		16	.500		210	12.35		222.35	250	
2150	1" size		14	.571		255	14.10		269.10	300	
2160	1-½" size		11	.727		365	17.95		382.95	430	
2170	2" size		8	1		430	25		455	510	
2180	2-½" size	Q-1	5	3.200		575	71		646	740	
2190	3" size		4.50	3.560		675	79		754	860	
2200	4" size		3	5.330		1,000	120		1,120	1,275	
2210	6" size	Q-2	3	8		1,775	185		1,960	2,225	
2220	8" size	"	2.50	9.600		3,300	220		3,520	3,950	
2260	For 300 lb., flanged, add					120%	15%				
2600	600 lb., flanged										
2620	½" size	1 Plum	16	.500	Ea.	375	12.35		387.35	430	
2640	¾" size		14	.571		400	14.10		414.10	460	
2650	1" size		12	.667		500	16.45		516.45	575	
2660	1-½" size		10	.800		575	19.75		594.75	660	
2670	2" size		7	1.140		900	28		928	1,025	
2680	2-½" size	Q-1	4	4		3,600	89		3,689	4,100	
2690	3" size		3.60	4.440		3,800	99		3,899	4,325	
2700	4" size		2.50	6.400		5,775	140		5,915	6,575	
2710	6" size	Q-2	2.60	9.230		9,675	215		9,890	11,000	
2720	8" size		2.10	11.430		25,000	265		25,265	27,900	
2730	10" size		1.70	14.120		27,000	325		27,325	30,200	
2740	12" size		1.20	20		34,000	460		34,460	38,100	
3100	Globe, OS&Y, 150 lb., flanged										
3120	½" size	1 Plum	18	.444	Ea.	195	11		206	230	
3140	¾" size		16	.500		220	12.35		232.35	260	
3150	1" size		14	.571		260	14.10		274.10	305	
3160	1-½" size		11	.727		390	17.95		407.95	455	
3170	2" size		8	1		485	25		510	570	
3180	2-½" size	Q-1	5	3.200		775	71		846	960	
3190	3" size		4.50	3.560		1,050	79		1,129	1,275	
3200	4" size		3	5.330		1,275	120		1,395	1,575	
3210	6" size	Q-2	3	8		2,200	185		2,385	2,700	
990 0010	**VALVES, SEMI-STEEL**										990
1020	Lubricated plug valve, threaded										
1030	½" pipe size	1 Plum	18	.444	Ea.	71	11		82	94	
1040	¾" pipe size		16	.500		71	12.35		83.35	96	
1050	1" pipe size		14	.571		85	14.10		99.10	115	
1060	1-¼" pipe size		12	.667		100	16.45		116.45	135	
1070	1-½" pipe size		11	.727		110	17.95		127.95	150	
1080	2" pipe size		8	1		130	25		155	180	

151 | Pipe and Fittings

151 950 | Valves

			CREW	DAILY OUTPUT	MAN-HOURS	UNIT	BARE COSTS MAT.	LABOR	EQUIP.	TOTAL	TOTAL INCL O&P	
990	1090	2-½" pipe size	Q-1	5	3.200	Ea.	200	71		271	325	990
	1100	3" pipe size	"	4.50	3.560	"	245	79		324	385	
	6990	Flanged										
	7000	2" pipe size	1 Plum	8	1	Ea.	150	25		175	200	
	7010	2-½" pipe size	Q-1	5	3.200		230	71		301	360	
	7020	3" pipe size		4.50	3.560		280	79		359	425	
	7030	4" pipe size	↓	3	5.330		350	120		470	560	
	7040	6" pipe size	Q-2	3	8		585	185		770	915	
	7050	8" pipe size		2.50	9.600		1,050	220		1,270	1,475	
	7060	10" pipe size		2.20	10.910		1,550	250		1,800	2,075	
	7070	12" pipe size	↓	1.70	14.120	↓	2,325	325		2,650	3,050	

152 | Plumbing Fixtures

152 100 | Fixtures

			CREW	DAILY OUTPUT	MAN-HOURS	UNIT	BARE COSTS MAT.	LABOR	EQUIP.	TOTAL	TOTAL INCL O&P	
101	0010	**FIXTURES** Includes trim fittings unless otherwise noted										101
	0080	For rough-in, supply, waste, and vent, see add for each type										
	0120	For electric water coolers, see Division 153-105	C8.1 -401									
	0160	For color, unless otherwise noted, add				Ea.	20%					
104	0010	**BATHS**										104
	0100	Tubs, recessed porcelain enamel on cast iron, with trim										
	0140	42" x 37"	B8.1 -410 Q-1	5	3.200	Ea.	535	71		606	695	
	0180	48" x 42"		4	4		855	89		944	1,075	
	0220	72" x 36"		3	5.330		910	120		1,030	1,175	
	0300	Mat bottom, 4' long		5.50	2.910		700	65		765	865	
	0340	4'-6" long		5	3.200		460	71		531	610	
	0380	5' long		4.40	3.640		276	81		357	425	
	0420	5'-6" long		4	4		665	89		754	865	
	0480	Above floor drain, 5' long		4	4		515	89		604	700	
	0560	Corner 48" x 44"	↓	4.40	3.640	↓	980	81		1,061	1,200	
	0750	Add for color					25%					
	2000	Enameled formed steel, 4'-6" long	Q-1	5.80	2.760	Ea.	191	61		252	300	
	2200	5' long		5.50	2.910		176	65		241	290	
	2300	Above floor drain, 5' long	↓	5.50	2.910	↓	195	65		260	310	
	2350	Add for color					10%					
	4000	Soaking, acrylic with pop-up drain, 40" x 40"	Q-1	5.50	2.910	Ea.	210	65		275	325	
	4100	66" x 36" x 18-½" deep		5	3.200		1,050	71		1,121	1,250	
	4200	72" x 44" x 18" deep		4.80	3.330		1,175	74		1,249	1,400	
	4300	72" x 60" x 20" deep	↓	4.40	3.640	↓	2,445	81		2,526	2,800	
	4600	Module tub & showerwall surround, molded fiberglass										
	4610	5' long x 34" wide x 76" high	Q-1	4	4	Ea.	535	89		624	720	
	4750	Handicap with 1-½" OD grab bar, antiskid bottom										
	4760	60" x 32-¾" x 72" high	Q-1	4	4	Ea.	760	89		849	970	
	4770	75" x 40" x 76" high with molded seat	"	3.50	4.570	"	1,025	100		1,125	1,275	
	5000	Hospital type without trim (see 151-141)										
	5050	Bathing pool, porcelain enamel on cast iron, grab bars										
	5060	pop-up drain, 72" x 36"	Q-1	3	5.330	Ea.	1,065	120		1,185	1,350	
	5100	Perineal (sitz), vitreous china		3	5.330		700	120		820	945	
	5120	Pedestal, vitreous china		8	2		115	44		159	190	
	5180	Pier tub, porcelain enamel on cast iron, 66-¾" x 30"		3	5.330		1,315	120		1,435	1,625	
	5200	Base, porcelain enamel on cast iron	↓	8	2	↓	840	44		884	990	

152 | Plumbing Fixtures

152 100 | Fixtures

			DAILY	MAN-		\multicolumn{4}{c	}{BARE COSTS}	TOTAL	
		CREW	OUTPUT	HOURS	UNIT	MAT.	LABOR	EQUIP.	TOTAL	INCL O&P	
104	5300 Whirlpool, porcelain enamel on cast iron, 72" x 36"	Q-1	1	16	Ea.	2,990	355		3,345	3,825	104
	6000 Whirlpool, bath with vented overflow, molded fiberglass										
	6100 66" x 48" x 24"	Q-1	1	16	Ea.	1,930	355		2,285	2,650	
	6400 72" x 36" x 24"		1	16		1,855	355		2,210	2,575	
	6500 60" x 36" x 21"		1	16		1,490	355		1,845	2,175	
	6600 72" x 42" x 22"		1	16		2,215	355		2,570	2,975	
	6700 84" x 66"	↓	.30	53.330	↓	3,600	1,175		4,775	5,725	
	7000 Redwood tub system										
	7050 4' diameter x 4' deep	Q-1	1	16	Ea.	980	355		1,335	1,600	
	7100 5' diameter x 4' deep		1	16		1,110	355		1,465	1,750	
	7150 6' diameter x 4' deep		.80	20		1,330	445		1,775	2,125	
	7200 8' diameter x 4' deep		.80	20		1,670	445		2,115	2,500	
	9600 Rough-in, supply, waste and vent, for all above tubs, add	↓	2.07	7.730	↓	86.66	170		256.66	350	
108	0010 **BIDET**										108
	0180 Vitreous china, with trim on fixture	Q-1	5	3.200	Ea.	350	71		421	490	
	0200 With trim for wall mounting		5	3.200		350	71		421	490	
	9600 For rough-in, supply, waste and vent, add	↓	1.78	8.990	↓	71.84	200		271.84	375	
112	0010 **DENTAL FOUNTAIN**										112
	0020 Deck mounted, with cuspidor										
	0050 Stainless steel receptor	1 Plum	4	2	Ea.	156	49		205	245	
	0100 Enameled steel receptor		4	2		118	49		167	205	
	9600 For rough-in, supply and waste, add	↓	1.16	6.900	↓	63.26	170		233.26	320	
116	0010 **DRINKING FOUNTAIN** For connection to cold water supply										116
	0800 For remote water chiller, see division 153-101										
	1000 Wall mounted, non-recessed										
	1200 Aluminum,										
	1280 Dual bubbler type	1 Plum	3.20	2.500	Ea.	540	62		602	685	
	1400 Bronze, with no back		4	2		576	49		625	705	
	1600 Cast iron, enameled, low back, single bubbler		4	2		252	49		301	350	
	1640 Dual bubbler type		3.20	2.500		447	62		509	585	
	1680 Triple bubbler type		3.20	2.500		567	62		629	715	
	1800 Cast aluminum, enameled, for correctional institutions		4	2		381	49		430	490	
	2000 Fiberglass, 12" back, single bubbler unit		4	2		282	49		331	385	
	2040 Dual bubbler		3.20	2.500		440	62		502	575	
	2080 Triple bubbler		3.20	2.500		520	62		582	665	
	2200 Polymarble, no back, single bubbler		4	2		261	49		310	360	
	2240 Dual bubbler		3.20	2.500		402	62		464	535	
	2280 Triple bubbler		3.20	2.500		560	62		622	710	
	2400 Precast stone, no back		4	2		275	49		324	375	
	2700 Stainless steel, single bubbler, no back		4	2		550	49		599	680	
	2740 With back		4	2		261	49		310	360	
	2780 Dual handle & wheelchair projection type		4	2		306	49		355	410	
	2820 Dual level for handicapped type		3.20	2.500		620	62		682	775	
	2840 Vandal resistant type	↓	4	2	↓	267	49		316	365	
	3300 Vitreous china										
	3340 7" back	1 Plum	4	2	Ea.	225	49		274	320	
	3940 For vandal-resistant bottom plate, add					36			36	40	
	3960 For freeze-proof valve system, add	1 Plum	2	4		210	99		309	380	
	3980 For rough-in, supply and waste, add	"	2.21	3.620	↓	38.90	89		127.90	175	
	4000 Wall mounted, semi-recessed										
	4200 Poly-marble, single bubbler	1 Plum	4	2	Ea.	339	49		388	445	
	4300 Fountain and cuspidor combination		2	4		600	99		699	805	
	4600 Stainless steel, satin finish, single bubbler		4	2		300	49		349	405	
	4900 Vitreous china, single bubbler		4	2		275	49		324	375	
	5980 For rough-in, supply and waste, add	↓	1.83	4.370		38.90	110		148.90	205	
	6000 Wall mounted, fully recessed										

152 | Plumbing Fixtures

152 100 | Fixtures

			Crew	Daily Output	Man-Hours	Unit	Mat.	Labor	Equip.	Total	Total Incl O&P	
116	6400	Poly-marble, single bubbler	1 Plum	4	2	Ea.	435	49		484	550	116
	6440	For water glass filler, add					75			75	83	
	6800	Stainless steel, single bubbler	1 Plum	4	2		354	49		403	465	
	6900	Fountain and cuspidor combination		2	4		795	99		894	1,025	
	7560	For freeze-proof valve system, add		2	4		175	99		274	340	
	7580	For rough-in, supply and waste, add		1.83	4.370		38.90	110		148.90	205	
	7600	Floor mounted, pedestal type										
	7700	Aluminum, architectural style, C.I. base	1 Plum	2	4	Ea.	309	99		408	485	
	7780	Wheelchair handicap unit		2	4		625	99		724	835	
	8000	Bronze, architectural style		2	4		685	99		784	900	
	8040	Enameled steel cylindrical column style		2	4		650	99		749	860	
	8200	Precast stone/concrete, cylindrical column		1	8		410	200		610	745	
	8240	Wheelchair handicap unit		1	8		600	200		800	955	
	8400	Stainless steel, architectural style		2	4		690	99		789	905	
	8600	Enameled iron, heavy duty service, 2 bubblers		2	4		620	99		719	830	
	8660	4 bubblers		2	4		675	99		774	890	
	8880	For freeze-proof valve system, add		2	4		174	99		273	340	
	8900	For rough-in, supply and waste, add		1.83	4.370		38.90	110		148.90	205	
	9100	Deck mounted										
	9500	Stainless steel, circular receptor	1 Plum	4	2	Ea.	198	49		247	290	
	9540	14" x 9" receptor		4	2		144	49		193	230	
	9580	25" x 17" deep receptor, with water glass filler		3	2.670		126	66		192	235	
	9760	White enameled steel, 14" x 9" receptor		4	2		117	49		166	200	
	9860	White enameled cast iron, 24" x 16" receptor		3	2.670		141	66		207	255	
	9980	For rough-in, supply and waste, add		1.83	4.370		38.90	110		148.90	205	
120	0010	**HOT WATER DISPENSERS**										120
	0160	Commercial, 100 cup, 11.3 amp	1 Plum	14	.571	Ea.	232	14.10		246.10	275	
	3180	Household, 60 cup	"	14	.571	"	136	14.10		150.10	170	
124	0010	**INDUSTRIAL SAFETY FIXTURES** Rough-in not included										124
	1000	Eye wash fountain										
	1400	Plastic bowl, pedestal mounted	Q-1	4	4	Ea.	132	89		221	275	
	1600	Unmounted		4	4		84	89		173	225	
	1800	Wall mounted		4	4		90	89		179	230	
	2000	Stainless steel, pedestal mounted		4	4		185	89		274	335	
	2200	Unmounted		4	4		111	89		200	255	
	2400	Wall mounted		4	4		120	89		209	265	
	3000	Eye wash, portable, self-contained					260			260	285	
	4000	Eye and face wash, combination fountain										
	4200	Stainless steel, pedestal mounted	Q-1	4	4	Ea.	215	89		304	370	
	4400	Unmounted		4	4		145	89		234	290	
	4600	Wall mounted		4	4		155	89		244	300	
	5000	Shower, single head, drench, ball valve, pull, freestanding		4	4		165	89		254	315	
	5200	Horizontal or vertical supply		4	4		145	89		234	290	
	6000	Multi-nozzle, eye/face wash combination		4	4		340	89		429	505	
	6400	Multi-nozzle, 12 spray, shower only		4	4		675	89		764	875	
	6600	For freeze-proof, add		6	2.670		320	59		379	440	
	8000	Walk-thru decontamination with eye-face wash		2	8		1,480	180		1,660	1,900	
	8200	For freeze proof, add		4	4		320	89		409	485	
128	0010	**INTERCEPTORS**										128
	0150	Grease, cast iron, 4 GPM, 8 lb. fat capacity	1 Plum	4	2	Ea.	170	49		219	260	
	0200	7 GPM, 14 lb. fat capacity		4	2		235	49		284	330	
	1000	10 GPM, 20 lb. fat capacity		4	2		280	49		329	380	
	1040	15 GPM, 30 lb. fat capacity		4	2		410	49		459	525	
	1060	20 GPM, 40 lb. fat capacity		3	2.670		500	66		566	650	
	1080	25 GPM, 50 lb. fat capacity	Q-1	3.50	4.570		565	100		665	770	
	1100	35 GPM, 70 lb. fat capacity	"	3	5.330		700	120		820	945	

152 | Plumbing Fixtures

152 100 | Fixtures

		CREW	DAILY OUTPUT	MAN-HOURS	UNIT	MAT.	LABOR	EQUIP.	TOTAL	TOTAL INCL O&P	
128	1120	Fabricated steel, 50 GPM, 100 lb. fat capacity	Q-1	2	8	Ea.	1,490	180		1,670	1,900	128
	1140	75 GPM, 150 lb. fat capacity		2	8		1,645	180		1,825	2,075	
	1160	100 GPM, 200 lb. fat capacity		2	8		1,850	180		2,030	2,300	
	1180	150 GPM, 300 lb. fat capacity		2	8		2,055	180		2,235	2,525	
	1200	200 GPM, 400 lb. fat capacity		1.50	10.670		2,990	235		3,225	3,650	
	1220	250 GPM, 500 lb. fat capacity		1.30	12.310		3,640	275		3,915	4,400	
	1240	300 GPM, 600 lb. fat capacity		1	16		4,090	355		4,445	5,025	
	1260	400 GPM, 800 lb. fat capacity	Q-2	1.20	20		5,020	460		5,480	6,200	
	1280	500 GPM, 1000 lb. fat capacity	"	1	24		5,940	555		6,495	7,350	
	1560	For chemical add-port, add					40			40	44	
	1580	For seepage pan, add					5%					
	3000	Hair, cast iron, 1-¼" and 1-½" pipe connection	1 Plum	8	1		64	25		89	105	
	3100	For chrome-plated cast iron, add					48			48	53	
	3200	For polished bronze, add					55			55	61	
	3300	For chrome plated bronze, add					69			69	76	
	4000	Oil, fabricated steel, 10 GPM, 2" pipe size	1 Plum	4	2		360	49		409	470	
	4100	15 GPM, 2" or 3" pipe size		4	2		495	49		544	620	
	4120	20 GPM, 2" or 3" pipe size		3	2.670		600	66		666	760	
	4140	25 GPM, 2" or 3" pipe size	Q-1	3.50	4.570		645	100		745	860	
	4160	35 GPM, 2", 3", or 4" pipe size		3	5.330		790	120		910	1,050	
	4180	50 GPM, 2", 3", or 4" pipe size		2	8		1,060	180		1,240	1,425	
	4200	75 GPM, 3" pipe size		2	8		1,710	180		1,890	2,150	
	4220	100 GPM, 3" pipe size		2	8		1,855	180		2,035	2,300	
	4240	150 GPM, 4" pipe size		2	8		2,295	180		2,475	2,800	
	4260	200 GPM, 4" pipe size		1.50	10.670		3,240	235		3,475	3,925	
	4280	250 GPM, 5" pipe size		1.30	12.310		3,760	275		4,035	4,550	
	4300	300 GPM, 5" pipe size		1	16		4,255	355		4,610	5,200	
	4320	400 GPM, 6" pipe size	Q-2	1.20	20		5,460	460		5,920	6,700	
	4340	500 GPM, 6" pipe size	"	1	24		6,900	555		7,455	8,400	
	6000	Solids, precious metals recovery, C.I., 1-¼" to 2" pipe	1 Plum	4	2		97	49		146	180	
	6100	Dental Lab., large, C.I., 1-½" to 2" pipe	"	3	2.670		445	66		511	585	
132	0010	**LABORATORY EQUIPMENT,** Corrosion resistant										132
	7000	Tanks, covers included										
	7400	Halar E-CTFE, FRP casing, high chemical resistance										
	7410	Temperature range 110°F to 275°F										
	7420	7 gallon, 12" x 12" x 12"	Q-1	20	.800	Ea.	420	17.80		437.80	490	
	7430	15 gallon, 18" x 12" x 18"		17	.941		550	21		571	635	
	7440	30 gallon, 24" x 18" x 18"		12	1.330		970	30		1,000	1,100	
	7500	Polyethylene, neutralization & dilution										
	7510	Continuous use to 180°F, includes 4" inlet & outlet										
	7550	55 gallon, upright cylinder	Q-1	5	3.200	Ea.	695	71		766	870	
	7570	100 gallon, upright cylinder		4	4		840	89		929	1,050	
	7590	250 gallon, upright cylinder		3	5.330		1,440	120		1,560	1,750	
	7650	Polyethylene with ultra violet light inhibitor										
	7660	Continuous use to 180°F, includes saddle & fittings										
	7680	55 gallon 24" O.D. x 36" long	Q-1	10	1.600	Ea.	500	36		536	605	
	7700	200 gallon 33" O.D. x 65" long		6	2.670		825	59		884	995	
	7720	300 gallon 38" O.D. x 72" long		5	3.200		1,260	71		1,331	1,500	
	7740	500 gallon 48" O.D. x 75" long		3	5.330		2,220	120		2,340	2,625	
	7800	Polyethylene liner, fiberglass casing										
	7810	Continuous service to 220°F										
	7830	2 gallon, 8" x 8" x 8"	Q-1	20	.800	Ea.	129	17.80		146.80	170	
	7850	7 gallon, 12" x 12" x 12"		20	.800		168	17.80		185.80	210	
	7870	15 gallon, 24" x 12" x 12"		17	.941		276	21		297	335	
	8010	30 gallon, 24" x 18" x 18"		12	1.330		402	30		432	485	
	8070	45 gallon, 24" x 18" x 24"		10	1.600		470	36		506	570	
	8080	90 gallon, 36" x 24" x 24"		8	2		720	44		764	860	

152 | Plumbing Fixtures

152 100 | Fixtures

			Crew	Daily Output	Man-Hours	Unit	Mat.	Labor	Equip.	Total	Total Incl O&P	
132	8150	Polyethylene, heavy duty walls										132
	8160	Continuous service to 180°F										
	8180	5 gallon, 11" I.D. x 15" deep	Q-1	20	.800	Ea.	32	17.80		49.80	62	
	8210	15 gallon, 14" I.D. x 27" deep		17	.941		60	21		81	97	
	8230	55 gallon, 22" I.D. x 36" deep		10	1.600		129	36		165	195	
	8250	100 gallon 28" I.D. x 42" deep		8	2		263	44		307	355	
	8270	200 gallon 36" I.D. x 48" deep		6	2.670		388	59		447	515	
	8290	360 gallon 48" I.D. x 48" deep		5	3.200		628	71		699	795	
	8350	With fiberglass casing										
	8420	55 gallon tank size	Q-1	20	.800	Ea.	445	17.80		462.80	515	
	8440	100 gallon tank size		16	1		690	22		712	790	
	8460	200 gallon tank size		12	1.330		1,015	30		1,045	1,150	
	8480	360 gallon tank size		10	1.600		1,500	36		1,536	1,700	
136	0010	**LAVATORIES** With trim, white unless noted otherwise										136
	0500	Vanity top, porcelain enamel on cast iron										
	0600	20" x 18"	Q-1	6.40	2.500	Ea.	132	56		188	230	
	0640	26" x 18" oval		6.40	2.500		164	56		220	265	
	0680	19" x 16" oval		6.40	2.500		125	56		181	220	
	0720	18" round		6.40	2.500		122	56		178	215	
	0760	20" x 12" triangular bowl		6.40	2.500		132	56		188	230	
	0860	For color, add					25%					
	1000	Cultured marble, 19" x 17", single bowl	Q-1	6.40	2.500		85	56		141	175	
	1040	25" x 19", single bowl		6.40	2.500		100	56		156	190	
	1080	31" x 19", single bowl		6.40	2.500		110	56		166	205	
	1120	25" x 22", single bowl		6.40	2.500		107	56		163	200	
	1160	37" x 22", single bowl		6.40	2.500		129	56		185	225	
	1200	49" x 22", single bowl		6.40	2.500		157	56		213	255	
	1580	For color, same price										
	1900	Stainless steel, self-rimming, 25" x 22", single bowl, ledge	Q-1	6.40	2.500	Ea.	161	56		217	260	
	1960	17" x 22", single bowl		6.40	2.500		84	56		140	175	
	2040	18-¾" round		6.40	2.500		236	56		292	340	
	2600	Steel, enameled, 20" x 17", single bowl		5.80	2.760		78	61		139	175	
	2660	19" round		5.80	2.760		76	61		137	175	
	2720	18" round		5.80	2.760		70	61		131	170	
	2860	For color, add					10%					
	2900	Vitreous china, 20" x 16", single bowl	Q-1	5.40	2.960		170	66		236	285	
	2960	20" x 17", single bowl		5.40	2.960		135	66		201	245	
	3020	19" round, single bowl		5.40	2.960		132	66		198	245	
	3080	19" x 16", single bowl		5.40	2.960		140	66		206	250	
	3140	17" x 14", single bowl		5.40	2.960		132	66		198	245	
	3200	22" x 13", single bowl		5.40	2.960		146	66		212	260	
	3560	For color, add					20%					
	3580	Rough-in, supply, waste and vent for all above lavatories	Q-1	2.30	6.960		76.95	155		231.95	315	
	4000	Wall hung										
	4040	Porcelain enamel on cast iron, 16" x 14", single bowl	Q-1	8	2	Ea.	213	44		257	300	
	4060	18" x 15" single bowl		8	2		223	44		267	310	
	4120	19" x 17", single bowl		8	2		186	44		230	270	
	4180	20" x 18", single bowl		8	2		105	44		149	180	
	4240	22" x 19", single bowl		8	2		215	44		259	300	
	4580	For color, add					30%					
	6000	Vitreous china, 18" x 15", single bowl with backsplash	Q-1	7	2.290		151	51		202	240	
	6060	19" x 17", single bowl		7	2.290		100	51		151	185	
	6120	24" x 20", single bowl		7	2.290		204	51		255	300	
	6180	19" x 19", corner style		8	2		290	44		334	385	
	6210	28" x 21", wheelchair type		7	2.290		229	51		280	325	
	6500	For color, add					30%					
	6700	Hospital type, without trim (see 151-141)										

152 | Plumbing Fixtures

152 100 | Fixtures

			Daily Output	Man-Hours	Unit	Bare Costs Mat.	Bare Costs Labor	Bare Costs Equip.	Bare Costs Total	Total Incl O&P	
136	6710	20" x 18", contoured splash shield	Q-1	8	2	Ea.	137	44		181	215	136
	6720	26" x 20", patient, corner, side deck & back		7	2.290		345	51		396	455	
	6730	28" x 20", surgeon, side decks		8	2		419	44		463	525	
	6740	28" x 22", surgeon scrub-up, deep bowl		8	2		540	44		584	660	
	6750	20" x 27", patient, wheelchair		7	2.290		290	51		341	395	
	6760	30" x 22", all purpose		7	2.290		505	51		556	630	
	6770	30" x 22", plaster work		7	2.290		505	51		556	630	
	6820	20" x 24" clinic service, liquid/solid waste		6	2.670		620	59		679	770	
	6960	Rough-in, supply, waste and vent for above lavatories		1.66	9.640		126.45	215		341.45	455	
140	0010	**LAUNDRY SINKS** With trim										140
	0020	Porcelain enamel on cast iron, black iron frame										
	0050	24" x 20", single compartment	Q-1	6	2.670	Ea.	285	59		344	400	
	0100	24" x 23", single compartment		6	2.670		310	59		369	430	
	0200	48" x 20", double compartment		5	3.200		465	71		536	615	
	2000	Molded stone, on wall hanger or legs										
	2020	22" x 21", single compartment	Q-1	6	2.670	Ea.	137	59		196	240	
	2100	45" x 21", double compartment	"	5	3.200	"	218	71		289	345	
	3000	Plastic, on wall hanger or legs										
	3020	18" x 23", single compartment	Q-1	6.50	2.460	Ea.	100	55		155	190	
	3100	20" x 24", single compartment		6.50	2.460		120	55		175	215	
	3200	36" x 23", double compartment		5.50	2.910		135	65		200	245	
	3300	40" x 24", double compartment		5.50	2.910		187	65		252	300	
	5000	Stainless steel, counter top, 22" x 17" single compartment		6	2.670		222	59		281	330	
	5100	19" x 22", single compartment		6	2.670		247	59		306	360	
	5200	33" x 22", double compartment		5	3.200		259	71		330	390	
	9600	Rough-in, supply, waste and vent, for all laundry sinks		2.14	7.480		88.38	165		253.38	345	
144	0010	**PRISON/INSTITUTION FIXTURES**, Stainless steel										144
	1000	Lavatory, wall hung, push button filler valve										
	1100	Rectangular bowl	Q-1	8	2	Ea.	500	44		544	615	
	1200	Oval bowl		8	2		495	44		539	610	
	1240	Oval bowl, corner mount		8	2		615	44		659	740	
	1300	For lavatory rough-in, supply, waste and vent		1.50	10.670		71.54	235		306.54	430	
	1700	Service sink, with soap dish										
	1740	24" x 19" size	Q-1	3	5.330	Ea.	1,230	120		1,350	1,525	
	1790	For sink rough-in, supply, waste and vent	"	.89	17.980	"		400		400	595	
	1800	Shower cabinet, unitized										
	1840	36" x 36" x 88"	Q-1	2.20	7.270	Ea.	3,510	160		3,670	4,100	
	1900	Shower package for built-in										
	1940	Hot & cold valves, recessed soap dish	Q-1	6	2.670	Ea.	510	59		569	650	
	2000	Urinal, back supply and flush										
	2200	Wall hung	Q-1	4	4	Ea.	1,890	89		1,979	2,200	
	2240	Stall		2.50	6.400		2,265	140		2,405	2,700	
	2300	For urinal rough-in, supply, waste and vent		1.49	10.740		88.97	240		328.97	450	
	3000	Water closet, integral seat, back supply and flush										
	3300	Wall hung, wall outlet	Q-1	5.80	2.760	Ea.	1,730	61		1,791	2,000	
	3400	Floor mount, wall outlet		5.80	2.760		1,900	61		1,961	2,175	
	3440	Floor mount, floor outlet		5.80	2.760		1,980	61		2,041	2,275	
	3480	For recessed tissue holder, add					156			156	170	
	3500	For water closet rough-in, supply, waste and vent	Q-1	1.19	13.450		88.43	300		388.43	540	
	5000	Water closet and lavatory units, push button filler valves,										
	5010	soap & paper holders, seat										
	5300	Wall hung	Q-1	5	3.200	Ea.	1,790	71		1,861	2,075	
	5400	Floor mount		5	3.200		1,670	71		1,741	1,950	
	6300	For unit rough-in, supply, waste and vent		1	16		100.96	355		455.96	640	
148	0010	**SHOWERS**										148
	1500	Stall, with door and trim										

152 | Plumbing Fixtures

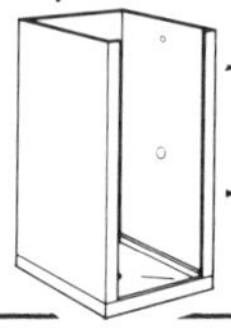

152 100 | Fixtures

			Crew	Daily Output	Man-Hours	Unit	Mat.	Labor	Equip.	Total	Total Incl O&P
148	1510	Baked enamel, molded stone receptor, 30" square	Q-1	2	8	Ea.	300	180		480	595	148
	1520	32" square		2	8		316	180		496	610
	1540	Terrazzo receptor, 32" square		2	8		515	180		695	830
	1560	36" square		1.80	8.890		555	200		755	905
	1580	36" corner angle		1.80	8.890		550	200		750	900
	1600	For color add					10%				
	3000	Fiberglass, one piece, with 3 walls, 32" x 32" square	Q-1	2.40	6.670		275	150		425	520
	3100	36" x 36" square	"	2.40	6.670		307	150		457	560
	3200	Handicap, 1-½" O.D. grab bars, nonskid floor									
	3210	48" x 34-½" x 72" corner seat	Q-1	2.40	6.670	Ea.	765	150		915	1,050
	3220	60" x 34-½" x 72" corner seat		2	8		795	180		975	1,150
	3230	36" x 34-½" x 72" fold up seat		2.20	7.270		1,170	160		1,330	1,525
	3250	64" x 65-¾" x 81-½" fold. seat, whlchr.		1.80	8.890		2,800	200		3,000	3,375
	4000	Polypropylene, with molded-stone floor, 30" x 30"		2	8		260	180		440	550
	4100	32" x 32"		2	8		266	180		446	555
	4960	Rough-in, supply, waste and vent for above showers		2.05	7.800		65.17	175		240.17	330
	5000	Built-in, head, arm, 4 GPM valve	1 Plum	4	2		89	49		138	170
	5200	Head, arm, by-pass, integral stops, handles		3.60	2.220		120	55		175	215
	5500	Head, water economizer, 3.0 GPM		24	.333		44.65	8.25		52.90	61
	5800	Mixing valve, Built-in		6	1.330		77	33		110	135
	5900	Exposed		6	1.330		295	33		328	375
	5950	Module, handicap, SS panel, fixed & hand held head, control									
	5960	valves, grab bar, curtain & rod, folding seat	1 Plum	4	2	Ea.	2,230	49		2,279	2,525
	6000	Group, w/valve, rough-in and rigging not included									
	6800	Column, 6 heads, no receptors, less partitions	Q-1	3	5.330	Ea.	1,450	120		1,570	1,775
	6900	With enameled partitions		1	16		2,725	355		3,080	3,525
	7600	5 heads, no receptors, less partitions		3	5.330		1,160	120		1,280	1,450
	7620	4 heads (1 handicap) no receptors, less partitions		3	5.330		1,750	120		1,870	2,100
	7700	With enameled partitions		1	16		2,625	355		2,980	3,425
	8000	Corner, 2 heads, no receptors, less partitions		4	4		1,072	89		1,161	1,300
	8100	With partitions		2	8		1,320	180		1,500	1,725
152	0010	**SINKS** With faucets and drain										152
	0050	Corrosion resistant									
	1000	Polyethylene, single sink, bench mounted, with									
	1020	plug & waste fitting with 1-½" straight threads									
	1030	2 drainboards, backnut & strainer									
	1050	18-½" x 15-½" x 12-½" sink, 54" x 24" O.D.	Q-1	3	5.330	Ea.	725	120		845	975
	1100	Single drainboard, backnut & strainer									
	1130	18-½" x 15-½" x 12-½" sink, 47" x 24" O.D.	Q-1	3	5.330	Ea.	670	120		790	915
	1150	18-½" x 15-½" x 12-½" sink, 70" x 24" O.D.	"	3	5.330	"	775	120		895	1,025
	1290	Flanged 1-¼" wide, rectangular with strainer									
	1300	plug & waste fitting, 1-½" straight threads									
	1320	12" x 12" x 8" sink, 14-½" x 14-½" O.D.	Q-1	4	4	Ea.	190	89		279	340
	1340	16" x 16" x 8" sink, 18-½" x 18-½" O.D.		4	4		220	89		309	375
	1360	21" x 18" x 10" sink, 23-½" x 20-½" O.D.		4	4		265	89		354	425
	1490	For rough-in, supply, waste & vent, add		2.02	7.920		79.21	175		254.21	350
	1600	Polypropylene									
	1620	Cup sink, oval, integral strainers									
	1640	6" x 3" I.D., 7" x 4" O.D.	Q-1	6	2.670	Ea.	94	59		153	190
	1660	9" x 3" I.D., 10" x 4-½" O.D.	"	6	2.670	"	106	59		165	205
	1720	Overflow standpipe									
	1740	1-½" diam. x 11" long				Ea.	27			27	30
	1980	For rough-in, supply, waste & vent, add	Q-1	1.70	9.410		58.21	210		268.21	375
	2000	Kitchen, counter top, P.E. on C.I., 24" x 21" single bowl		5.60	2.860		168	64		232	280
	2100	30" x 21" single bowl		5.60	2.860		191	64		255	305
	2200	32" x 21" double bowl		4.80	3.330		216	74		290	350
	2300	42" x 21" double bowl		4.80	3.330		336	74		410	480

152 | Plumbing Fixtures

152 100 | Fixtures

		Crew	Daily Output	Man-Hours	Unit	Mat.	Labor	Equip.	Total	Total Incl O&P	
152	3000 Stainless steel, self rimming, 19" x 18" single bowl	Q-1	5.60	2.860	Ea.	225	64		289	340	152
	3100 25" x 22" single bowl		5.60	2.860		249	64		313	370	
	3200 33" x 22" double bowl		4.80	3.330		350	74		424	495	
	3300 43" x 22" double bowl		4.80	3.330		385	74		459	535	
	3400 44" x 22" triple bowl		4.40	3.640		347	81		428	500	
	3500 44" x 24" corner double bowl		4.80	3.330		255	74		329	390	
	4000 Steel, enameled, with ledge, 24" x 21" single bowl		5.60	2.860		102	64		166	205	
	4100 32" x 21" double bowl		4.80	3.330		123	74		197	245	
	4960 For color sinks except stainless steel, add					10%					
	4980 For rough-in, supply, waste and vent, counter top sinks	Q-1	2.14	7.480		88.38	165		253.38	345	
	5000 Kitchen, raised deck, P.E. on C.I.										
	5100 32" x 21", dual level, double bowl	Q-1	2.60	6.150	Ea.	303	135		438	535	
	5200 42" x 21", double bowl & disposer well	"	2.20	7.270		420	160		580	700	
	5700 For color, add					20%					
	5790 For rough-in, supply, waste & vent, sinks	Q-1	1.85	8.650		88.38	190		278.38	380	
	6650 Service, floor, corner, P.E. on C.I., 28" x 28"	"	4.40	3.640		350	81		431	505	
	6750 Vinyl coated rim guard, add					46			46	51	
	6790 For rough-in, supply, waste & vent, floor service sinks	Q-1	1.64	9.760		135.73	215		350.73	470	
	7000 Service, wall, P.E. on C.I., roll rim, 22" x 18"		4	4		310	89		399	475	
	7100 24" x 20"		4	4		337	89		426	505	
	7600 For stainless steel rim guard, add					54			54	59	
	7800 For stainless steel rim guard, front only, add					28			28	31	
	8600 Vitreous china, 22" x 20"	Q-1	4	4		352	89		441	520	
	8960 For stainless steel rim guard, front or side, add					21			21	23	
	8980 For rough-in, supply, waste & vent, wall service sinks	Q-1	1.30	12.310		196.49	275		471.49	620	
160	0010 SINK WASTE TREATMENT System for commercial kitchens										160
	0100 includes clock timer, & fittings										
	0200 System less chemical, wall mounted cabinet	1 Plum	16	.500	Ea.	200	12.35		212.35	240	
	2000 Chemical, 1 gallon, add					33			33	36	
	2100 6 gallons, add					131			131	145	
	2200 15 gallons, add					296			296	325	
	2300 30 gallons, add					554			554	610	
	2400 55 gallons, add					948			948	1,050	
164	0010 TOILET SEATS										164
	0100 Molded composition, white										
	0150 Industrial, w/o cover, open front, regular bowl	1 Plum	24	.333	Ea.	15.45	8.25		23.70	29	
	0200 With self-sustaining hinge		24	.333		16.45	8.25		24.70	30	
	0220 With self-sustaining check hinge		24	.333		16.45	8.25		24.70	30	
	0240 Extra heavy, with check hinge		24	.333		22.40	8.25		30.65	37	
	0260 Elongated bowl, same price										
	0300 Junior size, w/o cover, open front										
	0320 Regular primary bowl, open front	1 Plum	24	.333	Ea.	22.55	8.25		30.80	37	
	0340 Regular baby bowl, open front, check hinge		24	.333		22.55	8.25		30.80	37	
	0380 Open back & front, w/o cover, reg. or elongated bowl		24	.333		23.40	8.25		31.65	38	
	0400 Residential										
	0420 Regular bowl, w/cover, closed front	1 Plum	24	.333	Ea.	23	8.25		31.25	38	
	0440 Open front	"	24	.333	"	23	8.25		31.25	38	
	0460 Elongated bowl, add					25%					
	0500 Self-raising hinge, w/o cover, open front										
	0520 Regular bowl	1 Plum	24	.333	Ea.	76	8.25		84.25	96	
	0540 Elongated bowl	"	24	.333	"	77.30	8.25		85.55	97	
	0600 Self-sustaining hinge, w/o cover, open front										
	0620 Regular bowl	1 Plum	24	.333	Ea.	76	8.25		84.25	96	
	0640 Elongated bowl	"	24	.333	"	77.30	8.25		85.55	97	
	0700 Molded wood, white, with cover										
	0720 Closed front, regular bowl, square back	1 Plum	24	.333	Ea.	6.80	8.25		15.05	19.70	
	0740 Extended back	"	24	.333	"	8.25	8.25		16.50	21	

152 | Plumbing Fixtures

152 100 | Fixtures

			CREW	DAILY OUTPUT	MAN-HOURS	UNIT	MAT.	LABOR	EQUIP.	TOTAL	TOTAL INCL O&P	
164	0780	Elongated bowl, square back	1 Plum	24	.333	Ea.	9.25	8.25		17.50	22	164
	0800	Open front, same price as closed front										
	0850	Decorator styles										
	0870	Cane top	1 Plum	24	.333	Ea.	11.45	8.25		19.70	25	
	0890	Vinyl top, patterned		24	.333		10.65	8.25		18.90	24	
	0900	Vinyl padded, plain colors, regular bowl		24	.333		10.65	8.25		18.90	24	
	0930	Elongated bowl		24	.333		17.20	8.25		25.45	31	
	1000	Solid plastic, white										
	1030	Industrial, w/o cover, open front, regular bowl	1 Plum	24	.333	Ea.	16.20	8.25		24.45	30	
	1080	Extra heavy, concealed check hinge		24	.333		22.55	8.25		30.80	37	
	1100	Self-sustaining hinge		24	.333		17.20	8.25		25.45	31	
	1150	Elongated bowl		24	.333		16.40	8.25		24.65	30	
	1170	Concealed check		24	.333		16.40	8.25		24.65	30	
	1190	Self-sustaining hinge, concealed check		24	.333		17.55	8.25		25.80	32	
	1220	Residential, with cover, closed front, regular bowl		24	.333		22	8.25		30.25	36	
	1240	Elongated bowl		24	.333		27.65	8.25		35.90	43	
	1260	Open front, regular bowl		24	.333		22	8.25		30.25	36	
	1280	Elongated bowl		24	.333		27.65	8.25		35.90	43	
168	0010	**URINALS**										168
	3000	Wall hung, vitreous china, with hanger & self-closing valve	Q-1	3	5.330	Ea.	318	120		438	525	
	3300	Rough-in, supply, waste & vent		2.83	5.650		66.02	125		191.02	260	
	5000	Stall type, vitreous china, includes valve		2.50	6.400		390	140		530	640	
	5100	3" seam cover, add		12	1.330		102	30		132	155	
	5200	6" seam cover, add		12	1.330		141	30		171	200	
	6980	Rough-in, supply, waste and vent		1.99	8.040		96.02	180		276.02	370	
172	0010	**WASH CENTER** Prefabricated, stainless steel, semirecessed										172
	0050	Lavatory, storage cabinet, mirror, light & switch, electric										
	0060	outlet, towel dispenser, waste receptacle & trim										
	0100	Foot water valve, cup & soap dispenser, 16" W x 54-¾" H	Q-1	8	2	Ea.	900	44		944	1,050	
	0200	Handicap, wrist blade handles, 17" W x 66-½" H		8	2		800	44		844	945	
	0220	20" W x 67-⅜" H		8	2		1,050	44		1,094	1,225	
	0300	Push button metering & thermostatic mixing valves										
	0320	Handicap 17" W x 27-½" H	Q-1	8	2	Ea.	880	44		924	1,025	
	0400	Rough-in, supply, waste and vent	"	2.10	7.620	"	50.04	170		220.04	305	
176	0010	**WASH FOUNTAINS** Rigging not included										176
	1900	Group, foot control										
	2000	Precast terrazzo, circular, 36" diam., 5 or 6 persons	Q-2	3	8	Ea.	1,130	185		1,315	1,525	
	2100	54" diameter for 8 or 10 persons		2.50	9.600		1,260	220		1,480	1,725	
	2400	Semi-circular, 36" diam. for 3 persons		3	8		1,040	185		1,225	1,425	
	2420	36" diam. for 3 persons in wheelchairs		3	8		1,685	185		1,870	2,125	
	2500	54" diam. for 4 or 5 persons		2.50	9.600		1,260	220		1,480	1,725	
	2520	54" diam. for 4 persons in wheelchairs		2.50	9.600		1,800	220		2,020	2,300	
	2700	Quarter circle (corner), 54" for 3 persons		3.50	6.860		1,225	160		1,385	1,575	
	2720	54" diam. for 3 persons in wheelchairs		3.50	6.860		1,475	160		1,635	1,850	
	3000	Stainless steel, circular, 36" diameter		3.50	6.860		1,255	160		1,415	1,625	
	3100	54" diameter		2.80	8.570		1,625	200		1,825	2,075	
	3400	Semi-circular, 36" diameter		3.50	6.860		1,090	160		1,250	1,425	
	3500	54" diameter		2.80	8.570		1,400	200		1,600	1,825	
	5000	Thermoplastic, pre-assembled, circular, 36" diameter		6	4		970	92		1,062	1,200	
	5100	54" diameter		4	6		1,125	140		1,265	1,450	
	5400	Semi-circular, 36" diameter		6	4		890	92		982	1,125	
	5600	54" diameter		4	6		1,085	140		1,225	1,400	
	5700	Rough-in, supply, waste and vent for above wash fountains	Q-1	1.82	8.790		106.29	195		301.29	405	
	6200	Duo for small washrooms, stainless steel		2	8		610	180		790	935	
	6400	Bowl with backsplash		2	8		705	180		885	1,050	
	6500	Rough-in, supply, waste & vent for duo fountains		2.02	7.920		52.57	175		227.57	320	

152 | Plumbing Fixtures

152 100 | Fixtures

				DAILY	MAN-			BARE COSTS			TOTAL	
			CREW	OUTPUT	HOURS	UNIT	MAT.	LABOR	EQUIP.	TOTAL	INCL O&P	
180	0010	**WATER CLOSETS**										180
	0020	For seats, see 152-164										
	0150	Tank type, vitreous china, incl. seat, supply pipe w/stop [B8.1 -470]										
	0200	Wall hung, one piece	Q-1	5.30	3.020	Ea.	495	67		562	645	
	0400	Two piece, close coupled [C8.1 -401]		5.30	3.020		339	67		406	470	
	0960	For rough-in, supply, waste, vent and carrier		2.60	6.150		137.90	135		272.90	355	
	1000	Floor mounted, one piece		5.30	3.020		418	67		485	560	
	1020	One piece, low profile		5.30	3.020		666	67		733	830	
	1050	One piece combination		5.30	3.020		645	67		712	810	
	1100	Two piece, close coupled, water saver		5.30	3.020		138	67		205	250	
	1150	With wall outlet		5.30	3.020		240	67		307	365	
	1200	With 18" high bowl		5.30	3.020		225	67		292	345	
	1960	For color, add					30%					
	1980	For rough-in, supply, waste and vent	Q-1	1.94	8.250		89.18	185		274.18	370	
	3000	Bowl only, with flush valve, seat										
	3100	Wall hung	Q-1	5.80	2.760	Ea.	260	61		321	375	
	3150	Hospital type, slotted rim for bed pan										
	3160	Elongated bowl	Q-1	5.80	2.760	Ea.	320	61		381	445	
	3200	For rough-in, supply, waste and vent, single WC		2.05	7.800		147.52	175		322.52	420	
	3300	Floor mounted		5.80	2.760		263	61		324	380	
	3350	With wall outlet		5.80	2.760		300	61		361	420	
	3360	Hospital type, slotted rim for bed pan										
	3370	Elongated bowl	Q-1	5	3.200	Ea.	265	71		336	395	
	3380	Elongated bowl, 18" high		5	3.200		296	71		367	430	
	3400	For rough-in, supply, waste and vent, single WC		1.80	8.890		98.80	200		298.80	400	
	3500	Gang side by side carrier system, rough-in, supply, waste & vent										
	3510	For single hook-up [B8.1 -510]	Q-1	1.97	8.120	Ea.	189.26	180		369.26	475	
	3520	For each additional hook-up, add	"	2.14	7.480	"	172.84	165		337.84	435	
	3550	Gang back to back carrier system, rough-in, supply, waste & vent										
	3560	For pair hook-up	Q-1	1.76	9.090	Pr.	281.93	200		481.93	610	
	3570	For each additional pair hook-up, add	"	1.81	8.840	"	265.57	195		460.57	585	
	4000	Water conserving systems										
	4100	2-½ gallon flush	Q-1	5.40	2.960	Ea.	220	66		286	340	
	4900	1 gallon flush		5.40	2.960		275	66		341	400	
	4980	For rough-in, supply, waste and vent		1.94	8.250		89.18	185		274.18	370	
	5100	2 quart flush		4.60	3.480		545	77		622	715	
	5200	For remote valve, add		24	.667		96	14.80		110.80	130	
	5300	For residential air compressor		6	2.670		610	59		669	760	
	5400	For light industrial air compressor		4	4		800	89		889	1,000	
	5500	For heavy duty industrial air compressor		1	16		1,460	355		1,815	2,125	
	5600	For dual compressor alternator		20	.800		235	17.80		252.80	285	
184	0010	**WATER FILTERS** Purification and treatment										184
	1000	Cartridge style, under sink, dirt and rust type	1 Plum	12	.667	Ea.	36	16.45		52.45	64	
	1200	Replacement cartridge		32	.250		4.03	6.20		10.23	13.60	
	1600	Taste and odor type		12	.667		43	16.45		59.45	72	
	1700	Replacement cartridge		32	.250		9.80	6.20		16	19.95	
	3000	Household unit, complete dwelling, 3 GPM		4	2		325	49		374	430	
	3100	Replacement cartridge		20	.400		13.15	9.90		23.05	29	
	3400	4 GPM		4	2		490	49		539	610	
	3600	Replacement cartridge		20	.400		19.25	9.90		29.15	36	
	4300	Oxidizing, removes iron, sulphur, manganese										
	4400	5 GPM	1 Plum	1	8	Ea.	375	200		575	705	
	5200	Neutralizing acid water										
	5400	5 GPM	1 Plum	1	8	Ea.	310	200		510	635	
	6200	Sediment, removal of suspended particles										
	6400	5 GPM	1 Plum	1	8	Ea.	300	200		500	625	
	7200	Carbon filter, to remove taste & odor										

152 100 | Fixtures

			CREW	DAILY OUTPUT	MAN-HOURS	UNIT	BARE COSTS MAT.	BARE COSTS LABOR	BARE COSTS EQUIP.	BARE COSTS TOTAL	TOTAL INCL O&P	
184	7400	5 GPM	1 Plum	1	8	Ea.	350	200		550	680	184
	8000	Commercial, fully automatic or push button automatic										
	8200	Iron removal, 660 GPH, 1″ pipe size	Q-1	1.50	10.670	Ea.	960	235		1,195	1,400	
	8240	1500 GPH, 1-¼″ pipe size		1	16		1,450	355		1,805	2,125	
	8280	2340 GPH, 1-½″ pipe size		.80	20		2,075	445		2,520	2,950	
	8320	3420 GPH, 2″ pipe size		.60	26.670		2,990	595		3,585	4,175	
	8360	4620 GPH, 2-½″ pipe size		.50	32		4,340	710		5,050	5,825	
	8500	Neutralizer for acid water, 780 GPH, 1″ pipe size		1.50	10.670		965	235		1,200	1,425	
	8540	1140 GPH, 1″ pipe size		1	16		1,130	355		1,485	1,775	
	8580	1740 GPH, 1-¼″ pipe size		.80	20		1,660	445		2,105	2,475	
	8620	2520 GPH, 2″ pipe size		.60	26.670		2,430	595		3,025	3,550	
	8660	3480 GPH, 2-½″ pipe size		.50	32		3,480	710		4,190	4,875	
	8800	Sediment removal, 780 GPH, 1″ pipe size		1.50	10.670		935	235		1,170	1,375	
	8840	1140 GPH, 1-¼″ pipe size		1	16		1,135	355		1,490	1,775	
	8880	1740 GPH, 1-½″ pipe size		.80	20		1,600	445		2,045	2,425	
	8920	2520 GPH, 2″ pipe size		3,400	.005		2,345	.10		2,345	2,575	
	8960	3480 GPH, 2-½″ pipe size		.50	32		3,360	710		4,070	4,750	
	9200	Taste and odor removal, 660 GPH, 1″ pipe size		1.50	10.670		920	235		1,155	1,375	
	9240	1500 GPH, 1-¼″ pipe size		1	16		1,660	355		2,015	2,350	
	9280	2340 GPH, 1-½″ pipe size		.80	20		2,430	445		2,875	3,325	
	9320	3420 GPH, 2″ pipe size		.60	26.670		3,415	595		4,010	4,625	
	9360	4620 GPH, 2-½″ pipe size	↓	.50	32	↓	4,735	710		5,445	6,275	

152 400 | Pumps

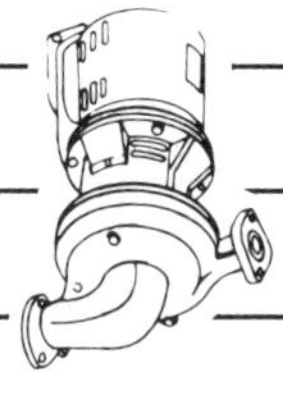

			CREW	DAILY OUTPUT	MAN-HOURS	UNIT	BARE COSTS MAT.	BARE COSTS LABOR	BARE COSTS EQUIP.	BARE COSTS TOTAL	TOTAL INCL O&P	
401	0010	**PUMPS** See also Division 154-145										401
410	0010	**PUMPS, CIRCULATING** Heated or chilled water application										410
	0600	Bronze, sweat connections, 1/40 HP, in line										
	0640	¾″ size	Q-1	16	1	Ea.	86	22		108	130	
	1000	Flange connection, ¾″ to 1-½″ size										
	1040	1/12 HP	Q-1	6	2.670	Ea.	209	59		268	320	
	1060	⅛ HP		6	2.670		350	59		409	475	
	1100	⅓ HP		6	2.670		385	59		444	510	
	1140	2″ size, ⅙ HP		5	3.200		440	71		511	590	
	1180	2-½″ size, ¼ HP		5	3.200		685	71		756	860	
	1220	3″ size, ¼ HP		4	4		715	89		804	920	
	1260	⅓ HP		4	4		870	89		959	1,100	
	1300	½ HP		4	4		890	89		979	1,100	
	1340	¾ HP		4	4		975	89		1,064	1,200	
	1380	1 HP	↓	4	4	↓	1,560	89		1,649	1,850	
	2000	Cast iron, flange connection										
	2040	¾″ to 1-½″ size, in line, 1/12 HP	Q-1	6	2.670	Ea.	138	59		197	240	
	2060	⅛ HP		6	2.670		215	59		274	325	
	2100	⅓ HP		6	2.670		250	59		309	365	
	2140	2″ size, ⅙ HP		5	3.200		265	71		336	395	
	2180	2-½″ size, ¼ HP		5	3.200		380	71		451	525	
	2220	3″ size, ¼ HP		4	4		382	89		471	550	
	2260	⅓ HP		4	4		515	89		604	700	
	2300	½ HP		4	4		530	89		619	715	
	2340	¾ HP		4	4		615	89		704	810	
	2380	1 HP	↓	4	4		885	89		974	1,100	
	2600	For non-ferrous impeller, add				↓	3%					
	3000	High head, bronze impeller										
	3030	1-½″ size ½ HP	Q-1	5	3.200	Ea.	430	71		501	580	
	3040	1-½″ size ¾ HP		5	3.200		515	71		586	670	
	3050	2″ size 1 HP		4	4		625	89		714	820	
	3090	2″ size 1-½ HP	↓	4	4	↓	730	89		819	935	
	4000	Close coupled, end suction, bronze impeller										

152 | Plumbing Fixtures

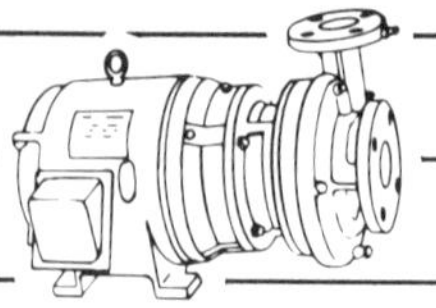

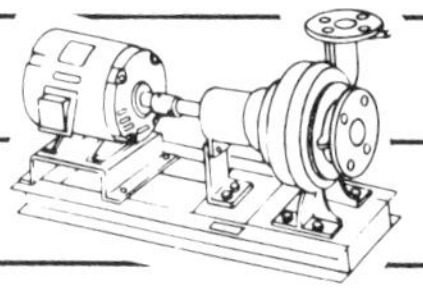

152 400 | Pumps

			CREW	DAILY OUTPUT	MAN-HOURS	UNIT	BARE COSTS MAT.	LABOR	EQUIP.	TOTAL	TOTAL INCL O&P	
410	4040	1-½" size, 1-½ HP, to 40 GPM	Q-1	3	5.330	Ea.	660	120		780	900	410
	4090	2" size, 2 HP, to 50 GPM		3	5.330		760	120		880	1,000	
	4100	2" size, 3 HP, to 90 GPM		2.30	6.960		1,200	155		1,355	1,550	
	4190	2-½" size, 3 HP, to 150 GPM		2	8		870	180		1,050	1,225	
	4300	3" size, 5 HP, to 225 GPM		1.80	8.890		1,015	200		1,215	1,400	
	4410	4" size, 5 HP, to 350 GPM		1.60	10		1,125	220		1,345	1,575	
	4420	4" size, 7-½ HP, to 350 GPM		1.60	10		1,370	220		1,590	1,825	
	4520	5" size, 10 HP, to 600 GPM	Q-2	1.70	14.120		1,710	325		2,035	2,375	
	4530	5" size, 15 HP, to 1000 GPM		1.70	14.120		2,010	325		2,335	2,700	
	4610	6" size, 20 HP, to 1350 GPM		1.50	16		2,370	370		2,740	3,150	
	4620	6" size, 25 HP, to 1550 GPM		1.50	16		2,660	370		3,030	3,475	
	5000	Base mounted, bronze impeller, coupling guard										
	5040	1-½" size, 1-½ HP, to 40 GPM	Q-1	2.30	6.960	Ea.	700	155		855	1,000	
	5090	2" size, 2 HP, to 50 GPM		2.30	6.960		765	155		920	1,075	
	5100	2" size, 3 HP, to 90 GPM		2	8		1,070	180		1,250	1,450	
	5190	2-½" size, 3 HP, to 150 GPM		1.80	8.890		830	200		1,030	1,200	
	5300	3" size, 5 HP, to 225 GPM		1.60	10		980	220		1,200	1,400	
	5410	4" size, 5 HP, to 350 GPM		1.50	10.670		1,000	235		1,235	1,450	
	5420	4" size, 7-½ HP, to 350 GPM		1.50	10.670		1,040	235		1,275	1,500	
	5520	5" size, 10 HP, to 600 GPM	Q-2	1.60	15		1,260	345		1,605	1,900	
	5530	5" size, 15 HP, to 1000 GPM		1.60	15		1,380	345		1,725	2,025	
	5610	6" size, 20 HP, to 1350 GPM		1.40	17.140		1,730	395		2,125	2,500	
	5620	6" size, 25 HP, to 1550 GPM		1.40	17.140		1,800	395		2,195	2,575	
	5800	The above pump capacities are based on 1800 RPM,										
	5810	at a 60 foot head. Increasing the RPM										
	5820	or decreasing the head will increase the GPM.										
430	0010	**PUMPS, GENERAL UTILITY** With motor, mounted on base										430
	0200	Multi-stage, horizontal split, for boiler feed applications										
	0300	Two stage, 3" discharge x 4" suction, 75 HP	Q-7	.30	107	Ea.	11,900	2,525		14,425	16,800	
	0340	Four stage, 3" discharge x 4" suction, 150 HP	"	.18	178	"	19,500	4,200		23,700	27,700	
	2000	Single stage										
	2060	End suction, 1"D. x 2"S., 3 HP	Q-1	.50	32	Ea.	2,900	710		3,610	4,250	
	2100	1-½"D. x 3"S., 10 HP	"	.40	40		3,100	890		3,990	4,725	
	2140	2"D. x 3"S., 15 HP	Q-2	.60	40		3,400	920		4,320	5,100	
	2180	3"D. x 4"S., 20 HP		.50	48		3,600	1,100		4,700	5,600	
	2220	4"D. x 6"S., 30 HP		.40	60		3,900	1,375		5,275	6,350	
	3000	Double suction, 2"D. x 2-½"S., 10 HP	Q-1	.30	53.330		4,000	1,175		5,175	6,150	
	3060	3"D. x 4"S., 15 HP	Q-2	.46	52.170		4,100	1,200		5,300	6,300	
	3100	4"D. x 5"S., 30 HP		.40	60		5,600	1,375		6,975	8,200	
	3140	5"D. x 6"S., 50 HP		.33	72.730		6,000	1,675		7,675	9,075	
	3180	6"D. x 8"S., 60 HP	Q-3	.30	107		6,750	2,525		9,275	11,200	
	8000	Vertical submerged, with non-submerged motor										
	8060	1"D., 3 HP	Q-1	.50	32	Ea.	4,200	710		4,910	5,675	
	8100	1-½"D., 10 HP	"	.30	53.330		4,400	1,175		5,575	6,600	
	8140	2"D., 15 HP	Q-2	.40	60		4,500	1,375		5,875	7,000	
	8180	3"D., 25 HP		.30	80		4,600	1,850		6,450	7,800	
	8220	4"D., 30 HP		.20	120		5,150	2,775		7,925	9,775	
440	0010	**PUMPS, GRINDER SYSTEM** Complete, includes check valve, tank,										440
	0020	standard controls. Excavation not included										
	0260	Simplex, 11 GPM at 40 PSIG, 60 gal. tank				Ea.	1,880			1,880	2,075	
	0300	For manway, 26" I.D., 18" high, add					360			360	395	
	0340	26" I.D., 36" high, add					480			480	530	
	0380	43" I.D., 4' high, add					595			595	655	
	0600	Simplex, 11 GPM at 40 PSIG, 120 gal. tank					2,410			2,410	2,650	
	0660	For manway 26" I.D., 18" high, add					305			305	335	
	0700	26" I.D., 36" high, add					435			435	480	
	0740	26" I.D., 4' high, add					556			556	610	

152 | Plumbing Fixtures

152 400 | Pumps

		CREW	DAILY OUTPUT	MAN-HOURS	UNIT	BARE COSTS MAT.	BARE COSTS LABOR	BARE COSTS EQUIP.	BARE COSTS TOTAL	TOTAL INCL O&P	
440	2000 Duplex, 22 GPM at 40 PSIG, 120 gal. tank				Ea.	3,960			3,960	4,350	440
	2060 For manway 43" I.D., 4' high, add					1,600			1,600	1,750	
	2400 For core only					1,460			1,460	1,600	
	2410 For salt water core, add				↓	134			134	145	
	2600 For addit. manway 5' to 10' high, 60 gal tank, per ft., add				V.L.F.	120			120	130	
	2620 For manways 5' to 10', 120 gal tank, add				Ea.	130			130	145	
450	0010 **PUMPS, PRESSURE BOOSTER SYSTEM** Constant speed										450
	0200 2 pump system with hydrocumulator										
	0300 100 GPM @ 50 psi	Q-2	.30	80	Ea.	9,930	1,850		11,780	13,700	
	0400 300 GPM @ 100 psi	"	.26	92.310	"	14,350	2,125		16,475	18,900	
	1000 3 pump system without hydrocumulator										
	1100 300 GPM @ 100 psi	Q-2	.23	104	Ea.	15,450	2,400		17,850	20,600	
	1200 1000 GPM @ 100 psi		.12	200		33,050	4,600		37,650	43,200	
	1300 5000 GPM @ 100 psi	↓	.08	300	↓	55,150	6,925		62,075	71,000	
460	0010 **PUMPS, PEDESTAL SUMP** With float control										460
	0400 Molded base, 42 GPM at 15' head, ⅓ HP	1 Plum	5	1.600	Ea.	96	40		136	165	
	0800 Iron base, 42 GPM at 15' head, ⅓ HP	"	5	1.600	"	116	40		156	185	
465	0010 **PUMPS, SEWAGE EJECTOR** With operating and level controls										465
	0100 Simplex, bitumastic coated steel tank, cover, 10' head, 230 volt										
	0600 Bronze pump										
	0640 70 GPM, ⅓ HP	Q-1	3	5.330	Ea.	1,310	120		1,430	1,625	
	0680 143 GPM, ½ HP	"	2.50	6.400	"	1,350	140		1,490	1,700	
	1040 Cast iron pump										
	1060 110 GPM, ½ HP	Q-1	2.50	6.400	Ea.	1,310	140		1,450	1,650	
	1080 173 GPM, ¾ HP		2	8		2,290	180		2,470	2,775	
	1100 218 GPM, 1 HP		1.60	10		2,315	220		2,535	2,875	
	1120 285 GPM, 2 HP		1.30	12.310		2,840	275		3,115	3,525	
	1140 325 GPM, 3 HP	Q-2	1.40	17.140		3,000	395		3,395	3,875	
	1160 370 GPM, 5 HP	"	1	24		3,395	555		3,950	4,550	
	1260 For fiberglass reinforced plastic tank, deduct				↓	10%					
	2000 Duplex, bitumastic coated steel tank, cover, 10' head, 230 volt										
	2640 Bronze pump										
	2660 70 GPM each pump, ⅓ HP	Q-1	2.50	6.400	Ea.	3,005	140		3,145	3,525	
	2700 143 GPM each pump, ½ HP	"	2	8	"	3,165	180		3,345	3,750	
	3040 Cast iron pump										
	3060 110 GPM each pump, ½ HP	Q-1	2	8	Ea.	2,930	180		3,110	3,475	
	3080 173 GPM each pump, ¾ HP	"	1.60	10		3,890	220		4,110	4,600	
	3100 218 GPM each pump, 1 HP	Q-2	1.20	20		4,150	460		4,610	5,250	
	3120 285 GPM each pump, 2 HP		1	24		4,530	555		5,085	5,800	
	3140 325 GPM each pump, 3 HP		.80	30		4,830	690		5,520	6,350	
	3160 370 GPM each pump, 5 HP	↓	.50	48		5,230	1,100		6,330	7,400	
	3260 For fiberglass reinforced plastic tank, deduct				↓	40%					
470	0010 **PUMPS, SPRINKLER** With check valve, steel base, 15' lift										470
	0100 37 GPM, ¾ HP	1 Plum	4	2	Ea.	335	49		384	440	
	0140 56 GPM, 1-½ HP	"	2	4		640	99		739	850	
	0180 68 GPM, 2 H.P.	Q-1	2	8		655	180		835	985	
480	0010 **PUMPS, SUBMERSIBLE** Dewatering										480
	0020 Sand & sludge, 20' head, starter & level control										
	0050 Cast iron										
	0100 2" discharge, 10 GPM	1 Plum	4	2	Ea.	360	49		409	470	
	0160 60 GPM		3	2.670		505	66		571	655	
	0200 120 GPM		2	4		965	99		1,064	1,200	
	1000 160 GPM	Q-1	1.50	10.670		1,955	235		2,190	2,500	
	1100 3" discharge, 220 GPM		1.20	13.330		2,390	295		2,685	3,075	
	1200 300 GPM		1	16		2,520	355		2,875	3,300	
	1360 4" discharge, 300 GPM	↓	.90	17.780		2,540	395		2,935	3,375	

152 | Plumbing Fixtures

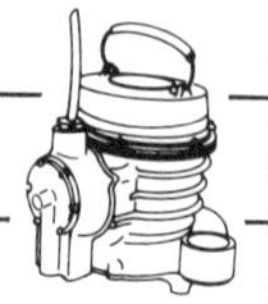

152 400 | Pumps

			CREW	DAILY OUTPUT	MAN-HOURS	UNIT	BARE COSTS MAT.	LABOR	EQUIP.	TOTAL	TOTAL INCL O&P
480	2000	Sewage & solids mixture, 8' head, automatic									480
	2020	Bronze, ½ HP									
	2100	75 GPM, 1-¼" or 1-½" NPT discharge	1 Plum	8	1	Ea.	350	25		375	420
	2140	120 GPM, 2" or 3" discharge	"	7	1.140	"	455	28		483	540
	2250	Cast iron									
	2300	122 GPM, ½ HP, 2" or 3" discharge	1 Plum	6	1.330	Ea.	325	33		358	405
	3000	Sewage & Solids mixture, high capacity, 20' head, non-automatic									
	3100	Cast iron, 3" flanged discharge									
	3140	40 GPM, ¾ HP	1 Plum	4	2	Ea.	1,200	49		1,249	1,400
	3160	100 GPM, 1 HP	"	3	2.670		1,290	66		1,356	1,525
	3180	175 GPM, 2 HP	Q-1	4.50	3.560		1,380	79		1,459	1,625
	3200	240 GPM, 3 HP		4	4		1,550	89		1,639	1,825
	3220	310 GPM, 5 HP		3	5.330		1,660	120		1,780	2,000
	3300	For tandem seal, add					120			120	130
	4000	Cast iron, 4" flanged discharge									
	4100	10 GPM, ¾ HP	1 Plum	4	2	Ea.	1,290	49		1,339	1,500
	4120	40 GPM, 1 HP	"	3	2.670		1,380	66		1,446	1,625
	4140	175 GPM, 2 HP	Q-1	4.50	3.560		1,465	79		1,544	1,725
	4160	275 GPM, 3 HP		4	4		1,640	89		1,729	1,925
	4180	450 GPM, 5 HP		3	5.330		1,755	120		1,875	2,100
	4240	For tandem seal, add					115			115	125
	5000	Sewage and solids, high head									
	5100	Bronze, 45 GPM at 25', ½ HP	1 Plum	6	1.330	Ea.	480	33		513	575
	5140	28 GPM at 50', 1 HP		5	1.600		585	40		625	700
	5160	25 GPM at 75', 1-½ HP		4	2		960	49		1,009	1,125
	5180	18 GPM at 100', 1-½ HP		4	2		960	49		1,009	1,125
	5500	Cast iron, 45 GPM at 25', ½ HP		6	1.330		390	33		423	480
	5540	28 GPM at 50', 1 HP		5	1.600		795	40		835	935
	5560	25 GPM at 75', 1-½ HP		4	2		860	49		909	1,025
	7000	Sump pump, 10' head, automatic									
	7100	Bronze, 22 GPM., ¼ HP, 1-¼" discharge	1 Plum	6	1.330	Ea.	225	33		258	295
	7140	68 GPM, ½ HP, 1-¼" or 1-½" discharge		5	1.600		365	40		405	460
	7160	94 GPM, ½ HP, 1-¼" or 1-½" discharge		5	1.600		500	40		540	610
	7180	105 GPM, ½ HP, 2" or 3" discharge		4	2		475	49		524	595
	7500	Cast iron, 23 GPM, ¼ HP, 1-¼" discharge		6	1.330		106	33		139	165
	7540	35 GPM, ⅓ HP, 1-¼" discharge		6	1.330		119	33		152	180
	7560	68 GPM, ½ HP, 1-¼" or 1-½" discharge		5	1.600		245	40		285	330
	7580	87 GPM, ½ HP, 2" or 3" discharge		4	2		260	49		309	360
490	0010	**PUMPS, WELL** Water system, with pressure control									490
	1000	Deep well, multi-stage jet, 42 gal. tank									
	1040	110' lift, 40 lb. discharge, 5 GPM, ¾ HP	1 Plum	.80	10	Ea.	475	245		720	890
	2000	Shallow well, reciprocating, 25 gal. tank									
	2040	25' lift, 5 GPM, ⅓ HP	1 Plum	2	4	Ea.	370	99		469	555
	3000	Shallow well, single stage jet, 42 gal. tank,									
	3040	15' lift, 40 lb. discharge, 16 GPM, ¾ HP	1 Plum	2	4	Ea.	365	99		464	550

153 | Plumbing Appliances

153 100 | Water Appliances

			CREW	DAILY OUTPUT	MAN-HOURS	UNIT	BARE COSTS MAT.	LABOR	EQUIP.	TOTAL	TOTAL INCL O&P
100	0010	**WASHER DRYER ACCESSORIES**									100
	1020	Valves ball type single lever									

153 | Plumbing Appliances

153 100 | Water Appliances

			CREW	DAILY OUTPUT	MAN-HOURS	UNIT	BARE COSTS MAT.	LABOR	EQUIP.	TOTAL	TOTAL INCL O&P	
100	1030	½" diam., IPS	1 Plum	21	.381	Ea.	21	9.40		30.40	37	100
	1040	½" diam., solder	"	21	.381	"	21	9.40		30.40	37	
	1050	Recessed box, 16 GA., two hose valves and drain										
	1060	½" size, 1-½" drain	1 Plum	18	.444	Ea.	30	11		41	49	
	1070	½" size, 2" drain	"	17	.471	"	31	11.60		42.60	51	
	1080	With grounding electric receptacle										
	1090	½" size, 1-½" drain	1 Plum	18	.444	Ea.	34	11		45	54	
	1100	½" size, 2" drain	"	17	.471	"	35	11.60		46.60	56	
	1110	With grounding and dryer recepacle										
	1120	½" size, 1-½" drain	1 Plum	18	.444	Ea.	40	11		51	60	
	1130	½" size, 2" drain	"	17	.471	"	41	11.60		52.60	62	
	1140	Recessed box 16 Ga., ball valves with single lever and drain										
	1150	½" size, 1-½" drain	1 Plum	19	.421	Ea.	50	10.40		60.40	70	
	1160	½" size, 2" drain	"	18	.444	"	51	11		62	72	
	1170	With grounding electric receptacle										
	1180	½" size, 1-½" drain	1 Plum	19	.421	Ea.	54	10.40		64.40	75	
	1190	½" size, 2" drain	"	18	.444	"	55	11		66	77	
	1200	With grounding and dryer receptacles										
	1210	½" size, 1-½" drain	1 Plum	19	.421	Ea.	60	10.40		70.40	81	
	1220	½" size, 2" drain	"	18	.444		61	11		72	83	
	1230	For duplex grounding receptacle add					5			5	5.50	
	1300	Recessed box 20 Ga. two hose valves and drain (economy type)										
	1310	½" size, 1-½" drain	1 Plum	19	.421	Ea.	21	10.40		31.40	39	
	1320	½" size, 2" drain		18	.444		22	11		33	40	
	1330	Box with drain only		24	.333		12	8.25		20.25	25	
	1340	½" size, 1-½" ABS/PVC drain		19	.421		20	10.40		30.40	37	
	1350	½" size, 2" ABS/PVC drain		18	.444		21	11		32	39	
	1360	Box with drain only		24	.333		11	8.25		19.25	24	
	1500	Dryer vent kit, recessed, 16 Ga.										
	1510	With door, electrical outlets, flex duct	1 Plum	20	.400	Ea.	105	9.90		114.90	130	
101	0010	WATER CHILLERS REMOTE, 80°F inlet										101
	0100	Aircooled, 50°F outlet, 115V, 4.1 GPH	1 Plum	6	1.330	Ea.	315	33		348	395	
	0200	5.7 GPH		5.50	1.450		447	36		483	545	
	0300	8.0 GPH		5	1.600		333	40		373	425	
	0400	10.3 GPH		4.50	1.780		470	44		514	580	
	0500	13.4 GPH		4	2		655	49		704	795	
	0600	19.5 GPH		3.60	2.220		735	55		790	890	
	0700	29 GPH	Q-1	5	3.200		770	71		841	955	
	1000	230V, 32 GPH	"	5	3.200		865	71		936	1,050	
	1200	For remote grill, add	1 Plum	16	.500		41.50	12.35		53.85	64	
105	0010	WATER COOLER										105
	0030	See line 153-105-9800 for rough-in, waste & vent										
	0040	for all water coolers										
	0100	Wall mounted, non-recessed										
	0140	4 GPH	Q-1	4	4	Ea.	291	89		380	450	
	0180	8.2 GPH		4	4		347	89		436	515	
	0220	14.3 GPH		4	4		367	89		456	535	
	0260	16.1 GPH		4	4		390	89		479	560	
	0600	For hot and cold water, add					160			160	175	
	0640	For stainless steel cabinet, add					41.50			41.50	46	
	1040	14.3 GPH	Q-1	3.80	4.210		504	94		598	695	
	1240	For stainless steel cabinet, add					78			78	86	
	2600	Wheelchair type, 8 GPH	Q-1	4	4		875	89		964	1,100	
	3000	Simulated recessed, 8 GPH		4	4		416	89		505	590	
	3040	11.5 GPH		4	4		440	89		529	615	
	3200	For glass filler in addition to bubbler, add					69			69	76	
	3240	For stainless steel cabinet, add					27			27	30	
	3300	Semi-recessed, 8.1 GPH	Q-1	4	4		468	89		557	645	

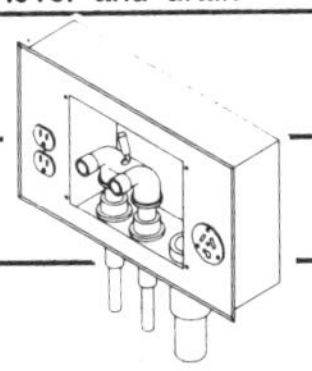

153 | Plumbing Appliances

153 100 | Water Appliances

			CREW	DAILY OUTPUT	MAN-HOURS	UNIT	BARE COSTS MAT.	LABOR	EQUIP.	TOTAL	TOTAL INCL O&P	
105	3320	12 GPH	Q-1	4	4	Ea.	490	89		579	670	105
	3340	For glass filler, add					69			69	76	
	3360	For stainless steel cabinet, add					27			27	30	
	3400	Full recessed, stainless steel, 8 GPH	Q-1	3.50	4.570		765	100		865	990	
	3420	11.5 GPH	"	3.50	4.570		825	100		925	1,050	
	3460	For glass filler, add					69			69	76	
	3600	For mounting can only					180			180	200	
	4600	Floor mounted, flush-to-wall										
	4640	4 GPH	1 Plum	3	2.670	Ea.	312	66		378	440	
	4680	8.2 GPH		3	2.670		354	66		420	485	
	4720	14.3 GPH		3	2.670		370	66		436	505	
	4960	For hot and cold water, add					132			132	145	
	4980	For stainless steel cabinet, add					65.50			65.50	72	
	5000	Dual height, 8.2 GPH	1 Plum	2	4		520	99		619	720	
	5040	14.3 GPH	1 Plum	2	4		540	99		639	740	
	5080	19.5 GPH	1 Plum	2	4		580	99		679	785	
	5120	For stainless steel cabinet, add					65.50			65.50	72	
	5600	Explosion Proof, 16 GPH	1 Plum	3	2.670		785	66		851	960	
	5640	For stainless steel cabinet, add					216			216	240	
	6000	Refrigerator Compartment Type, 4.5 GPH	1 Plum	3	2.670		735	66		801	905	
	6040	As above but hot and cold		3	2.670		830	66		896	1,000	
	6100	Bottle Supply, cold only, 1.0 GPH		4	2		545	49		594	675	
	6200	Hot and cold, 1.0 GPH		4	2		620	49		669	755	
	6600	Bottle Supply Type, 1.0 GPH		4	2		204	49		253	300	
	6640	Hot and cold, 1.0 GPH		4	2		276	49		325	375	
	7700	Cafeteria type, dual glass fillers, 27 GPH	Q-1	2.50	6.400		1,730	140		1,870	2,125	
	7800	For hot water, add					216			216	240	
	9800	For supply, waste & vent, all coolers	1 Plum	2.21	3.620		38.90	89		127.90	175	
110	0010	**WATER HEATERS**										110
	0020	For solar, see Division 155-471										
	1000	Residential, electric, glass lined tank, 10 gal., single element	1 Plum	2.30	3.480	Ea.	137	86		223	280	
	1040	20 gallon, single element		2.20	3.640		161	90		251	310	
	1060	30 gallon, double element		2.20	3.640		160	90		250	310	
	1080	40 gallon, double element		2	4		170	99		269	335	
	1100	52 gallon, double element		2	4		192	99		291	360	
	1120	66 gallon, double element		1.80	4.440		259	110		369	450	
	1140	80 gallon, double element		1.60	5		302	125		427	515	
	1180	120 gallon, double element		1.40	5.710		495	140		635	755	
	2000	Gas fired, glass lined tank, vent not incl., 20 gallon		2.10	3.810		170	94		264	325	
	2040	30 gallon		2	4		173	99		272	335	
	2060	40 gallon		1.90	4.210		188	105		293	360	
	2080	50 gallon		1.80	4.440		230	110		340	415	
	2100	75 gallon		1.50	5.330		412	130		542	650	
	2120	100 gallon		1.30	6.150		705	150		855	1,000	
	3000	Oil fired, glass lined tank, vent not included, 30 gallon		2	4		673	99		772	885	
	3040	50 gallon		1.80	4.440		910	110		1,020	1,175	
	3060	70 gallon		1.50	5.330		1,055	130		1,185	1,350	
	3080	85 gallon		1.40	5.710		1,525	140		1,665	1,875	
	4000	Commercial, 100° rise. NOTE: for each size tank, a range of										
	4010	heaters between the ones shown are available										
	4020	Electric										
	4100	5 gal., 3 KW, 12 GPH	1 Plum	2	4	Ea.	1,015	99		1,114	1,275	
	4120	10 gal., 6 KW, 25 GPH		2	4		1,125	99		1,224	1,375	
	4140	50 gal., 9 KW, 37 GPH		1.80	4.440		1,460	110		1,570	1,775	
	4160	50 gal., 36 KW, 148 GPH		1.80	4.440		2,230	110		2,340	2,625	
	4180	80 gal., 12 KW, 49 GPH		1.50	5.330		1,850	130		1,980	2,225	
	4200	80 gal., 36 KW, 148 GPH		1.50	5.330		2,560	130		2,690	3,000	
	4220	100 gal., 36 KW, 148 GPH		1.20	6.670		2,670	165		2,835	3,175	

153 | Plumbing Appliances

153 100 | Water Appliances

		CREW	DAILY OUTPUT	MAN-HOURS	UNIT	BARE COSTS MAT.	LABOR	EQUIP.	TOTAL	TOTAL INCL O&P	
4240	120 gal., 36 KW, 148 GPH	1 Plum	1.20	6.670	Ea.	2,780	165		2,945	3,300	110
4260	150 gal., 15 KW, 61 GPH		1	8		6,675	200		6,875	7,625	
4280	150 gal., 120 KW, 490 GPH		1	8		10,160	200		10,360	11,500	
4300	200 gal., 15 KW, 61 GPH	Q-1	1.70	9.410		7,290	210		7,500	8,325	
4320	200 gal., 120 KW, 490 GPH		1.70	9.410		10,650	210		10,860	12,000	
4340	250 gal., 15 KW, 61 GPH		1.50	10.670		7,510	235		7,745	8,625	
4360	250 gal., 150 KW, 615 GPH		1.50	10.670		11,775	235		12,010	13,300	
4380	300 gal., 30 KW, 123 GPH		1.30	12.310		8,300	275		8,575	9,525	
4400	300 gal., 180 KW, 738 GPH		1.30	12.310		12,900	275		13,175	14,600	
4420	350 gal., 30 KW, 123 GPH		1.10	14.550		8,900	325		9,225	10,300	
4440	350 gal, 180 KW, 738 GPH		1.10	14.550		13,200	325		13,525	15,000	
4460	400 gal., 30 KW, 123 GPH		1	16		10,050	355		10,405	11,600	
4480	400 gal., 210 KW, 860 GPH		1	16		15,700	355		16,055	17,800	
4500	500 gal., 30 KW, 123 GPH		.80	20		11,600	445		12,045	13,400	
4520	500 gal., 240 KW, 984 GPH		.80	20		18,550	445		18,995	21,100	
4540	600 gal., 30 KW, 123 GPH	Q-2	1.20	20		13,400	460		13,860	15,400	
4560	600 gal., 300 KW, 1230 GPH		1.20	20		21,800	460		22,260	24,700	
4580	700 gal., 30 KW, 123 GPH		1	24		14,050	555		14,605	16,300	
4600	700 gal., 300 KW, 1230 GPH		1	24		22,600	555		23,155	25,700	
4620	800 gal., 60 KW, 245 GPH		.90	26.670		15,400	615		16,015	17,900	
4640	800 gal., 300 KW, 1230 GPH		.90	26.670		23,250	615		23,865	26,500	
4660	1000 gal., 60 KW, 245 GPH		.70	34.290		16,800	790		17,590	19,700	
4680	1000 gal., 480 KW, 1970 GPH		.70	34.290		30,200	790		30,990	34,400	
4700	1250 gal., 60 KW, 245 GPH		.60	40		19,000	920		19,920	22,300	
4720	1250 gal., 480 KW, 1970 GPH		.60	40		31,100	920		32,020	35,600	
4740	1500 gal., 60 KW, 245 GPH		.50	48		25,200	1,100		26,300	29,400	
4760	1500 gal., 480 KW, 1970 GPH		.50	48		36,000	1,100		37,100	41,200	
5400	Modulating step control, 2-5 steps	1 Elec	5.30	1.510		845	37		882	985	
5440	6-10 steps		3.20	2.500		1,090	61		1,151	1,300	
5460	11-15 steps		2.70	2.960		1,340	72		1,412	1,575	
5480	16-20 steps		1.60	5		1,580	120		1,700	1,925	
5500	21-25 steps		.30	26.670		1,790	650		2,440	2,925	
5520	26-30 steps		.26	30.770		1,940	750		2,690	3,225	
6000	Gas fired, flush jacket, std. controls, vent not incl.										
6040	75 MBH input, 63 GPH	1 Plum	1.40	5.710	Ea.	748	140		888	1,025	
6060	96 MBH input, 81 GPH		1.40	5.710		920	140		1,060	1,225	
6080	120 MBH input, 101 GPH		1.20	6.670		975	165		1,140	1,325	
6100	115 MBH input, 110 GPH		1.10	7.270		1,215	180		1,395	1,600	
6120	135 MBH input, 130 GPH		1	8		1,365	200		1,565	1,800	
6140	155 MBH input, 150 GPH		.80	10		1,445	245		1,690	1,950	
6160	175 MBH input, 168 GPH		.70	11.430		1,600	280		1,880	2,175	
6180	200 MBH input, 192 GPH		.60	13.330		1,875	330		2,205	2,550	
6200	240 MBH input, 230 GPH		.50	16		2,290	395		2,685	3,100	
6220	295 MBH input, 278 GPH	Q-1	.80	20		2,960	445		3,405	3,925	
6240	365 MBH input, 374 GPH		.80	20		3,315	445		3,760	4,300	
6260	500 MBH input, 480 GPH		.70	22.860		4,540	510		5,050	5,750	
6280	600 MBH input, 576 GPH		.60	26.670		5,220	595		5,815	6,625	
6300	800 MBH input, 768 GPH		.50	32		6,225	710		6,935	7,900	
6320	1000 MBH input, 960 GPH		.50	32		7,275	710		7,985	9,050	
6340	1200 MBH input, 1150 GPH		.40	40		9,060	890		9,950	11,300	
6360	1500 MBH input, 1440 GPH	Q-2	.60	40		11,200	920		12,120	13,700	
6380	1800 MBH input, 1730 GPH		.50	48		12,650	1,100		13,750	15,600	
6400	2450 MBH input, 2350 GPH		.40	60		16,850	1,375		18,225	20,600	
6420	3000 MBH input, 2880 GPH		.30	80		20,550	1,850		22,400	25,300	
6440	3750 MBH input, 3600 GPH		.30	80		25,500	1,850		27,350	30,800	
6900	For low water cutoff, add	1 Plum	8	1		133	25		158	185	
6960	For bronze body hot water circulator, add	"	4	2		545	49		594	675	
8000	Oil fired, flush jacket, std. controls, vent not incl.										

153 | Plumbing Appliances

153 100	Water Appliances	CREW	DAILY OUTPUT	MAN-HOURS	UNIT	MAT.	LABOR	EQUIP.	TOTAL	TOTAL INCL O&P	
110	8060	103 MBH gross output, 116 GPH	1 Plum	1.10	7.270	Ea.	1,385	180		1,565	1,800	110
	8080	122 MBH gross output, 141 GPH		1	8		1,415	200		1,615	1,850	
	8100	137 MBH gross output, 161 GPH		.80	10		1,510	245		1,755	2,025	
	8120	168 MBH gross output, 192 GPH		.60	13.330		1,840	330		2,170	2,525	
	8140	195 MBH gross output, 224 GPH		.50	16		1,930	395		2,325	2,700	
	8160	225 MBH gross output, 256 GPH	Q-1	.80	20		2,210	445		2,655	3,100	
	8180	262 MBH gross output, 315 GPH		.70	22.860		2,500	510		3,010	3,500	
	8200	315 MBH gross output, 409 GPH		.70	22.860		3,290	510		3,800	4,375	
	8220	420 MBH gross output, 504 GPH		.60	26.670		3,775	595		4,370	5,025	
	8240	525 MBH gross output, 630 GPH		.50	32		4,840	710		5,550	6,375	
	8260	630 MBH gross output, 756 GPH		.50	32		5,400	710		6,110	7,000	
	8280	735 MBH gross output, 880 GPH		.40	40		6,650	890		7,540	8,625	
	8300	840 MBH gross output, 1000 GPH		.40	40		7,600	890		8,490	9,675	
	8320	1050 MBH gross output, 1260 GPH	Q-2	.60	40		9,250	920		10,170	11,500	
	8340	1365 MBH gross output, 1640 GPH		.50	48		11,900	1,100		13,000	14,700	
	8360	1680 MBH gross output, 2000 GPH		.40	60		13,950	1,375		15,325	17,400	
	8380	2310 MBH gross output, 2780 GPH		.30	80		18,060	1,850		19,910	22,600	
	8400	2835 MBH gross output, 3400 GPH		.30	80		22,450	1,850		24,300	27,400	
	8420	3150 MBH gross output, 3780 GPH		.20	120		25,250	2,775		28,025	31,900	
	8900	For low water cutoff, add	1 Plum	8	1		133	25		158	185	
	8960	For bronze body hot water circulator, add	"	4	2		545	49		594	675	
	8965	Point of use, electric, glass lined										
	8966	Residential										
	8967	6 gal. double element	1 Plum	2.50	3.200	Ea.	117	79		196	245	
	8968	10 gal. double element		2.50	3.200		122	79		201	250	
	8969	15 gal. double element		2.40	3.330		138	82		220	275	
	8970	20 gal. double element		2.40	3.330		148	82		230	285	
	8971	30 gal. double element		2.30	3.480		154	86		240	295	
	8973	Energy saver										
	8974	6 gal. double element	1 Plum	2.50	3.200	Ea.	133	79		212	265	
	8975	10 gal. double element		2.50	3.200		143	79		222	275	
	8976	15 gal. double element		2.40	3.330		154	82		236	290	
	8977	20 gal. double element		2.40	3.330		164	82		246	305	
	8978	30 gal. double element		2.30	3.480		186	86		272	330	
	8979	40 gal. double element		2.20	3.640		207	90		297	360	
	8981	Energy saver (ASHRAE std. 90)										
	8982	6 gallon	1 Plum	2.50	3.200	Ea.	186	79		265	320	
	8983	10 gallon		2.50	3.200		196	79		275	335	
	8984	15 gallon		2.40	3.330		207	82		289	350	
	8985	20 gallon		2.40	3.330		223	82		305	365	
	8986	30 gallon		2.30	3.480		245	86		331	395	
	8988	Commercial (ASHRAE energy std. 90)										
	8989	6 gallon	1 Plum	2.50	3.200	Ea.	196	79		275	335	
	8990	10 gallon		2.50	3.200		212	79		291	350	
	8991	15 gallon		2.40	3.330		223	82		305	365	
	8992	20 gallon		2.40	3.330		240	82		322	385	
	8993	30 gallon		2.30	3.480		260	86		346	415	
	8995	Under the sink, copper, w/bracket										
	8996	1 gallon	1 Plum	4	2	Ea.	280	49		329	380	
120	0010	**WATER HEATER PACKAGED SYSTEMS**										120
	1000	Car wash package, continuous duty, high recovery, gas fired										
	1040	100° rise, 180 MBH input, 174 GPH	1 Plum	3	2.670	Ea.	2,280	66		2,346	2,600	
	1060	280 MBH input, 270 GPH		2.50	3.200		2,540	79		2,619	2,900	
	1080	400 MBH input, 386 GPH		2.50	3.200		3,075	79		3,154	3,500	
	1100	480 MBH input, 464 GPH		2	4		3,500	99		3,599	4,000	
	1120	605 MBH input, 584 GPH		1.50	5.330		3,900	130		4,030	4,475	
	1140	700 MBH input, 676 GPH		1	8		4,100	200		4,300	4,800	

153 | Plumbing Appliances

153 100 | Water Appliances

		CREW	DAILY OUTPUT	MAN-HOURS	UNIT	MAT.	LABOR	EQUIP.	TOTAL	TOTAL INCL O&P
1160	1000 MBH input, 966 GPH	Q-1	1.60	10	Ea.	5,160	220		5,380	6,000
1180	1200 MBH input, 1159 GPH	↓	1.40	11.430		6,280	255		6,535	7,275
1200	1400 MBH input, 1353 GPH	↓	1.20	13.330	↓	6,730	295		7,025	7,850
3000	Combination dishwasher & general purpose, 2 temp. gas fired									
3040	124 GPH @ 140° rise; 434 GPH @ 40° rise	1 Plum	2	4	Ea.	2,540	99		2,639	2,950
3060	193 GPH @ 140° rise; 677 GPH @ 40° rise		1.60	5		3,020	125		3,145	3,500
3080	276 GPH @ 140° rise; 969 GPH @ 40° rise		1.40	5.710		3,550	140		3,690	4,125
3100	330 GPH @ 140° rise; 1160 GPH @ 40° rise		1.20	6.670		4,030	165		4,195	4,675
3120	417 GPH @ 140° rise; 1460 GPH @ 40° rise	↓	1	8		4,400	200		4,600	5,125
3140	481 GPH @ 140° rise; 1685 GPH @ 40° rise	Q-1	1.40	11.430		4,820	255		5,075	5,675
3160	688 GPH @ 140° rise; 2410 GPH @ 40° rise		1.20	13.330		5,780	295		6,075	6,800
3180	828 GPH @ 140° rise; 2790 GPH @ 40° rise		1	16		7,050	355		7,405	8,275
3200	965 GPH @ 140° rise; 3370 GPH @ 40° rise	↓	.80	20		7,525	445		7,970	8,925
3960	For unit base, add				↓	160			160	175
5000	Coin laundry units, gas fired, 100° rise									
5020	Single heater,									
5040	280 MBH input, 270 GPH	1 Plum	1.60	5	Ea.	2,940	125		3,065	3,425
5060	400 MBH input, 386 GPH		1.30	6.150		3,820	150		3,970	4,425
5080	480 MBH input, 464 GPH	↓	1	8		4,290	200		4,490	5,000
5100	605 MBH input, 584 GPH	Q-1	1.40	11.430		5,250	255		5,505	6,150
5120	700 MBH input, 676 GPH		1.20	13.330		5,325	295		5,620	6,300
5140	1000 MBH input, 966 GPH		1	16		6,520	355		6,875	7,700
5160	1200 MBH input, 1159 GPH		.90	17.780		7,840	395		8,235	9,200
5180	1400 MBH input, 1353 GPH	↓	.70	22.860	↓	8,480	510		8,990	10,100
6000	Multiple heater									
6040	560 MBH input, 540 GPH	1 Plum	1	8	Ea.	5,010	200		5,210	5,800
6060	800 MBH input, 772 GPH	Q-1	1.30	12.310		6,490	275		6,765	7,550
6080	960 MBH input, 928 GPH		1.20	13.330		7,975	295		8,270	9,200
6100	1210 MBH input, 1168 GPH		1	16		8,560	355		8,915	9,950
6120	1400 MBH input, 1352 GPH		1	16		9,040	355		9,395	10,500
6140	1700 MBH input, 1642 GPH		.80	20		10,450	445		10,895	12,200
6160	2000 MBH input, 1932 GPH		.70	22.860		11,350	510		11,860	13,200
6180	2400 MBH input, 2318 GPH	Q-2	.90	26.670		14,000	615		14,615	16,300
6200	2600 MBH input, 2512 GPH		.80	30		14,400	690		15,090	16,900
6220	2800 MBH input, 2706 GPH	↓	.70	34.290	↓	16,200	790		16,990	19,000
6800	Standard system sizing is based on									
6820	80% of the washers operating at one time.									
9010	Steam injection system heating of water and									
9020	water-miscible liquids to a preset temp.									
9030	Steam flow 100 psig to max. cap. indicated									
9040	Constant flow, threaded connections									
9050	30 GPM, 1-¼" NPT, 700 lb/hr	Q-1	1.60	10	Ea.	1,710	220		1,930	2,200
9054	90 GPM, 2" NPT, 1250 lb/hr		1.30	12.310		2,140	275		2,415	2,750
9058	140 GPM, 2-½" NPT, 2500 lb/hr		1	16		2,730	355		3,085	3,525
9062	230 GPM, 3" NPT, 5000 lb/hr		.71	22.540		3,680	500		4,180	4,800
9066	500 GPM, 4 NPT, 7500 lb/hr		.43	37.210		5,290	825		6,115	7,050
9070	500 GPM, 4" NPT, 10,000 lb/hr	↓	.38	42.110		5,710	935		6,645	7,675
9074	1400 GPM, 6" NPT, 15,000 lb/hr	Q-2	.50	48		7,730	1,100		8,830	10,100
9078	2400 GPM, 8 NPT, 20,000 lb/hr		.43	55.810		9,330	1,275		10,605	12,200
9082	2400 GPM, 8" NPT, 35,000 lb/hr		.38	63.160		11,075	1,450		12,525	14,300
9086	4000 GPM, 10" NPT, 50,000 lb/hr	↓	.34	70.590	↓	22,000	1,625		23,625	26,600
9100	For flanged ports on carbon steel									
9104	body (permits increased liquid									
9108	flow 200/300%), add				Ea.	35%				
9200	Variable flow, threaded connections									
9210	30 GPM, 1-¼" NPT, 700 lb/hr	Q-1	.82	19.510	Ea.	2,410	435		2,845	3,300
9214	90 GPM, 2" NPT, 1250 lb/hr		.67	23.880		2,680	530		3,210	3,725
9218	140 GPM, 2-½" NPT, 2500 lb/hr	↓	.52	30.770	↓	3,390	685		4,075	4,750

153 | Plumbing Appliances

153 100 | Water Appliances

			CREW	DAILY OUTPUT	MAN-HOURS	UNIT	MAT.	LABOR	EQUIP.	TOTAL	TOTAL INCL O&P	
120	9222	230 GPM, 3" NPT, 5000 lb/hr	Q-1	.37	43.240	Ea.	4,350	960		5,310	6,200	120
	9226	500 GPM, 4" NPT, 7,500 lb/hr		.22	72.730		6,210	1,625		7,835	9,225	
	9230	500 GPM, 4" NPT 10,000 lb/hr	↓	.20	80		7,870	1,775		9,645	11,300	
	9234	1400 GPM, 6" NPT, 15,000 lb/hr	Q-2	.26	92.310		9,080	2,125		11,205	13,100	
	9238	2400 GPM, 8" NPT, 20,000 lb/hr		.22	109		11,750	2,525		14,275	16,700	
	9242	2400 GPM, 8" NPT, 35,000 lb/hr		.19	126		14,750	2,900		17,650	20,500	
	9246	4000 GPM, 10" NPT, 50,000 lb/hr	↓	.17	141	↓	26,300	3,250		29,550	33,800	
	9290	For flanged ports on carbon steel										
	9294	body (permits increased liquid										
	9298	flow 200/300%), add				Ea.	40%					
	9400	Steam injector mixing chamber										
	9404	not including controls or instrumentation										
	9408	30 GPM, 1-¼" NPT, 700 lb/hr	Q-1	15	1.070	Ea.	445	24		469	525	
	9412	90 GPM, 2" NPT, 1250 lb/hr		12	1.330		880	30		910	1,000	
	9416	140 GPM, 2-½" NPT, 2500 lb/hr		9	1.780		1,335	40		1,375	1,525	
	9420	230 GPM, 3" NPT, 5000 lb/hr		6.60	2.420		1,980	54		2,034	2,250	
	9424	500 GPM, 4" NPT, 7500 lb/hr		4	4		3,010	89		3,099	3,450	
	9428	500 GPM, 4" NPT, 10,000 lb/hr	↓	3.50	4.570		3,420	100		3,520	3,925	
	9432	1400 GPM, 6" NPT, 15,000 lb/hr	Q-2	4.60	5.220		4,920	120		5,040	5,600	
	9436	2400 GPM, 8" NPT, 20,000 lb/hr		4	6		6,520	140		6,660	7,375	
	9440	2400 GPM, 8" NPT, 35,000 lb/hr		3.50	6.860		7,950	160		8,110	8,975	
	9444	4000 GPM, 10" NPT, 50,000 lb/hr	↓	3.20	7.500	↓	16,750	175		16,925	18,700	
	9448	For flanged ports on carbon steel										
	9452	body permit increased liquid										
	9456	flow (200/300%), add				Ea.	60%					
130	0010	**WATER HEATER STORAGE TANKS** 125 psi ASME										130
	1000	Copper, lined, 190 gal., 30" diam x 66" LOA	1 Plum	4	2	Ea.	2,990	49		3,039	3,350	
	1060	225 gal., 30" diam x 78" LOA	"	3	2.670		3,470	66		3,536	3,925	
	1080	325 gal., 36" diam x 81" LOA	Q-1	4	4		4,350	89		4,439	4,925	
	1100	460 gal., 42" diam x 84" LOA		3	5.330		6,070	120		6,190	6,850	
	1120	605 gal., 48" diam x 87" LOA		2.50	6.400		6,950	140		7,090	7,850	
	1140	740 gal., 54" diam x 91" LOA		2	8		8,240	180		8,420	9,325	
	1160	940 gal., 60" diam x 93" LOA		1.50	10.670		9,540	235		9,775	10,800	
	1180	1505 gal., 66" diam x 119" LOA	↓	1	16		12,300	355		12,655	14,100	
	1200	1615 gal., 72" diam x 110" LOA	Q-2	1.50	16		13,900	370		14,270	15,800	
	1220	2275 gal., 84" diam x 116" LOA		1	24		19,100	555		19,655	21,800	
	1240	3815 gal., 96" diam x 145" LOA		1	24		24,700	555		25,255	28,000	
	2000	Galvanized steel, 15 gal., 12" diam., 39" LOA	1 Plum	12	.667		390	16.45		406.45	455	
	2060	30 gal., 14" diam. x 40" LOA		11	.727		480	17.95		497.95	555	
	2080	75 gal., 18" diam. x 72" LOA		9	.889		635	22		657	730	
	2100	140 gal., 24" diam. x 75" LOA		6	1.330		945	33		978	1,100	
	2120	225 gal., 30" diam. x 78" LOA		4	2		1,325	49		1,374	1,525	
	2140	325 gal., 36" diam. x 81" LOA	↓	3	2.670		1,880	66		1,946	2,175	
	2160	460 gal., 36" diam. x 117" LOA	Q-1	4	4		2,625	89		2,714	3,025	
	2180	605 gal., 48" diam., x 87" LOA	"	3	5.330		4,240	120		4,360	4,850	
	3000	Glass lined, P.E., 80 gal., 20" diam. x 60" LOA	1 Plum	9	.889		735	22		757	840	
	3060	140 gal., 24" diam. x 80" LOA		6	1.330		1,150	33		1,183	1,325	
	3080	225 gal., 30" diam. x 78" LOA		4	2		1,325	49		1,374	1,525	
	3100	325 gal., 36" diam. x 81" LOA	↓	3	2.670		1,960	66		2,026	2,250	
	3120	460 gal., 42" diam. x 84" LOA	Q-1	4	4		2,490	89		2,579	2,875	
	3140	605 gal., 48" diam. x 87" LOA		3	5.330		3,550	120		3,670	4,075	
	3160	740 gal., 54" diam. x 91" LOA		3	5.330		4,050	120		4,170	4,625	
	3180	940 gal., 60" diam. x 93" LOA		2.50	6.400		4,820	140		4,960	5,525	
	3200	1330 gal., 66" diam. x 107" LOA		2	8		6,200	180		6,380	7,075	
	3220	1615 gal., 72" diam. x 110" LOA		1.50	10.670		7,230	235		7,465	8,300	
	3240	2275 gal., 84" diam. x 116" LOA	↓	1	16		10,350	355		10,705	11,900	
	3260	3815 gal., 96" diam. x 145" LOA	Q-2	1.50	16		14,750	370		15,120	16,800	

153 | Plumbing Appliances

153 100 | Water Appliances

			CREW	DAILY OUTPUT	MAN-HOURS	UNIT	BARE COSTS MAT.	LABOR	EQUIP.	TOTAL	TOTAL INCL O&P	
150	0010	**WATER TREATMENT, POTABLE**										150
	5800	Softener systems, automatic, intermediate sizes										
	5820	available, may be used in multiples.										
	6000	Hardness capacity between regenerations and flow										
	6100	150,000 grains, 37 GPM cont., 51 GPM peak	Q-1	1.20	13.330	Ea.	1,655	295		1,950	2,250	
	6200	300,000 grains, 81 GPM cont., 113 GPM peak		1	16		2,650	355		3,005	3,450	
	6300	750,000 grains, 160 GPM cont., 230 GPM peak		.80	20		5,490	445		5,935	6,700	
	6400	900,000 grains, 185 GPM cont., 270 GPM peak		.70	22.860		6,170	510		6,680	7,550	
160	0010	**WATER SUPPLY METERS**										160
	1000	Detector, serves dual systems such as fire and domestic or										
	1020	process water, wide range cap., UL and FM approved										
	1100	3" mainline x 2" by-pass, 400 GPM	Q-1	3.60	4.440	Ea.	2,110	99		2,209	2,475	
	1140	4" mainline x 2" by-pass, 700 GPM	"	2.50	6.400		2,320	140		2,460	2,775	
	1180	6" mainline x 3" by-pass, 1600 GPM	Q-2	2.60	9.230		3,080	215		3,295	3,700	
	1220	8" mainline x 4" by-pass, 2800 GPM		2.10	11.430		4,675	265		4,940	5,525	
	1260	10" mainline x 6" by-pass, 4400 GPM		2	12		8,125	275		8,400	9,350	
	1300	10"x12" mainlines x 6" by-pass, 5400 GPM		1.70	14.120		8,450	325		8,775	9,775	
	2000	Domestic/commercial, bronze										
	2020	Threaded										
	2060	5/8" diameter, to 20 GPM	1 Plum	16	.500	Ea.	45	12.35		57.35	68	
	2080	3/4" diameter, to 30 GPM		14	.571		86	14.10		100.10	115	
	2100	1" diameter, to 50 GPM		12	.667		104	16.45		120.45	140	
	2300	Threaded/flanged										
	2340	1-1/2" diameter, to 100 GPM	1 Plum	8	1	Ea.	237	25		262	295	
	2360	2" diameter, to 160 GPM	"	6	1.330	"	325	33		358	405	
	2600	Flanged, compound										
	2640	3" diameter, 320 GPM	Q-1	3	5.330	Ea.	1,165	120		1,285	1,450	
	2660	4" diameter, to 500 GPM		1.50	10.670		1,810	235		2,045	2,350	
	2680	6" diameter, to 1,000 GPM		1	16		3,520	355		3,875	4,400	
	2700	8" diameter, to 1,800 GPM		.80	20		6,800	445		7,245	8,150	
	7000	Turbine										
	7260	Flanged										
	7300	2" diameter, to 160 GPM	1 Plum	7	1.140	Ea.	370	28		398	450	
	7320	3" diameter, to 450 GPM	Q-1	3.60	4.440		560	99		659	765	
	7340	4" diameter, to 650 GPM	"	2.50	6.400		920	140		1,060	1,225	
	7360	6" diameter, to 1800 GPM	Q-2	2.60	9.230		1,825	215		2,040	2,325	
	7380	8" diameter, to 2500 GPM		2.10	11.430		2,720	265		2,985	3,375	
	7400	10" diameter, to 5500 GPM		1.70	14.120		4,000	325		4,325	4,875	

154 | Fire Extinguishing Systems

154 100 | Fire Systems

			CREW	DAILY OUTPUT	MAN-HOURS	UNIT	BARE COSTS MAT.	LABOR	EQUIP.	TOTAL	TOTAL INCL O&P	
101	0010	**AUTOMATIC FIRE SUPPRESSION SYSTEMS**										101
	0040	For detectors and control stations, see division 168-120										
	0100	Control panel, single zone with batteries (2 zones det., 1 suppr.)	1 Elec	1	8	Ea.	1,050	195		1,245	1,450	
	0150	Multizone (4) with batteries (8 zones det., 4 suppr.)	"	.50	16		2,150	390		2,540	2,950	
	1000	Dispersion nozzle, CO2, 3" x 5"	1 Plum	18	.444		68	11		79	91	
	1100	Halon, 1-1/2"	"	14	.571		50	14.10		64.10	76	
	2000	Extinguisher, CO2 system, high pressure, 75 lb. cylinder	Q-1	6	2.670		690	59		749	845	
	2100	100 lb. cylinder	"	5	3.200		780	71		851	965	
	2400	Halon system, filled, with mounting bracket										
	2460	26 lb. container	Q-1	8	2	Ea.	1,200	44		1,244	1,375	

154 | Fire Extinguishing Systems

154 100 | Fire Systems

			Crew	Daily Output	Man-Hours	Unit	Bare Costs Mat.	Labor	Equip.	Total	Total Incl O&P	
101	2480	44 lb. container	Q-1	7	2.290	Ea.	1,300	51		1,351	1,500	101
	2500	63 lb. container		6	2.670		1,400	59		1,459	1,625	
	2520	101 lb. container		5	3.200		1,720	71		1,791	2,000	
	2540	196 lb. container		4	4		2,200	89		2,289	2,550	
	3000	Electro/mechanical release	L-1	4	4		165	98		263	325	
	3400	Manual pull station	1 Plum	6	1.330		32	33		65	84	
	4000	Pneumatic damper release	"	8	1		85	25		110	130	
	6000	Average halon system, minimum				C.F.					.55	
	6020	Maximum				"					1.50	
115	0010	**FIRE EQUIPMENT CABINETS** Not equipped, 20 ga. steel box,										115
	0040	recessed, D.S. glass in door, box size given										
	1000	Portable extinguisher, single, 8" x 12" x 27", alum. door & frame	Q-12	8	2	Ea.	103	46		149	180	
	1100	Steel door and frame		8	2		52.50	46		98.50	125	
	1200	Stainless steel door and frame		8	2		185	46		231	270	
	2000	Portable extinguisher, large, 8" x 12" x 36", alum. door & frame		8	2		110	46		156	190	
	2100	Steel door and frame		8	2		75	46		121	150	
	2200	Stainless steel door and frame		8	2		238	46		284	330	
	3000	Hose rack assy., 1-½" valve & 100' hose, 24" x 40" x 5-½"										
	3100	Aluminum door and frame	Q-12	6	2.670	Ea.	144	62		206	250	
	3200	Steel door and frame		6	2.670		110	62		172	215	
	3300	Stainless steel door and frame		6	2.670		330	62		392	455	
	4000	Hose rack assy., 2-½" x 1-½" valve, 100' hose, 24" x 40" x 8"										
	4100	Aluminum door and frame	Q-12	6	2.670	Ea.	149	62		211	255	
	4200	Steel door and frame		6	2.670		116	62		178	220	
	4300	Stainless steel door and frame		6	2.670		337	62		399	460	
	5000	Hose rack assy., 2-½" x 1-½" valve, 100' hose										
	5010	and extinguisher, 30" x 40" x 8"										
	5100	Aluminum door and frame	Q-12	5	3.200	Ea.	156	74		230	280	
	5200	Steel door and frame		5	3.200		124	74		198	245	
	5300	Stainless steel door and frame		5	3.200		355	74		429	500	
	6000	Hose rack assy., 1-½" valve, 100' hose										
	6010	and 2-½" FD valve, 24" x 44" x 8"										
	6100	Aluminum door and frame	Q-12	5	3.200	Ea.	159	74		233	285	
	6200	Steel door and frame		5	3.200		132	74		206	255	
	6300	Stainless steel door and frame		5	3.200		348	74		422	495	
	7000	Hose rack assy., 1-½" valve & 100' hose, 2-½" FD valve										
	7010	and extinguisher, 30" x 44" x 8"										
	7100	Aluminum door and frame	Q-12	5	3.200	Ea.	170	74		244	295	
	7200	Steel door and frame		5	3.200		140	74		214	265	
	7300	Stainless steel door and frame		5	3.200		377	74		451	525	
	8000	Valve cabinet for 2-½" FD angle valve, 18" x 18" x 8"										
	8100	Aluminum door and frame	Q-12	12	1.330	Ea.	102	31		133	160	
	8200	Steel door and frame		12	1.330		58	31		89	110	
	8300	Stainless steel door and frame		12	1.330		189	31		220	255	
125	0010	**FIRE EXTINGUISHERS**										125
	0120	CO2, portable with swivel horn, 5 lb.				Ea.	48.50			48.50	53	
	0140	With hose and "H" horn, 10 lb.					94			94	105	
	0160	15 lb.					110			110	120	
	0180	20 lb.					150			150	165	
	0360	Wheeled type, cart mounted, 50 lb.					830			830	915	
	0380	100 lb. (two 50 lb. cylinders)					1,250			1,250	1,375	
	1000	Dry chemical, pressurized										
	1040	Standard type, portable, painted, 2-½ lb.				Ea.	16.50			16.50	18.15	
	1060	5 lb.					28.75			28.75	32	
	1080	10 lb.					42.50			42.50	47	
	1100	20 lb.					68			68	75	

154 | Fire Extinguishing Systems

154 100 | Fire Systems

			CREW	DAILY OUTPUT	MAN-HOURS	UNIT	BARE COSTS MAT.	LABOR	EQUIP.	TOTAL	TOTAL INCL O&P	
125	1300	Standard type, wheeled, 150 lb.				Ea.	1,250			1,250	1,375	125
	1360	350 lb.					2,200			2,200	2,425	
	2000	ABC all purpose type, portable, 2-½ lb.					17.35			17.35	19.10	
	2060	5 lb.					29			29	32	
	2080	9-½ lb.					42.50			42.50	47	
	2100	20 lb.					70			70	77	
	2300	Wheeled, 45 lb.					920			920	1,000	
	2360	150 lb.					1,250			1,250	1,375	
	3000	Dry chemical, outside cartridge to -65°F, painted, 9 lb.					130			130	145	
	3060	26 lb.					190			190	210	
	4000	Halon, painted, wall bracket, 2-½ lb.					35			35	39	
	4060	5 lb.					51			51	56	
	5000	Pressurized water, 2-½ gallon, stainless steel					44.50			44.50	49	
	5060	With anti-freeze					64.50			64.50	71	
	9400	Installation of extinguishers, 12 or more, on wood	1 Carp	30	.267			5.75		5.75	8.75	
	9420	On masonry or concrete	"	15	.533			11.50		11.50	17.50	
135	0010	**FIRE HOSE AND EQUIPMENT**										135
	0200	Adapters, rough brass, straight hose threads										
	0220	One piece, female to male, rocker lugs B8.2-310										
	0240	1" x 1"				Ea.	7.75			7.75	8.55	
	0260	1-½" x 1" B8.2-320					8.15			8.15	8.95	
	0280	1-½" x 1-½"					9			9	9.90	
	0300	2" x 1-½" B8.2-390					13.10			13.10	14.40	
	0320	2" x 2"					19.20			19.20	21	
	0340	2-½" x 1-½" C8.2-301					7			7	7.70	
	0360	2-½" x 2"					9.25			9.25	10.20	
	0380	2-½" x 2-½" C8.2-302					17.50			17.50	19.25	
	0400	3" x 2-½"					27			27	30	
	0420	3" x 3"					38.40			38.40	42	
	0500	For polished brass, add					25%					
	0520	For polished chrome, add					65%					
	0700	One piece, female to male, hexagon										
	0740	1-½" x ¾"				Ea.	6			6	6.60	
	0760	2" x 1"					15			15	16.50	
	0780	2-½" x 1"					29			29	32	
	0800	2-½" x 1-½"					17.50			17.50	19.25	
	0820	2-½" x 2"					17.50			17.50	19.25	
	0840	3" x 2-½"					25			25	28	
	0900	For chrome, add					60%					
	1100	Swivel, female to female, pin lugs										
	1120	1-½" x 1-½"				Ea.	16.50			16.50	18.15	
	1140	2" x 2"					45			45	50	
	1200	2-½ x 2-½"					31.25			31.25	34	
	1260	For polished brass, add					25%					
	1280	For polished chrome, add					55%					
	1400	Couplings, sngl & dbl jacket, pin lug or rocker lug, cast brass										
	1410	1-½"				Ea.	15.50			15.50	17.05	
	1420	2-½"					33			33	36	
	1500	For polished brass, add					20%					
	1520	For polished chrome, add					40%					
	1580	Reducing, F x F, interior installation, cast brass										
	1590	2" x 1-½"				Ea.	21			21	23	
	1600	2-½" x 1-½"					7.50			7.50	8.25	
	1680	For polished brass, add					50%					
	1720	For polished chrome, add					75%					
	1900	Escutcheon plate, for angle valves, polished brass, 1-½"					7.50			7.50	8.25	
	1920	2-½"					14			14	15.40	
	1940	3"					16.50			16.50	18.15	

154 | Fire Extinguishing Systems

154 100 | Fire Systems

			DAILY	MAN-		\multicolumn{4}{c}{BARE COSTS}	TOTAL
		CREW	OUTPUT	HOURS	UNIT	MAT.	LABOR	EQUIP.	TOTAL	INCL O&P
1980	For polished chrome, add				Ea.	15%				
2200	Hose, less couplings									
2260	Synthetic jacket, lined, 300 lb. test, 1-½" diameter				L.F.	1.20			1.20	1.32
2280	2-½" diameter					1.82			1.82	2
2360	High strength, 500 lb. test, 1-½" diameter					1.27			1.27	1.40
2380	2-½" diameter					2.18			2.18	2.40
2600	Hose rack, swinging, for 1-½" diameter hose,									
2620	Enameled steel, 50' & 75' lengths of hose	Q-12	20	.800	Ea.	24	18.45		42.45	54
2640	100' and 125' lengths of hose		20	.800		25	18.45		43.45	55
2680	Chrome plated, 50' and 75' lengths of hose		20	.800		35	18.45		53.45	66
2700	100' and 125' lengths of hose		20	.800		36	18.45		54.45	67
2780	For hose rack nipple, 1-½" polished brass, add					8			8	8.80
2820	2-½" polished brass, add					16			16	17.60
2840	1-½" polished chrome, add					9			9	9.90
2860	2-½" polished chrome, add					18			18	19.80
2990	Hose reel, swinging, for 1-½" polyester neoprene lined hose									
3000	50' long	Q-12	14	1.140	Ea.	47.50	26		73.50	92
3020	100' long		14	1.140		55	26		81	100
3060	For 2-½" cotton rubber hose, 75' long		14	1.140		57.50	26		83.50	105
3100	150' long		14	1.140		80	26		106	125
3750	Hydrants, wall, w/caps, single, flush, polished brass									
3800	2-½" x 2-½"	Q-12	5	3.200	Ea.	72	74		146	190
3840	2-½" x 3"		5	3.200		105	74		179	225
3860	3" x 3"		4.80	3.330		91	77		168	215
3900	For polished chrome, add					15%				
3950	Double, flush, polished brass									
4000	2-½" x 2-½" x 4"	Q-12	5	3.200	Ea.	252	74		326	385
4040	2-½" x 2-½" x 6"		4.60	3.480		410	80		490	570
4080	3" x 3" x 4"		4.90	3.270		384	75		459	535
4120	3" x 3" x 6"		4.50	3.560		445	82		527	610
4200	For polished chrome, add					9%				
4350	Double, projecting, polished brass									
4400	2-½" x 2-½" x 4"	Q-12	5	3.200	Ea.	110	74		184	230
4450	2-½" x 2-½" x 6"	"	4.60	3.480	"	202	80		282	340
4460	Valve control, dbl. flush/projecting hydrant, cap &									
4470	chain, ext. rod & cplg., escutcheon, polished brass	Q-12	8	2	Ea.	125	46		171	205
4480	Four-way square, flush, polished brass									
4540	2-½"(4) x 6"	Q-12	3.60	4.440	Ea.	1,100	105		1,205	1,375
4600	Vertical, flush, cast brass									
4620	Two-way, 2-½" x 2-½" x 4"	Q-12	5	3.200	Ea.	530	74		604	695
4640	Three-way, 2-½" x 2-½" x 2-½" x 6"		4.60	3.480		810	80		890	1,000
4720	Four-way, 2-½"(4) x 6"		3.80	4.210		1,050	97		1,147	1,300
4780	For polished chrome, add					10%			21	23
5000	Nipples, straight hose to tapered iron pipe, brass									
5040	Female to female, 1" x 1"				Ea.	19			19	21
5060	1-½" x 1-½"					6.50			6.50	7.15
5080	2" x 2"					30.50			30.50	34
5100	2-½" x 2-½"					13			13	14.30
5200	Double male or male to female, 1" x 1"					6.50			6.50	7.15
5220	1-½" x 1"					18			18	19.80
5230	1-½" x 1-½"					4.50			4.50	4.95
5240	2" x 1"					25.50			25.50	28
5260	2" x 1-½"					25.50			25.50	28
5270	2" x 2"					12			12	13.20
5280	2-½" x 1-½"					20			20	22
5300	2-½" x 2"					21			21	23
5310	2-½" x 2-½"					10.50			10.50	11.55
5340	For polished chrome, add					75%				

154 | Fire Extinguishing Systems

154 100 | Fire Systems

		CREW	DAILY OUTPUT	MAN-HOURS	UNIT	BARE COSTS MAT.	LABOR	EQUIP.	TOTAL	TOTAL INCL O&P
5600	Nozzles, brass									
5620	Adjustable fog, ¾" booster line				Ea.	64.75			64.75	71
5630	1" booster line					64.75			64.75	71
5640	1-½" leader line					67.75			67.75	75
5660	2-½" direct connection					136			136	150
5680	2-½" playpipe nozzle					110			110	120
5780	For chrome plated, add					8%				
5850	Electrical fire, adjustable fog, no shock									
5900	1-½"				Ea.	201			201	220
5920	2-½"					259			259	285
5980	For polished chrome, add					6%				
6200	Heavy duty, comb. adj. fog and str. stream, with handle									
6210	1" booster line				Ea.	186			186	205
6240	1-½"					196			196	215
6260	2-½", for playpipe					213			213	235
6280	2-½" direct connection					252			252	275
6300	2-½" playpipe combination					350			350	385
6480	For polished chrome, add					7%				
6500	Plain fog, polished brass, 1-½"					53.50			53.50	59
6540	Chrome plated, 1-½"					55.50			55.50	61
6700	Plain stream, polished brass, 1-½" x 10"					18			18	19.80
6740	1-½" x 12" x ⅝"					15.75			15.75	17.35
6760	2-½" x 15" x ⅞" or 1-½"					55			55	61
6860	For polished chrome, add					20%				
7000	Underwriters playpipe, 2-½" x 30" with 1-⅛" tip					120			120	130
7040	Less tip					96			96	105
7140	Standpipe connections, wall, w/plugs & chains									
7160	Single, flush, brass, 2-½" x 2-½"	Q-12	5	3.200	Ea.	86	74		160	205
7180	2-½" x 3"	"	5	3.200		98	74		172	220
7240	For polished chrome, add					3%				
7280	Double, flush, polished brass									
7300	2-½" x 2-½" x 4"	Q-12	5	3.200	Ea.	232	74		306	365
7330	2-½" x 2-½" x 6"		4.60	3.480		300	80		380	450
7340	3" x 3" x 4"		4.90	3.270		375	75		450	525
7370	3" x 3" x 6"		4.50	3.560		450	82		532	615
7400	For polished chrome, add					10%				
7440	For sill cock combination, add					30			30	33
7580	Double projecting, polished brass									
7600	2-½" x 2-½" x 4"	Q-12	5	3.200	Ea.	206	74		280	335
7630	2-½" x 2-½" x 6"	"	4.60	3.480		290	80		370	440
7680	For polished chrome, add					15%				
7900	Three way, flush, polished brass									
7920	2-½" (3) x 4"	Q-12	4.80	3.330	Ea.	710	77		787	895
7930	2-½" (3) x 6"	"	4.80	3.330		740	77		817	930
8000	For polished chrome, add					9%				
8020	Three way, projecting, polished brass									
8040	2-½"(3) x 4"	Q-12	4.80	3.330	Ea.	360	77		437	510
8070	2-½" (3) x 6"	"	4.60	3.480		405	80		485	565
8100	For polished chrome, add					5%				
8200	Four way, square, flush, polished brass,									
8240	2-½"(4) x 6"	Q-12	3.60	4.440	Ea.	1,100	105		1,205	1,375
8300	For polished chrome, add				"	7%				
8550	Wall, vertical, flush, cast brass									
8600	Two way, 2-½" x 2-½" x 4"	Q-12	5	3.200	Ea.	530	74		604	695
8660	Four way, 2-½"(4) x 6"		3.80	4.210		1,060	97		1,157	1,300
8680	Six way, 2-½"(6) x 6"		3.40	4.710		1,430	110		1,540	1,725
8700	For polished chrome, add					10%				
8800	Sidewalk siamese unit, polished brass, two way									

154 | Fire Extinguishing Systems

154 100 | Fire Systems

			CREW	DAILY OUTPUT	MAN-HOURS	UNIT	BARE COSTS MAT.	LABOR	EQUIP.	TOTAL	TOTAL INCL O&P	
135	8820	2-½" x 2-½" x 4"	Q-12	2.50	6.400	Ea.	275	150		425	525	135
	8850	2-½" x 2-½" x 6"		2	8		400	185		585	715	
	8860	3" x 3" x 4"		2.50	6.400		360	150		510	615	
	8890	3" x 3" x 6"		2	8		480	185		665	805	
	8940	For polished chrome, add					3%					
	9100	Sidewalk siamese unit, polished brass, three way										
	9120	2-½" x 2-½" x 2-½" x 6"	Q-12	2	8	Ea.	635	185		820	975	
	9160	For polished chrome, add					10%					
	9200	Storage house, hose only, primed steel					377			377	415	
	9220	Aluminum					800			800	880	
	9280	Hose and hydrant house, primed steel					423			423	465	
	9300	Aluminum					950			950	1,050	
	9340	Tools, crowbar and brackets	1 Carp	12	.667		33.25	14.40		47.65	58	
	9360	Combination hydrant wrench and spanner					18			18	19.80	
	9380	Fire axe and brackets										
	9400	6 lb.	1 Carp	12	.667	Ea.	33.25	14.40		47.65	58	
145	0010	**FIRE PUMPS** Including controller, fittings and relief valve										145
	0030	Diesel										
	0050	500 GPM, 50 psi, 40 HP, 4" pump	Q-13	.64	50	Ea.	25,400	1,225		26,625	29,800	
	0100	500 GPM, 100 psi, 68 HP, 4" pump		.60	53.330		26,500	1,300		27,800	31,100	
	0150	500 GPM, 125 psi, 103 HP, 4" pump		.56	57.140		27,500	1,400		28,900	32,300	
	0200	750 GPM, 50 psi, 40 HP, 5" pump		.60	53.330		26,700	1,300		28,000	31,300	
	0250	750 GPM, 100 psi, 99 HP, 5" pump		.56	57.140		29,650	1,400		31,050	34,700	
	0300	750 GPM, 165 psi, 188 HP, 5" pump		.52	61.540		39,350	1,500		40,850	45,500	
	0350	1000 GPM, 50 psi, 53 HP, 5" pump		.58	55.170		26,800	1,350		28,150	31,500	
	0400	1000 GPM, 100 psi, 99 HP, 5" pump		.56	57.140		30,400	1,400		31,800	35,500	
	0450	1000 GPM, 150 psi, 188 HP, 6" pump		.48	66.670		42,500	1,625		44,125	49,200	
	0470	1000 GPM, 200 psi, 238 HP, 6" pump		.40	80		43,250	1,950		45,200	50,500	
	0500	1500 GPM, 50 psi, 81 HP, 6" pump		.50	64		28,050	1,575		29,625	33,200	
	0550	1500 GPM, 100 psi, 188 HP, 6" pump		.46	69.570		35,400	1,700		37,100	41,500	
	0600	1500 GPM, 150 psi, 213 HP, 6" pump		.42	76.190		43,850	1,875		45,725	51,000	
	0650	1500 GPM, 200 psi, 288 HP, 6" pump		.38	84.210		49,700	2,075		51,775	57,500	
	0700	2000 GPM, 100 psi, 188 HP, 6" pump		.34	94.120		34,750	2,300		37,050	41,700	
	0750	2000 GPM, 150 psi, 292 HP, 6"pump		.30	107		39,150	2,625		41,775	47,000	
	0800	2500 GPM, 100 psi, 255 HP, 8" pump		.32	100		33,600	2,450		36,050	40,600	
	0820	2500 GPM, 150 psi, 427 HP, 8" pump		.26	123		40,700	3,025		43,725	49,300	
	0850	3000 GPM, 100 psi, 288 HP, 8"pump		.28	114		45,050	2,800		47,850	53,500	
	0900	3000 GPM, 150 psi, 534 HP, 10" pump		.20	160		92,850	3,925		96,775	108,000	
	0950	3500 GPM, 100 psi, 320 HP, 10" pump		.24	133		44,550	3,275		47,825	54,000	
	1000	3500 GPM, 150 psi, 534 HP, 10" pump		.20	160		90,800	3,925		94,725	105,500	
	3000	Electric										
	3100	250 GPM, 40 psi, 15 HP, 3550 RPM, 3" pump	Q-13	.70	45.710	Ea.	9,490	1,125		10,615	12,100	
	3200	500 GPM, 50 psi, 30 HP, 3550 RPM, 4" pump		.68	47.060		10,150	1,150		11,300	12,900	
	3250	500 GPM, 100 psi, 75 HP, 1770 RPM, 4" pump		.66	48.480		13,400	1,200		14,600	16,500	
	3300	500 GPM, 125 psi, 100 HP, 1770 RPM, 4" pump		.62	51.610		13,750	1,275		15,025	17,000	
	3350	750 GPM, 50 psi, 50 HP, 1770 RPM, 5" pump		.64	50		11,750	1,225		12,975	14,700	
	3400	750 GPM, 100 psi, 100 HP, 1770 RPM, 5" pump		.58	55.170		13,500	1,350		14,850	16,900	
	3450	750 GPM, 165 psi, 125 HP, 1770 RPM, 5" pump		.56	57.140		19,850	1,400		21,250	23,900	
	3500	1000 GPM, 50 psi, 50 HP 1770 RPM, 5" pump		.60	53.330		11,750	1,300		13,050	14,900	
	3550	1000 GPM, 100 psi, 125 HP, 1770 RPM, 5" pump		.54	59.260		14,500	1,450		15,950	18,100	
	3600	1000 GPM, 150 psi, 200 HP, 1770 RPM, 6" pump		.50	64		26,800	1,575		28,375	31,800	
	3650	1000 GPM, 200 psi, 250 HP, 1770 RPM, 6" pump		.36	88.890		29,800	2,175		31,975	36,000	
	3700	1500 GPM, 50 psi, 75 HP, 1770 RPM, 6" pump		.50	64		13,550	1,575		15,125	17,200	
	3750	1500 GPM, 100 psi, 150 HP, 1770 RPM, 6" pump		.46	69.570		16,850	1,700		18,550	21,100	
	3800	1500 GPM, 150 psi, 200 HP, 1770 RPM, 6" pump		.36	88.890		28,850	2,175		31,025	35,000	
	3850	1500 GPM, 200 psi, 250 HP, 1770 RPM, 6" pump		.32	100		31,800	2,450		34,250	38,600	
	3900	2000 GPM, 100 psi, 200 HP, 1770 RPM, 6" pump		.34	94.120		17,950	2,300		20,250	23,200	
	3950	2000 GPM, 150 psi, 300 HP, 1770 RPM, 6" pump		.28	114		26,000	2,800		28,800	32,800	

154 | Fire Extinguishing Systems

154 100 | Fire Systems

		CREW	DAILY OUTPUT	MAN-HOURS	UNIT	MAT.	LABOR	EQUIP.	TOTAL	TOTAL INCL O&P	
4000	2500 GPM, 100 psi, 250 HP, 1770 RPM, 8" pump	Q-13	.30	107	Ea.	24,900	2,625		27,525	31,300	145
4040	2500 GPM, 135 psi, 350 HP, 1770 RPM, 8" pump		.26	123		28,400	3,025		31,425	35,700	
4100	3000 GPM, 100 psi, 250 HP, 1770 RPM, 8" pump		.28	114		27,050	2,800		29,850	33,900	
4150	3000 GPM, 140 psi, 450 HP, 1770 RPM, 10" pump		.24	133		37,050	3,275		40,325	45,600	
4200	3500 GPM, 100 psi, 300 HP, 1770 RPM, 10" pump		.26	123		30,950	3,025		33,975	38,500	
4250	3500 GPM, 140 psi, 450 HP, 1770 RPM, 10" pump		.24	133		35,200	3,275		38,475	43,600	
5000	For jockey pump 1", 3 HP, add	Q-12	2	8		1,325	185		1,510	1,725	
0010	**FIRE VALVES**										160
0020	Angle, combination pressure adjustable/restricting, rough brass										
0030	1-½"	1 Spri	12	.667	Ea.	32	17.10		49.10	61	
0040	2-½"	"	7	1.140		71.50	29		100.50	120	
0050	For polished brass, add					30%					
0060	For polished chrome, add					40%					
0080	Wheel handle, 300 lb., 1-½"	1 Spri	12	.667		22.50	17.10		39.60	50	
0090	2-½"	"	7	1.140		51	29		80	100	
0100	For polished brass, add					35%					
0110	For polished chrome, add					50%					
1000	Ball drip, automatic, rough brass, ½"	1 Spri	20	.400		6	10.25		16.25	22	
1010	¾"	"	20	.400		7.50	10.25		17.75	24	
1100	Butterfly, 175 lb., sprinkler system, FM/UL, threaded, bronze										
1120	Slow close										
1150	1" size	1 Spri	19	.421	Ea.	45.50	10.80		56.30	66	
1160	1-¼" size		15	.533		51.30	13.70		65	77	
1170	1-½" size		13	.615		66.25	15.80		82.05	96	
1180	2" size		11	.727		86.60	18.65		105.25	125	
1190	2-½" size	Q-12	15	1.070		124	25		149	175	
1230	For supervisory switch kit, all sizes										
1240	One circuit, add	1 Spri	48	.167	Ea.	43.80	4.28		48.08	55	
1250	Two circuits, add	"	40	.200	"	52	5.15		57.15	65	
1280	Quarter turn for trim										
1300	½" size	1 Spri	22	.364	Ea.	4.70	9.35		14.05	19.05	
1310	¾" size		20	.400		7.20	10.25		17.45	23	
1320	1" size		19	.421		9.40	10.80		20.20	26	
1330	1-¼" size		15	.533		15.60	13.70		29.30	38	
1340	1-½" size		13	.615		19.50	15.80		35.30	45	
1350	2" size		11	.727		24.10	18.65		42.75	54	
1400	Caps, polished brass with chain, ¾"					15			15	16.50	
1420	1"					22			22	24	
1440	1-½"					7.50			7.50	8.25	
1460	2-½"					11			11	12.10	
1480	3"					20.50			20.50	23	
3000	Gate, hose, wheel handle, N.R.S., rough brass, 1-½"	1 Spri	12	.667		60	17.10		77.10	91	
3040	2-½", 300 lb.	"	7	1.140		76	29		105	125	
3080	For polished brass, add					40%					
3090	For polished chrome, add					50%					
3800	Hydrant, screw type, crank handle, brass										
3840	2-½" size	Q-12	11	1.450	Ea.	185	34		219	255	
3880	For chrome, same price										
4200	Hydrolator, vent and draining, rough brass, 1-½"	1 Spri	12	.667		37	17.10		54.10	66	
4220	2-½"	"	7	1.140		80	29		109	130	
4280	For polished brass, add					25%					
4290	For polished chrome, add					35%					
5000	Pressure restricting, adjustable rough brass, 1-½"	1 Spri	12	.667		52.75	17.10		69.85	83	
5020	2-½"	"	7	1.140		89.25	29		118.25	140	
5080	For polished brass, add					30%					
5090	For polished chrome, add					45%					
6000	Roof manifold, horiz., brass, with valves & caps										

154 | Fire Extinguishing Systems

154 100 | Fire Systems

			CREW	DAILY OUTPUT	MAN-HOURS	UNIT	BARE COSTS MAT.	LABOR	EQUIP.	TOTAL	TOTAL INCL O&P	
160	6040	2-½" x 2-½" x 4"	Q-12	4.80	3.330	Ea.	242	77		319	380	160
	6060	2-½" x 2-½" x 6"		4.60	3.480		268	80		348	415	
	6080	2-½" x 2-½" x 2-½" x 4"		4.60	3.480		340	80		420	495	
	6090	2-½" x 2-½" x 2-½" x 6"		4.60	3.480		355	80		435	510	
	7000	Sprinkler line tester, cast brass					16			16	17.60	
	8000	Wye, leader line, ball type, swivel female x male x male										
	8040	2-½" x 1-½" x 1-½" polished brass				Ea.	231			231	255	
	8060	2-½" x 1-½" x 1-½" polished chrome				"	239			239	265	
170	0010	**SPRINKLER SYSTEM COMPONENTS**										170
	0600	Accelerator	1 Spri	8	1	Ea.	225	26		251	285	
	0800	Air compressor for dry pipe system, automatic, complete B8.2-110										
	0820	200 gal. system capacity, ⅓ HP	1 Spri	1.30	6.150	Ea.	445	160		605	725	
	0840	350 gal. system capacity, ½ HP B8.2-120		1.30	6.150		465	160		625	745	
	0860	520 gal. system capacity, 1 HP		1.30	6.150		655	160		815	955	
	0900	Air compressor, with starting switch for manual operation B8.2-130										
	0910	200 gal. system capacity, ⅓ HP	1 Spri	1.30	6.150	Ea.	410	160		570	685	
	0920	350 gal. system capacity, ½ HP B8.2-140		1.30	6.150		430	160		590	710	
	0930	520 gal. system capacity, 1 HP		1.30	6.150		515	160		675	800	
	0960	Air pressure maintenance control B8.2-150		24	.333		81.50	8.55		90.05	100	
	1100	Alarm, electric pressure switch (circuit closer)		26	.308		52	7.90		59.90	69	
	1140	For explosion proof, max 20 PSI, contacts close or open		26	.308		164	7.90		171.90	190	
	1220	Water motor, complete with gong		4	2		100	51		151	185	
	1400	Deluge system, pressured monitoring panel, 120V C8.2-101		18	.444		310	11.40		321.40	360	
	1420	Explosion proof panel, not incl. enclosure		16	.500		230	12.85		242.85	270	
	1600	Dehydrator package, incl. valves and nipples C8.2-102		12	.667		172	17.10		189.10	215	
	1800	Firecycle system, controls, includes panel,										
	1820	batteries, solenoid valves and pressure switches C8.2-103	Q-13	1	32	Ea.	4,700	785		5,485	6,325	
	1980	Detector	1 Spri	16	.500		168	12.85		180.85	205	
	2000	Release, emergency, manual, for hydraulic or pneumatic system		12	.667		55	17.10		72.10	86	
	2060	Release, thermostatic, for hydraulic or pneumatic release line		20	.400		123	10.25		133.25	150	
	2200	Sprinkler cabinets, 6 head capacity		16	.500		20	12.85		32.85	41	
	2260	12 head capacity		16	.500		21.20	12.85		34.05	42	
	2340	Sprinkler head escutcheons, standard, brass tone, 1" size		40	.200		1	5.15		6.15	8.75	
	2360	Chrome, 1" size		40	.200		1.10	5.15		6.25	8.85	
	2400	Recessed type, brass tone		40	.200		2	5.15		7.15	9.85	
	2440	Chrome or white enamel		40	.200		1.45	5.15		6.60	9.25	
	2600	Sprinkler heads, not including supply piping										
	2640	Dry, pendent, ½" orifice, ¾" or 1" NPT										
	2660	1" to 4-¾" length	1 Spri	14	.571	Ea.	25.50	14.65		40.15	50	
	2670	5" to 6-¾" length		14	.571		25.50	14.65		40.15	50	
	2680	7" to 8-¾" length		14	.571		26.50	14.65		41.15	51	
	2690	9" to 10-¾" length		14	.571		28	14.65		42.65	53	
	2700	11" to 12-¾" length		14	.571		28	14.65		42.65	53	
	2710	13" to 14-¾" length		13	.615		31.50	15.80		47.30	58	
	2720	15" to 16-¾" length		13	.615		31.50	15.80		47.30	58	
	2730	17" to 18-¾" length		13	.615		35	15.80		50.80	62	
	2740	19" to 20-¾" length		13	.615		35	15.80		50.80	62	
	2750	21" to 22-¾" length		13	.615		36	15.80		51.80	63	
	2760	23" to 24-¾" length		13	.615		36	15.80		51.80	63	
	2780	25" to 26-¾" length		12	.667		36.50	17.10		53.60	66	
	2790	27" to 28-¾" length		12	.667		38.50	17.10		55.60	68	
	2800	For each inch or fraction over 29", add					1.17			1.17	1.29	
	2900	For recessed fitting, add					1.47			1.47	1.62	
	3600	Foam-water, pendent or upright, ½" NPT	1 Spri	12	.667		23	17.10		40.10	51	
	3630	On-off (automatic), 165°, 212°F										
	3640	Pendent, brass	1 Spri	12	.667	Ea.	43	17.10		60.10	73	
	3650	Chrome		12	.667		43	17.10		60.10	73	
	3660	Flush, chrome or brass		10	.800		54	21		75	90	

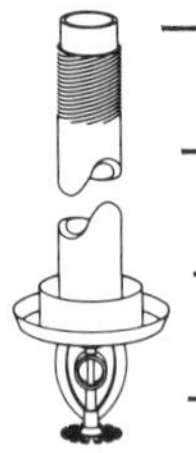

154 | Fire Extinguishing Systems

154 100 | Fire Systems

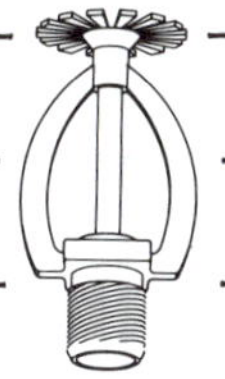

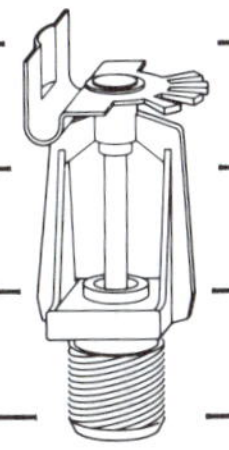

			Crew	Daily Output	Man-Hours	Unit	Bare Costs Mat.	Labor	Equip.	Total	Total Incl O&P
170	3700	Standard spray, pendent or upright, brass, 135° to 286°F										170
	3720	½″ NPT, ⅜″ orifice	1 Spri	16	.500	Ea.	4.05	12.85		16.90	24
	3730	½″ NPT, ⁷⁄₁₆″ orifice		16	.500		4.05	12.85		16.90	24
	3740	½″ NPT, ½″ orifice		16	.500		3.37	12.85		16.22	23
	3760	½″ NPT, ¹⁷⁄₃₂″ orifice		16	.500		3.87	12.85		16.72	23
	3780	¾″ NPT, ¹⁷⁄₃₂″ orifice		16	.500		3.87	12.85		16.72	23
	3800	For open sprinklers, deduct					.15			.15	.17
	3840	For chrome, add				Ea.	.50			.50	.55
	3860	For wax and lead coating, add					2.10			2.10	2.31
	3880	For wax coating, add					.60			.60	.66
	3900	For lead coating, add					1.30			1.30	1.43
	3920	For 360°F, same cost									
	3930	For 400°F, add					4.46			4.46	4.91
	3940	For 500°F, add					4.46			4.46	4.91
	4200	Sidewall, vertical, brass, 135°-286°F									
	4220	½″ NPT, ⅜″ orifice	1 Spri	16	.500	Ea.	4.84	12.85		17.69	24
	4230	½″ NPT, ⁷⁄₁₆″ orifice		16	.500		4.84	12.85		17.69	24
	4240	½″ NPT, ½″ orifice		16	.500		3.98	12.85		16.83	23
	4260	½″ NPT, ¹⁷⁄₃₂″ orifice		16	.500		4.26	12.85		17.11	24
	4280	¾″ NPT, ¹⁷⁄₃₂″ orifice		16	.500		4.14	12.85		16.99	24
	4360	For satin chrome, add					.47			.47	.52
	4400	For 360°F, same cost									
	4410	For 400°F, add					4.42			4.42	4.86
	4420	For 500°F, add					4.42			4.42	4.86
	4500	Sidewall, horizontal, brass, 135° to 286°F									
	4520	½″ NPT, ½″ orifice	1 Spri	16	.500	Ea.	4.12	12.85		16.97	24
	4540	For 360°F, same cost				″					
	4800	Recessed pendent, brass, 135° to 286°F									
	4820	½″ NPT, ⅜″ orifice	1 Spri	10	.800	Ea.	6.05	21		27.05	37
	4830	½″ NPT, ⁷⁄₁₆″ orifice		10	.800		6.05	21		27.05	37
	4840	½″ NPT, ½″ orifice		10	.800		5.03	21		26.03	36
	4860	½″ NPT, ¹⁷⁄₃₂″ orifice		10	.800		5.56	21		26.56	37
	4900	For satin chrome, add					.36			.36	.40
	5000	Recessed-vertical sidewall, brass, 135°-286°F									
	5020	½″ NPT, ⅜″ orifice	1 Spri	10	.800	Ea.	5.52	21		26.52	37
	5030	½″ NPT, ⁷⁄₁₆″ orifice		10	.800		5.52	21		26.52	37
	5040	½″ NPT, ½″ orifice		10	.800		4.73	21		25.73	36
	5060	½″ NPT, ¹⁷⁄₃₂″ orifice		10	.800		4.87	21		25.87	36
	5100	For bright nickel, same cost									
	5600	Concealed, complete with cover plate									
	5620	½″ NPT, ½″ orifice, 135°F to 212°F	1 Spri	9	.889	Ea.	7.43	23		30.43	42
	5800	Window, brass, ½″ NPT, ¼″ orifice		16	.500		8.30	12.85		21.15	28
	5810	½″ NPT, ⁵⁄₁₆″ orifice		16	.500		8.30	12.85		21.15	28
	5820	½″ NPT, ⅜″ orifice		16	.500		8.30	12.85		21.15	28
	5830	½″ NPT, ⁷⁄₁₆″ orifice		16	.500		8.30	12.85		21.15	28
	5840	½″ NPT, ½″ orifice		16	.500		8.75	12.85		21.60	29
	5860	For polished chrome, add					1.25			1.25	1.38
	5880	¾″ NPT, ⅝″ orifice	1 Spri	16	.500		9.20	12.85		22.05	29
	5890	¾ NPT, ¾″ orifice	″	16	.500		9.20	12.85		22.05	29
	6000	Sprinkler head guards, red					5.10			5.10	5.60
	6020	Bright zinc					1.65			1.65	1.82
	6025	Residential sprinkler components, (one and two family)									
	6026	Water motor alarm, with strainer	1 Spri	4	2	Ea.	100	51		151	185
	6027	Fast response, glass bulb, 135° to 155° f.									
	6028	½″ NPT, pendent, brass	1 Spri	16	.500	Ea.	5.55	12.85		18.40	25
	6029	½″ NPT, sidewall, brass		16	.500		6.35	12.85		19.20	26
	6030	½″ NPT, pendent, brass, extended coverage		16	.500		5.82	12.85		18.67	26
	6031	½″ NPT, sidewall, brass, extended coverage		16	.500		5.15	12.85		18	25

154 | Fire Extinguishing Systems

154 100 | Fire Systems

		CREW	DAILY OUTPUT	MAN-HOURS	UNIT	MAT.	LABOR	EQUIP.	TOTAL	TOTAL INCL O&P
170 6032	¾" NPT sidewall, brass, extended coverage	1 Spri	16	.500	Ea.	5.41	12.85		18.26	25
6033	For chrome, add					15%				
6034	For polyester/teflon coating add					20%				
6100	Sprinkler head wrenches, standard head				Ea.	6.40			6.40	7.05
6120	Recessed head				"	9.90			9.90	10.90
6200	Valves									
6210	Alarm, includes									
6220	retard chamber, trim, gauges, alarm line strainer									
6260	2-½" size	Q-12	3	5.330	Ea.	475	125		600	705
6280	4" size	"	2	8		495	185		680	820
6300	6" size	Q-13	4	8		530	195		725	875
6320	8" size	"	3	10.670		620	260		880	1,075
6500	Check, swing, C.I. body, brass fittings, auto. ball drip									
6520	4" size	Q-12	3	5.330	Ea.	86.75	125		211.75	280
6540	6" size	Q-13	4	8		190	195		385	500
6580	8" size	"	3	10.670		352	260		612	775
6800	Check, wafer, butterfly type, C.I. body, bronze fittings									
6820	4" size	Q-12	4	4	Ea.	216	92		308	375
6840	6" size	Q-13	5.50	5.820		313	145		458	555
6860	8" size		5	6.400		530	155		685	815
6880	10" size		4.50	7.110		690	175		865	1,025
6900	12" size		4	8		895	195		1,090	1,275
7000	Deluge, assembly, incl. trim, pressure									
7020	operated relief, emergency release, gauges									
7040	2" size	Q-12	2	8	Ea.	690	185		875	1,025
7060	3" size		1.50	10.670		815	245		1,060	1,275
7080	4" size		1	16		975	370		1,345	1,625
7100	6" size	Q-13	4	8		1,235	195		1,430	1,650
7300	Detector check, valve only, flanged,									
7320	4" size, painted	Q-12	4	4	Ea.	330	92		422	500
7340	6" size, painted	Q-13	5.50	5.820		500	145		645	760
7360	8" size, painted		5	6.400		765	155		920	1,075
7380	10" size, painted		4.50	7.110		1,500	175		1,675	1,900
7400	4" size, galvanized	Q-12	4	4		495	92		587	680
7420	6" size, galvanized	Q-13	5.50	5.820		640	145		785	915
7440	8" size, galvanized		5	6.400		985	155		1,140	1,325
7460	10" size, galvanized		4.50	7.110		1,620	175		1,795	2,050
7560	By-pass trim, not including meter									
7580	For ⅝" meter	1 Spri	6	1.330	Ea.	32	34		66	86
7600	For 1 meter		5.50	1.450		49	37		86	110
7620	For 1-½" meter		5	1.600		85	41		126	155
7800	Pneumatic actuator, bronze, required on all									
7820	pneumatic release systems, any size deluge	1 Spri	18	.444	Ea.	100	11.40		111.40	125
8000	Dry pipe air check valve, 3" size	Q-12	2	8		510	185		695	835
8200	Dry pipe valve, incl. trim and gauges, 3" size		2	8		665	185		850	1,000
8220	4" size		1	16		690	370		1,060	1,300
8240	6" size	Q-13	2	16		800	390		1,190	1,475
8280	For accelerator trim with gauges, add	1 Spri	8	1		226	26		252	285
8400	Firecycle package, includes swing check									
8420	and flow control valves with required trim									
8440	2" size	Q-12	2	8	Ea.	725	185		910	1,075
8460	3" size		1.50	10.670		1,155	245		1,400	1,625
8480	4" size		1	16		1,320	370		1,690	2,000
8500	6" size	Q-13	1.40	22.860		1,770	560		2,330	2,775
8800	Flow control valve, includes trim and gauges, 2" size	Q-12	2	8		645	185		830	985
8820	3" size	"	1.50	10.670		770	245		1,015	1,225
8840	4" size	Q-13	2.80	11.430		925	280		1,205	1,425
8860	6" size	"	2	16		1,190	390		1,580	1,900

154 | Fire Extinguishing Systems

	154 100	Fire Systems	CREW	DAILY OUTPUT	MAN-HOURS	UNIT	BARE COSTS MAT.	LABOR	EQUIP.	TOTAL	TOTAL INCL O&P	
170	9200	Pressure operated relief valve, brass body	1 Spri	18	.444	Ea.	88.50	11.40		99.90	115	170
	9600	Waterflow indicator, with recycling retard and										
	9610	two single pole retard switches, 2" thru 6" pipe size	1 Spri	8	1	Ea.	83	26		109	130	

155 | Heating

	155 100	Boilers	CREW	DAILY OUTPUT	MAN-HOURS	UNIT	BARE COSTS MAT.	LABOR	EQUIP.	TOTAL	TOTAL INCL O&P	
101	0010	**AVERAGE** Square foot and percent of total										101
	0020	job cost, see division 171										
105	0010	**BOILERS, GENERAL** Prices do not include flue piping, elec. wiring,										105
	0020	gas or oil piping, boiler base, pad, or tankless unless noted										
	0100	Boiler horsepower: 10 KW = 34 lbs/steam/hr = 33,475 BTU/hr.										
	0150	To convert SFR to BTU rating: Hot water, 150 x SFR;										
	0160	Forced hot water, 180 x SFR; steam, 240 x SFR										
110	0010	**BOILERS, ELECTRIC, ASME** Standard controls and trim										110
	1000	Steam, 6 KW, 20.5 MBH	Q-19	1.20	20	Ea.	2,810	460		3,270	3,775	
	1020	9 KW, 30.7 MBH		1.20	20		2,820	460		3,280	3,775	
	1040	12 KW, 40.9 MBH		1.20	20		2,825	460		3,285	3,800	
	1060	18 KW, 61.4 MBH		1.20	20		2,860	460		3,320	3,825	
	1080	24 KW, 81.8 MBH		1.10	21.820		3,020	500		3,520	4,075	
	1100	30 KW, 102 MBH		1.10	21.820		3,030	500		3,530	4,075	
	1120	36 KW, 123 MBH		1.10	21.820		3,200	500		3,700	4,250	
	2000	Hot water, 12 KW, 41 MBH		1.30	18.460		2,320	425		2,745	3,175	
	2020	15 KW, 52 MBH		1.30	18.460		2,330	425		2,755	3,200	
	2040	24 KW, 82 MBH		1.20	20		2,490	460		2,950	3,425	
	2060	30 KW, 103 MBH		1.20	20		2,540	460		3,000	3,475	
	2070	36 KW, 123 MBH		1.20	20		2,700	460		3,160	3,650	
	2080	45 KW, 154 MBH		1.10	21.820		2,720	500		3,220	3,725	
115	0010	**BOILERS, GAS FIRED** Natural or propane, standard controls										115
	1000	Cast iron, with insulated jacket										
	2000	Steam, gross output, 81 MBH	Q-7	1.40	22.860	Ea.	1,005	540		1,545	1,900	
	2020	102 MBH		1.30	24.620		1,160	580		1,740	2,150	
	2040	122 MBH		1	32		1,270	755		2,025	2,525	
	2060	163 MBH		.90	35.560		1,535	840		2,375	2,925	
	2080	203 MBH		.90	35.560		1,750	840		2,590	3,175	
	2100	240 MBH		.85	37.650		1,965	890		2,855	3,475	
	2120	280 MBH		.80	40		2,300	945		3,245	3,925	
	2140	320 MBH		.70	45.710		2,510	1,075		3,585	4,375	
	3000	Hot water, gross output, 80 MBH		1.46	21.920		895	520		1,415	1,750	
	3020	100 MBH		1.35	23.700		1,050	560		1,610	1,975	
	3040	122 MBH		1.10	29.090		1,155	690		1,845	2,300	
	3060	163 MBH		1	32		1,425	755		2,180	2,700	
	3080	203 MBH		1	32		1,640	755		2,395	2,925	
	3100	240 MBH		.95	33.680		1,855	795		2,650	3,225	
	3120	280 MBH		.90	35.560		2,130	840		2,970	3,600	
	3140	320 MBH		.80	40		2,335	945		3,280	3,975	
	6000	Hot water, including burner & one zone valve, gross output										
	6010	51.2 MBH	Q-6	2	12	Ea.	1,040	275		1,315	1,550	
	6020	72 MBH		2	12		1,330	275		1,605	1,875	
	6040	89 MBH		1.90	12.630		1,370	290		1,660	1,950	

155 | Heating

155 100 | Boilers

			CREW	DAILY OUTPUT	MAN-HOURS	UNIT	BARE COSTS MAT.	LABOR	EQUIP.	TOTAL	TOTAL INCL O&P	
115	6060	105 MBH	Q-6	1.80	13.330	Ea.	1,540	310		1,850	2,150	115
	6080	132 MBH		1.70	14.120		1,760	325		2,085	2,425	
	6100	155 MBH		1.50	16		2,030	370		2,400	2,775	
	6110	186 MBH		1.40	17.140		2,460	395		2,855	3,300	
	7000	For tankless water heater on smaller gas units, add					10%					
	7050	For additional zone valves up to 312 MBH add					70			70	77	
	7990	Special feature gas fired boilers										
	8000	Pulse combustion 44,000 BTU	Q-5	1.50	10.670	Ea.	1,570	240		1,810	2,075	
	8050	88,000 BTU		1.40	11.430		1,835	255		2,090	2,400	
	8080	134,000 BTU		1.20	13.330		2,625	295		2,920	3,325	
	9000	Wall hung, C.I., sealed combustion, direct vent										
	9010	Packaged, net output										
	9020	45,000 BTUH	Q-6	1.33	18.050	Ea.	1,040	415		1,455	1,775	
	9030	60,800 BTUH		1.33	18.050		1,160	415		1,575	1,900	
	9040	77,000 BTUH		1.33	18.050		1,275	415		1,690	2,025	
120	0010	**BOILERS, OIL FIRED** Standard controls, flame retention burner										120
	1000	Cast iron, with insulated flush jacket										
	2000	Steam, gross output, 109 MBH	Q-7	1.20	26.670	Ea.	1,320	630		1,950	2,400	
	2020	144 MBH		1.10	29.090		1,490	690		2,180	2,650	
	2040	173 MBH		1	32		1,670	755		2,425	2,950	
	2060	207 MBH		.90	35.560		1,810	840		2,650	3,250	
	3000	Hot water, same price as steam										
	4000	For tankless coil in smaller sizes, add				Ea.	15%					
	5000	Steel, insulated jacket, burner										
	6000	Steam, full water leg construction, gross output										
	6020	144 MBH	Q-6	1.60	15	Ea.	2,195	345		2,540	2,925	
	6040	198 MBH	"	1.40	17.140	"	2,390	395		2,785	3,225	
	6400	Larger sizes are same as steel, gas fired										
	7000	Hot water, gross output, 103 MBH	Q-6	1.90	12.630	Ea.	1,560	290		1,850	2,150	
	7020	122 MBH		1.80	13.330		1,580	310		1,890	2,200	
	7040	137 MBH		1.60	15		1,660	345		2,005	2,350	
	7060	168 MBH		1.50	16		2,000	370		2,370	2,750	
	7080	225 MBH		1.40	17.140		2,370	395		2,765	3,200	
	7340	For tankless coil in steam or hot water, add					7%					
150	0010	**SWIMMING POOL HEATERS** Not including wiring, external										150
	0020	piping, base or pad,										
	0060	Gas fired, gross output, 50 MBH	Q-6	3	8	Ea.	425	185		610	740	
	0100	80 MBH		2	12		545	275		820	1,000	
	0160	120 MBH		1.50	16		565	370		935	1,175	
	0180	145 MBH		1.30	18.460		650	425		1,075	1,350	
	0200	170 MBH		1	24		680	555		1,235	1,575	
	0220	200 MBH		.70	34.290		700	790		1,490	1,950	
	0240	280 MBH		.60	40		790	925		1,715	2,250	
	0260	450 MBH		.50	48		1,950	1,100		3,050	3,800	
	0280	500 MBH		.40	60		2,120	1,375		3,495	4,400	
	0300	600 MBH		.35	68.570		2,350	1,575		3,925	4,925	
	0320	750 MBH		.33	72.730		2,730	1,675		4,405	5,500	
	0340	890 MBH		.26	92.310		2,970	2,125		5,095	6,425	
	0360	965 MBH		.22	109		3,085	2,525		5,610	7,125	
	0370	1080 MBH		.21	114		3,440	2,650		6,090	7,700	
	0380	1312 MBH		.19	126		4,400	2,925		7,325	9,175	
	0400	1600 MBH		.14	171		5,660	3,950		9,610	12,100	
	0410	2100 MBH		.13	185		6,500	4,275		10,775	13,500	
	0420	2450 MBH		.11	218		6,900	5,050		11,950	15,100	
	0440	3000 MBH		.09	267		7,600	6,150		13,750	17,500	
	1000	Oil fired, gross output, 97 MBH		1.70	14.120		1,460	325		1,785	2,100	

155 | Heating

155 100 | Boilers

		CREW	DAILY OUTPUT	MAN-HOURS	UNIT	BARE COSTS MAT.	LABOR	EQUIP.	TOTAL	TOTAL INCL O&P	
150	1020 118 MBH	Q-6	1.70	14.120	Ea.	1,490	325		1,815	2,125	150
	1040 134 MBH		1.60	15		1,580	345		1,925	2,250	
	1060 161 MBH		1.30	18.460		1,930	425		2,355	2,750	
	1080 187 MBH		1.20	20		2,025	460		2,485	2,925	
	1100 214 MBH		1.10	21.820		2,320	505		2,825	3,300	
	1120 262 MBH		.89	26.970		2,610	625		3,235	3,800	
	1140 340 MBH		.68	35.290		3,450	815		4,265	5,000	
	1160 420 MBH		.58	41.380		3,970	955		4,925	5,775	
	1180 525 MBH		.46	52.170		5,080	1,200		6,280	7,375	
	1200 630 MBH		.41	58.540		5,670	1,350		7,020	8,250	
	1220 735 MBH		.35	68.570		6,980	1,575		8,555	10,000	
	1240 840 MBH		.33	72.730		7,980	1,675		9,655	11,300	
	1260 1050 MBH		.27	88.890		9,710	2,050		11,760	13,700	
	1280 1365 MBH		.21	114		12,500	2,650		15,150	17,700	
	1300 1680 MBH		.18	133		14,700	3,075		17,775	20,700	
	1320 2310 MBH		.13	185		18,950	4,275		23,225	27,200	
	1340 2835 MBH		.11	218		23,550	5,050		28,600	33,400	
	1360 3150 MBH		.09	267		26,500	6,150		32,650	38,300	
	2000 Electric, 12 KW, 4800 gallon pool	Q-19	3	8		1,050	185		1,235	1,425	
	2020 18 KW, 7200 gallon pool		2.80	8.570		1,080	195		1,275	1,475	
	2040 24 KW, 9600 gallon pool		2.40	10		1,140	230		1,370	1,600	
	2060 30 KW, 12,000 gallon pool		2	12		1,200	275		1,475	1,725	
	2080 36 KW, 14,400 gallon pool		1.60	15		1,310	345		1,655	1,950	
	2100 54 KW, 24,000 gallon pool		1.20	20		1,560	460		2,020	2,400	
	9000 To select pool heater: 12 BTUH x S.F. pool area										
	9010 X temperature differential =required output										
	9050 For electric, KW = gallons x 2.5 divided by 1000										
	9100 For family home type pool, double the										
	9110 Rated gallon capacity = ½°F rise per hour										

155 200 | Boiler Accessories

		CREW	DAILY OUTPUT	MAN-HOURS	UNIT	MAT.	LABOR	EQUIP.	TOTAL	TOTAL INCL O&P	
230	0010 **BURNERS**										230
	0990 Residential, conversion, gas fired, LP or natural										
	1000 Gun type, atmospheric input 35 to 180 MBH	Q-1	2.50	6.400	Ea.	157	140		297	385	
	1020 50 to 240 MBH	"	2	8	"	182	180		362	465	
	3000 Flame retention oil fired assembly, input										
	3020 .50 to 2.25 GPH	Q-1	2.40	6.670	Ea.	238	150		388	480	
	3040 2.0 to 5.0 GPH	"	2	8	"	385	180		565	685	
240	0010 **DRAFT CONTROLS, BAROMETRIC**										240
	5000 Vent damper, bi-metal, gas, 3" diameter	Q-9	24	.667	Ea.	38.80	14.60		53.40	65	
	5010 4" diameter		24	.667		44.20	14.60		58.80	71	
	5101 Electric, automatic, gas, 4" diameter		24	.667		111	14.60		125.60	145	
	5250 Automatic, oil, 4" diameter		24	.667		134	14.60		148.60	170	
250	0010 **FUEL OIL SPECIALTIES**										250
	0020 Foot valve, single poppet, metal to metal construction,										
	0040 bevel seat, ½" diameter	1 Stpi	20	.400	Ea.	31.25	9.90		41.15	49	
	0060 ¾" diameter		18	.444		32.85	11		43.85	52	
	1000 Oil filters, ⅜" IPT., 20 gal. per hour		20	.400		9.95	9.90		19.85	26	
	1800 Pump and motor sets										
	1810 Light fuel and diesel oils, 100 PSI										
	1820 25 GPH ¼ HP	Q-5	6	2.670	Ea.	395	59		454	525	
	2000 Remote tank gauging system, self contained										
	2020 30' transmission line										
	2100 30" pointer travel	1 Stpi	2	4	Ea.	1,090	99		1,189	1,350	
	2120 5" pointer travel	"	2.50	3.200	"	715	79		794	905	

155 | Heating

155 200 | Boiler Accessories

			DAILY	MAN-		\multicolumn{4}{c}{BARE COSTS}	TOTAL	
		CREW	OUTPUT	HOURS	UNIT	MAT.	LABOR	EQUIP.	TOTAL	INCL O&P	
250	2500	For each additional 10' transmission line, add				Ea.	13.25			13.25	14.60	250
	3000	Valve, ball check, globe type, ⅜" diameter	1 Stpi	24	.333		4.25	8.25		12.50	16.90	
	3500	Fusible, ⅜" diameter		24	.333		3.50	8.25		11.75	16.10	
	3600	½" diameter		24	.333		7.75	8.25		16	21	
	3610	¾" diameter		20	.400		14.55	9.90		24.45	31	
	3620	1" diameter		19	.421		50.25	10.40		60.65	71	
	4000	Nonfusible, ⅜" diameter		24	.333		5.75	8.25		14	18.55	
	4500	Shutoff, gate type, lever handle, spring-fusible kit										
	4520	¼" diameter	1 Stpi	14	.571	Ea.	9.45	14.15		23.60	31	
	4540	⅜" diameter		12	.667		8.60	16.50		25.10	34	
	4560	½" diameter		10	.800		11.75	19.80		31.55	42	
	4570	¾" diameter		8	1		15.50	25		40.50	54	
	5000	Vent alarm, whistling signal					16.80			16.80	18.50	
	5500	Vent protector/breather, 1-¼" diameter	1 Stpi	32	.250		4.20	6.20		10.40	13.80	

155 400 | Warm Air Systems

451	0010	**INFRA-RED UNIT**										451
	0020	Gas fired, unvented, electric ignition, 100% shutoff. Piping and										
	0030	wiring not included										
	0060	Input, 15 MBH	Q-5	7	2.290	Ea.	293	51		344	400	
	0100	30 MBH		6	2.670		315	59		374	435	
	0120	45 MBH		5	3.200		375	71		446	520	
	0140	50 MBH		4.50	3.560		400	79		479	560	
	0160	60 MBH		4	4		400	89		489	570	
	0180	75 MBH		3	5.330		475	120		595	700	
	0200	90 MBH		2.50	6.400		475	145		620	735	
	0220	105 MBH		2	8		510	180		690	825	
	0240	120 MBH		2	8		590	180		770	915	
	0500	For deep parabolic reflector, add					58			58	64	
	1000	For opt. screen, req'd. for hangar or garage install., add					8%					
	2000	Electric, single or three phase										
	2050	6 KW, 20,478 BTU	1 Elec	3	2.670	Ea.	330	65		395	460	
	2100	13.5 KW, 40,956 BTU		2.50	3.200		450	78		528	610	
	2150	24 KW, 81,912 BTU		2	4		850	97		947	1,075	
	3000	Oil fired, two stage pump, controls, solenoid valve, venter										
	3050	117,000 BTU, one burner	Q-5	2.50	6.400	Ea.	2,140	145		2,285	2,575	
	3080	234,000 BTU, two burner		2.25	7.110		3,940	160		4,100	4,575	
	3110	351,000 BTU, three burner		2	8		5,920	180		6,100	6,775	
	3140	468,000 BTU four burner		1.50	10.670		7,890	240		8,130	9,025	
	3200	Free air inlet per burner, add					120			120	130	
	3250	Prepurger per unit, add					50.60			50.60	56	
471	0010	**SOLAR ENERGY**										471
	0020	System/Package prices, not including connecting										
	0030	pipe, insulation, or special heating/plumbing fixtures										
	0150	For solar ultraviolet pipe insulation see Division 155-651-9290										
	0500	Hot water, standard package, low temperature										
	0540	2 collectors, circulator, fittings, no tank	Q-1	.50	32	Ea.	1,050	710		1,760	2,200	
	0580	2 collectors, circulator, fittings, 120 gal. tank		.40	40		1,730	890		2,620	3,225	
	0620	3 collectors, circulator, fittings, 120 gal. tank		.40	40		2,160	890		3,050	3,700	
	0700	Medium temperature package										
	0740	2 collectors, circulator, fittings, 80 gal. tank	Q-1	.40	40	Ea.	1,900	890		2,790	3,400	
	0780	3 collectors, circulator, fittings, 120 gal. tank	"	.30	53.330	"	2,410	1,175		3,585	4,400	
	0900	Commercial/process										
	0940	10 med. temp. collectors, fittings, 120 gal. tank	Q-2	.15	160	Ea.	6,780	3,700		10,480	12,900	
	0980	For each additional 120 gal. tank, add				"	670			670	735	
	1300	Solar assist package, for space heating and domestic										
	1340	hot water, 10 collectors, fittings	Q-2	.13	185	Ea.	6,975	4,250		11,225	14,000	

155 | Heating

155 400 | Warm Air Systems

			CREW	DAILY OUTPUT	MAN-HOURS	UNIT	BARE COSTS MAT.	LABOR	EQUIP.	TOTAL	TOTAL INCL O&P
471	1440	For heating, complete with heat pump, 9 collectors B8.3-710	Q-2	.12	200	Ea.	9,125	4,600		13,725	16,900	471
	1480	12 collectors		.10	240		10,700	5,525		16,225	20,000
	1540	18 collectors B8.3-720		.08	300		14,200	6,925		21,125	25,900
	2000	Seasonal pool heating package, fittings, 10 collectors		.30	80		2,920	1,850		4,770	5,950
	2250	Controller, liquid temperature B8.3-730	1 Plum	5	1.600		93.50	40		133.50	160
	2300	Circulators, air									
	2310	Blowers B8.3-740									
	2320	30 to 100 S.F. system, 1/20 HP	Q-9	16	1	Ea.	45	22		67	83
	2330	100-300 S.F. system, 1/10 HP		16	1		88	22		110	130
	2340	300-500 S.F. system, 1/6 HP		15	1.070		121	23		144	170
	2350	Two speed, 100-300 S.F., 1/10 HP		14	1.140		86	25		111	130
	2400	Reversible fan, 20" diameter, 2 speed		18	.889		77	19.50		96.50	115
	2480	Shutter mounted fan, 12" diameter, 650 CFM		14	1.140		100	25		125	150
	2520	Space & DHW system, less duct work		.50	32		1,190	700		1,890	2,375
	2550	Booster fan 5" diameter, 70 CFM		16	1		20	22		42	55
	2570	6" diameter, 90 CFM		16	1		23	22		45	58
	2580	8" diameter, 150 CFM		16	1		28	22		50	64
	2590	8" diameter, 250 CFM		14	1.140		38	25		63	80
	2600	8" diameter, 310 CFM		14	1.140		43	25		68	85
	2650	Rheostat		32	.500		9.95	10.95		20.90	28
	2660	Shutter/damper		12	1.330		27	29		56	74
	2670	Shutter motor		16	1		59	22		81	98
	2750	Circulators, liquid, 1/100 HP, 2 GPM	Q-1	14	1.140		86	25		111	130
	2770	1/100 HP, 3 GPM		14	1.140		84	25		109	130
	2800	1/25 HP, 5.3 GPM		14	1.140		95	25		120	140
	2820	1/20 HP, 17 GPM		12	1.330		73	30		103	125
	2850	1/20 HP, 17 GPM, stainless steel		12	1.330		156	30		186	215
	2870	1/12 HP, 30 GPM		10	1.600		135	36		171	200
	3000	Collector panels, air with aluminum absorber plate									
	3010	Wall or roof mount									
	3040	Flat black, plastic glazing									
	3080	4' x 8'	Q-9	6	2.670	Ea.	450	58		508	585
	3100	5' x 9'		5	3.200	"	550	70		620	710
	3200	Flush roof mount, 10' to 16' x 22" wide		96	.167	L.F.	54	3.65		57.65	65
	3210	Manifold, by L.F. width of collectors		160	.100	"	15	2.19		17.19	19.80
	3300	Collector panels, liquid with copper absorber plate									
	3320	Black chrome, tempered glass glazing									
	3330	Alum. frame, 3' x 8', 5/32" single glazing	Q-1	9.50	1.680	Ea.	335	37		372	425
	3360	Alum. frame, 3' x 8', 5/32" double glazing		9	1.780		365	40		405	460
	3390	Alum. frame, 4' x 8', 3/16" single glazing		6	2.670		680	59		739	835
	3440	Flat black									
	3450	Alum. frame, 3' x 8', 5/32" single glazing	Q-1	9	1.780	Ea.	325	40		365	415
	3500	Alum. frame, 3' x 8', 5/32" double glazing		5.50	2.910		345	65		410	475
	3520	Alum. frame, 3' x 10', plastic glazing		10	1.600		235	36		271	310
	3540	Alum. frame, 3' x 8', 1/8" tempered glass		5	3.200		380	71		451	525
	3550	Liquid with fin tube absorber plate									
	3560	Alum. frame 4' x 8' tempered glass	Q-1	10	1.600	Ea.	425	36		461	520
	3580	Liquid with vacuum tubes, 4' x 6'-10"		9	1.780		730	40		770	860
	3600	Liquid, full wetted, plastic, alum. frame, 3' x 10'		5	3.200		145	71		216	265
	3650	Collector panel mounting, flat roof or ground rack		7	2.290		125	51		176	215
	3670	Roof clamps		70	.229	Set	5	5.10		10.10	13.05
	3700	Roof strap, teflon	1 Plum	205	.039	L.F.	4.75	.96		5.71	6.65
	3900	Differential controller with two sensors									
	3930	Thermostat, hard wired	1 Plum	8	1	Ea.	93.50	25		118.50	140
	3950	Line cord and receptacle		12	.667		105	16.45		121.45	140
	4000	External adjustment		12	.667		94	16.45		110.45	130
	4050	Pool valve system, 2" pipe size (plastic)		2.50	3.200		245	79		324	385
	4070	1-1/2" pipe size (copper)		2	4		320	99		419	500

155 | Heating

155 400 | Warm Air Systems

		CREW	DAILY OUTPUT	MAN-HOURS	UNIT	BARE COSTS MAT.	LABOR	EQUIP.	TOTAL	TOTAL INCL O&P	
471	4080 Pool pump system, 2" pipe size	1 Plum	6	1.330	Ea.	155	33		188	220	471
	4100 Six station with digital read-out	"	3	2.670	"	300	66		366	430	
	4150 Sensors										
	4200 Brass plug, ½" MPT	1 Plum	32	.250	Ea.	15.50	6.20		21.70	26	
	4210 Brass plug, reversed		32	.250		14.30	6.20		20.50	25	
	4220 Freeze prevention		32	.250		15.50	6.20		21.70	26	
	4240 Screw attached		32	.250		9.85	6.20		16.05	20	
	4250 Brass, immersion		32	.250		24.50	6.20		30.70	36	
	4300 Heat exchanger										
	4310 Fluid to air coil										
	4330 Up flow, 45 MBH	Q-1	4	4	Ea.	97	89		186	240	
	4380 70 MBH		3.50	4.570		245	100		345	420	
	4400 80 MBH		3	5.330		355	120		475	565	
	4490 Horizontal, 110 MBH		2	8		195	180		375	480	
	4580 Fluid to fluid package includes two circulating pumps										
	4590 expansion tank, check valve, relief valve										
	4600 controller, high temperature cutoff and sensors	Q-1	2.50	6.400	Ea.	600	140		740	870	
	4650 Heat transfer fluid										
	4700 Propylene glycol, inhibited anti-freeze	1 Plum	28	.286	Gal.	7.39	7.05		14.44	18.60	
	4800 Solar storage tanks, knocked down										
	4810 Air, galvanized steel clad, double wall, 4" fiberglass										
	4820 insulation, 20 Mil PVC lining										
	4860 4' high, 3' x 3', = 36 C.F./250 gallons	Q-9	2.60	6.150	Ea.	1,080	135		1,215	1,400	
	4870 4' x 4', = 64 C.F./480 gallons		2	8		1,470	175		1,645	1,875	
	4880 5' x 5' = 100 C.F./750 gallons		1.50	10.670		1,910	235		2,145	2,450	
	4890 6' x 6' = 144 C.F./1000 gallons		1.30	12.310		2,410	270		2,680	3,050	
	4900 7' x 7' = 196 C.F./1450 gallons		1	16		3,080	350		3,430	3,925	
	5010 6'-3" high, 7' x 7' = 306 C.F./2000 gallons	Q-10	1.20	20		4,880	455		5,335	6,050	
	5020 7' x 10'-6" = 459 C.F./3000 gallons		.80	30		6,130	680		6,810	7,775	
	5030 7' x 14' = 613 C.F./4000 gallons		.60	40		7,390	910		8,300	9,500	
	5040 10'-6" x 10'-6" = 689 C.F./4500 gallons		.50	48		7,875	1,100		8,975	10,300	
	5050 10'-6" x 14' = 919 C.F./6000 gallons		.40	60		9,450	1,375		10,825	12,500	
	5060 14' x 14' = 1225 C.F./8000 gallons	Q-11	.40	80		11,350	1,850		13,200	15,300	
	5070 14' x 17'-6" = 1531 C.F./10,000 gallons		.30	107		13,100	2,475		15,575	18,200	
	5080 17'-6" x 17'-6" = 1914 C.F./12,500 gallons		.25	128		14,850	2,975		17,825	20,800	
	5090 17'-6" x 21' = 2297 C.F./15,000 gallons		.20	160		16,900	3,725		20,625	24,200	
	5100 21' x 21' = 2756 C.F./18,000 gallons		.18	178		19,350	4,125		23,475	27,500	
	5120 30 Mil reinforced Chemflex lining,										
	5130 4' high, 3' x 3' = 36 C.F./250 gallons	Q-9	2.60	6.150	Ea.	1,220	135		1,355	1,550	
	5140 4' x 4' = 64 C.F./480 gallons		2	8		1,620	175		1,795	2,050	
	5150 5' x 5' = 100 C.F./750 gallons		1.50	10.670		2,130	235		2,365	2,700	
	5160 6' x 6' = 144 C.F./1000 gallons		1.30	12.310		2,675	270		2,945	3,350	
	5170 7' x 7' = 196 C.F./1450 gallons		1	16		3,360	350		3,710	4,225	
	5190 6'-3" high, 7' x 7' = 306 C.F./2000 gallons	Q-10	1.20	20		5,290	455		5,745	6,500	
	5200 7' x 10'-6" = 459 C.F./3000 gallons		.80	30		6,590	680		7,270	8,275	
	5210 7' x 14' = 613 C.F./4000 gallons		.60	40		7,930	910		8,840	10,100	
	5220 10'-6" x 10'-6" = 689 C.F./4500 gallons		.50	48		8,430	1,100		9,530	10,900	
	5230 10'-6" x 14' = 919 C.F./6000 gallons		.40	60		10,150	1,375		11,525	13,200	
	5240 14' x 14' = 1225 C.F./8000 gallons	Q-11	.40	80		12,150	1,850		14,000	16,200	
	5250 14' x 17'-6" = 1531 C.F./10,000 gallons		.30	107		13,750	2,475		16,225	18,900	
	5260 17'-6" x 17'-6" = 1914 C.F./12,500 gallons		.25	128		15,750	2,975		18,725	21,800	
	5270 17'-6" x 21' = 2297 C.F./15,000 gallons		.20	160		17,950	3,725		21,675	25,400	
	5280 21' x 21' = 2756 C.F./18,000 gallons		.18	178		20,550	4,125		24,675	28,900	
	5290 30 Mil reinforced Hypalon lining, add					.02%					
	7000 Solar control valves and vents										
	7050 Air purger, 1" pipe size	1 Plum	12	.667	Ea.	16.50	16.45		32.95	43	
	7070 Air eliminator, automatic ¾" size		32	.250		9.95	6.20		16.15	20	
	7090 Air vent, automatic, ⅛" fitting		32	.250		5.65	6.20		11.85	15.40	

155 | Heating

155 400 | Warm Air Systems

			CREW	DAILY OUTPUT	MAN-HOURS	UNIT	MAT.	LABOR	EQUIP.	TOTAL	TOTAL INCL O&P	
471	7100	Manual, ⅛" NPT	1 Plum	32	.250	Ea.	1.43	6.20		7.63	10.75	471
	7120	Backflow preventer, ½" pipe size		16	.500		42.75	12.35		55.10	65	
	7130	¾" pipe size		16	.500		42.75	12.35		55.10	65	
	7150	Balancing valve, ¾" pipe size		20	.400		13.50	9.90		23.40	30	
	7180	Draindown valve, ½" copper tube		9	.889		150	22		172	200	
	7200	Flow control valve, ½" pipe size		22	.364		25.25	9		34.25	41	
	7220	Expansion tank, up to 5 gal.		32	.250		38.50	6.20		44.70	52	
	7250	Hydronic controller		8	1		36.50	25		61.50	77	
	7400	Pressure gauge, 2" dial		32	.250		8.35	6.20		14.55	18.35	
	7450	Relief valve, temp. and pressure ¾" pipe size		30	.267		16.50	6.60		23.10	28	
	7500	Solenoid valve, normally closed										
	7520	Brass, ¾" NPT, 24V	1 Plum	9	.889	Ea.	48	22		70	85	
	7530	1" NPT, 24V		9	.889		62	22		84	100	
	7750	Vacuum relief valve, ¾" pipe size		32	.250		25	6.20		31.20	37	
	7800	Thermometers										
	7820	Digital temperature monitoring, 4 locations	1 Plum	2.50	3.200	Ea.	110	79		189	240	
	7870	Indoor, outdoor		8	1		25	25		50	64	
	7890	In line, dial, ½" NPT		8	1		17	25		42	55	
	7900	Upright, ½" NPT		8	1		19	25		44	58	
	7970	Remote probe, 2" dial		8	1		27	25		52	66	
	7990	Stem, 2" dial, 9" stem		16	.500		16	12.35		28.35	36	
	8250	Water storage tank with heat exchanger and electric element										
	8260	66 gal. with 2" x ½ lb. density insulation	1 Plum	1.60	5	Ea.	515	125		640	750	
	8270	66 gal. with 2" x 2 lb. density insulation		1.60	5		545	125		670	785	
	8280	80 gal. with 2" x ½ lb. density insulation		1.60	5		575	125		700	815	
	8300	80 gal. with 2" x 2 lb. density insulation		1.60	5		590	125		715	830	
	8350	120 gal. with 2" x ½ lb. density insulation		1.40	5.710		645	140		785	920	
	8380	120 gal. with 2" x 2 lb. density insulation		1.40	5.710		660	140		800	935	
	8400	120 gal. with 2" x 2 lb. density insul., 40 S.F. heat coil		1.40	5.710		815	140		955	1,100	
	8500	Water storage module, plastic										
	8600	Tubular, 12" diameter, 4' high	1 Carp	48	.167	Ea.	50	3.60		53.60	60	
	8610	12" diameter, 8' high		40	.200		80	4.32		84.32	95	
	8620	18" diameter, 5' high		38	.211		90	4.55		94.55	105	
	8630	18" diameter, 10' high		32	.250		120	5.40		125.40	140	
	8640	58" diameter, 5' high	F-2	32	.500		350	10.80	.49	361.29	400	
	8650	Cap, 12" diameter					6.95			6.95	7.65	
	8660	18" diameter					7.95			7.95	8.75	

155 600 | Heating System Access.

			CREW	DAILY OUTPUT	MAN-HOURS	UNIT	MAT.	LABOR	EQUIP.	TOTAL	TOTAL INCL O&P	
601	0010	HEAT EXCHANGERS 4 pass, ¾" O.D. copper tubes,										601
	0020	C.I. heads, C.I. tube sheet, steel shell										
	0100	Hot water 40°F to 180°F, by steam at 10 PSI										
	0120	8 GPM	Q-5	6	2.670	Ea.	545	59		604	690	
	0140	10 GPM		5	3.200		830	71		901	1,025	
	0160	40 GPM		4	4		1,290	89		1,379	1,550	
	0500	For bronze head and tube sheet, add					50%					
	1000	Hot water 40°F to 140°F, by water at 200°F										
	1020	7 GPM	Q-5	6	2.670	Ea.	670	59		729	825	
	1040	16 GPM		5	3.200		965	71		1,036	1,175	
	1060	34 GPM		4	4		1,470	89		1,559	1,750	
	1080	55 GPM		3	5.330		2,120	120		2,240	2,500	
	1100	74 GPM		1.50	10.670		2,650	240		2,890	3,275	
	1120	86 GPM		1.40	11.430		3,620	255		3,875	4,350	
	1140	112 GPM	Q-6	2	12		4,600	275		4,875	5,475	
	1160	126 GPM		1.80	13.330		5,730	310		6,040	6,750	
	1180	152 GPM		1	24		7,320	555		7,875	8,875	

155 | Heating

155 600 | Heating System Access.

			CREW	DAILY OUTPUT	MAN-HOURS	UNIT	BARE COSTS MAT.	LABOR	EQUIP.	TOTAL	TOTAL INCL O&P	
630	0010	**HYDRONIC HEATING** Terminal units, not incl. main supply pipe										630
	1000	Radiation										
	1100	Panel, baseboard, C.I., including supports, no covers	Q-5	46	.348	L.F.	19.30	7.75		27.05	33	
	1310	Baseboard, pkgd, ½" copper tube, alum. fin, 7" high		60	.267		7.35	5.95		13.30	16.90	
	1320	¾" copper tube, alum. fin, 7" high	↓	58	.276	↓	7.70	6.15		13.85	17.60	
	1500	Note: fin tube may also require corners, caps, etc.										
	1990	Convector unit, floor recessed, flush, with trim										
	2000	for under large glass wall areas, no damper	Q-5	20	.800	L.F.	22.50	17.80		40.30	51	
	2100	For unit with damper, add				"	9.75			9.75	10.75	
	3000	Radiators, cast iron										
	3100	Free standing or wall hung, 6 tube, 25" high	Q-5	96	.167	Section	20.16	3.71		23.87	28	
	3150	4 tube 25" high		96	.167		15.08	3.71		18.79	22	
	3200	4 tube, 19" high	↓	96	.167	↓	14	3.71		17.71	21	
	3250	Adj. brackets, 2 per wall radiator up to 30 sections	1 Stpi	32	.250	Ea.	30.10	6.20		36.30	42	
	3500	Recessed, 20" high x 5" deep, without grille	Q-5	60	.267	Section	16.85	5.95		22.80	27	
	3600	For inlet grille, add				"	1.22			1.22	1.34	
	9500	To convert SFR to BTU rating: Hot water, 150 x SFR										
	9510	Forced hot water, 180 x SFR; steam, 240 x SFR										
640	0010	**HUMIDIFIERS**										640
	0030	Centrifugal atomizing										
	0050	5 lb. per hour	Q-5	12	1.330	Ea.	845	30		875	975	
	0100	10 lb. per hour		10	1.600		1,095	36		1,131	1,250	
	0120	24 lb. per hour	↓	8	2	↓	1,680	45		1,725	1,925	
651	0010	**INSULATION**										651
	0100	Rule of thumb, as a percentage of total mechanical costs				Job				10%		
	1000	Boiler, 1-½" calcium silicate, ½" cement finish	Q-14	50	.320	S.F.	3.03	6.90		9.93	13.95	
	1020	2" fiberglass	"	80	.200	"	1.95	4.31		6.26	8.80	
	2000	Breeching, 2" calcium silicate with ½" cement finish, no lath										
	2020	Rectangular	Q-14	50	.320	S.F.	4.22	6.90		11.12	15.25	
	2040	Round	"	40	.400	"	4.67	8.60		13.27	18.45	
	2300	Calcium silicate block, + 200° to + 1200°F										
	2340	1" thick	Q-14	30	.533	S.F.	2.38	11.50		13.88	20	
	2360	1-½" thick	"	25	.640	"	2.60	13.80		16.40	24	
	2900	Domestic water heater wrap kit										
	2920	1-½" with vinyl jacket, 20-60 gal.	1 Plum	8	1	Ea.	22.75	25		47.75	62	
	4000	Pipe covering										
	4040	Air cell, asbestos free corrugated felt, with cover										
	4100	3 ply, ½" iron pipe size	Q-14	145	.110	L.F.	.75	2.38		3.13	4.50	
	4130	¾" iron pipe size		145	.110		.85	2.38		3.23	4.61	
	4140	1" iron pipe size		145	.110		.90	2.38		3.28	4.66	
	4150	1-¼" iron pipe size		140	.114		1	2.46		3.46	4.90	
	4160	1-½" iron pipe size		140	.114		1.10	2.46		3.56	5	
	4170	2" iron pipe size		135	.119		1.20	2.55		3.75	5.25	
	4180	2-½" iron pipe size		135	.119		1.35	2.55		3.90	5.45	
	4190	3" iron pipe size		130	.123		1.50	2.65		4.15	5.75	
	4200	3-½" iron pipe size		130	.123		1.60	2.65		4.25	5.85	
	4210	4" iron pipe size		125	.128		1.95	2.76		4.71	6.40	
	4220	5" iron pipe size		120	.133		2.25	2.87		5.12	6.90	
	4230	6" iron pipe size		115	.139		2.40	3		5.40	7.25	
	4240	8" iron pipe size		105	.152		3.30	3.28		6.58	8.70	
	4250	10" iron pipe size		95	.168		3.90	3.63		7.53	9.90	
	4260	12" iron pipe size		90	.178		4.50	3.83		8.33	10.85	
	4300	4 ply, ½" iron pipe size		115	.139		1.06	3		4.06	5.80	
	4330	¾" iron pipe size		115	.139		1.20	3		4.20	5.95	
	4340	1" iron pipe size		115	.139		1.27	3		4.27	6	
	4350	1-¼" iron pipe size		110	.145		1.41	3.14		4.55	6.40	
	4360	1-½" iron pipe size	↓	110	.145	↓	1.55	3.14		4.69	6.55	

155 | Heating

155 600 | Heating System Access.

		Description	CREW	DAILY OUTPUT	MAN-HOURS	UNIT	BARE COSTS MAT.	LABOR	EQUIP.	TOTAL	TOTAL INCL O&P	
651	4370	2" iron pipe size	Q-14	105	.152	L.F.	1.69	3.28		4.97	6.90	651
	4380	2-½" iron pipe size		105	.152		1.90	3.28		5.18	7.15	
	4390	3" iron pipe size		100	.160		2.11	3.45		5.56	7.65	
	4400	3-½" iron pipe size		100	.160		2.32	3.45		5.77	7.85	
	4410	4" iron pipe size		95	.168		2.74	3.63		6.37	8.60	
	4420	5" iron pipe size		90	.178		3.17	3.83		7	9.40	
	4430	6" iron pipe size		90	.178		3.38	3.83		7.21	9.65	
	4440	8" iron pipe size		85	.188		4.64	4.06		8.70	11.35	
	4450	10" iron pipe size		75	.213		5.49	4.60		10.09	13.15	
	4460	12" iron pipe size		70	.229		6.33	4.93		11.26	14.55	
	4900	Calcium silicate, with cover										
	5100	1" wall, ½" iron pipe size	Q-14	170	.094	L.F.	1.97	2.03		4	5.30	
	5130	¾" iron pipe size		170	.094		1.98	2.03		4.01	5.30	
	5140	1" iron pipe size		170	.094		1.87	2.03		3.90	5.20	
	5150	1-¼" iron pipe size		165	.097		1.90	2.09		3.99	5.30	
	5160	1-½" iron pipe size		165	.097		1.93	2.09		4.02	5.35	
	5170	2" iron pipe size		160	.100		2.29	2.16		4.45	5.85	
	5180	2-½" iron pipe size		160	.100		2.46	2.16		4.62	6.05	
	5190	3" iron pipe size		150	.107		2.61	2.30		4.91	6.40	
	5200	4" iron pipe size		140	.114		3.05	2.46		5.51	7.15	
	5210	5" iron pipe size		135	.119		3.39	2.55		5.94	7.65	
	5220	6" iron pipe size		130	.123		3.81	2.65		6.46	8.30	
	5280	1-½" wall, ½" iron pipe size		150	.107		2.15	2.30		4.45	5.90	
	5310	¾" iron pipe size		150	.107		2.18	2.30		4.48	5.95	
	5320	1" iron pipe size		150	.107		2.37	2.30		4.67	6.15	
	5330	1-¼" iron pipe size		145	.110		2.55	2.38		4.93	6.50	
	5340	1-½" iron pipe size		145	.110		2.68	2.38		5.06	6.60	
	5350	2" iron pipe size		140	.114		2.92	2.46		5.38	7	
	5360	2-½" iron pipe size		140	.114		3.22	2.46		5.68	7.35	
	5370	3" iron pipe size		135	.119		3.36	2.55		5.91	7.65	
	5380	4" iron pipe size		125	.128		3.91	2.76		6.67	8.55	
	5390	5" iron pipe size		120	.133		4.39	2.87		7.26	9.25	
	5400	6" iron pipe size		110	.145		4.55	3.14		7.69	9.85	
	5460	2" wall, ½" iron pipe size		135	.119		3.25	2.55		5.80	7.50	
	5490	¾" iron pipe size		135	.119		3.48	2.55		6.03	7.75	
	5500	1" iron pipe size		135	.119		3.66	2.55		6.21	7.95	
	5510	1-¼" iron pipe size		130	.123		3.94	2.65		6.59	8.40	
	5520	1-½" iron pipe size		130	.123		4.14	2.65		6.79	8.65	
	5530	2" iron pipe size		125	.128		4.34	2.76		7.10	9	
	5540	2-½" iron pipe size		125	.128		5.22	2.76		7.98	10	
	5550	3" iron pipe size		120	.133		5	2.87		7.87	9.95	
	5560	4" iron pipe size		115	.139		5.87	3		8.87	11.10	
	5570	5" iron pipe size		110	.145		6.69	3.14		9.83	12.20	
	5580	6" iron pipe size		105	.152		7.51	3.28		10.79	13.30	
	5600	Calcium silicate, no cover										
	5720	1" wall, ½" iron pipe size	Q-14	180	.089	L.F.	1.83	1.92		3.75	4.96	
	5740	¾" iron pipe size		180	.089		1.83	1.92		3.75	4.96	
	5750	1" iron pipe size		180	.089		1.73	1.92		3.65	4.85	
	5760	1-¼" iron pipe size		175	.091		1.74	1.97		3.71	4.95	
	5770	1-½" iron pipe size		175	.091		1.76	1.97		3.73	4.98	
	5780	2" iron pipe size		170	.094		2.11	2.03		4.14	5.45	
	5790	2-½" iron pipe size		170	.094		2.24	2.03		4.27	5.60	
	5800	3" iron pipe size		160	.100		2.38	2.16		4.54	5.95	
	5810	4" iron pipe size		150	.107		2.80	2.30		5.10	6.60	
	5820	5" iron pipe size		145	.110		3.10	2.38		5.48	7.10	
	5830	6" iron pipe size		140	.114		3.48	2.46		5.94	7.65	
	5900	1-½" wall, ½" iron pipe size		160	.100		1.98	2.16		4.14	5.50	
	5920	¾" iron pipe size		160	.100		2	2.16		4.16	5.50	

155 | Heating

		155 600	Heating System Access.	CREW	DAILY OUTPUT	MAN-HOURS	UNIT	BARE COSTS MAT.	LABOR	EQUIP.	TOTAL	TOTAL INCL O&P	
651	5930		1" iron pipe size	Q-14	160	.100	L.F.	2.18	2.16		4.34	5.70	651
	5940		1-¼" iron pipe size		155	.103		2.35	2.23		4.58	6	
	5950		1-½" iron pipe size		155	.103		2.46	2.23		4.69	6.15	
	5960		2" iron pipe size		150	.107		2.69	2.30		4.99	6.50	
	5970		2-½" iron pipe size		150	.107		2.97	2.30		5.27	6.80	
	5980		3" iron pipe size		145	.110		3.08	2.38		5.46	7.05	
	5990		4" iron pipe size		135	.119		3.59	2.55		6.14	7.90	
	6000		5" iron pipe size		130	.123		4.02	2.65		6.67	8.50	
	6010		6" iron pipe size		120	.133		4.13	2.87		7	8.95	
	6020		7" iron pipe size		115	.139		4.94	3		7.94	10.05	
	6030		8" iron pipe size		105	.152		5.60	3.28		8.88	11.20	
	6040		9" iron pipe size		100	.160		6.72	3.45		10.17	12.70	
	6050		10" iron pipe size		95	.168		7.46	3.63		11.09	13.80	
	6060		12" iron pipe size		90	.178		8.84	3.83		12.67	15.65	
	6070		14" iron pipe size		85	.188		9.98	4.06		14.04	17.25	
	6080		16" iron pipe size		80	.200		11.19	4.31		15.50	18.95	
	6090		18" iron pipe size		75	.213		12.30	4.60		16.90	21	
	6120		2" wall, ½" iron pipe size		145	.110		3.14	2.38		5.52	7.10	
	6140		¾" iron pipe size		145	.110		3.26	2.38		5.64	7.25	
	6150		1" iron pipe size		145	.110		3.42	2.38		5.80	7.45	
	6160		1-¼" iron pipe size		140	.114		3.69	2.46		6.15	7.85	
	6170		1-½" iron pipe size		140	.114		3.88	2.46		6.34	8.05	
	6180		2" iron pipe size		135	.119		4.07	2.55		6.62	8.40	
	6190		2-½" iron pipe size		135	.119		4.93	2.55		7.48	9.35	
	6200		3" iron pipe size		130	.123		4.67	2.65		7.32	9.25	
	6210		4" iron pipe size		125	.128		5.50	2.76		8.26	10.30	
	6220		5" iron pipe size		120	.133		6.28	2.87		9.15	11.35	
	6230		6" iron pipe size		115	.139		7.05	3		10.05	12.40	
	6240		7" iron pipe size		110	.145		7.67	3.14		10.81	13.25	
	6250		8" iron pipe size		105	.152		8.44	3.28		11.72	14.35	
	6260		9" iron pipe size		100	.160		9.52	3.45		12.97	15.80	
	6270		10" iron pipe size		95	.168		10.54	3.63		14.17	17.20	
	6280		12" iron pipe size		90	.178		11.75	3.83		15.58	18.85	
	6290		14" iron pipe size		85	.188		12.95	4.06		17.01	21	
	6300		16" iron pipe size		80	.200		14.24	4.31		18.55	22	
	6310		18" iron pipe size		75	.213		15.54	4.60		20.14	24	
	6320		20" iron pipe size		65	.246		17.93	5.30		23.23	28	
	6330		22" iron pipe size		60	.267		19.30	5.75		25.05	30	
	6340		24" iron pipe size		55	.291		20.16	6.25		26.41	32	
	6360		3" wall, ½" iron pipe size		115	.139		4.37	3		7.37	9.45	
	6380		¾" iron pipe size		115	.139		5.72	3		8.72	10.90	
	6390		1" iron pipe size		115	.139		5.17	3		8.17	10.30	
	6400		1-¼" iron pipe size		110	.145		5.34	3.14		8.48	10.70	
	6410		1-½" iron pipe size		110	.145		5.68	3.14		8.82	11.10	
	6420		2" iron pipe size		105	.152		6.02	3.28		9.30	11.70	
	6430		2-½" iron pipe size		105	.152		7.22	3.28		10.50	13	
	6440		3" iron pipe size		100	.160		6.98	3.45		10.43	13	
	6450		4" iron pipe size		95	.168		9.14	3.63		12.77	15.65	
	6460		5" iron pipe size		90	.178		9.93	3.83		13.76	16.85	
	6470		6" iron pipe size		90	.178		11.19	3.83		15.02	18.20	
	6480		7" iron pipe size		85	.188		12.77	4.06		16.83	20	
	6490		8" iron pipe size		85	.188		13.27	4.06		17.33	21	
	6500		9" iron pipe size		80	.200		14.99	4.31		19.30	23	
	6510		10" iron pipe size		75	.213		16.02	4.60		20.62	25	
	6520		12" iron pipe size		70	.229		17.75	4.93		22.68	27	
	6530		14" iron pipe size		65	.246		19.89	5.30		25.19	30	
	6540		16" iron pipe size		60	.267		21.95	5.75		27.70	33	
	6550		18" iron pipe size		55	.291		24.23	6.25		30.48	36	

155 | Heating

155 600 | Heating System Access.

		CREW	DAILY OUTPUT	MAN-HOURS	UNIT	BARE COSTS MAT.	LABOR	EQUIP.	TOTAL	TOTAL INCL O&P	
651	6560	20" iron pipe size	Q-14	50	.320	L.F.	26.88	6.90		33.78	40	651
	6570	22" iron pipe size		45	.356		29.14	7.65		36.79	44	
	6580	24" iron pipe size	↓	40	.400	↓	31.34	8.60		39.94	48	
	6600	Fiberglass, with all service jacket										
	6640	½" wall, ½" iron pipe size	Q-14	250	.064	L.F.	.79	1.38		2.17	3	
	6660	¾" iron pipe size		240	.067		.87	1.44		2.31	3.18	
	6670	1" iron pipe size		230	.070		.92	1.50		2.42	3.32	
	6680	1-¼" iron pipe size		220	.073		1.01	1.57		2.58	3.53	
	6690	1-½" iron pipe size		220	.073		1.10	1.57		2.67	3.63	
	6700	2" iron pipe size		210	.076		1.18	1.64		2.82	3.83	
	6710	2-½" iron pipe size		200	.080		1.34	1.72		3.06	4.13	
	6720	3" iron pipe size		190	.084		1.50	1.82		3.32	4.45	
	6730	3-½" iron pipe size		180	.089		1.62	1.92		3.54	4.73	
	6740	4" iron pipe size		160	.100		1.92	2.16		4.08	5.45	
	6750	5" iron pipe size		150	.107		2.20	2.30		4.50	5.95	
	6760	6" iron pipe size		120	.133		2.31	2.87		5.18	6.95	
	6840	1" wall, ½" iron pipe size		240	.067		.93	1.44		2.37	3.24	
	6860	¾" iron pipe size		230	.070		1.07	1.50		2.57	3.49	
	6870	1" iron pipe size		220	.073		1.10	1.57		2.67	3.63	
	6880	1-¼" iron pipe size		210	.076		1.22	1.64		2.86	3.87	
	6890	1-½" iron pipe size		210	.076		1.33	1.64		2.97	3.99	
	6900	2" iron pipe size		200	.080		1.44	1.72		3.16	4.24	
	6910	2-½" iron pipe size		190	.084		1.60	1.82		3.42	4.56	
	6920	3" iron pipe size		180	.089		1.80	1.92		3.72	4.93	
	6930	3-½" iron pipe size		170	.094		1.97	2.03		4	5.30	
	6940	4" iron pipe size		150	.107		2.31	2.30		4.61	6.10	
	6950	5" iron pipe size		140	.114		2.68	2.46		5.14	6.75	
	6960	6" iron pipe size		120	.133		2.83	2.87		5.70	7.55	
	6970	7" iron pipe size		110	.145		3.50	3.14		6.64	8.70	
	6980	8" iron pipe size		100	.160		4.04	3.45		7.49	9.75	
	6990	9" iron pipe size		90	.178		4.40	3.83		8.23	10.75	
	7000	10" iron pipe size		90	.178		4.72	3.83		8.55	11.10	
	7010	12" iron pipe size		80	.200		5.38	4.31		9.69	12.55	
	7020	14" iron pipe size		80	.200		6.24	4.31		10.55	13.50	
	7030	16" iron pipe size		70	.229		7.41	4.93		12.34	15.75	
	7040	18" iron pipe size		70	.229		7.96	4.93		12.89	16.35	
	7050	20" iron pipe size		60	.267		8.88	5.75		14.63	18.65	
	7060	24" iron pipe size		60	.267		10.81	5.75		16.56	21	
	7080	1-½" wall, ½" iron pipe size		230	.070		1.89	1.50		3.39	4.39	
	7100	¾" iron pipe size		220	.073		1.97	1.57		3.54	4.59	
	7110	1" iron pipe size		210	.076		2.08	1.64		3.72	4.82	
	7120	1-¼" iron pipe size		200	.080		2.23	1.72		3.95	5.10	
	7130	1-½" iron pipe size		200	.080		2.37	1.72		4.09	5.25	
	7140	2" iron pipe size		190	.084		2.57	1.82		4.39	5.65	
	7150	2-½" iron pipe size		180	.089		2.81	1.92		4.73	6.05	
	7160	3" iron pipe size		170	.094		2.92	2.03		4.95	6.35	
	7170	3-½" iron pipe size		160	.100		3.18	2.16		5.34	6.80	
	7180	4" iron pipe size		140	.114		3.32	2.46		5.78	7.45	
	7190	5" iron pipe size		130	.123		3.72	2.65		6.37	8.20	
	7200	6" iron pipe size		110	.145		3.83	3.14		6.97	9.05	
	7210	7" iron pipe size		100	.160		4.40	3.45		7.85	10.15	
	7220	8" iron pipe size		90	.178		4.80	3.83		8.63	11.20	
	7230	9" iron pipe size		85	.188		5.47	4.06		9.53	12.25	
	7240	10" iron pipe size		80	.200		6.01	4.31		10.32	13.25	
	7250	12" iron pipe size		75	.213		6.56	4.60		11.16	14.30	
	7260	14" iron pipe size		70	.229		7.58	4.93		12.51	15.95	
	7270	16" iron pipe size		65	.246		8.53	5.30		13.83	17.55	
	7280	18" iron pipe size	↓	60	.267	↓	9.69	5.75		15.44	19.50	

155 | Heating

155 600	Heating System Access.	CREW	DAILY OUTPUT	MAN-HOURS	UNIT	BARE COSTS MAT.	BARE COSTS LABOR	BARE COSTS EQUIP.	BARE COSTS TOTAL	TOTAL INCL O&P
7290	20" iron pipe size	Q-14	55	.291	L.F.	10.28	6.25		16.53	21
7300	24" iron pipe size		50	.320		12	6.90		18.90	24
7320	2" wall, ½" iron pipe size		220	.073		2.96	1.57		4.53	5.70
7340	¾" iron pipe size		210	.076		3.07	1.64		4.71	5.90
7350	1" iron pipe size		200	.080		3.27	1.72		4.99	6.25
7360	1-¼" iron pipe size		190	.084		3.48	1.82		5.30	6.65
7370	1-½" iron pipe size		190	.084		3.65	1.82		5.47	6.80
7380	2" iron pipe size		180	.089		3.81	1.92		5.73	7.15
7390	2-½" iron pipe size		170	.094		4.09	2.03		6.12	7.65
7400	3" iron pipe size		160	.100		4.40	2.16		6.56	8.15
7410	3-½" iron pipe size		150	.107		4.74	2.30		7.04	8.75
7420	4" iron pipe size		130	.123		5.07	2.65		7.72	9.65
7430	5" iron pipe size		120	.133		5.71	2.87		8.58	10.70
7440	6" iron pipe size		100	.160		5.87	3.45		9.32	11.80
7450	7" iron pipe size		90	.178		6.72	3.83		10.55	13.30
7460	8" iron pipe size		80	.200		7.24	4.31		11.55	14.60
7470	9" iron pipe size		75	.213		7.99	4.60		12.59	15.90
7480	10" iron pipe size		70	.229		8.66	4.93		13.59	17.10
7490	12" iron pipe size		65	.246		9.55	5.30		14.85	18.70
7500	14" iron pipe size		60	.267		10.80	5.75		16.55	21
7510	16" iron pipe size		55	.291		11.84	6.25		18.09	23
7520	18" iron pipe size		50	.320		12.90	6.90		19.80	25
7530	20" iron pipe size		45	.356		14.29	7.65		21.94	28
7540	24" iron pipe size	↓	40	.400		16.02	8.60		24.62	31
7600	For fiberglass with standard canvas jacket, deduct				↓	5%				
7660	For fittings, add 3 L.F. for each fitting									
7680	plus 4 L.F. for each flange of the fitting									
7700	For equipment or congested areas, add				L.F.		20%			
7720	Finishes, for .010" aluminum jacket, add	Q-14	120	.133	S.F.	.42	2.87		3.29	4.89
7740	For .016" aluminum jacket, add		120	.133		.54	2.87		3.41	5
7760	For .010" stainless steel, add	↓	100	.160		.93	3.45		4.38	6.35
7780	For single layer of felt, add				↓	10%	10%			
7784	Polyethylene tubing, flexible closed cell foam									
7828	Standard temperature (-100° to 200° F)									
7830	⅜" wall, ⅛" iron pipe size	1 Asbe	130	.062	L.F.	.08	1.47		1.55	2.36
7831	¼" iron pipe size		130	.062		.11	1.47		1.58	2.39
7832	⅜" iron pipe size		130	.062		.12	1.47		1.59	2.40
7833	½" iron pipe size		126	.063		.16	1.52		1.68	2.52
7834	¾" iron pipe size		122	.066		.17	1.57		1.74	2.61
7835	1" iron pipe size		120	.067		.21	1.60		1.81	2.69
7836	1-¼" iron pipe size		118	.068		.24	1.62		1.86	2.77
7837	1-½" iron pipe size		118	.068		.27	1.62		1.89	2.80
7838	2" iron pipe size		116	.069		.32	1.65		1.97	2.90
7839	2-½" iron pipe size		114	.070		.38	1.68		2.06	3.01
7840	3" iron pipe size		112	.071		.46	1.71		2.17	3.14
7842	½" wall, ⅛" iron pipe size		120	.067		.13	1.60		1.73	2.60
7843	¼" iron pipe size		120	.067		.16	1.60		1.76	2.64
7844	⅜" iron pipe size		120	.067		.17	1.60		1.77	2.65
7845	½" iron pipe size		118	.068		.22	1.62		1.84	2.74
7846	¾" iron pipe size		116	.069		.25	1.65		1.90	2.82
7847	1" iron pipe size		114	.070		.30	1.68		1.98	2.92
7848	1-¼" iron pipe size		112	.071		.33	1.71		2.04	3
7849	1-½" iron pipe size		110	.073		.38	1.74		2.12	3.10
7850	2" iron pipe size		108	.074		.44	1.77		2.21	3.22
7851	2-½" iron pipe size		106	.075		.52	1.81		2.33	3.36
7852	3" iron pipe size		104	.077		.63	1.84		2.47	3.53
7855	¾" wall, ⅛" iron pipe size		110	.073		.25	1.74		1.99	2.96
7856	¼" iron pipe size	↓	110	.073	↓	.28	1.74		2.02	2.99

155 | Heating

155 600 | Heating System Access.

| | | | DAILY | MAN- | | \multicolumn{4}{c}{BARE COSTS} | TOTAL |
		CREW	OUTPUT	HOURS	UNIT	MAT.	LABOR	EQUIP.	TOTAL	INCL O&P
651	7857	3/8" iron pipe size	1 Asbe	108	.074	L.F.	.32	1.77		2.09	3.09	651
	7858	1/2" iron pipe size		106	.075		.40	1.81		2.21	3.22
	7859	3/4" iron pipe size		104	.077		.44	1.84		2.28	3.32
	7860	1" iron pipe size		102	.078		.49	1.88		2.37	3.43
	7861	1-1/4" iron pipe size		100	.080		.57	1.92		2.49	3.58
	7862	1-1/2" iron pipe size		100	.080		.62	1.92		2.54	3.63
	7863	2" iron pipe size		98	.082		.73	1.96		2.69	3.82
	7864	2-1/2" iron pipe size		96	.083		.85	2		2.85	4.01
	7868	1" wall, 1/4" iron pipe size		100	.080		.46	1.92		2.38	3.46
	7869	3/8" iron pipe size		98	.082		.52	1.96		2.48	3.58
	7870	1/2" iron pipe size		96	.083		.57	2		2.57	3.70
	7871	3/4" iron pipe size		94	.085		.66	2.04		2.70	3.87
	7872	1" iron pipe size		92	.087		.74	2.08		2.82	4.02
	7873	1-1/4" iron pipe size		90	.089		.79	2.13		2.92	4.15
	7874	1-1/2" iron pipe size		90	.089		.90	2.13		3.03	4.27
	7875	2" iron pipe size		88	.091		1.03	2.18		3.21	4.49
	7878	Contact cement, quart can				Ea.	5.95			5.95	6.55
	7879	Rubber tubing, flexible closed cell foam									
	7880	3/8" wall, 1/4" iron pipe size	1 Asbe	120	.067	L.F.	.22	1.60		1.82	2.70
	7900	3/8" iron pipe size		120	.067		.25	1.60		1.85	2.74
	7910	1/2" iron pipe size		115	.070		.28	1.67		1.95	2.87
	7920	3/4" iron pipe size		115	.070		.32	1.67		1.99	2.92
	7930	1" iron pipe size		110	.073		.36	1.74		2.10	3.08
	7940	1-1/4" iron pipe size		110	.073		.45	1.74		2.19	3.18
	7950	1-1/2" iron pipe size		110	.073		.53	1.74		2.27	3.27
	7960	2" iron pipe size		105	.076		.80	1.82		2.62	3.69
	7970	2-1/2" iron pipe size		100	.080		1.12	1.92		3.04	4.18
	7980	3" iron pipe size		100	.080		1.24	1.92		3.16	4.32
	7990	3-1/2" iron pipe size		100	.080		1.73	1.92		3.65	4.86
	8100	1/2" wall, 1/4" iron pipe size		90	.089		.33	2.13		2.46	3.64
	8120	3/8" iron pipe size		90	.089		.37	2.13		2.50	3.69
	8130	1/2" iron pipe size		89	.090		.41	2.15		2.56	3.77
	8140	3/4" iron pipe size		89	.090		.45	2.15		2.60	3.81
	8150	1" iron pipe size		88	.091		.50	2.18		2.68	3.90
	8160	1-1/4" iron pipe size		87	.092		.58	2.20		2.78	4.03
	8170	1-1/2" iron pipe size		87	.092		.70	2.20		2.90	4.16
	8180	2" iron pipe size		86	.093		.86	2.23		3.09	4.38
	8190	2-1/2" iron pipe size		86	.093		1.13	2.23		3.36	4.68
	8200	3" iron pipe size		85	.094		1.58	2.25		3.83	5.20
	8210	3-1/2" iron pipe size		85	.094		1.65	2.25		3.90	5.30
	8220	4" iron pipe size		80	.100		1.76	2.40		4.16	5.65
	8230	5" iron pipe size		80	.100		2.62	2.40		5.02	6.55
	8300	3/4" wall, 1/4" iron pipe size		90	.089		.49	2.13		2.62	3.82
	8320	3/8" iron pipe size		90	.089		.57	2.13		2.70	3.91
	8330	1/2" iron pipe size		89	.090		.67	2.15		2.82	4.05
	8340	3/4" iron pipe size		89	.090		.79	2.15		2.94	4.19
	8350	1" iron pipe size		88	.091		.94	2.18		3.12	4.39
	8360	1-1/4" iron pipe size		87	.092		1.26	2.20		3.46	4.78
	8370	1-1/2" iron pipe size		87	.092		1.42	2.20		3.62	4.96
	8380	2" iron pipe size		86	.093		1.67	2.23		3.90	5.25
	8390	2-1/2" iron pipe size		86	.093		2.23	2.23		4.46	5.90
	8400	3" iron pipe size		85	.094		2.75	2.25		5	6.50
	8410	3-1/2" iron pipe size		85	.094		2.99	2.25		5.24	6.75
	8420	4" iron pipe size		80	.100		3.18	2.40		5.58	7.20
	8430	5" iron pipe size		80	.100		3.83	2.40		6.23	7.90
	8440	6" iron pipe size		80	.100		6.46	2.40		8.86	10.80
	8680	Rubber insulation tape, 1/8" x 2" x 30'				Ea.	9.72			9.72	10.70
	8800	Urethane, with ASJ, -60°F to +225°F									

155 | Heating

155 600 | Heating System Access.

		CREW	DAILY OUTPUT	MAN-HOURS	UNIT	BARE COSTS MAT.	BARE COSTS LABOR	BARE COSTS EQUIP.	BARE COSTS TOTAL	TOTAL INCL O&P	
8960	1" wall, ½" iron pipe size	Q-14	240	.067	L.F.	1.05	1.44		2.49	3.38	651
8980	¾" iron pipe size		230	.070		1.05	1.50		2.55	3.47	
8990	1" iron pipe size		220	.073		1.63	1.57		3.20	4.21	
9000	1-¼" iron pipe size		210	.076		1.63	1.64		3.27	4.32	
9010	1-½" iron pipe size		210	.076		1.79	1.64		3.43	4.50	
9020	2" iron pipe size		200	.080		2.10	1.72		3.82	4.97	
9030	2-½" iron pipe size		190	.084		2.42	1.82		4.24	5.45	
9040	3" iron pipe size		180	.089		2.63	1.92		4.55	5.85	
9050	4" iron pipe size		150	.107		3.30	2.30		5.60	7.15	
9060	5" iron pipe size		140	.114		3.51	2.46		5.97	7.65	
9070	6" iron pipe size		120	.133		3.94	2.87		6.81	8.75	
9120	1-½" wall, ½" iron pipe size		230	.070		1.74	1.50		3.24	4.22	
9140	¾" iron pipe size		220	.073		1.74	1.57		3.31	4.33	
9150	1" iron pipe size		210	.076		1.84	1.64		3.48	4.55	
9160	1-¼" iron pipe size		200	.080		1.84	1.72		3.56	4.68	
9170	1-½" iron pipe size		200	.080		2.43	1.72		4.15	5.35	
9180	2" iron pipe size		190	.084		2.89	1.82		4.71	6	
9190	2-½" iron pipe size		180	.089		3.10	1.92		5.02	6.35	
9200	3" iron pipe size		170	.094		3.57	2.03		5.60	7.05	
9210	4" iron pipe size		140	.114		4.14	2.46		6.60	8.35	
9220	5" iron pipe size		130	.123		4.46	2.65		7.11	9	
9230	6" iron pipe size		110	.145		4.89	3.14		8.03	10.20	
9240	8" iron pipe size	↓	90	.178	↓	6.31	3.83		10.14	12.85	
9290	Urethane, with ultraviolet cover										
9310	1" wall, ½" pipe size	Q-14	216	.074	L.F.	1.16	1.60		2.76	3.74	
9320	¾" pipe size		207	.077		1.16	1.67		2.83	3.85	
9330	1" pipe size		198	.081		1.68	1.74		3.42	4.53	
9340	1-¼" pipe size		189	.085		1.68	1.82		3.50	4.66	
9350	1-½" pipe size		185	.086		1.95	1.86		3.81	5	
9360	2" pipe size		180	.089		2.31	1.92		4.23	5.50	
9400	1-½" wall, ½" pipe size		207	.077		1.95	1.67		3.62	4.72	
9410	¾" pipe size		198	.081		1.95	1.74		3.69	4.83	
9420	1" pipe size		189	.085		2.31	1.82		4.13	5.35	
9430	1-¼" pipe size		180	.089		2.31	1.92		4.23	5.50	
9440	1-½" pipe size		175	.091		2.68	1.97		4.65	6	
9450	2" pipe size	↓	171	.094	↓	3.10	2.02		5.12	6.50	
9500	Urethane, with ultraviolet cover, fittings										
9510	90° & 45° elbows, 1" wall thickness										
9520	½" pipe size	Q-14	108	.148	Ea.	3	3.19		6.19	8.20	
9530	¾" pipe size		104	.154		3	3.32		6.32	8.40	
9540	1" pipe size		99	.162		3.54	3.48		7.02	9.25	
9550	1-¼" pipe size		95	.168		3.54	3.63		7.17	9.50	
9560	1-½" pipe size		93	.172		4.06	3.71		7.77	10.20	
9570	2" pipe size	↓	90	.178	↓	4.75	3.83		8.58	11.15	
9650	90° & 45° elbows, 1-½" wall thickness										
9660	½" pipe size	Q-14	104	.154	Ea.	4.06	3.32		7.38	9.60	
9670	¾" pipe size		99	.162		4.06	3.48		7.54	9.85	
9680	1" pipe size		95	.168		4.75	3.63		8.38	10.85	
9690	1-¼" pipe size		90	.178		4.75	3.83		8.58	11.15	
9700	1-½" pipe size		88	.182		5.15	3.92		9.07	11.70	
9710	2" pipe size	↓	86	.186	↓	6.80	4.01		10.81	13.65	
9800	Tees & valves, 1" wall thickness										
9820	½" pipe size	Q-14	72	.222	Ea.	3.73	4.79		8.52	11.50	
9830	¾" pipe size		69	.232		3.73	5		8.73	11.80	
9840	1" pipe size		66	.242		4.59	5.25		9.84	13.10	
9850	1-¼" pipe size		63	.254		4.59	5.45		10.04	13.50	
9860	1-½" pipe size		62	.258		5.21	5.55		10.76	14.30	
9870	2" pipe size	↓	60	.267	↓	6.30	5.75		12.05	15.80	

155 | Heating

155 600 | Heating System Access.

		CREW	DAILY OUTPUT	MAN-HOURS	UNIT	BARE COSTS MAT.	LABOR	EQUIP.	TOTAL	TOTAL INCL O&P
651											651
9920	Tees & valves, 1-½" wall thickness									
9930	½" pipe size	Q-14	69	.232	Ea.	5.21	5		10.21	13.45
9940	¾" pipe size		66	.242		5.21	5.25		10.46	13.80
9950	1" pipe size		63	.254		6.30	5.45		11.75	15.35
9960	1-¼" pipe size		60	.267		6.30	5.75		12.05	15.80
9970	1-½" pipe size		58	.276		7.14	5.95		13.09	17
9980	2" pipe size	↓	57	.281	↓	9.46	6.05		15.51	19.75
671											671
0010	**TANKS**									
0020	Fiberglass, underground, U.L. listed, not including									
0030	manway or hold-down strap									
0040	550 gallon capacity	Q-6	3	8	Ea.	1,265	185		1,450	1,675
0100	1000 gallon capacity	"	2	12		1,600	275		1,875	2,175
0140	2000 gallon capacity	Q-7	2	16		2,340	380		2,720	3,125
0500	For manway, fittings and hold-downs, add				↓	20%	15%			
1020	Fiberglass, underground, double wall, U.L. listed,									
1030	includes manways, not incl. hold-down straps									
1040	550 gallon capacity	Q-6	3	8	Ea.	3,725	185		3,910	4,375
1050	1000 gallon capacity	"	2	12		4,790	275		5,065	5,675
1060	2500 gallon capacity	Q-7	2	16		6,215	380		6,595	7,400
1140	For hold-down straps, add				↓	2%	10%			
1500	Plastic, corrosion resistant, see Div. 152-132									
2000	Steel, liquid expansion, ASME, painted, 15 gallon capacity	Q-5	17	.941	Ea.	217	21		238	270
2020	24 gallon capacity		14	1.140		220	25		245	280
2040	30 gallon capacity		12	1.330		249	30		279	320
2060	40 gallon capacity		10	1.600		280	36		316	360
2360	Galvanized									
2370	15 gallon capacity	Q-5	17	.941	Ea.	405	21		426	475
2380	24 gallon capacity		14	1.140		440	25		465	520
2390	30 gallon capacity		12	1.330		510	30		540	605
3000	Steel ASME expansion, rubber diaphragm, 19 gal. cap. accept.		12	1.330		710	30		740	825
3020	31 gallon capacity		8	2		925	45		970	1,075
3040	61 gallon capacity	↓	6	2.670	↓	1,300	59		1,359	1,525
4000	Steel, storage, above ground, including supports, coating,									
4020	fittings, not including mat, pumps or piping									
4040	275 gallon capacity	Q-5	5	3.200	Ea.	225	71		296	355
4060	550 gallon capacity	"	4	4		1,050	89		1,139	1,275
4080	1000 gallon capacity	Q-7	4	8		1,350	190		1,540	1,775
4100	1500 gallon capacity		3.70	8.650		1,700	205		1,905	2,175
4120	2000 gallon capacity		3	10.670		1,700	250		1,950	2,250
5000	Steel underground, sti-P3, set in place, incl. hold-down bars.									
5500	Excavation, pad, pumps and piping not included									
5520	1000 gallon capacity, 7 gauge shell	Q-7	4	8	Ea.	1,500	190		1,690	1,925
5540	5000 gallon capacity, ¼" thick shell	"	1	32	"	5,000	755		5,755	6,625
6200	Steel, underground, 360°, double wall, U.L. listed,									
6210	with sti-P3 corrosion protection,									
6220	(dielectric coating, cathodic protection, electrical									
6230	isolation) 30 year warrantee,									
6240	not incl. manholes or hold-downs.									
6250	500 gallon capacity	Q-5	5	3.200	Ea.	2,200	71		2,271	2,525
6260	1000 gallon capactiy	Q-7	4	8		3,200	190		3,390	3,800
6270	2000 gallon capacity		3	10.670	↓	4,200	250		4,450	5,000
6280	3000 gallon capacity		2	16	↓	5,200	380		5,580	6,275
6400	For hold-downs 500-2000 gal, add		16	2	Set	270	47		317	365
6500	For manways, add				Ea.	400			400	440
673											673
0010	**TANK LEAK DETECTION SYSTEMS**, Liquid and vapor									
0100	For hydrocarbons and hazardous liquids/vapors									

155 | Heating

155 600 | Heating System Access.

		CREW	DAILY OUTPUT	MAN-HOURS	UNIT	BARE COSTS MAT.	LABOR	EQUIP.	TOTAL	TOTAL INCL O&P	
673	0120 Control master with alarm										**673**
	0140 For 1 or 2 probes				Ea.	725			725	800	
	0160 For up to 10 probes				"	1,350			1,350	1,475	
	0200 Probes										
	0210 Well, underground 2"				Ea.	650			650	715	
	0220 Underground 4"					760			760	835	
	0240 Vapor detector 2"				↓	615			615	675	
	0300 Surface										
	0310 In 4" pipe 30" tall				Ea.	575			575	635	
	0400 Steel double wall tank										
	0410 For 1-½" openings				Ea.	510			510	560	
	0420 For 2" openings				"	650			650	715	
	0500 Fiberglass double wall tank										
	0510 Dry annulus space				Ea.	470			470	515	
	0520 Dry annulus vapor detector				"	545			545	600	
	0600 Trench										
	0610 In 4" pipe 6' tall				Ea.	660			660	725	
	0700 Sump or manway					500			500	550	
	0800 Double wall piping				↓	500			500	550	
	1000 Cable										
	1010 4 conductor conduit				L.F.	.68			.68	.75	
	1020 4 conductor direct burial				"	.96			.96	1.06	
	1060 Data output with 4' connector				Ea.	26			26	29	
	2000 Accessories										
	2100 Adapter										
	2110 6" NPTF to 4" NPTM				Ea.	26			26	29	
	2120 2" NPTF to 4" NPTM					26			26	29	
	2200 Field test set				↓	285			285	315	
680	0010 **VENT CHIMNEY** Prefab metal, U.L. listed										**680**
	0020 Gas, double wall, galvanized steel										
	0080 3" diameter	Q-9	72	.222	V.L.F.	2.35	4.87		7.22	9.95	
	0100 4" diameter		68	.235		2.86	5.15		8.01	10.95	
	0120 5" diameter		64	.250		3.38	5.50		8.88	12	
	0140 6" diameter		60	.267		3.96	5.85		9.81	13.20	
	0160 7" diameter		56	.286		5.78	6.25		12.03	15.80	
	0180 8" diameter		52	.308		6.44	6.75		13.19	17.25	
	0200 10" diameter		48	.333		13.44	7.30		20.74	26	
	0220 12" diameter		44	.364		17.95	7.95		25.90	32	
	0240 14" diameter		42	.381		29.85	8.35		38.20	45	
	0260 16" diameter		40	.400		40.45	8.75		49.20	58	
	0280 18" diameter	↓	38	.421		52.20	9.25		61.45	71	
	0300 20" diameter	Q-10	36	.667		62	15.15		77.15	91	
	0320 22" diameter		34	.706		77.80	16.05		93.85	110	
	0340 24" diameter	↓	32	.750	↓	96	17.05		113.05	130	
	0600 For 4", 5" and 6" oval, add					50%					
	0650 Gas, double wall, galvanized steel, fittings										
	0660 Elbow 45°, 3" diameter	Q-9	36	.444	Ea.	5.80	9.75		15.55	21	
	0670 4" diameter		34	.471		6.80	10.30		17.10	23	
	0680 5" diameter		32	.500		8	10.95		18.95	25	
	0690 6" diameter		30	.533		9.55	11.70		21.25	28	
	0700 7" diameter		28	.571		13.80	12.50		26.30	34	
	0710 8" diameter		26	.615		15.90	13.50		29.40	38	
	0720 10" diameter		24	.667		39	14.60		53.60	65	
	0730 12" diameter		22	.727		49.40	15.95		65.35	78	
	0740 14" diameter		21	.762		68.25	16.70		84.95	100	
	0750 16" diameter		20	.800		85.75	17.55		103.30	120	
	0760 18" diameter	↓	19	.842		115	18.45		133.45	155	
	0770 20" diameter	Q-10	18	1.330		130	30		160	190	

155 | Heating

155 600 | Heating System Access.

		CREW	DAILY OUTPUT	MAN-HOURS	UNIT	MAT.	LABOR	EQUIP.	TOTAL	TOTAL INCL O&P
0780	22" diameter	Q-10	17	1.410	Ea.	195	32		227	265
0790	24" diameter	"	16	1.500		249	34		283	325
0950	Elbow 90°, adjustable, 3" diameter	Q-9	36	.444		10.45	9.75		20.20	26
0960	4" diameter		34	.471		11.80	10.30		22.10	29
0970	5" diameter		32	.500		13.60	10.95		24.55	32
0980	6" diameter		30	.533		16.45	11.70		28.15	36
0990	7" diameter		28	.571		25.80	12.50		38.30	47
1010	8" diameter		26	.615		27.40	13.50		40.90	51
1040	Roof flashing, 3" diameter		36	.444		4.02	9.75		13.77	19.15
1050	4" diameter		34	.471		5.50	10.30		15.80	22
1060	5" diameter		32	.500		6.10	10.95		17.05	23
1070	6" diameter		30	.533		8.55	11.70		20.25	27
1080	7" diameter		28	.571		9.90	12.50		22.40	30
1090	8" diameter		26	.615		11.65	13.50		25.15	33
1100	10" diameter		24	.667		31.50	14.60		46.10	57
1110	12" diameter		22	.727		40.25	15.95		56.20	68
1120	14" diameter		20	.800		48.80	17.55		66.35	80
1130	16" diameter		18	.889		60.40	19.50		79.90	96
1140	18" diameter	↓	16	1		81.75	22		103.75	125
1150	20" diameter	Q-10	18	1.330		107	30		137	165
1160	22" diameter		14	1.710		135	39		174	205
1170	24" diameter	↓	12	2		161	45		206	245
1200	Tee, 3" diameter	Q-9	27	.593		14.20	13		27.20	35
1210	4" diameter		26	.615		14.85	13.50		28.35	37
1220	5" diameter		25	.640		15.65	14.05		29.70	38
1230	6" diameter		24	.667		17.40	14.60		32	41
1240	7" diameter		23	.696		23.40	15.25		38.65	49
1250	8" diameter		22	.727		25.90	15.95		41.85	53
1260	10" diameter		21	.762		70	16.70		86.70	100
1270	12" diameter		20	.800		84.30	17.55		101.85	120
1280	14" diameter		18	.889		136	19.50		155.50	180
1290	16" diameter		16	1		192	22		214	245
1300	18" diameter	↓	14	1.140		240	25		265	300
1310	20" diameter	Q-10	17	1.410		330	32		362	410
1320	22" diameter		13	1.850		405	42		447	510
1330	24" diameter	↓	12	2		475	45		520	590
1460	Tee cap, 3" diameter	Q-9	45	.356		1.10	7.80		8.90	13
1470	4" diameter		42	.381		1.37	8.35		9.72	14.15
1480	5" diameter		40	.400		1.50	8.75		10.25	14.90
1490	6" diameter		37	.432		1.75	9.50		11.25	16.25
1500	7" diameter		35	.457		2.83	10		12.83	18.25
1510	8" diameter		34	.471		3.30	10.30		13.60	19.20
1520	10" diameter		32	.500		6.25	10.95		17.20	23
1530	12" diameter		30	.533		8.30	11.70		20	27
1540	14" diameter		28	.571		17.20	12.50		29.70	38
1550	16" diameter		25	.640		19.20	14.05		33.25	42
1560	18" diameter	↓	24	.667		22.50	14.60		37.10	47
1570	20" diameter	Q-10	27	.889		24.25	20		44.25	57
1580	22" diameter		22	1.090		27.70	25		52.70	68
1590	24" diameter	↓	21	1.140		31.20	26		57.20	74
1750	Top, 3" diameter	Q-9	46	.348		5.30	7.60		12.90	17.35
1760	4" diameter		44	.364		5.60	7.95		13.55	18.20
1770	5" diameter		42	.381		7.70	8.35		16.05	21
1780	6" diameter		40	.400		9.85	8.75		18.60	24
1790	7" diameter		38	.421		14.55	9.25		23.80	30
1800	8" diameter		36	.444		18.75	9.75		28.50	35
1810	10" diameter		34	.471		43.50	10.30		53.80	63
1820	12" diameter	↓	32	.500		65.50	10.95		76.45	89

155 | Heating

		155 600	Heating System Access.	CREW	DAILY OUTPUT	MAN-HOURS	UNIT	BARE COSTS MAT.	LABOR	EQUIP.	TOTAL	TOTAL INCL O&P	
680	1830		14" diameter	Q-9	30	.533	Ea.	74.20	11.70		85.90	99	680
	1840		16" diameter		28	.571		133	12.50		145.50	165	
	1850		18" diameter		26	.615		235	13.50		248.50	280	
	1860		20" diameter	Q-10	28	.857		263	19.50		282.50	320	
	1870		22" diameter		22	1.090		355	25		380	430	
	1880		24" diameter		20	1.200		445	27		472	530	
	3200	All fuel, pressure tight, double wall, U.L. listed, 1400°F.											
	3210	304 stainless steel liner, aluminized steel outer jacket											
	3220		6" diameter	Q-9	60	.267	L.F.	45.70	5.85		51.55	59	
	3221		8" diameter		52	.308		52	6.75		58.75	67	
	3222		10" diameter		48	.333		58.30	7.30		65.60	75	
	3223		12" diameter		44	.364		66.60	7.95		74.55	85	
	3225		16" diameter		40	.400		84.60	8.75		93.35	105	
	3226		18" diameter		38	.421		95.70	9.25		104.95	120	
	3227		20" diameter	Q-10	36	.667		108	15.15		123.15	140	
	3228		24" diameter	"	32	.750		139	17.05		156.05	180	
	3260	For 316 stainless steel liner add						6%					
	3280	All fuel, pressure tight, double wall fittings											
	3284	304 stainless steel inner, aluminized steel jacket											
	3288	Adjustable 18"/30" section											
	3292		6" diameter	Q-9	30	.533	Ea.	140	11.70		151.70	170	
	3293		8" diameter		26	.615		159	13.50		172.50	195	
	3294		10" diameter		24	.667		181	14.60		195.60	220	
	3295		12" diameter		22	.727		206	15.95		221.95	250	
	3296		14" diameter		21	.762		232	16.70		248.70	280	
	3297		16" diameter		20	.800		265	17.55		282.55	320	
	3298		18" diameter		19	.842		306	18.45		324.45	365	
	3299		20" diameter	Q-10	18	1.330		345	30		375	425	
	3300		24" diameter	"	16	1.500		440	34		474	535	
	3326	For 316 stainless steel liner, add						15%					
	3350	Elbow 15° adjustable											
	3354		6" diameter	Q-9	30	.533	Ea.	240	11.70		251.70	280	
	3355		8" diameter		26	.615		272	13.50		285.50	320	
	3356		10" diameter		24	.667		305	14.60		319.60	360	
	3357		12" diameter		22	.727		350	15.95		365.95	410	
	3358		14" diameter		21	.762		395	16.70		411.70	460	
	3359		16" diameter		20	.800		445	17.55		462.55	515	
	3360		18" diameter		19	.842		500	18.45		518.45	580	
	3361		20" diameter	Q-10	18	1.330		570	30		600	675	
	3362		24" diameter	"	16	1.500		730	34		764	855	
	3380	For 316 stainless steel liner, add						20%					
	3400	Elbow 45°											
	3404		6" diameter	Q-9	30	.533	Ea.	152	11.70		163.70	185	
	3405		8" diameter		26	.615		172	13.50		185.50	210	
	3406		10" diameter		24	.667		195	14.60		209.60	235	
	3407		12" diameter		22	.727		220	15.95		235.95	265	
	3408		14" diameter		21	.762		250	16.70		266.70	300	
	3409		16" diameter		20	.800		280	17.55		297.55	335	
	3410		18" diameter		19	.842		320	18.45		338.45	380	
	3411		20" diameter	Q-10	18	1.330		360	30		390	440	
	3412		24" diameter	"	16	1.500		460	34		494	560	
	3430	For 316 stainless steel liner, add						20%					
	3450	Tee 90°											
	3454		6" diameter	Q-9	24	.667	Ea.	159	14.60		173.60	195	
	3455		8" diameter		22	.727		183	15.95		198.95	225	
	3456		10" diameter		21	.762		214	16.70		230.70	260	
	3457		12" diameter		20	.800		251	17.55		268.55	305	
	3458		14" diameter		18	.889		285	19.50		304.50	345	

155 | Heating

155 600 | Heating System Access.

			DAILY	MAN-		BARE COSTS				TOTAL
		CREW	OUTPUT	HOURS	UNIT	MAT.	LABOR	EQUIP.	TOTAL	INCL O&P
3459	16" diameter	Q-9	16	1	Ea.	315	22		337	380
3460	18" diameter	"	14	1.140		370	25		395	445
3461	20" diameter	Q-10	17	1.410		430	32		462	520
3462	24" diameter	"	12	2		530	45		575	650
3480	For Tee Cap, add					35%	20%			
3500	For 316 stainless steel liner, add				↓	22%				
3520	Plate support, galvanized									
3524	6" diameter	Q-9	26	.615	Ea.	98	13.50		111.50	130
3525	8" diameter		22	.727		113	15.95		128.95	150
3526	10" diameter		20	.800		123	17.55		140.55	160
3527	12" diameter		18	.889		129	19.50		148.50	170
3528	14" diameter		17	.941		152	21		173	200
3529	16" diameter		16	1		161	22		183	210
3530	18" diameter	↓	15	1.070		169	23		192	220
3531	20" diameter	Q-10	16	1.500		177	34		211	245
3532	24" diameter	"	14	1.710		185	39		224	260
3570	Bellows, lined, 316 stainless steel only									
3574	6" diameter	Q-9	30	.533	Ea.	255	11.70		266.70	300
3575	8" diameter		26	.615		285	13.50		298.50	335
3576	10" diameter		24	.667		320	14.60		334.60	375
3577	12" diameter		22	.727		365	15.95		380.95	425
3578	14" diameter		21	.762		415	16.70		431.70	480
3579	16" diameter		20	.800		470	17.55		487.55	545
3580	18" diameter	↓	19	.842		530	18.45		548.45	610
3581	20" diameter	Q-10	18	1.330	↓	610	30		640	715
3600	Ventilated roof thimble, 304 stainless steel									
3620	6" diameter	Q-9	26	.615	Ea.	270	13.50		283.50	315
3624	8" diameter		22	.727		288	15.95		303.95	340
3625	10" diameter		20	.800		310	17.55		327.55	370
3626	12" diameter		18	.889		325	19.50		344.50	385
3627	14" diameter		17	.941		345	21		366	410
3628	16" diameter		16	1		360	22		382	430
3629	18" diameter	↓	15	1.070		380	23		403	455
3630	20" diameter	Q-10	16	1.500		400	34		434	490
3631	24" diameter	"	14	1.710	↓	445	39		484	550
3650	For 316 stainless steel, add					10%				
3670	Exit cone, 316 stainless steel only									
3674	6" diameter	Q-9	46	.348	Ea.	151	7.60		158.60	180
3675	8" diameter		42	.381		158	8.35		166.35	185
3676	10" diameter		40	.400		166	8.75		174.75	195
3677	12" diameter		38	.421		175	9.25		184.25	205
3678	14" diameter		37	.432		189	9.50		198.50	220
3679	16" diameter		36	.444		210	9.75		219.75	245
3680	18" diameter	↓	35	.457		258	10		268	300
3681	20" diameter	Q-10	28	.857		305	19.50		324.50	365
3682	24" diameter	"	26	.923	↓	405	21		426	475
3720	Roof support assy., incl. 30" pipe sect, 304 st. st.									
3724	6" diameter	Q-9	25	.640	Ea.	350	14.05		364.05	405
3725	8" diameter		21	.762		375	16.70		391.70	440
3726	10" diameter		19	.842		405	18.45		423.45	475
3727	12" diameter		17	.941		475	21		496	555
3728	14" diameter		16	1		480	22		502	560
3729	16" diameter		15	1.070		515	23		538	600
3730	18" diameter	↓	14	1.140		545	25		570	635
3731	20" diameter	Q-10	15	1.600		575	36		611	685
3732	24" diameter	"	13	1.850		640	42		682	765
3750	For 316 stainless steel, add				↓	20%				
3770	Stack cap, 316 stainless steel only									

155 | Heating

155 600 | Heating System Access.

		Description	CREW	DAILY OUTPUT	MAN-HOURS	UNIT	BARE COSTS MAT.	BARE COSTS LABOR	BARE COSTS EQUIP.	BARE COSTS TOTAL	TOTAL INCL O&P	
680	3774	6" diameter	Q-9	46	.348	Ea.	181	7.60		188.60	210	680
	3775	8" diameter		42	.381		210	8.35		218.35	245	
	3776	10" diameter		40	.400		245	8.75		253.75	285	
	3777	12" diameter		38	.421		285	9.25		294.25	325	
	3778	14" diameter		37	.432		325	9.50		334.50	370	
	3779	16" diameter		36	.444		365	9.75		374.75	415	
	3780	18" diameter	↓	35	.457		425	10		435	485	
	3781	20" diameter	Q-10	28	.857		480	19.50		499.50	555	
	3782	24" diameter	"	26	.923	↓	580	21		601	670	
	7800	All fuel, double wall, stainless steel, 6" diameter	Q-9	60	.267	V.L.F.	16.85	5.85		22.70	27	
	7802	7" diameter		56	.286		21.70	6.25		27.95	33	
	7804	8" diameter		52	.308		25.40	6.75		32.15	38	
	7806	10" diameter		48	.333		36.80	7.30		44.10	52	
	7808	12" diameter		44	.364		49.40	7.95		57.35	66	
	7810	14" diameter	↓	42	.381	↓	64.70	8.35		73.05	84	
	8000	All fuel, double wall, stainless steel fittings										
	8010	Roof support 6" diameter	Q-9	30	.533	Ea.	43.30	11.70		55	65	
	8020	7" diameter		28	.571		48.90	12.50		61.40	73	
	8030	8" diameter		26	.615		52.90	13.50		66.40	79	
	8040	10" diameter		24	.667		69.70	14.60		84.30	99	
	8050	12" diameter		22	.727		83.20	15.95		99.15	115	
	8060	14" diameter		21	.762		105	16.70		121.70	140	
	8100	Elbow 15°, 6" diameter		30	.533		37.70	11.70		49.40	59	
	8120	7" diameter		28	.571		42	12.50		54.50	65	
	8140	8" diameter		26	.615		48.30	13.50		61.80	74	
	8160	10" diameter		24	.667		63.25	14.60		77.85	92	
	8180	12" diameter		22	.727		76	15.95		91.95	110	
	8200	14" diameter		21	.762		90.80	16.70		107.50	125	
	8300	Insulated tee with insulated tee cap, 6" diameter		30	.533		71.20	11.70		82.90	96	
	8340	7" diameter		28	.571		93.50	12.50		106	120	
	8360	8" diameter		26	.615		105	13.50		118.50	135	
	8380	10" diameter		24	.667		148	14.60		162.60	185	
	8400	12" diameter		22	.727		207	15.95		222.95	250	
	8420	14" diameter		21	.762		272	16.70		288.70	325	
	8500	Joist shield, 6" diameter		30	.533		27.10	11.70		38.80	47	
	8510	7" diameter		28	.571		29	12.50		41.50	51	
	8520	8" diameter		26	.615		30.30	13.50		43.80	54	
	8530	10" diameter		24	.667		39	14.60		53.60	65	
	8540	12" diameter		22	.727		49	15.95		64.95	78	
	8550	14" diameter		21	.762		61	16.70		77.70	92	
	8600	Round top, 6" diameter		30	.533		24.80	11.70		36.50	45	
	8620	7" diameter		28	.571		33	12.50		45.50	55	
	8640	8" diameter		26	.615		44	13.50		57.50	69	
	8660	10" diameter		24	.667		79	14.60		93.60	110	
	8680	12" diameter		22	.727		113	15.95		128.95	150	
	8700	14" diameter		21	.762		151	16.70		167.70	190	
	8800	Adjustable roof flashing, 6" diameter		30	.533		28.70	11.70		40.40	49	
	8820	7" diameter		28	.571		32.80	12.50		45.30	55	
	8840	8" diameter		26	.615		35.70	13.50		49.20	60	
	8860	10" diameter		24	.667		45.80	14.60		60.40	72	
	8880	12" diameter		22	.727		58.50	15.95		74.45	88	
	8900	14" diameter	↓	21	.762	↓	72.80	16.70		89.50	105	
	9000	High temp. (2000° F), steel jacket, acid resist. refractory lining										
	9010	11 ga. galvanized jacket, U.L. listed										
	9020	Straight section, 48" long, 10" diameter	Q-10	13.30	1.800	V.L.F.	284	41		325	375	
	9030	12" diameter		11.20	2.140		309	49		358	415	
	9040	18" diameter		7.40	3.240		425	74		499	580	
	9050	24" diameter	↓	4.60	5.220	↓	585	120		705	825	

155 | Heating

155 600 | Heating System Access.

		CREW	DAILY OUTPUT	MAN-HOURS	UNIT	BARE COSTS MAT.	LABOR	EQUIP.	TOTAL	TOTAL INCL O&P
9120	Tee section, 10" diameter	Q-10	4.40	5.450	Ea.	475	125		600	710
9130	12" diameter		3.70	6.490		515	145		660	790
9140	18" diameter		2.40	10		710	225		935	1,125
9150	24" diameter		1.50	16		1,000	365		1,365	1,650
9220	Cleanout pier section, 10" diameter		3.50	6.860		500	155		655	785
9230	12" diameter		2.50	9.600		530	220		750	915
9240	18" diameter		1.90	12.630		720	285		1,005	1,225
9250	24" diameter		1.30	18.460		895	420		1,315	1,625
9320	For drain, add					53%				
9330	Elbow, 30° and 45°, 10" diameter	Q-10	6.60	3.640		268	83		351	420
9340	12" diameter		5.60	4.290		315	97		412	495
9350	18" diameter		3.70	6.490		485	145		630	755
9360	24" diameter		2.30	10.430		760	235		995	1,200
9430	For 60° and 90° elbow, add					112%				
9440	End cap, 10" diameter	Q-10	26	.923		565	21		586	655
9450	12" diameter		22	1.090		610	25		635	710
9460	18" diameter		15	1.600		830	36		866	970
9470	24" diameter		9	2.670		1,070	61		1,131	1,275
9540	Increaser (1 diameter), 10" diameter		6.60	3.640		397	83		480	560
9550	12" diameter		5.60	4.290		428	97		525	620
9560	18" diameter		3.70	6.490		585	145		730	865
9570	24" diameter		2.30	10.430		790	235		1,025	1,225
9600	For expansion joints, add to straight section					7%				
9610	For ¼" hot rolled steel jacket, add					157%				
9620	For 2950°F very high temperature, add					89%				
9630	26 ga. aluminized jacket, straight section, 48" long									
9640	10" diameter	Q-10	15.30	1.570	V.L.F.	131	36		167	200
9650	12" diameter		12.90	1.860		144	42		186	220
9660	18" diameter		8.50	2.820		222	64		286	340
9670	24" diameter		5.30	4.530		315	105		420	500
9700	Accessories (all models)									
9710	Guy band, 10" diameter	Q-10	32	.750	Ea.	41.80	17.05		58.85	72
9720	12" diameter		30	.800		49.30	18.20		67.50	82
9730	18" diameter		26	.923		63.75	21		84.75	100
9740	24" diameter		24	1		132	23		155	180
9810	Draw band, 11 gauge, 10" diameter		32	.750		33.25	17.05		50.30	62
9820	12" diameter		30	.800		34.20	18.20		52.40	65
9830	18" diameter		26	.923		51.30	21		72.30	88
9840	24" diameter		24	1		69.40	23		92.40	110
9910	Draw band, 26 gauge, 10" diameter		32	.750		13.30	17.05		30.35	40
9920	12" diameter		30	.800		13.30	18.20		31.50	42
9930	18" diameter		26	.923		15.20	21		36.20	48
9940	24" diameter		24	1		17.10	23		40.10	53

156 | HVAC Piping Specialties

156 200 | Heat/Cool Piping Misc.

		CREW	DAILY OUTPUT	MAN-HOURS	UNIT	BARE COSTS MAT.	LABOR	EQUIP.	TOTAL	TOTAL INCL O&P
0010	**AUTOMATIC AIR VENT**									
0020	Cast iron body, stainless steel internals, float type									
0180	½" NPT inlet, 250 psi	1 Stpi	10	.800	Ea.	155	19.80		174.80	200
0220	¾" NPT inlet, 250 psi	"	10	.800	"	155	19.80		174.80	200

156 | HVAC Piping Specialties

156 200 | Heat/Cool Piping Misc.

			CREW	DAILY OUTPUT	MAN-HOURS	UNIT	BARE COSTS MAT.	LABOR	EQUIP.	TOTAL	TOTAL INCL O&P	
201	0600	Forged steel body, stainless steel internals, float type										201
	0640	½" NPT inlet, 750 psi	1 Stpi	12	.667	Ea.	470	16.50		486.50	540	
	0680	¾" NPT inlet, 750 psi	"	12	.667	"	470	16.50		486.50	540	
	1100	Formed steel body, non corrosive										
	1110	⅛" NPT inlet 150 psi	1 Stpi	32	.250	Ea.	4.20	6.20		10.40	13.80	
	1120	¼" NPT inlet 150 psi		32	.250		16.45	6.20		22.65	27	
	1130	¾" NPT inlet 150 psi	↓	32	.250	↓	16.45	6.20		22.65	27	
	1300	Chrome plated brass, automatic/manual, for radiators										
	1310	⅛" NPT inlet, nickel plated brass	1 Stpi	32	.250	Ea.	2.76	6.20		8.96	12.20	
205	0010	**AIR CONTROL** With strainer										205
	0040	2" diameter	Q-5	6	2.670	Ea.	336	59		395	460	
	0080	2-½" diameter		5	3.200	↓	378	71		449	520	
	0100	3" diameter		4	4		580	89		669	770	
207	0010	**AIR PURGING SCOOP** with tappings										207
	0020	for air vent and expansion tank connection										
	0100	1" pipe size, threaded	1 Stpi	19	.421	Ea.	10.20	10.40		20.60	27	
	0110	1-¼" pipe size, threaded		15	.533		10.30	13.20		23.50	31	
	0120	1-½" pipe size, threaded		13	.615		22	15.25		37.25	47	
	0130	2" pipe size, threaded	↓	11	.727	↓	25	18		43	54	
220	0010	**CIRCUIT SETTER** Balance valve										220
	0018	Threaded										
	0019	½" pipe size	1 Stpi	22	.364	Ea.	33.60	9		42.60	50	
	0020	¾" pipe size	"	20	.400	"	35.70	9.90		45.60	54	
222	0010	**COCKS AND DRAINS**										222
	1000	Boiler drain										
	1010	Pipe thread to hose										
	1020	Bronze										
	1030	½" size	1 Stpi	36	.222	Ea.	4.32	5.50		9.82	12.90	
	1040	¾" size	"	34	.235	"	5.02	5.80		10.82	14.15	
	1100	Solder to hose										
	1110	Bronze										
	1120	½" size	1 Stpi	46	.174	Ea.	3.54	4.30		7.84	10.30	
	1130	¾" size	"	44	.182	"	4.03	4.50		8.53	11.10	
	1600	With built-in vacuum breaker										
	1610	½" IP or solder	1 Stpi	36	.222	Ea.	8.10	5.50		13.60	17.05	
	1630	With tamper proof vacuum breaker										
	1640	½" IP or solder	1 Stpi	36	.222	Ea.	11.65	5.50		17.15	21	
	1650	¾" IP or solder	"	34	.235	"	11.90	5.80		17.70	22	
	3000	Cocks										
	3010	Air, lever or tee handle										
	3020	Bronze, single thread										
	3030	⅛" size	1 Stpi	52	.154	Ea.	3.93	3.81		7.74	9.95	
	3040	¼" size		46	.174		4.43	4.30		8.73	11.25	
	3050	⅜" size		40	.200		4.73	4.95		9.68	12.55	
	3060	½" size		36	.222	↓	4.83	5.50		10.33	13.45	
	3100	Bronze, double thread										
	3110	⅛" size	1 Stpi	26	.308	Ea.	5.28	7.60		12.88	17.10	
	3120	¼" size		22	.364		5.15	9		14.15	19	
	3130	⅜" size		18	.444		5.60	11		16.60	22	
	3140	½" size	↓	15	.533	↓	6.75	13.20		19.95	27	
225	0010	**EXPANSION JOINTS** Bellows type, neoprene cover, flanged spool										225
	0100	6" face to face, ½" diameter	1 Stpi	14	.571	Ea.	183	14.15		197.15	220	
	0110	¾" diameter		14	.571		183	14.15		197.15	220	
	0120	1" diameter		13	.615		183	15.25		198.25	225	
	0140	1-¼" diameter		11	.727		183	18		201	230	
	0160	1-½" diameter	↓	10.60	.755		193	18.70		211.70	240	

156 | HVAC Piping Specialties

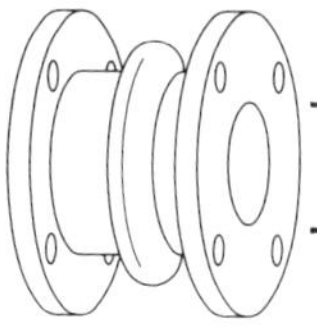

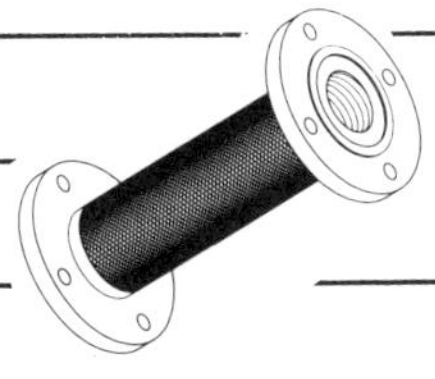

156 200 | Heat/Cool Piping Misc.

		CREW	DAILY OUTPUT	MAN-HOURS	UNIT	BARE COSTS MAT.	LABOR	EQUIP.	TOTAL	TOTAL INCL O&P	
225	0180	2" diameter	Q-5	13.30	1.200	Ea.	196	27		223	255	225
	0200	3" diameter		11.40	1.400		218	31		249	285	
	0480	10" face to face, 2" diameter		13	1.230		250	27		277	315	
	0500	2-½" diameter		12	1.330		270	30		300	340	
	0520	3" diameter		11	1.450		277	32		309	355	
	0540	4" diameter		8	2		326	45		371	425	
	0560	5" diameter		7	2.290		365	51		416	475	
	0580	6" diameter		6	2.670		370	59		429	495	
	0600	8" diameter		5	3.200		455	71		526	605	
	0620	10" diameter		4.60	3.480		505	77		582	670	
	0640	12" diameter		4	4		570	89		659	760	
	0660	14" diameter		3.80	4.210		685	94		779	895	
235	0010	**FLEXIBLE METAL HOSE** Connectors, standard lengths										235
	0100	Bronze braided, bronze ends										
	0120	⅜" diameter x 12"	1 Stpi	26	.308	Ea.	15.25	7.60		22.85	28	
	0140	½" diameter x 12"		24	.333		19.90	8.25		28.15	34	
	0160	¾" diameter x 12"		20	.400		25.40	9.90		35.30	43	
	0180	1" diameter x 18"		19	.421		41.15	10.40		51.55	61	
	0200	1-½" diameter x 18"		13	.615		56.80	15.25		72.05	85	
	0220	2" diameter x 18"		11	.727		76.50	18		94.50	110	
	1000	Carbon steel ends										
	1020	¼" diameter x 12"	1 Stpi	28	.286	Ea.	10.95	7.05		18	23	
	1040	⅜" diameter x 12"		26	.308		13.50	7.60		21.10	26	
	1060	½" diameter x 12"		24	.333		17.80	8.25		26.05	32	
	1080	½" diameter x 24"		24	.333		21.25	8.25		29.50	36	
	1100	½" diameter x 36"		24	.333		24.70	8.25		32.95	39	
	1120	¾" diameter x 12"		20	.400		22.25	9.90		32.15	39	
	1140	¾" diameter x 24"		20	.400		27.40	9.90		37.30	45	
	1160	¾" diameter x 36"		20	.400		32.55	9.90		42.45	50	
	1180	1" diameter x 18"		19	.421		34.25	10.40		44.65	53	
	1200	1" diameter x 30"		19	.421		41.80	10.40		52.20	61	
	1220	1" diameter x 36"		19	.421		45.60	10.40		56	66	
	1240	1-¼" diameter x 18"		15	.533		40.30	13.20		53.50	64	
	1260	1-¼" diameter x 36"		15	.533		55.25	13.20		68.45	80	
	1280	1-½" diameter x 18"		13	.615		45.30	15.25		60.55	72	
	1300	1-½" diameter x 36"		13	.615		63.10	15.25		78.35	92	
	1320	2" diameter x 24"		11	.727		68.50	18		86.50	100	
	1340	2" diameter x 36"		11	.727		81	18		99	115	
	1360	2-½" diameter x 24"		9	.889		101	22		123	145	
	1380	2-½" diameter x 36"		9	.889		128	22		150	175	
	1400	3" diameter x 24"		7	1.140		117	28		145	170	
	1420	3" diameter x 36"		7	1.140		148	28		176	205	
	2000	Carbon steel braid, carbon steel solid ends										
	2100	½" diameter x 12"	1 Stpi	24	.333	Ea.	15.90	8.25		24.15	30	
	2120	¾" diameter x 12"		20	.400		19.60	9.90		29.50	36	
	2140	1" diameter x 12"		19	.421		24.20	10.40		34.60	42	
	2160	1-¼" diameter x 12"		15	.533		27.70	13.20		40.90	50	
	2180	1-½" diameter x 12"		13	.615		31.40	15.25		46.65	57	
	3000	Stainless steel braid, welded on carbon steel ends										
	3100	½" diameter x 12"	1 Stpi	24	.333	Ea.	20.80	8.25		29.05	35	
	3120	¾" diameter x 12"		20	.400		24.50	9.90		34.40	42	
	3140	¾" diameter x 24"		20	.400		29	9.90		38.90	47	
	3160	¾" diameter x 36"		20	.400		33.50	9.90		43.40	52	
	3180	1" diameter x 12"		19	.421		29.75	10.40		40.15	48	
	3200	1" diameter x 24"		19	.421		35.40	10.40		45.80	54	
	3220	1" diameter x 36"		19	.421		41.10	10.40		51.50	61	
	3240	1-¼" diameter x 12"		15	.533		33.90	13.20		47.10	57	
	3260	1-¼" diameter x 24"		15	.533		40.80	13.20		54	64	

156 | HVAC Piping Specialties

156 200 | Heat/Cool Piping Misc.

			CREW	DAILY OUTPUT	MAN-HOURS	UNIT	MAT.	LABOR	EQUIP.	TOTAL	TOTAL INCL O&P	
235	3280	1-¼" diameter x 36"	1 Stpi	15	.533	Ea.	47.70	13.20		60.90	72	235
	3300	1-½" diameter x 12"		13	.615		38.80	15.25		54.05	65	
	3320	1-½" diameter x 24"		13	.615		47.20	15.25		62.45	75	
	3340	1-½" diameter x 36"		13	.615		55.60	15.25		70.85	84	
237	0010	**FLOW CHECK CONTROL**										237
	0100	Bronze body, soldered										
	0110	¾" size	1 Stpi	20	.400	Ea.	25.75	9.90		35.65	43	
	0120	1" size	"	19	.421	"	30.90	10.40		41.30	49	
	0200	Cast iron body, threaded										
	0210	¾" size	1 Stpi	20	.400	Ea.	18.90	9.90		28.80	35	
	0220	1" size		19	.421		20.80	10.40		31.20	38	
	0230	1-¼" size		15	.533		24.50	13.20		37.70	47	
	0240	1-½" size		13	.615		41.60	15.25		56.85	68	
	0250	2" size		11	.727		59	18		77	92	
240	0010	**HEATING CONTROL VALVES**										240
	0050	Hot water, nonelectric, thermostatic										
	0100	Radiator supply, ½" diameter	1 Stpi	24	.333	Ea.	74.40	8.25		82.65	94	
	0120	¾" diameter	"	20	.400	"	79	9.90		88.90	100	
	1000	Manual, radiator supply										
	1010	½" pipe size, angle union	1 Stpi	24	.333	Ea.	21	8.25		29.25	35	
	1020	¾" pipe size, angle union	"	20	.400	"	26.40	9.90		36.30	44	
	1100	Radiator, balancing										
	1110	½" pipe size, angle union	1 Stpi	24	.333	Ea.	20.40	8.25		28.65	35	
	1120	¾" pipe size, angle union	"	20	.400	"	23.80	9.90		33.70	41	
	1200	Steam, radiator, supply										
	1210	½" pipe size, angle union	1 Stpi	24	.333	Ea.	20.50	8.25		28.75	35	
	1220	¾" pipe size, angle union	"	20	.400	"	21.30	9.90		31.20	38	
	8000	System balancing and shut-off										
	8020	Butterfly, quarter turn, calibrated, threaded or solder										
	8040	Bronze, -30° F to +350° F, pressure to 175 psi										
	8060	½" size	1 Stpi	22	.364	Ea.	7.80	9		16.80	22	
	8070	¾" size	"	20	.400	"	10.20	9.90		20.10	26	
244	0010	**MONOFLOW TEE FITTING**										244
	1100	For one pipe hydronic, supply and return										
	1110	Copper, soldered										
	1120	¾" x ½" size	1 Stpi	13	.615	Ea.	7.35	15.25		22.60	31	
	2100	Cast iron, threaded										
	2110	¾" x ½" size	1 Stpi	10	.800	Ea.	16.80	19.80		36.60	48	
245	0010	**MIXING VALVE** Automatic water tempering										245
	0050	¾" size	1 Stpi	18	.444	Ea.	255	11		266	295	
	0100	1" size		16	.500		367	12.40		379.40	420	
	0120	1-¼" size		13	.615		530	15.25		545.25	605	
	0140	1-½" size		10	.800		640	19.80		659.80	735	
	0160	2" size		8	1		800	25		825	915	
	0180	3" size		4	2		1,850	50		1,900	2,100	
260	0010	**PRESSURE REGULATOR**										260
	0100	Gas appliance regulators										
	0106	Main burner and pilot applications										
	0108	Rubber seat poppet type										
	0109	⅛" pipe size	1 Stpi	24	.333	Ea.	8.05	8.25		16.30	21	
	0110	¼" pipe size		24	.333		8.75	8.25		17	22	
	0112	⅜" pipe size		24	.333		9.80	8.25		18.05	23	
	0113	½" pipe size		24	.333		11	8.25		19.25	24	
	0114	¾" pipe size		20	.400		12.75	9.90		22.65	29	
	0122	Lever action type										
	0123	⅜" pipe size	1 Stpi	24	.333	Ea.	20.60	8.25		28.85	35	
	0124	½" pipe size	"	24	.333	"	20.60	8.25		28.85	35	

156 | HVAC Piping Specialties

156 200 | Heat/Cool Piping Misc.

			CREW	DAILY OUTPUT	MAN-HOURS	UNIT	BARE COSTS MAT.	BARE COSTS LABOR	BARE COSTS EQUIP.	BARE COSTS TOTAL	TOTAL INCL O&P	
260	0125	¾" pipe size	1 Stpi	20	.400	Ea.	37.90	9.90		47.80	56	260
	0126	1" pipe size	"	19	.421	"	46.70	10.40		57.10	67	
	0132	Double diaphragm type										
	0133	⅜" pipe size	1 Stpi	24	.333	Ea.	18.10	8.25		26.35	32	
	0134	½" pipe size		24	.333		28	8.25		36.25	43	
	0135	¾" pipe size		20	.400		50.90	9.90		60.80	71	
	0136	1" pipe size		19	.421		77.25	10.40		87.65	100	
	0137	1-¼" pipe size		15	.533		200	13.20		213.20	240	
	0138	1-½" pipe size		13	.615		375	15.25		390.25	435	
	0139	2" pipe size		11	.727		375	18		393	440	
	0140	2-½" pipe size	Q-5	15	1.070		730	24		754	840	
	0141	3" pipe size		13	1.230		730	27		757	845	
	0142	4" pipe size (flanged)		8	2		1,280	45		1,325	1,475	
	0160	Main burner only										
	0162	Straight-thru-flow design										
	0163	½" pipe size	1 Stpi	24	.333	Ea.	21.30	8.25		29.55	36	
	0164	¾" pipe size		20	.400		27.50	9.90		37.40	45	
	0165	1" pipe size		19	.421		39.80	10.40		50.20	59	
	0166	1-¼" pipe size		15	.533		39.80	13.20		53	63	
	0200	Oil, light, hot water, ordinary steam, threaded										
	0220	Bronze body, ¼" size	1 Stpi	24	.333	Ea.	90.60	8.25		98.85	110	
	0230	⅜" size		24	.333		97.80	8.25		106.05	120	
	0240	½" size		24	.333		122	8.25		130.25	145	
	0250	¾" size		20	.400		145	9.90		154.90	175	
	0260	1" size		19	.421		220	10.40		230.40	255	
	0270	1-¼" size		15	.533		298	13.20		311.20	345	
	0320	Iron body, ¼" size		24	.333		69.50	8.25		77.75	89	
	0330	⅜" size		24	.333		82.20	8.25		90.45	105	
	0340	½" size		24	.333		87	8.25		95.25	110	
	0350	¾" size		20	.400		105	9.90		114.90	130	
	0360	1" size		19	.421		137	10.40		147.40	165	
	0370	1-¼" size		15	.533		191	13.20		204.20	230	
	9000	For water pressure regulators, see Div. 151-955										
265	0010	**SEPARATORS** Entrainment eliminator, steel body, 150 PSIG										265
	0100	¼" size	1 Stpi	24	.333	Ea.	84	8.25		92.25	105	
	0120	½" size		24	.333		90	8.25		98.25	110	
	0140	¾" size		20	.400		95	9.90		104.90	120	
	0160	1" size		19	.421		142	10.40		152.40	170	
	0180	1-¼" size		15	.533		163	13.20		176.20	200	
	0200	1-½" size		13	.615		184	15.25		199.25	225	
	0220	2" size		11	.727		205	18		223	250	
274	0010	**SUCTION DIFFUSERS**										274
	0100	Cast iron body with integral straightening vanes, strainer										
	1000	Flanged										
	1010	2" inlet, 1-½" pump side	1 Stpi	6	1.330	Ea.	140	33		173	205	
	1020	2" pump side	"	5	1.600		147	40		187	220	
	1030	3" inlet, 2" pump side	Q-5	6.50	2.460		182	55		237	280	
275	0010	**THERMOFLO INDICATOR** For balancing										275
	1000	Sweat connections, 1-¼" pipe size	1 Stpi	12	.667	Ea.	245	16.50		261.50	295	
	1020	1-½" pipe size	"	10	.800	"	252	19.80		271.80	305	
278	0010	**VACUUM BREAKERS**										278
	0011	See also backflow preventers (151-105)										
	1000	Anti-siphon continuous pressure type										
	1010	Max. 150 PSI - 210°F										
	1020	Bronze body										
	1030	½" size	1 Stpi	24	.333	Ea.	102	8.25		110.25	125	

156 | HVAC Piping Specialties

156 200 | Heat/Cool Piping Misc.

			CREW	DAILY OUTPUT	MAN-HOURS	UNIT	MAT.	LABOR	EQUIP.	TOTAL	TOTAL INCL O&P	
278	1040	¾" size	1 Stpi	20	.400	Ea.	102	9.90		111.90	125	278
	1050	1" size		19	.421		105	10.40		115.40	130	
	1060	1-¼" size		15	.533		180	13.20		193.20	220	
	1070	1-½" size		13	.615		228	15.25		243.25	275	
	1080	2" size	↓	11	.727	↓	235	18		253	285	
	1200	Max. 125 PSI with atmospheric vent										
	1210	Brass, in-line construction										
	1220	¼" size	1 Stpi	24	.333	Ea.	19.15	8.25		27.40	33	
	1230	⅜" size	"	24	.333		19.15	8.25		27.40	33	
	1260	For polished chrome finish, add				↓	13%					
	2000	Anti-siphon, non-continuous pressure type										
	2010	Hot or cold water 125 PSI - 210° F										
	2020	Bronze body										
	2030	¼" size	1 Stpi	24	.333	Ea.	12.45	8.25		20.70	26	
	2040	⅜" size		24	.333		12.45	8.25		20.70	26	
	2050	½" size		24	.333		14.15	8.25		22.40	28	
	2060	¾" size		20	.400		16.75	9.90		26.65	33	
	2070	1" size		19	.421		26.10	10.40		36.50	44	
	2080	1-¼" size		15	.533		43.30	13.20		56.50	67	
	2090	1-½" size		13	.615		51	15.25		66.25	79	
	2100	2" size		11	.727		79.30	18		97.30	115	
	2110	2-½" size		8	1		228	25		253	290	
	2120	3" size	↓	6	1.330	↓	303	33		336	380	
	2150	For polished chrome finish, add					50%					
280	0010	**VENTURI FLOW** Measuring device										280
	0050	½" diameter	1 Stpi	24	.333	Ea.	75.60	8.25		83.85	95	
	0100	¾" diameter		20	.400		75.60	9.90		85.50	98	
	0120	1" diameter		19	.421		84.80	10.40		95.20	110	
	0140	1-¼" diameter		15	.533		93	13.20		106.20	120	
	0160	1-½" diameter		13	.615		102	15.25		117.25	135	
	0180	2" diameter	↓	11	.727		123	18		141	160	
	0200	2-½" diameter	Q-5	16	1		165	22		187	215	
	0220	3" diameter		14	1.140		209	25		234	270	
	0240	4" diameter	↓	11	1.450		262	32		294	335	
	0260	5" diameter	Q-6	4	6		333	140		473	570	
	0280	6" diameter		3.50	6.860		385	160		545	660	
	0300	8" diameter		3	8		580	185		765	910	
	0320	10" diameter	↓	2	12		1,450	275		1,725	2,000	
	0500	For meter, add				↓	965			965	1,050	
290	0010	**WATER LEVEL CONTROLS**										290
	3000	Low water cut-off for hot water boiler, 50 psi maximum										
	3100	1" top & bottom equalizing pipes, manual reset	1 Stpi	14	.571	Ea.	136	14.15		150.15	170	
	3200	1" top & bottom equalizing pipes		14	.571		136	14.15		150.15	170	
	3300	2-½" side connection for nipple-to-boiler	↓	14	.571	↓	114	14.15		128.15	145	

156 600 | Strainers

			CREW	DAILY OUTPUT	MAN-HOURS	UNIT	MAT.	LABOR	EQUIP.	TOTAL	TOTAL INCL O&P	
601	0010	**STRAINERS, BASKET TYPE** Perforated stainless steel basket										601
	0100	Brass or monel available										
	2000	Simplex style										
	2300	Bronze body										
	2320	Screwed, ⅜" pipe size	1 Stpi	22	.364	Ea.	106	9		115	130	
	2340	½" pipe size		20	.400		106	9.90		115.90	130	
	2360	¾" pipe size		17	.471		148	11.65		159.65	180	
	2380	1" pipe size		15	.533		148	13.20		161.20	180	
	2400	1-¼" pipe size		13	.615		237	15.25		252.25	285	
	2420	1-½" pipe size	↓	12	.667	↓	237	16.50		253.50	285	

156 | HVAC Piping Specialties

156 600 | Strainers

			DAILY	MAN-			BARE COSTS			TOTAL	
		CREW	OUTPUT	HOURS	UNIT	MAT.	LABOR	EQUIP.	TOTAL	INCL O&P	
601	2440	2" pipe size	1 Stpi	10	.800	Ea.	415	19.80		434.80	485	601
	2460	2-½" pipe size	Q-5	15	1.070		570	24		594	660	
	2480	3" pipe size	"	14	1.140		760	25		785	875	
	2600	Flanged, 2" pipe size	1 Stpi	6	1.330		535	33		568	635	
	2620	2-½" pipe size	Q-5	4.50	3.560		830	79		909	1,025	
	2640	3" pipe size		3.50	4.570		975	100		1,075	1,225	
	2660	4" pipe size	↓	3	5.330		1,650	120		1,770	2,000	
	2680	5" pipe size	Q-6	3.40	7.060		2,450	165		2,615	2,925	
	2700	6" pipe size	"	3	8	↓	2,890	185		3,075	3,450	
	3600	Iron body										
	3700	Screwed, ⅜" pipe size	1 Stpi	22	.364	Ea.	65.50	9		74.50	85	
	3720	½" pipe size		20	.400		65.50	9.90		75.40	87	
	3740	¾" pipe size		17	.471		84.20	11.65		95.85	110	
	3760	1" pipe size		15	.533		84.20	13.20		97.40	110	
	3780	1-¼" pipe size		13	.615		118	15.25		133.25	150	
	3800	1-½" pipe size		12	.667		142	16.50		158.50	180	
	3820	2" pipe size	↓	10	.800		175	19.80		194.80	220	
	3840	2-½" pipe size	Q-5	15	1.070		237	24		261	295	
	3860	3" pipe size	"	14	1.140		284	25		309	350	
	4000	Flanged, 2" pipe size	1 Stpi	6	1.330		262	33		295	335	
	4020	2-½" pipe size	Q-5	4.50	3.560		350	79		429	505	
	4040	3" pipe size		3.50	4.570		360	100		460	545	
	4060	4" pipe size	↓	3	5.330		508	120		628	735	
	4080	5" pipe size	Q-6	3.40	7.060		820	165		985	1,150	
	4100	6" pipe size		3	8		1,005	185		1,190	1,375	
	4120	8" pipe size		2.50	9.600		1,840	220		2,060	2,350	
	4140	10" pipe size		2.20	10.910		2,540	250		2,790	3,175	
	4160	12" pipe size		1.70	14.120		3,110	325		3,435	3,900	
	4180	14" pipe size		1.40	17.140		3,730	395		4,125	4,700	
	4200	16" pipe size	↓	1	24	↓	3,950	555		4,505	5,175	
	7000	Stainless steel body										
	7200	Screwed, 1" pipe size	1 Stpi	15	.533	Ea.	330	13.20		343.20	385	
	7220	1-½" pipe size		12	.667		470	16.50		486.50	540	
	7240	2" pipe size	↓	10	.800		705	19.80		724.80	805	
	7260	2-½" pipe size	Q-5	15	1.070		1,060	24		1,084	1,200	
	7280	3" pipe size	"	14	1.140		1,470	25		1,495	1,650	
	7400	Flanged, 2" pipe size	1 Stpi	6	1.330		1,000	33		1,033	1,150	
	7420	2-½" pipe size	Q-5	4.50	3.560		1,840	79		1,919	2,150	
	7440	3" pipe size		3.50	4.570		1,960	100		2,060	2,300	
	7460	4" pipe size	↓	3	5.330		2,870	120		2,990	3,325	
	7480	6" pipe size	Q-6	3	8		4,770	185		4,955	5,525	
	7500	8" pipe size	"	2.50	9.600		7,770	220		7,990	8,875	
	8100	Duplex style										
	8200	Bronze body										
	8240	Screwed, ¾" pipe size	1 Stpi	16	.500	Ea.	565	12.40		577.40	640	
	8260	1" pipe size		14	.571		565	14.15		579.15	640	
	8280	1-¼" pipe size		12	.667		1,070	16.50		1,086	1,200	
	8300	1-½" pipe size		11	.727		1,070	18		1,088	1,200	
	8320	2" pipe size	↓	9	.889		1,670	22		1,692	1,875	
	8340	2-½" pipe size	Q-5	14	1.140		1,670	25		1,695	1,875	
	8420	Flanged, 2" pipe size	1 Stpi	6	1.330		1,920	33		1,953	2,150	
	8440	2-½" pipe size	Q-5	4.50	3.560		1,960	79		2,039	2,275	
	8460	3" pipe size		3.50	4.570		2,690	100		2,790	3,100	
	8480	4" pipe size	↓	3	5.330		4,110	120		4,230	4,700	
	8500	5" pipe size	Q-6	3.40	7.060		6,710	165		6,875	7,625	
	8520	6" pipe size	"	3	8		9,290	185		9,475	10,500	
	8700	Iron body										
	8740	Screwed, ¾" pipe size	1 Stpi	16	.500	Ea.	305	12.40		317.40	355	

205

156 | HVAC Piping Specialties

156 600 | Strainers

		CREW	DAILY OUTPUT	MAN-HOURS	UNIT	BARE COSTS MAT.	LABOR	EQUIP.	TOTAL	TOTAL INCL O&P	
601	8760	1" pipe size	1 Stpi	14	.571	Ea.	305	14.15		319.15	355	**601**
	8780	1-1/4" pipe size		12	.667		530	16.50		546.50	605	
	8800	1-1/2" pipe size		11	.727		530	18		548	610	
	8820	2" pipe size	↓	9	.889		865	22		887	985	
	8840	2-1/2" pipe size	Q-5	14	1.140		865	25		890	990	
	9000	Flanged, 2" pipe size	1 Stpi	6	1.330		940	33		973	1,075	
	9020	2-1/2" pipe size	Q-5	4.50	3.560		965	79		1,044	1,175	
	9040	3" pipe size		3.50	4.570		1,250	100		1,350	1,525	
	9060	4" pipe size	↓	3	5.330		1,970	120		2,090	2,350	
	9080	5" pipe size	Q-6	3.40	7.060		3,260	165		3,425	3,825	
	9100	6" pipe size		3	8		3,990	185		4,175	4,675	
	9120	8" pipe size		2.50	9.600		7,880	220		8,100	9,000	
	9140	10" pipe size		2.20	10.910		11,000	250		11,250	12,500	
	9160	12" pipe size		1.70	14.120		12,250	325		12,575	14,000	
	9180	16" pipe size	↓	1	24	↓	16,300	555		16,855	18,800	
	9700	Stainless steel body										
	9740	Screwed, 1" pipe size	1 Stpi	14	.571	Ea.	1,670	14.15		1,684	1,850	
	9760	1-1/2" pipe size		11	.727		2,550	18		2,568	2,825	
	9780	2" pipe size		9	.889		4,100	22		4,122	4,550	
	9860	Flanged, 2" pipe size	↓	6	1.330		4,190	33		4,223	4,650	
	9880	2-1/2" pipe size	Q-5	4.50	3.560		4,450	79		4,529	5,025	
	9900	3" pipe size		3.50	4.570		6,930	100		7,030	7,775	
	9920	4" pipe size	↓	3	5.330		8,420	120		8,540	9,450	
	9940	6" pipe size	Q-6	3	8		15,000	185		15,185	16,800	
	9960	8" pipe size	"	2.50	9.600	↓	24,500	220		24,720	27,300	
608	0010	**STRAINERS, Y TYPE** Bronze body										**608**
	0050	Screwed, 150 lb., 1/4" pipe size	1 Stpi	24	.333	Ea.	16.80	8.25		25.05	31	
	0070	3/8" pipe size		24	.333		16.80	8.25		25.05	31	
	0100	1/2" pipe size		20	.400		20.10	9.90		30	37	
	0120	3/4" pipe size		19	.421		23.40	10.40		33.80	41	
	0140	1" pipe size		17	.471		33.60	11.65		45.25	54	
	0150	1-1/4" pipe size		15	.533		45	13.20		58.20	69	
	0160	1-1/2" pipe size		14	.571		62.40	14.15		76.55	90	
	0180	2" pipe size	↓	13	.615		97.80	15.25		113.05	130	
	0200	2-1/2" pipe size	Q-5	17	.941		200	21		221	250	
	0220	3" pipe size		16	1		395	22		417	470	
	0240	4" pipe size	↓	15	1.070		900	24		924	1,025	
	0500	For 300 lb. rating, add					15%					
	1000	Flanged, 150 lb., 1-1/2" pipe size	1 Stpi	11	.727		255	18		273	305	
	1020	2" pipe size	"	8	1		330	25		355	400	
	1040	3" pipe size	Q-5	4.50	3.560		630	79		709	810	
	1060	4" pipe size	"	3	5.330		955	120		1,075	1,225	
	1080	5" pipe size	Q-6	3.40	7.060		1,400	165		1,565	1,775	
	1100	6" pipe size		3	8		1,820	185		2,005	2,275	
	1120	8" pipe size	↓	2.50	9.600		5,750	220		5,970	6,650	
	1500	For 300 lb. rating, add				↓	40%					
612	0010	**STRAINERS, Y TYPE** Iron body										**612**
	0050	Screwed, 250 lb., 1/4" pipe size	1 Stpi	20	.400	Ea.	7.40	9.90		17.30	23	
	0070	3/8" pipe size		20	.400		7.40	9.90		17.30	23	
	0100	1/2" pipe size		20	.400		7.40	9.90		17.30	23	
	0120	3/4" pipe size		18	.444		8.55	11		19.55	26	
	0140	1" pipe size		16	.500		11.40	12.40		23.80	31	
	0150	1-1/4" pipe size		15	.533		15	13.20		28.20	36	
	0160	1-1/2" pipe size		12	.667		18	16.50		34.50	44	
	0180	2" pipe size	↓	8	1		27.90	25		52.90	67	
	0200	2-1/2" pipe size	Q-5	12	1.330		54.60	30		84.60	105	

156 | HVAC Piping Specialties

156 600 | Strainers

		CREW	DAILY OUTPUT	MAN-HOURS	UNIT	BARE COSTS MAT.	BARE COSTS LABOR	BARE COSTS EQUIP.	BARE COSTS TOTAL	TOTAL INCL O&P	
612	0220	3" pipe size	Q-5	11	1.450	Ea.	78.60	32		110.60	135	612
	0240	4" pipe size	"	5	3.200		252	71		323	385	
	0500	For galvanized body, add					50%					
	1000	Flanged, 125 lb., 1-½" pipe size	1 Stpi	11	.727		84.60	18		102.60	120	
	1020	2" pipe size	"	8	1		84.60	25		109.60	130	
	1030	2-½" pipe size	Q-5	5	3.200		81	71		152	195	
	1040	3" pipe size		4.50	3.560		93.60	79		172.60	220	
	1050	3-½" pipe size		4	4		184	89		273	335	
	1060	4" pipe size		3	5.330		184	120		304	380	
	1080	5" pipe size	Q-6	3.40	7.060		288	165		453	560	
	1100	6" pipe size		3	8		350	185		535	660	
	1120	8" pipe size		2.50	9.600		595	220		815	985	
	1140	10" pipe size		2	12		1,100	275		1,375	1,625	
	1160	12" pipe size		1.70	14.120		1,680	325		2,005	2,325	
	1170	14" pipe size		1.30	18.460		2,660	425		3,085	3,550	
	1180	16" pipe size		1	24		3,790	555		4,345	5,000	
	1500	For 250 lb. rating, add					20%					
	2000	For galvanized body, add					50%					
	2500	For steel body, add					40%					

157 | Air Conditioning/Ventilating

157 100 | A.C. & Vent. Units

		CREW	DAILY OUTPUT	MAN-HOURS	UNIT	BARE COSTS MAT.	BARE COSTS LABOR	BARE COSTS EQUIP.	BARE COSTS TOTAL	TOTAL INCL O&P	
160	0010	**HEAT PUMPS**										160
	1000	Air to air, split system, not including curbs or pads										
	1010	For curbs/pads see division 157-440										
	1015	1.5 ton cooling, 7 MBH heat @ 0°F	Q-5	1.22	13.110	Ea.	1,300	290		1,590	1,875	
	1020	2 ton cooling, 8.5 MBH heat @ 0°F		1.20	13.330		1,450	295		1,745	2,025	
	1030	2.5 ton cooling, 10 MBH heat @ 0°F		1	16		1,665	355		2,020	2,350	
	1040	3 ton cooling, 13 MBH heat @ 0°F		.80	20		1,885	445		2,330	2,725	
	1050	3.5 ton cooling, 18 MBH heat @ 0°F		.75	21.330		2,295	475		2,770	3,225	
	1054	4 ton cooling, 24 MBH heat @ 0°F		.60	26.670		2,550	595		3,145	3,675	
	1060	5 ton cooling, 27 MBH heat @ 0°F		.50	32		2,970	715		3,685	4,325	
	1300	Supplementary electric heat coil, included										
	1500	Single package, not including curbs, pads, or plenums										
	1510	1.5 ton cooling, 5 MBH heat @ 0°F	Q-5	1.55	10.320	Ea.	1,600	230		1,830	2,100	
	1520	2 ton cooling, 6.5 MBH heat @ 0°F		1.50	10.670		1,755	240		1,995	2,275	
	1540	2.5 ton cooling, 8 MBH heat @ 0°F		1.40	11.430		1,915	255		2,170	2,475	
	1560	3 ton cooling, 10 MBH heat @ 0°F		1.20	13.330		2,115	295		2,410	2,775	
	1570	3.5 ton cooling, 11 MBH heat @ 0°F		1	16		2,390	355		2,745	3,150	
	1580	4 ton cooling, 13 MBH heat @ 0°F		.96	16.670		2,650	370		3,020	3,475	
	1620	5 ton cooling, 27 MBH heat @ 0°F		.65	24.620		3,050	550		3,600	4,175	
	1640	7.5 ton cooling, 35 MBH heat @ 0°F		.40	40		5,740	890		6,630	7,625	
	1700	Supplementary electric heat coil, included										
	2000	Water source to air, single package										
	2100	1 ton cooling, 13 MBH heat @ 75°F	Q-5	2	8	Ea.	745	180		925	1,075	
	2120	1.5 ton cooling, 17 MBH heat @ 75°F		1.80	8.890		890	200		1,090	1,275	
	2140	2 ton cooling, 19 MBH heat @ 75°F		1.70	9.410		930	210		1,140	1,325	
	2160	2.5 ton cooling, 25 MBH heat @ 75°F		1.60	10		995	225		1,220	1,425	
	2180	3 ton cooling, 27 MBH heat @ 75°F		1.40	11.430		1,025	255		1,280	1,500	
	2190	3.5 ton cooling, 29 MBH heat @ 75°F		1.30	12.310		1,100	275		1,375	1,625	

157 | Air Conditioning/Ventilating

157 100 | A.C. & Vent. Units

		CREW	DAILY OUTPUT	MAN-HOURS	UNIT	BARE COSTS MAT.	LABOR	EQUIP.	TOTAL	TOTAL INCL O&P	
160	2200	4 ton cooling, 31 MBH heat @ 75°F	Q-5	1.20	13.330	Ea.	1,345	295		1,640	1,925	160
	2220	5 ton cooling, 29 MBH heat @ 75°F	"	.90	17.780		1,630	395		2,025	2,375	
	3960	For supplementary heat coil, add				↓	10%					
170	0010	**PACKAGED TERMINAL AIR CONDITIONER** Cabinet, wall sleeve,										170
	0100	louver, electric heat, thermostat, manual changeover, 208 V										
	0200	6,000 BTUH cooling, 8800 BTU heat	Q-5	6	2.670	Ea.	670	59		729	825	
	0220	9,000 BTUH cooling, 13,900 BTU heat		5	3.200		685	71		756	860	
	0240	12,000 BTUH cooling, 13,900 BTU heat		4	4		700	89		789	900	
	0260	15,000 BTUH cooling, 13,900 BTU heat	↓	3	5.330	↓	750	120		870	1,000	
195	0010	**WINDOW UNIT AIR CONDITIONERS**										195
	4000	Portable, 15 amp 125V grounded receptacle required										
	4020	Standard models										
	4050	4000 BTUH, 1 speed fan	1 Carp	8	1	Ea.	208	22		230	260	
	4060	4000 BTUH, 2 speed fan		8	1		240	22		262	295	
	4080	5000 BTUH, 2 speed fan		8	1		270	22		292	330	
	4100	For high efficiency (EER rating), add				↓	48			48	53	
	4250	Semi-permanent installation, 3 speed fan										
	4260	15 amp 125V grounded receptacle required										
	4280	Standard models, 2 way air direction										
	4320	5000 BTUH	1 Carp	8	1	Ea.	291	22		313	355	
	4340	6000 BTUH	"	8	1	"	334	22		356	400	
	4400	High efficiency models										
	4450	5900 BTUH, 2 way air direction	1 Carp	8	1	Ea.	355	22		377	425	
	4480	8000 BTUH, 4 way high thrust air		6	1.330		416	29		445	500	
	4500	10,000 BTUH, 4 way high thrust air	↓	6	1.330		520	29		549	615	
	4520	12,000 BTUH, 4 way high thrust air	L-2	8	2		575	38		613	690	
	4540	14,000 BTUH, 4 way high thrust air	"	8	2	↓	640	38		678	765	
	4600	15 amp 250V grounded receptacle required										
	4700	High efficiency, 4 way high thrust air										
	4740	15,000 BTUH	L-2	6	2.670	Ea.	605	51		656	745	
	4780	18,000 BTUH	"	6	2.670	"	680	51		731	825	
	4820	20 amp 250V grounded receptacle required										
	4840	High efficiency, 4 way high thrust air										
	4860	21,000 BTUH	L-2	6	2.670	Ea.	775	51		826	930	
	4900	30 amp 250V grounded receptacle required										
	4910	High efficiency, 4 way high thrust air										
	4940	25,000 BTUH	L-2	4	4	Ea.	830	77		907	1,025	
	4960	29,000 BTUH	"	4	4	"	940	77		1,017	1,150	

157 200 | System Components

		CREW	DAILY OUTPUT	MAN-HOURS	UNIT	MAT.	LABOR	EQUIP.	TOTAL	TOTAL INCL O&P	
210	0010	**COMPRESSORS**									210
	5000	Air, diaphragm, w/skid, motor, drive, valves, & protective devices									
	5030	Single stage, 220 psig, 0.47 CFM	Q-5	3.30	4.850	Ea.	20,550	110		20,660	22,800	
	5040	1.7 CFM		2	8		23,800	180		23,980	26,400	
	5050	3.5 CFM		1.50	10.670		27,050	240		27,290	30,100	
	5060	8.5 CFM	↓	1	16		38,950	355		39,305	43,400	
	5100	14 CFM	Q-6	1	24		46,500	555		47,055	52,000	
	5120	28 CFM		.60	40		65,950	925		66,875	74,000	
	5130	56 CFM	↓	.30	80		113,500	1,850		115,350	127,500	
	5150	Two stage, 3600 psig, 0.47 CFM	Q-5	2.50	6.400		31,400	145		31,545	34,800	
	5160	1.7 CFM		1.50	10.670		37,900	240		38,140	42,000	
	5170	3.5 CFM	↓	1.10	14.550		44,300	325		44,625	49,200	
	5180	8.5 CFM	Q-6	1.10	21.820		62,700	505		63,205	69,500	
	5190	14 CFM		.60	40		74,650	925		75,575	83,500	
	5200	28 CFM	↓	.30	80	↓	110,350	1,850		112,200	124,000	
	5250	Reciprocating air cooled heavy duty tank mounted										

157 | Air Conditioning/Ventilating

157 200 | System Components

			DAILY	MAN-		\multicolumn{4}{c}{BARE COSTS}	TOTAL
		CREW	OUTPUT	HOURS	UNIT	MAT.	LABOR	EQUIP.	TOTAL	INCL O&P
5600	2 stage pkg. motor starter, duplex, control panel, drain									
5650	3.6 CFM at 90 psi 1 HP, 60 gal tank	Q-5	3	5.330	Ea.	2,210	120		2,330	2,600
5670	11.5 CFM at 90 psi, 3 HP, 80 gal tank		1.50	10.670		3,300	240		3,540	3,975
5680	43.2 CFM at 90 psi, 10 HP, 250 gal tank	↓	.60	26.670		7,650	595		8,245	9,300
5690	105 CFM at 90 psi, 25 HP, 250 gal tank	Q-6	.60	40	↓	10,550	925		11,475	13,000
5800	Simplex, motor & starter, tank, drain									
5850	8 CFM at 90 psi, 2 HP, 80 gal tank	Q-6	3.50	6.860	Ea.	1,330	160		1,490	1,700
5860	51.6 CFM at 90 psi, 10 HP, 250 gal tank	"	.90	26.670	"	3,950	615		4,565	5,250
6000	Reciprocating water cooled heavy duty slow speed 100 psi									
6050	Lubricated, 73 CFM by 20 HP motor	Q-5	.80	20	Ea.	10,700	445		11,145	12,400
6060	100 CFM by 25 HP motor		.60	26.670		8,750	595		9,345	10,500
6070	132 CFM by 30 HP motor		.50	32		9,060	715		9,775	11,000
6080	185 CFM by 40 HP motor	↓	.40	40		14,200	890		15,090	16,900
6090	210 CFM by 50 HP motor	Q-6	.60	40		15,950	925		16,875	18,900
6100	246 CFM by 50 HP motor		.50	48		19,400	1,100		20,500	23,000
6110	330 CFM by 75 HP motor	↓	.30	80		22,500	1,850		24,350	27,500
6120	428 CFM by 100 HP motor	Q-7	.40	80		27,150	1,900		29,050	32,700
6130	557 CFM by 125 HP motor	"	.30	107		31,450	2,525		33,975	38,300
6200	Nonlubricated, 73 CFM by 20 HP motor	Q-5	.80	20		8,560	445		9,005	10,100
6210	100 CFM by 25 HP motor		.60	26.670		9,290	595		9,885	11,100
6220	132 CFM by 30 HP motor		.50	32		9,620	715		10,335	11,600
6230	185 CFM by 40 HP motor	↓	.40	40		15,950	890		16,840	18,900
6250	210 CFM by 50 HP motor	Q-6	.60	40		20,400	925		21,325	23,800
6260	246 CFM by 50 HP motor		.50	48		21,600	1,100		22,700	25,400
6270	330 CFM by 75 HP motor	↓	.30	80		24,850	1,850		26,700	30,100
6280	428 CFM by 100 HP motor	Q-7	.40	80		30,450	1,900		32,350	36,300
6290	557 CFM by 125 HP motor	"	.30	107	↓	34,800	2,525		37,325	42,000
6500	Rotary screw motor & starter aftercooler heavy duty,									
6550	Air cooled single stage, 100 CFM at 115 psi 25 HP	Q-5	2.60	6.150	Ea.	5,660	135		5,795	6,425
6560	120 CFM at 115 psi 30 HP		2	8		6,870	180		7,050	7,825
6570	160 CFM at 115 psi 40 HP		1.40	11.430		7,760	255		8,015	8,925
6580	215 CFM at 115 psi 50 HP in enclosure		1	16		11,750	355		12,105	13,500
6590	260 CFM at 115 psi 60 HP in enclosure	↓	.80	20		14,200	445		14,645	16,300
6600	330 CFM at 115 psi 75 HP in enclosure	Q-6	1	24		15,750	555		16,305	18,100
6610	490 CFM at 115 psi 100 HP		.90	26.670		21,200	615		21,815	24,200
6620	600 CFM at 115 psi 125 HP		.80	30		25,200	695		25,895	28,700
6630	710 CFM at 115 psi 150 HP		.60	40		27,350	925		28,275	31,500
6640	950 CFM at 100 psi 200 HP	Q-7	.80	40		38,700	945		39,645	44,000
6650	1000 CFM at 115 psi 250 HP		.70	45.710		43,800	1,075		44,875	49,800
6660	1250 CFM at 115 psi 300 HP		.60	53.330		50,650	1,250		51,900	57,500
6670	1500 CFM at 115 psi 350 HP		.50	64		60,050	1,525		61,575	68,500
6680	2000 CFM at 100 psi 400 HP		.40	80		72,300	1,900		74,200	82,500
6690	2000 CFM at 115 psi 450 HP	↓	.30	107		77,700	2,525		80,225	89,000
6800	Water cooled single stage, 100 CFM at 115 psi 25 HP	Q-5	1.60	10		5,760	225		5,985	6,675
6810	120 CFM at 115 psi 30 HP		1.40	11.430		6,870	255		7,125	7,925
6820	180 CFM at 100 psi 40 HP in enclosure		1	16		10,900	355		11,255	12,500
6830	235 CFM at 100 psi 50 HP in enclosure		.80	20		11,750	445		12,195	13,600
6840	285 CFM at 100 psi 60 HP in enclosure		.60	26.670		14,200	595		14,795	16,500
6850	355 CFM at 100 psi 75 HP in enclosure	Q-6	1	24		15,750	555		16,305	18,100
6860	515 CFM at 100 psi 100 HP		.80	30		20,600	695		21,295	23,700
6870	640 CFM at 100 psi 125 HP		.70	34.290		23,900	790		24,690	27,500
6880	750 CFM at 100 psi 150 HP	↓	.60	40		26,000	925		26,925	30,000
6900	950 CFM at 100 psi 200 HP	Q-7	.60	53.330		35,350	1,250		36,600	40,800
6910	1000 CFM at 115 psi 250 HP		.50	64		39,100	1,525		40,625	45,300
6920	1250 CFM at 115 psi 300 HP		.50	64		45,200	1,525		46,725	52,000
6930	1500 CFM at 115 psi 350 HP		.40	80		54,100	1,900		56,000	62,500
6940	2000 CFM at 100 psi 400 HP		.40	80		67,600	1,900		69,500	77,000
6950	2000 CFM at 115 psi 450 HP	↓	.30	107		71,200	2,525		73,725	82,000

157 | Air Conditioning/Ventilating

157 200 | System Components

		CREW	DAILY OUTPUT	MAN-HOURS	UNIT	BARE COSTS MAT.	LABOR	EQUIP.	TOTAL	TOTAL INCL O&P	
210	Tanks with mounted compressor add				Ea.						210
7150											
7180	60 gallon					345			345	380	
7190	80 gallon					394			394	435	
7200	120 gallon					470			470	515	
7210	200 gallon					735			735	810	
7220	240 gallon					955			955	1,050	
220 0010	**COMPRESSOR ACCESSORIES**										220
0100	Aftercooler										
0130	Air cooled, based on 100 psig and 250°F										
0140	Tank mounted single stage, 20 SCFM	Q-5	7.50	2.130	Ea.	490	48		538	610	
0150	46 SCFM		7	2.290		570	51		621	705	
0160	77 SCFM		6.50	2.460		950	55		1,005	1,125	
0170	Floor mounted horizontal draft, 36 SCFM		6.50	2.460		505	55		560	635	
0180	78 SCFM		6	2.670		625	59		684	775	
0190	190 SCFM		5.70	2.810		965	63		1,028	1,150	
0200	260 SCFM		5.20	3.080		1,090	69		1,159	1,300	
0210	440 SCFM		4	4		1,440	89		1,529	1,725	
0220	650 SCFM		3.50	4.570		1,570	100		1,670	1,875	
0230	Floor mounted vertical draft, 850 SCFM		2.50	6.400		2,700	145		2,845	3,175	
0260	2060 SCFM		2	8		4,440	180		4,620	5,150	
0280	3640 SCFM		1.70	9.410		10,850	210		11,060	12,200	
0300	Separator with automatic float trap										
0330	600 lb/hr drain cap. 125 psi ¾" conn.	Q-5	7.50	2.130	Ea.	245	48		293	340	
0340	1200 lb/hr drain cap. 125 psi 1" conn.		7	2.290		260	51		311	360	
0350	1200 lb/hr drain cap. 125 psi 1-½" conn.		6	2.670		295	59		354	415	
0360	1200 lb/hr drain cap. 125 psi 2" conn.		5	3.200		316	71		387	455	
0370	1500 CFM at 200 psi 2-½" conn.		4	4		750	89		839	955	
0380	4000 CFM at 200 psi 4" conn.		3	5.330		810	120		930	1,075	
0400	Water cooled, fixed tube at 250°F										
0430	52 CFM	Q-5	5	3.200	Ea.	315	71		386	450	
0440	104 CFM		4	4		370	89		459	540	
0450	182 CFM		3.50	4.570		570	100		670	780	
0460	312 CFM		3	5.330		635	120		755	875	
0480	494 CFM		2.80	5.710		1,330	125		1,455	1,650	
0490	702 CFM		2.40	6.670		1,780	150		1,930	2,175	
0500	806 CFM		2.20	7.270		2,090	160		2,250	2,550	
0510	1092 CFM		2	8		2,600	180		2,780	3,125	
0520	1430 CFM		1.50	10.670		3,060	240		3,300	3,725	
0600	Separator, horizontal										
0610	100 CFM	Q-5	15	1.070	Ea.	173	24		197	225	
0620	350 CFM		10	1.600		250	36		286	330	
0630	900 CFM		7	2.290		605	51		656	740	
0640	1500 CFM		5	3.200		675	71		746	850	
0650	2800 CFM		3.50	4.570		990	100		1,090	1,250	
0700	Dryers, air, deliquescent at 90 psi										
0730	21 CFM	Q-5	14	1.140	Ea.	515	25		540	605	
0740	63 CFM		12	1.330		940	30		970	1,075	
0750	140 CFM		8	2		1,670	45		1,715	1,900	
0760	335 CFM		5.50	2.910		2,260	65		2,325	2,575	
0770	525 CFM		5	3.200		2,960	71		3,031	3,350	
0780	760 CFM		3	5.330		4,140	120		4,260	4,725	
0790	1050 CFM		2.50	6.400		5,150	145		5,295	5,875	
0800	1340 CFM		2	8		6,050	180		6,230	6,925	
0810	1700 CFM		1.50	10.670		7,700	240		7,940	8,825	
0820	2550 CFM	Q-6	2	12		9,990	275		10,265	11,400	
0830	3550 CFM		1.50	16		12,550	370		12,920	14,400	
0840	4700 CFM		1	24		15,600	555		16,155	18,000	
0850	6100 CFM	Q-7	1	32		18,250	755		19,005	21,200	

157 | Air Conditioning/Ventilating

157 200 | System Components

		CREW	DAILY OUTPUT	MAN-HOURS	UNIT	BARE COSTS MAT.	LABOR	EQUIP.	TOTAL	TOTAL INCL O&P	
0860	8400 CFM	Q-7	.80	40	Ea.	22,600	945		23,545	26,300	220
0870	10200 CFM		.60	53.330		24,650	1,250		25,900	29,000	
0880	12100 CFM		.50	64		26,350	1,525		27,875	31,200	
0890	14200 CFM		.40	80		27,820	1,900		29,720	33,400	
0950	Desiccant 33 lb. bag					23.90			23.90	26	
0960	55 lb. bag					39			39	43	
0980	2200 lb. bulk bag 1 or 2					1,570			1,570	1,725	
0990	2200 lb. bulk bag 3 or 4					1,520			1,520	1,675	
1250	Refrigeration, 50°F pressure dewpoint										
1280	20 CFM	Q-5	7	2.290	Ea.	995	51		1,046	1,175	
1290	60 CFM		6	2.670		1,420	59		1,479	1,650	
1300	130 CFM		5.50	2.910		1,830	65		1,895	2,100	
1310	150 CFM		5	3.200		3,840	71		3,911	4,325	
1320	200 CFM		4.50	3.560		3,950	79		4,029	4,475	
1330	280 CFM		4	4		4,310	89		4,399	4,875	
1340	350 CFM		3.50	4.570		4,700	100		4,800	5,325	
1350	450 CFM		3	5.330		5,410	120		5,530	6,125	
1360	520 CFM		2.80	5.710		5,950	125		6,075	6,725	
1370	650 CFM		2.40	6.670		6,550	150		6,700	7,425	
1380	800 CFM		2.20	7.270		6,990	160		7,150	7,925	
1390	1000 CFM		2	8		9,010	180		9,190	10,200	
1400	1400 CFM		1.50	10.670		10,600	240		10,840	12,000	
1410	2000 CFM		1.20	13.330		12,900	295		13,195	14,600	
1420	2400 CFM		1	16		18,650	355		19,005	21,000	
1430	3000 CFM	Q-6	1.30	18.460		25,300	425		25,725	28,500	
1440	3600 CFM		1.20	20		28,500	460		28,960	32,000	
1450	4800 CFM		1	24		33,300	555		33,855	37,500	
1460	6000 CFM		.80	30		40,900	695		41,595	46,000	
1470	7200 CFM		.50	48		47,800	1,100		48,900	54,000	
1500	Package includes dryer & filtration systems										
1530	150 CFM	Q-5	4.20	3.810	Ea.	5,620	85		5,705	6,300	
1540	200 CFM		3.90	4.100		5,730	91		5,821	6,450	
1550	280 CFM		3.50	4.570		6,580	100		6,680	7,400	
1560	350 CFM		3.20	5		7,390	110		7,500	8,300	
1570	450 CFM		3	5.330		8,190	120		8,310	9,175	
1580	520 CFM		2.50	6.400		8,700	145		8,845	9,775	
1590	650 CFM		2.20	7.270		9,030	160		9,190	10,200	
1600	800 CFM		2	8		9,550	180		9,730	10,800	
1610	1000 CFM		1.80	8.890		12,300	200		12,500	13,800	
1620	1200 CFM		1.40	11.430		13,800	255		14,055	15,600	
1630	1400 CFM		1.20	13.330		15,050	295		15,345	17,000	
1640	2000 CFM		1	16		17,350	355		17,705	19,600	
1650	2400 CFM		.70	22.860		22,350	510		22,860	25,300	
2000	Regenerative adsorption with desiccant										
2030	50 CFM	Q-5	5	3.200	Ea.	3,265	71		3,336	3,700	
2040	75 CFM		4.50	3.560		3,480	79		3,559	3,950	
2050	100 CFM		4.20	3.810		3,810	85		3,895	4,325	
2060	125 CFM		4	4		4,140	89		4,229	4,675	
2070	170 CFM		3.70	4.320		4,490	96		4,586	5,075	
2080	240 CFM		3.40	4.710		5,440	105		5,545	6,150	
2090	350 CFM		3	5.330		6,000	120		6,120	6,775	
2100	520 CFM		2.50	6.400		6,960	145		7,105	7,875	
2110	650 CFM		2	8		7,990	180		8,170	9,050	
2120	800 CFM		1.50	10.670		10,050	240		10,290	11,400	
2130	1000 CFM		1.20	13.330		11,650	295		11,945	13,300	
2140	1200 CFM		1	16		12,300	355		12,655	14,100	
2150	1600 CFM		.80	20		15,300	445		15,745	17,500	
2160	2000 CFM		.70	22.860		17,500	510		18,010	20,000	

157 | Air Conditioning/Ventilating

157 200 | System Components

			CREW	DAILY OUTPUT	MAN-HOURS	UNIT	BARE COSTS MAT.	BARE COSTS LABOR	BARE COSTS EQUIP.	BARE COSTS TOTAL	TOTAL INCL O&P	
220	2170	2500 CFM	Q-5	.60	26.670	Ea.	21,600	595		22,195	24,600	220
	2180	3000 CFM	Q-6	.90	26.670		22,550	615		23,165	25,700	
	2190	3500 CFM		.70	34.290		32,650	790		33,440	37,100	
	2200	4000 CFM	↓	.50	48	↓	33,650	1,100		34,750	38,700	
	2300	Desiccant, 50 lb. bag					93			93	100	
	2330	350 lb. drum					650			650	715	
	3000	Filters Air										
	3100	Adsorptive, odors by glass fiber & carbon, 90 psi										
	3140	110 CFM	Q-5	8	2	Ea.	640	45		685	770	
	3150	190 CFM		7.50	2.130		730	48		778	875	
	3160	290 CFM		7	2.290		905	51		956	1,075	
	3170	380 CFM		6	2.670		1,220	59		1,279	1,425	
	3180	570 CFM		5	3.200		1,730	71		1,801	2,000	
	3190	870 CFM		4.50	3.560		1,960	79		2,039	2,275	
	3200	1160 CFM		4	4		2,520	89		2,609	2,900	
	3210	1450 CFM		3.50	4.570		2,950	100		3,050	3,400	
	3220	1740 CFM	↓	3	5.330	↓	3,280	120		3,400	3,775	
	3260	Coalescent system, liquids & solids 90 psi high purity										
	3300	110 CFM	Q-5	7	2.290	Ea.	2,390	51		2,441	2,700	
	3310	190 CFM		6.70	2.390		2,590	53		2,643	2,925	
	3320	290 CFM		6.50	2.460		2,750	55		2,805	3,100	
	3330	380 CFM		6	2.670		3,220	59		3,279	3,625	
	3340	570 CFM		4.50	3.560		4,030	79		4,109	4,550	
	3350	870 CFM		4	4		4,260	89		4,349	4,825	
	3360	1160 CFM		3.50	4.570		4,860	100		4,960	5,500	
	3370	1450 CFM		3	5.330		5,470	120		5,590	6,200	
	3380	1740 CFM		2.50	6.400		5,790	145		5,935	6,575	
	3390	2030 CFM	↓	2	8	↓	5,990	180		6,170	6,850	
290	0010	**FANS**										290
	2500	Ceiling fan, right angle, extra quiet, 0.10" S.P.										
	2520	95 CFM	Q-20	20	1	Ea.	140	22		162	190	
	2540	210 CFM		19	1.050		150	24		174	200	
	2560	385 CFM	↓	18	1.110		191	25		216	250	
	2640	For wall or roof cap, add	1 Shee	16	.500		85	12.20		97.20	110	
	2660	For straight thru fan, add					10%					
	2680	For speed control switch, add	1 Elec	16	.500	↓	46	12.20		58.20	69	
	6650	Residential, bath exhaust, grille, back draft damper										
	6660	50 CFM	Q-20	24	.833	Ea.	28	18.65		46.65	59	
	6670	110 CFM		22	.909		55	20		75	91	
	6680	Light combination, squirrel cage, 100 watt, 70 CFM	↓	24	.833	↓	61	18.65		79.65	95	
	6700	Light/heater combination, ceiling mounted										
	6710	70 CFM, 1450 watt	Q-20	24	.833	Ea.	96	18.65		114.65	135	
	6800	Heater combination, recessed, 70 CFM		24	.833		56	18.65		74.65	90	
	6820	With 2 infrared bulbs	↓	23	.870	↓	71	19.50		90.50	105	

157 400 | Accessories

			CREW	DAILY OUTPUT	MAN-HOURS	UNIT	MAT.	LABOR	EQUIP.	TOTAL	INCL O&P	
410	0010	**ANTI-FREEZE** Inhibited										410
	0900	Ethylene glycol concentrated										
	1000	55 gallon drums, small quantities				Gal.	7.61			7.61	8.35	
	1200	Large quantities					7.05			7.05	7.75	
	2000	Propylene glycol, for solar heat, small quantities					7.39			7.39	8.15	
	2100	Large quantities				↓	6.74			6.74	7.40	
420	0010	**CONTROL COMPONENTS**										420
	2000	Gauges, pressure or vacuum										
	2100	2" diameter dial	1 Stpi	32	.250	Ea.	8	6.20		14.20	18	
	2200	2-½" diameter dial		32	.250		9.40	6.20		15.60	19.50	
	2300	3-½" diameter dial		32	.250		12	6.20		18.20	22	
	2400	4-½" diameter dial	↓	32	.250	↓	16.50	6.20		22.70	27	

157 | Air Conditioning/Ventilating

157 400 | Accessories

			CREW	DAILY OUTPUT	MAN-HOURS	UNIT	BARE COSTS MAT.	LABOR	EQUIP.	TOTAL	TOTAL INCL O&P	
420	2700	Flanged iron case, black ring										420
	2800	3-½" diameter dial	1 Stpi	32	.250	Ea.	42.75	6.20		48.95	56	
	2900	4-½" diameter dial		32	.250		51.75	6.20		57.95	66	
	3000	6" diameter dial		32	.250		70.50	6.20		76.70	87	
	3300	For compound pressure-vacuum, add					18%					
	4000	Thermometers										
	4100	Dial type, 3-½" diameter, vapor type, union connection	1 Stpi	32	.250	Ea.	95	6.20		101.20	115	
	4120	Liquid type, union connection		32	.250		133	6.20		139.20	155	
	4500	Stem type, 6-½" case, 2" stem, ½" NPT		32	.250		24	6.20		30.20	36	
	4520	4" stem, ½" NPT		32	.250		33	6.20		39.20	45	
	4600	9" case, 3-½" stem, ¾" NPT		28	.286		40	7.05		47.05	54	
	4620	6" stem, ¾" NPT		28	.286		43	7.05		50.05	58	
	4640	8" stem, ¾" NPT		28	.286		49	7.05		56.05	64	
	4660	12" stem, 1" NPT		26	.308		55	7.60		62.60	72	
	6000	Valves, motorized zone										
	6100	Sweat connections, ½" C x C	1 Stpi	20	.400	Ea.	37.50	9.90		47.40	56	
	6110	¾" C x C		20	.400		37.50	9.90		47.40	56	
	6120	1" C x C		19	.421		41.90	10.40		52.30	62	
	6140	½" C x C, with end switch, 2 wire		20	.400		45.30	9.90		55.20	65	
	6150	¾" C x C, with end switch, 2 wire		20	.400		47.40	9.90		57.30	67	
	6160	1" C x C, with end switch, 2 wire		19	.421		52.60	10.40		63	73	
	6180	1-¼" C x C, w/end switch, 2 wire		15	.533		58.10	13.20		71.30	83	
440	0010	**CURBS/PADS PREFABRICATED**										440
	6000	Pad, fiberglass reinforced concrete with polystyrene foam core										
485	0010	**VIBRATION ABSORBERS**										485
	0100	Hangers, neoprene flex										
	0200	10-120 lb. capacity				Ea.	6.75			6.75	7.45	
	0220	75-550 lb. capacity					9.05			9.05	9.95	
	0240	250-1100 lb. capacity					17.40			17.40	19.15	
	0260	1000-4000 lb. capacity					48.30			48.30	53	
	0500	Spring flex, 60-450 lb. capacity					18.70			18.70	21	
	0520	85-450 lb. capacity					29.10			29.10	32	
	0540	600-900 lb. capacity					38.50			38.50	42	
	0560	1100-1300 lb. capacity					41.60			41.60	46	
	1000	Mounts, neoprene, 135-380 lb. capacity					6.75			6.75	7.45	
	1020	250-1100 lb. capacity					16.55			16.55	18.20	
	1040	1000-4000 lb. capacity					39.80			39.80	44	
	1100	Spring flex, 60-450 lb. capacity					22.60			22.60	25	
	1120	85-900 lb. capacity					34.30			34.30	38	
	1140	1100-1300 lb. capacity					37.20			37.20	41	
	1160	900-1800 lb. capacity					55.10			55.10	61	
	1180	2200-2600 lb. capacity					61.10			61.10	67	
	1200	1800-3600 lb. capacity					91			91	100	
	1220	4400-5200 lb. capacity					103			103	115	
	1240	3150-6300 lb. capacity					131			131	145	
	1260	5400-10,800 lb. capacity					228			228	250	
	1280	9600-14,400 lb. capacity					430			430	475	
	1300	12,000-18,000 lb. capacity					595			595	655	
	1320	17,600-20,800 lb. capacity					480			480	530	
	1340	22,000-26,000 lb. capacity					665			665	730	
	2000	Pads, cork rib, 18" x 18" x 1", 10-50 psi					65.50			65.50	72	
	2020	18" x 36" x 1", 10-50 psi					131			131	145	
	2100	Shear flexible pads, 18" x 18" x ⅜", 20-70 psi					27			27	30	
	2120	18" x 36" x ⅜", 20-70 psi					54			54	59	
	3000	Note overlap in capacities due to deflections										

157 | Air Conditioning/Ventilating

157 600 | Miscellaneous

		CREW	DAILY OUTPUT	MAN-HOURS	UNIT	BARE COSTS MAT.	LABOR	EQUIP.	TOTAL	TOTAL INCL O&P
0010	**EXHAUST SYSTEMS**									
0500	Engine exhaust, garage, in-floor system									
0510	Single tube outlet assemblies									
0520	For transite pipe ducting, self-storing tube									
0530	3" tubing adapter plate	1 Shee	16	.500	Ea.	186	12.20		198.20	225
0540	4" tubing adapter plate		16	.500		186	12.20		198.20	225
0550	5" tubing adapter plate		16	.500		188	12.20		200.20	225
0600	For vitrified tile ducting									
0610	3" tubing adapter plate, self-storing tube	1 Shee	16	.500	Ea.	172	12.20		184.20	210
0620	4" tubing adapter plate, self-storing tube		16	.500		172	12.20		184.20	210
0650	4" tube size opening, non-storing tube		16	.500		110	12.20		122.20	140
0660	5" tubing adapter plate, self-storing tube		16	.500		174	12.20		186.20	210
0700	For vitrified tile & transite pipe ducting									
0710	3" tube size opening, self-storing tube	1 Shee	16	.500	Ea.	150	12.20		162.20	185
0720	4" tube size opening, self-storing tube	"	16	.500	"	150	12.20		162.20	185
0800	Two tube outlet assemblies									
0810	For transite pipe ducting, self-storing tube									
0820	3" tubing, dual exhaust adapter plate	1 Shee	16	.500	Ea.	201	12.20		213.20	240
0850	For vitrified tile ducting									
0860	3" tubing, dual exhaust, self-storing tube	1 Shee	16	.500	Ea.	186	12.20		198.20	225
0870	3" tubing, double outlet, non-storing tubes	"	16	.500	"	165	12.20		177.20	200
0900	Accessories for metal tubing, (overhead systems also)									
0910	Adapters, for metal tubing end									
0920	3" tail pipe type				Ea.	38			38	42
0930	4" tail pipe type					40			40	44
0940	5" tail pipe type					41			41	45
0960	4" bail type					16.50			16.50	18.15
0970	5" bail type					17.50			17.50	19.25
0990	5" diesel stack type					47			47	52
1000	6" diesel stack type					66			66	73
1100	Bullnose (guide) required for in-floor assemblies									
1110	3" tubing size				Ea.	14			14	15.40
1120	4" tubing size					17			17	18.70
1130	5" tubing size					18			18	19.80
1150	Plain rings, for tubing end									
1160	3" tubing size				Ea.	8			8	8.80
1170	4" tubing size				"	13			13	14.30
1200	Tubing, galvanized, flexible, (for overhead sys. also)									
1210	3" ID				L.F.	4			4	4.40
1220	4" ID					5			5	5.50
1230	5" ID					7			7	7.70
1240	6" ID					10			10	11
1250	Stainless steel, flexible, (for overhead sys, also)									
1260	3" ID				L.F.	12			12	13.20
1270	4" ID					16			16	17.60
1280	5" ID					23			23	25
1290	6" ID					29			29	32
1500	Engine exhaust, garage, ovrhd. compon., for neoprene tubing									
1510	Alternate metal tubing & accessories see above									
1550	Adapters, for neoprene tubing end									
1560	3" tail pipe, adjustable, neoprene				Ea.	18			18	19.80
1570	3" tail pipe, heavy wall neoprene					14			14	15.40
1580	4" tail pipe, heavy wall neoprene					30			30	33
1590	5" tail pipe, heavy wall neoprene					35			35	39
1650	Connectors, tubing									
1660	3" interior, aluminum				Ea.	9.50			9.50	10.45
1670	4" interior, aluminum					11			11	12.10
1710	5" interior, neoprene					21			21	23

157 | Air Conditioning/Ventilating

157 600 | Miscellaneous

		CREW	DAILY OUTPUT	MAN-HOURS	UNIT	BARE COSTS MAT.	LABOR	EQUIP.	TOTAL	TOTAL INCL O&P
1750	3" spiralock, neoprene				Ea.	4.50			4.50	4.95
1760	4" spiralock, neoprene					7.50			7.50	8.25
1780	Y for 3" ID tubing, neoprene, dual exhaust					20			20	22
1790	Y for 4" ID tubing, aluminum, dual exhaust					29			29	32
1850	Elbows, aluminum, splice into tubing for strap									
1860	3" neoprene tubing size				Ea.	15			15	16.50
1870	4" neoprene tubing size				"	22			22	24
1900	Flange assemblies, connect tubing to overhead duct									
1910	For galvanized & stainless tubing									
1920	3" cast aluminum				Ea.	14			14	15.40
1930	4" cast aluminum					16.50			16.50	18.15
1940	5" cast aluminum					18			18	19.80
1950	6" cast aluminum					20			20	22
1960	For neoprene tubing									
1970	3" neoprene				Ea.	13			13	14.30
1980	4" cast aluminum				"	15			15	16.50
2000	Hardware and accessories									
2020	Cable, vinyl coated, 5/32" diameter				L.F.	.35			.35	.39
2040	Cleat, tie down cable or rope				Ea.	1			1	1.10
2060	Pulley					2.50			2.50	2.75
2080	Pulley hook, universal					2			2	2.20
2100	Rope, manila, 5/16" diameter				L.F.	.25			.25	.28
2120	Winch, 1" diameter				Ea.	45			45	50
2150	Lifting strap, mounts on neoprene									
2160	3" tubing size				Ea.	8			8	8.80
2170	4" tubing size					8			8	8.80
2180	5" tubing size					9			9	9.90
2190	6" tubing size					15			15	16.50
2200	Tubing, neoprene, 11' lengths									
2210	3" ID				L.F.	5.45			5.45	6
2220	4" ID					10.10			10.10	11.10
2230	5" ID					13.15			13.15	14.45
2500	Engine exhaust, thru-door outlet									
2510	3" for up to 1/4" thick door	1 Carp	16	.500	Ea.	41	10.80		51.80	61
2520	3" for over 1/4" thick door		16	.500		44	10.80		54.80	65
2530	4" for up to 1/4" thick door		16	.500		46	10.80		56.80	67
7500	Welding fume elimination accessories for garage exhaust systems									
7600	Cut off (blast gate)									
7610	3" tubing size, 3" x 6" opening	1 Shee	24	.333	Ea.	22	8.10		30.10	36
7620	4" tubing size, 4" x 8" opening		24	.333		24	8.10		32.10	39
7630	5" tubing size, 5" x 10" opening		24	.333		29	8.10		37.10	44
7700	Hoods, magnetic, with handle & screen									
7710	3" tubing size, 3" x 6" opening	1 Shee	24	.333	Ea.	113	8.10		121.10	135
7720	4" tubing size, 4" x 8" opening		24	.333		113	8.10		121.10	135
7730	5" tubing size, 5" x 10" opening		24	.333		126	8.10		134.10	150

160 | Raceways

160 200 | Conduits

		CREW	DAILY OUTPUT	MAN-HOURS	UNIT	BARE COSTS MAT.	LABOR	EQUIP.	TOTAL	TOTAL INCL O&P
0010	CUTTING AND DRILLING									
0100	Hole drilling to 10' high, concrete wall									

160 | Raceways

160 200 | Conduits

		CREW	DAILY OUTPUT	MAN-HOURS	UNIT	MAT.	LABOR	EQUIP.	TOTAL	TOTAL INCL O&P	
260	0110	8" thick, ½" pipe size	1 Elec	12	.667	Ea.		16.25		16.25	24	260
	0120	¾" pipe size		12	.667			16.25		16.25	24	
	0130	1" pipe size		9.50	.842			21		21	30	
	0140	1-¼" pipe size		9.50	.842			21		21	30	
	0150	1-½" pipe size		9.50	.842			21		21	30	
	0160	2" pipe size		4.40	1.820			44		44	65	
	0170	2-½" pipe size		4.40	1.820			44		44	65	
	0180	3" pipe size		4.40	1.820			44		44	65	
	0190	3-½" pipe size		3.30	2.420			59		59	87	
	0200	4" pipe size		3.30	2.420			59		59	87	
	0500	12" thick, ½" pipe size		9.40	.851			21		21	31	
	0520	¾" pipe size		9.40	.851			21		21	31	
	0540	1" pipe size		7.30	1.100			27		27	39	
	0560	1-¼" pipe size		7.30	1.100			27		27	39	
	0570	1-½" pipe size		7.30	1.100			27		27	39	
	0580	2" pipe size		3.60	2.220			54		54	80	
	0590	2-½" pipe size		3.60	2.220			54		54	80	
	0600	3" pipe size		3.60	2.220			54		54	80	
	0610	3-½" pipe size		2.80	2.860			70		70	100	
	0630	4" pipe size		2.50	3.200			78		78	115	
	0650	16" thick ½" pipe size		7.60	1.050			26		26	38	
	0670	¾" pipe size		7	1.140			28		28	41	
	0690	1" pipe size		6	1.330			32		32	48	
	0710	1-¼" pipe size		5.50	1.450			35		35	52	
	0730	1-½" pipe size		5.50	1.450			35		35	52	
	0750	2" pipe size		3	2.670			65		65	96	
	0770	2-½" pipe size		2.70	2.960			72		72	105	
	0790	3" pipe size		2.50	3.200			78		78	115	
	0810	3-½" pipe size		2.30	3.480			85		85	125	
	0830	4" pipe size		2	4			97		97	145	
	0850	20" thick ½" pipe size		6.40	1.250			30		30	45	
	0870	¾" pipe size		6	1.330			32		32	48	
	0890	1" pipe size		5	1.600			39		39	57	
	0910	1-¼" pipe size		4.80	1.670			41		41	60	
	0930	1-½" pipe size		4.60	1.740			42		42	62	
	0950	2" pipe size		2.70	2.960			72		72	105	
	0970	2-½" pipe size		2.40	3.330			81		81	120	
	0990	3" pipe size		2.20	3.640			89		89	130	
	1010	3-½" pipe size		2	4			97		97	145	
	1030	4" pipe size		1.70	4.710			115		115	170	
	1050	24" thick ½" pipe size		5.50	1.450			35		35	52	
	1070	¾" pipe size		5.10	1.570			38		38	56	
	1090	1" pipe size		4.30	1.860			45		45	67	
	1110	1-¼" pipe size		4	2			49		49	72	
	1130	1-½" pipe size		4	2			49		49	72	
	1150	2" pipe size		2.40	3.330			81		81	120	
	1170	2-½" pipe size		2.20	3.640			89		89	130	
	1190	3" pipe size		2	4			97		97	145	
	1210	3-½" pipe size		1.80	4.440			110		110	160	
	1230	4" pipe size		1.50	5.330			130		130	190	
	1500	Brick wall, 8" thick, ½" pipe size		18	.444			10.80		10.80	15.95	
	1520	¾" pipe size		18	.444			10.80		10.80	15.95	
	1540	1" pipe size		13.30	.602			14.65		14.65	22	
	1560	1-¼" pipe size		13.30	.602			14.65		14.65	22	
	1580	1-½" pipe size		13.30	.602			14.65		14.65	22	
	1600	2" pipe size		5.70	1.400			34		34	50	
	1620	2-½" pipe size		5.70	1.400			34		34	50	
	1640	3" pipe size		5.70	1.400			34		34	50	

160 | Raceways

160 200 | Conduits

		Crew	Daily Output	Man-Hours	Unit	Bare Costs Mat.	Bare Costs Labor	Bare Costs Equip.	Bare Costs Total	Total Incl O&P
1660	3-½" pipe size	1 Elec	4.40	1.820	Ea.		44		44	65
1680	4" pipe size		4	2			49		49	72
1700	12" thick, ½" pipe size		14.50	.552			13.45		13.45	19.75
1720	¾" pipe size		14.50	.552			13.45		13.45	19.75
1740	1" pipe size		11	.727			17.70		17.70	26
1760	1-¼" pipe size		11	.727			17.70		17.70	26
1780	1-½" pipe size		11	.727			17.70		17.70	26
1800	2" pipe size		5	1.600			39		39	57
1820	2-½" pipe size		5	1.600			39		39	57
1840	3" pipe size		5	1.600			39		39	57
1860	3-½" pipe size		3.80	2.110			51		51	75
1880	4" pipe size		3.30	2.420			59		59	87
1900	16" thick, ½" pipe size		12.30	.650			15.85		15.85	23
1920	¾" pipe size		12.30	.650			15.85		15.85	23
1940	1" pipe size		9.30	.860			21		21	31
1960	1-¼" pipe size		9.30	.860			21		21	31
1980	1-½" pipe size		9.30	.860			21		21	31
2000	2" pipe size		4.40	1.820			44		44	65
2010	2-½" pipe size		4.40	1.820			44		44	65
2030	3" pipe size		4.40	1.820			44		44	65
2050	3-½" pipe size		3.30	2.420			59		59	87
2070	4" pipe size		3	2.670			65		65	96
2090	20" thick, ½" pipe size		10.70	.748			18.20		18.20	27
2110	¾" pipe size		10.70	.748			18.20		18.20	27
2130	1" pipe size		8	1			24		24	36
2150	1-¼" pipe size		8	1			24		24	36
2170	1-½" pipe size		8	1			24		24	36
2190	2" pipe size		4	2			49		49	72
2210	2-½" pipe size		4	2			49		49	72
2230	3" pipe size		4	2			49		49	72
2250	3-½" pipe size		3	2.670			65		65	96
2270	4" pipe size		2.70	2.960			72		72	105
2290	24" thick, ½" pipe size		9.40	.851			21		21	31
2310	¾" pipe size		9.40	.851			21		21	31
2330	1" pipe size		7.10	1.130			27		27	40
2350	1-¼" pipe size		7.10	1.130			27		27	40
2370	1-½" pipe size		7.10	1.130			27		27	40
2390	2" pipe size		3.60	2.220			54		54	80
2410	2-½" pipe size		3.60	2.220			54		54	80
2430	3" pipe size		3.60	2.220			54		54	80
2450	3-½" pipe size		2.80	2.860			70		70	100
2470	4" pipe size		2.50	3.200			78		78	115
3000	Knockouts to 8' high, metal boxes & enclosures									
3020	With hole saw, ½" pipe size	1 Elec	53	.151	Ea.		3.68		3.68	5.40
3040	¾" pipe size		47	.170			4.14		4.14	6.10
3050	1" pipe size		40	.200			4.87		4.87	7.15
3060	1-¼" pipe size		36	.222			5.40		5.40	7.95
3070	1-½" pipe size		32	.250			6.10		6.10	8.95
3080	2" pipe size		27	.296			7.20		7.20	10.60
3090	2-½" pipe size		20	.400			9.75		9.75	14.35
4010	3" pipe size		16	.500			12.20		12.20	17.90
4030	3-½" pipe size		13	.615			15		15	22
4050	4" pipe size		11	.727			17.70		17.70	26
4070	With hand punch set, ½" pipe size		40	.200			4.87		4.87	7.15
4090	¾" pipe size		32	.250			6.10		6.10	8.95
4110	1" pipe size		30	.267			6.50		6.50	9.55
4130	1-¼" pipe size		28	.286			6.95		6.95	10.25
4150	1-½" pipe size		26	.308			7.50		7.50	11.05

160 | Raceways

160 200 | Conduits

		CREW	DAILY OUTPUT	MAN-HOURS	UNIT	BARE COSTS MAT.	LABOR	EQUIP.	TOTAL	TOTAL INCL O&P	
260	4170	2" pipe size	1 Elec	20	.400	Ea.		9.75		9.75	14.35	260
	4190	2-½" pipe size		17	.471			11.45		11.45	16.85	
	4200	3" pipe size		15	.533			13		13	19.10	
	4220	3-½" pipe size		12	.667			16.25		16.25	24	
	4240	4" pipe size		10	.800			19.50		19.50	29	
	4260	With hydraulic punch, ½" pipe size		44	.182			4.43		4.43	6.50	
	4280	¾" pipe size		38	.211			5.15		5.15	7.55	
	4300	1" pipe size		38	.211			5.15		5.15	7.55	
	4320	1-¼" pipe size		38	.211			5.15		5.15	7.55	
	4340	1-½" pipe size		38	.211			5.15		5.15	7.55	
	4360	2" pipe size		32	.250			6.10		6.10	8.95	
	4380	2-½" pipe size		27	.296			7.20		7.20	10.60	
	4400	3" pipe size		23	.348			8.45		8.45	12.45	
	4420	3-½" pipe size		20	.400			9.75		9.75	14.35	
	4440	4" pipe size		18	.444			10.80		10.80	15.95	
275	0010	**MOTOR CONNECTIONS**										275
	0020	Flexible conduit and fittings, up to 1 HP motor, 115 volt, 1 phase	1 Elec	8	1	Ea.	2.75	24		26.75	39	
	0050	2 HP motor		6.50	1.230		2.75	30		32.75	47	
	0100	3 HP motor		5.50	1.450		4.05	35		39.05	57	
	0120	230 volt, 10 HP motor, 3 phase		4.20	1.900		4.83	46		50.83	74	
	0150	15 HP motor		3.30	2.420		8.72	59		67.72	96	
	0200	25 HP motor		2.70	2.960		9.45	72		81.45	115	
	0400	50 HP motor		2.20	3.640		25.20	89		114.20	160	
	0600	100 HP motor		1.50	5.330		65	130		195	265	

163 | Starters, Boards and Switches

163 100 | Starters & Controls

		CREW	DAILY OUTPUT	MAN-HOURS	UNIT	BARE COSTS MAT.	LABOR	EQUIP.	TOTAL	TOTAL INCL O&P	
130	0010	**MOTOR STARTERS & CONTROLS**										130
	0050	Magnetic, FVNR, with enclosure and heaters, 480 volt										
	0080	2 HP, size 00	1 Elec	3.50	2.290	Ea.	115	56		171	210	
	0100	5 HP, size 0		2.30	3.480		135	85		220	275	
	0200	10 HP, size 1		1.60	5		147	120		267	340	
	0300	25 HP, size 2		1.10	7.270		278	175		453	565	
	0400	50 HP, size 3		.90	8.890		454	215		669	820	
	0500	100 HP, size 4		.60	13.330		1,026	325		1,351	1,600	
	0600	200 HP, size 5		.45	17.780		2,360	435		2,795	3,225	
	0610	400 HP, size 6		.40	20		6,640	485		7,125	8,025	
	0620	NEMA 7, 5 HP, size 0		1.60	5		515	120		635	745	
	0630	10 HP, size 1		1.10	7.270		535	175		710	850	
	0640	25 HP, size 2		.90	8.890		845	215		1,060	1,250	
	0650	50 HP, size 3		.60	13.330		1,256	325		1,581	1,850	
	0660	100 HP, size 4		.45	17.780		2,000	435		2,435	2,825	
	0670	200 HP, size 5		.25	32		4,770	780		5,550	6,400	
	0700	Combination, with motor circuit protectors, 5 HP, size 0		1.80	4.440		427	110		537	630	
	0800	10 HP, size 1		1.30	6.150		444	150		594	710	
	0900	25 HP, size 2		1	8		629	195		824	980	
	1000	50 HP, size 3		.66	12.120		895	295		1,190	1,425	
	1200	100 HP, size 4		.40	20		1,940	485		2,425	2,850	
	1220	NEMA 7, 5 HP, size 0		1.30	6.150		880	150		1,030	1,200	

163 | Starters, Boards and Switches

163 100 | Starters & Controls

			CREW	DAILY OUTPUT	MAN-HOURS	UNIT	BARE COSTS MAT.	LABOR	EQUIP.	TOTAL	TOTAL INCL O&P	
130	1230	10 HP, size 1	1 Elec	1	8	Ea.	900	195		1,095	1,275	130
	1240	25 HP, size 2		.66	12.120		1,220	295		1,515	1,775	
	1250	50 HP, size 3		.40	20		1,990	485		2,475	2,900	
	1260	100 HP, size 4		.30	26.670		3,100	650		3,750	4,375	
	1270	200 HP, size 5		.20	40		6,680	975		7,655	8,775	
	1400	Combination, with fused switch, 5 HP, size 0		1.80	4.440		352	110		462	545	
	1600	10 HP, size 1		1.30	6.150		367	150		517	625	
	1800	25 HP, size 2		1	8		562	195		757	905	
	2000	50 HP, size 3		.66	12.120		928	295		1,223	1,450	
	2200	100 HP, size 4		.40	20		1,725	485		2,210	2,625	
	3500	Magnetic FVNR with NEMA 12, enclosure & heaters, 480 volt										
	3600	5 HP, size 0	1 Elec	2.20	3.640	Ea.	173	89		262	320	
	3700	10 HP, size 1		1.50	5.330		189	130		319	400	
	3800	25 HP, size 2		1	8		350	195		545	670	
	3900	50 HP, size 3		.80	10		530	245		775	940	
	4000	100 HP, size 4		.50	16		1,250	390		1,640	1,950	
	4100	200 HP, size 5		.40	20		2,990	485		3,475	4,000	
	4200	Combination with motor circuit protectors, 5 HP, size 0		1.70	4.710		505	115		620	725	
	4300	10 HP, size 1		1.20	6.670		520	160		680	810	
	4400	25 HP, size 2		.90	8.890		715	215		930	1,100	
	4500	50 HP, size 3		.60	13.330		1,020	325		1,345	1,600	
	4600	100 HP, size 4		.37	21.620		2,290	525		2,815	3,300	
	4700	Combination with fused switch, 5 HP, size 0		1.70	4.710		422	115		537	635	
	4800	10 HP, size 1		1.20	6.670		440	160		600	725	
	4900	25 HP, size 2		.90	8.890		658	215		873	1,050	
	5000	50 HP, size 3		.60	13.330		1,040	325		1,365	1,625	
	5100	100 HP, size 4		.37	21.620		2,110	525		2,635	3,100	
	5200	Factory installed controls, adders to size 0 thru 5										
	5300	Start-stop push button	1 Elec	32	.250	Ea.	29	6.10		35.10	41	
	5400	Hand-off-auto-selector switch		32	.250		29	6.10		35.10	41	
	5500	Pilot light		32	.250		53	6.10		59.10	67	
	5600	Start-stop-pilot		32	.250		79	6.10		85.10	96	
	5700	Auxiliary contact, NO or NC		32	.250		39	6.10		45.10	52	
	5800	NO-NC		32	.250		74	6.10		80.10	90	

163 300 | Switches

			CREW	DAILY OUTPUT	MAN-HOURS	UNIT	MAT.	LABOR	EQUIP.	TOTAL	INCL O&P	
320	0010	CONTROL STATIONS										320
	0050	NEMA 1, heavy duty, stop/start	1 Elec	8	1	Ea.	41	24		65	81	
	0100	Stop/start, pilot light		6.20	1.290		98	31		129	155	
	0200	Hand/off/automatic		6.20	1.290		48	31		79	99	
	0400	Stop/start/reverse		5.30	1.510		86	37		123	150	
	0500	NEMA 7, heavy duty, stop/start		6	1.330		119	32		151	180	
	0600	Stop/start, pilot light		4	2		254	49		303	350	

168 | Special Systems

168 100 | Special Systems

			CREW	DAILY OUTPUT	MAN-HOURS	UNIT	MAT.	LABOR	EQUIP.	TOTAL	INCL O&P	
120	0010	DETECTION SYSTEMS										120
	0100	Burglar alarm, battery operated, mechanical trigger	1 Elec	4	2	Ea.	185	49		234	275	
	0200	Electrical trigger		4	2		222	49		271	315	
	0400	For outside key control, add		8	1		52	24		76	93	

168 | Special Systems

168 100 | Special Systems

		CREW	DAILY OUTPUT	MAN-HOURS	UNIT	MAT.	LABOR	EQUIP.	TOTAL	TOTAL INCL O&P	
120	0600	For remote signaling circuitry, add	1 Elec	8	1	Ea.	83	24		107	125	120
	0800	Card reader, flush type, standard		2.70	2.960		625	72		697	795	
	1000	Multi-code		2.70	2.960		800	72		872	985	
	3600	Fire, sprinkler & standpipe alarm, control panel, 4 zone		2	4		700	97		797	915	
	3800	8 zone		1	8		975	195		1,170	1,350	
	4000	12 zone		.66	12.120		1,400	295		1,695	1,975	
	4020	Alarm device		8	1		93	24		117	140	
	4050	Actuating device		8	1		225	24		249	285	
	4200	Battery and rack		4	2		530	49		579	655	
	4400	Automatic charger		8	1		340	24		364	410	
	4600	Signal bell		8	1		37	24		61	77	
	4800	Trouble buzzer or manual station		8	1		27	24		51	66	
	5000	Detector, rate of rise		8	1		26	24		50	64	
	5100	Fixed temperature		8	1		21	24		45	59	
	5200	Smoke detector, ceiling type		6.20	1.290		47	31		78	98	
	5400	Duct type		3.20	2.500		191	61		252	300	
	5600	Light and horn		5.30	1.510		81	37		118	145	
	5800	Fire alarm horn		6.70	1.190		27	29		56	72	
	6000	Door holder, electro-magnetic		4	2		57	49		106	135	
	6200	Combination holder and closer		3.20	2.500		330	61		391	455	
	6400	Code transmitter		4	2		530	49		579	655	
	6600	Drill switch		8	1		66	24		90	110	
	6800	Master box		2.70	2.960		1,500	72		1,572	1,750	
	7000	Break glass station		8	1		37	24		61	77	
	7800	Remote annunciator, 8 zone lamp		1.80	4.440		183	110		293	360	
	8000	12 zone lamp		1.30	6.150		227	150		377	470	
	8200	16 zone lamp		1.10	7.270		278	175		453	565	
130	0010	**ELECTRIC HEATING**										130
	0200	Snow melting for paved surface embedded mat heaters & controls	1 Elec	130	.062	S.F.	4.55	1.50		6.05	7.20	
	0400	Cable heating, radiant heat plaster, no controls, in South		130	.062		5.50	1.50		7	8.25	
	0600	In North		90	.089		5.50	2.16		7.66	9.25	
	0800	Cable on ½" board, not incl. controls, tract housing		90	.089		4.55	2.16		6.71	8.20	
	1000	Custom housing		80	.100		5.20	2.44		7.64	9.30	
	1100	Rule of thumb: Baseboard units, including control		4.40	1.820	KW	56.80	44		100.80	130	
	1200	Duct heaters, including controls		5.30	1.510	"	46.50	37		83.50	105	
	1300	Baseboard heaters, 2' long, 375 watt		8	1	Ea.	29.70	24		53.70	69	
	1400	3' long, 500 watt		8	1		37	24		61	77	
	1600	4' long, 750 watt		6.70	1.190		45.63	29		74.63	93	
	1800	5' long, 935 watt		5.70	1.400		60.77	34		94.77	115	
	2000	6' long, 1125 watt		5	1.600		67.98	39		106.98	130	
	2200	7' long, 1310 watt		4.40	1.820		83.40	44		127.40	155	
	2400	8' long, 1500 watt		4	2		90.64	49		139.64	170	
	2600	9' long, 1680 watt		3.60	2.220		103	54		157	195	
	2800	10' long, 1875 watt		3.30	2.420		103	59		162	200	
	2950	Wall heaters with fan, 120 to 277 volt										
	2970	surface mounted, residential, 750 watt	1 Elec	7	1.140	Ea.	48.15	28		76.15	94	
	2980	1000 watt		7	1.140		62	28		90	110	
	2990	1250 watt		6	1.330		75	32		107	130	
	3000	1500 watt		5	1.600		80	39		119	145	
	3160	Recessed, residential, 750 watt		6	1.330		63	32		95	115	
	3170	1000 watt		6	1.330		70	32		102	125	
	3180	1250 watt		5	1.600		100	39		139	165	
	3190	1500 watt		4	2		100	49		149	180	
	3600	Thermostats, integral		16	.500		23	12.20		35.20	43	
	3800	Line voltage, 1 pole		8	1		23	24		47	61	
	3810	2 pole		8	1		23	24		47	61	
	3820	Low voltage, 1 pole		8	1		19	24		43	57	

168 | Special Systems

168 100	Special Systems	CREW	DAILY OUTPUT	MAN-HOURS	UNIT	BARE COSTS MAT.	LABOR	EQUIP.	TOTAL	TOTAL INCL O&P
4000	Heat trace system, 400 degree									
4020	115V, 2.5 watts per L.F.	1 Elec	530	.015	L.F.	4.05	.37		4.42	5
4030	5 watts per L.F.		530	.015		4.05	.37		4.42	5
4050	10 watts per L.F.		530	.015		4.05	.37		4.42	5
4060	220V, 4 watts per L.F.		530	.015		4.05	.37		4.42	5
4080	480V, 8 watts per L.F.		530	.015		4.05	.37		4.42	5
4200	Heater raceway									
4220	⅝"w x ⅜" H	1 Elec	200	.040	L.F.	2.60	.97		3.57	4.29
4240	⅝"w x ½" H	"	190	.042	"	3.64	1.03		4.67	5.50
4260	Heat transfer cement									
4280	1 gallon				Ea.	36			36	40
4300	5 gallon				"	145			145	160
4320	Snap band, clamp									
4340	¾" pipe size	1 Elec	470	.017	Ea.		.41		.41	.61
4360	1" pipe size		444	.018			.44		.44	.65
4380	1-¼" pipe size		400	.020			.49		.49	.72
4400	1-½" pipe size		355	.023			.55		.55	.81
4420	2" pipe size		320	.025			.61		.61	.90
4440	3" pipe size		160	.050			1.22		1.22	1.79
4460	4" pipe size		100	.080			1.95		1.95	2.87
4480	Single pole thermostat NEMA 4, 30 amp		8	1		135	24		159	185
4500	NEMA 7, 30 amp		7	1.140		140	28		168	195
4520	Double pole, NEMA 4, 30 amp		7	1.140		232	28		260	295
4540	NEMA 7, 30 amp		6	1.330		278	32		310	355
4560	Thermostat/contactor combination, NEMA 4									
4580	30 amp 4 pole	1 Elec	3.60	2.220	Ea.	408	54		462	530
4600	50 amp 4 pole		3	2.670		413	65		478	550
4620	75 amp 3 pole		2.50	3.200		489	78		567	655
4640	75 amp 4 pole		2.30	3.480		846	85		931	1,050
4680	Control transformer, 50 VA		4	2		57	49		106	135
4700	75 VA		3.10	2.580		62	63		125	160
4720	Expediter fitting		11	.727		13	17.70		30.70	40
5000	Radiant heating ceiling panels, 2' x 4', 500 watt		16	.500		108	12.20		120.20	135
5050	750 watt		16	.500		120	12.20		132.20	150
5200	For recessed plaster frame, add		32	.250		21	6.10		27.10	32
5300	Infra-red quartz heaters, 120 volts, 1000 watts		6.70	1.190		72	29		101	120
5350	1500 watt		5	1.600		72	39		111	135
5400	240 volts, 1500 watt		5	1.600		72	39		111	135
5450	2000 watt		4	2		72	49		121	150
5500	3000 watt		3	2.670		104	65		169	210
5550	4000 watt		2.60	3.080		104	75		179	225
5570	Modulating control		.80	10		46	245		291	410
5600	Unit heaters, heavy duty, with fan & mounting bracket									
5650	Single phase, 208-240-277 volt, 3 KW	1 Elec	3.20	2.500	Ea.	170	61		231	275
5700	4 KW		2.80	2.860		179	70		249	300
5750	5 KW		2.40	3.330		179	81		260	315
5800	7 KW		1.90	4.210		268	105		373	445
5850	10 KW		1.30	6.150		309	150		459	560
5900	13 KW		1	8		400	195		595	725
5950	15 KW		.90	8.890		462	215		677	825
6000	480 volt, 3KW		3.30	2.420		245	59		304	355
6020	4 KW		3	2.670		262	65		327	385
6040	5 KW		2.60	3.080		280	75		355	420
6060	7 KW		2	4		361	97		458	540
6080	10 KW		1.40	5.710		440	140		580	690
6100	13 KW		1.10	7.270		452	175		627	760
6120	15 KW		1	8		572	195		767	915
6140	20 KW		.90	8.890		767	215		982	1,150

168 | Special Systems

168 100 | Special Systems

		CREW	DAILY OUTPUT	MAN-HOURS	UNIT	BARE COSTS MAT.	BARE COSTS LABOR	BARE COSTS EQUIP.	BARE COSTS TOTAL	TOTAL INCL O&P	
130	6300	3 phase, 208-240 volt, 5 KW	1 Elec	2.40	3.330	Ea.	201	81		282	340	130
	6320	7 KW		1.90	4.210		282	105		387	460	
	6340	10 KW		1.30	6.150		344	150		494	600	
	6360	15 KW		.90	8.890		515	215		730	885	
	6380	20 KW		.70	11.430		740	280		1,020	1,225	
	6400	25 KW		.50	16		830	390		1,220	1,475	
	6500	480 volt, 5 KW		2.60	3.080		288	75		363	425	
	6520	7 KW		2	4		349	97		446	525	
	6540	10 KW		1.40	5.710		420	140		560	665	
	6560	13 KW		1.10	7.270		450	175		625	755	
	6580	15 KW		1	8		556	195		751	900	
	6600	20 KW		.90	8.890		756	215		971	1,150	
	6800	Vertical discharge heaters, with fan										
	6820	Single phase, 208-240-277 volt, 10 KW	1 Elec	1.30	6.150	Ea.	493	150		643	765	
	6840	15 KW		.90	8.890		666	215		881	1,050	
	6900	3 phase, 208-240 volt, 10 KW		1.30	6.150		493	150		643	765	
	6920	15 KW		.90	8.890		577	215		792	955	
	6940	20 KW		.70	11.430		830	280		1,110	1,325	
	7100	480 volt, 10 KW		1.40	5.710		593	140		733	855	
	7120	15 KW		1	8		683	195		878	1,050	
	7140	20 KW		.90	8.890		834	215		1,049	1,225	
	7160	25 KW		.60	13.330		952	325		1,277	1,525	
	7900	Cabinet convector heaters, 240 volt										
	7920	2' long, 1000 watt	1 Elec	5.30	1.510	Ea.	257	37		294	335	
	7940	1500 watt		5.30	1.510		278	37		315	360	
	7960	2000 watt		5.30	1.510		309	37		346	395	
	7980	3' long, 1500 watt		4.60	1.740		298	42		340	390	
	8000	2250 watt		4.60	1.740		329	42		371	425	
	8020	3000 watt		4.60	1.740		381	42		423	480	
	8040	4' long, 2000 watt		4	2		368	49		417	475	
	8060	3000 watt		4	2		389	49		438	500	
	8080	4000 watt		4	2		484	49		533	605	
	8100	Available also in 208 or 277 volt										
	8200	Cabinet unit heaters, 120 to 277 volt, 1 pole,										
	8220	wall mounted, 2000 watt	1 Elec	4.60	1.740	Ea.	780	42		822	920	
	8230	3000 watt		4.60	1.740		800	42		842	940	
	8240	4000 watt		4.40	1.820		845	44		889	995	
	8250	5000 watt		4.40	1.820		870	44		914	1,025	
	8260	6000 watt		4.20	1.900		895	46		941	1,050	
	8270	8000 watt		4	2		910	49		959	1,075	
	8280	10,000 watt		3.80	2.110		930	51		981	1,100	
	8290	12,000 watt		3.50	2.290		1,100	56		1,156	1,300	
	8300	13,500 watt		2.90	2.760		1,230	67		1,297	1,450	
	8310	16,000 watt		2.70	2.960		1,395	72		1,467	1,650	
	8320	20,000 watt		2.30	3.480		1,425	85		1,510	1,700	
	8330	24,000 watt		1.90	4.210		1,500	105		1,605	1,800	
	8350	Recessed, 2000 watt		4.40	1.820		835	44		879	985	
	8370	3000 watt		4.40	1.820		865	44		909	1,025	
	8380	4000 watt		4.20	1.900		910	46		956	1,075	
	8390	5000 watt		4.20	1.900		940	46		986	1,100	
	8400	6000 watt		4	2		965	49		1,014	1,125	
	8410	8000 watt		3.80	2.110		980	51		1,031	1,150	
	8420	10,000 watt		3.50	2.290		1,010	56		1,066	1,200	
	8430	12,000 watt		2.90	2.760		1,185	67		1,252	1,400	
	8440	13,500 watt		2.70	2.960		1,285	72		1,357	1,525	
	8450	16,000 watt		2.30	3.480		1,440	85		1,525	1,700	
	8460	20,000 watt		1.90	4.210		1,485	105		1,590	1,775	
	8470	24,000 watt		1.60	5		1,545	120		1,665	1,875	

168 | Special Systems

		168 100	Special Systems	CREW	DAILY OUTPUT	MAN-HOURS	UNIT	BARE COSTS MAT.	LABOR	EQUIP.	TOTAL	TOTAL INCL O&P	
130	8490		Ceiling mounted, 2000 watt	1 Elec	3.20	2.500	Ea.	780	61		841	950	130
	8510		3000 watt		3.20	2.500		805	61		866	975	
	8520		4000 watt		3	2.670		845	65		910	1,025	
	8530		5000 watt		3	2.670		865	65		930	1,050	
	8540		6000 watt		2.80	2.860		900	70		970	1,100	
	8550		8000 watt		2.40	3.330		910	81		991	1,125	
	8560		10,000 watt		2.20	3.640		940	89		1,029	1,175	
	8570		12,000 watt		2	4		1,120	97		1,217	1,375	
	8580		13,500 watt		1.50	5.330		1,240	130		1,370	1,550	
	8590		16,000 watt		1.30	6.150		1,275	150		1,425	1,625	
	8600		20,000 watt		.90	8.890		1,340	215		1,555	1,800	
	8610		24,000 watt		.60	13.330		1,435	325		1,760	2,050	
	8630		208 to 480 volt, 3 pole										
	8650		Wall mounted, 2000 watt	1 Elec	4.60	1.740	Ea.	765	42		807	905	
	8670		3000 watt		4.60	1.740		790	42		832	930	
	8680		4000 watt		4.40	1.820		845	44		889	995	
	8690		5000 watt		4.40	1.820		880	44		924	1,025	
	8700		6000 watt		4.20	1.900		900	46		946	1,050	
	8710		8000 watt		4	2		915	49		964	1,075	
	8720		10,000 watt		3.80	2.110		940	51		991	1,100	
	8730		12,000 watt		3.50	2.290		1,030	56		1,086	1,225	
	8740		13,500 watt		2.90	2.760		1,220	67		1,287	1,450	
	8750		16,000 watt		2.70	2.960		1,335	72		1,407	1,575	
	8760		20,000 watt		2.30	3.480		1,425	85		1,510	1,700	
	8770		24,000 watt		1.90	4.210		1,530	105		1,635	1,825	
	8790		Recessed, 2000 watt		4.40	1.820		840	44		884	990	
	8810		3000 watt		4.40	1.820		870	44		914	1,025	
	8820		4000 watt		4.20	1.900		915	46		961	1,075	
	8830		5000 watt		4.20	1.900		945	46		991	1,100	
	8840		6000 watt		4	2		970	49		1,019	1,150	
	8850		8000 watt		3.80	2.110		980	51		1,031	1,150	
	8860		10,000 watt		3.50	2.290		1,010	56		1,066	1,200	
	8870		12,000 watt		2.90	2.760		1,090	67		1,157	1,300	
	8880		13,500 watt		2.70	2.960		1,235	72		1,307	1,475	
	8890		16,000 watt		2.30	3.480		1,410	85		1,495	1,675	
	8900		20,000 watt		1.90	4.210		1,440	105		1,545	1,725	
	8920		24,000 watt		1.60	5		1,545	120		1,665	1,875	
	8940		Ceiling mount, 2000 watt		3.20	2.500		765	61		826	930	
	8950		3000 watt		3.20	2.500		785	61		846	955	
	8960		4000 watt		3	2.670		845	65		910	1,025	
	8970		5000 watt		3	2.670		880	65		945	1,075	
	8980		6000 watt		2.80	2.860		905	70		975	1,100	
	8990		8000 watt		2.40	3.330		910	81		991	1,125	
	9000		10,000 watt		2.20	3.640		940	89		1,029	1,175	
	9020		13,500 watt		1.50	5.330		1,234	130		1,364	1,550	
	9030		16,000 watt		1.30	6.150		1,370	150		1,520	1,725	
	9040		20,000 watt		.90	8.890		1,425	215		1,640	1,875	
	9060		24,000 watt		.60	13.330		1,510	325		1,835	2,150	
170	0010	**RESIDENTIAL WIRING**											170
	0020		20' avg. runs and #14/2 wiring incl. unless otherwise noted										
	1000		Service & panel, includes 24' SE-AL cable, service eye, meter,										
	1010		Socket, panel board, main bkr., ground rod, 15 or 20 amp										
	1020		1-pole circuit breakers, and misc. hardware										
	1100		100 amp, with 10 branch breakers	1 Elec	1.19	6.720	Ea.	260	165		425	525	
	1110		With PVC conduit and wire		.92	8.700		280	210		490	620	
	1120		With RGS conduit and wire		.73	10.960		369	265		634	800	
	1150		150 amp, with 14 branch breakers		1.03	7.770		430	190		620	750	
	1170		With PVC conduit and wire		.82	9.760		460	240		700	855	

223

168 | Special Systems

168 100 | Special Systems

		CREW	DAILY OUTPUT	MAN-HOURS	UNIT	MAT.	LABOR	EQUIP.	TOTAL	TOTAL INCL O&P
1180	With RGS conduit and wire	1 Elec	.67	11.940	Ea.	565	290		855	1,050
1200	200 amp, with 18 branch breakers		.90	8.890		530	215		745	900
1220	With PVC conduit and wire		.73	10.960		565	265		830	1,025
1230	With RGS conduit and wire		.62	12.900		755	315		1,070	1,300
1800	Lightning surge suppressor for above services, add	↓	32	.250	↓	29	6.10		35.10	41
2000	Switch devices									
2100	Single pole, 15 amp, Ivory, with a 1-gang box, cover plate,									
2110	Type NM (Romex) cable	1 Elec	17.10	.468	Ea.	5.50	11.40		16.90	23
2120	Type MC (BX) cable		14.30	.559		10.40	13.60		24	31
2130	EMT & wire		5.71	1.400		13.25	34		47.25	65
2150	3-way, #14/3, type NM cable		14.55	.550		9.10	13.40		22.50	30
2170	Type MC cable		12.31	.650		12.30	15.80		28.10	37
2180	EMT & wire		5	1.600		14.45	39		53.45	73
2200	4-way, #14/3, type NM cable		14.55	.550		17.85	13.40		31.25	39
2220	Type MC cable		12.31	.650		20.95	15.80		36.75	46
2230	EMT & wire		5	1.600		22.50	39		61.50	82
2250	S.P., 20 amp, #12/2, type NM cable		13.33	.600		10.20	14.60		24.80	33
2270	Type MC cable		11.43	.700		14.30	17.05		31.35	41
2280	EMT & wire		4.85	1.650		17.10	40		57.10	78
2300	S.P. rotary dimmer, 600W, type NM cable		14.55	.550		12.65	13.40		26.05	34
2320	Type MC cable		12.31	.650		17.65	15.80		33.45	43
2330	EMT & wire		5	1.600		20.45	39		59.45	80
2350	3-way rotary dimmer, type NM cable		13.33	.600		18.60	14.60		33.20	42
2370	Type MC cable		11.43	.700		22.30	17.05		39.35	50
2380	EMT & wire	↓	4.85	1.650	↓	24.45	40		64.45	86
2400	Interval timer wall switch, 20 amp, 1-30 min., #12/2			.550						
2410	Type NM cable	1 Elec	14.55	.550	Ea.	18.60	13.40		32	40
2420	Type MC cable		12.31	.650		23.35	15.80		39.15	49
2430	EMT & wire	↓	5	1.600	↓	26.50	39		65.50	86
2500	Decorator style									
2510	S.P., 15 amp, type NM cable	1 Elec	17.10	.468	Ea.	7.80	11.40		19.20	25
2520	Type MC cable		14.30	.559		12.95	13.60		26.55	34
2530	EMT & wire		5.71	1.400		15.80	34		49.80	68
2550	3-way, #14/3, type NM cable		14.55	.550		10.85	13.40		24.25	32
2570	Type MC cable		12.31	.650		15.45	15.80		31.25	40
2580	EMT & wire		5	1.600		17.45	39		56.45	77
2600	4-way, #14/3, type NM cable		14.55	.550		20	13.40		33.40	42
2620	Type MC cable		12.31	.650		23.60	15.80		39.40	49
2630	EMT & wire		5	1.600		25.70	39		64.70	86
2650	S.P., 20 amp, #12/2, type NM cable		13.33	.600		14.35	14.60		28.95	37
2670	Type MC cable		11.43	.700		18.30	17.05		35.35	45
2680	EMT & wire		4.85	1.650		21.30	40		61.30	83
2700	S.P., slide dimmer, type NM cable		17.10	.468		17.50	11.40		28.90	36
2720	Type MC cable		14.30	.559		22.70	13.60		36.30	45
2730	EMT & wire		5.71	1.400		26	34		60	79
2750	S.P., touch dimmer, type NM cable		17.10	.468		24	11.40		35.40	43
2770	Type MC cable		14.30	.559		29	13.60		42.60	52
2780	EMT & wire		5.71	1.400		32	34		66	85
2800	3-way touch dimmer, type NM cable		13.33	.600		34	14.60		48.60	59
2820	Type MC cable		11.43	.700		38	17.05		55.05	67
2830	EMT & wire	↓	4.85	1.650	↓	40	40		80	105
3000	Combination devices									
3100	S.P. switch/15 amp recpt., Ivory, 1-gang box, plate									
3110	Type NM cable	1 Elec	11.43	.700	Ea.	11	17.05		28.05	37
3120	Type MC cable		10	.800		19.65	19.50		39.15	50
3130	EMT & wire		4.40	1.820		22.70	44		66.70	90
3150	S.P. switch/pilot light, type NM cable		11.43	.700		10.90	17.05		27.95	37
3170	Type MC cable	↓	10	.800	↓	15.40	19.50		34.90	46

168 | Special Systems

168 100 | Special Systems

		Crew	Daily Output	Man-Hours	Unit	Bare Costs Mat.	Labor	Equip.	Total	Total Incl O&P	
170	3180 EMT & wire	1 Elec	4.43	1.810	Ea.	18.20	44		62.20	85	170
	3200 2-S.P. switches, 2-#14/2, type NM cables		10	.800		14.15	19.50		33.65	44	
	3220 Type MC cable		8.89	.900		21.60	22		43.60	56	
	3230 EMT & wire		4.10	1.950		20.55	48		68.55	93	
	3250 3-way switch/15 amp recpt., #14/3, type NM cable		10	.800		19.55	19.50		39.05	50	
	3270 Type MC cable		8.89	.900		22.70	22		44.70	57	
	3280 EMT & wire		4.10	1.950		25	48		73	97	
	3300 2-3 way switches, 2-#14/3 type NM cables		8.89	.900		25	22		47	60	
	3320 Type MC cable		8	1		29	24		53	68	
	3330 EMT & wire		4	2		28	49		77	100	
	3350 S.P. switch/20 amp recpt., #12/2 type NM cable		10	.800		18	19.50		37.50	48	
	3370 Type MC cable		8.89	.900		22.70	22		44.70	57	
	3380 EMT & wire		4.10	1.950		25	48		73	97	
	3400 Decorator style										
	3410 S.P. switch/15 amp recpt., type NM cable	1 Elec	11.43	.700	Ea.	18.30	17.05		35.35	45	
	3420 Type MC cable		10	.800		19.45	19.50		38.95	50	
	3430 EMT & wire		4.40	1.820		22.60	44		66.60	90	
	3450 S.P. switch/pilot light, type NM cable		11.43	.700		15.60	17.05		32.65	42	
	3470 Type MC cable		10	.800		19.95	19.50		39.45	51	
	3480 EMT & wire		4.40	1.820		24	44		68	92	
	3500 2-S.P. switches, 2-#14/2 type NM cables		10	.800		17.70	19.50		37.20	48	
	3520 Type MC cable		8.89	.900		25	22		47	60	
	3530 EMT & wire		4.10	1.950		24	48		72	96	
	3550 3-way/15 amp recpt., #14/3 type NM cable		10	.800		23	19.50		42.50	54	
	3570 Type MC cable		8.89	.900		26	22		48	61	
	3580 EMT & wire		4.10	1.950		28	48		76	100	
	3650 2-3 way switches, 2-3 #14/3 type NM cables		8.89	.900		30	22		52	65	
	3670 Type MC cable		8	1		34	24		58	73	
	3680 EMT & wire		4	2		33	49		82	110	
	3700 S.P. switch/20 amp recpt., #12/2 type NM cable		10	.800		21	19.50		40.50	52	
	3720 Type MC cable		8.89	.900		26	22		48	61	
	3730 EMT & wire		4.10	1.950		28	48		76	100	
	4000 Receptacle devices										
	4010 Duplex outlet, 15 amp recpt., Ivory, 1-gang box, plate										
	4015 Type NM cable	1 Elec	12.31	.650	Ea.	5.50	15.80		21.30	29	
	4020 Type MC cable		12.31	.650		9.90	15.80		25.70	34	
	4030 EMT & wire		5.33	1.500		12.80	37		49.80	68	
	4050 With #12/2 type NM cable		12.31	.650		6.60	15.80		22.40	31	
	4070 Type MC cable		10.67	.750		11.85	18.25		30.10	40	
	4080 EMT & wire		4.71	1.700		13.65	41		54.65	76	
	4100 20 amp recpt., #12/2 type NM cable		12.31	.650		8.95	15.80		24.75	33	
	4120 Type MC cable		10.67	.750		13.10	18.25		31.35	41	
	4130 EMT & wire		4.71	1.700		15.95	41		56.95	78	
	4140 For GFI see line 4300 below										
	4150 Decorator style, 15 amp recpt., type NM cable	1 Elec	14.55	.550	Ea.	6.70	13.40		20.10	27	
	4170 Type MC cable		12.31	.650		11.10	15.80		26.90	36	
	4180 EMT & wire		5.33	1.500		13.90	37		50.90	69	
	4200 With #12/2 type NM cable		12.31	.650		7.90	15.80		23.70	32	
	4220 Type MC cable		10.67	.750		12.10	18.25		30.35	40	
	4230 EMT & wire		4.71	1.700		14.90	41		55.90	77	
	4250 20 amp recpt. #12/2 type NM cable		12.31	.650		11.30	15.80		27.10	36	
	4270 Type MC cable		10.67	.750		14.40	18.25		32.65	43	
	4280 EMT & wire		4.71	1.700		18.70	41		59.70	81	
	4300 GFI, 15 amp recpt., type NM cable		12.31	.650		27	15.80		42.80	53	
	4320 Type MC cable		10.67	.750		31	18.25		49.25	61	
	4330 EMT & wire		4.71	1.700		34	41		75	98	
	4350 GFI with #12/2 type NM cable		10.67	.750		28	18.25		46.25	58	
	4370 Type MC cable		9.20	.870		32	21		53	66	

168 | Special Systems

168 100	Special Systems	CREW	DAILY OUTPUT	MAN-HOURS	UNIT	MAT.	LABOR	EQUIP.	TOTAL	TOTAL INCL O&P
4380	EMT & wire	1 Elec	4.21	1.900	Ea.	35	46		81	105
4400	20 amp recpt., #12/2 type NM cable		10.67	.750		30	18.25		48.25	60
4420	Type MC cable		9.20	.870		34	21		55	69
4430	EMT & wire		4.21	1.900		36	46		82	110
4500	Weather-proof cover for above receptacles, add		32	.250		3.40	6.10		9.50	12.70
4550	Air conditioner outlet, 20 amp-240 volt recpt.									
4560	30' of #12/2, 2 pole circuit breaker									
4570	Type NM cable	1 Elec	10	.800	Ea.	25	19.50		44.50	56
4580	Type MC cable		9	.889		30	22		52	65
4590	EMT & wire		4	2		41	49		90	115
4600	Decorator style, type NM cable		10	.800		27	19.50		46.50	58
4620	Type MC cable		9	.889		32	22		54	67
4630	EMT & wire		4	2		42	49		91	120
4650	Dryer outlet, 30 amp-240 volt recpt., 20' of #10/3									
4660	2 pole circuit breaker									
4670	Type NM cable	1 Elec	6.41	1.250	Ea.	41	30		71	90
4680	Type MC cable		5.71	1.400		42	34		76	96
4690	EMT & wire		3.48	2.300		39	56		95	125
4700	Range outlet, 50 amp-240 volt recpt., 30' of #8/3									
4710	Type NM cable	1 Elec	4.21	1.900	Ea.	69	46		115	145
4720	Type MC cable		4	2		67	49		116	145
4730	EMT & wire		2.96	2.700		56	66		122	160
4750	Central vacuum outlet		6.40	1.250		51	30		81	100
4770	Type MC cable		5.71	1.400		36	34		70	90
4780	EMT & wire		3.48	2.300		47	56		103	135
4800	30 amp-110 volt locking recpt., #10/2 circ. bkr.									
4810	Type NM cable	1 Elec	6.20	1.290	Ea.	44	31		75	95
4830	EMT & wire	"	3.20	2.500	"	43	61		104	135
4900	Low voltage outlets									
4910	Telephone recpt., 20' of 4/C phone wire	1 Elec	26	.308	Ea.	5	7.50		12.50	16.55
4920	TV recpt., 20' of RG59U coax wire, F type connector	"	16	.500	"	7.60	12.20		19.80	26
4950	Door bell chime, transformer, 2 buttons, 60' of bellwire									
4970	Economy model	1 Elec	11.50	.696	Ea.	43	16.95		59.95	72
4980	Custom model		11.50	.696		88	16.95		104.95	120
4990	Luxury model, 3 buttons		9.50	.842		190	21		211	240
6000	Lighting outlets									
6050	Wire only (for fixture) type NM cable	1 Elec	32	.250	Ea.	3.30	6.10		9.40	12.60
6070	Type MC cable		24	.333		6.50	8.10		14.60	19.10
6080	EMT & wire		10	.800		8.80	19.50		28.30	38
6100	Box (4") and wire (for fixture), type NM cable		25	.320		5.70	7.80		13.50	17.75
6120	Type MC cable		20	.400		10.20	9.75		19.95	26
6130	EMT & wire		11	.727		12.35	17.70		30.05	40
6200	Fixtures (use with lines 6050 or 6100 above)									
6210	Canopy style, economy grade	1 Elec	40	.200	Ea.	18.70	4.87		23.57	28
6220	Custom grade		40	.200		34	4.87		38.87	45
6250	Dining room chandelier, economy grade		19	.421		56	10.25		66.25	77
6260	Custom grade		19	.421		165	10.25		175.25	195
6270	Luxury grade		15	.533		370	13		383	425
6310	Kitchen fixture (fluorescent), economy grade		30	.267		38	6.50		44.50	51
6320	Custom grade		25	.320		122	7.80		129.80	145
6350	Outdoor, wall mounted, economy grade		30	.267		21.80	6.50		28.30	34
6360	Custom grade		30	.267		75	6.50		81.50	92
6370	Luxury grade		25	.320		170	7.80		177.80	200
6410	Outdoor Par floodlights, 1 lamp, 150 watt		20	.400		14.55	9.75		24.30	30
6420	2 lamp, 150 watt each		20	.400		24.25	9.75		34	41
6430	For infrared security sensor, add		32	.250		75	6.10		81.10	91
6450	Outdoor, quartz-halogen, 300 watt flood		20	.400		27	9.75		36.75	44
6600	Recessed downlight, round, pre-wired, 50 or 75 watt trim		30	.267		26	6.50		32.50	38

168 | Special Systems

168 100 | Special Systems

		CREW	DAILY OUTPUT	MAN-HOURS	UNIT	MAT.	LABOR	EQUIP.	TOTAL	TOTAL INCL O&P
6610	With shower light trim	1 Elec	30	.267	Ea.	31	6.50		37.50	44
6620	With wall washer trim		28	.286		38	6.95		44.95	52
6630	With eye-ball trim		28	.286		36	6.95		42.95	50
6640	For direct contact with insulation, add					1.10			1.10	1.21
6700	Porcelyn lamp holder	1 Elec	40	.200		2.60	4.87		7.47	10.05
6710	With pull switch		40	.200		2.90	4.87		7.77	10.35
6750	Fluorescent strip, 1-20 watt tube, wrap around diffuser, 24"		24	.333		39	8.10		47.10	55
6770	2-40 watt tubes, 48"		20	.400		65	9.75		74.75	86
6780	With 0° ballast		20	.400		68	9.75		77.75	89
6800	Bathroom heat lamp, 1-250 watt		28	.286		22.90	6.95		29.85	35
6810	2-250 watt lamps		28	.286		38	6.95		44.95	52
6820	For timer switch, see line 2400									
6900	Outdoor post lamp, incl. post, fixture, 35' of #14/2									
6910	Type NMC cable	1 Elec	3.50	2.290	Ea.	135	56		191	230
6920	Photo-eye, add		27	.296		22	7.20		29.20	35
6950	Clock dial time switch, 24 hr., w/enclosure, type NM cable		11.43	.700		38	17.05		55.05	67
6970	Type MC cable		11	.727		43	17.70		60.70	73
6980	EMT & wire		4.85	1.650		45	40		85	110
7000	Alarm systems									
7050	Smoke detectors, box, #14/3 type NM cable	1 Elec	14.55	.550	Ea.	20.80	13.40		34.20	43
7070	Type MC cable		12.31	.650		25	15.80		40.80	51
7080	EMT & wire		5	1.600		37	39		76	98
7090	For relay output to security system, add					8.70			8.70	9.55
8000	Residential equipment									
8050	Disposal hook-up, incl. switch, outlet box, 3' of flex									
8060	20 amp-1 pole circ. bkr., and 25' of #12/2									
8070	Type NM cable	1 Elec	10	.800	Ea.	16.90	19.50		36.40	47
8080	Type MC cable		8	1		20.15	24		44.15	58
8090	EMT & wire		5	1.600		21.80	39		60.80	81
8100	Trash compactor or dishwasher hook-up, incl. outlet box,									
8110	3' of flex, 15 amp-1 pole circ. bkr., and 25' of #14/2									
8120	Type NM cable	1 Elec	10	.800	Ea.	11.40	19.50		30.90	41
8130	Type MC cable		8	1		14.10	24		38.10	51
8140	EMT & wire		5	1.600		16.90	39		55.90	76
8150	Hot water sink dispensor hook-up, use line 8100									
8200	Vent/exhaust fan hook-up, type NM cable	1 Elec	32	.250	Ea.	3.30	6.10		9.40	12.60
8220	Type MC cable		24	.333		6.60	8.10		14.70	19.20
8230	EMT & wire		10	.800		8.80	19.50		28.30	38
8250	Bathroom vent fan, 50 CFM (use with above hook-up)									
8260	Economy model	1 Elec	15	.533	Ea.	17.30	13		30.30	38
8270	Low noise model		15	.533		22.80	13		35.80	44
8280	Custom model		12	.667		82	16.25		98.25	115
8300	Bathroom or kitchen vent fan, 110 CFM									
8310	Economy model	1 Elec	15	.533	Ea.	43.70	13		56.70	67
8320	Low noise model	"	15	.533	"	57	13		70	82
8350	Paddle fan, variable speed (w/o lights)									
8360	Economy model (AC motor)	1 Elec	10	.800	Ea.	68	19.50		87.50	105
8370	Custom model (AC motor)		10	.800		119	19.50		138.50	160
8380	Luxury model (DC motor)		8	1		242	24		266	300
8390	Remote speed switch for above, add		12	.667		15.60	16.25		31.85	41
8500	Whole house exhaust fan, ceiling mount, 36", variable speed									
8510	Remote switch, incl. shutters, 20 amp-1 pole circ. bkr.									
8520	30' of #12/2/ type NM cable	1 Elec	4	2	Ea.	354	49		403	460
8530	Type MC cable		3.50	2.290		362	56		418	480
8540	EMT & wire		3	2.670		377	65		442	510
8600	Whirlpool tub hook-up, incl. timer switch, outlet box									
8610	3' of flex, 20 amp-1 pole GFI circ. bkr.									
8620	30' of #12/2 type NM cable	1 Elec	10	.800	Ea.	58	19.50		77.50	92

168 | Special Systems

			DAILY	MAN-		BARE COSTS				TOTAL	
168 100	**Special Systems**	CREW	OUTPUT	HOURS	UNIT	MAT.	LABOR	EQUIP.	TOTAL	INCL O&P	
170	8630	Type MC cable	1 Elec	8	1	Ea.	61	24		85	105	170
	8640	EMT & wire	"	4	2	"	63	49		112	140	
	8650	Hot water heater hook-up, incl. 1-2 pole circ. bkr. box;										
	8660	3' of flex, 20' of #10/2 type NM cable	1 Elec	10	.800	Ea.	11.40	19.50		30.90	41	
	8670	Type MC cable		8	1		14	24		38	51	
	8680	EMT & wire	↓	5	1.600	↓	16.60	39		55.60	76	
	9000	Heating/air conditioning										
	9050	Furnace/boiler hook-up, incl. firestat, local on-off switch										
	9060	Emergency switch, and 40' of type NM cable	1 Elec	4	2	Ea.	28	49		77	100	
	9070	Type MC cable		3.50	2.290		33.80	56		89.80	120	
	9080	EMT & wire	↓	1.50	5.330	↓	38	130		168	235	
	9100	Air conditioner hook-up, incl. local 60 amp disc. switch										
	9110	3' Sealtite, 40 amp, 2 pole circuit breaker										
	9130	40' of #8/2 type NM cable	1 Elec	3.50	2.290	Ea.	99	56		155	190	
	9140	Type MC cable		3	2.670		104	65		169	210	
	9150	EMT & wire	↓	1.30	6.150	↓	105	150		255	335	
	9200	Heat pump hook-up, 1-40 & 1-100 amp 2 pole circ. bkr.										
	9210	Local disconnect switch, 3' Sealtite										
	9220	40' of #8/2 & 30' of #3/2										
	9230	Type NM cable	1 Elec	1.30	6.150	Ea.	245	150		395	490	
	9240	Type MC cable		1.08	7.410		250	180		430	540	
	9250	EMT & wire	↓	.94	8.510	↓	240	205		445	570	
	9500	Thermostat hook-up, using low voltage wire										
	9520	Heating only	1 Elec	24	.333	Ea.	3.30	8.10		11.40	15.60	
	9530	Heating/cooling	"	20	.400	"	3.60	9.75		13.35	18.30	

171 | S.F., C.F. and % of Total Costs

				UNIT COSTS			% OF TOTAL			
171 000	**S.F. & C.F. Costs**		UNIT	¼	MEDIAN	¾	¼	MEDIAN	¾	
010	0010	APARTMENTS Low Rise (1 to 3 story)	C14.1-000 S.F.	34.40	43.25	57.85				010
	0020	Total project cost	C.F.	3.09	4.07	5.02				
	2720	Plumbing	S.F.	2.69	3.53	4.51	6.80%	9%	10.20%	
	2770	Heating, ventilating, air conditioning		1.71	2.08	3.11	4.20%	5.80%	7.60%	
	2900	Electrical		1.99	2.66	3.71	5.20%	6.70%	8.70%	
	3100	Total: Mechanical & Electrical	↓	6	7.35	9.70	15.90%	18.30%	22.80%	
	9000	Per apartment unit, total cost	Apt.	27,700	39,700	60,300				
	9500	Total: Mechanical & Electrical	"	5,000	7,225	10,200				
020	0010	APARTMENTS Mid Rise (4 to 7 story)	S.F.	44	54.50	67.50				020
	0020	Total project costs	C.F.	3.56	5	5.90				
	2720	Plumbing	S.F.	2.69	3.39	4.58	6.20%	7.20%	8.90%	
	2900	Electrical		3.06	4.11	5.05	6.60%	7.20%	8.90%	
	3100	Total: Mechanical & Electrical	↓	8.45	10.65	12.90	17.90%	20.10%	22.30%	
	9000	Per apartment unit, total cost	Apt.	41,500	51,700	66,500				
	9500	Total: Mechanical & Electrical	"	10,100	11,800	17,300				
030	0010	APARTMENTS High Rise (8 to 24 story)	S.F.	51.90	61.20	73.40				030
	0020	Total project costs	C.F.	4.29	6	7.30				
	2720	Plumbing	S.F.	3.33	4.52	5.65	6.70%	9.10%	10.40%	
	2900	Electrical		3.74	4.61	6.15	6.80%	7.60%	9.10%	
	3100	Total: Mechanical & Electrical		10.60	13.05	16.50	18.70%	22.30%	24.50%	
	9000	Per apartment unit, total cost	Apt.	49,300	57,100	62,800				

171 | S.F., C.F. and % of Total Costs

171 000 | S.F. & C.F. Costs

			UNIT	UNIT COSTS ¼	UNIT COSTS MEDIAN	UNIT COSTS ¾	% OF TOTAL ¼	% OF TOTAL MEDIAN	% OF TOTAL ¾	
030	9500	Total: Mechanical & Electrical	Apt.	11,700	13,400	14,300				030
040	0010	**AUDITORIUMS**	S.F.	52	73.40	93.95				040
	0020	Total project costs	C.F.	3.45	4.70	6.55				
	2720	Plumbing	S.F.	3.34	4.45	5.75	5.70%	6.80%	8.40%	
	2770	Heating, ventilating, air conditioning		6.95	16.85	19.55	6.90%	16%	19.80%	
	2900	Electrical		4.27	6.15	8.25	6.80%	8.80%	11%	
	3100	Total: Mechanical & Electrical		8.85	11.75	20.40	14.70%	18.50%	23.60%	
050	0010	**AUTOMOTIVE SALES**	↓	36.30	45.95	59.90				050
	0020	Total project costs	C.F.	2.72	3.16	4.10				
	2720	Plumbing	S.F.	1.82	2.54	3.45	2.80%	5.90%	6.40%	
	2770	Heating, ventilating, air conditioning		2.65	4.35	6.30	6.30%	10.20%	10.70%	
	2900	Electrical		3.11	5.45	7.25	7.30%	9.90%	12.30%	
	3100	Total: Mechanical & Electrical		6.55	12.35	14.70	15.40%	19.10%	30.30%	
060	0010	**BANKS**	↓	79.95	100	132				060
	0020	Total project costs	C.F.	5.65	7.65	10.10				
	2720	Plumbing	S.F.	2.60	3.75	5.55	2.90%	4%	5%	
	2770	Heating, ventilating, air conditioning		5.05	6.90	9.80	5.20%	7.40%	8.70%	
	2900	Electrical		7.75	10.15	13.55	8.30%	10.30%	12.30%	
	3100	Total: Mechanical & Electrical		12.95	17.95	25.60	14.20%	18.20%	23.50%	
130	0010	**CHURCHES**	↓	53.10	66.50	84.55				130
	0020	Total project costs	C.F.	3.40	4.26	5.55				
	2720	Plumbing	S.F.	2.11	3.02	4.44	3.60%	4.90%	6.30%	
	2770	Heating, ventilating, air conditioning		4.99	6.50	9.30	7.80%	10%	12.20%	
	2900	Electrical		4.39	5.90	7.80	7.20%	8.70%	10.80%	
	3100	Total: Mechanical & Electrical		9.55	13.85	18.60	16.40%	21.80%	26.50%	
150	0010	**CLUBS, COUNTRY**	↓	53.70	64.50	84.35				150
	0020	Total project costs	C.F.	4.57	5.55	7.80				
	2720	Plumbing	S.F.	3.29	4.60	8.35	5.40%	8.90%	10%	
	2770	Heating, ventilating, air conditioning		3.17	6.85	10.20	6.70%	10%	10.70%	
	2900	Electrical		3.83	6.75	8.40	7%	9.70%	11%	
	3100	Total: Mechanical & Electrical		10.40	15.85	23.60	17.20%	23.70%	30.90%	
170	0010	**CLUBS, SOCIAL** Fraternal	↓	46.10	63.45	82.95				170
	0020	Total project costs	C.F.	2.82	4.23	5.20				
	2720	Plumbing	S.F.	2.16	3.42	3.91	4.90%	6.70%	7.80%	
	2770	Heating, ventilating, air conditioning		4.09	6.05	6.85	8.20%	10.90%	14.40%	
	2900	Electrical		3.23	5.55	6.30	6.70%	9.50%	11.40%	
	3100	Total: Mechanical & Electrical		10	13.35	18.15	18.50%	28.70%	33.10%	
180	0010	**CLUBS, Y.M.C.A.**	↓	53.65	68.15	82.35				180
	0020	Total project costs	C.F.	2.61	4.35	5.20				
	2720	Plumbing	S.F.	3.87	5.85	8	6%	8.40%	11%	
	2900	Electrical		3.74	5.30	6.90	6%	7.80%	10.10%	
	3100	Total: Mechanical & Electrical	↓	10.75	16.25	25.30	17.10%	27.90%	32.10%	
190	0010	**COLLEGES** Classrooms & Administration	S.F.	66.90	88.05	113				190
	0020	Total project costs	C.F.	4.63	6.60	9.80				
	2720	Plumbing	S.F.	3.48	4.70	7.50	4%	6.40%	8%	
	2770	Heating, ventilating, air conditioning		7	11.15	16.50	8.70%	12.20%	14.60%	
	2900	Electrical		5.10	8.30	12.55	7.70%	9.80%	11.50%	
	3100	Total: Mechanical & Electrical		14.65	24.40	32.30	19.70%	28%	34.30%	
210	0010	**COLLEGES** Science, Engineering, Laboratories	↓	77.95	106	126				210
	0020	Total project costs	C.F.	5.70	7.90	9.10				
	2720	Plumbing	S.F.	3.74	5.60	7.80	5.90%	6.80%	8%	
	2770	Heating, ventilating, air conditioning		5.85	12	14.15	8.20%	14.40%	19.10%	
	2900	Electrical		7.20	10.45	14.40	7.80%	9.60%	12%	
	3100	Total: Mechanical & Electrical		24.25	33.95	50.55	25.40%	34%	38.70%	
230	0010	**COLLEGES** Student Unions	↓	68.10	94.70	112				230
	0020	Total project costs	C.F.	3.85	4.86	6.40				

171 | S.F., C.F. and % of Total Costs

171 000 | S.F. & C.F. Costs

			UNIT	UNIT COSTS ¼	UNIT COSTS MEDIAN	UNIT COSTS ¾	% OF TOTAL ¼	% OF TOTAL MEDIAN	% OF TOTAL ¾	
230	2720	Plumbing	S.F.	4.19	5.45	6.95	4.20%	5.20%	8.60%	230
	2770	Heating, ventilating, air conditioning		10.30	12	17.40	10.90%	14.10%	17.40%	
	2900	Electrical		5.45	8.05	10.90	7.90%	9.70%	10.70%	
	3100	Total: Mechanical & Electrical		17.70	25.50	30.50	22.90%	26.20%	31.70%	
250	0010	COMMUNITY CENTERS	↓	56.15	68.80	87.35				250
	0020	Total project costs	C.F.	3.50	5	6.50				
	2720	Plumbing	S.F.	2.92	4.71	6.40	5.40%	6.90%	9.10%	
	2770	Heating, ventilating, air conditioning		4.68	6.65	8.90	7.60%	10.20%	12.90%	
	2900	Electrical		4.75	6.05	8.55	7.50%	9.20%	11.10%	
	3100	Total: Mechanical & Electrical		11.45	17.75	24.20	19.50%	26.30%	30.90%	
280	0010	COURT HOUSES	↓	74.65	91.85	113				280
	0020	Total project costs	C.F.	6.05	6.85	7.95				
	2720	Plumbing	S.F.	3.85	5.25	6.15	3.90%	6.30%	7.40%	
	2770	Heating, ventilating, air conditioning		10.20	11.40	16.75	10.30%	11.90%	14.80%	
	2900	Electrical		7.10	8.95	14.15	8.40%	9.80%	12%	
	3100	Total: Mechanical & Electrical		16.35	23.85	33.60	20.10%	26%	29.70%	
300	0010	DEPARTMENT STORES	↓	30.40	40.55	46.30				300
	0020	Total project costs	C.F.	1.37	2	2.65				
	2720	Plumbing	S.F.	.99	1.38	1.79	2.80%	3.90%	5.30%	
	2770	Heating, ventilating, air conditioning		3.16	4.20	6.35	8.30%	11.80%	14.80%	
	2900	Electrical		3.47	4.71	5.80	10.40%	11.90%	13.60%	
	3100	Total: Mechanical & Electrical		6.55	11.50	13.20	22.10%	26.70%	32.30%	
310	0010	DORMITORIES Low Rise (1 to 3 story)	↓	49.45	66.60	86.05				310
	0020	Total project costs	C.F.	3.77	6.05	7.75				
	2720	Plumbing	S.F.	3.42	4.29	5.75	8%	8.90%	9.60%	
	2770	Heating, ventilating, air conditioning		3.61	4.15	5.75	4.60%	7.60%	9.90%	
	2900	Electrical		3.50	5.10	6.30	6.40%	8.70%	9.50%	
	3100	Total: Mechanical & Electrical	↓	8.25	13.85	18.90	18.40%	22.50%	28.40%	
	9000	Per bed, total cost	Bed	10,300	16,800	26,200				
320	0010	DORMITORIES Mid Rise (4 to 8 story)	S.F.	72.50	85.05	105				320
	0020	Total project costs	C.F.	6.40	8.40	10				
	2720	Plumbing	S.F.	5.60	6.55	8.25	6.40%	10%	10.30%	
	2900	Electrical		5.80	8.10	9.90	8%	8.90%	10.10%	
	3100	Total: Mechanical & Electrical	↓	15.15	18.70	26.65	18.10%	22.20%	30.60%	
	9000	Per bed, total cost	Bed	14,000	17,000	22,400				
340	0010	FACTORIES	S.F.	25.40	35.50	60.85				340
	0020	Total project costs	C.F.	1.87	2.45	3.50				
	2720	Plumbing	S.F.	2.68	3.15	4.73	4.80%	4.90%	10.40%	
	2770	Heating, ventilating, air conditioning		2.46	3.97	4.42	5%	6.90%	7.90%	
	2900	Electrical		3.87	7.90	8.85	8.90%	11.50%	15.80%	
	3100	Total: Mechanical & Electrical		9.55	15.60	21.55	22.10%	28.60%	34%	
360	0010	FIRE STATIONS	↓	53.10	71.25	86.35				360
	0020	Total project costs	C.F.	3.39	4.53	5.70				
	2720	Plumbing	S.F.	3.41	5.30	7.20	5.90%	7.30%	9.50%	
	2770	Heating, ventilating, air conditioning		2.92	4.70	7.45	4.80%	7.30%	9.20%	
	2900	Electrical		3.99	6.65	9.50	7.20%	9.60%	11.90%	
	3100	Total: Mechanical & Electrical		10.10	15.75	21.40	17.50%	22.60%	27.50%	
370	0010	FRATERNITY HOUSES And Sorority Houses	↓	52.45	62.60	69.85				370
	0020	Total project costs	C.F.	5	6.10	6.75				
	2720	Plumbing	S.F.	3.96	4.63	6.15	5.90%	8%	10.80%	
	2900	Electrical		3.45	4.56	8.25	6.50%	8.80%	10.40%	
	3100	Total: Mechanical & Electrical	↓	9.80	13.90	16.75	14.60%	20.70%	24.20%	
380	0010	FUNERAL HOMES	S.F.	49.90	63	91.95				380
	0020	Total project costs	C.F.	3.53	5.05	6.30				
	2720	Plumbing	S.F.	1.98	2.74	3	4.10%	4.40%	4.70%	
	2770	Heating, ventilating, air conditioning	"	4.40	4.44	5.35	7%	9.20%	10.40%	

171 | S.F., C.F. and % of Total Costs

171 000	S.F. & C.F. Costs	UNIT	UNIT COSTS ¼	MEDIAN	¾	% OF TOTAL ¼	MEDIAN	¾	
380	2900	Electrical	S.F.	3.30	4.47	6.40	5.90%	7.70%	11%	380
	3100	Total: Mechanical & Electrical		9	11.95	13.80	17.80%	20.80%	27.10%	
390	0010	GARAGES, COMMERCIAL (service)	↓	30.20	47.75	62.40				390
	0020	Total project costs	C.F.	1.92	2.82	4.02				
	2720	Plumbing	S.F.	1.93	3.05	6.10	4.90%	7.30%	11%	
	2730	Heating & ventilating		2.84	3.91	4.71	5.20%	7.20%	9.50%	
	2900	Electrical		2.68	4.45	6.15	7.10%	9%	11.10%	
	3100	Total: Mechanical & Electrical		6.25	11.05	15.95	15.50%	21.90%	27.80%	
400	0010	GARAGES, MUNICIPAL (repair)	↓	32.65	51.15	75.10				400
	0020	Total project costs	C.F.	2.38	3.33	4.44				
	2720	Plumbing	S.F.	2.01	3.78	6.20	4.10%	6.90%	8.70%	
	2730	Heating & ventilating		2.52	4.51	6.80	6.10%	7.80%	11.60%	
	2900	Electrical		2.90	4.54	6.45	6.60%	8.30%	10.50%	
	3100	Total: Mechanical & Electrical		6.95	15.15	21.35	16%	24.40%	32.40%	
410	0010	GARAGES, PARKING	↓	17.25	21.75	36.50				410
	0020	Total project costs	C.F.	1.49	1.99	3.26				
	2720	Plumbing	S.F.	.31	.61	.88	2.10%	2.80%	3.80%	
	2900	Electrical		.73	1.06	1.72	4.20%	5.20%	6.50%	
	3100	Total: Mechanical & Electrical		1.26	1.70	2.54	7.10%	8.30%	9.50%	
	9000	Per car, total cost	Car	5,525	7,550	10,600				
	9500	Total: Mechanical & Electrical	"	395	590	730				
430	0010	GYMNASIUMS	S.F.	45.45	61.15	78.30				430
	0020	Total project costs	C.F.	2.27	3.15	4.02				
	2720	Plumbing	S.F.	2.80	3.82	4.82	4.80%	7.20%	8.50%	
	2770	Heating, ventilating, air conditioning		2.98	5.15	8.45	7.40%	9.70%	14%	
	2900	Electrical		3.82	4.66	6.95	6.50%	8.90%	10.70%	
	3100	Total: Mechanical & Electrical		8.25	12.85	16.85	16.60%	21.80%	27%	
460	0010	HOSPITALS	↓	100	121	163				460
	0020	Total project costs	C.F.	7.40	8.85	11.85				
	2720	Plumbing	S.F.	8.85	11.30	15.30	7.50%	9.10%	10.70%	
	2770	Heating, ventilating, air conditioning		9.60	16	22.05	8.40%	13%	16.60%	
	2900	Electrical		10.35	13.85	21.05	10%	12.30%	15.10%	
	3100	Total: Mechanical & Electrical		30.35	41.35	61.15	28.20%	36.60%	40.30%	
	9000	Per bed or person, total cost	Bed	27,100	54,300	69,700				
480	0010	HOUSING For the Elderly	S.F.	48.75	61.20	76.25				480
	0020	Total project costs	C.F.	3.44	4.77	6.20				
	2720	Plumbing	S.F.	3.69	5.10	7.46	8.30%	9.70%	10.90%	
	2730	Heating, ventilating, air conditioning		1.65	2.56	3.60	3.20%	5.60%	7.10%	
	2900	Electrical		3.59	5.05	7.05	7.50%	9%	10.60%	
	2910	Electrical incl. electric heat		4.10	7.70	9.15	9.60%	11%	13.30%	
	3100	Total: Mechanical & Electrical	↓	8.95	12.60	16.40	18.40%	22%	24.80%	
	9000	Per rental unit, total cost	Unit	43,600	51,100	56,300				
	9500	Total: Mechanical & Electrical	"	8,600	10,700	12,700				
500	0010	HOUSING Public (low-rise)	S.F.	37.05	51.35	69.95				500
	0020	Total project costs	C.F.	3.10	4.07	5.15				
	2720	Plumbing	S.F.	2.68	3.76	4.75	6.80%	9%	11.50%	
	2730	Heating, ventilating, air conditioning		1.43	2.78	3.04	4.20%	6%	6.40%	
	2900	Electrical		2.36	3.36	4.76	4.90%	6.40%	8.10%	
	3100	Total: Mechanical & Electrical	↓	7	10	14	14.90%	19.10%	22.20%	
	9000	Per apartment, total cost	Apt.	40,900	46,400	57,900				
	9500	Total: Mechanical & Electrical	"	6,875	9,425	11,800				
510	0010	ICE SKATING RINKS	S.F.	34.95	48.80	80.05				510
	0020	Total project costs	C.F.	1.98	2.48	2.92				
	2720	Plumbing	S.F.	1.05	1.55	2.36	3.10%	3.20%	4.60%	
	2900	Electrical	"	2.75	3.61	5	5.70%	7%	10.10%	

171 | S.F., C.F. and % of Total Costs

171 000 | S.F. & C.F. Costs

			UNIT	UNIT COSTS ¼	UNIT COSTS MEDIAN	UNIT COSTS ¾	% OF TOTAL ¼	% OF TOTAL MEDIAN	% OF TOTAL ¾	
510	3100	Total: Mechanical & Electrical	S.F.	5	7.10	10.65	12.40%	16.40%	25.90%	510
520	0010	**JAILS**	S.F.	112	127	152				520
	0020	Total project costs	C.F.	8.30	10.70	12.90				
	2720	Plumbing	S.F.	6.55	11.25	13.60	7%	8.30%	12%	
	2770	Heating, ventilating, air conditioning		6.60	11.90	17.25	6.30%	9.40%	12.10%	
	2900	Electrical		10.30	12.65	16.35	7.80%	10.10%	12.40%	
	3100	Total: Mechanical & Electrical		25.10	35.35	48.25	23.20%	29.60%	35.30%	
530	0010	**LIBRARIES**		63.15	77.80	97.85				530
	0020	Total project costs	C.F.	4.53	5.35	6.65				
	2720	Plumbing	S.F.	2.55	3.60	4.80	3.60%	4.50%	5.80%	
	2770	Heating, ventilating, air conditioning		6.40	9.05	11.80	8.70%	11%	13.20%	
	2900	Electrical		6.50	8.20	10.50	8.40%	10.90%	12.20%	
	3100	Total: Mechanical & Electrical		13.95	19.05	26.95	19.40%	24.50%	29.40%	
550	0010	**MEDICAL CLINICS**		60.80	74.80	93.15				550
	0020	Total project costs	C.F.	4.55	6.10	7.85				
	2720	Plumbing	S.F.	4.18	5.75	7.90	6.10%	8.40%	10.10%	
	2770	Heating, ventilating, air conditioning		5.05	6.60	9.60	6.70%	9%	11.90%	
	2900	Electrical		5.55	7.30	9.60	8.10%	9.90%	11.90%	
	3100	Total: Mechanical & Electrical		13.20	17.05	23.85	19%	24.30%	29.70%	
570	0010	**MEDICAL OFFICES**		56.45	70.35	85.40				570
	0020	Total project costs	C.F.	4.30	5.80	7.70				
	2720	Plumbing	S.F.	3.42	5.05	7.05	5.70%	6.90%	9.40%	
	2770	Heating, ventilating, air conditioning		3.95	5.95	7.70	6.50%	8%	10.40%	
	2900	Electrical		4.71	6.80	9.05	7.60%	9.70%	11.70%	
	3100	Total: Mechanical & Electrical		10.90	15.70	20.55	17.30%	22.40%	27.10%	
590	0010	**MOTELS**		40.75	54.90	74.10				590
	0020	Total project costs	C.F.	3.91	5.40	8.30				
	2720	Plumbing	S.F.	3.68	4.59	5.60	9.40%	10.50%	12.50%	
	2770	Heating, ventilating, air conditioning		1.94	3.34	6	4.90%	5.60%	10%	
	2900	Electrical		3.39	4.17	5.25	7.10%	8.10%	10.40%	
	3100	Total: Mechanical & Electrical		8.05	10.60	14.15	18.50%	23.10%	26.10%	
	9000	Per rental unit, total cost	Unit	14,600	27,800	38,700				
	9500	Total: Mechanical & Electrical	"	4,025	5,700	6,150				
600	0010	**NURSING HOMES**	S.F.	56.05	74.10	90.25				600
	0020	Total project costs	C.F.	4.55	5.95	7.80				
	2720	Plumbing	S.F.	4.98	6.10	9.05	9.30%	10.30%	14.10%	
	2770	Heating, ventilating, air conditioning		5.33	7.70	9.05	10.60%	11.70%	11.80%	
	2900	Electrical		5.75	7.15	9.25	9.80%	11.40%	12.80%	
	3100	Total: Mechanical & Electrical		13.35	17.45	26.35	22.30%	28.30%	33.20%	
	9000	Per bed or person, total cost	Bed	22,000	28,500	38,600				
610	0010	**OFFICES** Low-Rise (1 to 4 story)	S.F.	46	59	78				610
	0020	Total project costs	C.F.	3.39	4.75	6.35				
	2720	Plumbing	S.F.	1.75	2.64	3.77	3.60%	4.50%	6%	
	2770	Heating, ventilating, air conditioning		3.72	5.20	7.65	7.20%	10.40%	11.90%	
	2900	Electrical		3.85	5.35	7.35	7.40%	9.50%	11%	
	3100	Total: Mechanical & Electrical		8.05	11.95	17.25	14.80%	20.80%	26.80%	
620	0010	**OFFICES** Mid-Rise (5 to 10 story)		51.70	63.50	85.20				620
	0020	Total project costs	C.F.	3.55	4.60	6.45				
	2720	Plumbing	S.F.	1.56	2.38	3.41	2.80%	3.60%	4.50%	
	2770	Heating, ventilating, air conditioning		3.85	5.50	8.80	7.60%	9.30%	11%	
	2900	Electrical		3.28	4.70	7.95	6.50%	8%	10%	
	3100	Total: Mechanical & Electrical		9.25	11.90	20.10	16.70%	20.50%	26%	
630	0010	**OFFICES** High-Rise (11 to 20 story)		61.20	78.45	97.40				630
	0020	Total project costs	C.F.	3.92	5.55	7.90				
	2900	Electrical	S.F.	3.06	4.48	6.85	5.80%	7.80%	10.50%	
	3100	Total: Mechanical & Electrical	"	11.20	14.20	25.95	16.90%	21.40%	29.70%	

171 | S.F., C.F. and % of Total Costs

171 000 | S.F. & C.F. Costs

			UNIT	UNIT COSTS ¼	UNIT COSTS MEDIAN	UNIT COSTS ¾	% OF TOTAL ¼	% OF TOTAL MEDIAN	% OF TOTAL ¾	
640	0010	POLICE STATIONS	S.F.	76.55	98.25	125				640
	0020	Total project costs	C.F.	5.60	7.30	9.65				
	2720	Plumbing	S.F.	4.32	6.10	10.05	5.70%	6.80%	10.60%	
	2770	Heating, ventilating, air conditioning		6.15	8.30	11.80	7%	10.50%	11.90%	
	2900	Electrical		7.65	11.95	15.35	9.40%	11.60%	14.50%	
	3100	Total: Mechanical & Electrical		20.75	25.90	33.35	22.60%	27.50%	33%	
650	0010	POST OFFICES		61.65	74.40	97.20				650
	0020	Total project costs	C.F.	3.44	4.49	5.35				
	2720	Plumbing	S.F.	2.65	3.35	4.25	4.20%	5.30%	5.60%	
	2770	Heating, ventilating, air conditioning		3.84	5.15	7.80	6.60%	8%	9.80%	
	2900	Electrical		4.87	6.90	8.15	7.30%	9.40%	11%	
	3100	Total: Mechanical & Electrical		10.75	14.75	20.50	16.50%	21.40%	26.30%	
660	0010	POWER PLANTS		317	533	783				660
	0020	Total project costs	C.F.	10	18.40	51				
	2900	Electrical	S.F.	21.50	56.35	91.60	9.20%	12.70%	18.40%	
	8100	Total: Mechanical & Electrical		49.80	140	314	25.50%	32.50%	52.60%	
670	0010	RELIGIOUS EDUCATION		47.10	55.15	68.30				670
	0020	Total project costs	C.F.	2.72	3.88	5.10				
	2720	Plumbing	S.F.	1.98	2.93	4.20	4.10%	5.10%	7.10%	
	2770	Heating, ventilating, air conditioning		4.53	5.40	7.10	8.10%	9.90%	11.20%	
	2900	Electrical		3.54	4.70	6.15	6.90%	8.60%	10.20%	
	3100	Total: Mechanical & Electrical		7.85	11.05	16.05	14.90%	20.50%	24.60%	
690	0010	RESEARCH Laboratories and facilities		65.65	100	148				690
	0020	Total project costs	C.F.	3.90	7.60	11.85				
	2720	Plumbing	S.F.	6.80	9.30	13.05	5.20%	8.30%	10.80%	
	2770	Heating, ventilating, air conditioning		6.60	21.55	25.40	7.20%	16.40%	17.70%	
	2900	Electrical		7.85	11.65	24.55	9.10%	11.40%	16.20%	
	3100	Total: Mechanical & Electrical		17.10	33.45	63.85	20.60%	31.70%	41.90%	
700	0010	RESTAURANTS		66.55	87.65	113				700
	0020	Total project costs	C.F.	5.80	7.60	9.65				
	2720	Plumbing	S.F.	5.50	6.95	9.45	6%	8.20%	9.30%	
	2770	Heating, ventilating, air conditioning		7.60	10.30	13.20	9.60%	12.30%	13.30%	
	2900	Electrical		7.20	9.10	12.20	8.30%	10.50%	12%	
	3100	Total: Mechanical & Electrical		16.10	21.50	29	18.30%	23.20%	32%	
	9000	Per seat unit, total cost	Seat	2,150	3,110	4,080				
	9500	Total: Mechanical & Electrical	"	480	629	975				
720	0010	RETAIL STORES	S.F.	31.30	42.60	56.30				720
	0020	Total project costs	C.F.	2.18	3.09	4.29				
	2720	Plumbing	S.F.	1.21	1.95	3.46	3.20%	4.50%	6.80%	
	2770	Heating, ventilating, air conditioning		2.55	3.49	5.45	6.70%	8.50%	10.20%	
	2900	Electrical		2.95	3.99	5.85	7.40%	10%	11.90%	
	3100	Total: Mechanical & Electrical		5.40	8.20	11.80	14.90%	19%	24.20%	
740	0010	SCHOOLS Elementary		52.80	64.65	77.60				740
	0020	Total project costs	C.F.	3.53	4.46	5.70				
	2720	Plumbing	S.F.	3.07	4.43	5.90	5.60%	7.10%	9.20%	
	2730	Heating & ventilating		4.54	7.35	10.10	8.10%	10.80%	15.10%	
	2900	Electrical		4.78	6.10	7.95	8.40%	10%	11.80%	
	3100	Total: Mechanical & Electrical		11	16.05	20.75	20%	26.20%	32%	
	9000	Per pupil, total cost	Ea.	4,650	7,150	9,725				
	9500	Total: Mechanical & Electrical	"	1,400	2,025	3,300				
760	0010	SCHOOLS Junior High & Middle	S.F.	55.20	64.50	77.50				760
	0020	Total project costs	C.F.	3.42	4.29	5.05				
	2720	Plumbing	S.F.	3.22	3.89	5.05	5.40%	6.90%	8.10%	
	2770	Heating, ventilating, air conditioning		3.96	7.55	10.65	8.70%	11.50%	17.40%	
	2900	Electrical		5.30	6.35	7.35	8%	9.50%	10.60%	
	3100	Total: Mechanical & Electrical		11.65	16	23.50	19.30%	27.10%	32.50%	
	9000	Per pupil, total cost	Ea.	5,525	7,350	9,650				

171 | S.F., C.F. and % of Total Costs

171 000 | S.F. & C.F. Costs

			UNIT	UNIT COSTS ¼	UNIT COSTS MEDIAN	UNIT COSTS ¾	% OF TOTAL ¼	% OF TOTAL MEDIAN	% OF TOTAL ¾	
780	0010	**SCHOOLS** Senior High	S.F.	54.65	64.55	86.75				780
	0020	Total project costs	C.F.	3.48	4.25	5.50				
	2720	Plumbing	S.F.	2.88	4.84	7.75	5%	6.50%	8%	
	2770	Heating, ventilating, air conditioning		6.60	7.40	10.65	8.90%	11.50%	14.20%	
	2900	Electrical		5.55	7.25	10.95	8.30%	10%	12.30%	
	3100	Total: Mechanical & Electrical	↓	11.65	18.50	23.90	16.90%	25.60%	29.70%	
	9000	Per pupil, total cost	Ea.	5,625	9,050	11,800				
800	0010	**SCHOOLS** Vocational	S.F.	45.50	61.35	82.10				800
	0020	Total project costs	C.F.	2.83	3.90	5.35				
	2720	Plumbing	S.F.	3.05	4.48	6.45	5.40%	7%	8.50%	
	2770	Heating, ventilating, air conditioning		5.75	7.95	13.25	9.30%	12.50%	17%	
	2900	Electrical		4.89	6.60	9.95	9.50%	11.80%	13.90%	
	3100	Total: Mechanical & Electrical	↓	11.35	16.45	24.95	21.10%	29.70%	36%	
	9000	Per pupil, total cost	Ea.	2,800	16,800	24,800				
	9500	Total: Mechanical & Electrical	"	1,125	2,275	5,825				
830	0010	**SPORTS ARENAS**	S.F.	39.85	50.20	64.05				830
	0020	Total project costs	C.F.	2.16	3.95	5				
	2720	Plumbing	S.F.	2.04	3.50	6.25	4.30%	6.30%	8.50%	
	2770	Heating, ventilating, air conditioning		4.25	5.90	7.65	5.80%	10.20%	13.50%	
	2900	Electrical		3.29	5.50	6.75	7.10%	9.70%	12.20%	
	3100	Total: Mechanical & Electrical		7.30	12.95	16.65	13.40%	22.50%	30.80%	
850	0010	**SUPERMARKETS**	↓	36.70	42.35	49.05				850
	0020	Total project costs	C.F.	2.02	2.39	3.10				
	2720	Plumbing	S.F.	1.97	2.59	3.04	5%	6%	6.90%	
	2770	Heating, ventilating, air conditioning		3.03	3.61	4.41	8.50%	8.50%	9.50%	
	2900	Electrical		4.29	5.25	6.40	10.40%	12.40%	13.60%	
	3100	Total: Mechanical & Electrical		7.10	10.30	12.65	18.40%	22.40%	27.70%	
860	0010	**SWIMMING POOLS**	↓	56	72.45	102				860
	0020	Total project costs	C.F.	4.88	5.70	6.65				
	2720	Plumbing	S.F.	3.92	6.45	9	4.60%	9.60%	12.40%	
	2900	Electrical		4.25	6	9.10	6.50%	7.60%	7.90%	
	3100	Total: Mechanical & Electrical	↓	9.85	17.75	34.80	17.50%	24.90%	31%	
870	0010	**TELEPHONE EXCHANGES**	S.F.	80.95	111	147				870
	0020	Total project costs	C.F.	4.90	7.35	10.50				
	2720	Plumbing	S.F.	2.80	4.82	7.10	3.50%	5.70%	6.60%	
	2770	Heating, ventilating, air conditioning		6.80	15.65	19.45	11.70%	16%	18.40%	
	2900	Electrical		7.40	12.70	23.05	10.70%	13.90%	17.80%	
	3100	Total: Mechanical & Electrical		16.45	23.10	44.50	19.80%	30.80%	34.70%	
890	0010	**TERMINALS** Bus	↓	36.85	55.90	66.95				890
	0020	Total project costs	C.F.	1.82	3.15	4.04				
	2720	Plumbing	S.F.	1.22	2.75	4.25	2.30%	7.20%	8.80%	
	2900	Electrical		1.90	2.54	7.25	3.90%	7.50%	11.80%	
	3100	Total: Mechanical & Electrical	↓	1.93	5.90	9.40	8.30%	16.90%	19.50%	
910	0010	**THEATERS**	S.F.	45.85	59.95	90.65				910
	0020	Total project costs	C.F.	2.43	3.60	5.05				
	2720	Plumbing	S.F.	1.55	1.80	5.40	2.90%	4.60%	6.10%	
	2770	Heating, ventilating, air conditioning		4.31	5.80	6.65	7.30%	11.60%	13.30%	
	2900	Electrical		4.36	5.85	11.40	8%	9.30%	12.20%	
	3100	Total: Mechanical & Electrical		10.30	12.20	22.60	17.10%	24.90%	27.40%	
940	0010	**TOWN HALLS** City Halls & Municipal Buildings	↓	56.40	70.55	92.65				940
	0020	Total project costs	C.F.	3.83	5.60	7.15				
	2720	Plumbing	S.F.	1.97	3.87	6.75	4.20%	5.90%	7.90%	
	2770	Heating, ventilating, air conditioning		4.20	8.35	9.55	7%	9%	13.20%	
	2900	Electrical		4.47	6.65	9.20	7.90%	9.40%	11.60%	
	3100	Total: Mechanical & Electrical	↓	9.35	14.95	22.60	15.60%	21.10%	29.10%	

171 | S.F., C.F. and % of Total Costs

		171 000	S.F. & C.F. Costs	UNIT	UNIT COSTS ¼	UNIT COSTS MEDIAN	UNIT COSTS ¾	% OF TOTAL ¼	% OF TOTAL MEDIAN	% OF TOTAL ¾	
970	0010		WAREHOUSES And Storage Buildings	S.F.	20.30	28.25	43.05				970
	0020		Total project costs	C.F.	1.06	1.66	2.75				
990	0010		WAREHOUSE & OFFICES Combination	S.F.	24.90	32.20	44.45				990
	0020		Total project costs	C.F.	1.30	1.89	2.83				
	2720		Plumbing	S.F.	.97	1.66	2.59	3.60%	4.60%	6.20%	
	2770		Heating, ventilating, air conditioning		1.53	2.42	3.41	4.90%	5.60%	9.50%	
	2900		Electrical		1.69	2.49	3.91	5.70%	7.70%	9.90%	
	3100		Total: Mechanical & Electrical		3.51	5.50	8.35	11.70%	16.40%	22.10%	

HOW TO USE ASSEMBLIES COST TABLES

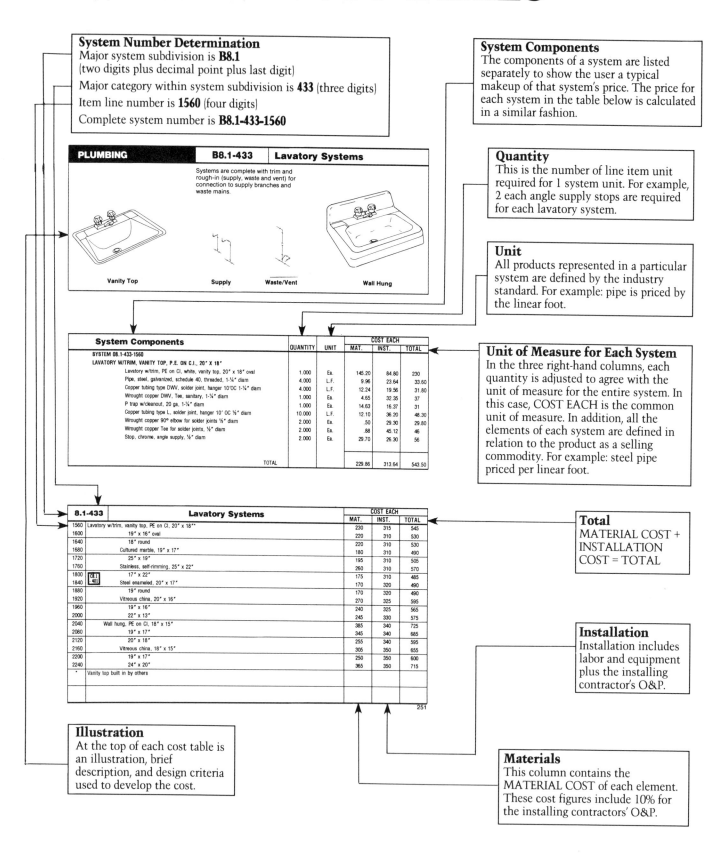

System Number Determination
Major system subdivision is **B8.1**
(two digits plus decimal point plus last digit)
Major category within system subdivision is **433** (three digits)
Item line number is **1560** (four digits)
Complete system number is **B8.1-433-1560**

System Components
The components of a system are listed separately to show the user a typical makeup of that system's price. The price for each system in the table below is calculated in a similar fashion.

Quantity
This is the number of line item unit required for 1 system unit. For example, 2 each angle supply stops are required for each lavatory system.

Unit
All products represented in a particular system are defined by the industry standard. For example: pipe is priced by the linear foot.

Unit of Measure for Each System
In the three right-hand columns, each quantity is adjusted to agree with the unit of measure for the entire system. In this case, COST EACH is the common unit of measure. In addition, all the elements of each system are defined in relation to the product as a selling commodity. For example: steel pipe priced per linear foot.

Total
MATERIAL COST + INSTALLATION COST = TOTAL

Installation
Installation includes labor and equipment plus the installing contractor's O&P.

Materials
This column contains the MATERIAL COST of each element. These cost figures include 10% for the installing contractors' O&P.

Illustration
At the top of each cost table is an illustration, brief description, and design criteria used to develop the cost.

SECTION B
ASSEMBLIES COSTS

TABLE OF CONTENTS

Section B of this book provides the costs of construction "assemblies" made up by combining unit prices, including overhead and profit, from Section A.

The System Components at the head of each table show typical unit price elements that are combined to create the single total cost for each line in the table.

By choosing the Systems lines with characteristics nearest to those required by your job, an accurate estimate can be compiled quickly.

Assemblies Estimates are especially useful for preparing budget estimates, preparing feasibility studies, comparing the cost of optional construction methods, and checking the magnitude of unit price estimates.

REF. NO.		PAGE
B8.1-000	**PLUMBING**	238
B8.1-010	Example of Plumbing Calculation	238
B8.1-100	**Hot Water**	239
B8.1-110	Electric Residential	239
B8.1-120	Gas Residential	240
B8.1-130	Oil Residential	241
B8.1-160	Electric Commercial	242
B8.1-170	Gas Commercial	243
B8.1-180	Oil Commercial	244
B8.1-300	**Storm Drainage**	245
B8.1-310	Roof Drains	245
B8.1-400	**Plumbing Fixtures**	247
B8.1-410	Bathtub	247
B8.1-420	Drinking Fountain	248
B8.1-431	Kitchen sink	249
B8.1-432	Laundry sink	250
B8.1-433	Lavatory	251
B8.1-434	Laboratory & Service Sink	252
B8.1-440	Shower	254
B8.1-450	Urinal	255
B8.1-460	Water Cooler	256
B8.1-470	Water Closet	257
B8.1-500	**Gang/Group Fixtures**	258
B8.1-510	Water Closets	258
B8.1-530	Urinals	259
B8.1-560	Wash Fountains	260
B8.1-580	Lavatories	261

REF. NO.		PAGE
B8.1-600	**Bathroom Systems**	262
B8.1-620	Two Fixture	262
B8.1-630	Three Fixture	263
B8.1-640	Four Fixture	264
B8.1-650	Five Fixture	265
B8.2-000	**FIRE PROTECTION**	266
B8.2-100	**Sprinkler Systems**	266
B8.2-110	Wet Pipe	266
B8.2-120	Dry Pipe	269
B8.2-130	Preaction	272
B8.2-140	Deluge	275
B8.2-150	Firecycle	278
B8.2-300	**Standpipe Systems**	281
B8.2-310	Wet Standpipe Risers	281
B8.2-320	Dry Standpipe Risers	283
B8.2-390	Standpipe Equipment	285
B8.2-800	**Special Systems**	286
B8.2-810	Halon Fire Suppression	286
B8.3-000	**HEATING**	287
B8.3-100	**Hydronic Systems**	287
B8.3-110	Electric Boilers Residential	287
B8.3-151	Fin Tube Residential	288
B8.3-600	**Solar Systems Domestic Hot Water**	289
B8.3-610	Closed Loop Hot Water, Immersed Exchanger	290
B8.3-620	Closed Loop Hot Water, External Exchanger	292

REF. NO.		PAGE
B8.3-630	Drainback Hot Water	294
B8.3-640	Draindown Hot Water	296
B8.3-650	Recirculation Hot Water	298
B8.3-660	Thermosyphon Hot Water	300
B8.3-700	**Solar Systems Space Heat and Special**	302
B8.3-710	Closed Loop	302
B8.3-720	Swimming Pool Heater	304
B8.3-730	Air to Water Exchanger Hot Water	306
B8.3-740	Air to Water Exchanger Space/H.W.	308
B8.5-000	**SPECIAL SYSTEMS**	310
B8.5-110	Garage Exhaust	310
B12.3-000	**Utilities**	311
B12.3-110	Trenching	311
B12.3-310	Pipe Bedding	314
B12.3-510	Drainage & Sewage Piping	316
B12.3-520	Gas Service Piping	318
B12.3-530	Subdrainage Piping	319
B12.3-540	Water Distribution Piping	320
B12.3-710	Manholes & Catch Basins	321
B12.3-900	Septic Systems	323
B12.3-922	Fire Hydrants	324
B12.3-925	Water Service	326
B12.7-910	Site Irrigation	328
B12.7-950	Swimming Pools	331

PLUMBING — B8.1-010 — Sample Estimate

Example of Plumbing Cost Calculations: The bathroom system includes the individual fixtures such as bathtub, lavatory, shower and water closet. These fixtures are listed below as separate items merely as a checklist.

8.1-010 Plumbing Systems 20 Unit, 2 Story Apartment Building

	FIXTURE	SYSTEM	LINE	QUANTITY	UNIT	COST EACH		
						MAT.	INST.	TOTAL
0440	Bathroom	B8.1-630	3640	20	Ea.	18,200	22,900	41,100
0480	Bathtub							
0520	Booster pump[1]	not req'd.						
0560	Drinking fountain							
0600	Garbage disposal[1]	not incl.						
0660								
0680	Grease interceptor							
0720	Water heater	B8.1-170	2140	1	Ea.	3,750	1,425	5,175
0760	Kitchen sink	B8.1-431	1960	20	Ea.	9,800	7,350	17,150
0800	Laundry sink	B8.1-432	1840	4	Ea.	2,475	1,450	3,925
0840	Lavatory							
0900								
0920	Roof drain, 1 floor	B8.1-310	4200	2	Ea.	485	755	1,240
0960	Roof drain, add'l floor	B8.1-310	4240	20	L.F.	88	190	278
1000	Service sink	B8.1-434	4300	1	Ea.	575	510	1,085
1040	Sewage ejector[1]	not req'd.						
1080	Shower							
1100								
1160	Sump pump							
1200	Urinal							
1240	Water closet							
1320								
1360	SUB TOTAL					35,400	34,500	69,900
1480	Water controls	C8.1-031		10%[2]		3,550	3,450	7,000
1520	Pipe & fittings[3]	C8.1-031		30%[2]		10,600	10,400	21,000
1560	Other							
1600	Quality/complexity	C8.1-031		15%[2]		5,300	5,175	10,475
1680								
1720	TOTAL					55,000	53,500	108,500

[1] **Note:** Cost for items such as booster pumps, backflow preventers, sewage ejectors, water meters, etc., may be obtained from Sections 15.1, 15.2 and 15.3. Water controls, pipe and fittings, and the Quality/Complexity factors come from Table C8.1-031.

[2] Percentage of sub total.

[3] Long easily discernable runs of pipe would be more accurately priced from Section 15.1. If this is done, reduce the miscellaneous percentage in proportion.

PLUMBING — B8.1-110 — Electric Water Heaters - Resi.

Installation includes piping and fittings within 10' of heater. Electric water heaters do not require venting.

1 Kilowatt hour will raise:

Gallons of Water	Degrees F	Gallons of Water	Degrees F
4.1	100°	6.8	60°
4.5	90	8.2	50
5.1	80	10.0	40
5.9	70		

System Components	QUANTITY	UNIT	COST EACH MAT.	COST EACH INST.	COST EACH TOTAL
SYSTEM 08.1-110-1780					
ELECTRIC WATER HEATER, RESIDENTIAL, 100° F RISE					
10 GALLON TANK, 7 GPH					
Water heater, residential electric, glass lined tank, 10 Gal	1.000	Ea.	150.70	129.30	280
Copper tubing, type L, solder joint, hanger 10' OC ½" diam	30.000	L.F.	36.30	108.60	144.90
Wrought copper 90° elbow for solder joints ½" diam.	4.000	Ea.	1	58.60	59.60
Wrought copper Tee for solder joints, ½" diam	2.000	Ea.	.88	45.12	46
Wrought copper union for soldered joints, ½" diam	2.000	Ea.	4.16	30.84	35
Valve, gate, bronze, 125 lb, NRS, soldered ½" diam	2.000	Ea.	23.98	24.02	48
Relief valve, bronze, press & temp, self-close, ¾" IPS	1.000	Ea.	48.40	10.60	59
Wrought copper adapter, CTS to MPT ¾" IPS	1.000	Ea.	.83	13.97	14.80
Copper tubing, type L, solder joints, ¾" diam	1.000	L.F.	1.82	3.83	5.65
Wrought copper 90° elbow for solder joints ¾" diam	1.000	Ea.	.57	15.43	16
TOTAL			268.64	440.31	708.95

8.1-110	Electric Water Heaters - Residential Systems	MAT.	INST.	TOTAL
1760	Electric water heater, residential, 100° F rise			
1780	10 gallon tank, 7 GPH	270	440	710
1820	20 gallon tank, 7 GPH	325	470	795
1860	30 gallon tank, 7 GPH	355	490	845
1900	40 gallon tank, 8 GPH	405	545	950
1940	52 gallon tank, 10 GPH	430	550	980
1980	66 gallon tank, 13 GPH	630	625	1,255
2020	80 gallon tank, 16 GPH	685	650	1,335
2060	120 gallon tank, 23 GPH	1,100	765	1,865

PLUMBING — B8.1-120 — Gas Fired Water Htrs. - Resi.

Installation includes piping and fittings within 10' of heater. Gas heaters require vent piping (not included with these units).

System Components	QUANTITY	UNIT	COST EACH MAT.	COST EACH INST.	TOTAL
SYSTEM 08.1-120-2220					
GAS FIRED WATER HEATER, RESIDENTIAL, 100° F RISE					
20 GALLON, 25 GPH					
Water heater, residential, gas, glass lined tank, 20 Gal	1.000	Ea.	187	138	325
Copper tubing, type L, solder joint, hanger 10' OC, ¾" diam	32.000	L.F.	58.24	122.56	180.80
Wrought copper 90° elbow for solder joints ¾" diam	5.000	Ea.	2.85	77.15	80
Wrought copper Tee for solder joints, ¾" diam	2.000	Ea.	2	48	50
Wrought copper union for soldered joints, ¾" diam	2.000	Ea.	5.46	32.54	38
Valve, bronze, 125 lb, NRS, soldered ¾" diam	2.000	Ea.	31.68	30.32	62
Relief valve, press & temp, bronze, self-close, ¾" IPS	1.000	Ea.	48.40	10.60	59
Wrought copper, adapter, CTS to MPT ¾" IPS	1.000	Ea.	.83	13.97	14.80
Pipe steel black, schedule 40, threaded, ½" diam	10.000	L.F.	9.90	46.60	56.50
Pipe, 90° elbow, malleable iron black, 150 lb, threaded, ½" diam	2.000	Ea.	1.12	38.88	40
Pipe, union with brass seat, malleable iron black, ½" diam	1.000	Ea.	2.19	20.81	23
Valve, gas stop w/o check, brass, ½" IPS	1.000	Ea.	8.09	11.91	20
TOTAL			357.76	591.34	949.10

8.1-120	Gas Fired Water Heaters - Residential Systems	COST EACH MAT.	COST EACH INST.	TOTAL
2200	Gas fired water heater, residential, 100° F rise			
2220	20 gallon tank, 25 GPH	360	590	950
2260	30 gallon tank, 32 GPH [C8.1-102]	365	600	965
2300	40 gallon tank, 32 GPH	420	675	1,095
2340	50 gallon tank, 63 GPH	470	680	1,150
2380	75 gallon tank, 63 GPH	725	765	1,490
2420	100 gallon tank, 63 GPH	1,050	800	1,850

PLUMBING — B8.1-130 — Oil Fired Water Heaters - Resi.

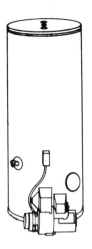

Installation includes piping and fittings within 10' of heater. Oil fired heaters require vent piping (not included in these prices).

System Components	QUANTITY	UNIT	COST EACH MAT.	COST EACH INST.	TOTAL
SYSTEM 08.1-130-2220 OIL FIRED WATER HEATER, RESIDENTIAL, 100° F RISE 30 GALLON TANK, 103 GPH					
Water heater, residential, oil glass lined tank, 30 Gal	1.000	Ea.	740.30	144.70	885
Copper tubing, type L, solder joint, hanger 10' O.C. ¾" diam	33.000	L.F.	60.06	126.39	186.45
Wrought copper 90° elbow for solder joints ¾" diam	5.000	Ea.	2.85	77.15	80
Wrought copper Tee for solder joints, ¾" diam	2.000	Ea.	2	48	50
Wrought copper union for soldered joints, ¾" diam	2.000	Ea.	5.46	32.54	38
Valve, gate, bronze, 125 lb, NRS, soldered ¾" diam	2.000	Ea.	31.68	30.32	62
Relief valve, bronze, press & temp, self-close, ¾" IPS	1.000	Ea.	48.40	10.60	59
Wrought copper adapter, CTS to MPT, ¾" IPS	1.000	Ea.	.83	13.97	14.80
Copper tubing, type L, solder joint, hanger 10' OC ⅜" diam	10.000	L.F.	10.90	34.90	45.80
Wrought copper 90° elbow for solder joints ⅜" diam	2.000	Ea.	1.32	26.68	28
Valve, globe, fusible, ⅜" diam	1.000	Ea.	3.85	12.25	16.10
TOTAL			907.65	557.50	1,465.15

8.1-130	Oil Fired Water Heaters - Residential Systems	MAT.	INST.	TOTAL
2200	Oil fired water heater, residential, 100° F rise			
2220	30 gallon tank, 103 GPH	910	560	1,470
2260	50 gallon tank, 145 GPH	1,200	640	1,840
2300	70 gallon tank, 164 GPH	1,425	705	2,130
2340	85 gallon tank, 181 GPH	1,950	715	2,665

PLUMBING — B8.1-160 — Elec. Water Htrs. - Comm.

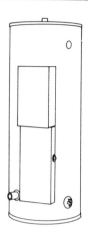

Systems below include piping and fittings within 10' of heater. Electric water heaters do not require venting.

System Components	QUANTITY	UNIT	MAT.	INST.	TOTAL
SYSTEM 08.1-160-1820					
ELECTRIC WATER HEATER, COMMERCIAL, 100° F RISE					
50 GALLON TANK, 9 KW, 37 GPH					
Water heater, commercial, electric, 50 Gal, 9 KW, 37 GPH	1.000	Ea.	1,606	169	1,775
Copper tubing, type L, solder joint, hanger 10' OC, ¾" diam	34.000	L.F.	61.88	130.22	192.10
Wrought copper 90° elbow for solder joints ¾" diam	5.000	Ea.	2.85	77.15	80
Wrought copper Tee for solder joints, ¾" diam	2.000	Ea.	2	48	50
Wrought copper union for soldered joints, ¾" diam	2.000	Ea.	5.46	32.54	38
Valve, gate, bronze, 125 lb, NRS, soldered ¾" diam	2.000	Ea.	31.68	30.32	62
Relief valve, bronze, press & temp, self-close, ¾" IPS	1.000	Ea.	48.40	10.60	59
Wrought copper adapter, copper tubing to male, ¾" IPS	1.000	Ea.	.83	13.97	14.80
TOTAL			1,759.10	511.80	2,270.90

8.1-160	Electric Water Heaters - Commercial Systems	MAT.	INST.	TOTAL
1800	Electric water heater, commercial, 100° F rise			
1820	50 gallon tank, 9 KW 37 GPH	1,750	510	2,260
1860	80 gal, 12 KW 49 GPH	2,275	620	2,895
1900	36 KW 147 GPH	3,125	665	3,790
1940	120 gal, 36 KW 147 GPH	3,350	725	4,075
1980	150 gal, 120 KW 490 GPH	11,500	810	12,310
2020	200 gal, 120 KW 490 GPH	12,000	775	12,775
2060	250 gal, 150 KW 615 GPH	13,400	935	14,335
2100	300 gal, 180 KW 738 GPH	14,600	995	15,595
2140	350 gal, 30 KW 123 GPH	10,200	1,100	11,300
2180	180 KW 738 GPH	15,000	1,075	16,075
2220	500 gal, 30 KW 123 GPH	13,200	1,250	14,450
2260	240 KW 984 GPH	20,900	1,300	22,200
2300	700 gal, 30 KW 123 GPH	16,000	1,450	17,450
2340	300 KW 1230 GPH	25,400	1,450	26,850
2380	1000 gal, 60 KW 245 GPH	19,400	2,050	21,450
2420	480 KW 1970 GPH	34,200	2,025	36,225
2460	1500 gal, 60 KW 245 GPH	28,700	2,525	31,225
2500	480 KW 1970 GPH	40,600	2,425	43,025

PLUMBING — B8.1-170 — Gas Fired Water Htrs. - Comm.

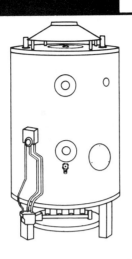

Units may be installed in multiples for increased capacity.

Included below is the heater with self-energizing gas controls, safety pilots, insulated jacket, hi-limit aquastat and pressure relief valve.

Installation includes piping and fittings within 10' of heater. Gas heaters require vent piping (not included in these prices).

System Components	QUANTITY	UNIT	COST EACH MAT.	COST EACH INST.	COST EACH TOTAL
SYSTEM 08.1-170-1780					
GAS FIRED WATER HEATER, COMMERCIAL, 100° F RISE					
75.5 MBH INPUT, 63 GPH					
Water heater, commercial, gas, 75.5 MBH, 63 GPH	1.000	Ea.	822.80	202.20	1,025
Copper tubing, type L, solder joint, hanger 10' OC, 1-¼" diam	30.000	L.F.	101.40	152.10	253.50
Wrought copper 90° elbow for solder joints 1-¼" diam	4.000	Ea.	10.52	77.48	88
Wrought copper Tee for solder joints, 1-¼" diam	2.000	Ea.	11	65	76
Wrought copper union for soldered joints, 1-¼" diam	2.000	Ea.	13.64	42.36	56
Valve, gate, bronze, 125 lb, NRS, soldered 1-¼" diam	2.000	Ea.	50.60	39.40	90
Relief valve, bronze, press & temp, self-close, ¾" IPS	1.000	Ea.	48.40	10.60	59
Copper tubing, type L, solder joints, ¾" diam	8.000	L.F.	14.56	30.64	45.20
Wrought copper 90° elbow for solder joints ¾" diam	1.000	Ea.	.57	15.43	16
Wrought copper, adapter, CTS to MPT, ¾" IPS	1.000	Ea.	.83	13.97	14.80
Pipe steel black, schedule 40, threaded, ¾" diam	10.000	L.F.	11.60	47.90	59.50
Pipe, 90° elbow, malleable iron black, 150 lb threaded, ¾" diam	2.000	Ea.	1.24	42.76	44
Pipe, union with brass seat, malleable iron black, ¾" diam	1.000	Ea.	2.23	22.77	25
Valve, gas stop w/o check, brass, ¾" IPS	1.000	Ea.	8.86	13.14	22
TOTAL			1,098.25	775.75	1,874

8.1-170	Gas Fired Water Heaters - Commercial Systems	MAT.	INST.	TOTAL
1760	Gas fired water heater, commercial, 100° F rise			
1780	75.5 MBH input, 63 GPH	1,100	775	1,875
1860	100 MBH input, 91 GPH	1,350	825	2,175
1980	155 MBH input, 150 GPH	1,875	940	2,815
2060	200 MBH input, 192 GPH	2,425	1,150	3,575
2140	300 MBH input, 278 GPH	3,750	1,425	5,175
2180	390 MBH input, 374 GPH	4,225	1,425	5,650
2220	500 MBH input, 480 GPH	5,600	1,550	7,150
2260	600 MBH input, 576 GPH	6,325	1,675	8,000
2300	800 MBH input, 768 GPH	7,450	1,850	9,300
2340	1000 MBH input, 960 GPH	8,750	1,875	10,625
2420	1500 MBH input, 1440 GPH	13,400	2,400	15,800
2460	1800 MBH input, 1730 GPH	15,000	2,725	17,725
2500	2450 MBH input, 2350 GPH	19,600	3,125	22,725
2540	3000 MBH input, 2880 GPH	23,700	3,750	27,450
2580	3750 MBH input, 3600 GPH	29,500	3,900	33,400

PLUMBING B8.1-180 Oil Fired Water Htrs. - Comm.

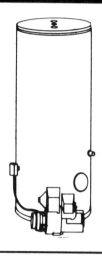

Units may be installed in multiples for increased capacity.

Included below is the heater, wired-in flame retention burners, cadmium cell primary controls, hi-limit controls, ASME pressure relief valves, draft controls, and insulated jacket.

Oil fired water heater systems include piping and fittings within 10' of heater. Oil fired heaters require vent piping (not included in these systems).

Systems Components	QUANTITY	UNIT	COST EACH		
			MAT.	INST.	TOTAL
SYSTEM 08.1-180-1820					
OIL FIRED WATER HEATER, COMMERCIAL, 100° F RISE					
103 MBH OUTPUT, 116 GPH					
Water heater, commercial, oil, 103 MBH	1.000	Ea.	1,523.50	276.50	1,800
Copper tubing, type L, solder joint, hanger 10' OC, ¾" diam	34.000	L.F.	61.88	130.22	192.10
Wrought copper 90° elbow for solder joints ¾" diam	5.000	Ea.	2.85	77.15	80
Wrought copper Tee for solder joints, ¾" diam	2.000	Ea.	2	48	50
Wrought copper union for soldered joints, ¾" diam	2.000	Ea.	5.46	32.54	38
Valve, bronze, 125 lb, NRS, soldered ¾" diam	2.000	Ea.	31.68	30.32	62
Relief valve, bronze, press & temp, self-close, ¾" IPS	1.000	Ea.	48.40	10.60	59
Wrought copper adapter, copper tubing to male, ¾" IPS	1.000	Ea.	.83	13.97	14.80
Copper tubing, type L, solder joint, hanger 10' OC, ⅜" diam	10.000	L.F.	10.90	34.90	45.80
Wrought copper 90° elbow for solder joints ⅜" diam	2.000	Ea.	1.32	26.68	28
Valve, globe, fusible, ⅜" IPS	1.000	Ea.	3.85	12.25	16.10
TOTAL			1,692.67	693.13	2,385.80

8.1-180		Oil Fired Water Heaters - Commercial Systems	COST EACH		
			MAT.	INST.	TOTAL
1800		Oil fired water heater, commercial, 100° F rise			
1820		103 MBH output, 116 GPH	1,700	695	2,395
1900	C8.1-101	134 MBH output, 161 GPH	1,925	870	2,795
1940		161 MBH output, 192 GPH	2,300	1,025	3,325
1980	C8.1-102	187 MBH output, 224 GPH	2,475	1,150	3,625
2060		262 MBH output, 315 GPH	3,100	1,325	4,425
2100		341 MBH output, 409 GPH	4,075	1,425	5,500
2140		420 MBH output, 504 GPH	4,625	1,525	6,150
2180		525 MBH output, 630 GPH	5,875	1,725	7,600
2220		630 MBH output, 756 GPH	6,500	1,750	8,250
2260		735 MBH output, 880 GPH	8,000	2,000	10,000
2300		840 MBH output, 1000 GPH	9,050	2,000	11,050
2340		1050 MBH output, 1260 GPH	10,900	2,025	12,925
2380		1365 MBH output, 1640 GPH	13,800	2,325	16,125
2420		1680 MBH output, 2000 GPH	16,400	2,950	19,350
2460		2310 MBH output, 2780 GPH	20,900	3,650	24,550
2500		2835 MBH output, 3400 GPH	25,700	3,600	29,300
2540		3150 MBH output, 3780 GPH	27,775	5,025	32,800

PLUMBING — B8.1-310 — Storm Drainage - Roof Drains

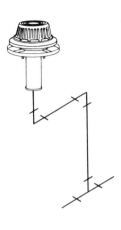

Design Assumptions: Vertical conductor size is based on a maximum rate of rainfall of 4" per hour. To convert roof area to other rates multiply "Max S.F. Roof Area" shown by four and divide the result by desired local rate. The answer is the local roof area that may be handled by the indicated pipe diameter.

Basic cost is for roof drain, 10' of vertical leader and 10' of horizontal, plus connection to the main.

Pipe Dia.	Max. S.F. Roof Area	Gallons per Min.
2"	544	23
3"	1610	67
4"	3460	144
5"	6280	261
6"	10,200	424
8"	22,000	913

System Components	QUANTITY	UNIT	COST EACH MAT.	INST.	TOTAL
SYSTEM 081-310-1880					
ROOF DRAIN, DWV PVC PIPE, 2" DIAM., 10' HIGH					
Drain, roof, main, PVC, dome type 2" pipe size	1.000	Ea.	38.50	37.50	76
Clamp, roof drain, underdeck	1.000	Ea.	10.18	21.82	32
Pipe, Tee, PVC DWV, schedule 40, 2" pipe size	1.000	Ea.	1.60	31.40	33
Pipe, PVC, DWV, schedule 40, 2" diam.	20.000	L.F.	28	179	207
Pipe, elbow, PVC schedule 40, 2" diam.	2.000	Ea.	2.14	37.66	39.80
TOTAL			80.42	307.38	387.80

8.1-310	Roof Drain Systems	COST PER SYSTEM MAT.	INST.	TOTAL
1880	Roof drain, DWV PVC, 2" diam., piping, 10' high	80	305	385
1920	For each additional foot add	1.40	8.95	10.35
1960	3" diam., 10' high	115	370	485
2000	For each additional foot add	2.54	9.95	12.49
2040	4" diam., 10' high	150	415	565
2080	For each additional foot add	3.52	11	14.52
2120	5" diam., 10' high	320	445	765
2160	For each additional foot add	5.25	12.25	17.50
2200	6" diam., 10' high	405	530	935
2240	For each additional foot add	6.50	13.50	20
2280	8" diam., 10' high	660	850	1,510
2320	For each additional foot add	10.50	17.50	28
3940	C.I., soil, single hub, service wt., 2" diam. piping, 10' high	170	320	490
3980	For each additional foot add	2.42	8.40	10.82
4120	3" diam., 10' high	210	350	560
4160	For each additional foot add	3.42	8.80	12.22
4200	4" diam., 10' high	245	375	620
4240	For each additional foot add	4.42	9.60	14.02
4280	5" diam., 10' high	320	420	740
4320	For each additional foot add	6	10.80	16.80
4360	6" diam., 10' high	415	450	865
4400	For each additional foot add	7.15	11.25	18.40
4440	8" diam., 10' high	680	930	1,610
4480	For each additional foot add	11.85	19.15	31
6040	Steel galv. sch 40 threaded, 2" diam. piping, 10' high	210	310	520
6080	For each additional foot add	3.88	8.20	12.08

PLUMBING — B8.1-310 Storm Drainage - Roof Drains

8.1-310 Roof Drain Systems

		MAT.	INST.	TOTAL
6120	3" diam., 10' high	335	440	775
6160	For each additional foot add	8.15	11.85	20
6200	4" diam., 10' high	460	570	1,030
6240	For each additional foot add	12.40	14.60	27
6280	5" diam., 10' high	770	725	1,495
6320	For each additional foot add	23	20	43
6360	6" diam, 10' high	995	900	1,895
6400	For each additional foot add	29	27	56
6440	8" diam., 10' high	1,550	1,225	2,775
6480	For each additional foot add	42	31	73

(Cost Per System)

PLUMBING — B8.1-410 Bathtub Systems

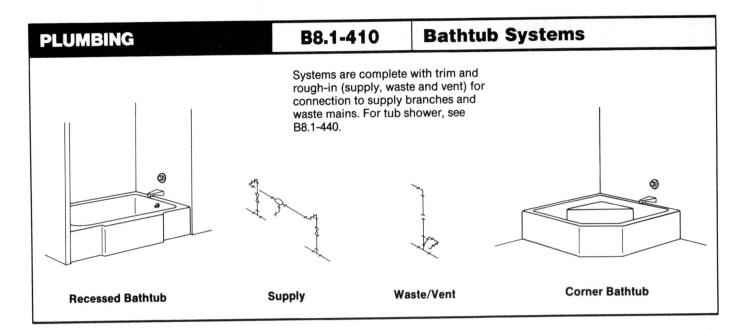

Systems are complete with trim and rough-in (supply, waste and vent) for connection to supply branches and waste mains. For tub shower, see B8.1-440.

Recessed Bathtub   Supply   Waste/Vent   Corner Bathtub

System Components	QUANTITY	UNIT	COST EACH MAT.	COST EACH INST.	TOTAL
SYSTEM 08.1-410-1960					
BATHTUB RECESSED, PORCELAIN ENAMEL ON CAST IRON, 42" X 37"					
Bath tub, porcelain enamel on cast iron, w/fittings, 42" x 37"	1.000	Ea.	588.50	106.50	695
Pipe, steel, galvanized, schedule 40, threaded, 1-¼" diam	4.000	L.F.	9.96	23.64	33.60
Pipe, CI, soil, no hub, w/coupling 10' OC, hanger 5' OC, 4" diam	3.000	L.F.	16.74	27.36	44.10
Combination Y and ⅛ bend for C.I. soil pipe, no hub, 4" pipe size	1.000	Ea.	12.15		12.15
Drum trap, 3" x 5", copper, 1-½" diam	1.000	Ea.	18.26	18.74	37
Copper tubing, type L, solder joints, hangers 10' OC ½" diam	10.000	L.F.	12.10	36.20	48.30
Wrought copper 90° elbow for solder joints, ½" diam	2.000	Ea.	.50	29.30	29.80
Wrought copper Tee for solder joints, ½" diam	2.000	Ea.	.88	45.12	46
Stop, angle supply, ½" diam	2.000	Ea.	29.70	26.30	56
Copper tubing type DWV, solder joint, hanger 10' OC 1-½" diam	3.000	L.F.	11.34	16.26	27.60
Pipe coupling, standard, C.I. soil no hub, 4" pipe size	2.000	Ea.	6.80	32	38.80
TOTAL			706.93	361.42	1,068.35

8.1-410	Bathtub Systems	MAT.	INST.	TOTAL
1960	Bathtub, recessed, P.E. on CI., 42" x 37"	705	360	1,065
2000	48" x 42"	1,050	390	1,440
2040	72" x 36"	1,125	430	1,555
2080	Mat bottom, 5' long	420	375	795
2120	5'-6" long	850	390	1,240
2160	Corner, 48" x 42"	1,200	375	1,575
2200	Formed steel, enameled, 4'-6" long	330	345	675
2240	5' long	310	350	660

PLUMBING — B8.1-420 — Drinking Fountain Systems

Systems are complete with trim and rough-in (supply, waste and vent) to connect to supply branches and waste mains.

Wall Mounted, No Back

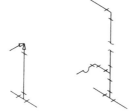

Supply   **Waste/Vent**

Wall Mounted, Low Back

System Components	QUANTITY	UNIT	MAT.	INST.	TOTAL
SYSTEM 08.1-420-1800					
DRINKING FOUNTAIN, ONE BUBBLER, WALL MOUNTED					
NON RECESSED, BRONZE, NO BACK					
Drinking fountain, wall mount, bronze, 1 bubbler	1.000	Ea.	633.60	71.40	705
Copper tubing, type L, solder joint, hanger 10' OC ⅜" diam	5.000	L.F.	5.45	17.45	22.90
Stop, supply, straight, chrome, ⅜" diam	1.000	Ea.	3.58	12.22	15.80
Wrought copper 90° elbow for solder joints ⅜" diam	1.000	Ea.	.66	13.34	14
Wrought copper Tee for solder joints, ⅜" diam	1.000	Ea.	1.60	21.40	23
Copper tubing, DWV, solder joint, hanger 10' OC 1-¼" diam	4.000	L.F.	12.24	19.56	31.80
P trap, standard, copper drainage, 1-¼" diam	1.000	Ea.	14.63	16.37	31
Wrought copper, DWV, Tee, sanitary, 1-¼" diam	1.000	Ea.	4.65	32.35	37
TOTAL			676.41	204.09	880.50

8.1-420	Drinking Fountain Systems	MAT.	INST.	TOTAL
1740	Drinking fountain, one bubbler, wall mounted			
1760	Non recessed			
1800	Bronze, no back	675	205	880
1840	Cast iron, enameled, low back	320	205	525
1880	Fiberglass, 12" back	355	205	560
1920	Stainless steel, no back	650	210	860
1960	Semi-recessed, poly marble	415	205	620
2040	Stainless steel	375	210	585
2080	Vitreous china	345	205	550
2120	Full recessed, poly marble	520	205	725
2200	Stainless steel	430	210	640
2240	Floor mounted, pedestal type, aluminum	385	280	665
2320	Bronze	795	280	1,075
2360	Stainless steel	800	280	1,080

PLUMBING — B8.1-431 — Kitchen Sink Systems

Systems are complete with trim and rough-in (supply, waste and vent) to connect to supply branches and waste mains.

Countertop Single Bowl

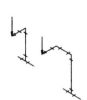
Supply

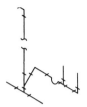
Waste/Vent

Countertop Double Bowl

System Components	QUANTITY	UNIT	MAT.	INST.	TOTAL
SYSTEM 08.1-431-1720					
KITCHEN SINK W/TRIM, COUNTERTOP, P.E. ON C.I., 24" X 21", SINGLE BOWL					
Kitchen sink, counter top, PE on CI, 1 bowl, 24" x 21" OD	1.000	Ea.	184.80	95.20	280
Pipe, steel, galvanized, schedule 40, threaded, 1-¼" diam	4.000	L.F.	9.96	23.64	33.60
Copper tubing, type DWV, solder, hangers 10' OC 1-½" diam	6.000	L.F.	22.68	32.52	55.20
Wrought copper, DWV, Tee, sanitary, 1-½" diam	1.000	Ea.	4.28	36.72	41
P trap, standard, copper, 1-½" diam	1.000	Ea.	17.11	16.89	34
Copper tubing, type L, solder joints, hangers 10' OC ½" diam	10.000	L.F.	12.10	36.20	48.30
Wrought copper 90° elbow for solder joints ½" diam	2.000	Ea.	.50	29.30	29.80
Wrought copper Tee for solder joints, ½" diam	2.000	Ea.	.88	45.12	46
Stop, angle supply, ½" diam	2.000	Ea.	29.70	26.30	56
TOTAL			282.01	341.89	623.90

8.1-431	Kitchen Sink Systems	MAT.	INST.	TOTAL
1720	Kitchen sink w/trim, countertop, PE on CI, 24"x21", single bowl	280	340	620
1760	30" x 21" single bowl	305	340	645
1800	[C8.1-201] 32" x 21" double bowl	340	370	710
1840	42" x 21" double bowl	480	375	855
1880	[C8.1-202] Stainless steel, 19" x 18" single bowl	345	340	685
1920	25" x 22" single bowl	370	345	715
1960	[C8.1-102] 33" x 22" double bowl	490	370	860
2000	43" x 22" double bowl	530	375	905
2040	44" x 22" triple bowl	495	385	880
2080	44" x 24" corner double bowl	390	370	760
2120	Steel, enameled, 24" x 21" single bowl	210	340	550
2160	32" x 21" double bowl	240	365	605
2240	Raised deck, PE on CI, 32" x 21", dual level, double bowl	440	465	905
2280	42" x 21" dual level, triple bowl	575	505	1,080

PLUMBING — B8.1-432 — Laundry Sink Systems

Systems are complete with trim and rough-in (supply, waste and vent) for connection to supply branches and waste mains.

Single Compartment Sink — **Supply** — **Waste/Vent** — **Double Compartment Sink**

System Components	QUANTITY	UNIT	MAT.	INST.	TOTAL
SYSTEM 08.1-432-1760					
LAUNDRY SINK W/TRIM, PE ON CI, BLACK IRON FRAME					
24" X 20" OD, SINGLE COMPARTMENT					
Laundry sink PE on CI w/trim & frame, 24" x 20" OD, 1 compartment	1.000	Ea.	313.50	86.50	400
Pipe, steel, galvanized, schedule 40, threaded, 1-¼" diam	4.000	L.F.	9.96	23.64	33.60
Copper tubing, type DWV, solder joint, hanger 10' OC 1-½" diam	6.000	L.F.	22.68	32.52	55.20
Wrought copper, DWV, Tee, sanitary, 1-½" diam	1.000	Ea.	4.28	36.72	41
P trap, standard, copper, 1-½" diam	1.000	Ea.	17.11	16.89	34
Copper tubing type L, solder joints, hangers 10' OC, ½" diam	10.000	L.F.	12.10	36.20	48.30
Wrought copper 90° elbow for solder joints ½" diam	2.000	Ea.	.50	29.30	29.80
Wrought copper Tee for solder joints, ½" diam	2.000	Ea.	.88	45.12	46
Stop, angle supply, ½" diam	2.000	Ea.	29.70	26.30	56
TOTAL			410.71	333.19	743.90

8.1-432	Laundry Sink Systems	MAT.	INST.	TOTAL
1740	Laundry sink w/trim, PE on CI, black iron frame			
1760	24" x 20", single compartment	410	335	745
1800	[C8.1-401] 24" x 23" single compartment	440	335	775
1840	48" x 21" double compartment	615	360	975
1920	Molded stone, on wall, 22" x 21" single compartment	250	335	585
1960	45" x 21" double compartment	345	365	710
2040	Plastic, on wall or legs, 18" x 23" single compartment	205	325	530
2080	20" x 24" single compartment	230	330	560
2120	36" x 23" double compartment	255	355	610
2160	40" x 24" double compartment	310	350	660
2200	Stainless steel, countertop, 22" x 17" single compartment	340	330	670
2240	19" x 22" single compartment	370	335	705
2280	33" x 22" double compartment	390	365	755

PLUMBING — B8.1-433 — Lavatory Systems

Systems are complete with trim and rough-in (supply, waste and vent) for connection to supply branches and waste mains.

Vanity Top   **Supply**   **Waste/Vent**   **Wall Hung**

System Components	QUANTITY	UNIT	COST EACH		
			MAT.	INST.	TOTAL
SYSTEM 08.1-433-1560					
LAVATORY W/TRIM, VANITY TOP, P.E. ON C.I., 20" X 18"					
Lavatory w/trim, PE on CI, white, vanity top, 20" x 18" oval	1.000	Ea.	145.20	84.80	230
Pipe, steel, galvanized, schedule 40, threaded, 1-¼" diam	4.000	L.F.	9.96	23.64	33.60
Copper tubing type DWV, solder joint, hanger 10'OC 1-¼" diam	4.000	L.F.	12.24	19.56	31.80
Wrought copper DWV, Tee, sanitary, 1-¼" diam	1.000	Ea.	4.65	32.35	37
P trap w/cleanout, 20 ga, 1-¼" diam	1.000	Ea.	14.63	16.37	31
Copper tubing type L, solder joint, hanger 10' OC ½" diam	10.000	L.F.	12.10	36.20	48.30
Wrought copper 90° elbow for solder joints ½" diam	2.000	Ea.	.50	29.30	29.80
Wrought copper Tee for solder joints, ½" diam	2.000	Ea.	.88	45.12	46
Stop, chrome, angle supply, ½" diam	2.000	Ea.	29.70	26.30	56
TOTAL			229.86	313.64	543.50

8.1-433	Lavatory Systems	COST EACH		
		MAT.	INST.	TOTAL
1560	Lavatory w/trim, vanity top, PE on CI, 20" x 18"*	230	315	545
1600	19" x 16" oval	220	310	530
1640	18" round	220	310	530
1680	Cultured marble, 19" x 17"	180	310	490
1720	25" x 19"	195	310	505
1760	Stainless, self-rimming, 25" x 22"	260	310	570
1800	17" x 22"	175	310	485
1840	Steel enameled, 20" x 17"	170	320	490
1880	19" round	170	320	490
1920	Vitreous china, 20" x 16"	270	325	595
1960	19" x 16"	240	325	565
2000	22" x 13"	245	330	575
2040	Wall hung, PE on CI, 18" x 15"	385	340	725
2080	19" x 17"	345	340	685
2120	20" x 18"	255	340	595
2160	Vitreous china, 18" x 15"	305	350	655
2200	19" x 17"	250	350	600
2240	24" x 20"	365	350	715
*	Vanity top built in by others			

PLUMBING — B8.1-434 — Laboratory Sink Systems

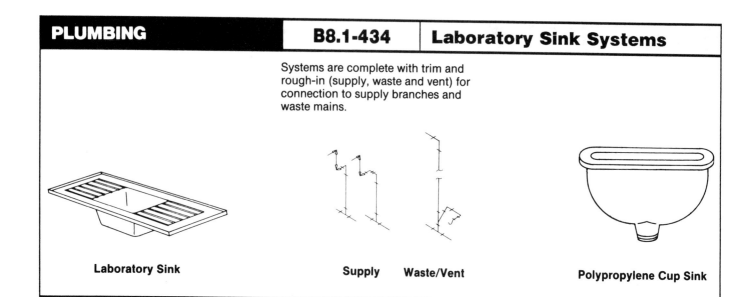

Systems are complete with trim and rough-in (supply, waste and vent) for connection to supply branches and waste mains.

Laboratory Sink — Supply — Waste/Vent — Polypropylene Cup Sink

System Components	QUANTITY	UNIT	MAT.	INST.	TOTAL
SYSTEM 08.1-434-1600					
LABORATORY SINK W/TRIM, POLYETHYLENE, SINGLE BOWL					
DOUBLE DRAINBOARD, 54" X 24" OD					
Sink w/trim, polyethylene, 1 bowl, 2 drainboards 54" x 24" OD	1.000	Ea.	797.50	177.50	975
Pipe, polypropylene, schedule 40, acid resistant 1-½" diam	10.000	L.F.	17.10	77.40	94.50
Tee, sanitary, polypropylene, acid resistant, 1-½" diam	1.000	Ea.	8.53	29.47	38
P trap, polypropylene, acid resistant, 1-½" diam	1.000	Ea.	18.37	17.63	36
Copper tubing type L, solder joint, hanger 10' OC ½" diam	10.000	L.F.	12.10	36.20	48.30
Wrought copper 90° elbow for solder joints ½" diam	2.000	Ea.	.50	29.30	29.80
Wrought copper Tee for solder joints, ½" diam	2.000	Ea.	.88	45.12	46
Stop, angle supply, chrome, ½" diam	2.000	Ea.	29.70	26.30	56
TOTAL			884.68	438.92	1,323.60

8.1-434	Laboratory Sink Systems	MAT.	INST.	TOTAL
1580	Laboratory sink w/trim, polyethylene, single bowl,			
1600	Double drainboard, 54" x 24" O.D.	885	440	1,325
1640	Single drainboard, 47" x 24" O.D.	825	440	1,265
1680	70" x 24" O.D.	940	435	1,375
1760	Flanged, 14-½" x 14-½" O.D.	295	390	685
1800	18-½" x 18-½" O.D.	330	395	725
1840	23-½" x 20-½" O.D.	380	395	775
1920	Polypropylene, cup sink, oval, 7" x 4" O.D.	165	345	510
1960	10" x 4-½" O.D.	180	350	530

PLUMBING — B8.1-434 Service Sink Systems

Service sink systems are complete with trim and rough-in (supply, waste and vent) to connect to supply branches and waste mains.

Wall Hung

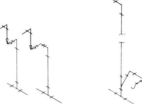

Supply   Waste/Vent

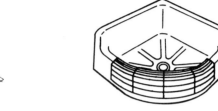

Corner, Floor

System Components	QUANTITY	UNIT	COST EACH MAT.	COST EACH INST.	COST EACH TOTAL
SYSTEM 08.1-434-4260					
SERVICE SINK, PE ON CI, CORNER FLOOR, 28"X28", W/RIM GUARD & TRIM					
Service sink, corner floor, PE on CI, 28" x 28", w/rim guard & trim	1.000	Ea.	385	120	505
Copper tubing type DWV, solder joint, hanger 10'OC 3" diam	6.000	L.F.	50.70	54.60	105.30
Copper tubing type DWV, solder joint, hanger 10'OC 2" diam	4.000	L.F.	20.08	26.72	46.80
Wrought copper DWV, Tee, sanitary, 3" diam	1.000	Ea.	15.57	75.43	91
P trap with cleanout & slip joint, copper 3" diam	1.000	Ea.	42.90	27.10	70
Copper tubing, type L, solder joints, hangers 10' OC, ½" diam	10.000	L.F.	12.10	36.20	48.30
Wrought copper 90° elbow for solder joints ½" diam	2.000	Ea.	.50	29.30	29.80
Wrought copper Tee for solder joints, ½" diam	2.000	Ea.	.88	45.12	46
Stop, angle supply, chrome, ½" diam	2.000	Ea.	29.70	26.30	56
TOTAL			557.43	440.77	998.20

8.1-434	Service Sink Systems	MAT.	INST.	TOTAL
4260	Service sink w/trim, PE on CI, corner floor, 28" x 28", w/rim guard	555	440	995
4300	Wall hung w/rim guard, 22" x 18"	575	510	1,085
4340	24" x 20"	605	510	1,115
4380	Vitreous china, wall hung 22" x 20"	625	510	1,135

C8.1-401

PLUMBING — B8.1-440 — Shower Systems

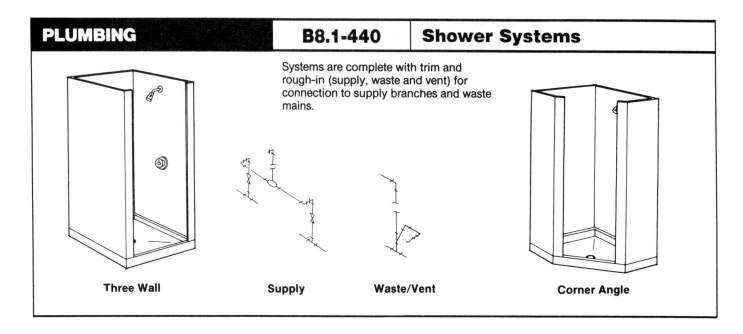

Systems are complete with trim and rough-in (supply, waste and vent) for connection to supply branches and waste mains.

Three Wall | Supply | Waste/Vent | Corner Angle

System Components	QUANTITY	UNIT	MAT.	INST.	TOTAL
SYSTEM 08.1-440-1560					
SHOWER, STALL, BAKED ENAMEL, MOLDED STONE RECEPTOR, 30" SQUARE					
Shower stall, enameled steel, molded stone receptor, 30" square	1.000	Ea.	330	265	595
Copper tubing type DWV, solder joints, hangers 10'OC, 1-½" diam	6.000	L.F.	22.68	32.52	55.20
Wrought copper DWV, Tee, sanitary, 1-½" diam	1.000	Ea.	4.28	36.72	41
Trap, standard, copper 1-½" diam	1.000	Ea.	17.11	16.89	34
Copper tubing type L, solder joint, hanger 10' OC ½" diam	16.000	L.F.	19.36	57.92	77.28
Wrought copper 90° elbow for solder joints ½" diam	3.000	Ea.	.75	43.95	44.70
Wrought copper Tee for solder joints, ½" diam	2.000	Ea.	.88	45.12	46
Stop and waste, straightway, bronze, solder joint ½" diam	2.000	Ea.	6.60	24.40	31
TOTAL			401.66	522.52	924.18

8.1-440	Shower Systems	MAT.	INST.	TOTAL
1560	Shower, stall, baked enamel, molded stone receptor, 30" square	400	525	925
1600	32" square	420	520	940
1640	Terrazzo receptor, 32" square	640	520	1,160
1680	36" square	680	550	1,230
1720	36" corner angle	675	555	1,230
1800	Fiberglass one piece, three walls, 32" square	375	475	850
1840	36" square	410	480	890
1880	Polypropylene, molded stone receptor, 30" square	360	520	880
1920	32" square	365	520	885
1960	Built-in head, arm, bypass, stops and handles	185	35	220

PLUMBING B8.1-450 Urinal Systems

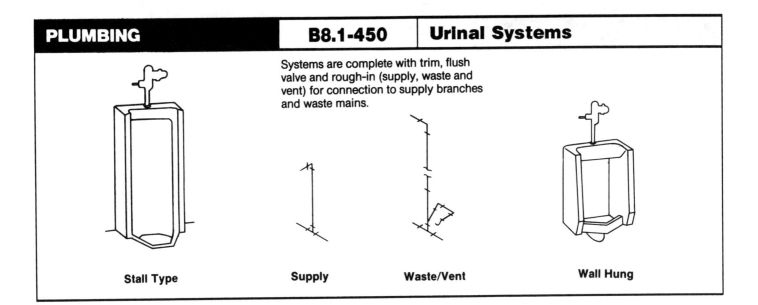

Systems are complete with trim, flush valve and rough-in (supply, waste and vent) for connection to supply branches and waste mains.

Stall Type — **Supply** — **Waste/Vent** — **Wall Hung**

System Components	QUANTITY	UNIT	COST EACH MAT.	COST EACH INST.	COST EACH TOTAL
SYSTEM 08.1-450-2000					
URINAL, VITREOUS CHINA, WALL HUNG					
Urinal, wall hung, vitreous china, incl. hanger	1.000	Ea.	349.80	175.20	525
Pipe, steel, galvanized, schedule 40, threaded, 1-½" diam	5.000	L.F.	15.05	32.95	48
Copper tubing type DWV, solder joint, hangers 10'OC, 2" diam	3.000	L.F.	15.06	20.04	35.10
Combination Y & ⅛ bend for Cl soil pipe, no hub, 3" diam	1.000	Ea.	6.60		6.60
Pipe, Cl, no hub, cplg 10' OC, hanger 5' OC, 3" diam	4.000	L.F.	16.40	33	49.40
Pipe coupling standard, Cl soil, no hub, 3" diam	3.000	Ea.	8.85	41.70	50.55
Copper tubing type L, solder joint, hanger 10' OC ¾" diam	5.000	L.F.	9.10	19.15	28.25
Wrought copper 90° elbow for solder joints ¾" diam	1.000	Ea.	.57	15.43	16
Wrought copper Tee for solder joints, ¾" diam	1.000	Ea.	1	24	25
TOTAL			422.43	361.47	783.90

8.1-450	Urinal Systems	COST EACH MAT.	COST EACH INST.	COST EACH TOTAL
2000	Urinal, vitreous china, wall hung	420	360	780
2040	Stall type	535	415	950
	C8.1-401			

PLUMBING — B8.1-460 Water Cooler Systems

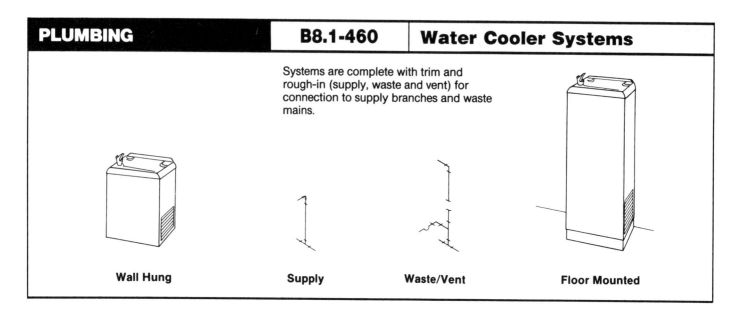

Systems are complete with trim and rough-in (supply, waste and vent) for connection to supply branches and waste mains.

Wall Hung | Supply | Waste/Vent | Floor Mounted

System Components	QUANTITY	UNIT	COST EACH MAT.	COST EACH INST.	COST EACH TOTAL
SYSTEM 08.1-460-1840					
WATER COOLER, ELECTRIC, SELF CONTAINED, WALL HUNG, 8.2 GPH					
Water cooler, wall mounted, 8.2 GPH	1.000	Ea.	381.70	133.30	515
Copper tubing type DWV, solder joint, hanger 10'OC 1-¼" diam	4.000	L.F.	12.24	19.56	31.80
Wrought copper DWV, Tee, sanitary 1-¼" diam	1.000	Ea.	4.65	32.35	37
P trap, copper drainage, 1-¼" diam	1.000	Ea.	14.63	16.37	31
Copper tubing type L, solder joint, hanger 10' OC ⅜" diam	5.000	L.F.	5.45	17.45	22.90
Wrought copper 90° elbow for solder joints ⅜" diam	1.000	Ea.	.66	13.34	14
Wrought copper Tee for solder joints, ⅜" diam	1.000	Ea.	1.60	21.40	23
Stop and waste, straightway, bronze, solder, ⅜" diam	1.000	Ea.	3.58	12.22	15.80
TOTAL			424.51	265.99	690.50

8.1-460	Water Cooler Systems	MAT.	INST.	TOTAL
1840	Water cooler, electric, wall hung, 8.2 GPH	425	265	690
1880	Dual height, 14.3 GPH	595	275	870
1920	Wheelchair type, 7.5 G.P.H.	1,000	270	1,270
1960	Semi recessed, 8.1 G.P.H.	560	265	825
2000	Full recessed, 8 G.P.H.	885	280	1,165
2040	Floor mounted, 14.3 G.P.H.	450	230	680
2080	Dual height, 14.3 G.P.H.	635	280	915
2120	Refrigerated compartment type, 1.5 G.P.H.	850	230	1,080
2160	Cafeteria type, dual glass fillers, 27 G.P.H.	1,950	355	2,305

PLUMBING — B8.1-470 — Water Closet Systems

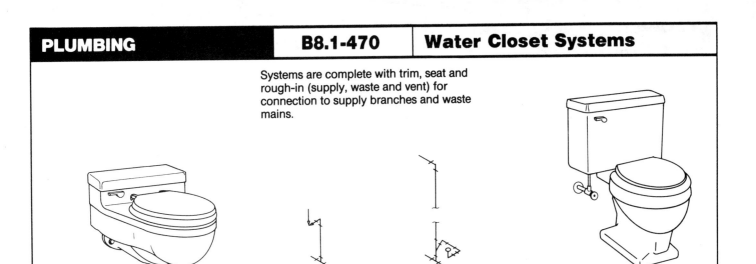

Systems are complete with trim, seat and rough-in (supply, waste and vent) for connection to supply branches and waste mains.

One Piece Wall Hung · Supply · Waste/Vent · Floor Mount

System Components	QUANTITY	UNIT	MAT.	INST.	TOTAL
SYSTEM 08.1-470-1840					
WATER CLOSET, VITREOUS CHINA, ELONGATED					
TANK TYPE, WALL HUNG, ONE PIECE					
Wtr closet tank type vit china wall hung 1 pc w/seat supply & stop	1.000	Ea.	544.50	100.50	645
Pipe steel galvanized, schedule 40, threaded, 2" diam	4.000	L.F.	15.52	32.88	48.40
Pipe, CI soil, no hub, cplg 10' OC, hanger 5' OC, 4" diam	2.000	L.F.	11.16	18.24	29.40
Pipe, coupling, standard coupling, CI soil, no hub, 4" diam	2.000	Ea.	6.80	32	38.80
Copper tubing type L, solder joint, hanger 10'OC, ½" diam	6.000	L.F.	7.26	21.72	28.98
Wrought copper 90° elbow for solder joints ½" diam	2.000	Ea.	.50	29.30	29.80
Wrought copper Tee for solder joints ½" diam	1.000	Ea.	.44	22.56	23
Support/carrier, for water closet, siphon jet, horiz, single, 4" waste	1.000	Ea.	110	50	160
TOTAL			696.18	307.20	1,003.38

8.1-470	Water Closet Systems	MAT.	INST.	TOTAL
1800	Water closet, vitreous china, elongated			
1840	Tank type, wall hung, one piece	695	305	1,000
1880	Close coupled two piece	525	305	830
1920	Floor mount, one piece	560	330	890
1960	One piece low profile	830	330	1,160
2000	Two piece close coupled	250	330	580
2040	Bowl only with flush valve			
2080	Wall hung	450	310	760
2120	Floor mount	400	335	735

PLUMBING — 8.1-510 — Water Closets, Group

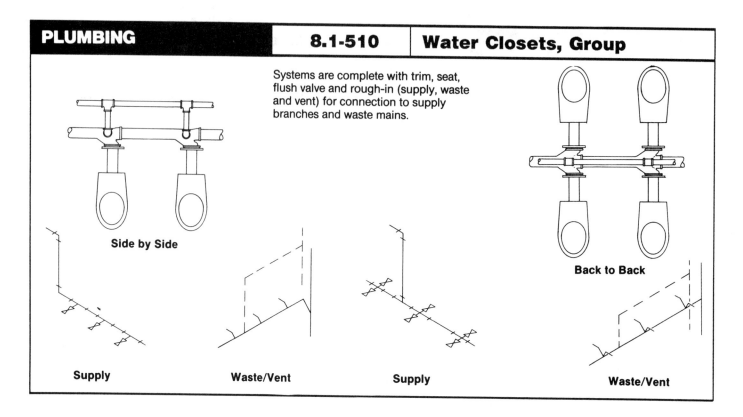

Systems are complete with trim, seat, flush valve and rough-in (supply, waste and vent) for connection to supply branches and waste mains.

Side by Side

Back to Back

Supply | Waste/Vent | Supply | Waste/Vent

System Components	QUANTITY	UNIT	MAT.	INST.	TOTAL
SYSTEM 08.1-510-1760					
WATER CLOSETS, BATTERY MOUNT, WALL HUNG, SIDE BY SIDE, FIRST CLOSET					
Water closet, bowl only w/flush valve, seat, wall hung	1.000	Ea.	286	89	375
Pipe, CI soil, no hub, cplg 10' OC, hanger 5' OC, 4" diam	3.000	L.F.	16.74	27.36	44.10
Coupling, standard, CI, soil, no hub, 4" diam	2.000	Ea.	6.80	32	38.80
Copper tubing type L, solder joints, hangers 10' OC, 1" diam	6.000	L.F.	15.12	25.98	41.10
Copper tubing, type DWV, solder joints, hangers 10'OC, 2" diam	6.000	L.F.	30.12	40.08	70.20
Wrought copper 90° elbow for solder joints 1" diam	1.000	Ea.	1.36	18.34	19.70
Wrought copper Tee for solder joints, 1" diam	1.000	Ea.	3.47	29.53	33
Support/carrier, siphon jet, horiz, adjustable single, 4" pipe	1.000	Ea.	110	50	160
Valve, gate, bronze, 125 lb, NRS, soldered 1" diam	1.000	Ea.	19.25	15.75	35
Wrought copper, DWV, 90° elbow, 2" diam	1.000	Ea.	5.37	29.63	35
TOTAL			494.23	357.67	851.90

8.1-510	Water Closets, Group	MAT.	INST.	TOTAL
1760	Water closets, battery mount, wall hung, side by side, first closet	495	360	855
1800	Each additional water closet, add	475	335	810
3000	[C8.1-401] Back to back, first pair of closets	880	480	1,360
3100	Each additional pair of closets, back to back	865	470	1,335

PLUMBING — B8.1-530 — Urinals, Battery Mount

Systems are complete with trim, flush valve and rough-in (supply, waste and vent) for connection to supply branches and waste mains.

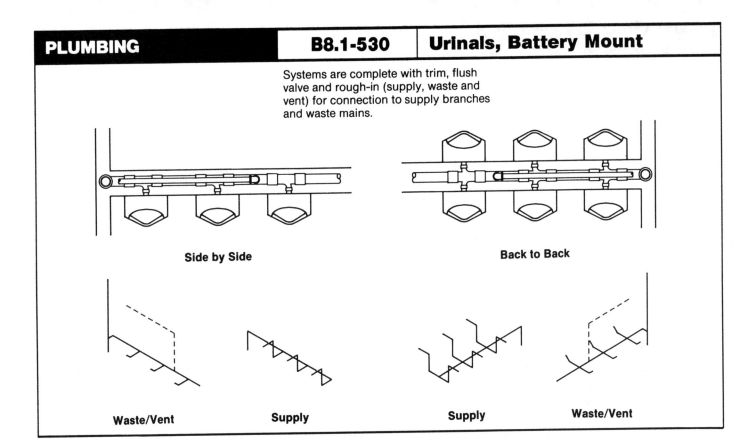

Side by Side / Back to Back / Waste/Vent / Supply / Supply / Waste/Vent

System Components	QUANTITY	UNIT	COST EACH MAT.	INST.	TOTAL
SYSTEM 08.1-530-1760					
URINALS, BATTERY MOUNT, WALL HUNG, SIDE BY SIDE, FIRST URINAL					
Urinal, wall hung, vitreous china, with hanger & trim	1.000	Ea.	349.80	175.20	525
No hub cast iron soil pipe, 3" diameter	4.000	L.F.	16.40	33	49.40
No hub cast iron sanitary tee, 3" diameter	1.000	Ea.	5		5
No hub coupling, 3" diameter	2.000	Ea.	5.90	27.80	33.70
Copper tubing, type L, ¾" diameter	5.000	L.F.	9.10	19.15	28.25
Copper tubing, type DWV, 2" diameter	2.000	L.F.	10.04	13.36	23.40
Copper 90° elbow, ¾" diameter	2.000	Ea.	1.14	30.86	32
Copper 90° elbow, type DWV, 2" diameter	2.000	Ea.	10.74	59.26	70
Galvanized steel pipe, 1-½" diameter	5.000	L.F.	15.05	32.95	48
Cast iron drainage elbow, 90°, 1-½" diameter	1.000	Ea.	5.25	29.75	35
TOTAL			428.42	421.33	849.75

8.1-530	Urinal Systems, Battery Mount	COST EACH MAT.	INST.	TOTAL
1760	Urinals, battery mount, side by side, first urinal	430	420	850
1800	Each additional urinal, add	410	375	785
2000	Back to back, first pair of urinals [C8.1-401]	805	635	1,440
2100	Each additional pair of urinals, back to back	760	500	1,260

PLUMBING — B8.1-560 — Group Wash Fountains

Systems are complete with trim and rough-in (supply, waste and vent) for connection to supply branches and waste mains.

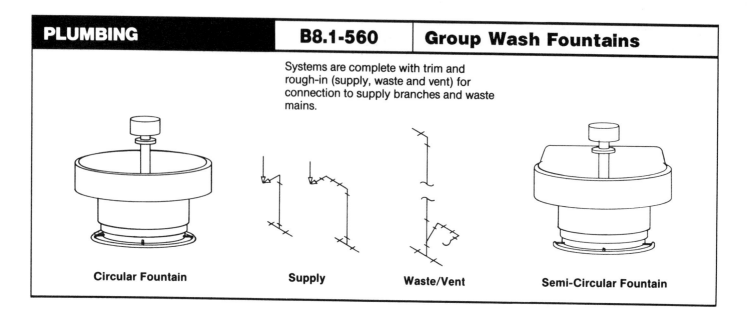

Circular Fountain — Supply — Waste/Vent — Semi-Circular Fountain

System Components	QUANTITY	UNIT	MAT.	INST.	TOTAL
SYSTEM 08.1-560-1760 GROUP WASH FOUNTAIN, PRECAST TERRAZZO CIRCULAR, 36" DIAMETER					
Wash fountain, group, precast terrazzo, foot control 36" diam	1.000	Ea.	1,243	282	1,525
Copper tubing type DWV, solder joint, hanger 10'OC, 2" diam	10.000	L.F.	50.20	66.80	117
P trap, standard, copper, 2" diam	1.000	Ea.	33	20	53
Wrought copper, Tee, sanitary, 2" diam	1.000	Ea.	7.92	42.08	50
Copper tubing type L, solder joint, hanger 10' OC ½" diam	20.000	L.F.	24.20	72.40	96.60
Wrought copper 90° elbow for solder joints ½" diam	3.000	Ea.	.75	43.95	44.70
Wrought copper Tee for solder joints, ½" diam	2.000	Ea.	.88	45.12	46
TOTAL			1,359.95	572.35	1,932.30

8.1-560	Group Wash Fountain Systems	MAT.	INST.	TOTAL
1740	Group wash fountain, precast terrazzo			
1760	Circular, 36" diameter	1,350	570	1,920
1800	54" diameter [C8.1-401]	1,500	630	2,130
1840	Semi-circular, 36" diameter	1,250	570	1,820
1880	54" diameter	1,500	630	2,130
1960	Stainless steel, circular, 36" diameter	1,500	535	2,035
2000	54" diameter	1,900	580	2,480
2040	Semi-circular, 36" diameter	1,325	515	1,840
2080	54" diameter	1,650	575	2,225
2160	Thermoplastic, circular, 36" diameter	1,175	425	1,600
2200	54" diameter	1,350	505	1,855
2240	Semi-circular, 36" diameter	1,100	435	1,535
2280	54" diameter	1,300	495	1,795

PLUMBING — 8.1-580 — Lavatories, Battery Mount

Systems are complete with trim, flush valve and rough-in (supply, waste and vent) for connection to supply branches and waste mains.

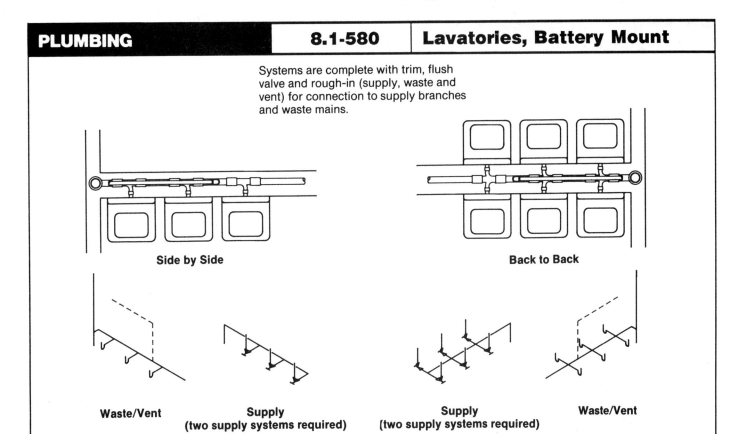

Side by Side — Back to Back — Waste/Vent — Supply (two supply systems required) — Supply (two supply systems required) — Waste/Vent

SYSTEM COMPONENTS	QUANTITY	UNIT	MAT.	INST.	TOTAL
SYSTEM 08.1-580-1760					
LAVATORIES, BATTERY MOUNT, WALL HUNG, SIDE BY SIDE, FIRST LAVATORY					
Lavatory w/trim wall hung PE on CI 20" x 18"	1.000	Ea.	115.50	64.50	180
Stop, chrome, angle supply, 3/8" diameter	2.000	Ea.	26.40	23.60	50
Concealed arm support	1.000	Ea.	77	48	125
P trap w/cleanout, 20 ga. C.P., 1-1/4" diameter	1.000	Ea.	10.78	16.22	27
Copper tubing, type L, 1/2" diameter	10.000	L.F.	12.10	36.20	48.30
Copper tubing, type DWV, 1-1/4" diameter	4.000	L.F.	12.24	19.56	31.80
Copper 90° elbow, 1/2" diameter	2.000	Ea.	.50	29.30	29.80
Copper tee, 1/2" diameter	2.000	Ea.	.88	45.12	46
DWV copper sanitary tee, 1-1/4" diameter	2.000	Ea.	9.30	64.70	74
Galvanized steel pipe, 1-1/4" diameter	4.000	L.F.	9.96	23.64	33.60
Black cast iron 90° elbow, 1-1/4" diameter	1.000	Ea.	2.04	23.96	26
TOTAL			241.68	199.92	441.60

8.1-580	Lavatory Systems, Battery Mount	MAT.	INST.	TOTAL
1760	Lavatories, battery mount, side by side, first lavatory	240	200	440
1800	Each additional lavatory, add	235	165	400
2000	Back to back, first pair of lavatories	425	315	740
2100	Each additional pair of lavatories, back to back	420	280	700

PLUMBING B8.1-620 Two Fixture Bathrooms

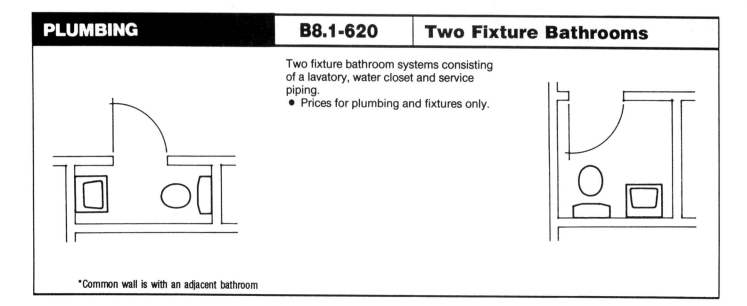

Two fixture bathroom systems consisting of a lavatory, water closet and service piping.
- Prices for plumbing and fixtures only.

*Common wall is with an adjacent bathroom

System Components	QUANTITY	UNIT	COST EACH MAT.	COST EACH INST.	COST EACH TOTAL
SYSTEM 08.1-620-1180					
BATHROOM, LAVATORY & WATER CLOSET, 2 WALL PLUMBING, STAND ALONE					
Water closet, 2 Pc close cpld vit china flr mntd w/seat, supply & stop	1.000	Ea.	151.80	98.20	250
Water closet, rough-in waste & vent	1.000	Set	98.10	271.90	370
Lavatory w/ftngs, wall hung, white, PE on CI, 20" x 18"	1.000	Ea.	115.50	64.50	180
Lavatory, rough-in waste & vent	1.000	Set	139.10	315.90	455
Copper tubing type L, solder joint, hanger 10' OC ½" diam	10.000	L.F.	12.10	36.20	48.30
Pipe, steel, galvanized, schedule 40, threaded, 2" diam	12.000	L.F.	46.56	98.64	145.20
Pipe, CI soil, no hub, coupling 10' OC, hanger 5' OC, 4" diam	7.000	L.F.	30.94	67.06	98
TOTAL			594.10	952.40	1,546.50

8.1-620	Two Fixture Bathroom, Two Wall Plumbing	MAT.	INST.	TOTAL
1180	Bathroom, lavatory & water closet, 2 wall plumbing, stand alone	595	950	1,545
1200	Share common plumbing wall*	545	835	1,380

8.1-620	Two Fixture Bathroom, One Wall Plumbing	MAT.	INST.	TOTAL
2220	Bathroom, lavatory & water closet, one wall plumbing, stand alone	560	865	1,425
2240	Share common plumbing wall*	505	750	1,255

PLUMBING B8.1-630 Three Fixture Bathrooms

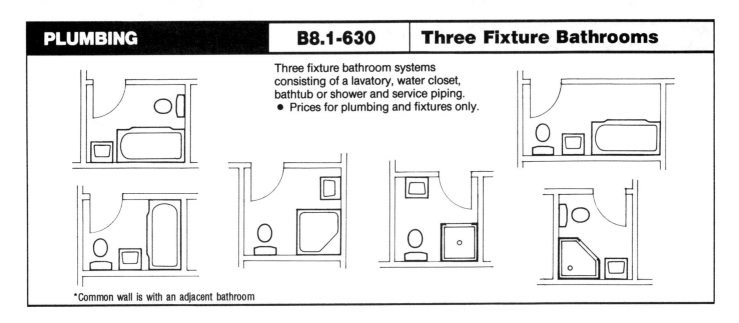

Three fixture bathroom systems consisting of a lavatory, water closet, bathtub or shower and service piping.
- Prices for plumbing and fixtures only.

*Common wall is with an adjacent bathroom

System Components	QUANTITY	UNIT	MAT.	INST.	TOTAL
SYSTEM 08.1-630-1170					
BATHROOM, LAVATORY, WATER CLOSET & BATHTUB					
ONE WALL PLUMBING, STAND ALONE					
Wtr closet, 2 pc close cpld vit china flr mntd w/seat supply & stop	1.000	Ea.	151.80	98.20	250
Water closet, rough-in waste & vent	1.000	Set	98.10	271.90	370
Lavatory w/ftngs, wall hung, white, PE on CI, 20" x 18"	1.000	Ea.	115.50	64.50	180
Lavatory, rough-in waste & vent	1.000	Set	139.10	315.90	455
Bathtub, white PE on CI, w/ftgs, mat bottom, recessed, 5' long	1.000	Ea.	303.60	121.40	425
Baths, rough-in waste and vent	1.000	Set	85.80	229.20	315
TOTAL			893.90	1,101.10	1,995

8.1-630	Three Fixture Bathroom, One Wall Plumbing	MAT.	INST.	TOTAL
1150	Bathroom, three fixture, one wall plumbing			
1160	Lavatory, water closet & bathtub			
1170	Stand alone	895	1,100	1,995
1180	Share common plumbing wall *	770	825	1,595

8.1-630	Three Fixture Bathroom, Two Wall Plumbing	MAT.	INST.	TOTAL
2130	Bathroom, three fixture, two wall plumbing			
2140	Lavatory, water closet & bathtub			
2160	Stand alone	900	1,125	2,025
2180	Long plumbing wall common *	810	910	1,720
3610	Lavatory, bathtub & water closet			
3620	Stand alone	970	1,250	2,220
3640	Long plumbing wall common *	910	1,150	2,060
4660	Water closet, corner bathtub & lavatory			
4680	Stand alone	1,675	1,125	2,800
4700	Long plumbing wall common *	1,575	875	2,450
6100	Water closet, stall shower & lavatory			
6120	Stand alone	990	1,400	2,390
6140	Long plumbing wall common *	945	1,325	2,270
7060	Lavatory, corner stall shower & water closet			
7080	Stand alone	1,175	1,300	2,475
7100	Short plumbing wall common *	1,075	965	2,040

PLUMBING — B8.1-640 — Four Fixture Bathrooms

Four fixture bathroom systems consisting of a lavatory, water closet, bathtub, shower and service piping.
- Prices for plumbing and fixtures only.

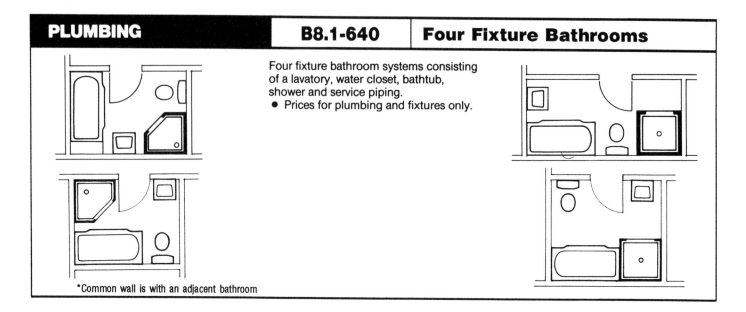

*Common wall is with an adjacent bathroom

System Components	QUANTITY	UNIT	MAT.	INST.	TOTAL
SYSTEM 08.1-640-1160					
BATHROOM, BATHTUB, WATER CLOSET, STALL SHOWER & LAVATORY					
TWO WALL PLUMBING, STAND ALONE					
Wtr closet, 2 pc close cpld vit china flr mntd w/seat supply & stop	1.000	Ea.	151.80	98.20	250
Water closet, rough-in waste & vent	1.000	Set	98.10	271.90	370
Lavatory w/ftngs, wall hung, white PE on CI, 20" x 18"	1.000	Ea.	115.50	64.50	180
Lavatory, rough-in waste & vent	1.000	Set	13.91	31.59	45.50
Bathtub, white PE on CI, w/ftgs, mat bottom, recessed, 5' long	1.000	Ea.	303.60	121.40	425
Baths, rough-in waste and vent	1.000	Set	95.33	254.67	350
Shower stall, bkd enam, molded stone receptor, door & trim 32" sq.	1.000	Ea.	347.60	262.40	610
Shower stall, rough-in supply, waste & vent	1.000	Set	71.69	258.31	330
TOTAL			1,197.53	1,362.97	2,560.50

8.1-640	Four Fixture Bathroom, Two Wall Plumbing	MAT.	INST.	TOTAL
1140	Bathroom, four fixture, two wall plumbing			
1150	Bathtub, water closet, stall shower & lavatory			
1160	Stand alone	1,200	1,375	2,575
1180	Long plumbing wall common *	1,100	1,100	2,200
2260	Bathtub, lavatory, corner stall shower & water closet			
2280	Stand alone	1,450	1,400	2,850
2320	Long plumbing wall common *	1,350	1,150	2,500
3620	Bathtub, stall shower, lavatory & water closet			
3640	Stand alone	1,325	1,650	2,975
3661	Long plumbing wall (opposite door) common*	1,225	1,400	2,625

8.1-640	Four Fixture Bathroom, Three Wall Plumbing	MAT.	INST.	TOTAL
4680	Bathroom, four fixture, three wall plumbing			
4700	Bathtub, stall shower, lavatory & water closet			
4720	Stand alone	1,650	1,825	3,475
4760	Long plumbing wall (opposite door) common *	1,600	1,700	3,300

PLUMBING B8.1-650 Five Fixture Bathrooms

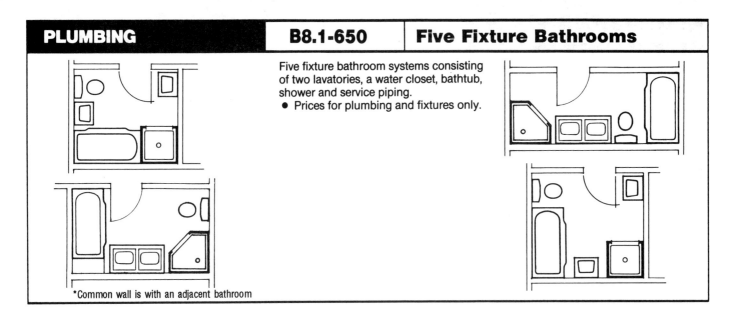

Five fixture bathroom systems consisting of two lavatories, a water closet, bathtub, shower and service piping.
● Prices for plumbing and fixtures only.

*Common wall is with an adjacent bathroom

System Components	QUANTITY	UNIT	COST EACH MAT.	INST.	TOTAL
SYSTEM 08.1-650-1360					
BATHROOM, BATHTUB, WATER CLOSET, STALL SHOWER & TWO LAVATORIES					
TWO WALL PLUMBING, STAND ALONE					
Wtr closet, 2 pc close cpld vit china flr mntd incl seat, supply & stop	1.000	Ea.	151.80	98.20	250
Water closet, rough-in waste & vent	1.000	Set	98.10	271.90	370
Lavatory w/ftngs, wall hung, white PE on CI, 20" x 18"	2.000	Ea.	231	129	360
Lavatory, rough-in waste & vent	2.000	Set	278.20	631.80	910
Bathtub, white PE on CI, w/ftgs, mat bottom, recessed, 5' long	1.000	Ea.	303.60	121.40	425
Baths, rough-in waste and vent	1.000	Set	95.33	254.67	350
Shower stall, bkd enam molded stone receptor, door & ftng, 32" sq.	1.000	Ea.	347.60	262.40	610
Shower stall, rough-in supply, waste & vent,	1.000	Set	71.69	258.31	330
TOTAL			1,577.32	2,027.68	3,605

8.1-650	Five Fixture Bathroom, Two Wall Plumbing	COST EACH		
		MAT.	INST.	TOTAL
1320	Bathroom, five fixture, two wall plumbing			
1340	Bathtub, water closet, stall shower & two lavatories			
1360	Stand alone	1,575	2,025	3,600
1400	One short plumbing wall common *	1,475	1,775	3,250
1440				
1500	Bathtub, two lavatories, corner stall shower & water closet			
1520	Stand alone	1,825	2,050	3,875
1540	Long plumbing wall common*	1,650	1,675	3,325

8.1-650	Five Fixture Bathroom, Three Wall Plumbing	COST EACH		
		MAT.	INST.	TOTAL
2360	Bathroom, five fixture, three wall plumbing			
2380	Water closet, bathtub, two lavatories & stall shower			
2400	Stand alone	1,825	2,050	3,875
2440	One short plumbing wall common *	1,750	1,800	3,550

8.1-650	Five Fixture Bathroom, One Wall Plumbing	COST EACH		
		MAT.	INST.	TOTAL
4080	Bathroom, five fixture, one wall plumbing			
4100	Bathtub, two lavatories, corner stall shower & water closet			
4120	Stand alone	1,750	1,875	3,625
4160	Share common wall *	1,500	1,250	2,750

FIRE PROTECTION — B8.2-110 — Wet Pipe Sprinkler Systems

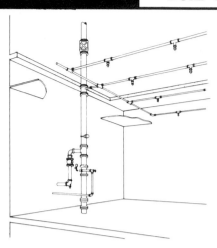

Wet pipe system. A system employing automatic sprinklers attached to a piping system containing water and connected to a water supply so that water discharges immediately from sprinklers opened by heat from a fire.

All areas are assumed to be open.

System Components	QUANTITY	UNIT	COST EACH MAT.	COST EACH INST.	COST EACH TOTAL
SYSTEM 08.2-110-0580					
WET PIPE SPRINKLER, STEEL, BLACK, SCH. 40 PIPE					
LIGHT HAZARD, ONE FLOOR, 2000 S.F.					
Valve, gate, iron body, 125 lb, OS&Y, flanged, 4" diam	1.000	Ea.	177.38	130.13	307.51
Valve, swing check, bronze, 125 lb, regrinding disc, 2-½" pipe size	1.000	Ea.	59.40	26.85	86.25
Valve, angle, bronze, 150 lb, rising stem, threaded, 2" diam	1.000	Ea.	81.68	19.58	101.26
*Alarm valve, 2-½" pipe size	1.000	Ea.	391.88	136.88	528.76
Alarm, water motor, complete with gong	1.000	Ea.	82.50	56.25	138.75
Valve, swing check, w/balldrip CI with brass trim 4" pipe size	1.000	Ea.	71.57	138.43	210
Pipe, steel, black, schedule 40, 4" diam	10.000	L.F.	55.88	116.63	172.51
*Flow control valve, trim & gauges, 4" pipe size	1.000	Set	763.13	305.63	1,068.76
Fire alarm horn, electric	1.000	Ea.	22.28	31.73	54.01
Pipe, steel, black, schedule 40, threaded, cplg & hngr 10'OC, 2-½" diam	20.000	L.F.	77.55	157.95	235.50
Pipe, steel, black, schedule 40, threaded, cplg & hngr 10'OC, 2" diam	12.500	L.F.	29.81	77.06	106.87
Pipe, steel, black, schedule 40, threaded, cplg & hngr 10'OC, 1-¼" diam	37.500	L.F.	56.81	166.78	223.59
Pipe steel, black, schedule 40, threaded cplg & hngr 10'OC, 1" diam	112.000	L.F.	136.08	464.52	600.60
Pipe Tee, malleable iron black, 150 lb threaded, 4" pipe size	2.000	Ea.	52.80	194.70	247.50
Pipe Tee, malleable iron black, 150 lb threaded, 2-½" pipe size	2.000	Ea.	18.90	87.60	106.50
Pipe Tee, malleable iron black, 150 lb threaded, 2" pipe size	1.000	Ea.	4.02	35.73	39.75
Pipe Tee, malleable iron black, 150 lb threaded, 1-¼" pipe size	5.000	Ea.	11.06	142.69	153.75
Pipe Tee, malleable iron black, 150 lb threaded, 1" pipe size	4.000	Ea.	5.46	108.54	114
Pipe 90° elbow, malleable iron black, 150 lb threaded, 1" pipe size	6.000	Ea.	5.22	102.78	108
Sprinkler head, standard spray, brass 135°-286°F ½" NPT, ⅜" orifice	12.000	Ea.	40.14	175.86	216
Valve, gate, bronze, NRS, class 150, threaded, 1" pipe size	1.000	Ea.	12.38	11.63	24.01
*Standpipe connection, wall, single, flush w/plug & chain 2-½"x2-½"	1.000	Ea.	70.95	82.80	153.75
TOTAL			2,226.88	2,770.75	4,997.63
COST PER S.F.			1.11	1.39	2.50

*Not included in systems under 2000 S.F.

8.2-110	Wet Pipe Sprinkler Systems	COST PER S.F. MAT.	COST PER S.F. INST.	COST PER S.F. TOTAL
0520	Wet pipe sprinkler systems, steel, black, sch. 40 pipe			
0530	Light hazard, one floor, 500 S.F.	.71	1.38	2.09
0560	1000 S.F.	1.05	1.43	2.48
0580	2000 S.F.	1.11	1.39	2.50
0600	5000 S.F.	.56	.99	1.55
0620	10,000 S.F.	.38	.83	1.21

FIRE PROTECTION — B8.2-110 — Wet Pipe Sprinkler Systems

8.2-110 Wet Pipe Sprinkler Systems

		\multicolumn{3}{c}{COST PER S.F.}		
		MAT.	INST.	TOTAL
0640	50,000 S.F.	.30	.76	1.06
0660	Each additional floor, 500 S.F.	.40	1.15	1.55
0680	1000 S.F.	.36	1.04	1.40
0700	2000 S.F.	.31	.93	1.24
0720	5000 S.F.	.24	.81	1.05
0740	10,000 S.F.	.23	.75	.98
0760	50,000 S.F.	.26	.72	.98
1000	Ordinary hazard, one floor, 500 S.F.	.81	1.53	2.34
1020	1000 S.F.	1.03	1.37	2.40
1040	2000 S.F.	1.16	1.48	2.64
1060	5000 S.F.	.60	1.07	1.67
1080	10,000 S.F.	.47	1.10	1.57
1100	50,000 S.F.	.41	1.08	1.49
1140	Each additional floor, 500 S.F.	.51	1.30	1.81
1160	1000 S.F.	.34	1.02	1.36
1180	2000 S.F.	.36	1.03	1.39
1200	5000 S.F.	.36	.98	1.34
1220	10,000 S.F.	.33	1.02	1.35
1240	50,000 S.F.	.31	.95	1.26
1500	Extra hazard, one floor, 500 S.F.	2.76	2.55	5.31
1520	1000 S.F.	1.68	2.07	3.75
1540	2000 S.F.	1.23	1.92	3.15
1560	5000 S.F.	.85	1.72	2.57
1580	10,000 S.F.	.74	1.57	2.31
1600	50,000 S.F.	.75	1.48	2.23
1660	Each additional floor, 500 S.F.	.58	1.55	2.13
1680	1000 S.F.	.57	1.47	2.04
1700	2000 S.F.	.48	1.47	1.95
1720	5000 S.F.	.41	1.32	1.73
1740	10,000 S.F.	.43	1.18	1.61
1760	50,000 S.F.	.41	1.09	1.50
2020	Grooved steel, black sch. 40 pipe, light hazard, one floor, 2000 S.F.	1.21	1.20	2.41
2060	10,000 S.F.	.51	.75	1.26
2100	Each additional floor, 2000 S.F.	.41	.75	1.16
2150	10,000 S.F.	.29	.63	.92
2200	Ordinary hazard, one floor, 2000 S.F.	1.24	1.28	2.52
2250	10,000 S.F.	.53	.93	1.46
2300	Each additional floor, 2000 S.F.	.44	.83	1.27
2350	10,000 S.F.	.38	.84	1.22
2400	Extra hazard, one floor, 2000 S.F.	1.37	1.64	3.01
2450	10,000 S.F.	.74	1.21	1.95
2500	Each additional floor, 2000 S.F.	.63	1.20	1.83
2550	10,000 S.F.	.54	1.07	1.61
3050	Grooved steel black sch. 10 pipe, light hazard, one floor, 2000 S.F.	1.18	1.19	2.37
3100	10,000 S.F.	.42	.71	1.13
3150	Each additional floor, 2000 S.F.	.38	.74	1.12
3200	10,000 S.F.	.27	.62	.89
3250	Ordinary hazard, one floor, 2000 S.F.	1.21	1.27	2.48
3300	10,000 S.F.	.50	.91	1.41
3350	Each additional floor, 2000 S.F.	.41	.82	1.23
3400	10,000 S.F.	.35	.82	1.17
3450	Extra hazard, one floor, 2000 S.F.	1.35	1.63	2.98
3500	10,000 S.F.	.68	1.19	1.87
3550	Each additional floor, 2000 S.F.	.61	1.19	1.80
3600	10,000 S.F.	.50	1.05	1.55
4050	Copper tubing, type M, light hazard, one floor, 2000 S.F.	1.21	1.19	2.40
4100	10,000 S.F.	.49	.72	1.21
4150	Each additional floor, 2000 S.F.	.43	.75	1.18

FIRE PROTECTION — B8.2-110 — Wet Pipe Sprinkler Systems

8.2-110	Wet Pipe Sprinkler Systems	COST PER S.F.		
		MAT.	INST.	TOTAL
4200	10,000 S.F.	.34	.64	.98
4250	Ordinary hazard, one floor, 2000 S.F.	1.27	1.33	2.60
4300	10,000 S.F.	.58	.85	1.43
4350	Each additional floor, 2000 S.F.	.49	.84	1.33
4400	10,000 S.F.	.42	.75	1.17
4450	Extra hazard, one floor, 2000 S.F.	1.41	1.65	3.06
4500	10,000 S.F.	1.09	1.30	2.39
4550	Each additional floor, 2000 S.F.	.67	1.21	1.88
4600	10,000 S.F.	.68	1.15	1.83
5050	Copper tubing, type M, T-drill system, light hazard, one floor			
5060	2000 S.F.	1.22	1.11	2.33
5100	10,000 S.F.	.46	.60	1.06
5150	Each additional floor, 2000 S.F.	.43	.67	1.10
5200	10,000 S.F.	.32	.52	.84
5250	Ordinary hazard, one floor, 2000 S.F.	1.23	1.13	2.36
5300	10,000 S.F.	.56	.76	1.32
5350	Each additional floor, 2000 S.F.	.43	.68	1.11
5400	10,000 S.F.	.42	.68	1.10
5450	Extra hazard, one floor, 2000 S.F.	1.29	1.35	2.64
5500	10,000 S.F.	.92	.96	1.88
5550	Each additional floor, 2000 S.F.	.58	.92	1.50
5600	10,000 S.F.	.52	.81	1.33

FIRE PROTECTION B8.2-120 Dry Pipe Sprinkler Systems

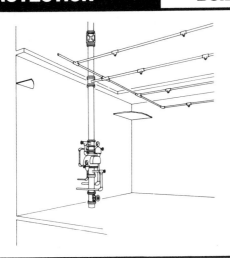

Dry Pipe System: A system employing automatic sprinklers attached to a piping system containing air under pressure, the release of which as from the opening of sprinklers permits the water pressure to open a valve known as a "dry pipe valve". The water then flows into the piping system and out the opened sprinklers.

All areas are assumed to be open.

System Components	QUANTITY	UNIT	COST EA. MAT.	COST EA. INST.	COST EA. TOTAL
SYSTEM 08.2-120-0580					
DRY PIPE SPRINKLER, STEEL BLACK, SCH. 40 PIPE					
LIGHT HAZARD, ONE FLOOR, 2000 S.F.					
Valve, gate, iron body 125 lb, OS&Y, flanged, 4" pipe size	1.000	Ea.	177.38	130.13	307.51
Valve, swing check, bronze, 125 lb, regrinding disc, 2-½" pipe size	1.000	Ea.	59.40	26.85	86.25
Valve, angle, bronze, 150 lb, rising stem, threaded, 2" pipe size	1.000	Ea.	81.68	19.58	101.26
*Alarm valve, 2-½" pipe size	1.000	Ea.	391.88	136.88	528.76
Alarm, water motor, complete with gong,	1.000	Ea.	82.50	56.25	138.75
Fire alarm horn, electric	1.000	Ea.	22.28	31.73	54.01
Valve swing check w/balldrip CI with brass trim, 4" pipe size	1.000	Ea.	71.57	138.43	210
Pipe, steel, black, schedule 40, 4" diam	10.000	L.F.	55.88	116.63	172.51
Dry pipe valve, trim & gauges, 4" pipe size	1.000	Ea.	569.25	405.75	975
Pipe, steel, black, schedule 40, threaded, cplg & hngr 10'OC 2-½" diam	20.000	L.F.	77.55	157.95	235.50
Pipe, steel, black, schedule 40, threaded, cplg & hngr 10'OC 2" diam	12.500	L.F.	29.81	77.06	106.87
Pipe, steel, black, schedule 40, threaded, cplg & hngr 10'OC 1-¼" diam	37.500	L.F.	56.81	166.78	223.59
Pipe, steel, black, schedule 40, threaded, cplg & hngr 10'OC 1" diam	112.000	L.F.	136.08	464.52	600.60
Pipe Tee, malleable iron black, 150 lb threaded, 4" pipe size	2.000	Ea.	52.80	194.70	247.50
Pipe Tee, malleable iron black, 150 lb threaded, 2-½" pipe size	2.000	Ea.	18.90	87.60	106.50
Pipe Tee, malleable iron black, 150 lb threaded, 2" pipe size	1.000	Ea.	4.02	35.73	39.75
Pipe Tee, malleable iron black, 150 lb threaded, 1-¼" pipe size	5.000	Ea.	11.06	142.69	153.75
Pipe Tee, malleable iron black, 150 lb threaded, 1" pipe size	4.000	Ea.	5.46	108.54	114
Pipe 90° elbow malleable iron black, 150 lb threaded, 1" pipe size	6.000	Ea.	5.22	102.78	108
Sprinkler head dry ½" orifice 1" NPT, 3" to 4-¾" length	12.000	Ea.	252.45	197.55	450
Air compressor, 200 Gal sprinkler system capacity, ⅛ HP	1.000	Ea.	367.13	176.63	543.76
*Standpipe connection, wall, flush, brs w/plug & chain 2-½"x2-½"	1.000	Ea.	70.95	82.80	153.75
Valve gate bronze, 300 psi, NRS, class 150, threaded, 1" pipe size	1.000	Ea.	12.38	11.63	24.01
TOTAL			2,612.44	3,069.19	5,681.63
COST PER S.F.			1.31	1.53	2.84

*Not included in systems under 2000 S.F.

8.2-120	Dry Pipe Sprinkler Systems	COST PER S.F. MAT.	COST PER S.F. INST.	COST PER S.F. TOTAL
0520	Dry pipe sprinkler systems, steel, black, sch. 40 pipe			
0530	Light hazard, one floor, 500 S.F.	2.83	2.71	5.54
0560	1000 S.F.	1.57	1.58	3.15
0580	2000 S.F.	1.31	1.53	2.84
0600	5000 S.F.	.71	1.06	1.77
0620	10,000 S.F.	.50	.87	1.37

FIRE PROTECTION

8.2-120 Dry Pipe Sprinkler Systems

8.2-120	Dry Pipe Sprinkler Systems	COST PER S.F.		
		MAT.	INST.	TOTAL
0640	50,000 S.F.	.39	.78	1.17
0660	Each additional floor, 500 S.F.	.65	1.31	1.96
0680	1000 S.F.	.50	1.06	1.56
0700	2000 S.F.	.42	.95	1.37
0720	5000 S.F.	.35	.82	1.17
0740	10,000 S.F.	.33	.76	1.09
0760	50,000 S.F.	.29	.68	.97
1000	Ordinary hazard, one floor, 500 S.F.	2.83	2.71	5.54
1020	1000 S.F.	1.56	1.56	3.12
1040	2000 S.F.	1.39	1.64	3.03
1060	5000 S.F.	.78	1.14	1.92
1080	10,000 S.F.	.63	1.14	1.77
1100	50,000 S.F.	.57	1.12	1.69
1140	Each additional floor, 500 S.F.	.65	1.31	1.96
1160	1000 S.F.	.53	1.15	1.68
1180	2000 S.F.	.50	1.05	1.55
1200	5000 S.F.	.45	.91	1.36
1220	10,000 S.F.	.41	.89	1.30
1240	50,000 S.F.	.39	.82	1.21
1500	Extra hazard, one floor, 500 S.F.	3.78	3.33	7.11
1520	1000 S.F.	2.19	2.40	4.59
1540	2000 S.F.	1.53	2.08	3.61
1560	5000 S.F.	.92	1.57	2.49
1580	10,000 S.F.	.90	1.43	2.33
1600	50,000 S.F.	.90	1.35	2.25
1660	Each additional floor, 500 S.F.	.80	1.57	2.37
1680	1000 S.F.	.78	1.49	2.27
1700	2000 S.F.	.70	1.49	2.19
1720	5000 S.F.	.59	1.32	1.91
1740	10,000 S.F.	.63	1.17	1.80
1760	50,000 S.F.	.63	1.09	1.72
2020	Grooved steel, black, sch. 40 pipe, light hazard, one floor, 2000 S.F.	1.40	1.35	2.75
2060	10,000 S.F.	.55	.76	1.31
2100	Each additional floor, 2000 S.F.	.52	.76	1.28
2150	10,000 S.F.	.39	.64	1.03
2200	Ordinary hazard, one floor, 2000 S.F.	1.47	1.43	2.90
2250	10,000 S.F.	.69	.97	1.66
2300	Each additional floor, 2000 S.F.	.58	.84	1.42
2350	10,000 S.F.	.52	.86	1.38
2400	Extra hazard, one floor, 2000 S.F.	1.67	1.80	3.47
2450	10,000 S.F.	.97	1.26	2.23
2500	Each additional floor, 2000 S.F.	.85	1.22	2.07
2550	10,000 S.F.	.75	1.09	1.84
3050	Grooved steel black sch. 10 pipe, light hazard, one floor, 2000 S.F.	1.38	1.34	2.72
3100	10,000 S.F.	.53	.75	1.28
3150	Each additional floor, 2000 S.F.	.49	.75	1.24
3200	10,000 S.F.	.37	.63	1
3250	Ordinary hazard, one floor, 2000 S.F.	1.44	1.42	2.86
3300	10,000 S.F.	.65	.95	1.60
3350	Each additional floor, 2000 S.F.	.56	.83	1.39
3400	10,000 S.F.	.49	.84	1.33
3450	Extra hazard, one floor, 2000 S.F.	1.65	1.79	3.44
3500	10,000 S.F.	.91	1.24	2.15
3550	Each additional floor, 2000 S.F.	.82	1.22	2.04
3600	10,000 S.F.	.72	1.08	1.80
4050	Copper tubing, type M, light hazard, one floor, 2000 S.F.	1.41	1.34	2.75
4100	10,000 S.F.	.60	.76	1.36
4150	Each additional floor, 2000 S.F.	.53	.76	1.29

FIRE PROTECTION

8.2-120 Dry Pipe Sprinkler Systems

		COST PER S.F.		
		MAT.	INST.	TOTAL
4200	10,000 S.F.	.44	.65	1.09
4250	Ordinary hazard, one floor, 2000 S.F.	1.50	1.49	2.99
4300	10,000 S.F.	.74	.90	1.64
4350	Each additional floor, 2000 S.F.	.70	.88	1.58
4400	10,000 S.F.	.57	.77	1.34
4450	Extra hazard, one floor, 2000 S.F.	1.71	1.81	3.52
4500	10,000 S.F.	1.33	1.35	2.68
4550	Each additional floor, 2000 S.F.	.89	1.23	2.12
4600	10,000 S.F.	.90	1.17	2.07
5050	Copper tubing, type M, T-drill system, light hazard, one floor			
5060	2000 S.F.	1.41	1.26	2.67
5100	10,000 S.F.	.58	.64	1.22
5150	Each additional floor, 2000 S.F.	.54	.68	1.22
5200	10,000 S.F.	.42	.53	.95
5250	Ordinary hazard, one floor, 2000 S.F.	1.46	1.28	2.74
5300	10,000 S.F.	.72	.81	1.53
5350	Each additional floor, 2000 S.F.	.57	.69	1.26
5400	10,000 S.F.	.53	.66	1.19
5450	Extra hazard, one floor, 2000 S.F.	1.59	1.51	3.10
5500	10,000 S.F.	1.17	1.01	2.18
5550	Each additional floor, 2000 S.F.	.77	.94	1.71
5600	10,000 S.F.	.74	.83	1.57

FIRE PROTECTION — B8.2-130 — Preaction Sprinkler Systems

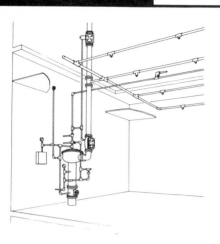

Pre-Action System: A system employing automatic sprinklers attached to a piping system containing air that may or may not be under pressure, with a supplemental heat responsive system of generally more sensitive characteristics than the automatic sprinklers themselves, installed in the same areas as the sprinklers; actuation of the heat responsive system, as from a fire, opens a valve which permits water to flow into the sprinkler piping system and to be discharged from those sprinklers which were opened by heat from the fire.

All areas are assumed to be open.

System Components	QUANTITY	UNIT	COST EACH MAT.	COST EACH INST.	COST EACH TOTAL
SYSTEM 08.2-130-0580					
PREACTION SPRINKLER SYSTEM, STEEL BLACK SCH. 40 PIPE					
LIGHT HAZARD, 1 FLOOR, 2000 S.F.					
Valve, gate, iron body 125 lb, OS&Y, flanged, 4" pipe size	1.000	Ea.	177.38	130.13	307.51
*Valve, swing check w/ball drip CI with brass trim 4" pipe size	1.000	Ea.	71.57	138.43	210
Valve, swing check, bronze, 125 lb, regrinding disc, 2-½" pipe size	1.000	Ea.	59.40	26.85	86.25
Valve, angle, bronze, 150 lb, rising stem, threaded, 2" pipe size	1.000	Ea.	81.68	19.58	101.26
*Alarm valve, 2-½" pipe size	1.000	Ea.	391.88	136.88	528.76
Alarm, water motor, complete with gong	1.000	Ea.	82.50	56.25	138.75
Fire alarm horn, electric	1.000	Ea.	22.28	31.73	54.01
Thermostatic release for release line	2.000	Ea.	202.95	22.05	225
Pipe, steel, black, schedule 40, 4" diam	10.000	L.F.	55.88	116.63	172.51
Dry pipe valve, trim & gauges, 4" pipe size	1.000	Ea.	569.25	405.75	975
Pipe, steel, black, schedule 40, threaded, cplg & hngr 10'OC 2-½" diam	20.000	L.F.	77.55	157.95	235.50
Pipe steel black, schedule 40, threaded, cplg & hngr 10'OC 2" diam	12.500	L.F.	29.81	77.06	106.87
Pipe, steel, black, schedule 40, threaded, cplg & hngr 10'OC 1-¼" diam	37.500	L.F.	56.81	166.78	223.59
Pipe, steel, black, schedule 40, threaded, cplg & hngr 10'OC 1" diam	112.000	L.F.	136.08	464.52	600.60
Pipe, Tee, malleable iron, black, 150 lb threaded, 4" diam	2.000	Ea.	52.80	194.70	247.50
Pipe, Tee, malleable iron, black, 150 lb threaded, 2-½" pipe size	2.000	Ea.	18.90	87.60	106.50
Pipe, Tee, malleable iron, black, 150 lb threaded, 2" pipe size	1.000	Ea.	4.02	35.73	39.75
Pipe, Tee, malleable iron, black, 150 lb threaded, 1-¼" pipe size	5.000	Ea.	11.06	142.69	153.75
Pipe, Tee, malleable iron, black, 150 lb threaded, 1" pipe size	4.000	Ea.	5.46	108.54	114
Pipe, 90° elbow, malleable iron, blk, 150 lb threaded, 1" pipe size	6.000	Ea.	5.22	102.78	108
Sprinkler head, std spray, brass 135°-286°F ½" NPT, ⅜" orifice	12.000	Ea.	40.14	175.86	216
Air compressor auto complete 200 Gal sprinkler sys cap, ⅓ HP	1.000	Ea.	367.13	176.63	543.76
*Standpipe conn., wall, flush, brass w/plug & chain 2-½" x 2-½"	1.000	Ea.	70.95	82.80	153.75
Valve, gate, bronze, 300 psi, NRS, class 150, threaded, 1" pipe size	1.000	Ea.	12.38	11.63	24.01
TOTAL			2,603.08	3,069.55	5,672.63
COST PER S.F.			1.30	1.53	2.83

*Not included in systems under 2000 S.F.

8.2-130	Preaction Sprinkler Systems	COST PER S.F. MAT.	COST PER S.F. INST.	COST PER S.F. TOTAL
0520	Preaction sprinkler systems, steel, black, sch. 40 pipe			
0530	Light hazard, one floor, 500 S.F.	2.74	2.16	4.90
0560	1000 S.F.	1.54	1.61	3.15
0580	2000 S.F.	1.30	1.53	2.83

FIRE PROTECTION — 8.2-130 Preaction Sprinkler Systems

8.2-130 Preaction Sprinkler Systems

		COST PER S.F.		
		MAT.	INST.	TOTAL
0600	5000 S.F.	.67	1.06	1.73
0620	10,000 S.F.	.47	.87	1.34
0640	50,000 S.F.	.37	.77	1.14
0660	Each additional floor, 500 S.F.	.60	1.17	1.77
0680	1000 S.F.	.46	1.05	1.51
0700	2000 S.F.	.42	.95	1.37
0720	5000 S.F.	.32	.82	1.14
0740	10,000 S.F.	.30	.75	1.05
0760	50,000 S.F.	.31	.70	1.01
1000	Ordinary hazard, one floor, 500 S.F.	1.02	1.55	2.57
1020	1000 S.F.	1.52	1.56	3.08
1040	2000 S.F.	1.40	1.64	3.04
1060	5000 S.F.	.72	1.13	1.85
1080	10,000 S.F.	.56	1.14	1.70
1100	50,000 S.F.	.49	1.10	1.59
1140	Each additional floor, 500 S.F.	.71	1.32	2.03
1160	1000 S.F.	.45	1.03	1.48
1180	2000 S.F.	.41	1.04	1.45
1200	5000 S.F.	.43	.98	1.41
1220	10,000 S.F.	.40	1.02	1.42
1240	50,000 S.F.	.37	.96	1.33
1500	Extra hazard, one floor, 500 S.F.	3.72	2.92	6.64
1520	1000 S.F.	2.06	2.18	4.24
1540	2000 S.F.	1.41	2.07	3.48
1560	5000 S.F.	.90	1.69	2.59
1580	10,000 S.F.	.82	1.59	2.41
1600	50,000 S.F.	.81	1.51	2.32
1660	Each additional floor, 500 S.F.	.79	1.57	2.36
1680	1000 S.F.	.67	1.48	2.15
1700	2000 S.F.	.58	1.48	2.06
1720	5000 S.F.	.49	1.33	1.82
1740	10,000 S.F.	.50	1.18	1.68
1760	50,000 S.F.	.47	1.08	1.55
2020	Grooved steel, black, sch. 40 pipe, light hazard, one floor, 2000 S.F.	1.40	1.35	2.75
2060	10,000 S.F.	.52	.76	1.28
2100	Each additional floor of 2000 S.F.	.51	.76	1.27
2150	10,000 S.F.	.36	.64	1
2200	Ordinary hazard, one floor, 2000 S.F.	1.43	1.43	2.86
2250	10,000 S.F.	.61	.97	1.58
2300	Each additional floor, 2000 S.F.	.54	.84	1.38
2350	10,000 S.F.	.45	.85	1.30
2400	Extra hazard, one floor, 2000 S.F.	1.56	1.79	3.35
2450	10,000 S.F.	.84	1.25	2.09
2500	Each additional floor, 2000 S.F.	.73	1.21	1.94
2550	10,000 S.F.	.61	1.07	1.68
3050	Grooved steel, black, sch. 10 pipe light hazard, one floor, 2000 S.F.	1.37	1.34	2.71
3100	10,000 S.F.	.50	.75	1.25
3150	Each additional floor, 2000 S.F.	.49	.75	1.24
3200	10,000 S.F.	.34	.63	.97
3250	Ordinary hazard, one floor, 2000 S.F.	1.40	1.42	2.82
3300	10,000 S.F.	.53	.94	1.47
3350	Each additional floor, 2000 S.F.	.52	.83	1.35
3400	10,000 S.F.	.42	.83	1.25
3450	Extra hazard, one floor, 2000 S.F.	1.54	1.78	3.32
3500	10,000 S.F.	.77	1.22	1.99
3550	Each additional floor, 2000 S.F.	.71	1.20	1.91
3600	10,000 S.F.	.58	1.06	1.64
4050	Copper tubing, type M, light hazard, one floor, 2000 S.F.	1.40	1.34	2.74

FIRE PROTECTION

8.2-130 Preaction Sprinkler Systems

8.2-130	Preaction Sprinkler Systems	COST PER S.F.		
		MAT.	INST.	TOTAL
4100	10,000 S.F.	.58	.76	1.34
4150	Each additional floor, 2000 S.F.	.53	.76	1.29
4200	10,000 S.F.	.36	.64	1
4250	Ordinary hazard, one floor, 2000 S.F.	1.46	1.48	2.94
4300	10,000 S.F.	.67	.89	1.56
4350	Each additional floor, 2000 S.F.	.53	.78	1.31
4400	10,000 S.F.	.45	.70	1.15
4450	Extra hazard, one floor, 2000 S.F.	1.60	1.80	3.40
4500	10,000 S.F.	1.18	1.33	2.51
4550	Each additional floor, 2000 S.F.	.78	1.22	2
4600	10,000 S.F.	.76	1.16	1.92
5050	Copper tubing, type M, T-drill system, light hazard, one floor			
5060	2000 S.F.	1.41	1.26	2.67
5100	10,000 S.F.	.55	.64	1.19
5150	Each additional floor, 2000 S.F.	.53	.68	1.21
5200	10,000 S.F.	.39	.52	.91
5250	Ordinary hazard, one floor, 2000 S.F.	1.42	1.28	2.70
5300	10,000 S.F.	.65	.80	1.45
5350	Each additional floor, 2000 S.F.	.54	.70	1.24
5400	10,000 S.F.	.49	.68	1.17
5450	Extra hazard, one floor, 2000 S.F.	1.48	1.50	2.98
5500	10,000 S.F.	1.01	.99	2
5550	Each additional floor, 2000 S.F.	.66	.93	1.59
5600	10,000 S.F.	.59	.82	1.41

FIRE PROTECTION — B8.2-140 — Deluge Sprinkler Systems

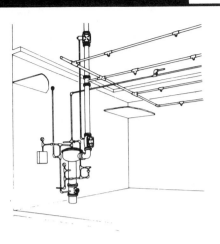

Deluge System: A system employing open sprinklers attached to a piping system connected to a water supply through a valve which is opened by the operation of a heat responsive system installed in the same areas as the sprinklers. When this valve opens, water flows into the piping system and discharges from all sprinklers attached thereto.

All areas are assumed to be open.

System Components	QUANTITY	UNIT	COST EA. MAT.	COST EA. INST.	COST EA. TOTAL
SYSTEM 08.2-140-0580					
DELUGE SPRINKLER SYSTEM, STEEL BLACK SCH. 40 PIPE					
LIGHT HAZARD, 1 FLOOR, 2000 S.F.					
Valve, gate, iron body 125 lb, OS&Y, flanged, 4" pipe size	1.000	Ea.	177.38	130.13	307.51
Valve, swing check w/ball drip, CI w/brass ftngs, 4" pipe size	1.000	Ea.	71.57	138.43	210
Valve, swing check, bronze, 125 lb, regrinding disc, 2-½" pipe size	1.000	Ea.	59.40	26.85	86.25
Valve, angle, bronze, 150 lb, rising stem, threaded, 2" pipe size	1.000	Ea.	81.68	19.58	101.26
*Alarm valve, 2-½" pipe size	1.000	Ea.	391.88	136.88	528.76
Alarm, water motor, complete with gong	1.000	Ea.	82.50	56.25	138.75
Fire alarm horn, electric	1.000	Ea.	22.28	31.73	54.01
Thermostatic release for release line	2.000	Ea.	202.95	22.05	225
Pipe, steel, black, schedule 40, 4" diam	10.000	L.F.	55.88	116.63	172.51
Deluge valve trim, pressure relief, emergency release, gauge, 4" pipe size	1.000	Ea.	804.38	414.38	1,218.76
Deluge system pressured monitoring panel, 120V	1.000	Ea.	255.75	14.25	270
Pipe, steel, black, schedule 40, threaded, cplg & hngr 10'OC 2-½" diam	20.000	L.F.	77.55	157.95	235.50
Pipe, steel, black, schedule 40, threaded, cplg & hngr 10'OC 2" diam	12.500	L.F.	29.81	77.06	106.87
Pipe, steel, black, schedule 40, threaded, cplg & hngr 10'OC 1-¼" diam	37.500	L.F.	56.81	166.78	223.59
Pipe, steel, black, schedule 40, threaded, cplg & hngr 10'OC 1" diam	112.000	L.F.	136.08	464.52	600.60
Pipe, Tee, malleable iron, black, 150 lb threaded, 4" pipe size	2.000	Ea.	52.80	194.70	247.50
Pipe, Tee, malleable iron, black, 150 lb threaded, 2-½" pipe size	2.000	Ea.	18.90	87.60	106.50
Pipe, Tee, malleable iron, black, 150 lb threaded, 2" pipe size	1.000	Ea.	4.02	35.73	39.75
Pipe, Tee, malleable iron, black, 150 lb threaded, 1-¼" pipe size	5.000	Ea.	11.06	142.69	153.75
Pipe, Tee, malleable iron, black, 150 lb threaded, 1" pipe size	4.000	Ea.	5.46	108.54	114
Pipe, 90° elbow, malleable iron, black, 150 lb threaded 1" pipe size	6.000	Ea.	5.22	102.78	108
Sprinkler head, std spray, brass 135°-286°F ½" NPT, ⅜" orifice	9.720	Ea.	32.51	142.45	174.96
Air compressor, auto, complete, 200 Gal sprinkler sys cap, ⅓ HP	1.000	Ea.	367.13	176.63	543.76
*Standpipe connection, wall, flush w/plug & chain 2-½"x2-½"	1.000	Ea.	70.95	82.80	153.75
Valve, gate, bronze, 300 psi, NRS, class 150, threaded, 1" pipe size	1.000	Ea.	12.38	11.63	24.01
TOTAL			3,086.33	3,059.02	6,145.35
COST PER S.F.			1.54	1.53	3.07

*Not included in systems under 2000 S.F.

8.2-140	Deluge Sprinkler Systems		COST PER S.F. MAT.	COST PER S.F. INST.	COST PER S.F. TOTAL
0520	Deluge sprinkler systems, steel, black, sch. 40 pipe				
0530	Light hazard, one floor, 500 S.F.		3.29	2.16	5.45
0560	C8.2-101 C8.2-102 C8.2-103 1000 S.F.		1.80	1.53	3.33
0580	2000 S.F.		1.54	1.53	3.07

FIRE PROTECTION — B8.2-140 Deluge Sprinkler Systems

8.2-140 Deluge Sprinkler Systems

		COST PER S.F.		
		MAT.	INST.	TOTAL
0600	5000 S.F.	.77	1.04	1.81
0620	10,000 S.F.	.51	.86	1.37
0640	50,000 S.F.	.37	.76	1.13
0660	Each additional floor, 500 S.F.	.60	1.15	1.75
0680	1000 S.F.	.46	1.05	1.51
0700	2000 S.F.	.41	.93	1.34
0720	5000 S.F.	.31	.80	1.11
0740	10,000 S.F.	.30	.74	1.04
0760	50,000 S.F.	.30	.69	.99
1000	Ordinary hazard, one floor, 500 S.F.	3.60	2.48	6.08
1020	1000 S.F.	1.79	1.55	3.34
1040	2000 S.F.	1.64	1.63	3.27
1060	5000 S.F.	.81	1.11	1.92
1080	10,000 S.F.	.60	1.12	1.72
1100	50,000 S.F.	.52	1.09	1.61
1140	Each additional floor, 500 S.F.	.70	1.30	2
1160	1000 S.F.	.44	1.01	1.45
1180	2000 S.F.	.41	1.02	1.43
1200	5000 S.F.	.39	.88	1.27
1220	10,000 S.F.	.36	.88	1.24
1240	50,000 S.F.	.34	.86	1.20
1500	Extra hazard, one floor, 500 S.F.	4.27	2.91	7.18
1520	1000 S.F.	2.48	2.25	4.73
1540	2000 S.F.	1.65	2.04	3.69
1560	5000 S.F.	.90	1.53	2.43
1580	10,000 S.F.	.81	1.38	2.19
1600	50,000 S.F.	.80	1.32	2.12
1660	Each additional floor, 500 S.F.	.78	1.54	2.32
1680	1000 S.F.	.66	1.45	2.11
1700	2000 S.F.	.58	1.45	2.03
1720	5000 S.F.	.49	1.30	1.79
1740	10,000 S.F.	.51	1.20	1.71
1760	50,000 S.F.	.50	1.12	1.62
2000	Grooved steel, black, sch. 40 pipe, light hazard, one floor			
2020	2000 S.F.	1.64	1.34	2.98
2060	10,000 S.F.	.57	.74	1.31
2100	Each additional floor, 2,000 S.F.	.51	.74	1.25
2150	10,000 S.F.	.36	.63	.99
2200	Ordinary hazard, one floor, 2000 S.F.	1.42	1.41	2.83
2250	10,000 S.F.	.66	.95	1.61
2300	Each additional floor, 2000 S.F.	.54	.82	1.36
2350	10,000 S.F.	.45	.83	1.28
2400	Extra hazard, one floor, 2000 S.F.	1.80	1.77	3.57
2450	10,000 S.F.	.89	1.19	2.08
2500	Each additional floor, 2000 S.F.	.73	1.18	1.91
2550	10,000 S.F.	.60	1.04	1.64
3000	Grooved steel, black, sch. 10 pipe, light hazard, one floor			
3050	2000 S.F.	1.44	1.27	2.71
3100	10,000 S.F.	.55	.73	1.28
3150	Each additional floor, 2000 S.F.	.48	.73	1.21
3200	10,000 S.F.	.34	.61	.95
3250	Ordinary hazard, one floor, 2000 S.F.	1.64	1.41	3.05
3300	10,000 S.F.	.58	.92	1.50
3350	Each additional floor, 2000 S.F.	.51	.81	1.32
3400	10,000 S.F.	.42	.81	1.23
3450	Extra hazard, one floor, 2000 S.F.	1.77	1.76	3.53
3500	10,000 S.F.	.81	1.19	2
3550	Each additional floor, 2000 S.F.	.71	1.17	1.88

FIRE PROTECTION — B8.2-140 Deluge Sprinkler Systems

8.2-140 Deluge Sprinkler Systems

Line	Description	MAT.	INST.	TOTAL
3600	10,000 S.F.	.57	1.03	1.60
4000	Copper tubing, type M, light hazard, one floor			
4050	2000 S.F.	1.64	1.33	2.97
4100	10,000 S.F.	.62	.74	1.36
4150	Each additional floor, 2000 S.F.	.52	.74	1.26
4200	10,000 S.F.	.36	.62	.98
4250	Ordinary hazard, one floor, 2000 S.F.	1.70	1.47	3.17
4300	10,000 S.F.	.71	.87	1.58
4350	Each additional floor, 2000 S.F.	.52	.76	1.28
4400	10,000 S.F.	.44	.68	1.12
4450	Extra hazard, one floor, 2000 S.F.	1.84	1.78	3.62
4500	10,000 S.F.	1.24	1.28	2.52
4550	Each additional floor, 2000 S.F.	.77	1.19	1.96
4600	10,000 S.F.	.75	1.12	1.87
5000	Copper tubing, type M, T-drill system, light hazard, one floor			
5050	2000 S.F.	1.65	1.25	2.90
5100	10,000 S.F.	.60	.62	1.22
5150	Each additional floor, 2000 S.F.	.55	.65	1.20
5200	10,000 S.F.	.38	.51	.89
5250	Ordinary hazard, one floor, 2000 S.F.	1.66	1.27	2.93
5300	10,000 S.F.	.69	.78	1.47
5350	Each additional floor, 2000 S.F.	.53	.67	1.20
5400	10,000 S.F.	.48	.66	1.14
5450	Extra hazard, one floor, 2000 S.F.	1.72	1.48	3.20
5500	10,000 S.F.	1.05	.96	2.01
5550	Each additional floor, 2000 S.F.	.65	.89	1.54
5600	10,000 S.F.	.59	.78	1.37

FIRE PROTECTION — B8.2-150 — Firecycle Sprinkler Systems

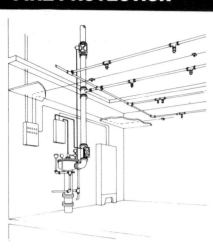

Firecycle is a fixed fire protection sprinkler system utilizing water as its extinguishing agent. It is a time delayed, recycling, preaction type which automatically shuts the water off when heat is reduced below the detector operating temperature and turns the water back on when that temperature is exceeded.

The system senses a fire condition through a closed circuit electrical detector system which controls water flow to the fire automatically. Batteries supply up to 90 hour emergency power supply for system operation. The piping system is dry (until water is required) and is monitored with pressurized air. Should any leak in the system piping occur, an alarm will sound, but water will not enter the system until heat is sensed by a Firecycle detector.

All areas are assumed to be open.

System Components	QUANTITY	UNIT	COST EACH MAT.	COST EACH INST.	COST EACH TOTAL
SYSTEM 08.2-150-0580					
FIRECYCLE SPRINKLER SYSTEM, STEEL BLACK SCH. 40 PIPE					
LIGHT HAZARD, ONE FLOOR, 2000 S.F.					
Valve, gate, iron body 125 lb, OS&Y, flanged, 4" pipe size	1.000	Ea.	177.38	130.13	307.51
Valve, angle, bronze, 150 lb, rising stem, threaded, 2" pipe size	1.000	Ea.	81.68	19.58	101.26
Valve, swing check, bronze, 125 lb, regrinding disc, 2-½" pipe size	1.000	Ea.	59.40	26.85	86.25
*Alarm valve, 2-½" pipe size	1.000	Ea.	391.88	136.88	528.76
Alarm, water motor, complete with gong	1.000	Ea.	82.50	56.25	138.75
Pipe, steel, black, schedule 40, 4" diam	10.000	L.F.	55.88	116.63	172.51
Fire alarm, horn, electric	1.000	Ea.	22.28	31.73	54.01
Pipe, steel, black, schedule 40, threaded, cplg & hngr 10'OC 2-½" diam	20.000	L.F.	77.55	157.95	235.50
Pipe, steel, black, schedule 40, threaded, cplg & hngr 10'OC 2" diam	12.500	L.F.	29.81	77.06	106.87
Pipe, steel, black, schedule 40, threaded, cplg & hngr 10'OC 1-¼" diam	37.500	L.F.	56.81	166.78	223.59
Pipe, steel, black, schedule 40, threaded, cplg & hngr 10'OC 1" diam	112.000	L.F.	136.08	464.52	600.60
Pipe, Tee, malleable iron, black, 150 lb threaded, 4" pipe size	2.000	Ea.	52.80	194.70	247.50
Pipe, Tee, malleable iron, black, 150 lb threaded, 2-½" pipe size	2.000	Ea.	18.90	87.60	106.50
Pipe, Tee, malleable iron, black, 150 lb threaded, 2" pipe size	1.000	Ea.	4.02	35.73	39.75
Pipe, Tee, malleable iron, black, 150 lb threaded, 1-¼" pipe size	5.000	Ea.	11.06	142.69	153.75
Pipe, Tee, malleable iron, black, 150 lb threaded, 1" pipe size	4.000	Ea.	5.46	108.54	114
Pipe, 90° elbow, malleable iron, black, 150 lb threaded, 1" pipe size	6.000	Ea.	5.22	102.78	108
Sprinkler head std spray, brass 135°-286°F ½" NPT, ⅜" orifice	12.000	Ea.	40.14	175.86	216
Firecycle controls, incls panel, battery, solenoid valves, press switches	1.000	Ea.	3,877.50	866.25	4,743.75
Detector, firecycle system	2.000	Ea.	277.20	30.30	307.50
Firecycle pkg, swing check & flow control valves w/trim 4" pipe size	1.000	Ea.	1,089	411	1,500
Air compressor, auto, complete, 200 Gal sprinkler sys cap, ⅛ HP	1.000	Ea.	367.13	176.63	543.76
*Standpipe connection, wall, flush, brass w/plug & chain 2-½"x2-½"	1.000	Ea.	70.95	82.80	153.75
Valve, gate, bronze, 300 psi, NRS, class 150, threaded, 1" diam	1.000	Ea.	12.38	11.63	24.01
TOTAL			7,003.01	3,810.87	10,813.88
COST PER S.F.			3.50	1.91	5.41

*Not included in systems under 2000 S.F.

8.2-150	Firecycle Sprinkler Systems	COST PER S.F. MAT.	COST PER S.F. INST.	COST PER S.F. TOTAL
0520	Firecycle sprinkler systems, steel black sch. 40 pipe			
0530	Light hazard, one floor, 500 S.F.	11.60	4.28	15.88
0560	1000 S.F.	5.95	2.67	8.62
0580	2000 S.F.	3.50	1.91	5.41

FIRE PROTECTION — B8.2-150 Firecycle Sprinkler Systems

8.2-150 Firecycle Sprinkler Systems

Code	Description	MAT.	INST.	TOTAL
0600	5000 S.F.	1.57	1.21	2.78
0620	10,000 S.F.	.94	.95	1.89
0640	50,000 S.F.	.49	.79	1.28
0660	Each additional floor of 500 S.F.	.68	1.18	1.86
0680	1000 S.F.	.50	1.06	1.56
0700	2000 S.F.	.38	.94	1.32
0720	5000 S.F.	.35	.83	1.18
0740	10,000 S.F.	.34	.76	1.10
0760	50,000 S.F.	.34	.71	1.05
1000	Ordinary hazard, one floor, 500 S.F.	11.70	4.43	16.13
1020	1000 S.F.	5.95	2.62	8.57
1040	2000 S.F.	3.55	2	5.55
1060	5000 S.F.	1.61	1.28	2.89
1080	10,000 S.F.	1.03	1.22	2.25
1100	50,000 S.F.	.70	1.25	1.95
1140	Each additional floor, 500 S.F.	.78	1.33	2.11
1160	1000 S.F.	.48	1.04	1.52
1180	2000 S.F.	.47	.95	1.42
1200	5000 S.F.	.42	.90	1.32
1220	10,000 S.F.	.38	.89	1.27
1240	50,000 S.F.	.37	.84	1.21
1500	Extra hazard, one floor, 500 S.F.	12.55	5.05	17.60
1520	1000 S.F.	6.45	3.23	9.68
1540	2000 S.F.	3.61	2.44	6.05
1560	5000 S.F.	1.70	1.71	3.41
1580	10,000 S.F.	1.27	1.66	2.93
1600	50,000 S.F.	1.01	1.80	2.81
1660	Each additional floor, 500 S.F.	.86	1.58	2.44
1680	1000 S.F.	.71	1.49	2.20
1700	2000 S.F.	.62	1.49	2.11
1720	5000 S.F.	.52	1.33	1.85
1740	10,000 S.F.	.54	1.19	1.73
1760	50,000 S.F.	.52	1.12	1.64
2020	Grooved steel, black, sch. 40 pipe, light hazard, one floor			
2030	2000 S.F.	3.60	1.72	5.32
2060	10,000 S.F.	1	.85	1.85
2100	Each additional floor, 2000 S.F.	.55	.76	1.31
2150	10,000 S.F.	.40	.65	1.05
2200	Ordinary hazard, one floor, 2000 S.F.	3.63	1.80	5.43
2250	10,000 S.F.	1.19	1.10	2.29
2300	Each additional floor, 2000 S.F.	.58	.84	1.42
2350	10,000 S.F.	.49	.86	1.35
2400	Extra hazard, one floor, 2000 S.F.	3.76	2.16	5.92
2450	10,000 S.F.	1.29	1.31	2.60
2500	Each additional floor, 2000 S.F.	.77	1.22	1.99
2550	10,000 S.F.	.65	1.08	1.73
3050	Grooved steel, black, sch. 10 pipe light hazard, one floor,			
3060	2000 S.F.	3.57	1.71	5.28
3100	10,000 S.F.	.98	.82	1.80
3150	Each additional floor, 2000 S.F.	.52	.75	1.27
3200	10,000 S.F.	.38	.63	1.01
3250	Ordinary hazard, one floor, 2000 S.F.	3.60	1.79	5.39
3300	10,000 S.F.	1.06	1.02	2.08
3350	Each additional floor, 2000 S.F.	.55	.83	1.38
3400	10,000 S.F.	.46	.84	1.30
3450	Extra hazard, one floor, 2000 S.F.	3.74	2.15	5.89
3500	10,000 S.F.	1.23	1.29	2.52
3550	Each additional floor, 2000 S.F.	.75	1.21	1.96

FIRE PROTECTION — B8.2-150 Firecycle Sprinkler Systems

8.2-150 Firecycle Sprinkler Systems

Line	Description	MAT.	INST.	TOTAL
3600	10,000 S.F.	.62	1.07	1.69
4060	Copper tubing, type M, light hazard, one floor, 2000 S.F.	3.60	1.71	5.31
4100	10,000 S.F.	1.05	.83	1.88
4150	Each additional floor, 2000 S.F.	.57	.77	1.34
4200	10,000 S.F.	.45	.65	1.10
4250	Ordinary hazard, one floor, 2000 S.F.	3.66	1.85	5.51
4300	10,000 S.F.	1.14	.97	2.11
4350	Each additional floor, 2000 S.F.	.56	.78	1.34
4400	10,000 S.F.	.48	.69	1.17
4450	Extra hazard, one floor, 2000 S.F.	3.80	2.17	5.97
4500	10,000 S.F.	1.68	1.42	3.10
4550	Each additional floor, 2000 S.F.	.81	1.23	2.04
4600	10,000 S.F.	.80	1.16	1.96
5060	Copper tubing, type M, T-drill system, light hazard, one floor 2000 S.F.	3.61	1.63	5.24
5100	10,000 S.F.	1.02	.71	1.73
5150	Each additional floor, 2000 S.F.	.63	.70	1.33
5200	10,000 S.F.	.43	.53	.96
5250	Ordinary hazard, one floor, 2000 S.F.	3.62	1.65	5.27
5300	10,000 S.F.	1.12	.88	2
5350	Each additional floor, 2000 S.F.	.57	.69	1.26
5400	10,000 S.F.	.53	.69	1.22
5450	Extra hazard, one floor, 2000 S.F.	3.68	1.87	5.55
5500	10,000 S.F.	1.48	1.06	2.54
5550	Each additional floor, 2000 S.F.	.69	.93	1.62
5600	10,000 S.F.	.63	.82	1.45

FIRE PROTECTION — B8.2-310 — Wet Standpipe Risers

Diagram: Wet standpipe riser showing Roof, Roof connections with hose gate valves (for combustible roof), Hose connections on each floor (size based on class of service), Siamese inlet connections (for fire department use), and Check Valve.

System Components	QUANTITY	UNIT	COST PER FLOOR MAT.	INST.	TOTAL
SYSTEM 082-310-0560					
WET STANDPIPE RISER, CLASS I, STEEL, BLACK, SCH. 40 PIPE, 10' HEIGHT					
4" DIAMETER PIPE, ONE FLOOR					
Pipe, steel, black, schedule 40, threaded, 4" diam	20.000	L.F.	210.40	289.60	500
Pipe, Tee, malleable iron, black, 150 lb threaded, 4" pipe size	2.000	Ea.	70.40	259.60	330
Pipe, 90° elbow, malleable iron, black, 150 lb threaded 4" pipe size	1.000	Ea.	25.30	89.70	115
Pipe, nipple, steel, black, schedule 40, 2-½" pipe size x 3" long	2.000	Ea.	13.42	66.58	80
Fire valve, gate, 300 lb, brass w/handwheel, 2-½" pipe size	1.000	Ea.	83.60	41.40	125
Fire valve, pressure restricting, adj, rgh brs, 2-½" pipe size	1.000	Ea.	196.36	83.64	280
Valve, swing check, w/ball drip, CI w/brs ftngs, 4" pipe size	1.000	Ea.	95.43	184.57	280
Standpipe conn wall dble flush brs w/plugs & chains 2-½"x2-½"x4"	1.000	Ea.	255.20	109.80	365
Valve, swing check, bronze, 125 lb, regrinding disc, 2-½" pipe size	1.000	Ea.	79.20	35.80	115
Roof manifold, fire, w/valves & caps, horiz/vert brs 2-½"x2-½"x4"	1.000	Ea.	266.20	113.80	380
Fire, hydrolator, vent & drain, 2-½" pipe size	1.000	Ea.	88	42	130
Valve, gate, iron body 125 lb, OS&Y, threaded, 4" pipe size	1.000	Ea.	269.50	50.50	320
TOTAL			1,653.01	1,366.99	3,020

8.2-310	Wet Standpipe Risers, Class I	MAT.	INST.	TOTAL
0550	Wet standpipe risers, Class I, steel black sch. 40, 10' height			
0560	4" diameter pipe, one floor	1,650	1,375	3,025
0580	Additional floors	425	465	890
0600	6" diameter pipe, one floor	2,550	2,250	4,800
0620	Additional floors	640	665	1,305
0640	8" diameter pipe, one floor	3,550	2,725	6,275
0660	Additional floors	800	810	1,610

8.2-310	Wet Standpipe Risers, Class II	MAT.	INST.	TOTAL
1030	Wet standpipe risers, Class II, steel black sch. 40, 10' height			
1040	2" diameter pipe, one floor	590	495	1,085
1060	Additional floors	230	205	435
1080	2-½" diameter pipe, one floor	795	710	1,505
1100	Additional floors	250	240	490

FIRE PROTECTION

B8.2-310 Wet Standpipe Risers

8.2-310 Wet Standpipe Risers, Class III

		MAT.	INST.	TOTAL
1530	Wet standpipe risers, Class III, steel black sch. 40, 10' height			
1540	4" diameter pipe, one floor	1,700	1,375	3,075
1560	Additional floors	355	390	745
1580	6" diameter pipe, one floor	2,600	2,250	4,850
1600	Additional floors	665	665	1,330
1620	8" diameter pipe, one floor	3,600	2,725	6,325
1640	Additional floors	820	810	1,630

(COST PER FLOOR)

FIRE PROTECTION   B8.2-320   Dry Standpipe Risers

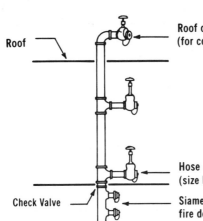

Roof connections with hose gate valves (for combustible roof)

Hose connections on each floor (size based on class of service)

Check Valve

Siamese inlet connections (for fire department use)

Costs for large jobs and those using prefabrications will run 15 to 25% less than these.

All areas are assumed to be open.

System Components	QUANTITY	UNIT	COST PER FLOOR		
			MAT.	INST.	TOTAL
SYSTEM 08.2-320-0540					
DRY STANDPIPE RISER, CLASS I, PIPE, STEEL, BLACK, SCH 40, 10' HEIGHT					
4" DIAMETER PIPE, ONE FLOOR					
Pipe, steel, black, schedule 40, threaded, 4" diam	20.000	L.F.	210.40	289.60	500
Pipe, Tee, malleable iron, black, 150 lb threaded, 4" pipe size	2.000	Ea.	70.40	259.60	330
Pipe, 90° elbow, malleable iron, black, 150 lb threaded 4" pipe size	1.000	Ea.	25.30	89.70	115
Pipe, nipple, steel, black, schedule 40, 2-½" pipe size x 3" long	2.000	Ea.	13.42	66.58	80
Fire valve gate NRS 300 lb, brass w/handwheel, 2-½" pipe size	1.000	Ea.	83.60	41.40	125
Fire valve, pressure restricting, adj, rgh brs, 2-½" pipe size	1.000	Ea.	98.18	41.82	140
Standpipe conn wall dble flush brs w/plugs & chains 2-½"x2-½"x4"	1.000	Ea.	255.20	109.80	365
Valve swing check w/ball drip Cl w/brs ftngs, 4"pipe size	1.000	Ea.	95.43	184.57	280
Roof manifold, fire, w/valves & caps, horiz/vert brs 2-½"x2-½"x4"	1.000	Ea.	266.20	113.80	380
TOTAL			1,118.13	1,196.87	2,315

8.2-320	Dry Standpipe Risers, Class I	COST PER FLOOR		
		MAT.	INST.	TOTAL
0530	Dry standpipe riser, Class I, steel black sch. 40, 10' height			
0540	4" diameter pipe, one floor	1,125	1,200	2,325
0560	Additional floors	335	425	760
0580	6" diameter pipe, one floor	1,925	1,850	3,775
0600	Additional floors	555	620	1,175
0620	8" diameter pipe, one floor	2,650	2,250	4,900
0640	Additional floors	710	770	1,480

8.2-320	Dry Standpipe Risers, Class II	COST PER FLOOR		
		MAT.	INST.	TOTAL
1030	Dry standpipe risers, Class II, steel black sch. 40, 10' height			
1040	2" diameter pipe, one floor	520	555	1,075
1060	Additional floor	190	180	370
1080	2-½" diameter pipe, one floor	590	650	1,240
1100	Additional floors	210	215	425

FIRE PROTECTION — B8.2-320 Dry Standpipe Risers

8.2-320 Dry Standpipe Risers, Class III

		COST PER FLOOR		
		MAT.	INST.	TOTAL
1530	Dry standpipe risers, Class III, steel black sch. 40, 10' height			
1540	4" diameter pipe, one floor	1,125	1,200	2,325
1560	Additional floors	275	385	660
1580	6" diameter pipe, one floor	1,950	1,850	3,800
1600	Additional floors	575	620	1,195
1620	8" diameter pipe, one floor	2,650	2,250	4,900
1640	Additional floor	730	770	1,500

FIRE PROTECTION — B8.2-390 Standpipe Equipment

8.2-390 Standpipe Equipment

Line	Description	MAT.	INST.	TOTAL
0100	Adapters, reducing, 1 piece, FxM, hexagon, cast brass, 2-½" x 1-½"	19.25		19.25
0200	Pin lug, 1-½" x 1"	8.95		8.95
0250	3" x 2-½"	30		30
0300	For polished chrome, add 75% mat.			
0400	Cabinets, D.S. glass in door, recessed, steel box, not equipped			
0500	Single extinguisher, steel door & frame	58	67	125
0550	Stainless steel door & frame	205	67	272
0600	Valve, 2-½" angle, steel door & frame	64	46	110
0650	Aluminum door & frame	110	48	158
0700	Stainless steel door & frame	210	47	257
0750	Hose rack assy, 2-½" x 1-½" valve & 100' hose, steel door & frame	130	92	222
0800	Aluminum door & frame	165	91	256
0850	Stainless steel door & frame	370	89	459
0900	Hose rack assy, & extinguisher, 2-½"x1-½" valve & hose, steel door & frame	135	110	245
0950	Aluminum	170	110	280
1000	Stainless steel	390	110	500
1550	Compressor, air, dry pipe system, automatic, 200 gal., ⅓ H.P.	490	235	725
1600	520 gal., 1 H.P.	565	235	800
1650	Alarm, electric pressure switch (circuit closer)	57	11.80	68.80
2500	Couplings, hose, rocker lug, cast brass, 1-½"	17.05		17.05
2550	2-½"	36		36
3000	Escutcheon plate, for angle valves, polished brass, 1-½"	8.25		8.25
3050	2-½"	15.40		15.40
3500	Fire pump, electric, w/controller, fittings, relief valve			
3550	4" pump, 30 H.P., 500 G.P.M.	11,200	1,725	12,925
3600	5" pump, 40 H.P., 1000 G.P.M.	12,900	1,975	14,875
3650	5" pump, 100 H.P., 1000 G.P.M.	16,000	2,150	18,150
3700	For jockey pump system, add	1,450	270	1,720
5000	Hose, per linear foot, synthetic jacket, lined,			
5100	300 lb. test, 1-½" diameter	1.32		1.32
5150	2-½" diameter	2		2
5200	500 lb. test, 1-½" diameter	1.40		1.40
5250	2-½" diameter	2.40		2.40
5500	Nozzle, plain stream, polished brass, 1-½" x 10"	19.80		19.80
5550	2-½" x 15" x ¹³⁄₁₆" or 1-½"	61		61
5600	Heavy duty combination adjustable fog and straight stream w/handle 1-½"	215		215
5650	2-½" direct connection	275		275
6000	Rack, for 1-½" diameter hose 100 ft. long, steel	28	28	56
6050	Brass	40	27	67
6500	Reel, steel, for 50 ft. long 1-½" diameter hose	52	40	92
6550	For 75 ft. long 2-½" diameter hose	63	42	105
7050	Siamese, w/plugs & chains, polished brass, sidewalk, 4" x 2-½" x 2-½"	305	225	530
7100	6" x 2-½" x 2-½"	440	275	715
7200	Wall type, flush, 4" x 2-½" x 2-½"	255	110	365
7250	6" x 2-½" x 2-½"	330	120	450
7300	Projecting, 4" x 2-½" x 2-½"	225	110	335
7350	6" x 2-½" x 2-½"	320	120	440
7400	For chrome plate, add 15% mat.			
8000	Valves, angle, wheel handle, 300 Lb., rough brass, 1-½"	25	25	50
8050	2-½"	56	44	100
8100	Combination pressure restricting, 1-½"	35	26	61
8150	2-½"	79	41	120
8200	Pressure restricting, adjustable, satin brass, 1-½"	58	25	83
8250	2-½"	98	42	140
8300	Hydrolator, vent and drain, rough brass, 1-½"	41	25	66
8350	2-½"	88	42	130
8400	Cabinet assy, incls. 2-½" valve, adapter, rack, hose, nozzle & hydrolator	465	205	670

FIRE PROTECTION — B8.2-810 — Halon Fire Suppression

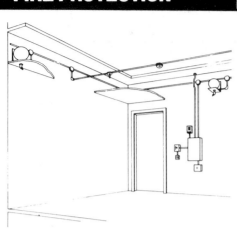

General: Automatic fire protection (suppression) systems other than water sprinklers may be desired for special environments, high risk areas, isolated locations or unusual hazards. Some typical applications would include:

Paint dip tanks
Securities vaults
Electronic data processing
Tape and data storage
Transformer rooms
Spray booths
Petroleum storage
High rack storage

Piping and wiring costs are dependent on the individual application and must be added to the component costs shown below.

All areas are assumed to be open.

8.2-810	Unit Components	MAT.	INST.	TOTAL
0020	Detectors with brackets			
0040	Fixed temperature heat detector	23	36	59
0060	Rate of temperature rise detector	29	35	64
0080	Ion detector (smoke) detector	52	46	98
0100				
0200	Extinguisher agent			
0240	200 lb halon, container	2,425	130	2,555
0280	75 lb carbon dioxide cylinder	760	86	846
0300				
0320	Dispersion nozzle			
0340	Halon 1-½" dispersion nozzle	55	21	76
0380	Carbon dioxide 3" x 5" dispersion nozzle	75	16.20	91.20
0400				
0420	Control station			
0440	Single zone control station with batteries	1,150	295	1,445
0470	Multizone (4) control station with batteries	2,375	585	2,960
0490				
0500	Electric mechanical release	180	145	325
0520				
0550	Manual pull station	35	49	84
0570				
0640	Battery standby power 10" x 10" x 17"	585	72	657
0700				
0740	Bell signalling device	41	36	77

8.2-810	Halon Systems	MAT.	INST.	TOTAL
0820	Average halon system, minimum			.60
0840	Maximum			1.65

HEATING — B8.3-110 — Hydronic, Electric Boilers

Boiler   **Baseboard Radiation**

Small Electric Boiler System Considerations:

1. Terminal units are fin tube baseboard radiation rated at 720 BTU/hr with 200° water temperature or 820 BTU/hr steam.
2. Primary use being for residential or smaller supplementary areas, the floor levels are based on 7-1/2' ceiling heights.
3. All distribution piping is copper for boilers through 205 MBH. All piping for larger systems is steel pipe.

System Components	QUANTITY	UNIT	MAT.	INST.	TOTAL
SYSTEM 08.3-110-1120					
SMALL HEATING SYSTEM, HYDRONIC, ELECTRIC BOILER					
1,480 S.F., 61 MBH, STEAM, 1 FLOOR					
Boiler, electric steam, standard controls & trim, 18 KW, 61.4 MBH	1.000	Ea.	3,146	679	3,825
Copper tubing type L, solder joint, hanger 10'OC, 1-1/4" diam	160.000	L.F.	540.80	811.20	1,352
Radiation, 3/4" copper tube w/alum fin baseboard pkg 7" high	60.000	L.F.	508.20	547.80	1,056
Rough in baseboard panel or fin tube with valves & traps	10.000	Set	1,094.70	2,755.30	3,850
Boiler room fittings and valves	1.000	System	314.60	67.90	382.50
Pipe covering, calcium silicate w/cover 1" wall 1-1/4" diam	160.000	L.F.	334.40	513.60	848
Low water cut-off, quick hookup, in gage glass tappings	1.000	Ea.	110	20	130
TOTAL			6,048.70	5,394.80	11,443.50
COST PER S.F.			4.09	3.65	7.74

8.3-110	Small Heating Systems, Hydronic, Electric Boilers	MAT.	INST.	TOTAL
1100	Small heating systems, hydronic, electric boilers			
1120	Steam, 1 floor, 1480 S.F., 61 M.B.H.	4.08	3.64	7.72
1160	3,000 S.F., 123 M.B.H.	2.87	3.19	6.06
1200	5,000 S.F., 205 M.B.H.	2.47	2.93	5.40
1240	2 floors, 12,400 S.F., 512 M.B.H.	2.20	2.91	5.11
1280	3 floors, 24,800 S.F., 1023 M.B.H.	2.20	2.88	5.08
1360	Hot water, 1 floor, 1,000 S.F., 41 M.B.H.	5.45	2.02	7.47
1400	2,500 S.F., 103 M.B.H.	3.81	3.63	7.44
1440	2 floors, 4,850 S.F., 205 M.B.H.	3.73	4.37	8.10
1480	3 floors, 9,700 S.F., 410 M.B.H.	3.75	4.54	8.29

HEATING B8.3-151 Fin Tube Radiation, Resi.

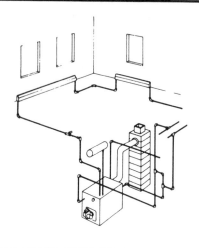

Basis for Heat Loss Estimate, Apartment Type Structures:

1. Masonry walls and flat roof are insulated. U factor is assumed at .08.
2. Window glass area taken as BOCA minimum, 1/10th of floor area. Double insulating glass with 1/4" air space, U = .65.
3. Infiltration = 0.3 C.F. per hour per S.F. of net wall.
4. Concrete floor loss is 2 BTUH per S.F.
5. Temperature difference taken as 70° F.
6. Ventilating or makeup air has not been included and must be added if desired. Air shafts are not used.

System Components	QUANTITY	UNIT	COST EACH MAT.	COST EACH INST.	COST EACH TOTAL
SYSTEM 08.3-151-1760					
HEATING SYSTEM, FIN TUBE RADIATION, FORCED HOT WATER					
1,000 S.F. AREA, 10,000 C.F. VOLUME					
Boiler, oil fired, CI, burner, controls & insulation 109 MBH	1.000	Ea.	1,452	948	2,400
Circulating pump, CI flange connection, 1/12 HP	1.000	Ea.	151.80	88.20	240
Expansion tank, painted steel, ASME 18 Gal capacity	1.000	Ea.	781	44	825
Storage tank, steel, above ground, 275 Gal capacity w/supports	1.000	Ea.	247.50	107.50	355
Copper tubing type L, solder joint, hanger 10' OC, 3/4" diam	100.000	L.F.	182	383	565
Radiation, 3/4" copper tube w/alum fin baseboard pkg, 7" high	30.000	L.F.	254.10	273.90	528
Pipe covering, calcium silicate w/cover, 1" wall, 3/4" diam	100.000	L.F.	217	313	530
Boiler room fittings and valves	1.000	System	726	474	1,200
Boiler breeching	1.000	System	72.60	47.40	120
Fuel oil piping system	1.000	System	290.40	189.60	480
TOTAL			4,374.40	2,868.60	7,243
COST PER S.F.			4.37	2.87	7.24

8.3-151	Apartment Building Heating - Fin Tube Radiation	COST PER S.F. MAT.	COST PER S.F. INST.	COST PER S.F. TOTAL
1740	Heating systems, fin tube radiation, forced hot water			
1760	1,000 S.F. area, 10,000 C.F. volume	4.37	2.87	7.24
1800	10,000 S.F. area, 100,000 C.F. volume	1.37	1.70	3.07

HEATING - SOLAR — B8.3-600 — General

Many styles of active solar energy systems exist. Those shown on the following page represent the majority of systems now being installed in different regions of the country.

The five active domestic hot water (DHW) systems which follow are typically specified as two or three panel systems with additional variations being the type of glazing and size of the storage tanks. Various combinations have been costed for the user's evaluation and comparison. The basic specifications from which the following systems were developed satisfy the construction detail requirements specified in the HUD Intermediate Minimum Property Standards (IMPS). If these standards are not complied with, the renewable energy system's costs could be significantly lower than shown.

To develop the system's specifications and costs it was necessary to make a number of assumptions about the systems. Certain systems are more appropriate to one climatic region than another or the systems may require modifications to be usable in particular locations. Specific instances in which the systems are not appropriate throughout the country as specified, or in which modification will be needed include the following:

- The freeze protection mechanisms provided in the DHW systems vary greatly. In harsh climates, where freeze is a major concern, a closed-loop indirect collection system may be more appropriate than a direct collection system.

- The thermosyphon water heater system described cannot be used when temperatures drop below 32°F.

- In warm climates it may be necessary to modify the systems installed to prevent overheating.

For each renewable resource (solar) system a schematic diagram and descriptive summary of the system is provided along with a list of all the components priced as part of the system. The costs were developed based on these specifications.

Considerations affecting costs which may increase or decrease beyond the estimates presented here include the following:

- Special structural qualities (allowance for earthquake, future expansion, high winds, and unusual spans or shapes);

- Isolated building site or rough terrain that would affect the transportation of personnel, material, or equipment;

- Unusual climatic conditions during the construction process;

- Substitution of other materials or system components for those used in the system specifications.

HEATING - SOLAR — B8.3-610 — Closed Loop, Immersed Exch.

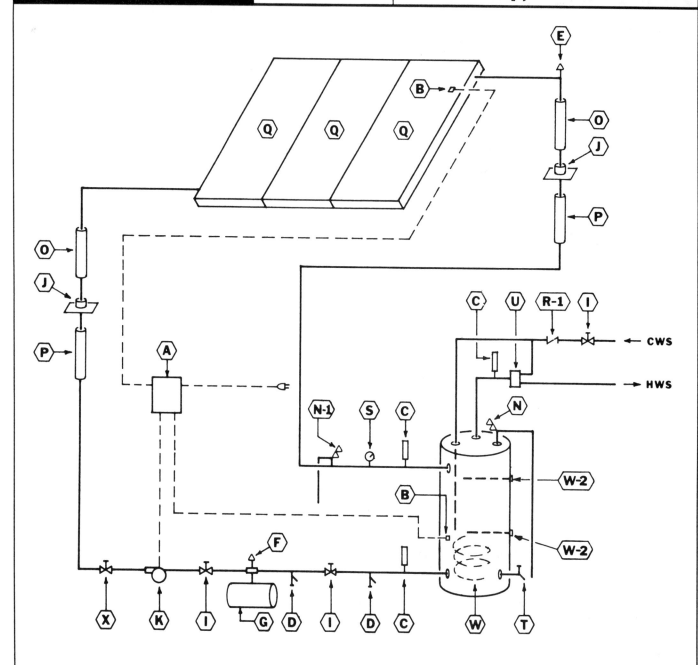

In this closed-loop indirect collection system, fluid with a low freezing temperature, such as propylene glycol, transports heat from the collectors to water storage. The transfer fluid is contained in a closed-loop consisting of collectors, supply and return piping, and a heat exchanger immersed in the storage tank. A typical two-or-three panel system contains 5 to 6 gallons of heat transfer fluid.

When the collectors become approximately 20° F warmer than the storage temperature, a controller activates the circulator. The circulator moves the fluid continuously through the collectors until the temperature difference between the collectors and storage is such that heat collection no longer occurs; at that point, the circulator shuts off. Since the heat transfer fluid has a very low freezing temperature, there is no need for it to be drained from the collectors between periods of collection.

HEATING - SOLAR — B8.3-610 — Closed Loop, Immersed Exch.

System Components	QUANTITY	UNIT	COST EACH MAT.	COST EACH INST.	COST EACH TOTAL
SYSTEM 08.3-610-2760					
SOLAR, CLOSED LOOP, HOT WATER SYSTEM, IMMERSED HEAT EXCHANGER					
¾" TUBING, THREE 3' X 7' BLACK CHROME COLLECTORS					
A, B — Differential controller, 2 sensors, thermostat, solar energy system	1.000	Ea.	115.50	24.50	140
C — Thermometer 2" dial	3.000	Ea.	52.80	55.20	108
D, T — Fill and drain valves, brass, ¾" connection	3.000	Ea.	14.85	36.60	51.45
E — Air vent, manual, ⅛" fitting	1.000	Ea.	1.57	9.18	10.75
F — Air purger	1.000	Ea.	18.15	24.85	43
G — Expansion tank	1.000	Ea.	42.35	9.65	52
I — Valve, gate, bronze, NRS, soldered ¾" diam	3.000	Ea.	47.52	45.48	93
J — Neoprene vent flashing	2.000	Ea.	12.76	29.24	42
K — Circulator, solar heated liquid, 1/25 HP	1.000	Ea.	104.50	35.50	140
N-1, N — Relief valve, temp & press 150 psi 210°F self-closing ¾" IPS	2.000	Ea.	36.30	19.70	56
O — Pipe covering, urethane ultraviolet cover, 1" wall, ¾" diam	20.000	L.F.	25.60	51.40	77
P — Pipe covering, fiberglass, all service jacket, 1" wall, ¾" diam	50.000	L.F.	59	115.50	174.50
Roof clamps for solar energy collector panel	3.000	Set	16.50	22.65	39.15
Q — Collector panel solar blk chrome on copper, ⅛" temp glass, 3'x7'	3.000	Ea.	1,105.50	169.50	1,275
R-1 — Valve, swing check, bronze, regrinding disc, ¾" diam, soldered	1.000	Ea.	11.99	15.01	27
S — Pressure gauge, 60 psi, 2-½" dial	1.000	Ea.	9.19	9.16	18.35
U — Valve, water tempering, bronze, sweat connections, ¾" diam	1.000	Ea.	31.90	15.10	47
W-2, W — Tank, water storage immersed heat exchr elec elem 2"x2# insul 120 Gal	1.000	Ea.	726	209	935
X — Valve, globe, bronze, rising stem, ¾" diam, soldered	1.000	Ea.	18.21	14.79	33
Copper tubing type L, solder joint, hanger 10' OC ¾" diam	20.000	L.F.	36.40	76.60	113
Copper tubing, type M, solder joint, hanger 10' OC ¾" diam	70.000	L.F.	91.70	261.80	353.50
Sensor wire, #22-2 conductor multistranded	.500	C.L.F.	5.23	14.28	19.51
Solar energy heat transfer fluid, propylene glycol, anti-freeze	6.000	Gal.	48.78	62.82	111.60
Wrought copper fittings & solder, ¾" diam	76.000	Ea.	43.32	1,172.68	1,216
TOTAL			2,675.62	2,500.19	5,175.81

8.3-610	Solar, Closed Loop, Hot Water Systems	MAT.	INST.	TOTAL
2550	Solar, closed loop, hot water system, immersed heat exchanger			
2560	⅜" tubing, 3 ea. 4' x 4'-4" vacuum tube collectors, 80 gal. tank	3,825	2,250	6,075
2580	½" tubing, 4 ea. 4' x 4'-4" vacuum tube collectors, 80 gal. tank	4,625	2,425	7,050
2600	120 gal. tank	4,700	2,450	7,150
2640	2 ea. 3'x7' black chrome collectors, 80 gal. tank	2,125	2,300	4,425
2660	120 gal. tank	2,200	2,325	4,525
2700	2 ea. 3'x7' flat black collectors, 120 gal. tank	2,175	2,325	4,500
2720	3 ea. 3'x7' flat black collectors, 120 gal. tank	2,550	2,400	4,950
2760	¾" tubing, 3 ea. 3'x7' black chrome collectors, 120 gal. tank	2,675	2,500	5,175
2780	3 ea. 3'x7' flat black collectors, 120 gal. tank	2,650	2,500	5,150
2800	2 ea. 4'x9' flat black w/plastic glazing collectors 120 gal. tank	2,325	2,525	4,850
2840	1" tubing, 4 ea. 2'x9' plastic absorber & glazing collectors 120 gal. tank	3,575	2,800	6,375
2860	4 ea. 3'x7' black chrome collectors, 120 gal. tank	3,175	2,825	6,000
2880	4 ea. 3'x7' flat black absorber collectors, 120 gal. tank	3,150	2,825	5,975

HEATING - SOLAR — B8.3-620 — Closed Loop, External Exch.

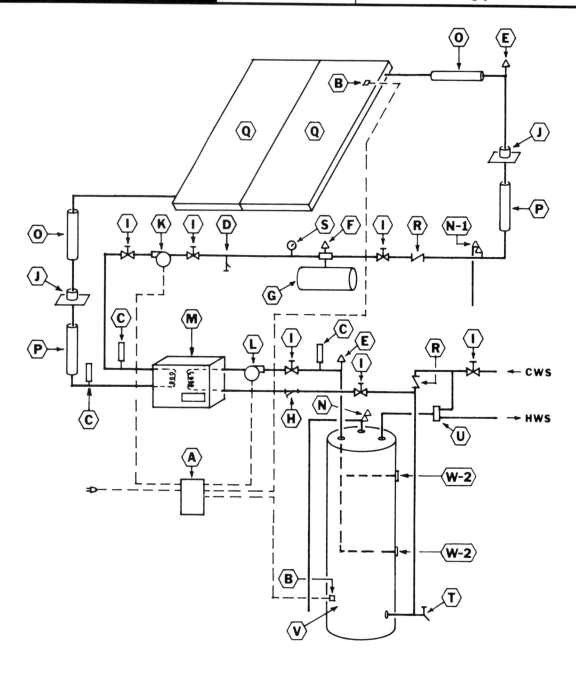

In this closed-loop indirect collection system, fluid with a low freezing temperature, such as propylene glycol, transports heat from the collectors to water storage. The transfer fluid is contained in a closed-loop consisting of collectors, supply and return piping, and a remote heat exchanger. The heat exchanger transfers heat energy from the fluid in the collector loop to potable water circulated in a storage loop. A typical two-or-three panel system contains 5 to 6 gallons of heat transfer fluid.

When the collectors become approximately 20°F warmer than the storage temperature, a controller activates the circulator on the collector and storage loops. The circulators will move the fluid and potable water through the heat exchanger until heat collection no longer occurs. At that point, the system shuts down. Since the heat transfer medium is a fluid with a very low freezing temperature, there is no need for it to be drained from the system between periods of collection.

HEATING - SOLAR B8.3-620 Closed Loop, External Exch.

System Components

System Components	QUANTITY	UNIT	MAT.	INST.	TOTAL
SYSTEM 08.3-620-2760					
SOLAR, CLOSED LOOP, ADD-ON HOT WATER SYSTEM, EXTERNAL HEAT EXCHANGER					
¾″ TUBING, TWO 3′X7′ BLACK CHROME COLLECTORS					
A, B, G, L, K, M Heat exchanger fluid-fluid pkg incl 2 circulators, expansion tank, Check valve, relief valve, controller, hi temp cutoff, & 2 sensors	1.000	Ea.	660	210	870
C Thermometer, 2″ dial	3.000	Ea.	52.80	55.20	108
D, T Fill and drain valve, brass, ¾″ connection	1.000	Ea.	4.95	12.20	17.15
E Air vent, manual, ⅛″ fitting	2.000	Ea.	3.14	18.36	21.50
F Air purger	1.000	Ea.	18.15	24.85	43
H Strainer, Y type, bronze body, ¾″ IPS	1.000	Ea.	25.74	15.26	41
I Valve, gate, bronze, NRS, soldered ¾″ diam	6.000	Ea.	95.04	90.96	186
J Neoprene vent flashing	2.000	Ea.	12.76	29.24	42
N-1, N Relief valve temp & press, 150 psi 210°F self-closing ¾″ IPS	1.000	Ea.	18.15	9.85	28
O Pipe covering, urethane, ultraviolet cover, 1″ wall ¾″ diam	20.000	L.F.	25.60	51.40	77
P Pipe covering, fiberglass, all service jacket, 1″ wall, ¾″ diam	50.000	L.F.	59	115.50	174.50
Q Collector panel solar energy blk chrome on copper, ⅛″ temp glass 3′x7′	2.000	Ea.	737	113	850
Roof clamps for solar energy collector panels	2.000	Set	11	15.10	26.10
R Valve, swing check, bronze, regrinding disc, ¾″ diam	2.000	Ea.	23.98	30.02	54
S Pressure gauge, 60 psi, 2″ dial	1.000	Ea.	9.19	9.16	18.35
U Valve, water tempering, bronze, sweat connections, ¾″ diam	1.000	Ea.	31.90	15.10	47
W-2, V Tank water storage w/heating element, drain, relief valve, existing	1.000	Ea.			
Copper tubing type L, solder joint, hanger 10′ OC ¾″ diam	20.000	L.F.	36.40	76.60	113
Copper tubing, type M, solder joint, hanger 10′ OC ¾″ diam	70.000	L.F.	91.70	261.80	353.50
Sensor wire, #22-2 conductor multistranded	.500	C.L.F.	5.23	14.28	19.51
Solar energy heat transfer fluid, propylene glycol anti-freeze	6.000	Gal.	48.78	62.82	111.60
Wrought copper fittings & solder, ¾″ diam	76.000	Ea.	43.32	1,172.68	1,216
TOTAL			2,013.83	2,403.38	4,417.21

8.3-620 Solar, Closed Loop, Add-on Hot Water Systems

		MAT.	INST.	TOTAL
2550	Solar, closed loop, add-on hot water system, external heat exchanger			
2570	⅜″ tubing, 3 ea. 4′ x 4′-4″ vacuum tube collectors	3,600	2,250	5,850
2580	½″ tubing, 4 ea 4 x 4′-4″ vacuum tube collectors	4,400	2,425	6,825
2600	2 ea 3′x7′ black chrome collectors	1,900	2,300	4,200
2620	3 ea 3′x7′ black chrome collectors	2,275	2,350	4,625
2640	2 ea 3′x7′ flat black collectors	1,875	2,300	4,175
2660	3 ea 3′x7′ flat black collectors	2,250	2,350	4,600
2700	¾″ tubing, 3 ea 3′x7′ black chrome collectors	2,400	2,475	4,875
2720	3 ea 3′x7′ flat black absorber plate collectors	2,350	2,475	4,825
2740	2 ea 4′x9′ flat black w/plastic glazing collectors	2,025	2,475	4,500
2760	2 ea 3′x7′ black chrome collectors	2,025	2,400	4,425
2780	1″ tubing, 4 ea 2′x9′ plastic absorber & glazing collectors	3,325	2,800	6,125
2800	4 ea 3′x7′ black chrome absorber collectors	2,925	2,800	5,725
2820	4 ea 3′x7′ flat black absorber collectors	2,875	2,800	5,675

HEATING - SOLAR B8.3-630 Drainback, Immersed Exch.

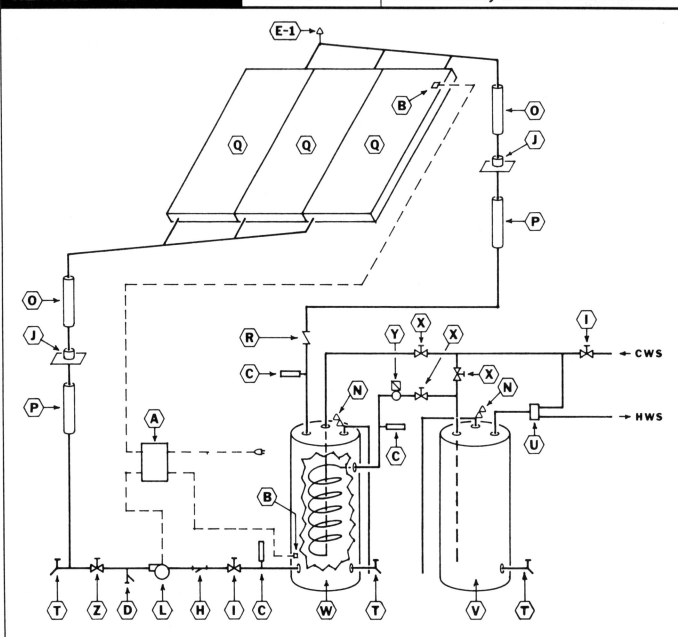

In the drainback indirect-collection system, the heat transfer fluid is distilled water contained in a loop consisting of collectors, supply and return piping, and an unpressurized holding tank. A large heat exchanger containing incoming potable water is immersed in the holding tank. When a controller activates solar collection, the distilled water is pumped through the collectors and heated and pumped back down to the holding tank. When the temperature differential between the water in the collectors and water in storage is such that collection no longer occurs, the pump turns off and gravity causes the distilled water in the collector loop to drain back to the holding tank. All the loop piping is pitched so that the water can drain out of the collectors and piping and not freeze there. As hot water is needed in the home, incoming water first flows through the holding tank with the immersed heat exchanger and is warmed and then flows through a conventional heater for any supplemental heating that is necessary.

HEATING - SOLAR B8.3-630 Drainback, Immersed Exch.

System Components	QUANTITY	UNIT	COST EACH MAT.	COST EACH INST.	TOTAL
SYSTEM 08.3-630-2760					
SOLAR, DRAINBACK, ADD ON, HOT WATER, IMMERSED HEAT EXCHANGER					
¾" TUBING, THREE EA 3'X7' BLACK CHROME COLLECTOR					
A, B Differential controller 2 sensors, thermostat, solar energy system	1.000	Ea.	115.50	24.50	140
C Thermometer 2" dial	3.000	Ea.	52.80	55.20	108
D, T Fill and drain valve, brass, ¾" connection	1.000	Ea.	4.95	12.20	17.15
E-1 Automatic air vent ⅛" fitting	1.000	Ea.	6.22	9.18	15.40
H Strainer, Y type, bronze body, ¾" IPS	1.000	Ea.	25.74	15.26	41
I Valve, gate, bronze, NRS, soldered ¾" diam	2.000	Ea.	31.68	30.32	62
J Neoprene vent flashing	2.000	Ea.	12.76	29.24	42
L Circulator, solar heated liquid, 1/20 HP	1.000	Ea.	80.30	44.70	125
N Relief valve temp. & press. 150 psi 210°F self-closing ¾" IPS	1.000	Ea.	18.15	9.85	28
O Pipe covering, urethane, ultraviolet cover, 1" wall, ¾" diam	20.000	L.F.	25.60	51.40	77
P Pipe covering, fiberglass, all service jacket, 1" wall, ¾" diam	50.000	L.F.	59	115.50	174.50
Q Collector panel solar energy blk chrome on copper, ⅛" temp glas 3'x7'	3.000	Ea.	1,105.50	169.50	1,275
Roof clamps for solar energy collector panels	3.000	Set	16.50	22.65	39.15
R Valve, swing check, bronze, regrinding disc, ¾" diam	1.000	Ea.	11.99	15.01	27
U Valve, water tempering, bronze sweat connections, ¾" diam	1.000	Ea.	31.90	15.10	47
W Tank, water storage immersed heat exchr elec 2"x1/2# insul 120 gal	1.000	Ea.	709.50	210.50	920
V Tank, water storage w/heating element, drain, relief valve, existing	1.000	Ea.			
X Valve, globe, bronze, rising stem, ¾" diam, soldered	3.000	Ea.	54.63	44.37	99
Y Flow control valve	1.000	Ea.	27.78	13.22	41
Z Valve, ball, bronze, solder ¾" diam, solar loop flow control	1.000	Ea.	7.87	15.13	23
Copper tubing, type L, solder joint, hanger 10' OC ¾" diam	20.000	L.F.	36.40	76.60	113
Copper tubing, type M, solder joint, hanger 10' OC ¾" diam	70.000	L.F.	91.70	261.80	353.50
Sensor wire, #22-2 conductor, multistranded	.500	C.L.F.	5.23	14.28	19.51
Wrought copper fittings & solder, ¾" diam	76.000	Ea.	43.32	1,172.68	1,216
TOTAL			2,575.02	2,428.19	5,003.21

8.3-630	Solar, Drainback, Hot Water Systems	MAT.	INST.	TOTAL
2550	Solar, drainback, hot water, immersed heat exchanger			
2560	⅜" tubing, 3 ea. 4' x 4'-4" vacuum tube collectors	3,725	2,175	5,900
2580	½" tubing, 4 ea 4' x 4'-4" vacuum tube collectors, 80 gal tank	4,525	2,350	6,875
2600	120 gal tank	4,575	2,375	6,950
2640	2 ea. 3'x7' blk chrome collectors, 80 gal tank	2,025	2,225	4,250
2660	3 ea. 3'x7' blk chrome collectors, 120 gal tank	2,475	2,325	4,800
2700	2 ea. 3'x7' flat blk collectors, 120 gal tank	2,075	2,250	4,325
2720	3 ea. 3'x7' flat blk collectors, 120 gal tank	2,450	2,325	4,775
2760	¾" tubing, 3 ea 3'x7' black chrome collectors, 120 gal tank	2,575	2,425	5,000
2780	3 ea. 3'x7' flat black absorber collectors, 120 gal tank	2,550	2,425	4,975
2800	2 ea. 4'x9' flat blk w/plastic glazing collectors 120 gal tank	2,225	2,450	4,675
2840	1" tubing, 4 ea. 2'x9' plastic absorber & glazing collectors, 120 gal tank	3,525	2,750	6,275
2860	4 ea. 3'x7' black chrome absorber collectors, 120 gal tank	3,125	2,775	5,900
2880	4 ea. 3'x7' flat black absorber collectors, 120 gal tank	3,075	2,775	5,850

HEATING - SOLAR — B8.3-640 — Draindown, Direct Collection

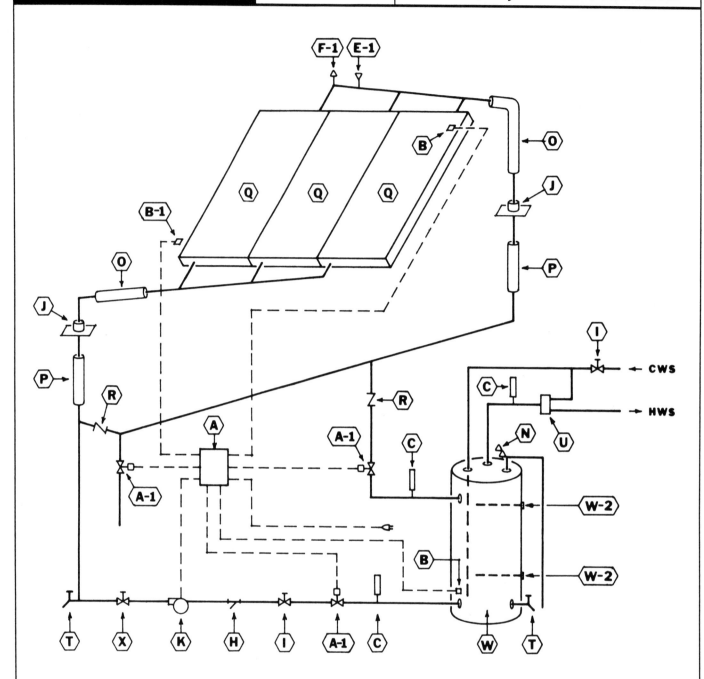

In the draindown direct-collection system, incoming domestic water is heated in the collectors. When the controller activates solar collection, domestic water is first heated as it flows through the collectors and is then pumped to storage. When conditions are no longer suitable for heat collection, the pump shuts off and the water in the loop drains down and out of the system by means of solenoid valves and properly pitched piping.

HEATING - SOLAR — B8.3-640 — Draindown, Direct Collection

System Components		QUANTITY	UNIT	COST EACH MAT.	COST EACH INST.	COST EACH TOTAL
	SYSTEM 08.3-640-2760					
	SOLAR, DRAINDOWN, HOT WATER, DIRECT COLLECTION					
	¾" TUBING, THREE 3'X7' BLACK CHROME COLLECTORS					
A, B	Differential controller, 2 sensors, thermostat, solar energy system	1.000	Ea.	115.50	24.50	140
A-1	Solenoid valve, solar heating loop, brass, ¾" diam, 24 volts	3.000	Ea.	158.40	96.60	255
B-1	Solar energy sensor, freeze prevention	1.000	Ea.	17.05	8.95	26
C	Thermometer, 2" dial	3.000	Ea.	52.80	55.20	108
E-1	Vacuum relief valve, ¾" diam	1.000	Ea.	27.50	9.50	37
F-1	Air vent, automatic, ⅛" fitting	1.000	Ea.	6.22	9.18	15.40
H	Strainer, Y type, bronze body, ¾" IPS	1.000	Ea.	25.74	15.26	41
I	Valve, gate, bronze, NRS, soldered, ¾" diam	2.000	Ea.	31.68	30.32	62
J	Vent flashing neoprene	2.000	Ea.	12.76	29.24	42
K	Circulator, solar heated liquid, 1/25 HP	1.000	Ea.	104.50	35.50	140
N	Relief valve temp & press 150 psi 210°F self-closing ¾" IPS	1.000	Ea.	18.15	9.85	28
O	Pipe covering, urethane, ultraviolet cover, 1" wall, ¾" diam	20.000	L.F.	25.60	51.40	77
P	Pipe covering, fiberglass, all service jacket, 1" wall, ¾" diam	50.000	L.F.	59	115.50	174.50
	Roof clamps for solar energy collector panels	3.000	Set	16.50	22.65	39.15
Q	Collector panel solar energy blk chrome on copper, ⅛" temp glass 3'x7'	3.000	Ea.	1,105.50	169.50	1,275
R	Valve, swing check, bronze, regrinding disc, ¾" diam, soldered	2.000	Ea.	23.98	30.02	54
T	Drain valve, brass, ¾" connection	2.000	Ea.	9.90	24.40	34.30
U	Valve, water tempering, bronze, sweat connections, ¾" diam	1.000	Ea.	31.90	15.10	47
W-2, W	Tank, water storage elec elem 2"x1/2# insul 120 gal	1.000	Ea.	709.50	210.50	920
X	Valve, globe, bronze, rising stem, ¾" diam, soldered	1.000	Ea.	18.21	14.79	33
	Copper tubing, type L, solder joints, hangers 10' OC ¾" diam	20.000	L.F.	36.40	76.60	113
	Copper tubing, type M, solder joints, hangers 10' OC ¾" diam	70.000	L.F.	91.70	261.80	353.50
	Sensor wire, #22-2 conductor, multistranded	.500	C.L.F.	5.23	14.28	19.51
	Wrought copper fittings & solder, ¾" diam	76.000	Ea.	43.32	1,172.68	1,216
	TOTAL			2,747.04	2,503.32	5,250.36

8.3-640	Solar, Draindown, Hot Water Systems	MAT.	INST.	TOTAL
2550	Solar, draindown, hot water			
2560	⅜" tubing, 3 ea. 4' x 4'-4" vacuum tube collectors, 80 gal tank	3,900	2,375	6,275
2580	½" tubing, 4 ea. 4' x 4'-4" vacuum tube collectors, 80 gal tank	4,700	2,425	7,125
2600	120 gal tank	4,750	2,475	7,225
2640	2 ea 3'x7' black chrome collectors, 80 gal tank	2,225	2,300	4,525
2660	3 ea 3'x7' black chrome collectors, 120 gal tank	2,650	2,400	5,050
2700	2 ea 3'x7' flat black collectors, 120 gal tank	2,250	2,350	4,600
2720	3 ea 3'x7' flat black collectors, 120 gal tank	2,600	2,400	5,000
2760	¾" tubing, 3 ea 3'x7' black chrome collectors, 120 gal tank	2,750	2,500	5,250
2780	3 ea 3'x7' flat collectors, 120 gal tank	2,725	2,500	5,225
2800	2 ea. 4'x9' flat black & plastic glazing collectors, 120 gal tank	2,400	2,525	4,925
2840	1" tubing, 4 ea. 2'x9' plastic absorber & glazing collectors, 120 gal tank	3,725	2,825	6,550
2860	4 ea 3'x7' black chrome absorber collectors, 120 gal tank	3,325	2,850	6,175
2880	4 ea 3'x7' flat black absorber collectors, 120 gal tank	3,275	2,850	6,125

HEATING - SOLAR   B8.3-650   Recirculation, Hot Water

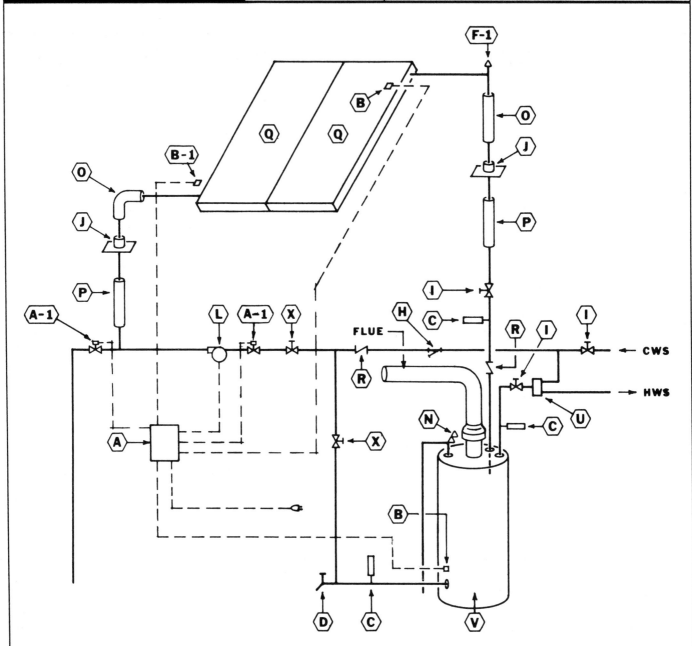

In the recirculation system, (a direct-collection system), incoming domestic water is heated in the collectors. When the controller activates solar collection, domestic water is heated as it flows through the collectors and then it flows back to storage. When conditions are not suitable for heat collection, the pump shuts off and the flow of the water stops. In this type of system, water remains in the collector loop at all times. A "frost sensor" at the collector activates the circulation of warm water from storage through the collectors when protection from freezing is required.

HEATING - SOLAR — B8.3-650 — Recirculation, Hot Water

System Components	QUANTITY	UNIT	COST EACH MAT.	COST EACH INST.	COST EACH TOTAL
SYSTEM 08.3-650-2820					
SOLAR, RECIRCULATION, HOT WATER					
¾" TUBING, TWO 3'X7' BLACK CHROME COLLECTORS					
A, B Differential controller 2 sensors, thermostat, for solar energy system	1.000	Ea.	115.50	24.50	140
A-1 Solenoid valve, solar heating loop, brass, ¾" IPS, 24 volts	2.000	Ea.	105.60	64.40	170
B-1 Solar energy sensor freeze prevention	1.000	Ea.	17.05	8.95	26
C Thermometer, 2" dial	3.000	Ea.	52.80	55.20	108
D Drain valve, brass, ¾" connection	1.000	Ea.	4.95	12.20	17.15
F-1 Air vent, automatic, ⅛" fitting	1.000	Ea.	6.22	9.18	15.40
H Strainer, Y type, bronze body, ¾" IPS	1.000	Ea.	25.74	15.26	41
I Valve, gate, bronze, 125 lb, soldered ¾" diam	3.000	Ea.	47.52	45.48	93
J Vent flashing, neoprene	2.000	Ea.	12.76	29.24	42
L Circulator, solar heated liquid, ½₀ HP	1.000	Ea.	80.30	44.70	125
N Relief valve, temp & press 150 psi 210°F self-closing ¾" IPS	2.000	Ea.	36.30	19.70	56
O Pipe covering, urethane, ultraviolet cover, 1" wall, ¾" diam	20.000	L.F.	25.60	51.40	77
P Pipe covering, fiberglass, all service jacket, 1" wall ¾" diam	50.000	L.F.	59	115.50	174.50
Q Collector panel solar energy blk chrome on copper, ⅛" temp glass 3'x7'	2.000	Ea.	737	113	850
Roof clamps for solar energy collector panels	2.000	Set	11	15.10	26.10
R Valve, swing check, bronze, 125 lb, regrinding disc, soldered ¾" diam	2.000	Ea.	23.98	30.02	54
U Valve, water tempering, bronze, sweat connections, ¾" diam	1.000	Ea.	31.90	15.10	47
V Tank, water storage, w/heating element, drain, relief valve, existing	1.000	Ea.			
X Valve, globe, bronze, 125 lb, ¾" diam	2.000	Ea.	36.42	29.58	66
Copper tubing, type L, solder joints, hangers 10' OC ¾" diam	20.000	L.F.	36.40	76.60	113
Copper tubing, type M, solder joints, hangers 10' OC ¾" diam	70.000	L.F.	91.70	261.80	353.50
Wrought copper fittings & solder, ¾" diam	76.000	Ea.	43.32	1,172.68	1,216
Sensor wire, #22-2 conductor, multistranded	.500	C.L.F.	5.23	14.28	19.51
TOTAL			1,606.29	2,223.87	3,830.16

8.3-650	Solar Recirculation, Domestic Hot Water Systems	MAT.	INST.	TOTAL
2550	Solar recirculation, hot water			
2560	⅜" tubing, 3 ea. 4' x 4'-4" vacuum tube collectors	3,200	2,075	5,275
2580	½" tubing, 4 ea. 4' x 4'-4" vacuum tube collectors	4,000	2,250	6,250
2640	2 ea. 3'x7' black chrome collectors	1,500	2,125	3,625
2660	3 ea. 3'x7' black chrome collectors	1,875	2,175	4,050
2700	2 ea. 3'x7' flat black collectors	1,475	2,125	3,600
2720	3 ea. 3'x7' flat black collectors	1,850	2,175	4,025
2760	¾" tubing, 3 ea. 3'x7' black chrome collectors	1,975	2,300	4,275
2780	3 ea. 3'x7' flat black absorber plate collectors	1,950	2,300	4,250
2800	2 ea. 4'x9' flat black w/plastic glazing collectors	1,625	2,300	3,925
2820	2 ea. 3'x7' black chrome collectors	1,600	2,225	3,825
2840	1" tubing, 4 ea. 2'x9' black plastic absorber & glazing collectors	2,950	2,600	5,550
2860	4 ea. 3'x7' black chrome absorber collectors	2,550	2,625	5,175
2880	4 ea. 3'x7' flat black absorber collectors	2,525	2,625	5,150

HEATING - SOLAR B8.3-660 Thermosyphon, Hot Water

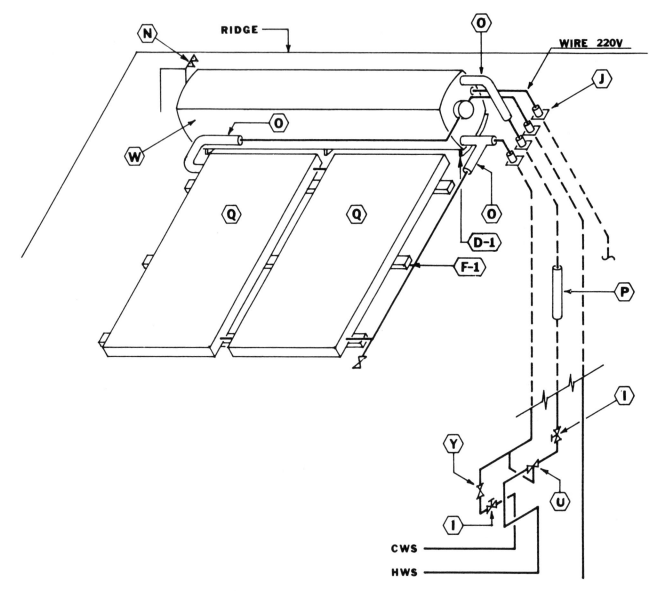

The thermosyphon domestic hot water system, a direct collection system, operates under city water pressure and does not require pumps for system operation. An insulated water storage tank is located above the collectors. As the sun heats the collectors, warm water in them rises by means of natural convection; the colder water in the storage tank flows into the collectors by means of gravity. As long as the sun is shining the water continues to flow through the collectors and to become warmer.

To prevent freezing, the system must be drained or the collectors covered with an insulated lid when the temperature drops below 32°F.

HEATING - SOLAR — B8.3-660 — Thermosyphon, Hot Water

System Components	QUANTITY	UNIT	MAT.	INST.	TOTAL
SYSTEM 08.3-660-0940					
SOLAR, THERMOSYPHON, WATER HEATER					
¾" TUBING, TWO 3'X7' BLACK CHROME COLLECTORS					
D-1 Framing lumber, fir, 2" x 6" x 8', tank cradle	.008	M.B.F.	3.30	3.46	6.76
F-1 Framing lumber, fir, 2" x 4" x 24', sleepers	.016	M.B.F.	6.60	10.20	16.80
I Valve, gate, bronze, 125 lb, soldered ½" diam	2.000	Ea.	23.98	24.02	48
J Vent flashing, neoprene	4.000	Ea.	25.52	58.48	84
O Pipe covering, urethane, ultraviolet cover, 1" wall, ½" diam	40.000	L.F.	51.20	98.40	149.60
P Pipe covering fiberglass all service jacket 1" wall ½" diam	160.000	L.F.	163.20	355.20	518.40
Q Collector panel solar, blk chrome on copper, 3/16" temp glass 3'-8" x 6'	2.000	Ea.	715	115	830
Y Flow control valve, globe, bronze, 125#, soldered, ½" diam	1.000	Ea.	15.29	12.71	28
U Valve, water tempering, bronze, sweat connections, ½" diam	1.000	Ea.	27.50	12.50	40
W Tank, water storage, solar energy system, 80 Gal, 2" x ½ lb insul	1.000	Ea.	632.50	182.50	815
Copper tubing type L, solder joints, hangers 10' OC ½" diam	150.000	L.F.	181.50	543	724.50
Copper tubing type M, solder joints, hangers 10' OC ½" diam	50.000	L.F.	44	174.50	218.50
Sensor wire, #22-2 gauge multistranded	.500	C.L.F.	5.23	14.28	19.51
Wrought copper fittings & solder, ½" diam	75.000	Ea.	18.75	1,098.75	1,117.50
TOTAL			1,933.37	2,721.59	4,654.96

C8.3-601

HEATING - SOLAR   B8.3-710   Closed Loop, Space/Hot Water

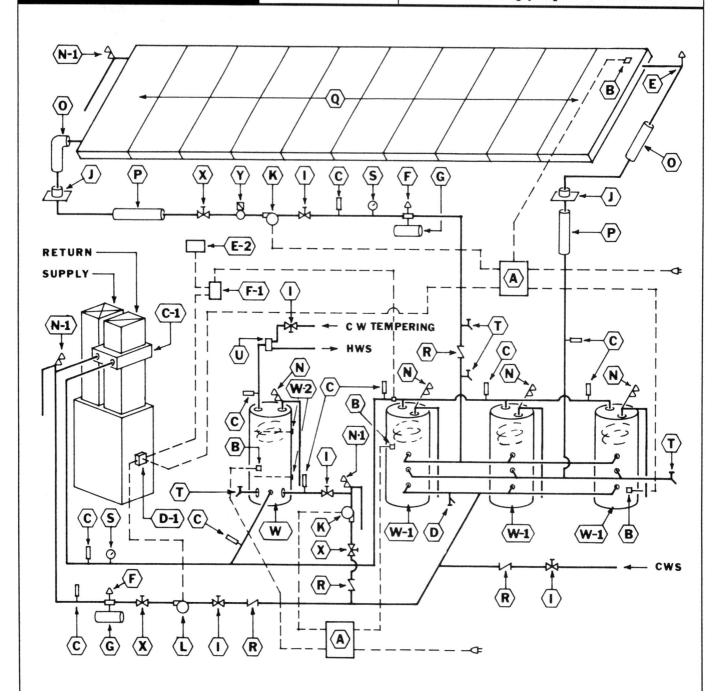

In this closed-loop indirect collection system, fluid with a low freezing temperature, such as propylene glycol, transports heat from the collectors to water storage. The transfer fluid is contained in a closed-loop consisting of collectors, supply and return piping, and a heat exchanger immersed in the storage tank.

When the collectors become approximately 20°F warmer than the storage temperature, the controller activates the circulator. The circulator moves the fluid continuously until the temperature difference between fluid in the collectors and storage is such that the collection will no longer occur and then the circulator turns off. Since the heat transfer fluid has a very low freezing temperature, there is no need for it to be drained from the collectors between periods of collection.

HEATING - SOLAR — B8.3-710 — Closed Loop, Space/Hot Water

System Components — SYSTEM 08.3-710-2750

SOLAR, CLOSED LOOP, SPACE/HOT WATER
1" TUBING, TEN 3'X7' BLK CHROME ON COPPER ABSORBER COLLECTORS

Ref	Description	Quantity	Unit	Mat.	Inst.	Total
A, B	Differential controller 2 sensors, thermostat, solar energy system	2.000	Ea.	231	49	280
C	Thermometer, 2" dial	10.000	Ea.	176	184	360
C-1	Heat exchanger, solar energy system, fluid to air, up flow, 80 MBH	1.000	Ea.	390.50	174.50	565
D, T	Fill and drain valves, brass, ¾" connection	5.000	Ea.	24.75	61	85.75
D-1	Fan center	1.000	Ea.	104.50	65.50	170
E	Air vent, manual, ⅛" fitting	1.000	Ea.	1.57	9.18	10.75
E-2	Thermostat, 2 stage for sensing room temperature	1.000	Ea.	55.22	36.78	92
F	Air purger	2.000	Ea.	36.30	49.70	86
F-1	Controller, liquid temperature, solar energy system	1.000	Ea.	102.85	57.15	160
G	Expansion tank	2.000	Ea.	84.70	19.30	104
I	Valve, gate, bronze, 125 lb, soldered, 1" diam	5.000	Ea.	96.25	78.75	175
J	Vent flashing, neoprene	2.000	Ea.	12.76	29.24	42
K	Circulator, solar heated liquid, $1/25$ HP	2.000	Ea.	209	71	280
L	Circulator, solar heated liquid, $1/20$ HP	1.000	Ea.	80.30	44.70	125
N	Relief valve, temp & pressure 150 psi 210°F self-closing	4.000	Ea.	72.60	39.40	112
N-1	Relief valve, pressure poppet, bronze, 30 psi, ¾" IPS	3.000	Ea.	45.21	32.79	78
O	Pipe covering, urethane, ultraviolet cover, 1" wall, 1" diam	50.000	L.F.	64	128.50	192.50
P	Pipe covering, fiberglass, all service jacket, 1" wall, 1" diam	60.000	L.F.	70.80	138.60	209.40
Q	Collector panel solar energy blk chrome on copper ⅛" temp glass 3'x7'	10.000	Ea.	3,685	565	4,250
	Roof clamps for solar energy collector panel	10.000	Set	55	75.50	130.50
R	Valve, swing check, bronze, 125 lb, regrinding disc, ¾" & 1" diam	4.000	Ea.	62.92	61.08	124
S	Pressure gage, 0-60 psi, for solar energy system	2.000	Ea.	18.38	18.32	36.70
U	Valve, water tempering, bronze, sweat connections, ¾" diam	1.000	Ea.	31.90	15.10	47
W-2, W-1, W	Tank, water storage immersed heat xchr elec elem 2"x1/2# ins 120 gal	4.000	Ea.	2,838	842	3,680
X	Valve, globe, bronze, 125 lb, rising stem, 1" diam	3.000	Ea.	89.10	45.90	135
Y	Valve, flow control	1.000	Ea.	27.78	13.22	41
	Copper tubing type M, solder joint, hanger 10' OC, 1" diam	110.000	L.F.	200.20	459.80	660
	Copper tubing, type L, solder joint, hanger 10' OC ¾" diam	20.000	L.F.	36.40	76.60	113
	Wrought copper fittings & solder, ¾" & 1" diam	121.000	Ea.	164.56	2,219.14	2,383.70
	Sensor, wire, #22-2 conductor, multistranded	.700	C.L.F.	7.32	19.99	27.31
	Ductwork, galvanized steel, for heat exchanger	8.000	Lb.	9.52	28.08	37.60
	Solar energy heat transfer fluid propylene glycol, anti-freeze	25.000	Gal.	203.25	261.75	465
	TOTAL			9,286.87	5,977.34	15,264.21

8.3-710 Solar, Closed Loop, Space/Hot Water Systems

Code	Description	Mat.	Inst.	Total
2540	Solar, closed loop, space/hot water			
2550	½" tubing, 12 ea. 4'x4'4" vacuum tube collectors	14,900	5,525	20,425
2600	¾" tubing, 12 ea. 4'x4'4" vacuum tube collectors	15,100	5,700	20,800
2650	10 ea. 3' x 7' black chrome absorber collectors	9,175	5,575	14,750
2700	10 ea. 3' x 7' flat black absorber collectors	9,050	5,575	14,625
2750	1" tubing, 10 ea. 3' x 7' black chrome absorber collectors	9,275	5,975	15,250
2800	10 ea. 3' x 7' flat black absorber collectors	9,175	5,975	15,150
2850	6 ea. 4' x 9' flat black w/plastic glazing collectors	7,850	5,950	13,800
2900	12 ea. 2' x 9' plastic absorber and glazing collectors	11,200	6,050	17,250

HEATING - SOLAR B8.3-720 Swimming Pool Heater

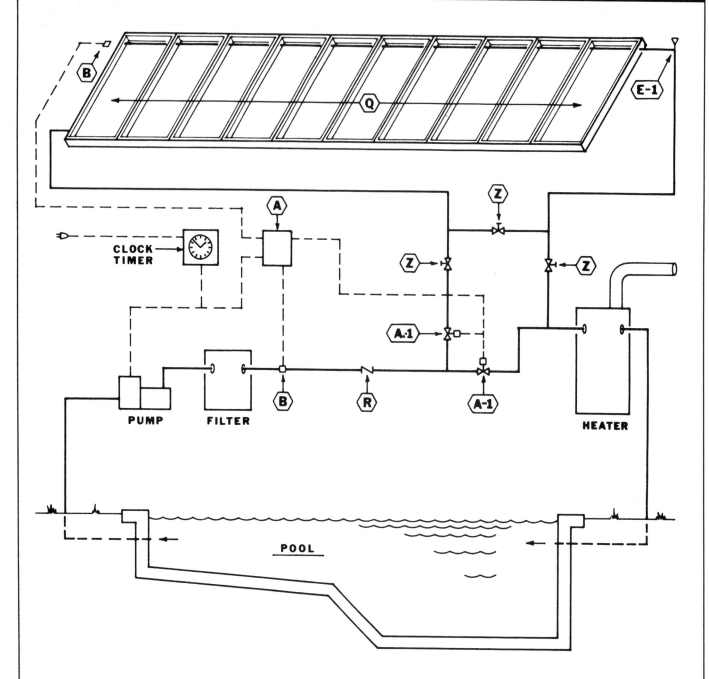

This draindown pool system uses a differential thermostat similar to those used in solar domestic hot water and space heating applications. To heat the pool, the pool water passes through the conventional pump-filter loop and then flows through the collectors. When collection is not possible, or when the pool temperature is reached, all water drains from the solar loop back to the pool through the existing piping. The modes are controlled by solenoid valves or other automatic valves in conjunction with a vacuum breaker relief valve, which facilitates draindown.

HEATING - SOLAR

B8.3-720 Swimming Pool Heater

System Components	QUANTITY	UNIT	COST EACH		
			MAT.	INST.	TOTAL
SYSTEM 08.3-720-2640					
SOLAR SWIMMING POOL HEATER, ROOF MOUNTED COLLECTORS					
TEN 4' X 10' FULLY WETTED UNGLAZED PLASTIC ABSORBERS					
A Differential thermostat/controller, 110V, adj pool pump system	1.000	Ea.	352	148	500
A-1 Solenoid valve, PVC, normally 1 open 1 closed, (included)	2.000	Ea.			
B Sensor, thermistor type, (included)	2.000	Ea.			
E-1 Valve, vacuum relief	1.000	Ea.	27.50	9.50	37
Q Collector panel, solar energy, plastic, liquid full wetted, 4' x 10'	10.000	Ea.	1,595	1,055	2,650
R Valve, ball check, PVC, socket, 1-½" diam	1.000	Ea.	46.20	14.80	61
Z Valve, ball, PVC, socket, 1-½" diam	3.000	Ea.	46.20	43.80	90
Pipe, PVC, sch 40, 1-½" diam	80.000	L.F.	89.60	650.40	740
Pipe fittings, PVC sch 40, socket joint, 1-½" diam	10.000	Ea.	6.80	183.20	190
Sensor wire, #22-2 conductor, multistranded	.500	C.L.F.	5.23	14.28	19.51
Roof clamps for solar energy collector panels	10.000	Set	55	75.50	130.50
Roof strap, teflon for solar energy collector panels	26.000	L.F.	135.98	36.92	172.90
TOTAL			2,359.51	2,231.40	4,590.91

8.3-720 Solar Swimming Pool Heater Systems

		COST EACH		
		MAT.	INST.	TOTAL
2530	Solar swimming pool heater systems, roof mounted collectors			
2540	10 ea. 3'x7' black chrome absorber, ⅛" temp. glass	4,450	1,750	6,200
2560	10 ea. 4'x8' black chrome absorber, 3/16" temp. glass	8,250	2,050	10,300
2580	10 ea. 3'8"x6' flat black absorber, 3/16" temp. glass	4,350	1,750	6,100
2600	10 ea. 4'x9' flat black absorber, plastic glazing	4,550	2,125	6,675
2620	10 ea. 2'x9' rubber absorber, plastic glazing	10,200	2,300	12,500
2640	10 ea. 4'x10' fully wetted unglazed plastic absorber	2,350	2,225	4,575
2660	Ground mounted collectors			
2680	10 ea. 3'x7' black chrome absorber, ⅛" temp. glass	4,575	2,000	6,575
2700	10 ea. 4'x8' black chrome absorber, 3/16" temp glass	8,375	2,300	10,675
2720	10 ea. 3'8"x6' flat blk absorber, 3/16" temp. glass	4,475	2,000	6,475
2740	10 ea. 4'x9' flat blk absorber, plastic glazing	4,675	2,375	7,050
2760	10 ea. 2'x9' rubber absorber, plastic glazing	10,200	2,475	12,675
2780	10 ea. 4'x10' fully wetted unglazed plastic absorber	2,475	2,475	4,950

HEATING - SOLAR | B8.3-730 | Air To Water Heat Exchange

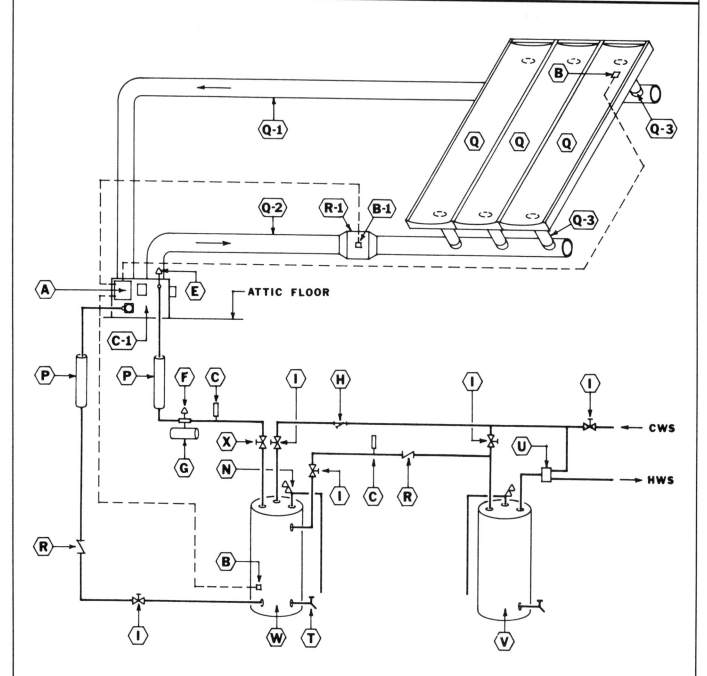

This domestic hot water pre-heat system includes heat exchanger with a circulating pump, blower, air-to-water, coil and controls, mounted in the upper collector manifold. Heat from the hot air coming out of the collectors is transferred through the heat exchanger. For each degree of DHW preheating gained, one degree less heating is needed from the fuel fired water heater. The system is simple, inexpensive to operate and can provide a substantial portion of DHW requirements for modest additional cost.

HEATING - SOLAR B8.3-730 Air To Water Heat Exchange

System Components

		QUANTITY	UNIT	COST EACH MAT.	COST EACH INST.	COST EACH TOTAL
	SYSTEM 08.3-730-2560					
	SOLAR, HOT WATER, AIR TO WATER HEAT EXCHANGE					
	THREE COLLECTORS, OPTICAL BLACK ON ALUMINUM, 10'X2', 80GAL TANK					
A, B	Differential controller, 2 sensors, thermostat, solar energy system	1.000	Ea.	115.50	24.50	140
C	Thermometer, 2" dial	2.000	Ea.	35.20	36.80	72
C-1	Heat exchanger, air to fluid, up flow 70 MBH	1.000	Ea.	269.50	150.50	420
E	Air vent, manual, for solar energy system 1/8" fitting	1.000	Ea.	1.57	9.18	10.75
F	Air purger	1.000	Ea.	18.15	24.85	43
G	Expansion tank	1.000	Ea.	42.35	9.65	52
H	Strainer, Y type, bronze body, 1/2" IPS	1.000	Ea.	22.11	14.89	37
I	Valve, gate, bronze, 125 lb, NRS, soldered 1/2" diam	5.000	Ea.	59.95	60.05	120
N	Relief valve, temp & pressure solar 150 psi 210°F self-closing	1.000	Ea.	18.15	9.85	28
P	Pipe covering, fiberglass, all service jacket, 1" wall, 1/2" diam	60.000	L.F.	61.20	133.20	194.40
Q	Collector panel solar energy, air, black on alum plate, flush mount, 10'x2'	30.000	L.F.	1,782	168	1,950
B-1, R-1	Shutter damper with shutter motor	1.000	Ea.	94.60	77.40	172
R	Backflow preventer for solar energy system, 1/2" diam	2.000	Ea.	94.06	35.94	130
T	Drain valve, brass, 3/4" connection	1.000	Ea.	4.95	12.20	17.15
U	Valve, water tempering, bronze, sweat connections, 1/2" diam	1.000	Ea.	27.50	12.50	40
W	Tank, water storage, solar energy system, 80 Gal, 2" x 2 lb insul	1.000	Ea.	649	181	830
V	Tank, water storage, w/heating element, drain, relief valve, existing	1.000	System			
X	Valve, globe, bronze, 125 lb, rising stem, 1/2" diam	1.000	Ea.	15.29	12.71	28
	Copper tubing type M, solder joints, hangers 10' OC 1/2" diam	50.000	L.F.	44	174.50	218.50
	Copper tubing type L, solder joints, hangers 10' OC 1/2" diam	10.000	L.F.	12.10	36.20	48.30
	Wrought copper fittings & solder, 1/2" diam	10.000	Ea.	2.50	146.50	149
	Sensor wire, #22-2 conductor multistranded	.500	C.L.F.	5.23	14.28	19.51
Q-1, Q-2	Ductwork, fiberglass, aluminzed jacket, 1-1/2" thick, 8" diam	32.000	S.F.	104.32	94.08	198.40
Q-3	Manifold for flush mount solar energy collector panels, air	6.000	L.F.	99	19.80	118.80
	TOTAL			3,595.28	1,467.53	5,062.81

8.3-730	Solar Hot Water, Air To Water Heat Exchange	COST EACH MAT.	COST EACH INST.	COST EACH TOTAL
2550	Solar hot water, air to water heat exchange			
2560	Three collectors, optical black on aluminum, 10' x 2', 80 Gal tank	3,600	1,475	5,075
2580	Four collectors, optical black on aluminum, 10' x 2', 80 Gal tank	4,225	1,550	5,775
2600	Four collectors, optical black on aluminum, 10' x 2', 120 Gal tank	4,300	1,575	5,875

HEATING - SOLAR   B8.3-740   Air To Water Heat Exchange

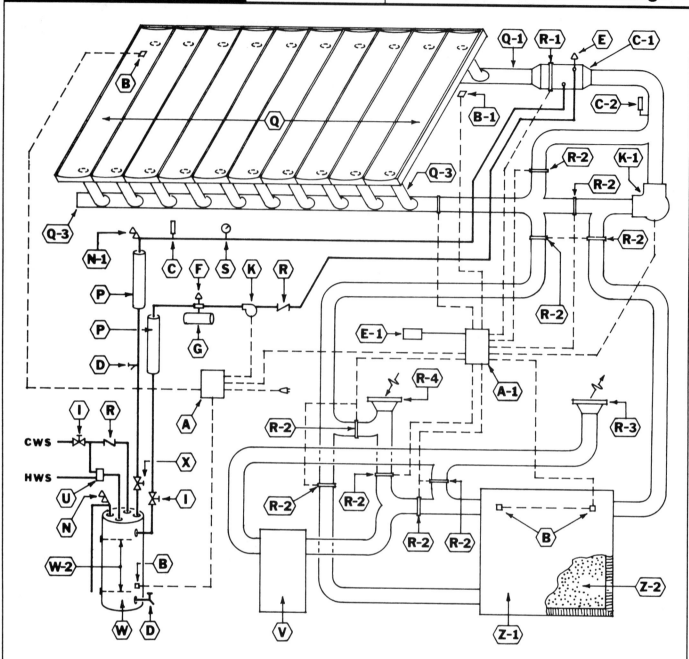

The complete Solar Air Heating System provides maximum savings of conventional fuel with both space heating and year-round domestic hot water heating. It allows for the home air conditioning to operate simultaneously and independently from the solar domestic water heating in summer. The system's modes of operation are:

Mode 1: The building is heated directly from the collectors with air circulated by the Solar Air Mover.

Mode 2: When heat is not needed in the building, the dampers change within the air mover to circulate the air from the collectors to the rock storage bin.

Mode 3: When heat is not available from the collector array and is available in rock storage, the air mover draws heated air from rock storage and directs it into the building. When heat is not available from the collectors or the rock storage bin, the auxiliary heating unit will provide heat for the building. The size of the collector array is typically 25% the size of the main floor area.

HEATING - SOLAR B8.3-740 Air To Water Heat Exchange

System Components		QUANTITY	UNIT	COST EACH MAT.	COST EACH INST.	COST EACH TOTAL
	SOLAR, SPACE/HOT WATER, AIR TO WATER HEAT EXCHANGE					
A, B	Differential controller 2 sensors thermos., solar energy sys liquid loop	1.000	Ea.	115.50	24.50	140
A-1, B	Differential controller 2 sensors 6 station solar energy sys air loop	1.000	Ea.	330	100	430
B-1	Solar energy sensor, freeze prevention	1.000	Ea.	17.05	8.95	26
C	Thermometer for solar energy system, 2″ dial	2.000	Ea.	35.20	36.80	72
C-1	Heat exchanger, solar energy system, air to fluid, up flow, 70 MBH	1.000	Ea.	269.50	150.50	420
D	Drain valve, brass, ¾″ connection	2.000	Ea.	9.90	24.40	34.30
E	Air vent, manual, for solar energy system ⅛″ fitting	1.000	Ea.	1.57	9.18	10.75
E-1	Thermostat, 2 stage for sensing room temperature	1.000	Ea.	55.22	36.78	92
F	Air purger	1.000	Ea.	18.15	24.85	43
G	Expansion tank, for solar energy system	1.000	Ea.	42.35	9.65	52
I	Valve, gate, bronze, 125 lb, NRS, soldered ¾″ diam	2.000	Ea.	31.68	30.32	62
K	Circulator, solar heated liquid, ½₆ HP	1.000	Ea.	104.50	35.50	140
N	Relief valve temp & press 150 psi 210°F self-closing, ¾″ IPS	1.000	Ea.	18.15	9.85	28
N-1	Relief valve, pressure, poppet, bronze, 30 psi, ¾″ IPS	1.000	Ea.	15.07	10.93	26
P	Pipe covering, fiberglass, all service jacket, 1″ wall, ¾″ diam	60.000	L.F.	70.80	138.60	209.40
Q-3	Manifold for flush mount solar energy collector panels	20.000	L.F.	330	66	396
Q	Collector panel solar energy, air, black on alum. plate, flush mount 10′x2′	100.000	L.F.	5,940	560	6,500
R	Valve, swing check, bronze, 125 lb, regrinding disc, ¾″ diam	2.000	Ea.	23.98	30.02	54
S	Pressure gage, 2″ dial, for solar energy system	1.000	Ea.	9.19	9.16	18.35
U	Valve, water tempering, bronze, sweat connections, ¾″ diam	1.000	Ea.	31.90	15.10	47
W-2, W	Tank, water storage, solar, elec element 2″x1/2# insul, 80 Gal	1.000	Ea.	632.50	182.50	815
X	Valve, globe, bronze, 125 lb, soldered, ¾″ diam	1.000	Ea.	18.21	14.79	33
	Copper tubing type L, solder joints, hangers 10′ OC ¾″ diam	10.000	L.F.	18.20	38.30	56.50
	Copper tubing type M, solder joints, hangers 10′ OC ¾″ diam	60.000	L.F.	78.60	224.40	303
	Wrought copper fittings & solder, ¾″ diam	26.000	Ea.	14.82	401.18	416
	Sensor wire, #22-2 conductor multistranded	1.200	C.L.F.	12.54	34.26	46.80
Q-1	Duct work, rigid fiberglass, rectangular	400.000	S.F.	276	944	1,220
	Ductwork, transition pieces	8.000	Ea.	129.84	174.16	304
R-2	Shutter/damper for solar heater circulator	9.000	Ea.	267.30	398.70	666
K-1	Shutter motor for solar heater circulator blower	9.000	Ea.	584.10	297.90	882
K-1	Fan, solar energy heated air circulator, space & DHW system	1.000	Ea.	1,309	1,066	2,375
Z-1	Tank, solar energy air storage, 6′-3″H 7′x7′ = 306 CF/2000 Gal	1.000	Ea.	5,368	682	6,050
Z-2	Crushed stone 1-½″	11.000	C.Y.	176.66	43.34	220
C-2	Thermometer, remote probe, 2″ dial	1.000	Ea.	29.70	36.30	66
R-1	Solenoid valve	1.000	Ea.	52.80	32.20	85
V, R-4, R-3	Furnace, supply diffusers, return grilles, existing	1.000	Ea.			
	TOTAL			16,261.32	5,857.78	22,119.10

C8.3-601

SPECIAL B8.5-110 Garage Exhaust

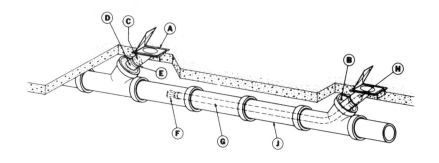
Vitrified Clay Garage Exhaust System

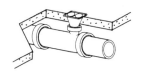
Dual Exhaust System

System Components	QUANTITY	UNIT	COST EACH MAT.	COST EACH INST.	COST EACH TOTAL
SYSTEM 085-110-1040					
GARAGE, EXHAUST, SINGLE OUTLET, 3" EXHAUST, CARS & LIGHT TRUCKS					
A Outlet top assembly for engine exhaust system, 3" diam	1.000	Ea.	107.84	11.86	119.70
B Tile adapter ring for engine exhaust system, 3" diam	1.000	Ea.	47.30	5.20	52.50
C Tubing adapter plate for engine exhaust system, 3" diam	1.000	Ea.	7.57	.83	8.40
D Outlet extension for engine exhaust system, 3" diam	1.000	Ea.	24.60	2.70	27.30
E Extension clamp for engine exhaust system, 3" diam	1.000	Ea.	1.89	.21	2.10
F Bullnose (guide) for engine exhaust system, 3" diam	1.000	Ea.	15.40		15.40
G Galvanized flexible tubing for engine exhaust system, 3" diam	8.000	L.F.	35.20		35.20
H Adapter for metal tubing end of engine exhaust system, 3" tail pipe	1.000	Ea.	42		42
J Pipe, sewer, vitrified clay, premium joint, 8" diam.	18.000	L.F.	52.92	86.58	139.50
Excavate utility trench w/chain trencher, 12 H.P., oper. walking	18.000	L.F.		15.84	15.84
Backfill utility trench by hand, incl. compaction, 8" wide 24" deep	18.000	L.F.		23.94	23.94
Stand for blower, concrete over polystyrene core, 6" high	1.000	Ea.	3.69	9.21	12.90
AC&V duct spiral reducer 10"x8"	1.000	Ea.	14.52	16.48	31
AC&V duct spiral reducer 12"x10"	1.000	Ea.	15.84	22.16	38
AC&V duct spiral preformed 45° elbow 8" diam	1.000	Ea.	52.47	18.53	71
AC&V utility fan, belt drive, 3 phase, 2000 CFM, 1 HP	2.000	Ea.	935	295	1,230
Safety switch, heavy duty fused, 240V, 3 pole, 30 amp	1.000	Ea.	68.20	91.80	160
TOTAL			1,424.44	600.34	2,024.78

8.5-110	Garage Exhaust Systems	COST PER BAY MAT.	COST PER BAY INST.	COST PER BAY TOTAL
1040	Garage, single exhaust, 3" outlet, cars & light trucks, one bay	1,425	600	2,025
1060	Additional bays up to seven bays	310	91	401
1500	4" outlet, trucks, one bay	1,450	600	2,050
1520	Additional bays up to six bays	325	91	416
1600	5" outlet, diesel trucks, one bay	1,475	600	2,075
1650	Additional single bays up to six	360	105	465
1700	Two adjoining bays	1,475	600	2,075
2000	Dual exhaust, 3" outlets, pair of adjoining bays	1,650	670	2,320
2100	Additional pairs of adjoining bays	505	105	610

SITE WORK — B12.3-110 Trenching

Trenching systems are shown on a cost per linear foot basis. the systems include excavation; backfill placed and compaction for various depths and trench bottom widths. Side slopes vary from 0:1 to 2:1

The expanded System Listing shows trenching systems that range from 2' to 12' in width. Depths range from 2' to 24'.

System Components	QUANTITY	UNIT	EQUIP.	LABOR	TOTAL
SYSTEM 12.3-110-1310					
TRENCHING, BACKHOE, 0 TO 1 SLOPE, 2' WIDE, 2' DP, ⅜ C.Y. BUCKET					
Excavation, trench, hyd. backhoe, track mtd., ⅜ C.Y. bucket	.174	C.Y.	.23	.55	.78
Backfill and load spoil, from stockpile	.174	C.Y.	.10	.16	.26
Compaction by rammer tamper, 8" lifts, 4 passes	.014	C.Y.	.01	.02	.03
Compaction by rammer tamper, 8" lifts, 4 passes	.014	C.Y.	.01	.02	.03
Remove excess spoil, 6 C.Y. dump truck, 2 mile roundtrip	.160	C.Y.	.40	.28	.68
TOTAL			.74	1.01	1.75

12.3-110	Trenching	EQUIP.	LABOR	TOTAL
1310	Trenching, backhoe, 0 to 1 slope, 2' wide, 2' deep, ⅜ C.Y. bucket	.74	1.01	1.75
1320	3' deep, ⅜ C.Y. bucket	.95	1.50	2.45
1330	4' deep, ⅜ C.Y. bucket	1.16	2	3.16
1340	6' deep, ⅜ C.Y. bucket	1.68	2.57	4.25
1350	8' deep, ½ C.Y. bucket	2.02	3.30	5.32
1360	10' deep, 1 C.Y. bucket	3.03	3.99	7.02
1400	4' wide, 2' deep, ⅜ C.Y. bucket	1.54	2.03	3.57
1410	3' deep, ⅜ C.Y. bucket	2.19	3.01	5.20
1420	4' deep, ½ C.Y. bucket	2.45	3.13	5.58
1430	6' deep, ½ C.Y. bucket	3.36	4.81	8.17
1440	8' deep, ½ C.Y. bucket	5.15	6.30	11.45
1450	10' deep, 1 C.Y. bucket	6.25	7.85	14.10
1460	12' deep, 1 C.Y. bucket	7.95	10.05	18
1470	15' deep, 1-½ C.Y. bucket	6.85	8.60	15.45
1480	18' deep, 2-½ C.Y. bucket	9.75	12.35	22.10
1520	6' wide, 6' deep, ⅝ C.Y. bucket	5.75	6.50	12.25
1530	8' deep, ¾ C.Y. bucket	7.75	8.10	15.85
1540	10' deep, 1 C.Y. bucket	9.20	9.80	19
1550	12' deep, 1-¼ C.Y. bucket	8.10	7.65	15.75
1560	16' deep, 2 C.Y. bucket	13.20	8.70	21.90
1570	20' deep, 3-½ C.Y. bucket	15.10	15.85	30.95
1580	24' deep, 3-½ C.Y. bucket	25	27	52
1640	8' wide, 12' deep, 1-¼ C.Y. bucket	11.85	10.40	22.25
1650	15' deep, 1-½ C.Y. bucket	14	12.85	26.85
1660	18' deep, 2-½ C.Y. bucket	20	12.95	32.95
1680	24' deep, 3-½ C.Y. bucket	34	35	69
1730	10' wide, 20' deep, 3-½ C.Y. bucket	27	27	54
1740	24' deep, 3-½ C.Y. bucket	43	44	87
1780	12' wide, 20' deep, 3-½ C.Y. bucket	33	32	65
1790	25' deep, bucket	57	59	116
1800	½ to 1 slope, 2' wide, 2' deep, ⅜ C.Y. bucket	.98	1.28	2.26
1810	3' deep, ⅜ C.Y. bucket	1.41	2.17	3.58

UTILITIES — B12.3-110 Trenching

12.3-110 Trenching

Line	Description	EQUIP.	LABOR	TOTAL
1820	4' deep, ⅜ C.Y. bucket	1.86	3.22	5.08
1840	6' deep, ⅜ C.Y. bucket	3.26	5	8.26
1860	8' deep, ½ C.Y. bucket	4.73	7.75	12.48
1880	10' deep, 1 C.Y. bucket	8.40	10.85	19.25
2300	4' wide, 2' deep, ⅜ C.Y. bucket	1.63	2.15	3.78
2310	3' deep, ⅜ C.Y. bucket	2.69	3.54	6.23
2320	4' deep, ½ C.Y. bucket	3.15	3.83	6.98
2340	6' deep, ½ C.Y. bucket	4.78	6.70	11.48
2360	8' deep, ½ C.Y. bucket	7.90	9.30	17.20
2380	10' deep, 1 C.Y. bucket	11.25	13.80	25.05
2400	12' deep, 1 C.Y. bucket	12.50	14.80	27.30
2430	15' deep, 1-½ C.Y. bucket	15.30	18.40	33.70
2460	18' deep, 2-½ C.Y. bucket	26	22	48
2840	6' wide, 6' deep, ⅝ C.Y. bucket	6.60	7.40	14
2860	8' deep, ¾ C.Y. bucket	10.75	11.20	21.95
2880	10' deep, 1 C.Y. bucket	13.85	14.75	28.60
2900	12' deep, 1-¼ C.Y. bucket	13	12.30	25.30
2940	16' deep, 2 C.Y. bucket	20	19.80	39.80
2980	20' deep, 3-½ C.Y. bucket	33	34	67
3020	24' deep, 3-½ C.Y. bucket	60	64	124
3100	8' wide, 12' deep, 1-¼ C.Y. bucket	17.20	14.85	32.05
3120	15' deep, 1-½ C.Y. bucket	22	20	42
3140	18' deep, 2-½ C.Y. bucket	35	22	57
3180	24' deep, 3-½ C.Y. bucket	69	72	141
3270	10' wide, 20' deep, 3-½ C.Y. bucket	42	43	85
3280	24' deep, 3-½ C.Y. bucket	78	81	159
3370	12' wide, 20' deep, 3-½ C.Y. bucket	48	47	95
3380	25' deep, 3-½ C.Y. bucket	91	94	185
3500	1 to 1 slope, 2' wide, 2' deep, ⅜ C.Y. bucket	1.14	1.51	2.65
3520	3' deep, ⅜ C.Y. bucket	1.82	2.68	4.50
3540	4' deep, ⅜ C.Y. bucket	2.43	4.09	6.52
3560	6' deep, ⅜ C.Y. bucket	4.44	6.60	11.04
3580	8' deep, ½ C.Y. bucket	6.65	10.55	17.20
3600	10' deep, 1 C.Y. bucket	13.85	17.20	31.05
3800	4' wide, 2' deep, ⅜ C.Y. bucket	1.95	2.57	4.52
3820	3' deep, ⅜ C.Y. bucket	3.43	4.51	7.94
3840	4' deep, ½ C.Y. bucket	3.75	4.27	8.02
3860	6' deep, ½ C.Y. bucket	5.90	8.05	13.95
3880	8' deep, ½ C.Y. bucket	10.70	12.30	23
3900	10' deep, 1 C.Y. bucket	14.95	17.70	32.65
3920	12' deep, 1 C.Y. bucket	22	26	48
3940	15' deep, 1-½ C.Y. bucket	21	24	45
3960	18' deep, 2-½ C.Y. bucket	38	29	67
4030	6' wide, 6' deep, ⅝ C.Y. bucket	8	8.95	16.95
4040	8' deep, ¾ C.Y. bucket	13.45	14.50	27.95
4050	10' deep, 1 C.Y. bucket	18	20	38
4060	12' deep, 1-¼ C.Y. bucket	17.55	18.15	35.70
4070	16' deep, 2 C.Y. bucket	35	26	61
4080	20' deep, 3-½ C.Y. bucket	48	54	102
4090	24' deep, 3-½ C.Y. bucket	91	105	196
4500	8' wide, 12' deep, 1-¼ C.Y. bucket	22	20	42
4550	15' deep, 1-½ C.Y. bucket	29	29	58
4600	18' deep, 2-½ C.Y. bucket	48	34	82
4650	24' deep, 3-½ C.Y. bucket	99	110	209
4800	10' wide, 20' deep, 3-½ C.Y. bucket	59	62	121
4850	24' deep, 3-½ C.Y. bucket	105	120	225
4950	12' wide, 20' deep, 3-½ C.Y. bucket	64	66	130
4980	25' deep, 3-½ C.Y. bucket	130	145	275

UTILITIES		B12.3-110	Trenching		
12.3-110	Trenching		COST PER L.F.		
			EQUIP.	LABOR	TOTAL
5000	1-½ to 1 slope, 2' wide, 2' deep, ⅜ C.Y. bucket		1.33	1.75	3.08
5020	3' deep, ⅜ C.Y. bucket		2.20	3.15	5.35
5040	4' deep, ⅜ C.Y. bucket		2.95	4.79	7.74
5060	6' deep, ⅜ C.Y. bucket		5.40	7.70	13.10
5080	8' deep, ½ C.Y. bucket		8.20	12.40	20.60
5100	10' deep, 1 C.Y. bucket		15.30	17.80	33.10
5300	4' wide, 2' deep, ⅜ C.Y. bucket		1.84	2.42	4.26
5320	3' deep, ⅜ C.Y. bucket		3.34	4.38	7.72
5340	4' deep, ½ C.Y. bucket		4.43	5	9.43
5360	6' deep, ½ C.Y. bucket		6.95	9.10	16.05
5380	8' deep, ½ C.Y. bucket		12.75	13.95	26.70
5400	10' deep, 1 C.Y. bucket		18	20	38
5420	12' deep, 1 C.Y. bucket		27	30	57
5450	15' deep, 1-½ C.Y. bucket		26	26	52
5480	18' deep, 2-½ C.Y. bucket		47	31	78
5660	6' wide, 6' deep, ⅝ C.Y. bucket		9.20	10	19.20
5680	8' deep, ¾ C.Y. bucket		15.65	16.20	31.85
5700	10' deep, 1 C.Y. bucket		21	23	44
5720	12' deep, 1-¼ C.Y. bucket		20	19.25	39.25
5760	16' deep, 2 C.Y. bucket		42	27	69
5800	20' deep, 3-½ C.Y. bucket		58	61	119
5840	24' deep, 3-½ C.Y. bucket		110	120	230
6020	8' wide, 12' deep, 1-¼ C.Y. bucket		26	22	48
6050	15' deep, 1-½ C.Y. bucket		35	32	67
6080	18' deep, 2-½ C.Y. bucket		57	36	93
6140	24' deep, 3-½ C.Y. bucket		120	125	245
6300	10' wide, 20' deep, 3-½ C.Y. bucket		70	69	139
6350	24' deep, 3-½ C.Y. bucket		130	130	260
6450	12' wide, 20' deep, 3-½ C.Y. bucket		76	73	149
6480	25' deep, 3-½ C.Y. bucket		155	160	315
6600	2 to 1 slope, 2' wide, 2' deep, ⅜ C.Y. bucket		1.85	1.61	3.46
6620	3' deep, ⅜ C.Y. bucket		2.50	3.47	5.97
6640	4' deep, ⅜ C.Y. bucket		3.34	5.30	8.64
6660	6' deep, ⅜ C.Y. bucket		5.80	8.25	14.05
6680	8' deep, ½ C.Y. bucket		9.30	13.95	23.25
6700	10' deep, 1 C.Y. bucket		17.40	20	37.40
6900	4' wide, 2' deep, ⅜ C.Y. bucket		1.84	2.41	4.25
6920	3' deep, ⅜ C.Y. bucket		3.43	4.51	7.94
6940	4' deep, ½ C.Y. bucket		4.86	5.30	10.16
6960	6' deep, ½ C.Y. bucket		7.65	9.85	17.50
6980	8' deep, ½ C.Y. bucket		14.10	15.30	29.40
7000	10' deep, 1 C.Y. bucket		20	22	42
7020	12' deep, 1 C.Y. bucket		30	33	63
7050	15' deep, 1-½ C.Y. bucket		29	30	59
7080	18' deep, 2-½ C.Y. bucket		53	35	88
7260	6' wide, 6' deep, ⅝ C.Y. bucket		10.05	10.65	20.70
7280	8' deep, ¾ C.Y. bucket		17.05	17.40	34.45
7300	10' deep, ¾ C.Y. bucket		23	25	48
7320	12' deep, 1-¼ C.Y. bucket		23	22	45
7360	16' deep, 2 C.Y. bucket		47	30	77
7400	20' deep, 3-½ C.Y. bucket		65	69	134
7440	24' deep, 3-½ C.Y. bucket		125	135	260
7620	8' wide, 12' deep, 1-¼ C.Y. bucket		29	24	53
7650	15' deep, 1-½ C.Y. bucket		39	35	74
7680	18' deep, 2-½ C.Y. bucket		64	40	104
7740	24' deep, 3-½ C.Y. bucket		135	140	275
7920	10' wide, 20' deep, 3-½ C.Y. bucket		77	76	153
7940	24' deep, 3-½ C.Y. bucket		140	145	285

UTILITIES — B12.3-310 Pipe Bedding

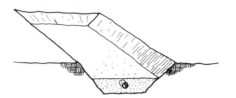

The Pipe Bedding System is shown for various pipe diameters. Compacted dead sand is used for pipe bedding and to fill 12″ over the pipe. No backfill is included. Various side slopes are shown to accommodate different soil conditions.

System Components	QUANTITY	UNIT	COST PER L.F. MAT.	COST PER L.F. INST.	COST PER L.F. TOTAL
SYSTEM 12.3-310-1440					
PIPE BEDDING, SIDE SLOPE 0 TO 1, 1′ WIDE, PIPE SIZE 6″ DIAMETER					
Borrow, bank sand, 2 mile haul, machine spread	.067	C.Y.	.24	.27	.51
Compaction, vibrating plate	.067	C.Y.		.06	.06
TOTAL			.24	.33	.57

12.3-310	Pipe Bedding	MAT.	INST.	TOTAL
1440	Pipe bedding, side slope 0 to 1, 1′ wide, pipe size 6″ diameter	.24	.33	.57
1460	2′ wide, pipe size 8″ diameter	.54	.73	1.27
1480	Pipe size 10″ diameter	.55	.75	1.30
1500	Pipe size 12″ diameter	.57	.78	1.35
1520	3′ wide, pipe size 14″ diameter	.93	1.27	2.20
1540	Pipe size 15″ diameter	.94	1.30	2.24
1560	Pipe size 16″ diameter	.95	1.31	2.26
1580	Pipe size 18″ diameter	.98	1.34	2.32
1600	4′ wide, pipe size 20″ diameter	1.41	1.93	3.34
1620	Pipe size 21″ diameter	1.42	1.95	3.37
1640	Pipe size 24″ diameter	1.46	2	3.46
1660	Pipe size 30″ diameter	1.49	2.04	3.53
1680	6′ wide, pipe size 32″ diameter	2.61	3.57	6.18
1700	Pipe size 36″ diameter	2.68	3.67	6.35
1720	7′ wide, pipe size 48″ diameter	3.49	4.77	8.26
1740	8′ wide, pipe size 60″ diameter	4.35	5.95	10.30
1760	10′ wide, pipe size 72″ diameter	6.30	8.60	14.90
1780	12′ wide, pipe size 84″ diameter	8.55	11.70	20.25
2140	Side slope ½ to 1, 1′ wide, pipe size 6″ diameter	.51	.70	1.21
2160	2′ wide, pipe size 8″ diameter	.85	1.16	2.01
2180	Pipe size 10″ diameter	.92	1.26	2.18
2200	Pipe size 12″ diameter	.98	1.35	2.33
2220	3′ wide, pipe size 14″ diameter	1.41	1.93	3.34
2240	Pipe size 15″ diameter	1.45	1.98	3.43
2260	Pipe size 16″ diameter	1.49	2.04	3.53
2280	Pipe size 18″ diameter	1.58	2.16	3.74
2300	4′ wide, pipe size 20″ diameter	2.08	2.86	4.94
2320	Pipe size 21″ diameter	2.13	2.92	5.05
2340	Pipe size 24″ diameter	2.29	3.13	5.42
2360	Pipe size 30″ diameter	2.57	3.51	6.08
2380	6′ wide, pipe size 32″ diameter	3.78	5.15	8.93
2400	Pipe size 36″ diameter	4.04	5.55	9.59
2420	7′ wide, pipe size 48″ diameter	5.55	7.55	13.10
2440	8′ wide, pipe size 60″ diameter	7.20	9.85	17.05

UTILITIES — B12.3-310 Pipe Bedding

12.3-310 Pipe Bedding

Line	Description	MAT.	INST.	TOTAL
2460	10' wide, pipe size 72" diameter	10.05	13.75	23.80
2480	12' wide, pipe size 84" diameter	13.40	18.35	31.75
2620	Side slope 1 to 1, 1' wide, pipe size 6" diameter	.78	1.06	1.84
2640	2' wide, pipe size 8" diameter	1.17	1.61	2.78
2660	Pipe size 10" diameter	1.29	1.76	3.05
2680	Pipe size 12" diameter	1.41	1.93	3.34
2700	3' wide, pipe size 14" diameter	1.89	2.58	4.47
2720	Pipe size 15" diameter	1.96	2.68	4.64
2740	Pipe size 16" diameter	2.03	2.78	4.81
2760	Pipe size 18" diameter	2.18	2.99	5.17
2780	4' wide, pipe size 20" diameter	2.76	3.78	6.54
2800	Pipe size 21" diameter	2.84	3.89	6.73
2820	Pipe size 24" diameter	3.11	4.25	7.36
2840	Pipe size 30" diameter	3.63	4.97	8.60
2860	6' wide, pipe size 32" diameter	4.95	6.80	11.75
2880	Pipe size 36" diameter	5.40	7.40	12.80
2900	7' wide, pipe size 48" diameter	7.55	10.35	17.90
2920	8' wide, pipe size 60" diameter	10.05	13.75	23.80
2940	10' wide, pipe size 72" diameter	13.85	18.95	32.80
2960	12' wide, pipe size 84" diameter	18.25	25	43.25
3000	Side slope 1-½ to 1, 1' wide, pipe size 6" diameter	1.05	1.43	2.48
3020	2' wide, pipe size 8" diameter	1.49	2.04	3.53
3040	Pipe size 10" diameter	1.65	2.26	3.91
3060	Pipe size 12" diameter	1.83	2.51	4.34
3080	3' wide, pipe size 14" diameter	2.37	3.24	5.61
3100	Pipe size 15" diameter	2.46	3.38	5.84
3120	Pipe size 16" diameter	2.57	3.51	6.08
3140	Pipe size 18" diameter	2.79	3.82	6.61
3160	4' wide, pipe size 20" diameter	3.44	4.71	8.15
3180	Pipe size 21" diameter	3.55	4.86	8.41
3200	Pipe size 24" diameter	3.93	5.40	9.33
3220	Pipe size 30" diameter	4.72	6.45	11.17
3240	6' wide, pipe size 32" diameter	6.10	8.35	14.45
3260	Pipe size 36" diameter	6.75	9.25	16
3280	7' wide, pipe size 48" diameter	9.60	13.15	22.75
3300	8' wide, pipe size 60" diameter	12.85	17.60	30.45
3320	10' wide, pipe size 72" diameter	17.65	24	41.65
3340	12' wide, pipe size 84" diameter	23	32	55
3400	Side slope 2 to 1, 1' wide, pipe size 6" diameter	1.34	1.84	3.18
3420	2' wide, pipe size 8" diameter	1.80	2.47	4.27
3440	Pipe size 10" diameter	2.01	2.76	4.77
3460	Pipe size 12" diameter	2.25	3.08	5.33
3480	3' wide, pipe size 14" diameter	2.84	3.89	6.73
3500	Pipe size 15" diameter	2.96	4.05	7.01
3520	Pipe size 16" diameter	3.10	4.25	7.35
3540	Pipe size 18" diameter	3.39	4.65	8.04
3560	4' wide, pipe size 20" diameter	4.11	5.65	9.76
3580	Pipe size 21" diameter	4.26	5.85	10.11
3600	Pipe size 24" diameter	4.75	6.50	11.25
3620	Pipe size 30" diameter	5.80	7.95	13.75
3640	6' wide, pipe size 32" diameter	7.30	10	17.30
3660	Pipe size 36" diameter	8.10	11.15	19.25
3680	7' wide, pipe size 48" diameter	11.60	15.90	27.50
3700	8' wide, pipe size 60" diameter	15.70	22	37.70
3720	10' wide, pipe size 72" diameter	21	29	50
3740	12' wide, pipe size 84" diameter	28	38	66

UTILITIES — B12.3-510 Drainage & Sewage Piping

12.3-510 Drainage & Sewage Piping

Line	Description	MAT.	INST.	TOTAL
2000	Piping, excavation & backfill excluded, bituminous fiber, plain			
2130	4" diameter	1.63	1.09	2.72
2150	6" diameter	3.09	1.23	4.32
2160	8" diameter	7.25	1.39	8.64
2900	Box culvert, precast, 8' long			
3000	6' x 3'	155	17.70	172.70
3020	6' x 7'	210	20	230
3040	8' x 3'	200	16.80	216.80
3060	8' x 8'	285	24	309
3080	10' x 3'	220	24	244
3100	10' x 8'	315	30	345
3120	12' x 3'	325	24	349
3140	12' x 8'	425	39	464
4000	Concrete, nonreinforced			
4150	6" diameter	3.25	4.75	8
4160	8" diameter	3.58	4.82	8.40
4170	10" diameter	3.96	5.55	9.51
4180	12" diameter	4.84	5.55	10.39
4200	15" diameter	5.60	5.75	11.35
4220	18" diameter	7	5.75	12.75
4250	24" diameter	10.45	6.25	16.70
4400	Reinforced, no gasket			
4580	12" diameter	5.70	5.05	10.75
4600	15" diameter	7.15	6.20	13.35
4620	18" diameter	9.15	7.85	17
4650	24" diameter	14.85	11.15	26
4670	30" diameter	20	26	46
4680	36" diameter	29	35	64
4690	42" diameter	38	38	76
4700	48" diameter	48	42	90
4720	60" diameter	72	58	130
4730	72" diameter	100	69	169
4740	84" diameter	165	87	252
4800	With gasket			
4980	12" diameter	6.90	4.57	11.47
5000	15" diameter	8.25	5.50	13.75
5020	18" diameter	10.40	6.40	16.80
5050	24" diameter	16.30	9.70	26
5070	30" diameter	22	24	46
5080	36" diameter	31	30	61
5090	42" diameter	41	29	70
5100	48" diameter	51	36	87
5120	60" diameter	81	55	136
5130	72" diameter	140	56	196
5140	84" diameter	200	100	300
5150				
5160				
5170				
5700	Corrugated metal, alum. or galv. bit. coated			
5760	8" diameter	5.45	2.15	7.60
5770	10" diameter	6.90	2.72	9.62
5780	12" diameter	8.40	3.38	11.78
5800	15" diameter	10.35	4.56	14.91
5820	18" diameter	12.20	5.05	17.25
5850	24" diameter	19.55	6.45	26
5870	30" diameter	23	7.55	30.55
5880	36" diameter	36	10.05	46.05
5900	48" diameter	47	21	68

UTILITIES — B12.3-510 | Drainage & Sewage Piping

12.3-510 Drainage & Sewage Piping

		COST PER L.F.		
		MAT.	INST.	TOTAL
5920	60" diameter	71	28	99
5930	72" diameter	105	47	152
6000	Plain			
6060	8" diameter	3.80	2	5.80
6070	10" diameter	5.10	2.53	7.63
6080	12" diameter	5.65	3.23	8.88
6100	15" diameter	7.05	4.36	11.41
6120	18" diameter	8.35	4.69	13.04
6140	24" diameter	14.20	5.45	19.65
6170	30" diameter	16.95	7.05	24
6180	36" diameter	27	15.75	42.75
6200	48" diameter	37	18.95	55.95
6220	60" diameter	57	27	84
6230	72" diameter	120	84	204
6300	Steel or alum. oval arch, coated & paved			
6400	15" equivalent diam	11.90	5.40	17.30
6420	18" equivalent diam	14.05	6.95	21
6450	24" equivalent diam	22	8.85	30.85
6470	30" equivalent diam	26	10.70	36.70
6480	36" equivalent diam	39	21	60
6490	42" equivalent diam	45	24	69
6500	48" equivalent diam	52	29	81
6600	Plain			
6700	15" equivalent diam	7.80	4.84	12.64
6720	18" equivalent diam	9.25	6.20	15.45
6750	24" equivalent diam	14.75	7.25	22
6770	30" equivalent diam	18.45	9.55	28
6780	36" equivalent diam	35	19.60	54.60
6790	42" equivalent diam	43	22	65
6800	48" equivalent diam	39	28	67
8000	Polyvinyl chloride SDR 35			
8130	4" diameter	.63	1.89	2.52
8150	6" diameter	1.34	2.03	3.37
8160	8" diameter	1.93	2.12	4.05
8170	10" diameter	3.08	2.92	6
8180	12" diameter	4.35	3	7.35
8200	15" diameter	6.75	5.05	11.80
9000	Vitrified clay, C-2000, premium joint			
9030	4" diameter	1.13	2.68	3.81
9050	6" diameter	1.88	3.57	5.45
9060	8" diameter	2.94	4.81	7.75
9070	10" diameter	4.87	5.05	9.92
9080	12" diameter	6.45	6.40	12.85
9100	15" diameter	12	9	21
9120	18" diameter	18.05	10.95	29
9150	24" diameter	34	21	55
9170	30" diameter	39	35	74
9180	36" diameter	60	55	115

UTILITIES — B12.3-520 Gas Service Piping

12.3-520 Gas Service Piping

Line	Description	MAT.	INST.	TOTAL
2000	Piping, excavation & backfill excluded, polyethylene			
2070	1-¼" diam, SDR 10	.67	1.78	2.45
2090	2" diam, SDR 11	1.19	1.97	3.16
2110	3" diam, SDR 11.5	2.26	2.37	4.63
2130	4" diam, SDR 11	3.85	3.70	7.55
2150	6" diam, SDR 21	4.29	4.01	8.30
2160	8" diam, SDR 21	7.80	4.79	12.59
3000	Steel, schedule 40, plain end, tarred & wrapped			
3060	1" diameter	3.26	3.89	7.15
3090	2" diameter	3.71	4.14	7.85
3110	3" diameter	7.15	4.49	11.64
3130	4" diameter	10.25	8	18.25
3140	5" diameter	14.75	9.25	24
3150	6" diameter	18.80	11.20	30
3160	8" diameter	28	14.80	42.80
3170	10" diameter	40	20	60

UTILITIES

B12.3-530 Subdrainage Piping

12.3-530	Subdrainage Piping	COST PER L.F.		
		MAT.	INST.	TOTAL
2000	Piping, excavation & backfill excluded, bituminous fiber, perforated			
2110	3" diameter	1.32	.89	2.21
2130	4" diameter	1.65	.93	2.58
2140	5" diameter	2.86	.99	3.85
2150	6" diameter	3.19	1.04	4.23
3000	Metal alum. or steel, perforated asphalt coated			
3150	6" diameter	5.25	1.87	7.12
3160	8" diameter	5.95	1.91	7.86
3170	10" diameter	7.30	2.68	9.98
3180	12" diameter	8.55	3.37	11.92
3220	18" diameter	12.95	4.67	17.62
4000	Porous wall concrete			
4130	4" diameter	1.65	2.12	3.77
4150	6" diameter	1.76	2.25	4.01
4160	8" diameter	2.86	3.09	5.95
4180	12" diameter	6	3.35	9.35
4200	15" diameter	6.90	4.17	11.07
4220	18" diameter	9.10	5.80	14.90
5000	Vitrified clay C-211, perforated			
5130	4" diameter	1.27	1.78	3.05
5150	6" diameter	1.85	2.25	4.10
5160	8" diameter	2.88	2.47	5.35
5180	12" diameter	6	3.50	9.50

UTILITIES — B12.3-540 Water Distribution Piping

12.3-540 Water Distribution Piping

		MAT.	INST.	TOTAL
2000	Piping. excav. & backfill excl., ductile iron class 250, mech. joint			
2130	4" diameter	7.15	4.95	12.10
2150	6" diameter	8.80	5.65	14.45
2160	8" diameter	12	9	21
2170	10" diameter	15.85	11.15	27
2180	12" diameter	19.90	13.10	33
2210	16" diameter	27	21	48
2220	18" diameter	31	29	60
3000	Tyton joint			
3130	4" diameter	6.50	4.51	11.01
3150	6" diameter	8.10	5.15	13.25
3160	8" diameter	11.35	8.10	19.45
3170	10" diameter	15.15	9.85	25
3180	12" diameter	18.70	12.30	31
3210	16" diameter	26	17.80	43.80
3220	18" diameter	29	25	54
3230	20" diameter	35	25	60
3250	24" diameter	45	27	72
4000	Copper tubing, type K			
4050	¾" diameter	2.70	1.95	4.65
4060	1" diameter	2.92	2.13	5.05
4080	1-½" diameter	4.73	2.42	7.15
4090	2" diameter	7.15	2.80	9.95
4110	3" diameter	14.25	3.95	18.20
4130	4" diameter	25	4.59	29.59
4150	6" diameter	74	36	110
5000	Polyvinyl chloride class 160, S.D.R. 26			
5130	1-½" diameter	.39	2.37	2.76
5150	2" diameter	.61	2.84	3.45
5160	4" diameter	2.15	3.55	5.70
5170	6" diameter	4.62	3.93	8.55
5180	8" diameter	10.45	6	16.45
6000	Polyethylene 160 psi, S.D.R. 7			
6050	¾" diameter	.17	1.35	1.52
6060	1" diameter	.23	1.46	1.69
6080	1-½" diameter	.55	1.58	2.13
6090	2" diameter	.88	1.95	2.83

UTILITIES B12.3-710 Manholes And Catch Basins

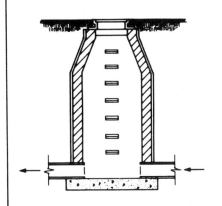

Manhole

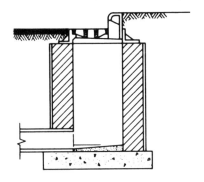

Catch Basin

The Manhole and Catch Basin System includes: excavation with a backhoe; a formed concrete footing; frame and cover; cast iron steps and compacted backfill.

The Expanded System Listing shows manholes that have a 4', 5' and 6' inside diameter riser. Depths range from 4' to 14'. Construction material shown is either concrete, concrete block, precast concrete, or brick.

System Components	QUANTITY	UNIT	COST PER EACH		
			MAT.	INST.	TOTAL
SYSTEM 12.3-710-1920					
MANHOLE/CATCH BASIN, BRICK, 4' I.D. RISER, 4' DEEP					
Excavation, hydraulic backhoe, ⅜ C.Y. bucket	14.815	C.Y.		65.33	65.33
Trim sides and bottom of trench	64.000	S.F.		28.16	28.16
Forms in place, manhole base, 4 uses	20.000	SFCA	8.40	49.40	57.80
Reinforcing in place footings, #4 to #7	.019	Tons	11.75	11.05	22.80
Concrete, 3000 psi, incl. place and vibrate under 1 CY, direct chute	.925	C.Y.	54.58	23.13	77.71
Catch basin or MH, brick, 4' ID, 4' deep	1.000	Ea.	415.80	469.20	885
Catch basin or MH steps; heavy galvanized cast iron	1.000	Ea.	7.59	6.61	14.20
Catch basin or MH frame and cover	1.000	Ea.	189.20	110.80	300
Backfill with wheeled front end loader	12.954	C.Y.		17.36	17.36
Backfill compaction, 12" lifts, air tamp	12.954	C.Y.		54.54	54.54
TOTAL			687.32	835.58	1,522.90

12.3-710	Manholes & Catch Basins	COST PER EACH		
		MAT.	INST.	TOTAL
1920	Manhole/catch basin, brick, 4' I.D. riser, 4' deep	685	835	1,520
1940	6' deep	865	1,175	2,040
1960	8' deep	1,025	1,600	2,625
1980	10' deep	1,250	1,975	3,225
3000	12' deep	1,450	2,075	3,525
3020	14' deep	1,650	3,050	4,700
3200	Block, 4' I.D. riser, 4' deep	545	680	1,225
3220	6' deep	655	965	1,620
3240	8' deep	780	1,325	2,105
3260	10' deep	935	1,650	2,585
3280	12' deep	1,100	2,125	3,225
3300	14' deep	1,250	2,600	3,850
4620	Concrete, cast-in-place, 4' I.D. riser, 4' deep	625	800	1,425
4640	6' deep	765	1,075	1,840
4660	8' deep	930	1,525	2,455
4680	10' deep	1,100	1,900	3,000
4700	12' deep	1,300	2,400	3,700

UTILITIES — B12.3-710 Manholes And Catch Basins

12.3-710 Manholes & Catch Basins

		MAT.	INST.	TOTAL
4720	14' deep	1,475	2,925	4,400
5820	Concrete, precast, 4' I.D. riser, 4' deep	555	580	1,135
5840	6' deep	680	785	1,465
5860	8' deep	790	1,100	1,890
5880	10' deep	945	1,350	2,295
5900	12' deep	1,100	1,675	2,775
5920	14' deep	1,250	2,175	3,425
6000	5' I.D. riser, 4' deep	730	700	1,430
6020	6' deep	895	975	1,870
6040	8' deep	1,075	1,325	2,400
6060	10' deep	1,275	1,700	2,975
6080	12' deep	1,475	2,150	3,625
6100	14' deep	1,675	2,650	4,325
6200	6' I.D. riser, 4' deep	1,025	910	1,935
6220	6' deep	1,250	1,225	2,475
6240	8' deep	1,500	1,725	3,225
6260	10' deep	1,800	2,200	4,000
6280	12' deep	2,125	2,775	4,900
6300	14' deep	2,425	3,375	5,800

SITE WORK — B12.3-900 — Septic Systems

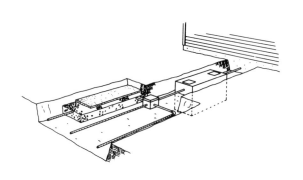

The Septic System includes: a septic tank; leaching field; concrete distribution boxes; plus excavation and gravel backfill.

The Expanded System Listing shows systems with tanks ranging from 1000 gallons to 5000 gallons. Tanks are either concrete or fiberglass. Cost is on a complete unit basis.

Systems Components	QUANTITY	UNIT	COST EACH		
			MAT.	INST.	TOTAL
SYSTEM 12.3-900-2010					
1000 GALLON TANK, LEACHING FIELD, 300 S.F., 50' FROM BLDG.					
Septic tank, precast, 1000 gallon	1.000	Ea.	462	118	580
Distribution box, precast, 5 outlets	1.000	Ea.	55	26	81
Perforated pipe, PVC, 4" diameter	60.000	L.F.	37.80	113.40	151.20
Sch. 40 sewer pipe, PVC, 4" diameter	40.000	L.F.	25.20	75.60	100.80
Sch. 40 fitting, wye, & tee, PVC, 4" diameter	4.000	Ea.	97.92	30.08	128
Excavation, hydraulic backhoe, backfill & load spoil	90.000	C.Y.		274.50	274.50
Stone fill, ¾" to 1-½", machine spread	15.000	C.Y.	243.75	273	516.75
Haul spoil, 12 C.Y. dump truck, 2 mile round trip	25.000	C.Y.		71	71
TOTAL			921.67	981.58	1,903.25

12.3-900	Septic Systems	COST EACH		
		MAT.	INST.	TOTAL
2010	1000 gal. septic tank, leaching field, 300 S.F., 50' from bldg.	920	980	1,900
2110	200' from bldg.	1,075	1,425	2,500
2210	6' deep precast pit, one at 6'-6" diameter, 50' from bldg.	1,125	1,125	2,250
2310	200' from bldg.	1,250	1,550	2,800
2410	4' deep precast galley, 12' long, 50' from bldg.	1,325	1,175	2,500
2510	200' from bldg.	1,475	1,600	3,075
3010	1250 gal. septic tank, leaching field, 400 S.F., 50' from bldg.	1,075	1,150	2,225
3110	200' from bldg.	1,225	1,575	2,800
3210	6' deep precast pit, one at 8'-0" diameter, 50' from bldg.	1,600	1,300	2,900
3310	200' from bldg.	1,750	1,725	3,475
3410	4' deep precast galley, 16' long, 50' from bldg.	1,600	1,275	2,875
3510	200' from bldg.	1,775	1,775	3,550
4010	1500 gal. septic tank, leaching field, 500 S.F., 50' from bldg.	935	1,250	2,185
4110	200' from bldg.	1,075	1,700	2,775
4210	6' deep precast pit, two at 6'-6" diameter, 50' from bldg.	2,050	1,900	3,950
4310	200' from bldg.	2,200	2,350	4,550
4410	4' deep precast galley, 20' long, 50' from bldg.	1,950	1,575	3,525
4510	200' from bldg.	2,100	2,000	4,100
5010	2000 gal. septic tank, leaching field, 600 S.F., 50' from bldg.	1,200	1,500	2,700
5110	200' from bldg.	1,350	1,950	3,300
5210	6' deep precast pit, two at 8'-0" diameter, 50' from bldg.	2,950	2,325	5,275
5310	200' from bldg.	3,100	2,750	5,850
5410	4' deep precast galley, 24 ft. long, 50' from bldg.	2,425	1,900	4,325
5510	200' from bldg.	2,575	2,325	4,900

SITE WORK — B12.3-922 — Fire Hydrants

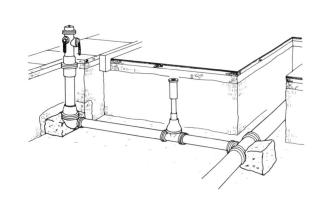

The Fire Hydrant Systems include: four different hydrants with three different lengths of offsets, at several depths of trenching. Excavation and backfill is included with each system as well as thrust blocks as necessary and pipe bedding. Finally spreading of excess material and fine grading complete the components.

System Components	QUANTITY	UNIT	COST PER EACH MAT.	COST PER EACH INST.	COST PER EACH TOTAL
SYSTEM 12.3-922-1500					
HYDRANT, 4-½" VALVE SIZE, TWO WAY, 10' OFFSET, 2' DEEP					
Excavation, trench, 1 C.Y. hydraulic backhoe	3.556	C.Y.		15.68	15.68
Sleeve, 12" x 6"	1.000	Ea.	1,094.50	55.50	1,150
Offset pipe, 6", CL, 250, ductile iron	8.000	L.F.	70.40	45.20	115.60
Gate valve, 6"	1.000	Ea.	495	50	545
Gate box	1.000	Ea.	89.10	35.90	125
Hydrant, incl. lower barrel and shoe	1.000	Ea.	891	94	985
Thrust blocks, at valve, shoe and sleeve	1.600	C.Y.	133.76	154.24	288
Compacted backfill and drainage stone	4.089	C.Y.	69.76	41.23	110.99
Spread excess excavated material	.204	C.Y.		3.87	3.87
Fine grade, hand	400.000	S.F.		121.45	121.45
TOTAL			2,843.52	617.07	3,460.59

12.3-922	Fire Hydrants	MAT.	INST.	TOTAL
1000	Hydrant, 4-½" valve size, two way, 0' offset, 2' deep	2,775	405	3,180
1100	4' deep	2,850	410	3,260
1200	6' deep	2,925	460	3,385
1300	8' deep	3,025	480	3,505
1400	10' deep	3,125	515	3,640
1500	10' offset, 2' deep	2,850	615	3,465
1600	4' deep	2,925	740	3,665
1700	6' deep	3,000	995	3,995
1800	8' deep	3,100	1,350	4,450
1900	10' deep	3,175	2,075	5,250
2000	20' offset, 2' deep	2,925	835	3,760
2100	4' deep	3,025	1,025	4,050
2200	6' deep	3,100	1,400	4,500
2300	8' deep	3,175	1,900	5,075
2400	10' deep	3,275	2,600	5,875
2500	Three way, 0' offset, 2' deep	2,825	410	3,235
2600	4' deep	2,925	420	3,345
2700	6' deep	3,000	470	3,470
2800	8' deep	3,100	490	3,590
2900	10' deep	3,200	530	3,730
3000	Hydrant, 4-½" valve size, three way, 10' offset, 2' deep	2,900	625	3,525
3100	4' deep	3,000	750	3,750

SITE WORK — B12.3-922 Fire Hydrants

12.3-922	Fire Hydrants	MAT.	INST.	TOTAL
3200	6' deep	3,075	1,000	4,075
3300	8' deep	3,175	1,350	4,525
3400	10' deep	3,275	2,100	5,375
3500	20' offset, 2' deep	3,000	840	3,840
3600	4' deep	3,075	1,050	4,125
3700	6' deep	3,175	1,425	4,600
3800	8' deep	3,275	1,925	5,200
3900	10' deep	3,350	2,625	5,975
5000	5-1/4" valve size, two way, 0' offset, 2' deep	2,850	410	3,260
5100	4' deep	2,950	405	3,355
5200	6' deep	3,075	445	3,520
5300	8' deep	3,200	480	3,680
5400	10' deep	3,225	500	3,725
5500	10' offset, 2' deep	2,925	625	3,550
5600	4' deep	3,025	735	3,760
5700	6' deep	3,150	985	4,135
5800	8' deep	3,275	1,350	4,625
5900	10' deep	3,300	2,075	5,375
6000	20' offset, 2' deep	3,025	840	3,865
6100	4' deep	3,125	1,025	4,150
6200	6' deep	3,225	1,400	4,625
6300	8' deep	3,375	1,900	5,275
6400	10' deep	3,400	2,600	6,000
6500	Three way, 0' offset, 2' deep	2,925	420	3,345
6600	4' deep	3,050	410	3,460
6700	6' deep	3,150	455	3,605
6800	8' deep	3,300	490	3,790
6900	10' deep	3,325	515	3,840
7000	10' offset, 2' deep	3,000	630	3,630
7100	4' deep	3,100	740	3,840
7200	6' deep	3,225	875	4,100
7300	8' deep	3,375	1,350	4,725
7400	10' deep	3,400	2,075	5,475
7500	20' offset, 2' deep	3,075	850	3,925
7600	4' deep	3,200	915	4,115
7700	6' deep	3,300	1,400	4,700

SITE WORK — B12.3-925 — Water Service

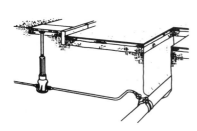

The Water Service Systems are for copper service taps from 1" to 2" diameter into pressurized mains from 6" to 8" diameter. Costs are given for two offsets with depths varying from 2' to 10'. Included in system components are excavation and backfill and required curb stops with boxes.

System Components	QUANTITY	UNIT	MAT.	INST.	TOTAL
SYSTEM 12.3-925-1000					
WATER SERVICE, 6" MAIN, 1" COPPER SERVICE, 10' OFFSET, 2' DEEP					
Trench excavation, ½ C.Y. backhoe, 1 laborer	2.220	C.Y.		8.68	8.68
Drill & tap pressurized main, 6", 1" to 2" service	1.000	Ea.		175	175
Corporation, brass, 1" diameter	1.000	Ea.	20.68	18.32	39
Saddle, cast iron, 1" diameter	1.000	Ea.	30		30
Copper tubing, type K, 1" diameter	11.000	L.F.	32.12	23.43	55.55
Curb stop, brass, 1" diameter	1.000	Ea.	26.13	17.87	44
Curb box, cast iron, 1" diameter	1.000	Ea.	32.07	24.93	57
Backfill by hand, no compaction, heavy soil	2.220	C.Y.		2.97	2.97
Compaction, vibrating plate	2.220	C.Y.		6.59	6.59
TOTAL			141	277.79	418.79

12.3-925	Water Service	MAT.	INST.	TOTAL
1000	Water service, 6" main, 1" copper service, 10' offset, 2' deep	140	280	420
1040	4' deep	140	310	450
1060	6' deep	140	350	490
1080	8' deep	140	405	545
1100	10' deep	140	430	570
1200	20' offset, 2' deep	170	315	485
1240	4' deep	170	380	550
1260	6' deep	170	465	635
1280	8' deep	170	575	745
1300	10' deep	170	705	875
2000	1-½" copper service, 10' offset, 2' deep	280	305	585
2040	4' deep	280	335	615
2060	6' deep	280	375	655
2080	8' deep	280	430	710
2100	10' deep	280	500	780
2200	20' offset, 2' deep	330	345	675
2240	4' deep	330	405	735
2260	6' deep	330	490	820
2280	8' deep	330	600	930
2300	10' deep	330	735	1,065
3000	6" main, 2" copper service, 10' offset, 2' deep	390	315	705
3040	4' deep	390	345	735

SITE WORK — B12.3-925 Water Service

12.3-925 Water Service

		MAT.	INST.	TOTAL
3060	6' deep	390	385	775
3080	8' deep	390	440	830
3100	10' deep	390	510	900
3200	20' offset, 2' deep	460	360	820
3240	4' deep	460	420	880
3260	6' deep	460	505	965
3280	8' deep	460	615	1,075
3300	10' deep	460	750	1,210
4000	8" main, 1" copper service, 10' offset, 2' deep	140	295	435
4040	4' deep	140	325	465
4060	6' deep	140	365	505
4080	8' deep	140	420	560
4100	10' deep	140	490	630
4200	20' offset, 2' deep	170	330	500
4240	4' deep	170	395	565
4260	6' deep	170	480	650
4280	8' deep	170	590	760
4300	10' deep	170	720	890
5000	1-½" copper service, 10' offset, 2' deep	280	320	600
5040	4' deep	280	350	630
5060	6' deep	280	390	670
5080	8' deep	280	445	725
5100	10' deep	280	515	795
5200	20' offset, 2' deep	330	360	690
5240	4' deep	330	420	750
5260	6' deep	330	505	835
5280	8' deep	330	615	945
5300	10' deep	330	750	1,080
6000	2" copper service, 10' offset, 2' deep	390	330	720
6040	4' deep	390	360	750
6060	6' deep	390	400	790
6080	8' deep	390	455	845
6100	10' deep	390	525	915
6200	20' offset, 2' deep	460	375	835
6240	4' deep	460	435	895
6260	6' deep	460	520	980
6280	8' deep	460	630	1,090
6300	10' deep	460	765	1,225

SITE WORK   B12.7-910   Site Irrigation

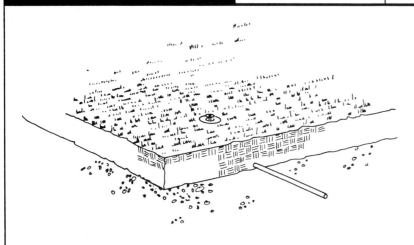

There are three basic types of Site Irrigation Systems: pop-up, riser mounted and quick coupling. Sprinkler heads are spray, impact or gear driven. Each system includes: the hardware for spraying the water; the pipe and fittings needed to deliver the water; and all other accessory equipment such as valves, couplings, heads, nipples, and nozzles. Excavation and backfill costs are also included in the system.

The Expanded System Listing shows a wide variety of Site Irrigation Systems.

System Components	QUANTITY	UNIT	COST PER S.F.		
			MAT.	INST.	TOTAL
SYSTEM 12.7-910-1000					
SITE IRRIGATION, POP UP SPRAY, PLASTIC, 10' RADIUS, 1000 S.F., PVC PIPE					
Excavation, chain trencher	54.000	L.F.		20.52	20.52
Pipe, plastic, PVC, schedule 40, 1" diameter	54.000	L.F.	47.52	127.98	175.50
Fittings PVC plastic	8.100	L.F.	7.13	19.20	26.33
Nipples, long PVC plastic, 1" diameter x 12" long	5.000	Ea.	4.40	11.85	16.25
Tees, PVC plastic, high pressure schedule, 40, 1" diameter	5.000	Ea.	11.55	188.45	200
Couplings PVC plastic, high pressure, 1" diameter	5.000	Ea.	1.45	81.30	82.75
Valves, bronze, globe, 125 lb. rising stem, threaded, 1" diameter	1.000	Ea.	29.70	15.30	45
Head & nozzle, pop-up spray, PVC plastic	5.000	Ea.	16	44.75	60.75
Backfill by hand with compaction	54.000	L.F.		17.82	17.82
Total cost per 1,000 S.F.			117.75	527.17	644.92
Total cost per S.F.			.12	.53	.65

12.7-910	Site Irrigation	COST PER S.F.		
		MAT.	INST.	TOTAL
1000	Site irrigation, pop up spray, plastic, 10' radius, 1000 S.F., PVC pipe	.12	.53	.65
1100	Polyethylene pipe	.08	.40	.48
1200	14' radius, 8000 S.F., PVC pipe	.05	.24	.29
1300	Polyethylene pipe	.03	.18	.21
1400	18' square, 1000 S.F. PVC pipe	.10	.40	.50
1500	Polyethylene pipe	.07	.27	.34
1600	24' square, 8000 S.F., PVC pipe	.03	.14	.17
1700	Polyethylene pipe	.02	.13	.15
1800	4' x 30' strip, 200 S.F., PVC pipe	.38	1.49	1.87
1900	Polyethylene pipe	.29	1.19	1.48
2000	6' x 40' strip, 800 S.F., PVC pipe	.12	.50	.62
2100	Polyethylene pipe	.08	.39	.47
2200	Economy brass, 11' radius, 1000 S.F., PVC pipe	.13	.53	.66
2300	Polyethylene pipe	.09	.40	.49
2400	14' radius, 8000 S.F., PVC pipe	.05	.24	.29
2500	Polyethylene pipe	.04	.18	.22
2600	3' x 28' strip, 200 S.F., PVC pipe	.42	1.49	1.91
2700	Polyethylene pipe	.33	1.19	1.52
2800	7' x 36' strip, 1000 S.F., PVC pipe	.10	.40	.50
2900	Polyethylene pipe	.08	.32	.40

SITE WORK — B12.7-910 Site Irrigation

12.7-910 Site Irrigation

		COST PER S.F.		
		MAT.	INST.	TOTAL
3000	Hd brass, 11' radius, 1000 S.F., PVC pipe	.15	.53	.68
3100	Polyethylene pipe	.11	.40	.51
3200	14' radius, 8000 S.F., PVC pipe	.06	.24	.30
3300	Polyethylene pipe	.05	.18	.23
3400	Riser mounted spray, plastic,10'radius, 1000S.F., PVC pipe	.11	.53	.64
3500	Polyethylene pipe	.07	.40	.47
3600	12' radius, 5000 S.F., PVC pipe	.06	.31	.37
3700	Polyethylene pipe	.04	.24	.28
3800	19' square, 2000 S.F., PVC pipe	.04	.17	.21
3900	Polyethylene pipe	.03	.13	.16
4000	24' square, 8000 S.F., PVC pipe	.02	.14	.16
4100	Polyethylene pipe	.02	.13	.15
4200	5' x 32' strip, 300 S.F., PVC pipe	.24	1	1.24
4300	Polyethylene pipe	.18	.79	.97
4400	6' x 40' strip, 800 S.F., PVC pipe	.11	.50	.61
4500	Polyethylene pipe	.08	.39	.47
4600	Brass, 11' radius, 1000 S.F., PVC pipe	.11	.53	.64
4700	Polyethylene pipe	.08	.40	.48
4800	14' radius, 8000 S.F., PVC pipe	.04	.24	.28
4900	Polythylene pipe	.03	.18	.21
5000	Pop up gear drive stream type,plastic, 30'radius, 10,000 S.F.,PVC pipe	.05	.26	.31
5020	Polyethylene pipe	.03	.09	.12
5040	40,000 S.F., PVC pipe	.05	.26	.31
5060	Polyethylene pipe	.03	.08	.11
5080	Riser mounted gear drive stream type,plas.,30'rad.,10,000S.F.,PVC pipe	.05	.26	.31
5100	Polyethylene pipe	.03	.09	.12
5120	40,000 S.F., PVC pipe	.04	.26	.30
5140	Polyethylene pipe	.03	.08	.11
5200	Q.C. valve thread type w/impact head,brass,75'rad,20,000S.F.,PVC pipe	.02	.10	.12
5250	Polyethylene pipe	.02	.03	.05
5300	100,000 S.F., PVC pipe	.03	.16	.19
5350	Polyethylene pipe	.02	.04	.06
5400	Q.C. valve lug type w/impact head,brass, 75'rad, 20,000 S.F., PVC pipe	.02	.10	.12
5450	Polyethylene pipe	.02	.03	.05
5500	100,000 S.F. PVC pipe	.03	.16	.19
5550	Polyethylene pipe	.02	.04	.06
6000	Site irrigation,pop up impact type,plastic,40'rad.,10000 S.F.,PVC pipe	.03	.17	.20
6100	Polyethylene pipe	.02	.05	.07
6200	45,000 S.F., PVC pipe	.03	.18	.21
6300	Polyethylene pipe	.02	.05	.07
6400	High medium volume brass, 40' radius, 10000 S.F., PVC pipe	.03	.17	.20
6500	Polyethylene pipe	.02	.05	.07
6600	45,000 S.F. PVC pipe	.03	.18	.21
6700	Polyethylene pipe	.02	.05	.07
6800	High volume brass, 60' radius, 25,000 S.F., PVC pipe	.03	.13	.16
6900	Polyethylene pipe	.02	.03	.05
7000	100,000 S.F., PVC pipe	.03	.13	.16
7100	Polyethylene pipe	.02	.03	.05
7200	Riser mounted part/full impact type,plas.,40'rad.,10,000 S.F.,PVC pipe	.03	.17	.20
7300	Polyethylene pipe	.02	.10	.12
7400	45,000 S.F., PVC pipe	.03	.18	.21
7500	Polyethylene	.02	.05	.07
7600	Low medium volume brass, 40' radius, 10,000 S.F., PVC pipe	.03	.17	.20
7700	Polyethylene pipe	.02	.05	.07
7800	45,000 S.F., PVC pipe	.03	.18	.21
7900	Polyethylene pipe	.02	.05	.07
8000	Medium volume brass, 50' radius, 30,000 S.F., PVC pipe	.03	.14	.17
8100	Polyethylene pipe	.01	.04	.05

SITE WORK — B12.7-910 Site Irrigation

12.7-910 Site Irrigation

		COST PER S.F.		
		MAT.	INST.	TOTAL
8200	70,000 S.F., PVC pipe	.04	.22	.26
8300	Polyethylene pipe	.02	.06	.08
8400	Riser mounted full only impact type, plas., 40' rad., 10000 S.F., PVC pipe	.03	.17	.20
8500	Polyethylene pipe	.01	.05	.06
8600	45,000 S.F., PVC pipe	.03	.18	.21
8700	Polyethylene pipe	.01	.05	.06
8800	Low medium volume brass, 40' radius, 10,000 S.F., PVC pipe	.03	.17	.20
8900	Polyethylene pipe	.02	.05	.07
9000	45,000 S.F., PVC pipe	.03	.18	.21
9100	Polyethylene pipe	.02	.05	.07
9200	High volume brass, 80' radius, 75,000 S.F., PVC pipe	.02	.10	.12
9300	Polyethylene pipe	.01	.02	.03
9400	150,000 S.F., PVC pipe	.02	.09	.11
9500	Polyethylene pipe	.01	.02	.03
9600	Very high volume brass, 100' radius, 100,000 S.F., PVC pipe	.02	.07	.09
9700	Polyethylene pipe	.01	.02	.03
9800	200,000 S.F., PVC pipe	.02	.07	.09
9900	Polyethylene pipe	.01	.02	.03

SITE WORK — B12.7-950 — Swimming Pools

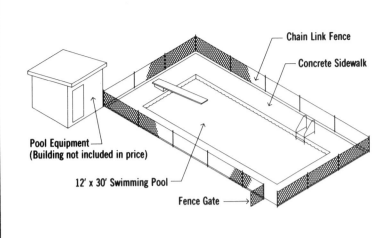

- Chain Link Fence
- Concrete Sidewalk
- Pool Equipment (Building not included in price)
- 12' x 30' Swimming Pool
- Fence Gate

The Swimming Pool System is a complete package. Everything from excavation to deck hardware is included in system costs. Below are three basic types of pool systems: residential, motel, and municipal. Systems elements include: excavation, pool materials, installation, deck hardware, pumps and filters, sidewalk, and fencing.

The Expanded System Listing shows three basic types of pools with a variety of finishes and basic materials. These systems are either vinyl lined with metal sides; gunite shell with a cement plaster finish or tile finish; or concrete sided with vinyl lining. Pool sizes listed here vary from 12' x 30' to 60' x 82.5'. All costs are on a per unit basis.

System Components	QUANTITY	UNIT	COST EACH MAT.	COST EACH INST.	COST EACH TOTAL
SYSTEM 12.7-950-1000					
SWIMMING POOL, RESIDENTIAL, CONC. SIDES, VINYL LINED, 12' X 30'					
Swimming pool, residential, in ground including equipment	360.000	S.F.	3,000	3,000	6,000
4" thick reinforced concrete sidewalk, broom finish, no base	400.000	S.F.	400	476	876
Chain link fence, residential, 3' high	124.000	L.F.	395.56	161.20	556.76
Fence gate, chain link	1.000	Ea.	33	54	87
TOTAL			3,828.56	3,691.20	7,519.76

12.7-950	Swimming Pools	MAT.	INST.	TOTAL
1000	Swimming pool, residential class, concrete sides, vinyl lined, 12' x 30'	3,830	3,690	7,520
1100	16' x 32'	5,205	5,050	10,255
1200	20' x 40'	7,780	7,600	15,380
2000	Metal sides, vinyl lined, 12' x 30'	2,990	2,850	5,840
2100	16' x 32'	3,990	3,840	7,830
2200	20' x 40'	5,880	5,700	11,580
3000	Gunite shell, cement plaster finish, 12' x 30'	5,870	5,730	11,600
3100	16' x 32'	8,085	7,930	16,015
3200	20' x 40'	7,485	7,305	14,790
3500	Tile finish, 12' x 30'	8,445	9,475	17,920
3600	16' x 32'	11,350	12,685	24,035
3700	20' x 40'	12,105	14,025	26,130
4000	Motel class, concrete sides, vinyl lined, 20' x 40'	7,785	7,605	15,390
4100	28' x 60'	15,560	15,320	30,880
5000	Metal sides, vinyl lined, 20' x 40'	5,885	5,705	11,590
5100	28' x 60'	11,570	11,330	22,900
6000	Gunite shell, cement plaster finish, 20' x 40'	15,085	14,905	29,990
6100	28' x 60'	30,890	30,650	61,540
6500	Tile finish, 20' x 40'	19,705	21,625	41,330
6600	28' x 60'	39,930	43,800	83,730
7000	Municipal class, gunite shell, cement plaster finish, 42' x 75'	64,910	64,600	129,510
7100	60' x 82.5'	101,270	100,900	202,170
7500	Tile finish, 42' x 75'	80,710	87,590	168,300
7600	60' x 82.5'	124,200	134,300	258,500
7700	Tile finish and concrete gutter, 42' x 75'	92,700	87,600	180,300
7800	60' x 82.5'	138,700	134,300	273,000
7900	Tile finish and stainless gutter, 42' x 75'	113,610	87,600	201,210
8000	60' x 82.5'	164,100	134,300	298,400

SECTION C
REFERENCE TABLES

Section C is made up of plumbing and related items, technical data, codes, sizing information and general data.

REF. NO.		PAGE
8.1-000	**PLUMBING**	334
8.1-030	**Piping**	334
8.1-031	Piping Approximations	334
8.1-032	Pipe Material Considerations	334
8.1-033	Domestic/Imported Pipe and Fitting Cost	334
8.1-080	**Valves**	335
8.1-100	**Hot Water**	338
8.1-101	Building Type Demands	338
8.1-102	Fixture Demands	338
8.1-200	**Sanitary Waste & Vent**	339
8.1-201	Fixture D.F.U. Requirements	339
8.1-202	Branch & Stack D.F.U. Requirements	339
8.1-400	**Plumbing Fixtures**	340
8.1-401	Minimum Fixture Requirements	340
8.1-402	Fixture Installation Time	341
8.1-403	Water Cooler Application	341
8.2-000	**FIRE PROTECTION**	342
8.2-100	**Sprinkler Systems**	342
8.2-101	Sprinkler Systems Automatic	342
8.2-102	Sprinkler Occupancy Classification	343
8.2-103	Sprinkler/Pipe Ratio	344
8.2-104	Adjustment for Sprinkler/Standpipe Installations	344
8.2-300	**Standpipe Systems**	345
8.2-301	Standpipe Systems Definition	345
8.2-302	Basic Standpipe Design	345

REF. NO.		PAGE
8.3-600	**Solar Heat**	346
8.3-601	Solar Heating Collector Data	346
8.3-602	Swimming Pools	346
10.1-000	**GENERAL REQUIREMENTS**	347
10.1-100	**Design & Engineering**	347
10.1-103	Mechanical and Electrical Engineering Fees	347
10.1-300	**Insurance & Bonds**	347
10.1-301	New England Builder's Insurance Rates	347
10.1-302	Performance Bonds	347
10.2-200	**Workers' Compensation**	348
10.2-201	Insurance Rates by Trade	348
10.2-202	Insurance Rates by State	348
10.2-203	Workers' Compensation by State	349
10.2-204	Workers' Compensation (Canada)	350
10.2-300	**Unemployment & Social Security**	351
10.2-301	Unemployment Taxes and Social Security	351
10.2-400	**Overtime**	351
10.2-401	Overtime: Production Efficiency	351
10.3-100	**Sales Tax**	351
10.3-101	Sales Tax by State	351
10.3-200	**Overhead & Profit**	352
10.3-201	Installing Contractor's Overhead & Profit	352
10.3-300	**Rental Rates**	353
10.3-301	Contractor Equipment	353

REF. NO.		PAGE
10.3-302	Steel Tubular Scaffolding	354
12.1-000	**SITE WORK**	355
12.1-100	**Site Shoring**	355
12.1-101	Wood Sheet Piling	355
12.1-102	Steel Sheet Piling	356
12.1-200	**Site Dewatering**	357
12.1-201	Wellpoints	357
12.3-100	**Excavation, Trench**	357
14.1-000	**SQUARE FOOT COSTS**	358
14.1-100	Square Foot and Cubic Foot Building Costs	358
14.1-101	Unit Gross Area Requirements	358
14.1-102	Square Foot Project Size Modifier	359
15.2-000	**REFERENCE AIDS**	360
15.2-100	**Area Requirement**	360
15.2-101	Floor Area Ratios	360
15.2-300	**Building Code Requirements**	360
15.2-301	Occupancy Determinations	360
15.2-400	General	
15.2-401	Contractor's Overhead	361
15.2-402	Main Office Expense	361
15.3-500	General	
15.3-501	Weather Data and Design Conditions	362
15.3-502	Maximum Depth of Frost Penetration in Inches	363
15.9-100	General	364
15.9-101	Metric Conversion Factors	364
15.9-102	Weights & Measures	365
18.1-000	**REPAIR & REMODELING**	365
18.1-101	Repair & Remodeling	365

PLUMBING C8.1-030 Piping

Table 8.1-031 Plumbing Approximations for Quick Estimating

Water Control
Water Meter; Backflow Preventer;
Shock Absorbers; Vacuum Breakers; .... 10 to 15% of Fixtures
Mixer.

Pipe And Fittings: .... 30 to 60% of Fixtures

> **Note:** Lower percentage for compact buildings or larger buildings with plumbing in one area.
> Larger percentage for large buildings with plumbing spread out.
> In extreme cases pipe may be more than 100% of fixtures.
> Percentages **do not** include special purpose or process piping.

Plumbing Labor:
1 & 2 Story Residential .... Rough-in Labor = 80% of Materials
Apartment Buildings .... Rough-in Labor = 90 to 100% of Materials
Labor for handling and placing fixtures is approximately 25 to 30% of fixtures.

Quality/Complexity Multiplier (For all installations)
Economy installation, add .... 0 to 5%
Good quality, medium complexity, add .... 5 to 15%
Above average quality and complexity, add .... 15 to 25%

Table 8.1-032 Pipe Material Consideration

1. Malleable fittings should be used for gas service.
2. Malleable fittings are used where there are stresses/strains due to expansion and vibration.
3. Cast fittings may be broken as an aid to disassembling of heating lines frozen by long use, temperature and minerals.
4. Cast iron pipe is extensively used for underground and submerged service.
5. Type M (light wall) copper tubing is available in hard temper only and is used for low pressure and less severe applications than K and L.
6. Type L (medium wall) copper tubing, available hard or soft for interior service.
7. Type K (heavy wall) copper tubing, available in hard or soft temper for use where conditions are severe. For underground and interior service.
8. Hard drawn tubing requires fewer hangers or supports but should not be bent. Silver brazed fittings are recommended, however soft solder is normally used.
9. Type DWV (very light wall) copper designed for drainage, waste and vent and other non critical pressure services.

Table 8.1-033 Domestic/Imported Pipe and Fittings Cost

The prices shown in this publication for steel/cast iron pipe and steel, cast iron, malleable iron fittings are based on domestic production sold at the normal trade discounts. The above listed items of foreign manufacture may be available at prices of 1/3 to 1/2 those shown. Some imported items after minor machining or finishing operations are being sold as domestic to further complicate the system.

Caution: Most pipe prices in this book also include a coupling and pipe hangers which for the larger sizes can add significantly to the per foot cost and should be taken into account when comparing "book cost" with quoted supplier's cost.

PLUMBING — C8.1-080 | Valves

Table 8.1-081 Valve Selection Considerations

INTRODUCTION: In any piping application, valve performance is critical. Valves should be selected to give the best performance at the lowest cost.

The following is a list of performance characteristics generally expected of valves.
1. Stopping flow or starting it.
2. Throttling flow (Modulation).
3. Flow direction changing.
4. Checking backflow (Permitting flow in only one direction).
5. Relieving or regulating pressure.

In order to properly select the right valve, some facts must be determined.

A. What liquid or gas will flow through the valve?
B. Does the fluid contain suspended particles?
C. Does the fluid remain in liquid form at all times?
D. Which metals does fluid corrode?
E. What are the pressure and temperature limits? (As temperature and pressure rise, so will the price of the valve.)
F. Is there constant line pressure?
G. Is the valve merely an on-off valve?
H. Will checking of backflow be required?
I. Will the valve operate frequently or infrequently?

Valves are classified by design type into such classifications as Gate, Globe, Angle, Check, Ball, Butterfly and Plug. They are also classified by end connection, stem, pressure restrictions and material such as bronze, cast iron, etc. Each valve has a specific use. A quality valve used correctly will provide a lifetime of trouble free service, but a high quality valve installed in the wrong service, may require frequent attention.

VALVE MATERIALS

Bronze:
Bronze is one of the oldest materials used to make valves. It is most commonly used in hot and cold water systems and other non-corrosive services. It is often used as a seating surface in larger iron body valves to ensure tight closure.

Carbon Steel:
Carbon steel is a high strength material. Therefore, valves made from this metal are used in higher pressure services, such as steam lines up to 600 psi at 850°F. Many steel valves are available with butt-weld ends for economy and are generally used in high pressure steam service as well as other higher pressure non-corrosive services.

Forged Steel:
Valves from tough carbon steel are used in service up to 2000 psi and temperatures up to 1000°F in Gate, Globe and Check valves.

Iron:
Valves are normally used in medium to large pipe lines to control non-corrosive fluid and gases, where pressures do not exceed 250 psi at 450° or 500 psi cold water, oil or gas.

Stainless Steel:
Developed steel alloys can be used in over 90% corrosive services.

Plastic PVC:
This is used in a great variety of valves generally in high corrosive service with lower temperatures and pressures.

VALVE SERVICE PRESSURES

Pressure ratings on valves provide an indication of the safe operating pressure for a valve at some elevated temperature. This temperature is dependent upon the materials used and the fabrication of the valve. When specific data is not available, a good "rule-of-thumb" to follow is the temperature of saturated steam on the primary rating indicated on the valve body. Example, the valve has the number 150S printed on the side indicating 150 psi and hence, a maximum operating temperature of 367°F (temperature of saturated steam and 150 psi).

DEFINITIONS:

1. "WOG" - Water, oil, gas (cold working pressures).
2. "SWP" - Steam working pressure.
3. 100% area (full port) - means the area through the valve is equal to or greater than the area of standard pipe.
4. "Standard Opening" - means that the area through the valve is less than the area of standard pipe and therefore these valves should be used only where restriction of flow is unimportant.
5. "Round Port" - means the valve has a full round opening through the plug and body, of the same size and area as standard pipe.
6. "Rectangular Port" - valves have rectangular shaped ports through the plug body. The area of the port is either equal to 100% of the area of standard pipe, or restricted (standard opening). In either case it is clearly marked.
7. "ANSI" - American National Standards Institute.

PLUMBING — C8.1-080 | Valves

STEM TYPES
(OS & Y) - Rising Stem - Outside Screw and Yoke
Offers a visual indication of whether the valve is open or closed. Recommended where high temperatures, corrosives, and solids in the line might cause damage to inside-valve stem threads. The stem threads are engaged by the yoke bushing so the stem rises through the hand wheel as it is turned.

(R.S.) - Rising Stem - Inside Screw
Adequate clearance for operation must be provided because both the hand wheel and the stem rise.
The valve wedge position is indicated by the position of the stem and hand wheel.

(N.R.S.) - Non-Rising Stem - Inside Screw
A minimum clearance is required for operating this type of valve. Excessive wear or damage to stem threads inside the valve may be caused by heat, corrosion, and solids. Because the hand wheel and stem do not rise, wedge position cannot be visually determined.

VALVE TYPES
Gate Valves
Provide full flow, minute pressure drop, minimum turbulence and minimum fluid trapped in the line.
They are normally used where operation is infrequent.

Globe Valves
Globe valves are designed for throttling and/or frequent operation with positive shut-off. Particular attention must be paid to the several types of seating materials available to avoid unnecessary wear. The seats must be compatible with the fluid in service and may be composition or metal. The configuration of the Globe valve opening causes turbulence which results in increased resistance. Most bronze Globe valves are rising stem-inside screw, but they are also available on O.S. & Y.

Angle Valves
The fundamental difference between the Angle valve and the Globe valve is the fluid flow through the Angle valve. It makes a 90° turn and offers less resistance to flow than the Globe valve while replacing an elbow. An angle valve thus reduces the number of joints and installation time.

PLUMBING — C8.1-080 — Valves

Check Valves
Check valves are designed to prevent backflow by automatically seating when the direction of fluid is reversed.
Swing Check valves are generally installed with Gate-valves, as they provide comparable full flow.
Usually recommended for lines where flow velocities are low and should not be used on lines with pulsating flow. Recommended for horizontal installation, or in vertical lines only where flow is upward.

Lift Check Valves
These are commonly used with Globe and Angle valves since they have similar diaphragm seating arrangements and are recommended for preventing backflow of steam, air, gas and water, and on vapor lines with high flow velocities. For horizontal lines, horizontal lift checks should be used and vertical lift checks for vertical lines.

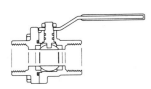

Ball Valves
Ball valves are light and easily installed, yet because of modern elastomeric seats, provide tight closure. Flow is controlled by rotating up to 90° a drilled ball which fits tightly against resilient seals. This ball seats with flow in either direction, and valve handle indicates the degree of opening. Recommended for frequent operation readily adaptable to automation, ideal for installation where space is limited.

Butterfly Valves
Butterfly valves provide bubble-tight closure with excellent throttling characteristics. They can be used for full-open, closed and for throttling applications.
The Butterfly valve consists of a disc within the valve body which is controlled by a shaft.
In its closed position, the valve disc seals against a resilient seat. The disc position throughout the full 90° rotation is visually indicated by the position of the operator.
A Butterfly valve is only a fraction of the weight of a Gate valve and requires no gaskets between flanges in most cases.
Recommended for frequent operation and adaptable to automation where space is limited.
Wafer and Lug type bodies when installed between two pipe flanges, can be easily removed from the line. The pressure of the bolted flanges holds the valve in place.
Locating lugs makes installation easier.

Plug Valves
Lubricated plug valves, because of the wide range of service to which they are adapted, may be classified as all purpose valves. They can be safely used at all pressure and vacuums, and at all temperatures up to the limits of available lubricants. They are the most satisfactory valves for the handling of gritty suspensions and many other destructive, erosive, corrosive and chemical solutions.

PLUMBING — C8.1-100 Hot Water

Table 8.1-101 Hot Water Consumption Rates

Type of Building	Size Factor	Maximum Hourly Demand	Average Day Demand
Apartment Dwellings	No. of Apartments:		
	Up to 20	12.0 Gal. per apt.	42.0 Gal. per apt.
	21 to 50	10.0 Gal. per apt.	40.0 Gal. per apt.
	51 to 75	8.5 Gal. per apt.	38.0 Gal. per apt.
	76 to 100	7.0 Gal. per apt.	37.0 Gal. per apt.
	101 to 200	6.0 Gal. per apt.	36.0 Gal. per apt.
	201 up	5.0 Gal. per apt.	35.0 Gal. per apt.
Dormitories	Men	3.8 Gal. per man	13.1 Gal. per man
	Women	5.0 Gal. per woman	12.3 Gal. per woman
Hospitals	Per bed	23 Gal. per patient	90 Gal. per patient
Hotels	Single room with bath	17 Gal. per unit	50 Gal. per unit
	Double room with bath	27 Gal. per unit	80 Gal. per unit
Motels	No. of units:		
	Up to 20	6.0 Gal. per unit	20.0 Gal. per unit
	21 to 100	5.0 Gal. per unit	14.0 Gal. per unit
	101 Up	4.0 Gal. per unit	10.0 Gal. per unit
Nursing Homes		4.5 Gal. per bed	18.4 Gal. per bed
Office buildings		0.4 Gal. per person	1.0 Gal. per person
Restaurants	Full meal type	1.5 Gal./max. meals/hr.	2.4 Gal. per meal
	Drive-in snack type	0.7 Gal./max. meals/hr.	0.7 Gal. per meal
Schools	Elementary	0.6 Gal. per student	0.6 Gal. per student
	Secondary & High	1.0 Gal. per student	1.8 Gal. per student

For evaluation purposes, recovery rate and storage capacity are inversely proportional. Water heaters should be sized so that the maximum hourly demand anticipated can be met in addition to allowance for the heat loss from the pipes and storage tank.

Table 8.1-102 Fixture Demands in Gallons Per Fixture Per Hour

Table below is based on 140°F final temperature except for dishwashers in public places (*) where 180°F water is mandatory.

Fixture	Apartment House	Club	Gym	Hospital	Hotel	Indust. Plant	Office	Private Home	School
Bathtubs	20	20	30	20	20			20	
Dishwashers, automatic	15	50-150*		50-150*	50-200*	20-100*		15	20-100*
Kitchen sink	10	20		20	30	20	20	10	20
Laundry, stationary tubs	20	28		28	28			20	
Laundry, automatic wash	75	75		100	150			75	
Private lavatory	2	2	2	2	2	2	2	2	2
Public lavatory	4	6	8	6	8	12	6		15
Showers	30	150	225	75	75	225	30	30	225
Service sink	20	20		20	30	20	20	15	20
Demand factor	0.30	0.30	0.40	0.25	0.25	0.40	0.30	0.30	0.40
Storage capacity factor	1.25	0.90	1.00	0.60	0.80	1.00	2.00	0.70	1.00

To obtain the probable maximum demand multiply the total demands for the fixtures (gal./fixture/hour) by the demand factor. The heater should have a heating capacity in gallons per hour equal to this maximum. The storage tank should have a capacity in gallons equal to the probable maximum demand multiplied by the storage capacity factor.

PLUMBING   C8.1-200   Requirements and Capacities

Table 8.1-201 Drainage Requirements

Drainage lines must have a slope to maintain flow for proper operation. This slope should not be less than 1/4" per foot for 3" diameter or smaller pipe and not less than 1/8" per foot for 4" diameter or larger pipe. The capacity of building drainage systems is calculated on a basis of "drainage fixture units" (d.f.u.) as per the following chart.

Type of Fixture	d.f.u. Value	Type of Fixture	d.f.u. Value
Automatic clothes washer (2" standpipe)	3	Service sink (trap standard)	3
Bathroom group (water closet, lavatory and		Service sink (P trap)	2
bathtub or shower) tank type closet	6	Urinal, pedestal, syphon jet blowout	6
Bathtub (with or without overhead shower)	2	Urinal, wall hung	4
Clinic sink	6	Urinal, stall washout	4
Combination sink & tray with food disposal	4	Wash sink (circ. or mult.) per faucet set	2
Dental unit or cuspidor	1	Water closet, tank operated	4
Dental lavatory	1	Water closet, valve operated	6
Drinking fountain	1/2	Fixtures not listed above	
Dishwasher, domestic	2	Trap size 1-1/4" or smaller	1
Floor drains with 2" waste	3	Trap size 1-1/2"	2
Kitchen sink, domestic with one 1-1/2" trap	2	Trap size 2"	3
Kitchen sink, domestic with food disposal	2	Trap size 2-1/2"	4
Lavatory with 1-1/4" waste	1	Trap size 3"	5
Laundry tray (1 or 2 compartment)	2	Trap size 4"	6
Shower stall, domestic	2		

For continuous or nearly continuous flow into the system from a pump, air conditioning equipment or other item, allow 2 fixture units for each gallon per minute of flow.

When the "drainage fixture units" (d.f.u.) for each horizontal branch or vertical stack is computed from the table above, the appropriate pipe size for each branch or stack is determined from the table below.

Table 8.1-202 Allowable Fixture Units (d.f.u.) for Branches and Stacks

Pipe Diam.	Horiz. Branch (not incl. drains)	Stack Size for 3 Stories or 3 Levels	Stack Size for Over 3 Levels	Maximum for 1 Story Building Stack
1-1/2"	3	4	8	2
2"	6	10	24	6
2-1/2"	12	20	42	9
3"	20*	48*	72*	20*
4"	160	240	500	90
5"	360	540	1100	200
6"	620	960	1900	350
8"	1400	2200	3600	600
10"	2500	3800	5600	1000
12"	3900	6000	8400	1500
15"	7000			

*Not more than two water closets or bathroom groups within each branch interval nor more than six water closets or bathroom groups on the stack.

Stacks sized for the total may be reduced as load decreases at each story to a minimum diameter of 1/2 the maximum diameter.

PLUMBING — C8.1-400 — Individual Fixture Systems

Table 8.1-401 Minimum Plumbing Fixture Requirements

TYPE OF BUILDING/USE	WATER CLOSETS Persons	WATER CLOSETS Fixtures	URINALS Persons	URINALS Fixtures	LAVATORIES Persons	LAVATORIES Fixtures	BATHTUBS OR SHOWERS Persons	BATHTUBS OR SHOWERS Fixtures	DRINKING FOUNTAIN Fixtures	OTHER Fixtures
Assembly Halls Auditoriums, Theater, Public assembly	1-100; 101-200; 201-400	1; 2; 3	1-200; 201-400; 401-600	1; 2; 3	1-200; 201-400; 401-750	1; 2; 3			1 for each 1000 persons	1 service sink
	Over 400 add 1 fixt. for ea. 500 men; 1 fixt. for ea. 300 women		Over 600 add 1 fixture for each 300 men		Over 750 add 1 fixture for each 500 persons					
Assembly Public Worship	300 men; 150 women	1; 1	300 men	1	men; women	1; 1			1	
Dormitories	Men: 1 for each 10 persons; Women: 1 for each 8 persons		1 for each 25 men, over 150 add 1 fixture for each 50 men		1 for ea. 12 persons; 1 separate dental lav. for each 50 persons recom.		1 for ea. 8 persons. For women add 1 additional for each 30. Over 150 persons add 1 for each 20.		1 for each 75 persons	Laundry trays 1 for each 50; serv. sink 1 for ea. 100
Dwellings Apartments and homes	1 fixture for each unit				1 fixture for each unit		1 fixture for each unit			
Hospitals Indiv. Room, Ward, Waiting room	8 persons	1; 1; 1			10 persons	1; 1; 1	20 persons	1	1 for 100 patients	1 service sink per floor
Industrial Mfg. plants, Warehouses	1-10; 11-25; 26-50; 51-75; 76-100	1; 2; 3; 4; 5	0-30; 31-80; 81-160; 161-240	1; 2; 3; 4	1-100; over 100	1 for ea. 10; 1 for ea. 15	1 Shower for each 15 persons subject to excessive heat or occupational hazard		1 for each 75 persons	
	1 fixture for each additional 30 persons									
Public Buildings Businesses, Offices	1-15; 16-35; 36-55; 56-80; 81-110; 111-150	1; 2; 3; 4; 5; 6	Urinals may be provided in place of water closets but may not replace more than 1/3 required number of men's water closets		1-15; 16-35; 36-60; 61-90; 91-125	1; 2; 3; 4; 5			1 for each 75 persons	1 service sink per floor
	1 fixture for ea. additional 40 persons				1 fixture for ea. additional 45 persons					
Schools Elementary	1 for ea. 30 boys; 1 for ea. 25 girls		1 for ea. 25 boys		1 for ea. 35 boys; 1 for ea. 35 girls		For gym or pool shower room 1/5 of a class		1 for each 40 pupils	
Schools Secondary	1 for ea. 40 boys; 1 for ea. 30 girls		1 for ea. 25 boys		1 for ea. 40 boys; 1 for ea. 40 girls		For gym or pool shower room 1/5 of a class		1 for each 50 pupils	

PLUMBING — C8.1-400 — Individual Fixture Systems

Table 8.1-402 Plumbing Fixture Installation Time

Item	Rough-In	Set	Total Hours	Item	Rough-In	Set	Total Hours
Bathtub	5	5	10	Shower head only	2	1	3
Bathtub and shower, cast iron	6	6	12	Shower drain	3	1	4
Fire hose reel and cabinet	4	2	6	Shower stall, slate		15	15
Floor drain to 4" diameter	3	1	4	Slop sink	5	3	8
Grease trap, single, cast iron	5	3	8	Test six fixtures			14
Kitchen gas range		4	4	Urinal, wall	6	2	8
Kitchen sink, single	4	4	8	Urinal, pedestal or floor	6	4	10
Kitchen sink, double	6	6	12	Water closet and tank	4	3	7
Laundry tubs	4	2	6	Water closet and tank, wall hung	5	3	8
Lavatory wall hung	5	3	8	Water heater, 45 gals. gas, automatic	5	2	7
Lavatory pedestal	5	3	8	Water heaters, 65 gals. gas, automatic	5	2	7
Shower and stall	6	4	10	Water heaters, electric, plumbing only	4	2	6

Fixtures in unit pricing are based on the cost per fixture set in place. The rough-in cost, which must be added for each fixture, includes carrier, if required, some supply, waste and vent pipe, connecting fittings and stops. The lengths of rough-in pipe are nominal runs which would connect to the larger runs and stacks.

The supply runs and DWV runs and stacks must be accounted for in separate entries. In the eastern half of the United States it is common for the plumber to carry these to a point 5' outside the building.

Table 8.1-403 Water Cooler Application

Type of Service	Requirement
Office, School or Hospital	12 persons per gallon per hour
Office, Lobby or Department Store	4 or 5 gallons per hour per fountain
Light manufacturing	7 persons per gallon per hour
Heavy manufacturing	5 persons per gallon per hour
Hot heavy manufacturing	4 persons per gallon per hour
Hotels	.08 gallons per hour per room
Theatre	1 gallon per hour per 100 seats

FIRE PROTECTION — C8.2-100 — General

Table 8.2-101 Sprinkler Systems (Automatic)

Sprinkler systems may be classified by type as follows:

1. **Wet Pipe System.** A system employing automatic sprinklers attached to a piping system containing water and connected to a water supply so that water discharges immediately from sprinklers opened by a fire.

2. **Dry Pipe System.** A system employing automatic sprinklers attached to a piping system containing air under pressure, the release of which as from the opening of sprinklers permits the water pressure to open a valve known as a "dry pipe valve". The water then flows into the piping system and out the opened sprinklers.

3. **Pre-Action System.** A system employing automatic sprinklers attached to a piping system containing air that may or may not be under pressure, with a supplemental heat responsive system of generally more sensitive characteristics than the automatic sprinklers themselves, installed in the same areas as the sprinklers; actuation of the heat responsive system, as from a fire, opens a valve which permits water to flow into the sprinkler piping system and to be discharged from any sprinklers which may be open.

4. **Deluge System.** A system employing open sprinklers attached to a piping system connected to a water supply through a valve which is opened by the operation of a heat responsive system installed in the same areas as the sprinklers. When this valve opens, water flows into the piping system and discharges from all sprinklers attached thereto.

5. **Combined Dry Pipe and Pre-Action Sprinkler System.** A system employing automatic sprinklers attached to a piping system containing air under pressure with a supplemental heat responsive system of generally more sensitive characteristics than the automatic sprinklers themselves, installed in the same areas as the sprinklers; operation of the heat responsive system, as from a fire, actuates tripping devices which open dry pipe valves simultaneously and without loss of air pressure in the system. Operation of the heat responsive system also opens approved air exhaust valves at the end of the feed main which facilitates the filling of the system with water which usually precedes the opening of sprinklers. The heat responsive system also serves as an automatic fire alarm system.

6. **Limited Water Supply System.** A system employing automatic sprinklers and conforming to these standards but supplied by a pressure tank of limited capacity.

7. **Chemical Systems.** Systems using halon, carbon dioxide, dry chemical or high expansion foam as selected for chemically special inhibiting flame propagation, suffocate flames ments. Agent may extinguish flames by by excluding oxygen, interrupting chemical action of oxygen uniting with fuel or sealing and cooling the combustion center.

8. **Firecycle System.** Firecycle is a fixed fire protection sprinkler system utilizing water as its extinguishing agent. It is a time delayed, recycling, preaction type which automatically shuts the water off when heat is reduced below the detector operating temperature and turns the water back on when that temperature is exceeded. The system senses a fire condition through a closed circuit electrical detector system which controls water flow to the fire automatically. Batteries supply up to 90 hour emergency power supply for system operation. The piping system is dry (until water is required) and is monitored with pressurized air. Should any leak in the system piping occur, an alarm will sound, but water will not enter the system until heat is sensed by a Firecycle detector.

Area coverage sprinkler systems may be laid out and fed from the supply in any one of several patterns as shown in Figure 8.2-101. It is desirable, if possible, to utilize a central feed and achieve a shorter flow path from the riser to the furthest sprinkler. This permits use of the smallest sizes of pipe possible with resulting savings.

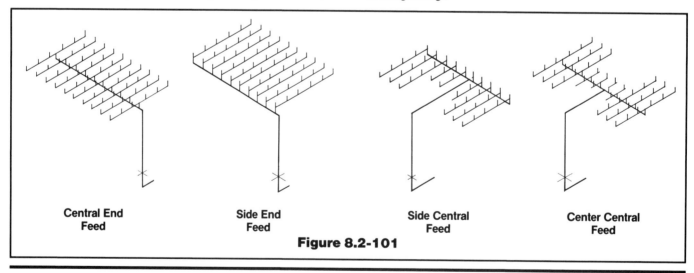

Central End Feed • Side End Feed • Side Central Feed • Center Central Feed

Figure 8.2-101

FIRE PROTECTION — C8.2-100 — General

Table 8.2-102 System Classification

SYSTEM CLASSIFICATION
Rules for installation of sprinkler systems vary depending on the classification of occupancy falling into one of three categories as follows:

LIGHT HAZARD OCCUPANCY
The protection area alloted per sprinkler should not exceed 200 S.F. with the maximum distance between lines and sprinklers on lines being 15'. The sprinklers do not need to be staggered. Branch lines should not exceed eight sprinklers on either side of a cross main. Each large area requiring more than 100 sprinklers and without a sub-dividing partition should be supplied by feed mains or risers sized for ordinary hazard occupancy.

Included in this group are:

Auditoriums	Museums
Churches	Nursing Homes
Clubs	Offices
Educational	Residential
Hospitals	Restaurants
Institutional	Schools
Libraries	Theaters
(except large stack rooms)	

ORDINARY HAZARD OCCUPANCY
The protection area allotted per sprinkler shall not exceed 130 S.F. of noncombustible ceiling and 120 S.F. of combustible ceiling. The maximum allowable distance between sprinkler lines and sprinklers on line is 15'. Sprinklers shall be staggered if the distance between heads exceed 12'. Branch lines should not exceed eight sprinklers on either side of a cross main.

Included in this group are:

Automotive garages	Electric generating stations
Bakeries	Feed mills
Beverage manufacturing	Grain elevators
Bleacheries	Ice manufacturing
Boiler houses	Laundries
Canneries	Machine shops
Cement plants	Mercantiles
Clothing factories	Paper mills
Cold storage warehouses	Printing and Publishing
Dairy products manufacturing	Shoe factories
Distilleries	Warehouses
Dry cleaning	Wood product assembly

EXTRA HAZARD OCCUPANCY
The protection area allotted per sprinkler shall not exceed 90 S.F. of noncombustible ceiling and 80 S.F. of combustible ceiling. The maximum allowable distance between lines and between sprinklers on lines is 12'. Sprinklers on alternate lines shall be staggered if the distance between sprinklers on lines exceeds 8'. Branch lines should not exceed six sprinklers on either side of a cross main.

Included in this group are:

Aircraft hangars	Paint shops
Chemical works	Shade cloth manufacturing
Explosives manufacturing	Solvent extracting
Linoleum manufacturing	Varnish works
Linseed oil mills	Volatile flammable
Oil refineries	Liquid manufacturing & use

FIRE PROTECTION — C8.2-100 — General

Table 8.2-103 Sprinkler Quantities for Various Size and Types of Pipe

Sprinkler Quantities: The table below lists the usual maximum number of sprinkler heads for each size of copper and steel pipe for both wet and dry systems. These quantities may be adjusted to meet individual structural needs or local code requirements. Maximum area on any one floor for one system is: light hazard and ordinary hazard 52,000 S.F., extra hazardous 25,000 S.F.

Pipe Size Diameter	Light Hazard Occupancy		Ordinary Hazard Occupancy		Extra Hazard Occupancy	
	Steel Pipe	Copper Pipe	Steel Pipe	Copper Pipe	Steel Pipe	Copper Pipe
1"	2 sprinklers	2 sprinklers	2 sprinklers	2 sprinklers	1 sprinklers	1 sprinklers
1-1/4"	3	3	3	3	2	2
1-1/2"	5	5	5	5	5	5
2"	10	12	10	12	8	8
2-1/2"	30	40	20	25	15	20
3"	60	65	40	45	27	30
3-1/2"	100	115	65	75	40	45
4"			100	115	55	65
5"			160	180	90	100
6"			275	300	150	170

Dry Pipe Systems: A dry pipe system should be installed where a wet pipe system is impractical, as in rooms or buildings which cannot be properly heated.

The use of an approved dry pipe system is more desirable than shutting off the water supply during cold weather.

Not more than 750 gallons of system capacity should be controlled by one dry pipe valve. Where two or more dry pipe valves are used, systems should preferably be divided horizontally.

Table 8.2-104 Adjustment for Sprinkler/Standpipe Installations

Quality/Complexity Multiplier (For all installations)
Economy installation, add .... 0 to 5%
Good quality, medium complexity, add .... 5 to 15%
Above average quality and complexity, add .... 15 to 25%

FIRE PROTECTION — C8.2-300 — General

Table 8.2-301 Standpipe Systems

The basis for standpipe system design is National Fire Protection Association NFPA 14, however, the authority having jurisdiction should be consulted for special conditions, local requirements and approval.

Standpipe systems, properly designed and maintained, are an effective and valuable time saving aid for extinguishing fires, especially in the upper stories of tall buildings, the interior of large commercial or industrial malls, or other areas where construction features or access make the laying of temporary hose lines time consuming and/or hazardous. Standpipes are frequently installed with automatic sprinkler systems for maximum protection.

There are three general classes of service for standpipe systems:

Class I for use by fire departments and personnel with special training for heavy streams (2-1/2" hose connections).

Class II for use by building occupants until the arrival of the fire department (1-1/2" hose connector with hose).

Class III for use by either fire departments and trained personnel or by the building occupants (both 2-1/2" and 1-1/2" hose connections or one 2-1/2" hose valve with an easily removable 2-1/2" by 1-1/2" adapter).

Standpipe systems are also classified by the way water is supplied to the system. The four basic types are:

Type 1: Wet standpipe system having supply valve open and water pressure maintained at all times.

Type 2: Standpipe system so arranged through the use of approved devices as to admit water to the system automatically by opening a hose valve.

Type 3: Standpipe system arranged to admit water to the system through manual operation of approved remote control devices located at each hose station.

Type 4: Dry standpipe having no permanent water supply.

Table 8.2-302 NFPA 14 Basic Standpipe Design

Class	Design-Use	Pipe Size Minimums	Water Supply Minimums
Class I	2½" hose connection on each floor. All areas within 30' of nozzle with 100' of hose. Fire Department Trained Personnel	Height to 100', 4" dia. Heights above 100', 6" dia. (275' max. except with pressure regulators 400' max.)	For each standpipe riser 500 GPM flow. For common supply pipe allow 500 GPM for first standpipe plus 250 GPM for each additional standpipe (2500 GPM max. total). 30 min. duration 65 PSI at 500 GPM
Class II	1½" hose connection with hose on each floor. All areas within 30' of nozzle with 100' of hose. Occupant personnel	Height to 50', 2" dia. Height above 50', 2½" dia.	For each standpipe riser 100 GPM flow. For multiple riser common supply pipe 100 GPM. 30 min. duration, 65 PSI at 100 GPM
Class III	Both of above. Class I valved connections will meet Class III with addition of 2½" by 1½" adapter and 1½" hose.	Same as Class I	Same as Class I

Combined Systems

Combined systems are systems where the risers supply both automatic sprinklers and 2-1/2" hose connection outlets for fire department use. In such a system the sprinkler spacing pattern shall be in accordance with NFPA 13 while the risers and supply piping will be sized in accordance with NFPA 14. When the building is completely sprinklered the risers may be sized by hydraulic calculation. The minimum size riser for buildings not completely sprinklered is 6".

The minimum water supply of a completely sprinklered, light hazard, high-rise occupancy building will be 500 GPM while the supply required for other types of completely sprinklered high-rise buildings is 1000 GPM.

General System Requirements

1. Approved valves will be provided at the riser for controlling branch lines to hose outlets.
2. A hose valve will be provided at each outlet for attachment of hose.
3. Where pressure at any standpipe outlet exceeds 100 PSI a pressure reducer must be installed to limit the pressure to 100 PSI. Note that the pressure head due to gravity in 100' of riser is 43.4 PSI. This must be overcome by city pressure, fire pumps, or gravity tanks to provide adequate pressure at the top of the riser.
4. Each hose valve on a wet system having linen hose shall have an automatic drip connection to prevent valve leakage from entering the hose.
5. Each riser will have a valve to isolate it from the rest of the system.
6. One or more fire department connections as an auxiliary supply shall be provided for each Class I or Class III standpipe system. In buildings having two or more zones, a connection will be provided for each zone.
7. There will be no shutoff valve in the fire department connection, but a check valve will be located in the line before it joins the system.
8. All hose connections street side will be identified on a cast plate or fitting as to purpose.

HEATING - SOLAR   C8.3-600   General

Table 8.3-601 Collector Tilt for Domestic Hot Water

Optimum collector tilt is usually equal to the site latitude. Variations of plus or minus 10 degrees are acceptable and orientation of 20 degrees on either side of true south is acceptable; however, local climate and collector type may influence the choice between east or west deviations.

Flat plate collectors consist of a number of components as follows: Insulation to reduce heat loss through the bottom and sides of the collector. The enclosure which contains all the components in this assembly is usually weatherproof and prevents dust, wind and water from coming in contact with the absorber plate. The cover plate usually consists of one or more layers of a variety of glass or plastic and reduces the reradiation. It creates an air space which traps the heat by reducing radiation losses between the cover plate and the absorber plate.

The absorber plate must have a good thermal bond with the fluid passages. The absorber plate is usually metallic and treated with a surface coating which improves absorptivity. Black or dark paints or selective coatings are used for this purpose, and the design of this passage and plate combination helps determine a solar system's effectiveness.

Heat transfer fluid passage tubes are attached above and below or integral with an asborber plate for the purpose of transferring thermal energy from the absorber plate to a heat transfer medium. The heat exchanger is a device for transferring thermal energy from one fluid to another. The rule of thumb of space heating sizing is one S.F. of collector per 2.5 S.F. of floor space.

For domestic hot water the rule of thumb is 3/4 S.F. of collector for one gallon of water used per day, on an average use twenty-five gallons per day per person, plus ten gallons per dishwasher or washing machine.

Table 8.3-602 Swimming Pool

Pool prices given per square foot of surface area include pool structure, filter and chlorination equipment where required, pumps, related piping, diving boards, ladders, maintenance kit, skimmer and vacuum system. Decks and electrical service to equipment are not included.

Residential in-ground pool construction can be divided into two categories: vinyl lined and gunite. Vinyl lined pool walls are constructed of different materials including wood, concrete, plastic or metal. The bottom is often graded with sand over which the vinyl liner is installed. Costs are generally in the $12 to $17 per S.F. range. Vermiculite or soil cement bottoms may be substituted for an added cost of $.72 per S.F. surface.

Gunite pool construction is used both in residential and municipal installations. These structures are steel reinforced for strength and finished with a white cement limestone plaster. Residential costs run from $16 to $28 per S.F. surface. Municipal costs vary from $35 to $51 because plumbing codes require more expensive materials, chlorination equipment and higher filtration rates.

Municipal pools greater than 1,600 S.F. require gutter systems to control waves. This gutter may be formed into the concrete wall. Often a vinyl, stainless steel gutter or gutter and wall system is specified, which will raise the pool cost an additional $51 to $180 per L.F. of gutter installed and up to $290 per L.F. if a gutter and wall system is installed.

Competition pools usually require tile bottoms and sides with contrasting lane striping. Add $12 per S.F. of wall or bottom to be tiled.

GENERAL REQUIREMENTS C10.1-100 Design & Engineering

Table 10.1-103 Mechanical and Electrical Engineering Fees

Typical **Mechanical and Electrical Engineering Fees** based on the size of the subcontract. These fees are included in Architectural Fees.

Type of Construction	Subcontract Size							
	$25,000	$50,000	$100,000	$225,000	$350,000	$500,000	$750,000	$1,000,000
Simple structures	6.4%	5.7%	4.8%	4.5%	4.4%	4.3%	4.2%	4.1%
Intermediate structures	8.0	7.3	6.5	5.6	5.1	5.0	4.9	4.8
Complex structures	12.0	9.0	9.0	8.0	7.5	7.5	7.0	7.0

For renovations, add 15% to 25% to applicable fee.

GENERAL REQUIREMENTS C10.1-300 Insurance & Bonds

Table 10.1-301 New England Builder's Insurance Rates

Builder's Risk Insurance is insurance on a building during construction. Premiums are paid by the owner or the contractor. Blasting, collapse and underground insurance would raise total insurance costs above those listed. Floater policy for materials delivered to the job runs $.75 to $1.25 per $100 value. Contractor equipment insurance runs $.50 to $1.50 per $100 value.

Tabulated below are New England Builder's Risk insurance rates in dollars per $100 value for $1,000 deductible. For $25,000 deductible, rates can be reduced 13% to 34%. On contracts over $1,000,000, rates may be lower than those tabulated. Policies are written annually for the total completed value in place. For "all risk" insurance (excluding flood, earthquake and certain other perils) add $.025 to total rates below.

Coverage	Frame Construction (Class 1)		Brick Construction (Class 4)		Fire Resistive (Class 6)	
	Range	Average	Range	Average	Range	Average
Fire Insurance	$.300 to .420	$.394	$.132 to .189	$.174	$.062 to .090	$.081
Extended Coverage	.115 to .150	.144	.080 to .105	.101	.081 to .105	.100
Vandalism	.012 to .016	.015	.008 to .011	.011	.008 to .011	.010
Total Annual Rate	$.427 to .586	$.553	$.220 to .305	$.286	$.151 to .206	$.191

Table 10.1-302 Performance Bond

This table shows the cost of a Performance Bond for a construction job scheduled to be completed in 12 months. Add 1% of the premium cost per month for jobs requiring more than 12 months to complete. The rates are "preferred" rates offered to contractors that the bonding company considers financially sound and capable of doing the work. The rates quoted below are suggested averages. Actual rates vary from contractor to contractor and from bonding company to bonding company. Contractors should prequalify through a bonding agency before submitting a bid on a contract that requires a bond.

Contract Amount	Building Construction Class B Projects	Highways & Bridges	
		Class A New Construction	Class A-1 Highway Resurfacing
First $ 100,000 bid	$25.00 per M	$15.00 per M	$ 9.40 per M
Next 400,000 bid	$ 2,500 plus $15.00 per M	$ 1,500 plus $10.00 per M	$ 940 plus $7.20 per M
Next 2,000,000 bid	8,500 plus 10.00 per M	5,500 plus 7.00 per M	3,820 plus 6.00 per M
Next 2,500,000 bid	28,500 plus 7.50 per M	19,500 plus 5.50 per M	15,820 plus 5.00 per M
Next 2,500,000 bid	47,250 plus 7.00 per M	33,250 plus 5.00 per M	28,320 plus 4.50 per M
Over 7,500,000 bid	64,750 plus 6.00 per M	45,750 plus 4.50 per M	39,570 plus 4.00 per M

GENERAL REQUIREMENTS C10.2-200 | Workers' Compensation

Table 10.2-201 Insurance Rates by Trade

The table below tabulates the national averages for Workers' Compensation insurance rates by trade and type of building. The average "Insurance Rate" is multiplied by the "% of Building Cost" for each trade. This produces the "Workers' Compensation Cost" by % of total labor cost, to be added for each trade by building type to determine the weighted average Workers' Compensation rate for the building types analyzed.

Trade	Insurance Rate (% of Labor Cost)		% of Building Cost			Workers' Compensation Cost		
	Range	Average	Office Bldgs.	Schools & Apts.	Mfg.	Office Bldgs.	Schools & Apts.	Mfg.
Excavation, Grading, etc.	3.5% to 26.8%	9.7%	4.8%	4.9%	4.5%	.46%	.47%	.44%
Piles & Foundations	5.0 to 52.0	23.7	7.1	5.2	8.7	1.68	1.23	2.06
Concrete	5.0 to 32.7	13.9	5.0	14.8	3.7	.69	2.06	.51
Masonry	3.6 to 36.3	12.6	6.9	7.5	1.9	.87	.94	.24
Structural Steel	5.0 to 118.4	30.2	10.7	3.9	17.6	3.23	1.18	5.31
Miscellaneous & Ornamental Metals	2.7 to 27.4	10.0	2.8	4.0	3.6	.28	.40	.36
Carpentry & Millwork	5.0 to 40.1	15.1	3.7	4.0	0.5	.56	.60	.08
Metal or Composition Siding	5.0 to 34.2	12.7	2.3	0.3	4.3	.29	.04	.55
Roofing	5.0 to 86.2	27.6	2.3	2.6	3.1	.63	.72	.85
Doors & Hardware	3.5 to 20.9	9.0	0.9	1.4	0.4	.08	.13	.04
Sash & Glazing	3.2 to 22.5	11.1	3.5	4.0	1.0	.39	.44	.11
Lath & Plaster	3.3 to 38.5	12.2	3.3	6.9	0.8	.40	.84	.10
Tile, Marble & Floors	2.6 to 23.3	7.6	2.6	3.0	0.5	.20	.23	.04
Acoustical Ceilings	3.1 to 22.3	9.2	2.4	0.2	0.3	.22	.02	.03
Painting	4.2 to 32.2	11.3	1.5	1.6	1.6	.17	.18	.18
Interior Partitions	5.0 to 40.1	15.1	3.9	4.3	4.4	.59	.65	.66
Miscellaneous Items	2.1 to 98.0	13.7	5.2	3.7	9.7	.71	.51	1.33
Elevators	2.2 to 15.8	7.2	2.1	1.1	2.2	.15	.08	.16
Sprinklers	2.2 to 15.1	7.2	0.5	—	2.0	.04	—	.14
Plumbing	2.5 to 14.2	6.7	4.9	7.2	5.2	.33	.48	.35
Heat., Vent., Air Conditioning	3.2 to 20.4	9.4	13.5	11.0	12.9	1.27	1.03	1.21
Electrical	2.3 to 10.9	5.5	10.1	8.4	11.1	.55	.46	.61
Total	2.1% to 118.4%	—	100.0%	100.0%	100.0%	13.79%	12.69%	15.36%
Overall Weighted Average								13.95%

Table 10.2-202 Insurance Rates by States

The table below lists the weighted average Workers' Compensation base rate for each state with a factor comparing this with the national average of 13.7%.

State	Weighted Average	Factor	State	Weighted Average	Factor	State	Weighted Average	Factor
Alabama	11.4%	83	Kentucky	13.1%	96	North Dakota	8.0%	58
Alaska	22.6	165	Louisiana	12.6	92	Ohio	8.9	65
Arizona	13.9	101	Maine	18.8	137	Oklahoma	12.3	90
Arkansas	10.0	73	Maryland	15.3	112	Oregon	27.6	201
California	15.6	114	Massachusetts	22.1	161	Pennsylvania	14.7	107
Colorado	21.9	160	Michigan	14.9	109	Rhode Island	18.4	134
Connecticut	23.3	170	Minnesota	24.9	182	South Carolina	10.5	77
Delaware	12.0	88	Mississippi	9.9	72	South Dakota	9.1	66
District of Columbia	19.7	144	Missouri	7.6	55	Tennessee	7.7	56
Florida	22.3	163	Montana	31.8	232	Texas	19.0	139
Georgia	13.9	101	Nebraska	7.8	57	Utah	8.5	62
Hawaii	16.7	122	Nevada	14.7	107	Vermont	9.0	66
Idaho	10.8	79	New Hampshire	18.6	136	Virginia	9.0	66
Illinois	19.1	139	New Jersey	7.5	55	Washington	9.7	71
Indiana	4.9	36	New Mexico	18.3	134	West Virginia	7.8	57
Iowa	11.3	82	New York	9.6	70	Wisconsin	12.6	92
Kansas	8.6	63	North Carolina	6.4	47	Wyoming	5.4	39
Weighted Average for U.S. is 13.9% of payroll = 100								

Rates in the following table are the base or manual costs per $100 of payroll for Workers' Compensation in each state. Rates are usually applied to straight time wages only and not to premium time wages and bonuses.

The weighted average skilled worker rate for 35 trades is 13.7%. For bidding purposes, apply the full value of Workers' Compensation directly to total labor costs, or if labor is 32%, materials 48% and overhead and profit 20% of total cost, carry 32/80 x 13.7% = 5.5% of cost (before overhead and profit) into overhead. Rates vary not only from state to state but also with the experience rating of the contractor.

Rates are the most current available at the time of publication.

GENERAL REQUIREMENTS C10.2-200 | Workers' Compensation

Table 10.2-203 Workers' Compensation by Trade and State

STATE	CARPENTRY — 3 stories or less	CARPENTRY — interior cab. work	CARPENTRY — general	CONCRETE WORK — NOC	CONCRETE WORK — flat (flr, sdwk.)	ELECTRICAL WIRING — inside	EXCAVATION — earth NOC	EXCAVATION — rock	GLAZIERS	INSULATION WORK	LATHING	MASONRY	PAINTING & DECORATING	PILE DRIVING	PLASTERING	PLUMBING	ROOFING	SHEET METAL WORK (HVAC)	STEEL ERECTION — door & sash	STEEL ERECTION — inter. ornam.	STEEL ERECTION — structure	STEEL ERECTION — NOC	TILE WORK — (interior ceramic)	WATERPROOFING	WRECKING
	5651	5437	5403	5213	5221	5190	6217	6217	5462	5479	5443	5022	5474	6003	5480	5183	5551	5538	5102	5102	5040	5057	5348	9014	5701
AL	12.08	6.90	11.44	11.27	5.85	5.16	8.26	8.26	10.22	9.01	7.34	10.05	12.08	25.98	9.49	5.27	20.27	10.95	8.05	8.05	18.72	16.86	7.20	3.74	16.86
AK	17.73	13.92	16.51	22.61	8.87	8.23	11.95	11.95	19.72	21.17	15.09	13.35	10.05	43.86	21.09	11.06	34.15	16.45	27.44	27.44	63.02	48.73	10.07	5.66	63.02
AZ	15.92	9.02	21.28	11.57	10.10	7.88	5.95	5.95	10.08	21.31	8.37	15.61	9.51	24.13	16.24	5.69	22.05	9.38	12.82	12.82	26.59	13.56	6.59	5.53	13.56
AR	12.93	5.26	11.87	9.51	5.41	3.53	6.99	6.99	9.26	8.34	6.10	7.51	9.36	15.67	7.50	4.05	15.49	8.62	5.49	5.49	33.76	12.71	4.74	4.43	33.76
CA	18.94	7.82	18.94	9.02	9.02	6.64	7.55	7.55	15.45	22.32	8.17	14.33	15.20	22.19	14.11	8.92	34.84	10.47	10.42	10.42	26.67	24.84	7.24	15.20	24.84
CO	22.81	13.43	19.38	20.39	14.20	6.56	13.75	13.75	11.58	20.41	10.43	26.22	17.00	36.16	38.54	11.54	48.70	12.88	12.23	12.23	52.23	30.77	10.81	9.24	30.77
CT	18.58	20.34	25.91	26.78	15.09	8.87	12.75	12.75	21.83	25.42	15.47	28.35	17.77	42.59	21.19	10.09	51.57	15.49	16.81	16.81	50.82	26.21	9.81	4.61	50.82
DE	11.44	13.73	11.44	9.20	6.25	5.71	8.49	8.49	11.11	11.44	10.45	9.77	13.30	11.50	10.45	5.32	22.88	10.11	10.09	10.09	26.31	10.09	7.46	9.77	25.47
DC	9.56	9.67	13.72	25.53	11.93	10.89	15.71	15.71	13.07	12.77	9.93	22.79	10.97	34.61	11.41	14.19	30.49	10.42	19.07	19.07	43.86	43.00	23.30	5.35	43.86
FL	17.65	13.65	22.18	32.70	14.79	10.53	16.55	16.55	16.41	17.96	18.84	20.28	21.13	32.88	23.56	11.36	41.30	15.61	15.68	15.68	39.23	40.67	9.96	8.38	39.23
GA	16.35	10.45	18.42	11.02	8.82	5.62	12.30	12.30	9.00	16.39	11.48	11.45	9.02	31.28	14.73	5.65	24.39	9.78	6.64	6.64	19.06	23.00	5.70	7.28	23.00
HI	14.35	8.50	32.61	11.42	12.15	9.98	10.55	10.55	15.27	16.95	8.37	17.18	8.25	24.52	16.13	7.27	38.99	8.30	11.55	11.55	29.18	30.59	6.86	8.96	29.18
ID	13.97	5.85	13.39	9.79	5.11	4.02	8.45	8.45	9.94	10.63	7.06	12.26	12.87	17.11	9.30	3.64	25.78	8.23	6.61	6.61	15.27	13.75	5.78	5.89	15.27
IL	15.80	8.01	13.60	20.08	8.88	7.38	8.09	8.09	13.83	12.40	11.35	17.27	14.02	32.69	9.60	8.91	27.22	12.22	13.06	13.06	59.49	70.93	11.92	4.52	70.93
IN	6.17	3.53	5.56	5.49	3.28	2.27	3.49	3.49	4.96	4.14	3.09	3.86	4.32	8.98	5.19	2.50	8.81	3.62	2.71	2.71	5.98	9.98	2.61	2.77	9.98
IA	6.61	5.61	11.50	13.82	4.98	4.02	7.05	7.05	6.80	10.86	5.86	10.19	8.96	15.80	6.39	6.77	19.85	6.73	7.17	7.17	27.31	40.65	4.95	4.24	27.31
KS	9.06	5.97	8.60	7.56	5.72	3.47	5.02	5.02	6.41	14.67	7.59	7.50	6.11	16.47	6.55	4.01	16.08	6.27	4.50	4.50	10.88	20.45	4.16	4.75	20.45
KY	14.27	6.19	14.56	11.42	7.61	4.67	7.40	7.40	8.65	10.16	10.07	13.10	12.37	28.02	9.53	5.21	23.87	9.76	9.85	9.85	30.22	23.44	7.65	4.39	30.22
LA	16.33	10.25	16.12	8.59	7.84	5.59	9.61	9.61	12.34	8.20	7.25	7.74	13.24	37.62	8.86	6.29	20.21	7.76	7.91	7.91	24.13	13.43	6.64	6.06	24.13
ME	9.22	9.22	27.88	20.42	9.29	6.90	13.98	13.98	15.52	14.51	10.56	14.07	14.00	36.58	14.43	8.92	37.32	11.36	12.69	12.69	44.04	41.81	10.13	5.88	44.04
MD	12.59	12.33	10.70	17.28	9.77	7.64	12.85	12.85	18.78	12.60	8.29	12.40	9.07	19.45	10.26	9.40	32.69	13.58	11.27	11.27	26.18	32.54	9.59	4.30	37.63
MA	12.60	9.42	26.89	25.38	11.56	4.99	9.76	9.76	17.27	12.69	11.51	21.62	14.97	19.73	14.61	7.41	86.25	10.81	16.38	17.38	62.84	50.08	9.94	7.16	49.11
MI	11.40	7.35	12.74	12.71	9.27	5.75	12.42	12.42	14.56	15.48	9.32	16.14	13.24	26.48	14.23	7.23	26.63	8.70	11.42	11.42	29.17	20.06	8.13	NA	29.17
MN	20.86	20.86	36.23	21.03	14.74	6.95	21.20	21.20	17.38	22.76	22.29	17.84	17.92	35.90	22.29	11.77	45.20	14.86	16.41	16.41	51.17	54.54	12.08	9.34	51.17
MS	10.19	6.87	12.79	8.41	4.70	4.93	8.18	8.18	8.45	6.92	7.85	6.29	6.64	22.56	9.94	3.36	15.30	7.80	6.98	6.98	22.27	13.33	6.72	3.86	22.27
MO	7.25	4.96	6.94	7.22	4.52	3.44	5.53	5.53	5.65	8.52	5.61	7.13	5.32	20.51	5.71	3.21	14.46	5.11	5.83	5.83	13.42	10.04	3.50	3.76	10.04
MT	22.82	12.41	40.15	31.40	20.18	9.53	26.82	26.82	22.53	18.61	17.04	36.26	32.24	46.83	25.12	12.45	71.78	15.57	15.45	15.45	118.44	40.61	13.49	12.82	118.44
NE	5.66	4.36	8.40	9.99	5.22	3.17	5.75	5.75	7.75	5.62	5.68	7.63	6.30	10.93	5.96	3.24	13.55	5.82	3.70	3.70	9.92	26.40	3.55	5.92	26.40
NV	13.65	13.65	12.16	10.39	10.39	5.83	12.16	12.16	10.35	12.91	12.54	10.79	11.45	10.51	12.54	8.99	19.46	20.38	12.16	12.16	30.59	30.59	9.97	10.51	30.59
NH	15.33	9.51	18.26	25.79	13.04	5.10	12.72	12.72	10.14	14.36	11.47	14.29	13.08	51.99	18.07	8.94	59.75	11.04	11.78	11.78	31.10	16.32	8.84	6.18	31.10
NJ	6.47	4.92	6.47	5.71	5.00	2.41	6.10	6.10	4.21	6.72	6.47	7.34	7.94	9.23	6.47	3.21	15.08	4.25	6.39	6.39	22.51	9.91	3.13	3.19	25.90
NM	14.96	11.73	19.31	24.57	9.63	5.95	10.09	10.09	16.15	14.70	11.32	16.70	11.44	49.12	16.45	10.09	37.80	12.36	18.46	18.46	21.61	25.84	10.07	7.75	21.61
NY	8.34	4.78	8.34	11.27	9.57	4.39	8.35	8.35	8.27	6.74	7.87	10.79	8.57	13.14	9.78	6.31	NA	7.30	6.52	6.52	18.70	18.64	7.03	4.55	16.93
NC	6.34	5.99	8.28	6.46	3.47	3.22	4.48	4.48	4.26	6.28	3.86	4.23	4.25	12.33	6.21	3.28	9.32	5.04	3.47	3.47	21.60	6.26	3.64	2.87	21.60
ND	7.46	7.46	7.46	5.92	5.92	2.60	6.09	6.09	9.15	4.46	3.35	3.63	5.45	15.78	3.35	7.56	9.55	7.56	7.46	7.46	15.78	15.78	3.25	9.55	NA
OH	7.64	7.64	7.64	8.33	8.33	2.98	8.33	8.33	8.74	6.79	6.79	8.06	8.74	8.33	6.79	4.38	16.28	9.78	NA	NA	8.33	8.33	3.87	16.28	NA
OK	13.33	8.25	11.24	10.59	7.22	4.41	10.61	10.61	9.62	10.28	7.69	7.75	8.16	24.75	10.26	5.35	24.61	8.14	7.36	7.36	30.49	23.00	4.97	5.89	30.49
OR	34.23	14.01	33.37	26.01	19.95	8.49	20.99	20.99	15.10	28.80	13.90	24.25	24.82	53.64	26.62	11.10	60.89	14.90	16.80	16.80	48.90	36.45	23.07	17.85	48.90
PA	12.37	11.26	12.37	18.19	7.71	5.46	9.56	9.56	9.99	12.37	12.65	12.69	14.59	14.75	12.65	6.66	27.07	10.31	15.41	15.41	39.44	15.41	7.85	12.69	60.05
RI	13.05	8.78	15.18	16.40	13.86	6.94	10.84	10.84	15.17	12.80	9.77	13.70	15.02	32.93	13.58	5.78	32.54	8.38	11.83	11.83	65.56	48.77	7.80	6.72	65.56
SC	14.28	7.39	15.32	7.64	6.55	6.30	7.43	7.43	11.77	11.46	6.85	10.01	9.36	14.13	9.58	3.44	17.21	8.84	4.23	4.23	11.28	24.72	8.80	4.44	11.28
SD	7.41	5.12	12.00	10.46	4.87	3.67	6.81	6.81	7.12	10.23	5.43	6.33	6.97	14.86	7.35	6.12	27.69	5.36	6.02	6.02	15.63	12.14	4.37	3.40	15.63
TN	7.71	5.62	8.49	6.38	5.15	3.31	6.18	6.18	6.27	8.69	5.21	8.03	8.26	14.85	5.15	3.89	12.53	6.50	5.19	5.19	13.53	10.11	3.71	3.35	13.53
TX	22.09	15.58	22.09	18.49	14.60	9.81	14.91	14.91	13.54	20.74	9.35	16.27	14.06	30.47	14.57	12.00	38.41	16.85	11.50	11.50	39.93	21.52	8.82	7.96	38.04
UT	NA	NA	8.00	8.76	4.49	4.49	5.56	5.56	6.09	6.00	7.18	11.66	8.20	14.04	7.46	5.05	18.12	5.10	5.26	5.26	NA	22.11	4.24	2.73	22.11
VT	7.51	4.70	9.70	10.10	4.96	2.91	6.99	6.99	7.16	7.32	6.28	9.70	6.93	15.84	7.74	4.04	15.45	5.88	5.33	5.33	16.43	23.55	4.72	4.02	16.43
VA	7.28	5.90	9.08	9.23	6.29	3.45	5.52	5.52	8.03	8.84	6.87	7.69	8.54	9.24	5.64	4.72	25.24	7.11	5.10	5.10	21.59	15.51	3.78	3.34	21.59
WA	9.33	9.33	9.33	8.53	7.21	2.94	6.44	6.44	9.81	7.53	9.33	11.43	7.52	18.40	9.73	4.14	8.94	4.99	7.95	7.95	15.67	15.67	7.33	8.28	10.88
WV	8.34	8.34	8.34	11.46	11.46	3.08	6.52	6.52	3.18	3.18	12.16	5.41	12.16	7.62	12.16	2.71	9.93	3.18	7.64	7.64	6.12	7.64	5.41	2.10	6.12
WI	9.52	7.70	12.85	10.02	5.11	5.21	7.34	7.34	11.14	13.29	7.54	11.74	10.03	25.49	11.62	6.50	21.13	6.64	9.76	9.76	29.41	26.79	8.53	4.82	46.42
WY	5.00	5.00	5.00	5.00	5.00	5.00	5.00	5.00	5.00	5.00	5.00	5.00	5.00	5.00	5.00	5.00	5.00	5.00	5.00	5.00	5.00	5.00	5.00	5.00	5.00
AVG.	12.69	8.97	15.09	13.86	8.72	5.53	9.71	9.71	11.06	12.38	9.19	12.65	11.28	23.67	12.18	6.74	27.64	9.44	9.97	9.97	30.18	24.37	7.62	6.54	31.44

GENERAL REQUIREMENTS C10.2-200 | Workers' Compensation

Table 10.2-204 Workers' Compensation (cont.) (Canadian dollars)

PROVINCE		Alberta	British Columbia	Manitoba	Ontario	New Brunswick	Newfndld & Labrador	Northwest Territories	Nova Scotia	Prince Edward Island	Quebec	Saskatchewan	Yukon
CARPENTRY—3 stories or less	Rate Code	4.78 8-04	2.65 060412	4.62 401	4.20 062-08	3.60 403	5.00 403	4.25 4-41	2.42 4013	5.10 401	17.84 42272	5.25 B12-02	2.00 4-052
CARPENTRY—interior cab. work	Rate Code	4.78 8-04	2.65 060412	4.62 401	4.20 062-08	3.60 403	5.00 403	4.25 4-41	2.42 4013	5.10 401	17.84 42272	4.50 B11-25	2.00 4-042
CARPENTRY—general	Rate Code	4.78 8-04	2.65 060412	4.62 401	4.20 062-08	3.60 403	5.00 403	4.25 4-41	2.42 4013	5.10 401	17.84 42272	5.25 B12-02	2.00 4-052
CONCRETE WORK—NOC	Rate Code	4.72 6-01	5.46 070604	4.62 401	9.09 744-09	3.60 403	5.00 403	4.25 4-41	2.42 4222	5.10 401	13.22 42225	8.65 B14-04	2.50 2-032
CONCRETE WORK—flat (flr., sidewalk)	Rate Code	4.72 6-01	5.46 070604	4.62 401	9.09 744-09	3.60 403	5.00 403	4.25 4-41	2.42 4222	5.10 401	13.22 42225	8.65 B14-04	2.50 2-032
ELECTRICAL Wiring—inside	Rate Code	2.26 6-06	2.05 071100	2.50 402	5.17 864-07	3.60 403	2.40 400	3.00 4-46	1.21 4261	2.65 402	6.63 42612	4.50 B11-05	2.00 4-041
EXCAVATION—earth NOC	Rate Code	4.60 6-07	3.94 072607	6.56 407	13.18 753-13	3.60 403	5.00 403	4.75 4-43	2.48 4214	5.10 401	9.99 42141	5.65 R11-06	2.50 2-016
EXCAVATION—rock	Rate Code	4.60 6-07	3.94 072607	6.56 407	13.18 753-13	3.60 403	5.00 403	4.75 4-43	2.48 4214	5.10 401	9.99 42141	5.65 R11-06	2.50 2-016
GLAZIERS	Rate Code	3.83 6-03	1.59 060236	4.62 401	9.41 873-11	3.60 403	2.50 402	4.25 4-41	2.42 4233	2.65 402	15.42 42355	7.35 B13-04	2.00 4-042
INSULATION WORK	Rate Code	4.98 6-03	7.23 070504	4.62 401	9.41 873-11	3.60 403	2.50 402	4.25 4-41	2.42 4234	5.10 401	8.43 42561	5.25 B12-07	2.50 2-035
LATHING	Rate Code	4.13 6-03	7.23 070500	4.62 401	9.81 854-12	3.60 403	2.50 402	4.25 4-41	2.42 4271	2.65 402	9.51 42755	7.35 B13-02	2.50 2-036
MASONRY	Rate Code	5.09 6-04	5.46 070602	4.62 401	9.81 854-12	3.60 403	5.00 403	4.25 4-41	2.42 4231	5.10 401	15.42 42355	11.50 B15-01	2.50 2-032
PAINTING & DECORATING	Rate Code	4.35 6-03	7.23 070501	4.62 401	9.41 873-11	3.60 403	2.50 402	3.00 4-49	2.42 4275	2.65 402	9.51 42755	5.25 B12-01	2.50 2-036
PILE DRIVING	Rate Code	4.72 6-01	12.85 072502	6.56 407	10.96 836-13	3.60 403	5.50 404	4.75 4-43	2.75 4221	5.10 401	13.22 42225	5.25 B12-10	2.50 2-030
PLASTERING	Rate Code	4.13 6-03	7.23 070502	4.62 401	9.81 854-12	3.60 403	2.50 402	4.25 4-41	2.42 4271	2.65 402	9.51 42711	7.35 B13-02	2.50 2-036
PLUMBING	Rate Code	2.41 6-02	2.60 070712	2.50 402	5.17 864-07	3.60 403	2.50 401	3.00 4-46	1.79 4241	2.65 402	7.98 42555	4.50 B11-01	2.00 4-039
ROOFING	Rate Code	9.45 6-05	5.46 070600	7.40 404	9.81 854-12	3.60 403	5.00 403	4.25 4-41	2.42 4235	5.10 401	15.46 42356	11.50 B15-02	2.50 2-031
SHEET METAL WORK (HVAC)	Rate Code	2.25 6-02	2.60 070714	7.40 404	5.17 864-07	3.60 403	2.50 401	4.25 4-41	2.42 4236	2.65 402	7.98 42555	4.50 B11-07	2.00 4-040
STEEL ERECTION—door & sash	Rate Code	4.13 8-03	12.85 072509	11.00 405	11.22 827-09	3.60 403	5.50 404	4.25 4-41	2.42 4223	5.10 401	13.26 42229	11.50 B15-03	2.50 2-012
STEEL ERECTION—inter., ornam.	Rate Code	4.72 6-01	12.85 072509	11.00 405	11.22 827-09	3.60 403	5.00 403	4.25 4-41	2.42 4223	5.10 401	13.26 42229	11.50 B15-03	2.50 2-012
STEEL ERECTION—structure	Rate Code	10.86 6-08	12.85 072509	11.00 405	23.11 809-14	3.60 403	5.50 404	4.25 4-44	4.57 4227	5.10 401	13.26 42229	11.50 B15-04	2.50 2-012
STEEL ERECTION—NOC	Rate Code	10.86 6-08	12.85 072509	11.00 405	11.22 827-09	3.60 403	5.50 404	4.25 4-41	4.57 4227	5.10 401	13.26 42229	11.50 B15-03	2.50 2-012
TILE WORK—inter. (ceramic)	Rate Code	3.92 6-03	7.23 070506	4.62 401	5.17 864-07	3.60 403	2.50 402	3.00 4-49	2.42 4276	2.65 402	9.51 42755	7.35 B13-01	2.50 2-034
WATERPROOFING	Rate Code	3.41 6-02	1.59 060237	6.56 407	9.41 873-11	3.60 403	5.00 403	4.25 4-41	2.42 4239	2.65 402	15.42 42355	4.50 B11-17	2.50 2-030
WRECKING	Rate Code	10.86 6-08	5.46 070600	4.62 401	29.01 859-15	3.60 403	5.00 403	4.75 4-43	2.42 4211	5.10 401	13.22 42225	8.65 B14-07	2.50 2-030

GENERAL REQUIREMENTS C10.2-300 Unemployment & Social Security

Table 10.2-301 Unemployment Taxes and Social Security Taxes

Mass. State Unemployment tax ranges from 1.4% to 5.6% plus an experience rating assessment the following year, on the first $7,000 of wages. Federal Unemployment tax is 5.4% of the first $7,000 of wages. This is reduced by a credit for payment to the state. The minimum Federal Unemployment tax is .8% after all credits.

Combined rates in Mass. thus vary from 2.2% to 6.4% of the first $7,000 of wages. Combined average U.S. rate is about 6.2% of the first $7,000. Contractors with permanent workers will pay less since the average annual wages for skilled workers is $22.10 x 2,000 hours or about $44,200 per year. The average combined rate for U.S. would thus be 6.2% x $7,000 ÷ $44,200 = .98% of total wages for permanent employees.

Rates not only vary from state to state but also with the experience rating of the contractor.

Social Security (FICA) for 1990 is estimated at time of publication to be 7.56% of wages up to $48,000.

GENERAL REQUIREMENTS C10.2-400 Overtime

Table 10.2-401 Overtime: Production Efficiency

One way to improve the completion date of a project or eliminate negative float from a schedule, is to compress activity duration times. This can be achieved by increasing the crew size or working overtime with the proposed crew.

To determine the costs of working overtime to compress activity duration times, consider the following examples. Below is an overtime efficiency and cost chart based on a five, six, or seven day week with an eight through twelve hour day. Payroll percentage increases for time and one half and double time are shown for the various working days.

Days per Week	Hours per Day	Production Efficiency					Payroll Cost Factors	
		1 Week	2 Weeks	3 Weeks	4 Weeks	Average 4 Weeks	@ 1-1/2 Times	@ 2 Times
5	8	100%	100%	100%	100%	100%	100%	100%
	9	100	100	95	90	96.25	105.6	111.1
	10	100	95	90	85	91.25	110.0	120.0
	11	95	90	75	65	81.25	113.6	127.3
	12	90	85	70	60	76.25	116.7	133.3
6	8	100	100	95	90	96.25	108.3	116.7
	9	100	95	90	85	92.50	113.0	125.9
	10	95	90	85	80	87.50	116.7	133.3
	11	95	85	70	65	78.75	119.7	139.4
	12	90	80	65	60	73.75	122.2	144.4
7	8	100	95	85	75	88.75	114.3	128.6
	9	95	90	80	70	83.75	118.3	136.5
	10	90	85	75	65	78.75	121.4	142.9
	11	85	80	65	60	72.50	124.0	148.1
	12	85	75	60	55	68.75	126.2	152.4

GENERAL REQUIREMENTS C10.3-100 Sales Tax

Table 10.3-101 Sales Tax by State

State sales tax on materials is tabulated below (5 states have no sales tax). Many states allow local jurisdictions, such as a county or city, to levy additional sales tax.

Some projects may be sales tax exempt, particularly those constructed with public funds.

State	Tax	State	Tax	State	Tax	State	Tax
Alabama	4%	Illinois	5%	Montana	0%	Rhode Island	6%
Alaska	0	Indiana	5	Nebraska	4	South Carolina	5
Arizona	5	Iowa	4	Nevada	5.50	South Dakota	4
Arkansas	4	Kansas	4	New Hampshire	0	Tennessee	5.5
California	6	Kentucky	5	New Jersey	6	Texas	6
Colorado	3	Louisiana	4	New Mexico	4.75	Utah	6
Connecticut	7.5	Maine	5	New York	4	Vermont	4
Delaware	0	Maryland	5	North Carolina	3	Virginia	4.5
District of Columbia	6	Massachusetts	5	North Dakota	5.5	Washington	6.5
Florida	6	Michigan	4	Ohio	5	West Virginia	5
Georgia	3	Minnesota	6	Oklahoma	4	Wisconsin	6
Hawaii	4	Mississippi	6	Oregon	0	Wyoming	3
Idaho	5	Missouri	4.225	Pennsylvania	6	Average	4.41%

GENERAL REQUIREMENTS C10.3-200 | Overhead & Profit

Table 10.3-201 Installing Contractor's Overhead and Profit

Listed below in the last two columns are **average** billing rates for the installing contractor's labor.

The Base Rates are averages for the building construction industry and include the usual negotiated fringe benefits. Workers' Compensation is a national average of state rates established for each trade. Average Fixed Overhead is a total of average rates for U.S. and State Unemployment, 6.2%; Social Security (FICA), 7.56%; Builders' Risk, 0.34%; and Public Liability, 1.55%. These are analyzed in ② and ⑤. All the rates except Social Security vary from state to state as well as from company to company. The installing contractor's overhead presumes annual billing of $500,000 and up. Overhead percentages may increase with smaller annual billing.

Overhead varies greatly within each trade. Some controlling factors are annual volume, job type, job size, location, local economic conditions, engineering and logistical support staff and equipment requirements. All factors should be examined carefully for each job.

Abbr.	Trade	Base Rate Incl. Fringes		Workers' Comp. Ins.	Average Fixed Overhead	Overhead	Profit	Total Overhead & Profit		Rate with O & P	
		Hourly	Daily					%	Amount	Hourly	Daily
Skwk	Skilled Workers Average (35 trades)	$22.10	$176.80	13.7%	15.7%	12.8%	10%	52.2%	$11.55	$33.65	$269.20
	Helpers Average (5 trades)	16.75	134.00	15.0		13.0		53.7	9.00	25.75	206.00
	Foremen Average, Inside (50¢ over trade)	22.60	180.80	13.7		12.8		52.2	11.80	34.40	275.20
	Foremen Average, Outside ($2.00 over trade)	24.10	192.80	13.7		12.8		52.2	12.60	36.70	293.60
Clab	Common Building Laborers	17.15	137.20	15.1		11.0		51.8	8.90	26.05	208.40
Asbe	Asbestos Workers	23.95	191.60	12.4		16.0		54.1	12.95	36.90	295.20
Boil	Boilermakers	24.35	194.80	8.7		16.0		50.4	12.25	36.60	292.80
Bric	Bricklayers	22.15	177.20	12.6		11.0		49.3	10.90	33.05	264.40
Brhe	Bricklayer Helpers	17.25	138.00	12.6		11.0		49.3	8.50	25.75	206.00
Carp	Carpenters	21.60	172.80	15.1		11.0		51.8	11.20	32.80	262.40
Cefi	Cement Finishers	21.05	168.40	8.7		11.0		45.4	9.55	30.60	244.80
Elec	Electricians	24.35	194.80	5.5		16.0		47.2	11.50	35.85	286.80
Elev	Elevator Constructors	24.55	196.40	7.2		16.0		48.9	12.00	36.55	292.40
Eqhv	Equipment Operators, Crane or Shovel	22.90	183.20	9.7		14.0		49.4	11.30	34.20	273.60
Eqmd	Equipment Operators, Medium Equipment	22.10	176.80	9.7		14.0		49.4	10.90	33.00	264.00
Eqlt	Equipment Operators, Light Equipment	21.10	168.80	9.7		14.0		49.4	10.40	31.50	252.00
Eqol	Equipment Operators, Oilers	18.80	150.40	9.7		14.0		49.4	9.30	28.10	224.80
Eqmm	Equipment Operators, Master Mechanics	23.60	188.80	9.7		14.0		49.4	11.65	35.25	282.00
Glaz	Glaziers	22.10	176.80	11.1		11.0		47.8	10.55	32.65	261.20
Lath	Lathers	21.65	173.20	9.2		11.0		45.9	9.95	31.60	252.80
Marb	Marble Setters	22.00	176.00	12.6		11.0		49.3	10.85	32.85	262.80
Mill	Millwrights	22.40	179.20	9.2		11.0		45.9	10.30	32.70	261.60
Mstz	Mosaic and Terrazzo Workers	21.50	172.00	7.6		11.0		44.3	9.50	31.00	248.00
Pord	Painters, Ordinary	20.30	162.40	11.3		11.0		48.0	9.75	30.05	240.40
Psst	Painters, Structural Steel	21.00	168.00	38.1		11.0		74.8	15.70	36.70	293.60
Pape	Paper Hangers	20.35	162.80	11.3		11.0		48.0	9.75	30.10	240.80
Pile	Pile Drivers	21.80	174.40	23.7		16.0		65.4	14.25	36.05	288.40
Plas	Plasterers	21.35	170.80	12.2		11.0		48.9	10.45	31.80	254.40
Plah	Plasterer Helpers	17.55	140.40	12.2		11.0		48.9	8.60	26.15	209.20
Plum	Plumbers	24.70	197.60	6.7		16.0		48.4	11.95	36.65	293.20
Rodm	Rodmen (Reinforcing)	23.30	186.40	24.4		14.0		64.1	14.95	38.25	306.00
Rofc	Roofers, Composition	19.85	158.80	27.6		11.0		64.3	12.75	32.60	260.80
Rots	Roofers, Tile & Slate	19.90	159.20	27.6		11.0		64.3	12.80	32.70	261.60
Rohe	Roofer Helpers (Composition)	14.75	118.00	27.6		11.0		64.3	9.50	24.25	194.00
Shee	Sheet Metal Workers	24.35	194.80	9.4		16.0		51.1	12.45	36.80	294.40
Spri	Sprinkler Installers	25.65	205.20	7.2		16.0		48.9	12.55	38.20	305.60
Stpi	Steamfitters or Pipefitters	24.75	198.00	6.7		16.0		48.4	12.00	36.75	294.00
Ston	Stone Masons	22.05	176.40	12.6		11.0		49.3	10.85	32.90	263.20
Sswk	Structural Steel Workers	23.45	187.60	30.2		14.0		69.9	16.40	39.85	318.80
Tilf	Tile Layers (Floor)	21.55	172.40	7.6		11.0		44.3	9.55	31.10	248.80
Tilh	Tile Layer Helpers	17.15	137.20	7.6		11.0		44.3	7.60	24.75	198.00
Trlt	Truck Drivers, Light	17.80	142.40	12.7		11.0		49.4	8.80	26.60	212.80
Trhv	Truck Drivers, Heavy	18.10	144.80	12.7		11.0		49.4	8.95	27.05	216.40
Sswl	Welders, Structural Steel	23.45	187.60	30.2		14.0		69.9	16.40	39.85	318.80
Wrck	*Wrecking	17.15	137.20	31.4	↓	11.0	↓	68.1	11.70	28.85	230.80

*Not included in Averages.

GENERAL REQUIREMENTS C10.3-300 | Rental Rates

Table 10.3-301 Contractor Equipment

Rental Rates shown in the front of the book pertain to late model high quality machines in excellent working condition, rented from equipment dealers. Rental rates from contractors may be substantially lower than the rental rates from equipment dealers depending upon economic conditions. For older, less productive machines, reduce rates by a maximum of 15%. Any overtime must be added to the base rates. For shift work, rates are lower. Usual rule of thumb is 150% of one shift rate for two shifts; 200% for three shifts.

For periods of less than one week, operated equipment is usually more economical to rent than renting bare equipment and hiring an operator.

Equipment moving and mobilization costs must be added to rental rates where applicable. A large crane, for instance, may take two days to erect and two days to dismantle.

Rental rates vary throughout the country with larger cities generally having lower rates. Lease plans for new equipment are available for periods in excess of six months with a percentage of payments applying toward purchase.

Monthly rental rates vary from 2% to 5% of the cost of the equipment depending on the anticipated life of the equipment and its wearing parts. Weekly rates are about 1/3 the monthly rates and daily rental rates about 1/3 the weekly rate.

The hourly operating costs for each piece of equipment includes costs to the user such as fuel, oil, lubrication, normal expendables for the equipment, and a percentage of mechanic's wages chargeable to maintenance. The hourly operating costs listed do not include the operator's wages.

The daily cost for equipment used in the standard crews (foreword) is figured by dividing the weekly rate by five, then adding eight times the hourly operating cost to give the total daily equipment cost, not including the operator. This figure is in the right hand column of Division 016 under Crew Equip. Cost.

Pile Driving rates shown for pile hammer and extractor do not include leads, crane, boiler or compressor. Vibratory pile driving requires an added field specialist at $310 per day during set-up and pile driving operation for the electric model. The hydraulic model requires a field specialist for set-up only. Up to 125 reuses of sheet piling are possible using vibratory drivers. For normal conditions, crane capacity for hammer type and size are as follows.

Crane Capacity	Hammer Type and Size		
	Air or Steam	Diesel	Vibratory
25 ton	to 8,750 ft.-lb.		70 H.P.
40 ton	15,000 ft.-lb.	to 32,000 ft.-lb.	170 H.P.
60 ton	25,000 ft.-lb.		300 H.P.
100 ton		112,000 ft.-lb.	

Cranes should be specified for the job by size, building and site characteristics, availability, performance characteristics, and duration of time required.

Backhoes & Shovels rent for about the same as equivalent size cranes but maintenance and operating expense is higher. Crane operators rate must be adjusted for high boom heights as follows: for 150' boom add 55¢ per hour; over 185', add $1.05 per hour; over 210', add $1.30 per hour; over 250', add $2.00 per hour and over 295', add $2.80 per hour.

Tower Cranes

Capacity in Kip-Feet	Typical Jib Length in Feet	Speed at Maximum Reach and Load	Purchase Price (New)		Monthly Rental, to 6 mo.	
			Crane & 80' Mast	Mast Sections	Crane & 80' Mast	Mast Sections
725	100	350 FPM	$200,000	$495/L.F.	$ 5,150	$14/L.F.
900	100	500	240,000	575	5,675	15
*1100	130	1000	328,000	655	8,250	19
1450	150	1000	458,000	915	11,850	22
2150	200	1000	577,000	1,125	14,900	26
3000	200	1000	811,000	1,200	19,500	31

*Most widely used.

Tower Cranes of the climbing or static type have jibs from 50' to 200' and capacities at maximum reach range from 4,000 to 14,000 pounds. Lifting capacities increase up to maximum load as the hook radius decreases.

Typical rental rates, based on purchase price are about 2% to 3% per month.

Erection and dismantling run between $11,100 and $70,600. Climbing operation takes three men three hours per 20' climb. Crane dead time is about five hours per 40' climb. If crane is bolted to side of the building add cost of ties and extra mast sections. Mast sections cost $500 to $1,200 per vertical foot or can be rented at 2% to 3% of purchase price per month. Contractors using climbers claim savings of $1.75 per C.Y. of concrete placed, plus 15¢ per S.F. of formwork. Climbing cranes have from 80' to 180' of mast while static cranes have 80' to 800' of mast.

Truck Cranes can be converted to tower cranes by using tower attachments. Mast heights over 400' have been used. See Division 016-460 for rental rates of high boom cranes.

A single 100' high material **Hoist and Tower** can be erected and dismantled for about $13,000; a double 100' high hoist and tower for about $20,000. Erection costs for additional heights are $100 and $120 per vertical foot respectively up to 150' and $100 to $160 per vertical foot over 150' high. A 40' high portable Buck hoist costs about $4,700 to erect and dismantle. Additional heights run $73 per vertical foot to 80' and $100 per vertical foot for the next 100'. Most material hoists do not meet local code requirements for carrying personnel.

A 150' high **Personnel Hoist** requires about 500 to 800 man-hours to erect and dismantle with costs ranging from $11,500 to $25,200. Budget erection cost is $130 per vertical foot for all trades. Local code requirements or labor scarcity requiring overtime can add up to 50% to any of the above erection costs.

Earthmoving Equipment: The selection of earthmoving equipment depends upon the type and quantity of material, moisture content, haul distance, haul road, time available, and equipment available. Short haul cut and fill operations may require dozers only, while another operation may require excavators, a fleet of trucks, and spreading and compaction equipment. Stockpiled material and granular material is easily excavated with front end loaders. Scrapers are most economically used with hauls between 300' and 1-1/2 miles if adequate haul roads can be maintained. Shovels are often used for blasted rock and any material where a vertical face of 8' or more can be excavated. Special conditions may dictate the use of draglines, clamshells, or backhoes. Spreading and compaction equipment must be matched to the soil characteristics, the compaction required and the rate the fill is being supplied.

GENERAL REQUIREMENTS C10.3-300 Rental Rates

Table 10.3-302 Steel Tubular Scaffolding

On new construction, tubular scaffolding is efficient up to 60' high or five stories. Above this it is usually better to use a hung scaffolding if construction permits.

In repairing or cleaning the front of an existing building the cost of tubular scaffolding per S.F. of building front increases as the height increases above the first tier. The first tier cost is relatively high due to leveling and alignment. Swing scaffolding operations may interfere with tenants. In this case the tubular is more practical at all heights.

The minimum efficient crew for erection is three men. For heights over 50', a four-man crew is more efficient. Use two or more on top and two at the bottom for handing up or hoisting. Four men can erect and dismantle about nine frames per hour up to five stories. From five to eight stories they will average six frames per hour. With 7' horizontal spacing this will run about 300 S.F. and 200 S.F. of wall surface, respectively. Time for placing planks must be added to the above. On heights above 50', five planks can be placed per man-hour.

The cost per 1,000 S.F. of building front in the table below was developed by pricing the materials required for a typical tubular scaffolding system eleven frames long and two frames high. Planks were figured five wide for standing plus two wide for materials.

Frames are 2', 4' and 5' wide and usually spaced 7' O.C. horizontally. Sidewalk frames are 6' wide. Rental rates will be lower for jobs over three months duration.

For jobs under twenty-five frames, figure rental at $6.00 per frame. For jobs over one hundred frames, rental can go as low as $2.65 per frame. These figures do not include accessories which are listed separately below. Large quantities for long periods can reduce rental rates by 20%.

Item	Unit	Purchase, Each		Monthly Rent, Each		Per 1,000 S.F. of Building Front	
		Regular	Heavy Duty	Regular	Heavy Duty	No. of Frames	Rental per Mo.
5' Wide Frames, 3' High	Ea.	$55	$ —	$3.65	$ —	—	—
*5'-0" High		70	—	3.65	—	—	—
*6'-6" High		85	—	3.65	—	24	$ 87.60
2' & 4' Wide, 5' High		—	75	—	3.75	—	—
6'-0" High		—	85	—	3.75	—	—
6' Wide Frame, 7'-6" High		130	155	7.95	10	—	—
Sidewalk Bracket, 20"		20	—	1.60	—	12	19.20
Guardrail Post		15	—	1.10	—	12	13.20
Guardrail, 7' section		7	—	.80	—	11	8.80
Cross Braces		15	17	.75	.75	44	33.00
Screw Jacks & Plates		20	30	2.00	2.50	24	48.00
8" Casters		50	—	5.75	—	—	—
16' Plank, 2" x 10"		22	—	5.10	—	35	178.50
8' Plank, 2" x 10"		11	—	3.75	—	7	26.25
1' to 6' Extension Tube		—	70	—	2.50	—	—
Shoring Stringers, steel, 10' to 12' long	L.F.	—	7	—	.40	—	—
Aluminum, 12' to 16' long		—	16	—	.60	—	—
Aluminum joists with nailers, 10' to 22' long		—	12.50	—	.50	—	—
Flying Truss System, Aluminum	S.F.C.A.	—	10	—	.60	—	—
						Total	$414.55
						2 Use/Mo.	$207.28

*Most commonly used

Scaffolding is often used as falsework over 15' high during construction of cast-in-place concrete beams and slabs. Two ft. wide scaffolding is generally used for heavy beam construction. The span between frames depends upon the load to be carried with a maximum span of 5'.

Heavy duty scaffolding with a capacity of 10,000#/leg can be spaced up to 10' O.C. depending upon form support design and loading.

Scaffolding used as horizontal shoring requires less than half the material required with conventional shoring.

On new construction, erection is done by carpenters.

Rolling towers supporting horizontal shores can reduce labor and speed the job. For maintenance work, catwalks with spans up to 70' can be supported by the rolling towers.

SITE WORK — C12.1-100 Site Shoring

Table 12.1-101 Wood Sheet Piling

Wood sheet piling may be used for depths to 20' where there is no ground water. If moderate ground water is encountered Tongue & Groove sheeting will help to keep it out. When considerable ground water is present, steel sheeting must be used.

For estimating purposes on trench excavation, sizes are as follows:

Depth	Sheeting	Wales	Braces	B.F. per S.F.
To 8'	3 x 12's	6 x 8's, 2 line	6 x 8's, @ 10'	4.0 @ 8'
8' x 12'	3 x 12's	10 x 10's, 2 line	10 x 10's, @ 9'	5.0 average
12' to 20'	3 x 12's	12 x 12's, 3 line	12 x 12's, @ 8'	7.0 average

Sheeting to be toed in at least 2' depending upon soil conditions. A five man crew with an air compressor and sheeting driver can drive and brace 440 SF/day at 8' deep, 360 SF/day at 12' deep, and 320 SF/day at 16' deep. For normal soils, piling can be pulled in 1/3 the time to install. Pulling difficulty increases with the time in the ground. Production can be increased by high pressure jetting. Figures below assume 50% of lumber is salvaged and includes pulling costs. Some jurisdictions require an equipment operator in addition to Crew B-31.

Sheeting Pulled

Daily Cost Crew B-31	M.H./Day	Hourly Cost	Daily Cost	8' Depth, 440 S.F./Day		16' Depth, 320 S.F./Day	
				To Drive (1 Day)	To Pull (1/3 Day)	To Drive (1 Day)	To Pull (1/3 Day)
1 Foreman	8	$19.15	$153.20	$ 153.20	$ 51.07	$ 153.20	$ 51.07
3 Laborers	24	17.15	411.60	411.60	137.20	411.60	137.20
1 Carpenter	8	21.60	172.80	172.80	57.60	172.80	57.60
1 Air Compressor			84.00	84.00	28.00	84.00	28.00
1 Sheeting Driver			8.80	8.80	2.93	8.80	2.93
2-50 Ft. Air Hoses, 1-1/2" Diam.			9.60	9.60	3.20	9.60	3.20
Lumber (50% salvage)				1.76 MBF 378.40		2.24 MBF 481.60	
Total			$840.00	$1,218.40	$280.00	$1,321.60	$280.00
Total/S.F.				$ 2.77	$ .64	$ 4.13	$ .88
Total (Drive and Pull)/S.F.				$ 3.41		$ 5.01	

Sheeting Left in Place

Daily Cost	8' Depth 440 S.F./Day	10' Depth 400 S.F./Day	12' Depth 360 S.F./Day	16' Depth 320 S.F./Day	18' Depth 305 S.F./Day	20' Depth 280 S.F./Day
Crew B-31	$ 840.00	$ 840.00	$ 840.00	$ 840.00	$ 840.00	$ 840.00
Lumber	1.76M 756.80	1.8M 774.00	1.8M 774.00	2.24M 963.20	2.1M 903.00	1.9M 817.00
Total in Place	$1,596.80	$1,614.00	$1,614.00	$1,803.20	$1,743.00	$1,657.00
Total/S.F.	$ 3.63	$ 4.04	$ 4.48	$ 5.64	$ 5.71	$ 5.92
Total/M.B.F.	$ 907.27	$ 896.67	$ 896.67	$ 805.00	$ 830.00	$ 872.11

SITE WORK — C12.1-100 — Site Shoring

Table 12.1-102 Steel Sheet Piling

Limiting weights are 22 to 38#/S.F. of wall surface with 27#/S.F. average for usual types and sizes. (Weights of piles themselves are from 30.7#/L.F. to 57#/L.F. but they are 15" to 21" wide.) Lightweight sections 12" to 28" wide from 3 ga. to 12 ga. thick are also available for shallow excavations. Piles may be driven two at a time with an impact or vibratory hammer (use vibratory to pull) hung from a crane without leads. A reasonable estimate of the life of steel sheet piling is 10 uses with up to 125 uses possible if a vibratory hammer is used. Used piling costs from 50% to 80% of new piling depending on location and market conditions. Sheet piling and H piles can be rented for about 30% of the delivered mill price for the first month and 5% per month thereafter. Allow 1 man-hour per pile for cleaning and trimming after driving. These costs increase with depth and hydrostatic head. Vibratory drivers are faster in wet granular soils and are excellent for pile extraction. Pulling difficulty increases with the time in the ground and may cost more than driving. It is often economical to abandon the sheet piling, especially if it can be used as the outer wall form. Allow about 1/3 additional length or more, for toeing into ground. Add bracing, waler and strut costs. Waler costs can equal the cost per ton of sheeting.

	Cost of Sheet Piling & Production Rate by Ton & S.F.					
Depth of Excavation	15' Depth		20' Depth		25' Depth	
Description of Pile	22 psf = 90.9 S.F./Ton		27 psf = 74 S.F./Ton		38 psf = 52.6 S.F./Ton	
Type of operation: Left in Place or Removed	Drive & Left	Drive & Extract*	Drive & Left	Drive & Extract*	Drive & Left	Drive & Extract*
Labor & Equip. to Drive 1 ton	$282.31	$423.47	$235.66	$353.49	$160.62	$239.36
Piling (75% Salvage)	690.00	172.50	690.00	172.50	690.00	172.50
Cost/Ton in Place	$972.31	$595.97	$925.66	$525.99	$850.62	$411.86
Production Rate, Tons/Day	10.81	7.22	12.95	8.65	19.00	12.75
Cost/S.F. in Place (incl. 33% toe in)	$10.70	$6.56	$12.51	$7.11	$16.17	7.83
Production Rate, S.F./Day (incl. 33% toe-in)	983.00	656.00	960.00	640.00	1,000.00	670.00

Crew B-40	Bare Costs		Inc. Subs O & P	
	Hr.	Daily	Hr.	Daily
1 Pile Driver Foreman	$23.80	$190.40	$39.35	$314.80
4 Pile Drivers	21.80	697.60	36.05	1,153.60
2 Equip. Oper. (crane)	22.90	366.40	34.20	547.20
1 Equip. Oper. Oiler	18.80	150.40	28.10	224.80
1 Crane, 40 Ton		630.40		693.45
Vibratory Hammer & Gen.		1,016.60		1,118.25
64 M.H., Daily Totals		$3,051.80		$4,052.10

Installation Cost per ton
for 15' Deep Excavation plus 33% toe-in
$3,051.80 per day ÷ 10.81 tons = $282 per ton

Installation Cost per S.F.

$$\frac{2000\#}{22\#/S.F.} = 90.9 \text{ S.F.} \times 10.81 \text{ tons} = 983 \text{ S.F. per day}$$

$3,051.80 ÷ 983 S.F. per day = $3.10 per S.F.

*For driving & extracting two mobilizations & demobilizations will be necessary.

SITE WORK — C12.1-200 | Site Dewatering

Table 12.1-201 Wellpoints

A single stage wellpoint system is usually limited to dewatering an average 15' depth below normal ground water level. Multi-stage systems are employed for greater depth with the pumping equipment installed only at the lowest header level. Ejectors, with unlimited lift capacity, can be economical when two or more stages of wellpoints can be replaced or when horizontal clearance is restricted, such as in deep trenches or tunneling projects, and where low water flows are expected.

Wellpoints are usually spaced on 2-1/2' to 10' centers along a header pipe. Wellpoint spacing, header size, and pump size are all determined by the expected flow, as dictated by soil conditions.

In almost all soils encountered in wellpoint dewatering, the wellpoints may be jetted into place. Cemented soils and stiff clays may require sand wicks about 12" in diameter around each wellpoint to increase efficiency and eliminate weeping into the excavation. These sand wicks require 1/2 to 3 C.Y. of washed filter sand and are installed by using a 12" diameter steel casing and hole puncher jetted into the ground 2' deeper than the wellpoint. Rock may require predrilled holes.

Labor required for the complete installation and removal of a single stage wellpoint system is in the range of 3/4 to 2 man-hours per linear foot of header, depending upon jetting conditions, wellpoint spacing, etc.

Continuous pumping is necessary except in some free draining soil where temporary flooding is permissible (as in trenches which are backfilled after each day's work). Good practice requires provision of a stand-by pump during the continuous pumping operation.

Systems for continuous trenching below the water table should be installed three to four times the length of expected daily progress to insure uninterrupted digging, and header pipe size should not be changed during the job.

For pervious free draining soils, deep wells in place of wellpoints may be economical because of lower installation and maintenance costs. Daily production ranges between two to three wells per day, for 25' to 40' depths, to one well per day for depths over 50'.

Detailed analysis and estimating for any dewatering problem is available at no cost from wellpoint manufacturers. Major firms will quote "sufficient equipment" quotes or their affiliates offer lump sum proposals to cover complete dewatering responsibility.

	Description for 200' System with 8" Header	Quantities	1st Month Unit	1st Month Total	Thereafter Unit	Thereafter Total
Equipment & Material	Wellpoints 25' long, 2" diameter @ 5' O.C.	40 Each	$ 25.00	$ 1,000	$ 17.75	$ 710
	Header pipe, 8" diameter	200 L.F.	3.68	736	1.80	361
	Discharge pipe, 8" diameter	100 L.F.	2.70	270	1.11	111
	8" valves	3 Each	110.40	331	66.24	199
	Combination Jetting & Wellpoint pump (standby)	1 Each	1,975.00	1,975	1,402.25	1,402
	Wellpoint pump, 8" diameter	1 Each	1,800.00	1,800	1,080.00	1,080
	Transportation to and from site	1 day	491.20	491		
	Fuel 30 days x 60 gal./day	1800 Gallons	1.20	2,160	1.20	2,160
	Lubricants for 30 days x 16 lbs./day	480 Lbs.	.72	346	.72	346
	Sand for points	40 C.Y.	20.25	810		
	Equipment and Materials Sub Total			$ 9,919		$ 6,368
Labor	Technician to supervise installation	1 Week	$1,275.00	$ 1,275		
	Labor for installation and removal of system	300 Man-hours	17.15	5,145		
	4 Operators straight time 40 hrs./wk. for 4.33 wks.	693 Hrs.	21.10	14,622	$ 21.10	$14,622
	4 Operators overtime 2 hrs./wk. for 4.33 wks.	35 Hrs.	42.20	1,477	42.20	1,477
	Labor Sub Total			$22,519		$16,099
	Total Cost			$32,438		$22,467
	Monthly Cost/L.F. Header			$ 162		$ 112

SITE WORK — C12.3-100 | Excavation, Trench

Example 12.3-102

Example: Find the cost per L.F. for excavating, bedding, and backfilling a 36" diameter pipe 10' deep in damp sandy loam.

Method: From trench bottom widths for various size pipe, Table 12.3-101, a 36" diameter pipe uses a 6' wide trench bottom.

					6' Wide Bottom of Trench			
					Slope 1/2 to 1	Slope 1 to 1	Slope 1-1/2 to 1	Slope 2 to 1
Excavation & Backfill	For 1/2 to 1 slope see:	Trench Excavation	System	12.3-110-2880	$28.61			
	1 to 1 slope			-4050		$38.23		
	For 1-1/2 to 1 slope	Trench Excavation		-5700			$43.75	
	2 to 1 slope			-7300				$48.44
Pipe Bedding	For 1/2 to 1 slope see:	Trench Pipe Bedding	System	12.3-310-2400	$ 9.50			
	1 to 1 slope			-2880		$12.79		
	For 1-1/2 to 1 slope	Trench Pipe Bedding		-3260			$16.02	
	2 to 1 slope			-3660				$19.25
	Total Cost per L.F. (not including cost of pipe)*				$38.19	$51.02	$59.77	$67.69

*For Costs of pipe see Systems (12.3-510)

SQUARE FOOT — C14.1-000 — General

Table 14.1-001 Square Foot and Cubic Foot Building Costs

The cost figures in division 171 were derived from more than 11,500 projects contained in the Means Data Bank of Construction Costs and include the contractor's overhead and profit, but do not include architectural fees or land costs. The figures have been adjusted to January 1, 1990. New projects are added to our files each year and projects over ten years old are discarded. For this reason, certain costs may not show a uniform annual progression. In no case are all subdivisions of a project listed.

These projects were located throughout the U.S. and reflect tremendous differences in S.F. and C.F. costs. This is due to both differences in labor and material costs, plus differences in the owner's requirements. For instance, a bank in a large city would have different features than one in a rural area. This is true of all different types of buildings analyzed. As a general rule, the projects on the low side did not include any site work or equipment, but the projects on the high side may include both equipment and site work. The median figures do not generally include site work.

None of the figures "go with" any others. All individual cost items were computed and tabulated separately. Thus the sum of the median figures for Plumbing, HVAC and Electrical will not normally total up to the total Mechanical and Electrical costs arrived at by separate analysis and tabulation of the projects.

Each building was analyzed as to total and component costs and percentages. The figures were arranged in ascending order with the results tabulated as shown. The 1/4 column shows that 25% of the projects had lower costs, 75% higher. The 3/4 column shows that 75% of the projects had lower costs, 25% had higher. The median column shows that 50% of the projects had lower costs, 50% had higher.

There are two times when square foot costs are useful. The first is in the conceptual stage when no details are available. Then square foot costs make a useful starting point. The second is after the bids are in and the costs can be worked back into their appropriate units for information purposes. As soon as details become available in the project design, the square foot approach should be discontinued and the project priced as to its particular components. When more precision is required or for estimating the replacement cost of specific buildings, the "Means Square Foot Costs 1990" should be used.

In using the figures in division 171, it is recommended that the median column be used for preliminary figures if no additional information is available. The median figures, when multiplied by the total city construction cost index figures (see Appendix) and then multiplied by the project size modifier on the preceding page, should present a fairly accurate base figure, which would then have to be adjusted in view of the estimator's experience, local economic conditions, code requirements and the owner's particular requirements. There is no need to factor the percentage figures as these should remain constant from city to city. All tabulations mentioning air conditioning had at least partial air conditioning.

The editors of this book would greatly appreciate receiving cost figures on one or more of your recent projects which would then be included in the averages for next year. All cost figures received will be kept confidential except that they will be averaged with other similar projects to arrive at S.F. and C.F. cost figures for next year's book. See the last two pages of the book for details and the discount available for submitting one or more of your projects.

SQUARE FOOT — C14.1-100 — S.F., C.F., & % of Total Costs

The figures in the table below indicate typical ranges in square feet as a function of the "occupant" unit. This table is best used in the preliminary design stages to help determine the probable size requirement for the total project. See next page for the typical total size ranges for various types of buildings.

Table 14.1-101 Unit Gross Area Requirements

Building Type	Unit	Gross Area in S.F.		
		1/4	Median	3/4
Apartments	Unit	660	860	1100
Auditorium & Play Theaters	Seat	18	25	38
Bowling Alleys	Lane		940	
Churches & Synagogues	Seat	20	28	39
Dormitories	Bed	200	230	275
Fraternity & Sorority Houses	Bed	220	315	370
Garages, Parking	Car	325	355	385
Hospitals	Bed	685	850	1075
Hotels	Rental Unit	475	600	710
Housing for the Elderly	Unit	515	635	755
Housing, Public	Unit	700	875	1030
Ice Skating Rinks	Total	27,000	30,000	36,000
Motels	Rental Unit	360	465	620
Nursing Homes	Bed	290	350	450
Restaurants	Seat	23	29	39
Schools, Elementary	Pupil	65	77	90
Junior High & Middle	↓	85	110	129
Senior High		102	130	145
Vocational		110	135	195
Shooting Ranges	Point		450	
Theaters & Movies	Seat		15	

SQUARE FOOT — C14.1-100 — S.F., C.F., & % of Total Costs

Table 14.1-102 Square Foot Project Size Modifier

One factor that affects the S.F. cost of a particular building is the size. In general, for buildings built to the same specifications in the same locality, the larger building will have the lower S.F. Cost. This is due mainly to the decreasing contribution of the exterior walls plus the economy of scale usually achievable in larger buildings. The Area Conversion Scale shown below will give a factor to convert costs for the typical size building to an adjusted cost for the particular project.

The Square Foot Base Size lists the median costs, most typical project size in our accumulated data and the range in size of the projects.

The Size Factor for your project is determined by dividing your project area in S.F. by the typical project size for the particular Building Type. With this factor, enter the Area Conversion Scale at the appropriate Size Factor and determine the appropriate cost multiplier for your building size.

Example: Determine the cost per S.F. for a 100,000 S.F. Mid-rise apartment building.

$$\frac{\text{Proposed building area} = 100{,}000 \text{ S.F.}}{\text{Typical size from below} = 50{,}000 \text{ S.F.}} = 2.00$$

Enter Area Conversion scale at 2.0, intersect curve, read horizontally the appropriate cost multiplier of 0.94. Size adjusted cost becomes 0.94 x $54.50=$51.23 based on national average costs.

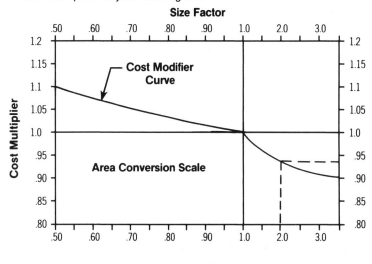

Note: For Size Factors less than .50, the Cost Multiplier is 1.1
For Size Factors greater than 3.5, the Cost Multiplier is .90

Building Type	Median Cost per S.F.	Typical Size Gross S.F.	Typical Range Gross S.F.	Building Type	Median Cost per S.F.	Typical Size Gross S.F.	Typical Range Gross S.F.
Apartments, Low Rise	$ 43.25	21,000	9,700 - 37,200	Jails	$127.00	13,700	7,500 - 28,000
Apartments, Mid Rise	54.50	50,000	32,000 - 100,000	Libraries	77.80	12,000	7,000 - 31,000
Apartments, High Rise	61.20	310,000	100,000 - 650,000	Medical Clinics	74.80	7,200	4,200 - 15,700
Auditoriums	73.40	25,000	7,600 - 39,000	Medical Offices	70.35	6,000	4,000 - 15,000
Auto Sales	45.95	20,000	10,800 - 28,600	Motels	54.90	27,000	15,800 - 51,000
Banks	100.00	4,200	2,500 - 7,500	Nursing Homes	74.10	23,000	15,000 - 37,000
Churches	66.50	9,000	5,300 - 13,200	Offices, Low Rise	59.00	8,600	4,700 - 19,000
Clubs, Country	64.50	6,500	4,500 - 15,000	Offices, Mid Rise	63.50	52,000	31,300 - 83,100
Clubs, Social	63.45	10,000	6,000 - 13,500	Offices, High Rise	78.45	260,000	151,000 - 468,000
Clubs, YMCA	68.15	28,300	12,800 - 39,400	Police Stations	98.25	10,500	4,000 - 19,000
Colleges (Class)	88.05	50,000	23,500 - 98,500	Post Offices	74.40	12,400	6,800 - 30,000
Colleges (Science Lab)	106.00	45,600	16,600 - 80,000	Power Plants	533.00	7,500	1,000 - 20,000
College (Student Union)	94.70	33,400	16,000 - 85,000	Religious Education	55.15	9,000	6,000 - 12,000
Community Center	68.80	9,400	5,300 - 16,700	Research	100.00	19,000	6,300 - 45,000
Court Houses	91.85	32,400	17,800 - 106,000	Restaurants	87.65	4,400	2,800 - 6,000
Dept. Stores	40.55	90,000	44,000 - 122,000	Retail Stores	42.60	7,200	4,000 - 17,600
Dormitories, Low Rise	66.60	24,500	13,400 - 40,000	Schools, Elementary	64.65	41,000	24,500 - 55,000
Dormitories, Mid Rise	85.05	55,600	36,100 - 90,000	Schools, Jr. High	64.50	92,000	52,000 - 119,000
Factories	35.50	26,400	12,900 - 50,000	Schools, Sr. High	64.55	101,000	50,500 - 175,000
Fire Stations	71.25	5,800	4,000 - 8,700	Schools, Vocational	61.35	37,000	20,500 - 82,000
Fraternity Houses	62.60	12,500	8,200 - 14,800	Sports Arenas	50.20	15,000	5,000 - 40,000
Funeral Homes	63.00	7,800	4,500 - 11,000	Supermarkets	42.35	20,000	12,000 - 30,000
Garages, Commercial	47.75	9,300	5,000 - 13,600	Swimming Pools	72.45	13,000	7,800 - 22,000
Garages, Municipal	51.15	8,300	4,500 - 12,600	Telephone Exchange	111.00	4,500	1,200 - 10,600
Garages, Parking	21.75	163,000	76,400 - 225,300	Terminals, Bus	55.90	11,400	6,300 - 16,500
Gymnasiums	61.15	19,200	11,600 - 41,000	Theaters	59.95	10,500	8,800 - 17,500
Hospitals	121.00	55,000	27,200 - 125,000	Town Halls	70.55	10,800	4,800 - 23,400
House (Elderly)	61.20	37,000	21,000 - 66,000	Warehouses	28.25	25,000	8,000 - 72,000
Housing (Public)	51.35	36,000	14,400 - 74,400	Warehouse & Office	32.20	25,000	8,000 - 72,000
Ice Rinks	48.80	29,000	27,200 - 33,600				

REFERENCE AIDS — C15.2-100 — Area Requirements

Table 15.2-101 Floor Area Ratios: commonly used gross to net area and net to gross area ratios expressed in % for various building types.

Building Type	Gross to Net Ratio	Net to Gross Ratio	Building Type	Gross to Net Ratio	Net to Gross Ratio
Apartment	156	64	School Buildings (campus type)		
Bank	140	72	Administrative	150	67
Church	142	70	Auditorium	142	70
Courthouse	162	61	Biology	161	62
Department Store	123	81	Chemistry	170	59
Garage	118	85	Classroom	152	66
Hospital	183	55	Dining Hall	138	72
Hotel	158	63	Dormitory	154	65
Laboratory	171	58	Engineering	164	61
Library	132	76	Fraternity	160	63
Office	135	75	Gymnasium	142	70
Restaurant	141	70	Science	167	60
Warehouse	108	93	Service	120	83
			Student Union	172	59

The gross area of a building is the total floor area based on outside dimensions.
The net area of a building is the usable floor area for the function intended and excludes such items as stairways, corridors and mechanical rooms. In the case of a commercial building, it might be considered as the "leasable area."

REFERENCE AIDS — C15.2-300 — Building Code Requirements

Table 15.2-301 Occupancy Determinations

Description		S.F. Required Per Person*			
		BBC	BOCA	SBC	UBC
Assembly Areas	Fixed Seats	6	**	6	7
	Movable Seats	15		15	15
	Concentrated		7		
	Unconcentrated		15		
	Standing Space		3		
Educational	Unclassified	40			
	Classrooms		20	40	20
	Shop Areas		50	100	50
Institutional	Unclassified	150		125	
	In-Patient Areas		240		
	Sleeping Areas		120		
Mercantile	Basement	30	30	30	20
	Ground Floor	30	30	30	30
	Upper Floors	60	60	60	50
Office		100	100	100	100

* BBC=Basic Building Code
  BOCA=Building Officials & Code Administrators
  SBC=Southern Building Code
  UBC=Uniform Building Code

** The occupancy load for assembly area with fixed seats shall be determined by the number of fixed seats installed.

REFERENCE AIDS C15.2-400 | General

Table 15.2-401 Contractor's Overhead

The table below shows a contractor's overhead as a percentage of direct cost in two ways. The figures on the right are for the overhead, markup based on both material and labor. The figures on the left are based on the entire overhead applied only to the labor. This figure would be used if the owner supplied the materials or if a contract is for labor only.

Items of General Contractor's Indirect Costs	% of Direct Costs	
	As a Markup of Labor Only	As a Markup of Both Material and Labor
Field Supervision	6.0%	2.4%
Main Office Expense (see details below)	9.2	7.7
Tools and Minor Equipment	1.0	0.4
Workers' Compensation & Employers' Liability. See C10.2-200	13.9	5.6
Field Office, Sheds, Photos, Etc.	2.0	0.8
Performance and Payment Bond, 0.5% to 0.9%. See C10.1-302	0.7	0.7
Unemployment Tax See C10.2-301 (Combined Federal and State)	6.2	2.5
Social Security and Medicare (7.56% of first $48,000)	7.6	3.0
Sales Tax — add if applicable 48/80 x % as markup of total direct costs including both material and labor. See C10.3-101		
Sub Total	46.6%	23.1%
*Builder's Risk Insurance ranges from 0.151% to 0.586%. See C10.1-301	0.3	0.3
*Public Liability Insurance	1.5	1.5
Grand Total	48.4%	24.9%

*Paid by Owner or Contractor

Table 15.2-402 Main Office Expense

A General Contractor's main office expense consists of many items not detailed in the front portion of the book. The percentage of main office expense declines with increased annual volume of the contractor. Typical main office expense ranges from 2% to 20% with the median about 7.2% of total volume. This equals about 7.7% of direct costs. The following are approximate percentages of total overhead for different items usually included in a General Contractor's main office overhead. With different accounting procedures, these percentages may vary.

Item	Typical Range	Average
Managers', clerical and estimators' salaries	40% to 55%	48%
Profit sharing, pension and bonus plans	2 to 20	12
Insurance	5 to 8	6
Estimating and project management (not including salaries)	5 to 9	7
Legal, accounting and data processing	0.5 to 5	3
Automobile and light truck expense	2 to 8	5
Depreciation of overhead capital expenditures	2 to 6	4
Maintenance of office equipment	0.1 to 1.5	1
Office rental	3 to 5	4
Utilities including phone and light	1 to 3	2
Miscellaneous	5 to 15	8
Total		100%

REFERENCE AIDS — C15.3-500 — General

Table 15.3-501 Weather Data and Design Conditions

City	Latitude (1) 0	Latitude (1) 1'	Winter Temperatures (1) Med. of Annual Extremes	Winter Temperatures (1) 99%	Winter Temperatures (1) 97½%	Winter Degree Days (2)	Summer (Design Dry Bulb) Temperatures and Relative Humidity 1%	2½%	5%
UNITED STATES									
Albuquerque, NM	35	0	6	12	16	4,400	96/61	94/61	92/61
Atlanta, GA	33	4	14	17	22	3,000	95/74	92/74	90/73
Baltimore, MD	39	2	12	14	17	4,600	94/75	92/75	89/74
Birmingham, AL	33	3	17	17	21	2,600	97/74	94/75	93/74
Bismarck, ND	46	5	-31	-23	-19	8,800	95/68	91/68	88/67
Boise, ID	43	3	0	3	10	5,800	96/65	93/64	91/64
Boston, MA	42	2	-1	6	9	5,600	91/73	88/71	85/70
Burlington, VT	44	3	-18	-12	-7	8,200	88/72	85/70	83/69
Charleston, WV	38	2	1	7	11	4,400	92/74	90/73	88/72
Charlotte, NC	35	1	13	18	22	3,200	96/74	94/74	92/74
Casper, WY	42	5	-20	-11	-5	7,400	92/58	90/57	87/57
Chicago, IL	41	5	-5	-3	2	6,600	94/75	91/74	88/73
Cincinnati, OH	39	1	2	1	6	4,400	94/73	92/72	90/72
Cleveland, OH	41	2	-2	1	5	6,400	91/73	89/72	86/71
Columbia, SC	34	0	16	20	24	2,400	98/76	96/75	94/75
Dallas, TX	32	5	14	18	22	2,400	101/75	99/75	97/75
Denver, CO	39	5	-9	-5	1	6,200	92/59	90/59	89/59
Des Moines, IA	41	3	-13	-10	-5	6,600	95/75	92/74	89/73
Detroit, MI	42	2	0	3	6	6,200	92/73	88/72	85/71
Great Falls, MT	47	3	-29	-21	-15	7,800	91/60	88/60	85/59
Hartford, CT	41	5	-4	3	7	6,200	90/74	88/73	85/72
Houston, TX	29	5	24	28	33	1,400	96/77	94/77	92/77
Indianapolis, IN	39	4	-2	-2	2	5,600	93/74	91/74	88/73
Jackson, MS	32	2	17	21	25	2,200	98/76	96/76	94/76
Kansas City, MO	39	1	-2	2	6	4,800	100/75	97/74	94/74
Las Vegas, NV	36	1	18	25	28	2,800	108/66	106/65	104/65
Lexington, KY	38	0	0	3	8	4,600	94/73	92/72	90/72
Little Rock, AR	34	4	13	15	20	3,200	99/76	96/77	94/77
Los Angeles, CA	34	0	38	41	43	2,000	94/70	90/70	87/69
Memphis, TN	35	0	11	13	18	3,200	98/77	96/76	94/76
Miami, FL	25	5	39	44	47	200	92/77	90/77	89/77
Milwaukee, WI	43	0	-11	-8	-4	7,600	90/74	87/73	84/71
Minneapolis, MN	44	5	-19	-16	-12	8,400	92/75	89/74	86/71
New Orleans, LA	30	0	29	29	33	1,400	93/78	91/78	90/77
New York, NY	40	5	6	11	15	5,000	94/74	91/73	88/72
Norfolk, VA	36	5	18	20	22	3,400	94/77	91/76	89/76
Oklahoma City, OK	35	2	4	9	13	3,200	100/74	97/74	95/73
Omaha, NE	41	2	-12	-8	-3	6,600	97/76	94/75	91/74
Philadelphia, PA	39	5	7	10	14	4,400	93/75	90/74	87/72
Phoenix, AZ	33	3	25	31	34	1,800	108/71	106/71	104/71
Pittsburgh, PA	40	3	1	3	7	6,000	90/72	88/71	85/70
Portland, ME	43	4	-14	-6	-1	7,600	88/72	85/71	81/69
Portland, OR	45	4	17	17	23	4,600	89/68	85/67	81/65
Portsmouth, NH	43	1	-8	-2	2	7,200	88/73	86/71	83/70
Providence, RI	41	4	0	5	9	6,000	89/73	86/72	83/70
Rochester, NY	43	1	-5	1	5	6,800	91/73	88/71	85/70
Salt Lake City, UT	40	5	-2	3	8	6,000	97/62	94/62	92/61
San Francisco, CA	37	5	38	38	40	3,000	80/63	77/62	83/61
Seattle, WA	47	4	22	22	27	5,200	81/68	79/66	76/65
Sioux Falls, SD	43	4	-21	-15	-11	7,800	95/73	92/72	89/71
St. Louis, MO	38	4	1	3	8	5,000	96/75	94/75	92/75
Tampa, FL	28	0	32	36	40	680	92/77	91/77	90/76
Trenton, NJ	40	1	7	11	14	5,000	92/75	90/74	87/73
Washington, DC	38	5	12	14	17	4,200	94/75	92/74	90/74
Wichita, KS	37	4	-1	3	7	4,600	102/72	99/73	96/73
Wilmington, DE	39	4	6	10	14	5,000	93/74	93/74	87/74
ALASKA									
Anchorage	61	1	-29	-23	-18	10,800	73/59	70/58	67/56
Fairbanks	64	5	-59	-51	-47	14,280	82/62	78/60	75/59
CANADA									
Edmonton, Alta.	53	3	-30	-29	-25	11,000	86/66	83/65	80/63
Halifax, N.S.	44	4	-4	1	5	8,000	83/66	80/65	77/64
Montreal, Que.	45	3	-20	-16	-10	9,000	88/73	86/72	84/71
Saskatoon, Sask.	52	1	-35	-35	-31	11,000	90/68	86/66	83/65
St. Johns, Nwf.	47	4	1	3	7	8,600	79/67	77/65	75/64
Saint John, N.B.	45	2	-15	-12	-8	8,200	81/67	79/65	77/64
Toronto, Ont.	43	4	-10	-5	-1	7,000	90/73	87/72	85/71
Vancouver, B.C.	49	1	13	15	19	6,000	80/67	78/66	76/65
Winnipeg, Man.	49	5	-31	-30	-27	10,800	90/73	87/71	84/70

(1) Handbook of Fundamentals, ASHRAE, Inc., NY 1972/1985
(2) Local Climatological Annual Survey, USDC Env. Science Services Administration, Ashville, NC

REFERENCE AIDS | **C15.3-500** | **General**

Table 15.3-502 Maximum Depth of Frost Penetration in Inches

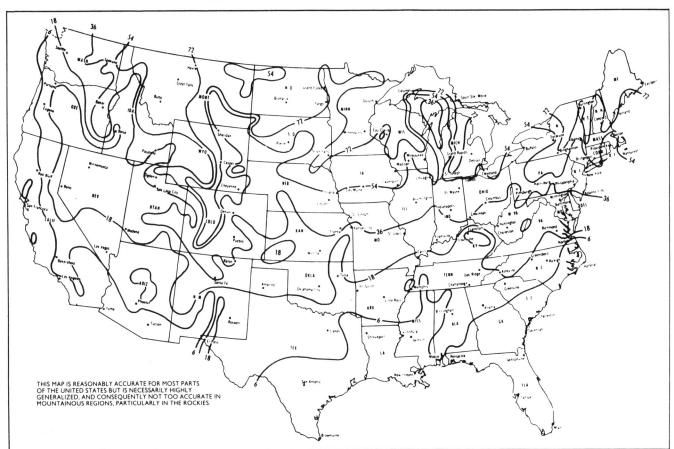

REFERENCE AIDS — C15.9-100 — General

Description: This table is primarily for converting customary U.S. units in the left hand column to SI metric units in the right hand column. In addition, conversion factors for some commonly encountered Canadian and non-SI metric units are included.

Table 15.9-101 Metric Conversion Factors

	If You Know		Multiply By		To Find
Length	Inches	x	25.4[a]	=	Millimeters
	Feet	x	0.3048[a]	=	Meters
	Yards	x	0.9144[a]	=	Meters
	Miles (statute)	x	1.609	=	Kilometers
Area	Square inches	x	645.2	=	Square millimeters
	Square feet	x	0.0929	=	Square meters
	Square yards	x	0.8361	=	Square meters
Volume (Capacity)	Cubic inches	x	16,387	=	Cubic millimeters
	Cubic feet	x	0.02832	=	Cubic meters
	Cubic yards	x	0.7646	=	Cubic meters
	Gallons (U.S. liquids)[b]	x	0.003785	=	Cubic meters[c]
	Gallons (Canadian liquid)[b]	x	0.004546	=	Cubic meters[c]
	Ounces (U.S. liquid)[b]	x	29.57	=	Milliliters[c,d]
	Quarts (U.S. liquid)[b]	x	0.9464	=	Liters[c,d]
	Gallons (U.S. liquid)[b]	x	3.785	=	Liters[c,d]
Force	Kilograms force[d]	x	9.807	=	Newtons
	Pounds force	x	4.448	=	Newtons
	Pounds force	x	0.4536	=	Kilograms force[d]
	Kips	x	4448	=	Newtons
	Kips	x	453.6	=	Kilograms force[d]
Pressure, Stress, Strength (Force per unit area)	Kilograms force per square centimeter[d]	x	0.09807	=	Megapascals
	Pounds force per square inch (psi)	x	0.006895	=	Megapascals
	Kips per square inch	x	6.895	=	Megapascals
	Pounds force per square inch (psi)	x	0.07031	=	Kilograms force per square centimeter[d]
	Pounds force per square foot	x	47.88	=	Pascals
	Pounds force per square foot	x	4.882	=	Kilograms force per square meter[d]
Bending Moment Or Torque	Inch-pounds force	x	0.01152	=	Meter-kilograms force[d]
	Inch-pounds force	x	0.1130	=	Newton-meters
	Foot-pounds force	x	0.1383	=	Meter-kilograms force[d]
	Foot-pounds force	x	1.356	=	Newton-meters
	Meter-kilograms force[d]	x	9.807	=	Newton-meters
Mass	Ounces (avoirdupois)	x	28.35	=	Grams
	Pounds (avoirdupois)	x	0.4536	=	Kilograms
	Tons (metric)	x	1000[a]	=	Kilograms
	Tons, short (2000 pounds)	x	907.2	=	Kiloprams
	Tons, short (2000 pounds)	x	0.9072	=	Megagrams[e]
Mass per Unit Volume	Pounds mass per cubic foot	x	16.02	=	Kilograms
	Pounds mass per cubic yard	x	0.5933	=	Kilograms
	Pounds mass per gallon (U.S. liguid)[b]	x	119.8	=	Kilograms per cubic meter
	Pounds mass per gallon (Canadian liquid)[b]	x	99.78	=	Kilograms per cubic meter
Temperature	Degrees Fahrenheit	(F-32)/1.8		=	Degrees Celsius
	Degrees Fahrenheit	(F+459.67)/1.8		=	Degrees Kelvin
	Degrees Celsius	C+273.15		=	Degrees Kelvin

[a] The factor given is exact
[b] One U.S. gallon = 0.8327 Canadian gallon
[c] 1 liter = 1000 milliliters = 1000 cubic centimeters
  1 cubic decimeter = 0.001 cubic meter
[d] Metric but not SI unit
[e] Called "tonne" in England and "metric ton" in other metric countries

REFERENCE AIDS — C15.9-100 | General

Table 15.9-102 Weights and Measures

Measures of Length
1 Mile = 1760 Yards = 5280 Feet
1 Yard = 3 Feet = 36 inches
1 Foot = 12 Inches
1 Mil = 0.001 Inch
1 Fathom = 2 Yards = 6 Feet
1 Rod = 5.5 Yards = 16.5 Feet
1 Hand = 4 Inches
1 Span = 9 Inches
1 Micro-inch = One Millionth Inch or 0.000001 Inch
1 Micron = One Millionth Meter + 0.00003937 Inch

Surveyor's Measure
1 Mile = 8 Furlongs = 80 Chains
1 Furlong = 10 Chains = 220 Yards
1 Chain = 4 Rods = 22 Yards = 66 Feet = 100 Links
1 Link = 7.92 inches

Square Measure
1 Square Mile = 640 Acres = 6400 Square Chains
1 Acre = 10 Square Chains = 4840 Square Yards = 43,560 Sq. Ft.
1 Square Chain = 16 Square Rods = 484 Square Yards
   = 4356 Sq. Ft.
1 Square Rod = 30.25 Square Yards = 272.25 Square Feet = 625 Square Lines
1 Square Yard = 9 Square Feet
1 Square Foot = 144 Square Inches
An Acre equals a Square 208.7 Feet per Side

Cubic Measure
1 Cubic Yard = 27 Cubic Feet
1 Cubic Foot = 1728 Cubic Inches
1 Cord of Wood = 4 x 4 x 8 Feet = 128 Cubic Feet
1 Perch of Masonry = 16½ x 1½ x 1 Foot = 24.75 Cubic Feet

Avoirdupois or Commercial Weight
1 Gross or Long Ton = 2240 Pounds
1 Net or Short Ton = 2000 Pounds
1 Pound = 16 Ounces = 7000 Grains
1 Ounce = 16 Drachms = 437.5 Grains
1 Stone = 14 Pounds

Shipping Measure
For Measuring Internal Capacity of a Vessel:
   1 Register Ton = 100 Cubic Feet

For Measurement of Cargo:
   Approximately 40 Cubic Feet of Merchandise is considered a Shipping Ton, unless that bulk would weigh more than 2000 Pounds, in which case Freight Charge may be based upon weight.

40 Cubic Feet = 32.143 U.S. Bushels = 31.16 Imp. Bushels

Liquid Measure
1 Imperial Gallon = 1.2009 U.S. Gallon = 277.42 Cu. In.
1 Cubic Foot = 7.48 U.S. Gallons

Table 18.1-101 Repair and Remodeling

Cost figures in MEANS PLUMBING COST DATA are based on new construction utilizing the most cost-effective combination of labor, equipment and material with the work scheduled in proper sequence to allow the various trades to accomplish their work in an efficient manner.

The costs for repair and remodeling work must be modified due to the following factors that may be present in any given repair and remodeling project:

1. Equipment usage curtailment due to the physical limitations of the project, with only hand-operated equipment being used.
2. Increased requirement for shoring and bracing to hold up the building while structural changes are being made and to allow for temporary storage of construction materials on above-grade floors.
3. Material handling becomes more costly due to having to move within the confines of an enclosed building. For multi-story construction, low capacity elevators and stairwells may be the only access to the upper floors.
4. Large amount of cutting and patching and attempting to match the existing construction is required. It is often more economical to remove entire walls rather than create many new door and window openings. This sort of trade-off has to be carefully analyzed.
5. Cost of protection of completed work is increased since the usual sequence of construction usually can not be accomplished.
6. Economies of scale usually associated with new construction may not be present. If small quantities of components must be custom fabricated due to job requirements, unit costs will naturally increase. Also, if only small work areas are available at a given time, job scheduling between trades becomes difficult and subcontractor quotations may reflect the excessive start-up and shut-down phases of the job.
7. Work may have to be done on other than normal shifts and may have to be done around an existing production facility which has to stay in production during the course of the repair and remodeling.
8. Dust and noise protection of adjoining non-construction areas can involve substantial special protection and alter usual construction methods.
9. Job may be delayed due to unexpected conditions discovered during demolition or removal. These delays ultimately increase construction costs.
10. Piping and ductwork runs may not be as simple as for new construction. Wiring may have to be snaked through walls and floors.
11. Matching "existing construction" may be impossible because materials may no longer be manufactured. Substitutions may be expensive.
12. Weather protection of existing structure requires additional temporary structures to protect building at opening.
13. On small projects, because of local conditions, it may be necessary to pay a tradesman for a minimum of four hours for a task that is completed in one hour.

All of the above areas can contribute to increased costs for a repair and remodeling project. Each of the above factors should be considered in the planning, bidding and construction stage in order to minimize the increased costs associated with repair and remodeling jobs.

SECTION D
APPENDIX

TABLE OF CONTENTS

Historical Cost Index	368
City Cost Indexes	369
Abbreviations	378
Index	381

CITY COST INDEXES

Historical Cost Indexes

The table below lists both the Means City Cost Index based on Jan. 1, 1975 = 100 as well as the computed value of an index based on January 1, 1990 costs. Since the Jan. 1, 1990 figure is estimated, space is left to write in the actual index figures as they become available thru either the quarterly "Means Construction Cost Indexes" or as printed in the "Engineering News-Record". To compute the actual index based on Jan. 1, 1990 = 100, divide the Quarterly City Cost Index for a particular year by the actual Jan. 1, 1990 Quarterly City Cost Index. Space has been left to advance the index figures as the year progresses.

Year	"Quarterly City Cost Index" Jan. 1, 1975 = 100		Current Index Based on Jan. 1, 1990 = 100		Year	"Quarterly City Cost Index" Jan. 1, 1975 = 100	Current Index Based on Jan. 1, 1990 = 100		Year	"Quarterly City Cost Index" Jan. 1, 1975 = 100	Current Index Based on Jan. 1, 1990 = 100	
	Est.	Actual	Est.	Actual		Actual	Est.	Actual		Actual	Est.	Actual
Oct. 1990					July 1977	113.3	53.1		July 1961	45.4	21.3	
July 1990					1976	107.3	50.3		1960	45.0	21.1	
April 1990					1975	102.6	48.1		1959	44.2	20.7	
Jan. 1990	213.4		100.0	100.0	1974	94.7	44.4		1958	43.0	20.1	
July 1989		210.9	98.8		1973	86.3	40.4		1957	42.2	19.8	
1988		205.7	96.4		1972	79.7	37.3		1956	40.4	18.9	
1987		200.7	94.0		1971	73.5	34.4		1955	38.1	17.9	
1986		192.8	90.3		1970	65.8	30.8		1954	36.7	17.2	
1985		189.1	88.6		1969	61.6	28.9		1953	36.2	17.0	
1984		187.6	87.9		1968	56.9	26.7		1952	35.3	16.5	
1983		183.5	86.0		1967	53.9	25.3		1951	34.4	16.1	
1982		174.3	81.7		1966	51.9	24.3		1950	31.4	14.7	
1981		160.2	75.1		1965	49.7	23.3		1949	30.4	14.2	
1980		144.0	67.5		1964	48.6	22.8		1948	30.4	14.2	
1979		132.3	62.0		1963	47.3	22.2		1947	27.6	12.9	
1978		122.4	57.4		1962	46.2	21.6		1946	23.2	10.9	

City Cost Indexes

Tabulated on the following pages are average construction cost indexes for 162 major U.S. and Canadian cities. Index figures for both material and installation are based on the 30 major city average of 100 and represent the cost relationship as of July 1, 1989. The index for each division is computed from representative material and labor quantities for that division. The weighted average for each city is a weighted total of the components listed above it, but does not include relative productivity between trades or cities.

The material index for the weighted average includes about 100 basic construction materials with appropriate quantities of each material to represent typical "average" building construction projects.

The installation index for the weighted average includes the contribution of about 30 construction trades with their representative man-days in proportion to the material items installed. Also included in the installation costs are the representative equipment costs for those items requiring equipment.

Since each division of the book contains many different items, any particular item multiplied by the particular city index may give incorrect results. However, when all the book costs for a particular division are summarized and then factored, the result should be very close to the actual costs for that particular division for that city.

If a project has a preponderance of materials from any particular division (say structural steel), then the weighted average index should be adjusted in proportion to the value of the factor for that division.

Adjustments to Costs

Time Adjustment using the Historical Cost Indexes:

$$\frac{\text{Index for Year A}}{\text{Index for Year B}} \times \text{Cost in Year B} = \text{Cost in Year A}$$

Location Adjustment using the City Cost Indexes:

$$\frac{\text{Index for City A}}{\text{Index for City B}} \times \text{Cost in City B} = \text{Cost in City A}$$

Adjustment from the National Average:

$$\text{National Average Cost} \times \frac{\text{Index for City A}}{100} = \text{Cost in City A}$$

Note: The City Cost Indexes for Canada can be used to convert U.S. national averages to local costs in Canadian dollars.

CITY COST INDEXES

	DIVISION	ALABAMA													ALASKA			ARIZONA		
		BIRMINGHAM			HUNTSVILLE			MOBILE			MONTGOMERY			ANCHORAGE			PHOENIX		
		MAT.	INST.	TOTAL	MAT.	INST.	TOTAL	MAT.	INST.	TOTAL	MAT.	INST.	TOTAL	MAT.	INST.	TOTAL	MAT.	INST.	TOTAL
2	SITE WORK	100.0	89.7	95.4	119.6	87.4	105.3	122.6	86.6	106.6	91.9	85.8	89.2	159.1	127.5	145.1	92.5	94.6	93.4
3.1	FORMWORK	97.6	71.5	77.4	103.4	62.2	71.4	106.5	73.4	80.9	112.4	65.4	76.0	124.3	138.8	135.6	108.6	87.0	91.8
3.2	REINFORCING	94.5	71.7	85.2	95.8	64.4	83.1	82.9	71.7	78.4	82.9	71.7	78.3	117.8	130.2	122.8	111.1	92.2	103.4
3.3	CAST IN PLACE CONC.	89.2	91.6	90.6	101.9	89.8	94.6	99.9	92.9	95.7	101.1	89.2	93.9	225.7	111.9	156.8	105.4	92.7	97.7
3	CONCRETE	92.0	81.9	85.6	100.8	76.7	85.5	97.4	83.4	88.5	99.3	78.3	86.0	181.8	124.1	145.3	107.3	90.4	96.6
4	MASONRY	81.7	70.3	73.0	88.4	63.6	69.5	93.9	77.2	81.2	86.6	52.0	60.2	150.2	136.5	139.7	93.3	79.0	82.3
5	METALS	95.5	78.4	89.5	100.0	73.4	90.7	93.4	79.1	88.4	95.7	78.3	89.6	116.3	122.8	118.5	99.1	92.4	96.7
6	WOOD & PLASTICS	92.0	72.8	81.3	107.5	65.2	84.0	92.0	75.6	82.9	101.7	69.3	83.6	117.9	135.1	127.5	99.2	85.4	91.5
7	MOISTURE PROTECTION	84.5	60.6	76.9	92.1	58.7	81.6	87.3	62.1	79.3	88.6	58.9	79.2	102.6	135.6	113.0	92.7	85.0	90.3
8	DOORS, WINDOWS, GLASS	90.7	72.2	81.1	101.0	60.2	80.0	98.4	73.1	85.4	98.1	66.8	81.9	128.5	128.0	128.3	103.1	83.4	92.9
9.2	LATH & PLASTER	95.8	69.3	75.7	91.1	67.6	73.2	91.8	79.3	82.3	108.3	68.0	77.7	120.3	137.7	133.5	93.5	90.9	91.5
9.2	DRYWALL	100.7	71.9	87.3	108.6	64.4	88.0	92.6	75.7	84.8	100.9	69.2	86.1	122.0	136.9	128.9	90.6	85.4	88.2
9.5	ACOUSTICAL WORK	97.7	72.2	83.8	100.1	64.3	80.6	93.1	74.7	83.1	93.1	68.2	79.5	124.0	136.4	130.8	103.7	84.4	93.1
9.6	FLOORING	112.0	73.3	101.6	97.4	63.7	88.4	114.0	78.8	104.6	100.8	46.3	86.2	117.3	137.1	122.6	93.1	88.4	91.9
9.9	PAINTING	104.2	68.1	75.4	110.6	66.8	75.6	121.4	77.3	86.2	119.7	75.9	84.8	123.2	141.3	137.6	96.3	80.7	83.8
9	FINISHES	103.2	70.5	85.8	105.3	65.3	84.0	100.3	76.6	87.7	102.3	69.7	84.9	121.2	138.4	130.4	92.8	84.2	88.2
10-14	TOTAL DIV. 10-14	100.0	75.3	92.7	100.0	74.4	92.5	100.0	78.3	93.6	100.0	73.8	92.3	100.0	127.7	108.1	100.0	89.4	96.9
15	MECHANICAL	96.5	71.2	83.9	99.3	71.6	85.5	97.3	73.9	85.7	99.0	69.0	84.1	107.3	123.9	115.5	98.4	86.6	92.5
16	ELECTRICAL	94.9	72.1	79.2	92.6	71.2	77.8	90.5	75.8	80.4	91.6	61.3	70.7	105.7	137.1	127.9	105.4	79.1	87.3
1-16	WEIGHTED AVERAGE	94.9	74.5	84.0	100.2	70.6	84.4	97.8	77.5	87.0	96.9	68.6	81.8	125.7	129.9	127.9	99.1	85.6	91.9

	DIVISION	ARIZONA			ARKANSAS						CALIFORNIA								
		TUCSON			FORT SMITH			LITTLE ROCK			ANAHEIM			BAKERSFIELD			FRESNO		
		MAT.	INST.	TOTAL	MAT.	INST.	TOTAL	MAT.	INST.	TOTAL	MAT.	INST.	TOTAL	MAT.	INST.	TOTAL	MAT.	INST.	TOTAL
2	SITE WORK	110.3	96.8	104.3	100.0	89.8	95.5	106.9	92.0	100.3	104.7	112.2	108.1	97.2	110.9	103.3	94.7	120.7	106.2
3.1	FORMWORK	109.0	86.8	91.8	111.3	65.0	75.4	103.5	64.9	73.6	104.5	122.7	118.6	124.7	122.8	123.2	110.0	124.5	121.3
3.2	REINFORCING	95.1	92.2	93.9	124.5	65.6	100.6	117.8	60.6	94.6	99.3	129.4	111.5	96.0	129.4	109.6	106.5	129.4	115.8
3.3	CAST IN PLACE CONC.	105.5	97.3	100.5	90.4	90.3	90.3	98.4	90.7	93.7	109.3	109.5	109.4	103.2	109.6	107.1	92.9	108.6	102.4
3	CONCRETE	103.9	92.7	96.8	102.1	78.2	87.0	103.7	77.9	87.4	106.1	116.4	112.7	105.8	116.5	112.6	99.3	116.7	110.3
4	MASONRY	92.2	79.0	82.1	95.4	71.9	77.5	88.8	71.9	75.9	108.6	130.2	125.1	100.8	115.2	111.8	119.8	113.0	114.6
5	METALS	90.9	94.0	92.0	96.5	74.5	88.8	106.2	71.5	94.1	99.3	121.7	107.1	99.3	122.0	107.2	94.9	123.3	104.9
6	WOOD & PLASTICS	106.1	84.9	94.3	107.2	66.2	84.4	94.8	66.2	78.9	96.2	118.1	108.3	95.3	118.1	107.9	96.9	121.7	110.7
7	MOISTURE PROTECTION	105.5	75.4	96.0	84.8	63.4	78.1	84.3	63.4	77.7	107.9	130.0	114.9	84.9	116.5	94.9	107.5	112.6	109.1
8	DOORS, WINDOWS, GLASS	88.2	83.4	85.7	92.7	59.3	75.5	95.1	59.4	76.7	93.3	122.6	108.4	99.9	117.4	108.9	101.1	120.1	110.9
9.2	LATH & PLASTER	109.0	87.7	92.8	93.0	71.8	76.9	98.4	71.8	78.2	97.2	130.8	122.7	92.3	101.4	99.2	102.1	116.3	112.9
9.2	DRYWALL	82.1	85.4	83.6	95.1	64.8	81.0	114.8	64.8	91.5	97.4	123.4	109.5	98.0	112.9	104.9	98.9	120.9	109.1
9.5	ACOUSTICAL WORK	113.6	84.4	97.7	83.7	65.0	73.5	83.7	65.0	73.5	81.3	118.7	101.7	93.2	118.7	107.1	96.6	122.6	110.8
9.6	FLOORING	110.0	84.2	103.1	89.5	72.8	85.0	88.7	72.8	84.4	117.5	118.7	118.0	111.8	102.6	109.3	88.7	101.7	92.2
9.9	PAINTING	98.5	79.7	83.5	111.0	50.1	62.4	104.7	63.3	71.6	108.3	120.3	117.9	120.1	122.1	121.7	107.9	100.0	101.6
9	FINISHES	93.0	83.4	87.9	94.5	60.7	76.5	105.2	65.3	83.9	101.6	122.7	112.9	102.8	115.2	109.3	97.4	112.2	105.3
10-14	TOTAL DIV. 10-14	100.0	88.6	96.6	100.0	71.2	91.5	100.0	71.8	91.7	100.0	126.2	107.7	100.0	123.7	106.9	100.0	144.6	113.1
15	MECHANICAL	98.7	91.5	95.1	97.2	64.4	80.9	96.8	68.3	82.6	96.8	123.0	109.8	94.9	97.2	96.1	92.7	113.9	103.2
16	ELECTRICAL	103.2	83.9	89.9	100.1	70.7	79.8	94.2	74.0	80.3	99.5	120.6	114.1	107.1	103.0	104.3	110.6	97.5	101.6
1-16	WEIGHTED AVERAGE	99.0	87.4	92.8	97.2	70.5	82.9	98.9	72.0	84.5	101.0	122.0	112.3	99.1	111.4	105.7	99.6	114.8	107.7

	DIVISION	CALIFORNIA																	
		LOS ANGELES			OXNARD			RIVERSIDE			SACRAMENTO			SAN DIEGO			SAN FRANCISCO		
		MAT.	INST.	TOTAL	MAT.	INST.	TOTAL	MAT.	INST.	TOTAL	MAT.	INST.	TOTAL	MAT.	INST.	TOTAL	MAT.	INST.	TOTAL
2	SITE WORK	97.8	115.7	105.7	102.0	104.3	103.0	98.8	111.3	104.3	86.5	105.6	95.0	95.2	108.3	101.0	102.1	116.8	108.6
3.1	FORMWORK	111.3	123.1	120.5	98.4	123.2	117.6	113.9	122.8	120.8	110.0	128.2	124.1	105.1	122.2	118.8	103.2	138.5	130.5
3.2	REINFORCING	87.2	129.4	104.3	99.3	129.4	111.5	124.5	129.4	126.5	99.3	129.4	111.5	118.4	129.4	122.9	123.7	129.4	126.0
3.3	CAST IN PLACE CONC.	96.7	112.5	106.3	102.3	110.2	107.1	102.3	109.8	106.9	115.9	107.8	111.0	99.4	104.6	102.6	100.3	118.1	111.1
3	CONCRETE	97.5	118.2	110.6	100.9	117.0	111.1	109.5	116.6	114.0	111.0	117.7	115.3	104.8	114.0	110.6	106.1	127.1	119.4
4	MASONRY	108.7	130.2	125.1	100.8	124.3	118.8	105.3	117.5	114.6	103.2	114.6	111.9	110.3	109.9	110.0	126.5	148.5	143.3
5	METALS	101.6	122.7	109.0	105.3	122.0	111.1	99.2	121.8	107.1	111.1	123.3	115.3	99.1	120.7	106.7	104.0	126.3	111.8
6	WOOD & PLASTICS	99.7	119.1	110.5	92.7	119.0	107.3	94.6	118.0	107.7	78.4	126.4	105.1	96.2	118.1	108.4	93.1	137.7	117.9
7	MOISTURE PROTECTION	103.9	131.8	112.7	90.1	129.6	102.6	90.6	125.0	102.6	85.3	122.1	96.9	94.6	110.3	99.6	100.4	134.9	111.3
8	DOORS, WINDOWS, GLASS	102.8	122.6	113.0	102.6	122.6	112.9	103.1	122.6	113.2	91.8	120.7	106.7	107.4	121.3	114.6	113.6	134.2	124.2
9.2	LATH & PLASTER	96.4	130.9	122.5	97.6	123.5	117.2	97.6	126.1	119.2	99.1	128.1	121.1	102.1	111.8	109.4	101.7	146.8	135.9
9.2	DRYWALL	89.2	123.4	105.2	98.7	120.7	109.0	94.8	123.4	108.1	97.4	126.4	110.9	99.8	119.4	108.9	81.1	140.4	108.7
9.5	ACOUSTICAL WORK	98.9	118.7	109.7	87.5	118.7	104.5	87.5	118.7	104.5	85.6	127.3	108.4	100.8	118.9	110.7	100.8	139.5	121.9
9.6	FLOORING	96.3	128.0	104.8	95.8	128.0	104.4	95.8	128.0	104.4	85.9	130.1	97.7	98.3	131.6	107.2	107.1	136.7	115.0
9.9	PAINTING	83.9	124.6	116.3	92.2	115.1	110.5	100.7	120.3	116.3	112.9	130.6	126.9	91.5	126.5	119.4	102.1	146.3	137.4
9	FINISHES	91.2	124.2	108.8	96.5	119.3	108.7	95.1	122.4	109.7	95.4	128.3	113.0	98.8	122.2	111.3	91.0	142.5	118.4
10-14	TOTAL DIV. 10-14	100.0	126.5	107.7	100.0	126.1	107.6	100.0	126.0	107.6	100.0	146.3	113.6	100.0	124.1	107.0	100.0	152.3	115.3
15	MECHANICAL	97.6	125.4	111.4	98.5	122.6	110.5	96.5	125.9	111.1	97.9	118.6	108.2	102.9	123.6	113.2	101.1	172.8	136.7
16	ELECTRICAL	102.0	125.4	118.1	99.5	116.1	110.9	99.0	124.6	116.6	110.6	93.6	98.8	105.8	106.3	106.1	108.0	153.1	139.2
1-16	WEIGHTED AVERAGE	99.3	123.9	112.4	99.4	120.0	110.4	99.6	121.1	111.1	99.8	117.0	109.0	101.7	115.9	109.3	103.3	144.8	125.5

CITY COST INDEXES

DIVISION		CALIFORNIA									COLORADO						CONNECTICUT		
		SANTA BARBARA			STOCKTON			VALLEJO			COLO SPRINGS			DENVER			BRIDGEPORT		
		MAT.	INST.	TOTAL	MAT.	INST.	TOTAL	MAT.	INST.	TOTAL	MAT.	INST.	TOTAL	MAT.	INST.	TOTAL	MAT.	INST.	TOTAL
2	SITE WORK	125.3	112.0	119.4	121.0	114.0	117.9	107.0	115.5	110.8	98.8	92.7	96.1	105.6	99.5	102.9	121.2	98.2	111.0
3.1	FORMWORK	115.0	122.9	121.1	106.6	124.5	120.4	113.6	137.7	132.3	103.4	70.9	78.2	94.4	80.4	83.6	122.5	87.6	95.4
3.2	REINFORCING	99.3	129.4	111.5	83.4	129.4	102.0	99.3	129.4	111.5	96.0	87.1	92.4	108.0	87.1	99.5	112.7	113.6	113.1
3.3	CAST IN PLACE CONC.	125.6	121.6	123.2	102.9	108.2	106.1	102.9	107.8	105.9	113.8	95.4	102.7	123.0	92.4	104.5	102.9	100.0	101.1
3	CONCRETE	117.6	122.8	120.9	99.3	116.5	110.1	104.2	121.5	115.1	107.8	85.0	93.4	114.0	87.2	97.1	108.9	96.3	100.9
4	MASONRY	118.4	123.7	122.4	112.4	114.6	114.1	109.8	140.2	133.0	106.0	83.3	88.7	104.3	83.7	88.6	106.2	96.9	99.1
5	METALS	96.2	125.6	106.5	91.6	123.0	102.6	88.8	123.2	100.9	91.4	89.1	90.6	95.6	88.2	93.0	91.8	107.8	97.4
6	WOOD & PLASTICS	108.6	118.7	114.2	86.2	121.8	106.0	99.3	138.1	120.9	86.3	70.3	77.4	91.4	82.0	86.2	107.1	84.5	94.6
7	MOISTURE PROTECTION	89.9	108.0	95.6	89.3	114.6	97.3	87.6	129.5	100.9	85.5	79.0	83.5	116.2	81.0	105.1	100.1	114.9	104.8
8	DOORS, WINDOWS, GLASS	103.9	122.6	113.5	95.3	118.6	107.3	99.1	134.2	117.2	98.2	79.1	88.4	90.7	82.8	86.6	102.1	98.5	100.3
9.2	LATH & PLASTER	104.4	115.0	112.4	100.2	118.8	114.3	100.2	124.9	118.9	101.9	91.3	93.8	88.0	94.7	93.1	106.1	93.3	96.4
9.2	DRYWALL	122.6	121.0	121.9	107.2	121.0	113.6	107.9	133.7	119.9	93.1	77.5	85.9	88.2	88.2	88.2	113.0	82.5	98.8
9.5	ACOUSTICAL WORK	87.5	118.7	104.5	85.6	122.6	105.8	88.5	139.5	116.3	94.6	69.2	80.8	96.4	81.7	88.4	105.9	84.4	94.2
9.6	FLOORING	101.8	126.1	108.3	84.9	107.3	90.9	84.3	136.7	98.3	108.0	77.9	100.0	99.5	100.5	99.7	85.1	97.6	88.4
9.9	PAINTING	119.0	115.1	115.9	102.9	103.4	103.3	105.9	130.6	125.6	117.5	75.9	84.3	104.2	90.6	93.4	121.4	82.2	90.1
9	FINISHES	114.5	118.8	116.8	100.0	114.0	107.4	100.8	132.8	117.8	99.2	77.2	87.4	92.9	89.8	91.2	106.9	84.3	94.9
10-14	TOTAL DIV. 10-14	100.0	124.4	107.1	100.0	144.8	113.1	100.0	149.1	114.4	100.0	90.3	97.1	100.0	93.1	97.9	100.0	104.2	101.2
15	MECHANICAL	98.5	122.4	110.4	96.9	113.5	105.2	95.8	137.7	116.6	97.8	87.5	92.7	97.0	88.0	92.5	103.6	98.9	101.3
16	ELECTRICAL	98.7	116.3	110.8	101.3	113.9	110.0	110.8	126.8	121.9	98.7	81.9	87.1	95.8	82.7	86.8	103.8	92.8	96.2
1-16	WEIGHTED AVERAGE	105.3	120.9	113.6	99.2	116.8	108.6	99.4	131.3	116.4	98.6	84.1	90.8	101.1	86.9	93.5	104.1	96.7	100.1

DIVISION		CONNECTICUT											DELAWARE			D.C.		
		HARTFORD			NEW HAVEN			STAMFORD			WATERBURY			WILMINGTON			WASHINGTON		
		MAT.	INST.	TOTAL	MAT.	INST.	TOTAL	MAT.	INST.	TOTAL	MAT.	INST.	TOTAL	MAT.	INST.	TOTAL	MAT.	INST.	TOTAL
2	SITE WORK	100.3	98.5	99.5	116.9	96.5	107.8	124.8	100.0	113.8	109.2	97.5	104.0	115.2	101.2	109.0	89.9	92.9	91.2
3.1	FORMWORK	111.3	90.4	95.1	110.7	89.3	94.1	112.1	85.7	91.2	101.9	89.2	92.1	105.1	103.3	103.7	106.8	86.9	91.3
3.2	REINFORCING	115.2	113.6	114.5	112.7	113.6	113.1	130.7	113.6	123.8	115.2	113.6	114.5	112.7	103.3	108.9	109.2	82.7	98.5
3.3	CAST IN PLACE CONC.	98.4	100.0	99.3	95.1	99.4	97.7	117.8	100.4	107.2	114.9	100.0	105.9	99.0	114.0	108.1	102.7	89.8	94.9
3	CONCRETE	104.7	97.4	100.1	102.1	96.7	98.7	119.5	95.5	104.4	112.4	97.0	102.6	103.2	108.9	106.8	104.9	88.0	94.2
4	MASONRY	99.6	97.1	97.7	122.7	97.0	103.0	122.5	98.1	103.9	109.6	97.0	100.0	101.7	92.6	94.7	92.7	94.8	94.3
5	METALS	92.6	107.8	97.9	85.2	107.8	93.1	85.8	107.8	93.5	88.1	107.8	95.0	85.7	106.7	93.1	103.0	87.1	97.4
6	WOOD & PLASTICS	114.3	88.0	99.7	115.4	87.1	99.6	111.2	81.7	94.8	107.4	86.8	95.9	103.5	103.4	103.4	105.4	88.9	96.2
7	MOISTURE PROTECTION	101.2	98.5	100.3	88.2	101.5	92.4	87.9	104.2	93.1	88.7	98.3	91.7	89.0	113.9	96.9	106.6	90.8	101.6
8	DOORS, WINDOWS, GLASS	92.4	100.5	96.6	98.8	99.3	99.1	94.9	97.0	96.0	88.8	99.3	94.2	86.8	103.3	95.3	99.7	89.6	94.5
9.2	LATH & PLASTER	113.6	95.7	100.0	121.4	89.4	97.1	98.7	96.5	97.1	113.7	95.5	99.9	94.1	92.8	93.2	98.8	103.9	102.6
9.2	DRYWALL	108.2	87.1	98.4	113.0	82.4	98.8	117.9	82.3	101.4	113.4	86.1	100.7	102.5	103.1	102.8	121.4	88.6	106.1
9.5	ACOUSTICAL WORK	105.9	88.1	96.2	105.9	86.3	95.2	105.1	81.0	92.0	86.6	86.3	86.4	90.8	103.5	97.7	107.3	89.9	97.2
9.6	FLOORING	94.5	98.2	95.5	97.2	97.9	97.4	96.0	98.2	96.6	102.0	97.9	100.9	85.2	95.4	88.0	94.5	98.9	95.7
9.9	PAINTING	107.3	99.0	100.6	121.2	98.4	103.0	121.2	112.8	114.5	114.4	78.1	85.4	100.6	96.4	97.2	98.2	97.5	97.6
9	FINISHES	105.0	92.6	98.4	110.0	89.7	99.2	112.0	94.7	102.8	108.9	84.8	96.0	97.4	99.6	98.6	111.5	93.3	101.8
10-14	TOTAL DIV. 10-14	100.0	105.0	101.4	100.0	104.6	101.3	100.0	104.9	101.4	100.0	103.5	101.0	100.0	103.4	101.0	100.0	91.6	97.5
15	MECHANICAL	101.4	96.0	98.7	101.9	98.4	100.2	101.4	105.9	103.6	100.5	93.8	97.1	100.0	99.2	99.6	101.8	87.9	94.9
16	ELECTRICAL	100.1	94.4	96.2	93.8	92.4	92.8	95.6	122.2	113.9	92.4	77.4	82.0	106.2	98.4	100.8	97.4	86.6	90.0
1-16	WEIGHTED AVERAGE	100.6	97.2	98.8	101.4	96.8	99.0	104.3	102.3	103.3	100.8	93.6	97.0	98.8	101.6	100.3	101.8	89.8	95.4

DIVISION		FLORIDA															GEORGIA		
		FT LAUDERDALE			JACKSONVILLE			MIAMI			ORLANDO			TAMPA			ATLANTA		
		MAT.	INST.	TOTAL	MAT.	INST.	TOTAL	MAT.	INST.	TOTAL	MAT.	INST.	TOTAL	MAT.	INST.	TOTAL	MAT.	INST.	TOTAL
2	SITE WORK	108.4	85.8	98.4	117.9	82.8	102.4	97.3	82.7	90.8	97.2	88.4	93.3	109.9	90.2	101.2	103.7	92.5	98.7
3.1	FORMWORK	107.3	74.5	81.9	104.4	71.3	78.7	108.9	74.2	82.0	103.8	71.9	79.1	99.7	75.4	80.9	85.8	74.5	77.1
3.2	REINFORCING	100.1	83.8	93.5	87.3	70.3	80.4	100.1	83.8	93.5	100.1	72.3	88.8	100.1	82.8	93.1	85.8	77.5	82.4
3.3	CAST IN PLACE CONC.	91.5	93.9	93.0	96.9	89.9	92.7	88.6	97.5	94.0	94.3	91.4	92.5	99.1	109.2	105.2	88.4	95.1	92.5
3	CONCRETE	96.5	85.4	89.5	96.3	80.9	86.5	95.2	87.1	90.1	97.5	82.0	87.7	99.5	93.6	95.7	87.3	85.5	86.2
4	MASONRY	99.0	88.1	90.7	90.6	61.5	68.3	92.9	74.5	78.8	93.7	62.2	69.6	96.9	77.9	82.3	89.2	75.6	78.8
5	METALS	87.0	86.5	86.8	94.8	78.3	89.0	86.7	89.4	87.6	86.7	79.4	84.1	98.0	92.4	96.0	110.2	83.7	100.9
6	WOOD & PLASTICS	107.0	80.0	92.0	102.7	74.6	87.0	107.7	79.1	91.8	102.6	72.9	86.1	102.2	79.2	89.4	89.4	77.5	82.8
7	MOISTURE PROTECTION	88.1	78.4	85.0	87.4	70.6	82.1	86.3	79.2	84.1	87.5	69.7	81.9	104.5	64.9	92.0	98.0	72.9	90.1
8	DOORS, WINDOWS, GLASS	86.6	76.4	81.3	89.7	69.6	79.3	93.2	76.4	84.5	88.3	69.1	78.4	96.5	66.7	81.2	92.3	75.4	83.6
9.2	LATH & PLASTER	100.8	87.5	90.7	103.0	66.9	75.6	104.1	78.3	84.5	102.3	64.7	73.8	100.9	67.1	75.3	112.0	77.2	85.6
9.2	DRYWALL	103.2	78.4	91.7	107.1	73.4	91.4	102.8	78.0	91.2	103.2	68.5	87.0	96.9	78.1	88.1	115.5	75.6	96.9
9.5	ACOUSTICAL WORK	91.0	78.4	84.1	91.0	73.6	81.5	100.1	78.4	88.2	91.0	71.9	80.6	92.8	78.4	84.9	91.9	76.5	83.5
9.6	FLOORING	104.1	88.9	100.0	104.1	64.7	93.6	105.5	76.9	97.9	102.9	65.0	92.8	100.2	79.3	94.6	101.4	82.5	96.4
9.9	PAINTING	113.1	68.7	77.7	102.7	67.2	74.4	111.8	68.7	77.4	100.1	72.0	77.7	108.6	65.0	73.8	95.1	84.3	86.4
9	FINISHES	103.4	76.2	88.9	104.7	70.2	86.3	104.1	74.7	88.5	101.8	69.5	84.6	98.6	73.0	84.9	108.4	79.3	92.9
10-14	TOTAL DIV. 10-14	100.0	86.7	96.1	100.0	76.1	93.0	100.0	86.3	95.9	100.0	79.1	93.8	100.0	80.8	94.3	100.0	78.8	93.7
15	MECHANICAL	100.7	82.1	91.5	99.9	76.7	88.4	97.5	91.0	94.3	96.8	78.7	87.8	97.2	82.0	89.6	102.7	81.3	92.1
16	ELECTRICAL	99.0	82.6	87.7	100.3	71.2	80.2	100.7	92.4	94.9	93.6	72.4	79.0	93.6	78.3	83.0	95.6	86.2	89.1
1-16	WEIGHTED AVERAGE	97.6	83.3	90.0	98.6	73.8	85.3	96.2	84.4	89.9	95.4	74.9	84.5	99.2	81.9	90.0	99.1	81.6	89.7

CITY COST INDEXES

DIVISION		GEORGIA								HAWAII			IDAHO			ILLINOIS		
		COLUMBUS			MACON			SAVANNAH		HONOLULU			BOISE			CHICAGO		
		MAT.	INST.	TOTAL	MAT.	INST.	TOTAL	MAT.	INST.	TOTAL	MAT.	INST.	TOTAL	MAT.	INST.	TOTAL	MAT.	INST.	TOTAL
2	SITE WORK	122.8	85.6	106.3	115.9	88.7	103.8	117.8	87.9	104.5	132.7	104.5	120.2	92.9	98.2	95.3	104.6	105.3	104.9
3.1	FORMWORK	105.2	58.1	68.7	98.7	65.8	73.2	101.2	68.6	75.9	132.2	109.7	114.7	110.3	93.9	97.6	80.9	110.9	104.1
3.2	REINFORCING	97.1	77.5	89.2	86.2	77.5	82.7	107.1	71.0	92.5	117.8	99.8	110.5	117.8	83.0	103.7	106.3	108.8	107.3
3.3	CAST IN PLACE CONC.	108.2	86.5	95.1	102.4	99.4	100.5	94.8	101.7	99.0	113.7	101.9	106.5	96.5	99.2	98.1	101.7	99.6	100.5
3	CONCRETE	105.1	74.5	85.8	98.0	84.2	89.3	98.8	86.0	90.7	118.2	104.8	109.7	104.0	95.7	98.7	98.7	104.9	102.6
4	MASONRY	92.7	48.3	58.8	84.4	55.9	62.6	92.2	68.1	73.8	125.6	111.9	115.1	101.8	83.7	88.0	97.3	106.3	104.2
5	METALS	95.6	82.9	91.2	90.7	87.2	89.4	100.6	83.7	94.7	110.2	100.8	106.9	93.3	88.6	91.7	89.7	105.6	95.3
6	WOOD & PLASTICS	103.4	60.5	79.5	92.5	67.8	78.7	102.5	70.2	84.5	121.4	111.3	115.8	92.4	92.5	92.5	93.7	110.1	102.8
7	MOISTURE PROTECTION	92.8	65.0	84.0	92.6	66.7	84.4	90.8	61.6	81.5	107.6	113.9	109.6	105.6	87.6	99.9	97.7	112.4	102.4
8	DOORS, WINDOWS, GLASS	89.7	61.9	75.4	93.3	67.4	80.0	91.3	63.8	77.1	114.0	105.4	109.6	104.9	82.3	93.2	110.1	108.6	109.3
9.2	LATH & PLASTER	103.3	54.1	66.0	102.9	60.7	70.9	97.6	55.9	66.0	116.9	118.0	117.7	114.3	92.3	97.7	107.2	108.0	107.8
9.2	DRYWALL	91.9	59.2	76.7	91.9	65.8	79.7	111.9	68.7	91.8	151.6	112.8	133.5	94.7	93.1	94.0	98.3	109.9	103.7
9.5	ACOUSTICAL WORK	101.4	59.0	78.3	101.4	66.6	82.4	101.6	69.1	83.9	118.7	111.2	114.6	112.9	92.3	101.6	98.6	110.3	105.0
9.6	FLOORING	82.2	51.0	73.8	88.2	58.7	80.3	95.8	70.0	88.9	132.6	115.1	127.9	93.9	90.8	93.1	98.8	104.1	100.2
9.9	PAINTING	117.1	56.5	68.7	116.5	69.0	78.6	116.8	58.2	70.1	124.1	119.8	120.7	100.4	68.9	75.3	92.8	103.4	101.3
9	FINISHES	93.3	57.3	74.1	94.5	66.1	79.4	107.7	64.5	84.6	141.3	115.5	127.6	97.0	84.5	90.3	98.1	107.2	102.9
10-14	TOTAL DIV. 10-14	100.0	73.8	92.3	100.0	75.5	92.8	100.0	72.1	91.8	100.0	113.4	103.9	100.0	85.4	95.7	100.0	107.8	102.3
15	MECHANICAL	98.4	65.0	81.8	98.7	70.0	84.4	98.4	71.5	85.0	111.3	106.7	109.0	96.5	93.0	94.8	96.5	100.1	98.3
16	ELECTRICAL	97.8	59.7	71.5	108.4	69.6	81.7	101.6	74.3	82.7	106.0	102.1	103.3	96.7	77.3	83.3	94.1	104.8	101.5
1-16	WEIGHTED AVERAGE	99.1	65.1	80.9	97.7	72.1	84.0	99.9	74.3	86.2	115.3	107.5	111.1	98.9	88.4	93.3	98.1	105.1	101.8

DIVISION		ILLINOIS								INDIANA								
		PEORIA			ROCKFORD			SPRINGFIELD		EVANSVILLE			FORT WAYNE			GARY		
		MAT.	INST.	TOTAL	MAT.	INST.	TOTAL	MAT.	INST.	TOTAL	MAT.	INST.	TOTAL	MAT.	INST.	TOTAL	MAT.	INST.	TOTAL
2	SITE WORK	114.4	97.0	106.7	112.3	102.4	107.9	109.0	96.3	103.4	103.6	97.8	101.0	97.6	96.6	97.2	111.4	95.2	104.2
3.1	FORMWORK	117.2	96.2	100.9	124.9	103.3	108.1	104.3	95.0	97.1	105.7	93.4	96.2	119.0	91.1	97.3	113.6	102.0	104.6
3.2	REINFORCING	112.7	91.8	104.3	112.9	108.9	111.3	92.8	82.7	88.7	93.8	100.3	96.4	93.8	98.1	95.6	93.8	99.8	96.2
3.3	CAST IN PLACE CONC.	86.7	82.5	84.2	97.4	102.4	100.4	101.7	97.7	99.3	113.7	95.9	102.9	91.7	94.4	93.3	97.2	112.2	106.3
3	CONCRETE	98.5	88.7	92.3	106.3	103.3	104.4	100.2	95.3	97.1	107.7	95.3	99.9	97.5	93.4	94.9	99.7	107.1	104.4
4	MASONRY	99.3	90.0	92.2	89.9	98.9	96.8	107.0	85.1	90.3	88.1	96.3	94.4	95.4	85.1	87.5	95.4	107.0	104.2
5	METALS	87.8	86.9	87.5	108.1	106.5	107.5	93.0	87.5	91.1	93.9	96.7	94.8	99.8	97.9	99.1	89.6	103.7	94.5
6	WOOD & PLASTICS	113.7	96.5	104.1	107.1	101.1	103.8	103.2	94.9	98.6	93.1	92.7	92.9	102.9	91.6	96.6	113.0	103.9	107.9
7	MOISTURE PROTECTION	93.6	101.2	96.0	101.0	106.9	107.0	99.0	92.6	97.0	88.0	96.0	90.5	96.3	87.0	93.4	93.7	107.8	98.1
8	DOORS, WINDOWS, GLASS	93.8	90.5	92.1	100.5	99.4	100.0	105.4	86.5	95.7	106.9	91.8	99.1	98.1	87.6	92.7	98.7	97.8	98.2
9.2	LATH & PLASTER	104.0	96.2	98.0	105.2	98.4	100.0	103.8	89.0	92.6	101.2	89.1	92.0	101.9	77.2	83.2	117.4	96.3	101.4
9.2	DRYWALL	110.2	96.0	103.6	94.7	101.0	97.6	116.2	94.3	106.0	113.5	92.1	103.5	100.8	91.0	96.2	100.3	103.7	101.9
9.5	ACOUSTICAL WORK	84.0	96.4	90.8	83.9	101.3	93.4	83.9	94.7	89.8	103.9	92.4	97.6	85.0	91.3	88.4	90.3	104.1	97.8
9.6	FLOORING	105.0	93.1	101.8	123.4	95.6	116.0	115.2	88.5	108.1	97.7	92.8	96.4	98.8	88.0	95.9	100.7	109.2	103.0
9.9	PAINTING	115.8	93.1	97.7	96.9	100.1	99.4	90.8	82.5	84.2	103.5	92.0	94.3	95.2	84.4	86.5	92.5	95.7	95.0
9	FINISHES	107.4	94.8	100.7	100.7	100.2	100.4	110.6	89.6	99.4	108.0	91.9	99.4	98.6	87.6	92.7	99.2	100.9	100.1
10-14	TOTAL DIV. 10-14	100.0	89.6	96.9	100.0	100.7	100.2	100.0	89.7	97.0	100.0	95.7	98.7	100.0	98.3	99.5	100.0	100.6	100.1
15	MECHANICAL	96.0	90.1	93.1	101.6	95.9	98.8	97.0	84.0	90.5	98.0	93.5	95.8	98.3	83.7	91.1	97.5	92.6	95.1
16	ELECTRICAL	94.8	88.2	90.3	93.6	95.3	94.8	95.4	81.1	85.5	95.1	96.2	95.8	97.4	80.2	85.5	101.4	96.8	98.3
1-16	WEIGHTED AVERAGE	98.4	90.6	94.2	102.5	99.8	101.1	100.7	88.3	94.1	99.6	94.9	97.1	98.2	88.3	92.9	98.6	101.0	99.9

DIVISION		INDIANA								IOWA						KANSAS		
		INDIANAPOLIS			SOUTH BEND			TERRE HAUTE		DAVENPORT			DES MOINES			TOPEKA		
		MAT.	INST.	TOTAL	MAT.	INST.	TOTAL	MAT.	INST.	TOTAL	MAT.	INST.	TOTAL	MAT.	INST.	TOTAL	MAT.	INST.	TOTAL
2	SITE WORK	101.2	94.6	98.3	101.3	98.3	100.0	92.3	86.5	89.8	107.9	88.9	99.4	103.5	91.5	98.2	110.0	84.8	98.8
3.1	FORMWORK	113.8	97.4	101.1	108.9	92.2	96.0	115.4	87.0	93.4	103.9	93.9	96.1	112.8	79.4	86.9	101.3	69.9	76.9
3.2	REINFORCING	110.5	100.4	106.4	106.0	90.7	99.8	93.8	93.4	93.7	97.8	88.6	94.1	101.8	78.6	92.4	87.6	97.6	91.7
3.3	CAST IN PLACE CONC.	83.5	95.2	90.6	90.0	103.8	98.4	92.8	95.2	94.2	91.6	96.9	94.8	115.3	93.0	101.8	91.8	94.9	93.7
3	CONCRETE	95.4	96.5	96.1	97.3	98.1	97.8	97.5	91.8	93.9	95.4	95.0	95.1	111.8	86.4	95.7	92.8	85.3	88.0
4	MASONRY	100.5	96.5	97.4	94.1	92.5	92.8	86.8	95.9	93.7	115.5	85.1	92.3	101.3	80.2	85.2	100.1	75.8	81.5
5	METALS	98.9	98.6	98.8	101.2	95.3	99.1	91.6	94.5	92.6	88.9	90.9	89.6	88.7	82.7	86.6	101.5	96.8	99.8
6	WOOD & PLASTICS	100.4	98.6	99.4	106.8	92.3	98.7	109.2	87.3	97.0	105.3	95.7	100.0	104.5	78.4	90.1	94.7	69.4	80.6
7	MOISTURE PROTECTION	92.6	96.3	93.8	90.1	93.3	91.1	93.3	85.6	90.8	90.5	91.5	90.8	87.4	76.1	83.8	96.6	75.8	90.1
8	DOORS, WINDOWS, GLASS	109.7	98.8	104.1	104.9	84.2	94.3	99.0	89.2	93.9	92.1	84.5	88.2	89.0	80.8	84.8	98.5	76.3	87.0
9.2	LATH & PLASTER	96.7	96.3	96.4	105.9	89.9	93.8	107.5	86.3	91.4	100.3	86.1	89.5	106.1	73.8	81.6	87.1	73.9	77.1
9.2	DRYWALL	89.6	97.8	93.4	101.1	91.1	96.4	100.9	86.5	94.2	102.6	91.9	97.6	115.9	76.4	97.5	91.3	68.1	80.5
9.5	ACOUSTICAL WORK	101.1	98.1	99.5	88.4	91.4	90.0	91.3	86.8	88.8	91.1	92.3	91.8	104.3	77.6	89.7	97.4	65.3	79.9
9.6	FLOORING	107.9	98.7	105.4	103.6	83.7	98.3	107.8	95.5	104.5	107.8	79.1	100.1	93.2	70.5	87.1	107.4	75.1	98.8
9.9	PAINTING	91.3	90.2	90.4	97.5	75.4	79.9	120.4	83.5	91.0	103.2	90.9	93.4	104.2	80.2	85.0	89.7	76.4	79.1
9	FINISHES	94.9	95.1	95.0	100.4	85.1	92.2	103.8	86.1	94.4	102.9	90.3	96.2	108.5	77.2	91.8	94.8	71.8	82.5
10-14	TOTAL DIV. 10-14	100.0	95.2	98.6	100.0	91.3	97.4	100.0	94.1	98.2	100.0	84.1	95.3	100.0	83.1	95.0	100.0	88.2	96.5
15	MECHANICAL	100.7	94.4	97.5	98.1	87.5	92.8	98.0	90.7	94.4	99.7	81.0	90.4	96.4	84.0	90.3	99.3	76.7	88.0
16	ELECTRICAL	99.9	99.1	99.4	98.0	87.6	90.8	109.1	91.2	96.8	98.0	85.0	89.1	99.4	84.4	89.0	98.7	76.8	83.6
1-16	WEIGHTED AVERAGE	99.0	96.4	97.6	98.7	91.3	94.8	97.8	91.2	94.3	98.6	87.7	92.8	99.5	83.1	90.7	98.5	79.5	88.4

CITY COST INDEXES

DIVISION		KANSAS WICHITA			KENTUCKY LEXINGTON			KENTUCKY LOUISVILLE			LOUISIANA BATON ROUGE			LOUISIANA NEW ORLEANS			LOUISIANA SHREVEPORT		
		MAT.	INST.	TOTAL	MAT.	INST.	TOTAL	MAT.	INST.	TOTAL	MAT.	INST.	TOTAL	MAT.	INST.	TOTAL	MAT.	INST.	TOTAL
2	SITE WORK	114.2	92.1	104.4	92.4	90.0	91.3	106.8	92.3	100.4	98.6	77.4	89.2	101.8	86.3	94.9	106.3	79.2	94.3
3.1	FORMWORK	102.0	65.2	73.5	107.4	73.2	80.9	100.3	75.6	81.1	122.5	70.1	81.9	94.0	79.6	82.8	102.7	63.3	72.2
3.2	REINFORCING	87.6	100.3	92.8	101.3	92.1	97.6	117.8	92.1	107.4	100.4	64.7	86.0	95.0	74.9	86.8	100.4	63.6	85.5
3.3	CAST IN PLACE CONC.	94.4	100.2	97.9	83.8	92.4	89.0	77.9	102.8	93.0	97.2	86.2	90.5	90.6	88.0	89.0	86.4	88.8	87.8
3	CONCRETE	94.4	86.4	89.3	92.3	84.8	87.6	91.2	91.2	91.2	102.9	78.0	87.1	92.3	83.5	86.7	92.7	76.6	82.5
4	MASONRY	96.7	71.4	77.4	89.4	77.1	80.0	92.0	70.8	75.8	105.6	86.7	91.2	103.4	80.1	85.6	114.6	63.3	75.4
5	METALS	98.1	100.3	98.9	83.7	92.5	86.8	79.9	95.4	85.3	104.9	71.7	93.3	94.8	78.5	89.1	92.4	72.9	85.5
6	WOOD & PLASTICS	94.1	66.3	78.6	105.8	73.0	87.6	102.1	75.6	87.4	104.3	72.6	86.6	95.7	81.3	87.7	87.8	66.8	76.1
7	MOISTURE PROTECTION	97.0	65.9	87.2	84.8	72.8	81.0	84.9	73.8	81.4	111.2	71.1	98.5	111.3	71.1	98.6	87.0	63.9	79.7
8	DOORS, WINDOWS, GLASS	93.1	74.3	83.4	103.1	74.2	88.2	99.1	77.3	87.8	89.4	65.4	77.0	97.6	80.5	88.8	102.6	61.9	81.7
9.2	LATH & PLASTER	94.6	66.9	73.5	87.9	76.5	79.2	95.7	79.9	83.7	88.1	75.8	78.8	89.3	79.1	81.5	103.1	69.0	77.3
9.2	DRYWALL	90.8	66.1	79.3	92.1	72.9	83.1	90.3	74.5	83.0	100.3	71.3	86.8	88.2	79.7	84.3	91.0	65.4	79.1
9.5	ACOUSTICAL WORK	85.8	65.2	74.6	85.1	72.1	78.0	89.9	74.7	81.7	80.0	71.6	75.4	105.6	80.4	91.9	100.4	64.7	80.9
9.6	FLOORING	97.9	72.3	91.1	104.2	70.1	95.1	113.1	72.7	102.3	94.7	86.8	92.6	96.8	72.1	90.2	98.6	65.1	89.6
9.9	PAINTING	104.7	67.8	75.3	120.4	66.4	77.3	110.6	63.9	73.3	115.5	60.8	71.9	112.2	70.4	78.8	107.2	55.8	66.2
9	FINISHES	93.4	67.1	79.4	97.0	70.6	82.9	97.5	71.0	83.4	98.7	69.1	82.9	93.9	76.0	84.3	95.3	62.3	77.7
10-14	TOTAL DIV. 10-14	100.0	77.4	93.3	100.0	85.7	95.8	100.0	86.1	95.9	100.0	68.4	90.7	100.0	80.7	94.3	100.0	69.8	91.1
15	MECHANICAL	96.9	73.6	85.3	100.3	78.4	89.4	101.0	83.6	92.4	96.6	68.7	82.7	99.0	77.9	88.5	95.9	77.9	87.0
16	ELECTRICAL	103.2	73.3	82.6	103.0	78.6	86.2	100.9	78.4	85.4	98.1	82.1	87.0	97.4	81.2	86.2	95.4	75.7	81.8
1-16	WEIGHTED AVERAGE	97.9	77.2	86.8	95.6	79.8	87.2	95.8	81.7	88.3	100.3	75.5	87.0	98.3	80.2	88.6	96.8	71.7	83.4

DIVISION		MAINE LEWISTON			MAINE PORTLAND			MARYLAND BALTIMORE			MASSACHUSETTS BOSTON			MASSACHUSETTS LAWRENCE			MASSACHUSETTS LOWELL		
		MAT.	INST.	TOTAL	MAT.	INST.	TOTAL	MAT.	INST.	TOTAL	MAT.	INST.	TOTAL	MAT.	INST.	TOTAL	MAT.	INST.	TOTAL
2	SITE WORK	98.1	95.7	97.0	101.1	106.2	103.3	100.6	86.7	94.4	108.6	103.5	106.3	107.4	102.6	105.3	102.9	100.6	101.9
3.1	FORMWORK	107.2	83.5	88.8	107.2	83.5	88.8	111.7	86.5	92.2	105.5	124.8	120.5	119.1	110.7	112.6	111.5	110.8	111.0
3.2	REINFORCING	117.8	83.3	103.8	117.8	83.3	103.8	104.8	96.6	101.5	118.6	120.0	119.2	98.2	113.4	104.4	116.2	117.9	116.9
3.3	CAST IN PLACE CONC.	92.7	93.1	92.9	92.7	93.5	93.2	123.5	92.7	104.9	114.5	121.1	118.5	111.5	107.3	108.9	108.3	107.3	107.7
3	CONCRETE	101.1	88.4	93.1	101.1	88.7	93.2	117.0	90.6	100.3	113.7	122.5	119.2	110.0	109.2	109.5	110.7	109.6	110.0
4	MASONRY	94.0	65.4	72.1	94.2	65.4	72.2	85.3	91.5	90.0	110.3	127.9	123.8	105.7	126.9	121.9	110.2	126.9	122.9
5	METALS	94.0	89.8	92.5	107.3	89.8	101.2	97.3	94.6	96.4	110.8	119.3	113.8	96.1	110.6	101.2	93.7	113.4	100.6
6	WOOD & PLASTICS	108.4	84.0	94.8	105.0	84.0	93.3	102.0	88.2	94.3	105.1	125.6	116.5	112.8	108.0	110.1	110.5	108.0	109.1
7	MOISTURE PROTECTION	88.3	63.8	80.5	86.8	63.8	79.5	92.2	84.2	89.7	106.9	133.3	115.2	98.8	130.8	108.9	99.3	130.8	109.3
8	DOORS, WINDOWS, GLASS	107.1	72.7	89.4	95.2	72.7	83.6	96.8	93.7	95.2	105.4	123.5	114.7	107.0	106.9	107.0	101.4	107.8	104.7
9.2	LATH & PLASTER	107.3	79.5	86.2	108.2	79.8	86.7	114.1	89.0	95.1	129.5	122.6	124.3	99.3	121.8	116.4	97.1	110.5	107.2
9.2	DRYWALL	106.0	90.8	98.9	106.0	90.8	98.9	112.1	87.3	100.6	123.5	117.5	120.7	105.7	107.1	106.4	106.8	107.1	106.9
9.5	ACOUSTICAL WORK	94.8	84.2	89.0	94.8	84.2	89.0	100.6	87.6	93.5	87.3	126.6	108.8	105.9	109.1	107.6	105.9	109.1	107.6
9.6	FLOORING	104.3	69.6	95.0	102.0	69.6	93.4	103.4	97.4	101.8	118.1	130.5	121.4	97.5	127.5	105.4	103.5	127.2	109.8
9.9	PAINTING	98.3	49.9	59.7	102.3	49.9	60.5	94.6	86.4	88.1	115.2	141.2	136.0	101.1	111.4	109.3	96.7	125.9	120.0
9	FINISHES	104.0	73.9	88.0	103.9	74.0	87.9	107.6	87.8	97.1	118.7	127.7	123.5	103.3	111.1	107.4	104.7	115.4	110.4
10-14	TOTAL DIV. 10-14	100.0	83.0	95.0	100.0	83.0	95.0	100.0	92.3	97.7	100.0	121.0	106.1	100.0	119.0	105.5	100.0	119.9	105.8
15	MECHANICAL	96.5	95.0	95.8	96.5	95.0	95.7	100.4	90.2	95.3	104.0	120.5	112.2	98.7	113.5	106.1	98.3	102.9	100.6
16	ELECTRICAL	94.4	72.7	79.4	97.8	72.7	80.5	101.2	97.4	98.5	99.0	121.3	114.4	101.0	91.5	94.4	101.0	91.4	94.4
1-16	WEIGHTED AVERAGE	98.2	81.4	89.2	98.9	81.9	89.8	101.6	91.3	96.1	107.5	122.7	115.6	102.5	111.2	107.2	102.0	109.9	106.2

DIVISION		MASSACHUSETTS SPRINGFIELD			MASSACHUSETTS WORCESTER			MICHIGAN ANN ARBOR			MICHIGAN DETROIT			MICHIGAN FLINT			MICHIGAN GRAND RAPIDS		
		MAT.	INST.	TOTAL	MAT.	INST.	TOTAL	MAT.	INST.	TOTAL	MAT.	INST.	TOTAL	MAT.	INST.	TOTAL	MAT.	INST.	TOTAL
2	SITE WORK	96.2	101.8	98.7	105.5	103.9	104.8	98.6	101.5	99.9	92.5	104.9	98.0	98.0	97.7	97.8	81.9	88.2	84.7
3.1	FORMWORK	113.8	101.2	104.0	114.6	110.9	111.7	110.4	92.6	96.6	96.3	116.0	111.6	112.9	82.4	89.2	120.6	80.8	89.8
3.2	REINFORCING	98.2	112.4	104.0	98.2	117.9	106.2	109.2	112.1	110.4	88.7	112.1	98.2	109.2	112.1	110.4	117.8	81.2	103.0
3.3	CAST IN PLACE CONC.	99.4	106.8	103.9	106.2	104.1	104.9	88.9	104.3	98.2	110.9	113.1	112.2	103.7	96.0	99.0	96.2	93.6	94.6
3	CONCRETE	102.0	105.1	103.9	106.1	108.0	107.3	97.6	100.4	99.4	103.1	114.1	110.1	106.7	92.0	97.4	105.8	87.5	94.2
4	MASONRY	112.8	105.1	106.9	102.8	125.6	120.2	98.5	112.0	108.8	102.4	115.1	112.1	107.9	101.0	102.6	94.6	70.9	76.5
5	METALS	96.1	108.3	100.4	95.1	113.4	101.5	91.7	113.4	99.3	105.5	117.0	109.6	91.2	110.2	97.8	104.6	87.4	98.5
6	WOOD & PLASTICS	98.1	98.8	98.5	114.5	108.0	110.9	119.2	87.9	101.8	93.7	115.9	106.1	111.5	80.5	94.3	115.8	81.1	96.5
7	MOISTURE PROTECTION	97.8	97.7	97.8	99.9	121.7	106.8	90.6	104.5	95.0	94.9	118.4	102.3	85.1	86.6	85.6	111.5	71.6	98.9
8	DOORS, WINDOWS, GLASS	98.5	98.8	98.7	109.5	115.3	112.5	104.0	91.0	97.3	103.7	110.8	107.3	107.2	83.7	95.1	103.8	73.1	88.0
9.2	LATH & PLASTER	96.1	89.3	90.9	93.6	105.4	102.5	87.0	115.7	108.7	96.9	111.9	108.3	90.2	80.1	82.5	91.3	76.9	80.4
9.2	DRYWALL	104.8	91.6	98.6	106.8	105.6	106.2	88.0	98.2	92.7	89.5	115.4	101.5	111.8	77.7	95.9	114.9	78.1	97.8
9.5	ACOUSTICAL WORK	116.1	98.5	106.5	108.9	109.1	109.0	80.0	87.4	84.1	99.6	116.3	108.7	97.1	79.8	87.7	105.1	80.4	91.6
9.6	FLOORING	96.6	106.8	99.4	115.1	108.3	113.3	89.2	111.4	95.1	111.9	108.4	111.0	89.4	95.9	91.1	101.5	69.4	92.9
9.9	PAINTING	105.4	102.9	103.4	112.5	104.2	105.8	106.9	109.8	109.2	117.9	109.8	111.4	92.3	83.3	85.1	104.3	65.2	73.1
9	FINISHES	103.7	97.0	100.1	109.1	105.6	107.2	89.5	103.4	96.9	98.2	112.8	106.0	103.3	81.3	91.5	109.6	73.2	90.2
10-14	TOTAL DIV. 10-14	100.0	98.1	99.4	100.0	106.0	101.7	100.0	102.9	100.8	100.0	105.2	101.5	100.0	99.4	99.8	100.0	84.0	95.3
15	MECHANICAL	97.5	93.5	95.5	101.1	89.9	95.5	99.7	99.3	99.5	103.6	109.6	106.6	99.0	96.9	98.0	98.1	79.5	88.8
16	ELECTRICAL	95.4	96.4	96.1	97.3	107.7	104.4	99.3	77.9	84.5	100.1	110.1	107.0	99.3	101.6	100.9	97.9	61.8	73.0
1-16	WEIGHTED AVERAGE	99.6	100.1	99.9	102.6	107.7	105.4	97.5	99.4	98.5	101.0	112.1	106.9	100.1	94.9	97.3	101.6	77.5	88.7

CITY COST INDEXES

DIVISION		MICHIGAN									MINNESOTA						MISSISSIPPI		
		KALAMAZOO			LANSING			SAGINAW			DULUTH			MINNEAPOLIS			JACKSON		
		MAT.	INST.	TOTAL	MAT.	INST.	TOTAL	MAT.	INST.	TOTAL	MAT.	INST.	TOTAL	MAT.	INST.	TOTAL	MAT.	INST.	TOTAL
2	SITE WORK	96.3	92.3	94.6	115.5	93.6	105.8	114.0	93.3	104.8	123.6	90.5	108.9	119.4	102.9	112.1	101.5	80.9	92.3
3.1	FORMWORK	115.1	76.8	85.4	116.5	90.7	96.5	106.2	82.2	87.6	120.7	81.8	90.5	90.8	100.4	98.2	102.6	62.6	71.6
3.2	REINFORCING	117.8	81.2	103.0	117.8	112.1	115.5	109.2	112.1	110.4	105.3	91.8	99.9	75.5	96.6	84.1	103.9	63.6	87.6
3.3	CAST IN PLACE CONC.	98.0	94.5	95.9	95.0	85.2	89.0	91.2	95.3	93.7	95.8	97.7	97.0	98.8	96.9	97.6	96.9	87.7	91.3
3	CONCRETE	105.8	86.4	93.5	104.3	89.7	95.1	98.2	91.7	94.1	102.8	90.9	95.3	92.0	98.2	95.9	99.6	75.7	84.5
4	MASONRY	97.8	75.8	81.0	106.8	78.7	85.3	98.5	74.9	80.5	110.0	88.0	93.2	100.2	97.8	98.4	101.9	61.5	71.0
5	METALS	101.4	87.3	96.5	110.4	106.4	109.0	100.1	110.2	103.6	105.3	94.1	101.4	95.8	95.8	95.8	85.9	72.4	81.1
6	WOOD & PLASTICS	96.8	75.3	84.8	114.4	92.3	102.1	107.1	80.5	92.3	100.9	80.6	89.6	99.6	99.1	99.3	93.2	65.8	77.9
7	MOISTURE PROTECTION	89.3	76.4	85.2	111.0	82.3	101.9	93.3	86.4	91.2	94.6	87.9	92.5	90.4	104.2	94.8	83.4	61.3	76.4
8	DOORS, WINDOWS, GLASS	95.1	73.3	83.9	109.1	90.9	99.7	98.5	82.6	90.3	94.7	81.6	88.0	105.0	97.4	101.1	98.3	62.2	79.7
9.2	LATH & PLASTER	89.1	74.4	77.9	90.3	83.3	85.0	99.9	81.1	85.6	105.9	84.6	89.7	90.1	102.0	99.1	117.8	60.7	69.5
9.2	DRYWALL	107.8	75.0	92.5	116.5	85.0	101.8	94.4	77.7	86.6	107.2	79.7	94.4	99.6	99.9	99.7	114.8	63.0	90.6
9.5	ACOUSTICAL WORK	99.5	75.3	86.3	99.5	92.0	95.4	104.4	79.8	91.0	96.0	79.9	87.2	97.7	99.5	98.7	88.2	63.9	75.0
9.6	FLOORING	97.3	70.2	90.0	102.6	77.4	95.9	101.5	72.1	93.6	93.4	86.0	91.4	92.3	99.9	94.3	99.0	63.3	89.4
9.9	PAINTING	110.2	76.3	83.2	111.8	85.0	90.4	121.2	72.2	82.1	119.8	94.3	99.4	108.1	100.9	102.4	114.9	54.7	66.9
9	FINISHES	104.6	75.1	88.9	111.0	84.9	97.1	99.6	75.8	86.9	104.5	85.5	94.3	98.5	100.3	99.5	108.8	60.1	82.8
10-14	TOTAL DIV. 10-14	100.0	89.7	97.0	100.0	98.3	99.5	100.0	97.3	99.2	100.0	87.1	96.2	100.0	98.0	99.4	100.0	67.5	90.4
15	MECHANICAL	97.9	85.1	91.5	99.7	86.2	93.0	99.7	81.1	90.5	98.9	89.6	94.3	101.0	96.9	99.0	99.5	61.4	80.6
16	ELECTRICAL	94.1	80.2	84.5	100.6	87.2	91.4	99.3	95.1	96.4	97.9	89.3	91.9	93.7	103.6	100.5	95.5	64.0	73.8
1-16	WEIGHTED AVERAGE	99.1	82.0	90.0	105.5	87.9	96.1	99.9	86.5	92.7	102.2	88.7	95.0	98.9	99.0	99.0	97.9	66.4	81.1

DIVISION		MISSOURI						MONTANA						NEBRASKA					
		KANSAS CITY			ST LOUIS			BILLINGS			GREAT FALLS			LINCOLN			OMAHA		
		MAT.	INST.	TOTAL	MAT.	INST.	TOTAL	MAT.	INST.	TOTAL	MAT.	INST.	TOTAL	MAT.	INST.	TOTAL	MAT.	INST.	TOTAL
2	SITE WORK	91.4	104.4	97.2	83.5	96.7	89.3	99.5	95.0	97.5	94.1	94.1	94.1	103.9	87.9	96.8	113.8	94.6	105.3
3.1	FORMWORK	100.2	97.8	98.4	94.5	106.7	104.0	104.1	77.5	83.5	124.5	78.0	88.5	116.2	62.4	74.5	102.9	73.4	80.0
3.2	REINFORCING	78.7	97.6	86.3	83.1	102.8	91.1	112.5	79.5	99.1	112.7	79.5	99.3	107.4	69.4	92.0	96.8	69.4	85.7
3.3	CAST IN PLACE CONC.	95.2	94.9	95.0	81.7	101.1	93.4	103.3	94.3	97.8	115.0	93.7	102.1	104.6	91.9	96.9	93.6	93.6	93.6
3	CONCRETE	92.5	96.3	94.9	84.5	103.4	96.5	105.5	86.4	93.4	116.4	86.3	97.3	107.5	78.3	89.0	96.2	83.5	88.1
4	MASONRY	101.5	95.7	97.0	94.9	107.1	104.2	109.1	84.7	90.5	120.1	88.6	96.0	100.7	54.3	65.3	105.9	72.8	80.6
5	METALS	104.5	96.1	101.6	101.2	101.9	101.4	95.5	84.0	91.5	88.8	84.0	87.1	85.7	77.0	82.6	108.6	77.1	97.6
6	WOOD & PLASTICS	110.3	97.2	103.0	85.2	104.1	95.7	89.8	76.1	82.2	99.1	76.6	86.6	103.4	60.0	79.2	101.0	73.5	85.7
7	MOISTURE PROTECTION	102.1	102.1	102.1	93.4	103.9	96.7	100.1	75.4	92.3	102.2	74.7	93.5	88.5	63.3	80.5	105.7	72.4	95.2
8	DOORS, WINDOWS, GLASS	93.1	100.1	96.7	101.4	115.0	108.4	89.8	71.0	80.1	101.3	71.7	86.0	98.7	67.6	82.7	111.5	73.9	92.1
9.2	LATH & PLASTER	105.9	93.3	96.4	113.4	103.0	105.5	104.6	71.9	79.8	109.6	72.9	81.7	96.7	67.9	74.9	91.1	76.4	80.0
9.2	DRYWALL	97.5	96.4	97.0	95.0	104.0	99.2	103.5	73.3	89.4	106.0	74.0	91.1	90.1	65.5	78.7	92.0	73.9	83.6
9.5	ACOUSTICAL WORK	107.2	96.7	101.5	101.1	104.4	102.9	100.1	75.2	86.5	100.8	75.8	87.1	88.8	58.5	72.3	93.9	72.6	82.3
9.6	FLOORING	96.0	102.4	97.7	101.7	103.8	102.3	97.9	73.8	91.4	105.6	85.2	100.1	110.3	58.9	96.5	103.8	71.2	95.1
9.9	PAINTING	74.7	97.2	92.7	99.6	107.1	105.6	121.0	72.4	82.2	115.8	74.0	82.5	101.3	66.9	73.9	89.0	66.9	71.4
9	FINISHES	95.9	96.9	96.4	97.8	105.1	101.7	103.7	73.1	87.4	106.5	74.9	89.7	95.7	65.1	79.4	94.4	71.3	82.1
10-14	TOTAL DIV. 10-14	100.0	99.3	99.3	100.0	103.4	101.0	100.0	86.3	95.9	100.0	86.4	96.0	100.0	78.4	93.6	100.0	80.7	94.3
15	MECHANICAL	102.6	98.8	100.7	97.6	109.4	103.5	99.3	93.6	96.5	98.8	88.0	93.4	99.7	61.2	80.6	99.9	74.3	87.2
16	ELECTRICAL	104.4	100.4	101.7	103.2	115.4	111.6	98.8	87.0	90.6	98.3	86.2	89.9	96.5	75.1	81.7	92.3	77.7	82.2
1-16	WEIGHTED AVERAGE	99.2	98.1	98.6	95.5	107.0	101.6	100.1	85.2	92.1	102.5	84.4	93.0	98.5	69.0	82.8	101.5	77.4	88.6

DIVISION		NEVADA						NEW HAMPSHIRE						NEW JERSEY					
		LAS VEGAS			RENO			MANCHESTER			NASHUA			JERSEY CITY			NEWARK		
		MAT.	INST.	TOTAL	MAT.	INST.	TOTAL	MAT.	INST.	TOTAL	MAT.	INST.	TOTAL	MAT.	INST.	TOTAL	MAT.	INST.	TOTAL
2	SITE WORK	90.5	108.0	98.3	90.5	104.7	96.8	91.8	88.8	90.4	98.6	93.2	96.2	113.0	106.1	109.9	107.2	106.4	106.8
3.1	FORMWORK	112.6	111.6	111.8	109.1	104.3	105.4	113.1	78.5	86.3	111.9	79.1	86.5	113.7	111.6	112.1	123.6	111.7	114.4
3.2	REINFORCING	118.4	128.4	122.4	77.4	128.4	98.0	117.8	85.6	104.7	117.8	85.6	104.7	109.2	134.4	119.4	109.2	134.4	119.4
3.3	CAST IN PLACE CONC.	98.8	108.9	104.9	109.3	106.1	107.4	93.1	85.3	88.4	100.5	95.9	97.7	98.9	104.7	102.4	105.6	98.9	101.5
3	CONCRETE	105.9	111.7	109.5	102.1	107.4	105.4	102.5	82.6	89.9	106.6	88.4	95.1	104.1	110.0	107.9	109.9	107.1	108.1
4	MASONRY	108.5	96.3	99.2	123.8	90.2	98.1	103.1	78.0	83.9	107.1	78.0	84.9	106.8	98.6	100.6	110.6	100.7	103.0
5	METALS	110.9	121.7	114.7	97.8	121.6	106.2	100.6	85.3	95.3	88.1	88.9	88.4	100.9	123.9	108.9	98.3	122.5	106.7
6	WOOD & PLASTICS	88.5	109.7	100.3	88.0	102.8	96.2	105.2	77.1	89.5	110.7	78.6	92.9	111.7	109.3	110.4	109.5	109.5	109.5
7	MOISTURE PROTECTION	88.8	113.4	96.6	102.9	108.5	104.6	96.6	110.1	100.9	102.2	110.2	104.7	118.0	115.6	117.2	105.1	112.4	107.4
8	DOORS, WINDOWS, GLASS	94.5	111.2	103.1	99.9	106.8	103.5	101.9	80.5	90.9	96.5	80.5	88.3	98.9	117.0	108.2	100.7	115.6	108.4
9.2	LATH & PLASTER	86.8	107.8	102.7	101.5	105.7	104.7	110.6	77.8	85.7	110.4	77.6	85.5	108.1	107.4	107.6	99.7	101.5	101.0
9.2	DRYWALL	92.6	109.7	100.6	99.4	112.7	105.6	113.5	73.9	95.0	114.7	73.9	95.7	108.1	107.4	107.8	100.7	109.7	108.8
9.5	ACOUSTICAL WORK	110.0	110.1	110.1	101.3	102.9	102.2	106.3	76.2	89.9	106.3	76.2	89.9	100.6	109.6	105.5	100.6	109.8	105.6
9.6	FLOORING	118.5	100.6	113.7	98.6	85.3	95.1	83.7	79.7	82.6	88.5	79.7	86.1	105.4	102.6	104.6	98.7	104.4	100.2
9.9	PAINTING	105.5	112.9	111.4	114.8	99.1	102.3	126.8	63.1	76.0	105.7	63.1	71.7	92.7	112.3	108.4	89.7	112.3	107.7
9	FINISHES	100.9	110.1	105.8	101.0	104.8	103.0	107.6	71.0	88.1	107.2	71.0	87.9	105.2	109.1	107.3	104.4	108.8	106.7
10-14	TOTAL DIV. 10-14	100.0	104.3	101.2	100.0	128.7	108.4	100.0	90.3	97.1	100.0	90.3	97.1	100.0	105.5	101.6	100.0	105.3	101.5
15	MECHANICAL	100.0	107.2	103.6	102.9	102.6	102.8	97.0	83.4	90.3	98.5	83.5	91.0	99.9	104.0	101.9	97.1	101.7	99.4
16	ELECTRICAL	103.2	108.4	106.8	108.6	108.7	108.6	101.9	76.7	84.5	98.0	76.7	83.3	96.6	113.7	108.4	97.4	111.0	106.8
1-16	WEIGHTED AVERAGE	100.7	108.0	104.6	102.0	105.4	103.8	100.2	81.6	90.3	100.5	83.2	91.3	103.5	108.4	106.1	102.5	107.0	104.9

CITY COST INDEXES

		NEW JERSEY						NEW MEXICO			NEW YORK								
	DIVISION	PATERSON			TRENTON			ALBUQUERQUE			ALBANY			BINGHAMTON			BUFFALO		
		MAT.	INST.	TOTAL	MAT.	INST.	TOTAL	MAT.	INST.	TOTAL	MAT.	INST.	TOTAL	MAT.	INST.	TOTAL	MAT.	INST.	TOTAL
2	SITE WORK	116.2	105.2	111.3	107.0	107.3	107.1	108.5	91.1	100.8	103.3	101.1	102.3	92.8	87.4	90.4	99.7	99.3	99.5
3.1	FORMWORK	109.5	108.3	108.6	124.3	110.1	113.3	125.7	75.4	86.7	117.2	94.1	99.3	111.7	82.5	89.1	122.2	115.9	117.3
3.2	REINFORCING	108.8	134.4	119.2	109.2	112.1	110.4	117.8	75.0	100.4	80.1	90.4	84.3	80.1	86.1	82.6	97.1	104.5	100.1
3.3	CAST IN PLACE CONC.	102.2	102.0	102.1	89.1	103.1	97.6	101.9	100.4	100.9	77.7	99.8	91.1	91.1	98.3	95.5	108.8	100.0	103.5
3	CONCRETE	105.1	107.3	106.5	100.5	106.7	104.4	110.1	88.3	96.3	86.0	96.7	92.8	92.7	91.0	91.7	108.8	106.7	107.5
4	MASONRY	110.0	128.3	124.0	105.2	100.5	101.6	103.0	74.7	81.4	87.7	92.6	91.4	100.5	81.8	86.2	99.4	116.2	112.3
5	METALS	96.1	123.9	105.8	98.2	110.4	102.5	107.5	83.4	99.1	97.1	95.6	96.6	99.2	89.9	96.0	104.4	103.2	104.0
6	WOOD & PLASTICS	117.5	109.5	113.0	120.2	110.4	114.8	100.3	77.9	87.8	96.8	92.7	94.5	103.8	79.6	90.3	112.4	117.2	115.1
7	MOISTURE PROTECTION	114.4	111.0	113.3	102.9	119.3	108.1	97.5	66.6	87.7	105.8	94.9	102.4	97.5	87.4	94.3	100.7	109.6	103.5
8	DOORS, WINDOWS, GLASS	98.8	121.7	110.6	104.9	113.0	109.1	99.6	73.4	86.1	104.3	86.6	95.1	99.5	76.2	87.5	96.2	108.8	102.7
9.2	LATH & PLASTER	99.6	108.1	106.1	115.4	104.7	107.3	119.1	75.5	86.0	106.2	92.9	96.1	109.1	83.4	89.6	111.0	107.6	108.4
9.2	DRYWALL	113.1	107.5	110.5	109.5	107.2	108.4	85.5	76.8	81.5	106.0	92.1	99.5	113.6	78.6	97.3	123.7	117.8	121.0
9.5	ACOUSTICAL WORK	100.6	109.8	105.6	97.0	109.3	103.7	92.1	77.1	83.9	111.2	92.4	101.0	110.6	78.9	93.3	116.1	118.3	117.3
9.6	FLOORING	90.8	128.9	101.0	101.1	104.2	101.9	104.0	69.4	94.7	86.0	86.6	86.2	99.4	83.4	95.1	104.0	109.5	105.4
9.9	PAINTING	100.0	112.3	109.8	96.5	112.3	109.1	110.2	69.8	78.0	116.9	88.8	94.5	103.5	78.8	83.8	112.4	109.5	110.1
9	FINISHES	105.6	110.9	108.4	105.5	108.8	107.2	93.3	73.8	82.9	103.1	90.6	96.4	109.1	79.3	93.2	117.3	113.8	115.4
10-14	TOTAL DIV. 10-14	100.0	106.0	101.7	100.0	114.7	104.3	100.0	82.9	95.0	100.0	93.7	98.1	100.0	89.3	96.8	100.0	102.3	100.6
15	MECHANICAL	99.9	104.0	101.9	99.7	111.5	105.6	100.4	89.7	95.1	95.8	88.9	92.4	100.1	76.4	88.3	97.4	96.2	96.8
16	ELECTRICAL	96.6	122.2	114.3	94.7	123.9	114.9	94.8	84.1	87.4	92.3	89.7	90.5	92.1	78.7	82.9	99.1	104.2	102.6
1-16	WEIGHTED AVERAGE	103.4	113.5	108.8	101.6	110.4	106.3	101.7	82.7	91.5	96.8	92.5	94.5	98.7	82.9	90.3	102.7	106.2	104.6

		NEW YORK															NORTH CAROLINA		
	DIVISION	NEW YORK			ROCHESTER			SYRACUSE			UTICA			YONKERS			CHARLOTTE		
		MAT.	INST.	TOTAL	MAT.	INST.	TOTAL	MAT.	INST.	TOTAL	MAT.	INST.	TOTAL	MAT.	INST.	TOTAL	MAT.	INST.	TOTAL
2	SITE WORK	118.2	124.9	121.2	108.2	96.6	103.1	97.1	94.6	96.0	116.4	93.6	106.3	123.4	113.3	118.9	115.4	84.3	101.6
3.1	FORMWORK	111.0	156.3	146.1	107.8	106.4	106.7	110.5	88.1	93.1	113.5	75.0	83.7	115.5	120.5	119.3	109.8	60.8	71.8
3.2	REINFORCING	101.7	171.9	130.2	106.5	103.5	105.3	106.5	100.0	103.8	106.5	82.9	96.9	80.1	128.9	99.9	87.8	65.7	78.8
3.3	CAST IN PLACE CONC.	152.5	112.3	128.1	126.8	99.2	110.1	103.1	78.3	88.1	84.0	96.1	91.3	116.4	103.5	108.6	110.7	94.2	100.7
3	CONCRETE	133.0	134.9	134.2	118.5	102.4	108.3	105.3	84.1	91.9	94.8	86.6	89.6	108.1	112.4	110.8	105.4	78.5	88.4
4	MASONRY	104.4	145.0	135.4	102.1	108.3	106.9	102.1	84.3	88.5	100.0	78.7	83.7	122.7	109.1	112.3	90.1	48.8	58.5
5	METALS	104.7	148.3	119.9	102.0	101.1	101.7	103.1	92.1	99.3	103.9	89.2	98.7	97.5	121.3	105.8	100.3	79.1	92.9
6	WOOD & PLASTICS	111.8	155.3	136.0	98.1	106.2	102.6	107.2	85.8	95.3	112.7	74.2	91.3	103.5	122.8	114.2	104.9	63.3	81.7
7	MOISTURE PROTECTION	110.1	157.2	125.0	97.4	108.7	101.0	96.6	100.8	98.0	97.6	96.6	97.2	105.7	141.6	117.0	88.7	46.2	75.3
8	DOORS, WINDOWS, GLASS	98.2	155.5	127.7	97.0	100.8	99.0	98.0	86.0	91.8	103.6	75.2	88.9	105.3	129.8	117.9	96.0	60.0	77.5
9.2	LATH & PLASTER	87.9	127.8	118.2	107.7	97.3	99.8	106.2	97.5	99.6	109.4	80.1	87.2	93.6	115.7	110.4	100.0	52.2	63.7
9.2	DRYWALL	119.4	147.5	132.5	94.2	100.0	96.9	108.7	85.0	97.7	110.4	73.0	93.0	97.5	123.6	109.6	88.1	61.7	75.8
9.5	ACOUSTICAL WORK	102.6	157.7	132.7	115.7	106.6	110.8	98.8	85.3	91.4	115.7	73.3	92.6	115.7	123.6	120.0	92.2	62.0	75.7
9.6	FLOORING	99.0	136.9	109.1	93.6	101.9	95.8	86.3	78.4	84.2	87.8	73.5	84.0	102.3	117.9	106.4	90.6	47.9	79.2
9.9	PAINTING	118.2	139.4	135.1	98.2	104.7	103.3	103.2	87.9	91.0	108.6	90.2	93.9	107.7	86.9	91.1	96.8	61.4	68.6
9	FINISHES	112.8	143.6	129.2	96.5	102.1	99.5	102.4	86.3	93.8	105.6	79.4	91.6	100.9	110.0	105.8	90.1	60.1	74.1
10-14	TOTAL DIV. 10-14	100.0	116.1	104.7	100.0	103.1	100.9	100.0	97.3	99.2	100.0	92.5	97.8	100.0	111.1	103.2	100.0	69.7	91.1
15	MECHANICAL	99.3	149.7	124.4	97.2	99.7	98.5	100.8	90.3	95.6	99.2	85.3	92.3	96.5	110.8	103.6	97.1	65.1	81.2
16	ELECTRICAL	95.7	151.3	134.1	98.3	102.6	101.3	98.7	90.2	92.8	95.7	78.4	83.8	104.0	111.0	108.8	98.0	60.0	71.8
1-16	WEIGHTED AVERAGE	108.1	143.4	126.9	102.0	102.7	102.4	101.0	88.3	94.2	100.9	83.6	91.7	103.9	113.6	109.1	98.6	65.3	80.8

		NORTH CAROLINA						OHIO											
	DIVISION	GREENSBORO			RALEIGH			AKRON			CANTON			CINCINNATI			CLEVELAND		
		MAT.	INST.	TOTAL	MAT.	INST.	TOTAL	MAT.	INST.	TOTAL	MAT.	INST.	TOTAL	MAT.	INST.	TOTAL	MAT.	INST.	TOTAL
2	SITE WORK	90.6	88.6	89.7	99.3	91.9	96.1	117.0	99.8	109.4	105.1	98.0	101.9	92.8	101.5	96.6	121.8	107.1	115.3
3.1	FORMWORK	99.8	60.8	69.6	104.3	60.8	70.6	111.4	104.7	106.2	110.2	99.6	102.0	99.9	97.9	98.4	120.4	118.6	119.0
3.2	REINFORCING	82.2	68.1	76.5	93.8	68.1	83.4	98.2	111.1	103.4	98.2	93.4	96.3	106.3	94.7	101.6	85.4	111.1	95.8
3.3	CAST IN PLACE CONC.	99.5	91.9	94.9	107.2	96.8	100.9	89.7	101.4	96.7	89.7	100.8	96.4	87.5	97.8	93.7	93.7	111.9	104.7
3	CONCRETE	95.7	77.6	84.3	103.6	80.1	88.7	95.8	103.5	100.7	95.6	99.7	98.2	94.1	97.6	96.3	97.1	114.5	108.1
4	MASONRY	103.0	48.8	61.6	89.4	48.8	58.4	93.4	102.3	100.2	107.6	98.3	100.5	74.6	91.5	87.5	95.4	115.8	111.0
5	METALS	91.2	79.7	87.2	91.1	81.4	87.7	99.0	105.8	101.4	99.0	95.2	97.7	98.5	95.0	97.3	105.0	110.0	106.7
6	WOOD & PLASTICS	91.8	63.3	75.9	95.1	63.3	77.4	104.6	105.0	104.8	103.2	100.1	101.5	109.0	96.2	101.9	142.9	116.5	128.2
7	MOISTURE PROTECTION	86.7	46.2	73.9	87.2	46.2	74.2	99.0	105.6	101.1	99.0	104.7	100.8	96.1	102.3	98.0	108.3	120.6	112.2
8	DOORS, WINDOWS, GLASS	91.0	61.5	75.8	85.4	61.5	73.1	101.0	110.5	105.9	88.8	88.8	88.8	96.9	93.1	95.0	94.2	114.8	104.8
9.2	LATH & PLASTER	97.8	63.2	71.5	106.6	56.9	68.9	116.1	103.9	106.8	112.3	89.7	95.1	103.1	95.1	97.0	105.1	117.2	114.3
9.2	DRYWALL	86.0	61.7	74.7	95.6	61.7	79.8	112.9	104.8	109.1	110.9	96.7	104.3	98.2	95.8	97.1	101.3	116.4	108.3
9.5	ACOUSTICAL WORK	97.7	62.0	78.2	108.8	62.0	83.3	82.6	105.1	94.9	101.6	100.1	100.8	96.6	96.2	96.4	98.2	116.9	108.4
9.6	FLOORING	90.0	47.9	78.8	102.0	47.9	87.6	82.3	100.4	87.2	114.1	93.6	108.6	91.1	94.3	92.0	84.9	116.9	93.4
9.9	PAINTING	91.0	61.4	67.4	90.4	61.4	67.3	107.7	103.8	104.6	101.5	93.8	95.3	103.0	90.9	93.3	104.5	117.0	114.5
9	FINISHES	88.5	60.7	73.7	97.8	60.4	77.8	103.3	104.1	103.7	110.0	95.3	102.2	97.1	94.0	95.4	97.8	116.7	107.9
10-14	TOTAL DIV. 10-14	100.0	71.5	91.6	100.0	71.8	91.7	100.0	102.9	100.8	100.0	99.9	99.9	100.0	93.6	98.1	100.0	111.5	103.3
15	MECHANICAL	95.6	65.3	80.5	97.0	65.3	81.2	99.2	96.9	98.1	99.3	85.4	92.4	99.3	92.5	95.9	101.3	106.5	103.9
16	ELECTRICAL	97.5	63.9	74.3	99.4	63.9	74.9	94.4	96.5	95.8	93.3	88.2	89.7	99.9	90.3	93.3	96.3	106.7	103.5
1-16	WEIGHTED AVERAGE	94.3	66.1	79.2	96.3	66.8	80.6	99.9	101.7	100.9	99.6	94.3	96.8	96.5	94.2	95.3	101.9	112.0	107.3

CITY COST INDEXES

DIVISION		OHIO - COLUMBUS			OHIO - DAYTON			OHIO - LORAIN			OHIO - TOLEDO			OHIO - YOUNGSTOWN			OKLAHOMA - OKLAHOMA CITY		
		MAT.	INST.	TOTAL	MAT.	INST.	TOTAL	MAT.	INST.	TOTAL	MAT.	INST.	TOTAL	MAT.	INST.	TOTAL	MAT.	INST.	TOTAL
2	SITE WORK	89.6	104.4	96.2	91.4	98.0	94.3	104.9	100.8	103.1	124.2	99.7	113.4	97.2	99.5	98.2	122.8	86.5	106.7
3.1	FORMWORK	105.2	93.7	96.3	118.7	92.5	98.4	110.5	99.7	102.2	116.5	108.8	110.5	108.4	95.3	98.3	116.1	72.6	82.4
3.2	REINFORCING	116.3	99.0	109.3	98.2	93.4	96.3	98.2	111.1	103.4	98.2	99.4	98.7	98.2	95.2	97.0	94.3	65.6	82.7
3.3	CAST IN PLACE CONC.	96.4	96.8	96.7	105.9	98.6	101.4	95.4	99.3	97.7	92.8	100.4	97.4	82.4	100.1	93.1	100.6	90.3	94.4
3	CONCRETE	102.6	95.8	98.3	106.7	95.7	99.8	99.0	100.5	99.9	98.7	103.6	101.8	91.0	97.8	95.3	102.2	81.2	88.9
4	MASONRY	90.3	95.6	94.3	86.2	91.9	90.6	101.6	93.7	95.6	109.6	94.5	98.0	95.9	92.5	93.3	99.9	82.6	86.7
5	METALS	101.6	98.0	100.3	101.0	95.0	98.9	98.8	107.9	102.0	98.8	98.6	98.7	98.4	96.5	97.7	94.3	74.6	87.4
6	WOOD & PLASTICS	107.2	92.7	99.1	108.8	91.7	99.3	99.6	98.7	99.1	119.4	111.4	114.9	106.4	93.5	99.2	115.2	76.3	93.6
7	MOISTURE PROTECTION	98.8	96.6	98.1	100.8	92.4	98.1	97.6	111.5	102.0	91.5	102.9	95.1	101.1	98.9	100.4	94.4	72.2	87.4
8	DOORS, WINDOWS, GLASS	97.2	92.2	94.6	107.9	86.5	96.9	96.3	106.7	101.7	100.3	100.6	100.5	97.7	92.9	95.2	103.1	72.0	87.1
9.2	LATH & PLASTER	91.4	92.1	91.9	110.9	92.8	97.1	110.5	93.3	97.4	115.1	98.5	102.5	115.6	93.3	98.6	99.5	78.2	83.3
9.2	DRYWALL	105.7	92.5	99.6	112.7	92.6	103.3	108.0	98.3	103.5	109.8	110.7	110.2	96.3	92.9	94.7	108.6	75.2	93.0
9.5	ACOUSTICAL WORK	101.8	92.9	96.9	86.8	91.2	89.2	91.8	98.7	95.5	115.0	111.1	112.9	95.5	93.2	94.3	86.8	75.5	80.6
9.6	FLOORING	95.9	89.6	94.3	113.6	87.1	106.5	118.5	96.7	112.7	99.7	94.0	98.1	88.2	92.6	89.3	107.1	80.1	99.9
9.9	PAINTING	105.6	98.5	99.9	84.3	93.3	91.5	103.4	117.0	114.2	115.1	92.2	96.8	74.6	98.1	93.3	105.7	76.9	82.7
9	FINISHES	102.9	94.4	98.4	108.0	92.3	99.6	108.6	104.4	106.4	108.6	102.4	105.3	92.7	94.7	93.8	106.1	76.3	90.2
10-14	TOTAL DIV. 10-14	100.0	97.0	99.1	100.0	93.3	98.0	100.0	108.3	102.4	100.0	104.1	101.2	100.0	97.1	99.1	100.0	79.3	93.9
15	MECHANICAL	102.1	97.7	99.9	98.8	88.9	93.9	99.0	89.7	94.4	99.0	98.3	98.7	99.8	90.0	95.0	94.2	78.5	86.4
16	ELECTRICAL	92.5	93.3	93.0	98.2	91.0	93.2	97.3	90.2	92.4	99.1	97.7	98.2	97.3	94.0	95.0	102.8	81.3	87.9
1-16	WEIGHTED AVERAGE	99.5	95.9	97.6	100.9	92.3	96.3	100.2	98.0	99.0	102.0	100.1	100.9	97.3	94.5	95.8	100.7	79.5	89.4

DIVISION		OKLAHOMA - TULSA			OREGON - EUGENE			OREGON - PORTLAND			PENNSYLVANIA - ALLENTOWN			PENNSYLVANIA - ERIE			PENNSYLVANIA - HARRISBURG		
		MAT.	INST.	TOTAL	MAT.	INST.	TOTAL	MAT.	INST.	TOTAL	MAT.	INST.	TOTAL	MAT.	INST.	TOTAL	MAT.	INST.	TOTAL
2	SITE WORK	90.5	91.9	91.2	96.7	105.8	100.7	110.4	102.3	106.8	126.5	99.8	114.6	120.3	97.2	110.0	97.6	97.5	97.6
3.1	FORMWORK	125.2	71.8	83.8	120.7	94.4	100.3	122.5	96.2	102.1	110.5	111.1	111.0	90.4	95.0	94.0	113.6	90.4	95.6
3.2	REINFORCING	91.4	65.6	80.9	101.3	104.9	102.8	101.3	104.9	102.8	114.7	117.0	115.6	117.6	90.8	106.7	114.7	105.5	111.0
3.3	CAST IN PLACE CONC.	88.4	95.1	92.4	100.7	124.1	114.8	116.8	99.9	106.5	103.2	100.8	101.7	83.4	99.2	93.0	104.4	103.2	103.7
3	CONCRETE	96.3	83.3	88.1	104.7	110.7	108.5	114.4	98.9	104.6	107.2	106.3	106.6	92.4	96.8	95.2	108.5	98.4	102.1
4	MASONRY	95.8	71.7	77.4	114.6	93.2	98.3	126.7	98.5	105.2	86.0	105.8	101.1	105.4	94.1	96.8	82.6	88.8	87.3
5	METALS	104.9	76.0	94.8	103.4	111.8	106.3	107.0	103.0	105.6	104.7	109.7	106.5	100.9	92.9	98.1	96.6	105.0	99.3
6	WOOD & PLASTICS	116.9	75.5	93.8	92.2	92.2	92.2	89.2	94.4	92.1	104.2	113.1	109.2	89.4	94.6	92.3	110.1	91.7	99.8
7	MOISTURE PROTECTION	96.7	71.0	88.6	86.6	86.4	86.5	86.5	91.1	88.0	96.8	116.4	103.0	97.4	98.2	97.6	79.2	91.7	83.2
8	DOORS, WINDOWS, GLASS	100.5	70.3	84.9	101.9	95.4	98.6	107.6	96.4	101.8	102.5	101.0	101.7	92.2	90.7	91.5	104.1	89.7	96.7
9.2	LATH & PLASTER	99.7	74.1	80.3	113.1	86.7	93.1	117.9	93.1	99.1	99.5	96.6	97.3	110.4	88.8	94.0	96.5	86.8	89.1
9.2	DRYWALL	111.7	74.3	94.3	112.0	87.9	100.8	110.2	89.6	100.6	107.0	101.1	104.2	94.0	93.9	94.0	107.3	90.9	99.6
9.5	ACOUSTICAL WORK	86.8	74.6	80.1	110.5	91.9	100.4	110.5	94.2	101.6	100.6	113.4	107.6	100.2	94.2	96.9	98.8	91.2	94.7
9.6	FLOORING	111.0	82.6	103.4	123.2	95.3	115.7	102.8	98.7	101.7	97.1	104.0	98.9	102.7	85.9	98.2	97.0	85.7	94.0
9.9	PAINTING	79.1	76.6	77.1	119.8	82.4	90.0	97.5	82.4	85.5	104.6	98.9	100.0	88.7	79.4	81.3	91.5	75.1	78.4
9	FINISHES	106.1	75.7	89.9	115.2	86.8	100.0	107.5	88.3	97.3	103.9	101.3	102.5	96.3	88.0	91.9	102.5	84.8	93.1
10-14	TOTAL DIV. 10-14	100.0	77.5	93.4	100.0	91.6	97.5	100.0	100.9	100.2	100.0	100.9	100.2	100.0	93.0	97.9	100.0	91.4	97.4
15	MECHANICAL	96.8	81.8	89.4	98.7	94.1	96.4	98.2	96.7	97.4	100.3	101.8	101.1	99.8	89.1	94.5	101.1	91.4	96.3
16	ELECTRICAL	100.4	76.6	84.0	102.7	86.8	91.7	102.7	103.7	103.4	98.5	82.0	87.1	90.3	94.9	93.4	92.9	82.9	86.0
1-16	WEIGHTED AVERAGE	99.1	78.3	88.0	101.9	97.3	99.4	104.5	98.0	101.0	102.7	101.6	102.1	98.6	93.3	95.8	98.8	91.6	95.0

DIVISION		PENNSYLVANIA - PHILADELPHIA			PENNSYLVANIA - PITTSBURGH			PENNSYLVANIA - READING			PENNSYLVANIA - SCRANTON			RHODE ISLAND - PROVIDENCE			SOUTH CAROLINA - CHARLESTON		
		MAT.	INST.	TOTAL	MAT.	INST.	TOTAL	MAT.	INST.	TOTAL	MAT.	INST.	TOTAL	MAT.	INST.	TOTAL	MAT.	INST.	TOTAL
2	SITE WORK	103.3	108.8	105.7	128.5	100.4	116.0	87.2	97.2	91.7	102.8	105.2	103.8	83.6	104.4	92.9	122.0	83.5	104.9
3.1	FORMWORK	93.4	122.6	116.0	103.1	97.9	99.1	110.9	86.4	91.9	107.5	91.2	94.9	115.9	118.0	117.5	104.4	54.9	66.0
3.2	REINFORCING	83.3	117.0	96.9	83.1	106.1	92.4	114.7	104.6	110.6	114.7	102.9	109.9	117.8	111.8	115.4	96.0	65.6	83.7
3.3	CAST IN PLACE CONC.	92.5	106.2	100.8	111.1	95.6	101.7	98.0	96.5	97.1	92.4	123.5	111.2	87.5	106.1	98.8	100.8	87.3	92.6
3	CONCRETE	90.6	113.6	105.2	103.3	97.4	99.6	104.2	93.2	97.3	100.3	109.0	105.8	99.8	111.3	107.1	100.4	72.6	82.8
4	MASONRY	90.8	117.0	110.8	100.3	102.7	102.1	90.2	87.8	88.4	105.3	87.8	91.9	101.1	96.2	97.3	92.2	51.0	60.7
5	METALS	103.3	115.3	107.5	100.8	103.2	101.6	96.3	102.2	98.3	98.3	110.8	102.7	111.6	105.6	109.5	99.0	74.5	90.4
6	WOOD & PLASTICS	92.0	122.7	109.1	110.8	98.6	104.0	100.3	86.3	92.5	101.8	88.6	94.5	91.4	111.2	102.4	98.7	58.5	76.3
7	MOISTURE PROTECTION	102.8	124.1	109.5	96.4	104.7	99.0	88.0	109.0	94.6	98.7	95.5	97.7	106.2	104.1	105.5	91.1	58.5	80.8
8	DOORS, WINDOWS, GLASS	94.1	121.5	108.2	101.0	104.7	102.9	103.8	86.4	94.8	92.9	85.7	89.2	110.3	102.9	106.5	101.0	57.0	78.3
9.2	LATH & PLASTER	97.3	120.2	114.7	106.4	95.9	98.4	95.1	80.0	83.7	101.0	84.1	88.2	106.3	96.3	98.7	94.0	55.1	64.5
9.2	DRYWALL	110.9	123.4	116.7	113.3	98.3	106.3	109.3	80.0	95.7	104.5	84.6	95.3	95.9	104.7	100.0	108.0	57.0	84.3
9.5	ACOUSTICAL WORK	92.9	124.0	109.8	103.1	98.3	100.7	99.8	85.6	91.6	99.7	88.0	93.3	103.8	111.6	108.1	95.0	57.0	74.3
9.6	FLOORING	97.0	107.9	99.9	113.0	101.9	110.0	103.1	83.6	97.9	100.4	83.9	96.0	88.7	98.3	91.3	89.0	52.0	79.1
9.9	PAINTING	121.7	120.3	120.6	82.6	104.7	100.2	90.0	85.2	86.2	109.5	88.4	92.7	105.5	97.0	98.7	112.0	61.4	71.6
9	FINISHES	107.2	121.1	114.6	109.2	100.6	104.7	104.9	82.5	93.0	103.6	86.1	94.3	96.1	101.7	99.1	102.9	58.1	79.0
10-14	TOTAL DIV. 10-14	100.0	112.8	103.7	100.0	98.7	99.6	100.0	97.4	99.2	100.0	93.6	98.1	100.0	104.4	101.2	100.0	70.1	91.2
15	MECHANICAL	96.1	110.5	103.3	98.5	96.4	97.5	99.3	102.2	100.7	99.1	90.1	94.6	99.8	91.8	95.8	98.4	61.3	80.0
16	ELECTRICAL	98.2	114.6	109.5	95.3	93.6	94.1	94.4	89.6	91.1	98.4	88.7	91.7	99.4	94.7	96.1	98.5	55.6	68.9
1-16	WEIGHTED AVERAGE	98.1	115.1	107.2	102.5	98.9	100.6	98.3	93.3	95.6	99.9	94.9	97.2	100.5	101.0	100.8	100.1	62.8	80.2

CITY COST INDEXES

DIVISION		SOUTH CAROLINA COLUMBIA			SOUTH DAKOTA SIOUX FALLS			TENNESSEE CHATTANOOGA			TENNESSEE KNOXVILLE			TENNESSEE MEMPHIS			TENNESSEE NASHVILLE		
		MAT.	INST.	TOTAL	MAT.	INST.	TOTAL	MAT.	INST.	TOTAL	MAT.	INST.	TOTAL	MAT.	INST.	TOTAL	MAT.	INST.	TOTAL
2	SITE WORK	111.8	89.5	101.9	93.5	83.5	89.1	98.4	86.2	93.0	102.5	93.2	98.4	86.5	90.9	88.5	84.1	88.9	86.2
3.1	FORMWORK	89.6	59.1	65.9	105.1	58.8	69.2	106.2	71.7	79.5	107.0	65.9	75.1	88.5	70.8	74.8	88.1	69.5	73.7
3.2	REINFORCING	91.4	65.6	81.0	105.0	64.0	88.4	98.2	70.4	87.0	98.2	64.8	84.7	97.1	68.6	85.5	97.1	67.0	84.9
3.3	CAST IN PLACE CONC.	81.1	91.9	87.7	98.6	81.6	88.3	81.7	90.5	87.0	85.8	88.7	87.5	93.3	92.9	93.0	85.2	85.6	85.4
3	CONCRETE	85.1	76.7	79.8	101.3	71.1	82.2	90.2	81.4	84.6	92.7	77.6	83.1	93.2	82.1	86.1	88.4	77.6	81.6
4	MASONRY	87.3	51.3	59.8	106.9	68.0	77.2	78.8	78.2	78.4	79.9	69.0	71.6	86.5	73.2	76.3	92.5	74.7	78.9
5	METALS	104.6	76.5	94.8	107.2	70.5	94.4	91.6	76.7	86.4	103.3	73.2	92.8	91.0	75.8	85.7	99.1	73.8	90.2
6	WOOD & PLASTICS	86.0	63.6	73.6	97.9	57.9	75.7	105.8	74.3	88.3	107.3	68.1	85.5	83.9	72.4	77.5	107.7	72.1	87.9
7	MOISTURE PROTECTION	102.0	57.5	88.0	98.4	61.7	86.8	103.2	67.8	92.0	87.8	61.5	79.5	96.7	73.7	89.4	101.6	68.5	91.1
8	DOORS, WINDOWS, GLASS	102.4	59.4	80.2	103.4	54.6	78.2	103.7	68.7	85.6	107.4	61.8	83.9	95.2	75.4	85.0	94.1	70.7	82.0
9.2	LATH & PLASTER	104.7	54.8	66.8	110.2	64.9	75.8	93.8	70.9	76.4	92.0	68.5	74.2	90.3	79.4	82.1	89.7	69.1	74.1
9.2	DRYWALL	83.5	60.2	72.7	105.9	55.6	82.5	109.6	73.1	92.6	107.6	67.4	88.9	96.3	80.7	89.0	102.8	70.7	87.8
9.5	ACOUSTICAL WORK	93.9	62.3	76.7	101.8	55.8	76.7	97.7	73.4	84.4	89.9	67.1	77.5	99.6	71.5	84.2	99.5	70.9	83.9
9.6	FLOORING	94.7	52.6	83.4	111.8	68.0	100.1	109.0	79.5	101.1	100.9	69.3	92.5	100.7	66.2	91.5	129.0	76.0	114.8
9.9	PAINTING	121.2	61.4	73.5	112.8	53.8	65.7	91.0	66.8	71.7	94.6	72.0	76.5	91.4	79.5	81.9	94.4	69.5	74.5
9	FINISHES	91.0	59.9	74.4	107.7	56.5	80.4	106.3	71.3	87.6	103.1	69.1	85.0	96.9	78.4	87.0	107.2	70.6	87.7
10-14	TOTAL DIV. 10-14	100.0	70.2	91.2	100.0	74.2	92.4	100.0	75.1	92.7	100.0	73.6	92.2	100.0	79.4	93.9	100.0	73.7	92.2
15	MECHANICAL	99.8	62.6	81.3	99.2	57.9	78.7	99.0	73.1	86.2	99.9	70.3	85.2	100.2	81.1	90.7	97.2	72.8	85.1
16	ELECTRICAL	104.4	58.7	72.8	96.7	67.0	76.2	94.5	74.2	80.5	96.1	72.8	80.0	108.7	87.3	94.0	100.0	67.8	77.7
1-16	WEIGHTED AVERAGE	97.8	65.1	80.3	101.2	65.6	82.2	97.2	76.0	85.9	98.1	72.4	84.4	96.2	80.1	87.6	96.9	73.8	84.5

DIVISION		TEXAS AMARILLO			TEXAS AUSTIN			TEXAS BEAUMONT			TEXAS CORPUS CHRISTI			TEXAS DALLAS			TEXAS EL PASO		
		MAT.	INST.	TOTAL	MAT.	INST.	TOTAL	MAT.	INST.	TOTAL	MAT.	INST.	TOTAL	MAT.	INST.	TOTAL	MAT.	INST.	TOTAL
2	SITE WORK	117.5	85.0	103.1	88.4	83.9	86.4	126.9	93.7	112.2	112.9	85.5	100.8	114.3	87.3	102.3	107.6	100.2	104.3
3.1	FORMWORK	97.8	70.3	76.4	108.0	76.1	83.3	94.4	87.9	89.3	106.2	62.1	72.0	82.8	76.3	77.8	106.1	53.0	64.9
3.2	REINFORCING	113.6	72.6	97.0	97.1	77.2	89.0	93.8	85.5	90.5	104.4	65.2	88.5	97.1	67.9	85.2	117.8	74.7	100.3
3.3	CAST IN PLACE CONC.	114.1	90.8	100.0	96.6	91.6	93.5	111.2	94.5	101.1	106.1	89.1	95.8	97.8	91.9	94.3	92.1	80.7	85.2
3	CONCRETE	110.8	81.1	92.0	98.9	84.2	89.6	104.1	91.1	95.9	105.7	76.4	87.2	94.7	83.7	87.7	100.5	69.3	80.8
4	MASONRY	106.6	67.9	77.0	104.3	80.6	86.2	111.8	96.9	100.4	107.6	66.7	76.4	102.7	71.7	79.0	96.1	55.5	65.1
5	METALS	99.8	80.2	92.9	91.0	83.0	88.2	97.8	89.4	94.9	97.8	75.0	89.8	91.2	77.9	86.6	104.3	77.2	94.8
6	WOOD & PLASTICS	94.1	72.5	82.1	96.6	79.9	87.3	94.6	92.1	93.2	101.9	64.7	81.2	96.5	80.9	87.8	91.8	49.4	68.2
7	MOISTURE PROTECTION	94.0	57.8	82.6	97.5	65.6	87.4	95.9	76.4	89.8	97.1	61.1	85.8	102.8	70.5	92.6	98.3	56.1	84.9
8	DOORS, WINDOWS, GLASS	92.5	65.7	78.7	96.7	75.9	86.0	102.7	83.7	92.9	101.1	60.1	79.9	103.6	80.7	91.8	99.8	53.4	75.9
9.2	LATH & PLASTER	92.7	78.3	81.8	80.9	79.8	80.1	86.0	81.7	82.8	92.1	70.0	75.3	90.5	81.6	83.8	90.6	53.3	62.3
9.2	DRYWALL	85.0	74.3	80.0	84.9	78.9	82.1	90.3	86.7	88.6	87.1	65.6	77.1	78.7	79.5	79.1	87.3	48.8	69.3
9.5	ACOUSTICAL WORK	91.7	72.5	81.2	94.3	79.1	86.0	94.3	90.7	92.4	90.2	63.4	75.6	96.0	79.8	87.1	90.6	47.6	67.1
9.6	FLOORING	104.1	70.2	95.0	102.6	71.8	94.4	102.6	98.5	101.5	94.6	63.4	86.3	88.7	75.4	85.1	104.2	55.8	91.3
9.9	PAINTING	103.9	55.8	65.6	108.6	58.9	69.0	105.0	82.6	87.2	96.9	61.4	68.6	100.1	79.4	83.6	89.6	46.1	54.9
9	FINISHES	91.8	67.8	79.0	91.8	71.6	81.0	94.7	86.2	90.1	90.1	64.1	76.2	84.7	79.3	81.8	91.6	48.5	68.6
10-14	TOTAL DIV. 10-14	100.0	79.1	93.8	100.0	80.4	94.2	100.0	87.7	96.4	100.0	80.4	94.2	100.0	84.1	95.3	100.0	69.4	91.0
15	MECHANICAL	98.9	74.8	86.9	98.7	77.9	88.4	98.7	81.2	90.0	98.6	63.9	81.4	99.5	73.5	86.6	101.5	63.5	82.6
16	ELECTRICAL	104.2	70.6	81.0	102.4	74.0	82.8	105.7	88.5	93.8	100.2	62.5	74.2	97.6	82.6	87.2	94.3	64.2	73.5
1-16	WEIGHTED AVERAGE	101.2	73.8	86.6	97.2	78.7	87.3	102.0	84.4	94.7	100.5	68.8	83.5	98.1	78.9	87.8	99.6	63.6	80.4

DIVISION		TEXAS FORT WORTH			TEXAS HOUSTON			TEXAS LUBBOCK			TEXAS SAN ANTONIO			UTAH SALT LAKE CITY			VERMONT BURLINGTON		
		MAT.	INST.	TOTAL	MAT.	INST.	TOTAL	MAT.	INST.	TOTAL	MAT.	INST.	TOTAL	MAT.	INST.	TOTAL	MAT.	INST.	TOTAL
2	SITE WORK	114.4	88.6	103.0	114.0	89.3	103.0	121.8	93.2	109.1	79.0	90.6	84.1	84.9	95.2	89.4	97.6	90.5	94.5
3.1	FORMWORK	101.7	76.6	82.2	98.5	74.0	79.5	108.7	67.8	77.0	94.4	69.7	75.3	113.9	77.4	85.6	116.0	76.9	85.7
3.2	REINFORCING	101.0	67.9	87.5	113.4	71.7	96.5	106.6	71.4	92.3	101.9	69.3	88.7	133.4	88.9	115.4	111.5	85.6	101.0
3.3	CAST IN PLACE CONC.	109.0	91.7	98.5	112.7	88.9	98.3	99.3	90.1	93.7	73.4	104.9	92.5	87.7	93.9	91.5	101.1	100.8	100.9
3	CONCRETE	105.8	83.6	91.8	110.1	81.5	92.0	102.8	79.7	88.2	83.9	87.9	86.4	103.0	86.9	92.9	106.3	90.0	96.0
4	MASONRY	108.6	71.7	80.4	114.5	81.0	88.9	113.2	64.3	75.9	97.5	71.3	77.5	97.2	85.3	88.1	110.8	60.9	72.6
5	METALS	97.2	77.4	90.2	93.4	77.7	87.9	88.9	79.5	85.6	93.3	83.2	89.7	106.5	94.5	102.3	103.5	92.6	99.7
6	WOOD & PLASTICS	99.2	81.5	89.4	104.1	75.4	88.2	91.3	71.6	80.3	88.3	72.5	79.5	83.6	76.5	79.6	119.7	76.6	95.7
7	MOISTURE PROTECTION	95.4	73.0	88.4	89.4	72.9	84.2	93.5	70.4	86.2	85.8	61.1	78.0	90.2	80.8	87.2	87.9	79.5	85.3
8	DOORS, WINDOWS, GLASS	99.2	80.7	89.6	103.2	74.4	88.3	99.0	65.9	82.0	103.0	72.4	87.2	100.2	77.7	88.6	105.6	66.5	85.4
9.2	LATH & PLASTER	101.5	84.6	88.7	92.9	80.9	83.8	92.1	69.7	75.1	95.1	71.0	76.9	117.9	72.6	83.5	91.2	65.4	71.7
9.2	DRYWALL	101.9	79.5	91.5	105.7	76.4	92.1	86.1	69.1	78.2	87.4	71.2	79.9	92.2	74.8	84.1	108.6	71.0	91.1
9.5	ACOUSTICAL WORK	91.7	79.8	85.2	96.8	74.5	84.6	91.7	70.5	80.1	97.9	71.7	83.6	99.1	75.7	86.4	99.0	76.0	86.4
9.6	FLOORING	105.2	76.4	97.5	94.2	76.8	89.6	106.7	66.7	96.0	91.1	72.1	86.1	100.1	69.2	91.9	109.2	64.5	97.2
9.9	PAINTING	98.9	87.4	89.7	103.6	79.8	84.6	102.7	55.0	64.6	96.2	57.5	65.3	97.5	77.4	81.5	110.2	64.6	73.8
9	FINISHES	101.5	82.3	91.3	102.0	77.7	89.0	92.9	64.2	77.6	90.1	66.6	77.6	95.6	75.2	84.8	107.7	69.0	87.1
10-14	TOTAL DIV. 10-14	100.0	84.1	95.3	100.0	81.3	94.5	100.0	80.9	94.4	100.0	78.3	93.6	100.0	86.9	96.1	100.0	81.4	94.5
15	MECHANICAL	99.9	72.3	86.1	100.4	76.7	88.6	99.7	72.0	85.9	100.4	82.5	91.5	104.0	81.5	92.8	100.0	72.1	86.5
16	ELECTRICAL	98.8	77.4	84.0	103.5	89.5	93.9	101.7	72.5	81.5	108.5	66.8	79.7	102.4	91.3	94.7	101.5	67.7	78.2
1-16	WEIGHTED AVERAGE	101.5	78.4	89.2	102.4	80.6	90.8	100.1	73.1	85.7	94.3	77.4	85.3	99.6	84.9	91.7	102.4	75.6	88.1

CITY COST INDEXES

DIVISION		VIRGINIA													WASHINGTON					
		NEWPORT NEWS			NORFOLK			RICHMOND			ROANOKE			SEATTLE			SPOKANE		
		MAT.	INST.	TOTAL	MAT.	INST.	TOTAL	MAT.	INST.	TOTAL	MAT.	INST.	TOTAL	MAT.	INST.	TOTAL	MAT.	INST.	TOTAL
2	SITE WORK	120.8	84.2	104.6	111.0	82.7	98.4	83.1	86.7	84.7	100.5	84.3	93.4	101.1	99.4	100.3	108.1	101.3	105.1
3.1	FORMWORK	102.5	65.8	74.0	106.9	65.7	74.9	99.3	64.6	72.4	105.0	58.7	69.1	82.9	100.9	96.8	106.3	97.1	99.1
3.2	REINFORCING	100.9	71.3	88.9	100.9	71.3	88.9	96.9	75.9	88.4	105.8	78.6	94.8	109.2	104.9	107.5	112.9	104.9	109.7
3.3	CAST IN PLACE CONC.	115.4	85.9	97.6	113.2	88.2	98.1	109.5	88.1	96.5	111.6	87.3	96.9	96.7	110.1	104.8	108.3	99.1	102.8
3	CONCRETE	109.7	76.7	88.8	109.3	77.9	89.4	104.7	77.8	87.7	109.0	75.3	87.7	96.8	106.0	102.6	108.9	98.8	102.5
4	MASONRY	104.1	66.3	75.2	103.7	66.3	75.1	101.0	77.5	83.1	102.5	60.7	70.6	125.3	102.4	107.8	115.5	92.6	98.0
5	METALS	86.7	76.4	83.1	86.7	76.9	83.3	96.1	75.9	89.0	96.8	82.0	91.6	105.9	106.0	105.9	102.9	102.6	102.8
6	WOOD & PLASTICS	103.9	69.0	84.5	103.6	69.0	84.3	103.3	67.5	83.4	102.6	60.1	79.0	76.5	98.1	88.5	101.8	95.9	98.5
7	MOISTURE PROTECTION	85.5	50.9	74.6	86.8	50.9	75.5	108.7	49.8	90.1	85.8	50.7	74.7	111.8	108.3	110.7	96.1	101.1	97.7
8	DOORS, WINDOWS, GLASS	90.6	67.3	78.6	89.5	67.3	78.0	90.1	63.5	76.4	94.6	60.9	77.2	94.3	97.3	95.9	100.2	94.9	97.5
9.2	LATH & PLASTER	113.7	66.7	78.1	98.3	67.1	74.6	105.5	67.6	76.8	107.5	55.3	67.9	99.5	103.7	102.7	115.5	92.2	97.8
9.2	DRYWALL	87.4	66.3	77.6	87.5	66.3	77.6	97.8	66.8	83.4	91.9	58.3	76.2	80.6	100.6	89.9	96.3	95.4	95.9
9.5	ACOUSTICAL WORK	97.4	67.7	81.2	94.6	67.7	79.9	104.3	66.5	83.7	96.8	58.5	75.9	99.0	97.9	98.4	105.0	96.2	100.2
9.6	FLOORING	98.8	64.2	89.6	94.5	64.2	86.4	88.0	77.9	85.3	103.3	57.2	91.0	90.1	99.6	92.7	106.2	96.6	103.6
9.9	PAINTING	91.0	58.5	65.1	101.7	61.8	69.9	96.7	56.4	64.5	90.8	53.3	60.9	83.8	102.5	98.7	101.0	95.2	96.3
9	FINISHES	91.7	63.6	76.7	91.3	64.8	77.1	96.2	64.0	79.0	95.0	56.3	74.4	84.9	101.1	93.6	100.1	95.3	97.5
10-14	TOTAL DIV. 10-14	100.0	71.2	91.5	100.0	71.4	91.6	100.0	75.3	92.7	100.0	71.0	91.5	100.0	106.5	101.9	100.0	101.4	100.4
15	MECHANICAL	102.9	65.7	84.4	102.6	67.6	85.2	101.6	64.2	83.0	103.3	68.6	86.1	99.6	104.1	101.8	103.1	106.8	104.9
16	ELECTRICAL	106.0	59.1	73.7	106.0	59.1	73.6	103.2	69.7	80.1	102.3	60.1	73.2	106.6	95.8	99.2	104.1	102.5	103.0
1-16	WEIGHTED AVERAGE	100.3	68.4	83.2	99.6	69.0	83.3	99.6	71.3	84.5	100.2	66.9	82.4	100.4	102.6	101.6	103.5	99.7	101.5

DIVISION		WASHINGTON			WEST VIRGINIA						WISCONSIN						WYOMING		
		TACOMA			CHARLESTON			HUNTINGTON			MADISON			MILWAUKEE			CHEYENNE		
		MAT.	INST.	TOTAL	MAT.	INST.	TOTAL	MAT.	INST.	TOTAL	MAT.	INST.	TOTAL	MAT.	INST.	TOTAL	MAT.	INST.	TOTAL
2	SITE WORK	104.8	97.7	101.7	119.2	99.0	110.3	124.3	102.0	114.4	83.5	98.6	90.2	75.2	100.2	86.3	109.7	89.9	100.9
3.1	FORMWORK	113.4	99.6	102.7	117.8	93.7	99.1	99.1	91.6	93.3	108.9	79.8	86.3	105.0	101.0	101.9	110.3	71.3	80.0
3.2	REINFORCING	100.7	104.9	102.4	120.8	90.4	108.5	116.4	96.5	108.3	106.2	83.0	96.8	105.0	107.3	106.0	103.3	75.0	91.8
3.3	CAST IN PLACE CONC.	100.5	101.2	100.9	117.7	97.3	105.4	114.3	98.2	104.5	100.1	103.3	102.0	80.5	95.8	89.8	98.2	91.4	94.1
3	CONCRETE	103.1	100.9	101.7	118.4	95.3	103.8	111.8	95.4	101.4	103.2	92.2	96.3	90.8	98.8	95.9	101.7	82.0	89.3
4	MASONRY	123.2	97.1	103.2	90.7	91.9	91.6	102.7	88.7	92.0	101.4	80.9	85.8	103.7	100.8	101.5	112.1	65.1	76.2
5	METALS	99.2	102.7	100.4	111.7	92.8	105.1	102.5	96.4	100.3	96.7	90.0	94.4	95.4	102.5	97.9	87.4	81.5	85.3
6	WOOD & PLASTICS	101.8	97.5	99.4	118.0	95.4	105.4	103.4	90.9	96.4	99.9	78.2	87.9	95.4	98.9	97.3	96.6	72.2	83.0
7	MOISTURE PROTECTION	110.4	106.9	109.3	89.8	92.4	90.6	89.2	93.2	90.5	87.4	83.0	86.0	103.3	96.0	101.0	89.1	69.8	83.0
8	DOORS, WINDOWS, GLASS	103.1	97.1	100.0	106.7	87.7	96.9	112.2	87.4	99.4	97.6	80.1	88.6	95.2	99.4	97.3	108.4	74.5	91.0
9.2	LATH & PLASTER	108.2	103.0	104.2	118.7	93.8	99.8	116.0	94.0	99.3	105.4	77.2	84.0	103.4	95.4	97.3	108.0	93.0	96.7
9.2	DRYWALL	99.8	100.3	100.0	100.7	93.7	97.4	98.1	91.9	95.2	109.2	77.2	94.3	95.3	98.9	97.0	95.5	80.6	88.6
9.5	ACOUSTICAL WORK	105.0	97.4	100.9	108.8	94.3	100.9	110.6	91.2	100.0	108.5	77.4	91.5	99.9	99.2	99.5	95.4	71.2	82.2
9.6	FLOORING	98.1	88.7	95.6	85.4	94.5	87.8	81.3	90.4	83.7	96.7	79.4	92.1	102.6	91.6	99.7	93.3	67.5	86.4
9.9	PAINTING	109.9	102.5	104.0	124.0	79.7	88.7	114.6	85.5	91.4	99.0	81.5	85.1	103.4	93.1	95.2	100.4	92.1	93.7
9	FINISHES	101.0	100.2	100.6	100.6	89.0	94.4	97.4	89.6	93.3	105.3	78.9	91.2	98.3	96.2	97.2	95.8	83.6	89.3
10-14	TOTAL DIV. 10-14	100.0	106.4	101.8	100.0	94.2	98.3	100.0	94.5	98.3	100.0	86.9	96.1	100.0	90.7	97.2	100.0	83.6	95.2
15	MECHANICAL	101.7	105.5	103.6	101.6	86.0	93.8	104.1	90.0	97.1	101.7	88.0	94.9	100.2	94.6	97.4	102.9	70.4	86.8
16	ELECTRICAL	104.1	109.8	108.1	95.5	89.2	91.1	98.5	90.6	93.1	88.9	90.5	90.0	93.7	102.0	99.4	98.6	76.4	83.3
1-16	WEIGHTED AVERAGE	103.5	102.3	102.9	104.5	91.2	97.4	104.1	92.0	97.6	98.3	87.1	92.3	96.3	98.3	97.3	100.1	76.3	87.4

DIVISION		CANADA																	
		EDMONTON			MONTREAL			QUEBEC			TORONTO			VANCOUVER			WINNIPEG		
		MAT.	INST.	TOTAL	MAT.	INST.	TOTAL	MAT.	INST.	TOTAL	MAT.	INST.	TOTAL	MAT.	INST.	TOTAL	MAT.	INST.	TOTAL
2	SITE WORK	107.5	101.1	104.7	96.6	97.5	97.0	101.6	72.7	88.8	117.4	104.1	111.5	116.3	103.9	110.8	109.3	102.1	106.1
3.1	FORMWORK	120.8	100.7	105.2	120.7	102.2	106.4	113.9	102.2	104.8	118.9	125.9	124.3	109.5	112.2	111.5	108.0	94.4	97.5
3.2	REINFORCING	119.7	97.1	110.5	119.5	89.0	107.1	117.8	89.0	106.1	80.1	114.3	94.0	100.1	103.6	101.5	117.9	88.1	105.8
3.3	CAST IN PLACE CONC.	119.1	99.4	107.2	109.1	99.8	103.4	145.6	75.4	103.1	164.1	103.9	127.6	117.1	104.5	109.5	108.5	111.6	110.4
3	CONCRETE	119.6	99.7	107.0	113.7	99.8	104.9	133.2	87.1	104.1	136.5	113.5	121.9	111.9	107.4	109.0	110.5	102.8	105.6
4	MASONRY	112.9	89.7	95.2	117.8	101.8	105.6	108.8	101.8	103.4	123.4	110.7	113.7	125.6	106.7	111.2	128.6	93.5	101.8
5	METALS	102.1	97.7	100.5	88.9	97.4	91.9	86.7	88.6	87.4	103.6	111.3	106.3	104.7	101.7	103.7	108.4	102.5	106.3
6	WOOD & PLASTICS	93.8	99.9	97.2	109.8	102.5	105.7	106.7	102.5	104.3	104.6	126.6	116.8	93.4	109.2	102.2	94.6	96.9	95.9
7	MOISTURE PROTECTION	99.0	100.6	99.5	92.9	104.0	96.4	92.3	104.0	96.0	97.6	110.3	101.6	106.6	113.9	108.9	103.7	92.8	100.3
8	DOORS, WINDOWS, GLASS	100.8	98.2	99.5	101.4	88.3	94.6	102.1	88.2	94.9	95.8	117.5	107.0	107.8	106.3	107.0	111.5	90.3	100.6
9.2	LATH & PLASTER	109.3	99.0	101.5	99.0	96.6	97.1	94.9	96.6	96.2	100.2	97.1	97.9	111.4	110.0	110.3	111.9	91.1	96.1
9.2	DRYWALL	108.5	99.6	104.4	111.6	96.7	104.7	114.5	96.7	106.2	107.3	111.3	109.2	112.3	109.5	111.0	105.6	93.0	99.7
9.5	ACOUSTICAL WORK	80.0	100.0	90.9	101.5	102.6	102.1	101.5	102.6	102.1	101.5	127.9	115.9	83.1	109.5	97.5	100.6	96.2	98.2
9.6	FLOORING	99.7	95.6	98.6	92.2	104.4	95.5	88.9	104.4	93.0	95.8	107.2	98.8	99.9	109.4	102.5	109.4	92.6	104.9
9.9	PAINTING	112.4	98.0	100.9	124.3	101.2	105.9	134.3	101.2	107.9	117.8	109.8	111.4	121.2	127.3	126.0	115.8	91.6	96.5
9	FINISHES	104.7	98.8	101.5	107.5	99.3	103.1	109.3	99.3	104.0	105.2	111.0	108.3	108.1	115.7	112.2	107.2	92.7	99.5
10-14	TOTAL DIV. 10-14	100.0	97.2	99.1	100.0	100.5	100.1	100.0	100.5	100.1	100.0	95.0	98.5	100.0	104.5	101.3	100.0	94.0	98.2
15	MECHANICAL	99.4	92.3	95.9	101.1	94.0	97.5	100.1	93.9	97.1	103.4	113.0	108.2	97.9	98.7	98.3	98.8	97.6	98.2
16	ELECTRICAL	108.2	95.9	99.7	104.1	95.4	98.1	106.0	95.4	98.6	104.6	102.9	103.4	100.8	100.8	100.8	111.5	101.1	104.3
1-16	WEIGHTED AVERAGE	104.8	96.1	100.2	102.6	97.8	100.0	105.1	93.6	99.0	109.0	110.4	109.8	105.7	105.3	105.5	106.0	97.3	101.5

ABBREVIATIONS

A	Area Square Feet; Ampere	C/C	Center to Center	Demob.	Demobilization
ABS	Acrylonitrile Butadiene Styrene; Asbestos Bonded Steel	Cab.	Cabinet	d.f.u.	Drainage Fixture Units
A.C.	Alternating Current; Air Conditioning; Asbestos Cement	Cair.	Air Tool Laborer	D.H.	Double Hung
		Calc	Calculated	DHW	Domestic Hot Water
		Cap.	Capacity	Diag.	Diagonal
		Carp.	Carpenter	Diam.	Diameter
A.C.I.	American Concrete Institute	C.B.	Circuit Breaker	Distrib.	Distribution
Addit.	Additional	C.C.A.	Chromate Copper Arsenate	Dk.	Deck
Adj.	Adjustable	C.C.F.	Hundred Cubic Feet	D.L.	Dead Load; Diesel
af	Audio-frenquency	cd	Candela	Do.	Ditto
A.G.A.	American Gas Association	cd/sf	Candela per Square Foot	Dp.	Depth
Agg.	Aggregate	CD	Grade of Plywood Face & Back	D.P.S.T.	Double Pole, Single Throw
A.H.	Ampere Hours	CDX	Plywood, grade C&D, exterior glue	Dr.	Driver
A hr	Ampere-hour	Cefi.	Cement Finisher	Drink.	Drinking
A.H.U.	Air Handling Unit	Cem.	Cement	D.S.	Double Strength
A.I.A.	American Institute of Architects	CF	Hundred Feet	D.S.A.	Double Strength A Grade
AIC	Ampere Interrupting Capacity	C.F.	Cubic Feet	D.S.B.	Double Strength B Grade
Allow.	Allowance	CFM	Cubic Feet per Minute	Dty.	Duty
alt.	Altitude	c.g.	Center of Gravity	DWV	Drain Waste Vent
Alum.	Aluminum	CHW	Chilled Water	DX	Deluxe White, Direct Expansion
a.m.	Ante Meridiem	C.I.	Cast Iron	dyn	Dyne
Amp.	Ampere	C.I.P.	Cast in Place	e	Eccentricity
Anod.	Anodized	Circ.	Circuit	E	Equipment Only; East
Approx.	Approximate	C.L.	Carload Lot	Ea.	Each
Apt.	Apartment	Clab.	Common Laborer	E.B.	Encased Burial
Asb.	Asbestos	C.L.F.	Hundred Linear Feet	Econ.	Economy
A.S.B.C.	American Standard Building Code	CLF	Current Limiting Fuse	EDP	Electronic Data Processing
Asbe.	Asbestos Worker	CLP	Cross Linked Polyethylene	E.D.R.	Equiv. Direct Radiation
A.S.H.R.A.E.	American Society of Heating, Refrig. & AC Engineers	cm	Centimeter	Eq.	Equation
		CMP	Corr. Metal Pipe	Elec.	Electrician; Electrical
A.S.M.E.	American Society of Mechanical Engineers	C.M.U.	Concrete Masonry Unit	Elev.	Elevator; Elevating
		Col.	Column	EMT	Electrical Metallic Conduit; Thin Wall Conduit
A.S.T.M.	American Society for Testing and Materials	CO_2	Carbon Dioxide		
		Comb.	Combination	Eng.	Engine
Attchmt.	Attachment	Compr.	Compressor	EPDM	Ethylene Propylene Diene Monomer
Avg.	Average	Conc.	Concrete		
A.W.G.	American Wire Gauge	Cont.	Continuous; Continued	Eqhv.	Equip. Oper., heavy
Bbl.	Barrel	Corr.	Corrugated	Eqlt.	Equip. Oper., light
B.&B.	Grade B and Better; Balled & Burlapped	Cos	Cosine	Eqmd.	Equip. Oper., medium
		Cot	Cotangent	Eqmm.	Equip. Oper., Master Mechanic
B.&S.	Bell and Spigot	Cov.	Cover	Eqol.	Equip. Oper., oilers
B.&W.	Black and White	CPA	Control Point Adjustment	Equip.	Equipment
b.c.c.	Body-centered Cubic	Cplg.	Coupling	ERW	Electric Resistance Welded
BE	Bevel End	C.P.M.	Critical Path Method	Est.	Estimated
B.F.	Board Feet	CPVC	Chlorinated Polyvinyl Chloride	esu	Electrostatic Units
Bg. Cem.	Bag of Cement	C. Pr.	Hundred Pair	E.W.	Each Way
BHP	Boiler Horse Power Brake Horse Power	CRC	Cold Rolled Channel	EWT	Entering Water Temperature
		Creos.	Creosote	Excav.	Excavation
B.I.	Black Iron	Crpt.	Carpet & Linoleum Layer	Exp.	Expansion
Bit.; Bitum.	Bituminous	CRT	Cathode-ray Tube	Ext.	Exterior
Bk.	Backed	CS	Carbon Steel	Extru.	Extrusion
Bkrs.	Breakers	Csc	Cosecant	f.	Fiber stress
Bldg.	Building	C.S.F.	Hundred Square Feet	F	Fahrenheit; Female; Fill
Blk.	Block	CSI	Construction Specification Institute	Fab.	Fabricated
Bm.	Beam			FBGS	Fiberglass
Boil.	Boilermaker	C.T.	Current Transformer	F.C.	Footcandles
B.P.M.	Blows per Minute	CTS	Copper Tube Size	f.c.c.	Face-centered Cubic
BR	Bedroom	Cu	Cubic	f'c.	Compressive Stress in Concrete; Extreme Compressive Stress
Brg.	Bearing	Cu. Ft.	Cubic Foot		
Brhe.	Bricklayer Helper	cw	Continuous Wave	F.E.	Front End
Bric.	Bricklayer	C.W.	Cool White; Cold Water	FEP	Fluorinated Ethylene Propylene (Teflon)
Brk.	Brick	Cwt.	100 Pounds		
Brng.	Bearing	C.W.X.	Cool White Deluxe	F.G.	Flat Grain
Brs.	Brass	C.Y.	Cubic Yard (27 cubic feet)	F.H.A.	Federal Housing Administration
Brz.	Bronze	C.Y./Hr.	Cubic Yard per Hour	Fig.	Figure
Bsn.	Basin	Cyl.	Cylinder	Fin.	Finished
Btr.	Better	d	Penny (nail size)	Fixt.	Fixture
BTU	British Thermal Unit	D	Deep; Depth; Discharge	Fl. Oz.	Fluid Ounces
BTUH	BTU per Hour	Dis.; Disch.	Discharge	Flr.	Floor
BX	Interlocked Armored Cable	Db.	Decibel	F.M.	Frequency Modulation; Factory Mutual
c	Conductivity	Dbl.	Double		
C	Hundred; Centigrade	DC	Direct Current	Fmg.	Framing

ABBREVIATIONS

Fndtn.	Foundation	Insul.	Insulation	Mat; Mat'l.	Material
Fori.	Foreman, inside	I.P.	Iron Pipe	Max.	Maximum
Fount.	Fountain	I.P.S.	Iron Pipe Size	MBF	Thousand Board Feet
FPM	Feet per Minute	I.P.T.	Iron Pipe Threaded	MBH	Thousand BTU's per hr.
FPT	Female Pipe Thread	I.W.	Indirect Waste	MC	Metal Clad Cable
Fr.	Frame	J	Joule	M.C.F.	Thousand Cubic Feet
F.R.	Fire Rating	J.I.C.	Joint Industrial Council	M.C.F.M.	Thousand Cubic Feet per Minute
FRK	Foil Reinforced Kraft	K	Thousand; Thousand Pounds; Heavy Wall Copper Tubing	M.C.M.	Thousand Circular Mils
FRP	Fiberglass Reinforced Plastic			M.C.P.	Motor Circuit Protector
FS	Forged Steel	K.A.H.	Thousand Amp. Hours	MD	Medium Duty
FSC	Cast Body; Cast Switch Box	K.D.A.T.	Kiln Dried After Treatment	M.D.O.	Medium Density Overlaid
Ft.	Foot; Feet	kg	Kilogram	Med.	Medium
Ftng.	Fitting	kG	Kilogauss	MF	Thousand Feet
Ftg.	Footing	kgf	Kilogram force	M.F.B.M.	Thousand Feet Board Measure
Ft. Lb.	Foot Pound	kHz	Kilohertz	Mfg.	Manufacturing
Furn.	Furniture	Kip.	1000 Pounds	Mfrs.	Manufacturers
FVNR	Full Voltage Non Reversing	KJ	Kiljoule	mg	Milligram
FXM	Female by Male	K.L.	Effective Length Factor	MGD	Million Gallons per Day
Fy.	Minimum Yield Stress of Steel	Km	Kilometer	MGPH	Thousand Gallons per Hour
g	Gram	K.L.F.	Kips per Linear Foot	MH	Manhole; Metal Halide; Man-Hour
G	Gauss	K.S.F.	Kips per Square Foot	MHz	Megahertz
Ga.	Gauge	K.S.I.	Kips per Square Inch	Mi.	Mile
Gal.	Gallon	K.V.	Kilo Volt	MI	Malleable Iron; Mineral Insulated
Gal./Min.	Gallon Per Minute	K.V.A.	Kilo Volt Ampere	mm	Millimeter
Galv.	Galvanized	K.V.A.R.	Kilovar (Reactance)	Mill.	Millwright
Gen.	General	KW	Kilo Watt	Min.	Minimum
G.F.I.	Ground Fault Interrupter	KWh	Kilowatt-hour	Misc.	Miscellaneous
Glaz.	Glazier	L	Labor Only; Length; Long; Medium Wall Copper Tubing	ml	Milliliter
GPD	Gallons per Day			M.L.F.	Thousand Linear Feet
GPH	Gallons per Hour	Lab.	Labor	Mo.	Month
GPM	Gallons per Minute	lat	Latitude	Mobil.	Mobilization
GR	Grade	Lath.	Lather	Mog.	Mogul Base
Gran.	Granular	Lav.	Lavatory	MPH	Miles per Hour
Grnd.	Ground	lb.; #	Pound	MPT	Male Pipe Thread
H	High; High Strength Bar Joist; Henry	L.B.	Load Bearing; L Conduit Body	MRT	Mile Round Trip
		L. & E.	Labor & Equipment	ms	Millisecond
H.C.	High Capacity	lb./hr.	Pounds per Hour	M.S.F.	Thousand Square Feet
H.D.	Heavy Duty; High Density	lb./L.F.	Pounds per Linear Foot	Mstz.	Mosaic & Terrazzo Worker
H.D.O.	High Density Overlaid	lbf/sq in.	Pound-force per Square Inch	M.S.Y.	Thousand Square Yards
Hdr.	Header	L.C.L.	Less than Carload Lot	Mtd.	Mounted
Hdwe.	Hardware	Ld.	Load	Mthe.	Mosaic & Terrazzo Helper
Help.	Helper average	L.F.	Linear Foot	Mtng.	Mounting
HEPA	High Efficiency Particulate Air Filter	Lg.	Long; Length; Large	Mult.	Multi; Multiply
Hg	Mercury	L. & H.	Light and Heat	M.V.A.	Million Volt Amperes
H.O.	High Output	L.H.	Long Span High Strength Bar Joist	M.V.A.R.	Million Volt Amperes Reactive
Horiz.	Horizontal	L.J.	Long Span Standard Strength Bar Joist	MV	Megavolt
H.P.	Horsepower; High Pressure			MW	Megawatt
H.P.F.	High Power Factor	L.L.	Live Load	MXM	Male by Male
Hr.	Hour	L.L.D.	Lamp Lumen Depreciation	MYD	Thousand yards
Hrs./Day	Hours Per Day	lm	Lumen	N	Natural; North
HSC	High Short Circuit	lm/sf	Lumen per Square Foot	nA	Nanoampere
Ht.	Height	lm/W	Lumen Per Watt	NA	Not Available; Not Applicable
Htg.	Heating	L.O.A.	Length Over All	N.B.C.	National Building Code
Htrs.	Heaters	log	Logarithm	NC	Normally Closed
HVAC	Heating, Ventilating & Air Conditioning	L.P.	Liquefied Petroleum; Low Pressure	N.E.M.A.	National Electrical Manufacturers Association
Hvy.	Heavy	L.P.F.	Low Power Factor	NEHB	Bolted Circuit Breaker to 600V.
HW	Hot Water	LR	Long Radius	N.L.B.	Non-Load-Bearing
Hyd.; Hydr.	Hydraulic	L.S.	Lump Sum	NM	Non-metallic Cable
Hz.	Hertz (cycles)	Lt.	Light	nm	Nanometer
I.	Moment of Inertia	Lt. Ga.	Light Gauge	No.	Number
I.C.	Interrupting Capacity	L.T.L.	Less than Truckload Lot	NO	Normally Open
ID	Inside Diameter	Lt. Wt.	Lightweight	N.O.C.	Not Otherwise Classified
I.D.	Inside Dimension; Identification	L.V.	Low Voltage	Nose.	Nosing
		M	Thousand; Material; Male; Light Wall Copper Tubing	N.P.T.	National Pipe Thread
I.F.	Inside Frosted			NQOB	Bolted Circuit Breaker to 240V.
I.M.C.	Intermediate Metal Conduit	m/hr	Man-hour	N.R.C.	Noise Reduction Coefficient
In.	Inch	mA	Milliampere	N.R.S.	Non Rising Stem
Incan.	Incandescent	Mach.	Machine	ns	Nanosecond
Incl.	Included; Including	Mag. Str.	Magnetic Starter	nW	Nanowatt
Int.	Interior	Maint.	Maintenance	OB	Opposing Blade
Inst.	Installation	Marb.	Marble Setter		

ABBREVIATIONS

OC	On Center	R.H.W.	Rubber, Heat & Water Resistant; Residential Hot Water	T.E.M.	Transmission Electron Microscopy
OD	Outside Diameter			TFE	Tetrafluoroethylene (Teflon)
O.D.	Outside Dimension	rms	Root Mean Square	T. & G.	Tongue & Groove; Tar & Gravel
ODS	Overhead Distribution System	Rnd.	Round		
O & P	Overhead and Profit	Rodm.	Rodman	Th.; Thk.	Thick
Oper.	Operator	Rofc.	Roofer, Composition	Thn.	Thin
Opng.	Opening	Rofp.	Roofer, Precast	Thrded	Threaded
Orna.	Ornamental	Rohe.	Roofer Helpers (Composition)	Tilf.	Tile Layer Floor
O.S.&Y.	Outside Screw and Yoke	Rots.	Roofer, Tile & Slate	Tilh.	Tile Layer Helper
Ovhd.	Overhead	R.O.W.	Right of Way	THW.	Insulated Strand Wire
OWG	Oil, Water or Gas	RPM	Revolutions per Minute	THWN; THHN	Nylon Jacketed Wire
Oz.	Ounce	R.R.	Direct Burial Feeder Conduit	T.L.	Truckload
P.	Pole; Applied Load; Projection	R.S.	Rapid Start	Tot.	Total
p.	Page	RT	Round Trip	T.S.	Trigger Start
Pape.	Paperhanger	S.	Suction; Single Entrance; South	Tr.	Trade
P.A.P.R.	Powered Air Purifying Respirator			Transf.	Transformer
PAR	Weatherproof Reflector	Scaf.	Scaffold	Trhv.	Truck Driver, Heavy
Pc.	Piece	Sch.; Sched.	Schedule	Trlr.	Trailer
P.C.	Portland Cement; Power Connector	S.C.R.	Modular Brick	Trlt.	Truck Driver, Light
		S.D.R.	Standard Dimension Ratio	TV	Television
P.C.M.	Phase Contrast Microscopy	S.E.	Surfaced Edge	T.W.	Thermoplastic Water Resistant Wire
P.C.F.	Pounds per Cubic Foot	S.E.R.; S.E.U.	Service Entrance Cable		
P.E.	Professional Engineer; Porcelain Enamel; Polyethylene; Plain End	S.F.	Square Foot	UCI	Uniform Construction Index
		S.F.C.A.	Square Foot Contact Area	UF	Underground Feeder
		S.F.G.	Square Foot of Ground	U.H.F.	Ultra High Frequency
Perf.	Perforated	S.F. Hor.	Square Foot Horizontal	U.L.	Underwriters Laboratory
Ph.	Phase	S.F.R.	Square Feet of Radiation	Unfin.	Unfinished
P.I.	Pressure Injected	S.F.Shlf.	Square Foot of Shelf	URD	Underground Residential Distribution
Pile.	Pile Driver	S4S	Surface 4 Sides		
Pkg.	Package	Shee.	Sheet Metal Worker	V	Volt
Pl.	Plate	Sin.	Sine	V.A.	Volt Amperes
Plah.	Plasterer Helper	Skwk.	Skilled Worker	V.A.C.	Vinyl Composition Tile
Plas.	Plasterer	SL	Saran Lined	VAV	Variable Air Volume
Pluh.	Plumbers Helper	S.L.	Slimline	Vent.	Ventilating
Plum.	Plumber	Sldr.	Solder	Vert.	Vertical
Ply.	Plywood	S.N.	Solid Neutral	V.F.	Vinyl Faced
p.m.	Post Meridiem	S.P.	Static Pressure; Single Pole; Self Propelled	V.G.	Vertical Grain
Pord.	Painter, Ordinary			V.H.F.	Very High Frequency
pp	Pages	Spri.	Sprinkler Installer	VHO	Very High Output
PP; PPL	Polypropylene	Sq.	Square; 100 square feet	Vib.	Vibrating
P.P.M.	Parts per Million	S.P.D.T.	Single Pole, Double Throw	V.L.F.	Vertical Linear Foot
Pr.	Pair	S.P.S.T.	Single Pole, Single Throw	Vol.	Volume
Prefab.	Prefabricated	SPT	Standard Pipe Thread	W	Wire; Watt; Wide; West
Prefin.	Prefinished	Sq. Hd.	Square Head	w/	With
Prop.	Propelled	S.S.	Single Strength; Stainless Steel	W.C.	Water Column; Water Closet
PSF; psf	Pounds per Square Foot	S.S.B.	Single Strength B Grade	W.F.	Wide Flange
PSI; psi	Pounds per Square Inch	Sswk.	Structural Steel Worker	W.G.	Water Gauge
PSIG	Pounds per Square Inch Gauge	Sswl.	Structural Steel Welder	Wldg.	Welding
PSP	Plastic Sewer Pipe	St.; Stl.	Steel	W. Mile	Wire Mile
Pspr.	Painter, Spray	S.T.C.	Sound Transmission Coefficient	W.R.	Water Resistant
Psst.	Painter, Structural Steel	Std.	Standard	Wrck.	Wrecker
P.T.	Potential Transformer	STP	Standard Temperature & Pressure	W.S.P.	Water, Steam, Petroleum
P. & T.	Pressure & Temperature	Stpi.	Steamfitter, Pipefitter	WT, Wt.	Weight
Ptd.	Painted	Str.	Strength; Starter; Straight	WWF	Welded Wire Fabric
Ptns.	Partitions	Strd.	Stranded	XFMR	Transformer
Pu	Ultimate Load	Struct.	Structural	XHD	Extra Heavy Duty
PVC	Polyvinyl Chloride	Sty.	Story	XHHW; XLPE	Cross-linked Polyethylene Wire Insulation
Pvmt.	Pavement	Subj.	Subject		
Pwr.	Power	Subs.	Subcontractors	Y	Wye
Q	Quantity Heat Flow	Surf.	Surface	yd	Yard
Quan.; Qty.	Quantity	Sw.	Switch	yr	Year
Q.C.	Quick Coupling	Swbd.	Switchboard	Δ	Delta
r	Radius of Gyration	S.Y.	Square Yard	%	Percent
R	Resistance	Syn.	Synthetic	~	Approximately
R.C.P.	Reinforced Concrete Pipe	Sys.	System	∅	Phase
Rect.	Rectangle	t.	Thickness	@	At
Reg.	Regular	T	Temperature; Ton	#	Pound; Number
Reinf.	Reinforced	Tan	Tangent	<	Less Than
Req'd.	Required	T.C.	Terra Cotta	>	Greater Than
Resi	Residential	T & C	Threaded and Coupled		
Rgh.	Rough	T.D.	Temperature Difference		

INDEX

A

Abandon catch basin	12
Abatement asbestos	14
ABC extinguisher	171
ABS DWV pipe	82
Absorber vibration	213
Accelerator sprinkler system	176
Accessory bathroom	35
fuel oil	181
Acetal insert fitting	90
pipe-fitting	91
Acid resistant pipe	72
Adapter fire hose swivel	171
pipe-fitting	70
polybutylene	90
Adjustment factor	1
Adsorption air-dryer	211
Adsorptive desiccant	212
filter	212
Aeration sewage	27
Aerial lift	7
survey	3
Aftercooler air-cooled	210
compressor	210
separator	210
water-cooled	210
Aggregate spreader	7
Air cell pipe-covering	186
cock	200
compressor	7, 208
compressor dental	41
compressor package	209
compressor sprinkler system	176
conditioner cooling & heating	208
conditioner packaged terminal	208
conditioner receptacle	226
conditioner thru-wall	208
conditioner window	208
conditioner wiring	228
control	200
filter	212
filtration	14
hose	8
purger solar-energy-system	184
sampling	14
scoop	200
tool	8
vent automatic	199
vent solar-energy-system	184
Air-conditioner portable	208
Air-conditioning ventilating	208, 214-215
Air-dryer adsorption	211
compressor	210
deliquescent	210
refrigeration	211
regenerative	211
Airless sprayer	14
Alarm burglar	219
fire	176
residential	227
sprinkler	220
standpipe	220
valve sprinkler	178
vent	182
water motor	176
All fuel chimney	196-198
service jacket insulation	189
Alteration fee	1
Aluminum corrugated pipe	317
flashing	32, 55
pipe	23, 25, 56-57
salvage	13
weld rod	30
Anchor pipe-conduit casing	131
Angle framing	30
valve	139, 145
Anti-freeze inhibited	212
Anti-siphon device	203
water	55
Apartment bldg. heat fin-tube	288
S.F. & C.F.	228
Appliance	38
plumbing	162-165, 167-168, 256
residential	37, 227
Architectural fee	1
woodwork	31
Area clean-up	16
Arena sport S.F. & C.F.	234
Asbestos abatement	14
demolition	15
disposal	15
removal	15
Ash receiver	36
Asphalt flashing	32
Aspirator dental	41
Atomizer water	14
Atomizing humidifier	186

Auditorium S.F. & C.F.	229
Auger	7
Auto park drain	45
Automatic fire suppression	169
flush	49
washing machine	39
Automotive equipment	38
exhaust system	310
lift	38
sales S.F. & C.F.	229
Autopsy equipment	41
Axe fire	174

B

B and S pipe gaskets	65
Backfill	19
trench	18, 314-315
Backflow preventer	43
preventer solar	185
Backhoe excavation	17
rental	7
trenching	311
Backup control sewer	48
Backwater valve	47
Bag glove	15
Bags disposable	14
Balance valve circuit setter	200
Balancing hydronic	203
valve solar-energy-system	185
Ball valve	139, 145-146
Ball-check valve	146
Band vent-chimney	199
Bank S.F. & C.F.	229
Baptistry	37
Bar front	38
grab	36
towel	36
tub	36
Barber equipment	37
Barometric draft control	181
Barrel	8
Barricade	5, 8
Barrier separation	14
Base cabinet	31
sink	31
vanity	32
Baseboard fin-tube heating	288
heater electric	220
heating	186
Bath	149
communal	150
exhaust fan	212
faucet	49
heater & fan	212
hospital	149
paraffin	41
perineal	149
redwood	150
shower	254
soaking	149
steam	42
whirlpool	41, 150
Bathroom accessory	35
fixture	149, 153-154, 156, 158, 247, 251
system	262-265
Bathtub	149
bar	36
enclosure	35
pier	149
removal	13
system	247
Battery mount water-closet	258
Beam wide flange	30
Bedding pipe	19, 314-315
Bedpan cleanser	49
Bell & spigot pipe	61
Bellow expansion joint pipe	200
Bidet	150
rough-in	150
Bituminous coated metal pipe	316
coating	20
fiber perforated pipe	319
fiber pipe	24, 316
pipe	22
pipe-coating	73
Block manhole	23
manhole/catch basin	321
Bloodbank refrigeration	41
Boiler cut-off low water	204
drain	200
electric	179
electric steam	179
feed pump	160
gas fired	179
gas pulse	180

Boiler general	179
hot water	179-180
insulation	186
oil fired	180
steam	179-180
steam electric	287
wall hung	180
Bolt & gasket set	116
Bond performance	3, 347
Boom lift	7
Booth painting	38
Boring horizontal	19
Borosilicate pipe	77
Bottled water-cooler	164
Bowl wash	251
water-closet	257-258
Box culvert precast	316
distribution	27
Bracket pipe	132
Braided bronze hose	201
steel hose	201
Brass pipe	58
pipe fitting	58, 60
salvage	13
valve	138
Break glass station	220
Breaker vacuum	55, 203
Breeching insulation	186
Brick catch basin	23
manhole/catch basin	321
Bridge sidewalk	5
Bronze body strainer	206
butterfly valve	139
valve	139
Bubbler	150
drinking	150-151
flood	28
Bucket crane	7
Buffalo roadway box	21
Builder insurance	347
risk insurance	2
Building air supported	4
permit	3
portable	6
sitework	321
sprinkler	176
temporary	6
Built-in range	38
shower	155
Burglar alarm	219
Burner gas conversion	181
gun type	181
oil	181
residential	181
Bus terminal S.F. & C.F.	234
Butterfly valve	142, 144
valve bronze	139
valve grooved-joint	128
valve slow close	175
valve stainless	147

C

Cabinet convector heater	222
fire equipment	170
hose rack	170
hotel	37
kitchen	31
laboratory	40
medicine	37
shower	34
unit heater	222-223
valve	170
Cable heating	220
jack	10
Cafeteria water-cooler	256
Calcium silicate insulation	186
silicate pipe-covering	187
Cap vent	182
Car-wash water-heater	166
Carbon dioxide extinguisher	169-170
Carpentry rough	31
Carrier fixture	52
pipe	133, 136
Cart mounted extinguisher	170
Casing anchor pipe-conduit	131
Cast iron drain	45
iron manhole cover	23
iron pipe	61
iron pipe fitting	62, 105
iron pipe gaskets	65
iron radiator	186
iron trap	53
iron weld rod	30
Cast-iron pipe-fitting	63, 65, 107-109, 115

Catch basin	23
basin and manhole	322
basin frame and cover	24
basin masonry	23
basin removal	12
basin/manhole	321
basin/manhole system	321
Catwalk	5
Ceiling fan	212
heater	39
Cell prison	38
Cement lining	27
Centrifugal humidifier	186
pump	8
Chain hoist	10, 43
link fence	5
saw	9
trencher	7
Chair barber	37
dental	41
hydraulic	41
Chalkboard	33
Chamber decontamination	14
Channel framing	30
slotted	30
Characteristics pipe	332
Check swing valve	139, 143
valve	148, 178
valve ball	146
valve silent	141, 144
valve wafer	141, 144
Check-lift valve	144
Checkered plate	31
Chemical dry extinguisher	170
storage tank	153
toilet	9
water closet	27
Chiller remote water	163
Chimney all fuel	196-198
metal	198-199
positive pressure	196-198
prefabricated metal	196-198
vent	194
vent fitting	198
China cabinet	31
Chlorination system	42
Church equipment	37
S.F. & C.F.	229
Chute rubbish	12
CI roof drain system	245
Circuit setter	200
Circular saw	9
Circulating pump	159
Circulator air solar-energy	183
solar-energy-system	183
City hall S.F. & C.F.	234
Clamp pipe	132, 138
riser	133
valve	145
Clamshell bucket	7
Clay pipe	23, 26
pipe vitrified	26
Clean-up area	16
Cleaning up	11
Cleanout pipe	44
tee	45
Clevis pipe hanger	135
Climbing crane	9
jack	10
Clinic service-sink	154
Clock timer	227
Clothes dryer commercial	37
dryer residential	39
Club country S.F. & C.F.	229
S.F. & C.F.	229
Coal tar pipe-coating	73
Coalescent filter	212
Coat hook	36
Coating & wrapping	73
bituminous	20
corrosion-resistant	73
epoxy	20
polyethylene	20
Cock air	200
pet	200
Coffee maker	35
Coin-laundry water-heater	167
Collector solar-energy	182
solar-energy-system	183
College S.F. & C.F.	229
Combination device	224
Comfort station	42
Command dog	6
Commercial water heater	164-166, 242-244
Communal bath	150
Community center S.F. & C.F.	230
Compact fill	19

381

INDEX

C

Compactor earth 7
Companion flange 116
Compensation worker 348
   worker's 2
Component sprinkler system 176
Compression tanks 193
Compressor accessories 210
   aftercooler 210
   air 7, 208
   air package 209
   air-dryer 210
   diaphragm 208
   filter 212
   reciprocating 208
   reciprocating hermetic 208
   rotary screw 209
Concrete catch basin 23
   cutting 11
   drill 11-12
   drilling 216
   finishing 29
   footing 29
   formwork 29
   foundation 29
   hole cutting 217
   hole drilling 216
   in place 29
   insert hanger 134
   manhole 23
   nonreinforced pipe 316
   pipe 22, 24-25
   pipe removal 12
   placing 29
   porous wall pipe 319
   reinforced pipe 316
   septic tank 27
   side/vinyl lined pool 331
   utility vault 20
Conduit & fitting flexible 218
   pipe prefabricated 129, 131
Conduit-fitting pipe 130
Connection motor 218
   standpipe 173
Connector flexible 45
   water copper tubing 45
Conserving water-closet 158
Construction cost index 1
   management 1
   special 41
   time 1
Contingencies 1
Contract closeout 11
   overhead 358
Contractor equipment 7
   overhead 1, 11
   pump 8
Control & motor starter 218
   air 200
   component 212
   flow check 202
   hand/off/automatic 219
   package firecycle 176
   pressure sprinkler 176
   station 219
   station stop/start 219
   valve heating 202, 213
   valve solar-energy-system 184
   water level 204
Control-component 213
Controller solar-energy-system 183
Convector cabinet heater 222
   heating unit 186
Cooking equipment 39
   range 38
Cooler beverage 39
   water 163, 256
Cooling & heating air conditioner 208
Copper ACR tubing 68
   drum trap 54
   DWV tubing 68
   flashing 32, 56
   in trench pipe 320
   pipe 67-68
   pipe-fitting 70
   salvage 13
   tubing oxygen class 67
   type K tubing 320
Core drill 11-12
Cornice drain 45
Corrosion resistant pipe 71
   resistant pipe fitting 73-74
   resistant sink 252
Corrosion-resistant backflow preven 43
   coating 73
   lab equipment 152
   lined fittings 75

Corrosion-resistant pipe 72-73
   pipe-fitting 75-76
   sink 155
   tank 193
   trap 54
   valve 144
Corrugated metal coated pipe 316
   metal pipe 25
   metal plain pipe 317
   oval arch coated pipe 317
   oval arch plain pipe 317
   pipe 23
Cost mark up 2
   plumbing average 43
Countertop sink 155, 249
Country club S.F. & C.F. 229
Coupling fire-hose 171
   mechanical 123
   plastic 88
Courthouse S.F. & C.F. 230
Cover manhole 24
   stair tread 4
   weather protection 3
Covering protection saddle 137
CPVC pipe 82
   valve 146-147
Crane 9
   bucket 7
   climbing 9
   crawler 9
   hydraulic 10
   material handling 9, 43
   tower 9
Crew 1
Crowbar fire 174
Cubic foot building cost 228
Cubicle shower 155
   toilet 33
Culvert box precast 316
   end 25
   reinforced 24
Cup sink 155, 252
Curb prefabricated 213
Curtain rod 35
Cut-off low water boiler 204
Cutting torch 9

D

Darkroom equipment 40
Deck drain 45
   roof 31
Decontamination chamber 14
   enclosure 14-15
   equipment 14
Decorator device 224
   switch 224
Deep seal trap 54
   well pump 162
Dehumidifier 38
Dehydrator package sprinkler 176
Deliquescent air-dryer 210
   desiccant 211
Deluge sprinkler 275-277
   sprinkler monitoring panel 176
   sprinkler system 275-277
   valve assembly sprinkler 178
Demolition 13
   asbestos 15
   enclosure 16
   hammer 7
   plumbing 13
Dental equipment 41
   fountain 150
   fountain rough-in 150
   metal interceptor 152
Department store S.F. & C.F. 230
Derrick 10
   guyed 10
   stiffleg 10
Desiccant dryer 211-212
Detection system 219
Detector meter water supply 169
   smoke 220
   temperature rise 220
   valve sprinkler 178
Detention equipment 38
Device anti-siphon 203
   combination 224
   decorator 224
   GFI 225
   receptacle 225
   residential 224
Dewater 10, 17
   pump 161
   pumping 16-17
Diaphragm compressor 208

Diaphragm pump 9
   valve 145
Dielectric union 48
Diesel fire pump 174
Diffusers pump suction 203
Dimmer switch 224
Dirt and rust water filter 158
Discharge hose 8
Dishwasher 38-39
   water-heater 167
Dispenser hot water 151
   hot-water 164
   napkin 36
   soap 36
   toilet tissue 36
   towel 36
Dispersion nozzle 169
Disposable bags 14
Disposal asbestos 15
   field 27
Disposer garbage 39
Distiller water 41
Distribution box 27
Ditching 16
Dog command 6
Dome drain 47
Domestic hot-water 239-241
Door bell residential 226
   fire 220
   shower 35
Dormitory S.F. & C.F. 230
Draft control barometric 181
   damper vent 181
Drain 45-47
   boiler 200
   cast iron 45
   deck 45
   dome 47
   expansion joint roof 47
   flexible bellows roof 47
   floor 45
   gutter 46
   main 47
   oil-interceptor 46
   pipe 17
   pool 46
   roof 47
   scupper 47
   shower 46
   system roof 246
   terrace 47
   trap 47
   trench 47
Drainage & sewage piping 316-317
   fitting 113-114
   pipe 24-26, 71, 77, 84
   requirements 339
   site 23
   trap 53-54
Draindown valve solar-energy-system 185
Drill concrete 11-12
   core 11-12
   hammer 8
   horizontal 19
   steel 8
Drilling concrete 216
Drinking bubbler 150-151
   fountain 150-151, 163
   fountain deck rough-in 151
   fountain floor rough-in 151
   fountain handicap 150
   fountain refrigerated 256
   fountain support 52
   fountain system 248
   fountain wall rough-in 150-151
Drum trap 54
   trap copper 54
Dry chemical extinguisher 171
   pipe sprinkler 269
   pipe sprinkler head 176
   pipe sprinkler system 269-271
Dryer accessories washer 163
   clothes 39
   commercial clothes 37
   desiccant 211-212
   hand 36
   receptacle 226
   residential 37
   system 211
   vent 39, 163
Duck tarpaulin 6
Duct humidifier 186
Ductile iron fitting 21
   iron in trench pipe 320
   iron pipe 20
Dump truck 7, 19
Dumpster 12
Duplex style strainer 205-206

Dust partition 12
DWV pipe ABS 82
   PVC pipe 82
   tubing copper 68

E

Earth compactor 7
   vibrator 18
Earthwork 17, 19
   equipment 7
Economizer shower-head water 155
Education religious S.F. & C.F. 233
Ejector pump 161
Elbow pipe 126
Elderly housing S.F. & C.F. 231
Electric baseboard heater 220
   boiler 179, 287
   cabinet heater 222
   fire pump 174
   generator 8
   heat 220
   heater 39
   hot-air heater 222
   infra-red heater 182
   pool heater 181
   unit heater 220-222
   water cooler 256
   water heater 164, 165, 239, 242
Electrical fee 1
   installation drilling 216
   knockouts 217
   laboratory 40
Elementary school S.F. & C.F. 233
Elevator construction 10
   fee 1
Employer liability 2
Encapsulation 16
   pipe 16
Enclosure bathtub 35
   decontamination 14-15
   demolition 16
   shower 35
   tub 35
End culvert 25
Engine exhaust-elimination 214
Engineering fee 1, 347
   fees 332
Entrainment eliminator 203
Entrance screen 34
Epoxy coating 20
   fiberglass wound pipe 71
Equipment 7, 37
   earthwork 7
   fire 171, 285
   formwork 29
   foundation 29
   general 2
   hospital 41
   insurance 2
   laundry 37
   medical 41
   rental 9, 332, 353
   standpipe 285
Escutcheon plate 171
Estimate electrical heating 220
   plumbing 238
Ethylene glycol 212
Excavation 19
   backhoe 17
   hand 18
   septic tank 27
   trench 18, 311-313, 357
Exchanger heat 184-185
Exhaust hood 39
   system 214
   system garage 310
Exhaust-elimination engine 214
   garage 214
Expansion joint 200
   joint roof drain 47
   tank 193
   tank solar-energy-system 185
Expense office 2
Exterior sprinkler 28
Extinguisher fire 169-170
   installation 171
Extra work 2
Extractor industrial 37
Eye wash fountain 151
   wash portable 151

INDEX

F

Fabrication metal	31
Face wash fountain	151
Factor	1
Factory S.F. & C.F.	230
Fan	212
bath exhaust	212
ceiling	212
paddle	227
residential	227
ventilation	227
wiring	227
Faucet & fitting	49
bath	49
gooseneck	49
Faucets medical	49
Fee architectural	1
engineering	1, 347
Fees engineering	332
Fence chain link	5
plywood	5
temporary	5
wire	5
Fiberglass insulation	186
panel	3
pipe covering	189-190
septic tank	27
shower stall	35
tank	193
Field disposal	27
office	6
Fill	19
gravel	19
Fillet weld	30
Film equipment	40
Filter air	212
compressor	212
iron removal	159
odor	212
oil	181
swimming pool	42
water	158
water neutralizing	158
Filtration air	14
equipment	43
Fin tube heating residential	288
Fin tube heating system	287
Finishing concrete	29
floor	29
Fire alarm	176, 220
call pullbox	220
crowbar	174
door	220
equipment	171
equipment cabinet	170
extinguisher	169-170
extinguishing	266-274, 276-281, 283-286
extinguishing system	169, 171-174, 176-178
horn	220
hose	172
hose adapter	171
hose gate valve	175
hose nozzle	173
hose storage cabinet	170
hose valve	175
hose wye	176
hydrants	20, 172, 324-325
protection classification	343
protection kitchen	39
pump	174
retardent pipe	72
signal bell	220
sprinkler head	176
sprinkler sizing	344
sprinkler system	266-280
standpipe	345
station S.F. & C.F.	230
suppression automatic	169
suppression halon	286
tool	174
valve	175
valve hydrant	175
Fire-hose coupling	171
nipple	172
storage house	174
Firecycle sprinkler	279
sprinkler system	278-280
system control package	176
valve package	178
Firestop wood	31
Fitting drainage	113-114
flanged	116
galvanized	114
gas vent	194-195
Fitting grooved joint pipe	126
monoflow	202
pipe	43, 106-107, 110-111, 113-116, 120
pipe-covering	192
tee	21
vent chimney	194, 195, 198-199
water pipe	21
weld	120
wye	21
Fittings corrosion-resistant lined	75
Fixture bathroom	149, 153-154, 156, 158, 247, 251
carrier	52
demands	338
institution	154
plumbing	149-162, 248-253, 255, 257
prison	154
removal	13
residential	226
support handicap	52
support/carrier	52
units (d.f.u.)	339
Flange companion	116
gasket	116
grooved-joint	128
polybutylene	91
PVC	89
stainless-steel	99
steel	128
steel weld-on	120
threaded	117
Flanged fitting	116
pipe	103-104
Flashing	32
aluminum	55
asphalt	32
copper	32, 56
galvanized	56
neoprene	56
stainless	33
vent	55
vent chimney	195, 198
Flatbed truck	7
Flexible bellows roof drain	47
conduit & fitting	218
connector	45
metal hose	201
Floater equipment	2
Flood bubbler	28
Floodback sewer control	48
Floodlight	8
Floor area ratios	357
cleaning	11
cleanout	44
drain	45
finishing	29
receptor	50
scupper	47
sink	253
Flow check control	202
fitting hydronic	202
meter	204
Flue chimney metal	194
prefab metal	194
Fluid heat transfer	184
Flush automatic	49
valve	49
Foam pipe covering	191-192
Foam-water sprinkler head	176
Folding door shower	35
Food service equipment	39
Foot valve	147
valve oil	181
Footing concrete	29
Forged steel pipe-fitting	120, 122
Formwork concrete	29
equipment	29
Foundation concrete	29
equipment	29
mat	29
Fountain	28
dental	150
drinking	150-151, 163
eye wash	151
face wash	151
wash	157
Framing lightweight	30
metal	30
Fraternal club S.F. & C.F.	229
Fraternity house S.F. & C.F.	230
Freezer	39
Frost penetration	360
Fuel-oil gauge	181
pump	181

Fuel-oil specialties	181
valve	182
Fume elimination welding	215
Funeral home S.F. & C.F.	230
Fusible oil valve	182
Fusion pipe-fitting	91

G

Galvanized fitting	114
pipe fitting	114
Gantry crane	43
Garage exhaust system	310
exhaust-elimination	214
S.F. & C.F.	231
Garbage disposer	39
Gas connector	45
conversion burner	181
fired boiler	179
fired infra-red heater	182
fired pool heater	180
pipe	22
pressure regulators	202-203
pulse combustion	180
regulators	203
service and distribution	22
stop valve	138
vent	194
vent fitting	194-195
water heater	165
Gas-fired water-heater	240, 243
Gas-service piping	318
polyethylene pipe	318
Gasket & bolt set	116
flange	116
joint pipe	61
joint pipe fitting	63-65
Gaskets B and S pipe	65
cast iron pipe	65
Gasoline pump	38
Gate valve	142, 148
valve grooved-joint	128
valve soldered	140
Gauge fuel-oil	181
oil tank	181
pressure	212
pressure solar-energy-system	185
pressure/vacuum	212
vacuum	212
Gear driven sprinkler	28
General equipment	2
Generator construction	11
steam	41, 179
GFI receptacle	225
Gland seal pipe-conduit	129
Glass door shower	35
filler	164
lined water heater	39
mirror	36
P trap	54
pipe	77
pipe fitting	78
process supply pipe	77
shower stall	35
Glassware washer	40
Globe valve	140, 143, 148
Glove bag	15
Glycol ethylene	212
Gooseneck faucet	49
Grab bar	36
Gradall	7
Grading	19
Grass sprinkler	28
Grating sewer	23
Gravel fill	19
pack well	21
Grease interceptor	151
Grinder pump system	160
Groove cut labor steel	128
roll labor steel	128
Grooved joint pipe	124
reducers	127
Grooved joint flange	128
pipe	125
Ground box hydrant	51
post hydrant	51
Group shower	155
wash fountain	157, 260
Guard service	5
sprinkler head	177
Guardrail temporary	5
Guide pipe	134
Gunite shell pool	331
Gutter drain	46
swimming pool	42
Guyed derrick	10

Gymnasium S.F. & C.F.	231

H

Hair interceptor	152
Halon fire extinguisher	169
fire suppression	286
fire suppression system	286
Hammer demolition	7
drill	8
Hand dryer	36
excavation	18-19
hole	20
Hand/off/automatic control	219
Handicap drinking fountain	150
fixture support	52
lavatory	154
shower	155
tub/shower	149
wash-center	157
washfountain	157
water cooler	163, 256
Hanger & support pipe	132-135, 137-138
clevis	135
plastic pipe	138
rod pipe	135
rod socket	137
roll	136
trapeze	136
U-bolt pipe	138
U-hook	138
vibration absorbing	213
Hardboard cabinet	31
Hat and coat strip	36
Hazardous waste cleanup	13
waste disposal	13
Head sprinkler	28, 176
Header pipe	11
Heads springler	28
Heat electric	220
exchanger	184-185
exchanger solar-energy-system	184
pump	207
pump residential	228
radiant	220
temporary	4
therapy	41
trace system	221
transfer fluid	184
Heater & fan bath	212
cabinet convector	222
ceiling mount unit	223
contractor	8
electric	39
electric baseboard	220
electric hot-air	222
electric wall	220
infra-red	182
infra-red quartz	221
raceway	221
sauna	42
swimming pool	180, 305
swimming pool solar	305
terminal	182
vertical discharge	222
wall mounted	222
water	39, 164-166
Heating	179-187, 189-194, 198
baseboard	186
cable	220
control transformer	221
control valve	202
estimate electrical	220
fin-tube residential	288
forced hot-water	288
hot water solar	295
hydronic	179-180, 186
hydronic system	287-288
industrial	179
insulation	186
panel radiant	221
solar-energy	305, 307, 309
system	303
system oil-fired	288
unit convector	186
High impact pipe	79
school S.F. & C.F.	233-234
temperature vent chimney	198, 199
Historical cost index	2
Hoist	43
and tower	10
automotive	38
contractor	10
electric	43

383

INDEX

H

Hoist lift equipment	9
personnel	10
Holding tank	27
Hole cutting electrical	217
drilling electrical	216
Hood fire protection	39
range	39
Hook coat	36
robe	36
type pipe outlets	123
Horizontal auger	7
boring	19
drill	19
Horn fire	220
Hose & hydrant house	174
adapter fire	171
air	8
braided bronze	201
braided stainless-steel	201
braided steel	201
discharge	8
equipment	171, 173
fire	172
metal flexible	201
nozzle	173
rack	172
rack cabinet	170
reel	172
suction	8
valve cabinet	170
water	8
Hospital bath	149
equipment	41
lavatory	154
S.F. & C.F.	231
sink	154
water closets	158
whirlpool	150
Hot & cold polybutylene pipe	84
tub	150
water boiler	179-180
water consumption	338
water dispenser	151
water heating	179, 186
water/water exchange	185
Hot-air heater electric	222
Hot-water boiler	179
commercial	242-244
dispenser	164
domestic	239-241
heating forced	288
solar-energy	291, 293, 295, 297, 299, 301, 303, 307, 309
system	239-244
Hotel cabinet	37
House fire-hose storage	174
hose & hydrant	174
Household water filter	158
Housing for the elderly S.F. & C.F.	231
public S.F. & C.F.	231
Hubbard tank	41
Humidifier	39
centrifugal	186
duct	186
HVAC piping specialties	199, 201, 203-207
Hydrant fire	20, 172, 324-325
ground box	51
ground post	51
removal	12
screw type valve	175
tool	174
water	50
Hydrants fire	20
Hydraulic chair	41
crane	10, 43
jack	10
Hydrocumulator	161
Hydrolator valve	175
Hydronic balancing	203
flow fitting	202
heating	179-180, 186

I

Ice cube maker	39
skating rink S.F. & C.F.	231
Icemaker	39
Impact sprinkler	28
wrench	8
Imported pipe costs	334
Increaser vent chimney	199
Index construction cost	1
Indicator thermoflo	203
valves post	20
Industrial heating	179
Industrial safety fixture	151
Infra-red heater	182
heater gas fired	182
quartz heater	221
Insert fitting acetal	90
hanger concrete	134
pipe-fitting	90
Installation extinguisher	171
Institution fixture	154
Insulation	186, 188, 190-192
all service jacket	189
boiler	186
breeching	186
calcium silicate	186
fiberglass	186
pipe	186, 191-192
polyethylene	190-191
removal	15
water heater	186
Insurance	2
builder	347
builder risk	2
equipment	2
public liability	2
Interceptor grease	151
metal recovery	152
oil	151
Interval timer	224
Intrusion system	219
Invert manhole	24
Iron alloy mechanical joint pipe	71
body valve	142-143
ductile mech joint pipe	320
ductile tyton joint pipe	320
removal filter	159
Irrigation shrub	28
site	328
system	28

J

J hook clamp w/nail	138
Jack cable	10
hydraulic	10
Jackhammer	8
Jacking	19
Jail equipment	38
S.F. & C.F.	232
Jet water system	162
Jetting pump	10
Job condition	2
Jockey pump fire	175

K

Kettle	39
Kitchen cabinet	31
equipment	39
equipment fee	1
sink	155
sink faucet	49
sink system	249
Knee action mixing valve	49
Knockouts electrical	217

L

Labor index	2
pipe groove cut	128
pipe groove roll	128
pipe threading steel	104
pipe weld stainless-steel	95
pipe weld steel	105
Laboratory equip corrosion-resist	152
equipment	40
plumbing fixture	152
research S.F. & C.F.	233
sink	40, 155
sink system	252
tank	152
tank casing	153
Ladder	8
rolling	5
towel	36
Landscaping fee	1
Laundry equipment	37
faucet	49
sink system	250
tray	154
water-heater	167
Lavatories battery	261
group	261
Lavatory faucet	49
handicap	154
hospital	154
Lavatory sink	251
support	52
vanity top	153
Lavatorys	251
Lawn sprinkler	28, 328
Leaching field	323
field chamber	27
pit	27
Lead flashing	33
salvage	13
Leader line wye	176
Liability employer	2
Library S.F. & C.F.	232
Lift aerial	7
automotive	38
scissor	43
Light dental	41
stand	14
temporary	4
tower	8
underwater	42
Lighting outdoor	8
outlet	226
residential	226
Lightning suppressor	224
Lightweight framing	30
Lined fittings	75
pipe	72
valve	144
Lining cement	27
pipe	27
Loadcenter residential	223
Loader vacuum	14
Locking receptacle	226
Lube equipment	38
Lubricated plug valve	148

M

Machine valves washing	163
welding	9
Magnetic motor starter	218
Main drain	47
office expense	2, 358
Malleable iron pipe fitting	110-111, 112-113, 122, 124
Management construction	1
fee	1
Manhole	23
cover	24
invert	24
removal	12
step	24
Manhole/catch basin system	321
Manifold roof fire valve	175
Marble screen	34
shower stall	35
sink	251
toilet partition	33
Mark-up cost	2
Masonry catch basin	23
flashing	32
manhole	23
saw	9
Mat foundation	29
Material hoist	10
index	3
Mechanical cost	43
coupling	123
fee	1
Mechanical-joint pipe-fitting	122, 124
Medical clean copper tubing	67
clinic S.F. & C.F.	232
equipment	41
faucets	49
office S.F. & C.F.	232
Medicine cabinet	37
Melting snow	220
Metal chimney	198-199
fabrication	31
flexible hose	201
flue chimney	194
framing	30
perforated coated pipe	319
pipe	20, 25
plumbing fixture	154
recovery interceptor	152
screen	34
toilet partition	33
Meter trim	20
venturi flow	204
water supply	169
water supply detector	169
water supply domestic	169
Metric conversion	361
Mirror	36
Mixing valve	202
Mixing-valve shower	155
Modification to cost	2
Module tub/shower	149
Moil point	8
Monoflow fitting	202
Monument survey	3
Mop holder strip	36
sink	156
Motel pool	331
S.F. & C.F.	232
Motor connection	218
generator	8
starter	218
starter & control	218
starter magnetic	218
starter w/circuit protector	218
starter w/fused switch	219
Motor-starter enclosed & heated	218
Motorized zone valve	213
Mount vibration absorbing	213
Movie S.F. & C.F.	234
Municipal pool	331
Mylar tarpaulin	6

N

Nailer wood	31
Napkin dispenser	36
Needle valve	147
Neoprene flashing	56
Neutralizing water filter	158
Nipple fire-hose	172
No-hub pipe	61
Nonfusible oil valve	182
Nozzle dispersion	169
fire hose	173
fog	173
playpipe	173
Nursing home S.F. & C.F.	232

O

Oakum	61
Observation well	21
Occupancy determination	357
Odor filter	212
Off highway truck	7
Office expense	2
field	6
medical S.F. & C.F.	232
S.F. & C.F.	232
trailer	6
Oil burner	181
filter	181
fired boiler	180
heater temporary	8
interceptor	151-152
shut-off valve	182
tank	193
water heater	164-165
Oil-fired infra-red heater	182
pool heater	180
water-heater	241, 244
Oil-interceptor drain	46
Omitted work	2
Operating cost equipment	7
OSHA testing	16
Outdoor lighting	8
Outlet lighting	226
Oven	38-39
Overhaul	13, 19
Overhead	1
and profit	3, 352
contract	358
contractor	1, 11
hoist	43
Overtime	2-3
efficiency	351
Oxygen lance cutting	14

P

P trap	53-54
P&T relief valve	141
Packaging waste	15
Pad prefabricated	213
vibration absorbing	213
Paddle fan	227
Painting booth	38
swimming pool	43
Pan shower	33
Panel collecting	183
fire	220
radiant heat	221

INDEX

P

Paperholder	36
Paraffin bath	41
Parking garage S.F. & C.F.	231
Partition dust	12
shower	34
toilet	33-34
Perforated pipe	23
PVC pipe	23
Performance bond	3, 347
Perineal bath	149
Permit building	3
Personal respirator	14
Personnel hoist	10
Pet cock	200
Photography	4
time lapse	4
Pickup truck	9
Pier bathtub	149
Pilaster toilet partition	34
Piling sheet	355
Pipe	23
& fittings	44-45, 47, 49-54, 56-60, 62-63, 66-70, 72-88
acid resistant	72
aluminum	23, 25, 56-57
bedding	19, 314-315
bedding trench	19
bellow expansion joint	200
bituminous	22
bituminous coated metal	316
bituminous fiber	24, 316
bituminous fiber perforated	319
brass	58
carrier	136
cast iron	61
characteristics	332
clamp plastic	138
clay	23
cleanout	44
concrete	22, 24-25
concrete nonreinforced	316
concrete porous wall	319
concrete reinforced	316
conduit-fitting	130
copper	67-68
copper in trench	320
corrosion resistant	71-73
corrugated	23
corrugated metal coated	316
corrugated metal plain	317
corrugated oval arch coated	317
corrugated oval arch plain	317
costs imported	334
covering	186, 189
covering fiberglass	189-190
covering foam	191-192
covering ultraviolet	192
covering urethane	191
CPVC	82
drain	17
drainage	24-26, 71
ductile iron in trench	320
DWV ABS	82
DWV PVC	82
encapsulation	16
epoxy fiberglass wound	71
fire retardant	72
fitting	43, 106-107, 110-111, 113-116, 120
fitting brass	58
fitting cast iron	62, 65, 105
fitting copper	69
fitting corrosion resistant	73-74
fitting DWV	87
fitting galvanized	114
fitting gasket joint	64
fitting glass	78
fitting grooved joint	126
fitting malleable iron	110-111
fitting no-hub	65
fitting pitched	113-114
fitting plastic	86, 88
fitting soil	61
fitting steel	105, 115, 117
fitting steel carbon	117
fitting weld steel	117
fitting, gasket joint	63-65
flanged	103-104
gas	22
glass	77
groove cut labor	128
groove roll labor	128
grooved joint	124, 125
Pipe hanger & support	132-135, 137-138
hanger clevis	135
hanger plastic	138
hanger strap	137
hanger u-bolt	138
header	11
high impact	79
high pressure PVC	80
hot & cold polybutylene	84
in trench	316-320
insulation	186, 191-192
iron alloy mechanical joint	71
iron ductile mech joint	320
iron ductile tyton joint	320
lined	72
lining	27
materials	334
metal	25
metal perforated coated	319
no-hub	61
perforated	23
plastic	79-80, 82-84
polybutylene	83
polyethylene	22
polyethylene gas-service	318
polyethylene in trench	320
polypropylene	72
polyvinyl chloride	317
polyvinylidene fluoride	72
prefabricated conduit	129
process pressure	77
protection external	73
proxylene	72
PVC	26, 82
PVC in trench	320
PVC pressure	81
quick coupling	11
relay	17
removal	12
ring hanger	134
sewage	24-26
shock absorber	51
single hub	61
soil	61
stainless steel	92-94, 96
steel	22-23, 25, 101-103, 105
steel gas-service	318
steel plastic lined	72
steel tarred & wrapped	318
subdrainage	22-23
support saddle	136
threading steel labor	104
use	332
vitrified clay	26
vitrified clay perforated	319
vitrified clay premium joint	317
weld joint	92, 94-95, 102, 104
weld stainless-steel labor	95
weld steel labor	105
wrapping	20
Pipe-coating bituminous	73
coal tar	73
polyethylene	73
Pipe-conduit prefabricated	129-132
system	129-130
Pipe-covering	188
calcium silicate	187
fitting	192
Pipe-fitting acetal	91
adapter	70
brass	60
cast-iron	63, 65, 107-109, 115
copper	70
corrosion-resistant	75-76
flanged cast-iron	115
forged steel	120, 122
fusion	91
insert	90
malleable iron	112-113, 122, 124
mechanical-joint	122, 124
plastic	84-85, 87, 89
polybutylene	89-91
stainless-steel	97-98, 100-101
steel	120, 122
steel carbon	119
welded steel	122
Piped utilities	19
Piping drainage & sewage	316-317
elevated installation	56
excavation	311
gas-service	318
hydrant	20
polyethylene water	320
removal	13
specialties HVAC	201, 203-207
subdrainage	319
water distribution	320
Pit cover	31
leaching	27
sump	16
Pitched pipe fitting	113-114
Placing concrete	29
Plant power S.F. & C.F.	233
Plastic coupling	88
pipe	79-80, 82-84
pipe clamp	138
pipe fitting	86-88
pipe hanger	138
pipe-fitting	84-85, 87, 89
sink	155, 252
tank	152
trap	54-55
tubing	22
valve	145
Plate checkered	31
escutcheon	171
Platform checkered plate	31
trailer	9
Playpipe fire-hose	173
Plug valve	145, 148
Plumbing	43
appliance	162-165, 167-169, 256
approximations	334
average cost	43
demolition	13
fixture	149-162, 247-253, 255, 257
fixture labor	341
fixture metal	154
fixture requirements	340
laboratory	40
system estimate	238
Plywood fence	5
sidewalk	6
Point moil	8
of use water heater	166
Police station S.F. & C.F.	233
Polybutylene adapter	90
flange	91
pipe	83
pipe hot & cold	84
pipe-fitting	89-91
Polyethylene coating	20
gas-service pipe	318
in trench pipe	320
insulation	190-191
pipe	22, 84, 328
pipe-coating	73
sink	155
tank	152
tarpaulin	6
Polypropylene pipe	72
sink	155
valve	146
Polyvinyl chloride pipe	317
tarpaulin	6
Polyvinylidene fluoride pipe	72
Pool concrete side/vinyl lined	331
drain	46
gunite shell	331
heater electric	181
heater gas fired	180
heater oil-fired	180
heater solar-energy	305
motel swimming	331
municipal swimming	331
residential swimming	331
swimming	42
swimming S.F. & C.F.	234
tile lined	331
Pop up sprinkler	28
Porcelain enamel sink	251, 253
Porous wall concrete pipe	319
Portable air compressor	7
air-conditioner	208
building	6
eye wash	151
fire extinguisher	170
heater	8
Positive pressure chimney	196-198
Post indicator valves	20
office S.F. & C.F.	233
Potable water-treatment	169
Power plant S.F. & C.F.	233
temporary	4
Preaction sprinkler system	272-274
Precast catch basin	23
manhole	23
manhole/catch basin	321
receptor	35
septic tank	27
Prefabricated comfort station	
metal chimney	196-198
pipe-conduit	129-132
Preparation site	16
Pressure booster system	161
Pressure gauge	212
pipe	81
pipe process	77
pipe PVC	81
regulator	203
regulator oil	202
regulators gas	202-203
relief valve	141
restricting valve	175
valve relief	141
Pressure/vacuum gauge	212
Pressurized fire extinguisher	171
Primer trap	55
Prison fixture	154
S.F. & C.F.	232
toilet	38
Process supply pipe glass	77
Project overhead	3
size modifier	356
Promenade drain	45
Property line survey	3
Propylene glycol	212
Protection winter	3
worker	14
Proxylene pipe	72
Public housing S.F. & C.F.	231
Pulse boiler gas	180
Pump	160-162
circulating	159
contractor	16
diaphragm	9
fire	174
fuel-oil	181
gasoline	38
heat	207
jetting	10
operator	17
rental	9
shallow well	162
sprinkler	161
submersible	8, 161-162
sump	39, 161-162
trash	9
water	8, 11, 21, 159
wellpoint	11
Pumping	16
dewater	16-17
station	26
Putlog	5
PVC DWV pipe	82
PVC flange	89
PVC in trench pipe	320
pipe	21, 26, 80, 82, 328
pipe high pressure	80
roof drain system	245
sdr35 pipe	317
PVC union	89
PVC valve	145, 147
Pyrex pipe	77

Q

Quartz heater	221
Quick coupling sprinkler	28

R

Raceway	215-218
for heater cable	221
Rack hose	172
Radiant heat	220
heating panel	221
Radiator air vent	200
cast iron	186
supply valve	202
Railing temporary	5
Rain curtain	28
Ramp temporary	6
Range cooking	38
hood	39
receptacle	226
Receptacle air conditioner	226
device	225
dryer	226
GFI	225
locking	226
range	226
telephone	226
television	226
waste	36
weatherproof	226
Receptor floor	
shower	35, 50, 155
Reciprocating compressor	208
hermetic compressor	208
Recirculating chemical toilet	27

INDEX

R

Reducers grooved	127
Redwood bath	150
Refrigerated drinking fountain	256
Refrigeration air-dryer	211
bloodbank	41
commercial	39
tubing	68
Refrigerator compartment/cooler	164
Regenerative air-dryer	211
Regulator oil pressure	202
pressure	203
Regulators gas	203
Reinforced concrete pipe	24-25
culvert	24
Relay pipe	17
Release emergency sprinkler	176
Relief pressure valve	141
valve P&T	141
valve pressure	141
water vacuum	55
Religious education S.F. & C.F.	233
Remote oil gauge	181
Removal asbestos	15
catch basin	12
hydrant	12
insulation	15
piping	13
sidewalk	12
Rental equipment	9, 332, 353
equipment rate	4, 7
generator	8
Repair and remodeling	362
Research laboratory S.F. & C.F.	233
Residential alarm	227
appliance	37, 227
burner	181
device	224
door bell	226
dryer	37
fan	227
fin tube heating	288
fixture	226
heat pump	228
lighting	226
loadcenter	223
pool	331
service	223
smoke detector	227
sprinkler	177
switch	224
washer	37
water heater	164, 228, 239-241
wiring	223, 227
Resistant sink corrosion	252
Respirator	14
personal	14
Rest room fixture	255, 258
Restaurant S.F. & C.F.	233
Retail store S.F. & C.F.	233
Ring hanger pipe	134
Riser clamp	133
mounted sprinkler	28
standpipe	281, 284
Road temporary	6
Roadway box buffalo	21
Robe hook	36
Rod curtain	35
pipe hanger	135
socket	137
weld	29
Roll hanger	136
Rolling ladder	5
tower	5
Roof drain	47
drain system	245-246
drain system steel	246
flashing vent chimney	198
Rotary hammer drill	8
screw compressor	209
Rough carpentry	31
Rough-in bidet	150
dental fountain	150
drinking fountain deck	151
drinking fountain floor	151
drinking fountain wall	150-151
sink corrosion-resistant	155
sink countertop	156
sink cup	155
sink raised deck	156
sink service floor	156
sink service wall	156
tub	150
Rubber pipe insulation	191
Rubbish chute	12
handling	12
Running trap	53

S

S trap	53
S.F. & C.F. costs	358
Saddle covering protection	137
pipe support	136
Safety equipment laboratory	40
fixture industrial	151
shower	151
Salamander	9
Sales tax	3, 351
Sampling air	14
Sand backfill	314
Sauna	41
Saw	9
chain	9
circular	9
masonry	9
Scaffold steel tubular	4
Scaffolding and staging	354
specialties	5
stair	5
tubular	4
School elementary S.F. & C.F.	233
S.F. & C.F.	233
Scissor lift	43
Scoop air	200
Screen entrance	34
urinal	34
Scrub station	41
Scupper drain	47
Seal pipe-conduit gland	129
Seat toilet	156
water-closet	156
Secondary treatment plant	27
Sediment bucket drain	46
strainer trap	55
strainer y valve	147
Self propelled crane	10
Self-closing relief valve	141
Semi-steel valve	148
Sentry dog	6
Separation barrier	14
Separator	203
aftercooler	210
Septic system	323
tank	27, 323
trench	323
Service residential	223
sink	156
sink faucet	49
sink system	253
station equipment	38
tap	326
water	326-327
Service-sink clinic	154
Setter circuit	200
Sewage aeration	27
holding tank	27
municipal waste system	27
pipe	24-26
piping	316
pump	161-162
pumping station	26
sitework	321
treatment plant	26
Sewer backup control	48
control floodback	48
control system	48
grating	23
Sewerage and drainage	22
Sheet piling	355
piling steel	332
piling wood	332
Sheeting wood	17
Shelf bathroom	36
Shift work	3
Shock absorber pipe	51
Shower arm	155
built-in	155, 254
by-pass valve	50
door	35
drain	46
enclosure	35
group	155
handicap	155
mixing-valve	155
pan	33
partition	34
receptor	35, 50, 155
safety	151
stall	154
surround	35
system	254
Shower-head water economizer	155
Shrub irrigation	28
Shut-off valve oil	182
Siamese	172
Sidewalk bridge	5
removal	12
temporary	6
Sign	6
Signal bell fire	220
Silent check valve	141, 144
Sillcock	50
Simplex style strainer	204
Single hub pipe	61
Sink barber	37
base	31
corrosion-resistant	155
corrosion-resistant rough-in	155
countertop	155
countertop rough-in	156
cup	252
cup rough-in	155
darkroom	40
floor	253
hospital	154
kitchen	249
laboratory	40, 155, 252
laundry	154, 250
lavatory	153, 251
plastic	155
polyethylene	155
polypropylene	155
raised deck rough-in	156
removal	13
service	156
service floor rough-in	156
service wall rough-in	156
support	52
waste treatment	156
Site drainage	23
improvements	28
irrigation	328-330
preparation	16
removal	12
utility	314
Sitework catch basin system	321
manhole system	321-322
swimming pool system	331-332
trenching system	311-313
Skating rink S.F. & C.F.	231
Slab on grade	29
support	4
Sliding door shower	35
mirror	37
Slop sink	154, 156
Slotted channel	30
Slow close butterfly valve	175
Small tool	3
Smoke detector	220
vent chimney	194
Snow melting	220
Soaking bath	149
Soap dispenser	36
holder	36
tank	36
Social club S.F. & C.F.	229
security tax	351
Socket hanger rod	137
Softener water	39, 169
Soil compactor	7
pipe	61
Solar backflow preventer	185
draindown hot water	297
energy system	291, 293, 299, 301, 303
hot water	346
Solar-energy	182-185
circulator air	183
heating	305
hot-water	291, 293, 295, 297, 299, 301, 303, 307, 309
pool heater	305
space-heater	303
system	293
water-heater	303, 307, 309
Solar-energy-hot water heating	183
Solar-energy-system air purger	184
air vent	184
balancing valve	185
circulator	183
collector	183
control valve	184
controller	183
draindown valve	185
expansion tank	185
gauge pressure	185
heat exchanger	184
storage tank	184
thermometer	185
vacuum relief	185
Solar-system solenoid valve	185
Solenoid valve solar-system	185
Sorority house S.F. & C.F.	230
Spa bath	150
Space heater rental	8
Space-heater solar-energy	303
Special construction	41
electrical system	219
systems	221-223
Specialties	36
fuel-oil	181
piping HVAC	200-201, 203, 205-206
scaffolding	5
Sport arena S.F. & C.F.	234
Spotter	19
Spray substrate	16
Sprayer airless	14
Springler heads	28
Sprinkler alarm	220
building	176
butterfly valve	175
cabinet	176
control pressure	176
cost adjustment	344
dehydrator package	176
deluge	275-277
deluge system	275-277
detector valve	178
dry pipe	269
dry pipe system	269-271
firecycle	279
firecycle system	278-280
flow control valve	178
head	28, 176-177
head guard	177
head wrench	178
lawn	28, 328
line tester	176
monitoring panel deluge	176
preaction system	272-273
pump	161
release emergency	176
residential	177
system	28, 342
system accelerator	176
system component	176
trim valve	175
valve	178
wet pipe system	266-268
residential	177
Square foot building cost	228
Stainless butterfly valve	147
flashing	33
screen	34
steel pipe	92, 94
steel shelf	36
steel sink	249, 251
steel weld rod	30
Stainless-steel flange	99
pipe	93-96
pipe-fitting	97-98, 100-101
valve	147-148
Stair scaffolding	5
temporary protection	4
Stall shower	154
toilet	33
urinal	157
Standpipe alarm	176, 220
classification	345
connection	173
equipment	285
fire	345
riser dry system	283-284
riser wet system	281
Starter motor	218
Starters boards & switches	218-219
Station control	219
hospital	41
Steam bath	42
bath residential	42
boiler	179-180
boiler electric	179, 287
boiler system	287
generator	179
injection water heaters	167-168
jacketed kettle	39
radiator valve	202
water heaters	167-168
Steel carbon pipe-fitting	119
cutting	13
drill	8
flange	120, 128
gas-service pipe	318
oval arch corrugated pipe	317
pipe	22-23, 25, 101-103, 105
pipe fitting	105, 117

INDEX

S

Steel pipe removal	12
pipe-fitting	120, 122
plastic lined pipe	72
roof drain system	245-246
salvage	13
sheet piling	332
sink	249, 251
tank	193
tarred & wrapped pipe	318
weld rod	29
welding	29
Step manhole	24
Sterilizer barber	37
dental	41
medical	41
Stiffleg derrick	10
Stop water supply	50
Stop/start control station	219
Storage building S.F. & C.F.	235
tank chemical	153
tank solar-energy-system	184
tank water-heater	168
van	6
Store retail S.F. & C.F.	230, 233
Storm drainage system	245-246
Strainer basket type	204-205
bronze body	206
duplex style	205-206
simplex style	204
Y type	206
Strap pipe hanger	137
Strapless outlets	124
Structural fee	1
Subcontractor O & P	3
Subdrainage pipe	22-23
piping	319
Submersible pump	8, 22, 160-162
Submittal	3
Suction diffusers pump	203
hose	8
Sump hole construction	17
pit	16
pump	39, 161-162
Supermarket S.F. & C.F.	234
Support drinking fountain	52
lavatory	52
pipe	132
slab	4
Support/carrier fixture	52
Suppressor lightning	224
Surfactant	16
Surround shower	35
tub	35
Survey aerial	3
monument	3
property line	3
topographic	3
Swimming pool	42, 346
pool equipment	42
pool heater	180, 305
pool motel	331
pool municipal	331
pool painting	43
pool residential	331
pool S.F. & C.F.	234
pool solar heater	305
Swing check valve	139
Switch decorator	224
dimmer	224
residential	224
sprinkler alarm	176
Switchboard electric	219
Swivel adapter fire hose	171
System bathroom	262-265
bathtub	247
boiler steam	287
catch basin/manhole	321
deluge sprinkler	275-277
drinking fountain	248
dry pipe sprinkler	269-271
dryer	211
estimate plumbing	238
exhaust	214
fin-tube heating	287
fire extinguishing	171-174, 176-178
fire sprinkler	266-280
firecycle sprinkler	278-280
grinder pump	160
halon fire suppression	286
heat trace	221
heating	303
heating hydronic	287-288
hot-water	239-244

System irrigation	28
kitchen sink	249
laboratory sink	252
laundry sink	250
lavatory	251
manhole/catch basin	321
oil-fired heating	288
packaged water-heater	166
pipe-conduit	129-131
plumbing estimate	238
preaction sprinkler	272-274
riser dry standpipe	283-284
riser wet standpipe	281
roof drain	245
service sink	253
sewer control	48
shower	254
sitework catch basin	321
sitework manhole	321-322
sitework swimming pool	331-332
sitework trenching	311-313
solar-energy	291, 293, 295, 297, 299, 301, 303, 305, 307
sprinkler	28, 176, 178
standpipe riser dry	283-284
standpipe riser wet	281
storm drainage	245
urinal	255
wash-fountain	260
water-closet	257-258
water-cooler	256
wet pipe sprinkler	266-268

T

Tamper	8, 18
Tank casing laboratory	153
corrosion-resistant	193
darkroom	40
expansion	193
fiberglass	193
gauge oil	181
holding	27
hubbard	41
laboratory	152
oil & gas	193
plastic	152
septic	27
soap	36
steel	193
water	193
water storage solar	185
water-heater storage	168
Tanks compression	193
Tarpaulin	3, 6
duck	6
mylar	6
polyethylene	6
polyvinyl	6
Tax	3
sales	3, 351
social security	3
unemployment	3, 351
Tee cleanout	45
fitting	21
pipe	126
Telephone exchange S.F. & C.F.	234
receptacle	226
Television receptacle	226
Temperature relief valve	141
rise detector	220
Tempering valve	142
valve water	202
Temporary building	6
construction	4
facility	5
guardrail	5
heat	4
oil heater	8
toilet	9
Terminal air conditioner packaged	208
heater	182
S.F. & C.F.	234
Terne coated flashing	33
Terrace drain	47
Terrazzo receptor	35
Test well	21
Tester sprinkler line	176
Testing OSHA	16
Theater S.F. & C.F.	234
Thermoflo indicator	203
Thermometer	213
solar-energy-system	185
wells	124
Thermostat contactor combination	221
integral	220
wiring	228

Threaded flange	117
Threading labor steel	104
Thru-wall air conditioner	208
air-conditioner	208
Tile lined pool	331
Time lapse photography	4
Timer clock	227
interval	224
Toilet	27
accessory	36
bowl	158
chemical	9
partition	33-34
partition removal	14
prison	38
seat	156
stall	33
temporary	9
tissue dispenser	36
trailer	9
Tool air	8
fire	174
hydrant	174
small	3
Topographic survey	3
Torch cutting	9, 13
Towel bar	36
dispenser	36
Tower crane	9
hoist	10
light	8
rolling	5
Town hall S.F. & C.F.	234
Tractor	18
truck	9
Trailer office	6
platform	9
toilet	9
truck	7, 9
Transformer heating control	221
Translucent pipe	77
Transparent pipe	77
Trap cast iron	53
corrosion-resistant	54
drain	47
drainage	53-54
grease	151
plastic	54-55
primer	55
sediment strainer	55
Trapeze hanger	136
Trash pump	9
Tray laundry	154, 250
Treatment plant secondary	27
Tree watering	28
Trench backfill	18, 314-315
cover	31
drain	47
excavation	18-19, 357
Trencher	7
chain	7
Trenching	16, 312-313
Truck dump	7
flatbed	7
mounted crane	9
off highway	7
pickup	9
rental	7
tractor	9
trailer	7, 9
Trucking	19
Tub bar	36
bath	149
enclosure	35
hot	150
redwood	150
rough-in	150
soaking	149
surround	35
laundry	250
Tub/shower handicap	149
module	149
Tubing copper	67
copper type k	320
plastic	22
Tubular scaffolding	4
Tumbler holder	36
Turbine water meter	169

U

U-bolt pipe hanger	138
U-hook hanger	138
Ultraviolet pipe covering	192
Underdrain	23
Underground piping	314
tank	193

Underwater light	42
Unemployment tax	3, 351
Union dielectric	48
PVC	89
Unit heater cabinet	222-223
heater electric	220-222
Urethane pipe covering	191
Urinal removal	13
screen	34
stall	157
support	52
system	255
Urinals battery mount	259
group	259
Use pipe	332
Utensil washer medical	41
Utilities piped	19
Utility excavation	311
pump	160
structure	321
trench	18
vault	20

V

Vacuum breaker	55, 203
cleaning	37
gauge	212
loader	14
relief solar-energy-system	185
relief water	55
Valve	56, 139-140, 142-143, 145-146, 148
angle	139, 145
assembly dry pipe sprinkler	178
assembly sprinkler deluge	178
backwater	47
balancing & shut off	202
ball	139, 145-146
ball-check	146
brass	138
bronze	139
bronze butterfly	139
butterfly	142, 144
cabinet	170
cap fire	175
check	148, 178
check swing	143
check-lift	144
circuit setter balance	200
clamp	145
control solar-energy-system	184
corrosion-resistant	144
CPVC	146
diaphragm	145
fire	175
fire hose	175
flush	49
foot	147
foot oil	181
fuel-oil	182
fusible oil	182
gas stop	138
gate	142, 148
globe	140, 143, 148
grooved-joint butterfly	128
grooved-joint gate	128
heating control	202, 213
hot water radiator	202
hydrant fire	175
hydrant screw type	175
hydrolator	175
iron body	142-143
lined	144
lubricated plug	148
mixing	202
mixing shower	155
motorized zone	213
needle	147
nonfusible oil	182
oil shut-off	182
package firecycle	178
plastic	145
plug	145, 148
polypropylene	146
pressure relief	141
PVC	145
radiator supply	202
selection	335
semi-steel	148
shower by-pass	50
slow close butterfly	175
soldered gate	140
sprinkler	178
sprinkler alarm	178
sprinkler butterfly	175
sprinkler flow control	178
sprinkler trim	175

387

INDEX

V

Valve stainless butterfly 147
   stainless-steel 147-148
   steam radiator 202
   swing check 139
   tempering 142
   water pressure 141
   water supply 50
   water tempering 202
   Y sediment strainer 147
   Y-check 147
Valves 335
Van storage 6
Vanity base 32
   top lavatory 153, 251
Vault utility 20
Vent air automatic 200
   alarm 182
   automatic air 199
   cap 182
   chimney 194, 198
   chimney all fuel 198
   chimney fitting 198-199
   chimney flashing 198
   chimney high temperature 199
   chimney increaser 199
   draft damper 181
   dryer 39, 163
   flashing 55
   metal chimney 194
   radiator air 200
   dryer 163
Vent-chimney 195, 199
   band 199
   fitting 194-195
   flashing 195
   high temperature 198
Ventilating air-conditioning . 208, 214-215
Ventilation fan 227
   garage 214
Venturi flow meter 204
Vibration absorber 213
   absorbing pad 213
Vibrator earth 18
Vibratory equipment 7
Vitreous china lavatory 251
   china urinal 255
Vitreous-china service sink 253
   water-closet 257
Vitrified clay perforated pipe ... 319
   clay pipe 23, 26
   clay premium joint pipe 317
Vocational school S.F. & C.F. 234

W

Wafer butterfly valve 144
   check valve 141, 144
Wall heater 39
   heater electric 220
   hung boiler 180
   hydrant 50, 172
   urn ash receiver 36
Warehouse S.F. & C.F. 235
Wash bowl 153, 251
   center prefabricated 157
   fountain 157
   fountain group 260
Wash-center handicap 157
Wash-fountain system 260
Washer commercial 37
   darkroom 40
   dryer accessories 163
   residential 37, 39
Wash fountain handicap 157
Washing machine automatic 39
   machine valves 163
Waste packaging 15
   receptacle 36
   treatment sink 156
Wastewater treatment system 27
Watchdog 6
Watchman service 6
Water anti-siphon 55
   atomizer 14
   bubbler 248
   chiller remote 163
   closet 158
   closet chemical 27
   closet removal 13
   closet support 52-53
   closets group 258
   closets hospital 158
   cooler 163, 256
   cooler handicap 163
   cooler sizing 341

Water cooler support 53
   copper tubing connector 45
   dispenser hot 151, 164
   distiller 41
   distribution piping 320
   distribution system 20
   filter 158
   flow indicator 179
   fountain removal 13
   heater 39, 165, 228
   heater commercial 164-166
   heater electric 164
   heater gas 165
   heater insulation 186
   heater oil 164-165
   heater removal 13
   heater residential 240
   heater wrap kit 186
   heater, point of use 166
   heater, under the sink 166
   heaters steam 167-168
   heating hot 179, 186
   heating solar-energy-hot 183
   hose 8
   hydrant 50
   level control 204
   meter turbine 169
   motor alarm 176
   neutralizing filter 158
   piping polyethylene 320
   pressure relief valve 141
   pressure valve 141
   pump 8, 11, 21, 39, 159, 161
   pump fire 174
   pumping 16
   purification 158
   service 326-327
   softener 39, 169
   storage solar tank 185
   supply detector meter 169
   supply domestic meter 169
   supply meter 169
   supply valve 50
   tank 193
   tempering valve 142, 202
   treatment potable 158
   vacuum relief 55
   well 21
Water-closet 258
   battery mount 258
   bowl 257-258
   conserving 158
   seat 156
   system 257-258
   tank type 257
Water-cooler bottled 164
   cafeteria 256
   electric 256
   handicap 256
   system 256
Water-heater 166
   car-wash 166
   coin-laundry 167
   commercial 242-244
   dishwasher 167
   electric 165, 239, 242
   gas-fired 240, 243
   laundry 167
   oil-fired 241, 244
   residential 239, 241
   solar-energy . 291, 293, 295, 297, 299,
                    301, 303, 307, 309
   storage tank 168
   system packaged 166
Water-treatment potable 169
Watering tree 28
Weather data 359
Weatherproof receptacle 226
Weights and measures 362
Weld fillet 30
   fitting 120
   joint pipe 92, 94-95, 102, 104
   rod 29
   rod aluminum 30
Weld-on flange steel 120
Welded steel pipe-fitting 122
Welding 30
   fume elimination 215
   labor stainless-steel 95
   labor steel 105
   machine 9
   steel 29
Well 17, 21
   gravel pack 21
   pump deep 162
   pump shallow 162
Wellpoint 17, 357
   equipment 10

Wellpoint header pipe 10
   pump 11
Wellpoints 332
Wells thermometer, ... 124
Wet pipe sprinkler system 266-268
Wheelbarrow 9
Whirlpool bath 41, 150
Wide flange beam 30
Window air conditioner 208
   wall framing 30
Winter protection 3
Wire fence 5
Wiring air conditioner 228
   fan 227
   residential 223, 227
   thermostat 228
Wood firestop 31
   nailer 31
   sheet piling 332
   sheeting 17
Woodwork architectural 31
Work extra 2
Worker compensation 348
   protection 14
Worker's compensation 2
Wrapping & coating 73
   pipe 20
Wrench impact 8
   sprinkler head 178
Wye fire hose 176
   fitting 21

Y

Y sediment strainer valve 147
   type iron body strainer 206
Y-check valve 147
YMCA club S.F. & C.F. 229

Z

Zinc flashing 33

Means Construction Cost Indexes 1990

(Individual and back issues available at $38.50 per copy)

The index service providing updated cost adjustment factors

Whether updating construction costs from Means cost manuals, or data from other sources, the construction cost index service is the efficient way to ensure 90-day cost accuracy.

Published quarterly (January, April, July, October), this handy report provides cost adjustment factors for the preparation of more precise estimates no matter how late in the year. It's also the ideal method for making continuous cost revisions on on-going projects as the year progresses.

The report is organized in four unique sections

- breakdowns for 209 major cities
- national averages for 30 key cities
- five large city averages
- historical construction cost indexes

Book No. 60140 $154.00/year   (U.S. Funds)

Means Forms for Building Construction Professionals

First Edition
Over 325 Pages
Three-ring Binder

Don't waste time trying to compose forms—we've done the job for you!

- Forms can be customized with your company name and reproduced on your copier or at your local instant printer.
- Forms for all primary construction activities—estimating, designing, project administration, scheduling, appraising.
- Many optional variations—condensed, detailed versions.
- Forms compatible with Means annual cost books and other typical user systems.
- Ideal for standardizing estimating and project management function at low cost.
- Full size forms on durable reproduction paper presented in a sturdy three-ring binder.

ISBN 0-911950-87-7 $69.95/copy
Book No. 67231   U.S. Funds

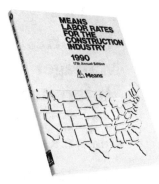

Means Labor Rates for the Construction Industry 1990

17th Annual Edition
Over 325 Pages

CITY•STATE•NATIONAL

- detailed wage rates by trade for over 300 U.S. and Canadian cities.
- forty-six construction trades listed by local union number in each city
- base hourly wage rates plus fringe benefit package costs gathered from reliable sources
- dependable estimates for the trade wage rates not reported at press time
- effective dates for newly negotiated union contracts for both 1989 and 1990
- factors for comparing each trade rate by city, state, and national averages
- historical 1988–1989 wage rates also included for comparison purposes
- each city chart is alphabetically arranged with handy visual flip tabs for quick reference

ISBN 0-87629-161-2 $132.00/copy
Book No. 60120   U.S. Funds

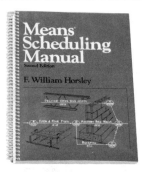

Means Scheduling Manual

By F. William Horsley

2nd Edition
Over 200 Pages
Illustrated

For experienced schedulers . . . project managers . . . understudies

Fast, convenient expertise for keeping your scheduling skills right in step with today's cost-conscious times.

This concisely written scheduling handbook shows you the entire scheduling process far faster than any reference of its kind.

You'll benefit from all the information provided on traditional bar charts, pert and CPM . . . and home in on the precision offered by *Precedence Scheduling*.

You're taken through all aspects of scheduling visually. You work with fold-out spread sheets, charts, sample schedules.

ISBN 0-911950-36-2 $44.95/copy
Book No. 67152   U.S. Funds

Planning and Managing Interior Projects

By Carol E. Farren

200 Pages
Illustrated
Hardcover

NOW, *a clearly defined working guide to project management functions of interior installations*

You can rely on the expertise in *Planning and Managing Interior Projects* because it's been tested and proved out *on the job!* The author draws upon the fruits of experience to give you a better working knowledge of each area of interior project management.

If your situation requires you to be competent in *any or all phases of carrying out interior projects*—working with the client, working with building managers, contractors, movers, telephone installers and suppliers, as well as preparing designs and plans, this book will be *the best investment you can make for doing a better, more professional job!*

ISBN 0-87629-097-7　　　　　　　　　　$54.95/copy
Book No. 67245　　　　　　　　　　　　U.S. Funds

Facilities Maintenance Management

By Gregory H. Magee, P.E.

Over 250 Pages
Illustrated
Hardcover

Provocative—instructive—you'll benefit from new ideas for planning and managing maintenance functions in your organization

This comprehensive reference will guide you through important aspects of facilities maintenance management.

It gives you ideas for staffing, estimating, budgeting, scheduling, and controlling work to produce a more efficient, cost-effective maintenance department.

No matter what your need or problem, you're sure to find direction for solving it in this authoritative book—written by a professional who's conquered every kind of challenge—*including the one on your desk right now!*

ISBN 0-87629-100-0　　　　　　　　　　$54.95/copy
Book No. 67249　　　　　　　　　　　　U.S. Funds

Means Facilities Maintenance Standards

Over 575 Pages
205 Tables, Checklists,
and Diagrams
Hardcover

A definitive reference addressing thousands of facilities maintenance problems

Means Facilities Maintenance Standards is a working encyclopedia which points the way to solutions to every kind of maintenance and repair dilemma.

The book guides you to the underlying causes of material deterioration, shows you how to analyze its effects, and steps you through the appropriate methods of repair.

All of the checklists in this reference are organized in the order you need them. You'll never have to worry about overlooking an important consideration or crucial step in repairs again!

ISBN 0-87629-096-9　　　　　　　　　　$119.95/copy
Book No. 67246　　　　　　　　　　　　U.S. Funds

The Facilities Manager's Reference

• Management • Building Audits
• Planning　　• Estimating

By Harvey H. Kaiser, Ph.D.

200 Pages with Prototype
Forms and Line Art
Graphics, Hardcover

Here's your one-step source for newly developed facilities management methods being used successfully by both large and small operations

Until now, no management authority has taken up the challenge of producing a book that describes how to manage facilities in the "real world" of modern organizations.

That's not surprising when you consider the constraints and the diverse "hats" a facilities manager must wear as organizer, planner, estimator, supervisor, motivator and decision-maker.

Now you can consult with one of the nation's top facilities professionals—have access to a huge collection of genuinely fresh ideas, methods and tools you can use *immediately* to build up your level of performance and funding!

ISBN 0-87629-142-6　　　　　　　　　　$54.95/copy
Book No. 67264　　　　　　　　　　　　U.S. Funds

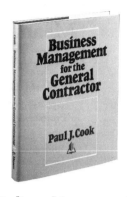

Business Management for the General Contractor

By Paul J. Cook
First Edition
Over 200 Pages
Illustrated/Hardcover

It's direct. It's current. And it's relevant to your needs.

Introducing *Business Management for the General Contractor*, authored by Paul J. Cook, one of the nation's leading construction consultants and writers.

The book's overriding priority is to give the contractor a basic working knowledge of all aspects of business management. With this dependable reference, you won't need bundles of cash or battalions of experts to solve your everyday problems.

You'll refer to this remarkable source book again and again because the ideas it provides will be of continuous value to your career and your company's progress! You'll find efficient methods and strategies to help you handle almost any kind of management problem typical to contractors.

ISBN 0-87629-098-5
Book No. 67250
$49.95/copy
U.S. Funds

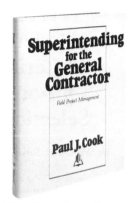

Superintending for the General Contractor

Field Project Management

By Paul J. Cook
First Edition
250 Pages
Illustrated
Hardcover

A landmark guide to the effective on-site management of construction projects

At last there is a guide to on-site construction management that goes beyond textbook theory and simplistic discussion. Paul J. Cook's *Superintending for the General Contractor* is a fully developed, well organized working handbook. It delves deeply into every area of the superintendent's job, probing, elaborating . . . pointing out the do's and don'ts of managing manpower, materials, equipment and paperwork.

Contains hundreds of valuable insights for dealing with clients, subcontractors, foremen, suppliers and workers . . . anyone who works on the project . . . so it gets done at targeted quality, cost and deadlines.

ISBN 0-87629-063-2
Book No. 67233
$49.95/copy
U.S. Funds

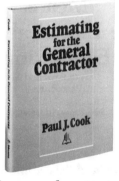

Estimating for the General Contractor

By Paul J. Cook
Over 225 Pages
Illustrated
Hardcover

For general contractors . . . breathe new life into your estimates and profits

Light on theory, heavy on practical estimating methods and ideas, here's powerful help for the contractor/estimator who wants to evaluate and polish every aspect of estimating procedures.

Estimators at all levels of experience will appreciate this comprehensive package of indispensable methods and procedures.

Through the use of clear explanations as well as detailed examples, tables, and graphs, the reader is shown how estimating may be done with *maximum efficiency*—without sacrificing *quality*.

ISBN 0-87629-110-8
Book No. 67160
$54.95/copy
U.S. Funds

Bidding for the General Contractor

By Paul J. Cook
First Edition
Over 225 Pages
With Graphics
Hardcover

The techniques of successful bidding and how to apply them in your own construction business

Now you can have a truly comprehensive guide for making competitive bids—methods and guidelines for all job sizes, up to multimillion dollar projects.

It sheds new light on bidding procedures and techniques . . . at last you can see and compare your approach with other successful bidders. You'll have in-depth discussion and illustrations covering every step of the bid management process, beginning the first moment you get the sponsor's bid package.

ISBN 0-911950-77-X
Book No. 67180
$49.95/copy
U.S. Funds

HVAC: Design Criteria, Options, Selection

By William H. Rowe, III, A.I.A., P.E.

Over 250 Pages
Illustrated, Hardcover

For a total understanding of HVAC systems ...

If you're new to HVAC systems design, or simply want to make certain you're right in step with the newest HVAC design concepts and equipment, you'll benefit from this highly recommended resource.

HVAC: Design Criteria, Options, Selection is a masterful book, providing a thorough understanding of modern heating, ventilating, cooling, and air conditioning (HVAC) systems.

It gives you a comprehensive overview of the basic functions of HVAC, with emphasis on the design and costs of effective integrated climate control systems.

ISBN 0-87629-102-7 $54.95/copy
Book No. 67251 U.S. Funds

Means Mechanical Estimating

Standards and Procedures

374 Pages
Illustrated
Hardcover

For HVAC/Plumbing/Fire Protection estimating ... from takeoff through pricing, bidding and scheduling

Means Mechanical Estimating examines each mechanical contracting activity, pointing out the best ways to predict material and installation costs. It evaluates, analyzes, and integrates every key estimating procedure from interpreting contract documents to the final minutes of the bid.

This is a comprehensive, no-nonsense reference that offers frank discussion of how to evaluate mechanical plans and estimate all cost components ... right down to the last installed pipe hanger.

It will help you estimate better, understand mechanical work better, and develop the most cost efficient approaches to achieve your goals.

ISBN 0-87629-066-7 $49.95/copy
Book No. 67235 U.S. Funds

Hazardous Material and Hazardous Waste:

A Construction Reference Manual

By F.J. Hopcroft, P.E.
D.L. Vitale, M. Ed.
D.L. Anglehart, Esq.

300 Pages
Illustrated, Hardcover

With OSHA, EPA and other agencies stepping up compliance inspections at construction sites, contractors can no longer afford to put off installing programs for informing and training their workers on the proper handling and disposal of hazardous materials.

You're given a full explanation of the laws as they pertain to construction work and what you—as an employer—are expected to do.

This includes suggested methods for storing and using hazardous materials, and then disposing of hazardous wastes, all in accordance with Federal and State regulations.

ISBN 0-87629-136-1 $69.95/copy
Book No. 67258 U.S. Funds

Means Electrical Estimating

Standards and Procedures

306 Pages, Illustrated
Hardcover

Even experienced estimators applaud the countless ways this superb guidebook helps them!

This eye-opening book breaks electrical installations down into modules and explains how to estimate each of them using the Means Electrical Cost Data manual.

- gives you instant electrical estimating help for specific types of installations
- gives you the combined experience of the Means staff plus top designers and electrical contractors
- covers electrical estimating in full—from takeoff to overhead and profit

80 electrical estimating modules illustrate and explain each step in the estimating process ... units of measure for labor and materials, typical job conditions, takeoff procedures, cost modifications ... and a great deal more!

ISBN 0-911950-83-4 $49.95/copy
Book No. 67230 U.S. Funds

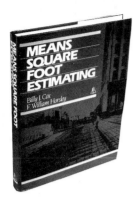

Means Square Foot Estimating

By Billy J. Cox &
F. William Horsley

First Edition
Over 300 Pages
Hardcover

A new generation of techniques for conceptual and design-stage cost planning

Doing an effective job at the drawing board and estimating desk takes time. Too often, the time to carefully explore alternatives and evaluate different ideas is limited.

Means Square Foot Estimating is devoted to helping you accomplish more in less time. It steps you through the entire square foot cost process, pointing out faster, better ways to relate the design to the budgets.

In all, *Means Square Foot Estimating* provides clearer, better knowledge of how to greatly upgrade the *efficiency* and *effectiveness* of square foot cost estimating in the project's early stages.

ISBN 0-87629-090-X $52.95/copy
Book No. 67145 U.S. Funds

Means Unit Price Estimating

First Edition
Over 350 Pages
Hardcover

Direct, immediate help for preparing better unit cost estimates—no matter how much experience you have!
Indispensable for strengthening your unit cost estimating.

Means Unit Price Estimating directs you to the right answers to your unit cost procedural questions—and directs you fast! It describes the most productive, universally-accepted ways to estimate, and uses checklists and charts to unearth shortcuts and time-savers. The strategy of bidding is explained, and up-to-date guidance is provided to assist in evaluation of your own approach.

A model estimate for a multi-story office building is included to demonstrate procedures. The book provides proven systems and special pointers to guide you through the building process.

ISBN 0-87629-027-6 $49.95/copy
Book No. 67232 U.S. Funds

Quantity Takeoff for the General Contractor

By Paul J. Cook

225 Pages
Illustrated, Hardcover

How to put more speed and accuracy into your quantity takeoff work—

If you're new to quantity takeoff estimating, or simply want to be sure you're using the latest takeoff techniques, this book is "must" reading.

It gives you a concise overview of the process—the quantity estimator's role, the tools he or she uses, how the project is broken down, and the rules to follow which help to ensure accuracy.

You will see how to evaluate plans for the site, footings, foundation, slab, floor, wall, framing, and roof, to calculate the quantity of materials and installing labor.

If you've ever had any doubts about how to do a better, faster job making quantity takeoffs—this book will help you do just that—**by pointing out ways to make error-free takeoff estimates for every project.**

ISBN 0-87629-141-8 $54.95/copy
Book No. 67262 U.S. Funds

Means Repair and Remodeling Estimating

(Formerly
*Estimating & Analysis for
Commercial Renovation*)

by Edward B. Wetherill
Over 450 Pages
Illustrated, Hardcover

- Authoritative
- Easy to understand
- Follows CSI format
- Sample estimates

Means Repair and Remodeling Estimating focuses on the unique problems of estimating renovations of existing structures. It helps you determine the true costs of remodeling through careful evaluation of architectural details and a site visit.

This, coupled with a CSI division-by-division discussion of potential pitfalls, and two sample estimates, gives you a real foundation for estimating remodeling work.

Although designed primarily for contractors and architects, the concepts in *Means Repair and Remodeling Estimating* apply to anyone who wants to enhance their renovation estimating skills.

ISBN 0-87629-144-2 $52.95/copy
Book No. 67265 U.S. Funds

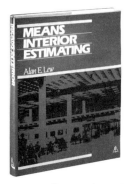

Means Interior Estimating

Over 370 Pages
Illustrated
Hardcover

Four complete estimating manuals in one comprehensive reference

This book provides in-depth discussion and illustrations covering every type of interior construction...

- **Readable.** Tightly written, easy to read.
- **Illustrated.** Dozens of easy-to-follow prototype estimating forms and diagrams of interior assemblies and building plans.
- **Answers.** Each fact-filled chapter is a gold mine of answers to your questions.
- **Comprehensive.** Virtually anyone whose work involves interior estimating will benefit from this book.
- **Authoritative.** Authored and edited by a team of interior estimating experts, this information is based on actual experience and proven techniques.
- Hands-on application of *Means Interior Cost Data*.

ISBN 0-87629-067-5
Book No. 67237
$49.95/copy
U.S. Funds

Means Structural Steel Estimating

By S. Paul Bun'ea
275 Pages
Illustrated
Hardcover

Written by one of the nation's most highly regarded steel fabrication and erection specialists

Now, a reference that offers you methods, standards, and just plain know-how for estimating structural steel, miscellaneous iron, and ornamental metal used in construction.

- setting up a steel fabrication plant
- evaluating the bid package
- structural steel takeoff
- steel erection techniques
- contracts, bonds, insurance
- estimating miscellaneous iron and ornamental metals

As a steel subcontractor, general contractor, estimator, or architect/engineer, we urge you to see this book. It may well be one of the most important references you'll ever use.

ISBN 0-87629-069-1
Book No. 67241
$59.95/copy
U.S. Funds

Means Landscape Estimating

By Sylvia H. Fee

First Edition
Over 275 Pages
Illustrated
Hardcover

Everything you've ever wanted to know about preparing competitive landscape construction estimates...

Here's the important new landscape estimating reference that gives you the tools you need to solve your landscape pricing problems.

Means Landscape Estimating is a thorough, easy-reading, well organized working guide that "talks you through" every step of preparing effective bids and estimates—in a minimum of time. Written by a highly respected landscape designer and contractor.

Everything you want to know about landscape estimating is right here—including marketing your services, performing the takeoff, bidding and planning the job.

ISBN 0-87629-064-0
Book No. 67239
$52.95/copy
U.S. Funds

Roofing: Design Criteria, Options, Selection

By R.D. Herbert, III

Over 200 Pages
Illustrated, Hardcover

This authoritative new guide is overflowing with fresh, practical know-how for professionals involved in roof construction—architects, contractors, owners, facilities managers and roofing installers.

Now you can avoid roofing problems and choose the most cost-effective system—this easy-reading book helps you see the opportunities and pitfalls of modern roofing construction.

All types of roofing are covered... built-up, single-ply, modified bitumens, metal, sprayed-in-place, slate, tile, shingles and shakes, as well as all types of seals and accessories.

ISBN 0-87629-104-3
Book No. 67253
$54.95/copy
U.S. Funds

Plans, Specs and Contracts for Building Professionals

By Waller S. Poage, AIA, CSI, CCS

First Edition
Over 325 Pages
Illustrated
Hardcover

A practical, in-depth approach to managing construction documents ...

Major features of this one-of-a-kind guide:

- dozens of detailed discussions of contract components ... addenda, conditions, supplements, specs, plans
- directions for preparing specifications and technical requirements ... description writing, proprietary and performance specs, standards
- pointers for contract administration ... duties and responsibilities in the OPC (owner, design professional, contractor) relationship, meetings, transmittals, shop drawings, mock-ups, the "punch" list, payments

ISBN 0-87629-068-3
Book No. 67243

$49.95/copy
U.S. Funds

Cost Control in Building Design

By Roger A. Killingsworth

Over 200 Pages
Illustrated
Hardcover

Expert methods for the total construction planning process

Direct from the practical experience of a highly respected estimating consultant and educator.

Cost Control in Building Design examines every step of the early construction planning and estimating process ... pointing out reliable new ways to budget and control costs as the design moves into sharp focus.

It explains—evaluates—integrates every key step into a total COST CONTROL SYSTEM that can help you bring projects to completion within 5% of budget.

ISBN 0-87629-103-5
Book No. 67252

$53.95/copy
U.S. Funds

Project Planning and Control for Construction

By David R. Pierce, Jr.
Over 275 Pages, Illustrated
Includes Sample Project
Hardcover

Here for the first time is a comprehensive action-guide to results-oriented project management

Project Planning and Control for Construction is designed specifically to help construction project managers work more effectively ... and profitably. It is a guide to the best, most up-to-date techniques for:

- pre-construction planning
- determining activity sequence
- scheduling
- monitoring and controlling
- managing submittal data
- managing resources
- accelerating the project
- cost control

This guide allows you to compare your current methods with those recommended by one of the nation's most highly respected project management consultants.

ISBN 0-87629-099-3
Book No. 67247

$53.95/copy
U.S. Funds

Cost Effective Design/Build Construction

By Anthony J. Branca, P.E.

420 Pages
Illustrated
Hardcover

For contractors, architects, engineers ... any professional who wants to get into the design/build business

If you've been thinking about moving into design/build construction work, this book can be invaluable for helping you make your decision.

As a contractor, architect, engineer or other construction professional, perhaps you've been intrigued by the prospect of getting into design/build construction—maybe even founding your own firm.

Cost Effective Design/Build Construction takes you through every step in the business ... including what it takes to start your own firm. Learn how to market yourself, understand client needs to prepare presentations, and how to manage projects using the design/build method. You'll find everything needed to understand exactly how design/build works.

ISBN 0-87629-088-8
Book No. 67242

$49.95/copy
U.S. Funds

Bidding and Managing Government Construction

By
Theodore J. Trauner, Jr.,
P.E., P.P., and
Michael H. Payne, Esq.

Here's the straight-talking new book that answers your questions about successfully winning and administrating government construction contracts.

Why this book will be of immense value to you in your government construction work.

- It provides you with plain language explanations of the laws that control government construction and the complex and often inconsistent requirements of government contracts.
- It explains the bidding process, pointing out the reasons for disqualification based on nonresponsive or irresponsible submissions.
- It clarifies how various government agencies administer and manage construction, pointing out your rights, responsibilities and interests.
- It describes in detail the procedures and pricing methods for changes in construction contracts.

ISBN 0-87629-111-6　　　　　　　　$53.95/copy
Book No. 67257　　　　　　　　　　U.S. Funds

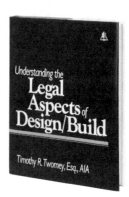

Understanding the Legal Aspects of Design/Build

By Timothy R. Twomey,
Esq., AIA

First Edition
Over 370 Pages
Illustrated

This practical design/build guide will help you:

- **Evaluate and compare** various design/build methods
- **Analyze** the strengths and weaknesses of design/build systems
- **Understand** your role, responsibilities and liabilities as contractor, designer or client
- **Gain insight** into the types of clients most likely to use these services
- **Survey** the legal issues surrounding errors, acts, and omissions
- **See how** traditional legal concepts apply differently to design/build
- **Use** prototype design/build contracts
- **Answer** insurance, bonding and licensing questions

ISBN 0-87629-137-X　　　　　　　　$64.95/copy
Book No. 67259　　　　　　　　　　U.S. Funds

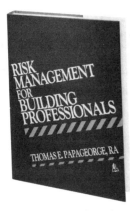

Risk Management for Building Professionals

By Thomas E. Papageorge, R.A.

First Edition
Over 200 Pages
Illustrated, Hardcover

How well do you manage the complex risks of building design and construction?

If you've suffered losses of time, money, reputation ... harm to workers, or damage to projects because risks went unnoticed— **we have very important information for you.**

Risk Management for Building Professionals provides you with a master plan for phasing risk management functions into every department of your firm.

The goal is to provide a practical framework for recognizing potential risks and planning out how they will be handled *before* they occur.

ISBN 0-87629-106-X　　　　　　　　$49.95/copy
Book No. 67254　　　　　　　　　　U.S. Funds

Contractor's Business Handbook

- Accounting
- Finance
- Tax Management
- Cost Control

by Michael S. Milliner

First Edition
300 Pages
Illustrated, Hardcover

Here it is—your action guide for new growth and profits through streamlined financial controls

This handbook is designed for contractors who want to put their business on a firmer financial footing and plan for future development.

In plain language, the book describes and demonstrates how to use the contractor's most powerful financial management tool— *an efficient financial control system.*

In nine wide-ranging chapters, the book delves deeply into accounting systems, design, financial analysis and forecasting, asset and debt management, tax reduction strategies, and computer-based control.

A convenient Glossary defines financial terminology used in the text.

ISBN 0-87629-105-1　　　　　　　　$53.95/copy
Book No. 67255　　　　　　　　　　U.S. Funds

Means Man-Hour Standards for Construction

2nd Edition
over 750 Pages
Hardcover

The "professional's choice" for uncompromised trade and labor productivity data

Here is the working encyclopedia of labor productivity information for construction professionals ... *Means Man-Hour Standards for Construction*, revised 2nd Edition.

The efficient format permits rapid comparisons of labor requirements for thousands of construction functions in the new CSI format.

You'll find every bit of labor data you may need ... *all in a superb layout with "quick-find" indexes, and handy visual flip tabs.*

ISBN 0-87629-089-6
Book No. 67236

$119.95/copy
U.S. Funds

Means Graphic Construction Standards

1st Edition
Over 500 Pages
Illustrated

Create construction concepts/designs and new insights and approaches

Means Graphic Construction Standards assists you in making preliminary "audits" of your designs. It simplifies the review of construction methods, helping you sort out potential problems. You decide visually which elements are essential and which offer you the most cost-effective alternatives.

The book illustrates and discusses the relationships between various building systems. Because each construction assembly gives you extensive design data, you're able to leap from rough concepts to workable plans quickly. You don't waste time working backwards from costs to designs. The book gives you the freedom to maximize your creativity within time and budget goals.

ISBN 0-911950-79-6
Book No. 67210

$99.95/copy
U.S. Funds

Means Illustrated Construction Dictionary

Over 575 Pages
Illustrated
Hardcover

A working handbook of over 12,000 construction terms—explained and illustrated

Here's the on-the-job reference even the most experienced professionals can turn to for immediate answers about construction terms.

The Means Dictionary is packed with thousands of up-to-date explanations of construction terminology. It covers every area of construction from design right on through everyday lingo used by tradesmen. It's "alive" with entries covering every conceivable new technique, product.

Its no-nonsense guidance, illustrations, abbreviations, and easy-to-use format will serve you for years to come.

ISBN 0-911950-82-6
Book No. 67190

$79.95/copy
U.S. Funds

Fundamentals of the Construction Process

By K.K. Bentil, A.I.C.
Over 350 Pages
Illustrated, Hardcover

The first and only book designed specifically to introduce the basics of building construction

Fundamentals of the Construction Process has been prepared for executives overseeing, budgeting, or otherwise involved in building or facilities construction. Because construction processes are often highly technical, it focuses on providing simplified information.

It provides extensive coverage of the pre-construction phases, including an overview of project types, contract documents, cost estimating, contract procurement, bonding, scheduling and mobilization.

The greater part of the book is devoted to describing and illustrating the components of actual construction—materials, building methods, installation techniques—the differences between various construction "assemblies".

ISBN 0-87629-138-8
Book No. 67260

$54.95/copy
U.S. Funds

Construction Paperwork:
An Efficient Management System

By J. Edward Grimes
First Edition
Over 300 Pages
Illustrated, Hardcover

For project managers, office managers, facilities managers, design/build professionals, subcontractors...

The author, J. Edward Grimes, is a project manager with 20 years of experience, and an arbitrator of construction disputes for the American Arbitration Association.

Construction Paperwork: An Efficient Management System cuts through theory to give you practical, instantly usable techniques—with immediate payback. It is the first book designed specifically to help project administrators manage paperwork more efficiently and profitably.

ISBN 0-87629-147-7
Book No. 67268

$59.95/copy
U.S. Funds

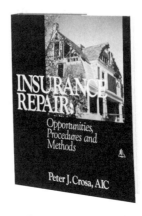

Insurance Repair:
Opportunities, Procedures and Methods

By Peter J. Crosa, AIC
First Edition
Over 200 Pages
Illustrated, Hardcover

Advice for getting into the business of insurance repair—based on first-hand experience

As a contractor or subcontractor interested in expansion, you might be considering working with claims adjusters and insurance companies to repair damaged properties.

The fact is that billions of dollars are paid out annually by insurance companies ... mostly without fierce competitive bidding.

The business is also highly stable—going on in both good times and bad.

Insurance Repair: Opportunities, Procedures and Methods gives you the information you need to evaluate insurance repair, including the benefits and pitfalls.

ISBN 0-87629-146-9
Book No. 67267

$49.95/copy
U.S. Funds

Means Legal Reference for Design & Construction

By Charles R. Heuer, Esq., AIA
First Edition
Over 450 Pages
Hardcover

At last—authoritative help for recognizing and understanding the legal issues in design and construction

Design and construction law is a large topic to grasp. With this in mind, the *Means Legal Reference For Design & Construction* has been prepared to enable its users to sort out and see the legal implications of each stage of project delivery.

Each section is illustrated and explained with examples and visuals. These make it easy for you to compare various legal documents, contracts, and situations to better understand the issues.

The large Appendix and Glossary include a comprehensive list of legal terms, names and addresses of trade associations, and samples of standard form contracts commonly used in the industry.

ISBN 0-87629-145-0
Book No. 67266

$99.95/copy
U.S. Funds

Home Improvement Cost Guide

Second Edition
Over 225 Pages
Illustrated

How to plan and price home improvements quickly, easily—projects large and small

**Planning a home improvement?
Maintenance project? Read this.**

Prior to planning your next home improvement, wouldn't it make sense for you to talk with several expert builders who have done the same project many times before?

Suppose these professionals happily shared their insights, warned you of potential dangers, pointed out ways for you to get the most for your money ... and then provided you with a **reliable estimate** of what you'd expect to pay for the improvement—even if you did some of the work yourself?

You'd welcome this kind of advice with open arms, of course. Anyone would.

Well, that's exactly what the new **Means Home Improvement Cost Guide** does for you.

ISBN 0-87629-173-6
Book No. 67280

$29.95/copy
U.S. Funds

DataSource

Plug into the Means database

Now you can access over 20,000 lines of Means construction cost information right at your PC...

... with new Means DataSource.™

Say "goodbye" to the tedious inputting of cost data. ... and say "hello" to Means **DataSource**—an advanced innovation from Means that allows you to **electronically** access the Building Construction Cost Database as well as other Means databases (see order form for details). With **DataSource,** you can depend on the same reliable, proven Means information you've always relied on—except now you can **get what you need in mere seconds** ... right on your computer screen. **DataSource** allows you to **instantly call up data** (in the familiar CSI MASTERFORMAT) and to handle your estimating tasks with more speed, ease and precision than ever before.

Now instead of spending hours inputting and creating your own database, you can tackle the big (and little) jobs the easy way—with **DataSource. DataSource** enables you to load the entire Building Construction Cost Data file into your IBM AT, XT or IBM compatible PC with MS-DOS 2.0 or higher. You then select out the unit prices needed for your estimate, enter in quantities, and transfer the data to your spreadsheet. **There's no need to change your present software!**

As a result, you can dramatically reduce the time it takes to complete your estimates. You can streamline your operation with an easy-to-learn, **easy-to-use** tool. And you can make your business **more efficient** than ever before.

Plus, with **DataSource,** you get:

- The ability to select specific line items and transfer them to any program that accepts ASCII files (including Lotus 1-2-3, dBASE III, and many others)

- An available feature to extend quantities and calculate costs; and

- Extensive reporting capabilities ... enabling you to choose from a menu of standard report formats, or to use your existing reporting features in your current spreadsheet programs.

JUST THINK OF THE BENEFITS...

- no more tedious inputting of cost data
- no more risk of obsolete prices
- no more fumbling through old estimates, bills and price sheets
- no more price data "miscues"
- no more frustration creating and maintaining your own cost files
- no more productivity and man-hour guesswork for unfamiliar construction

---

Whether you're a contractor, engineer or architect, you're bound to agree that **DataSource** is an extremely useful cost estimating tool—a tool that combines computerized technology with the accuracy and reliability of R.S. Means cost data. (Over 250,000 professionals regularly use our cost information.)

You can also get substantial multiple discounts of up to 25% or more—call us for details, and use our convenient 800 number found on the order form.

IBM is a trademark of International Business Machines, Inc.
Lotus 1-2-3 is a registered trademark of Lotus Development Corp.
dBASE is a trademark of Ashton-Tate
DataSource is a trademark of R.S. Means Company, Inc.

NOTE: DataSource is designed for transfer to standard spreadsheet programs used for estimating. It will not work with dedicated estimating programs.

Means Pulsar System

The most significant advance in construction management systems since Means invented the cost book.

PULSAR is a fully integrated single user micro computer-based construction estimating and planning system for Facilities Managers, Owners and Owners Representatives.

Over 40,000 line items are included covering all aspects of repair and remodeling, new construction, and building maintenance in the CSI MASTERFORMAT.

There are four approaches to access cost data with diverse report-generating capabilities including area specific adjustment factors for 162 cities.

Integrated multi-project management reporting is provided by the PLANTRAC Scheduling/Project Management Module.

Together PULSAR and PLANTRAC provide the most complete estimating and planning package available today for the facilities management professional.

BENEFITS
- Ease of access to database by simple English terms using the 16 Division CSI MASTERFORMAT
- User friendly—Minimal learning curve reduces user frustration
- Estimates using MEANS data can be adjusted for specific locations
- Specification checklist to ensure accuracy and completeness of estimates
- Easy and quick generation of project schedules DIRECTLY from an estimate
- Flexible reporting with ability to schedule variable work week and holidays
- Histograms showing available vs. required resources
- Generate payment estimate and revenue projection graph

Unit Price Cost Standards

Specific construction cost standards help you create detailed estimates

Rapidly changing costs in the construction industry are no longer a problem thanks to a series of specific building information standards from R.S. Means Company, Inc. The Unit Price Cost Standards provide you with up-to-date cost data in several different contractor and subcontractor construction categories. This information eliminates much of the uncertainty of creating detailed estimates and bids.

These cost data standards, which can be purchased together or separately, contain thousands of thoroughly-researched unit prices for labor, materials and installation. They can be used in conjunction with Means estimating systems to determine construction costs in specific building applications, including mechanical, electrical, site work and more.

Each construction task is defined by providing productivity and crew make-up assumptions as well as material costs. These can be easily adjusted to reflect your marketplace needs.

The Unit Price Cost Standards provide the estimator with quick access to the cost figures he needs in the CSI format. National average union labor rates and equipment rental rates are included. The standards save time and money on the preparation of estimates and give you the confidence of knowing that your bid is as accurate as it can be.

R.S. Means also provides you with valuable annual update service for these important Unit Price Cost Standards. Each priced item is checked and adjusted as needed before the standards are sent to you each year.

The Unit Price Cost Standards can be changed and modified to your estimate without sacrificing accuracy.

UNIT PRICE COST STANDARDS
- Building Construction
- Facilities
- Repair and Remodeling
- Mechanical
- Plumbing
- Electrical
- Concrete
- Site Work
- Interiors
- Heavy and Highway

Means Unit Price Estimating System

ASTRO

Now you can depend on the speed and accuracy of your computer to simplify your estimating process. Using known construction costs that reflect your marketplace, the ASTRO can access any of the Means Standard Unit Cost Data Files or help you develop your own cost data file.

In addition to accessing unit cost information, ASTRO enables you to create assemblies. An assembly is a collection of related unit cost information grouped under one code. You have complete control over the composition of the assembly for ease in creating conceptual estimates.

Means now offers three ASTRO estimating packages to suit your individual needs

ASTRO—offers fast, standardized unit cost and assemblies estimating for cost control and construction planning. The construction professional who wants to specialize in one division of the Means Cost Data can choose any one cost data file to go with this package.

ASTRO PLUS—includes the benefits of the standard ASTRO software with the added benefits of specification review and the Building Construction Cost Data, Mechanical, Electrical Cost Data Files, and pre-built assemblies.

ASTRO XL—with specification review, pre-built assemblies and the complete Means Cost Data Files, combines estimating with scheduling for the bidding phase.

With the choice of these three packages, Means has provided an estimating option for all of our customers.

BENEFITS

- Easy to operate
- Saves hours of tedious calculating
- Creates customized assemblies
- Download to most common spreadsheets
- Access up to 55,000 lines of Means Cost Data
- Develop 5,000 user cost lines
- Specification review for rapid conceptual budgetary estimates
- Flawless accuracy in calculations
- Access over 400 pre-built assemblies
- Create critical path from estimate data
- Quick conceptual schedule with cash flow

GALAXY

The GALAXY system combines quantity takeoff and estimating, utilizing a computer and an electronic digitizer board. Quantities from drawings are transferred directly from the digitizer board via an electronic stylus to the computer, where costs from the MEANS database are applied to each task.

Electronic takeoff can reduce your estimating time by 50% or more. In addition to having access to the MEANS standard cost data, the user can call up data from their own custom data file up to 5,000 lines, or from the pre-built assembly file of over 400 assemblies.

GALAXY comes complete with a 36 x 48 digitizer board, Means complete cost data base (over 50,000 cost lines), pre-built assemblies, and two days of training.

BENEFITS

- Saves valuable time doing quantity takeoffs
- Instant access to cost lines and assemblies with the touch of the stylus
- Earthwork module compares existing and proposed contour lines from site plan and calculates cubic yards of cut and fill
- Easily calculates areas, volumes, lengths, widths, counts and perimeters simply by touching points of the drawing with the stylus pen
- Automatic recalculation of quantity by changing the units of measure on the digitizer menu

Means Computer Estimating Services and Electronic Data

INFORMATION/DEMO DISKETTES

I am interested in:

☐ ASTRO ☐ ASTRO PLUS ☐ ASTRO XL

☐ GALAXY ☐ PULSAR

Please send me the following Demonstration Diskette(s):

☐ ASTRO @ $45.00 ☐ PULSAR @ $50.00

DataSource

Please send me the following DataSource product(s):

Quantity	Price		Total
_____	x $395	Building Construction	$ _____
_____	x $395	Mechanical	_____
_____	x $395	Electrical	_____
_____	x $395	Repair & Remodeling	_____
_____	x $195	Light Commercial (10,000 line items)	_____
Disk Size		Massachusetts residents add 5% state sales tax:	_____
☐ 3½" ☐ 5¼"		Total	_____

*Discounts on Multiple DataSource Orders ... **starting at 25%** CALL US FOR DETAILS AT 1-800-448-8182

DataSource is a trademark of R.S. Means Company, Inc.

Prices are for U.S. delivery only. Canadian customers should write for current prices.

Call toll free 1-800-448-8182, or mail this request today to:

**R.S. Means Company, Inc.
100 Construction Plaza
P.O. Box 800
Kingston, MA 02364-0800**

☐ Yes, please tell me more about the computer services exclusively designed for the construction industry.

☐ I have a _____ computer. Disk Size: ☐ 3½" ☐ 5¼"
         make/model

☐ Check enclosed, payable to R.S. Means Company, Inc. (*Save shipping and handling charges.*)

☐ Charge order to: ☐ American Express ☐ VISA ☐ MasterCard

_____   _____
Account Number   Expiration Date

_____   ☐ Bill me (P.O. No. _____)
Cardholder's Signature

Name _____

Title _____

Company _____

Address _____

City/State/Zip _____

Telephone _____

Means Assemblies Cost Data 1990

**15th Annual Edition
Over 550 Pages
Illustrated**

For planning and design stage estimating and a fast, dependable way to develop construction cost strategies

Means Assemblies Cost Data 1990 enables you to compare quickly the most desirable construction approaches using "pre-grouped" component costs called assemblies.

Each assembly includes a complete grouping of materials and associated installation costs including the installing contractor's overhead and profit.

Alternate component price selections are shown together with each system so it is possible to fine tune an assembly to meet specific use or cost goals.

The result? A fast, simple way to price preliminary designs to meet cost constraints or to evaluate and check unit price estimates.

What you'll find packed into the 1990 edition:

- detailed illustrations, descriptions, specifications, and costs for every conceivable building assembly
- energy use and conservation data including heat loss for roof and wall assemblies, recommended insulation levels, climatic condition charts
- solar energy assemblies with installation cost and special operating requirements
- loading factors for support assemblies including snow and wind loads for all U.S. regions
- fire rating, protection, and suppression information
- HVAC assemblies costs
- space-planning data for various building uses
- design ideas with related costs
- square foot and cubic foot costs for design and planning purposes
- explicit directions, worked-out examples, discussion of how to use the manual most effectively

ISBN 0-87629-155-8   Book No. 60060 $95.95/copy U.S. Funds

Means Construction Seminars 1990

During the year, R.S. Means offers a series of 2-day seminars oriented to a wide range of construction-related topics. All seminars include comprehensive workbooks, current Means Cost Books plus proven techniques for estimating and scheduling.

REPAIR AND REMODELING ESTIMATING

Repair and remodeling work is becoming increasingly competitive as more professionals enter the market. Recycling existing buildings can pose difficult estimating problems. Labor costs, energy use concerns, building codes, and the limitations of working with an existing structure place enormous importance on the development of accurate estimates. Using the exclusive techniques associated with Means' widely-acclaimed *Repair & Remodeling Cost Data*, this seminar sorts out and discusses solutions to the problems of building alteration estimating. Attendees will receive two intensive days of eye-opening methods for handling virtually every kind of repair and remodeling situation . . . from demolition and removal to final restoration.

MECHANICAL AND ELECTRICAL ESTIMATING

This seminar is tailored to fit the needs of those seeking to develop or improve their skills and to have a better understanding of how mechanical and electrical estimates are prepared during the conceptual, planning, budgeting and bidding stages. Learn how to avoid costly omissions and overlaps between these two interrelated specialties by preparing complete and thorough cost estimates for both trades. Featured are order of magnitude, assemblies, and unit price estimating. In combination with the use of *Means Mechanical Cost Data*, *Means Plumbing Cost Data* and *Means Electrical Cost Data*, this seminar will ensure more accurate and complete Mechanical/Electrical estimates for both unit price and preliminary estimating proedures.

CONSTRUCTION ESTIMATING– THE UNIT PRICE APPROACH

This seminar shows how today's advanced estimating techniques and cost information sources can be used to develop more reliable unit price esimates for projects of any size. It demonstrates how to organize data, use plans efficiently, and avoid embarrassing errors by using better methods of checking.

You'll get down-to-earth help and easy-to-apply guidance for:
- making maximum use of construction cost information sources
- organizing estimating procedures in order to save time and reduce mistakes
- sorting out and identifying unusual job requirements to prevent underestimates.

SQUARE FOOT COST ESTIMATING

Learn how to make better preliminary estimates with a limited amount of budget and design information. You will benefit from examples of a wide range of systems estimates with specifications limited to building use requirements, budget, building codes, and type of building. And yet, with minimal information, you will obtain a remarkable degree of accuracy.

Workshop sessions will provide you with model square foot estimating problems and other skill-building exercises. The exclusive Means building assemblies square foot cost approach shows how to make very reliable estimates using "bare bones" budget and design information.

SCHEDULING AND PROJECT MANAGEMENT

This seminar helps you successfully establish project priorities, develop realistic schedules, and apply today's advanced management techniques to your construction projects. Hands-on exercises familiarize participants with network approaches such as Critical Path or Precedence Diagram Methods. Special emphasis is placed on cost control; including use of computer based systems. Through this seminar you'll perfect your scheduling and management skills, ensuring completion of your projects *on time* and *within budget*. Includes hands-on application of *Means Scheduling Manual* and *Building Construction Cost Data*.

THE CONSTRUCTION PROCESS– METHODS & MATERIALS

This survey course provides an overview of the basic construction process from the time an idea/need is identified until the final move-in. Participants will learn about the components of construction and how they are assembled to build a project.

Also provided are guidelines for reading the plans and specifications to identify the key elements of a building. Attendees will achieve a thorough understanding of the construction process, from concept through completion, and with a practical overview of the methods and materials used in construction. If you are new to the construction industry or just want to know more about the complex process of converting a need for a building project into a reality, this course is for you!

AVOIDING AND RESOLVING CONSTRUCTION CLAIMS

Construction claims are a common and costly problem in the construction industry. This course provides you with insight and practical recommendations for dealing with claims. The hands-on approach focuses on recognizing and responding to problems as they arise, preparing documentation and formal reports, analyzing causation, calculating damages, evaluating responsibility and defending against unmeritorious claims. Special emphasis will be given to determining schedule and cost impact of project delays. You'll perfect your skills in negotiation to resolve disputes in order to avoid the risks of trial or arbitration. In addition, the program provides realistic approaches to minimizing and avoiding the problems which lead to claims. This course is a must for those responsible for the management and administration of construction projects.

1990 Means Seminar Schedule

SPRING & SUMMER

New York City, NY	January 22–25	Chicago, IL	April 30–May 3
Las Vegas, NV	February 26–March 1	Denver, CO	May 14–17
Washington, DC	March 5–8	Los Angeles, CA	May 21–24
Seattle, WA	March 12–15	Tarrytown, NY	June 4–7
San Francisco, CA	March 19–22	Detroit, MI	June 11–14
Atlantic City, NJ	March 26–29	Washington, DC	June 25–28
Houston, TX	April 2–5	San Jose, CA	July 9–12
Boston, MA	April 9–12	Buffalo, NY	July 23–26
Atlanta, GA	April 9–12	St. Louis, MO	August 13–16
Baltimore, MD	April 23–26	Minneapolis/St. Paul, MN	August 27–30

FALL

Hyannis, MA	September 10–13	Dallas, TX	November 5–8
Washington, DC	September 17–20	Raleigh-Durham, NC	November 12–15
San Diego, CA	September 24–27	Tarrytown, NY	November 26–29
Philadelphia, PA	October 1–4	Long Beach, CA	December 3–6
Cincinnati, OH	October 22–25	Orlando, FL	December 10–13
San Francisco, CA	October 29–November 1		

For a complete schedule of courses offered at each location, call our Seminar Registrar at 1-800-448-8182.

Registration Information

How to Register
To register, call our Seminar Registrar, Marcia Crosby today. Means toll-free number for making reservations is:
1-800-448-8182.

Registration Fees
- One seminar registration — $795 per person
- Two to four seminar registrations — $745 per person
- Five or more seminar registrations — $695 per person
- Ten or more seminar registrations — call for pricing

Special Offer
Sign up for two separate courses at the same location at the same time and pay only $1,295. You get the second course for only $500. (a 40% discount) Payment must be received at least ten days prior to seminar dates to confirm attendance.

Cancellations
Cancellations will be accepted up to ten days prior to the seminar start. After that time a 2-day seminar cancellation is subject to a $150 cancellation fee. The fee may be applied to any Means seminar within one calendar year of cancellation. Substitutions can be made at any time before the session starts. No-shows are subject to the full seminar fee.

AACE Approved Courses
The R.S. Means Construction Estimating and Management Seminars described and offered to you here have each been approved for 14 hours (1.4 CEU) of credit by the American Association of Cost Engineers (AACE) Inc. Certification Board toward meeting the continuing education requirements for re-certification as a Certified Cost Engineer/Certified Cost Consultant.

Daily Course Schedule
The first day of each seminar session begins at 8:30 A.M. and ends at 4:30 P.M. The second day is 8:00–4:00. Participants are urged to bring a hand-held calculator since many actual problems will be worked out in each session.

Continental Breakfast
Your registration includes the cost of a continental breakfast, a morning coffee break, and an afternoon cola break. These informal segments will allow you to discuss topics of mutual interest with other members of the seminar. (You are free to make your own lunch and dinner arrangements.)

Hotel/Transportation Arrangements
R.S. Means has arranged to hold a block of rooms at each hotel hosting a seminar. To take advantage of special group rates when making your reservation be sure to mention that you are attending the Means Seminar. You are of course free to stay at the lodging place of your choice. (Hotel reservations and transportation arrangements should be made directly by seminar attendees.)

Important
Class sizes are limited, so please register as soon as possible.

Registration Form

Please register the following people for the Means Construction Seminars as shown here. Full payment or deposit is enclosed, and we understand that we must make our own hotel reservations if overnight stays are necessary.

☐ Full payment of $ _____ enclosed.
☐ Deposit of $ _____ enclosed.
   Balance due is $ _____
   U.S. FUNDS

Name of Registrant(s)
(To appear on certificate of completion)

Firm Name _____
Address _____
City/State/Zip _____
Telephone Number _____
☐ Charge our registration(s) to:
   ☐ American Express ☐ Visa ☐ MasterCard
Account No. _____ Expiration Date _____
CARDHOLDER'S SIGNATURE
Seminar Name   City   Dates

Please mail check to: R.S. MEANS COMPANY, INC., 100 Construction Plaza, P.O. Box 800, Kingston, MA 02364-0800 USA

Means In-House Training 1990

Discover the cost savings and added benefits of bringing Means proven training programs to your facility ...

WHO GOES TO A MEANS IN-HOUSE TRAINING SEMINAR?

Facility, Design, and Construction Professionals who want to improve their estimating, project management, and negotiation skills

WHAT MAKES UP AN IN-HOUSE TRAINING SEMINAR?

One or more MEANS Training Courses (as described on the preceding page)

Normally, each two-day course runs 8 AM to 4 PM on two consecutive days

The intensive training includes conceptual work and practice exercises

Students gain valuable insight and learn the most current estimating and scheduling methods and how to use the MEANS Cost Data Books.

IN-HOUSE TRAINING SEMINAR VS. PUBLIC SEMINAR

For 10–12 people (or more), the In-House Seminar costs less

The In-House Seminar conducted at the client's facility will not require additional travel expenses and will minimize the time away from work

An In-House Seminar (IHS) program is more flexible and responsive to client needs and requirements

The IHS students benefit from the synergy of a uniform student body. Everyone sees and hears the same thing and participates together

Improving their skills and broadening their knowledge simultaneously, students return immediate benefits to their work place

Build team spirit and boost morale

IN-HOUSE TRAINING SEMINAR CLASS SIZE

The cost effective break-even point is 10–12 people; most seminars have from 15 to 25 students; class size is limited to 35 students

Occasionally, to satisfy their needs or to reduce their per student training cost, a client invites outside personnel with a similar background to attend their MEANS Seminar.

SCHEDULING THE IN-HOUSE TRAINING SEMINAR

You can choose the dates and location that best fit "your" schedule

Consult with Means professional training advisor to design the most effective course for your organization

COMPREHENSIVE MATERIALS

Each participant receives a comprehensive workbook and current Means cost book. The materials reinforce program content and serve as a valuable reference for the future.

CERTIFICATES & CEU's

A certificate of completion is awarded by R.S. Means Co., Inc. to those who complete the program. Continuing Education Units (CEU's) are also awarded through the American Association of Cost Engineers (AACE).

GUARANTEE

R.S. Means stands behind its in-house seminars.

You will deal with real problems, not theoretical situations. If your in-house seminar does not give you the tools you need to grow in the subject covered, just tell us why and we'll give you credit toward another seminar.

Partial list of companies and organizations that have brought Mean's Training in-house:

- Army Corp. of Engineers
- AT&T
- Bell Research Lab
- Bell Operating Companies
- Boston Edison
- Digital Equipment Corporation
- Eastman Kodak
- General Motors
- General Services Administration
- Housing and Urban Development
- IBM
- Internal Revenue Service
- Jacksonville Electric Authority
- Marine Corp.
- National Guard
- Penn State University
- Port Authority of NY/NJ
- State of Missouri
- State of Virginia
- U.S. Air Force
- U.S. Army
- U.S. Navy
- University of Massachusetts
- Westinghouse Electric Authority

How to find out MORE—
Call Roger J. Grant at (617) 585-7880

Means Mechanical Cost Data 1990

- HVAC
- Controls

13th Annual Edition
440 Pages, Illustrated

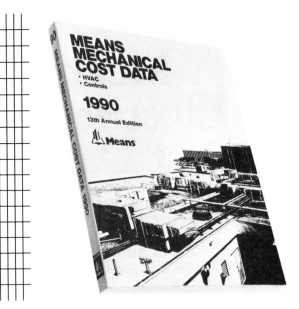

Gives you comprehensive prices for HVAC and mechanical estimating . . .

For contractors and designers who must estimate costs for mechanical installations, Means "mechanical book" is a cost tool of *increasing value* each year.

Now, we are pleased to announce the latest cost information for heating, ventilation, air conditioning and related mechanical construction in *Means Mechanical Cost Data 1990*.

Plumbing and fire protection cost information has been improved and expanded, and is now published separately in *Means Plumbing Cost Data 1990*.

There are so many benefits from using this storehouse of mechanical cost information.

The new *Means Mechanical Cost Data 1990* enables you to answer every kind of HVAC and related mechanical cost question. Use it to:

- estimate better
- compare and analyze methods/costs
- check ratings, outputs, sizing information
- locate items faster
- assist pre-bid scheduling

More valuable to you than ever—focused exclusively on HVAC, controls . . . all related piping, ductwork, accessories and construction

Offered in 1990

- Many price changes for copper, steel and other metal fabrications used in HVAC
- Extensive HVAC CLASSIFICATIONS including:
  - purging scoops
  - cocks and drains
  - liquid drainers—several types
  - flow check controls
  - suction diffusers
  - multi-purpose valves
  - mono-flow tee fittings
  - vacuum breakers
  - direct digital controls
  - flue heat reclaim
  - commercial kitchen ventilation
- Plus price coverage for:
  - polyethylene foam closed cell sheet and tubing
  - gas appliance regulators
  - more types of steam traps
  - more air control vents
  - more control system components
  - more water and steam coils
  - more silent check valves

ISBN 0-87629-164-7   Book No. 60020 $61.95/copy U.S. Funds

Means Electrical Cost Data 1990

13th Annual Edition
400 Pages, Illustrated

Complete in every way—your trusted price book for electrical estimating

Why *Means Electrical Cost Data 1990* is the "tool of choice" for your electrical estimating

Means Electrical Cost Data has become a trusted and well-used guide by your fellow electrical estimating, contracting and design professionals.

This year is no exception. Particularly in light of the important price changes in recent months.

In fact, 1990 electrical estimating can hold some pricing surprises. Here's where Means value really shines. The Means staff of experts have done their homework—so you can steer clear of the pitfalls *and take advantage* of the opportunities ahead.

This is a powerful, easy-to-use resource dedicated solely to electrical estimating.

With *Means Electrical Cost Data 1990* **you'll make estimates with a price source you can trust.**

Many Important Electrical Unit Price Changes for 1990. You'll have them all in *Means Electrical Cost Data 1990*

Complete Unit Prices

- Crews, daily output, man-hours, bare costs for material, labor, equipment, O&P and more. Over 15,000 in all.

- Includes general requirements, site work, specialties, architectural equipment, special construction.

Electrical Systems Costs included

- 40 Electrical assemblies with illustrations

Helpful Electrical Estimating References

- Mechanical, electrical, KW value/cost determination, lighting, AC, H.V. line poles, workers comp, overtime (lost productivity), cost indexes and 28 unit cost procedure models.

- City cost modifications, square foot costs, repair and remodeling factors.

ISBN 0-87629-157-4   Book No. 60030 $61.95/copy U.S. Funds

Means Square Foot Costs 1990

Commercial/Residential
Industrial/Institutional
11th Annual Edition
435 Pages, Illustrated

*Quoting accurate square foot prices
is vital to construction planning and budgeting*

Take a close look at what you get in Means Square Foot Costs 1990

- **New, highly reliable adjustments for local construction costs.**
- **More costs for Common Additives** in the commercial/industrial/institutional sections.
- **More precise HVAC assemblies costs and expanded HVAC options** in the Unit-in-Place (assemblies) section.
- 1990 square foot prices for all types of building construction
- four levels of residential construction quality: economy, average, custom and luxury

- 70 types of typical commercial, industrial and institutional buildings with illustrations
- illustrated "building assemblies"—costs broken down by materials and installation costs
- regional cost adjustment factors for local labor and materials price differences by zip code
- helpful prototype estimating forms and worksheets
- abundant illustrations, worked out examples

You can have reliable square foot prices for any building construction you're planning in minutes

Means Square Foot Costs 1990 is the annually updated source of cost facts that covers every situation you're likely to handle—residential, commercial, industrial and institutional construction of all types.

The convenient tables enable you to simply flip to the building type under consideration, and select an appropriate square foot price in just a few minute's time.

The "Unit-in-Place" assemblies style construction prices give you the ability to prepare more detailed square foot costs through the analysis of individual construction assemblies. These pages are suited perfectly to comparing and selecting various design schemes according to predetermined budgets.

ISBN 0-87629-170-1   Book No. 60050 $69.95/copy U.S. Funds

Means Repair & Remodeling Cost Data 1990

Commercial/Residential
11th Annual Edition
Over 400 Pages
Illustrated

Revised and updated ... the comprehensive resource for estimating commercial and residential remodeling ...

No matter what kind of renovation cost problem you may face, *Means Repair & Remodeling Cost Data 1990* will give you the *special prices* you're looking for ...

- selective demolition
- gutting interiors
- debris removal
- foundation rebuilding
- supports/reinforcements
- masonry repairs
- interior replacements
- cleaning/restoration
- M/E upgrades
- interior finishes
- asbestos removal
- dust/noise protection
- testing services
- subsurface investigation
- structure moving

plus hundreds more renovation costs

This is the Means cost guide that's specifically prepared for your renovation estimating

Means Repair & Remodeling Cost Data 1990 conforms to the Construction Specifications Institute's (CSI) MASTERFORMAT so you can prepare your estimates more efficiently.

- Make your repair and remodeling estimates more reliable and precise. *Means Repair & Remodeling Cost Data 1990* is written especially to help you save time and take the worry and inconsistencies out of estimating.

- All pricing information is obtained through extensive research from contractors, builders, and suppliers throughout the country.

- PLUS ... you can get hundreds of cost and time-saving tips, hints, and advice based on the expertise and background of R.S. Means—over 47 years in the construction estimating business.

ISBN 0-87629-167-1   Book No. 60040 $61.95/copy U.S. Funds

Means Facilities Cost Data 1990

5th Annual Edition
900 Pages, Illustrated

A cost planning tool for facilities construction and maintenance!

More reasons than ever to use *Means Facilities Cost Data 1990* for your facilities estimating projects!

If you are involved in facilities renovations, new construction, or maintenance as a contractor bidding for jobs or a manager planning them, there is tremendous pressure on you to justify your expenditures and to make your estimates reliable.

Means Facilities Cost Data 1990 can help you do just that. This *ultra-complete reference source* makes your estimating more precise and cuts down dramatically on the time you have to spend checking other job costs and calling subs and vendors.

You can use this book to adjust national average data to specific locations.

There are hundreds of other ways you can use this guide. With well over 40,000 unit prices, assembly costs and square foot costs, it is actually five books wrapped into one.

Here is a brief look at what it contains:

New Facilities Construction:
Unit prices of thousands of line items not found anywhere else ... not even in our other books! These unit prices are broken down into crew, daily crew output, man-hours, material, labor, equipment, overhead and profit.

Everything imaginable is covered, from site work, drainage, and caissons to HVAC assemblies, computer rooms, electrical components, and furnishings.

Renovation, Retrofitting and Restoration:
Often you have to take an existing space and redesign it for a different use. These extensive sections can make this job easier and more efficient. They cover everything from demolition and asbestos removal to furnishings and carpets.

Facilities Maintenance:
Both interior and exterior maintenance are covered with frequency tables and dozens of money-saving tips.

ISBN 0-87629-158-2   Book No. 60200 $173.95/copy U.S. Funds

Means Electrical Change Order Cost Data 1990

2nd Annual Edition
400 Pages

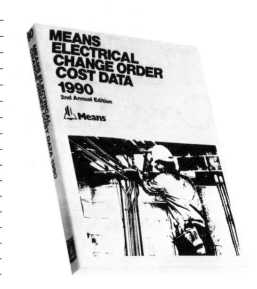

How to accurately price and document electrical change orders—making sure the costs are recoverable!

Consider the countless ways
Means Electrical Change Order Cost Data will help you . . .

1. Compare your change order prices with national averages for the same work.
2. Check to make sure you've included all labor and materials cost components.
3. Determine the impact on other segments of the project.
4. Shop for installation alternatives by comparing "apples with apples" change order prices.
5. Make faster estimates using uniform price data.
6. Give the client/owner reliably priced change order options without dangerous guesstimating.
7. Price change orders at any stage of construction.
8. Quickly check out change order prices from subcontractors.
9. Analyze the impact in installation efficiency, crew orientation, materials prices, man-hours, overtime.
10. Justify your change order pricing with a highly reliable national construction cost authority.

As an electrical contractor, project manager, or engineer, pricing and documenting change orders is surely a key part of your job.

Change orders—or project "extras"—are the source of conflicts, lost time, and sometimes serious disputes.

This guide provides you with electrical unit prices *exclusively* for pricing change orders—based on the recent, direct experience of contractors and suppliers throughout North America.

The costs are broken down into two comprehensive sections: *pre-installation* and *post-installation* changes.

For the first time, you can analyze and check your own change order estimates against the experience others have had *doing exactly the same work!*

ISBN 0-87629-172-8   Book No. 60230 $65.95/copy U.S. Funds

Means Residential Cost Data 1990

9th Annual Edition
Over 470 Pages
Illustrated

Residential costs—from a simple one-story "economy" house to a luxurious 4-unit townhouse

More valuable to you than ever with newly detailed S.F. models—new SUPER-ACCURATE adjustments for local price conditions.

Thousands of Unit Prices
From stone work and insulation to painting and wall coverings, these unit prices are individually figured so you can select the items you need for very exacting estimates. All in the CSI MASTERFORMAT.

Over Eighty Building Assemblies
Fully illustrated and described assemblies can save you hours of estimating time. Each assembly lists the materials and labor needed and the total costs. They give you an outstanding overview of what is needed to complete each job.

Square Foot Costs
Square Foot Costs help you verify your figures and "ballpark" estimates for all popular types of residential construction.

PLUS ... Reference Notes section with added information on how unit costs were figured.

ISBN 0-87629-168-X   Book No. 60170 $59.95/copy U.S. Funds

Means Light Commercial Cost Data 1990

9th Annual Edition
Over 500 Pages
Illustrated

For the special estimating needs of light commercial contractors and architects

Easy to use, reliable price information about light commercial cost planning for adjusters, architects, contractors, planners and project managers.

No better resource for estimating commercial construction with current price information.

If you're still estimating commercial construction with hard to follow price sheets, bills for old jobs, or "guesstimates," we have good news for you.

Means new *Light Commercial Cost Data 1990* is totally dedicated to your special estimating needs as a commercial designer or builder.

It's simple to use, provides instantaneous price quotes, and is reliable for your 1990 cost planning. With a copy on your desk, you'll have the price data you need in *one convenient place*—not stacks of file folders, bills or wrinkled computer printouts.

Yes, here in *one manual* is all the 1990 cost data you're likely to need in three estimating formats—unit prices, assembly prices and square foot costs.

ISBN 0-87629-163-9   Book No. 60180 $59.95/copy U.S. Funds

Means Concrete Cost Data 1990

8th Annual Edition
Over 450 Pages
Illustrated

Arranged in the CSI MASTERFORMAT

Included in the new 1990 edition of *Means Concrete Cost Data* are cost facts for every concrete estimating problem—from complicated formwork to lavish brickwork.

The comprehensive unit cost section shows crew, daily output, man-hour information with bare costs for materials, labor, equipment, overhead and profit for over 15,000 individual items.

The "most-popular" assemblies cost section actually describes the concrete or masonry assembly with drawings and diagrams.

ISBN 0-87629-156-6   Book No. 60110 $59.95/copy U.S. Funds

Means Open Shop Building Construction Cost Data 1990

6th Annual Edition
Over 450 Pages

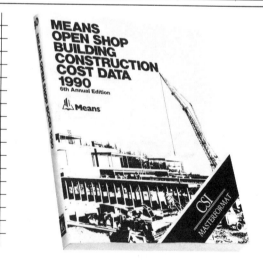

With so many important price changes in the last 12 months, this is "must have" information for your estimating

You depend on BCCD for union labor . . . now you can have the same comprehensive prices for open shop work.

One flip through your copy of *Means Open Shop Building Construction Cost Data 1990* will convince you of its value to your estimating process.

Here at last are over 20,000 reliable unit cost entries based on non-union skilled and trade labor costs. No longer will you need to use time-consuming, inefficient ways to get these prices. The Open Shop BCCD gives you every price you need in the familiar Means layout.

The labor cost data is broken down into man-hours, crew, bare labor, equipment, overhead and profit.

You can break out labor cost facts in any way you need for substitutions, comparisons, and adjustments.

ISBN 0-87629-165-5   Book No. 60150 $69.95/copy U.S. Funds

Means Plumbing Cost Data 1990

- Piping
- Fixtures
- Fire Protection

13th Annual Edition
350 Pages
Illustrated

New—comprehensive unit and assemblies prices for every imaginable plumbing installation

Here's your all-inclusive price guide for efficiently and accurately estimating plumbing work and fire protection installations—

Tanks, filtration equipment, pipe, fittings, valves, fixtures, pumps, appliances, sprinkler and standpipe systems . . . *all related construction*

60 Illustrated Plumbing and Fire Protection Assemblies Costs

This estimating manual gives you instant access to current materials and trade labor prices for virtually all types of contemporary plumbing and fire protection contracting.

One glance through this massive guide—containing thousands of "one stop" costs for piping, fittings, valves, support structures, fire protection systems, appliances—will convince you of its great value to your pricing work.

Whether you use it for a complete unit price plumbing estimate, plumbing design concept, or for a sprinkler system quick price check, it will give you the estimating data you need.

ISBN 0-87629-166-3   Book No. 60210 $61.95/copy U.S. Funds

Building Construction Cost Data Western Edition 1990

3rd Annual Edition
Over 500 Pages
Illustrated

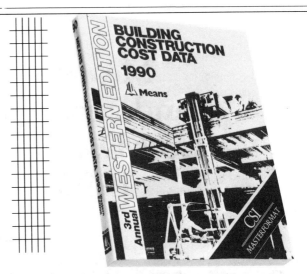

For Western contractors, estimators, architects, engineers, builders, facilities professionals

This regional edition of *Building Construction Cost Data* is specifically designed to give you more precise cost information for the West. It also provides greater information on the construction assemblies which are common in the West.

Based on western methods of construction, this edition makes unit cost information **easier to understand and use.**

Indexes are broken down into major construction components and subtrades.

The Western Edition has information regarding western practices and situations which are not found in our national edition. It helps you estimate more precisely because it has 30 different Western locations, nearly **twice as many** as currently offered in our national edition!

ISBN 0-87629-171-X   Book No. 60220 $69.95/copy U.S. Funds

Means Interior Cost Data 1990

7th Annual Edition
460 Pages, Illustrated

For estimating partitions, ceilings, floors, finishes and furnishings

Estimating interior construction can be a lot easier with this new guide

Due to constantly changing styles and new design directions, thousands of new materials and hardware items for interior construction are introduced each year. Few designers and estimators can keep up with this avalanche of price options for finish work.

But now, you can keep up with—and stay ahead of—the infinite varieties of specialized materials and installation expenses involved in commercial and industrial interior construction... thanks to *Means Interior Cost Data 1990*.

Here, in one all-inclusive resource, are all the prices and help you could ever hope to have for making accurate interior work estimates.

Comprehensive unit prices, illustrated assembly costs, supplemental references—complete guidance for your interior estimating.

ISBN 0-87629-160-4   Book No. 60090 $59.95/copy U.S. Funds

Means Landscape Cost Data 1990

3rd Annual Edition
Over 350 Pages
Illustrated

Estimate landscape and related hard construction faster, easier— and with complete reliability.

Means Landscape Cost Data 1990 is for busy landscape designers, contractors, facilities managers and other professionals needing accurate prices for landscape projects. Cost data arranged in CSI MASTERFORMAT.

Here you have a landscape cost book that will give you direct, reliable answers for your landscape and outdoor improvements estimating.

Means Landscape Cost Data 1990 includes Standard Landscape Crew Tables with hourly, daily costs, and productivities. Also includes a 162 City Cost Index for the U.S. and Canada showing price variations for materials and labor from region to region, hardiness zones, special plant uses and adaptability, scientific and common plant names, unit conversions, and complete subject index and appendix.

ISBN 0-87629-162-0   Book No. 60190 $64.95/copy U.S. Funds

Means Site Work Cost Data 1990

9th Annual Edition
Over 350 Pages
Illustrated

Dedicated to the special problems of site work estimating ...

Here are just a few of the ways *Means Site Work Cost Data 1990* will help you

- estimate crews, equipment and man-hours required for any site work operation ... earthwork hauling, underground installations
- use the price data to compare and select designs and specifications in the project's conceptual stages
- verify your prices and estimates with the manual's national averages
- use it for the hard-to-find costs and site work installations unfamiliar to you
- double-check on subcontractor bids and estimates
- get expert guidance for complicated site work estimating problems

Much new data to help you ...

- More accurate local materials, labor and equipment price adjustment factors.
- More site work assembly cost tables for conceptual estimating.
- Additional new reference tables for calculating quantities, pricing site work.

ISBN 0-87629-169-8   Book No. 60070 $61.95/copy U.S. Funds

Means Heavy Construction Cost Data 1990

4th Annual Edition
350 Pages, Illustrated

Now—heavy construction costs for utilities, public works, earthwork, roadways, airports, pipelines, sewerage, railroads, marine work and more!

Now you have cost data for heavy construction in the convenient Means format.

Means Heavy Construction Cost Data 1990 is designed for contractors and engineers responsible for estimating heavy construction projects with high reliability.

It's an estimating tool that provides prices based on painstaking research into the actual costs for heavy construction throughout North America in the past 12 months. The heavy construction unit and systems cost entries are supplemented with preparation, mobilization and finishing costs for most projects.

The book can be used to price out an entire estimate or used to quickly verify estimates with cost data based on national averages, adjusted for locations in the U.S. and Canada.

The unit price entries are organized in the popular Means line item system containing crew make-up, crew productivity, man-hour data, and bare costs for materials, labor, and equipment ... with and without overhead and profit.

ISBN 0-87629-159-0   Book No. 60160 $64.95/copy U.S. Funds

1990 ORDER FORM

Means
R.S. Means Company, Inc.
100 Construction Plaza, P. O. Box 800, Kingston, MA 02364-0800
617-585-7880

IN THE U.S. . . .
CALL TOLL FREE
1-800-448-8182

QTY.	BOOK NO.	TITLE	UNIT PRICE	TOTAL
	60010	Building Construction Cost Data 1990	$ 59.95	
	60020	Means Mechanical Cost Data 1990	61.95	
	60030	Means Electrical Cost Data 1990	61.95	
	60040	Means Repair and Remodeling Cost Data 1990	61.95	
	60050	Means Square Foot Costs 1990	69.95	
	60060	Means Assemblies Cost Data 1990	95.95	
	60070	Means Site Work Cost Data 1990	61.95	
	60090	Means Interior Cost Data 1990	59.95	
	60110	Means Concrete Cost Data 1990	59.95	
	60120	Means Labor Rates for the Const. Industry 1990	132.00	
	60140	Means Construction Cost Indexes	154.00	
	60140A	Means Construction Cost Index–January	38.50	
	60140B	Means Construction Cost Index–April	38.50	
	60140C	Means Construction Cost Index–July	38.50	
	60140D	Means Construction Cost Index–October	38.50	
	60150	Means Open Shop Building Construction Cost Data 1990	69.95	
	60160	Means Heavy Construction Cost Data 1990	64.95	
	60170	Means Residential Cost Data 1990	59.95	
	60180	Means Light Commercial Cost Data 1990	59.95	
	60190	Means Landscape Cost Data 1990	64.95	
	60200	Means Facilities Cost Data 1990	173.95	
	60210	Means Plumbing Cost Data 1990	61.95	
	60220	Building Construction Cost Data–Western Edition 1990	69.95	
	60230	Means Electrical Change Order Cost Data 1990	65.95	
	67145	Means Square Foot Estimating	52.95	
	67152	Means Scheduling Manual–2nd Ed.	44.95	
	67160	Estimating for the General Contractor	54.95	
	67180	Bidding for the General Contractor	49.95	
	67190	Means Illustrated Construction Dictionary	79.95	
	67210	Means Graphic Construction Standards	99.95	
	67230	Means Electrical Estimating	49.95	
	67231	Means Forms for Building Construction Professionals	69.95	
	67232	Means Unit Price Estimating	49.95	
	67233	Superintending for the General Contractor	49.95	
	67235	Means Mechanical Estimating	49.95	
	67236	Means Man-Hour Standards for Construction–2nd Ed.	119.95	
	67237	Means Interior Estimating	49.95	

QTY.	BOOK NO.	TITLE	UNIT PRICE	TOTAL
	67239	Means Landscape Estimating	$ 52.95	
	67241	Means Structural Steel Estimating	59.95	
	67242	Cost Effective Design/Build Construction	49.95	
	67243	Plans, Specs & Contracts for Building Professionals	49.95	
	67245	Planning and Managing Interior Projects	54.95	
	67246	Means Facilities Maintenance Standards	119.95	
	67247	Project Planning and Control for Construction	53.95	
	67249	Facilities Maintenance Management	54.95	
	67250	Business Management for the General Contractor	49.95	
	67251	HVAC: Design Criteria, Options, Selection	54.95	
	67252	Cost Control in Building Design	53.95	
	67253	Roofing: Design Criteria, Options, Selection	54.95	
	67254	Risk Management for Building Professionals	49.95	
	67255	Contractor's Business Handbook	53.95	
	67257	Bidding & Managing Government Construction	53.95	
	67258	Hazardous Material & Hazardous Waste	69.95	
	67259	Understanding the Legal Aspects of Design/Build	64.95	
	67260	Fundamentals of the Construction Process	54.95	
	67262	Quantity Takeoff for the General Contractor	54.95	
	67264	The Facilities Manager's Reference	54.95	
	67265	Means Repair & Remodeling Estimating	52.95	
	67266	Means Legal Reference for Design & Construction	99.95	
	67267	Insurance Repair	49.95	
	67268	Construction Paperwork	59.95	
	67280	Means Home Improvement Cost Guide–2nd Ed.	29.95	
			TOTAL	

NOTE: Prices subject to change without notice.
MA residents add 5% state sales tax.
Prices are for U.S. delivery only. Canadian customers should write for current prices. (U.S. Funds)
Postage and handling extra when billed.
Send your check with your order to save shipping and handling charges!
1990 editions available December 1989.

SEND ORDER TO:
Name (PLEASE PRINT) _____
Company _____
☐ Company
☐ Home Address _____
City/State/Zip _____
P.O. # _____ Phone # ( ) _____

(MUST ACCOMPANY ALL ORDERS BEING BILLED)

Means will bill you or accept MasterCard, Visa, and American Express

MA57

Building Construction Cost Data 1990

**48th Annual Edition
Over 450 Pages
Illustrated**

America's foremost construction cost information guide with over 20,000 unit prices for labor, materials and installation

---

Building Construction Cost Data, now in its 48th year of publication, offers the reliability of over 20,000 thoroughly researched unit prices, plus the efficient, easy-to-use CSI MASTERFORMAT. Even the most complicated estimates can be accurately prepared in less time than with comparable references.

Astute construction professionals prefer *Building Construction Cost Data* as their primary estimating resource. It's the original, most sought-after book of its kind ... known and depended upon by its users for unparalleled accuracy and versatility ... a cost resource prepared with you—the user—in mind.

Unit prices are based on the actual experience of contractors ... coast to coast

Price information shown in *Building Construction Cost Data 1990* is carefully gathered from the recent, actual experience of contractors throughout the United States and Canada.

Labor prices are based on union negotiated trade rates for the year.

Completely updated for 1990

- materials, fixtures, hardware, and equipment items included in each section
- all items updated to reflect 1990 costs and construction techniques
- unit prices divided into material and installation costs with overhead and profit shown separately
- hourly and daily wage rates for installation crews and crew sizes, equipment, and average daily crew output listed
- city cost adjustment factors for material and labor costs in 19 categories for each of 162 major U.S. and Canadian metro areas
- factors to compute historical costs for all cities dating back to 1946
- square foot and cubic foot cost section showing range and medium costs for 59 common building types with plumbing, HVAC, and electrical percentages tabulated separately
- easiest-to-use format
- costs are the national average and can be easily adjusted for local wage scales
- special cost advantages such as owned equipment, low-cost materials purchases, and low overhead can be identified and computed separately
- over 19 index pages for quick item location and cross-reference
- helpful examples, instructions, illustrations, and explanations of how costs were developed for each major division

ISBN 0-87629-154-X   Book No. 60010 $59.95/copy U.S. Funds

1991 ORDER FORM

Means
R.S. Means Company, Inc.
100 Construction Plaza, P. O. Box 800, Kingston, MA 02364-0800
617-585-7880

**IN THE U.S. . . .
CALL TOLL FREE
1-800-448-8182**

Means will bill you or accept MasterCard, Visa, and American Express

QTY.	BOOK NO.	TITLE	UNIT PRICE	TOTAL
	60011	Building Construction Cost Data 1991	$ 65.95	
	60021	Means Mechanical Cost Data 1991	67.95	
	60031	Means Electrical Cost Data 1991	67.95	
	60041	Means Repair and Remodeling Cost Data 1991	67.95	
	60051	Means Square Foot Costs 1991	76.95	
	60061	Means Assemblies Cost Data 1991	105.95	
	60071	Means Site Work Cost Data 1991	67.95	
	60091	Means Interior Cost Data 1991	65.95	
	60111	Means Concrete Cost Data 1991	65.95	
	60121	Means Labor Rates for the Const. Industry 1991	145.00	
	60141	Means Construction Cost Indexes	169.00	
	60141A	Means Construction Cost Index–January	42.25	
	60141B	Means Construction Cost Index–April	42.25	
	60141C	Means Construction Cost Index–July	42.25	
	60141D	Means Construction Cost Index–October	42.25	
	60151	Means Open Shop Building Construction Cost Data 1991	76.95	
	60161	Means Heavy Construction Cost Data 1991	71.95	
	60171	Means Residential Cost Data 1991	65.95	
	60181	Means Light Commercial Cost Data 1991	65.95	
	60191	Means Landscape Cost Data 1991	71.95	
	60201	Means Facilities Cost Data 1991	190.95	
	60211	Means Plumbing Cost Data 1991	67.95	
	60221	Building Construction Cost Data–Western Edition 1991	76.95	
	60231	Means Electrical Change Order Cost Data 1991	72.95	
	67145	Means Square Foot Estimating	57.95	
	67152	Means Scheduling Manual–2nd Ed.	49.95	
	67160	Estimating for the General Contractor	59.95	
	67180	Bidding for the General Contractor	54.95	
	67190	Means Illustrated Construction Dictionary	87.95	
	67210	Means Graphic Construction Standards	109.95	
	67230	Means Electrical Estimating	54.95	
	67231	Means Forms for Building Construction Professionals	76.95	
	67232	Means Unit Price Estimating	54.95	
	67233	Superintending for the General Contractor	54.95	
	67235	Means Mechanical Estimating	54.95	
	67236	Means Man-Hour Standards for Construction–2nd Ed.	131.95	
	67237	Means Interior Estimating	54.95	

QTY.	BOOK NO.	TITLE	UNIT PRICE	TOTAL
	67239	Means Landscape Estimating	$ 57.95	
	67241	Means Structural Steel Estimating	65.95	
	67242	Cost Effective Design/Build Construction	54.95	
	67243	Plans, Specs & Contracts for Building Professionals	54.95	
	67245	Planning and Managing Interior Projects	59.95	
	67246	Means Facilities Maintenance Standards	131.95	
	67247	Project Planning and Control for Construction	58.95	
	67249	Facilities Maintenance Management	59.95	
	67250	Business Management for the General Contractor	54.95	
	67251	HVAC: Design Criteria, Options, Selection	59.95	
	67252	Cost Control in Building Design	58.95	
	67253	Roofing: Design Criteria, Options, Selection	59.95	
	67254	Risk Management for Building Professionals	54.95	
	67255	Contractor's Business Handbook	58.95	
	67257	Bidding & Managing Government Construction	58.95	
	67258	Hazardous Material & Hazardous Waste	76.95	
	67259	Understanding the Legal Aspects of Design/Build	71.95	
	67260	Fundamentals of the Construction Process	59.95	
	67262	Quantity Takeoff for the General Contractor	59.95	
	67264	The Facilities Manager's Reference	59.95	
	67265	Means Repair & Remodeling Estimating	57.95	
	67266	Means Legal Reference for Design & Construction	109.95	
	67267	Insurance Repair	54.95	
	67268	Construction Paperwork	65.95	
	67280	Means Home Improvement Cost Guide–2nd Ed.	32.95	
			TOTAL (U.S. Funds)	

MA57

NOTE: Prices subject to change without notice.
MA residents add 5% state sales tax.
Prices are for U.S. delivery only. Canadian customers should write for current prices.
Postage and handling extra when billed.
Send your check with your order to save shipping and handling charges!
1991 editions available December 1990.

SEND ORDER TO:
Name (PLEASE PRINT) _____
Company _____
☐ Company ☐ Home Address _____
City/State/Zip _____
P.O. # _____ Phone # ( ) _____

(MUST ACCOMPANY ALL ORDERS BEING BILLED)